For Reference

Not to be taken from this room

The American Economy

The American Economy

A HISTORICAL ENCYCLOPEDIA
Revised Edition

Volume Two: Essays and Primary Source Documents

Cynthia L. Clark
Editor

ABC-CLIO

Santa Barbara, California • Denver, Colorado • Oxford, England

Library of Congress Cataloging-in-Publication Data

The American economy : a historical encyclopedia / Cynthia L. Clark, editor. — Rev. ed.
    p. cm.
  Includes bibliographical references and index.
  ISBN 978–1–59884–461–0 (hbk. : alk. paper) — ISBN 978–1–59884–462–7 (ebook)
1. United States—Economic policy—Encyclopedias. 2. United States—Economic conditions—Encyclopedias.
3. United States—Social policy—Encyclopedias. 4. United States—Social conditions—Encyclopedias.
I. Northrup, Cynthia L. Clark, 1959–
HC102.A66   2011
330.973003—dc22   2010024504

ISBN: 978–1–59884–461–0
EISBN: 978–1–59884–462–7

15 14 13 12 11   1 2 3 4 5

This book is also available on the World Wide Web as an eBook.
Visit www.abc-clio.com for details.

ABC-CLIO, LLC
130 Cremona Drive, P.O. Box 1911
Santa Barbara, California 93116-1911

This book is printed on acid-free paper ∞

Manufactured in the United States of America

Contents

List of Short Entries

List of Essays and Primary Source Documents

The American Economy

A HISTORICAL ENCYCLOPEDIA
Revised Edition

Volume Two: Essays and Primary Source Documents

Essays

Advertising

Christopher A. Preble

Advertising is an essential element of a classical-liberal economic system that is founded on the principle of individual choice. In the early stages of economic development, advertising informs consumers about the different products and services available to them. As the range of consumer choices expands, manufacturers and retailers use advertising to differentiate their products and services from those of their competitors. The history of advertising in the United States demonstrates this evolution and shows how advertising styles have changed over time.

The Early Period: Colonial Times to the Early 1800s

Advertising has been a persistent feature of American life since colonial times. Printed handbills, one of the earliest forms of advertising, promoted emigration to the New World. Lured to the barren wilderness with promises of fortune, the new immigrants established businesses, which used outdoor advertising—principally signs—to call attention to their operations.

Some of the first newspapers in the New World, including Benjamin Franklin's *Philadelphia Gazette* and John Peter Zenger's *New York Weekly Journal*, contained advertising within their pages. On the whole, however, early newspapers remained an ineffective advertising medium. The 300 or so newspapers published around the turn of the nineteenth century reached only a limited number of readers in a handful of small cities. Paper in the New World was expensive, and printing presses had only a limited capacity for altering the layout of pages to include advertising. Early advertisements provided information only, making advertising copy generally boring and unpersuasive. It was also repetitious; some ads remained unchanged for a year or longer as many newspapers provided discounts to advertisers who printed the same ad repeatedly.

Given these and other limitations, newspapers derived only about one-third of their revenues from advertising, with the balance coming from readers. The ratio of advertising revenue to other revenue proved even less for the small number of print magazines operating during the early republic period of the United States. Many publishers viewed advertising as a sign of financial weakness, an embarrassment, a sign that the literary value of their particular work failed to spark sufficient interest to merit readers' attention and money.

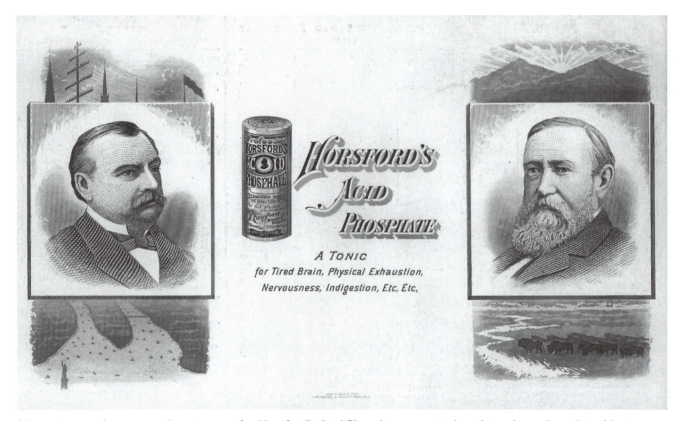

A late-nineteenth-century advertisement for Horsford's Acid Phosphate, a tonic that claimed to relieve "tired brain, physical exhaustion, nervousness, indigestion, etc. etc." At the time, there were no regulations protecting the public from the dangers of untested patent medicine. (Library of Congress.)

Mid- to Late Nineteenth Century: Rise of the Agency

Beginning in the 1830s and 1840s, technological changes opened new opportunities for newspaper publishers and advertisers alike. As the cost of paper declined, and as other improvements in printing technology reduced production costs, innovators experimented with changing the relationship between advertising copy and the rest of the text. James Gordon Bennett Sr., publisher of the *New York Herald*, insisted that advertisements change every day, just as the news changed every day. This innovation, combined with the growth in the number of pages in most newspapers, resulted in an explosion in the sheer volume of advertising space available for filling the pages of the newspaper.

The advertising agent emerged to solve this unique problem for newspaper publishers. According to industry historian Ralph Hower, the role of advertising agents evolved in a series of four stages. In the first stage, the agent served the newspaper, selling space on the publisher's behalf and earning a commission for orders taken. In the second stage, the agent played the role of space jobber, selling to advertisers on a piecemeal basis, buying space as necessary from publishers, and earning a profit on the difference between the buying price and the selling price. The space wholesaler carried the role of the space jobber one step further, buying advertising space in large quantities and then reselling the space in smaller quantities to advertisers for a profit. Finally, in the last stage in the evolution of the agent's role, the agent as concessionaire acted as the sole agent for given publications and then presented advertisers wishing to promote their products and services with a list of the publications for which he held a concession.

The first advertising agent, Volney Palmer, established operations in Philadelphia around 1843 and, by 1849, claimed to represent 1,300 newspapers. Palmer was an early evangelist for advertising, communicating the importance of advertising to his clients and emphasizing the use of advertising to develop new markets.

George P. Rowell started in advertising by selling space for the *Boston Post*. He then established an independent agency in Boston and later in New York. Initially, Rowell filled a role similar to that of a typical space wholesaler, but he also set about to validate circulation figures, which publishers inflated notoriously. *Rowell's American Newspaper Directory*, first published in 1869, included information on 5,000 newspapers in the United States and another 300 in Canada. Rowell's other main innovation involved the institution of the open contract in 1875. Under the open contract, Rowell agreed to serve the advertiser instead of the publisher.

Other advertising agencies copied Rowell's efforts. Francis Wayland Ayer improved upon several of Rowell's innovations to become the leading advertising agent at the end of the nineteenth century. Ayer opened his agency, N. W. Ayer and Son, in Philadelphia with his father in 1866. Like Rowell, Ayer also produced a listing of publications, *Ayer and Son's Manual for Advertisers*, and, again following Rowell's lead, Ayer adopted a variation of the open contract. Ayer further cemented his relationship as an agent for the advertiser, not the publisher, by establishing an exclusive arrangement with his clients for a fixed period of time.

The makers of patent medicines spent far more money on advertising than did any other industry through most of the nineteenth century, providing substantial revenue for publishers and agents alike. Sales of patent medicines increased when advertising expenditures rose, which suggested the effectiveness of advertising in general. But the untruthfulness of the patent-medicine ads tarnished the reputation of advertising. Some publications quietly pocketed the cash and looked the other way, but others balked at carrying advertisements of dubious veracity. Magazines, in particular, resisted advertising altogether to avoid being associated with patent-medicine makers and other hucksters.

Opposition to advertising changed during the latter half of the nineteenth century as new advertisers, promoting a diverse array of products and services, eventually displaced patent medicines as the engine of growth in the advertising business. For example, ad spending by retailers matched that of patent-medicine manufacturers by the late 1800s. Department store pioneer John Wanamaker used outdoor advertising liberally, including 12-foot-high billboards all over Philadelphia, and he distributed handbills at fairs to promote his store. In the case of print advertising, Wanamaker initiated the use of full-page advertisements, with ads that included detailed descriptions of products and prices. Other retailers quickly copied

Wanamaker's methods. Department store advertising provided a steady stream of revenue for newspapers in the late 1800s.

Consumer goods manufacturers also began appealing directly to buyers for their business in the late 1800s; for example, Levi Strauss jeans, designed for durability, were promoted through catalogs. Although these manufacturers capitalized on expanding production capacity and an extended sales and marketing network to reach a mass market, they remained motivated primarily by the desire to alter the power relationship between themselves and the middlemen—wholesalers and retailers—who controlled the point of sale. During most of the nineteenth century, manufacturers depended on these middlemen to deliver and market products to consumers. In this context, wholesalers could play one manufacturer against another, using price pressures to extract the maximum possible profit for themselves while squeezing manufacturers economically. Advertising enabled manufacturers to shift this power relationship by appealing directly to consumers, who in turn pressured the middlemen to carry certain products they had seen advertised.

Much of this advertising appeared in newspapers, but another print medium, the magazine, became a popular advertising vehicle in that same period. Although a few magazines existed in the United States in the early 1800s, only a small number of them depended on advertising for income. This pattern continued through most of the nineteenth century until three men popularized the use of magazines as advertising media. J. Walter Thompson did so from the agency side of the business, developing an expertise in the placement of ads in magazines that propelled his namesake agency to its place as one of the largest and most successful agencies of the twentieth century. Cyrus H. K. Curtis expanded the role of magazines as advertising media from the publishing side by dramatically boosting circulation of his magazines, first the *Ladies' Home Journal* and later the *Saturday Evening Post*, and reaping the financial rewards through increased advertising revenues. Finally, Frank Munsey moved the revolution in magazine advertising a step further by drastically reducing the cover price of his magazines (such as *Golden Argosy* and *Munsey's Magazine*) to boost circulation, recouping the lost revenue through advertising. Munsey's tactics made him one of the most despised men in publishing in the late 1800s, but his competitors were forced to follow suit. By the beginning of the twentieth century, advertising generated an ever-greater revenue for magazines that previously refused to accept ads for fear that doing so would cheapen their genteel, literary image.

The Progressive Era and World War I: Advances in Style

The volume of advertising increased 10-fold in the last 30 years of the nineteenth century and advertising expenditures in the United States totaled over 3 percent of gross national product by 1900. Advertising agencies, building on the example of Rowell's and Ayer's open contract, developed new services for their clients, including copywriting and other creative capabilities.

Albert D. Lasker of the Lord and Thomas (L&T) agency in Chicago developed a distinctive copywriting style—often known as *reason-why advertising*—that vaulted

Advertisement for Arm & Hammer baking soda, ca. 1900. (Library of Congress.)

his agency to a leading place within the industry. Lasker believed that advertising equaled salesmanship in print. He also believed that customers must see a specific reason for purchasing a particular product. Star copywriter Claude C. Hopkins further refined the reason-why style, attracting prominent new clients to L&T and becoming one of the highest-paid men in advertising. Advertisers remember him as one of the greatest copywriters of all time.

By the early 1900s, advertising agencies employed more scientific methods to gauge consumer opinion, such as questionnaires and surveys. Business schools began to teach advertising: New York University offered the first such course in 1906, adding still further evidence of the industry's rising professional stature. Meanwhile, trade journals such as *Printers' Ink* provided a respected public voice for the industry.

Along with the growing influence of advertising came an increased interest on the part of consumers and politicians to control or limit it. In the early 1900s, the threat of governmental action prompted the move toward self-regulation, carried out primarily by industry trade groups including the Associated Advertising Clubs of America (later the World) (AACA/AACW), established in 1905; the Association of National Advertisers (ANA), established in 1915; and the American Association of Advertising Agencies (AAAA), formed in 1917. The relative ineffectiveness of self-regulation later haunted the industry as consumer groups gained more power and influence in Washington, D.C.

Highs and Lows: The Roaring Twenties and the Great Depression

Efforts to force changes in advertising practices did not come to fruition until the early 1930s. In the meantime, advertising experienced its period of greatest growth and influence in the years immediately after World War I.

The maturation of the advertising business began during World War I with George Creel's Committee on Public Information. *Printers' Ink* boasted that advertising had earned its credentials as an implement of war. This somewhat dubious distinction did not become a liability until the 1930s, when critics raised new questions about U.S. involvement in the war and cast a skeptical eye on the propagandizing efforts of the Creel Committee.

In the years immediately after World War I, the federal government inadvertently provided the impetus for the single greatest explosion of ad spending in the nation's history when Congress failed to swiftly revoke the wartime excess-profits tax. Threatened by this confiscatory levy, businesses chose instead to spend their extra income on advertising. The results proved dramatic. Total advertising spending *doubled* in less than two years, from $1.5 billion in 1918 to nearly $3 billion in 1920.

This expansion in advertising spending coincided with the introduction of new and improved products into the market. Popular culture glorified advertising and politicians celebrated it, including President Calvin Coolidge, who praised advertisers for changing and adapting cultural norms and habits and for ministering to "the spiritual side of trade" in 1926. Another prominent politician, New York Governor Franklin D. Roosevelt, stated that he would have chosen a career in advertising if he could live his life over again.

Advertising styles varied during the 1920s. Pioneered by Theodore F. MacManus, a star copywriter for General Motors, the "atmospheric" or "impressionistic" style emphasized building an image of durable quality rather than pitching the merits of a particular product. Helen Resor of J. Walter Thompson combined the MacManus style with Lasker's reason-why style to create many memorable campaigns, including the one for Woodbury Soap with the slightly suggestive slogan "A Skin You Love to Touch."

The up-and-coming agency Batten, Barton, Durstine and Osborn (BBDO), founded in 1919, also used the MacManus style. Bruce Barton, one of the founders of the new firm, authored *The Man Nobody Knows* (1924), a book that presented a contemporary view of Jesus Christ. Although critics satirized Barton's "Christ as Adman" story, the book sold 250,000 copies in 18 months, securing Barton's public image, an image that he later parlayed into a brief career in politics.

Not all "admen" (as they were called at the time) embraced the MacManus style. Albert Lasker stubbornly resisted the shift away from reason-why advertising, and he attracted many new clients, including George Washington Hill's American Tobacco Company, by stressing reason-why principles. The campaign L&T created for Hill's

Lucky Strike cigarette brand—"Reach for a Lucky Instead of a Sweet"—aroused the ire of the Federal Trade Commission (FTC), but the campaign helped to make Lucky Strike the number-one-selling cigarette brand, earning L&T millions of dollars in the process.

Advertising agencies took the lead in exploiting the first of the broadcast media—radio—despite early resistance to the commercialization of the airwaves. Initially, agencies remained reluctant to use the overt sales pitches used in print for years, and radio executives feared that advertising would harm the medium's reputation. In response to these and other concerns, both agents and networks opted for the soft-sell approach, allowing sponsors to underwrite the production of on-air programs, such as Pepsodent's *Amos 'n' Andy Show* and *The Fleischmann Yeast Hour* featuring Rudy Vallee.

But just as agencies and their clients were learning about the effectiveness of radio as a marketing vehicle, the bottom dropped out of the economy. Advertising, like most industries, was devastated financially during the depression: From a high of $3.4 billion in total billings in 1929, ad spending bottomed out at only $1.3 billion, 38 percent of the pre-depression level, in 1933.

Advertising also suffered from an image problem in the 1930s. In 1927, Stuart Chase and Frederick J. Schlink published *Your Money's Worth*, a broad-based indictment of modern selling practices. The authors singled out advertising for special blame, arguing that falling production costs, which should have resulted in lower prices for consumers, had been offset by fat advertising budgets, which kept prices artificially high. Selling well over 100,000 copies, *Your Money's Worth* spawned the creation of Consumer Research, a grassroots organization, the ranks of which swelled from a mere 1,200 members in 1929 to over 45,000 in 1933. The organization refocused public scrutiny on the advertising business.

Several prominent proponents of Franklin Roosevelt's New Deal, including presidential adviser Harry Hopkins and Assistant Secretary of Agriculture Rexford Tugwell, aligned with consumer activists in seeking greater governmental oversight of advertising. Hopkins wondered aloud if the government should take over advertising completely, while Tugwell favored moving the regulation of food and drug advertising away from the FTC and into the Agriculture Department. The New Dealers gained the support of Senator Royal Copeland (D–NY), who introduced legislation extending regulations governing product labels to advertising and broadening the definition of false advertising in 1933.

The admen countered these threats by again pledging to regulate themselves. This time, however, they failed to thwart more stringent government regulations, especially revisions to the Federal Trade Commission Act of 1938 (Wheeler-Lea amendments). In the two years following passage of these revisions, the FTC handed down 18 injunctions against the industry, forcing advertisers to revise claims the FTC deemed "deceptive acts of commerce."

This external pressure posed the greatest challenge to advertisers in the nation's history to date, but the news was not all bad for the advertising business. The decade witnessed the emergence of Young and Rubicam (Y&R), one of the most creative agencies in the history of American advertising. Raymond Rubicam set the tone for the agency by combining a respect for the science of advertising with an eye for the MacManus image style. Rubicam demonstrated his fealty to scientific method by hiring George Gallup to conduct polling for the agency. By decade's end, Y&R became the second-largest agency in the country.

Meanwhile radio broadcasting and radio advertising continued to grow, spawning new creative outlets and innovative revenue opportunities for advertising agencies and clients alike. Radio audiences swelled as people sought a temporary escape from economic hardship. By 1938, radio surpassed magazines in total advertising revenues. Print media continued to lose ground to broadcasting in the years to come.

Agencies and advertisers retained much control over production of radio programs through the 1930s and into the 1940s. The agencies hired the writers and established the rules, while the networks provided the technical vehicle for delivering product messages. After World War II, this relationship carried over to the next great broadcasting medium—television.

The 1950s: The Golden Age of Television

Advertising grew modestly during World War II, but the industry enjoyed one of its greatest periods of growth immediately after the war, when total advertising expenditures nearly doubled from $2.9 billion in 1945 to $5.7 billion in 1950.

The growth of television in the early 1950s presented the greatest challenges and the greatest opportunities for the advertising business. Although television debuted in the late 1930s, the adoption of the new technology slowed, first because of World War II and later because of a Federal Communication Commission (FCC) decision to freeze the granting of new television licenses over concerns involving signal interference. Despite this freeze, television ad spending grew at a rate faster than that of radio during its formative years: From $12.3 million in 1949, ad spending on television soared to $40.8 million in 1950, then to $128 million in 1951.

When the FCC lifted the freeze in 1952, the agencies soon gained control of programming as they had with radio, using sponsors to underwrite production costs. Sponsors' control over programming proved sometimes ridiculous—for example, DeSoto asked a game show contestant named Ford to use a different last name on its program. But overall, sponsors and advertising agencies alike remained motivated to create popular, enjoyable, quality programs, which earned the respect and support of the viewing public.

Meanwhile, the agencies battled with the networks for control of television programming. As the number of viewers expanded, the cost of advertising and sponsorship skyrocketed. Many advertisers found themselves priced out of the market altogether; many who remained chose to use repetitive, hard-sell commercials to get their messages across. Customers quickly grew weary of these outspoken sales pitches. The success of Blab-Off, a device that enabled television users to turn off the sound for commercials, portended challenging times ahead for agencies and their clients as viewers resorted to technical devices to limit their exposure to advertising.

In the late 1950s, after the revelation that unscrupulous sponsors of quiz shows had manipulated the games to further their perceived commercial ends, the trend toward network control over television programming was sealed. The networks used these scandals as a pretext for assuming complete control over programming. After the collapse of the original sponsorship system, ratings, based on questionnaires completed by households, determined programming decisions. The quality of the programming no longer was the primary concern.

Although the advertising industry enjoyed great prosperity in the years after World War II, widespread criticism of the admen of Madison Avenue also existed during this era. Vance Packard's book *The Hidden Persuaders*, published in 1957, questioned the use of motivation research (MR) to manipulate consumer behavior. Meanwhile, fictionalized accounts of the advertising business, including Frederic Wakeman's *The Hucksters* (1946) and Sloan Wilson's *The Man in the Gray Flannel Suit* (1955), painted an unflattering picture of admen wrought by self-doubt and guilt and driven by the pursuit of the almighty dollar to the point of burnout and deteriorating health.

The 1960s through the 1980s: Cycles of Change

Advertising styles fluctuated in the 1960s, 1970s, and 1980s as the industry struggled to capture the attention of a consuming public routinely bombarded by marketing messages from all directions. In the 1960s, new personalities emerged to move advertising through another period of creativity. Characters such as the Marlboro Man, the Pillsbury Doughboy, and the celebrated "Think Small" campaign created by Doyle Dane Bernbach (DDB) for German automaker Volkswagen are remembered as some of the most memorable campaigns and images in the history of advertising.

Cute and memorable campaigns notwithstanding, the advertising business became subject to repeated and persistent criticism during the 1960s and 1970s; many of these criticisms related to the broader social and cultural changes of the era. For example, feminists, emboldened by Betty Friedan's critique of advertising in her book *The Feminine Mystique*, objected to advertisers' use of sex to sell products, a practice dating at least as far back as Helen Resor's famous Woodbury Soap campaigns. Feminists also questioned why so few women held senior-level positions in the advertising business. The underrepresentation of racial and ethnic minorities not only in agencies but also in advertisements proved equally troubling. Finally, the industry was criticized for promoting values that celebrated the consumption of goods at the expense of other concerns and for foisting this value system on citizens at a very young age by targeting advertising at children.

Government efforts to regulate advertising proceeded on several fronts during the 1960s, with executive agencies such as the Federal Communications Commission and the Federal Trade Commission taking the lead. In 1969, industry critics Ralph Nader and Aileen Coward called on the FTC to verify claims made in various commercials and advertisements. The FTC complied, ordering advertisers to provide additional information and scrutinizing advertisements by considering the intent, as well as the literal truthfulness, of a number of ads.

Congress also imposed new regulations on cigarette advertising. Following the *Surgeon General Report of 1964*, Congress mandated the placing of warning labels on cigarettes in 1965. Two years later, an FCC ruling applied the fairness doctrine to cigarette advertising by requiring television stations to donate airtime for anti-smoking messages to counter advertisements paid for by cigarette makers. In 1970, Congress ordered a complete ban on all cigarette advertising on television. None of these efforts, however, had the effect intended by smoking foes—cigarette makers shifted their ad spending to print media, and sales of their products continued to grow.

In the face of government action, the industry responded once again with self-regulation. The National Association of Broadcasters banned ads featuring actors dressed up as doctors to promote products, a practice with roots in the patent-medicine print advertisements of the mid-nineteenth century. Meanwhile, advertising groups allied with the Better Business Bureau to form the National Advertising Review Board (NARB) in 1971. This body commanded the attention of advertisers, hearing nearly 1,900 cases in 10 years and forcing the revision or discontinuation of campaigns in 42 percent of the cases. By this time, government action dwarfed any amount of self-regulation, with an estimated 20 different federal agencies exercising oversight of advertising.

A tight economy in the 1970s challenged advertisers to demonstrate more measurable results from advertising expenditures, prompting a return to the hard-sell, reason-why style. These economic pressures continued as a wave of mergers altered the competitive landscape into the 1980s. The merger mania among the top agencies brought renewed emphasis on creativity as a host of boutique agencies developed some truly memorable ad campaigns. The king of the upstart creative agencies was Chiat/Day. The agency's greatest success involved the famed "1984" commercial for computer-maker Apple, considered by many as one of the most important advertisements of all time. The ad was renowned for its juxtaposition of Apple's futuristic Mac computers against the bleak future envisioned in George Orwell's famous book *1984*, in which "Big Brother" (the government) used technology to watch individuals.

Beyond the creativity of Apple's "1984" commercial, which featured the filmmaking talents of acclaimed director Ridley Scott, the ad also marked an important watershed in the history of advertising because it aired only once—in 1984—during the third quarter of football's Super Bowl XIX that January. In subsequent years, advertisers aimed at grabbing the attention of otherwise passive viewers by broadcasting high-profile—and costly—commercials during the most-watched television event of the year. By the late 1990s, the excitement over Super Bowl advertising often generated more attention than the exploits of the players on the field.

The Emergence of New Media: Advertising and the Internet

Advertising flourishes when consumers become introduced to new products in new situations. Such was the case in the late 1990s when a host of Internet companies, the "dot-coms," created a series of flashy TV and print ads that variously shocked, amused, or amazed the viewing audience. At the height of the Internet boom in January 2000, 17 of the 36 companies that advertised during the Super Bowl were Internet companies. At a cost of $2.2 million for a 30-second advertisement, many of these new ventures reveled in seemingly wasteful ad spending. An ad by Internet brokerage firm e*trade featured a trained monkey dancing on top of a garbage can and concluded with the open-ended question, "We just wasted $2 million dollars. What are you doing with your money?" Some advertisers use pop-up ads to grab the attention of Internet users, but most often the pop-up ad is considered annoying. Banner ads (ads placed at the top of Web sites) are somewhat less annoying. Another technique is the use of cookies, which let computers track who visits a particular site; this information is then utilized for similar sites based on tracking behaviors.

Such self-deprecating humor involved more than simply tongue-in-cheek satire. The high cost of television advertising paradoxically appealed to the fledgling dot-coms because these companies sought respectability through ad spending. To devote hundreds of thousands, or millions, of dollars to an ad campaign sent a message to customers, competitors, and company personnel alike: "We've arrived. Take us seriously."

The ultimate demise of so many Internet firms, which collectively spent hundreds of millions of dollars on advertising in the space of three to four years, raised questions about the wisdom of spending for spending's sake. These questions emerged amid growing doubts about the effectiveness of television advertising. Average ad recall rates, in which consumers identified a company that advertised during a television program they just watched, fell by over 70 percent during the last 30 years of the twentieth century.

Advertisers responded by becoming more intrusive and more ubiquitous, by flooding media markets with brand messages of all types. The sheer volume of advertising on television alone rose dramatically during the 1980s and 1990s, with commercial breaks consuming between 20 and 30 percent of every programming hour, three to four times longer than in 1960.

The increasing din of advertising messages in the late twentieth century coincided with information overload, or what David Shenk (1997) called "data smog." In 1999, one industry observer likened the use of advertising to narcotics—in essence, consumers required greater and greater "doses" to overcome "immunity" to ad repetition. Another scholar analyzing advertising and consumer trends in the post–World War II years envisioned advertisers and consumers engaged in a technological war. At the beginning of the twenty-first century, consumers remained less inclined than ever before to spend their most precious resource—time—on advertising, and advertising agencies and their clients scrambled for new ways to get out their messages.

The vast majority of advertising spending throughout U.S. history has been directed at convincing people to take a particular action—namely, to spend money on a particular advertiser's product or service. Although political advertising encourages people to perform a noncommercial transaction such as voting, the history of political advertising shows some similarities to commercial advertising in that political advertising has remained subject to persistent scrutiny by consumers (voters) and to repeated attempts at regulation on the part of the government.

Political advertising has existed throughout American history. Richard S. Tedlow argued that image advertising dated at least to Andrew Jackson's presidential race in 1828 and was also a feature of the 1858 Senate campaign between Stephen "The Little Giant" Douglas and Abraham "The Rail Splitter" Lincoln. Stephen Fox wrote that advertising proved instrumental in the movement to draft Theodore Roosevelt in 1916, and he also pointed out that the use of advertising by Oliver Wendell Holmes and Woodrow Wilson in that same year prompted Congress to consider limitations on political advertising as early as 1917.

Efforts to restrict or regulate political advertising persisted throughout the twentieth century, with a host of reforms enacted in the years following the Nixon-era Watergate political scandal. The 1976 Supreme Court ruling in *Buckley v. Vallejo* found that some of these reforms violated the free speech provisions of the First Amendment, but proponents of restrictions on political advertising continued to offer legislative solutions because of ever-increasing amounts of money being spent on political campaigns. Candidates spent an estimated $3 billion on political advertising in 2000, approximately 1.2 percent of all advertisement spending in that year.

Partly out of concern that negative advertising on television had contributed to a deepening cynicism among the electorate, Congress passed the Bipartisan Campaign Reform Act (McCain-Feingold Act) of 2002. Although the law's supporters sought to limit the influence of money in politics, the act included no restrictions on print advertising. Instead, the law focused on "issue advertising" on television, prohibiting such messages within 60 days of a general election or within 30 days of a primary election.

After passage of the act, the Supreme Court ruled on several cases challenging the constitutionality of all or part of the law. In December 2003, the Supreme Court upheld most of the Bipartisan Campaign Reform Act of 2002 in its ruling in *McConnell v. Federal Election Commission*. Following the Court's ruling, a sharp increase occurred in the number of "527 organizations," called such because they claim tax-exemption as a political organization under Section 527 of the Internal Revenue Code but not as "political committees" as defined in the Federal Election Campaign Act, which uses a different definition. In May 2004, the Federal Election Commission voted to not change its rules in regards to 527 organizations but did require that at least half of the funds they used for advertising in support of a particular candidate be "hard money" and required them to register with the Federal Election Commission as "political committees" and abide by the contribution limits set by the Bipartisan Campaign Reform Act of 2002. In June 2007, the Supreme Court rendered its decision in *Federal Election Commission v. Wisconsin Right to Life, Inc.*, ruling that the Bipartisan Campaign Reform Act's limit on corporations or unions funding of issue ads within 60 days of a general election and 30 days prior to a primary election was unconstitutional since such ads only appealed to voters to support a particular candidate. In 2008, the Supreme Court handed down its ruling in *Davis v. Federal Election Commission*, in which the "millionaires amendment" of the campaign reform act, which included a provision increasing the limit of contributions for a candidate running against another candidate who used more than $350,000 of his or her own personal wealth to pay for campaign costs in order to equalize the economic effect that would create. Finally, on January 21, 2010, the Supreme Court ruled in the case of *Citizens United v. Federal Election Commission*, which involved a ban of the airing of "Hillary, the Movie" during the presidential primaries leading up to the election of 2008 on the grounds that the company producing the movie violated the Bipartisan Campaign Reform Act by expressing opinions about candidate Hillary Clinton. The Supreme Court declared that the government may not ban political spending by corporations during candidate elections since it violates the First Amendment rights of corporations, which the court recognized as a "person" just as much as an individual.

While politicians continue using televised political campaign ads still, during the presidential primaries and general election of 2008, Democrat candidate Barack Obama's campaign capitalized on the escalating advertising potential of the Internet. In 2009, around 73 percent of American adults were online and social network sites have more and more adults in their 30s and older logging on to them regularly; more than half of the users on Facebook are over the age of 35. Correspondingly, ad spending and revenues generated have skyrocketed over the past several years with estimated advertisement spending on social networks worldwide being $2.2 billion and in the United States estimated at $1.3 billion for 2010. That figure represents a 71 percent increase from the 2009 U.S. social network ad expenditure level. Facebook, one of the largest social networks, offers several forms of advertisement options including engagement, display, search, and self-serve ads, the latter of which is utilized primarily by small and local businesses. Revenues generated are projected at $1 billion in 2010, up from $550 million in 2009. Estimates for ad spending on Facebook for 2009 amount to $435 million, with a 39 percent increase up to $605 million projected for 2010.

Internet video ads are also on the rise. The number one ranked video Internet site, YouTube, has over 345 million monthly visitors worldwide, with 80 million monthly visitors from the United States. In 2008, YouTube sold ads against 3 percent of its video views and 9 percent in 2009, a 6 percent increase in one year. It is estimated that YouTube's ad revenue for 2009 ranges between $120 million and $500 million. Advertising cost for video ads average $4 per 1,000 views. Although video ads only account for 4.6 percent of the total Internet revenue, that equates to $587 million compared to search-related revenue of $10.7 billion and display ad revenue of $4.6 billion in 2009. According to a recent Television Bureau of Advertising Internet and Revenue report, total video ad revenue, estimated at $699 million for 2009, is projected to reach $1 billion in 2010. The cost for an average CPM (cost per thousand views) is $42 for video ads, compared to $15 for display ads. Comparing video ads to television ads, in terms of advertising dollars per hour per user to cost per hour per viewer, video ads generate 17 cents to television's 13 cents of revenue generated.

Conclusion

Advertising of all types, including ads encouraging people to "buy" or "spend" as well as ads asking people to "vote for" or "support," has changed over the course of

U.S. history, but several trends have remained clear. First, the history of advertising in the United States demonstrates the evolution in the uses of advertising—from informing the customer of the range of new products and services available to them, to an effort to differentiate similar products and services within the marketplace—and also shows how advertising styles have changed over time in service of these different ends. These stylistic changes often coincided with technological innovations, especially the introduction of new media or changes to existing media in which advertising appeared.

Another recurrent theme throughout the history of U.S. advertising concerns its economic and social effects. Advertising does have some effects on popular culture, but its effects are ambiguous and occasionally contradictory. Given that advertising is only one of many factors contributing to the success or failure of a given product, and given that advertising can rarely be shown to have a direct effect on sales, it is not clear—as the critics of advertising have repeatedly claimed—that advertising causes consumers to buy things they do not want or need. Likewise, the extent to which advertising has or has not contributed to the rise of a consumer culture on a grand scale is difficult to establish.

Finally, the history of advertising reveals the persistent role played by political institutions. Government regulations inflicted a persistent, if frequently ineffectual, influence on advertising, particularly in the twentieth century. Those working within the industry often complained of the harmful effects of such efforts, but the federal government, with total ad spending in excess of $1.2 billion in 2000 (placing it number 18 on a list of the top 100 advertisers), pumped billions of dollars into the advertising business in the latter half of the twentieth century. In the future, advertisers and consumers alike should expect to see contradictory trends of the government spending money on advertising while simultaneously placing restrictions on advertising.

References

Applegate, Edd. *Personalities and Products: A Historical Perspective on Advertising in America*. Westport, CT: Greenwood Press, 1998.

Baker, C. Edwin. *Advertising and a Democratic Press*. Princeton, NJ: Princeton University Press, 1994.

Buckley v. Valeo, 424 U.S. 1 (1976).

Citizens United v. Federal Election Commission, 558 U.S. – 2010).

Davis v. Federal Election Commission, No. 7-320 (June 26, 2008).

eMarketer. "Newspapers Join in Twitter Conversation." Available: http://www.emarketer.com/Article.aspx?R=1007442; accessed December 28, 2009.

Federal Election Commission v. Wisconsin Right to Life, Inc., 551 U.S. 449 (2007).

Fox, Stephen. *The Mirror Makers: A History of American Advertising and Its Creators*. Chicago: University of Illinois Press, 1997.

Hower, Ralph M. *The History of an Advertising Agency: N. W. Ayer and Son at Work, 1869–1949*. Cambridge, MA: Harvard University Press, 1949.

Laird, Pamela Walker. *Advertising Progress: American Business and the Rise of Consumer Marketing*. Baltimore, MD: Johns Hopkins University Press, 1998.

McConnell v. Federal Election Commission 540 U.S. 93 (2003).

Rotzoll, Kim B., and James E. Haefner, with Steven R. Hall. *Advertising in Contemporary Society: Perspectives toward Understanding*. 3rd ed. Chicago: University of Illinois Press, 1996.

Sacharin, Ken. *Attention: How to Interrupt, Yell, Whisper, and Touch Consumers*. New York: John Wiley and Sons, 2001.

Samuel, Lawrence R. *Brought to You By: Postwar Television Advertising and the American Dream*. Austin: University of Texas Press, 2001.

Schudson, Michael. *Advertising, the Uneasy Persuasion: Its Dubious Impact on American Society*. New York: Basic Books, 1984.

Shenk, David. *Data Smog: Surviving the Information Glut*. San Francisco: Harper Edge, 1997.

Shiffman, Denise. "Obama's Rivals Should Steal From His Social Playbook: Web Strategy Forges Deep, Wide Connections," Advertising Act. Available: http://adage.com/campaigntrail/post?article_id=126336; accessed December 28, 2009.

Tedlow, Richard S. "Advertising and Public Relations." In Glenn Porter, ed., *Encyclopedia of American Economic History, Volume 2*. New York: Scribner's, 1980.

"Watching YouTube: News, Research, and Statistics about Online Video and the 'Tube." Available: http://www.strangelove.com/blog/2009/08/video-ad-spending-projected-699-million-2009/; accessed December 28, 2009.

Williamson, Debra Aho. "Social Network Advertising: Trends for 2010." *eMarketer*. Available: http://www.emarketer.com/blog/index.php/social-network-advertising-trends-2010/; accessed December 28, 2009.

Agricultural Policy

Karen A. J. Miller

Discussions of agricultural policy in the United States focus typically on price support systems established through the Department of Agriculture. These programs certainly deserve a position at the center of any analysis of agricultural policy, since they have fostered substantial budgetary outlays and large administrative bureaucracies. However, this focus can be somewhat misleading. The roots of federal agricultural policy extend back to the early days of the republic when priorities established in the nineteenth century set the course for modern agricultural development in America. Federal agricultural policy has embraced a broad range of regulation, with the acts designed to improve the quality of life for American farmers.

During the nineteenth century, federal efforts to promote agriculture concentrated on opening the frontier to agricultural development. The encouragement for American farmers to move westward provided them significant economic opportunities but also weakened the legitimacy of Indian claims to frontier land and deterred foreign nations from encroaching on American territory.

Complicating the agricultural development of the frontier was a fundamental philosophical debate over the true nature of American farming. Proponents of agricultural development included those who, on the one hand, adopted the cultural rhetoric of the individualistic yeoman farmer and those who, on the other hand, lauded plantations based on slave labor. The absence of a single set of cultural values made western development a contentious political issue in the antebellum period, but it did not halt the transformation of frontier land into farms. Rather, the debate led to unsystematic development, with the influx of settlers into the frontier punctuated by delays triggered by policy debates.

Frontier development had very different implications for the economic health of the various states. Splits emerged between older and newer states over the speed of agricultural expansion into the frontier, with older states fearing the loss of workers to the frontier as well as the eventual rise of agricultural competition from more fertile regions in the west. Volatile divisions arose over the issue of extending slavery into the territories. By the eve of the Civil War, contentious debate controlled the formation of agricultural policy.

Despite these sporadic political barriers to agricultural development, technological breakthroughs steadily pushed Americans westward. By the 1840s, farmers and educators, particularly in the northern states, became very interested in German scientific agriculture, with its emphasis on soil chemistry and hybridization studies. These advocates of scientific methodology sought to reform American education to include agricultural science in the curriculum of existing colleges. This movement for academic reform had important policy implications, as reformers began to lobby for the creation of new public colleges dedicated to the scientific study of agriculture. Although the national government did not enact legislative changes in higher education before the Civil War, it did charge the U.S. Commissioner of Patents with the responsibility of gathering, compiling, and distributing information concerning agricultural technology.

Advances in transportation technology also served to propel federal agricultural policy. The establishment of railroads enabled the development of land not served by navigable rivers. This improved access to bulk transportation encouraged the expansion of market networks and facilitated the creation of urban processing centers, such as Cincinnati, Ohio, and Chicago, Illinois. As the role of railroads in interstate commerce became clear in the 1850s, members of Congress began to use railroad development in the federal territories as a means to direct agricultural expansion. The most important tool in this effort—the transfer of federal land to the railroad companies—spearheaded expansion into the frontier. Before the Civil War, the federal government had authorized railroad land grants in 11 western states and territories. This aid to railroad companies prompted the development of over 6 million acres in slave-worked areas and nearly 16 million acres in free soil areas.

The federal government's commitment to agricultural development in the west was most clearly demonstrated by the transfer of federal lands to individuals. Federal land remained one of the most valuable assets of the national government in its first 100 years. Proceeds from the sale of public lands consistently provided a major portion of annual national revenue. Nonetheless, from the time of the Louisiana Purchase (1803), the federal government steadily changed its land-sale rules to make public land more affordable to its citizens. This policy brought about a consistent pattern of reducing the per-acre price of land for sale. It also included the more subtle process of reducing the size of parcels, undercutting land speculators (the only ones able to afford such large parcels) who could profit from subdividing and reselling land on the frontier.

The Civil War provided the Union Congress with an opportunity to define the ideological goals for the agricultural development of the frontier. Suddenly able to build a policy coalition around antislavery, Congress constructed a complex agricultural development policy that reflected the ideals of Northern politicians, particularly those from the newer western states. Congress passed the Morrill Act, which provided for the creation of land-grant colleges dedicated to the study of agriculture. It authorized the first transcontinental railroad, not only providing for economic development of the central Great Plains but also setting a precedent for the expansion of a massive railroad network throughout the undeveloped west. The policy substantially liberalized the transfer of public lands to individuals through the Homestead Act, which permitted families to take title to up to 160 acres of federal land without payment after five years of occupancy and improvements. Recognizing that agriculture was being propelled into a more active political and economic role, Congress created the Department of Agriculture as a means of facilitating the expansion of scientific farming. Congress designed these policy initiatives to promote an agricultural system dominated by prosperous family-owned farms integrated into a national market system.

Throughout the late nineteenth century, agricultural policy remained dominated by these principles set by the Union government during the Civil War. The policy proved sufficient to facilitate the development of federal land by individual family farms while encouraging the dissemination of information regarding scientific farming, and it also reinforced a larger economic transition occurring after the Civil War.

Post–Civil War

As large numbers of farmers began to populate the areas west of the Mississippi River after the Civil War, patterns of land ownership underwent a shift that continued well into the twentieth century. In the mid-nineteenth century, agriculture in the west included substantial numbers of very large properties, worked by hired labor or tenants in the North and slaves in the South. During the Gilded Age—a term coined by Mark Twain to denote the outward appearance of wealth and commonly applied to the period from the 1870s to the 1890s—the number of farms increased and the average size of these farms decreased. Policies regarding western land development, combined with economic forces, led first to a period when tenant farmers and homesteaders dominated agriculture, then later to an evolution into an agricultural culture dominated by family-owned farms in the early twentieth century. The Deep South, where sharecropping continued to dominate rural society until the 1930s, remained the only region not affected by this transition.

The pre–Civil War policy to promote a national railroad network expanded tremendously during the Gilded Age, with the number of miles of track nearly tripling between 1870 and 1890. The expansion of the rail system created a national market and fostered the emergence of regional specialization in agricultural production. The Cotton Belt, stretching from eastern Texas to the South Carolina shore, existed since the antebellum period, and single-crop production continued to be the rule in the region. This pattern of regional specialization expanded in the Gilded Age: Examples were the Corn Belt that emerged in the Midwest between Iowa and Indiana and the Wheat Belt that came to dominate a north-south axis from North Dakota to Kansas. Regional specialization provided a more efficient means of producing these key commodities but also made farmers reliant on shipping contractors and agricultural processors. When agricultural prices began to fall as a result of increased mechanization and improved planting techniques, farmers focused their anger on the middlemen who offered unsatisfactory prices for crops.

As the agricultural economy became more sophisticated, so did the political organization of farming interests. In the closing years of the Gilded Age, farmers in the Midwest became skilled in the formation of organizations dedicated to lobbying for railroad regulation and antimonopoly legislation. This pressure did help in the creation of the Interstate Commerce Commission and the passage of the Sherman Anti-Trust Act. Although these nineteenth-century efforts proved ineffective in producing a strong federal regulatory effort, they at least created a framework for changes in federal regulatory policy in the twentieth century.

The growing urbanization in the United States created a natural market for increasing agricultural production. Urban consumers drove the demand for mass-processed flour and meat and created regional markets for perishable fruits and vegetables. As a result, prices for farm goods rose by 89 percent in the first decade of the twentieth century.

Farmers became vocal advocates of paved roads needed to connect them to local markets and major transportation networks. These roads not only helped the farmers move commodities to market but also helped increasing numbers of farm children attend high schools in nearby towns. The federal government responded to this interest in education through the Smith-Lever Act, which authorized the U.S. Department of Agriculture (USDA) to initiate education programs in scientific farming and home-making, and the Smith-Hughes Act, which funded vocational agriculture programs in high schools. The cumulative impact of these forces led farm families to embrace modern life and adopt urban consumer standards.

World War I

High demand for American agricultural production received a further stimulus after the outbreak of World War I, as growing European purchases matched U.S. domestic consumption. To meet the increasing demand, the government encouraged expansion of agricultural output. During the war, American farmers put more fallow land into production, took on more debt to purchase agricultural machinery, and broke records for production levels of beef, pork, wheat, and corn. In addition, farmers paid higher taxes as the assessed value of farm property soared.

As long as European demand held, the high price of agricultural products enabled farmers to prosper despite new levels of debt and taxes. However, after the 1918 armistice, the European Allies could no longer justify large-scale agricultural imports that skewed their national trade balances. By spring 1921, prices for wheat, corn, beef, and pork all plummeted by nearly one-half.

The economic impact of collapsing farm prices severely affected farmers, who began to default on equipment loans, tax payments, and mortgages. For the previous 20 years, farmers earned incomes comparable to those of urban blue-collar workers; that pattern was now suddenly broken, with no apparent prospects for resolution. Farm communities quickly mobilized to pressure state and federal governments for relief. In 1921, a group of congressmen from the Midwest and South formed the Agricultural Bloc, the first bipartisan congressional bloc to operate openly as a special interest group. Members of the Agricultural Bloc sought pragmatic legislative change to restore the earning power of the American farmer.

Enacting a legislative solution to the farm crisis proved complex in the 1920s. Even within the Agricultural Bloc, no clear consensus existed for constructing a response to the farm problem. If the farm crisis proved simply a manifestation of the European postwar economic crisis, then Congress could restore farm incomes by authorizing the War Finance Corporation to facilitate the sale of grains and meat in Europe and by engaging in efforts to rebuild the European economy. Alternatively, if the farm crisis resulted from overspecialization and an inability to adjust to changes in consumer demand, then Congress could provide farmers with loans for diversification, and farm cooperatives could develop more sophisticated techniques for marketing and advertising. One group argued that the farm crisis did not occur because of a mismatch between production and market demand but because of the unfair actions of foreign governments that subsidized their own farmers and refused to compete in a free market arena with American agriculture. The solution to this threat included initiating American protectionist measures designed to bar foreign competition from the U.S. domestic market.

These three perspectives all provoked legislation in the 1920s. More important, they formed the foundation of all subsequent debates over farm policy. Federal agricultural policy became grounded in the presumption that farm problems remained essentially market problems and that the federal government was responsible for rectifying them.

Congress took substantial action in responding to the farm crisis of the 1920s. Both the Departments of Commerce and Agriculture became aggressive promoters of farm exports. Legislators couched much of the rationale for the refinancing of Allied war debt and extension of credit to Germany in terms of restoring markets for American agriculture. The Capper-Volstead Act (1920) strengthened American agricultural marketing cooperatives by exempting them from antitrust prosecution for price fixing. The 1922 Fordney-McCumber Tariff Act (and later the 1930 Hawley-Smoot Tariff Act) set barriers against agricultural competition. These efforts at federal assistance proved most effective in emerging sectors of the agricultural market: Tobacco for cigarettes, milk for ice cream, and oranges for the breakfast table all experienced improvement in the 1920s. Federal intervention remained remarkably unsuccessful in the more established sectors such as wheat, beef, and cotton.

As low prices continued to weaken key sectors, proponents of farm relief began to support a plan proposed by two former members of the War Production Board—George Peek, an adviser on agricultural imports, and Hugh Johnson, head of the National Recovery Administration in 1933. Peek and Johnson argued that the American economy remained healthy only when farmers' income achieved parity with that of factory workers and that the government must intervene to restore the economic status of the American farmer. To accomplish this, the government needed to establish an agency responsible for defining key agricultural products and then set a price for those products so farmers could earn a parity income. Farmers could sell their crops to the federal government, which would then release them into the domestic market at a sufficiently slow rate to maintain the parity income price. The federal government could sell anticipated surpluses on the world market at a loss to prevent excessive stockpiling.

Senator Charles McNary (R–OR) and Representative Gilbert Haugen (R–IA) promoted the Peek-Johnson plan. Congress voted against the first McNary-Haugen bill in 1924, but the two congressmen continued to build support for the idea. In both

1927 and 1928, Congress passed the McNary-Haugen bill, but President Calvin Coolidge vetoed it.

The farm policy debates reached a stalemate by the end of the 1920s. When the Great Depression began to stagnate the economy as a whole, the collapse of farm prices continued. By the 1933 inauguration of Franklin Roosevelt, the farm crisis became so critical that Roosevelt identified it as one of the primary targets for reform in his noted "100 Days," a group of sweeping reform measures planned for immediate implementation that addressed the banking crisis and attempted to put the unemployed to work on government projects such as the Civilian Conservation Corps and the Civil Works Administration.

The plan adopted by the Roosevelt administration borrowed heavily from the ideas promoted by Peek and Johnson a decade earlier. The Agricultural Adjustment Act (AAA), which authorized the secretary of agriculture to set minimum prices for key agricultural products and reduce overproduction, became the cornerstone of New Deal agricultural policy. Like the earlier McNary-Haugen proposed legislation, the AAA sought to restore the earning power of American farmers to pre–World War I levels. However, the AAA departed from earlier notions by placing heavy emphasis on the federal government's authority to limit annual production of key commodities. Although the government might tolerate temporary disparities between domestic and world prices for crops, it would not dump surplus U.S. production on the world market.

Although the primary goal of New Deal agriculture policy remained the commitment to prevent overproduction, the means of attaining that goal did change over time. The Supreme Court declared the first AAA unconstitutional because of its payment system. This prompted the government to adopt a policy of "nonrecourse loans." The USDA would set target prices for key commodities and loan money to participating farmers based on a formula using past production levels, land held out of production that year, and the target price. If the market price exceeded the target price, farmers could simply repay the loan. If it did not, the farmer would give his crops to the government to repay the loan in full and owe nothing more. The government would store these crops used as payment for the nonrecourse loans to sell later after prices rebounded. This system unrealistically assumed that surplus goods could be stored for months, thus limiting the Agriculture Department's ability to support farmers who specialized in highly perishable crops.

By the end of the New Deal, Congress fixed certain principles in federal policy toward agriculture. The government adopted a permanent role in the regulation of prices for key agricultural products as a means of protecting farm income. This role as a market regulator included the power to limit production of farm goods to prevent oversupply, provide crop insurance to farmers to offset natural catastrophes, and store grain in reserve in the event of unanticipated demand.

In addition to these foundation principles concerning the regulation of oversupply, other New Deal legislation included important provisions for farmers. The larger purpose of the Tennessee Valley Authority (TVA) focused on stabilizing the economy of the Tennessee River Valley, one of the poorest rural regions in the United States. Dams constructed by the TVA improved navigation and controlled flooding on the river. These dams generated hydroelectric power that the TVA then sold to the general public, providing inexpensive electricity to rural areas and enabling farmers to make use of electricity-based technology such as refrigeration and water pumping systems. In addition, the TVA sponsored experimentation in the scientific use of fertilizers, crop rotation, and adoption of hybrid strains of plant crops.

New Deal legislation also improved the quality of life for farmers. In 1936, Congress created the Rural Electrification Authority (REA), an agency designed to enable rural communities to form cooperatives for the management of electricity generation and distribution. The REA permitted rural areas to initiate electrification programs and provide low-cost electricity to regions left undeveloped by commercial power companies. Congress also created the Farm Security Administration to assist farmers to move out of poverty by helping them to adopt more modern farm practices.

The cumulative legacy of the New Deal programs remains enormous. The federal government recognized the necessity of maintaining the opportunity for rural prosperity. Farmers should have incomes similar to those of urban workers; they should have access to the advantages of modern technology; they should embrace the same consumer values held by those who lived in cities and suburbs. However, this commitment to the prosperity of rural America contained important conundrums. To balance supply and demand for farm products, farmers needed to reduce the acreage in production to prevent oversupply. To maximize the income of individual rural families, farmers needed to embrace scientific farming, thus maximizing productivity per acre. Farmers with the capital and the will to modernize along the lines of the New Deal prospered. At the same time, the New Deal policies drove sharecroppers from marginal land in the South into an already large pool of unskilled, unemployed workers. Those farmers who could not or would not embrace technology failed.

The New Deal's objectives of making farms more efficient facilitated the U.S. government's response to the outbreak of war in Europe in 1939. Under the Agricultural Adjustment Act, the U.S. government provided subsidies to farmers who agreed to not plant some of their acreage or to prevent the reproduction of their livestock. This program remained in effect until 1941, when the United States implemented the Lend-Lease program. Although much of the focus of the Lend-Lease program transferred manufactured goods to Great Britain and other U.S. Allies, agricultural production proved an important aspect of Lend-Lease support. The Department of Agriculture raised the basic price supports for key commodities to increase supplies of those goods requested by the Allies. To further stimulate production, the government created a second classification of price supports for those agricultural products destined for the export market. Through these methods, the federal government accommodated the increased demand triggered by the war. Congress, very carefully, reserved the right to draw down production to prevent an oversupply of farm goods in the postwar economy.

World War II Farm Security Administration poster from 1942. (Library of Congress.)

Agricultural surpluses emerged as the most intractable problem of farm policy in the post–World War II period. The general prosperity of the postwar U.S. economy facilitated the widespread adoption of technology in every aspect of farming. Yields improved enormously, with per-acre production of wheat doubling between 1945 and 1985, and some crops experiencing as much as a fourfold increase in productivity.

After World War II, agricultural policy became increasingly dependent on export markets. In 1947, the United States became a participant in the General Agreement on Tariffs and Trade (GATT), an agreement among 25 nations designed to lower barriers on imported goods. Efficiency of farm production placed U.S. agriculture in a particularly strong position within the GATT system; American farmers could easily compete against foreign producers in a more liberalized trade system. Postwar reconstruction programs, which provided funds or credit for the purchase of American food, also promoted the export of agricultural goods.

In 1954, the federal government adopted a long-term policy of linking the practice of using agricultural exports to absorb overproduction with improving American political stature in developing countries. Under the Agricultural Trade Development and Assistance Act (ATDAA, Public Law 480), Congress could designate surplus American agricultural products for emergency food relief to friendly nations. To further facilitate foreign purchases of American agricultural goods, trade provisions permitted the use of foreign currencies in lieu of American dollars or gold. The ATDAA served as a bulwark of both U.S. foreign policy toward less developed regions and U.S. domestic policy toward continued stabilization of farm income.

Even with U.S. commitment to a strong export policy, the problem of agricultural overproduction continued. In an effort to curb the amount of acreage in production, the Eisenhower administration called for passage of the Soil Bank Program in 1956. The program permitted farmers and ranchers to reserve land specifically for conservation purposes, the first use of environmental policy as a tool to curb overproduction.

Improvements in farm efficiency during the postwar period placed important constraints on agricultural policy, but they also contained important political implications. As farms became more efficient, the number of farmers declined; only 8.7 percent of Americans lived on farms in 1960, compared with 23.2 percent in 1940. As the number of farmers declined, it became increasingly difficult to justify price support policies for such a small segment of the population.

In an effort to build a larger political constituency in the 1960s, politicians from rural districts began searching for political alliances with other segments of the population. The most successful of these initiatives linked farm price support legislation with efforts to improve nutritional standards for the urban poor.

In the period after the New Deal, Congress based farm policy on the objectives of guaranteeing the prosperity of American farming by curbing overproduction of agricultural goods. In the 1960s, Congress added another objective—to reduce food prices enough so that all Americans could eat nutritionally sound diets. By creating programs such as food stamps and expanding the school lunch program, the USDA broaden the domestic market for food production. This improved the health of the poor, provided the government with another tool for curbing overproduction, and strengthened public support for agricultural price support systems.

At the time of its creation in 1964, the Department of Agriculture, not the Department of Health, Education, and Welfare, administered the food stamp program. This followed the 1939 precedent in which Congress placed the school lunch program under USDA authority, and also demonstrated the power held by members of Congress from rural constituencies and their desire to form political alliances in urban America. However, the strategy to expand the constituency of the USDA served to divert attention from guaranteeing the prosperity of farmers. By 1974, USDA expenditures to improve nutrition surpassed the amount of money spent on farm subsidies and agricultural research combined.

The idea of a farmer-consumer coalition proved problematic in the 1970s. Throughout the 1960s, members of Congress, representing farm constituencies, faced demands to limit subsidies. This pressure intensified in the 1970s as several successful policy initiatives produced unanticipated consequences. The USDA's efforts to encourage agricultural exports, combined with the Nixon administration's desire to strengthen its détente policy of establishing friendlier relations with the USSR, culminated in the important 1972 grain agreement with the Soviet Union. The sudden export of $750 million worth of American grain substantially reduced reserve grain stocks, driving up domestic food prices. This pattern continued for the rest of the decade, with large foreign sales causing higher costs for American consumers. This inflation of food prices occurred simultaneously with the inflationary pressures generated by the 1973 oil embargo implemented by the Organization of Petroleum Exporting Countries (OPEC, a group of foreign nations, many in the Middle East, created for the purpose of controlling world oil production). This combination of events provoked substantial consumer hostility toward the American farmer, who continued to reap high prices in foreign markets while foreign producers restricted the importation of foreign oil.

The Agriculture and Consumer Protection Act of 1973 marked a substantial retrenchment of farmer interests. As general inflationary pressures increased at the beginning of the decade, Americans pressed politicians to reduce both government expenditures and taxes. Even within the USDA, defenders of price supports faced substantial competition from the food stamp program, which expanded steadily throughout the decade. These pressures forced changes in the new price supports system created by the 1973 legislation. Under the new system, the government established a target price, and participants in the program received compensation only when the domestic market price fell below the target price. This "deficiency payment system" became effective only in years when world market demand proved too weak to drive up domestic prices. Although nonrecourse loans continued, the price guarantees remained so low that they constituted a departure from the New Deal objective of encouraging rural prosperity.

The pattern of high prices for grain and meat continued until 1980 when the Carter administration placed an embargo on grain sales to the Soviet Union as a response to the USSR's invasion of Afghanistan. Two other factors, combined with this sudden loss of foreign sales, further complicated farm policies until the late 1980s. The long-term impact of the OPEC oil embargo weakened the ability of developing nations to purchase food from the United States. In addition, the European Economic Community (EEC, which became the European Union in 1993) made a dual commitment to subsidize European agricultural production and to encourage the exportation of food, and these policies provided the American farmer with substantial competition.

As farm prices fell in the 1980s, the agricultural sector faced significant economic burdens. During the prosperous 1970s, farmers borrowed extensively to purchase new equipment. Farmers experienced the rising costs for interest payments along with the rapid appreciation of land values coupled with inflationary mortgage rates. As long as inflation remained a force in the economy, this debt burden was manageable for most farmers. However, when the Federal Reserve Bank decided to limit inflation forcefully in the 1980s, by initiating inflation-control fiscal policies, farmers found themselves trapped between declining income and high overhead costs.

In this economic climate, the Reagan administration possessed only a limited ability to make major changes to agricultural price support policy. Both the Agriculture and Food Act of 1981 and the Food Security Act of 1985 continued the basic pattern of farm legislation set in 1973. The deficiency payment system continued, farmers received inducements to reserve ecologically fragile land, and Congress maintained nonrecourse loan provisions. The 1985 farm legislation, however, did include an important policy departure with its strong commitment to spur agricultural exports. The Export Enhancement Program, which provided bonuses to exporters who sought inroads in specified foreign markets, became the hallmark of this new direction. Congress designed this program primarily to open the EEC to agricultural exports, thus challenging the main U.S. competitor in the EEC's home markets. In addition, the United States began aggressively using the GATT to create a more favorable environment for American agricultural exports.

For most involved parties, agricultural policy of the 1970s and 1980s proved unsatisfactory in its construction and implementation. As other sectors of the federal budget experienced substantial cuts, farm price subsidies remained high and served as a force in driving up budget deficits. Politicians committed to fiscal conservatism pushed for agricultural reform to force farmers into a free market system. This effort, facilitated by budget reconciliation legislation, reduced the influence of the congressional agriculture committees.

During the late twentieth century, a market revolution occurred in American farming. International trade in agricultural goods transformed the landscape of farming and placed a premium on economies of scale and adoption of new technology. This provided a substantial advantage to corporate farming, which mustered greater capital resources than small family farms. To survive in this environment, some family farms were reconstructed into family corporations determined to possess a share of this highly competitive market. Others became subcontractors for larger corporations. The least successful survived by supplementing farm income with nonfarm employment.

In this context, conservative politicians began to call for abandonment of the New Deal objectives for agricultural policy and for adoption of the concept of "freedom-to-farm." Conservatives argued that the price supports system unintentionally bolstered overproduction by removing risk in the production of goods such as wheat, corn, and cotton. Unfettered market forces would encourage farmers to diversify in response to changing demand. The appeal of this argument proved widespread. It simultaneously evoked the nineteenth-century image of the farmer as resourceful individualist and the more modern characterization of the farmer as scientific planner.

As fiscal conservatives gained more strength in Congress during the 1990s, the concept of freedom-to-farm wielded greater influence in the construction of agricultural policy. Congress designed the Agricultural Improvement and Reform Act of 1996 to end the New Deal concept of government protection of key farm prices. Under the provisions of the act, the government no longer directly intervened to protect the five crops that dominated the deficiency payment system established in

1973—wheat, corn, soybeans, rice, and cotton. Congress limited supports substantially for other commodities as well.

The transformation of American agricultural policy proved more difficult than the advocates of freedom-to-farm supposed. When commodity prices slumped at the end of the 1990s, Congress demonstrated its willingness to protect farmers with emergency aid expenditures. There remains in American culture a strong sense of compassion for farmers, particularly those confronting an economic crisis. A thriving agricultural sector means the availability of inexpensive food for all Americans. Since 1996, congressional negotiations over agricultural policy continued to demonstrate an unwillingness to abandon the defense of American farmers' opportunity to prosper.

References

Browne, William P. *Private Interests, Public Policy, and American Agriculture*. Lawrence: University Press of Kansas, 1988.

Cochrane, Willard W., and C. Ford Runge. *Reforming Farm Policy: Toward a National Agenda*. Ames: Iowa State University Press, 1992.

Cochrane, Willard W., and Mary E. Ryan. *American Farm Policy, 1948–1973*. Minneapolis: University of Minnesota Press, 1976.

Fite, Gilbert C. *Cotton Fields No More: Southern Agriculture, 1865–1980*. Lexington: University Press of Kentucky, 1984.

Gates, Paul Wallace. *Agriculture and the Civil War*. New York: Alfred A. Knopf, 1965.

Hansen, John Mark. *Gaining Access: Congress and the Farm Lobby, 1919–1981*. Chicago: University of Chicago Press, 1991.

Holt, Marilyn Irvin. *Linoleum, Better Babies, and the Modern Farm Woman, 1890–1930*. Albuquerque: University of New Mexico Press, 1995.

Kulikoff, Allan. *The Agrarian Origins of American Capitalism*. Charlottesville: University Press of Virginia, 1992.

Neth, Mary C. *Preserving the Family Farm: Women, Community, and the Foundations of Agribusiness in the Midwest, 1900–1940*. Baltimore, MD: Johns Hopkins University Press, 1995.

Sanders, Elizabeth. *Roots of Reform: Farmers, Workers, and the American State, 1877–1917*. Chicago: University of Chicago Press, 1999.

Sheingate, Adam D. *The Rise of the Agricultural Welfare State: Institutions and Interest Group Power in the United States, France, and Japan*. Princeton, NJ: Princeton University Press, 2001.

Antitrust Legislation

Thibaut Kleiner

Antitrust legislation is a central tenet of U.S. economic policy and indeed a major force in U.S. economic history. For more than a century, it shaped the face of modern capitalism and promoted the idea that free markets and free competition are beneficial to society and even to democracy. At the same time, the framework and development of U.S. antitrust legislation was fraught with controversies, confrontations, and changes. Starting from a political objective to guarantee economic freedom, antitrust legislation evolved toward a legal and economic discipline, promoting consumer welfare and economic efficiency, and using sophisticated analytical tools to monitor economic behavior. Growing with U.S. economic expansion, it became an essential element of most governments' economic policy, and continues to contribute to spreading the model of liberal democracy and free markets to the world.

The Origins of Regulation

Antitrust legislation dates back to the Sherman Anti-Trust Act of 1890 (reproduced in the Documents section of this volume), a turning point in U.S. economic history because it signals the start of federal government intervention into the economy. It is important to understand the historical context of this legislation to realize how it was the product of the economic and political conditions of the 1880s.

This period was one of rapid economic and social transformation of the country. Population increased from 31.5 million inhabitants in 1860 to 76 million in 1900. An economic index created by Edwin Frickey, an economist, established a basis of 100 for 1899; with these calculations, the index was 16 for 1860, 31 for 1872, and 79 for 1892. In May 1869, the first transcontinental railroad was completed. This corresponded to the railroad mania: there were 28,900 railroad miles in 1860, 53,000 miles in 1870, 120,000 miles in 1882, and 165,000 miles in 1890. Before the Civil War, businesses were mostly networks of independent merchants, with only a limited number of employees and operated in a limited geographic area. After the war and the abolition of slavery, the economy underwent major structural change, becoming more industrial. New technologies, and notably railroads, brought about economies of scale in production, distribution, and marketing. Reduced transportation costs boosted interstate trade, which led to the growth of large, bureaucratic companies.

Antitrust legislation cartoon from 1902. (Library of Congress.)

Attendant to this growing economy and population, a new era emerged: the era of unbridled capitalism, with its billionaires such as Andrew Carnegie, the steel magnate, and John D. Rockefeller, founder of the Standard Oil Company. The dominant economic thinking of the time remained in the vein of Adam Smith's belief in the "invisible hand"—in the capacity of markets to self-organize in a way that also benefited society as a whole. Therefore, the success of large companies was seen as being consistent with a belief in individual self-determination, free enterprise, and limited state power and intervention.

However, competition from large industrial firms was often fatal for smaller businesses, and big business began to dominate most economic sectors. In most regions, railroads enjoyed a transportation monopoly and thus possessed the ability to charge high prices to the farmers and merchants who relied on the rail system to carry their goods. To enhance and protect their position, railroad firms sometimes engaged in political corruption. Americans often perceived large industrial firms as not only distorting economic life and destroying small business but also as corrupting political life. In addition, one effect of the new technologies was excess capacity: Because of their increased productivity, industrial plants were much larger than necessary to satisfy demand. This prompted some firms to seek ways to regulate their output in order to manage excess capacity, avoid price wars, and maintain their profit margins. But establishing cartels was not always easy, especially given the temptation for businessmen to gain market share instead of maintaining high prices. In 1882, Rockefeller created the Standard Oil trust, in which the shareholders of 40 U.S. oil companies exchanged their shares for shares of Standard Oil; nine trustees managed the entire group. Through the trust arrangement, therefore, competing companies were combined in restraint of trade by the transfer of controlling stock interest in them to the board of trustees for integrated, noncompetitive operations. Within a short period of time, sugar, seeds, oil, whiskey, and other industries were forming trusts. Many Americans began denouncing the trusts as the enemy of civil society and free enterprise, the press described Standard Oil as a menacing octopus with tentacles stretching across the country, and political unrest exacerbated the need for government intervention. Congress responded with the Sherman Anti-Trust Act of July 2, 1890, which it subsequently strengthened with the Clayton Anti-Trust Act and Federal Trade Commission Act in 1914, the Robinson-Patman Act of 1936, and revisions to the antimerger provisions of the Clayton Act in 1950 (Celler-Kefauver amendments).

The Sherman Anti-Trust Act

The exact political and economic objectives of Congress in passing the Sherman Anti-Trust Act remain the subject of much academic and legal analysis. In the U.S. Senate debate of 1890, a substantial amount of discussion focused on small producers and what constituted fair competition, but little was said about economics, with economic efficiency as an issue not in play. Some scholars argue that consumer welfare was the prime objective of the act. However, the 1880s was a period of unprecedented growth and increased efficiency, achieved through the promotion of new means of production and technologies. Moreover, prices declined during this period, even in the very industries where trusts operated: From 1880 to 1890, the price of refined petroleum fell by 61 percent, and sugar prices by 18 percent. For that reason, some observers claim the Sherman Anti-Trust Act was intended as a protection for small producers against big and more efficient firms. Others claim it was intended as a general protection against large firms with too much political power, which endangered the American ideal that free market and free entrepreneurship enabled individuals to develop their business, compete on their own merits, and flourish.

Furthermore, legal analysts note some parallels between the wording of the Sherman Anti-Trust Act and that of the common law then in place. Before the legislation, restraint of trade and monopoly was addressed by the common law in Great Britain and the United States. Under common law, invalid restraints of trade were those contracts, agreements, or combinations deemed unreasonable and therefore void and unenforceable at the bar; those that were reasonable remained valid and enforceable. A "reasonable restraint" accorded with "public policy" or with the "public interest" or "public welfare." On its face, the Sherman Anti-Trust Act superseded the common law in two respects: First, it made restraints of trade found to contravene public policy criminally illegal, as misdemeanors, punishable by the government; second, it rendered perpetrators of such restraints liable to private civil suits for treble damages. Therefore, the act was simultaneously in harmony with the common law yet revolutionary because it opened a new chapter of legal proceedings.

Section one of the Sherman Anti-Trust Act established that "every contract, combination in the form of trust or otherwise, or conspiracy, in restraint of trade or commerce among the several States, or with foreign nations" was illegal. "Every person who shall make any contract or engage in any combination or conspiracy hereby declared to be illegal shall be deemed guilty of a felony and, on conviction thereof, shall be punished by fine not exceeding $10,000,000 if a corporation, or, if any other person, $350,000, or by imprisonment not exceeding three years, or by both said punishments, in the discretion of the court." Section two of the act addressed monopolization, attempted monopolization, and conspiracies to monopolize. It stipulated that "every person who shall monopolize, or attempt to monopolize, or combine or conspire with any other person or persons, to monopolize any part of the trade or commerce among the several States, or with foreign nations, shall be deemed guilty of a felony," with the same punishments as listed in section one as a consequence.

From 1890 to 1911, the Early Years: The Rule-of-Reason Controversy

To many scholars, the wording of the Sherman Anti-Trust Act, and especially the parallels to wording in the common law, left unresolved some of the issues that surrounded its enactment in Congress. Thus, the courts were implicitly given the task of clarifying the precise scope of the articles and giving them some legal certainty. For instance, the act did not define "fair competition," debated by Senators John Kenna (D–WV) and Sherman Hoar (D–MA), in particular, before its passage. What was unfair competition? Was it an individual's aggressive pursuit of wealth through any means possible? Or was it also ruthless efficiency, which could drive competitors to extinction? Likewise, was the meaning of "monopoly" in section two so obvious that it needed no further explanation? Or was the meaning of "every" so all-encompassing that it meant literally *every* restraint of trade? As a result, and from a legal point of view, controversies ensued during the first years following passage of the Sherman Anti-Trust Act, with much of the debate focused on meaning of the wording and its implications for the legality of certain business transactions.

From a political point of view, the first years of implementation of the act were not particularly successful. The first Supreme Court decision interpreting it, *United States v. E. C. Knight Co.* (1895), which concerned a trust combination of producers, held that the trust affected only manufacturing and did not affect interstate commerce, thus the business structure could not be prohibited.

In fact, early applications of the Sherman Anti-Trust Act were used as a tool against labor unions, an ironic twist which strayed far from the ideological foundations of its original supporters. Between 1890 and 1897, 12 of the first 13 convictions under the act were against unions and the monopoly they exercised by using 100 percent of their members (in essence a monopoly) as striking workers to stop interstate trade. Consequently, Congress updated antitrust law in section 6 of the Clayton Act

(1914) and later in the Norris-LaGuardia Act (1932) to exempt most labor organizing from the antitrust laws. Furthermore, the Sherman Anti-Trust Act did not prevent big business from flourishing. In fact, a wave of mergers ensued: Entrepreneurs took the view that the act prohibited cartels and other restrictive agreements but not tighter acquisitions of assets or creation of holdings.

On the legal front, controversy surrounded interpretation of the Sherman Anti-Trust Act. Until the *Standard Oil Co. v. United States* case in 1911, U.S. Supreme Court opinions revealed some confusion about the relationship of section one of the act and the prohibition in common-law notions of "restraint of trade." The Literalists, as they were called, took the Sherman Anti-Trust Act at its word, prohibiting literally every contract in restraint of trade. Supreme Court Justice Rufus Peckham, for instance, embracing the Jeffersonian ideal of independent farmers and small businesses, saw motives of individual or corporate aggrandizement as against the public interest. Literalists, therefore, sought to prohibit not only price-fixing cartels but also partnership agreements and even simple contracts for the sale of goods—in short, contracts perfectly legal under the common law. In 1897, with its decision in *United States v. Trans-Missouri Freight Association et al.*, the Supreme Court declared illegal both reasonable and unreasonable restraints of trade. But other justices issued opinions based on the "rule of reason" (Rule of Reasonists), arguing that the Sherman Anti-Trust Act did not invalidate the continuance of old contracts by which former competitors united in the past. According to Justice Oliver Wendell Holmes, Congress did not intend to enact the vision of Herbert Spencer, an English philosopher who viewed everything in terms of Social Darwinism (according to which individuals and firms were the subject of natural selection through competition); on the contrary, the Sherman Anti-Trust Act was meant to prohibit the ferocious extreme of competition with others, to rein in the sinister power that firms or agreements exercised to keep rivals out of the business and to ruin those who already were in business. In addition, public criticism increased in the period between 1897 and 1911, coming from economists, capitalists, labor leaders, and President Theodore Roosevelt himself, who at some point suggested updating the law.

In *Standard Oil Co. v. United States* (1911) and *United States v. American Tobacco Company* (1911), the Supreme Court condemned the use of holding companies under both sections one and two of the Sherman Anti-Trust Act. It held that the statute must be read against its common-law background to forbid only "contracts or acts" having a "monopolistic tendency" and hence only unreasonable restraints of interstate or foreign commerce. The Court expressed the view that it would consider economic evidence to determine whether a restrictive agreement unduly hampered competition, which meant freely competitive markets, adequate supplies of quality goods, and services at reasonable prices. These cases introduced a new test of legality as to whether the restraint of trade merely regulated and thereby promoted competition or whether it could suppress or even destroy competition. But even as the "rule of reason" became the dominant framework for antitrust legislation, the Court also declared in subsequent rulings that certain forms of conduct were violations of the statute per se, because of their pernicious effect on competition and lack of any redeeming virtue, so that no economic evidence would be received as to the precise harm they caused or the business rationale for their use. The principal categories declared per se unlawful by the Supreme Court were agreements between competitors to fix prices, limit production, divide markets or customers, and boycott other businesses.

From 1914 to 1933: Consolidation and Hesitation

By 1914, it became clear that the Sherman Anti-Trust Act did not specify sufficiently what constituted unfair and unethical business practice, and many analysts started to believe that the rule of reason was greatly weakening the act. The new Wilson administration responded with the Clayton Anti-Trust Act and the Federal Trade Commission Act in 1914 (both reproduced in the Documents section of this volume). The Clayton Act listed four business practices deemed illegal if their effect "may be substantially to lessen competition or tend to create a monopoly." Section two of the Clayton Act outlawed price discrimination or the use of price differences not justified by cost differentials to lessen competition or create a monopoly. This section was intended to prevent firms from engaging in "predatory pricing" to exclude competitors or attempt to monopolize a market, which happened in railroads and certain retail chain stores. Section 3 of the act also forbade "tying" contracts and exclusive dealerships if a reasonable probability existed that these arrangements might substantially lessen competition in any line of business. (A *tying contract* is an agreement between seller and buyer that requires the buyer of one product or service to purchase some other product or service from the same producer. An *exclusive dealership* is an agreement between a manufacturer and its dealers that forbids the dealers from handling other manufacturers' products.) Section six of the act created an exemption for labor organizing.

Section seven of the Clayton Act was an important development, since it condemned mergers on a far more aggressive standard than applied under the Sherman Anti-Trust Act, thus filling a gap in the regulation. Section seven forbade a merger (the acquisition by a firm of a competitor's stock or physical assets) if the effect of the merger reduced competition substantially. Additional merger restrictions enacted in 1950 (Celler-Kefauver amendments) brought vertical mergers, the joining of two or more companies that perform different stages of the same production process, within the Clayton Act's reach. Finally, section 8 of the act prohibited interlocking directorates if they substantially reduced competition, even though this regulation was never enforced actively.

The Federal Trade Commission Act created the Federal Trade Commission (FTC), an administrative body authorized to initiate government action in the courts when it suspected unfair methods of competition. The legislation empowered the agency to investigate cases of industrial espionage, bribery for obtaining business secrets, and boycotts. The FTC was also granted the authority to attack practices it regarded as anticompetitive, even if they did not violate any existing antitrust law.

With this new regulatory package, antitrust was firmly established as a key component of government economic action.

In addition, the new provisions and the recognition of the rule of reason promoted the role of economists and of economic theory as instruments to determine whether business conduct was illegal or not. During the nineteenth century, both law and economics started to develop theories of competition and ideological defenses of competition as social goods, but it was some time before economic concepts became integrated with these theories. Competition was defined as the individual acting in self-interest in order to gain the most from others and to surrender the least. Anticompetitive conduct was a restraint on individual freedom, not mere interference with a relationship between prices and costs. This view changed with Alfred Marshall's *Principles of Economics* (1890). According to Marshall's theory, restraint was present and harmed competition on the market not when the agreement eliminated someone's freedom, but when it allowed the price to be higher than if the unhampered play of supply and demand remained in force; whereas restraint was not present when the agreement gave no one that power or even took it away from those who held it. In other words, apart from restraints being per se illegal, economic theory offered a tool for evaluating whether or not agreements were regarded as reasonable. Of course, economics was bound to play an increasing role in the history of antitrust legislation. However, in the aftermath of World War I, when antitrust regulation was suppressed to enable coordination of the war effort, it was not always so obvious to economists and politicians that competition and the free market were the best way to organize production.

The political consensus against cartels and similar business arrangements produced an economic rationale in the United States. The country enjoyed a huge domestic market, a fairly stable state, and a growing economy; with no real output problem, competition was the means to stimulate efficiency and innovation. But the situation was different in other parts of the world. After World War I, Europe lost a large number of workers, killed during the conflict, and experienced demographic stagnation. National markets were limited and, after 1921, the problems with the gold standard created wildly fluctuating currencies, making trade difficult. Because of the war, government assumed control over the economy. The 1920s was a decade when economic regulation on the international front gained support; government intervention and cartelization abroad were regarded as means to promote economic stability and avoid destructive competition. Indeed, U.S. policy toward international cartels was quite different from what prevailed in America, where advocacy was for competition. The 1918 Webb-Pomerene Act allowed American producers in the same line of business to form joint companies to manage their exports. This act, originally designed to facilitate a joint effort of American firms in export markets, became a useful instrument for the creation of international cartels, and American copper producers promptly used the law to function as such a cartel. The practice became even more common after the FTC expressed the view in a letter to the Silver Producers Committee, a trade association, that the only test of legality for cooperative agreements with a foreign corporation for the sole purpose of operation in a foreign market was that these arrangements must have no effect "upon domestic conditions within the United States." Producers took the FTC letter as a grant of permission to engage in cartels outside the United States. The 1920s and 1930s saw the rise of a number of cartels involving U.S. firms and German firms. For instance, after some mergers, DuPont and Allied Chemical in the United States, Imperial Chemical Industries (ICI) in Britain, and IG Farbenindustrie (IG Farben) in Germany became heavyweight firms in their respective countries and reached a number of cartel agreements among themselves in international markets. IG Farben was at the center of these chemical cartels, which were based on, alternatively, patent rights, market sharing, and price fixing. IG Farben also entered into agreements in the petrochemical field with Standard Oil of New Jersey, the world's largest oil company. Another famous international cartel involved General Electric in the field of electric lamps (the Phoebus cartel).

From 1933 to 1948: The First and Second New Deals, from Attempted Centralization to Antitrust Revival

The Great Depression and the country's unprecedented economic collapse threw millions out of work in the 1930s and propelled Franklin D. Roosevelt into the White House, with a radical platform of economic reform—the New Deal. The political climate of the time was one of great skepticism toward big business, which was accused of causing the economic failure and trying to gain political power at the expense of democracy. At the same time, economic theory, when used to analyze the crisis, suggested that price competition was inefficient and that the free market was failing; the forward path called for regulation, planning, and freedom from antitrust prosecution for joint ventures and cartels. In Europe, some countries began implementing such policies: in Italy, Spain, and Germany where fascism had taken over, and in the Soviet Union. Consequently, scholars portrayed the Roosevelt era as having two periods in terms of its antitrust policy. The first period involved an attempt to get rid of the antitrust provisions. Herbert Hoover, as secretary of commerce and then as president, indulged in the political economy of blessing associationalism (collective efforts within an industry). But Roosevelt went even further: The National Industrial Recovery Act (NIRA) of 1933 authorized industrial codes of ethics to organize American business and labor. The act attempted to bring together the various industry, trade, and interest groups—including trade unions—to suggest and seek government approval of "codes of fair competition," which virtually legalized various forms of collusion and suppressed what was called "destructive competition." Under the FTC, practices that violated the codes were punished. However, the NIRA instead led to general confusion and conflicting goals: some businesspeople believed that cooperation led to bureaucratic socialism, and some government officials feared it would result in fascism or economic oppression.

In 1935, the Supreme Court declared the NIRA unconstitutional in its decision in *Schechter Poultry v. United States*. This case marked the start of the second New Deal and a change in Roosevelt's attitude toward antitrust legislation. In 1936, Congress passed the Robinson-Patman Act, which amended section two of the Clayton Act to limit the ability of firms to charge lower prices to large customers than they did to smaller ones. In 1938, Thurman Arnold, newly appointed as head of the Department of Justice's (DOJ) antitrust division, began pursuing a vigorous antitrust policy. The DOJ increased its staff, filed a number of cases involving not only restrictive agreements but also vertical integration, cartels, and even tacit collusion between oligopolistic firms. The DOJ also used the Robinson-Patman Act to protect small business against more efficient and larger firms. This crackdown on big business was related to the general political climate of the pre–World War II period. In 1941, press reports exposed that U.S. companies were linked with German firms through a number of cartel and other types of agreements. The press claimed, for instance, that the royalties paid to German firms for Plexiglas were financing the Nazi war effort. Other agreements were vilified, such as the IG Farben and Standard Oil arrangement, which was castigated as the cause of a shortage of synthetic rubber so much needed in wartime.

On the political scene, some analysts equated Nazism with a dictatorship of monopoly capitalism. Fascism was called the necessary result of excessive power in the hands of big business, and antitrust law was then called for to protect economic democracy in the place of small businesses. The 1948 *U.S. v. Aluminum Company of America* (Alcoa) case illustrated this attitude. Alcoa was admittedly in a monopoly position in the United States, but it had neither increased prices nor restrained output, and it was subject to competition from imports, so the market theoretically remained competitive. However, the Supreme Court held that Alcoa's power to exclude competitors, even if it had no specific intent to do so, was illegal, because it contravened the spirit of antitrust law as a way to keep alive a system of small producers, independent of one other. However, not all antitrust activity was so radical during the New Deal. In addition, the war effort accommodated some of the antitrust rhetoric and led business to pay greater attention to efficiencies.

From 1948 to 1967: The Maturation of Antitrust Legislation

The postwar period became the turning point of antitrust legislation and marked its transition to modern practice. The opportunity arose to establish antitrust regulation as a generic model for government-business relationships, in contrast to communistic collectivization. Throughout the war, the DOJ had prepared litigation against international cartels and had 19 cases ready for filing by 1945. As a consequence, few of the 1930s international cartels escaped the action of U.S. Courts. In addition, the Allied occupation of Germany and Japan, where cartels and trusts—in the form of *Konzerns* or *zaibatsu*—played a notorious and somber role in the fascist era, was seized as a unique opportunity to expand the influence of antitrust provisions. These countries imposed decartelization and deconcentration policies in 1947 and 1948 and passed U.S.-style antitrust laws, actions which were a step toward establishing antitrust and free trade as an international policy line. The 1959 treaty for the European Coal and Steel Community, precursor to the European Economic Community (now the European Union), also contained antitrust provisions. As antitrust expanded worldwide and the number of U.S. cases increased, it became evident that economic theory was increasingly important in the analysis of restraints in competition.

Economic theory of the postwar era emphasized analysis of market power as a source for the absence of competition, either because of one firm's dominance or because of collusion among the members of an oligopoly. The so-called Harvard School was primarily responsible for updating the conceptual fabric of antitrust law, with a focus on the structure-conduct-performance framework. The National Committee to Study the Antitrust Laws, in its 1955 report, advocated stricter merger standards, relying on structural factors and largely disregarding efficiencies arising from merger. Joe Bain provided the intellectual basis for market power analysis in the 1950s, especially in his *Barriers to New Competition* (1956). Carl Kaysen and Donald Turner, in their influential *Antitrust Policy: An Economic and Legal Analysis* (1959), formalized this approach for the purpose of antitrust considerations. The Harvard School incorporated concepts from classical economics (demand curve, relation between prices and costs) and derived regularities from the market structure to infer conduct by businesses. This approach led to generally negative views toward concentration; tying and leveraging arrangements whenever a firm had market power over one product were condemned particularly. There were also very restrictive views about entry barriers.

In the *DuPont* (GM) case (1957), the DOJ tried to reverse a stock purchase by the DuPont family in General Motors, which had taken place 40 years earlier, on the basis of some vertical relations between the firms. In the 1962 *Brown Shoe* case, the merger between Brown and Kinner was prohibited, despite a rather small share of the national market (5 percent), because the Supreme Court reasoned that due to the resulting higher efficiency and lower prices, the merger would lead to other consolidations in a fragmented market and therefore harm "viable, small and locally owned businesses" in a fragmented industry. In *FTC v. Procter and Gamble*, the FTC expressed the view that potential efficiencies from Procter's acquisition of Clorox could raise barriers to entry, and that Procter's market power through advertising expenses to Clorox would further damage competition.

The 1960s are now regarded as the "dark age" of antitrust because of a series of cases in which only low concentration levels were tolerated and small business was systematically protected, even deeming superior efficiencies of larger firms a detrimental element, and using speculative views about the ability to transfer market power from one market to another. In fact, the rhetoric of the time was not so different from that elaborated in previous periods of antitrust legislation. Furthermore, the period provided the occasion to introduce economic reasoning more firmly in the analysis.

From 1968 to 2000: The Modern Era of Antitrust Legislation

The modern era of U.S. antitrust coincides with an almost philosophical twist in the purpose of antitrust legislation, away from the protection of small competitors and toward more purely economic objectives, such as promotion of efficiency. At the origins of this shift in policy was an intellectual reaction to the Harvard School's structural presumptions about competition and its impact on case law. In the 1950s, Aaron Director (a professor at Chicago University), Judge Richard Posner, Edmund Kitch (a law professor at the University of Virginia), Judge Robert Bork, and George Stigler (a Nobel Prize winner in economics) started to question the usually accepted antitrust scenarios. Why should predatory prices—that is, below cost—be forbidden? After all, they benefit customers and stimulate rivalry between firms. Why should a tie-in be regarded as a means to extend monopoly from one market to another market? Even in a monopoly situation, there is only one production and price combination that maximizes profit, and tying two monopoly products would not consequently increase that profit level. Do these practices have no other reason than the destruction of competition? A firm generally maximizes its profits upstream and downstream; it does not necessarily have incentives to restrain supply or foreclose access to vertical markets. When markets are described as anticompetitive, can people really be sure that entry barriers are as high as imagined and that no other firm will enter in case prices are raised? There must be barriers that are artificial and that do not result from superior efficiency.

For the Chicago School, most markets are competitive, and when in doubt, government should refrain from intervening in the market. Even with high degrees of concentration and with product differentiation, one should remain cautious about showing restriction of competition. Business firms maximize their profits, and one must prove that firms will have incentive to reduce competition when they can. This rhetoric of skepticism in Chicago analysis brought some healthy rejuvenation to antitrust after the previous period of restrictive policies. Moreover, numerous studies, conducted during the 1960s, found that practices considered anticompetitive actually were not so.

The influence of the Chicago School was soon felt. In 1968, the DOJ's antitrust division published merger guidelines, explaining its enforcement policy and coming to terms with acceptable levels of concentration that the agency would not normally challenge. A series of Supreme Court cases after 1969 and throughout the 1970s progressively reversed the case holdings of the 1960s. In *Fortner Enterprises, Inc.* (1969) and *General Dynamics* (1974), simply having a high market share was not deemed to equate with market power; in *Falstaff Brewing* (1973) and *Marine Bancorporation* (1974), the "potential competition" doctrine was refined to consider reasonable economic factors and incentives rather than intent. In the field of mergers, the Hart-Scott-Rodino Act (1976) was passed to organize and simplify the reporting of merger transactions.

With the election of Ronald Reagan on a free market platform and deregulation, starting in the late 1970s, the 1980s were marked by rhetoric of free competition and economic laissez-faire doctrine. The FTC's actions, which had been considered too zealous, witnessed a shift in approach from "social" considerations toward "economic" ones. The promotion of business efficiency was established as the primary objective of antitrust. No criticism on the theoretical or academic level succeeded in totally dismantling the Chicago School propositions, which became the generally accepted view toward markets. Subsequent developments in antitrust legislation were mostly refinements and adjustments to its key principles.

The DOJ issued new merger guidelines in 1982 and 1984, which largely followed the dominant Chicago School line. They shed some light on the difficult issue of market definition, which is the preamble to any assessment of market power. The guidelines also introduced a new concentration index, the Herfindahl-Hirschman Index (HHI), to measure the degree of concentration in a market. These measures emphasized the importance of nonstructural factors, clarified that foreign competition should be taken into account analogously to domestic competition, and indicated that efficiencies should be taken into account in relevant cases. In 1992, the FTC and the DOJ jointly issued new horizontal-merger guidelines, adding further refinements to their analysis. Theories of anticompetitive effects were fleshed out in greater detail through the analysis of unilateral and coordinated interaction. With the Clinton administration, the enforcement became somewhat more stringent, the more so as economic thinking developed some theories that countered certain Chicago School propositions, especially about what constituted collusion, exclusionary practices, tying, and predatory pricing. These new theories, relating to sometimes quite complex game-theory models, have not been incorporated fully in the case law yet.

The 2001 *Microsoft* case, which was opened by the FTC in 1990 and eventually closed by the DOJ in 2002, led to much publicity and controversy. It involved the claim that Microsoft, the massive software company founded by Bill Gates, had monopolized, attempted to monopolize, and restrained trade in software markets. On August 20, 1993, the FTC closed a three-year investigation after the five commissioners twice deadlocked and were unable to decide on issuing an administrative complaint. The DOJ took over the case, together with 20 states. In 1994, Microsoft entered a consent decree agreeing to eliminate certain restrictions on PC (personal computer) manufacturers. However, in 1997, the DOJ and the European Commission sued Microsoft, claiming it violated the 1994 consent decree. The process became an embarrassment to the enforcement powers of the agency, nonetheless, because of Gates's attitude and arrogance throughout the proceedings and in his 1999 trial testimony. In 2002, the case was closed in the United States through behavioral remedies, with Microsoft also appointing a compliance officer to monitor its enforcement. Meanwhile, in 1997, the FTC and DOJ published joint guidelines insisting on efficiencies and explaining that the agencies would not challenge a merger if efficiencies were of a character and magnitude such that the merger would not likely be anticompetitive in any relevant market.

Conclusion: Toward a Global Competition Policy?

The history of U.S. antitrust legislation reached a mature stage now where it is highly valued by business and government alike. There were variations over time, both in the theory and in the vigor of enforcement but antitrust became a beacon for prosperity and economic welfare and was embraced by an increasing number of nations. At present, more than 120 countries have some antitrust legislation, and these laws accompany the globalization of the free market and democratic ideals. New actors around the world emerged in the antitrust field, notably the European Commission, which in 2001 prohibited the merger of General Electric and Honeywell and which is now recognized as an important influence in the development of international antitrust policies. With the creation of the International Competition Network in 2001, an organization established to provide authorities across the globe with information on antitrust activities, the world is equipped with a new forum to develop global competition policy capable of meeting the challenge of a globalized business world. To that extent, U.S. antitrust legislation may well advance outside American borders.

References

Amato, Giulano. *Antitrust and the Bounds of Power: The Dilemma of Liberal Democracy in the History of the Market.* Oxford: Hart Publishing, 1997.

Bain, Joe. *Barriers to New Competition.* Cambridge, MA: Harvard University Press, 1956.

Bittlingmayer, George. "Economics and 100 Years of Antitrust: Introduction." *Economic Inquiry*, vol. 30, no. 2 (1992): 203–206.

Clayton Anti-Trust Act (1914). See Primary Source Documents section, this volume.

Duggan, Michael A. *Antitrust and the U.S. Supreme Court, 1829–1980: A Compendium of Supreme Court Decisions Dealing with Restraint of Trade and Monopoly.* New York: Federal Legal Publications, 1981.

Fox, Elaine. "The Modernization of Antitrust: A New Equilibrium." *Cornell Law Review*, vol. 66 (1981): 1140–1156.

Hazlett, Thomas. "The Legislative History of the Sherman Act Re-Examined." *Economic Inquiry*, vol. 30, no. 2 (1992): 263–276.

Hovenkamp, Herbert. *Enterprise and American Law, 1836–1937.* Cambridge, MA: Harvard University Press, 1991.

Hovenkamp, Herbert. *Federal Antitrust Policy: The Law of Competition and Its Practice.* St. Paul, MN: West Group, 1999.

Kaspi, André. *Les Américains.* Paris: Le Seuil, 1998.

Kaufman, Burton I. *The Oil Cartel Case.* Westport, CT: Greenwood Press, 1978.

Kaysen, Carl, and Donald Turner. *Antitrust Policy: An Economic and Legal Analysis.* Cambridge, MA: Harvard University Press, 1959.

Kovacic, William E. "The Influence of Economics on Antitrust Law." *Economic Inquiry*, vol. 30, no. 2 (1992): 294–306.

Libecap, Gary D. "The Rise of the Chicago Packers and the Origins of Meat Inspection and Antitrust." *Economic Inquiry*, vol. 30, no. 2 (1992): 242–262.

Marshall, Alfred. *Principles of Economics.* New York: Macmillan, 1890.

McKenzie, Richard B. *Trust on Trial: How the Microsoft Case Is Reframing the Rules of Competition.* Cambridge, MA: Perseus Publishing, 2001.

Mueller, Dennis C. "Lessons from the United States' Antitrust History." *International Journal of Industrial Organization*, vol. 14 (1996): 415–445.

Posner, Richard A. *Antitrust Cases, Economic Notes, and Other Materials.* St. Paul, MN: West Publishing, 1981.

Sherman Anti-Trust Act (1890). See Primary Source Documents section, this volume.

Sklar, Martin J. *The Corporate Reconstruction of American Capitalism, 1890–1916: The Market, the Law, and Politics.* New York: Cambridge University Press, 1988.

U.S. Department of Justice. "Public Comments and Plaintiff's Response: *United States of America v. Aluminum Company of America and Alumax, Inc.*" No date. Available: http://www.usdoj.gov/atr/cases/f1900/1948.htm; accessed July 15, 2003.

U.S. Department of Justice Antitrust Case Filings. "*United States v. Microsoft Current Case.*" No date. Available: http://www.usdoj.gov/atr/cases/ms_index.htm; accessed July 14, 2003.

Wells, Wyatt C. *Antitrust and the Formation of the Postwar World.* New York: Columbia University Press, 2002.

Williamson, Oliver E. *Antitrust Economics: Mergers, Contracting, and Strategic Behavior.* Oxford: Blackwell, 1987.

Banking

Michael V. Namarato

A financial intermediary is an institution that serves as an intermediary between savers and investors or between depositors and borrowers. Broadly conceived, financial intermediaries can and have appeared in a variety of guises, such as banks, insurance companies, credit unions, savings and loans (thrifts), and other commercial entities. Traditionally, banks assumed the prominent role among financial intermediaries, and there is no question that banks (commercial and savings) played a vital role in the development of U.S. business and the economy.

How Banks Developed

Banking has a very long tradition, and although evidence indicates it was practiced in Babylonia, ancient Greece, and Rome, not until the Middle Ages did the more modern banking practices of today appear. During this period, gold and silver (specie—meaning "in-kind") were used as money or media of exchange. Since people wanted to protect their precious metals, they stored their specie (gold) with goldsmiths who possessed strongboxes to hold and protect it.

Initially, goldsmiths kept the specie deposits and charged a fee for the service. When depositors wanted their gold, the goldsmith gave it to them. However, it soon became apparent that depositors could still use their gold without actually withdrawing it every time they wanted to buy goods or services. Goldsmiths began to issue written orders to pay for purchases the gold depositors made, and these orders were then traded for the purchases. In time, the orders included names and a specific amount of specie—the precursor of checks. These written orders thereby facilitated trade. A new problem arose because a goldsmith could not readily provide the exact amount of the purchase, since measurements in ounces did not always equal the precise purchase price. Goldsmiths, moreover, soon realized that their depositors did not use their entire deposit all of the time. The result was that the goldsmiths began to extend loans, issue notes, or exchange notes—all of which led to today's modern concept of fractional reserve banking.

In time, early banks began to appear. In Europe, banking developed along centralized lines. The Bank of England and similar central banking institutions not only grew but also became quite powerful within the national economies in which they existed. In contrast, banking development took a different route in the English North American colonies and, later, the independent United States.

The Bank of North America

During the colonial period, roughly from 1607 to 1776, financial intermediation was primitive at best. Money itself was practically nonexistent except for Spanish gold coins or other similar means of exchange. Colonial merchants used bills of exchange and traded them as if they were money. However, the colonies did not trust or even like each other much, and typically, money in one colony might not be accepted at face value in another colony. Discounting money was common practice by Chesapeake Bay planters or northern merchants, whose economies differed, one being agricultural and the other based on trade. By the time of the American Revolution, the colonies' financial system was so primitive that creative financing was required to pay for the Revolutionary War. In this regard, Robert Morris, the "financier of the American Revolution," left his imprint. As debts mounted and financial problems multiplied, Morris established the Bank of North America in 1781. Centered in Philadelphia, the bank held government deposits used by Morris to provide credit services to the central government and merchants operating within the European commission system. Merchants who once relied upon English merchants for credit turned to Morris's Bank of North America, which replaced the English merchants and facilitated the growth of banks in general.

Although the Bank of North America was successful in helping the Congress of the Articles of Confederation, the loosely organized institution was not the answer for a growing, independent country such as the United States whose future seemed to point in a different direction. Even though early state banks were appearing, the new nation needed a bank that could provide economic stability, a national currency, and assistance to the central government, not only for its daily operations but also in international economic exchanges. Here, the genius of Alexander Hamilton came to the fore.

First and Second Banks of the United States, 1791–1836

Alexander Hamilton was primarily responsible for developing and implementing George Washington's first domestic program. Hamilton saw America's future in industrial pursuits rather than in agriculture and believed that a central banking mechanism was of the utmost importance. Working through Washington and compromising with Thomas Jefferson, Hamilton had Congress charter the First Bank of the United States in 1791.

The belief was that a central banking mechanism would provide a uniform currency and enhance the stability of the economy, and thus the bank would help in creating the new federal government's credit at home and abroad as well as in providing long-term financing for industry. The original charter guaranteed that the bank exercised a monopoly, a life span of 20 years, and a capitalization of $10 million (one-fourth in specie and three-fourths in U.S. securities). The federal government, moreover, was to participate in the bank's profits, be a recipient of bank loans, and place a major share of its revenue in the bank. With its main branch in Philadelphia and eight additional branches scattered around the country, the bank collected the largest specie reserve in the United States. By using its capital resources, it effectively regulated the currency and provided stability for the growing American economy.

Unanticipated by Hamilton and his followers, however, was the opposition of state politicians, farmers, and businessmen who were controlled by the bank. By 1811, the furor reached such a pitch that Congress did not renew the Bank's charter, and between then and 1816, the United States had no central bank. This was particularly unfortunate because the War of 1812 broke out and America's financial needs were critical. With finances in ruin and the nation undergoing a depression in 1815, Congress again acted to create another central bank, chartering the Second Bank of the United States in 1816.

Like its predecessor, the Second Bank of the United States was given a monopoly, a 20-year life span, and governmental securities for capitalization, set at $35 million. The Second Bank paid the federal government $1.5 million for its charter and agreed to let the president of the United States appoint five of the 25 directors. Compared with the First Bank, the Second Bank was better capitalized, held more governmental revenue as the sole depository of federal funds, and operated more branches (28 in all). Moreover, its president, Nicholas Biddle, led the institution effectively.

Unfortunately, like the First Bank, the Second Bank also had its opponents, including Wall Street, businessmen, state politicians, state banks, and farmers. A prominent opponent was President Andrew Jackson, who, after the 1832 election, successfully attacked and destroyed the bank. By 1841, despite Biddle's efforts to save it, the Second Bank ceased to exist under a state charter from Pennsylvania. With the demise of the Second Bank, America's venture into central banking ended until it was resurrected with the creation of the Federal Reserve System in 1913.

State and "Free" Banking

Although centralized banking was a highly important development in America's financial history, its duration was relatively short, only 40 years. To fill the void, another state-supported form of banking appeared.

With the demise of the Bank of North America in 1784, both New York and Massachusetts incorporated banks. Modeled on the Bank of North America, both were designed to serve as commercial banks, make loans, and facilitate banking services. Although both banks were (relatively) prosperous, they were not the only ones in existence. Under Alexander Hamilton's guidance, the Bank of New York was used to support Federalists on the political front, with the inevitable result being creation of a rival. In 1799, with the political chicanery of Aaron Burr, the Manhattan Company Bank was incorporated to aid Jeffersonian Democratic Republicans.

Political-oriented banking was not extensive, however. In fact, state banks grew noticeably only after the charter of the First Bank of the United States expired in 1811. From that point on, the states entered banking with enthusiasm. Regionally, state banks were highly uniform. Eastern state banks were supported by legislatures so as to make enough profit and thereby reduce taxes. So desirous of incorporation were individual banks that they usually paid the states for their charters. However, the eastern banks had limited importance for American industrial development, since European investment

Nicholas Biddle became president of the Second Bank of the United States in 1823. Under Biddle's leadership, the bank expanded and gained the public's confidence by providing a stable currency and restraining state banks from engaging in unsound business practices. (Library of Congress.)

was so readily available. In the west, on the other hand, state loans and investment were substantial in banking. Typically, states would provide nearly half of the capital and appoint half of the directors in the chartered state banks. The express purpose of their commitment was to make profits, which were available for investing in northern industry.

Perhaps the most unusual state banks were established in the south. Essentially mercantile, southern state banks were mortgage banks—that is, private stockholders subscribed to them by tendering mortgages on their land. Obviously, banks of this sort had low liquidity, and bank runs were disastrous. For that reason, southern state legislatures were the mainstay of these banks.

By the 1830s and 1840s, states began withdrawing from the banking business and turned instead to passing "free" banking laws, with most states experimenting with free banking from 1835 to 1860. The laws typically allowed individuals or groups to set up banks as long as they backed their note issues with securities kept on deposit with the banking authority within their state. If the bank thereafter failed to honor its debts, the state could then exercise the right to sell the bank's securities and pay off depositors and note holders. Some states, such as Louisiana, had very successful free banking systems. Others, such as Michigan, did not. On average, however, free banking was not as troublesome as one might think. Losses from bankrupt banks were relatively small compared with total aggregate wealth.

As the free banks showed, issuance of notes was a serious problem. In an attempt to resolve it, in 1818, the Suffolk Bank of Boston was established with the objective of redeeming the notes of banks and clearing all accounts, provided that each member bank maintained a balance at the Suffolk of $5,000 plus enough to cover note redemption. In every respect, the Suffolk was to act as a banker's bank. Yet the principal weakness of the Suffolk was that it represented only one bank. A more substantial institution was needed, and it came with the establishment of the New York Clearinghouse in 1853. Clerks from individual banks met, conducted note payment and redemption, and received clearinghouse certificates in return (representing deposits of specie by member banks at the clearinghouse). Clearinghouses, of course, remained a fundamental advance in providing a uniform currency and in stabilizing interbank relations.

Amid these developments, banking stability became a chief concern of the states. Some states sought to provide it through legislative edict. In 1829, the New York Safety Fund Act was passed, which thereafter required all banks in the state to pay each year a sum equal to one-half percent of their capital into a fund used to repay note holders of defaulting banks. A commission was also established to inspect contributing banks and to take legal action against the insolvent ones. In a similar vein, the Louisiana Banking Act of 1842 drew sharp distinctions among types of loans a bank could make while also establishing a reserve fund to meet bank needs. There is no question that both of these laws were advances in banking, yet they also represented the weakness of any state plan—lack of uniformity. Not until the federal government passed the National Bank Act (1863) and the Federal Reserve Act (1913) did uniformity prevail. Thereafter, the federal government regulated banking for all the states.

Commercial Banking and Administration

Commercial banking was practically nonexistent in colonial America, which had no need for the commercial bank's function of discounting notes and conducting exchange operations. After the Revolutionary War, commercial banking grew, at first serving merchants with short-term loans. As banking developed and as more Americans became dependent on a money economy, commercial banking spread; to the extent it existed, both the central banks and state banks were part of it. However, problems developed with note issuance, and these were resolved only after the Suffolk system and the clearinghouses appeared. To ensure confidence about making long- and short-term loans, commercial banking needed stability, and states tried to provide it with legislation.

From an administrative viewpoint, however, commercial banking was significant. The cashier in the commercial banks was the first professional banker in the United States. He administered bank procedures and oversaw the bank's day-to-day management and operation. Before 1820, the president of a bank and the board of directors, meeting only once a week, made decisions on loans, deposits, and discounting. In turn, the cashier carried out their decisions. The cashier, however, lost his distinguished position once bank presidents exerted more authority. Nicholas Biddle, president of the Second Bank of the United States, was the leader in this respect. He set the example, which others followed, of making the cashier a salaried manager and of establishing committees to run various aspects of the bank's affairs. From then on, cashiers and tellers (who had considerable power since they controlled the keys to the vaults) became professionals on the middle and lower levels of administration.

Savings and Investment Banking

Originally, savings banks were designed to help the poor improve their economic station in life. Founded around the period from 1815 to 1820, savings banks were intended to help the poor save money and to lighten the relief load of local governments. By the 1820s, the philanthropic purpose of these institutions changed. Professional managers appeared and redirected the purposes of the savings banks. Emphasizing growth and expansion, these managers were responsible for appealing to all income groups and serving all clientele. Loans were more readily extended so as to make a profit. With profit maximization as its objective, the savings bank thereafter developed more rapidly.

Investment banking, in contrast, involved selling securities on a commission basis and/or purchasing securities for sale to the general public. Originating in England, investment banks there consisted of English-merchant syndicates buying treasury securities at auctions. In the United States, however, investment banking grew only slowly in the 1820s and 1830s and only after individuals such as John Jacob Astor and Stephen Girard delved into purchasing securities from individual states, which were trying to finance transportation projects. Still, these activities were financially insignificant. Investment banking would not really blossom until the railroads and financiers such as Jay Gould and J. P. Morgan rose to prominence in the years after the Civil War.

The National Banking System

In banking, the federal government brought some stability to the industry by passing the National Bank Act of 1863, amended in 1864. Essentially, the act gave the federal government the power to grant state banks charters to become national banks through the Office of the Comptroller of the Currency. These new national banks were required to have a minimum capital of $200,000 in cities of 50,000 people, $100,000 in cities with between 6,000 and 50,000 people, or $50,000 in cities of 6,000 people or less. Each bank was required to deposit with the Comptroller bonds equal to one-third its capital, but not less than $30,000. In exchange, the bank received national bank notes equal to 90 percent of the par (market) value of the deposited bonds. Country banks, which serviced larger regions and primarily extended mortgage notes to farmers, were required to maintain a 15 percent reserve, three-fifths of which they could deposit in a larger city bank with a more diversified portfolio of loans. Finally, a tax of 1 percent was levied semiannually against the national bank's note circulation.

By providing a stable currency and banking system, the National Bank Act definitely increased the number of banks in the United States, although their success depended upon the region in which they were located. The law also created the dual U.S. banking system of national and state banks. As for the success of the system itself, questions immediately were raised. The South did not fare well under this new system. Devastated financially by the Civil War, the southern states reverted to a primitive system of financial intermediation in which the merchants became dominant, not only controlling the money supply and interest rates but also becoming so powerful as to take possession of southern lands through a form of foreclosure. Nor did the national banking system prevent major banking and economic crises thereafter. Still, the system worked well enough that it was not replaced until Congress passed the Federal Reserve Act in 1913.

The Federal Reserve System, 1913 to 1933

As the United States experienced seemingly uncontrollable financial panics and economic depressions, frustration with America's financial system intensified. The depression of the 1890s was especially severe in its impact on unemployment, prices, and economic productivity. Scarcity of currency became a serious problem, as businessmen sought to protect themselves against economic uncertainty by withdrawing their funds from banks. Bank suspensions commonly ensued until Congress passed the Aldrich-Vreeland Act of 1908, which provided for the organization of national currency associations. The law also set up a National Monetary Commission to study the currency problem. It was through such studies that Congress finally acted to create the Federal Reserve System in 1913. (The legislation appears in the Documents section of this volume.)

Originally, the Federal Reserve (the Fed) divided the United States into 12 regional districts with a Federal Reserve Bank in each. Headed by a Federal Reserve Board, the system was controlled by the member banks, with some, such as the New York Federal Reserve, exerting significant authority and influence. The system was particularly attractive because member banks regulated each other and exercised authority to issue Federal Reserve notes, which served as a national currency. Undoubtedly, this arrangement was a major improvement over what existed before.

Between the time of its founding and the outbreak of the Great Depression in 1929, the Fed made a decent showing. It did fairly well during World War I in stabilizing economic activity and government borrowing. Between 1923 and 1929, the Fed also used open market operations, discount rate changes, and reserve limits to stabilize the growing economy of the decade. Problems, however, soon appeared when the stock market embarked on a highly speculative bull run. Today, most economic historians agree that the Fed stood by and did practically nothing to stave off the impending catastrophe. The inevitable result was that the U.S. economy, through a convergence of several factors, began to decline rapidly, and the U.S. banking system eventually fell so low that total disintegration was on the horizon. By 1932, bank

A crowd protests in the rain outside New York City's Bank of the United States after its failure in 1931. Signs carried by the demonstrators call for government intervention to protect the assets of small depositors in what was then the largest bank failure in American history. (Library of Congress.)

insolvencies were so widespread that state governors were closing banks whether or not they thought they had the authority to do so. Herbert Hoover attempted to help the economy recover through such programs as the Reconstruction Finance Corporation, but these efforts were too feeble. By 1932 the American people wanted a change, and they gave a mandate to the governor of New York, Franklin D. Roosevelt, who promised them a New Deal if he was elected.

Banking in the New Deal

The New Deal was a haphazard and multifaceted attempt, at times successful, to address the Great Depression, but it would fail in the end to alleviate the economic distress. Nevertheless, it brought significant reform to the U.S. banking system. No sooner did Roosevelt take the oath of office than he immediately closed all the banks for a four-day period with his famous "bank holiday," when bank operations were suspended until authorities examined them for sound banking practices. Congress soon gave the president the authority he needed by passing the Emergency Banking Act of 1933. More important, Roosevelt acted quickly to seize the opportunity presented to him and endorsed the Glass-Steagall Banking Act of 1933. Considered today as among the most important pieces of legislation affecting U.S. banking, Glass-Steagall created the Federal Deposit Insurance Corporation (FDIC), separated commercial and investment banking, and implemented the well-known Regulation Q of the Federal Reserve Act to strictly regulated interest rate ceilings. These restrictions remained in effect until 1986. This the end of the New Deal's banking reform.

Realizing that the Fed must bear some responsibility for the Great Depression and the banking crisis, Roosevelt, through his adviser Marriner Eccles, persuaded Congress to pass the Banking Act of 1935. This law eliminated the original Federal Reserve Board and replaced it with the Board of Governors. It also centralized all authority in the Board of Governors, thereby reducing the power of member banks. The Fed was definitely starting to act like America's third central bank.

Although these reforms were positive advances in the banking industry, they did not necessarily resolve all economic and banking problems. For example, there was the 1937–1938 recession, which was brought on by Roosevelt's policies and programs and the use of deficit spending to provide relief for individuals. If nothing else, the recession showed that still more change was needed.

During World War II, the Fed helped the federal government by agreeing to buy government securities in order to maintain the interest rate that the government paid on its debt. This practice remained in existence until the Fed stopped buying government bonds in 1952. During the Eisenhower presidency, moreover, the Fed ceased intervening in the economy to maintain a governmentally favorable interest rate. Politically, Fed leaders and U.S. presidents battled each other constantly as each financial crisis occurred, often with the political leaders demanding that the Fed bail them out.

American Banking since 1945

After World War II, U.S. banking was definitely influenced by the Fed and by the numerous regulatory laws passed by Congress. During the 1950s, the Fed concentrated its attention on inflation control; in the 1960s, it focused more on monetary policy decisions in money market strategies. The Fed itself underwent internal changes, as professional economists began to sit on the board or serve as chairman of the Board of Governors, with Alan Greenspan ultimately becoming one of the longest-reigning Fed chairmen. Throughout the 1970s, 1980s, and 1990s, the Fed advanced in power, influence, and authority. As the economy grew and underwent its own internal changes—for example, the appearance of the military-industrial complex, the

Vietnam War, the Reagan supply-side revolution—the Fed adjusted not only to economic events but to political changes as well. Slowly and gradually, the Fed ascended to such a level that today it controls America's money supply and economy.

These events do not mean that all has gone well for American banking and America's third central bank. Witness the serious economic crises that erupted since 1960 alone—the Penn Central Railroad crisis (1970), the Franklin National Bank crisis (1974), the Hunt brothers silver speculation (1980s), the stock market crash (1987), the savings and loan debacle (1980s), and the stock market–Dow Jones problems (1990s), many of these attributable to the dot-com bust and the corruption uncovered in corporate America. Yet it is significant that as financial crises occurred, the U.S. banking system and the Fed responded, often in very satisfactory ways.

After 1945, banking regulation became more focused on very specific issues. In 1956, the Bank Holding Company Act was passed, prohibiting interstate acquisitions by banks unless the state approved them. In 1961, Congress passed the Interest Rate Adjustment Act, which sought to extend Regulation Q to the thrift industry. In 1970, the Bank Holding Company Act was extended to place restrictions on bank holding companies.

Era of Banking Deregulation and Its Consequences

During the 1980s and 1990s, Congress passed several pieces of legislation gradually lifting restrictions on the banking and financial services industries, which allowed for the unprecedented growth of financial institutions during the first decade of the twenty-first century and contributed to the scale of the banking crisis that hit the U.S. economy in 2008.

In 1980, the Depository Institutions Deregulation and Monetary Control Act (DIDMCA) was passed, phasing out interest rate regulations and giving the Fed authority over reserve requirements for practically all banking institutions. All banks and thrifts could participate and use Fed services for a fee, and FDIC insurance was increased. Two years later, Congress passed the Garn–St. Germain Act, which permitted money market accounts and allowed interstate mergers among banks. One year later, in 1983, the International Lending Supervisory Act gave regulatory agencies the authority to establish capital requirements for banks. During the mid-1980s, a savings and loan crisis, in which numerous savings and loan as well as thrift institutions failed, led Congress to pass the 1989 Financial Institutions Reform, Recovery, and Enforcement Act (FIRREA), which restructured the FDIC, established the Resolution Trust Corporation to close hundreds of thrifts, moved oversight responsibility for these institutions to the Office of Thrift Supervision (OTS) under the U.S. Department of Treasury, and increased insurance premiums. Two years later, in 1991, the Federal Deposit Insurance Corporation Improvement Act gave the FDIC the authority to monitor troubled banks. Still more was to come.

In 1999, Congress passed and President William Clinton signed into law the Financial Services Modernization Act (also referred to as the Gramm-Leach-Bliley Act). Comprehensive in scope and intent, the law removed restrictions on banks affiliating with securities firms, created a new "financial holding company," provided for state regulation of insurance, streamlined governmental restrictions on bank holding companies generally, and included a host of other reforms governing savings and loans and other financial intermediaries. However, some congressional members and economic analysts of the Financial Services Modernization Act criticized the act on the basis that it removed restrictions placed on the banking industry during the Great Depression, measures designed to prevent a reoccurrence of another financial crisis like the one that the nation had experienced during the 1930s. One of the more outspoken opponents of the measure was Senator Byron L. Dorgan (D-NB), who warned of the potential for a future banking crisis in which financial institutions would become "too big to fail" if banks, insurance, and investment firms were allowed to engage in unrestricted mergers and acquisitions.

Shortly after the passage of the Financial Services Modernization Act, several mergers took place and, over the course of the next decade, banking institutions became very big—"too big to fail." When the Housing Bubble burst in August 2007, a liquidity crisis and cash crunch shook the banking industry to its core over the next year. In March 2008, the fifth-largest U.S. investment firm of Bear Stearns teetered on the verge of bankruptcy because of the enormous amount of toxic securities in two of its hedge funds, which were invested heavily in the subprime mortgage market. With the financial markets already reeling from the subprime mortgage crisis and investor confidence shaken, the Federal Reserve and the Department of the Treasury stepped in to prevent the collapse of Bear Stearns. A government-brokered sale of Bear Stearns to JPMorgan Chase was negotiated on March 17. Under the terms of the agreement, the government provided JPMorgan Chase $29 billion, thereby basically assuming the liability for the less liquid assets of Bear Stearns.

Although a financial shockwave on Wall Street was averted temporarily, there was no stopping the storm that broke following the government takeover of the mortgage government-sponsored enterprises (GSEs) of Fannie Mae and Freddie Mac on September 7, 2008. With financial institutions so heavily invested in mortgage-backed securities, which were proving more toxic as home foreclosures skyrocketed throughout 2008, the crisis hit Wall Street with an unexpected severity. During the week of September 8 to 12, four of the largest financial institutions in the country—investment firms of Lehman Brothers and Merrill Lynch, insurance giant American International Group (A.I.G.), and Washington Mutual Bank—found themselves on the verge of collapse unless the government stepped in to prevent that from occurring through government-brokered agreements or bailouts. Over the weekend, Federal Reserve and Treasury officials met with financial institution executives in New York to discuss measures to address the worst week of financial crisis on Wall Street since the Stock Market Crash in October 1929. Federal Reserve and Treasury officials sought a plan that would not require more and more bailouts by the federal government, especially when there was the potential of the crisis deepening further in the months ahead. Failing to reach any agreement, the talks ended. In a move designed to prevent the firm from getting pulled under by the fallout of the crisis, Merrill Lynch, the nation's largest and oldest investment firm with more than

$1.4 trillion in its investment portfolio, voluntarily sold itself to Bank of America for $50.3 billion in stock; the company was worth $100 billion a year earlier. Merrill Lynch issued the announcement was on Sunday, September 14. On Monday, September 15, Lehman Brothers announced it was filing for bankruptcy, making it the largest failure of an investment firm in U.S. history. Tuesday, September 16, witnessed another financial institutions giant brought to its knees as the government was forced to step in with an $85 billion bailout of the insurance giant A.I.G., the 18th-largest public company in the world; the agreement was signed on September 23.

The announcement of the A.I.G. bailout did not restore investor confidence and the stock market dropped nearly 500 points anyway on September 16. Two days later, Treasury Secretary Henry S. Paulson issued a three-page $700 billion proposal to allow the federal government to buy the toxic securities from the nation's largest banks, thereby shoring up the banking industry and restoring confidence in the U.S. financial system. While Congress was stilling debating the proposal, federal bank regulators seized the assets of Washington Mutual Bank on September 25, selling its assets to JPMorgan Chase that same day. The next day, Washington Mutual filed for bankruptcy, resulting in the largest bank failure in U.S. history.

On September 29, the U.S. House of Representatives rejected Paulson's proposal, causing the S&P 500 stocks to drop 90 percent in value that same day—the worst day on the stock market since the height of the savings and loan crisis, which took place on October 19, 1987. On October 1, the Senate prepared a revised version of the House bill on Paulson's $700 billion program. The Senate version, which included tax credits, other compromises, and earmarks, passed that day by a vote of 74 to 25. Two days later, the House passed the bill by a vote of 263 to 171. The act established the Troubled Asset Relief Program (TARP). Even after the passage of the $700 billion program, bank failures continued to occur. In December 2008, the government was forced to provide a $2.33 billion bailout to CIT Group, which was the lender to hundreds of small and medium-size banks.

Prior to the subprime mortgage crisis of 2007, there were no bank failures in the United States during 2005 and 2006. In 2007, only three banks failed. The number of bank failures rose to 25 in 2008, before skyrocketing to 140 failures in 2009. Much debate has taken place concerning the cause of the financial crisis. Many agreed with the prediction made by Senator Byron L. Dorgan in his speech on the floor of the Senate just before passage of the Financial Services Modernization Act of 1999 when he warned that the lifting of restrictions on bank mergers and allowing them to transact business across state lines would allow banks to become "too big to fail," which did indeed become the doctrine governing the financial crisis of 2007. Government bailouts added $900 billion to the federal debt in 2008 and another $787 billion in 2009. Bank failures still continue unabated.

References
Blackford, Mansel, and Austin Kerr. *Business Enterprise in American History.* 2nd ed. New York: Houghton Mifflin, 1990.

Carosso, Vincent P. *Investment Banking in America: A History.* Cambridge, MA: Harvard University Press, 1970.

Fogel, Robert William, and Stanley Engerman, eds. *A Reinterpretation of American Economic History.* New York: Harper and Row, 1971.

Friedman, Milton, and Anna J. Schwartz. *A Monetary History of the United States, 1867–1960.* Princeton, NJ: Princeton University Press, 1963.

Galbraith, John Kenneth. *The Great Crash, 1929.* Boston: Houghton Mifflin, 1972.

Hammond, Bray. *Banks and Politics in America from the Revolution to the Civil War.* Princeton, NJ: Princeton University Press, 1957.

Kindleberger, Charles. *Manias, Panics, and Crashes: A History of Financial Crises.* New York: Basic Books, 1978.

Krooss, Herman, and Martin Blyn. *A History of Financial Intermediaries.* New York: Random House, 1971.

Redlich, Fritz. *The Molding of American Banking: Men and Ideas.* New York: Hafner, 1947 and 1951.

Schweikart, Larry. *Banking in the American South from the Age of Jackson to Reconstruction.* Baton Rouge: Louisiana State University Press, 1988.

Stein, Herbert. *The Fiscal Revolution in America.* Rev. ed. Washington, DC: American Enterprise Institute, 1990.

Sylla, Richard. "American Banking and Growth in the Nineteenth Century: A Partial View of the Terrain." *Explorations in Economic History*, vol. 9 (1971–1972): 197–227.

Temin, Peter. *Did Monetary Forces Cause the Great Depression?* New York: Norton, 1976.

Wicker, Elmus. *Federal Reserve and Monetary Policy, 1917–1933.* New York: Random House, 1966.

Big Business and Government Relationships

Henry B. Sirgo

The adoption of the U.S. Constitution put an end to the practice of states imposing tariffs on one another, a practice that prevented development of the national economy before 1789. A robust national economy as envisioned by Alexander Hamilton required a strong centralized government, and the founding fathers laid the constitutional groundwork for this national authority in article 1, section 8, with enumerated powers granted to Congress. They perceived these powers as indispensable for the development of enterprise on a large scale, including the powers to establish a postal system to unite the nation through communication, to grant copyright protection, and to regulate interstate and foreign commerce; perhaps most important was the power granted exclusively to Congress to coin money. A major argument for adopting the U.S. Constitution involved relief for creditors who had to pay back their loans with inflated state paper money.

Business and Government: The Search for Balance

Efforts were made to promote economic growth even before the U.S. Constitution was adopted. For example, the Northwest Ordinance of 1787 emphasized public education and development of the intracoastal waterway system, which subsidized the barge industry until the late 1970s. The purpose of the waterway was to enable the nation to connect commercially and politically, and the ordinance decreed that the waterways remain forever free. Efforts to impose fees on barge operators to defray costs began during the administration of Franklin D. Roosevelt but did not succeed until Jimmy Carter's presidency, even though the policy change was supported by all intervening presidents. In addition, the ordinance provided that the U.S. government turn over large tracts of land to territories on condition they establish public schools.

Another measure dealing with education was the Morrill Act (1862), a more explicitly economically oriented measure authored by Republican U.S. Senator Justin Morrill of Vermont. The act provided land grants for the establishment of agricultural and mechanical colleges (which came to be known as A&M schools).

The government also participated in the development of railroads, granting the railroad industry huge land subsidies to foster its growth. Indeed, the Republican Party in the nineteenth century, including President Abraham Lincoln and U.S. Senator

Leland Stanford of California, promoted such subsidies. The aftermath of the Civil War brought continued expansion of the railroads and of other industry in general. Opinion about government involvement was not uniform, however. In the second half of the nineteenth century, debate surrounded the opposing views held by big business and small farmers about the desirability of national government activism. Initially, monied interests saw a strong national government as overwhelmingly desirable, since the U.S. Treasury paid creditors in hard currency, Congress imposed high tariffs on foreign goods to diminish potentially fatal competition, and the government established a strong national bank. In contrast, the typical small yeoman farmer initially saw few advantages and many disadvantages in a strong national government, especially after small farmers became dependent on the railroads and grain elevator operators. In an about-face, however, the farmers ultimately sought federal regulation of these businesses, which held exploitative power over the small enterprises, which remained no match for the railroads or any other big business.

As Adam Smith concluded in *The Wealth of Nations* (1776), the last thing anyone in business wants is competition. The "invisible hand" of competition might produce the greatest good for the greatest number, but collusion is attractive to most people. With this realization in mind, Congress passed the Sherman Anti-Trust Act of 1890, but the U.S. Supreme Court considerably weakened the act in two famous cases.

In the first case, the Court held that *manufacturing* trusts were not engaged in commerce and, therefore, only states could regulate them (*United States v. E. C. Knight Co.*, 156 U.S. 1 [1895]). In the second case, the Court laid down the "rule of reason" by which not *every* combination in restraint of trade (as Congress had explicitly stated in the Act) was illegal, but only those "unreasonably" so (*Standard Oil Co. v. United States*, 221 U.S. 1 [1910]).

To overcome these rulings, which weakened the act, Congress passed the Clayton Act in 1914. Still, until 1937, the Supreme Court continued to act as defender of the status quo by finding unconstitutional statutes intended to ameliorate the worst effects of industrialization, as it did with its holding in *Hammer v. Dagenhart* (247 U.S. 251 [1918]), which voided a statute prohibiting child labor. Although the judiciary lagged in its response to the undesirable side-effects of industrialization, such as sweatshops and unsanitary conditions as depicted in Upton Sinclair's *The Jungle*, the executive branch during the administration of President Theodore Roosevelt became activist, undertaking antitrust actions and promoting such measures as the Pure Food and Drug Act and the Meat Inspection Act.

Other administrations were activist to some degree until the 1920s. President William Howard Taft pursued trust-busting with even more fervor than Theodore Roosevelt exhibited. President Woodrow Wilson signed the Clayton Anti-Trust Act, which forbade abuses that tended to weaken competition, restricted corporations from acquiring stock in competing firms or building interlocking directorates, made corporate officers individually liable for violations, and facilitated civil suit procedures by injured parties. Subsequently, Presidents Warren G. Harding and Calvin Coolidge heralded, respectively, "a return to normalcy" and "that the business of America is business." During the "roaring twenties" in industrialized America, stock market speculation soared, and the policy of laissez-faire held sway during President Coolidge's tenure.

Although conditions appeared robust in the realm of big business, by the mid-1920s depression descended on the farms. When the stock market crashed in October 1929, heralding economic decline in the industrial sector, the lessons learned by policymakers from the last depression of the nineteenth century appeared inapplicable to the current crisis. Clement Studebaker, president of the Studebaker Corporation, and many others blamed President Herbert Hoover for causing the depression by lowering tariff duties. Consequently, Congress responded initially to the Great Depression by passing the Hawley-Smoot Tariff Act of 1930, which raised the average tariff duty to approximately 60 percent and provoked retaliatory actions from other nations.

Approaches to trade remained a major point of contention among government policymakers over positions taken with respect to the General Agreement on Tariffs and Trade (GATT). This is evident in the excerpts reprinted here from letters written by Louisiana's Democratic U.S. Senator J. Bennett Johnston Jr. and Democratic U.S. Representative Jimmy Hayes, in December 1994. Political scientist David B. Truman explained in a 1956 article in the *American Political Science Review* that party identification and state of residence accounted for most of the variation in how members of a congressional delegation voted. Yet these excerpts offer quite different perspectives on GATT. (As a side note, about a year after these letters were written, Jimmy Hayes switched his membership to the Republican Party and subsequently ran unsuccessfully for the U.S. Senate seat, which J. Bennett Johnston Jr. had vacated.) U.S. Senator J. Bennett Johnston Jr. wrote the following on December 12, 1994 (letter to author):

Thank you for contacting me to express your thoughts on the GATT legislation. I joined Presidents Reagan, Bush and Clinton in supporting GATT.

I voted for it because it will greatly benefit the economy of the United States in general and Louisiana, in particular. GATT will promote sales of Louisiana's agricultural commodities and chemicals, and will enable smaller manufacturers to break into foreign markets. Louisiana is a trade state. We have more ports and exports per capita than any state in the nation. They are the source of thousands of Louisiana jobs. We are in a strategic location to ship the increased cargo that will result from GATT from across the United States to overseas markets.

U.S. Representative Jimmy Hayes expressed concerns in a letter written December 7, 1994, which led him to vote against GATT. He stated that he opposed the fast-track procedure in principle,

I could not support the attachment of completely unrelated (and potentially destructive) provisions.

I was also concerned about . . . the dispute resolution process. Under the proposal, the United States will have the power to enforce fair-trading practices on offending countries, while losing our power to block decisions made against our trading practices. Without blocking power, the United States could suffer trade penalties from those countries disputing our trading practices unless we change our laws to suit their demands.

The Regulatory Cycle

The interrelationship between the U.S. government and big business in international relations became evident when the United States and Britain joined forces in attacking targets in Afghanistan on October 7, 2001, in the aftermath of terrorist attacks on the World Trade Center in New York City. The twin towers housed thousands of employees of big businesses, including Morgan Stanley. The terrorists also provoked retaliatory attacks by targeting the Pentagon.

War resulted commonly in increased collaboration between business leaders and government. Business leaders played a role in planning U.S. deployments in both World War I and World War II. Charles Erwin "Engine Charlie" Wilson left his position as president of General Motors to serve as U.S. Secretary of Defense in the Eisenhower administration, during which legislation beneficial to big business was passed, including the Interstate Highway and Defense Act of 1956. In addition, Robert S. McNamara, taking with him a number of other "whiz kids," moved from the Ford Motor Company into the position of U.S. Secretary of Defense during the Kennedy and Johnson administrations.

The prominence of automobile executives in the Defense Department was unsurprising, since automobile factories manufactured Jeeps, aircraft, and tanks during World War II. Some government policies tremendously benefited the automobile industry, such as the construction of the U.S. and interstate highway systems, but others threatened corporate profits. General Motors, in its 1979 annual report, complained that its net income had fallen to only 4.4 percent, whereas its profits amounted to 10.3 percent in 1965. From its perspective, the government should reduce spending, regulation, and the size of the national deficit. Interestingly, regulation of the automobile industry, at least as it applied to automobile safety, occurred as the result of actions taken by General Motors in 1965. In 1956, Ford Motor Company introduced a deep-dish steering wheel, which allegedly was less likely to crush a driver's chest in the event of an accident, but no profits to the company clearly resulted. In ensuing years, a Democratic congressman from Alabama studied automobile safety yet made relatively little headway. But, in 1965, an obscure lawyer named Ralph Nader published *Unsafe at Any Speed*. The book lambasted automobile manufacturers for their lack of emphasis on safety, as evidenced by the production of hardtops, cars lacking center roof pillars, which crushed easily during rollovers. Nader also identified one vehicle not sold in a hardtop version, the rear-engine Chevrolet Corvair, which rolled over easily due to a weak rear axle design. General Motors responded by hiring private detectives to investigate Nader's personal life. This grotesque invasion of his privacy made Nader a household name and led to his testifying before a transportation safety committee chaired by Democratic U.S. Senator Abraham Ribicoff of Connecticut. Following lengthy testimony, which included a grisly X-ray photograph of a boy with a 1951 Mercury hood ornament embedded in his skull, Congress passed the National Highway Traffic Safety Act of 1965.

Regulation hit its peak during the administration of Richard M. Nixon when Congress established the Environmental Protection Agency, the Occupational Safety and Health Administration, and the Consumer Product Safety Commission. Then, in the late 1970s, the government began deregulating industries in an effort to increase competition and provide consumers with lower prices.

Era of Deregulation

In the late 1970s, Americans placed great emphasis on airline deregulation, and later Clinton economist appointee Alfred Kahn led the charge. Efforts also ensued to deregulate financial institutions, particularly the savings and loan industry, and this activity accelerated during the administration of Ronald W. Reagan during the early 1980s. During the mid- to late-1980s, many of the savings and loan associations failed in the aftermath of deregulation changes, with hundreds of billions of tax-payers' dollars required to ameliorate the meltdown.

During the 1980s and 1990s, the deregulation of the banking and financial services institutions occurred. In 1980, the Depository Institutions Deregulation and Monetary Control Act (DIDMCA) phased out interest rate regulations and all banking institutions were placed under the control of the Federal Reserve. In 1982, Congress passed the Garn–St. Germain Act, which allowed for the creation of money market accounts and interstate mergers among banks. In 1983, the International Lending Supervisory Act gave regulatory agencies the authority to establish capital requirements for banks. In the aftermath of the Savings and Loan crisis of the late 1980s, Congress passed the Financial Institutions Reform, Recovery, and Enforcement Act (FIRREA) of 1989, which restructured the FDIC, established the Resolution Trust Corporation to close hundreds of thrifts, moved oversight responsibility for these institutions to the Office of Thrift Supervision (OTS) under the U.S. Department of Treasury, and increased insurance premiums. In 1991, the Federal Deposit Insurance Corporation Improvement Act granted the FDIC the authority to monitor troubled banks. Then, in 1999, Congress passed the Financial Services Modernization Act (also referred to as the Gramm-Leach-Bliley Act), which removed restrictions on banks affiliating with securities firms, created a new "financial holding company," provided for state regulation of insurance, streamlined governmental restrictions on bank holding companies generally, and included a host of other reforms governing savings and loans and other financial intermediaries.

The deregulation of the financial services institutions resulted in numerous mergers between banks, insurance, and investment firms during the early years of the first decade of the twenty-first century. These giant firms were deemed "too big to fail" by the Federal Reserve and Department of Treasury when the financial crisis of 2007 hit. The number of financial institutions that failed went from 0 in 2005 and 2006 to 3 in 2007, before climbing to 25 in 2008, and jumping to 140 in 2009. The government brokered the sale of the fifth-largest U.S. investment firm of Bear Stearns to JPMorgan Chase, providing $29 billion to cover the less liquid assets of the firm, in March 2009. By September, the Federal Reserve and Department of Treasury bailed out the two mortgage giants Fannie Mae and Freddie Mac, with the federal government receiving

79 percent ownership, in preferred stock, of the two institutions. Later that month, Merrill Lynch was forced to voluntarily sell itself to Bank of America when the government refused to provide a bailout for the company. Lehman Brothers, another investment firm, could not find a buyer and was forced into bankruptcy, the largest bankruptcy of an investment firm in U.S. history up to that time. On September 23, the government was forced to bailout the worldwide insurance giant American International Group (A.I.G.) with an $85 billion credit facility in exchange for 79 percent of the company in preferred stock. Two days later, bank regulators seized and sold the assets of Washington Mutual Bank to JPMorgan Chase. The next day, Washington Mutual filed for bankruptcy, the largest bank failure in U.S. history. In December 2008, the government also bailed out another financial giant, CIT Group.

Despite the creation of the Troubled Asset Relief Program (TARP), which allocated $700 billion for the purchase of toxic securities from the nation's bank portfolios in exchange for preferred stocks in the institutions, the number of bank failures continued to escalate throughout 2009. In all, there were 168 bank failures from 2007 through 2009.

As a result of the deregulation of the financial services industry, the relationship between the federal government and big business became more interwoven than ever before. In 2010, the government owns the majority of many banks, investment, and insurance firms. In addition, the government also brokered deals with the two auto giants General Motors and Chrysler in which the government received majority control of the stock in exchange for financial bailouts. Since that time, both companies filed and came out of bankruptcy within a relatively quick period of time, approximately two months, in the first half of 2009.

Government ownership of controlling interests in many of the nation's largest businesses led to much debate concerning the role of the federal government in the private sector. No doubt this debate will continue long after the financial crisis passes.

References

Critchlow, Donald T. *Studebaker: The Life and Death of an American Corporation.* Bloomington: Indiana University Press, 1996.

"Economic Report of the President." Washington, DC: U.S. Government Printing Office, 1999.

Flippen, J. Brooks. *Nixon and the Environment.* Albuquerque: University of New Mexico Press, 2000.

Hayes, Jimmy, to author. Letter in possession of author. December 7, 1994.

Johnston, J. Bennett, to author. Letter in possession of author. December 12, 1994.

Niemark, Marilyn Kleinberg. *The Hidden Dimensions of Annual Reports: Sixty Years of Social Conflict at General Motors.* Princeton, NJ: Markus Wiener, 1995.

Plano, Jack C., and Milton Greenberg. *The American Political Dictionary.* 11th ed. Fort Worth, TX: Harcourt College Publishers, 2002.

Reid, T. R. *Congressional Odyssey: The Saga of a Senate Bill.* San Francisco: W. H. Freeman, 1980.

Communications

Ann Harper Fender

Recognizing the importance of communications among citizens of the newly-formed United States, the Continental Congress appointed Benjamin Franklin the country's first postmaster general in 1775. In the eighteenth century, letters were the primary means of communication for those separated by space, and the country's founders realized that timely delivery of mail would help to bind the new nation together, facilitate commerce, and encourage the flow of ideas and information. In making mail service the responsibility of the federal government, these officials implicitly recognized that private markets were unlikely to generate optimal outcomes in the provision of this communication service.

From an economic perspective, an industry generates maximum social benefits if production expands until the cost of producing one more unit of output just equals the benefit derived from producing that additional unit. Further, all costs of production are incurred by the producer, so no external costs fall on those not privy to the decision to produce the good or service in question. All benefits of production fall to the consumers who purchase the product; thus, those not privy to the decision to purchase recognize no external benefits. In other words, costs and benefits are private. Theoretical analysis suggests that competitive markets generate, via the self-interest of the producing and consuming parties, an outcome whereby the net social benefits of production are maximized. Economic efficiency exists in that there is no dead-weight loss—that is, there is no difference between the maximum net social benefits and the actual net benefits generated by the industry outcome. This conclusion—the optimality of competitive outcomes—holds only for perfect competition in static contexts with no spillover (additional) effects or externalities (external, uncontrolled) effects. Such ideal conditions are unlikely to be met by any real-world markets, of course. But in many cases, actual conditions are close enough to this ideal and the difficulties of attempting any effective public policy intervention are pervasive enough that relatively unregulated markets, which bring together private buyers and sellers, function reasonably well in allocating society's scarce resources.

Historically, three conditions particular to the communications industry have seemed sufficiently far from the competitive ideal to warrant intervention. Although those conditions especially apply to telecommunications, they arguably typify mail communications as well. First, the industry exhibits network effects. With network effects, externalities occur because of interdependent demands. For instance, the benefit each consumer enjoys from using telephone service depends on the number of other people using that service: A single subscriber to a telephone service obtains no benefit (other than status perhaps) without being able to call others. But with network effects, all consumers benefit by interconnectivity, so that each consumer can reach every other consumer. This interconnectivity does not necessarily require the offering of service by only one provider, but it does require that different providers use compatible equipment—in essence, that there be a single, networkwide standard. Network effects also provide an efficiency rationale for universal service.

A second condition warranting intervention stems from economies of scale, which occur when a proportional increase of all inputs raises output by a greater proportion. When economies of scale are extensive relative to market demand, a single firm can supply the market at a lower cost per unit of output than can multiple firms. Competition is unlikely to exist as a dominant firm expands to take advantage of the lower average costs that come with high output.

The third condition occurs with economies of scope, when more than a single product or service is produced. Telecommunications firms, for example, produce multiple services, such as long-distance and local calling. With economies of scope, a firm can produce a given quantity of both services at a lower total cost than could two firms, each specializing in the production of one of the services.

Given the existence of these three conditions, modern public policymakers deem telecommunications likely to operate monopolistically or even a natural monopoly, which controls the market through increased efficiency in the industry. Eighteenth-century public policy makers came to a similar conclusion about mail service. Believing that the private delivery of mail would not generate as much service as was socially desirable, they set up a public firm to handle this responsibility.

Technological change dramatically altered the delivery of communications services in the two centuries following Franklin's appointment. Public policy changed, albeit not always smoothly or quickly, in response to this evolving technology, but communications remained a target for collective ownership or oversight and regulation.

Postal Service

Even before Franklin's appointment as postmaster general, the North American colonies experimented with both privately and publicly funded mail delivery schemes. During a time when transportation by sea was much cheaper than transportation over land, communication between England and North America dominated colonial mail service. In 1639, Richard Fairbanks's Boston tavern was named the receiving site for this overseas mail, and it became the location from which colonial distribution emanated. In 1673, the New York governor established a short-lived monthly mail service between New York and Boston, and William Penn set up Pennsylvania's first mail service 10 years later. In 1691, the British Crown contracted with a private organization to establish central mail delivery and then purchased control of the

Postman delivering mail, rural mail route, York County, Maine. Photo by George W. Ackerman, August 26, 1930. (National Archives and Records Administration.)

system in 1707. In the 1730s, long before his Continental Congress appointment, Franklin served as postmaster in Philadelphia under the British system, and he became one of the two joint postmasters general for the British in the colonies. Under his leadership, the postal service reported its first surplus in 1760. After Franklin was dismissed in 1763, Postmaster William Goddard instituted the Constitutional Post to provide mail service among the colonies, with the funding obtained by subscription and revenues used to improve the services offered. When the colonies revolted, Franklin chaired the Committee of Investigation to formulate a mail system. Under the 1781 Articles of Confederation, Congress had the sole right to create and regulate post offices. Initially, letter recipients paid the postage costs but, in 1847, the post office issued stamps purchased by the senders of mail.

Facing little or no competition in providing communications, the postal service grew with the new country, and new technology complemented this service. In

1832, the postal service entered into tentative contracts for transporting correspondence by rail. An 1838 act designated all U.S. railroad routes as postal routes; soon postal agents accompanied the mail on the rails, and 1862 witnessed the first post office on wheels. The westward movement of the railroad preempted a brief but memorable effort at an express, horse-based mail service between Missouri and California. The Pony Express operated between April 1860 and October 1861, when telegraph lines reached the West Coast. In 1911, with the development of air transportation, the postal service began to ship mail by plane.

The public provision of mail service was partly motivated by considerations of economic efficiency. The political interest in tying the country together also encouraged this service. Concerns about fairness likely affected post office decisions about rates and interacted with the goal of providing universal service. The postal service introduced free city delivery in 1863, the same year it established uniform postage rates within the country, regardless of distance. Rural free delivery followed 29 years later.

During Andrew Jackson's administration, the postal service attained Cabinet status, but the 1970 Postal Reorganization Act, motivated by large deficits in the post office budget, removed the service from the Cabinet and streamlined its operations.

Telegraph Service

The application of electricity to communications was described at least as early as 1753, with published suggestions for an electric telegraph. The early-nineteenth-century development of the electrochemical battery and the discovery of the relationship between magnetism and electricity led the way to a working prototype, which Samuel Morse demonstrated in 1837. Like the postal service, the telegraph industry made use of the railroads, for telegraph lines were strung along the right-of-way for the rail lines' roadbeds. In 1844, the first workable telegraph line of significant distance was strung for 40 miles along the Baltimore and Ohio Railroad tracks between Baltimore and Washington, D.C. The usefulness of telegraphy, especially when vast distances separated people and activities, led to its rapid adoption, and in less than 20 years from their initial commercial use, telegraphs lines connected the Atlantic and Pacific Coasts. By the end of the American Civil War, international telegraph service linked the United States with Europe.

The telegraph industry displayed at least some of the attributes of a natural monopoly. Most European countries set up government-owned monopolies to provide telegraph service, and they restricted entry into the industry, just as they would do for telephone service. But in the United States, policymakers instead were confronted with a private monopoly when the many competing companies merged into the Western Union Telegraph Company in 1865.

The lively minds of nineteenth-century scientists, fascinated by electricity, developed the basic elements of the writing telegraph, a rudimentary facsimile machine. The scientists also experimented with wireless electrical communication systems. Successful commercial applications of these technologies did not emerge until well into the twentieth century.

Office of E. T. Holmes, headquarters of the first business telephone system serving Boston, Massachusetts, in 1877. (Library of Congress.)

Telephone Service

In the 1974 antitrust case brought by the U.S. Department of Justice against American Telephone and Telegraph (AT&T), the company argued that the regulated monopoly structure of the U.S. telephone industry served consumers well. AT&T's defense rested upon its contention that telephone service, as a network industry, worked best when a single firm connected all consumers, handled both local and long-distance calls, provided equipment of the necessary quality and compatibility, and developed new equipment and services for the future. Hence, the company contended, the vertically integrated structure of the telephone industry—with a single company controlling equipment manufacturing (through Western Electric), providing long-distance service (through long lines), interconnecting with local operating companies (through wholly owned operating subsidiaries), and undertaking research (through Bell Laboratories)—generated good outcomes. It provided consumers one-stop shopping for telephone service, at prices that made local service almost universal, and it compared favorably with the state-owned monopoly telephone companies common in most other countries of the world.

In contrast, the Antitrust Division of the Justice Department contended that AT&T used its position to monopolize the industry in violation of the Sherman Anti-Trust Act and to forestall potential competitors' entry into the field. Eight years later, in 1982, the parties settled the case via a consent decree, issuing the modified final judgment that resulted in the largest divestiture in antitrust history and the breakup of the Bell system. As the new millennium dawned, the consequences of this breakup, the effects in the United States of a new telecommunications law, and the forces of changing technology continued to modify the structure of the telecommunications industry, and few commentators were brave enough to predict the future of that structure. In 2005, Southwestern Bell Corporation acquired and merged together 10 of the 22 regional Bell companies under the name of AT&T.

Economic Characteristics of the Telephone Industry

Because the telecommunications industry exhibits network effects and because economies of scale and scope occur in production, perfectly competitive markets are unlikely to exist in this field. In some countries, policymakers responded to the failure of the private market in telephony by providing the service publicly, thereby substituting public monopoly for private monopoly. In other nations, most notably the United States, policymakers severely limited entry into the industry by granting a single franchise to a private provider of telecommunications services and then regulating that supplier, presumably to protect consumer interests. As technological change occurred during and after World War II, the relationship of effective telecommunications to military policy added a defense concern to the policy goals. Whatever the benefits or costs of past public policy, evolving telecommunications technology during the last half century led to pressures for policy change.

History of the Telephone Industry in the United States

In 1876 and 1877, Alexander Graham Bell received patents on basic telephone equipment, besting Elisha Gray's similar patent filing. Bell offered to sell his patent rights to Western Union for $100,000, an offer which was refused. Western Union soon attempted to enter the telephone industry on its own, using equipment developed by the Thomas Edison labs. The new manager of the Boston Bell Patent Association, Theodore Vail, forced Western Union to back out of the telephone field by threatening to sue for patent infringement. The American Bell Company made money by assigning exclusive franchises to companies in separate geographic areas, taking an equity stake in each. In 1881, Bell purchased Western Electric, the equipment manufacturer, and four years later established a toll company, the long lines which connected the local Bell operating companies. Thus, by the time that the original Bell patents expired in 1893 and 1894, the vertically integrated structure of the Bell system was in place.

The now-public American Bell Company faced competitors attracted to the industry by the company's high profits even before Bell's patents expired—and despite its practices designed to control the market. For example, Bell required customers to lease all telephone equipment from the company. It also refused to provide interconnection for competitors to its long-distance service; thus, customers who wanted such service and non-Bell local service needed two telephones. In addition, the company proceeded to buy up its competitors. Its increasing dominance of the telephony industry as the twentieth century dawned resulted from economies of scale and scope and efficiencies derived from central control of the network. The dominance also stemmed, however, from deliberate strategies to drive efficient competitors from the field through predatory pricing, financial market connections, and manipulation of the regulatory environment. Through its ownership of the Empire Subway Company in New York City, for instance, AT&T refused its potential local-service competitors access to underground conduits. It also agreed to limit its entry into telegraphy in return for Western Union's commitment not to lease pole space to telephone competitors. Despite such efforts, however, independents did manage to establish local companies, especially in the Midwest, and they also set up regional networks. Some contend that, in response, AT&T strategically set prices below the average variable cost in local markets, using profits from its monopolized markets to subsidize short-term losses in its competitive markets. This predatory pricing hurt the competition, deterred potential competitors, and reduced buyout prices. The regional independents had neither AT&T's profits from monopolized markets nor the company's access to New York financial markets to sustain their own short-term losses. The panic of 1907 further exacerbated the financial problems of the independents.

To avoid scrutiny of its purchases of rival operations in terms of antitrust violations, AT&T sometimes used third parties to make acquisitions on its behalf. For example, in 1909, AT&T provided the R. L. Day Company $7.3 million to purchase the United States Company, a Midwestern independent whose assets were valued at almost $13 million. The only legal action that AT&T faced from its operations in competition with the United States Company came from minority stockholders in Central Union, AT&T's regional operating company. In the 1909 case *Read et al. v. Central Union*, these individuals filed suit against the majority stockholders when Central Union consistently incurred losses in its attempt to drive the independent firm from the market. The judge in the case ruled that Central Union's predatory actions harmed the plaintiffs, and he ordered AT&T to sell its holdings in the company. Before this judgment was effected, however, the parties settled out of court, with AT&T purchasing the minority shares at prices well above market value and par value (the amount paid to the investor at maturity).

AT&T also took advantage of state regulations to enter local markets on more favorable terms than the incumbents (companies already in the market) faced and to deny its competitors access to valuable facilities. For example, as a precondition for entry into the local market, New York required companies to offer long-distance connections to all cities within 1,000 miles that had more than 4,000 residents and to present contracts providing this service within six months of receiving a New York franchise.

By 1910, AT&T, under the leadership of Theodore Vail (who had resigned from the company in the 1880s but returned early in the twentieth century), consolidated its hold on the telephone industry. Economic historians note that during the competitive period following patent expiration and lasting roughly until 1910, telephone connections grew at an annual rate of 20.6 percent, as compared with 3 percent to 5 percent in the preceding and succeeding years. They point out that, in 1920, only 35 percent of all households had telephones and that both the proportion and the number of farms having phones fell in the 1920s and 1930s.

Foreshadowing current debates about the relationship between telecommunications and broadcasting via broadband, AT&T briefly maintained interests in radio broadcasting after World War I. Italian scientist Guglielmo Marconi's experiments with radio waves in the early twentieth century led to commercial radio. The Pittsburgh-based Westinghouse Company, through its radio station KDKA, used amplitude modulation for the first U.S. public broadcast in 1920. Several other companies, including AT&T, soon set up their own stations. AT&T's radio station, WEAF, began broadcasting from New York in 1922. Westinghouse and General Electric (GE) established the Radio Corporation of America (RCA) as a patent-holding company and, in 1926, AT&T agreed to sell its interests in radio broadcasting to RCA.

Regulation of the Telecommunications Industry

Antitrust policy seeks to promote greater competition and the gains associated with it by prohibiting monopoly and specific practices considered likely to lead to monopoly. English common law long proscribed monopoly, but passage of the Sherman Anti-Trust Act in 1890 formally codified the federal position toward market control in the United States. When competitive markets are deemed unlikely to exist or unlikely to function in the interest of consumers, the U.S. policy response was to limit entry into the affected industry, to grant a franchise permitting entry to the successful applicant(s), and then to regulate the behavior of the licensed firm. Antitrust actions were brought numerous times against telephone service providers, especially AT&T, both by private plaintiffs and by the Antitrust Division of the Justice Department.

State regulation of telecommunications preceded federal involvement. Several southern states were the first to enact regulations in this field, and perhaps they tried to use low communications rates to entice business investment. In 1907, Wisconsin and New York became regulatory leaders. By 1914, 34 states and the District of Columbia were regulating such things as rates, licensing and interconnection requirements, and common-carrier status. Congress promulgated federal regulations with an amendment to the Mann-Elkins Act of 1910, which provided for Interstate Commerce Commission (ICC) oversight of the telephone industry. The postal service cast a covetous eye toward the industry, agreeing with Vail that it was a natural monopoly. Populists and monopolists joined forces to prohibit competition in the industry. Faced with the possibility of a government-owned telephone company, AT&T supported measures to make the industry a regulated monopoly. And with regulation, AT&T became somewhat immunized, at least for a while, from antitrust actions. The federal

Willis-Graham Act of 1921 shifted the regulatory oversight of telephone mergers and acquisitions from the Department of Justice to the ICC; as regulator of the telephone industry, the ICC primarily reacted to complaints. Economic concerns in the 1930s about problems with holding companies led to the 1934 passage of the Federal Communications Commission Act. This legislation set up the Federal Communications Commission (FCC) agency to regulate interstate telephony and set the dominant tone of regulation until the 1982 court-mandated breakup of the Bell system and the 1996 Telecommunications Act. The 1934 act further formalized the dual regulation of the telephone industry, with the Federal Communications Commission (FCC) responsible for long-distance service and state (and local) agencies responsible for local service. Because the services were supplied interdependently, with long-distance calls originating and terminating through the access lines of local service providers, the appropriate division of regulatory responsibilities was frequently questioned. A single company, AT&T, usually provided both local and long-distance services.

Although the Bell system initially did not rush to provide service outside major urban areas, it supported the regulatory goal of establishing universal service. To the extent that universal service took advantage of network effects, it augmented the value of telephone service to all users. Increasingly, however, universal service meant the provision of basic service at "affordable" rates. Regulatory agencies typically set rates to cover the costs of production, with a reasonable return on investment included. Although some of the costs of telephony were attributed to a particular service, ambiguity exists about how to divide other costs among the services offered. The Bell system, with regulatory oversight, met the requirement of providing affordable service by charging rates below the cost of production for some services; it then was permitted to charge rates above the cost of production on other, "nonbasic" services to offset the losses incurred on basic services. Over time, an elaborate system of cross-subsidization arose, with long-distance calls subsidizing local service, business customers subsidizing residential customers, and urban users subsidizing rural users. It is not clear that these subsidies redistributed real income from the rich to the poor, but without doubt they increasingly distorted economic decision making. And over time, the regulatory rate structure probably discouraged the use of the least-cost combination of resources to produce a given level of output.

The first public demonstration of microwave technology occurred in 1915, and American and British groups worked on its further development. By 1946, several U.S. firms sought FCC franchises for microwave telecommunications service in a number of eastern cities. Faced with this challenge, the Bell system undertook a massive R&D effort that enabled it to introduce a nationwide microwave system, which it had readied by 1950. With pressure from AT&T, the FCC excluded all other microwave competition until 1959, thereby transforming this arena of potential competition into an exclusive AT&T monopoly over both transmission and equipment. In 1959, the FCC issued its "above 890 megahertz" decision, which granted to private companies the use of that portion of the bandwidth for internal microwave operations. Finally, in 1969, the FCC allowed Micro-Wave, Inc. (MCI), after a six-year quest, to enter the long-distance service market, and it required AT&T to interconnect MCI with local operating companies. Entry into the long-distance market was particularly attractive because regulation led to high long-distance rates (presumably to subsidize universal local service). It is likely that these high rates unrealistically attracted multiple companies to enter the industry.

Space exploration led to yet another telecommunications technology. By the end of the 1960s, seven international satellites orbited the earth and possessed the potential to relay telecommunication signals. The FCC granted a franchised monopoly to Comsat, a mixed private corporation established in 1962, and the company partially succeeded in capturing the U.S. domestic satellite market. (A mixed private corporation is composed of diverse forms of public and private enterprises working together—for example, local police, agents from the Federal Bureau of Investigation [FBI], and Pinkerton detectives, all with policing authority.) Given the interest in this market and the political pressure for access to it, a 1970 White House initiative established a policy permitting all qualified applicants to send up satellites. Successful entry into the field still required interconnection with the Bell system, but regulatory moves made this more likely.

Antitrust Issues in the Telephone Industry

During AT&T's aggressive pursuit of its competitors in the early twentieth century, a number of independent companies complained to the newly formed Antitrust Division of the Justice Department. Reacting to these complaints, the division filed suit against AT&T, charging the dominant firm with monopolization. In response, AT&T entered into the so-called Kingsbury Commitment of 1913, agreeing to provide long-distance interconnections to its competitors and promising not to purchase further competitors without regulatory approval. The company also divested itself of Western Union through this agreement. However, AT&T continued to purchase noncompeting companies, and the 1921 Willis-Graham Act, which shifted merger oversight to the ICC, further lessened the constraints on the company's acquisition of competitors. But before AT&T could acquire 100 percent of the country's local telephone companies, it once more agreed to restrict additional acquisitions. For their part, the independents learned that, under regulation, they and the dominant firm shared an interest in restricting new entrants into the market, and the remaining independents and AT&T coexisted peacefully until 1982.

Although the regulation of telephony reduced the antitrust pressure on AT&T, it did not eliminate it. The vertical integration of telephone research, equipment manufacturing, and local and long-distance service continued to generate concerns about possible violations of antitrust laws. In particular, AT&T's control over the price of telephone-related equipment led to fears that the company was inflating these prices and thereby generating costs then built into average cost-regulated prices; thus, for instance, AT&T could shift profits from the telephone service stage to the equipment manufacturing stage. In 1949, the Antitrust Division filed suit, seeking Bell's divestiture of Western Electric. Ultimately, the 1956 settlement of this case did not require divestiture, but it constrained AT&T from entering industries other than regulated telecommunications (such as the computer industry), and it further stipulated that the company produce equipment only for its own use and license its patents for reasonable and nondiscriminatory royalties.

Further concerns about AT&T's restrictions on the use of telephone equipment soon arose. As a result of the 1956 case involving the Hush-a-Phone, a device that permitted private conversations in crowded rooms, AT&T was required to permit attachments to its phone networks. Similarly, the 1968 decision regarding the Carterfone, a device involving a two-way radio system, permitted a coupling device designed for attachment to a phone in order to connect phone users with radio devices. Eventually, AT&T's requirement that users of its services lease and use only Western Electric equipment to access those services was eroded.

Changing technology further challenged regulatory control of a monopolistically structured telecommunications industry. Many of the challenges occurred through antitrust cases and led to the 1974 case in which the Antitrust Division again charged AT&T with violation of the Sherman Anti-Trust Act. After years of proceedings, the case was settled in 1982 when a modification of final judgment of the 1956 consent decree was issued. Changing technology and the potential for more competition within the telecommunications industry led to the decree and affected its specific requirements.

Technological Change

No one can dispute that AT&T was responsible for impressive R&D advances over the years. As mentioned, the company established its research facilities, the Bell Laboratories, in the late nineteenth century. Although not particularly noted as a strong source of new technology in that era, the labs became increasingly involved in basic research as well as commercial development. They also played an important role in military-related research during and after World War II. Yet despite the success of the laboratories, it is not clear that AT&T pursued and implemented the most advanced telecommunications technology possible. Rather, the company may well have sought to protect its large capital investment, and at any given time, that investment was tied to a particular technology. Companies with market power, especially those with market power protected by legal barriers to the entry of competitors, are not under the same pressure to develop new technology as are firms that seek to enter the existing market. Thus, AT&T was not quick to develop microwave telecommunications technology, a potent alternative to fixed-line transmission. Similarly, the company did not lead in satellite developments, another potential source of competition, though national and regulatory policies influenced this outcome.

As computer technology developed after World War II, the military became increasingly interested in sharing information between computers separated by space, and transmission over telephone lines seemed a reasonable means to accomplish this goal. Defense leaders expressed concern as to whether AT&T could and would create the digital technology and equipment necessary for transmission of data to replace the older, slower analog system. The company assured the government that it would do so. However, it is not clear whether AT&T was more active in this arena than more competitive firms would have been.

Fiber-optic lines transmit many more messages than copper wire and allow faster transmission. Teleport, not AT&T, installed the first fiber-optic lines in New York City. Rapid advances in switching-equipment technology and the use of electronics generally accelerated in the 1990s, allowing more firms to compete in the industry. The fiber-optics industry increased the speed of transmitting information and allowed for the development of high-speed connections for computer-to-computer communications.

The advent of the personal computer (PC) produced a great economic impact on the United States. At first, PCs were used primarily for their word-processing and spreadsheet capabilities and communicated over telephone lines through dial-up modems. By the beginning of the twenty-first century, new technology was developed to provide improved services to the 161 million PC owners and almost 166 million Internet users. The new communication revolution resulted in the development of an online entertainment industry. In 2000, more than 220,000 people were employed in the online gaming industry. According to recent reports, the industry generated $10.5 billion to the U.S. economy that year. The Bureau of Economic Analysis notes that the growth rate for the industry was 14.9 percent in 2001, double the growth rate of the U.S. economy as a whole. These changes are attributed largely to Web sites where players can form teams and challenge one another with instant responses both in the game and in online chats.

The Internet, which allows easy access to an unlimited amount of information, and satellite cellular telephones are now the most widely used forms of communication. In 2000, Americans owned over 69 million cell phones. The affordability of these two forms of technology resulted in their widespread use. By 2006, the number of American cellular phone users jumped to 203 million, which equated to nearly one cell phone per person in the United States.

The dramatic increase in the use of cell phones occurred partly because of the development of new technological features, such as SMS (short message service), by the cellular service providers as well as new devices such as Bluetooth. Text messaging and "tweeting" on Twitter made real-time communication available on a massive scale. Even the majority of newspapers have at least one Twitter account and send out at least 1 or more tweets per day to those who sign up for their messages. The New York Times has almost 2 million subscribers to their Twitter messages and the newspaper sends up to almost 100 tweets per day, which are then re-forwarded or re-tweeted to other people.

Computer technology in the first decade of the twenty-first century also continued to expand communications. The development of portable laptop computers, wireless internet technology, WiFi services, and a wide array of mobile applications makes access to the information and communication through email, webcams, and other means readily available to the majority of Americans. Those without computers of their own can access the Internet through terminals located at most public libraries. In addition, the rise of social networks such as MySpace and Facebook as well as group specific sites categorized by ethnicity, gender, and political and religious orientation as well as many others expanded communication opportunities to unprecedented heights. In the United States, more than 80 million Americans per month on average visit the online video site YouTube, where they can watch videos covering topics from politics to comedy at the click of a mouse. The availability of videos online plays a significant role in the dissemination of information and has broken the government stranglehold on information not only in the United States but also around the world. For example, in December 2009, anti-regime protests in Iran turned violent and bloody yet the Iranian government denied that such events were transpiring, but its denials rung hallow when video showing protesters being beaten was uploaded onto YouTube for the whole world to see.

References

Alexander, Donald, ed. *Telecommunications Policy: Have Regulators Dialed the Wrong Number?* Westport, CT: Praeger, 1997.

Brock, Gerald. *Telecommunications Policy for the Information Age: From Monopoly to Competition.* Cambridge, MA: Harvard University Press, 1994.

Bureau of the Census. *Historical Statistics of the United States: Colonial Times to 1957.* Washington, DC: U.S. Government Printing Office, 1960.

Gabel, David. "Competition in a Network Industry: The Telephone Industry, 1894–1910." *Journal of Economic History*, vol. 54, no. 3 (September 1994): 543.

Harris, Robert G., and C. Jeffrey Kraft. "Meddling Through: Regulating Local Telephone Competition in the United States." *Journal of Economic Perspectives*, vol. 11, no. 4 (Fall 1997): 93–112.

Irwin, Manley, and James McConnaughey. "Telecommunications." In Walter Adams and James Brock, eds., *The Structure of American Industry.* Upper Saddle River, NJ: Prentice-Hall, 2001.

Johnson, Leland. "Technological Advance and Market Structure in Domestic Telecommunications." *American Economic Review*, vol. 60, no. 2 (May 1970): 204–208.

Kittross, John, ed. *Documents in American Telecommunications Policy.* 2 vols. New York: Arno Press, 1977.

Mitchell, Bridger, and Ingo Vogelsand. *Telecommunications Competition: The Last Ten Miles.* Cambridge, MA: MIT Press, 1997.

Olufs, Dick W., III. *The Making of Telecommunications Policy.* Boulder, CO: Lynne Rienner Publishers, 1999.

Peltzman, Sam, and Clifford Winston, eds. *Deregulation of Network Industries: What's Next?* Washington, DC: American Enterprise Institute and Brookings Institution Joint Center for Regulatory Studies, 2000.

Shiers, George, ed. *The Development of Wireless to 1920.* New York: Arno Press, 1977.

Shiers, George, ed. *The Electric Telegraph: An Historical Anthology.* New York: Arno Press, 1977.

Shiers, George, ed. *The Telephone: An Historical Anthology.* New York: Arno Press, 1977.

Viscusi, W. Kip, John M. Vernon, and Joseph E. Harrington Jr. *Economics of Regulation and Antitrust.* 3rd ed. Cambridge, MA: MIT Press, 2000.

Vogelsang, Ingo, and Glenn Woroch. "Local Telephone Service: A Complex Dance of Technology, Regulation, and Competition." In Larry Duetsch, ed., *Industry Studies.* Armonk, NY: M. E. Sharpe, 1998.

Wilcox, Clair, and William G. Shepherd. *Public Policies toward Business.* 5th ed. Homewood, IL: Richard D. Irwin, 1975.

Wilson, Kevin G. *Deregulating Telecommunications: U.S. and Canadian Telecommunications, 1840–1997.* Lanham, MD: Rowman and Littlefield, 2000.

Currency

Wyatt Wells

Currency—money—provides a common unit of value, which allows commerce to move beyond barter and enables financial markets to develop. The British colonies in North America inherited their currency from Europe, which had conducted transactions with gold and silver coins (specie) for thousands of years. Since the late medieval period, financial instruments (bills of exchange and banknotes) supplemented specie. Issuers promised to convert their notes into specie on demand, but they never had enough gold and silver on hand to redeem all of their paper and counted on their financial assets—debts others owed them—to back their notes. From the start, the value of paper money depended chiefly on the creditworthiness of its issuer.

Conditions in the British colonies in North America forced major changes in this system. The colonies suffered chronic trade deficits that they covered, in part, by exporting specie. Accordingly, the supply of gold and silver was generally insufficient to finance even current business, much less the rapid expansion of the colonial economy. And the colonies did not have banks to provide notes or bills of exchange.

Colonists responded to the shortage of currency in three ways. They constantly extended credit to each other, so domestic trade more often involved the exchange of promissory notes rather than cash. Some colonies used commodities as money. From the seventeenth century, Virginia levied taxes and paid public officials' salaries in tobacco, for which a ready market existed in Europe. Most notably, some colonial governments issued paper money, either to finance government deficits or through loan offices. Such issues contradicted the conventional wisdom, which ascribed paper money value only if it was convertible into specie. Nevertheless, the colonies' paper money worked well in most cases. Governments usually issued only limited quantities of paper and provided for its redemption, accepting notes for taxes or the repayment of loans. This guaranteed a steady demand for paper money, which traded at only a modest discount to specie.

The American Revolution overwhelmed these expedients. The war with Britain severely reduced American exports and foreign trade, exacerbating both the payments deficit and the shortage of gold and silver. The Continental Congress could not levy taxes to defray military expenses and instead issued large quantities of paper money, whose value fell rapidly. Several states followed this example. By the 1783

Peace of Paris, which secured American independence, the nation was awash in worthless paper money.

The new federal Constitution, which went into effect in 1789, addressed this problem. It lodged authority over the currency with the central government and specifically banned state governments from issuing paper money. George Washington's Treasury secretary, Alexander Hamilton, quickly asserted the federal government's power. In 1791, he persuaded Congress to charter the Bank of the United States (BUS) with $10 million in capital, consisting of specie and federal bonds. The BUS issued banknotes equal to its total capital, which it redeemed on demand in specie. As was always be the case, the quantity of notes exceeded the specie in reserve. Hamilton also organized a mint to coin gold and silver, but the shortage of specie limited its output. Most of the coins in circulation were from abroad, and American coins were only common several decades later.

Hamilton's program was controversial. Thomas Jefferson and James Madison argued that the Constitution did not authorize a bank and that the operations of the BUS infringed on the legitimate rights of states. A strong popular prejudice existed against banking, which critics believed profited by manipulating credit rather than from honest labor. Finally, many Americans considered corporations, with their limited liability and special powers, synonymous with monopoly and privilege, which the Revolution supposedly banished. Only the support of President Washington and the Federalists allowed Hamilton to secure congressional approval of the BUS's charter.

Meanwhile, states chartered their own banks. Like the BUS, these institutions issued banknotes, which were supposedly redeemable in specie on demand, to borrowers. At first, states generally chartered only one institution to provide a uniform local currency. Banks proved very profitable, however, and soon others demanded similar privileges for themselves. Although each bank charter still required a special legislative act, these institutions multiplied rapidly and, by the early 1800s, dozens of banks, each of which issued its own notes, operated throughout the country. In theory, all were supposed to redeem their notes on demand in specie, but in practice, merchants were reluctant to accept the notes of distant banks about which they knew little. The BUS provided uniformity by purchasing state banknotes at close to par (face value) and redeeming them for either specie or its own notes. The practice was unpopular with state bankers, who at any time might find the BUS demanding a large portion of their specie. However, it kept the value of the wide variety of notes in circulation fairly equal and forced state banks to maintain a conservative ratio between notes issued and specie in reserve.

The growth of banks contributed in another way to the development of currency. Most of these institutions took deposits and gave borrowers credit on their books as well as banknotes. Those with bank credit could transfer funds by check. In cities such as Boston, New York, Philadelphia, and Baltimore, many transactions occurred without any cash changing hands—banks simply moved money from one account to another. Although little remarked at the time, bank accounts were money just as much as banknotes were. As early as 1800, the value of accounts roughly equaled the notes in circulation, and the importance of accounts continued to increase throughout U.S.

history. By 2000, cash made up a relatively small portion of the total supply of money in the country.

Congress refused to recharter the BUS when its initial authorization expired in 1811. Hamilton was dead by that time, and Thomas Jefferson's Republicans were in power. Although 20 years of wise management won over some opponents, among them James Madison, many of the bank's critics remained unreconciled to it, and they could count on the support of certain state banks, which were irritated by the limits the BUS imposed on their operations.

The War of 1812 led at least some opponents of the BUS to reevaluate their stance. The war thoroughly disrupted foreign trade, which was, among other things, the chief source of tax revenue. Heavy military outlays further strained the government's credit, and throughout the war, Washington paid its bills slowly, if at all. The dislocation of international trade and government finances badly hurt banks. By 1814, most of them ceased redeeming their notes in specie. In effect, the country now possessed as many currencies as banks, with the notes of each institution valued according to the institution's reputation.

In 1816, the federal government created the Second Bank of the United States to remedy these problems. This bank was essentially a larger version of the First BUS, with $35 million in capital. Unfortunately, during the 1817–1818 boom, the new institution lent recklessly, and it suffered heavy losses in the 1819 panic. The Second BUS survived only by aggressively pressing its debtors for payment, driving many into bankruptcy and intensifying the economic hardship.

Nevertheless, by the mid-1820s, under the leadership of Langdon Cheves and Nicholas Biddle, the BUS managed to create a uniform currency. Supported by the U.S. Treasury, it gradually forced state banks to resume redeeming their notes in specie, and it followed the example of the First BUS in purchasing state notes at close to par and systematically cashing them in for gold or silver. The BUS also issued its own notes, which traded throughout the country at par. The bank provided another critical service by moving money around the country in response to seasonal changes in the demand for it. The United States was an overwhelmingly agricultural country, and many farmers and planters paid their bills once a year, when they sold their harvest. This created a regular jump in the demand for currency that, unless neutralized, could disrupt financial markets. The BUS systematically expanded its credits in the West and South during the fall, financing the movement of crops to market, and then reduced credits as the harvest was sold and borrowers repaid their debts. Inevitably, some state bankers resented the BUS's competition and the limits it placed on their ability to issue notes, but the business community as a whole appreciated the benefits of a stable, uniform currency.

In the 1830s, President Andrew Jackson struck a blow at federal control over the currency, causing damages not fully repaired for almost a century. In early 1832, he vetoed the bill renewing the charter of the BUS, and he withdrew the government's deposits from the institution, robbing it of its largest source of funds, in 1833. Opposition to the bank became the central issue around which the Democratic Party, the first political party formed in the United States in 1828, coalesced. In 1836, the

Second BUS ceased to exist when its charter expired. A variety of motives guided action in this regard. Some ambitious businesspeople opposed the limits the BUS imposed on their operations, as suggested earlier. This was particularly true of many New York bankers, who resented the power of the Philadelphia-based BUS. Further, many farmers and planters were suspicious of banking in general, seeing it as an essentially dishonest calling. Most telling, however, was the charge that the BUS was a corrupt aggregation of political and economic power resting on an exclusive government charter incompatible with political democracy. The bank's incompetent attempts to defeat Jackson in the 1832 presidential election reinforced this concern.

The demise of the Second BUS forced the nation to find other ways to regulate its currency. A few individuals, including Jackson himself at times, hoped to limit all transactions to specie, but the country did not have enough gold and silver for this. It needed banknotes. After a period of financial confusion, including two crises in 1837 and 1839 during which most banks stopped converting their notes into specie, a workable—if somewhat ramshackle—system emerged.

After the mid-1830s, states regulated banks and their notes. Policy varied considerably from state to state. Several states to the west and south (Indiana, Missouri, Mississippi) banned banking corporations altogether or chartered only one state-owned institution. Others, such as Louisiana and Massachusetts, strictly oversaw banks to guarantee they redeemed their notes in specie and, in general, conducted business in a sound fashion. New York devised the most important innovation: free banking. The Empire State automatically granted a banking charter to anyone with enough capital in bonds, allowing the individual to issue notes equal to the value of these bonds. This move legitimized banking by democratizing it, allowing anyone who met objective criteria to organize a bank and issue currency. Free banking also ended the need for the state legislature to authorize every banking charter, a process always contentious and often corrupt. By 1860, several other states adopted free banking, though it was hardly universal.

The federal government's Independent Treasury provided a practical brake on the issuance of notes by state banks. Authorized in 1840 and reauthorized in 1846, the Independent Treasury operated as Washington's financial agent, accepting tax receipts and making payments. It did business solely in specie. Consequently, taxpayers and buyers of public lands needed gold or silver, which they usually obtained by redeeming banknotes for specie. Such redemptions were not as systematic as those of the old BUS, but they did encourage banks to maintain a conservative ratio between notes issued and specie held in reserve.

Although the new system worked, it was not as efficient as the BUS. It had no mechanism to accommodate seasonal shifts in the demand for money and no device to keep banknotes at par. Indeed, discounting the hundreds of types of notes circulating in the United States became a significant part of most banks' business. The new system might not have worked at all had not the discovery of gold in California in the late 1840s injected a great deal of specie into the economy, partially compensating for the system's inflexibility.

California gold had another important implication for the currency. Although gold and silver served as money throughout most of history, in practice people used whichever was more plentiful for transactions and hoarded the other. During the early Republic, specie was largely silver. But the role of gold grew for several decades, and the influx from California largely drove silver from circulation. In the 1850s, the United States operated under a de facto gold standard, with the value of the dollar fixed at $20.67 to an ounce of gold. (The gold standard uses gold as the standard value for a nation's currency. Since 1971, when the United States left the gold standard, no country in the world has operated under this system. Instead, currencies are based on a floating rate set by market forces.)

The Civil War affected the currency as dramatically as it did most other aspects of American life. The military effort entailed unprecedented spending (several billion dollars), and to pay its bills, the federal government abandoned specie and issued $450 million worth of paper money known as "greenbacks." Greenbacks were a "fiat" currency that the government made legal tender for payment of debts. (A fiat currency is a worthless paper money that gains its value from confidence in the government's ability to meet its obligations.) The greenbacks were not convertible into specie, and many people feared that they would become worthless, as had paper money issued during the Revolution. But Washington also imposed heavy taxes and devised an extensive system of borrowing to pay most of its military expenses. The quantity of greenbacks was limited, and Washington created a demand for them by accepting them for federal bonds and most taxes. Accordingly, although greenbacks did depreciate against gold, bottoming out in 1864 at two and a half greenbacks to one gold dollar, they remained a viable currency. Gold still played a role, however. The federal government required importers to pay tariffs in the precious metal, and the holders of federal bonds received their interest in gold. Moreover, merchants conducted foreign trade in gold or sterling (Britain was on the gold standard, so its money was "as good as gold"). During and immediately after the Civil War, the United States possessed two currencies: gold and greenbacks.

Other reforms more than compensated for the confusion wrought by this two-tiered system. In 1863, Congress enacted the National Bank Act, which created a universal system of free banking. Anyone with enough capital, in the form of federal bonds, could receive a banking charter and the right to issue notes equal to the face value of these bonds. Banks deposited their bonds with the Treasury and promised to redeem notes on demand with greenbacks. Washington regularly audited national banks to guarantee they were sound. When state banks proved reluctant to convert to federal charters, the government imposed a prohibitive tax on their notes, forcing these institutions either to become federal banks or to stop issuing notes and become banks of deposit. However, the new system had weaknesses. The supply of money depended on the supply of federal bonds, not economic conditions. The financial system failed to adjust to seasonal shifts in the demand for money. And there was no mechanism to regulate deposits, which were twice as great as the supply of paper money by 1867. Nevertheless, Civil War–era banking reforms asserted federal control over the currency and, because greenbacks and national banknotes circulated interchangeably, gave the country its first genuinely uniform money.

With the end of the Civil War in 1865, most people expected the country to return swiftly to the gold standard. In fact, the process took 14 years and generated immense controversy. During the last third of the nineteenth century, prices fell steadily, in the United States and across the world. The decline did not impair American economic growth, but it did impose punishing burdens on debtors, who repaid loans in ever-more-valuable dollars. Debtors were naturally skeptical of returning to the gold standard, which entailed increasing the value of greenbacks to that of gold dollars—that is, more deflation (the devaluing of currency). The pressures for resumption were also strong, however. Many considered precious metals the only honest basis of currency. More important, during the 1870s, most Western European countries adopted the gold standard, which, by linking all currencies to gold, fixed their value in terms of each other, greatly facilitating international trade and investment. The United States conducted most of its foreign trade with these countries and relied on them for critical investment, and making the dollar "as good as gold" would strengthen these important relationships. After a long political debate, the United States returned to the gold standard in 1879, making greenbacks freely convertible into gold at the rate of $20.67 an ounce.

The return to the gold standard changed the currency in several important ways. Under that standard, the supply of money ultimately depended not on the quantity of federal bonds or greenbacks but on the country's gold reserve. This reserve, in turn, depended chiefly on the international balance of payments because countries paid their deficits in gold. If the United States ran a surplus, gold flowed in and the money supply expanded. A deficit drained gold and contracted the supply of money. The U.S. Treasury, which was responsible for redeeming greenbacks into the precious metal, held most of the country's gold reserve—a sharp contrast with the situation before 1861, when each bank held specie to cover its own notes.

Advocates of inflation did not give up after 1879 but instead turned their attention to silver. In 1873, Congress demonetized silver, which, because of plentiful gold supplies, did not actually circulated for decades. Although presented at the time as a rationalization measure to eliminate a type of money no one used, the initiative was intended to serve more significant objectives. The other industrial countries were abandoning silver for gold, and the United States sought to align its currency with those of its chief trading partners. Moreover, new discoveries of silver promised to vastly increase its supply; thus, if silver remained legal money, it would eventually replace less-plentiful gold, greatly expanding the money supply and unleashing inflation.

For these reasons, those hurt by falling prices began to call for "free silver"—the unlimited coinage of silver at the rate of 16 ounces of silver to 1 ounce of gold. Because the market price of silver was roughly one-thirtieth that of gold, this would effectively put the country on a silver standard and devalue the dollar, expand the money supply, and push prices upward. In the 1880s, Congress sought to appease silver interests by issuing fixed amounts of silver coins and silver certificates (notes backed by silver). Their limited quantity allowed the United States to maintain their

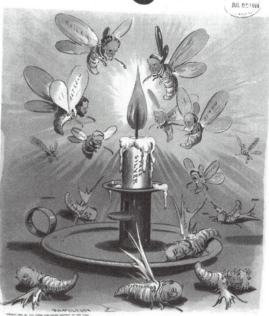

THE SILVER CANDLE AND THE MOTHS.

This free silver-gold standard controversy cartoon depicts John Peter Altgeld, Henry Teller, Ben Tillman, Boies Penrose, Richard Parks Bland, Adlai Stevenson, and Grover Cleveland as moths drawn to the flame of a candle labeled "free silver," and dying (1896). (Library of Congress.)

value against gold. But the severe financial panic from 1893 to 1897 increased the pressure for more currency and higher prices even as it created federal budget and national trade deficits, which drained the country's gold reserve. To limit the quantity of notes eligible for redemption, protect the reserve, and maintain the gold standard, Congress ended all silver coinage, a move which infuriated silverites (individuals who wanted to use silver as legal tender). In 1896, the Democrats nominated William Jennings Bryan for the presidency on a platform of free silver. The Republican candidate, William McKinley, took up the challenge, warning that an unlimited coinage of silver would drive gold from circulation, devalue the dollar against European currencies, and create financial chaos. The Republicans won a crushing victory, guaranteeing gold's central role in the currency for the next generation.

After 1900, debate on the currency shifted from its metallic basis to the structure of the banking system. The discovery of gold in Alaska and South Africa and the development of new techniques for refining it greatly increased the supply of the precious metal and inaugurated a period of mild but steady inflation worldwide, defusing pressures for silver currency and greenbacks. Moreover, the public increasingly recognized that most of the nation's money was in bank accounts, not coins or notes, and that the banking system had serious weaknesses. No mechanism existed to accommodate seasonal shifts in the demand for money, which were often severe during harvest time. In addition, reserves were scattered, so it was hard to mobilize money during a financial crisis. The inability to mobilize money meant that if depositors lost confidence in a bank and demanded cash for their deposits—that is, if they started a run—the bank might well fail even if its assets exceeded its liabilities. A severe financial panic in 1907 highlighted the need for reform.

The Federal Reserve Act, passed by Congress in 1913, altered the currency almost as drastically as Civil War–era reforms had. It established a dozen regional reserve banks in which all national banks and most leading state banks purchased stock. These Federal Reserve banks provided banks within their regions currency or credit in exchange for "real bills" (short-term commercial loans secured by goods), federal obligations (bonds), or gold. Commercial banks kept their reserves on deposit with the reserve banks, which, in a crisis, could advance funds to any institution in trouble. The Federal Reserve banks issued their own notes, gradually replacing the motley collection of greenbacks, notes from national banks, and silver certificates in circulation. In the long run, the supply of money still depended on the supply of gold, but reserve banks could cope with seasonal shifts in the demand for currency by purchasing (rediscounting) real bills from member banks to finance the movement of goods. The repayment of these loans resulted in the withdrawal of the money from circulation once it was no longer needed. A central board, appointed by the president and headquartered in Washington, was established to oversee the new Federal Reserve system (commonly referred to as "the Fed"). Bankers themselves largely authored these reforms, which were designed to reinforce the financial system, not remake it. But progressive reformers such as Bryan and the lawyer Louis Brandeis were able to insist that the politically appointed board in Washington have ultimate responsibility over the system.

World War I further changed the American and, indeed, the world monetary systems. The combatants abandoned the gold standard, and precious metal gravitated to the United States as the Allies used gold to pay for military supplies, greatly increasing both the supply of money and prices in the United States. After the country itself entered the conflict in 1917, Washington temporarily banned the export of gold, effectively suspending the gold standard. (Gold continued to circulate domestically.) To finance the country's military effort, the Federal Reserve purchased large quantities of federal bonds with its notes, further expanding the money supply and pushing prices upward. Overall, prices in the United States more than doubled between 1914 and 1920. The architects of the Federal Reserve assumed the gold standard would continue to govern international monetary relations and that real bills would constitute the majority of the Fed's assets. The war undermined both assumptions, forcing Fed officials to rethink monetary policy.

In the 1920s, the United States and leading European powers sought to re-create the monetary stability of the prewar era. The United States ended the embargo on gold exports in 1919, and a sharp recession in 1920 and 1921—a result, in part, of Fed efforts to halt inflation by raising interest rates—reversed some of the wartime rise in prices but other industrial nations only gradually followed the American example. They suffered more inflation than the United States and lost much of their gold reserves. Britain, the most important of these nations, returned to the gold standard only in 1925. Even after that year, the dollar held a special place in the international system. The United States possessed the world's strongest economy, and it consistently ran a surplus on its balance of payments (a statement which summarizes economic and financial transactions between banks, companies, private households, and public authorities in comparison with those of other nations on an annual basis). Dollars were at a premium, and some countries covered balance-of-payment deficits by transferring dollars rather than gold. The dollar partially replaced the precious metal in international finance. This freed the United States from the day-to-day limits the gold standard imposed on monetary policy and forced the Federal Reserve to devise new criteria for action. The central bank, working through the embryonic Open Market Committee (OMC), managed policy by trading federal securities in the open market. Purchases injected money into the financial system; sales sucked it out. But open market operations represented a tool, not a plan. In practice, Fed policy followed no hard-and-fast rule but the judgment of its leaders, who manipulated interest rates and the money supply in ways intended to promote economic growth and financial stability.

Their judgment proved unequal to the Great Depression. The stock market crash in the United States and comparable disasters in Europe deranged financial markets and set off a cascade of bankruptcies. Unsure how to respond and internally divided, the Fed vacillated between paralysis and adherence to the verities of the gold standard. In 1931, it raised interest rates to curtail gold exports, a move that helped choke off a recovery. The supply of money contracted by one-third between 1929 and 1933, hurting every type of business and forcing prices and production down sharply.

The disaster forced further changes in the currency. After taking office in 1933, President Franklin D. Roosevelt gradually devalued the dollar from $20.67 to an ounce of gold to $35, and his administration banned domestic ownership of gold entirely. Gold coins disappeared from circulation, replaced by paper. Though the precious metal continued, in theory, to back the currency, the link was tenuous. Gold mattered only for international transactions, and the Roosevelt administration overvalued the precious metal, so foreigners were eager to sell it to the United States at $35 an ounce. In practice, the dollar was a fiat currency, worth what it could buy in the marketplace. The federal government also insured deposits with commercial banks, largely eliminating the danger that bank runs could seriously damage financial markets. Finally, in 1935, Congress reformed the Federal Reserve system, centralizing authority in the Federal Reserve Board in Washington and giving the Open Market Committee formal authority over monetary policy.

During World War II, the Federal Reserve financed the American military effort by purchasing large quantities of federal bonds. This policy increased the money supply and drove prices up 50 percent between 1939 and 1948, but the increase was less than that during World War I because the federal government levied stiff taxes to pay for the war. The main wartime innovations in economics involved international finance. Most economists and government officials believed that in the 1930s the dislocation of international finance—devaluation, payments crises, and currency controls—contributed substantially to the Great Depression. Accordingly, the Allies devised a plan to rebuild the international monetary system once the war was over.

They sought stable exchange rates and readily convertible currencies but did not want to tie their money to the supply of gold—that is, they wanted the advantages of the gold standard without its disadvantages. To this end, the Allies adopted a system of "pegs," fixing the value of their currencies in terms of dollars, which were "as good as gold," and settling deficits and surpluses with the American currency. International agencies, most notably the International Monetary Fund (IMF), financed countries with deficits, and governments in dire circumstances regulated the flow of money across their borders. Other governments with accumulated dollars could convert them into gold at $35 an ounce.

This system worked fairly well for 20 years. The United States ran trade surpluses, which kept the dollar strong, and American foreign aid and investment allowed other countries to pay for imports and amass dollar reserves large enough to expand their own currencies in line with production. As a practical matter, dollars served the role that gold once served.

Domestic policy was less consistent. After 1945, the Fed kept the interest rates on government bonds low, purchasing them itself if private buyers would not. Although popular with the Treasury, this policy forced the Federal Reserve to expand the money supply rapidly if either the demand for credit or the government deficit rose sharply, thereby fueling inflation. That is exactly what happened after the outbreak of the Korean War in 1950. After long negotiations with the Treasury, the Fed changed its policy emphasis in 1951: Henceforth, it set interest rates and supply currency, first and foremost, to secure high employment and stable prices. The international balance of payments and government finances remained a significant, but secondary, consideration.

Between 1968 and 1973, a series of crises destroyed the international system. Rising prices in the United States (a side effect of heavy military and social spending, financed in part by currency expansion) as well as the growing efficiency of foreign competitors (chiefly Japan and Germany) created large payment deficits that Americans paid with dollars. Other countries accumulated stocks of the U.S. currency vastly greater than America's gold reserves. The United States could have raised interest rates and cut government spending to force prices down and eliminate the payments deficit, but no political support existed for this course, which would have entailed lower growth and employment rates, at least for a while. Further, the United States could not simply devalue its currency because the dollar was the centerpiece of the entire global financial system. In 1973, after a series of increasingly severe crises, the industrial democracies ended all pegs and allowed their currencies to float, or find their value in trading in financial markets. Washington formally severed the last link between the dollar and gold, ceasing to value its currency against the precious metal. After 1973, the United States replied on a fiat currency, worth only what it could buy in the marketplace. In 1975, Americans gained the right to own gold, with its price fluctuating like that of other commodities.

The dollar fared badly in the decade after 1973, during which consumer prices increased 130 percent—the most rapid rise in the country's peacetime history. Many factors conspired to push prices up, but ultimately, the problem reflected a lack of political will. The Federal Reserve could contain prices by raising interest rates and slowing the growth of the money supply, but in the short run, this approach would create a recession, which political leaders refused to tolerate.

Eventually, the pain of inflation eroded the resistance to strong measures. Starting in 1979, the Federal Reserve, under Chair Paul Volcker, embarked on a decisive campaign to tame inflation, raising interest rates to historical highs and strictly limiting expansion of the currency. However, this policy, in which the interest rate was linked to the money supply, produced unintended consequences since the switch took place right when the difficult components of the money supply were shifted when Congress allowed for the payment of interest on money market savings accounts, previously classified as part of M2 but which then combined with M1—the category to which Volcker's monetarist policy based interest rates on. This meant that the money supply figures were artificially increased and triggered higher than expected interest rate levels. These moves sparked a severe recession, which slowly recessed as inflation slowed and growth resumed after 1982 when the Federal Reserve abandoned its ineffective experimental monetarist policy. Although in its mechanisms quite different from the gold standard, this policy was designed with the same objective: establishing a stable currency.

Alan Greenspan, Volcker's successor, became Chairman of the Federal Reserve Board in 1987, serving in that capacity until 2006. During the remaining years of the 1980s and throughout the 1990s, he focused on monetary policies designed to fight inflation. During the 1990s, global trade changes resulted in countries such as China and other emerging developing countries initiated economic changes that increased their exports abroad, including to the United States and its other industrial trade partners. The U.S. dollar, along with the euro, served as the two international reserve currencies worldwide. Therefore, as China and the developing countries exported a rapidly increasing amount of goods to other countries, their reserve currency savings mounted to enormous levels. Between 2000 and 2005, these unintended reserve currency savings drove down the interest rate for long-term securities and helped to decouple the Federal Reserve's short-term interest rates, which regulated 30- and 60-day Treasury note rates and had remained in lockstep with long-term rates between 1971 and 2002, from the long-term rates on securities such as 30-year home mortgages.

Between the terrorist attacks of September 11, 2001 and June 2003, the Federal Reserve cut interest rates 13 times in an effort to stimulate an economy in a recession since March 2001. By late June 2003, Greenspan reported positive indications that the economy was improving but warned of some persisting weaknesses. When the Federal Reserve increased its short-time interest rate in 2004, Greenspan noted that the long-term rate did not respond accordingly and that the correlation between the two rates had "diminished to insignificance," attributing the change to the unintended reserve currency savings in China and other developing countries that continued to increase from the early 1990s until that time, which lowered long-term mortgage rates and allowed mortgage companies to expand the number of loans in their portfolios tremendously and also to offer a large portion of the loans in their portfolio to subprime borrowers with credit deemed insufficient for conventional loans at a higher interest rate. In 2005, as the number of mortgages climbed higher and higher, Greenspan warned Congress of his growing concern about the unprecedented growth of the nation's two giant mortgage government-sponsored enterprises (GSEs)—Fannie Mae and Freddie Mac—and the potential for a future financial crisis in the housing sector if the GSEs were not regulated more closely. By 2006, the long-term interest rate declined to single digits, according to Fed Chair Greenspan, for the first time in U.S. history that he was aware. These lower mortgage rates made home loans accessible to more and more marginal borrowers and drove the housing market frenzy.

In August 2007, American legislation, designed to impose trade sanctions against China in an attempt to revalue the Chinese *yuan*, was proposed. Two Chinese officials warned that if such legislation was enacted, the Chinese government, with its massive reserve currency savings, would sell a substantial amount of their reserves in America, with such actions significantly impacting the value of the dollar in a negative manner while also affecting the ability of the U.S. Treasury to attract additional short-term investments in government securities if so needed. The legislation was not enacted. However, that same month, the housing bubble, which had been driven by unprecedentedly low long-term rates, burst and the United States entered a recession.

During the recession, the Federal Reserve and Department of Treasury assumed an active role in ensuring that the financial markets did not fail. In March 2008, these efforts began with the government-brokered sale of Bear Stearns to JPMorgan Chase, under terms which included $29 billion from the government to cover the less liquid assets of the failing Bear Stearns. They continued through the September government bailouts of Fannie Mae and Freddie Mac as well as the insurance giant American International Group (A.I.G.), which were followed by the enactment of the $700 billion Troubled Relief Assets Program (TARP) in October. During late 2008, the dollar became stronger during the initial phase of the crisis. However, as retired Fed Chair Alan Greenspan noted, the dollar began to weaken again in early 2009 as countries such as China, Russia, and India with large reserve currencies in dollars began "moving away from the dollar to diversify their securities."

References

Broz, J. Lawrence. *The International Origins of the Federal Reserve System*. Ithaca, NY: Cornell University Press, 1997.

Chandler, Lester V. *Benjamin Strong, Central Banker*. New York: Arno Press, 1978.

Chernow, Ron. *The Warbugs: The Twentieth Century Odyssey of a Remarkable Jewish Family*. Ithaca, NY: Cornell University Press, 1993.

Friedman, Milton, and Anna J. Schwartz. *A Monetary History of the United States, 1867–1960*. Princeton, NJ: Princeton University Press, 1963.

Greenspan, Alan. "The Fed Didn't Cause the Housing Bubble," *Wall Street Journal*, March 11, 2009. Available: http://online.wsj.com/article/SB1236729650 66989281.html; accessed December 30, 2009.

Hammond, Bray. *Banks and Politics in America from the Revolution to the Civil War.* Princeton, NJ: Princeton University Press, 1957.

Hammond, Bray. *Sovereignty and an Empty Purse: Banks and Politics in the Civil War.* Princeton, NJ: Princeton University Press, 1970.

Kettl, Donald. *Leadership at the Fed.* New Haven, CT: Yale University Press, 1986.

Livingston, James. *Origins of the Federal Reserve System: Money, Class, and Corporate Capitalism, 1890–1913.* New York: Arno Press, 1978.

New York Times. "Greenspan Calls to Break Up Banks 'Too Big to Fail,' " October 5, 2009. Available: http://dealbook.blogs.nytimes.com/2009/10/15/greenspan-break-up-banks-too-big-to-fail/; accessed December 30, 2009.

Unger, Irwin. *The Greenback Era: A Social and Political History of America.* Princeton, NJ: Princeton University Press, 1964.

Woolley, John. *Monetary Politics: The Federal Reserve and the Politics of Monetary Policy.* New York: Cambridge University Press, 1984.

Economic Theories

Mary Stockwell

Although humans throughout time often wondered about the nature of buying and selling, only in the modern world did thinkers try to understand and explain this process in a systematic manner. The rise of economic theory developed when the world moved from ancient and medieval times into the modern era as the process of buying and selling became more complex. There seemed little mystery to economics in a world where the vast majority of men and women tilled the soil or brought wealth up from under the ground. A small group at the top—the emperors, kings, and nobles—drew the greatest benefit from this wealth. In this dual world, only the trader and the merchant who brought goods from distant lands seemed to hint at the existence of another reality. They pointed to an economics that moved past mere subsistence to the production of goods.

The steady stream of items shipped west by caravan and caravel from exotic places such as India, China, and Africa in late medieval and early modern times sparked a revolution that the best economic theorists of the last centuries have attempted to comprehend. Trade with the Orient and the subsequent rise of manufacturing in Western Europe paved the way for a new economic system, later known as capitalism. People once tied to the soil in subsistence agriculture could join the ranks of the middle class. Through trade and manufacturing, ambitious individuals could create more wealth for themselves and their nations than they had ever dreamed possible.

Just when the economy of Western Europe began changing so dramatically, British subjects founded the 13 original American colonies. Strung along the Atlantic shore from Massachusetts to Georgia, the people of these struggling colonies seemed to redefine economics every day just to survive. The first people who sailed west to Jamestown, Virginia, in 1607 remained very much a part of the old economic order. They hoped to find quick wealth in the New World and return to take their place as honored members in the English hierarchy. They came from a world still tied to its medieval past. Birth meant everything, and wealth served as a tool to move individuals into the highest reaches of the social order. So, ambitious young people headed for the James River, hoping to find the gold and silver to take back to England as noble heroes. Many traveled west reading the works of English geographer and author Richard Hakluyt, who wrote that even if the explorers failed to find gold and silver, surely they would discover a way west to the Orient and its wealth. They might even find a way to make exotic goods such as glass or silk in Virginia, and if nothing else, the fur trade would be profitable.

The Jamestown settlers quickly discovered the lack of precious metals in Virginia. Land offered the only opportunity for accumulating wealth, but the land required cultivation. Captain John Smith, a soldier of fortune who helped found Virginia and who explored Massachusetts, explained this new reality clearly. The English colonies in America would become a place where ambitious and hardworking men and women could make a good life for themselves as farmers, craftspeople, and traders. Although he could not phrase it as eloquently as later theorists, Captain Smith told the world that capitalism would rule the English colonies from the start.

For the next 150 years, the American colonists struggled to find the wealth in the land, as Smith first suggested. Freedmen and freedwomen, servants, and slaves carved out tobacco and rice plantations throughout the South; tight-knit communities of farmers in New England and larger family farms and trading towns in the Middle Colonies dotted the landscape throughout the north. To the west, the rich land stretched as far as the eye could see to the Mississippi River and beyond to the Rocky Mountains and the Pacific Ocean. With deep harbors and good forests all along the Atlantic shore, shipbuilding developed less than a generation after the founding of the first colonies. American vessels took the goods of the hardworking colonists— tobacco, rice, wheat, corn, fruit, livestock, and naval stores—not just to the English homeland but also to Africa, the Mediterranean, and the West Indies. When England tried to rein in its colonies economically during the 1760s through the Proclamation of 1763 and the enforcement of various acts of Parliament such as the Sugar and Stamp Acts, it was too late. The new economy had given rise to a new politics. The colonists declared their independence in 1776, and a new nation based on westward expansion, trade with the world, and the limitless production of goods was born.

Mercantilism versus Capitalism

It is not surprising that when European economists in the sixteenth and seventeenth centuries first confronted the new world of production, trade, and sale, they struggled mightily to understand it and generally interpreted it in light of the past. For a long time, wealth was derived from a limited supply of land and workers. However, large-scale farming, world trade, and manufacturing provided the keys to wealth. The first modern economic theorists, known as mercantilists, tried to comprehend the new economy in terms of the old. They argued that a limited amount of wealth existed in the world, and that every nation must do all in its power to acquire wealth, especially in gold and silver. Establishing colonies remained one of the best methods to attain wealth. These outposts provided raw materials and farm produce to the homeland, which, in turn, sold manufactured goods back to the colonies. The home country was assured of maintaining a favorable balance of trade by always exporting more goods than it imported. The colonies remained cash-poor to keep the gold and silver flowing home.

A group of French philosophers known as the Physiocrats first questioned the theory of mercantilism. Writing just as France lost its great empire in the New World, the Physiocrats argued that foreign trade was more a necessary evil than the prime factor in a strong economy. Even if much wealth was gained with trade between a home country and its colonies, the constant wars necessary to maintain the empire offset the gains, as the French learned all too well in the Seven Years' War. Even more important, the Physiocrats contended, mercantilists failed to grasp the essential fact of modern economic life: It is impossible to sell without buying at the same time. Similarly, individuals accumulated wealth more easily by manufacturing goods instead of just by hoarding gold and silver.

The Physiocrats remain famous to this day for coining the term *laissez-faire*. According to the laissez-faire doctrine, a government need not take strict control of every facet of the national economy. Instead, the entrepreneur must be allowed to develop production and other means of wealth as he or she sees fit, without the interference of the state. Likewise, the government must consider private property sacred, and the individual must control his or her own property. Ironically, the Physiocrats remained staunch supporters of absolute monarchy despite their call for respecting individual property rights.

The Physiocrats were the first to question mercantilism in theory, but the American colonists were the first to question it in practice. Britain's reinvigorated mercantilist policies of the 1760s and 1770s led a generation of political leaders in America to question their ties to the empire. They argued that the drive of settlers into the Ohio Country, the development of manufacturing in the Hudson River valley and northern Virginia, and trade on the high seas with the entire Atlantic world should not be stifled in service to Great Britain. Although these early leaders are most remembered for their demands for political liberty, they also argued for an end to mercantilist policies, which crushed the development of the American economy as a way to enrich the British Empire.

The founders of the American nation won the support of the Scottish political economist Adam Smith, the greatest economic theorist of his day, who published *The Wealth of Nations* in 1776—the very year the colonists declared their independence. Building on the work of the Physiocrats, Smith agreed that colonies drained a nation of wealth through constant wars, but he went even further by laying out the clearest explanation of how the modern economy in his era truly worked. He broke the last ties to the Middle Ages through his clear emphasis on production as the source of wealth. He reminded everyone that few people in the civilized world provided for all of their needs through their own labor. Most fulfilled their wants through the exchange of goods. Money was the necessary means of exchange in this world of changing goods. Further, he stated, the value of money was not a constant but instead depended on the supply and demand of goods. When supplies increased and demand decreased, prices went down. When the situation reversed, prices soared. The ever-fluctuating relationship between supply and demand was held in balance through a mysterious process that Smith described as the "invisible hand." In this new capitalistic world, he contended, the only role for government involved making certain that

Adam Smith, eighteenthth-century Scottish economist and father of the capitalist political-economic theory first articulated in his 1776 book *On the Wealth of Nations*. (Jupiter images.)

The Author of the Wealth of Nations

effective competition existed. Smith suggested that a government could do this through establishing equitable taxation and a solid banking system.

Smith's ideas launched the classical era in European economic thought as theorists joined the attempt to discover the underlying laws that governed the modern economy. David Ricardo emphasized the value of free trade and argued that no restrictions of any kind should be placed on it. In contrast, Thomas Malthus believed that the tie between reproduction and the food supply was the basis for the essential law governing economics. He believed that famine would inevitably occur, since population increased geometrically whereas the food supply only increased arithmetically. John Stuart Mill developed a utilitarian philosophy that stressed the development of the individual and the progress of all humanity. He taught that correct actions in every area of human life, including economics, increased both the quality and the quantity of human happiness. In economics, he argued that a new method to equalize the wealth of business owners and workers alike was needed.

In the United States, a politician, not a philosopher, embraced the challenge of trying to understand the modern economy. Alexander Hamilton, the first secretary of the Treasury, laid out a plan for the economic stability and growth of the United

States, which put the best theory of the day into practice. Like Smith, Hamilton saw a world where people no longer produced all they needed to survive. Even though most Americans still lived on farms, he envisioned a day when manufacturing would be equally important in the nation. Hamilton proposed measures for the national government to strengthen the changing economy that included paying the war debt of the nation and the individual states, establishing a national bank and a stable currency, and encouraging manufacturing through the use of high tariffs, premiums, and other means.

Protectionism, Free Trade, and Communism

From Hamilton's time onward, economic theory in the United States produced political implications. If economists could determine how the economy worked, then the government could pursue appropriate actions to foster its growth or refrain from actions that might do it harm. The first generation of American economists struggled to understand the economy and then to advise their nation on the best legislation for the future. Daniel Raymond, a Baltimore attorney, agreed with Hamilton that a distinction between national and personal wealth must exist. National wealth consisted of a country's ability to produce goods. The government must do all in its power to increase production through high tariffs. Frederick List, a German economist who spent several years in the United States, agreed with Raymond but added that once the nation could produce on its own, the government should pursue free trade policies and end all tariffs. Henry Carey, the son of Irish immigrants who settled in Philadelphia, believed in the need for a balance between land, labor, and capital. At first, Carey argued that the government ought to maintain the balance through free trade policies, but he later came to believe that only protectionist policies could preserve the balance.

Throughout the early national period, the debate over economics in the United States revolved almost exclusively around the issue of protectionism. Henry Clay's American System called for ever higher tariffs to encourage northern manufacturing along with government support for transportation projects in the West. In contrast, southern politicians depended almost exclusively on cotton production and export for their livelihood and thus demanded national free trade policies in order to import cheap manufactured goods into their states. The conflict over protectionism and free trade in part led to the Civil War, which ultimately strengthened the economy of the north while ruining the economy of the south.

As the war raged, few Americans realized that many economists in Europe had moved far beyond the question of protectionism versus free trade. The German philosopher Karl Marx proposed a new economic system known as communism, which could potentially overturn capitalism. Inspired by the metaphysics of Friedrich Hegel and with the help of fellow philosopher Friedrich Engels, Marx argued that history continues as a never ending struggle between the wealthiest and poorest classes. Periodically, the opposing classes destroy each other in a great synthesis, which once again gives rise to a new class struggle. By the nineteenth century, feudalism had collapsed and capitalism had taken its place. The class struggle now waged between the wealthy bourgeoisie and the poor workers, collectively known as the proletariat. Marx urged the proletariat to rise up against their bourgeois oppressors and take control of the means of production. Once the workers held total control over the economy, he argued, the class struggle would end at last, ushering in an era of permanent equality throughout the world.

From Civil War to World War

The American nation changed so much after the Civil War that some thinkers claimed they could barely recognize their own country anymore. Once a land of small farmers, the United States developed into a nation of heavy industry, massive immigration, and booming cities. The struggle that Marx predicted between capital and labor was played out seemingly in the many bitter strikes that plagued the nation's factories, mines, and railroads. Popular writers such as Mark Twain decried the shift from antebellum agrarian values to the new obsession with money, power, and confrontation. Twain dismissed the post–Civil War era as the "Gilded Age," in which the rich grew ever richer and the poor became even poorer. Henry George, another popular writer of the late nineteenth century, went further than Twain in analyzing why the American nation and underlying economy was apparently unraveling. In *Progress and Poverty*, published in 1879, George argued that the owners of real estate remained the principal cause of the imbalance in American society. They created the gap between the rich and the poor by raising rents, creating scarcity, and pursuing their own good at the expense of the nation's good. George proposed a single tax on rental income as a remedy for all modern ills; the tax could pay for the many government services desperately needed by the poorest workers. He also advocated government control of the railroads and all public utilities.

Although less well known in their own country than Mark Twain or Henry George, several American economists struggled with the same questions that plagued the more popular writers during the late nineteenth century and early twentieth century. These thinkers continued to lay out the best explanations possible for how capitalism actually worked, while at the same time offering opinions on whether the government should do anything to reduce the widening gap between the rich and the poor. One group of economists continued the traditional approach to these questions by seeking the underlying principles of buying and selling. Another group of theorists took a more critical look at capitalism and described it in terms of its institutional development over time. Still others sought to explain all economic transitions in terms of mathematical formulas.

A mathematician and astronomer named Simon Newcomb led the way in searching for the underlying principles that governed the modern economy. He became the first economist to distinguish between the flow of income and the fund of capital. He described this process as the "wheel of wealth," in which money flowed in one direction while goods and services flowed in another. Newcomb even formulated a mathematical equation of exchange that assisted later economists in their struggle to understand the modern economy. But despite his innovations in economic theory, he totally opposed any attempt to use the power of government to equalize wealth. A staunch supporter of laissez-faire economics, he described the brutal competition between the rich and poor in terms of the Social Darwinism popular in his day.

Like Newcomb, Francis A. Walker agreed it was necessary to develop economics as a true science and not simply a tool used by politicians and reformers. As the first president of the American Economic Association, he became famous for saying that economics was meant to teach and not to preach. However, Walker did believe that the government could take significant actions to end both unfair competition and the growing inequalities in American society. He advocated increasing the money supply in order to raise wages and thus alleviate poverty. He questioned the gold standard (whereby a nation's currency is valued on the price of gold), one of the first economists to do so. He believed that the limited supply of gold in the world could not be used to gauge wealth in such a rapidly developing economy.

Newcomb and Walker sought to discover the underlying principles of capitalism, but Thorstein Veblen took a historical and much more critical approach to modern economics. Influenced by the evolutionary science of Charles Darwin and the pragmatic philosophy of John Dewey, he argued that economists should study all economic institutions as they have developed over time. For Veblen, it was simply impossible to discover immutable laws at work in economics because human institutions constantly changed. Instead, he proposed a new kind of evolutionary economics that simply described past and present business practices, rather than searching for underlying philosophical or mathematical principles.

In his most famous work, entitled *The Theory of the Leisure Class*, published in 1899, Veblen explained how humanity had passed through the four great economic stages of savagery, barbarism, handicrafts, and the machine process. The last stage produced more wealth than ever before accumulated in human history. Wealthy factory owners acquired so much money that they no longer needed to work and instead became a leisure class. This new class maintained its position in society through conspicuous consumption of goods and services. Veblen held out no hope of ever toppling these captains of industry, since they constructed monopolies in order to keep a stranglehold on the economy and the nation. In his opinion, only a revolt of the technological engineering class could save America and the world from the total control of the leisure class.

Wesley C. Mitchell, another institutional economist, agreed with Veblen's distinction between the leisure class and the working class. However, unlike Veblen, Mitchell tried harder to explain how capitalism actually worked. He viewed the modern world as, first and foremost, a money economy. Money no longer served simply as a means of exchange but instead was an important kind of economic activity in and of itself. Wealth and poverty no longer simply represented productivity and hard work; rather, they were linked to an adequate or inadequate supply of income. Mitchell also studied modern business cycles and attempted to analyze the relationships between prices, costs, and profits. He tried to understand how these complex interrelationships led to the boom-and-bust cycle that plagued capitalism from the start.

John R. Commons, a professor of economics at the University of Wisconsin, became the third important institutional economist at work in the United States in the early twentieth century. He agreed with Veblen that economists needed to study economic institutions as they developed across time, but he added that it was also necessary to study the law as the counterpoint to a purely historical description. Commons also disagreed with any economist who tried to argue that economics operated as a pure science, devoid of any attachment to politics. Instead, he believed that economists must work hand in hand with elected officials to achieve a just society based on a more equitable distribution of wealth. Commons became an adviser to Wisconsin's progressive governor Robert LaFollette. He helped to craft legislation for the state that regulated the public utilities and provided worker's compensation and unemployment insurance. Above all, Commons hoped that economics would someday move beyond a mere description of commodities and exchange and become the study of real transactions between competing groups in a society.

Although the institutional economists made a name for themselves in the United States, two other American economists who ventured into the realm of pure mathematics won the attention of their European counterparts. John Bates Clark became the first American economist to receive worldwide attention for using mathematics to develop a marginal theory of value (an economic theory based on exchange rather than production or distribution). His theory operated as part of an overall attempt to explain economics in a more dynamic way than ever before. He proposed a synchronization economics in contrast to advanced economics by explaining that the existence of a capital fund makes it possible to consider production and consumption as synchronized. Irving Fisher took the drive toward mathematical formulas in economics even further, and most Europeans considered him the most important economist ever from the United States. He proposed and defended both a utility theory (in which utility determines value) and an operational theory of cardinal utility (in which total utility maximization determines value). He also advanced a quantity theory of money that stated the money in circulation times its velocity equaled the price level times the volume of trade. Business cycles could be explained in relation to monetary fluctuations.

The World According to Keynes

Although institutional economists such as Veblen raised concerns about the essential nature of capitalism, most American thinkers in the early twentieth century accepted the economic system as essentially sound. Their great concern involved the discovery of the proper descriptive and mathematical explanations necessary to understand how capitalism actually worked. Similarly, most Americans remained satisfied with an economic system that made an unending array of consumer durable items such as cars, radios, and household appliances available to them on easy credit terms. In contrast, many European thinkers were starting to doubt the future of capitalism and its ability to survive the many traumas of the new century. The shocks of World War I, the Russian Revolution, and the Great Depression only increased these doubts and sparked a desperate search to find a way to prop up an apparently failing system. Although history seemed to point to the inevitable downfall of capitalism and the slow rise of communism, economists and governments alike might yet find a way to make it a viable system for at least a while longer.

The English economist John Maynard Keynes became the towering figure in the drive to rescue capitalism in a chaotic world. He did this by analyzing nearly every political and economic crisis that plagued the British Empire from World War I to the beginnings of the Cold War. His analysis proved so powerful that his opinions became orthodox economic theory in most Western nations, including the United States. He reminded governments that their policies produced a profound effect on the overall strength of national economies and the world economy. The days of laissez-faire economics were over, and now governments must lay out their economic strategies carefully in order to keep capitalism on an even keel. He first made this point in *The Economic Consequences of the Peace*, published in 1920. Keynes argued that the heavy reparations required of Germany after World War I, along with the loan repayments demanded by the Allied powers, would lead the world economy to ruin. When the Great Depression struck, he urged governments to go off the gold standard and begin deficit spending in order to get their failed economies moving again. Finally, as World War II drew to a close, he advocated free trade among nations and even recommended the creation of a European economic union.

The Death and Rebirth of Capitalism

By the 1950s. the American economic system seemed to teeter on the brink of the world dominance that eluded it in the chaos of the Great Depression and World War II. The nation's industries successfully retooled, and consumer items once again poured out of the nation's factories. In the next 20 years, the economy was transformed into one driven by services as much as goods and through the development of computer technology that held the potential of implications for the growth of new businesses never before imagined. However, the triumph of capitalism was not a complete one, since communism still held sway in the Soviet Union, Eastern Europe, and China. Despite the dominant influence of the United States in world affairs, communism appeared to be on the rise in Asia, Latin America, and Africa.

Most American economists followed John Maynard Keynes without question and continued to search for ways in which governments could keep capitalism going in a world that seemed to threaten it more each year. Even economists who did not doubt the value of capitalism worried that some essential flaw in the system would someday bring it to ruin. Throughout the West in the postwar years, it became popular to quote the Austrian economist Joseph A. Schumpeter. In *Capitalism, Socialism, and Democracy*, published in the darkest days of World War II, Schumpeter predicted that capitalism would fail because of its very success. Uninspired managers and absentee stockholders would inevitably replace the entrepreneurial elite who gave rise to new ideas and new companies.. The creativity so necessary in capitalism would die out, he claimed, leaving aging companies run by salaried employees. Even worse, the new business leaders would help bring the whole system crashing down because they would prove equally poor political leaders as well.

Harvard professor John Kenneth Galbraith became the best-known American economist of the mid-twentieth century by joining the ranks of those who criticized capitalism. He openly declared that capitalism was not the great success story of the modern world. Instead, he contended that it had failed to prevent the dangerous concentration of power that plagued the world since the late nineteenth century. Monopolies gave way to oligopolies that only the countervailing power of labor unions, consumer groups, and government regulation could control. Galbraith scolded Americans who believed that their affluent society was the envy of the world. Although the nation remained wealthy in consumer goods, it was also increasingly poor in its lack of the public services that made life worth living. Following his mentor John Maynard Keynes, Galbraith remained a staunch advocate of government intervention to control the growing power of oligopolies and improve the quality of life for all citizens, especially the poor.

Although few economists supported or agreed with the work of the popular Galbraith, most remained staunchly in the Keynesian camp and continued to look for ways that governments could strengthen the overall economy and ease the burdens on the poorest citizens. Only the economists at the University of Chicago seemed willing to question the prevailing orthodoxy. Collectively known as the Chicago School, economists Frank H. Knight, Jacob Viner, Henry Simons, George Stigler, and Milton Friedman argued for an end to government intervention in the economy. Deeply influenced by the ideas of the Austrian economist Friedrich von Hayek, the Chicago School defended democracy and individual liberty as much as they defended capitalism. They argued governments could set monetary policies that controlled the money supply and interest rates, but beyond that, individuals remain able to trade freely and as they saw fit in the open marketplace.

Milton Friedman emerged as the most influential member of the Chicago School, especially after winning the Nobel Prize in economics in 1976. He consistently stressed that free markets and the freedom of the individual were inseparable. The complex modern economy could only work successfully if individuals made most of the decisions regarding their own private property. If governments exercised too much power, then capitalism and democracy would both be destroyed. Friedman urged politicians everywhere to abandon the economics of Marx and Keynes and let free markets peacefully link all the nations of the world in a new birth of capitalism and democracy.

At the beginning of the twenty-first century, the debate continues between economists who call for increasing government intervention and those who encourage a more laissez-faire approach. One area of agreement involves the growing reliance on the science of econometrics, which uses statistics and mathematical formulas to explain economic activity. But even with the great strides made in econometrics, there remains something indefinable about the complex system once known as capitalism and now called free market economics. If the past is indicative of future tendencies, then this system may continue to stay one step ahead of the best economists as they attempt to explain it.

References

Butkiewicz, James L., Kenneth J. Koford, and Jeffrey B. Miller, eds. *Keynes' Economic Legacy: Contemporary Economic Theories*. New York: Praeger, 1986.

Fry, Michael, ed. *Adam Smith's Legacy: His Place in the Development of Modern Economics*. New York: Routledge, 1992.

Reisman, David. *Economic Thought and Political Theory*. Boston: Kluwer Academic Publishers, 1994.

Spiegel, Henry William. *The Growth of Economic Thought*. Durham, NC: Duke University Press, 1994.

Education

David Treviño

Socioeconomic and political events from the 1700s to the 2000s dictated the relationship between the U.S. government and primary and secondary education. In the eighteenth and nineteenth centuries, the federal government did its best to avoid directly interfering with education, leaving it as a state and local priority. But by the middle of the twentieth century, the federal government assumed a more active and direct role in education; by the end of the century, it passed myriad laws that regulated education in the states and localities. It seemed that power increasingly shifted away from the states and localities over the years. The government's relationship with education involved continually changing policies, and educational policies grew piecemeal. Those policies were shaped by social, economic, and political events both at home and abroad and culminated in a large amount of legislation intended to complement both higher and lower education.

After the United States acquired its independence, people assumed that public education was an essential feature of a republican government based on the people's will. Indeed, the founding fathers believed that education was the backbone of republicanism. But despite their conviction, neither the Articles of Confederation nor the Constitution defined the government's role in education, and the government had no centralized educational plan during the late eighteenth century and throughout the nineteenth. However, the organization of public education developed when the nation expanded westward.

Education in the Colonial Period

Americans during the colonial period came to distrust the economic system of mercantilism. They struggled with issues of landownership, settlement, and taxation. The ideas of the Enlightenment, a broad European scientific and intellectual movement that pushed for a more rational approach to life, strengthened the colonists' ideas of free will, equality, and liberty and advanced the cause of education. Literacy grew in the colonies during the late colonial period. The Great Awakening, a religious/intellectual movement in the early to mid-1700s, also strengthened the colonists' educational ambitions. Negative changes in their economy on the eve of the American Revolution helped to undermine their views on traditional socioeconomic ideas and prepare them for revolution.

Localism existed in education during the years after independence. The founding fathers believed that education remained the responsibility of the state and municipal governments. Although, as mentioned, the U.S. Constitution contains no explicit reference to education, some of the state constitutions adopted before 1800 did. As the nation grew with the addition of more states, it became somewhat of a tradition to include educational provisions in the state constitutions. Still, the founding fathers feared that leaving education in the hands of private families, churches, and local communities was potentially dangerous to democracy. Since the Constitution was silent in this regard, the power to establish schools fell directly to the states.

Education in the Postindependence Period, 1776 to the Mid-1800s

The American Revolution and the subsequent market revolution of the early to mid-1800s called for new approaches to education and teaching. "Common schools" attempted to meet the social, political, and economic needs of the new nation. These schools promoted the values of patriotic nationalism that helped unite the colonies into a nation. Teachers in these schools taught students about competition, ambition, and achievement to prepare them for the business world. But Americans remained divided over the educational agenda. Some wanted a universal education that reinforced the tenets of liberty and equality for all; others believed that public education should control the selfish impulses of the individual and advocate the ideas of the Revolution.

The Land Ordinance of 1785 and the Northwest Ordinance of 1787 marked the beginning of the federal government's involvement in promoting public schools as a form of internal improvement. Some scholars questioned the government's motives in these two ordinances. Sponsors of the educational provisions embodied within these measures included Massachusetts residents who wanted to persuade fellow northerners to buy lands and migrate to the West. In the 1785 ordinance, the only reference to education was the general comment that it should be encouraged.

The Land Ordinance of 1785 provided for the division of the Northwest Territories (the area bordered by the Great Lakes and the Ohio River) into townships. The revenue earned from the sale of these lands helped support education. Throughout the 1800s, the federal government used land grants to fund public education, granting close to 100 million acres to the states for public schools. The Northwest Ordinance of 1787 reinforced the vital link between good government, schools, and morality. The legislation echoed the sentiments of the times with its edict that "Religion, Morality and Knowledge [were] necessary to good government and the happiness of mankind. Schools and the means of education shall forever be encouraged." But, by 1789, the United States ratified and was governed under the Constitution, which reshaped the goals of the nation. Federal support of public education became abstract and symbolic. Thus, the major responsibility for schools increasingly shifted to the states. The common school was considered fundamental to the success of the new nation, and the government advocated its extension.

Federal assistance to education in the nineteenth century did not follow a rational model of finance and governance. Rather, the movement of money from the government to education reflected the politics, ideological assumptions, and economic conditions prevalent in the United States at the time. During the early 1800s, changes in the economy convinced many Americans that educational reform was needed. The growth of the cash economy and the withering away of the barter and trade system made many citizens demand the establishment of universal public education so that everyone could take advantage of new opportunities. More Americans entered the cash-based market economy, and many believed that the future of the nation's children depended on an appreciation of hard work, competition, determination, and achievement. The original goal of teaching people how to function as good citizens in a new republic gave way to the goal of teaching them how to compete in the growing market society.

The changes in the economy affected members of the middle class most dramatically; for them, success and failure in that economy took on increased importance. They began to embrace the common school in droves. In general, working people, both skilled and unskilled, started to accept the idea of the common school and its emphasis on teaching the values of hard work and competition. Urban Americans acknowledged the value of a common school education because they lived in the market economy, and this helped change their attitudes about their children's future. They realized that sporadic and remedial education would not accomplish much within this new economy. To many, the common school made sound economic sense. But some businessmen believed it limited the pool of children available to work in factories, and they often opposed it for that reason.

Education in the Mid- and Late Nineteenth Century

More federal educational legislation was enacted during and after the American Civil War (1861–1865) and helped signal the start of a transition in education, which reached its peak during the first decades of the twentieth century. The government authorized public land grants to the states for the creation and maintenance of agricultural and mechanical colleges. Congress passed the Morrill Act, also called the Land-Grant College Act of 1862. The primary objective of this measure was to provide funding for institutions of higher learning in the states, and according to its terms, every state would receive 30,000 acres of federal land for the establishment of programs associated with agriculture and the mechanical arts, including engineering and home economics. (The Second Morrill Act of 1890 provided financial grants to support instruction in the agricultural and mechanical arts.) Unfortunately, things did not go as well as the government intended with the Morrill Act of 1862. Speculators bought a large portion of the allotted lands, which meant that the states received very little for their territory. Congress later reinforced the Morrill Act with similar measures in order to provide much-needed additional funding for the land-grant institutions.

The Morrill Act of 1862 donated public land to the states and territories, property available for use to set up colleges for the benefit of the agricultural and mechanical arts. Thereafter, the Second Morrill Act applied a portion of the proceeds of the sale of public lands to the more complete endowment and support of those colleges, as established under the provisions of Congress. The 1890 act created fewer land-grant institutions than the original measure, but it represented the first governmental effort to ensure vocational education. The government promoted vocational and industrial education because officials wanted to provide the nation with skilled workers and technicians. However, after the Morrill Acts, additional vocational education legislation was not introduced until the 1917 Smith-Hughes Act.

Higher education in the United States was transformed because of the land grant, which gave way to the state college. In these colleges, Americans developed institutions that sustained an agrarian economic, political, and social past. Like public primary schools, the number of public and private higher education institutions increased dramatically. The businesspeople of the age worked in league with the government to found universities; many bear the names of prominent industrialists—Cornell, Vanderbilt, Stanford, and Tulane, to name just a few.

In 1867, the federal government passed the Department of Education Act, which authorized the creation of the Department of Education (also known as the Office of Education). This department served as the source from which federal educational legislation emanated. Still, the Department of Education left much of the implementation and sometimes the revision of federal educational programs to the states and to individual localities. Its primary purpose involved collecting information on schools and teaching to aid the states in establishing effective educational systems. In short, the Department of Education sought to acquire information on what worked in the schools and provide that information to teachers and to educational policymakers.

After the Civil War, with the rise of industrial cities and the expansion of the economy, businesses sought workers who were better educated. The postwar economy became geared toward industrialization, especially in the north, and rapid economic changes occurred all the time. The schools therefore taught students to conform to the industrial system. The teaching of science was added to the more traditional subjects in order to supply industry with better-educated workers.

Immediately after the Civil War, early forms of vocational training included courses in bookkeeping and stenography. Before the war, vocational training was provided only at home and through apprenticeships. Among the early private trade schools were Cooper Union (founded in 1859) and the Pratt Institute (1887), both in New York City. African Americans could learn industrial, agricultural, and home economics at the Hampton Institute (1868) and the Tuskegee Institute (1881), among others. The University of Minnesota became the first established vocational higher education school and agricultural high school (1888). Its main emphasis was on public instruction of agriculture. Thereafter, the number of vocational schools greatly increased.

A major educational transition occurred during the last half of the 1800s. he country experienced a significant shift of its population from the countryside to the city. Agriculture became more mechanized; job opportunities for people on farms began to dissipate. Also, immigration from Europe dramatically increased, especially during the last 20 years of the century. With the broad economic changes that occurred, the common school proved unable to meet the challenges created by new multicultural situations. The question of race also surfaced. After the Civil War, 4 million slaves received their freedom and became integrated into American society. But the integration of southern society remained nearly impossible because of the difficulties associated with Reconstruction and racism in both the north and the south.

Educational reformers sought a new model of organization and found it in the graded school, with an administrative structure based on the American corporation. The structure of the American corporation was shaped by the development of railroads and canals in the first half of the 1800s, making the corporate model highly successful in the eyes of many Americans. In turn, educational reformers believed that if the school system mirrored the corporate model, perhaps some of the same success would be replicated within the educational arena.

Thus, the corporate model of education and the graded system arose in reaction to the successes and changing complexities of the American economy. As schools changed, state boards of education, school superintendents, and principals provided them with different levels of management. The teacher assumed the role of hired employee, instead of being responsible for running the entire school as well as teaching. In the common schools, the curriculum focused on the three Rs in the primary grades and classical languages in the secondary schools. With new socioeconomic demands, however, this type of instruction no longer applied to American society. Now, the expansion of science and technology and the influence of the United States in the world demanded the teaching of new subjects, including basic sciences, physics, chemistry, and similar fields.

Public schools increased in number by the end of the 1800s. Yet even though millions of dollars were spent on public education, at the beginning of the 1900s, the average American adult had very limited schooling. The state and nature of education changed as a result of the Industrial Revolution. The urban, corporate, and modern revolutions forced Americans to reconsider their earlier educational ideas and values as they applied to a new nation. Educators deemphasized the common school, and in the new educational form of the graded school, the curriculum was expanded. In addition, officials required that teachers in graded (or "normal") schools be licensed.

From 1785 to 1906, the federal government acquired discretionary powers over the land grants. The states remained in charge of the appropriation of funds, the subjects taught with federal money, and the filing of annual reports. Until the first decade of the twentieth century, grants provided for the advancement of general education. By 1906, however, the federal government earmarked funds for specific types of education, primarily vocational education. Federal aid to higher education in the nineteenth century moved from a broad program of endowment grants to a series of piecemeal efforts to aid education through a broad range of special interest programs. At the beginning of the twentieth century, the grants of federal funds were targeted at the adult worker. The land-grant colleges and the experimental agricultural stations associated with these colleges trained young adults for careers in agriculture or the mechanical arts.

Education in the Twentieth Century

During the first decades of the 1900s, special-interest groups with vocational educational objectives lobbied the government. In 1906, Congress approved the Adams Act, which increased the monies allotted for agricultural experimental stations. With passage of this act, the transition in federal aid to education was completed. Back in the 1780s, when the government gave grants to the states for educational purposes, federal assistance to education remained connected to the land. This situation changed over the years as grants consisted of funds derived from the sale of lands. The Adams Act required that grants to the agricultural experimental stations derive from monetary surpluses in the Treasury, thereby severing the connection between grants and land (and land sales). With the passage of this act, the idea of direct federal payments to the states for vocational purposes became more acceptable.

Later, Congress created the Commission on National Aid to Vocational Education to study federal aid for vocational schooling. The president appointed individuals to the commission, which was sanctioned by the Smith-Lever Act of 1914. This commission also developed guidelines for future legislation on federal aid to vocational education. In addition, it recommended a nationwide plan for vocational education; the training of teachers to instruct trade and industrial subjects, agriculture, and home economics; the payment of part of the salaries of such teachers; and the provision of assistance for day, part-time, and evening schools. All these recommendations formed the core of the subsequent Smith-Hughes Act of 1917.

The Smith-Hughes Act called for all the states to cooperate in the promotion of vocational education in order to avoid federal control. The money given to vocational education remained regulated as well. The emphasis was on more responsibility for the states and localities, which provided necessary plants and equipment for their schools. As with other educational bills, this measure was designed to prepare students over 14 years of age for useful employment.

The idea of granting educational benefits to veterans extends back to the beginning of the twentieth century. Congress promulgated the Rehabilitation Act of 1919, one of the first veterans' benefits packages passed after World War I. The act gave disabled veterans of the Great World War I monthly education assistance allowances as well as federal grants for rehabilitation through training. The Vocational Rehabilitation Act of 1943 provided assistance to disabled veterans. These rehabilitation programs remained high on the government's list of priorities, and the states received numerous grants for them.

The George-Reed Act of 1929 and the George-Deen Act of 1936 continued to outline the appropriations that vocational education received. They also dealt with such things as removing home economics from the trade and industrial sections of the Smith-Hughes Act and adding other occupations to the list of trades receiving certain appropriations. The George-Deen Act helped energize the economy, which was reeling from the Great Depression. The government allocated funds to step up vocational training in agriculture, trade, industrial, and home economics education and reserved money to assist in training employed workers in these occupations to help small businesses and encourage entrepreneurship.

The Bankhead-Jones Act of 1935 gave the states more funds for agricultural research. This act, like others before and after it, sought to improve the country's agricultural status by addressing issues related to "the development of new and improved methods of the production, marketing, distribution, processing, and utilization of plant and animal commodities at all stages from the original producer through to the ultimate consumer." The act also spurred research dealing with "the discovery, introduction, and breeding of new and useful agricultural crops, plants, and animals, both foreign and native, particularly for those crops and plants which may be adapted to utilization in chemical and manufacturing industries."

During World War II, the federal government passed legislation incorporating educational benefits for veterans. Congress passed the Servicemen's Readjustment Act of 1944, more commonly referred to as the GI Bill. Veterans' benefits packages existed in the past, as noted, but this act proved monumental, enabling millions of veterans to attend colleges and universities after World War II. President Franklin D. Roosevelt signed legislation, recognized generally as one of the most important acts of Congress. Over the decades, it led to the investment of billions of dollars in the education and training of millions of veterans of wars since 1944. It also changed the way the United States views its veterans and their education. Many veterans received farm training, which proved invaluable because large numbers of them came from agricultural families or wanted to pursue farming after their service in the military.

Before 1944, Congress was hesitant to pass educational legislation concerning veterans. In fact, before the GI Bill became a reality, Congress failed to act in response to over 600 bills regarding veterans and their educational welfare. The enactment of the GI Bill was attributable, in part, to a nationwide campaign for its passage. The American Legion is aptly credited for being the one organization responsible for creating the main features of the 1944 GI Bill. It also helped push the bill through Congress. In addition to education and training, the first GI Bill provided for loan guaranties for homes, farms, or businesses; unemployment pay of $20 a week for up to one year; assistance in finding jobs; top priority for building materials for Veterans Administration hospitals; and military review of dishonorable discharges. The 1944 legislation set the foundation for all subsequent bills concerning veterans by helping returning servicemen and servicewomen make a healthy transition into civilian life. In addition, veterans' legislation enticed young people to join the military forces.

Still, many Americans were opposed to the GI Bill. Its opponents complained about the possible ill effects on veterans and society alike. Critics, which included Congress and university educators, charged that the entire legislation package was absurdly expensive and argued it would result in educational laziness on the part of veterans. They were also concerned about the uncertainty of the post–World War II economy. Many people, both in and out of Congress, anticipated a postwar economy centered on unemployment and economic depression; the Great Depression of the 1930s was fresh in the minds of people across the nation. Shortly after the United

Harvard registration, Cambridge, Massachusetts, 1946. College enrollment increased following World War II because of the tuition assistance provided by the Servicemen's Readjustment Act of 1944. (Library of Congress.)

States entered the war in 1941, the White House established the National Planning Resources Board. This agency assumed the responsibility of anticipating the country's postwar economic problems and creating solutions for them. By summer 1943, the board recommended to the White House many programs for education and training, guided by the state of the economy and the education budget of the White House.

After World War II, the economic problems within the educational system became apparent. Rural districts were in financial straits. They suffered from low funding, poor facilities, teacher shortages, and obsolete teaching materials. Inequitable funding became a major issue. Furthermore, American schools reflected a racial bias. In many states, the institutionalization of racially separate schools existed, which meant black students received fewer months of schooling and were taught by instructors with less training and lower pay than their white peers.

Nonetheless, from 1941 to mid-1947, the federal government spent an estimated $187 million on programs for school construction and equipment, school maintenance and operation, and child care. In 1942, Congress authorized $5 million in loans to students in institutions of higher education studying medicine, dentistry, pharmacy, engineering, chemistry, and physics.

Congress approved the 1946 National School Lunch Act in hopes of improving the physical well-being of children through improved lunch programs. The act called for the encouragement of the consumption of nutritious agriculture products and other foods by children through grants-in-aid. Local governments and charitable agencies originated lunch programs as early as the mid-1800s, and similar acts were passed in later years. In 1970, for example, an amendment stipulated that any child living at the poverty level receive a free or reduced-price lunch, with priority for free lunches given to the neediest children.

Vocational education continued as a priority for the federal government after World War II. The George-Barden Act of 1946 expanded vocational education programs and transferred their administration to the Office of Education. Agricultural education taught people new ways of farming and how to preserve foods. The 1946 act focused on agricultural, industrial, and home economics training for high school students. It also provided for veterans' training in agricultural education. In the end, the George-Barden Act authorized $34 million for the programs outlined in the earlier George-Deen Act.

In the decades that followed World War II, the state of education in America was transformed. With subsequent federal legislation, the government forced institutionally segregated schools to integrate students of different races without the government taking direct control of these schools. The government worked in league with the states during these decades, as opposed to the previous system in which the localities worked with the states in setting the agenda for education. In addition, establishing education standards and curriculum became a federal matter in the post–World War II society.

By the beginning of the 1950s, the vitality of progressive education, initiated under the New Deal programs of the 1930s and continued into the war-torn years of the 1940s, lost momentum. Administrators no longer devoted their energies to reforming schools because individuals with little vision captured top-level positions. Seemingly, the teachers lost their desire to reform the schools as well. The anticommunist movement of the 1950s ended the educators' opportunities to wed the organization of teacher unions to the quest for a democratic society. The teachers moved away from teaching and advancing controversial social issues and increasingly focused on things such as salaries and working conditions.

The 1950s ushered in the Korean War, and Congress passed a new bill for GIs in 1952, the Veterans Readjustment Assistance Act. President Harry S Truman approved the act that July. The Korean GI Bill provided education and training benefits to veterans who served 90 days or more after June 27, 1950; who entered the service before February 1, 1955; and who received anything other than a dishonorable discharge. This bill also provided home, farm, and business loans to veterans. It differed in one aspect from its World War II predecessor—it made payment of unemployment compensation a state function. Millions of veterans received educational training because of this bill until Congress discontinued it in early 1965. The total cost of the measure's education and training program amounted to about $4.5 billion. In 1966 and 1967, Congress passed a permanent bill, extending benefits not only to veterans of the Vietnam War but also to all men and women who received an honorable discharge after six or more months of service in the armed forces after the original GI Bill expired in 1955.

One major event that changed the government's perception about education in the United States was the Soviet Union's launching of the satellite *Sputnik* into orbit in 1957. This event reawakened educational reform efforts, and a resurgence of interest in schools occurred, especially in terms of their ability to train scientists and engineers to surpass the Soviets in space technology and other fields. As a result of the *Sputnik* episode, Congress passed the National Defense Education Act of 1958. Thus, the focus of federal education legislation shifted in the late 1950s because of Cold War events. The government believed that schools provided the solution to the international crisis. The federal government provided money for better curriculum materials, for the training of better teachers, and for improved financing for future scientists and engineers.

The National Defense Education Act helped develop skilled technicians in fields requiring scientific knowledge, and encouraged vocational schools to train technicians. Furthermore, the state and local school systems strengthened instruction in science, mathematics, and modern foreign languages. The Defense Education Act also improved guidance, counseling, testing services, and training institutes. The government provided more assistance in terms of higher education student loans and fellowships. And colleges and universities began emphasizing foreign language study. In general, assistance was given to those fields either necessary or very important to the maintenance of the national defense.

In the 1960s, in response to traumatic social events at home and abroad, the educational agenda shifted from curricular to social concerns. Just like their predecessors in the early 1800s, educational reformers in the 1960s called for subject matter designed to prepare youths for the increasing complexity of technology and the economy. At the same time, the civil rights movement fostered a new concern for disadvantaged youths.

The civil rights movement of the 1960s greatly impacted federal legislation, beginning with President John F. Kennedy's administration and continuing through Lyndon B. Johnson's presidency. Both men lobbied for a more aggressive federal role in improving the nation's schools. Johnson called for the War on Poverty, which ultimately led to his Great Society programs. He believed that education was the key to improved economic opportunity.

During the 1960s, the Department of Labor and the Department of Education assumed control over vocational training under the Area Redevelopment Act. The Department of Labor identified occupations and selected individuals for training in fields specified under the act. After completing the program, the students received positions through the Labor Department. The Department of Education also provided training through existing vocational educational facilities or private institutions. The

Area Redevelopment Act was the first measure to provide vocational job training through the Department of Labor with 100 percent federal funding.

In 1963, President Kennedy appointed a panel to evaluate the state of vocational education programs in the country. The panel's recommendations led to the passage of the Vocational Education Act later that year. The act proved monumental for several reasons. To begin with, it broadened the definition of vocational and technical education and no longer required the categorization of occupations in these areas; funding for all was covered under the vocational category. It also required collaboration between state vocational agencies and employment agencies by calling for periodic reviews of state and local vocational programs. Funds were authorized for work-study programs and residential vocational educational schools, and monies were allocated for vocational research and experimental programs. Vocational education became available for high school students and for those who dropped out of high school, and people employed in vocational trades were provided the opportunity to retrain as well. The goal of the Vocational Education Act of 1963 was to reduce unemployment among youth groups and eliminate inequalities in terms of the opportunity to pursue vocational education. This act, and those that followed, aimed at encouraging the effectiveness and efficiency of the workforce.

In 1964, Congress inaugurated the Project Head Start program. During the 1960s, government leaders grew concerned about the cultural, social, and economical impact of poverty on children: The new program offered culturally and socially deprived children a head start through an enriched preschool experience. Health, nutrition, education, social, and other services were also provided to assist these children in attaining their full potential. In addition, the Civil Rights Act of 1964 helped to accelerate the pace of desegregation in public educational institutions.

The Higher Education Act of 1965 was designed to more broadly extent the opportunity for higher education among lower- and middle-income families by providing more scholarships and work-study programs for college students. It also gave financial assistance to smaller and less-developed colleges. Amendments in 1966 and 1968 reinforced the federal government's message about providing education for those who otherwise could not afford it and training instructors to become more effective teachers.

The 1965 Elementary and Secondary Education Act, passed under the Johnson administration, was pivotal in implementing a number of much-needed public school programs. Particular attention was paid to children of low-income families. The act authorized grant money for elementary and secondary school programs for needy children and school library resources, textbooks, and other instructional materials. It strengthened state education agencies, educational research, and research training.

Also in 1965 the health professions and higher education received additional assistance through federal legislation. The Health Professions Educational Assistance Amendments of 1965 provided scholarships to needy pupils in the health professions. The Higher Education Act of 1965 made grants available for university community service programs, library training and research, teacher training programs, and student instructional equipment. It also authorized insured student loans and provided for graduate teacher training fellowships.

The federal government provided more grants to institutions of higher education via the 1966 International Education Act. Congress earmarked these grants for the creation and operation of research and training centers in international studies and other fields that incorporated international aspects within the curricula. Marine education received a boost with the National Sea Grant College and Program Act of 1966. The act authorized the creation and operation of Sea Grant Colleges and programs by supporting education and research in the marine resources fields. Educational programs for adults, including the training of teachers in adult education, expanded under the Adult Education Act of 1966.

The arts and humanities were enriched with the National Foundation on the Arts and the Humanities Act of 1965. This measure gave grants and loans for projects in the creative and performing arts. It also gave assistance for research, training, and scholarly publications in the humanities. The National Technical Institute for the Deaf Act of 1965 called for the creation of a residential school for postsecondary and technical training of the deaf. The following year, legislators passed the Model Secondary School for the Deaf Act; this measure authorized the establishment and operation of Gallaudet College, which became a model secondary school for the deaf. The School Assistance in Disaster Areas Act guided educational agencies in disaster areas and helped them meet the high costs of reconstruction necessitated by major disasters.

In the 1970s, federal aid to education continued, but the guidelines and regulations of the entire application and grant approval process became more complex than ever before. Few new legislative acts that aided education passed during the presidency of Richard M. Nixon. However, President Gerald Ford signed an elementary and secondary education act into law when he first entered the White House. The federal assistance to education continued in spite of the economic recession of the 1970s, though there was less money to work with than in the previous decade. Middle-income students attending college or other postsecondary education institutions received financial assistance under the Middle Income Student Assistance Act of 1978.

In the 1980s, the Reagan administration reduced federal assistance to education. President Ronald Reagan believed that aid to education should be distributed in block grants to the states for redistribution to local school districts. This approach differed from the categorical grants of the past, which were created for specific purposes. During the George H. W. Bush presidency, a national commission on educational goals reported that American students were falling behind those in Europe and Asia, especially Japan, in science and mathematics. American students lacked the skills needed to function in the high-technology economy.

The Bush commission began to search for ways to remedy these problems. It set standards of achievement for elementary, middle, and high school students, and it urged state and local educational officials to improve both teaching methods and facilities. Unfortunately, two major problems existed. Bush's predecessor, Reagan, placed the top priority on defense, and education lost billions of dollars in support each year. Also, Bush lacked an effective plan to raise federal funds for local education. These circumstances hampered the Bush commission's ability to correct educational problems.

At the beginning of the twenty-first century, vocational education was significantly more advanced than in the past. Separate public schools devoted to various occupational fields developed over the years, and large training centers existed for the public. The schools and the industries and trades work together. Students are eligible for employment part-time in the vocational fields they are interested in while attending classes during the day or at night. Community colleges, in particular, provide vocational courses.

In the United States, education remains, first and foremost, the responsibility of the states and localities. Local communities establish schools and colleges, develop course curricula, and determine the requirements for enrollment and graduation. A vast majority of the money spent on education at all levels comes from state, local, and private sources: Of the roughly $650 billion spent on education at all levels throughout the nation, 91 percent comes from state, local, and private resources. The federal government, then, provides about 9 percent of the national expenditures on education. However, that 9 percent includes spending in other federal agencies as well, such as the Department of Health and Human Services' Head Start program and the Department of Agriculture's School Lunch program. Consequently, the Department of Education actually receives only about 6 percent of the total education spending, or about $42 billion a year.

Clearly, the economy affects education. But education also affects the economy. For instance, variation in the quality and quantity of education across countries is one factor contributing to differences in such economic indicators as worker productivity, capital investment, technical innovation, foreign trade, and government regulation. Education is a significant contributor to productivity growth and a major influence on the standard of living. In general, worker productivity in the United States increased almost continuously since the end of World War II, but growth slowed after 1973. Also since World War II, worker productivity grew more slowly in the United States than in other industrialized countries.

In the last half of the twentieth century, the amount of government involvement in education skyrocketed. Congress passed numerous laws that dealt with education. The Office of Education had grown considerably in size and influence. Educational legislation during that period provided a superb example of the formation of policies according to the temperament of the times. In the 1950s, 1960s, and 1970s, the country was deeply involved in the civil rights movement and the Cold War, both of which fostered insecurity at home and abroad. Federal legislation took into account the scientific and technical competition between the United States and the Soviet Union, as well as policies that eliminated discrimination in education on the basis of race, sex, or age.

In the 1990s, a movement arose that called for the creation of a school voucher system allowing for the use of federal tax dollars for nonpublic education. Proponents argued that the voucher system would encourage competition among schools and offer a choice in educational opportunities; opponents argued that the system would remove much-needed revenues from public institutions. On January 27, 2002, the Supreme Court upheld the validity, or constitutionality, of school vouchers. Currently, eight states—Minnesota, Colorado, Texas, Arizona, Indiana, Virginia, Alabama, and Utah—use vouchers.

Impact of Education on American Society

When the United States became a nation, schools taught republican values to students. Teachers in the common schools instructed students on the meaning of being a good republican and a hard worker in the changing economy of early-nineteenth-century America. By the latter half of the century, the land grants issued by the government established many institutions of higher learning. Vocational education became very popular in these colleges and universities, a development continued well into the twentieth century.

Industrialism emerged in the United States in the late 1800s. Its arrival signified the need for the federal government to undertake new approaches toward education. Public education followed the example of the successful American corporation, with a top-down administrative and employee structure. The graded school developed, a system that continues in the United States today. But because of political and economic events that occurred in the post–World War II era, the government placed an emphasis on scientific and mathematical subjects in order to compete in this new and uncertain world. The secondary schools, as well as colleges and universities, experienced another educational transition. The state of the economy affected, and continues to affect, educational policies and vice versa. Historically, the government used restraint in terms of intruding in the implementation of its educational policies. It was not until the late 1900s that the government took a more active, direct role in education. Economic and political events will undeniably determine future substantial educational transition and its significance in the shaping of American domestic policy.

References

Carlton, Frank Tracy. *Economic Influences upon Educational Progress in the United States, 1820–1850.* New York: Teachers College Press, 1966.

Cooperative State Research, Education, and Extension Service of USDA (REEUSDA). "Bankhead-Jones Act of 1935." June 29, 1935. Available: http://www.reeusda.gov/1700/legis/bkjones.htm; accessed December 21, 2002.

Department of Veterans Affairs (VA). "The GI Bill: From Roosevelt to Montgomery: GI Bill History." No date. Available: http://www.gibill.va.gov/education/GI_Bill.htm; accessed October 15, 2002.

Fraser, James W. *The School in the United States: A Documentary History.* Boston: McGraw-Hill, 2001.

Gutek, Gerald Lee. *Education and Schooling in America*. Englewood Cliffs, NJ: Prentice-Hall, 1988.

Herbst, Jurgen. *The Once and Future School: Three Hundred and Fifty Years of American Secondary Education*. New York: Routledge, 1996.

Higher Education Resource Hub (HERH). "Land-Grant Act: History and Institutions." No date. Available: http://www.higher-ed.org/resources/morrill_acts.htm; accessed March 1, 2002.

Kliebard, Herbert M. *Schooled to Work: Vocationalism and the American Curriculum, 1876–1946*. New York: Teachers College Press, 1999.

Lapati, Americo D. *Education and the Federal Government: A Historical Record*. New York: Mason/Charter, 1975.

McClure, Arthur F., James Riley Chrisman, and Perry Mock. *Education for Work: The Historical Evolution of Vocational and Distributive Education in America*. Rutherford, NJ: Fairleigh Dickinson University Press, 1985.

Meyer, Warren G., ed. *Vocational Education and the Nation's Economy*. Washington, DC: American Vocational Association, 1977.

Mississippi State University (MSSTATE), Department of Agricultural Information Science and Education. "Development of Vocational Education in Agriculture: The Smith-Hughes Act of 1917." Available: http://www.ais.msstate.edu/AEE/8593/unit4/tsld022.htm; accessed October 16, 1998.

National Center for Education Statistics (NCES). "Education and the Economy: An Indicators Report." 1997. Available: http://www.nces.ed.gov/pubs97/97939.html; accessed September 24, 2002.

National Center for Education Statistics (NCES). *Digest of Education Statistics, 2000*. Chapter 4, "Federal Programs for Education and Related Activities." 2000. Available: http://www.nces.ed.gov/pubsearch/digest/ch4.html#1; accessed September 24, 2002.

North Carolina State University (NCSU), Department of Agricultural and Extension Education. "More than Sows, Cows, and Plows." January 13, 1999. Available: http://www.cals.ncsu.edu/agexed/aee501/show2/tsld005.htm; accessed October 21, 2002.

Parkerson, Donald Hugh, and Jo Ann Parkerson. *Transitions in American Education: A Social History of Teaching*. New York: Routledge Falmer, 2001.

Pulliam, John D., and James Van Patten. *History of Education in America*. Englewood Cliffs, NJ: Merrill, 1995.

Rainsford, George N. *Congress and Higher Education in the Nineteenth Century*. Knoxville: University of Tennessee Press, 1972.

Ravitch, Diane. *The Troubled Crusade: American Education, 1945–1980*. New York: Basic Books, 1983.

Rudolph, Frederick. *The American College and University: A History.* New York: Alfred A. Knopf, 1968.

Texas A&M University, College of Education (TAMU). "Vocational Education Legislation from 1950–1990." 1990. Available: http://www.coe.tamu.edu/~epsy/cded/becky1.htm; accessed October 29, 2002.

Texas A&M University, College of Education (TAMU). "Summary of Selected Federal Legislation Preceding the Smith-Hughes Act of 1917 to 1946." 1997. Available: http://www.coe.tamu.edu/~epsy/cded/owre1.htm; accessed November 13, 2002.

Tyack, David B., Thomas James, and Aaron Benavot. *Law and the Shaping of Public Education, 1785–1954.* Madison: University of Wisconsin Press, 1987.

University of Kentucky (UKY). "The Morrill Act and the Land-Grant Colleges." No date. Available: http://www.uky.edu/CampusGuide/land-grant.html; accessed July 22, 2002.

U.S. Department of Education (ED). "The Federal Role in Education." April 2, 2003. Available: http://www.ed.gov/offices/OUS/fedrole.html; accessed April 5, 2003.

Wirt, Frederick M., and Grant Harman, eds. *Education, Recession, and the World Village: A Comparative Political Economy of Education.* London: Falmer Press, 1986.

Energy Policy

Keith L. Miller

Modern times began with the Industrial Revolution in England about 1750. The first industrial revolution owed its existence to another one—the energy revolution, which depended first on the mining of coal and then, by 1859, on the drilling for oil. Coal and oil production together gave birth to the fossil fuel era, which started in the mid-eighteenth century and continued through the nineteenth, twentieth, and early twenty-first centuries.

Some experts argue that the end of the fossil fuel era might occur within the next century for one very simple reason—the world's natural coal and oil resources are both nonrenewable and finite. Coal will last longer than oil. As of 1999, the estimated reserves of coal equaled 1,088 billion tons—sufficient to supply human needs for another 210 years at current production levels. From the date of Edwin L. Drake's discovery well in northwestern Pennsylvania in 1859, which ushered in what might be called the oil age, until the end of 1900, the earth produced 1.7 billion barrels of crude oil. Roughly 1 billion produced from wells in the United States.

With the twentieth century, a phenomenal transformation occurred in the oil industry. An enormous appetite for oil, first in the United States and soon thereafter in Western Europe, created a burgeoning demand for crude oil. The statistics of production make this observation clear. Through 1956, the world's cumulative production of oil reached 96 billion barrels, 58 percent of which (or 55.2 billion barrels) came from the United States.

Yet those numbers fail to even compare with the statistics of oil production after 1956. With the emergence of Third World countries—and particularly with their drive to industrialize in the second half of the twentieth century—the demand for oil worldwide skyrocketed. Once again, the production statistics tell the story. In just 41 years, from 1957 through 1997, the earth yielded 704 billion barrels of oil, a figure which amounts to 88 percent of all the crude produced in modern times.

Petroleum geologists, with a few exceptions, warned that, as a result, the world could experience an energy crisis if the earth's peoples do not soon reduce their heavy dependence on oil. The best estimates indicate that the world's supply of conventional oil (easily producible oil) will dwindle to almost nothing by 2050. L. F. Ivanhoe, a leading authority on petroleum exploration and its future, predicted in the November 1996 edition of *World Oil* that oil production capabilities will fail to meet supply demands by 2010 and that production levels will plummet to 5 billion barrels

Electric Tower at the Pan-American Exposition in Buffalo, New York, 1901. (Ridpath, John Clark, *Ridpath's History of the World*, 1901.)

by 2050. However, through 1997 America produced 175.6 billion barrels out of a global total of 800 billion barrels. That means the United States produced 22 percent of the world's oil, dating from the Drake well of 1859. During the first decade of the twenty-first century, U.S. oil production jumped to its highest peak since 1979. New oil reserves were opened in North Dakota as well as in the Gulf of Mexico. By the end of the decade, the continued production of oil within the United States appears positive for many more decades into the future.

The Electrical Revolution

Henry Ford (1863–1947) thought one might well refer to that period of years as the age of Edison, in honor of Thomas A. Edison, whom Ford considered the true founder of modern industry in the United States. In 1882, Edison constructed the first central electric power station in New York City for public use. Shortly thereafter, George Westinghouse improved on Edison's system by introducing the principle of an alternating current for electrical transmission. In 1895, building on that principle, Nikola Tesla invented a reliable motor driven by an alternating current. That motor design found its first practical application in the building of a 5,000-horsepower generator (one of three) driven by power derived from Niagara Falls. Soon thereafter, another of Tesla's innovations—his high-potential magnifying transmitter—made it possible to transport electric power for long distances from the electrical plant. That advance freed industry from the necessity of locating factories near sources of power.

Around the same time, steam power began to complement the production of hydroelectric power in American factories. In 1896, Westinghouse purchased the rights to the steam turbine, which was invented 12 years earlier in England. Such engines soon outmoded the old type, such as the ones first used at Niagara Falls. The new steam turbines revolutionized the situation through the production of immense quantities of low-cost electric power. Total primary power for factories, as applied by electric motors, increased from 5 percent in 1899 to 55 percent in 1919. By 1925, the figure stood at 73 percent.

Meanwhile, electricity began to find its way into American homes. Besides the ubiquitous light bulb, the first electric appliance (the flat iron) soon appeared, after its demonstration at the World's Fair in Chicago in 1893. Other appliances followed in the iron's wake until, by the 1920s, the electrically-equipped home was a reality.

Except for hydroelectric power, which remained important, the primary source of power for electric generation in home and factory came from coal—one of America's most abundant raw materials. Even though Americans used up much of that coal by the 1920s, the United States still possessed one-fourth of the world's reserves at the end of the twentieth century.

The Transportation Revolution

In addition to the electrical revolution, the United States also experienced a transportation revolution. Henry Ford founded the Ford Motor Company in 1903, the same year that Orville and Wilbur Wright launched the airplane. Ford receives much of the credit for making the motorized vehicle (particularly the automobile) the people's choice for transportation. He accomplished that feat in two ways. First, he revolutionized the technology of production by introducing the moving assembly line, which became fully operational in 1914. That innovation made it possible to assemble a Model T chassis in 1 hour and 33 minutes. By way of contrast, in 1913, the stationary assembly technique required 12 hours and 28 minutes to complete a chassis. The savings in time allowed for the mass production of the Model T at a lower unit cost, which greatly augmented the number of sales. Car sales jumped, in fact, from 261,000 to 803,000 from 1914 to 1918. By 1927, when Ford discontinued the

Model T, more than 15 million units were sold. Ford's second major innovation involved reducing the workday from nine to eight hours and doubling the basic daily wage to $5. In the process, he not only reduced worker turnover but also stimulated the growth of a mass market for the Model T. By the early 1920s, the Ford Motor Company produced 60 percent of all American automobiles and 50 percent of the world's total.

By the early twentieth century, motorized vehicles began to predominate not only on America's roads but also on its farms. Tractors made their appearances in ever larger numbers. Sales increased from 25,000 to 246,000 in 1915 and 1920, respectively. The number of trucks, which numbered only 25,000 in 1915, reached 139,000 by 1920. More and more farmers also bought cars, the numbers climbing from 472,000 to 2.1 million in 1915 and 1920, respectively.

All these land vehicles, other than some powered by steam or electricity, as well as airplanes received their energy from oil, at first primarily from gasoline but increasingly from kerosene and diesel fuel as well. Interestingly, refiners long considered gasoline a nuisance. In fact, before the advent of motorized vehicles powered by the internal combustion engine, gasoline was treated as a waste product and was often dumped into rivers near the refineries.

The Oil Revolution

Along with the electrical revolution and the transportation revolution, an intensification in the discovery and exploitation of America's oil wealth occurred. The golden age of crude production in the United States spanned the years from 1901 through 1950. During that period, the world's first great oil discovery of the twentieth century occurred in Texas. Three miles south of Beaumont, in Jefferson County along the Gulf Coast, Captain Anthony F. Lucas brought in the Spindletop gusher at a depth of 1,139 feet on January 10, 1901. The well yielded an estimated daily production of 75,000 barrels.

Many other great oil discoveries followed, mainly in states west of the Mississippi River. The heyday for discoveries occurred during the 10-year period from 1921 through 1930, when exploration yielded 24 oil fields, all west of the Mississippi; each produced over 100 million barrels through 1945. These fields culminated with the Daisy Bradford No. 3, the discovery well of the east Texas field—the greatest oil field ever found in the coterminous United States.

In the first half of the twentieth century, no country approached the United States in terms of oil production. By 1938, the United States produced a cumulative output of 21,187,141,000 barrels of oil, more than five times as much as the Soviet Union, its nearest rival. In fact, the United States produced almost 64 percent of the world's oil by 1938. In that year alone, Texas and California both produced more oil than any other country. Texas, with 475,614,000 barrels, and California, with 249,749,000 barrels, exceeded the Soviet Union's 202,290,000 barrels. In 1950, the United States still produced 52 percent of the world's oil.

By 1997, though, the U.S. share of world oil production plummeted to 10 percent. During the second half of the century, the United States found it increasingly necessary to import oil. In fact, the nation became a net importer of crude in 1948—a state of affairs that prevailed ever since. By 1999, this growing dependence on foreign oil, especially from the Organization of Petroleum Exporting Countries (OPEC), meant the importation of 50 percent of the oil used in the United States.

During the last 50-plus years, the United States offset this growing dependence on foreign oil, in large part through offshore drilling, particularly in the Gulf of Mexico and off the coast of California. In 1896, such boring for oil began off the coast of Summerland, California. Wooden piers, extending outward from the shore, permitted the drilling.

By 1946, offshore drilling came of age. Piers were no longer needed; the rigs stood in open water on rigid platforms. Oil companies drilled nine such wells in the Gulf of Mexico—five off the coast of Louisiana and four offshore from Texas by that same year.

New developments not only in the Gulf of Mexico but also elsewhere in the coastal waters of the United States became bogged down in a legal battle between the national and state governments. The dispute, which lasted from 1947 to 1953, hinged on the following question: Did the national government or the respective state governments with coastal waters have jurisdiction over offshore lands? In 1953, all parties reached a compromise—depending on the distance from the shoreline, both the national government and the state governments exercised jurisdiction.

In 1945, President Harry S Truman opened Pandora's box on this issue when he proclaimed that the national government held jurisdiction over all lands and natural resources seaward from the coastlines. The U.S. Supreme Court upheld Truman's proclamation in 1947, but protests by the coastal states led to congressional action intended to redress state grievances. The Submerged Lands Act of 1953 awarded the coastal states submerged lands seaward from their shorelines to a distance of 3 miles. A second 1953 law, the Outer Continental Shelf Lands Act, reserved the jurisdiction of the national government over submerged lands beyond the 3-mile limit. Decisions by the Supreme Court, however, gave Texas and Florida an extended limit—3 leagues (10.3 miles) seaward, not the 3 miles given to other coastal states.

In the aftermath of World War II, Americans realized that the abundant and usually cheap energy, made readily available in large part from America's production of oil, created a consumer culture. Experts characterized consumerism by the purchases of innumerable goods, including millions of motorized vehicles, electrical appliances, and the products of a new technology known as television. A large number of the products so consumed demanded enormous outlays of energy as well—so much so, in fact, that the United States (with only 6.1 percent of the world's population) utilized 44.5 percent of the earth's total production of energy in 1950.

Motorists remained the chief consumers of energy in the United States; in the 1950s, Americans became infatuated with the automobile. Known to one critic as the "dinosaur in the driveway," it remained heavy in weight, overpowered, and loaded with creature comforts, all of which contributed to its gas-guzzling nature. For example, in 1955 (the peak year for sales during the decade, with 7.9 million cars sold), the American automobile got an average of 12.7 miles per gallon. Taken together, American cars consumed 25 billion gallons of fuel in 1950 alone. Ten years later, they burned 42 billion gallons.

By the late 1950s, with the introduction of the compact American Rambler and the German Volkswagen in particular, more energy-efficient cars began to appear on the highways of the United States, but Americans still drove an exorbitant number of miles and burned excessive quantities of gasoline both for business and for pleasure. In addition, truck traffic, with its prodigious consumption of diesel fuel, increased the amount of oil consumed.

The U.S. government encouraged Americans to take to the road after 1956—the year Congress enacted the Federal-Aid Highway Act at the urging of President Dwight D. Eisenhower. The act created the largest public works project in history. Initially, it called for 41,000 miles of interstate highways scheduled for completion by 1972 at a cost of about $26 billion. But two decades after Eisenhower left office in 1961, this highway system (which was not yet finished) already cost nearly $100 billion.

In the 1960s, another development neared maturity as well. That development—the environmental movement in the United States—considerably impacted energy-related matters. One event involving the oil industry probably did more than anything else to invigorate the movement—the 1969 blowout of a well off the coast of Santa Barbara, California. Protests against the resultant oil spill, among other things, brought the passage into law of the National Environmental Policy Act of 1969. Other laws enacted by Congress in a similar vein followed in quick succession—the Marine Mammal Protection Act (1972), the Federal Water Protection Act (1972), the Endangered Species Act (1973), the Federal Land Policy and Management Act (1976), and the Alaska National Interest Lands Conservation Act (1980). With the adoption of the National Wilderness Preservation Act in 1964, before the furor raised by environmentalists five years later, the oil business and other extractive industries assumed a defensive position.

Another consequence of the barrage of legislation, along with the decisions of the Bureau of Land Management and the U.S. Forest Service, included the decision to severely curtail oil and gas exploration on federal lands. By 1990, out of a total of 688.3 million acres of nationally owned lands, 43.6 percent (or 301.5 million acres) remained off-limits to oil companies and on June 26, 1990, President George H. W. Bush placed a moratorium (the largest and longest thus far) on the leasing of 192 million acres of the Outer Continental Shelf—a moratorium slated to remain in effect from 1990 to 2003. This policy occurred at a time when the country experienced a decline in oil production, an increase in domestic oil consumption, and a substantial growth in the amount of imported crude oil. Since then, new offshore wells in the Gulf of Mexico and a major oil discovery now tapped in North Dakota resulted in a jump in U.S. oil production to peak 1979 levels.

Alternative Power Sources

Power from water, primarily hydroelectric, offers the most immediate dividends among the renewable energy sources. Even as long ago as the 1930s, the United

States constructed great dams across major bodies of water around the country, which provided almost 40 percent of the nation's electrical needs. Although the percentage for waterpower fell to 12 percent in the 1990s, hydroelectric power accounted for 98 percent of the electricity coming from renewable sources in the United States.

Hydroelectric Power

In the twenty-first century, if government officials focus on environmental concerns, hydroelectric power may well become the greatest source of renewable energy in the country. On the Columbia River system alone, 192 dams already exist. But problems remain. Dams create new bodies of water, which can destroy a variety of wildlife, from frogs to plants (and in the case of the Columbia River, many salmon). Changes in water levels can also affect habitats along shorelines and can reduce water temperatures downstream when dams release cold water. Dams can also affect the ecosystems of plants as well as animals, including mammals. Still, new dams will provide much-needed energy for the future.

Wind Power

The generation of wind power also a long and respectable history in the United States. By the close of the nineteenth century, almost 6.5 million windmills supplied energy for pumping water and grinding grain on farms across the nation. By the end of the twentieth century, more sophisticated devices, known as wind turbines, each with two blades shaped like airplane propellers, generated up to 5,000 kilowatts of power, which is enough power to furnish electricity for more than 1,000 homes.

Several states already have programs for a greater use of wind or are planning to implement them, chiefly by means of those powerful turbines. In that respect, California serves as the leader so far, beginning with commercial wind farms in operation since 1981. In the Lake Benton area of Minnesota, wind turbines already stand along a 30-mile swath of farmland called Buffalo Ridge, generating a great deal of electricity in addition to earning $2,000-a-year per turbine for the landowners. Other states—including Texas and Iowa, which experience powerful winds, but also unlikely places such as Pennsylvania, New York, and West Virginia—possess great potential in terms of the use of wind.

Bio-based Fuel Sources

The processing of plant life (biomass) into fuel, already begun worldwide, also holds great promise. In the United States alone, distilleries transform such organic products as corn, sorghum, and sugar beets into ethanol, which, when mixed with gasoline, forms what is known as gasohol, an efficient fuel. Brazil, which instituted its National Alcohol Program in 1975, serves as an example. By using sugarcane converted into ethanol, that country greatly reduced its dependence on foreign oil; Brazil imported

Ethanol production plant in South Dakota. (iStockPhoto.com.)

79.5 percent of its crude in 1975. Through the operations of its National Alcohol Program, the production of ethanol jumped dramatically from 147 million gallons to more than 2.5 billion gallons a year by the early 1980s. Although new oil off the coast of Brazil, discovered after 1989, began to compete with ethanol in price, the latter still accounted for one-fifth of the country's total use of fuel for road vehicles in 1995. Critics of biomass production question the wisdom of using food-producing land for fuel output, but there is little doubt about its future in the world's growing search for more energy.

Solar power, second only to hydroelectric power in its potential as a renewable source of energy in the United States, remains relatively expensive. Photovoltaic cells, for instance, which convert light from the sun into electric power, are not yet cost-effective in most applications. However, the Southern California Edison Company funded a photovoltaic plant built in 1981. As of 1999, it provided 1,000 kilowatts of power—an impressive output but a far cry from the million or more kilowatts generated by a typical coal- or nuclear-powered facility.

Solar technologies received a boost in the 1970s from the federal government. Congress passed the Solar Energy Research, Development and Demonstration Act of 1974, authorizing the Energy Research and Development Administration (which became the Department of Energy in 1977) to devote substantial manpower and money to innovations in the realm of solar energy. In 1974, Congress also earmarked $20 billion over a projected 10-year period to foster nonnuclear power facilities, mainly in response to the concerns of people who remained skeptical about the future of nuclear power in the nation's energy picture.

Since the 1970s, nuclear power experienced a difficult time, in the United States. For one thing, there is a great deal of concern, particularly among environmentalists, over the transport and disposal of nuclear wastes, not to mention nuclear safety. By 1990, the United States stored about 90 million gallons of radioactive debris in underground tanks near nuclear facilities in Washington, Idaho, and South Carolina. But those wastes must remain in storage for another 600 years. In addition, such a disposal system necessitates the replacement of the tanks periodically and may result in leaks. It is hoped that the Department of Energy will solve the problem. The radioactive wastes will be stored permanently in deep underground geologic formations, undisturbed by earthquakes for millions of years, namely, in slate, granite, basalt, or volcanic rocks.

Probably, though, the greatest fear of the American people has to do with the possibility of runaway nuclear reactors, such as the one at Three Mile Island near Middletown, Pennsylvania. On March 28, 1979, America's most serious accident in 22 years of commercial nuclear energy output began to unfold at that location. The reactor, suffering from a loss of coolant, formed a hydrogen bubble, which could have exploded. After a week, the danger passed, but the repercussions were considerable. Residents in the Middletown area were understandably shocked, and many other Americans across the country joined ranks with them in protesting further nuclear power developments in the United States.

The outcry was so great, in fact, that some officials talked of imposing a permanent moratorium on the construction of nuclear plants in the country. A commission established by the Carter administration considered the Three Mile Island debacle quite serious but stopped short of advancing such a recommendation. By early 1990, by which time the protests began to subside, the Nuclear Regulatory Commission (established in 1974), which superseded the Atomic Energy Commission, actually permitted construction to begin on a new test plant not far from Chattanooga, Tennessee. Even so, in the light of the Three Mile Island fiasco, the prospects for nuclear energy remain questionable in the United States.

On a positive note, geothermal sources of power may offer a promising alternative. With continued advances in technology, some experts predict that geothermal plants will soon exist in the United States and have a capacity to generate 24 million kilowatts of electricity. Two facilities in California demonstrated the potential for the future. A plant at Brawley, jointly owned by the Southern California Edison Company and the Union Oil Company of California, produces more than 10,000 kilowatts. But the biggest operation in the country, operated by the Pacific Gas and Electric Company and located just 90 miles north of San Francisco, harnessed steam to run turbines from a number of hot springs, known as The Geysers, which emitted hot water from deep in the earth for centuries. The steam-powered turbines generate nearly 2 million kilowatts of electricity.

References

Faulkner, Harold U. *The Decline of Laissez-Faire 1897–1917*. New York: Holt, Rinehart and Winston, 1951.

Herda, D. J., and Margaret L. Madden. *Energy Resources: Towards a Renewable Future*. New York: Franklin Watts, 1991.

Hubbert, M. King. *Nuclear Energy and the Fossil Fuels, in Drilling and Production Practice in 1956*. Washington, DC: American Petroleum Institute, 1957.

Jehl, Douglas. "Curse of the Winds Turns to Farmer's Blessing." *New York Times*, November 26, 2000.

Lugar, Richard G., and R. James Woolsey. "The New Petroleum." *Foreign Affairs*, vol. 78, no. 1 (January/February 1999): 88–103.

Marsh, G. Rogge. "The Environmental Realities of Petroleum Exploration." In Richard Steinmetz, ed., *The Business of Petroleum Exploration*. Tulsa, OK: American Association of Petroleum Geologists, 1992.

Mitchell, John G. "Urban Sprawl: The American Dream?" *National Geographic*, vol. 200, no. 1 (July 2001): 48–74.

O'Sullivan, John, and Edward F. Keuchel. *American Economic History: From Abundance to Constraint*. New York: Markus Wiener, 1989.

Porter, Edward. "Are We Running Out of Oil?" Discussion Paper no. 081. Washington, DC: American Petroleum Institute, 1995.

Schurr, Sam H., and Bruce C. Netschert. *Energy in the American Economy, 1850–1975: An Economic Study of Its History and Prospects*. Baltimore, MD: Johns Hopkins University Press, 1960.

Federal Reserve Bank

Simone Selva

The Federal Reserve Bank (Fed) is a key institution in America's economy and society, designed to provide financial stability by ensuring currency flexibility. As such, since its establishment, the Fed consistently played a vital role in U.S. economic and monetary policies.

The Federal Reserve Bank system was established in December 1913, so the history of the monetary policies and regulations of the Fed goes back only to the early years of the twentieth century. Prior to 1900, the United States did not have a central banking and financial system after the charter for the Second Bank of the United States expired in 1836, but debates on feasible banking reforms actually began in the mid-nineteenth century. Consequently, it is reasonable to divide the history of the Federal Reserve Bank system into two distinct phases. The first phase, covering the monetary history of the United States from the second half of the nineteenth century up to the early twentieth century, was dominated by intense discussions on the existing financial and banking structures and the attempts to reform them. Reform proposals advanced during this period laid the foundations of a banking system regulated by national control, as the Federal Reserve Bank system became within a few decades. In the second phase, beginning with the 1913 establishment of the Federal Reserve Bank system, the focus was on the Fed's role and functions in U.S. financial and economic arenas during the twentieth and early twenty-first centuries.

In nineteenth-century America, the banking system was shaken by several economic and financial crises, and the effects of these recurrent downturns shaped the debates and proposals that arose on how to reform the banking system. As such, most of the proposed and enacted reforms were thought of as ways to cope with current financial crises and to stabilize the currency.

Throughout the second half of the nineteenth century, there was an economic crisis almost every 10 years. The first one, which occurred in 1861, resulted from the Civil War's effects on the U.S. financial structure. To deal with this crisis, a reform was passed to give any national bank the right to issue paper currency on its own. What economists usually regard as a national system for chartering banks was thus established. This reform was also the first step toward instituting a coordinated and regulated monetary system. The second crisis, which occurred in 1873, was the product of the government's efforts to carry out a reform to redeem paper money with specie (payment in gold or silver only). In this case, the bank reserve system proved too weak to avoid an overall panic provoked by the demand for bank reserves. Yet another crisis occurred in the ensuing decade when, in 1884, the overall stability of the banking system was threatened by massive international pressures for payment in gold for the securities of U.S. companies owned by Europeans. Just nine years later, in 1893, another major economic and financial crisis began, caused by the demise of the Reading Railroad and the failure of the stock market shortly thereafter. The twofold collapse was followed by the failure of other prominent firms. This major economic distress stimulated, even more than in the past, discussions and controversies among economists and bankers on the best way to provide monetary stability within the U.S. banking system.

During the 1890s, two main proposals were brought before the business and political communities. The first proposed bank reform, presented at the 1894 American Bankers Association meeting by a banker from New York and another from Baltimore, was known as the Baltimore Plan and rested on the idea that financial and currency stability required the creation of a new currency backed by a central fund provided by the banking system. This central fund was intended to cope with financial panics and downward economic trends. The plan foresaw bank loans to the business community based solely on the gold standard, under which the only legal tender was gold. The second bank reform proposal arising out of discussions on the economic crisis of the 1890s came from a report presented at the 1897 Indianapolis Monetary Convention. According to the report's author, economist J. Lawrence Laughlin, it was critical for the system to be flexible in times of economic uncertainty. As Laughlin argued about a decade later while reflecting on the 1907 financial crisis, monetary stability required national control. And, in his view, some institution wholly free from politics or outside influence should exert this national control: By this, however, he did not mean a central bank, as was later established. Rather than a government-led institution, he proposed a sort of bank of banks, backed by the banking system and committed to regulated banking. This vision for the achievement of financial and currency stability was realized within 10 years when the U.S. economy fell in the grip of a fifth major economic slump.

A couple of observations should be made regarding these 1890s proposals to reform the banking system. First, both the Baltimore Plan and the Laughlin report did not have wide consensus within the business community. The former was sharply criticized and consistently opposed by many nationwide banks, whereas numerous state-chartered banks and some small banking institutions did not agree on the Laughlin report.

Second, both these monetary reforms ran counter to the cause of the silverites (those who wanted silver included as legal tender) and the silver principles underpinning the Populist protest movement that arose during these financial crises, especially among Midwestern agricultural sectors and greenbackers (who wanted paper currency used as legal tender) and against the financial elites and industrial development based in the East Coast. The 1896 general elections brought Republicans back to power. This political turnover stopped the rise of the Populist movement, whereas the two bank reforms proposed during the decade reassessed the role and strength of more traditional centers of power, such as the bankers and the eastern financial and business communities.

During the first decade of the twentieth century, there was, as mentioned, a fifth major economic and financial crisis, which accelerated the move toward a national coordination of monetary policy and an overall control of the stability and flexibility of the currency. In fact, the 1907 economic crisis, which cut the net national product by 11 percent in one year, looked like a sharp economic downturn with the potential to lead the country to the brink of a financial collapse.

In 1908, not only economists and the business community but also politicians and Congress began to approach the ongoing economic crisis by planning a reform of the banking system. For the first time, bank reform was on the top of the congressional agenda. A number of bills came out of this wider interest in the problem, and to bring into harmony as many reform views and interests as possible, a committee was established. Co-chaired by Nelson Aldrich from the Senate and Edward Vreeland from the House of Representatives, the committee produced a final bill known by historians and economists as the Aldrich-Vreeland Act. This act established the National Monetary Commission, which was led by Aldrich and Vreeland, appointed chair and vice-chair, respectively. The commission's work was pivotal to the founding of the Federal Reserve Bank system. In fact, the report produced by the commission, widely known as the Aldrich Plan, endorsed the series of reforms that resulted in the creation of the Fed. Extensively explained in a 24-volume publication, the Aldrich Plan required the establishment of the National Reserve Association—a body that included a Washington-based central administrative bureau and 15 regional districts that, in turn, were linked to local commercial banks through their local associations. Led by 46 directors recruited from among both the 15 districts and the reserve associations as well as the government, the National Reserve Association was responsible for determining the discount rate, issuing currency, and holding part of the member banks' reserves. According to Aldrich and Vreeland, this body, charged with controlling the banking and financial system, must operate free from political influence and not considered a central bank. On the contrary, it was conceived as a bank of banks—an entity owned by the commercial banks. Members of Congress debated extensively on the nature and meaning of this institution. In particular, controversy arose over whether it functioned like a central bank. The National Monetary Commission clearly stated that the structure of the institution not resemble that of European central banks. Nonetheless, a member in the House voiced the opinion that the National Reserve Association would, in fact, resemble the European central banks structurally.

The monetary institution outlined in the Aldrich Plan, a institutions supposedly free from political influences and working unlike a moneymaking institution, was met with interest and received approval from the most prominent banking and business players. The National Board of Trade, the American Bankers Association, and the most outstanding bankers endorsed the plan early on. The scheme was clearly opposed only by the Democrats, who depicted it as the product of conservative-minded Republicans.

In the end, the National Reserve Association envisioned by the Aldrich Plan was never established. In fact, as a result of the 1912 general elections, which brought in a Democrat administration, Democrats started shaping debates and legislation on the reform of the banking system. In his last message to Congress, the Republican president William Howard Taft recommended the National Reserve Association, but the new president, the Democrat Woodrow Wilson, and a Democrat-dominated Congress stopped the establishment and implementation of this economic institution. The new Congress worked over the bill establishing the Federal Reserve Bank system, and the House Committee on Banking and Currency was appointed to draft this measure. According to the committee president, Carter Glass, the government would not have had sufficient control over the National Reserve Association. He argued that instead of a bank of banks headed by bankers, what was needed was a central banking agency that coordinated the currency issue with the volume of business; it should be a public utility led by the nonprofit Federal Reserve Board.

As long as the bill was being worked over by the Senate and the House, controversy persisted among members of Congress on whether or not to tie the new institution and its governing board to American politics. Although legislators stressed that the Federal Reserve Board should work as a sort of public coordinator of all private banks, free from political control, many politicians argued that the Glass bill and the forthcoming institution would shape a monetary policy influenced by the presidency. Glass replied that the Fed was aimed at extending democratic control over the banking system. In other words, the Federal Reserve Board should be a board of control, working on behalf of the interests of citizens. Indeed, the basic principle underpinning most debates on bank reform in the past—that is, the establishment of an institution that could grant monetary and financial stability through a stable currency issue—was still at stake. In fact, according to Glass and his legislators, the Federal Reserve was consistent with the gold system precisely because the gold system and the real bills (backed by specie such as gold) could be coupled with and contribute to the regulation of the money supply: Glass's scheme granted every district reserve in the Federal Reserve system the right to discount only short-term loans to businesses that created products for sale. Such a discounting rule adjusted the money supply to the volume of business by providing as much money as necessary for commerce. By this monetary policy, the Fed could promote elasticity in the economy's money supply.

The birth of the U.S. central monetary institution stimulated discussions not only within the Congress but also, of course, among bankers and the business community at large. When the Glass bill was presented, not all the banks were keen to accept it. The eastern banks were ready to work in cooperation with a central bank dominated by bankers, whereas the Midwestern banks believed that only district reserve associations were necessary. Almost all bankers were skeptical about the banking system proposed by Glass because they regarded it as too dependent on the government. In any case, when the bill was finally passed in the Congress at the end of 1913, the opinion on the law held by bankers and banking associations had somewhat changed. They increasingly viewed it as a reasonable compromise.

What the Federal Reserve Act lacked was a clear distribution of power and monetary authority between the Federal Reserve Board and the Federal Reserve banks. This unresolved problem caused conflicts and controversies between these two bodies up to the 1930s. In fact, after the establishment of the Federal Reserve Bank system, each Federal Reserve bank member started setting its own discount rate; there was no national authority to coordinate the banks as the later Federal Open Market Committee on Monetary Policy (FOMC) did. In the beginning, the district banks prevailed on an individual basis. Among them, the most relevant was the Federal Reserve Bank of New York.

Because the most important commercial banks were concentrated in New York City, the New York district bank was able to challenge the Federal Reserve Board of Washington. In particular, the district banks challenged the Washington board by setting up their own organization, the Governors' Conference, whose members were the heads of their own institutions. Led by the New York Fed and its president, Benjamin Strong, the district banks tried to make open market purchases and sales of Treasury assets, which eventually caused a chaotic and uncoordinated situation. In 1922, urged by the Washington board to coordinate market sales and purchases, the Federal Reserve Bank of New York and four other eastern district reserve banks established a committee in New York City to make joint purchases and sales. From the early 1920s to the New Deal reforms of the 1930s, the balance of power between the Federal Reserve banks and the Washington Federal Reserve Board started shifting toward the latter. The progressive waning of influence on the part of the district banks, caused at least in part by the death of Benjamin Strong, was marked by the Federal Reserve Board's decision to regulate and limit the right of the Federal Reserve banks' committee to make open market purchases and sales. As a matter of fact, the Federal Reserve Board transformed that body committee into a system committee, known as the Open Market Investment Committee in 1923. Everything that the committee chose in terms of open market purchases and sales required approval by the Washington board before becoming effective. Nonetheless, the growing control over the open market operations did not end the long-term dispute between the board and the regional banks. At any rate, in 1930, just before the bank reforms of the 1930s, the Washington board once again changed the structure and functions of the Open Market Investment Committee—at this time, it was transformed into the Open Market Policy Conference, made up by all the Federal Reserve banks' governors. According to the new legislation, each district bank could leave the Open Market Policy Conference or choose not to work according to its policy, but the Federal Reserve Board updated on every choice in this regard.

When the United States faced the 1929 economic slump, the ongoing struggle between the Federal Reserve banks and the Federal Reserve Board and, above all, the incoherent and uncoordinated U.S. monetary policy that resulted were blamed for the economic crisis. This link between the fragmentation of the Federal Reserve Bank system and the Wall Street crash of 1929 was probably deepened and intensified by what happened to the Fed in the late 1920s, for the 1928 death of Benjamin Strong sharpened the system's incoherence by opening an internal struggle for power within the system.

During the 1930s, the Federal Reserve Bank system was widely reformed by the New Deal administration of President Franklin Roosevelt. Indeed, the Roosevelt administration and the New Deal era are renowned for the overall reforms achieved, so it is worth stressing how the Fed's reform was crucial and paramount to the New Deal reform process. A wide range of sectors in American society, from the federal government to labor, were affected by New Deal reforms, and the banking system and the Federal Reserve were on the top of the New Dealers' agenda. Such a discredited and criticized institution as the Fed could not avoid the Roosevelt administration's reform process. Broadly speaking, during the 1930s, the Federal Reserve system was made more independent of the banking system and more unified within itself. What is still discussed among scholars, however, is whether these reforms also made the Fed more independent of the government and the White House. The main cluster of reforms took place between 1933 and 1935. The Banking Act of 1933 transformed the Federal Open Market Committee into a statutory body; up to that time, its composition remained unchanged, still made up by the 12 heads of the banks. Furthermore, the Banking Act lengthened the term of appointment to the board of governors to 12 months. It also started augmenting the power of the Federal Reserve Board, another main feature of the Fed reforms taking place throughout the first half of the 1930s. The board's power was enlarged by the Thomas Amendment to the Agricultural Adjustment Act, which granted it the power to alter the reserve requirements (although this was an emergency power exercised only under the approval of the president).

In 1934. the Glass-Steagall Act required banks to choose between undertaking investment banking and specializing in commercial banking—that is, the taking of deposits and granting of loans. In turn, the 1934 act widened the lending power of the banks. Thereafter, any Federal Reserve member bank was allowed to make advances to all of its member banks on any good security whenever it wanted to do so.

All of the acts described thus far were important to the reform of the Federal Reserve Bank system, but the single most significant measure was the Banking Act of 1935, which encompassed all the main features of the reform process taking place during the 1930s. First, it changed the composition of both the Federal Reserve Board and the FOMC. The Washington board, renamed the Board of Governors of the Federal Reserve System, was still made up of seven appointed members, but their tenure was lengthened to 14 years; even more crucial, both the secretary of the Treasury and the comptroller of the currency were no longer ex-officio members of the board. Of course, the change made the Washington board and the Fed at large more independent of the administration. This reform was promoted by the Fed bureaucracy and in particular by the candidate for the board chair, Marriner Eccles, but the Roosevelt administration preferred that the secretary of the Treasury and the comptroller of the currency continue as ex-officio board members. Although the president was still in charge of appointing the Federal Reserve governors and designating the chair and vice-chair, the reformulation achieved by the Banking Act of 1935 established a Federal Reserve Board and a system at large independent of the government budget. As a matter of fact, one of the first results of these reforms was

The Federal Reserve System is headquartered in the Eccles Building on Constitution Avenue in Washington D.C. The building is named for Marriner Eccles, chair of the Federal Reserve from 1934 to 1948. (iStockPhoto.com.)

that the Fed became completely self-financing and did not work in accordance with either the president's or the Congress's budgetary policies. Further, the 1935 Banking Act strengthened the power and authority of the Federal Reserve Board not only in respect to the government but also with regard to the Federal Reserve banks. The restructuring of the Open Market Committee's composition was aimed at unifying the system and reducing fragmentation by strengthening the role of the board in Washington. The heads of the district banks were renamed presidents of the Federal Reserve banks, and the FOMC, which once included only the 12 men who headed the district banks, now included the seven members of the Washington board and five of the 12 presidents of the Federal Reserve banks. As such, this reform of the FOMC widened the influence and power of the Federal Reserve Board by granting it a voting majority on the FOMC. The Banking Act of 1935 consolidated the wider role of the Federal Reserve Board. First and foremost, the Board of Governors retained the right to determine the discount rate; consequently, the president of the Federal Reserve Bank of New York could not determine the discount rate on his own anymore. In addition, reserve banks could no longer carry out transactions on their own—each was now allowed to buy and sell government securities only on approval by or in accordance with the Federal Open Market Committee. Furthermore, the Board of Governors was charged with setting a ceiling to the interest rates paid by member banks. This provision, previously granted by the 1933 Banking Act and now confirmed, constrained the growth of saving accounts within the commercial banks. One more provision granted by the Banking Act of 1935 made it clear just how far these reforms went in consolidating the role of the Board of Governors as the most powerful and important body within the Federal Reserve system. The board's power to change the reserve requirements, initially established as an emergency power in 1933, was transformed into a permanent right; the board could change reserve requirements within a range spanning from the minimum percentages specified in 1917 to twice those percentages. Furthermore, as a result of the Securities Exchange Act of 1934, the board took over the regulation of credit advanced by banks to their customers for buying and carrying registered securities.

Even if the New Deal reforms are regarded as significant steps forward in terms of augmenting the Fed's independence and power, it is clear that in the following years and decades, the Federal Reserve system was weak both economically and politically. Its economic weakness resulted from the banking reforms of the 1930s, whereas its political weakness stemmed from long-term features of the system itself, deeply rooted in its origins and policy environment. In the following passages, the two areas are dealt with separately.

As mentioned, because its unity and cohesion was strengthened, the Federal Reserve system was not only more independent of the government and the district reserve banks but also more powerful in regard to the commercial banks and the banking system at large. However, although the 1930s' banking reforms granted it more power before the private banking system and more control over monetary policy, the Fed actually controlled a smaller monetary system after 1940. This weakness was the result of one of the banking reforms promulgated in the 1930s. Concerned with the failure of the banking system, the politicians adopted, as already shown, a number of provisions; the Fed's reform was just one of them. Another response was the promotion of and support given to the thrift (savings) industry. The Roosevelt administration provided the thrift industry with a number of direct and indirect subsidies, ranging from deposit insurance to public housing programs and from urban renewal plans to deductible and guaranteed mortgages. This set of provisions made the thrift industry grow very quickly shortly after the New Deal era. Still a marginal player in the 1940s, the industry became a giant by the 1960s. Throughout this period, the number of mutual savings banks and savings and loan associations rose, whereas the thrift industry took over more and more of the mortgage sector. In the long run, the miracle of the thrift industry widened a financial sector untouched by and far from the Federal Reserve Bank system. In fact, the thrift industry could rely on its own agencies: Registered with state authorities, they could fix their own reserve requirements, for they were not required to abide by the Fed's reserve requirements. In essence, these financial institutions were quite apart from the Federal Reserve system, and their growth and expansion reduced the size of the monetary system presided

President Ronald Reagan congratulates Alan Greenspan after his swearing in as new chair of the Federal Reserve Board on August 11, 1987. Greenspan, who served as chair until 2005, is often credited with improving the economy. (AP/Wide World Photos.)

over by the Federal Reserve Bank. By the 1950s and 1960s, only one-third of the American financial institutions participated in the Federal Reserve monetary system.

The Fed's independence of the political system was not achieved until two decades after the New Deal reforms. Throughout World War II, the Fed worked according to the financial needs of the Treasury and Congress. But during the postwar reconstruction period, its relationships with its political partners started changing. As a result of the inflation experienced in 1946 and 1947, the Council of Economic Advisers was established to assist the White House, and the federal government's control over economic issues was strengthened. Given this legislative context and economic situation, the Treasury thought that the Federal Reserve Bank should raise interest rates, especially on Treasury debt. But the Fed insisted on keeping interest rates low.

This controversy, which lasted at least until the onset of the Korean War in 1950, unfolded the dispute about who should take charge of monetary policy, and in late

1950 and 1951, the controversy became a top priority for the administration of President Harry S Truman. In 1951, Fed Chair Thomas McCabe resigned and President Truman intervened. A number of meetings among the Federal Reserve Board, the FOMC, the Treasury, and the Truman administration were held during 1951. Hearings and meetings led to the Treasury–Federal Reserve accord of 1951 and 1952, an agreement whereby the Fed was no longer required to support the Treasury interest rates. Instead, interest rates became a matter of consultation and agreement between the two players.

The accord can be regarded as a further step toward independence from politics for the Fed. But real independence was not reached clearly until as late as 1953, when a new administration came to power. This move toward greater independence, begun under Truman's watch and carried on by Eisenhower, was consistent with the history of the Federal Reserve Bank system to that point. Ever since Congress established the Fed in 1913, successive administrations granted the Fed more independence. Thus, the Federal Reserve's role and independence was consistently decided and guaranteed by a wide consensus within the political environment of which it was a part.

An overview of the Federal Reserve Bank system's history throughout the twentieth century shows that the institution followed a long route to clearer independence and a more stable organization and structure, mainly based on the crucial role played by the Federal Reserve Board. This trend toward developing into a more reliable economic institution charged with setting monetary policy continued even after World War II. At that time, the Fed could leave behind the war experience that temporarily tied it to political choices and budgetary issues. Throughout the post–World War II years, the economic institution continued to grow in terms of budgets, monetary policymaking, and reliability.

Nonetheless, under the Nixon administration in the 1970s, some disappointments arose in regard to inflation, and certain economists and presidential advisers were sympathetic to Milton Friedman's monetarist standpoint. (A monetarist is an economist who believes the money supply is the most important economic measure.) As happened in 1970, the Fed chair (in this case William Martin, whose tenure focused on low inflation and economic stability and a wide array of other economic indicators) was replaced by a monetarist policymaker (Arthur Burns). The Fed appeared poised on the brink of monetarism. Meanwhile, the inflation rate was climbing, and an even more significant wage-and-price control put in place. Monetarists used this inflationary tendency throughout the decade to criticize the Federal Reserve Bank system's structure and independence, and blamed the Fed for the inflationary tendency—its immobility and sovereignty were seen as causes for inflation. As such, the economic trends of the 1970s were regarded as a pretext to take on monetarism, a policy Paul Volcker pursued after being named Fed chair in 1979. Actually, the policy started to influence American policymaking only when Ronald Reagan became president in 1981.

During the first years of Reagan's administration, the Federal Reserve pursued a tight monetarism designed to tame inflation, at the expense of the New Deal's legacies. Throughout the 1980s, monetary policy making led to a sharp deregulation of the banking and financial services institutions. The Federal Reserve Bank dealt with a mild recession from 1990 to 1992 in which interest rates were reduced to help stimulate the economy. From 1992 until the recession of March 2001, the Federal Reserve worked on other issues, such as reducing the amount of "float" (financial transactions that take several days to process, most commonly involving checks). With the widespread use of direct deposits by employers and debit cards by consumers, the amount of float declined throughout the 1990s. In 1993, more than $19 billion of transactions were floating for one to three days. By 1995, that number dropped to $15.5 billion and the float amount plummeted to $774 million in 2000. The ability to credit funds instantly allowed money to circulate more freely.

After the recession of March 2001, which some economists believe ended by summer 2003, the Federal Reserve reduced interest rates to a 40-year low in an effort to stimulate the economy. With the prime interest rate at 1.25 percent, the economy showed some signs of recovery, but businesses, fearful of future terrorist attacks after September 11, 2001, remained cautious about reemploying laid-off workers or investing in more capital equipment. In 2004, the Federal Reserve increased interest rates. Fed Chair Alan Greenspan noted that, at that time, the correlation between the Fed's short-term interest rate for securities and the long-term interest rate for securities such as 30-year mortgages, were no longer linked. The decoupling of the two rates, which remained in lockstep between 1971 and 2002, was primarily the result of the accumulation of enormous unintended reserve currency savings by countries such as China and other emerging developing countries such as India and Russia which increased the amount of their exports suddenly and dramatically from the early 1990s on. These unintended reserve currency savings of dollars resulted in declining long-term securities interest rates and helped drive the frenzy in the U.S. housing market from 2000 to 2007. By 2006, the long-term interest rate declined into the single digits for the first time in U.S. history, according to Greenspan's observation. As the housing market grew to unprecedented proportions, the enormous expansion of the mortgage-backed portfolios of the government-sponsored enterprises of Fannie Mae and Freddie Mac ballooned into the trillions of dollars. Greenspan warned Congress of the potential of a future financial crisis in the housing market with potentially dire repercussions on the rest of the U.S. economy during congressional hearings held in 2006. However, Congress failed to heed the warning until it was too late. In 2006, Greenspan retired from his position as Chair of the Federal Reserve Board of Governor, replaced by incoming Fed Chair Ben Bernanke.

When the housing bubble burst in August 2007, the Federal Reserve worked in conjunction with the Department of Treasury as well as the Securities and Exchange Commission to address the expanding financial crisis. A liquidity crisis and cash crunch, which began affecting Wall Street banking, investment, and insurance institutions, developed in 2008. Bernanke assumed a high visibility role in the arrangement of a government-sponsored sale of Bear Stearns to JPMorgan Chase, which cost the federal government $29 billion to cover the less liquid assets in the Bear Stearns securities portfolio. Bernanke remained in the public eye as he worked through the Fannie Mae and Freddie Mac bailouts, which he finalized on September 7. He remained actively and visibly involved in the bailout of A.I.G. and Washington Mutual Bank later that same month. In a televised speech in September, Bernanke outlined a $700 billion proposal allowing the government to purchase toxic securities from the nation's banks, a proposal at first rejected by Congress and then approved after the $85 billion bailout of A.I.G. and the largest bank failure in U.S. history when Washington Mutual filed bankruptcy.

During the recession of 2007, the Federal Reserve kept interest rates low in an attempt to stimulate the U.S. economy. The performance of Fed Chair Bernanke during the crisis remained relatively positive overall but he is not without critics. Former Chair Greenspan recently wrote that the credibility of the Federal Reserve in the future will be difficult to repair as far as standing up to big business deemed "too big to fail" because during the recession, "when push came to shove, they didn't stand up." Greenspan was not the only one concerned about the future position and role of the Federal Reserve Bank. During Bernanke's renomination hearings in December 2009, many congressional members expressed the need for a new Chair of the Fed to replace Bernanke, a "hard money" chair able to stand up and resist attempts by some to get out of the current recession that occurred as a result of the housing bubble by pursuing an easy credit "soft money" policy that would, in effect, float another bubble and cause more financial damage in the future. Both the House of Representatives and the Senate began demanding greater transparency by the Federal Reserve and the Senate debated drafting legislation to redefine the central role of the bank in financial stability and take the power of supervising banks away from the Federal Reserve Bank. If such legislation ever passes, the traditional role played by the Federal Reserve Bank in the U.S. economy in the past will no longer remain.

When the economy no longer is in danger of economic weakness, the Federal Reserve will once again raise interest rates to counter inflationary tendencies.

References

Broz, J. Lawrence. *The International Origins of the Federal Reserve System*. Ithaca, NY: Cornell University Press, 1997.

Corder, J. Kevin. *Central Bank Autonomy: The Federal Reserve System in American Politics*. New York: Garland Publishing, 1998.

Friedman, Milton, and Anna Schwartz. *A Monetary History of the United States, 1867–1960*. Princeton, NJ: Princeton University Press, 1963.

Greider, William. *Secrets of the Temple: How the Federal Reserve Runs the Country*. New York: Simon and Schuster, 1987.

Greenspan, Alan. "The Fed Didn't Cause the Housing Bubble," *Wall Street Journal*, March 11, 2009. Available: http://online.wsj.com/article/SB1236729650 66989281.html; accessed December 30, 2009.

Hadjimichalakis, Michael. *The Federal Reserve, Money, and Interest Rates: The Volcker Years and Beyond*. New York: Praeger, 1984.

Havrilesky, Thomas. *The Pressures on American Monetary Policy*. Boston: Kluwer, 1993.

Johnson, Peter. *The Government of Money: Monetarism in Germany and the United States*. Ithaca, NY: Cornell University Press, 1998.

Kopcke, Richard, and Lynn Browne, eds. *The Evolution of Monetary Policy and the Federal Reserve System over the Past Thirty Years: A Conference in Honor of Frank E. Morris*. Boston: Federal Reserve Bank of Boston, 2000.

Mayer, Thomas. *Monetary Policy and the Great Inflation in the United States: The Federal Reserve and the Failure of Macroeconomic Policy, 1965–1979*. Northampton, MA: Edward Elgar, 1999.

McCulley, Richard. *Banks and Politics during the Progressive Era: The Origins of the Federal Reserve System, 1897–1913*. New York: Garland Publishing, 1997.

Morris, Irwin. *Congress, the President, and Federal Reserve: The Politics of American Monetary Policy-Making*. Ann Arbor: University of Michigan Press, 2000.

New York Times. "Greenspan Calls to Break Up Banks 'Too Big to Fail,' " October 5, 2009. Available: http://dealbook.blogs.nytimes.com/2009/10/15/greenspan-break-up-banks-too-big-to-fail/; accessed December 30, 2009.

Siegel, Barry, ed. *Money in Crisis: The Federal Reserve, the Economy, and the Monetary Reform*. San Francisco: Pacific Institute for Public Policy Research, 1984.

Stein, Herbert. *Presidential Economics: The Making of Economic Policy from Roosevelt to Clinton*. Washington, DC: American Enterprise Institute, 1994.

Timberlake, Richard. *Monetary Policy in the United States: An Intellectual and Institutional History*. Chicago: University of Chicago Press, 1993.

Timberlake, Richard. *The Origins of Central Banking in the United States*. Cambridge, MA: Harvard University Press, 1978.

Woodward, Bob. *Maestro: Greenspan's Fed and the American Boom*. New York: Simon and Schuster, 2001.

Woolley, John. *Monetary Politics: The Federal Reserve and the Politics of Monetary Policy*. New York: Cambridge University Press, 1984.

Wueschner, Silvano. *Charting Twentieth Century Monetary Policy: Herbert Hoover and Benjamin Strong, 1917–1927*. Westport, CT: Greenwood Press, 1999.

Foreign Policy

Keith A. Leitich

Since the founding of the United States, American foreign policy vacillated between isolationism, or the reluctance to become involved in global politics, and moralism, which dictates foreign policy justified on ethical principles. The uniqueness of this approach to foreign policy derives from the peculiar experiences and circumstances of the United States: its geographic isolation from the centers of world conflict during the nineteenth century, its tendency toward pacifism in international affairs, and the uniqueness of the American experiment.

When the founders broke constitutional ties with England, they were convinced of the need to develop a foreign policy distinct from that of the European powers—a position characterized by George Washington's admonition against entangling alliances. This retreat from European politics was a retreat from the power politics of the time, for political conflict was centered in Europe. This period of American foreign policy was a realistic period, an era in which when the United States understood that neutrality in international politics was necessitated by the national interest of the country.

The next phase of foreign policy, known as the ideological period, was guided by an approach that involved thinking in terms of moral principles yet acting in terms of power. In an era when the European powers struggled for colonial possessions through imperialistic ventures and wars of conquest in Africa and Asia, American foreign policy was influenced by the writings of Thomas Jefferson and John Quincy Adams, who described political interests in moral terms. The Monroe Doctrine and Manifest Destiny are the best examples of political interests couched in moral terminology. The ideological period ended during the latter half of the nineteenth century as the United States sought to become a great power, best exhibited by the U.S. annexation of the Philippines following the cessation of the Spanish-American War in 1898.

America entered a new phase of foreign policy, known as the utopian period, when moral principles no longer justified the country's national interest and foreign policy was divorced from political reality and dictated in terms of moral principles. This phase, best characterized by the political thought of Woodrow Wilson, opposed the pursuit of America's national interest—maintaining the balance of power in Europe—on moral grounds. Yet, when President Wilson led the United States into war with Germany, he pursued the right policy—again, maintaining the balance of

Harry S Truman became president of the United States on April 12, 1945, following the death of Franklin Roosevelt. As president, Truman oversaw the end of the World War II and made the decision to drop the atomic bomb. He then led the nation in the tumultuous early years of the Cold War that included the Berlin Airlift and the Korean War. (Library of Congress.)

power in Europe—for the wrong reason. Wilson could only respond to the national interests of the Allies in terms of his own moral principles. In the treaties of Paris and Versailles, the president agreed to a series of compromises that, in effect, meant a capitulation of those very principles.

The isolation of the interwar period was interrupted by America's entrance into World War II, primarily on moral grounds. The Axis powers were characterized as evil; thus, the goal of U.S. involvement in World War II was viewed as the destruction of evil.

Following the end of World War II, America's isolation from global politics ended, necessitated by a series of events that culminated with the onset of the Cold War against the Soviet Union. A globalist course of foreign policy, motivated by domestic values, was set in motion. America's foreign policy became based on the principles of maintaining the balance of power with the Soviet Union and assuming global responsibility. Threatening statements against Western-style capitalism by Soviet leader Joseph Stalin served as the guiding force of American foreign policy throughout the Cold War era. Put another way, America's global involvement was based on opposition to the Soviet Union.

With the breakdown of the Cold War consensus, as exemplified by America's defeat in Vietnam, succeeding administrations attempted to introduce a new foreign policy to replace the outdated containment strategy. The administration of President

Richard M. Nixon sought to reintroduce power politics to American foreign policy, whereas Jimmy Carter's tried to introduce a global politics approach. Ronald Reagan and his administration restored a foreign policy from an earlier era, and the Soviet Union and the threat of international communism became the centerpiece of American foreign policy until the collapse of the USSR in 1991. Following the Soviet Union's fall, the process of formulating American foreign policy objectives focused on economics. Changing technology, a growing population, and economic development necessitated the emphasis on economic needs.

In the post–World War II period, the foreign policy of the United States became directly entwined with foreign aid. In 1947, President Harry S Truman announced the Truman Doctrine, which provided funds for anticommunist forces in Greece and Turkey. The success of the Truman Doctrine resulted in the implementation of the Marshall Plan in late 1947, which provided $12 billion for the rebuilding of Western Europe (the plan was originally offered to the Soviet Union as well, but the Soviets refused to participate). During the 1950s and 1960s, the United States continued to divert foreign aid to areas on the verge of falling to communism, and it increased military expenditures in countries such as Korea and Vietnam. Funding went to the Afghanistan freedom fighters after the Soviets invaded that country in 1979, and aid was provided to the Contras in Nicaragua in an effort to topple the communist-backed Sandinista government in the 1980s. The United States also earmarked over $23 billion for the Strategic Defense Initiative (Star Wars) project, which ultimately resulted in a series of U.S.-Soviet treaties to limit missiles. After the Cold War ended with the fall of the Soviet Union in 1991, foreign policy expenditures took on a different function.

After the terrorist attacks of September 11, 2001, the United States augmented its financial support of countries with large Muslim populations in Southeast Asia. Increases in assistance to nations such as India, Pakistan, and the Philippines rose between 17 percent and 250 percent. Both Pakistan received $200 million and India received an increase of $25 million in 2002.

In 2002, the United States continued to provide foreign assistance to a number of countries and international organizations around the world, totaling $15.4 trillion. Israel received $720 million, Egypt $655 million, Jordan $150 million, East Timor $25 million, Mongolia $12 million, and the Sudan $10 million. Israel and Egypt also received $2,040,000 and $1,300,000 in military expenditures, respectively. In addition, the United States also spent $615 million in Eastern Europe and $795.5 million in the former Soviet Union. Another $318.5 million went for antiterrorism programs. Most of the balance of the foreign assistance budget focused on a variety of international programs such as the Peace Corps, the Export-Import Bank, the Trade and Development Agency, HIV and AIDS research, refugee services, technology research, and efforts to end international slavery.

The U.S. economic involvement in foreign policy continues to promote the peace and stability of a number of regions around the world. It also promotes American interests and attempts to address the needs of peoples in distress. As in the past, political, cultural, and social considerations determine the amount and availability of U.S. funds provided to countries around the world.

References

Bloomfield, Lincoln P. *In Search of American Foreign Policy.* New York: Oxford University Press, 1974.

Crabb, Cecil V., Jr. *Policymakers and Critics: Conflicting Theories of American Foreign Policy.* New York: Praeger, 1976.

Dallek, Robert. *The American Style of Foreign Policy: Cultural Politics and Foreign Affairs.* New York: Alfred A. Knopf, 1983.

Gilpin, Robert. *War and Change in World Politics.* New York: Cambridge University Press, 1981.

Holsti, Ole R., and James S. Rosenau. *American Leadership in World Affairs.* Boston: Allen and Unwin, 1984.

Legg, Keith R. *Politics and the International System: An Introduction.* New York: Harper and Row, 1971.

Leopold, Richard W. *The Growth of American Foreign Policy.* New York: Alfred A. Knopf, 1962.

Morganthau, Hans. *In Defense of the National Interest.* New York: Alfred A. Knopf, 1952.

Perkins, Dexter. *The American Approach to Foreign Policy.* Cambridge, MA: Harvard University Press, 1962.

Quester, George. *American Foreign Policy: The Lost Consensus.* New York: Praeger, 1982.

Government Domestic Economic Policies

David B. Sicilia

The federal government of the United States is a major promoter and regulator of the American economy. Vast bureaucratic agencies and commissions staffed with thousands of experts monitor the economy and adjust various fiscal and monetary levers in an ongoing and complicated effort to maintain a healthy economy. These institutions include, but certainly are not limited to, the White House, Congress, the Federal Reserve Bank, the Council of Economic Advisers, the U.S. Treasury, and the Federal Trade Commission (FTC).

The United States became the largest free market economy in the world in the late nineteenth century. But, it is hardly a "pure" capitalist system. Rather, government and the private sector together comprise a "mixed" economy, one in which government economic policy makers interact continually with entrepreneurs, corporations, workers, and consumers. This arrangement was especially true after the 1930s, when the role of government in the economy grew dramatically under President Franklin D. Roosevelt's New Deal. And since World War II, the scale and scope of the government's economic expertise, programs, and policies grew exponentially.

Throughout the history of the American Republic, and even during the colonial period, political leaders as well as ordinary citizens made sense of their economic lives by relying on metaphors, models, and other frameworks for understanding individual and collective economic behavior. Political leaders and economic policymakers shared a common set of goals since the U.S. Constitution was ratified and the new federal government became operational in 1789: robust growth of the economy, welfare for the citizenry, and low rates of unemployment and inflation. However, they often disagreed about the best policies for achieving these goals, and prevailing economic ideas changed dramatically over time.

The Era of Promotionalism: From Constitution to Civil War, 1787 to 1865

In 1776, the year the Declaration of Independence was signed, the Scottish political economist Adam Smith published *The Wealth of Nations*, a work that became one of the most influential economic treatises of modern times. Smith advocated governments limit themselves to maintaining security, leaving economic affairs in private hands. Markets, he argued, do a much better job of setting prices and maintaining quality than governments.

But Smith's vision was not reality in the British colonies of North America in 1776. Instead, the economies of the colonies were controlled by a variety of economic policies integral to the British imperialist system. Operating a global system of commerce designed to benefit the homeland, the British monarchy defined what products the American colonies could produce, export, and import. It also prohibited colonists from coining money. Although historians disagree about the precise economic toll these mercantilist controls exacted on the 13 colonies, there is little doubt that the American Revolution was, in large measure, a fight for greater economic independence.

The patriots who fought for independence faced, among other things, the practical problem of raising and funding an army without a central government. By 1775, the Continental Congress assumed many of the economic functions of an indigenous central government, such as forming a postal system, issuing paper currency (known as Continentals), and levying taxes on the states (but not individuals). However, some states refused to tax their citizens and issued their own paper currencies, which caused a massive devaluation of Continentals. The situation was stabilized when Congress retired the currency in 1781.

The U.S. Constitution not only defined a remarkable system of representative government but also held great economic significance. It empowered the central government to levy taxes and collect duties on imports, regulate domestic trade, grant patents, and coin money. To establish the new nation's credit on a firm footing, it provided for the redemption of all war debts. The Constitution also authorized a navy and army to defend the nation and to protect and expand commerce.

In the 1790s, the Federalists (led by Alexander Hamilton, the first secretary of the Treasury) and the Anti-Federalists (or Jeffersonian Democrat-Republicans, most notably Thomas Jefferson and James Madison) struggled over the issue of central government power. In the end, despite the fact that states retained a good deal of power and independence in economic affairs, the Federalists nevertheless made several important gains, although they did not achieve all of their aims. These gains included the establishment of a protective import tariff, national excise taxes, a stronger army and navy, and a national bank. Congress was also authorize to collect and publish statistics on the nation's population (the 10-year census), build lighthouses and harbor facilities, and support scientific exploration.

During the antebellum period (1790–1860), federal economic policy was most influential in four areas. One pertained to tariffs and subsidies. Among those benefiting from protective tariffs and subsidies were cod-fishing enterprises, telegraph companies, stagecoach lines, and small-arms manufacturers. Merchant shipping was an especially large beneficiary: Congress imposed discriminatory duties, offered mail contracts and generous subsidies ($14 million between 1845 and 1858), and excluded foreign competition in the coastal trade.

A second important dominion of federal economic policy was banking. At Hamilton's urging, Congress federally chartered the Bank of the United States

(BUS) in 1791. Capitalized at $10 million, BUS issued much-needed paper currency, provided loans to the Treasury and to responsible state banks, and served as the federal government's repository and fiscal agent in foreign exchange. Although BUS helped stabilize the nation's banking and currency and facilitated commerce, Jefferson and other Anti-Federalists declared it a threat to sound hard currency (gold and silver) and to agrarian interests, and they prevented a renewal of the bank's 20-year charter in 1811. The Second Bank of the United States (1816–1836) experienced a similar history, though on a larger scale. Expanded to 29 branches by its aggressive president, Philadelphia banker Nicholas Biddle, the Second BUS met strong opposition from President Andrew Jackson as well as from competing state and local banks. From the time the Second BUS's charter renewal was denied until the Civil War, there was no central bank in the United States. During that period, state banks, many of them reckless "wildcats," issued their own currencies, which often fluctuated wildly in value. But many state governments reined in such practices with various regulations—most notably, requirements that chartered banks hold a minimum percentage of specie (money in coins) for every paper dollar issued.

Third, the federal government played a major economic role through its land policies. Throughout the antebellum period, the government pursued an explicit strategy of territorial expansion, which involved purchasing or, in some cases, forcibly taking vast tracts of western lands. Large purchases from France in 1803 (the Louisiana Territory), from Spain in 1819 (Florida) and 1845 (Texas), and Great Britain in 1846 (Oregon) were supplemented by military takeovers of Mexico-controlled California and the Southwest in 1848 (at the end of the Mexican-American War) and of vast Indian lands. Federal government policies controlled the transition of new lands to the status of territories and then states.

To encourage the settlement and cultivation of new lands—the central aim of federal land policy—Congress passed several key laws. The Homestead Act offered a quarter section (160 acres) to any adult, whom never raised arms against the United States, who lived on and cultivated the land, at a price of just $1.25 per acre after six months or for free after five years of residency on the land. Subsequent legislation—the Timber Culture Act of 1873, the Desert Land Act of 1877, and the Timber and Stone Culture Act of 1878—offered landownership incentives to homesteaders who cleared or irrigated marginal lands. But these policies largely failed to achieve their intended goals. Of the 96 million acres distributed under the four acts, only one-sixth of them were distributed as gifts, and only 1 western farmer in 10 was a true homesteader. Rather, cheating and speculation were rampant as choice lands were gobbled up by large speculators and then divided and subdivided for profit.

Fourth, the federal government played a major role in building the nation's transportation infrastructure. In 1806, Congress authorized construction of the National Road to encourage western settlement and commerce. After an intense political battle, Cumberland, Maryland, was selected as the eastern terminus, and the road reached Wheeling, Ohio in 1819. Although Treasury Secretary Albert Gallatin spelled out an ambitious plan for federal turnpike and canal building in his *Report on Roads and Canals* (1808), his plan was scuttled by constitutional arguments

The Erie Canal was a major component of the development of the New York–New Jersey region. (Library of Congress.)

against a strong central government, rivalries among states and localities, and budgetary concerns.

Canals became major arteries for commerce in the post-War of 1812 period. The most successful was the Erie Canal, constructed between 1816 and 1825, when it connected Albany and Buffalo—and thus the East Coast—to the Great Lakes. The Erie Canal was built by the state of New York, with strong support from its governor, DeWitt Clinton, but financed by domestic and foreign private investors. It sparked many imitators in Pennsylvania, Ohio and elsewhere. The federal government provided surveyors and some land grants to the states for these projects but state governments played a more overt role by directly financing many of the projects. In the United States between 1815 and 1860, state public funds accounted for roughly three-quarters of the $190 million spent to build about 4,000 miles of canals, most of them linked to natural waterways. By the late 1840s, however, many of these projects defaulted on their loans, and several states revised their constitutions to ban debt-financed improvements. Nevertheless, these public-private projects dramatically lowered transportation costs in many parts of the Northeast and upper Midwest.

By this time, railroads, which appeared in the 1830s, began eclipsing canals. In Massachusetts, Pennsylvania, South Carolina, and Georgia, state governments financed the first rail companies. Although states turned away from direct investment in the railroads in the 1840s, they continued to grant generous charters, which often gave rail companies the power to seize land through eminent domain, and sometimes exempted them from taxation and rate regulation. Meanwhile, municipalities and counties played a growing promotional role, offering to build free terminals, subscribe to blocks of stock, and the like. For its part, the federal government made generous land grants to railroads, in part to encourage private investors to build rail lines and, in part, to reap the benefits, for railroad development boosted prices of nearby government lands. Together, state and federal governments granted about 200 million acres of land (an area roughly the size of Texas) to the railroads before the Civil War.

The Civil War wrought massive disruptions, many of them economic, which the federal government and the new Confederacy in the south struggled to overcome. Federal spending surged from $66.5 million in 1861 to $1.3 billion in 1865. Although in 1863 the government introduced a new income tax, which was repealed after the war, as well as new excise taxes, it financed most of its expenditures with loans and by issuing $400 million of greenbacks, a new paper currency. These actions contributed to runaway inflation, which seriously eroded the real buying power of northerners. Consumer prices roughly doubled in the north during the war, whereas wages for skilled and unskilled workers actually fell. However, the situation was far worse in the south. The Confederacy imposed no income tax until 1863. Rather, it printed more than $1 billion of new paper money, which became worthless with the south's surrender. By that time, the south owed more than $2 billion to domestic and foreign creditors. Although Confederate wages rose about 10-fold during the war, key prices climbed more than 30 fold.

More important, however, the Civil War assured Republican control of Congress when southern Democrats withdrew from the Union, ushering in a set of economic policies which favored many powerful economic interests in the north and often encouraged economic development. These measures included the aforementioned Homestead Act; a new wave of loans and land grants for railroads, including authorization of the first transcontinental railroad; the Morrill Land-Grant College Act, which supported agricultural education and research; a contract-labor law, which encouraged manufacturing investment; and a national banking system with the power to charter and regulate banks.

In these and other ways, federal, state, and local governments encouraged the economic development of the nation in the post-Civil War period. In general, government played a promotional role—protecting infant industries against cheap imports, opening new lands for settlement and cultivation, and encouraging investment in transportation and communication networks. But the government's efforts to foster a stable and adequate system of money and banking were uneven at best, and its control over the nation's natural resources too often led to speculation and

Under orders of the U.S. Marshal, worm-infested currants and raisins seized from Washington, D.C. bakeries under provisions of the Pure Food and Drug Act are destroyed on November 20, 1909. (Library of Congress.)

reckless exploitation. The federal government played virtually no direct role in the slave-based cotton economy of the south. Roughly every 20 years during the nineteenth century, the U.S. economy was plagued with a severe recession which left millions of urban and farm workers destitute, yet the federal government did little or nothing to correct these recessions. Very few people thought that government could or should do much to control economic cycles, other than continue to protect the sanctity of private property and remove obstacles to entrepreneurial investment.

The Era of Industrialism: Regulating Trusts and Competition, 1865 to 1914

In the generation after the Civil War, the United States emerged as the world's pre-eminent economic power. Its railroad networks possessed more track than existed in

Europe and Russia combined, and its behemoth iron, steel, and oil refineries far out-produced those of any foreign rival. Small and medium-sized firms persisted and multiplied, but national attention increasingly focused on the giant industrial corporations, which were defining the era. Yet it was glaringly apparent that rapid industrialization, for all of its benefits, also brought a host of economic and social problems. As a result, whereas government played a primarily promotional role before the Civil War, it took on a second, regulatory role as well in the post-Civil War era.

The regulation of business corporations typically began at the state level and later moved to the federal level. Railroads attracted the first intense regulatory scrutiny. Midwestern farmers and shippers were frustrated by secret rebates to large shippers and by complicated railroad rate schedules, especially those that forced them to pay higher rates per mile to ship commodities over short distances rather than long distances. Investors, large and small, were angered by the watering down of railroad stocks (diluting the stocks' value), bogus construction contracts, insider trading, and the bond defaults, which plagued many American railroads. All complained of the railroads' undue political influence. In the 1860s, Illinois, Iowa, Minnesota, and Wisconsin passed the first state laws regulating railroads, which were soon imitated in neighboring states. These Granger Laws were based on the principle that states should regulate railroads because they were indispensable "natural monopolies" affected with a "public interest." The Granger movement encountered opposition from railroad owners, who claimed the laws denied them their Fourteenth Amendment right to private property. The Supreme Court first upheld the Granger Laws in *Munn v. Illinois* (1877) and then reversed itself in the *Wabash* case (1886), in which the Court affirmed that only Congress had the power to regulate interstate commerce.

The *Wabash* ruling left the door open for federal regulation, which many railroad executives also advocated by this time. They wanted to eliminate the worse abuses of less responsible rivals, deal with a single set of federal commissioners rather than scores of different state regulators, and take a hand in defining the new regulation. The result was the Interstate Commerce Act of 1887, the first federal regulation of business in U.S. history. Its major provisions mandated "just and reasonable rates," outlawed price discrimination, prohibited pooling arrangements, and established the five-member Interstate Commerce Commission (ICC). Initially, the impact of the ICC remained nominal. It held no explicit powers of enforcement, and its language about "just and reasonable rates" was subject to broad interpretation. Moreover, the courts more often than not ruled in favor of the railroads. But, in the Progressive Era of the early twentieth century, several additional laws—the Elkins Act (1903), the Hepburn Act (1906), and the Mann-Elkins Act (1910)—gave the ICC investigative, enforcement, and rate-setting powers.

The second major federal regulation of corporations came with the passage of the Sherman Anti-Trust Act of 1890. This legislation was designed to deal with the growing problem of business concentration, especially in the manufacturing sector. State incorporation laws prohibited a corporation in one state from owning a corporation in another. However, giant firms saw this act as a great obstacle to expansion and interstate management of their assets. In 1882, a lawyer for Standard Oil devised the first "trust," a way of skirting the prohibition against interstate corporate ownership. Soon, several other industries consolidated as trusts. States responded with antitrust laws; 15 state laws were passed between 1888 and 1890. In 1889, New Jersey, hoping to attract more business, passed a holding-company law, which gave corporations a new way of legally consolidating their multistate operations.

The Sherman Anti-Trust Act of 1890 outlawed all "contracts, combinations, and conspiracies in restraint of trade." But, like the Interstate Commerce Act, it was vaguely worded, weakly enforceable, and usually interpreted by the courts in favor of big business. In one crucial Supreme Court ruling, the *Addyston Pipe* case (1898), the Court affirmed that collusion was illegal, but merger was legal. This ruling encouraged a massive wave of corporate mergers at the turn of the century. Congress finally put teeth in the antitrust law during the Progressive Era. In 1911, the Justice Department broke up two of the world's most powerful monopolies, Standard Oil and American Tobacco. In these cases, the Court articulated a "rule of reason," which distinguished between "good" trusts, which controlled a dominant market share but did not act anti-competitively, and "bad" ones, which interfered with competition. In 1914, antitrust law was significantly strengthened and expanded by passage of the Clayton Act, which created the Federal Trade Commission; the commission was given the power to investigate anticompetitive practices and issue "cease and desist" orders. The Clayton Act also outlawed interlocking directorships, selling and buying contracts, and price discrimination. In this way, U.S. antitrust policy became more a matter of administrative government rather than court interpretation.

In the late nineteenth and early twentieth centuries, progressivism—a constellation of reformers and reform movements struggling with the effects of industrialization, urbanization, and immigration—fostered the passage of a wave of economic legislation intended to reform business and improve labor conditions. The strengthening of railroad regulation and the antitrust legislation, were among the most important measures. Often, such reforms were pioneered at the state level before being emulated nationally. The so-called Progressive presidents, Theodore Roosevelt (1901–1908), William Howard Taft (1909–1912), and Woodrow Wilson (1913–1921), made the greatest strides. Roosevelt realized that big corporations could benefit society with their great efficiencies, but he also believed that government should exercise the power to rein in abusive firms. He believed in using a combination of publicity, antitrust law, and regulations to keep corporations in line. During 1906, his administration passed the Hepburn Act, the Pure Food and Drug Act, the Meat Inspection Act, and an employer-liability law for the District of Columbia. Roosevelt proposed even more ambitious measures such as a federal incorporation act and employer liability for all federal workers, but pro-business forces defeated them.

The Wilson administration's three major economic measures were the Clayton Act and the Federal Trade Commission Act as well as the Federal Reserve Act of 1913. The last of these measures created the U.S. Federal Reserve system (Fed) to address a number of weaknesses in the financial system, which plagued the economy since the demise of the Second Bank of the United States in 1836. The Fed operated 12 district banks distributed throughout key economic regions of the country.

Individual banks were encouraged to become members of the system by subscribing to a portion of the stock of their regional Fed. Boards of governors appointed by member banks and by the central Federal Reserve Board ran the regional Feds. Therefore, the system shared power between public and private interests and represented and served diverse regional economic interests.

To encourage responsible banking practices among its members, the Fed enforced minimum reserve requirements (the minimum cash on hand required of financial institutions under the law). To moderate business cycles, it raised or lowered the rediscount rate—the rate at which it loaned money to member banks. The Fed also acted as a clearinghouse for obligations among member banks and as the federal government's fiscal agent. In the 1920s, the Fed began to ease or tighten credit by buying or selling large blocks of government securities—its so-called open market operations. The Federal Reserve gave the nation a permanent and largely effective central bank.

The Progressives also instituted many new forms of national labor regulation. Up to this time, employee-employer relations were generally governed by the "fellow servant" rule, which left employers free of any responsibility for worker injury or death on the job. Moreover, Progressive legislation severely limited the widespread practice of using the Sherman Anti-Trust Act against labor unions (as organizations "in restraint of trade") rather than to control corporations. Progressive legislation also provided minimum-wage laws for women workers, restricted the hours and working conditions for child workers, and required pensions for indigent widows with children. In spite of these gains for industrial workers, however, local, state, and federal governments usually sided with employers during labor disputes. For instance, governors often called out state militias to help manufacturers put down strikes.

The rise of giant corporations after the Civil War encouraged the expansion of state and federal regulatory powers in response. Government policies continued to foster economic development in a variety of ways, from tariffs to liberal immigration laws to agricultural extension services, but the government now also played a larger role as the arbiter of disputes, enforcer of competition, and guardian of the industrial worker.

The Era of National Emergencies: Economic Policies in World War and Depression, 1914 to 1945

Three national crises—World War I (1917–1918), the Great Depression (1929–1939), and World War II (1941–1945)—ushered in a new era of relations between the government and the economy. To mobilize for war, to soften the economic disruptions of war, and to cope with the century's most severe economic depression, American citizens called on their government to dramatically expand its role in the nation's economic affairs. But this expansion often was curtailed or limited by continuing fears of a strong central government and by a continuing belief in the natural and inevitable character of business cycles.

When World War I began in Europe in August 1914, the United States was strongly isolationist. Although supplying the Allies with large quantities of war-related foodstuffs, raw materials, manufactured goods, and loans, the country did not begin to seriously mobilize for war until mid-1916, and it did not enter the war as a combatant until April 1917. But the mobilization process did not go smoothly. In 1916, it was handled mainly by the Council of National Defense (CND) and the U.S. Shipping Board, with the result that shortages of tanks, planes, bombs, and critical materials were commonplace. In July 1917, the CND created the War Industries Board (WIB) to set priorities and increase production of critical materials. This was the first formal attempt at central economic planning in U.S. history.

But the WIB did not possess clear, constitutional powers to compel manufacturers to abide by its priorities. Many companies did so voluntarily, motivated by patriotism, profit seeking, or both. The WIB did not become reasonably effective until 1918, when Wilson established a price-fixing board within the WIB and appointed as its head Wall Street tycoon Bernard Baruch. Structuring the WIB more like a corporation, Baruch staffed it with business leaders, established functional divisions, and instituted a range of controls over the production and distribution of food and fuel to discourage shortages, hoarding, and price discrimination. The WIB also operated adjustment boards to control wages, hours, and working conditions. In its most dramatic exercise of power, Baruch's board took over operation of the nation's railroad system in April 1918, followed by the telephone and telegraph systems. Although most businesspeople initially viewed these actions with alarm, the wartime business-government partnership proved to be mostly beneficial for American business. Corporate profits rose generously during the war. The government also relaxed antitrust enforcement.

The federal government financed about two-thirds of the war effort by levying new or increased excise, estate, and income taxes. The Sixteenth Amendment, passed in 1913, authorized a graduated personal income tax, which soon was instituted on a sharply progressive basis, ranging from 3 to 63 percent. Meanwhile, the country suffered from severe price inflation, brought on by a combination of heavy gold imports and liberal Federal Reserve credit policies.

The new enthusiasm among business leaders for a strong business-government partnership dissipated rather quickly with the return of peace. Under presidents Warren Harding (1921–1923) and Calvin Coolidge (1923–1929), the federal government raised tariffs, lowered taxes, made frequent antitrust exemptions, and staffed the FTC with business-friendly regulators but otherwise left big business alone. The gross national product (the total market value of the goods and services produced by the United States in a given year) rose 43 percent between 1920 and 1929, spurred by the mass production and mass marketing of automobiles, electricity, and consumer durables. The agricultural sector suffered severely during the 1920s, but the government acted only to expand credit and to encourage cooperative efforts of farmers.

When engineer-businessman Herbert Hoover was elected president in 1928, big business was held in high esteem, labor union membership was declining, and stock prices on Wall Street were skyrocketing. The stock market began a harrowing decline in October 1929 and did not hit bottom for three years. Hoover blamed speculators and foreigners for the Great Crash, and he called on business leaders to maintain wages and prices. Drawing lessons from World War I, business-government co-operation, and his own Quaker background, he advocated "associationalism," an approach by which business leaders voluntarily cooperated to control wages, prices, and output for the nation's good.

Although this approach proved naive, Hoover also took some concrete measures to revive the economy. The centerpiece of his efforts was the Reconstruction Finance Corporation, which ultimately loaned more than $3 billion to ailing railroads and financial institutions. He staunchly resisted direct government grants to either individuals or firms. Some of Hoover's economic policies were continued, in modified form, under the Democrat administration of President Franklin D. Roosevelt (1933–1945). Most notably, the National Industrial Recovery Act (NIRA) (1933) brought together leaders of big business to voluntarily set wages, prices, and output levels, reminiscent of Hoover's associationalism.

The federal government passed a dizzying array of economic legislation under Roosevelt's New Deal—15 major pieces of legislation in the first 100 days alone. To make sense of these many laws and the "alphabet agencies" Congress created, historians employ various organizing schemes. One views New Deal economic policies and programs in terms of three fundamental goals: relief, recovery, and reform. Relief programs, designed to help relieve the suffering of hard-hit groups such as farmers or unemployed laborers, included the Federal Emergency Relief Administration and the Public Works Administration, which created thousands of construction jobs. Recovery legislation, intended to lift the economy out of depression, similarly often involved job creation; among the projects such legislation spawned was the Tennessee Valley Authority, a massive regional land reclamation and electrification project. Reform legislation, designed to permanently correct structural flaws or weaknesses in the economy, focused on agriculture, public utilities, and banking. The New Deal separated investment and commercial banking and created the Securities and Exchange Commission to regulate Wall Street. Many programs were fashioned to achieve more than one of these goals.

The New Deal also expanded the federal government's role as a guardian of social welfare and organized labor. In 1935, the National Labor Relations (Wagner) Act ensured the rights of workers to organize and bargain collectively, and the Social Security Act provided old-age, unemployment, and other benefits. To some liberals, the New Deal did not go far enough: It virtually ignored certain groups, and it preserved the basic structure of American capitalism. Moreover, Roosevelt shared many of his predecessors' traditional values, as shown when he attempted to balance the budget in 1937, thereby bringing on a new recession. Still, the New Deal, whose dimensions are only suggested here, represented a dramatic expansion of federal economic power and activism.

World War II continued the trend. As Washington geared up for war in the late 1930s, many economic planners strove to avoid the production bottlenecks, shortages, and rampant inflation that had plagued the nation in World War I. As in that conflict, business executives played key managerial roles in the economy in the 1930s and 1940s, and as in the New Deal, Roosevelt again created scores of alphabet agencies. For war production, these agencies were the Office of Production Management (under General Motors' president William Knudsen) and the Supply, Priorities, and Allocations Board, both created in 1941. The U.S. economy converted to war production remarkably quickly, its wartime output surprising allies and enemies alike. From 1941, rationing and price controls were handled by the Office of Price Administration (OPA), which succeeded in holding inflation well below World War I levels. Labor unions sustained a no-strike policy through most of the war but, in 1943, Congress passed the War Labor Disputes Act, which strengthened the executive branch's power to stop strikes at government war plants. The federal budget soared between 1941 and 1945, with nearly 90 percent of the $318 billion in expenditures going directly to the war. This heavy price tag was funded by even heavier taxation, the large-scale sale of government bonds, and deficits that reached $55 billion a year by the war's end.

From Keynesians to Neoconservatism: Managing the Postwar Economy, 1945 to the Present

The wartime economy put into practice an economic theory that began to gain attention in the late 1930s. In 1936, British economist John Maynard Keynes published *The General Theory of Employment, Interest, and Money*, arguably the century's most influential economic treatise. In his analysis of business cycles, Keynes argued that recessions were potentially so severe that they would fail to self-correct, as consumers hoarded money in spite of falling prices. He contended that government deficit spending (spending more than the government received in taxes by borrowing money through the sale of treasury notes) was needed to spark recovery.

Keynes's ideas, which seemed to be validated by the wartime recovery, were widely accepted by postwar U.S. economists and policymakers. Often, too, they were oversimplified and "bastardized," that is, used as an excuse to justify policies that relied too heavily on short-term fiscal solutions. (In fact, Keynes recommended monetary controls for most economic conditions.) Still, Keynesian economics dominated until the late 1970s. Far more than even during the New Deal, the federal government was deemed responsible for the health of the economy. This expectation was reflected in the passage of the Employment Act of 1946, which created the Council of Economic Advisers (CEA), a body of economists charged with analyzing the economy and reporting on it to the president and Congress.

In the 1950s and 1960s, the economy performed extraordinarily well. New products and growing efficiencies deserved much of the credit, but so did the new variety of macroeconomic management that gained prominence after the war. Using new quantitative techniques from the emerging field of econometrics, economic policymakers began to speak of "fine-tuning" an economy from which major business cycles were virtually eliminated. Downturns became "corrections," and recessions were now known as "soft landings." Gone was the notion that business cycles were inevitable. In addition, heavy government spending on expanded social welfare programs and on the peacetime "military-industrial complex" (to support the nation's Cold War doctrine) provided a steady stimulus to the economy. The federal government also made major investments in the nation's wealth-producing capacity through the 1944 Serviceman's Readjustment Act, or GI Bill, and the 1956 Federal Highway Act.

Postwar prosperity encouraged rising expectations about the safety and quality of American life, which were translated into a new wave of regulation. The New Social Regulation included some three dozen major new laws regulating the environment, the workplace, and consumer products. These laws included the Clean Air Act (1967, with later amendments), the Occupational Safety and Health Act (1970), the Consumer Products Safety Act (1972), and the Toxic Substances Control Act (1976).

Growth rates remained high and unemployment and inflation were low until the mid-1960s, when—with the economy running close to capacity—President Lyndon Johnson resisted raising taxes to pay for the aggressive, simultaneous expansion of his Great Society social programs and the Vietnam War. Thus began the "great inflation" of the 1960s and 1970s. Historically, inflation and unemployment moved inversely but, by the early 1970s, both were topping 6 percent, leaving economists at a loss to explain "stagflation." In 1972, President Richard Nixon instituted wage-and-price controls, a remarkable step for the conservative Republican. Similarly, his successor in the White House, the liberal Democrat Jimmy Carter, began the broad-gauge deregulation of several major transportation, energy, communications, and manufacturing sectors: airlines, trucking, railroads, petroleum and natural gas, electricity, telecommunications, and financial services. Both presidents used unconventional measures in grappling with a seemingly intractable economic slump.

The time was ripe for change, politically and within the economics profession. In the late 1970s, new research suggested that overregulation (such as the New Social Regulation) and over-taxation contributed to economic slowdown. These ideas attracted the attention of some conservative Republican politicians, as did a theory proposed by University of Southern California economist Arthur Laffer, who argued that cutting taxes would actually increase tax revenues. Republican presidential candidate Ronald Reagan (1981–1989) ran on a supply-side economic platform, promising massive tax cuts to spur savings and investment, mild spending cuts, and a balanced budget. He and his successor, George H. W. Bush (1989–1993), cut taxes, scaled back health and safety and environmental regulation, and greatly reduced antitrust enforcement. Inflation fell, but the total national debt swelled to $4 trillion (rising from 23 percent to 69 percent of the gross domestic product [GDP], or the total market value of the goods and services produced by workers and capital within the United States in a year).

The administration of President Bill Clinton (1993–2001) followed a mainstream economic program, which was supported by a massive stock market boom, historically low energy prices, and large technology-related productivity gains. Since 1979 the economy also has benefited from excellent leadership at the Federal Reserve, under chairs Paul Volcker (from 1979 to 1987) and Alan Greenspan (since 1987 to 2005). The simultaneous high productivity rates, low inflation rates, and high employment rates of the late 1980s and 1990s proved to be as baffling to economists as stagflation had been, though certainly more welcome.

Since the 1980s, economic policymakers have strongly favored opening up business to ever greater levels of free market competition, both domestically and globally. President George W. Bush (2001–2009) prescribed supply-side policies much like those of his father during most of his presidency. However, Bush and his successor Barack Obama, who became president in 2009, reverted to Keynesian deficit spending on an all-time record scale when the U.S. economy plunged into a deep recession after the housing bubble burst in August 2007.

References

Bruchey, Stuart W. *Enterprise: The Dynamic Economy of a Free People*. Cambridge, MA: Harvard University Press, 1990.

Collins, Robert M. *More: The Politics of Economic Growth in Postwar America*. New York: Oxford University Press, 2000.

Engerman, Stanley L., and Robert E. Gallman, eds. *The Cambridge Economic History of the United States*. 3 vols. Cambridge: Cambridge University Press, 1996–2000.

Feldstein, Martin, ed. *American Economic Policy in the 1980s*. Chicago: University of Chicago Press, 1994.

Hughes, Jonathan R. T. *The Governmental Habit Redux: Economic Controls from Colonial Times to the Present*. Princeton, NJ: Princeton University Press, 1991.

Keller, Morton. *Regulating a New Economy: Public Policy and Economic Change in America, 1900–1933*. Cambridge, MA: Harvard University Press, 1990.

Krugman, Paul. *Peddling Prosperity*. New York: W. W. Norton, 1994.

Nettels, Curtis P. *The Emergence of a National Economy, 1775–1815*. New York: Holt, Rinehart and Winston, 1962.

Stein, Herbert. *Presidential Economics: The Making of Economic Policy from Roosevelt to Clinton*. Washington, DC: American Enterprise Institute, 1994.

Temin, Peter. *Lessons from the Great Depression*. Cambridge, MA: MIT Press, 1989.

Vietor, Richard. *Contrived Competition: Regulation and Deregulation in America*. Cambridge, MA: Harvard University Press, 1994.

Immigration Policy

John Barnhill

Immigrants provided labor and skills for America's economic development since the first British colonies in North American were established in the early 1600s. For nearly 400 years, the "unpeopled" continent of North America attracted Europeans who sought free land and the opportunity for advancement that came with it. From the time settlers arrived in Jamestown, Virginia, there was more available land than labor to work it, and even after land became scarce, workers still found employment in America's factories and mills. The nation's immigration policy, whether written or not, welcomed immigrants with open arms, then closed the door, and then welcomed them again.

Predominant tendencies allow a loose periodization of American immigration. Between 1776 and 1880, the United States welcomed immigrants, which was followed by a period of reduction from 1880 to World War I. A period of exclusion was formalized in 1924, and it lasted until 1965, when the United States once again opened its doors to refugees and other foreign immigrants.

Indians, Indentures, and Slaves

Early experiments in using the labor of Indians, a potential workforce numbering in the millions, failed because most of the native peoples disappeared into the countryside. Those who did not frequently died from various European diseases, and war reduced the native population to a small percentage of their pre-European contact level of 18 million people. Another attempt at increasing the labor pool by establishing tenants in a transplanted English manorial system proved unsuccessful because nobody wanted to work for someone else unless faced with no other choice. Those who lacked the means to get to the empty land or the tools to break off into the wilderness were forced by circumstances to sign work contracts, or indentures, to get their passage and a small grubstake at the end of the term, which varied from four to seven years. But, once in America, the indentures (indentured servants) displayed a disconcerting habit of heading off across the mountains into the wilderness or blended into a neighboring colony, with no questions asked. Indentured servitude brought between 100,000 and 300,000 people to America between 1607 and the early eighteenth century. By 1800, cheap transatlantic transportation largely ended the practice.

Slavery, a system that provided another source of labor, flourished in the plantation economy that gradually developed after the Jamestown settlers began cultivating tobacco instead of searching for gold. About 500,000 individuals were transported to America by the slave trade between 1619 and 1808. By comparison, between 3 and 4 million slaves were taken to the Caribbean, and the total for the four centuries of the trade equaled around 11 million slaves. By 1750, there were some 200,000 slaves in America; by 1860, the United States, primarily the south, consisted of a population of more than 3 million slaves. States such as Virginia, whose agricultural economy faded compared to the virgin soils of the frontier south, developed a highly profitable slave-breeding business. Slavery lasted until 1865, fueling the expansion of the cotton and textile industries, establishing the shippers and merchants of New England and the middle states, and providing the bulk of the foreign exchange available to the United States for 80 years. Involuntary immigrants made an immeasurable economic impact, and American policy, if not allowing it, at least tolerated it.

Immigration in the Early National Period

The mass of immigrants in early national period came voluntarily in wave after wave with the ups and downs of the European and American economies, and they provided the mudsill grunt labor. They usually rose through the ranks over time or returned home. All of this happened without a great deal of government involvement. The first immigration law, that of 1790, set a standard two-year residency for naturalization; Congress replaced the measure with a five-year residency requirement in 1795. Between 1790 and 1875, Congress enacted only a dozen more immigration laws. By contrast, twentieth-century Congresses enacted that many immigration laws each decade.

Congress formulated the first American immigration policy for political rather than economic reasons. After the American Revolution, France experienced an extremely chaotic period from the beginning of its own revolution in 1789 through the Napoleonic Wars, which ended in 1814. Wild swings in forms of government and a great deal of violence against those with different ideas led to an influx of French refugees in the United States, individuals who used the safety of the nation in America to agitate for their particular brand of politics. American political leaders were split between pro-French (Jeffersonian) and anti-French (Federalist) policies. When the anti-French were in power, they enacted the Alien and Sedition Acts, which eased deportation while increasing barriers to citizenship. America's first immigration policy sought to repress immigrants who deviated from the official definition of appropriate political ideas for good Americans.

The founding fathers also disagreed on the future structure of the United States. The Jeffersonian, pro-French faction included mostly small-government agrarians. The anti-French Federalists supported manufacturing as a means of attaining self-sufficiency, a need made evident by the economic difficulties arising from the European conflicts between 1789 and 1812. After the War of 1812, Henry Clay introduced his pro-immigrant American System, with its internal improvements designed to attract immigrants to the interior region as farmers. Whether Germans, Scots-Irish,

KNOW-NOTHINGISM IN BROOKLYN.
"None but citizens of the United States can be licensed to engage in any employment in this city."
Brooklyn Board of Aldermen.

Cartoon captioned "Know-Nothingism in Brooklyn. None but citizens of the United States can be licensed to engage in any employment in this city." The Know-Nothing Party, or American Party, gained widespread support in the 1850s. The party's platform called for restrictions on immigrants, including withdrawing their right to vote. When asked about the party's platform, members were supposed to reply that they knew nothing, hence the name. (Library of Congress.)

Huguenots, or other, these people dispersed or set themselves apart; they were mostly Protestant and similar to the old-stock Americans. The next wave of immigrants produced more friction than the handful of French who recently arrived.

The First Great Wave, 1830 to 1860

The first great wave of immigrants included over 4.9 million individuals. In 1860, some 13.2 percent of the total population of 31.4 million Americans claimed foreign birth. The 1830s saw the beginnings of a massive influx of Irish Catholics, who built the railroads and populated the cities. As the population of Ireland exploded beyond the capacity of the land in the early years of the nineteenth century, Irish began to immigrate in large numbers. Ship captains and owners encouraged the immigration of these people as substitutes for the slaves they transported before the slave trade was outlawed in 1808. Federal Passenger Acts in 1819, 1847, and 1855 set standards that made travel more attractive to Northern and Western Europeans. The 1855 act also drew the distinction between permanent and temporary immigrants.

With population pressure already great, the famine in Ireland in the mid-1840s forced a large number of Irish to flee their homeland. By the 1860s, the United States consisted of 2.5 million Catholic Irish, most of whom worked as manual laborers or domestic servants. Beginning in the 1850s, Germans, whose livelihoods fell prey to industrialization, provided another source of labor. Nearly a million of them migrated to the United States. And in the old Spanish Southwest, Mexicans arrived to work in agriculture, ranching, and railroad construction. In an unofficial expression of immigration policy, the American Party, more commonly known as the Know-Nothing Party, emerged in opposition to the influx of foreign competition.

Members of the Know-Nothing Party viewed immigrants and Catholics as threats to the Protestant United States. One of their goals focused on the exclusion of inassimilable immigrants. But growth, not nativism, remained their main policy. The Know-Nothings did not desire exclusion, except in the case of the Chinese, whose presence generated the first laws indicating that, to some Americans at least, economic growth should not continue if it meant accepting all types of people into American society. Ethnic difference mattered in the 1850s.

After the discovery of gold in California, 200,000 Asians, mainly Chinese, exercised the grand American right of going where opportunities existed. They built the transcontinental railroads and provided food, laundry, and other services for the '49ers, who failed to strike it rich but did strike against Asian workers. Although the number of Orientals remained small, a good number of people felt there was something "un-American" about their appearance and about their ability to work for less than European Americans. The big difference involved housing, not wages. The smaller quarters offered to Asian workers saved the employer as much as 10 to 20 percent and made Asians more appealing economically. Initially, local and state governments enacted head taxes on Asians as well as other discriminatory legislation. The anti-Asian movement culminated in federal legislation. Congress passed the Chinese Exclusion Act of 1882, which barred the entry of any Chinese citizens for 10 years. Exclusion became permanent in 1904, remaining in effect until the measure was rescinded in 1943.

The Chinese Exclusion Act became the first immigration restriction act since the Alien Act passed under the administration of John Adams; a later act, the 1906 Gentlemen's Agreement, extended exclusion to the Japanese. Filipinos, as American colonial subjects, remained exempt from exclusion.

The Great Wave and the New Immigrants, 1880 to 1914

The population of the United States in 1870 totaled 38.5 million, a number that continued to climb to over 100 million by 1914. Total immigration between 1860 and 1880 equaled 5.1 million; between 1880 and 1920, immigrants reached a peak of 27.5 million. Foreign-born persons comprised from 13 to 15 percent of the total population of the United States.

During the Civil War, the need for labor kept the military recruiters active. The United States even advertised in Irish papers for immigrants to join the war effort to replace dead or wounded soldiers. The economic boom that occurred after the war continued to attract immigrants, who helped build more railroads and farm the plains. During the Gilded Age, industrialization changed the nature of American work, eliminating the craftsmanship that once attracted the older English, Irish, German, and other Northern European immigrants. Those who wanted to farm found their efforts stymied by the disappearance of cheap arable land, made official by the closing of the frontier with the 1890 census and the final land runs in Oklahoma in 1889. The "good immigrants" stopped coming because better opportunity existed elsewhere.

Industrial labor proved mind-numbing, unskilled, and attractive only to those who intended to finance a better life in the old country or who left their homelands under duress. These individuals comprised the new immigrants—Slavs, southern Europeans, and even some Turks and Jews.

Americans encouraged mostly free and open immigration during the eighteenth and early nineteenth centuries. However, in the late nineteenth century, that approach slowly changed. Some of the states began to regulate immigration in the years after the Civil War. In 1875, the Supreme Court ruled that regulation of immigration remained the responsibility of the federal government alone. At the same time, the economy, especially in agriculture, began to sour. Still the immigrants continued to come. Congress began passing immigration legislation. The Chinese Exclusion Act of 1882 and laws on alien contract-labor passed in 1885 and 1887 prohibited specific categories of immigrants. The Immigration Act of 1882 levied a head tax of $.50 on each immigrant; it also prohibited immigration of "idiots," "lunatics," convicts, and persons likely to become public charges. Additional restrictive legislation, which was enacted in 1891, 1903, and 1907, barred entry to other so-called undesirable classes, including prostitutes, polygamists, carriers of infectious diseases, and individuals who espoused unpopular ideas.

As one source of people dwindled, others flourished. But instead of people from Anglo-Saxon stock (and the Irish fell within this category by that time), these immigrants included Jews in flight from the horrors of Russian and other Eastern European persecution. Italians came after their livelihoods failed due to overpopulation, industrialization, and a general need to escape the problems of their homeland and test the land of opportunity. Similarly, economic, political, and social dislocation brought masses of Poles, Hungarians, Czechs, and Slavs. Indeed, 13 million of these people arrived between around 1900 and 1913, with their peak year being 1907 when 1.28 million immigrated. Between 1890 and 1914, nearly 4 million Italians migrated to the United States, some to stay and many to return home but all to impact the American economy and society.

In 1891, Congress established an immigration service under the Department of the Treasury. The federal government began the task of processing the millions who migrated to the United States. Ellis Island, which processed 22 million people between 1892 and 1924, became the most important of the immigration stations. Aside from the inspection, detention, and hearing and administrative areas, the facility also housed hospitals, cafeterias, ticket offices, and space for the many immigrant aid societies. Of the 180 immigration service employees in 1893, there were 119 immigration employees working at Ellis Island.

Unlike the earlier immigrants who disappeared into the wide-open spaces and dispersed more broadly into inconspicuousness, the new immigrants swelled the ranks of the cities. Factories offered new opportunity, but immigrants remained restricted economically to the ghettos. Thus, these new immigrants were highly visible and very different, and their arrival resulted in a renewed nativism, the Red Scare, and the restrictions of the 1920s.

Exclusion, 1914 to 1965

In the aftermath of World War I, the combined effects of nativist restrictions, the Great Depression, and the Second World War reduced annual immigration to an average of less than 100,000. As overall population rose 50 percent to 150 million in 1950, the percentage of foreign-born individuals declined to 6.9 percent.

During the late nineteenth and early twentieth centuries, the United States fell under the influence of Social Darwinism, also known as the "White Man's Burden"—the distorted version of Charles Darwin's evolutionary theory. According to Social Darwinism, humanity consisted of various races, with the Nordic race superior and all others ranked in descending order by degree of inferiority. The new immigrants ranked low on the scale.

Between 1907 and 1910, the Dillingham Commission examined the rampant immigration of the previous few decades. Its report reiterated the alleged inferiority of the new immigrants and recommended a slowdown in the number of immigrants accepted by the United States. The new immigrants needed time to acculturate, and the United States needed time to Americanize them. Congress attempted to pass restrictive legislation several times up to 1915, but presidents William Howard Taft and Woodrow Wilson vetoed each attempt. However, the pressure became too great with the onset of the Americanization movement and the distraction of the World War I. The Immigration Act of 1917 required a literacy test for all immigrants over 16 years of age, expanded coverage of the Gentlemen's Agreement to almost totally stop immigration from Asia by creating the "Asiatic Barred Zone," and introduced the concept of guests, who were allowed short visits to the United States but not allowed to remain in the country.

World War I greatly reduced immigration and heated up the economy. The conflict, along with the Red Scare of 1919, led to the final closure of the open immigration policy. During World War I, the Creel Committee, along with various hyper-patriotic private organizations, placed intense pressure on those who displayed less than 100 percent loyalty to and zeal for America. Rabid patriots forced Germans to Americanize their names and habits. Congress passed legislation strongly reminiscent of the Alien and Sedition Acts of a century earlier. The antiforeigner fervor went unchecked and unshaken by the sudden end of the war. Fueled by the Russian Revolution and then the Bolshevik betrayal, the anti-immigrant sentiment grew through 1919.

In 1918, with hysteria and Americanism running wild and Wilson's government failing in leadership, the wartime economy shifted without plan and almost overnight. The helter-skelter demobilization and the too-rapid end of government controls over industry led to massive unemployment and a recession. Organized labor struck; black veterans refused to return to mudsill status. Frustrated patriots reacted with anger against nontraditional groups such as Russian Jews, and socialists and the radical labor organizations, which immigrants often dominated. Older, established American labor groups and earlier immigrants frequently found themselves included among these so-called undesirables. During this time, lynching, murder, riots, and suppression through violence and intimidation occurred. Immigrants became victims of government too: Several hundred were deported with only minimal due process in 1919.

During the isolationist and disillusioned 1920s, Congress acted. Decades of Social Darwinism, general racism, and nativism culminated in two major laws severely restricting immigration and attempting to reestablish the old immigrants at the expense of the new. The 1921 Quota Act (Johnson Act) established the first American immigration quotas. The act limited immigration to a number equal to 3 percent of the total number foreign-born residents of a given nationality in the 1910 census. Immigration from the Western Hemisphere remained unrestricted. The 1924 Immigration Act (Johnson-Reid Act) limited Eastern Hemisphere immigration to 154,227 individuals per year. Within this limit, Congress based the quota for each country on its U.S. population as of the 1920 census. As a result of these laws and easier immigration elsewhere, immigration fell from 800,000 in 1921 to less than 150,000 in 1929. By 1933, with the Great Depression in full force, America attracted only 23,000 immigrants from the entire world. As a result of the laws enacted in the 1920s, individuals from countries that encouraged immigration did not face restrictive quotas and people from countries with quotas did not desire to emigrate to the United States. The depression finished the work immigration restrictionists began 40 years earlier.

The restrictions of the 1920s produced an unfortunate effect before and during World War II. Some refugees fled to the United States—but not as many as might have come from among the millions affected by the racism and barbarism of the fascist regimes and the war. America still maintained a strong undercurrent of anti-Semitism in this period, and organized fascist and Nazi parties formed. The restrictions set into place in the 1920s meant that no adequate quota for the millions of persecuted Jews, Gypsies, and other dislocates existed. Yet America made room for approximately 100 Jewish German and Austrian physicists between 1932 and 1945. Five refugees—Peter Debye, Albert Einstein, Enrico Fermi, James Franck, and Victor F. Hess—all won Nobel Prizes before they arrived in the United States. In addition, Hans A. Bethe, Felix Bloch, Emilio G. Segre, Otto Stern, Eugene P. Wigner, and Maria Mayer earned Nobel Prizes while living in America. These immigrants proved vital to the nation's atomic weapons program.

As American men and women joined the military during World War II, the jobs they left behind went to women and blacks previously excluded from the labor force. The Bracero Program, which brought Mexican workers into the American Southwest, provided an additional source of labor. Mexican workers long served as field hands, miners, railroad workers, and in light industry, with 55,000 Mexicans having immigrated to the United States between 1850 and 1880. In the ensuing decade, the construction of a railway between the United States and Mexico employed a labor force in which up to 60 percent of the workers were Mexicans. Beginning in 1916, Mexico's economy declined after the Mexican Revolution. World War I drew unemployed Mexican workers into industry, trades, and service work within the United States, but American business exploited Mexican immigrants, leading Mexican president Venustiano Carranza to establish terms in 1920 by which Mexican workers could help American farmers and ranchers. Accordingly, immigrants held the right to have their families with them, but they needed to negotiate employment contracts before crossing the border; the contracts defined pay, work schedule, location of the work, and other conditions. In effect, the contracts served as the prototype for the Bracero program.

Meanwhile, in 1924, the United States created the Border Patrol and defined undocumented workers as illegal aliens. When the depression hit, American employers did not want Mexican workers. The United States denied visas to Mexicans without proven employment and deported those illegally residing in the United States. But the depression gave way to the war, and the demand for labor rose again. In 1942, the United States and Mexico signed the Bracero Treaty and, between 1942 and 1964, around 4 million Mexicans entered the United States as contract ranch and agricultural workers and as industrial laborers. At the conclusion of the war, the demand ended. Employers removed Mexicans, blacks, and women from the better-paying sectors of the economy. After the war, the mechanization of farming and increased immigration saturated the agricultural labor market. Although made permanent by law in 1951, the Bracero Program ended in 1964. The Border Patrol enforced immigration restrictions under a program known as Operation Wetback.

The McCarran-Walter Act, also known as the Immigration and Nationality Act of 1952, became law over the veto of President Harry S Truman. It retained the national origins quotas of the 1920s and the annual ceiling of 154,277 immigrants. It also repealed the anti-Asian laws and allowed 100 visas for each Asian country, and established a preference within the national quotas for relatives and skilled workers. Latin American and Caribbean immigrants remained exempt from the quotas.

The Recent Immigrants—Refugees, Asylum-Seekers, Legal or Illegal, 1965 to the Present

By 1970, the American population passed 200 million and the percentage of foreign-born residents fell to an all-time low of 4.7 percent. Once immigration was liberalized after 1965, legal and illegal immigration led to a doubling of the percentage of foreign-born residents, to over 10 percent by the end of the century.

The mid-1960s brought concern that the United States would lose the Cold War race to attract highly intelligent professionals. The solution called for bringing in people with education and technical skills through the Immigration Reform and Control Act of 1965 (IRCA). To liberals and President John F. Kennedy, immigration quotas remained unfair, disadvantaging some groups such as the Irish who wanted greater access to American visas, while other groups such as the English failed to use their allotted number of visas. Meanwhile, the fight over civil rights dominated the public agenda, and that meant agitation for the equal treatment of immigrants as well. Officials favored the immigration of talented and meritorious individuals regardless of country of origin. Reform dictated expanding the 1952 law by increasing the immigration of relatives and skilled individuals. The humane impulse and the economic impulse both led in the same direction because the reformers assumed that the new immigrants would migrate from the same places as earlier immigrants, albeit in different proportions. And the descendents of the old new immigrants thought their native lands would also benefit by Congress overturning the exclusions of the 1920s. They did not see that the United States no longer acted as an economic magnet, as both northern and southern Europe prospered in the 1960s. Instead, the 1965 law attracted a set of new immigrants, non-European in origin. The influx of Asian and Central American immigrants renewed the anti-immigrant feeling of the old, settled Americans, even among third-generation new immigrants. In fact, the demand far exceeded the available number of visas, and Congress began passing special refugee legislation periodically. Not until the Refugee Act of 1980 did the United States establish a policy on the admission of refugees.

European immigration did not disappear, but the largest numbers of immigrants were now from Latin America, Africa, and Asia. As others throughout American history, they left homelands plagued with economic, social, and political dislocation. As they could manage it, they brought members of their extended families. During the 10 years after the IRCA, European immigration dropped 38 percent, while Asian immigration rose by 663 percent. Overall, 60 percent more immigrants entered the United States. Simultaneously, legal Latin American immigration continued to accelerate. In 1976, Congress established quotas for Latin America and, 10 years later, began penalizing employers who hired illegal aliens, while at the same time amnestied illegal aliens residing in the United States since before 1982. After 1980, Congress persisted in broadening the definition of a refugee, increasing the number who qualified and entered the United States. This policy became a problem because refugees more often than not lacked economic assets or cultural tools.

For instance, Cubans fled Fidel Castro's regime after the revolution in 1958. In the initial wave, from 1959 to 1962, the Cuban refugees were anti-Castro leaders with education, skills, and resources. Those in the second wave still came from the middle class and arrived between 1965 and 1973. The third wave, made up of the Mariel boatpeople of 1980, appeared to many Americans as the dregs of Cuban society—prisoners and drug abusers, many of whom were black. Because the Marielitos tended to seek residence in the older Cuban communities, especially in Miami, they provoked conflict and hardship. Some Americans questioned the policy of having an open door for refugees from communist regimes.

With Cubans disturbing America's tranquility, along came the Haitians. Because the Haitian government remained a friend of the United States, immigration officials almost always denied Haitians asylum. U.S. policy assumed that refugees from communist countries were fleeing repression, whereas refugees from noncommunist allies were classified as economic immigrants. And economic immigrants were subject to quotas: The rejection rate neared 99 percent. Those who got in, most of whom were black and from lower-class backgrounds, crowded in close proximity to the Marielitos and previously established Haitians. They often placed a drain on the social and economic resources of the places where they settled.

The Vietnamese arrived next. The first wave, composed of those who arrived after the 1973 collapse of Saigon, possessed resources and a cultural affinity for America. People in the next wave possessed less of both. The final wave included the boatpeople. Problems in the U.S. economy, nose-diving from the oil crisis of 1973, created economic friction that affected even those in the second wave. Hard-working and ambitious, these immigrants conflicted with the Louisiana and Texas gulf communities in 1975. Americans suffered from stagflation. Living expenses rose rapidly, wages remained stagnant, and trawlers overfished the Gulf of Mexico. Into this economic malaise came the Vietnamese. They were "different," overfished and undercut, and had government assistance. Some Americans became increasingly upset that their government continued to help their competition, the Vietnamese and the Cubans, who seemed too alien to them in the first place.

The situation continued to worsen. For instance, some Americans felt that the Hmong, who came from Laos in the late 1970s and early 1980s, appeared markedly different and required a long time to assimilate. These Americans noted that the Hmong only developed a written language just a generation before; their illiteracy rate remained high; their culture was nonindustrial and Oriental; and they seemingly did not have the skills to make the transition, but were able to get on welfare. They clustered together and practiced their strange customs and their animistic religion (animism). Even their food seemed odd.

Colombians, Salvadorans, and others who sought sanctuary from right-wing political regimes seemed less conspicuous and controversial. Their cultural and economic values was similar to those of the surrounding communities, and they fit in nicely—when they could get in. Others, such as the new Irish, felt fully at home within the industrial West, but often ended up in the underground economy, frustrated by the insufficient numbers of visas needed for them to become legal, mainstream, fully employed workers utilizing their education, skills, and talents. The illegal aliens continued to cross the 2,000-mile-long border between poverty and opportunity. They came from Latin America and Mexico at a rate of 250,000 to 750,000 per year. They located first in California, Texas, and the Southwest, finding work as cheap labor and, some said, placing a burden on social services. Then, they moved to the Midwestern cities, medium and large. By the early years of the twenty-first century, evidence indicated that Europeans, Asians, and Africans as well as Latin Americans all used the southern route of entry.

Immigration restriction proved a hopeless policy. Demand did not falter, and the process did not improve despite amnesties in 1982, 1986, and the late 1990s. Among his first actions as president in 2001, George W. Bush proposed legalizing the 3 million illegal Mexicans already in the United States. Yet, as some saw it, amnesties did nothing more than legitimize huge numbers of illegal aliens. And the volume of illegal aliens did not seem to decrease. The continuing failure of policy and the accommodation of illegality increasingly outraged those who felt that the United States already was the home of a sufficient number of tired, poor, and huddled masses.

In the 1980s, the first major widespread backlash occurred. Broader than the Texas and Louisiana friction of the 1970s but based again in a time of economic downturn, this effort took several forms. Supporters of the English-only movement wanted to require English as the official language of government and business. The movement failed to achieve the passage of legislation, which caused some people to lose interest until the issue reemerged later.

In California and many other places, the problems of American society were obvious: crime, moral decay, increased income disparities, racial conflict, and a general malaise and cynicism. California set the pace for immigration restrictions and reforms, and the federal government changed the Immigration and Naturalization Service and immigration laws once again. Meanwhile, on one hand, some Californians fought to eliminate bilingual education, welfare for illegal aliens, social services, and what they perceived as the unfair tax burden, they were forced to assume paying for the support of illegal residents who seemed to steal their jobs. Pro-immigration advocates, on the other hand, managed to forestall the most drastic changes, which would adversely affected immigrants, arguing that the immigrants filled the low-end jobs and moved quickly out of social services to self-sufficiency: In fact, they rapidly brought more resources to California. Although reformers demanded change and supporters of change argued the economic benefits of either leaving the issue of reform alone or opening it up, Congress passed, on an average, one new reform law each year through the 1990s.

Illegal or legal, the immigrants still played a role in the American economy. They no longer built the railroads, but they replicated the patterns of the late nineteenth century. They moved into badly decayed neighborhoods. In New York City, they helped revitalize burned out neighborhoods in the south Bronx and east Brooklyn. Minority-owned businesses in New York grew between 1987 and 1992, with black businesses rising from 17,400 to almost 36,000; Hispanic from 10,000 to over 34,000; and Asian from 27,000 to 46,000. Approximately 90 percent of those businesses belonged to immigrants. They did not open manufacturing businesses already in a long decline. Rather, the emphasis remained on service businesses—delivery services, phone parlors, remittance shops, and import/export firms. Immigrants worked as day laborers and contractors—the dirty, low-profit, low-end counterparts to the stoop labor of the migrants who harvested the Southwest and the Midwest. Koreans ran grocery stores. Russians, then Haitians, Pakistanis, and Ethiopians, Dominicans, and Nigerians drove taxis. They even filled the niches, running jitneys after hours or in neighborhoods where the licensed cabs refused to operate. The multiplier of these tiny businesses came in the multi-shift operation, the gasoline and tires, and the ability of the stranded and unemployed to get out of the neighborhoods and move to where the jobs were. Entrepreneurial immigrants are also consumers of housing, transportation, and services.

Concern grew that illegal aliens were an increasing problem because American immigration policy did not match the economic needs of the country; this concern produced a strong immigration restriction movement late in the twentieth century. Although supporters of the movement were vocal, they failed to move policy, which remained an inconsistent hodgepodge of enforcement, amnesty, and other flip-flop measures.

The Federation for American Immigration Reform (FAIR), established in 1979, was the first of the immigration restriction organizations; in the late 1990s, it had approximately 70,000 members. Those who supported immigration restrictions also founded the Carrying Capacity Network, Californians for Population Stabilization,

An Air Force serviceman welds together border-fence panels along the U.S.-Mexico border in Yuma, Arizona, April 24, 2007. (USAF Photo/Senior Airman John Hughel Jr.)

Population-Environment Balance, and American Immigration Control Foundation. Groups of this sort did not espouse nativism. Their concerns were social and environmental. They pointed to problems of assimilation and the shortage of land or jobs and they cited pollution as a consequence of overcrowding. As did all, they noted how poorly the Immigration and Naturalization Service operated and how porous America's borders were, giving easy access to criminals and terrorists. FAIR cited an estimated cost for post-1969 immigrants of $65 billion in 1996, noting that other estimates reached upward of $80 billion. The group projected enforcement costs beyond $100 billion by 2006. The 10-year total equaled $866 billion. Limited immigration restriction movement success came in the 1990s, when Congress increased funding for the Border Patrol, tightened asylum rules, and increased the deportation of undesirables in 1996. Most notably, welfare reform took food stamps and disability payments from immigrants. Although state and federal governments restored some welfare benefits for pre-1996 immigrants, the U.S. Supreme Court upheld the welfare restriction laws in 2000.

Congress modified the rules in 1965, 1976, 1978, 1980, 1986, and 1990, each time enlarging the numbers of immigrants eligible to enter the United States. The

1976 Amendments to the Immigration and Nationality Act extended the preference system to all Western Hemisphere countries and established a ceiling of 20,000 immigrants from any one country. The 1978 amendments combined the Eastern and Western Hemisphere ceilings to a single worldwide quota of 290,000. The 1980 Refugee Act set a separate policy for refugees, eliminated the previous emphasis on anticommunism, set a refugee target of 50,000, and reduced the worldwide ceiling to 270,000.

The 1981 "Report of the Select Commission on Immigration and Refugee Policy" recommended stopping illegal immigration and called for a clearly defined, fair immigration policy and an efficient organization to carry it out. The 1986 Immigration Reform and Control Act provided amnesty and temporary status to all illegal aliens who lived in the United States continuously since before January 1, 1982; it extended a more lenient amnesty to farm workers and provided sanctions for employers of illegal aliens.

In the 1990s, the Diversity Lottery (through which 55,000 permanent resident visas granted per year on a lottery basis for people around the world) specifically targeted the underrepresented, including Africans. This step led to an influx of immigrants from countries previously underrepresented in American society, though the number was still minuscule compared with the number of illegal Hispanics. The total for the entire history of African immigration amounts to less than the number of illegal aliens in a single year. The Africans began moving to St. Paul, Minnesota and other cities and making the same positive contributions and creating the same dislocations of welfare and culture of other immigrants groups.

By 1990, the government began to cave in to pressures for change. The 1990 Immigration Act (IMMACT) increased the total number of visas approved annually to 700,000 and bumped up the number of available visas by 40 percent. The act kept the family reunion provision while doubling employment immigration. It also encouraged increased immigration from underrepresented areas to enhance diversity. Individuals seeking asylum also benefited as the law became more liberal almost every year in the 1990s.

As rules tightened and loosened, as funding fluctuated, as enforcement waxed and waned, the immigrants continued to come (see Table 1). The 1930s total was only 528,000. World War II brought just 120,000. But, by the 1970s, one year's immigration almost exceeded the two-decade total. By 1978, the annual legal number hit 600,000, which was the average for each year of the 1980s. The 1990s averaged a million per year, and the total of that decade remains the greatest of any decade in American history. On top of the legal millions, another 275,000 to 500,000 illegal aliens enter the United States annually.

America became more diverse after 1970. From 1970 to 1996, the percentage of nonnative-born residents rose from 4.8 percent to 9.3 percent. And America's immigrants—whether legal or illegal, refugees or asylum-seekers—were the world's migrants, not just those of Europe.

After the terrorist attacks of September 11, 2001, immigration difficult increased. The Customs Service, now part of the Department of Homeland Security, received additional resources to prevent illegal immigration across U.S. borders with Canada

Table 1. Nativity of the population and place of birth of the native population, 1850–1990

Year[*]	Total population	Native population						Foreign-born population
		Total	Born in the United States	Born abroad				
				Total	In outlying areas[†]	Of American parents		

Year[*]	Total population	Total	Born in the United States	Total	In outlying areas[†]	Of American parents	Foreign-born population
Number							
1990[‡]	248,709,873	228,942,557	225,695,826	3,246,731	1,382,446	1,864,285	19,767,316
1980[‡]	226,545,805	212,465,899	210,322,697	2,143,202	1,088,172	1,055,030	14,079,906
1970[‡§]	203,210,158	193,590,856	191,329,489	2,261,367	891,266	1,370,101	9,619,302
1960[‡**]	179,325,671	169,587,580	168,525,645	1,061,935	660,425	401,510	9,738,091
1950[‡]	150,216,110	139,868,715	139,442,390	426,325	329,970	96,355	10,347,395
1940	131,669,275	120,074,379	119,795,254	279,125	156,956	122,169	11,594,896
1930	122,775,046	108,570,897	108,304,188	266,709	136,032	130,677	14,204,149
1920	105,710,620	91,789,928	91,659,045	130,883	38,020	92,863	13,920,692
1910	91,972,266	78,456,380	78,381,104	75,276	7,365	67,911	13,515,886
1900	75,994,575	65,653,299	65,583,225	70,074	2,923	67,151	10,341,276
1890[*]	62,622,250	53,372,703	53,362,371	10,332	322	10,010	9,249,547
1880	50,155,783	43,475,840	43,475,498	342	51	291	6,679,943
1870	38,558,371	32,991,142	32,990,922	220	51	169	5,567,229
1860[**]	31,443,321	27,304,624	27,304,624	–[††]	–	–	4,138,697
1850[**]	23,191,876	20,947,274	20,947,274	–	–	–	2,244,602
Percent Distribution							
1990[‡]	100.0	92.1	90.7	1.3	0.6	0.7	7.9
1980[‡]	100.0	93.8	92.8	0.9	0.5	0.5	6.2
1970[‡§]	100.0	95.3	94.2	1.1	0.4	0.7	4.7
1960[‡**]	100.0	94.6	94.0	0.6	0.4	0.2	5.4
1950[‡]	100.0	93.1	92.8	0.3	0.2	0.1	6.9
1940	100.0	91.2	91.0	0.2	0.1	0.1	8.8
1930	100.0	88.4	88.2	0.2	0.1	0.1	11.6
1920	100.0	86.8	86.7	0.1	–	0.1	13.2
1910	100.0	85.3	85.2	0.1	–	0.1	14.7
1900	100.0	86.4	86.3	0.1	–	0.1	13.6
1890[*]	100.0	85.2	85.2	–	–	–	14.8
1880	100.0	86.7	86.7	–	–	–	13.3
1870	100.0	85.6	85.6	–	–	–	14.4
1860[**]	100.0	86.8	86.8	–	–	–	13.2
1850[**]	100.0	90.3	90.3	–	–	–	9.7

[*]Starting in 1960, figures include population of Alaska and Hawaii. For 1890, excludes population enumerated in the Indian Territory and on Indian reservations, for which information on most topics, including nativity, was not collected.

[†]Puerto Rico is the only outlying area for which the number has ever exceeded 100,000. The numbers for Puerto Rico are: 1,190,533 in 1990; 1,002,863 in 1980; 810,087 in 1970; 617,056 in 1960; 226,010 in 1950; 69,967 in 1940; 52,774 in 1930; 11,811 in 1920; 1,513 in 1910; and 678 in 1900.

[‡]Indicates sample data.

[§]The data shown in Table 1 are based on the 15 percent sample. For 1970, data based on the 5 percent sample show total population as 203,193,774, native population as 193,590,856, born in the United States as 191,836,655, born abroad as 1,617,396, in outlying areas as 873,241, of American parents as 744,155, and foreign-born population as 9,739,723.

[**]In 1850 and 1860, information on nativity was not collected for slaves. The data in the table assume, as was done in 1870 census reports, that all slaves in 1850 and 1860 were native. Of the total black population of 4,880,009 in 1870, 9,645, or 0.2 percent, were foreign-born (1870 Census, vol. I, Dubester #45, Table 22, pp. 606–615).

[††]Dash represents zero or rounds to zero.

Source: U.S. Census Bureau, Population Division, http://www.census/gov/population/www/documentation/twps0029/tab02/html.

and Mexico. In addition, Congress rejected a previously proposed amnesty for illegal immigrants who resided in the United States for more than five years.

References

Arthur, John A. *Invisible Sojourners: African Immigrant Diaspora in the United States*. Westport, CT: Praeger, 2000.

Bennett, David. *The Party of Fear: From Nativist Movements to the New Right in American History*. Chapel Hill: University of North Carolina Press, 1988.

Bodnar, John. *The Transplanted*. Bloomington: Indiana University Press, 1985.

Bureau of the Census. http://www.census.gov; accessed January 3, 2003.

Center for Immigration Studies. http://www.cis.org; accessed September 2, 2002.

Countryman, Edward. *Americans: A Collision of Histories*. New York: Hill and Wang, 1996.

Dinnerstein, Leonard, and David M. Reimers. *Ethnic Americans*. New York: Columbia University Press, 1999.

Federation for American Immigration Reform. http://www.fairus.org; accessed September 21, 2002.

Fleming, Donald, and Bernard Bailyn, eds. *The Intellectual Migration: Europe and America, 1930–1960*. Cambridge, MA: Harvard University Press, Belknap Press, 1969.

Handlin, Oscar. *The Uprooted*. Boston: Little, Brown, 1973.

Immigration and Nationalization Service. http://www.usdoj.gov/ins; accessed September 1, 2002.

Lacey, Dan. *The Essential Immigrant*. New York: Hippocrene Books, 1990.

Millman, Joel. *The Other Americans*. New York: Viking, 1997.

National Immigration Forum. http://www.immigrationforum.org; accessed September 1, 2002

Olson, James Stuart. *The Ethnic Dimension in American History*. New York: St. Martin's Press, 1979.

Portes, Alejandro, and Ruben G. Rumbaut. *Immigrant America*. Berkeley: University of California Press, 1990.

Reimers, David M. *Still the Golden Door: The Third World Comes to America*. New York: Columbia University Press, 1992.

Smith, Marian L. "Overview of INS History." In George T. Kurian, ed., *A Historical Guide to the U.S. Government*. New York: Oxford University Press, 1998.

Takaki, Ronald. *A Different Mirror*. Boston: Little, Brown, 1993.

Insurance

Dalit Baranoff

Insurance before 1810

The American insurance industries that developed during the late eighteenth and early nineteenth centuries were modeled on those already existing in England, where marine, fire, and life insurance all were well established by the eighteenth century. State oversight of the industry initially went little beyond the state chartering of insurance companies.

Marine Insurance

Marine insurance, the oldest form of insurance, dates back to ancient Greece or Babylonia, with modern marine insurance contracts appearing in the Italian city-states of the thirteenth and fourteenth centuries. As Britain became a commercial sea power in the seventeenth century, English merchants came to dominate the marine insurance field.

Until the nineteenth century, individual merchants, not companies, wrote most British insurance contracts. A regular, albeit informal, system whereby shippers and ship owners could acquire insurance revolved around London's coffeehouses, including Edward Lloyd's Coffeehouse (the predecessor of Lloyd's of London), which came to dominate the individual underwriting business by the middle of the eighteenth century.

Individual underwriting in the London style was quite common in eighteenth-century American seaports. Beginning in the 1720s, insurance "offices," where local merchants could underwrite individual voyages, began to appear in a number of port cities, north and south, centered in Philadelphia. But, the amount that Americans could cover was limited enough that when larger sums of insurance were needed, shippers and ship owners looked to the far better established London underwriting market.

Fire Insurance

Compared to marine insurance, fire insurance is a relatively recent innovation. The security it provides only became necessary once a certain level of both urbanization and wealth-holding was achieved. Vast, crowded cities, such as London in the mid- to late-seventeenth century, posed great fire risks. British fire insurance began to develop after the Great Fire of 1666, which burned nearly a square mile of the city and destroyed over 13,000 houses.

By the early eighteenth century, three different kinds of fire insurance companies were doing business in London: a limited number of firms granting royal charters; unincorporated companies (a form of the extended partnership); and mutual societies, in which each policyholder owned a share.

Although Americans were aware of these developments, the colonies generated little demand for fire insurance. Families and communities could usually meet the needs of those who were burned out of their homes. The first companies formed were mostly mutual companies, filling the need for insurance in a few urban centers where capital was concentrated. These were not considered moneymaking ventures but outgrowths of volunteer firefighting organizations.

Benjamin Franklin was the organizing force behind the first American mutual company, the Philadelphia Contributionship for the Insurance of Houses from Loss by Fire (known familiarly by the name of its symbol, the "hand in hand"). With over 15,000 residents, thousands of buildings, and scores of well-heeled citizens, Philadelphia, in the 1750s, was the most populous city in North America and one of the few places in the colonies where insurance seemed practicable.

By the 1780s, growing demand in other urban areas led to the formation of additional fire mutuals in Philadelphia, New York, Baltimore, Norwich (Connecticut), Charleston, Boston, Providence, and elsewhere. All buildings initially insured within one city and its immediate outskirts only, although some soon began employing agents to sell insurance in nearby cities. At least one Virginia fire mutual initially sold shares statewide, covering both town and country properties.

Mutual fire insurance companies played a crucial role in the economic development of the new nation, serving as sources of capital, routinely investing their surpluses in banks and other institutions, and making loans. In a capital-poor economy, insurance made a significant contribution to commercial and industrial expansion. Stock fire insurance companies, which soon entered the market, provided even greater flows of investment capital than the mutuals.

Joint-Stock Companies

Around the same time that the first mutual companies appeared, a few businesses were formed on another model—the joint-stock company, which raised capital through the sale of shares and distributed dividends. The defining characteristic of a joint-stock company was the limited liability that its charter affords to shareholders. After the Revolution, American insurers found it fairly easy to obtain charters from state legislatures eager to promote a domestic insurance industry, in contrast to the difficulty of securing British royal charters. Joint-stock companies first appeared in the marine sector, where both demand and the potential profit were greater. Not reliant on the fortunes of any one individual, joint-stock companies provided greater security than private underwriting. In addition to their premium income, they maintained a fixed amount of capital, allowing them to cover larger insurance policies.

In 1792, the first successful joint-stock company, the Insurance Company of North America, was formed in Philadelphia to sell marine, fire, and life insurance. By 1810, upwards of 70 such companies were chartered in the United States. Most of those incorporated prior to 1810 operated primarily in the marine sector, although they were often chartered to handle other lines.

Joint-stock companies further advanced the role of insurers as financial intermediaries, loaning money to their own shareholders and policyholders. In many ways, early insurance companies resembled the banks of the period, which were often established by merchants primarily for their personal use. In many cities, a bank and an insurance company might be closely aligned, sharing the same directors and owning each other's stock.

Investment income kept many insurers afloat during the periodic business disruptions that accompanied the Napoleonic Wars. Despite the profitability of blockade running, increased war premiums could not always cover the costs that were imposed on insurers when ships were seized. When President Thomas Jefferson declared an embargo on American shipping at the end of 1807, marine insurers' premiums dried up completely, forcing them to seek other sources of revenue. The Embargo Act and the War of 1812 also stimulated domestic industries such as textiles. Both the need for new sources of revenue and a growing demand moved many marine insurers toward fire insurance after 1810.

The same growth of demand also led to the formation of a few joint-stock companies that concentrated on fire coverage from the beginning, with little or no marine business. These differed from the mutual insurers in one significant way: They insured personal property as well as real estate, a growing necessity as Americans' personal wealth began to grow.

Life Insurance

Although life insurance also has ancient origins, it was often considered little more than a form of gambling through the eighteenth century. The sale of tontine insurance (whereby those who survived the longest received the benefits) and third-party policies taken out on the lives of famous people did little to discourage this impression. Marine insurers also sold life insurance to ship passengers, primarily to cover the payment of ransom in case they were captured.

The first American life insurance companies were semi-charitable institutions established by churches to insure the lives of ministers. In 1759, the Presbyterian synods in Philadelphia and New York created the Corporation for Relief of Poor and Distressed Widows and Children of Presbyterian Ministers. Ten years later, Episcopalian ministers established a similar corporation. A few joint-stock corporations also organized to sell life insurance in the years prior to 1810, but they sold few policies. None lasted more than a few years.

Insurance from 1810 to 1870

The fire and life insurance industries experienced tremendous growth during the middle years of the nineteenth century, as urbanization and industrialization transformed the risks that most individuals faced. An intensification of market activities resulted in more business and personal property needing protection. At the same time, myriad risks—business failure, disease, injury, and fire—loomed larger, particularly in the cities. Both the wealthy and the members of an emerging middle class drove the demand for products that could help them manage these risks.

By midcentury, most states adopted general incorporation laws, making it even easier to start an insurance company. At the same time, a regulatory framework began to take shape, with the creation of the first state insurance departments and the passage of laws focusing primarily on assuring the solvency of insurers.

Fire Insurance

During this period, fire insurance developed from a local industry to a national one. Prior to 1835, a number of states enacted legislation taxing out-of-state companies' premiums, which discouraged "foreign" companies from entering markets such as New York City. In that year, a devastating fire destroyed New York's business district, causing between $15 and $26 million in damage and bankrupting 23 of the 26 local fire insurance companies. Fire insurers learned a lesson they were not to forget. From that date on, geographic diversification of risks became a cornerstone of the business.

Diversification meant expanding into new markets under competitive conditions. To minimize costs, companies contracted with independent agents to sell their policies locally. Pioneered mainly by firms based in Hartford, Connecticut, and Philadelphia, the agency system did not become widespread until the 1850s. By 1860, the national company with networks of local agents replaced the purely local operation as the mainstay of the industry.

As the agency system grew, so, too, did competition. By the 1860s, fire insurance was a national affair, with individual firms competing in hundreds of local markets at once. Rate wars and business failures were common.

Marine Insurance

Marine insurance, although still a distinct field, increasingly became conflated with fire insurance for regulatory purposes. During the mid-nineteenth century, marine (and fire-and-marine) insurers served the growing river trade, selling inland marine policies on goods traveling by steamboat and other river conveyances. By the late 1870s, another subcategory of the insurance industry—the steam boiler inspection and insurance company—emerged to insure boilers on steamers and in factories, which were known for their tendency to explode.

Life Insurance

The life insurance industry experienced its first significant period of growth during the 1830s and 1840s. By the 1850s, nearly $100 million in policies were in force. Unlike the fire insurance industry, which spread insurance among hundreds of firms of different sizes, a few large firms wrote over half the life insurance in the country.

Two developments accounted for the growth of the life insurance industry during this period. The first was the passage of the Married Women's Acts in New York, Massachusetts, and other states, measures that recognized the insurable interest that married women held in their husbands' lives. These laws allowed women to enter into insurance contracts in their own names, thus protecting their insurance policies (up to a certain value) from their husbands' creditors.

The second factor was the development of mutual life insurance companies in the 1840s. Although this type of insurance existed in England since the 1760s, no American life insurers adopted this form of organization until the 1840s. But, following the panic of 1837, new joint-stock companies were unable to raise enough capital to begin operating. Mutuals, by contrast, could and did enter into business with little capital.

To have enough money to pay claims, mutual life insurers needed to sell large numbers of policies. To achieve the desired volume, the mutual companies promoted membership extensively through advertising and solicitation. Life insurance sales continued to grow during the 1860s, partly because of the Civil War. Although standard life policies excluded coverage for death caused by acts of war, a number of companies insured soldiers for an increased premium. The heightened awareness of mortality during the war further contributed to a surge in insurance purchases afterward. Dozens of new life insurance companies were created between 1865 and 1870 to meet the demand. As was the case in fire insurance, the late 1860s were years of intense competition.

Regulation

Until the middle of the nineteenth century, state oversight was limited primarily to matters of incorporation and taxation. Most states modeled their insurance regulations after those of either Massachusetts or New York, which established general insurance codes and created bodies to oversee the new laws in the 1840s and 1850s. The first general insurance law, passed in New York in 1849, required all insurers incorporating or doing business in the state to have a minimum capital stock of $100,000; an 1851 statute stipulated that all life insurance companies had to deposit $100,000 with the comptroller of New York. Such capitalization laws were intended to protect consumers from company failures. The measures were supported by the more established insurance companies, whose officers hoped they might block competition from new firms, especially from mutuals.

In 1853, New York passed separate statutes for fire and life insurance. Massachusetts codified all its insurance laws under a single statute in 1854. One year earlier, Massachusetts established a board of insurance commissioners. Made up of the secretary of state, the state auditor, and the state treasurer, the commission was charged with examining the annual returns filed by each insurance company operating in Massachusetts. In 1855, the state organized an insurance department.

Following these examples, other states codified their insurance laws and established insurance boards to supervise companies over the next few decades. As the laws governing insurance increased in number and complexity, states created separate insurance departments to oversee them. Following Massachusetts, those establishing insurance departments included Vermont (1852), New Hampshire (1852), and Rhode Island (1856). By 1870, they were joined by New York (1860), Connecticut (1865), Indiana (1865), California (1868), Maine (1868), West Virginia (1868), Missouri (1869), and Kentucky (1870). Eight other states supervised insurance without establishing separate departments by this time.

The U.S. Supreme Court affirmed state supervision of insurance in *Paul v. Virginia* (1868), which found insurance was not interstate commerce and thus not eligible for regulation by the federal government. Prior to the ruling, the insurance industry campaigned for federal regulation. For life as well as fire insurance firms, the variability of regulations in different states made doing business on a national scale increasingly complex. A Virginia fire insurance agent brought the test case, challenging the state's right to require all out-of-state insurance companies operating in Virginia to obtain a license by depositing special bonds with the state. As a result of *Paul v. Virginia*, insurance was not subject to any federal regulations over the coming decades.

Insurance from 1870 to 1920

During the late nineteenth and early twentieth century, as both industrialization and urbanization intensified, insurers expanded to meet the growing demand for their products. Regulation assumed a new urgency. By the early 1900s, nearly every state established an insurance department. The maturing fire and life insurance industries both sought to shape their own regulatory frameworks, which, in turn, were influenced by larger societal forces. By the 1920s, the foundations of modern insurance regulation were established.

Fire Insurance and Regulation

Rate competition proved disastrous for the fire insurance industry in the early 1870s. The Chicago fire of 1871 and the Boston fire of 1872 bankrupted some 100 companies, leaving policyholders with little or no recompense. After the fires, the industry began to organize in order to set rates collectively. By the mid-1880s, most fire insurance rates were set by boards of local agents, with regional organizations determining rates for areas outside local boards' jurisdictions. Unlike the attempts to set rates in the 1850s and 1860s, which always broke down, these agreements endured through both the economic boom of the 1880s and the downturn following the panic of 1893. By the early 1900s, local rate setting was entrenched.

At the end of the first decade of the 1900s, fire insurance was regulated as much by the companies as by state governments. This situation prevailed despite the passage of anti-compact legislation in 12 states between 1885 and 1900 (22 by 1908). Passed primarily in Populist strongholds in the Midwest and the central states, the laws featured in the larger national antitrust movement. But their effectiveness was limited. Where open collusion was outlawed, insurers established private rating bureaus to set "advisory" rates instead.

Among other regulations opposed by the fire insurance industry was valued-policy laws, which required payment of the face value of a policy in case of a total loss. Insurers argued that property was often insured for more than it was worth, but consumer lobbying pushed the legislation through, first in Wisconsin in 1874, and then in 22 other states between 1880 and the early 1900s.

By the 1910s, states began to abandon anti-compact laws in favor of rate regulation, meaning the state either set the rates itself or reviewed industry-set rates. Nearly 30 states established some form of rate regulation by the early 1920s. In 1909, Kansas became the first to adopt strict rate regulation, followed by Texas in 1910, and Missouri in 1911.

Contesting the constitutionality of the rate regulation law, the insurance industry took the state of Kansas to court. In 1914, *German Alliance Insurance Co. v. Ike Lewis, Superintendent of Insurance* was decided in the state's favor, with the U.S. Supreme Court declaring insurance a public good and thus subject to rate regulation.

In 1911, although the Kansas case was still pending, New York entered the rating arena with a much less restrictive law. New York's law was greatly influenced by a legislative investigation undertaken the previous year. The Merritt Committee concluded that cooperation between firms was often in the public interest and recommended that insurance boards continue to set rates. The law mandated state review of rates to prevent discrimination. It also required insurance companies to submit uniform statistics on premiums and losses for the first time. Other states soon adopted similar requirements.

New York's data-collection requirement resulted in far-reaching consequences for the entire fire insurance industry. Because every major insurer in the United States did business in New York (and often a great deal of it), any legislation passed there produced national implications. And once New York mandated that companies submit data, the imperative for a uniform classification system was born.

In 1914, the industry responded by creating the Actuarial Bureau within the National Board of Fire Underwriters, the industry's main national organization, to collect uniformly organized data and submit them to the states. Supported by the National Convention of Insurance Commissioners (today called the National Association of Insurance Commissioners, or NAIC), the Actuarial Bureau was soon able to establish uniform classification standards across the industry.

Related Lines

Casualty insurance regulation most closely resembled fire insurance regulation, with the states supervising or setting the rates that companies could charge. From a single firm offering accident insurance in 1864, casualty insurance developed into a full-fledged industry in the early 1900s. By 1910, a total of 23 companies sold liability policies.

In the early years of the twentieth century, both fire-and-marine insurers and casualty companies sold automobile insurance policies. Regulators determined that fire-and-marine companies could write auto policies covering property damage and casualty companies could cover the liability portion. Single forms were used to provide coverage in two companies.

Life Insurance and Regulation

As the demand for life insurance increased during the late nineteenth century, competition continued to rule the industry. To gain market share, life insurers introduced new products, which their agents marketed aggressively. New types of life insurance companies were also established, primarily to serve working-class Americans. A variety of consumer abuses led to calls for increased regulation, but real change did not occur until after 1906.

In the late 1860s, life insurers began selling tontine, or deferred-dividend policies, in which only part of each premium payment went directly toward an ordinary insurance policy. The rest was held in an investment fund for a set period of time (10, 15, or 20 years), with the benefits paid to those who survived the required period of time without letting his or her policy lapse. Insurers found these types of policies profitable because, unlike traditional policies, they did not pay yearly dividends to policyholders. They also did not require payment of the cash surrender value on forfeited policies, which Massachusetts began requiring in 1880. Policyholders bought the policies hoping for large returns. By 1905, an estimated two-thirds of life insurance policies featured deferred dividends.

Although tontine insurance grew in popularity, new types of insurance companies also formed to serve the emerging market for smaller insurance policies. One was the fraternal benefit society, a cooperative firm whose members contributed to pay death benefits when a member died. (Fraternal societies also sometimes provided sickness benefits, as did unions and employer-sponsored mutual benefit societies.) The other new type of company was the industrial life insurer (following the British model). Starting in the 1870s, a number of firms began to market low-value insurance policies (as small as $100) to working-class families. Premiums for these policies were collected on a door-to-door basis.

With the expansion of the industry came a number of problems, many associated with cutthroat competition: rebating (returning part of the premium to select customers), twisting (convincing people to trade in old policies with accrued cash value for new ones without), and exaggerated claims of future payments on tontine policies. Through local and regional organizations and a national body—the National Association of Life Underwriters (NALU), formed in 1890—the life insurance industry attempted to end these practices. But unlike their colleagues in the fire insurance industry, life underwriters did not succeed at self-regulation.

To raise revenues during the depression of the 1890s, a number of states tried to increase taxes on life insurers significantly. This was not the first time they attempted such legislation. During the 1870s, New York tried to raise taxes but met strong industry opposition. Midwestern states, including Missouri, Kansas, and Wisconsin, passed life insurance taxes during the 1880s and 1890s, as did Texas, although they were all eventually reduced or repealed. Texas and Kansas also led a movement in the 1890s to try to force insurance companies doing business in those states to invest locally. Despite public support for such measures, the life insurance lobby was strong enough to keep the laws from passing.

Three large New York firms—New York Life, the Equitable Life Assurance Society, and Metropolitan Life Insurance Company—dominated the life insurance industry of the late nineteenth century and early twentieth century. They successfully squashed most efforts at reform prior to 1906. Concerns about how the industry did business (including its high operating expenses and salaries, surreptitious financial procedures, and various consumer abuses) eventually led to an investigation of the industry. New York's Armstrong Committee investigation, which commenced in 1905, brought to light myriad improprieties, including political kickbacks, nepotism, extremely high salaries for top officials, and misuse of funds.

New York's investigation led many other states to conduct their own reviews. Their findings led to the passage of a number of life insurance reforms and resulted in strict supervision of the industry for the first time. In 1907, New York outlawed deferred-dividend policies, rebating, and twisting. The new law curtailed lobbying activities, eliminated proxy voting, and mandated standardized policy forms. Other states passed similar laws, but because companies operating in New York were required to follow the new regulations in any state where they did business (the so-called Appleton Rule), New York's life insurance statutes essentially became national.

Following the Armstrong investigation, the life insurance industry experienced another period of tremendous growth, with the number of companies nearly quadrupling between 1905 and 1914. In 1911, the Equitable Life Assurance Society wrote the first group insurance policy. By 1919, a total of 29 companies were writing policies that covered groups of employees, with states requiring a minimum of 50 or 100 individuals to constitute a group.

Related Lines

The first health insurance policies were sold in the 1890s. Between 1900 and 1918, the total amount of health insurance premiums collected annually grew from $500,000 to over $12 million. This coverage was expensive and excluded many common diseases. During the 1910s, the insurance industry fought a movement for compulsory health insurance, a movement that ultimately failed.

During World War I, the federal government began offering life and disability policies for active service members. State governments also recently got involved in another form of social insurance; during the 1910s, over 40 states mandated some type of workers' compensation coverage.

Insurance from 1920 to 1960

By the 1920s, insurance reached far beyond just the fire, marine, and life fields. With a variety of new products, fire and life evolved into property/casualty and life/health categories, each with its own set of regulations. With multiple lines and more sophisticated technology, insurance regulation became increasingly complex over the following decades. The most substantial changes prior to 1960 focused on property/casualty rating. Life insurance, meanwhile, remained a competitive market, as did the expanding health insurance industry. Starting in the 1930s, the federal government also became increasingly involved in social insurance, creating Social Security in 1935, and expanding it in 1939 and 1954.

Property/Casualty Insurance

Through the 1920s and 1930s, property insurance rating continued as it had before, with various rating bureaus determining the rates that insurers charged and the states reviewing or approving them. Casualty insurance rates were set in much the same way. But, in 1944, the Supreme Court struck a blow to the status quo, overturning *Paul v. Virginia*. In a case brought against the Southeastern Underwriters Association (SEUA), which set rates in a number of southern states, the Court decided that the SEUA was in violation of federal antitrust statutes. As a result of *U.S. v. South-Eastern Underwriters Association*, the industry became subject to federal regulation for the first time.

Within a year, to avoid conflicts between federal and state laws, Congress passed the McCarran-Ferguson Act, which allowed states to continue regulating insurance as long as they met certain federal requirements. Congress also granted the industry a limited exemption from antitrust law. The NAIC was given three years to develop model rating laws for the states to adopt.

In 1946, the NAIC adopted model rate laws for fire and casualty insurance, which required a state's "prior approval" of rates before the insurer could use them. Although most of the industry supported this requirement as a way to prevent competition, a group of independent insurers opposed prior approval and instead supported file and use rates, whereby insurers pay on the basis of use.

By the 1950s, all states passed rating laws, although not necessarily the model laws. Some allowed insurers to file deviations from bureau rates; others required bureau membership and strict prior approval of rates. Most regulatory activity through the late 1950s involved the industry's attempts to protect the bureau rating system.

The bureaus' tight hold on rates was soon to loosen, however. In 1959, an investigation into bureau practices by a U.S. Senate antitrust subcommittee (O'Mahoney Committee) found that competition should serve as the main regulator of the industry. As a result, states began to make it easier for insurers to deviate from prior approval rates.

Life/Health Insurance

The McCarran-Ferguson Act was a lot less influential on the life and health insurance industries. Because life insurance rates were based on standard mortality tables, no model rate laws were necessary. The main concern of regulators after 1920 was the solvency of life insurance companies and the assurance of adequate reserves.

Meanwhile, the health insurance industry began to grow. A plan offering a set level of hospital benefits for a monthly fee was first offered in 1929. Within a decade, such hospital plans were identified as Blue Cross plans. The first Blue Shield plan, which covered physician care for a similar monthly fee, was established in California in 1939. Group coverage in Blue Cross/Blue Shield plans and through traditional fee-for-service plans expanded between the 1940s and 1960s as organized labor was able to bargain for better benefit packages. The first health maintenance organizations (HMOs) also made an appearance by the 1960s.

Insurance since 1960

In recent decades, insurance evolved into an increasingly complex industry with a huge array of lines and products. The private sector of the industry expanded into new forms of risk management and financial services, and moreover, the federal and state governments became increasingly involved in providing insurance—often in areas where the private market has failed. Through an expansion of social insurance programs and the creation of guarantee funds provided by the states to compensate policyholders when companies fail, the government developed an ever growing level of protection. Most recently, the passage of the Gramm-Leach-Bliley Financial Services Modernization Act of 1999 and the Obama healthcare legislation of 2010 revived the debate over federal regulation of the insurance industry.

Property/Casualty Regulation

By the mid-1960s, two different systems of property/casualty regulation were beginning to develop. Although many states got rid of the prior approval requirement and began competitive rating, others strengthened strict rating laws. At the same time, the many rating bureaus that provided rates for different states began to consolidate. By the 1970s, the rates that these combined rating bureaus provided were officially only advisory. Insurers could choose whether to use them or develop their own rates.

Although membership in rating bureaus is no longer mandatory, these advisory organizations continue to play an important part in property/casualty insurance by providing required statistics to the states. They also allow new firms easy access to rating data. The Insurance Services Office (ISO), one of the largest "bureaus," became a for-profit corporation in 1997, and is no longer controlled by the insurance industry.

The end of bureau rates did not mean the end of state rating. A number of states continued to regulate rates for certain lines (such as automobile and workers' compensation coverage) and require prior approval, often as the result of rising insurance costs. Since the 1970s, states usually take into consideration companies' investment income when reviewing rates.

Since the 1960s, liability insurance became increasingly important, with liability components included in both commercial and personal policies. Automobile liability insurance is mandated by most states, and insurance companies are required to provide coverage (often through "assigned-risk pools") to high-risk drivers.

The federal government also expanded its involvement in property/casualty insurance, providing or guaranteeing coverage in a number of areas where the private market

President Lyndon B. Johnson signs the Medicare program into law on July 30, 1965. On the right is former President Harry Truman, who became the first person to apply for the federal health care program. (Lyndon B. Johnson Library.)

failed. The National Flood Insurance Act of 1968 made affordable flood insurance available to at-risk homeowners. Although the origins of the federal crop insurance program lie in the depression, the program expanded greatly in the 1980s, covering many more acres and crops. Most recently, in November 2002, Congress passed a bill providing up to $100 billion in reinsurance for the insurance industry over three years in case the country should experience another terrorist attack on the scale of that on September 11, 2001.

Life/Health Insurance Regulation

In 1965, the federal government entered the realm of health insurance with the establishment of Medicare and Medicaid. HMOs received a boost with the passage of the Health Maintenance Organization Act of 1973, which required insurers to offer an HMO option when they provided health insurance for their employees. By the 1980s, another form of managed care, the preferred provider network (PPO), was also offered.

Important health care legislation includes the Consolidated Omnibus Budget Reconciliation Act (COBRA) of 1986, which requires employers to provide continuation of coverage for a varied period of time when an employee leaves a job, and the Health Insurance Portability and Accountability Act (HIPAA) of 1996, which allows insurance benefits to be carried from job to job without a waiting period for coverage of preexisting conditions.

Gramm-Leach-Bliley

Gramm-Leach-Bliley (as the Financial Services Modernization Act of 1999, or GLB, is commonly known) went into effect in November 2000 and leaves state regulators in charge of the day-to-day regulation of insurance. However, it opens the door for federal regulation. GLB has the greatest impact on life insurance companies because of their involvement in the financial services sector, but provisions of the act have consequences for all lines of insurance.

GLB requires states to create uniform "producer" statutes for licensing agents and brokers in all lines. The law mandated that, by 2002, over half of the states were to adopt either uniform or reciprocal licensing, a condition that regulators have met. GLB also contains privacy provisions requiring policyholders to give permission before the insurer releases personal data, a condition that is particularly relevant to health insurance.

References

Baranoff, Dalit. "Shaped by Risk: Fire Insurance in America 1790–1920." PhD dissertation. Baltimore, MD, Johns Hopkins University, 2003.

Baranoff, Etti. *Risk Management and Insurance*. New York: John Wiley and Sons, 2003.

Fishback, Price V. "Workers' Compensation." In Robert Whaples, ed., *EH.Net Encyclopedia*. August 15, 2001. Available: http://www.eh.net/encyclopedia/fishback.workers.compensation.php; accessed February 2, 2002.

Grant, H. Roger. *Insurance Reform: Consumer Action in the Progressive Era*. Ames: Iowa State University Press, 1979.

Harrington, Scott E. "Insurance Rate Regulation in the 20th Century." *Journal of Risk and Insurance*, vol. 19, no. 2 (Winter 2000): 204–218.

Keller, Morton. *The Life Insurance Enterprise, 1885–1910: A Study in the Limits of Corporate Power*. Cambridge, MA: Belknap Press, 1963.

Lilly, Claude C. "A History of Insurance Regulation in the United States." *CPCU [Chartered Property Casualty Underwriter] Annals*, vol. 29 (June 1976): 99–115.

Merkel, Philip L. "Going National: The Life Insurance Industry's Campaign for Federal Regulation after the Civil War." *Business History Review*, vol. 65 (Autumn 1991): 528–553.

Murphy, Sharon Ann. "Life Insurance in the United States through World War I." In Robert Whaples, ed., *EH.Net Encyclopedia*. August 15, 2002. Available: http://www.eh.net/encyclopedia/murphy.life.insurance.us.php; accessed August 15, 2002.

Perkins, Edwin J. *American Public Finance and Financial Services, 1700–1815*. Columbus: Ohio State University Press, 1994.

Pomeroy, Earl, and Carole Olson Gates. "State and Federal Regulation of the Business of Insurance." *Journal of Risk and Insurance*, vol. 19, no. 2 (Winter 2000): 179–188.

Wagner, Tim. "Insurance Rating Bureaus." *Journal of Risk and Insurance*, vol. 19, no. 2 (Winter 2000): 189–203.

Intellectual Property

R. Jake Sudderth

Intellectual property is knowledge or expression owned by an individual or a corporate entity. Intellectual property consists of three customary domains: copyright, patent, and trademark. A fourth designation, trade secrets, emerged as a legal construct over the past two centuries. The term *intellectual property* became popular in legal doctrine, in congressional debate, and with U.S. computer specialists in the early 1980s. Europeans first used the term in the late nineteenth century to describe several disciplines of creative arts and design using a single, broad definition.

Intellectual Property in the Early Republic

The identification and cataloging of ideas across borders and within trading zones through legalized intellectual property protection grew from English tradition and slowly infiltrated common law in the American colonies in the seventeenth and eighteenth centuries. Federal standards for intellectual property protections expanded with the adoption of the U.S. Constitution in 1789. Interest in the protection of specific goods and services flourished in the nineteenth century as the American consumer market grew, new technologies spawned new products, and advertising methods promoted unique brands. Powerful trading organizations and lobbying groups called for international guidelines designed to mediate legal barriers to knowledge and expression. A growing business press, which recorded the economic impact of invention and chronicled the entrepreneurial development of products from inception to incarnation, fortified these efforts in nineteenth-century America.

U.S. copyright law protects original forms of expression, such as the movie *Star Wars* or the play *Rent*. Patent law protects commercial designs or formulas produced by inventors and the law is designed to dissuade other individuals or firms from copying their work. Patent law protects inventions and processes (via "utility" patents) and ornamental designs (via "design" patents). Patent protections developed long before copyrights became controversial. The first American patent was granted by a special 1641 act of the Massachusetts colonial government for the development of a saltworks. At the beginning of the twenty-first century, the United States granted utility patents for a period of 17 years and design patents for 14 years. Anyone can make, use, or sell the invention or design in question once the patent for an invention or design expires.

Trademarks and service marks include words, names, symbols, or devices used by manufacturers of goods and providers of services to identify their goods and services and to distinguish them from those manufactured and sold by others. The brand Taco Bell or the contours of a BMW hood ornament are examples of trademark designations. Historically, U.S. trademark law has not restricted the use of a trademark that is unlikely to cause confusion, mistake, or deception among consumers. However, the 1996 Lanham Act introduced legislation that protected famous marks from uses that dilute their distinctiveness, even in the absence of any likelihood of confusion or competition. Marks qualify as famous if they promote such powerful associations in the consumer's mind that even noncompeting uses can impinge on their value. Before November 1989, a U.S. trademark's owner could file a trademark application only after he or she actually used the trademark in commerce. U.S. law allows a person who has a bona fide intention to use a trademark in commerce to apply to register the trademark. Certificates of federal trademark registration usually remain in effect for 10 years. A federal registration may be renewed for any number of successive 10-year terms as long as the mark is still in use in commerce. The duration of state registration varies.

Trade-secret law only protects information that a company has tried but failed to conceal from competitors. Unique formulas for soft drinks and confidential marketing strategies are examples of trade secrets. Unlike the law in other areas of intellectual property, such as copyright or patent law, trade-secret law imposes liability only when the appropriator acquires, reveals, or uses secrets in a wrongful manner. A wide variety of materials may be protected by trade-secret law, including the following types of technical and business information: customer lists, designs, instructional methods, manufacturing processes, document-tracking processes, and formulas for producing products. Inventions and processes not patentable might also receive protection under trade-secret law. Patent applicants generally rely on trade-secret law to protect their inventions while the patent applications are pending.

Framers of the U.S. Constitution reviewed over 200 years of English law while formulating language addressing the rights of ideas and inventions. Merging European common law principles with American policies designed to promote individual rights proved difficult. In 1557, Queen Mary I assigned all printing and book sales to a single guild, the Stationers' Company. Guild members purchased manuscripts from writers and held the exclusive right to print and sell them forever. The Crown also granted exclusive rights to print the works of deceased writers, and the guild censored books it considered seditious or heretical. England's guild monopoly frustrated several writers, and eventually, Parliament withdrew royal monopolies. Stationers' Company officials responded by purchasing perpetual licenses to manuscripts. By the eighteenth century, the English considered the independent rights for authors a legitimate protection, and Parliament enacted the Statute of Anne, the first modern copyright law, in 1710. The act gave authors the rights to their work and limited the duration of protection to 14 years, a standard unchallenged until late in the twentieth century in Europe and the United States. The guild spent decades trying to recapture its legal monopoly by embarking on a series of lawsuits that maintained the Crown could not strip businesses of their property after 14 years or any other arbitrary length of time. In 1774, the House of Lords clarified that authors and publishers possessed no absolute property rights over their works. Members determined that rights to products of the mind remained temporary and should be in the public domain after a short period of time, available for use by all.

Framers of the U.S. Constitution considered the merits of independent state laws when assessing whether to define clear national policy or ignore provisions for intellectual property. Before 1787, state assemblies could grant rights to inventions or ideas, but South Carolina was the only state that passed general legislation allowing grants of patents without special acts of the legislature. Although discarding the ineffective Articles of Confederation and proceeding with a drafted version of the Constitution at the Constitutional Convention in Philadelphia, beginning on May 14, 1787, participants reviewed inconsistent decisions in respect to intellectual property. When searching for samples or templates of how to incorporate ideas and inventions as protected commodities, they found that England showcased a more consistent policy than any single American state.

The debate did not address provisions for ideas, inventions, or any other language now associated with intellectual property until the Committee Detail submitted its recommendations. Virginia's James Madison harked back to English law on August 18, 1787, and suggested adding the right "to secure to literary authors their copyrights for a limited time" (*Debates in the Federal Constitution*). On the same day, South Carolina delegate Charles Pinckney recommended a provision "to grant patents for useful inventions" and "to secure to authors exclusive rights" (*Debates in the Federal Constitution*). On August 31, the assembly referred these proposals and others to a committee composed of one member from each state. On September 5, 1787, the committee, which included Madison, reported that Congress should have the power "to promote the progress of science and useful arts, by securing for limited times to authors and inventors the exclusive right to their respective writings and discoveries." The clause surfaced verbatim in what became Article 1, Section 8, Clause 8 of the Constitution.

Madison's writings demonstrated his belief that federal oversight of ideas and inventions remained a necessary evil as the burgeoning national economy forced goods to pass across borders efficiently. His theories differed from those of Thomas Jefferson, who remained more interested in ensuring that inventions became available to the public. "The copyright of authors has been solemnly adjudged in Great Britain to be a right of common law. . . . The public good fully coincides . . . with the claims of individuals," Madison lectured (*Introduction to the Debates*). He believed that state leaders were poised to give up control of knowledge and ideas for the good of federalism. "The States cannot separately make effectual provision for either of the cases, and most of them have anticipated the decision of this point by law passed at the instance of Congress," he reminded his compatriots.

The pursuit of protection for intellectual property symbolized a national debate stirred by Thomas Jefferson, Alexander Hamilton, and James Madison during the late eighteenth century, after the American Revolution. As American lawmakers moved away from governance via a loose confederation of states managed by separate laws and added centralized control relying on English common law, a fusion of local and national intellectual property protections emerged. The framers of the Constitution pursued a middle ground that protected state autonomy while simultaneously promoting centralized banking, international trade, and interstate commerce. The result of this middle passage resulted in a collision of values and legal interpretations that shifted some power to state authorities and some to federal managers. Judicial interpretation expanded the federal oversight of copyrights and trademarks as the national economy grew and private investment in distant trade surged. American writers discovered new markets for their works, and large, private corporations prospered. Market expansion led independent trade groups and business interests to seek even broader protection for intellectual property ownership. At the twilight of the eighteenth century, the compromise position of part state and part federal protection articulated by American delegates to the Constitution Convention tilted toward a federal approach. Madison's call to "encourage by premiums and provisions, the advancement of useful knowledge and discoveries" trumped Jefferson's conclusion that products of the human mind "cannot, in nature, be a subject of property" (*Introduction to the Debates*).

Building from the language of England's Statute of Anne, the U.S. Copyright Act of May 31, 1790, provided creators of books, maps, and charts a 14-year copyright, with the option of renewing for another 14 years. The act became the first major legislative form of intellectual property protection in the United States. On February 3, 1831, the first general revision of the copyright law added music as a category of works protected against unauthorized printing and vending. The first term of copyright could also extend to 28 years, with the privilege of renewal for a term of 14 years. Until the middle of the nineteenth century, U.S. copyright owners enjoyed little more than protection against verbatim copying of language. A federal circuit court rejected the claim of Harriet Beecher Stowe that a German translation of *Uncle Tom's Cabin* infringed her copyright in 1853, finding the Constitution shielded literal text alone. Only 17 years later did Congress include translations (thereby allowing for legal interpretation of story lines or ideas borrowed from a written work in addition to literal copying) in the revised Copyright Act of July 8, 1870. The new law protected authors from infringement related to close approximations of plots or use of characters to create an unauthorized sequel, beginning a period of more liberal interpretation, championed by artists such as Mark Twain.

Intellectual Property in the Gilded Age

Copyright law was further refined in *Baker v. Selden* (1879), when the Supreme Court ruled that describing a system of accounting in a textbook did not confer copyright protection on the system itself. The Court wrote: "Recurring to the case before us, we observe that Charles Selden, by his books, explained and described a peculiar system of book-keeping, and illustrated his method by means of ruled lines and blank columns, with proper headings on a page, or on successive pages. Now, whilst no one has a right to print or publish his book, or any material part thereof, as a book intended to convey instruction in the art, any person may practice and use the art itself, which he has described and illustrated therein. The use of the art is a totally different thing from a publication of the book explaining it."

As the Supreme Court fine-tuned copyright law, established writers lobbied for continued protection. Mark Twain noted the publishers would not pay for works produced by unrecognized authors when they were not even required to pay famous authors for their works. He astutely co-opted Jefferson's public domain argument by suggesting that extending rights to major authors remained critical for preserving American icons and values. More recently, spokespersons at Disney and other corporations emulated his approach when advocating long-term control of icons such as Mickey Mouse. "It is not merely a question of copyright. . . . It is a question of maintaining in America a national literature, of preserving national sentiment, national politics, national thought, and national morals," announced Twain in the *New York Times*. On July 1, 1909, a third general revision of the copyright law became effective and extended the renewal term from 14 to 28 years. Generally, copyright standards have continued to be extended in respect to duration in America, and in the 1980s and 1990s, copyright doctrine also included detailed legal language addressing computer programs. The December 1, 1990, Computer Software Rental Amendment Act granted the owner of a copyright in computer programs exclusive rights to authorize or prohibit the rental, lease, or lending of the program for direct or indirect commercial purposes.

The U.S. government enacted the first federal patent law on April 10, 1790. The new law placed complete power over the granting of patents in the hands of the secretary of state, the secretary of war, and the attorney general. Secretary of State Thomas Jefferson personally examined each patent application filed. As the number of patents submitted for analysis increased, federal officials became overwhelmed. On February 11, 1793, Congress passed a new patent law, intended to place the burden of evaluating the validity of the claim of original invention on the courts and keep Cabinet officers, who lacked time, from having to examine patent submissions. The new law, which remained in effect until 1836, introduced the U.S. Patent Office. An inventor simply submitted a description of the invention, drawings, and a model and paid a fee. In 1842, Congress extended the reach of the patent statute to cover "new and original designs for articles of manufacture." The new act engaged inventor interest in various types of goods that had received little attention before that time. Products such as display racks received protection. In 1849, control over the Patent Office was transferred from the Department of State to the newly created Department of the Interior. The 1952 Patent Act made only general revisions to the law, not substantive changes.

Prior to the Civil War, manufacturers infrequently used trademarks on general merchandise. As a result, members of Congress paid little attention to the trademark issue. However, lobbying by private business interests began to reduce local government oversight of trade within cities and counties. New York State became the epicenter of this shift toward universal American trademark applications. Until the 1840s, the inspection of traded goods in New York cities was treated as a

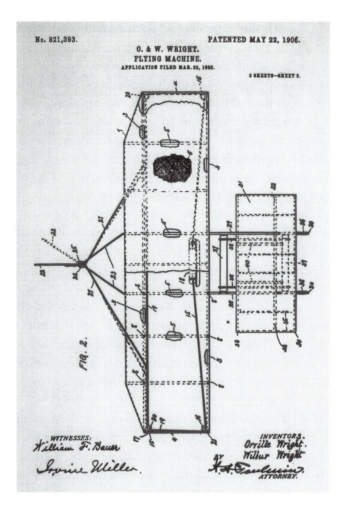

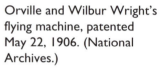

Orville and Wilbur Wright's flying machine, patented May 22, 1906. (National Archives.)

monopoly of the state government. By the middle of the decade, 372 inspectors and 109 weighers, who were responsible for part of the inspection process, occupied 22 percent of the 2,238 political appointee positions filled by the New York governor, and state inspections raised over 30 percent more revenues than state taxes. In response, business leaders lobbied for marks that would signal acceptable products, requiring no review or inspection. State leaders joined the businesspeople who claimed that the collection of inspection fees led to grotesque patronage and remained akin to imposing a commercial surcharge on goods and trade. Laws passed in 1844 and 1845 forbade private inspection in the city and county of New York and in Kings County. In 1845, New York became the first state to legislate private trademark protection for a variety of goods and services, enabling voluntary inspections overseen by company officials and municipal authorities. New York abolished all inspections and weighings in November 1846.

Federal trademark legislation, based on the copyright clause of the Constitution, surfaced in 1870. Averill Paints received the first mark under this act. However, the Supreme Court declared the measure unconstitutional in 1879 on the grounds that it impermissibly affected intrastate affairs. The Court held that the basis of any trademark rested on the commerce clause, which allowed for regulation of *interstate* commerce, not *intrastate* commerce. In response, New York business leaders sprang into action again, now calling for uniform trademark guidelines at the national level to reduce any trade restraints across the United States. Twelve New York industrialists founded the U.S. Trademark Association (USTA) in 1878 and lobbied for enactment of the Trademark Act of 1881, arguing that manufacturers should be able to protect their brands as a necessity of commerce when engaging in foreign trade.

By 1887, the association expanded its activities by publishing *The Bulletin* to circulate articles of interest to trademark owners and law students. Interaction with elected officials and campaign donations resulted in USTA's president, Francis Forbes, being appointed by President William McKinley to head a commission empowered to revise statutes relating to patents, trade, and other marks. The commission's report, submitted to Congress in 1900, made recommendations that formed the basis of the Trademark Act of 1905, a law adopted on the principle of prior ownership and use. Companies establishing marks in the previous 10 years received authorization to consolidate ownership through procedural registration. The new law precipitated 16,224 applications for the year, nearly a sevenfold increase from 1904. In 1906, USTA officials expanded the geographic scope of their advice and initiated trademark planning in other nations. Officials in Argentina were counseled to liberalize national law, and the association drafted trademark law for Ecuador in 1908, a model later used in other South American jurisdictions.

Intellectual Property in the Twentieth Century

The 1946 Trademark Act introduced legislation governing federal trademark registration. Thereafter, USTA officials launched a major campaign to reduce the effect of mandatory state trademark registration, which resulted in the 1949 Model State Trademark Bill, approved by the National Association of Secretaries of State and the Council of State Governments. Enactment in 46 states confirmed that all jurisdictions would incorporate uniform registration practices and share information. American state and federal trademarks shifted toward national, rather than regional, data management. In 1993, the USTA recast itself as the International Trademark Association and claimed approximately 3,000 members drawn from 110 countries.

Private business representatives did not have to work as hard when advocating legal protections for trade secrets. Nineteenth-century legal decisions regarding the shipment of goods established that packages, cases, and vessels containing commodities could shield their identity. Courts also mandated that imitations of goods as diverse as team uniforms and stationery remained unacceptable. Likewise, competitive companies could not distribute goods that caused consumer confusion or "tarnished" private trademarks. In the *Dow Jones* case, the Supreme Court of Illinois held that the Chicago Board of Trade (CBOT) could not develop a stock index futures contract keyed to the Dow Jones Industrial Average without first obtaining permission from the company that created the market index. Officials at the CBOT used similar reasoning to their advantage as they successfully argued that the organization's price quotations were "like a trade secret," thereby suppressing the sharing of insider pricing with potential competitors. Unlike patent, copyright, and trademark law, no private federal civil cause of action existed in U.S. trade-secret law. In 1979, the American Bar Association approved the Uniform Trade Secrets Act (UTSA) as a model for states to adopt.

Nineteenth- and twentieth-century American popular literature, commerce, and shopping introduced copyrighted books, patented industrial designs, and trademarked consumer goods to millions of consumers across the country. Business journals, engineering specialists, corporate officers, and government officials helped inventors and producers understand the legal terminology serving as the foundation of intellectual property. Marketing efforts ensured that consumers became aware of new brands as they entered the national marketplace, and independent inventors received inspiration from firms such as Munn and Company, the parent firm of *Scientific American Magazine*. Munn officials developed the first professional services organization in the United States dedicated to submitting patent applications. Thomas Edison, the quintessential American inventor and protector of special designs and schemes, was said to never miss an issue of *Scientific American* as a young boy. In 1877, he entered the New York offices of the magazine and demonstrated an early version of his phonograph to great fanfare.

Scientific American captured readers such as Edison by promoting the captivating nature of scientific curiosity and invention. Dreams and success stories dominated every issue, and creative capitalist enterprise abounded. The masthead of the first edition stated: "This paper is especially entitled to the patronage of Mechanics and Manufactures, being the only paper in America, devoted to the interest of those classes." Former painter, schoolmaster, and inventor Rufus Porter launched the magazine on August 28, 1845, and sold the publication to Alfred Ely Beach and Orson Desaix Munn the following year for a small profit.

Beach grew up as the son of Moses Yale Beach, who owned the *New York Sun* and developed the rag-cutting machine for the manufacture of paper. Munn, who had been one of Alfred's classmates at Monson Academy, ran a general store in Monson, Massachusetts, at the time of the purchase. Together, the two men increased the magazine's circulation to 10,000 by 1848, 20,000 by 1852, and 30,000 by 1853. The journal championed the growth in the number of people working in technology across the United States and promoted Munn and Company as the experts necessary for planning and protecting inventors' ideas and design concepts. At the end of 1845, the U.S. Patent Office had issued 4,347 patents throughout its history. By 1890, the number of patents accepted (approximately one-third as many additional applications were denied) by the same office numbered 402,166, and over 20,000 were being granted each year. During the early 1860s, Munn and Company generated one-third of all patents issued in America. By 1924, the firm's number of patents exceeded 200,000, more than one-seventh of all patents ever issued by the Patent Office to that time. Firm officials became active lobbyists. Throughout the 1850s, Beach, who secured several patents of his own (including one for a typewriter enhancement for the blind), traveled to the District of Columbia every two weeks to personally deliver applications. Munn and Company also opened a branch office in Washington, across the street from the Patent Office. Personnel from the firm wrote letters of advice to Congress members and U.S. presidents, and they tutored government officials interested in technology. The company also published several editions of a handbook specific to patent law. A former patent commissioner even became one of the company's attorneys.

As independent inventors became more sophisticated, corporate leaders followed suit. They received aid from court rulings that further eroded municipal controls over trade and business transactions. Courts ruled that cities could no longer regulate the hours of business within their confines. The Supreme Court decision in *Santa Clara v. Southern Pacific Railroad* (1886) finalized a legal revolution that resulted in corporations being declared "persons" entitled to the constitutional rights and protections guaranteed by the Fourteenth Amendment. Through the emergence of "substantive due process," corporations achieved "natural" economic status as ordinary, private, constitutionally protected enterprises rather than special, public creations of the state. Nineteenth-century corporate officials used these new legal findings to justify closely held control over ideas and inventions. For instance, the DuPont Company developed postemployment covenants designed to prevent the dissemination of knowledge, thereby restricting the spread of workplace knowledge outside the job site. When courts upheld these contracts, company officials drafted comprehensive agreements stipulating that firms legally owned the rights to any employee-developed ideas.

Nineteenth-century U.S. efforts to develop policy relating to ideas and knowledge-based products were consistently influenced by international advocates for protection. Many foreign exhibitors refused to attend the International Exhibition of Inventions in Vienna in 1873 because they were afraid their ideas would be stolen and exploited commercially in other countries. Ten years later, the Paris Convention for the Protection of Industrial Property led to the major international treaty of the same name, which was designed to help individuals in one nation obtain protection in other countries for their inventions, usually patents, trademarks, and industrial designs. The Paris Convention became codified in 1884 with 14 members, and it created an international bureau designed to organize policy across the world. The 1886 Bern Convention for the Protection of Literary and Artistic Works enhanced this effort. The meeting allowed nationals of member states to plan for international protection of their rights to control and receive payment for the use of creative works such as novels, stories, poems, plays, songs, operas, musicals, sonatas, drawings, paintings, sculptures, and architectural works. Emulating the Paris meeting, the Bern Convention established an international bureau to direct tasks. In conjunction with Paris Convention officials, the bureau formed an organization called the United International Bureau for the Protection of Intellectual Property (BIRPI). A staff of seven, based in Bern, Switzerland, preceded what became the World Intellectual Property Organization (WIPO) over 60 years later.

In the twentieth and twenty-first centuries, persistent market expansion and lobbying of government officials resulted in new U.S. law expanding the duration of knowledge protection and a greater focus on world trade standards. Intellectual property increasingly served as a key commodity that American inventors, artists, and business owners used to control uses of their products and to raise investment money. Intellectual property definitions increasingly became key underpinnings for general agreements on trade, drawing interest from business leaders and policymakers. In the wake of other new multilateral institutions dedicated to international economic cooperation, notably the Bretton Woods institutions (now known as the World Bank and the International Monetary Fund), the General Agreement on Tariffs and Trade (GATT) surfaced in 1946. Early GATT negotiations resulted in 45,000 tariff concessions affecting $10 billion—or about one-fifth—of world trade, and they began a worldwide transition toward detailed provisional rules governing trade. A special charter for the International Trade Organization (ITO), a short-lived agency of the United Nations, even set rules relating to employment, commodity agreements, restrictive business practices, and international investment. GATT, officially activated in January 1948, established a forum that world leaders used to develop international principles of trade and business, including intellectual property.

In 1960, BIRPI moved from Bern to Geneva, and a decade later, the organization became the World Intellectual Property Organization. In 1974, WIPO became a specialized agency of the United Nations and received a mandate to administer intellectual property matters recognized by members. GATT remained the only multilateral instrument governing international trade until the Marrakesh Agreement established the World Trade Organization (WTO) in 1994. The latter body established a council for trade-related aspects of intellectual property rights (TRIPS), operating under the guidance of the WTO's General Council. This interaction codified intellectual property rights within industrial nations in the same fashion the U.S. Constitution merged English law with state law in America. Today, WTO officials encourage global intellectual property provisions and agreement among major trading nations, and government leaders follow the organization's advice. When the European Union, in the mid-1990s, adopted the German copyright standard, which called for a duration based on the author's life plus 70 years, U.S. Congress members increased the U.S. duration from 50 to 70 years. In 1996, WIPO officials entered into a cooperative agreement with WTO administrators. At the beginning of the twenty-first century, the organization had 179 independent member states and a staff of over 800, representing 84 countries around the world.

U.S. corporations became huge supporters of a worldwide agreement regarding intellectual property standards and the protection of these business assets (the property itself) as their own business interests expanded into outlying markets. Federal spending on semiconductor research in northern California in the latter half of the twentieth century led to the rise of Silicon Valley and high-tech areas outside Boston. Other cities and metropolitan areas sought to capture high-tech growth industries fueled by technological expansion, and several cities and states promoted research labs and development centers sometimes affiliated with major universities. These growing R&D centers sprouted new technology designed to convert ideas and products into wealth. Firms relying on medicine, weaponry, and computing systems remained especially popular.

In the 1970s, *Popular Mechanics*, a magazine similar to *Scientific American*, provided inspiration to Microsoft founders Paul Allen and Bill Gates, who discovered the Altair, a home computer kit, in the pages of the magazine. Allen and Gates fastidiously programmed software for the machine and launched a vast empire designed to license ideas through software (Microsoft). As several other companies eschewed business models based on selling machines (hardware, in the case of computers) or services and consulting, licensing software to operate networks, computers, and manufacturing systems became accepted practice. Buying and selling software and technology as commodities, as opposed to using the technology to build something more tangible, was popularized, and the term *intellectual property* emerged as an American definition of knowledge-based assets such as copyrights, patents, trademarks, and trade secrets. Law schools began offering special programs for intellectual property studies, and the term consistently turned up in congressional debates and within proposed congressional bills in the 1980s. The term was eventually replaced by a shortened usage, *IP*, a popular expression incorporated by business executives, investors, technologists, and attorneys.

American venture capital firms seeding start-up companies with capital often focus more on the intellectual property associated with a business or idea than on the company itself. The intellectual property is treated as the critical asset behind the business and as the only tangible, valuable commodity. Intellectual property–related trade has grown into one of the largest economic sectors within the nation's economy. In 1998, high-tech industries accounted for 11 percent of the $12.5 trillion worth of goods produced in the United States, and they grew much faster than other sectors. Management of this growth mandated intense interest by private and public authorities in intellectual property. At the dawn of the twenty-first century, some estimates conclude that copyrighted material alone contributes over $400 billion to the U.S. economy each year, arguably making it the country's single most important export.

References

African Methodist Episcopal Church Review. Reprinted by the Ohio Historical Society, "The African-American Experience in Ohio, 1850–1920," vol. 6, no. 3 (January 1890). Available: http://dbs.ohiohistory.org/africanam/page.cfm?ID=2387.

Arber, Edward, ed. *A Transcript of the Registers of the Company of Stationers of London, 1554–1640* a.d. 5 vols. New York: P. Smith, 1950.

Chisum, Donald S. *Principles of Patent Law: Cases and Materials*. 2nd ed. New York: Foundation Press, 2001.

Cowan, Ruth Schwartz. *A Social History of American Technology*. New York: Oxford University Press, 1997.

The Debates in the Federal Constitution of 1787. Available: http://www.constitution.org/dfc/dfc_0818.htm; accessed June 27, 2003.

Dobyns, Kenneth W. *The Patent Office Pony: A History of the Early Patent Office*. Spotsylvania, VA: Sergeant Kirkland's Press, 1999.

Donner, Irah. "The Copyright Clause of the U.S. Constitution: Why Did the Framers Include It with Unanimous Approval?" *American Journal of Legal History*, vol. 36, no. 3 (1992): 361–378.

Fabian, Ann. *Card Sharps and Bucket Shops: Gambling in Nineteenth-Century America*. New York: Routledge, 1999.

Fisk, Catherine L. "Working Knowledge: Trade Secrets, Restrictive Covenants in Employment, and the Rise of Corporate Intellectual Property, 1800–1920." *Hastings Law Journal*, vol. 52 (2001): 441–535.

Hund, Gaillard, and James Brown Scott, eds. *Debates in the Federal Convention of 1787* reported by James Madison. In "The Avalon Project at the Yale Law School: Documents in Law, History, and Diplomacy." New York: Oxford University Press, 1920.

Introduction to the Debates in the Federal Convention of 1787 by James Madison. Available: http://www.constitution.org/dfc/dfc_0001.htm; accessed June 27, 2003.

Jaffe, Steven H. "Yale Moses Beach." In Kenneth T. Jackson, ed., *The Encyclopedia of New York History*. New Haven, CT: Yale University Press, 1995.

Kasson, John. *Civilizing the Machine: Technology and Republican Values in America, 1776–1900*. New York: Penguin, 1977.

Mann, Charles C. "Who Will Own Your Next Good Idea?" *Atlantic Monthly*, vol. 282, no. 3 (September 1998): 57–64.

Samuelson, Pamela. "The Originality Standard for Literary Works under U.S. Copyright Law." *American Journal of Comparative Law*, vol. 42 (1994): 393–397.

Session Laws of American States and Territories prior to 1900. Microfiche. Westport, CT: Redgrave Information Resources Corporation, 1998.

Sterk, Steward P. "Rhetoric and Reality in Copyright Law." *Michigan Law Review*, vol. 94, no. 5 (1996): 1197–1249.

Twain, Mark. Quoted in the *New York Times*, December 10, 1889.

United States Patent Act. U.S. Statutes at Large 1 (1793): 318–323.

United States Trademark Act. U.S. Statutes at Large 21 (1881): 502.

United States Trademark Act. U.S. Statutes at Large 33 (1905): 724.

U.S. Constitution, article 1, section 8, clause 8. Available: http://www.constitution/dfc/dfc_0905.htm.

Walterscheid, Edward C. *To Promote the Progress of Useful Arts: American Patent Law and Administration, 1798–1836*. Littleton, CO: Fred Rothman, 1998.

Judiciary

Robert C. Cottrell

Over the span of its history, now covering more than two centuries, the U.S. Supreme Court has ruled on a series of issues relating to economic matters. In delivering its decrees, the nation's highest judicial tribunal relied on a set of powers explicitly and implicitly drawn from the U.S. Constitution. Section 8 of Article 1 outlines many of those powers, authorizing Congress "to lay and collect taxes, duties, imposts, and excises, to pay the debts and provide for the common defense and general welfare of the United States." The Constitution mandates that all such "duties, imposts and excises shall be uniform throughout the United States." Additionally, it allows Congress "to borrow money on the credit of the United States" and "to regulate commerce with foreign nations, and among the several States, and with the Indian tribes." Furthermore, according to the Constitution, Congress possesses the authority "to establish ... uniform laws on the subject of bankruptcies throughout the United States," "to coin money, regulate the value thereof, and of foreign coin, and fix the standard of weights and measures," and "to provide for the punishment of counterfeiting the securities and current coin of the United States." Finally, Section 8 concludes with an arguably sweeping grant of power—stating that Congress possesses the authority "to make all laws which shall be necessary and proper for carrying into execution the foregoing powers, all other powers vested by this Constitution in the government of the United States, or in any department or officer thereof."

The founding fathers articulated other significant powers pertaining to commercial transactions in Sections 9 and 10 of Article 1. Section 9 mandates that "no capitation, or other direct, tax shall be laid, unless in proportion to the census or enumeration herein before directed to be taken" and that "no tax or duty shall be laid on articles exported from any State." Similarly, "no preference shall be given by any regulation of commerce or revenue to the ports of one State over those of another; nor shall vessels bound to, or from, one State, be obliged to enter, clear, or pay duties to another." Moreover, "no money shall be drawn from the treasury, but in consequence of appropriations made by law; and a regular statement and account of the receipts and expenditures of all public money shall be published from time to time." Article 10 denies all states the authority to "coin money; emit bills of credit; make anything but gold and silver a tender in payment of debts; pass any bill ... or law impairing the obligation of contracts." The states, absent congressional approval, are similarly not allowed "to lay any imposts or duties on imposts or exports, except what may be absolutely necessary for executing [their] inspection laws; and the net produce of all duties and imposts . . . shall be for the use of the treasury of the United States." Article 7 states that "all debts contracted and engagements entered into, before the adoption of this Constitution, shall be valid against the United States under this Constitution, as under the Confederation."

Justices, attorneys appearing before the Supreme Court, and legal scholars have argued about the specific nature of such clauses, with some contending that the language in the Constitution is exact and others declaring that it is ambiguous at best. Interpretations pertaining to economic policies and practices of the federal government, states, municipalities, corporations, and private individuals have varied with the passage of time. This essay will explore some of the most significant of those arguments, drawing on a series of seminal Supreme Court rulings.

Concerns about the new nation's chaotic economic makeup, along with fears that the experiment in republican government might not succeed, led to calls for a revision of the Articles of Confederation. The gathering that ensued, the 1787 Constitutional Convention in Philadelphia, resulted in the crafting of a new, national document that gave the central government broad powers, including powers in the economic realm. In fact, little debate occurred in Congress over the commerce clause, which later spawned more legislation than any other component of the U.S. Constitution. Moreover, the commerce clause long provided the chief means for strengthening federal power. However, the contracts clause, not the clause regarding commerce, occupied most of the U.S. Supreme Court's limited docket during its first years of operation. And that clause had been controversial from its inception, with concerns expressed that the provision would unnecessarily hamper the states. The due process clause and the takings clause of the Fifth Amendment (which declares that "no person shall be deprived of life, liberty, or property, without due process of law; nor shall private property be taken for public use without just compensation") also proved instrumental.

The Marshall Court, 1801 to 1835

Chief Justice John Marshall turned to both clauses to ensure the early primacy of judicial nationalism. In *Fletcher v. Peck* (1810), Marshall employed the contracts clause to prevent states from encroaching on property rights. To safeguard investors who had acquired land through state grants, he had to disregard past notorious financial dealings involving highly placed officials in Georgia, in the U.S. Senate, and on the federal bench. Avoiding the issue of those unsavory practices, Marshall asserted that the purchaser of land possessed "a title good at law, he is innocent, whatever may be the guilt of others, and equity will not subject him to the penalties attached to that guilt." Otherwise, "all titles would be insecure, and the intercourse between man and man would be very seriously obstructed, if this principle be overturned."

In *Dartmouth College v. Woodward* (1819), Marshall broadened the reach of the contracts clause to include corporate charters. The New Hampshire state legislature sought to revise a 1769 charter that had established Dartmouth College. Daniel Webster argued that the legislature's effort amounted to "impairing the Obligation

The U.S. Supreme Court building in Washington, D.C. The Supreme Court is the highest authority in the judicial branch of the U.S. government, with jurisdiction over cases relating to the U.S. Constitution, federal laws, and treaties involving the United States. (Franz Jantzen/Collection of the Supreme Court of the United States.)

of Contracts." Effectively accepting Webster's contention that the contracts clause precluded states from interfering with such charters, the chief justice thereby shielded private economic interests from government regulation. Marshall's subsequent effort to overturn a New York insolvency law that purportedly violated the contracts clause, delivered in the case of *Ogden v. Saunders* (1827), proved unavailing.

Marshall had been more successful three years earlier, when he employed the commerce clause for the first time to help nurture an expansive national economy. The case of *Gibbons v. Ogden* (1824) regarded a state-granted monopoly for steam navigation along the Hudson River. With sweeping prose, Marshall indicated that state law "must yield to the law of Congress" when a conflict arises. "Completely internal commerce of a state" was "reserved for the state itself." However, "the power to regulate; that is, to prescribe the rule by which commerce is to be governed . . . like all others vested in Congress, is complete in itself." Thus, he held, it "may be exercised to its utmost extent, and acknowledges not limitations, other than are prescribed in the constitution." Marshall overturned the state court's decree, which had sustained the monopoly for steamboats, and in the process encouraged the blossoming transportation revolution.

In *McCulloch v. Maryland* (1819), Marshall also employed the necessary and proper clause to further the principle of judicial nationalism. The case involved the establishment of state branches by the Second Bank of the United States. A Maryland statute leveled a tax on banks that operated in the state without legislative approval. In a unanimous ruling, Marshall declared that "the government of the United States . . . though limited in its powers, is supreme; and its laws, when made in pursuance of the Constitution, form the supreme law of the land." The Constitution implicitly authorized the establishment of the national bank, Marshall continued, as indicated in the necessary and proper clause. He wrote, "This provision is made in a constitution intended to endure for ages to come, and, consequently, to be adapted to the various crises of human affairs."

The Taney Court, 1836 to 1864

Roger Taney, a former attorney general and Jacksonian Democrat with a very different conception of judicial power, succeeded John Marshall as chief justice. The difference between the two men became starkly apparent in the case of *Charles River Bridge v. Warren Bridge* (1837), which involved a state charter for a toll bridge. A second corporation, the Warren Bridge Company, subsequently received a charter to construct another bridge close to the first one. That bridge would remain a toll bridge for six years only. Contending that its contractual rights had been violated, the Charles River Company sought injunctive relief. In a forcefully argued 4–3 decision, Chief Justice Taney insisted that "the object and end of all government is to promote the happiness and prosperity of the community." Thus, it could not be assumed "that the government intended to diminish its power of accomplishing the end for which it was created." The defendant's claim that a monopoly could be granted over "a line of traveling," Taney declared, would terminate technological innovations that "are now adding to the wealth and prosperity, and the convenience and comfort of every part of the civilized world." Justice Joseph Story, in his dissent, complained that the majority ruling "destroys the sanctity of contracts."

Another 1837 decision, *Briscoe v. Bank of the Commonwealth of Kentucky*, placed Story in dissent against a transformed Supreme Court. A state-owned public banking corporation in Kentucky had issued paper money, an act that Marshall, in *Craig v. Missouri* (1830), deemed unconstitutional. Now, the Court declared states' banknotes constitutional, while narrowly defining what constituted a "bill of credit" under Article 1, Section 10 of the Constitution.

A happier ruling in John Swift's estimation involved the unanimous decision handed down by the Supreme Court in *Swift v. Tyson* (1842). Written by Swift himself, this judicial determination involved the question of whether the Court would adhere to

Roger B. Taney was appointed chief justice of the U.S. Supreme Court by President Andrew Jackson in 1836 and served until his death in 1864. (Library of Congress.)

general commercial legal principles if they ran counter to state court decrees. Swift answered in the affirmative, thus allowing the federal judiciary to uphold "a general commercial law" related to judicial precedents. Thereby, interstate commerce could avoid local impediments that might otherwise have been established.

Another important case decided by the Taney court, *Cooley v. Board of Wardens of the Port of Philadelphia* (1852), provided a somewhat definitive ruling on the commerce clause's applicability regarding various state-federal issues. A Pennsylvania statute required boats using the port of Philadelphia to pay half of the pilotage fees if the captains did not use local pilots. The Supreme Court affirmed that "the grant of commercial power to Congress does not contain any terms which expressly exclude the States from exercising an authority over its subject matter." The Court then stated, "If they are excluded it must be because the nature of the power, thus granted to Congress, requires that a similar authority should not exist in the States."

The Chase Court, 1864 to 1873

The last third of the nineteenth century witnessed a series of monumental decisions by the U.S. Supreme Court regarding economic matters. During this period, the American economy underwent remarkable transformations. By the close of the nineteenth century, the United States had become the world's most productive country, surpassing Great Britain. Along with a soaring population, itself the by-product of a high natural birthrate and massive immigration from abroad, the American landscape possessed great natural abundance. Scientific and commercial ingenuity, technological innovations, a managerial revolution, and the flowering of corporate capitalism also proved significant. In a series of rulings, the Supreme Court provided judicial support for the economic boom that saw the gross national product increase 33-fold from 1859 to 1919. Many of the decisions made by this activist Court determinedly sustained the liberty of contract, due process of the laws, and equal protection in a legal sense.

The closely fought *Slaughterhouse Cases* (1873) sharply restricted the effectiveness of the privileges and immunities clause of the recently ratified Fourteenth Amendment (1868). The case involved state and local codes passed in Louisiana to safeguard public health. In a 5–4 ruling, the Court declared that the privileges and immunities clause precluded states from restricting only "the privileges or immunities of citizens of the United States," not those articulated by the states. An impassioned dissent presented by Justice Stephen J. Field declared that the Louisiana regulations placing restraints on butchers violated the Fourteenth Amendment's admonition regarding due process of law. Field's dissent planted the seeds for the constitutional theory of substantive due process, while championing the ideal of "inalienable individual liberties." He wrote, "Clearly among these must be placed the right to pursue a lawful employment in a lawful manner, without other restraint such as equally affects all persons." However, Field insisted, "grants of exclusive privileges, such as is made by the act in question, are opposed to the whole theory of free government, and it requires no aid from any bill of rights to render them void."

The Waite Court, 1874 to 1888

The conceptual thrust behind the *Slaughterhouse* dissent ultimately came to prevail in a series of Supreme Court decisions, with certain exceptions carved out along the way. In *Munn v. Illinois* (1877), for example, the Court declared valid the Illinois statute establishing rates for grain elevator operations. Once again, Justice Field tendered a strong dissent, stating that "if this is sound law, all property and all business in the state are held at the mercy of the Legislature." By contrast, Field joined the majority of the justices in the case of *Wabash, St. Louis & Pacific Railway Co. v. Illinois* (1886), when the Supreme Court asserted that the states lacked authority to regulate railroad rates involving interstate commerce. "Indirect" restraints—but not "direct" ones—on interstate transportation, the Court ruled, were permissible. In response to the *Wabash* ruling, the U.S. Congress passed the Interstate Commerce Act of 1887, which authorized the setting of interstate rail rates by the Interstate Commerce Commission. In 1890, the Sherman Anti-Trust Act also became law.

The Fuller Court, 1888 to 1910

In *United States v. E. C. Knight* (1895) and *Pollock v. Farmers' Loan & Trust Co.* (1895), decided within two months of one another, the Supreme Court placed substantial constraints on the ability of the federal government to curb corporate excesses and the power of a small band of individuals who had amassed great wealth during the period of rapid modernization. The case involved an attempt to restrict the growth of the American Sugar Refining Company, which controlled 98 percent of the market share. Chief Justice Melville W. Fuller all but eviscerated the efficacy of the Sherman Anti-Trust Act, drawing a distinction between manufacturing and commerce and declaring the Court should not consider the indirect effects on interstate commerce under that legislation. If the American Sugar Refining Company was a monopoly, Fuller contended, it involved manufacturing only. Justice John Marshall Harlan dissented, declaring that an unlawful restraint on trade impacted an entire state. Harlan wrote, "The general government is not placed by the Constitution in such a condition of helplessness that it must fold its arms and remain inactive while capital combines . . . to destroy competition . . . throughout the entire country, in the buying and selling of articles . . . that go into commerce among the states." In *Pollock*, the Court, with Fuller again delivering the majority ruling, invalidated major portions of the federal income tax law of 1894, which placed a 2 percent tax on incomes greater than $4,000. Fuller declared that "what was intended as a tax on capital would remain in substance a tax on occupations and labor." Justice Harlan dissented, terming the ruling a "judicial revolution that may sow the seeds of hate and distrust among the people of different sections of our common country." Justice Henry Billings Brown dismissed Fuller's opinion as "a surrender of the taxing power to the moneyed class."

Justice Field's determined belief in both freedom of contract and liberty of enterprise came to carry enormous weight with the Supreme Court during the latter stages of the nineteenth century. In 1890, the Court declared that due process required the judicial review of state regulations of railroad rates, but later in the decade, the Court determined that railroads were entitled to a fair profit. In the case of *Allgeyer v. Louisiana* (1897), the Court, relying on the doctrine of substantive due process, overturned a statute mandating that all companies conducting business in Louisiana pay state fees. Justice Rufus Peckham relied on the ideal of "liberty of contract," propounded by the British philosopher Herbert Spencer and other champions of laissez-faire, to invalidate the Louisiana law.

Peckham offered a still more striking justification of liberty of contract in *Lochner v. New York* (1905). In that case, he delivered a 5–4 ruling that overturned a New York law limiting bakers from toiling more than 10 hours a day or 60 hours a week. Peckham bluntly wrote, "There is not reasonable ground for interfering with the liberty of person or the right of free contract" in such a manner. The law in question, he continued, "involves neither the safety, the morals, nor the welfare, of the public, and . . . the interest of the public is not in the slightest degree affected by such an act." The intended design of the statute, Peckham declared, was "simply to regulate the hours of labor between the master and his employees . . . in a private business." Thus, in such a situation, the ability of the employer and the employee to contract freely with each other "cannot be prohibited or interfered with, without violating the Federal Constitution." In his dissent, Justice Oliver Wendell Holmes Jr. argued that state directives could interfere with the liberty of contract. Moreover, "the 14th Amendment does not enact Mr. Herbert Spencer's *Social Statics* . . . a Constitution is not intended to embody a particular economic theory, whether of paternalism and the organic relation of the citizen to the state or of *laissez faire*." In a companion dissent, Justice Harlan stated that "the liberty of contact may, within certain limits, be subjected to regulations designed and calculated to promote the general welfare, or to guard the public health, the public morals, or the public safety." Additionally, Harlan noted, "a legislative enactment, Federal or state, is never to be disregarded or held invalid unless it be, beyond question, plainly and palpably in excess of legislative power."

Despite such rulings as *E. C. Knight, Pollock, Allgeyer*, and *Lockner*, the U.S. Supreme Court sustained government regulations in certain instances. In *Champion v. Ames* (1903), Justice Holmes issued the 5–4 majority opinion upholding the lottery act of 1895. Holmes affirmed that "lottery tickets are subjects of traffic, and therefore are subjects of commerce, and the regulation of such tickets from state to state, at least by independent carriers, is a regulation of commerce among the several states." He went on to say "that the power of Congress to regulate commerce among the states is plenary, is complete in itself, and is subject to no limitations except such as may be found in the Constitution." In *McCray v. United States* (1904), Justice Edward E. White upheld an act of Congress that allowed for the regulation of the production of oleomargarine. Such an excise tax, White determined, remained constitutional, notwithstanding the rationale sustaining it. Justice Harlan, in *Northern Securities v. United States* (1904), backed the use of the Sherman Anti-Trust Act against a giant railroad company. The case of *Swift v. United States* (1905) saw Holmes deliver the Court's unanimous decision defending a sweeping interpretation of the commerce clause. In upholding antitrust action against the beef trust in that case, Holmes articulated the "current of commerce" doctrine. Commerce, he wrote, involved a practical legal matter, not a technical one. In another unanimous ruling, *Muller v. Oregon* (1908), the Court upheld an Oregon statute capping a workday at 10 hours for women who worked in factories or laundries. Influenced by the brief filed by labor lawyer Louis D. Brandeis, Justice David J. Brewer delivered the majority opinion. Brewer declared that a "woman's physical structure and the performance of maternal functions place her at a disadvantage in the struggle for subsistence."

The White Court, 1910 to 1921

Under Chief Justice White and his successor, William Howard Taft, the U.S. Supreme Court continued to cut a generally conservative swath, with some exceptions. White presented the unanimous ruling in *Standard Oil Co. v. United States* (1911), which declared that a court must resort to a "rule of reason" in determining whether it should apply the Sherman Anti-Trust Act in a particular instance. In that case and in *United States v. American Tobacco Co.* (1911), the Court did sustain government efforts to apply the Sherman Anti-Trust Act. Despite his concurrence in the *Standard Oil* ruling, Justice Harlan derided the "rule of reason" as amounting to judicial legislation. The Court also upheld federal legislation regarding the grain, meatpacking, and radio broadcasting industries.

The Supreme Court looked less favorably on social legislation. In *Hammer v. Dagenhart* (1918), Justice William R. Day delivered the 5–4 ruling that the 1916 Keating-Owen Child Labor Act was unconstitutional. Day stated, "Over interstate transportation, or its incidents, the regulatory power of Congress is ample, but the production of articles, intended for interstate commerce, is a matter of local regulation." Deeming the act in question "repugnant to the Constitution," Day declared that "it not only transcends the authority delegated to Congress over commerce but also exerts a power as to a purely local matter to which the federal authority does not extend." If Congress could affect such regulation, he insisted, "all freedom of commerce will be at an end, and the power of the states over local matters may be eliminated, and thus our system of government be practically destroyed." In his dissent, Justice Holmes noted that "it would be not be argued today that the power to regulate does not include the power to prohibit." In his estimation, "the power to regulate commerce and other constitutional powers could not be cut down or qualified by the fact that it might interfere with the carrying out of the domestic policy of any State."

The Taft Court, 1921 to 1930

The Taft court demonstrated its anti-labor basis in a series of rulings, including *Truax v. Corrigan* (1921). Chief Justice Taft delivered the 5–4 majority opinion, which invalidated an Arizona statute that restricted courts from issuing injunctions against striking workers. The measure, Taft determined, abridged the due process and equal protection clauses of the Fourteenth Amendment. In *Bailey v. Drexel Furniture Co.* (1922), the Court deemed the Child Labor Tax Law unconstitutional. The act, Taft declared, established a penalty with a "prohibitory and regulatory effect" that would "break down all constitutional limitation of the powers of Congress and completely wipe out the sovereignty of the States." Justice George Sutherland, in *Adkins v. Children's Hospital* (1923), invalidated another federal law, this one setting a minimum-wage standard for women workers in the District of Columbia. Such a measure, from Sutherland's perspective, violated the liberty of contract that was guaranteed under the Fifth Amendment's due process clause. To Sutherland, "freedom of contract [was] the general rule and restraint the exception." Chief Justice Taft dissented, arguing that legislators, wielding the police power, could limit freedom of contract to afford protection to women laborers. Justice Holmes condemned the liberty of contract doctrine, stating that "pretty much all law consists in forbidding men to do some things that they want to do."

The Hughes Court, 1930 to 1941

The liberal-conservative divide on the Court appeared perhaps starker still as the Great Depression unfolded, when unemployment mushroomed to unprecedented levels, soup kitchens and breadlines appeared across the land, and desperation and anger mounted. In a number of closely argued cases, the Supreme Court ruled on the constitutionality of a series of measures by the federal government designed to improve the nation's economy. Initially, the Court appeared close to adopting a different approach regarding substantive due process. In *Nebbia v. New York*, Justice Owen Roberts offered the Court's 5–4 majority opinion sustaining a New York law that regulated the dairy industry. Roberts asserted, "In the absence of other constitutional restriction, a state is free to adopt whatever economic policy may reasonably be deemed to promote public welfare, and to enforce that policy by legislation adapted to its purpose." Moreover, "if the laws passed are seen to have a reasonable relation to a proper legislative purpose, and are neither arbitrary nor discriminatory, the requirements of due process are satisfied." In his dissent, Justice James Clark McReynolds insisted otherwise: "We must inquire concerning its purpose and decide whether the means proposed have reasonable relation to something within legislative power—whether the end is legitimate and the means appropriate." In *Home Building & Loan Association v. Blaisdell* (1934), another 5–4 ruling, delivered by Chief Justice Charles Evans Hughes, the 1933 Minnesota Mortgage Moratorium Law was upheld. Hughes wrote, "While emergency does not create power, emergency may furnish the occasion for the exercise of power." Affirming that the commerce clause was not absolute, Hughes declared that states possessed the authority to protect the well-being of their residents. The dissenters decried the impairment of the obligation of contracts.

Increasingly, the arguments posed by the dissenters would become part of majority opinions that overturned legislation sponsored by the administration of Franklin Delano Roosevelt. In May 1935 alone, the Supreme Court declared four New Deal enactments unconstitutional. The most important of those cases, *Schechter Poultry v. United States* (1935), resulted in a unanimous ruling delivered by Chief Justice Hughes that effectively invalidated the National Industrial Recovery Act of 1933. That measure, intended to stimulate economic recovery, called for industry groups to establish codes of fair competition. In a crushing blow to the Roosevelt administration, Hughes declared that "extraordinary conditions do not create or enlarge constitutional power." Most tellingly, he argued that the act had unconstitutionally ceded legislative powers to the executive branch. In a 6–3 ruling in *United States v. Butler* (1936), Justice Owen Roberts tossed out various provisions of the Agricultural Adjustment Act of 1933, another centerpiece of the First New Deal. Roberts contested the notion that Article 1, Section 8 of the U.S. Constitution "grants power to provide for the general welfare, independently of the taxing power." In a sharply drawn dissent, Justice Harlan F. Stone termed Robert's decision "a tortured construction of the Constitution." Stone also warned that "courts are not the only agency of government that must be assumed to have capacity to govern. Congress and the courts both unhappily may falter or be mistaken in the performance of their constitutional duty.... The only check upon our own exercise of power is our own sense of self-restraint." Yet another 5–4 ruling, *Carter v. Carter Coal Co.* (1936), had Justice George Sutherland invalidate the Bituminous Coal Conservation Act of 1935. "Production," he exclaimed, "is not commerce but a step in preparation for commerce."

As the makeup of the Court began to change and Chief Justice Hughes became more consistently amenable to a liberal perspective, rulings more favorable to later New Deal legislation followed. Consequently, the Court upheld the progressive state laws and the cornerstones of the Second New Deal—the Social Security Act and the National Labor Relations Act (NLRA), both passed in 1935. Indeed, from 1937 through the duration of the Roosevelt administration, the Supreme Court did not overturn any major federal legislation. The case of *West Coast Hotel Co. v. Parrish* (1937) saw a 5–4 decision delivered by the chief justice, who upheld a statute setting a minimum-wage standard for women workers in Washington State. In overruling *Adkins*, Hughes asked, "What is this freedom? The Constitution does not speak of freedom of contract." In his dissent, Justice Sutherland contended that treating men and women differently under the law amounted to arbitrary discrimination. In *NLRB v. Jones & Laughlin Steel Corp.* (1937), yet another hard-fought 5–4 case, Chief Justice Hughes sustained the NLRA, which guaranteed the right of workers to bargain collectively. Hughes wrote: "The congressional authority to protect interstate commerce from burdens and obstructions is not limited to transactions which can be deemed to be an essential part of a 'flow' of interstate or foreign commerce.... Although activities may be intrastate in character when separately considered, if they have such a close and substantial relation to interstate commerce that their control is essential or appropriate to protect that commerce from burdens and obstructions, Congress cannot be denied the power to exercise that control."

In *Steward Machine Co. v. Davis* and in *Helvering v. Davis* (1937), the Court prevented the Social Security Act from being discarded. In still one more 5–4 ruling, Justice Benjamin Cardozo denied in *Steward Machine Co.* that the Constitution precluded the government "from assenting to conditions that will assure a fair and just requital for benefits received." In *Helvering*, Cardozo affirmed that "Congress may spend money in aid of the 'general welfare.'" Acknowledging that a distinction had to be made between particular and general welfare, Cardozo declared that "the discretion . . . is not confided to the courts. The discretion belongs to Congress, unless the choice is clearly wrong, a display of arbitrary power, not an exercise of judgment." Additionally, he said, "when money is spent to promote the general welfare, the concept of welfare or the opposite is shaped by Congress, not the states. So the concept be not arbitrary, the locality must yield."

The Stone Court, 1941 to 1946

In the 1941 ruling of *United States v. Darby Lumber Co.,* Chief Justice Harlan Stone overruled the *Dagenhart* decision in upholding the 1938 Fair Labor Standards Act, which established a 40-hour maximum workweek while mandating a minimum wage of $.40 an hour for workers "engaged in commerce or in the production of goods for commerce." Stone declared that "the shipment of manufactured goods interstate is such commerce and the prohibition of such shipment by Congress is indubitably a regulation of the commerce." Congress's power "over interstate commerce is not confined to the regulation of commerce among the states. It extends to those activities intrastate which so affect interstate commerce or the exercise of the power of Congress over it as to make regulation of them appropriate means to the attainment of a legitimate end, the exercise of the granted power of Congress to regulate interstate commerce."

The case of *Wickard v. Filburn* (1942) further extended the federal government's exercise of power through the commerce clause. In a unanimous ruling, Justice Robert Jackson sustained key provisions of the second Agricultural Adjustment Act, declaring that "the Court's recognition of the relevance of the economic effects in the application of the Commerce Clause ... has made the mechanical application of legal formulas no longer feasible." Thus, he wrote, "even if an appellee's activity be local and though it may not be regarded as commerce, it may still, whatever its nature, be reached by Congress if it exerts a substantial economic effect on interstate commerce and this irrespective of whether such effect is what might at some earlier time have been defined as 'direct' or 'indirect.' "

The Vinson Court, 1946 to 1953

The U.S. Supreme Court did rule against President Harry S Truman in the case of *Youngstown Sheet and Tube Company v. Sawyer* (1952). In the midst of the Korean War, Truman ordered Secretary of Commerce Charles Sawyer to take control of the steel mills during a nationwide strike by the United Steelworkers. In a 6–3 ruling, Justice Hugo Black declared that "the President's power, if any, to issue the order must stem either from an act of Congress or from the Constitution itself. There is no statute that expressly authorizes the President to take possession of the property as he did here."

The Warren Court, 1953 to 1969

Throughout the Cold War era, the Supreme Court repeatedly affirmed the authority of the federal government to rely on the commerce power. In *Heart of Atlanta Motel v. United States* (1964), Justice Thomas Clark upheld the constitutionality of Title II of the 1964 Civil Rights Act, which banned racial discrimination in public accommodations; that measure relied on the commerce clause. Quoting from an earlier ruling, Clark affirmed that "if it is interstate commerce that feels the pinch, it does not matter how local the operation which applies the squeeze." He declared, "Thus the power of Congress to promote interstate commerce also includes the power to regulate the local incidents thereof, including local activities in both the States of origin and destination, which might have a substantial and harmful effect upon the commerce."

The Burger Court, 1969 to 1986

In 1976, the Supreme Court, for the first time in four decades, declared unconstitutional legislation that relied on the commerce clause. In a 5–4 ruling in the case of

National League of Cities v. Usery, Justice William Rehnquist invalidated the 1974 amendments to the Fair Labor Standards Act that sought to extend minimum-wage and maximum-hour protections to most state and local public employees. Rehnquist insisted that "this Court has never doubted that there are limits upon the power of Congress to override state sovereignty, even when exercising its otherwise plenary powers to tax or to regulate commerce which are conferred by Article 1 of the Constitution." He declared, "We hold that insofar as the challenged amendments operate to directly displace the States' freedom to structure integral operations in areas of traditional governmental functions, they are not within the authority granted Congress by Art. 1, section 8." In his dissent, Justice William Brennan asserted that Rehnquist's decision amounted to a "patent usurpation of the role reserved for the political process." Brennan went on to say that "today's holding patently is in derogation of the sovereign power of the Nation to regulate interstate commerce."

Only nine years later, the Court overruled the decision in the case of *Garcia v. San Antonio Metropolitan Transit Authority*. Justice Harry Blackmun asserted that "the attempt to draw the boundaries of state regulatory immunity in terms of 'traditional government function' is not only unworkable but is inconsistent with established principles of federalism and, indeed, with those very federalism principles on which National League of Cities purported to rest." Therefore, he declared, "we . . . now reject, as unsound in principle and unworkable in practice, a rule of state immunity from federal regulation that turns on a judicial appraisal or whether a particular governmental function is 'integral' or 'traditional.' " In his dissent, Justice Lewis Powell contended that the decision "substantially alters the federal system embodied in the Constitution."

The Rehnquist Court, 1986 to 2005

In keeping with the *Garcia* case, most Supreme Court rulings following the 1937 "judicial revolution" afforded both the federal and state governments wide latitude in regulating the marketplace. During the 1990s, however, the Rehnquist court displayed a greater readiness than any high court since the mid-1930s to view congressional discretion in the economic realm more critically. In the hotly contested case of *United States v. Lopez* (1995), Chief Justice Rehnquist declared that a statute regulating private individuals exceeded Congress's authority under the commerce clause. The case focused on a congressional enactment that banned guns within 1,000 feet of schools. The 5–4 majority ruling declared that Congress had failed to demonstrate a "substantial" effect on interstate commerce.

In 2000, the U.S. Supreme Court heard an appeal from the Florida Supreme Court over the disputed election between presidential candidates George W. Bush and Al Gore and decided that the Florida recount was unconstitutional. Since 2000, the Rehnquist court maintained a conservative position on most issues, including upholding the validity of school vouchers. However, in 2003, the Court issued two

Justices of the U.S. Supreme Court photographed in 1997: (seated, left to right) Antonin Scalia, John Paul Stevens, William Rehnquist, Sandra Day O'Connor, Anthony Kennedy; (standing) Ruth Bader Ginsburg, David Souter, Clarence Thomas, Stephen Breyer. (Collection of the Supreme Court of the United States.)

decisions that deviated from this conservative position. First, in two cases brought against the University of Michigan, the Court split its decisions: It ruled that minority students applying for admission cannot receive an additional 20 points on the entrance application based on their race (an amount that exceeded the points given for a student's grade point average) but that the University of Michigan Law School could use race as a factor to achieve diversity within its student body. Second, on June 27, 2003, the Supreme Court struck down a Texas sodomy law that outlawed gay sex. With a Court deciding social issues on a liberal basis, many in Congress awaited the last day of the Supreme Court session in 2003 to see if any of the justices would retire, but none did.

Judiciary | 705

The Roberts Court, 2005 to the Present

The Roberts Court has heard arguments on numerous cases since 2005, some of which remain open still at the end of 2009. On July 15, 2008, a *writ of certiorari* was filed with the Supreme Court in the case of *al-Marri v. Pucciarelli*. Petitioner Ali Saleh Kahlah al-Marri was arrested in 2001 and brought up on two charges involving credit card fraud and assorted crimes of dishonesty in 2003. On June 23, 2003, President George W. Bush declared al-Marri an enemy combatant, asserting that he was a sleeper agent for the terrorist organization Al Qaeda sent to probe possible ways to disrupt U.S. financial systems, and therefore ordered him transferred to the custody of the Department of Defense. The Fourth Circuit Court of Appeals ruled that al-Marri, as a legal resident of the United States who was detained within the borders of the United States, cannot be held in military custody as an enemy combatant. When the case reached the Supreme Court, the Acting Solicitor General filed an application to transfer al-Marri from military custody to the custody of the Attorney General. On March 6, 2009, the case was dismissed as moot.

Another case, decided on January 21, 2010, is the case of *Citizens United v. Federal Election Commission*. The legal issue before the Supreme Court is whether *Hillary: The Movie*, a politically critical documentary of then-Senator, and Democrat presidential hopeful candidate, Hillary Clinton, violates the "campaign ad" restrictions of the Bipartisan Campaign Reform Act, often commonly called the McCain-Feingold Act. The Court first heard arguments on the case on March 24, 2009, and a ruling was expected sometime that following summer. However, on June 29, 2009, the Court ordered that the parties issue briefs and reargue the case on expanded legal issues, which took place on September 9, 2009. The Supreme Court declared that the government may not ban political spending by corporations during candidate elections since it violates the First Amendment rights of corporations, which the court recognized as a "person" just as much as an individual.

Another case before the Roberts Court, *Flores-Figueroa v. United States*, asked whether the law enhancing the sentence of identity theft requires proof that an individual had knowledge that the identity card or number he had used belonged to another actual person. The Supreme Court issued a unanimous decision on this case on May 4, 2009. The Court ruled that the law enhancing the sentence for identity theft required actual knowledge on the part of the defendant that the identity card or number used belonged to another actual person and that the mere use of the card or number did not constitute a sufficient connection to that individual.

References
Baum, Lawrence. *The Supreme Court*. Washington, DC: Congressional Quarterly Press, 2001.

Elder, Witt, ed. *The Supreme Court A to Z: A Ready Reference Encyclopedia*. Washington, DC: Congressional Quarterly Press, 1993.

Hall, Kermit L., ed. *The Oxford Companion to the Supreme Court of the United States*. New York: Oxford University Press, 1992.

Hall, Kermit L., ed. *The Oxford Guide to United States Supreme Court Decisions.* New York: Oxford University Press, 2001.

Horwitz, Morton J. *The Transformation of American Law, 1780–1860.* New York: Oxford University Press, 1992.

Horwitz, Morton J. *The Transformation of American Law, 1870–1960: The Crisis of Legal Orthodoxy.* New York: Oxford University Press, 1992.

Irons, Peter. *A People's History of the United States.* New York: Viking, 1999.

McCloskey, Robert G. *The American Supreme Court.* Chicago: University of Chicago Press, 2000.

McDonald, Forrest. *A Constitutional History of the United States.* New York: Franklin Watts, 1982.

Pacelle, Richard L., Jr. *The Transformation of the Supreme Court's Agenda: From the New Deal to the Reagan Administration.* Boulder, CO: Westview Press, 1991.

Schwartz, Bernard. *A History of the Supreme Court.* New York: Oxford University Press, 1993.

Steamer, Robert J. *The Supreme Court in Crisis: A History of Conflict.* Amherst: University of Massachusetts Press, 1971.

Labor

Albert Atkins

Economic resources are limited or scarce. In general, the term *economic resources* refers to all natural, human, and manufactured resources that go into the production of goods and services, including factory and farm buildings and all sorts of equipment, tools, and machinery used in the production of manufactured goods and agricultural products; a variety of transportation and communication facilities; innumerable types of labor; and, last but not least, land and mineral resources of all kinds. Resources fall into two general classifications: property resources, which include land, raw materials, and capital, and human resources, such as labor and entrepreneurial ability.

Labor is a broad term that the economist uses in referring to all the physical and mental talents people use in producing goods and services. Economists view entrepreneurial ability, with its special significance in capitalistic economies, separately from labor. Thus, the services of a ditch digger, retail clerk, machinist, teacher, professional football player, and nuclear physicist all fall under the general heading of labor.

Labor in the Colonial Period

In North America by 1775, the original 13 colonies unfurled the standard of revolt. A few of the non-rebel territories, such as Canada and Jamaica, were larger, wealthier, or more populous than the first 13 colonies. And even among the rebellious American colonies, dramatic differences in economic organization, social structure, and ways of life existed.

All the rebellious colonies possessed one outstanding feature in common: Their populations continued to grow rapidly. In 1700, the colonies contained fewer than 300,000 souls, with about 20,000 of African descent. By 1775, some 2.5 million persons inhabited the 13 colonies. Immigration accounted for roughly one-half of the increase. However, most of the spurt stemmed from the remarkable natural fertility of all Americans. To the amazement and dismay of the Europeans, the colonists doubled their numbers every 20 years. Beyond that, lower population densities in some areas slowed the spread of contagious microbes, making American death rates lower than those of the relatively crowded Old World. Colonial America served as a melting pot from the outset. Although basically English ethnically and linguistically, the population also contained sizable foreign groups.

Workers harvest tobacco in colonial Virginia, c. 1650. (Library of Congress.)

Researchers agree that crude frontier life did not permit the flagrant display of class distinctions, and the seventeenth-century colonial society had a simple sameness to it. Would-be American blue bloods resented the pretensions of those who were less fortunate than they were and passed laws to keep them in their place. Massachusetts in 1751, for example, prohibited poorer folk from "wearing gold or silver lace," and in eighteenth-century Virginia, a tailor could receive a fine or imprisonment for arranging to race his horse, a sport that was "only for gentlemen." In the southern colonies, landholding served as the passport to power, prestige, and wealth. The Virginia gentry proved remarkably adept at keeping the land in a small circle of families over several generations, largely because they parceled out their huge holdings among several children rather than just to the eldest son, as was the custom in England.

Luckless black slaves remained consigned to society's lowest class. Though enchained in all the colonies, blacks were heavily concentrated in the South, where their numbers rose dramatically throughout the eighteenth century. Blacks in the tobacco-growing Chesapeake region had a somewhat easier lot. Farms were closer together, which permitted more frequent contact with friends and relatives, and tobacco proved a less physically demanding crop to work than those of the deeper South.

A few of the blacks had been freed, but the vast majority remained condemned to a life under the lash. The universal passion for freedom vented itself during the colonial era in numerous incidents of arson, murder, and insurrection or near insurrection. Yet the Africans made a significant contribution to America's early development through their labor, chiefly the arduous toil of cleaning swamps, grubbing out trees, and other menial tasks. A few of them became artisans, carpenters, bricklayers, and tanners, thus refuting the common prejudice that assumed black people lacked the intelligence to perform skilled labor.

In addition to slaves, the labor force of the early colonies also consisted of indentured servants, or indentures. Receiving passage to the New World in exchange for a specified period of labor, usually five to seven years, indentured servants enjoyed the same rights as other colonists. During the period of employment, they performed tasks ranging from domestic chores to skilled labor, and in exchange, they received room and board. At the end of the indentures' contracts, employers provided them with clothes, tools of their trades, and other essentials to help them start out on their own. The system alleviated the overcrowding of orphanages in England and provided opportunities for poorer English people displaced by the Industrial Revolution. As slavery increased, the number of indentured servants declined. By the American Revolution, the system of indentured servitude had virtually disappeared.

Labor from Independence to 1815

Economic changes wrought by the War of Independence proved likewise noteworthy but not overwhelming. States seized control of former Crown lands, and although rich speculators had their way, many colonial officials confiscated Loyalist holdings and eventually cut them up into small farms. A sharp stimulus was given to manufacturing by the prewar non-importation agreements and later by the war itself. Goods that had formerly been imported from England were cut off for the most part, but the ingenious Yankees simply made their own replacements.

Economically speaking, independence had numerous drawbacks. Much of the coveted commerce of the home country was still reserved for the loyal parts of the empire; and now the independent Americans had to find new customers for the goods and services they produced. Fisheries were disrupted, and bounties for ships' stores abruptly ended. In some respects, the hated British Navigation Laws became even more disagreeable after independence.

New commercial outlets fortunately compensated, at least partially, for the loss of old ones. Americans could now trade freely with foreign nations, subject to local restrictions—a boon they had not enjoyed in the old days of mercantilism. Enterprising Yankee shippers ventured boldly and profitably into the Baltic and China Seas. In 1784, the empress of China, carrying a valuable weed (ginseng) that was highly prized by Chinese herb doctors as a cure for impotence, led the way into the East Asian markets.

Many researchers agree that war had spawned demoralizing extravagance, speculation, and profiteering, with profits as indecently high as 300 percent. Runaway inflation had been ruinous to middle-class citizens on fixed incomes, and Congress had failed in its feeble attempts to curb economic laws by fixing prices. In fact, the whole economic and social atmosphere was unhealthy. The controversy leading to the war had bred a keen distaste for taxes, and the wholesale seizure of Loyalist estates had encouraged disrespect for private property.

In 1791, the national debt had swelled to $75 million because of Alexander Hamilton's insistence on honoring the outstanding federal and state obligations alike. A man less determined to establish a healthy public credit could have sidestepped $13 million in back interest and could have avoided the state debts entirely. Where was the money to come from to pay interest on this huge debt and to run the government? Hamilton proposed customs duties derived from a tariff. Tariff revenues, in turn, depended on a vigorous foreign trade, another crucial link in Hamilton's overall economic strategy for the new Republic.

Congress passed the first tariff in 1789, a low one with rates of about 8 percent on the value of dutiable imports. Raising revenue was by far the main goal, but the measure also advocated the erection of a low protective wall around infant industries. Hamilton had the vision to see that the Industrial Revolution would soon reach America, and he argued strongly in favor of more protection for the well-to-do manufacturing groups, another vital element in his economic program. In his *Report on the Subject of Manufactures*, Hamilton urged the industrial development of the United States. He noted that since the country had a "scarcity of hands," meaning laborers, the establishment of industries would encourage immigration. It would also provide Americans, primarily women and children, with additional work that would benefit their families, especially during the winter season when agricultural work diminished. But Congress, still dominated by the agricultural and commercial interests, voted only two slight increases in the tariff during George Washington's presidency.

The War of 1812 was a small conflict, in which about 6,000 Americans were killed or wounded. Indeed, it became but a footnote to the mighty European conflagration in the same year. When Napoleon invaded Russia with about 500,000 men in 1812, President James Madison tried to invade Canada with about 5,000. However, if the American conflict was globally unimportant, its results proved highly significant to the United States.

Moreover, a new nation was welded in the fiery furnace of armed conflict. Sectionalism, now identified with discredited New England Federalists, was given a black eye. The painful events of the war glaringly revealed, as perhaps nothing else could have done, the folly of sectional disunity. In a sense, the most conspicuous casualty of the war was the Federalist Party. New war heroes emerged, men such as Andrew Jackson, William Henry Harrison, and Winfield Scott. All three became presidential candidates, two of them successful.

Hostile Indians of the south had been crushed by Jackson at Horseshoe Bend (1814) and those of the north by Harrison at the Battle of the Thames (1813). Left in the lurch by their British friends in the Treaty of Ghent, the Indians negotiated such terms as they could. They reluctantly consented, in a series of treaties, to relinquish vast areas of forested land north of the Ohio River.

Manufacturing increased behind the wall of the British blockade. In an economic sense as well as a diplomatic one, the War of 1812 could be regarded as the second War of Independence. The industries stimulated by the fighting rendered America less dependent on the workshops of Europe.

Labor from 1815 to the Civil War

The postwar upsurge of nationalism between 1815 and 1924 manifested itself in manufacturing. Patriotic Americans took pride in the factories that had recently mushroomed, largely as a result of the self-imposed embargo and the war. When hostilities ended in 1815, British competitors tried to recover lost ground. They began to dump the contents of their bulging warehouses on the United States, often cutting their prices below cost and thus forcing war baby factories out of business. The infant industries demanded protection.

In their view, a nationalist Congress responded by passing the Tariff of 1816. This tariff became the first in American history with protective aims. The rates ranged roughly from 20 to 25 percent on the value of dutiable imports—not high enough to provide complete protection but a bold beginning nonetheless.

The first textile factories employed young women and children, a labor force that worked for lower wages than men. These workers toiled long hours, sometimes up to 16 hours a day six days a week, in poorly lit factories with inadequate ventilation. Children performed menial tasks, such as changing out bobbins and running errands. Men rarely handled these duties, working instead on farms or at a particular craft.

Sectional tensions increased in 1819 when the territory of Missouri petitioned Congress for admission as a slave state. This fertile and well-watered area contained sufficient population to warrant statehood. However, the House of Representatives introduced the incendiary Tallmadge Amendment, which stipulated that no more slaves should be taken into Missouri and also provided for the gradual emancipation of children born to slave parents already there.

Southerners saw in the Tallmadge Amendment, subsequently defeated in the Senate, an ominous threat to the sectional balance and to the system of labor used in the South. When the Constitution was adopted in 1788, the north and south were running neck and neck in terms of wealth and population. However, with every passing decade, the north became wealthier and more thickly settled, an advantage reflected in an increasing northern majority in the House of Representatives. The future of the slave system caused southerners profound concern. Missouri became the first state entirely west of the Mississippi River that was carved out of the Louisiana Purchase, and the Missouri emancipation amendment might have set a damaging precedent for the rest of the area.

During the decade between 1840 and 1850, the railroad significantly contributed to a solution to one great American problem: distance. Railroads proved fast, reliable, and cheaper to construct than canals, and they did not freeze over in winter. Inevitably, the hoarse screech of the locomotive sounded the doom of various vested interests, who railed against progress in defense of their pocketbooks. Turnpike investors and tavern keepers did not relish the loss of business, and farmers feared for their hay-and-horse market. The canal backers became especially violent. Mass meetings were held along the Erie Canal and, in 1833, the legislature of New York, anxious to protect its canal investment, prohibited the railroads from carrying freight, at least temporarily.

Revolutionary advances in manufacturing and transportation brought increased prosperity to all Americans, but they also widened the gulf between the rich and the poor. Millionaires were rare on the eve of the Civil War, but several colossal financial successes existed.

Cities bred the greatest extremes of economic inequality. Unskilled workers, then as always, fared worst. Many of them made up a floating mass of "drifters," buffeted from town to town by the shifting prospects for menial jobs. These wandering workers accounted, at various times, for up to half the population of the sprawling industrial centers. Though their numbers grew big, they left little behind them but the simple fruits of their transient labor. Largely without stories and unsung themselves, they remain among the forgotten men and women of American history.

Ulrich B. Phillips made two key points in his study *American Negro Slavery* (1918) about the years leading up to the Civil War. He noted that slavery remained a relatively benign social system and that it had become a dying economic institution, unprofitable to the slaveowner and an obstacle to the economic development of the South as a whole. Phillips's study followed two different implications. First, the abolitionists had fundamentally misconstrued the nature of the "peculiar institution," as Southerners referred to their society's slave system. Second, the Civil War was probably unnecessary because slavery might eventually have expired from "natural economic causes."

For more than half a century, historians have debated these issues, sometimes heatedly. Despite the increasing sophistication of economic analysis, no consensus exists on the degree of slavery's profitability. In regard to the social character of the system, a large number of modern scholars refuse to concede that slavery functioned as a benign institution. However, much evidence confirms the health and vitality of black culture in slavery, as reflected in the strength of family ties, religious institutions, and cultural forms of all kinds.

Many historians could argue that historical treatments of the 1850s have long reflected the major controversy of that decade: whether the principal issue involved slavery itself or simply the expansion of slavery into the western territories. Historians have generally emphasized the geographic factor, describing a contest for control of the territories and for control of the central government that disposed of those territories. Recently, however, some analysts, probably reflecting the pro–civil rights agitation of the times, have stressed broader issues, including morality. In this view, the territorial question remains real enough, but it also is seen as symbolizing a pervasive threat posed by the slave power to the free, Northern way of life. In the end, the problems of southern slavery and "free soil" in the West proved inseparable and insoluble, except by war.

Labor from 1865 to 1900

Economic miracles wrought during the decades after the Civil War enormously increased the wealth of the Republic. The standard of living rose sharply, and well-fed American workers enjoyed more physical comforts than their counterparts in any other industrial nation. Urban centers prospered as the insatiable factories demanded more American labor and as immigrants poured into the vacuums created by new job openings.

The sweat of the laborer lubricated the vast new industrial machine. Yet the wageworkers did not share proportionately with their employers the benefits of the age of big business. The worker, suggestive of the Roman galley slave, became a lever-puller in a giant mechanism that placed more emphasis on manual skills. After the Civil War, the factory hand employed by a corporation became depersonalized, bodiless, soulless, and frequently conscienceless.

New machines often replaced workers. In the long run, the Second Industrial Revolution (1860–1890) created more jobs than it destroyed, but in the short run, the manual worker suffered. A glutted labor market, moreover, severely handicapped the wage earners. The vast new railroad network could shuttle unemployed workers, including blacks and immigrants, into areas where wages remained high. Immigrating Europeans further worsened conditions. During the 1880s and 1890s and later, the labor market had to absorb several thousand unskilled workers a year. Individual workers became powerless to battle single-handedly against giant industry. Forced to organize and fight for basic rights, they found the scenario to their disadvantage. The corporation could dispense with the individual worker much more easily than the worker could dispense with the corporation. A corporation might even own the "company town," with its high-priced grocery stores and easy credit. Often, the worker sank into perpetual debt, a status that strongly resembled serfdom.

The public, annoyed by recurrent strikes, grew deaf to the outcry of the worker. American wages were perhaps the highest in the world, although a dollar a day for pick-and-shovel labor does not seem excessive. Andrew Carnegie and John D. Rockefeller had battled their way to the top of the steel and oil industries by paying their workers the minimum wages necessary to survive. Big businesses might have combined into trusts to raise prices, but workers were not able to combine into unions to raise wages.

Labor unions, which had been few and disorganized in 1861, received a strong boost by the Civil War. By 1872, several hundred thousand organized workers and 32 national unions existed, including unions for bricklayers, typesetters, shoemakers, and other craftspeople. The National Labor Union, organized in 1866, represented a huge advance for workers. It lasted six years and attracted an impressive total of some 600,000 members, including skilled and unskilled workers as well as farmers. Its keynote involved social reform, although it agitated for such specific goals as the eight-hour day and the arbitration of industrial disputes. The devastating depression of the 1870s dealt it a knockout blow. Wage reductions in 1877 touched off a series of strikes on railroads, collectively known as the Great Railroad Strike of 1877, which became so violent that federal troops were used to restore order.

A new organization, the Knights of Labor, seized the torch dropped by the former National Labor Union. Officially known as the Noble and Holy Order of the Knights of Labor, the organization began inauspiciously in 1869 as a secret society, complete with a private ritual, passwords, and a grip. This secrecy, which continued until 1881, was intended to forestall possible reprisals by employers. Initially, the Knights of Labor conducted a series of significant strikes against the financier Jay Gould. When Gould hired Pinkerton detectives to thwart another strike in 1886, union members protested in Haymarket Square in Chicago. Violence erupted, several police officers were killed, and officials blamed the whole incident on the "socialist" union members. Because of the continued violence, the Knights organization had melted down to 100,000 members by 1890, and these remaining individuals gradually fused with other protest groups.

As the Knights of Labor declined in membership, Samuel Gompers organized skilled workers under the American Federation of Labor (AFL). Vowing to keep the union out of politics, Gompers increased membership and, by 1920, the total number of union members reached 4 million. The AFL managed to survive the public dissatisfaction that followed two violent strikes in the 1890s. In 1892, miners struck at Andrew Carnegie's Homestead steel plant. When negotiations between unionists and plant manager H. C. Frick failed, he hired 300 Pinkerton detectives to bust the union. As the detectives floated down the river toward the plant, the union members waited for them on the banks. Shots were fired, and a bloody battle ensured that resulted in the death of nine union members and seven Pinkerton detectives. Carnegie then asked for and received assistance from the National Guard. This pattern of government intervention continued until the twentieth century when President Theodore Roosevelt mediated the anthracite coal strike, which resulted in labor receiving an increase in wages. This strike and the president's intervention reversed the pattern of the government providing assistance to business only. The American public, already upset by the violence at the Homestead plant, witnessed another strike in 1894—this time involving the Pullman Sleeping Car Company. The panic of 1893 resulted in the railroad company laying off more than half of its workers and cutting the wages of the remaining crews by 25 to 40 percent. Meanwhile, the rent and prices in the company-controlled town and store remained the same. The president of the American Railroad Union, Eugene V. Debs, called for a general strike of all railroad workers. The strike did not turn violent, but the shutting down of the entire railway system forced the government to intervene, and it used the Sherman Anti-Trust Act against the union. Once again, the federal government sided with big business.

Labor in the Progressive Era

Nearly 76 million Americans greeted the new century in 1900. Of them, almost one in seven had been born in a foreign country. Theodore Roosevelt, though something of an imperialistic president, supported progressivism within the United States. He promised a "square deal" for capital, labor, and the public at large. Broadly speaking, his program embraced three Cs: control of the corporations, consumer protection, and conservation of natural resources.

The square deal for labor received its acid test in 1902 when a crippling strike broke out in the anthracite coal mines of Pennsylvania. Some 140,000 workers, many of them illiterate immigrants, had long been frightfully exploited and decimated by accidents. They demanded, among other improvements, a 20 percent increase in pay and a reduction of the working day from 10 to 9 hours.

Unsympathetic mine owners, confident that a chilled public would react against the miners, refused to arbitrate or even negotiate. As coal supplies dwindled, factories and schools shut down, and even hospitals felt the icy grip of winter. Desperately seeking a solution, Roosevelt summoned representatives of the striking miners and the mine owners to the White House. He finally resorted to his trusty big stick when he threatened to seize the mines and operate them with federal troops. Faced for the first time with a threat to use federal troops against capital rather than labor, the owners grudgingly consented to arbitration. A compromise decision ultimately gave the miners a 10 percent pay boost and a working day of nine hours.

Keenly aware of the mounting antagonisms between capital and labor, Roosevelt urged Congress to create the new Department of Commerce and Labor in 1903. (Ten years later, the department split into two different agencies.) An important arm of the newly formed department involved the Bureau of Corporations, which was authorized to probe businesses engaged in interstate commerce. However, the bureau also became highly useful in helping to break the stranglehold of monopoly and in clearing the road for the era of "trust busting" that lay ahead.

Labor in the Interwar Years

During World War I, labor worked in unison with the government to provide the supplies needed for the war. After the war, a brief period of labor unrest occurred, but the U.S. economy quickly converted from wartime to peacetime production. From 1922 to 1929, the country experienced prosperous times. The wages of workers continued to increase, with Henry Ford leading the way. Ford deviated from traditional business practices that called for paying workers subsistence-level wages. Instead, he believed that by paying his employees enough so that they could purchase automobiles themselves, he would increase his profits. Throughout the 1920s, the United States experienced prosperous times, with labor enjoying higher wages, better working conditions, and shorter work hours. Then the Great Depression hit in October 1929. By 1930, the depression had become a national calamity. Through no fault of their own, a host of industrious citizens lost everything. They wanted to work, but employers were not hiring. Herbert Hoover created the Reconstruction Finance Corporation, which provided funds to banks and businesses, based on the trickle-down philosophy that business would reinvest the money by hiring employees or purchasing capital goods. Unfortunately, those at the top of banks and companies kept the money to cover their own expenses. The situation grew worse when the Federal Reserve Bank raised interest rates and constricted the money supply.

After the election of Franklin D. Roosevelt (FDR), Congress approved a series of measures that helped labor. During his first 100 days, Congress created the Civilian Conservation Corps (CCC), which became the most popular of all the New Deal "alphabetical agencies." This program provided employment in fresh-air government

Jobless search postings at an employment agency in New York City, 1936. Photo by Arthur Rothstein. (Rothstein, Arthur. *The Depression Years As Photographed by Arthur Rothstein*. Dover Publications, Inc., 1978.)

camps for about 3 million uniformed young men. They worked on projects that included reforestation, fire fighting, flood control, and swamp drainage. The recruits helped their families by sending home most of their pay.

Congress also grappled with the millions of unemployed adults through the Federal Emergency Relief Act. Its chief aim was to provide immediate relief rather than long-range recovery. Immediate relief was also given to two large and hard-pressed special groups by the Hundred Days Congress. One section of the Agricultural Adjustment Act made many millions of dollars available to help farmers meet their mortgages. Another law created the House Owners Loan Corporation (HOLC). Designed to refinance mortgages on nonfarm homes, it ultimately assisted about a million badly pinched households and bailed out mortgage-holding banks.

Harassed by the continuing plague of unemployment, FDR himself established the Civil Works Administration (CWA) late in 1933. As a branch of the Federal Emergency Relief Administration designed to provide purely temporary jobs during the cruel winter emergency, it served a useful purpose. Tens of thousands of jobless people were put to work at leaf raking and other make-work tasks; they were dubbed "boondogglers." Because this kind of labor put a premium on shovel-leaning slow motion, the scheme received wide criticism.

Table 2. Federal minimum wage rates, 1938–2009

Year/Month	Minimum wage rate
10/1938	$0.25
10/1939	$0.30
10/1945	$0.40
01/1950	$0.75
03/1956	$1.00
09/1961	$1.15
09/1963	$1.25
01/1967	$1.40
02/1968	$1.60
05/1974	$2.00
01/1975	$2.10
01/1976	$2.30
01/1978	$2.30
01/1978	$2.65
01/1979	$2.90
01/1980	$3.10
01/1981	$3.35
04/1990	$3.80
04/1991	$4.25
10/1996	$4.75
09/1997	$5.15
07/2007	$5.85
07/2008	$6.55
07/2009	$7.25

Source: U.S. Department of Labor, Wage and Hour Division, 1938–2009.

The Emergency Congress authorized a daring attempt to stimulate a nationwide comeback with the passage of the National Recovery Administration (NRA) measure under the National Industrial Recovery Act (NIRA). This ingenious scheme became by far the most complex and far-reaching effort by the New Dealers to combine immediate relief with long-term recovery and reform. A triple-barreled approach, it assisted industry, labor, and the unemployed.

Labor, under the NRA, received additional benefits. Workers were formally guaranteed the right to organize and bargain collectively through representatives of their own choosing, not handpicked agents of the company's choosing, through Section 7A of the National Recovery Administration measure. The hated yellow-dog, or antiunion, contract remained expressively forbidden and certain safeguarding restrictions continued on the use of child labor.

Unskilled workers now pressed their advantage. A better deal for labor continued when Congress passed the memorable Fair Labor Standards Act (a wages and hours bill) in 1938. Industries involved in interstate commerce set up minimum-wage and maximum-hour levels. Though not immediately established, the specific goals were $.40 an hour (which was later raised) and a 40-hour week. Labor by children under 16 was forbidden (if the occupation involved more dangerous work, the age limit was 18). Many industrialists opposed these reforms, especially southern textile manufacturers who had profited from low-wage labor (see Table 2).

Labor in World War II

During the World War II period, the armed services enrolled more than 15 million men and women. The draft was tightened after Pearl Harbor, as millions of youngsters were plucked from their homes and clothed in "GI" (government-issue) uniforms. With the government keeping an eye on the long pull, key workers in industry and agriculture often received draft deferments. Women desk warriors came into their own. They had been used sparingly in 1917 and 1918, but now some 216,000 women were efficiently employed for noncombat duties, chiefly clerical. The best known of these "women in arms" were the army's WAACs (Women's Auxiliary Army Corps), the marines/navy's WAVES (Women Accepted for Volunteer Emergency Service), and the coast guard's SPARs, named after the coast guard motto "Semper Paratus" (Always Ready).

The "War of Survival" of 1941 to 1945, more than that of 1917 and 1918, became an all-out conflict. Old folks came out of retirement "for the duration" to serve in industry or as air-raid wardens in civilian defense. Western Union telegraph "boys" were often elderly men. Women left the home to work in the heavier industries such as shipbuilding, where Rosie the Riveter won laurels. Rosie also helped to build tanks and airplanes, and when the war ended, she was in no hurry to put down her tools. She and millions of her sisters wanted to keep on working outside the home, and many of them did. The war thus touched off a revolution in the roles played by women in American society.

Labor from the Postwar Years to the Present

During the years following World War II, the growing power of organized workers proved deeply disturbing to many conservatives. Asserting that big labor had become a menace just as big business had once been, die-hard industrialists demanded a showdown. The Republicans gained control of the Congress in 1947, for the first time in 14 years, and proceeded to call the tune. Balding, blunt-spoken Robert A. Taft of Ohio, son of the former president and one of the Republican big guns in the Senate, became the cosponsor of a controversial new labor law known as the Taft-Hartley Act. Congress passed the measure in June 1947, over President Harry S Truman's vigorous veto.

The new Taft-Hartley law promptly became the center of controversy. Partly designated to protect the public, this piece of legislation contained a number of provisions that caused labor leaders to condemn the entire act as a "slave labor law." The provisions outlawing the closed (all-union) shop while making unions liable for damages resulting from jurisdictional disputes among themselves proved especially problematic. The law also required union leaders to take an oath against communism, though employers did not have to comply with the new ruling. But despite labor's pained outcries, Taft-Hartleyism, though annoying, did not cripple the labor movement. By 1950, the AFL could boast 8 million members and the Congress of Industrial Organization (CIO) had 6 million.

Wretched housing became another grievance of labor, as indeed it was for much of the population. New construction had been slowed or halted by the war, while at the same time the country had experienced a baby boom. Tens of thousands of migrant

Table 3. Unemployment rates by month, 2007–2009

Month	2007	2008	2009
January	4.60	4.90	7.60
February	4.50	4.80	8.10
March	4.40	5.10	8.50
April	4.50	5.00	8.90
May	4.50	5.50	9.40
June	4.50	5.50	9.50
July	4.60	5.70	9.40
August	4.60	6.10	9.70
September	4.70	6.10	9.80
October	4.70	6.50	10.20
November	4.70	6.70	10.00
December	5.00	7.20	10.00

Source: U.S. Department of Labor, Bureau of Labor Statistics.

workers, moreover, had concentrated in housing around war industries. This trend was most conspicuous in northern industrial areas such as Detroit and along the Pacific Coast, notably in California, which experienced a spectacular increase of population.

In response to Truman's persistent prodding, Congress finally tackled the housing problem. It passed laws in 1948 and 1949 to provide federally financed construction, despite the protests of real estate promoters and other vested interests. However, these measures, though promising steps forward, fell far short of meeting the pressing need for more and better housing.

During the early 1960s, John F. Kennedy took office, with a narrow Democrat majority in Congress. President Kennedy faced strong opposition from southern Republicans, who put the ax to New Frontier proposals such as medical assistance for the aged and increased federal aid to education. Another vexing problem involved the economy. Kennedy had campaigned on the theme of getting the country moving again after the recession of the Eisenhower years. His administration helped negotiate a noninflationary wage agreement in the steel industry in early 1962.

The current labor force has changed significantly since the turbulent 1960s, the recessional 1970s, the internationally defiant 1980s, and the prosperous 1990s. Today's labor force includes more working women, single parents, workers of color, and older persons. Many companies hire contingent or part-time workers, often for shared jobs. The use of temporary and leased employees has also increased. Disabled employees are being included in the labor force in growing numbers, and this trend has accelerated because of the passage of the Americans with Disabilities Act. After the terrorist attacks of September 11, 2001, even temporary hiring declined sharply as employers downsized to maximize profits. Society may also exert pressures on corporate managers. Increasingly, firms must accomplish their purposes while meeting societal norms. Change continues to occur at an ever-increasing rate, and few firms operate today as they did even a decade ago.

A major concern to management is the effect technological changes have had and will have on business. In recent years, small and midsize companies have created

80 percent of the new jobs. Every year thousands of individuals motivated by a desire to be their own bosses, to earn better incomes, and to realize the American dream launch new business ventures. And many new immigrants from developing areas, especially Southeast Asia and Latin America, continue to swell the U.S. labor force.

During the recession of 2001 and after the terrorist attacks of September 11, many Americans lost their jobs as the recession worsened. Workers in the dot-com technologies sector were hit particularly hard during after the stock market bubble burst at the beginning of the twenty-first century. Early indications of a recovery appeared in June 2003, but with the slow economy, laborers continue to struggle. Many unemployed workers had their unemployment benefits extended under Social Security regulations that cover unemployment in states where the levels exceed normal rates due to crises. As the economic situation began to improve, laborers in some industries started to recover financially until oil prices unexpectedly and dramatically spiked during the first half of 2008. As energy and gasoline fuel prices doubled within a matter of months, many American workers, who were already living paycheck-to-paycheck and living beyond their means because of the availability of easy credit through credit cards, found themselves on the edge of financial disaster when businesses began laying off workers following the onset of the recession that began when the housing bubble burst in August 2007. Unemployment rates, which had remained steady at 4.6 percent from January through August 2007, began to creep up in September to 4.7 percent, reaching 5 percent in December. As the recession deepened, the unemployment rate continued to rise, reaching double digits (10.2 percent) in the October 2009 (see Table 3).

During the recent recession, laborers in the manufacturing sector have borne the heaviest burden, especially in the industrial Midwestern states of Michigan, Ohio, and Pennsylvania. Members of the United Auto Workers' Union (UAW) were forced to accept reductions in their retirement benefits, particularly in the amount they have to contribute or cover for continuing health care benefits. At the close of 2009, the immediate future of labor does not look optimistic at this time.

References

Curtin, Philip D. *The Rise and Fall of the Plantation Complex: Essays in Atlantic History.* New York: Cambridge University Press, 1990.

Laurie, Bruce. *Artisans into Workers: Labor in Nineteenth-Century America.* New York: Hill and Wang, 1989.

Nelson, Daniel. *Shifting Fortunes: The Rise and Decline of American Labor from the 1820s to the Present.* Chicago: I. R. Dee, 1997.

Reynolds, Morgan O. *The History and Economics of Labor Unions.* College Station: Texas A&M University Press, 1985.

U.S. Department of Labor Bureau of Labor Statistics. "Economic News Release: Employment Situation." Available: www.bls.gov; accessed December 24, 2009.

U.S. Department of Labor Wage and Hour Division. "History of Federal Minimum Wage Rates Under the Fair Labor Standards Act, 1938–2009." Available: www.dol.gov/whd/minwage/chart.htm; accessed December 12, 2009.

Land Policies

Cynthia L. Clark

In the original colonial charters, the king granted land to the joint-stock companies or proprietors who then organized the eastern seaboard. Prior to the formation of the United States, most settlers could purchase land, but the terms and quantities allotted to individuals varied with each colony. In Virginia, land could be acquired through outright purchase or under the headright system. Under that system, an individual who paid for the transatlantic passage of another person received 50 acres of land for free; the more passages that were paid for, the more land the individual received. In Massachusetts Bay, the local town officials parceled out the land. In New York, officials received large land grants in lieu of payment for their services. No uniform system of land disbursement existed.

After the formation of the government established under the Articles of Confederation, various states, especially Virginia, ceded land to the national government. Since the Articles did not grant the federal government the power to tax, land sales became the only available source of direct revenue, although states did receive requests for funds, which were usually ignored. The legislative representatives passed three acts that dealt with this territory. The Ordinance of 1784, proposed by Thomas Jefferson, divided the entire region into 10 self-governing districts that could apply for statehood once the population equaled the number of people living in the smallest state. The next year, Congress passed the Ordinance of 1785. This act established the method of selecting surveyors, the system of surveying the land, and the terms of the land sale. Surveyors mapped out seven east-west ranges of 6-mile townships located north of the Ohio River. Each of these townships was divided into 36 sections of 640 acres each. In each township, officials designated section 16 for educational purposes. In addition, the national government, until 1804, reserved the right to four other sections as well as one-third of the mines located in the area. Private individuals or speculators could purchase a minimum of 640 acres for $1 per acre plus any costs. Since the government desperately needed money, all sales had to be transacted in specie (coins) or the paper currency called Continentals. Most individuals could not afford to purchase $640 worth of land in cash all at once, so the early sales went to speculators, who then sold smaller plots to individual farmers at a higher rate per acre. Congress passed the final act under the Articles, the Northwest Ordinance of 1787, which united all of the territory into one administrative unit that could later be subdivided into three to five territories. When the population of the territory reached 60,000,

A settler stands outside his homestead cabin in Oregon's Umqua National Forest. The Homestead Act of 1862 honored claims on public land to anyone who would settle on it and work the land for five years. (Forest History Society.)

the territory could apply for admission as a state. A state constitution had to be drafted that guaranteed the freedom of religion and a right to trial by jury, and then Congress could approve admission. Although this last law did not deal directly with the sale of land, it did encourage investment and migration by promising that individuals who moved west would be treated just like every other American.

Land Policies in the Early Republic

After the ratification of the U.S. Constitution, the federal government continued its former land policies until 1796. That year, Congress allowed the sale of larger plots, ranging from 640 to 5,760 acres, on credit. An investor would purchase the land at $2 per acre and pay 5 percent down, 50 percent in 30 days, and the balance in a year. If the transaction was done in cash, the investor received a 5 percent discount. Four years later, Congress passed the Harrison Land Act of 1800. This legislation allowed for the sale of 320 acres at $2 per acre, with the payments due over four years. By 1804, the minimum size of plots that could be sold fell to 160 acres.

As a result of the smaller purchase requirements and the extension of credit, more speculators purchased land from the federal government, especially after the War of 1812. By 1819, the government held more than $24 million worth of notes, and then a panic hit the United States. Within a few months, the government began requiring cash payment for all future transactions. Congress also established the General Land Office, first under the Department of the Treasury and then under the Department of the Interior. At the same time, the minimum purchase requirement dropped to 80 acres and then fell to 40 by 1820. Nine years later, individuals could purchase public domain land for $1.25 per acre before any government auction.

As the country moved from a subsistence economy to a market economy, the amount of land sold dramatically increased. By 1840, the federal Treasury experienced a surplus from the profits and from higher tariffs. Henry Clay proposed that the national government disburse some of the funds to the states for internal improvements such as roads, canals, and land reclamation. The only stipulation he placed on his bill suspended the disbursements if the average tariff rate exceeded 20 percent. Since the rate went up the following year, only one disbursement payment was made. In 1841, Congress passed Clay's Land Distribution Bill, which granted citizens, individuals who had applied for citizenship, a head of household, or a male over the age of 21 the opportunity to claim 320 acres of land with one year to pay off the balance. Land sales boomed. Then, in 1854, Congress authorized the sale of unsold land after a 30-year period at the rate of $1.25 per acre. These low prices created a speculation fury. Veterans of the Mexican-American War also received military bounties in 1847, 1850, 1852, and 1855. Each veteran who had not already received land could receive 160 acres for his services. Many of these veterans redeemed the bounties and then sold the land to investors for a cheaper price than that asked by the government.

Land Acquisition (1803 to 1860)

By the time of the Civil War, the United States had acquired additional lands. The first major acquisition occurred when the government negotiated with France to buy the Louisiana Purchase in 1803. President Thomas Jefferson hoped to buy an island at the mouth of the Mississippi as a point of transshipment for American goods traveling from the interior down the Mississippi River. He sent special envoys to France to negotiate the agreement, but Napoleon had other plans for the land. He had hoped to use the Louisiana Territory to feed the slave population on Haiti. Once the Haitian revolutionary Toussaint-Louverture led a successful slave rebellion against the French, Napoleon proposed that the United States buy the approximately 529 million acres of the Louisiana Purchase for $15 million. Although Congress debated the agreement, it finally ratified the treaty, thereby increasing the public domain substantially.

The United States also increased the size of its territory in 1819 with the cession of lands from Spain under the Transcontinental Treaty. Then, in 1846, the United States and Great Britain finalized an agreement over the Oregon Territory. The United States obtained all the territory south of the forty-ninth parallel, adding an additional

Table 4. Major land acquisitions

	Year of acquisition
State cessions	1781–1802
Louisiana Purchase	1803
Transcontinental Treaty (Spain)	1819
Oregon	1846
Mexican-American War	1848
Texas	1850
Gadsden Purchase	1853
Alaska	1867

180,644,480 acres to the public domain. Two years later, at the conclusion of the Mexican-American War, the United States acquired most of the Southwest—another 338,680,690 acres in present-day Arizona, New Mexico, and California—in the Treaty of Guadalupe Hidalgo. In 1850, the U.S. Congress passed a joint resolution that allowed for the annexation of Texas. According to the Compromise of 1850, Congress agreed to pay the outstanding debts of Texas in exchange for a cession of land to New Mexico, and Texas became part of the United States. When Congress appropriated funds for the construction of the Transcontinental Railroad, the proposed route had to go through part of Mexico to achieve the best grade for the tracks. In 1853, Congress ratified a treaty with Mexico for the Gadsden Purchase, paying $15 million for 78,926,720 acres of land. The only other substantial acquisition of land occurred in 1867 when the United States purchased 375,303,680 acres in Alaska from Russia, at a cost of $7.2 million (see Table 4).

Land Policies from the Civil War through 1900

Between 1867 and 1879, Congress appropriated funds for four land surveys: the Hayden survey from 1867 to 1878, the King survey from 1867 to 1872, the Wheeler survey from 1869 to 1879, and the Powell survey from 1869 to 1879. In 1879, the United States established the U.S. Geological Survey and charged it with classifying public lands and studying the geology and natural resources of the public domain.

Prior to the Civil War, Congress debated several homestead acts and passed one that President James Buchanan vetoed in 1860. The South resisted the passage of such an act, but once Northern Republicans controlled Congress during the Civil War, they secured passage of the Homestead Act of 1862. The legislation allowed citizens, individuals in the process of becoming naturalized citizens, any head of household, Union veterans, and males over the age of 21 who had never been an enemy or aided an enemy of the United States to claim 160 acres for only a small filing fee. Before title could be transferred, the individual had to establish residency on the land for five years and improve the property. People could also pay for the land after six months instead of waiting out the five years. Smaller plots of 80 acres in alternate sections to railroad lands could also be settled. After the Civil War,

Congress allocated 160 acres for Union veterans, and two years later, the residency requirements for the veterans changed when Congress passed legislation that permitted the years of military service to be deducted from the five-year requirement. Congress also passed the Morrill Land-Grant College Act in 1862. Designed to encourage the growth of agricultural and mechanical schools (A&Ms), this legislation granted each state 30,000 acres for every representative it had in Congress. The land could be sold and the profits used to construct school buildings, or it could become the location of the institution.

During the 1870s, Congress actively promoted westward migration by passing several acts that helped persuade Americans to settle in the arid region west of Kansas. In 1873, the Timber Culture Act granted individuals 160 acres of land if they planted one-quarter of the property in trees. Five years later, Congress passed the Timber and Stone Culture Act, under which individuals could purchase land rich in timber and stone for $2.50 per acre. More Americans took advantage of these two acts than the third, the Desert Land Act of 1877. Hoping to entice Americans to settle the Great American Desert, the government offered 640 acres for irrigation at $.25 per acre at the time of filing and another $1 per acre at the end of two years. The sale of land under the Homestead, Timber Culture, Timber and Stone, and Desert Land Acts proved so successful that the superintendent of the census noted that by 1890, the frontier line had disappeared. However, during the 1870s, numerous fraudulent claims created the need to establish the Public Lands Commission to investigate land claims made under the Preemption and Homestead Laws that were sold to investors. Subsequently, Congress reformed land policies in 1891. Under the General Revision Act, legislators stopped government land auctions, repealed the Timber Culture Act, restricted the total number of acres available to one individual to 160 acres, and allowed the president to establish forest reserves.

Land Policies from 1891 to the Present

The General Revision Act of 1891 marks a transition point in federal land policies. Congress increased the size of the plots being sold to as high as 640 acres and lowered residency requirements to three years in 1912. Ranchers could receive an entire section of land if engaged in the raising of livestock. Other pieces of legislation dealt with restricting the use of the land or managing federal land reserves.

During the late nineteenth century, Presidents Benjamin Harrison, Grover Cleveland, William McKinley, and Theodore Roosevelt exercised their power under the General Revision Act to set aside 194 million acres of land as reserves. Roosevelt placed a tremendous emphasis on the scientific management of these lands, appointing Gifford Pinchot as his chief forester. He would also remove 172 million acres of forest from the land available for settlement, under the terms of the Forest Reserve Act of 1891. He, more than any other president, encouraged the shift from land disposal to conservation and the setting aside of reserves. By 1905, Congress created the Forest Service under the Department of the Interior and then the

Department of Agriculture to administer national forests. In 1916, the management of the national parks transferred to the National Park Service.

Although the federal government restricted the available land for sale to individuals, homestead grants continued at an escalated pace after the passage of the Forest Homestead Law of 1906, which opened up agricultural lands in forest reserves. Congress also passed a new policy in 1905 to encourage the sale and improvement of desert lands. The Newlands Reclamation Act allowed states to use 95 percent of the revenue generated by land sales in the western states to fund irrigation projects. The act proved more successful than the Desert Land Act of 1877.

By the Great Depression, the amount of land available for homesteading had declined dramatically. Yet some pockets remained. Then, in 1934, Congress passed the Taylor Grazing Act, which removed an additional 80 million acres of grazing lands in 22 western states from the property available to the public. Homesteading continued to decline from 1934 on, except in Alaska where Americans could claim land as late as 1986.

Beginning in the 1960s, Congress passed a series of acts designed to protect the natural resources of the country. The Wilderness Act of 1964 covered all wilderness areas. In the same year, Congress also approved the Land and Water Conservation Fund, which appropriated money for the creation and maintenance of outdoor recreational facilities. In 1965, legislators passed the Water Quality Act, establishing clean water standards on the federal level. And, by 1968, the Wild and Scenic Rivers Act allowed for the preservation of rivers with "remarkable recreational, geologic, fish and wildlife, historic, cultural, or other similar values."

The policies of the 1960s continued into the 1970s. At the beginning of the decade, the national government made the protection of the environment a priority by passing the National Environmental Policy Act of 1970. Three years later, Washington issued a list of threatened wildlife granted protection under the Endangered Species Act. In Alaska, 80 million acres of land were withdrawn from public use as forest reserves, wildlife refuges, and scenic areas, and by 1980, Congress had added an additional 47 million acres to the national park system in Alaska. Finally, in 1976, Congress approved the Federal Land Policy and Management Act (FLPMA) to retain all remaining public lands, to survey all natural resources on the land, and to manage the land. Following the passage of the FLPMA, Congress repealed the Homestead Act in the lower 48 states and in Alaska in 1986.

As of the year 2000, the United States no longer had a policy of free or cheap land for its citizens. Debate in the federal government continues to focus on issues such as controlled fires in the national parks and the preservation of endangered species (see Table 5).

Finances

The original intent of the founding fathers in selling land held in the public domain focused on generating revenue for the fledgling nation. Land sales comprised

Table 5. Land policy legislation

Homestead Act	1862
General Mining Law	1872
Timber Culture Act	1873
Desert Land Act	1877
Timber and Stone Act	1878
General Revision Act	1891
Forest Reserve Act	1891
Forest Management Act	1897
Newlands Reclamation Act	1902
Forest Homestead Act	1906
Enlarged Homestead Act	1909
Taylor Grazing Act	1934
Water Quality Act	1965
Wild and Scenic Rivers Act	1968
National Environmental Policy Act	1970
Alaska Native Claims Settlement Act	1971
Endangered Species Act	1973
Federal Land Policy and Management Act	1976
Alaska National Interest Lands Conservation Act	1980

between 1.3 and 9.1 percent of the total receipts of the government in 1801 and 1820, respectively. That amount jumped to a maximum of 49 percent in 1836. The percentage of income derived from the sale of land declined dramatically in the post–Civil War period, as high protective tariffs generated the majority of the federal revenues: By 1880, land receipts amounted to a mere 0.3 percent of the federal income. However, during this same period, the government initiated policies to encourage Americans to migrate westward by offering free or inexpensive land.

Since the amount of revenue generated from the sale of public lands continued to decline, the increased legislation that facilitated the disposal of the public domain occurred for other reasons. Congress was not interested in simply generating money to pay the federal debt. Other motivations include the need to address social problems, such as a wave of massive immigration, a rise in the number of squatters in the post–Civil War period as the country experienced several financial panics that left many Americans deeply in debt, and the rise of tenant farming in the South. By opening up western lands, the government solidified control over the West, and as the population increased in these areas, the territories completed the process of becoming states as specified in the Northwest Ordinance of 1787. In this respect, another of the original intentions of the founding fathers was fulfilled.

U.S. policies regarding land sales also created a variety of problems. First among these was the problem of incomplete record keeping. Although the General Land Office had the responsibility for recording sales, land agents failed to use a uniform system to document transactions. In addition, many people attempted to defraud the government by not fulfilling residency or improvement requirements. The American public, from the beginning, argued that the government policies benefited the

Table 6. Disposition of the public domain, 1781–2002

Type of disposition	Acres
Disposition by methods not elsewhere classified[*]	303,500,000
Granted or sold to homesteaders[†]	287,500,000
Total unclassified and homestead dispositions	**591,000,000**
Granted to states for:	
Support of common schools	77,630,000
Reclamation of swampland	64,920,000
Construction of railroads	37,130,000
Support of miscellaneous institutions[‡]	21,700,000
Purposes not elsewhere classified[§]	117,600,000
Canals and rivers	6,100,000
Construction of wagon roads	3,400,000
Total granted to states	**328,480,000**
Granted to railroad corporations	94,400,000
Granted to veterans as military bounties	61,000,000
Confirmed as private land claims[**]	34,000,000
Sold under timber and stone law[††]	13,900,000
Granted or sold under timber culture law[‡‡]	10,900,000
Sold under desert land law[§§]	10,700,000
Total miscellaneous dispositions	**224,900,000**
Granted to state of Alaska	
State selections[***]	90,100,000
Native selections[†††]	37,400,000
Total granted to state of Alaska	**127,500,000**
Grand total	**1,271,880,000**

[*]Chiefly public, private, and preemption sales, but includes mineral entries, scrip locations, and sales of townsites and townlots.

[†]The homestead laws generally provided for the granting of lands to homesteaders who settled on and improved vacant agricultural public lands. Payment for the lands was sometimes permitted, or required, under certain conditions.

[‡]Universities, hospitals, asylums, etc.

[§]For construction of various public improvements (individual items not specified in the granting acts), reclamation of desert lands, construction of water reservoirs, etc.

[**]The government has confirmed title to lands claimed under valid grants made by foreign governments prior to the acquisition of the public domain by the United States.

[††]The timber and stone laws provided for the sale of lands valuable for timber or stone and unfit for cultivation.

[‡‡]The timber culture laws provided for the granting of public lands to settlers if they planted and cultivated trees on the lands granted. Payments for the lands were permitted under certain conditions.

[§§]The desert land laws provided for the sale of arid agricultural public lands to settlers who irrigated them and brought them under cultivation. Some desert land patents are still being issued.

[***]Alaska Statehood Act of July 7, 1958 (72 Stat. 338), as amended.

[†††]Alaska Native Claims Settlement Act of December 18, 1971 (43 U.S.C. 1601).

Source: Bureau of Land Management; http://www.blm.gov/natacq/pls02/pl1-2_02.pdf; accessed June 29, 2003.

Note: Data are estimated from available records.

speculator more than the individual farmer. Some contended that the sale of public lands at auction allowed groups of investors to form combinations that could artificially hold down the prices. A huge outcry occurred as railroad companies, after receiving more than 64,900,000 acres in land grants, began charging high prices to transport the produce of farmers while providing rebates to large trusts such as Standard Oil.

Although historians do not agree on the exact motivations behind specific bills, they do find patterns indicating that the political parties influenced land policies. For instance, the Republican Party favored giving free land to homesteaders, the Whigs encouraged the sale of land and the disbursement of revenues to the states for internal improvements, and the Democrats promoted preemption. Other patterns concern the amount of land sold or granted during specific periods. Interestingly, the amount of land disposed of under the Homestead Act increased after the General Revision Act of 1891. Prior to the passage of the act, only 52 million acres had been claimed, whereas an additional 230 million acres fell under the Homestead Act provisions after 1891. The federal government's disposition of public land occurred in 1910, when approximately 25 million acres were sold or granted to individuals or the states. Table 6 illustrates how the government disposed of public lands.

The land policies of the U.S. government have influenced settlement patterns, facilitated the development of an internal land transportation system, and assisted states in creating recreation, education, and municipal areas. Since the 1970s, the government has increasingly focused on managing the remaining natural resources, and the disposition of the public domain has virtually ceased. Nonetheless, it is clear that the decisions made in the past continue to impact Americans today.

References

Czech, Brian, and Paul R. Krausman. *The Endangered Species Act: History, Conservation, Biology, and Public Policy.* Baltimore, MD: Johns Hopkins University Press, 2001.

Gates, Paul Wallace. *Public Land Policies: Management and Disposal.* New York: Arno Press, 1979.

Hibbard, Benjamin Horace. *A History of the Public Land Policies.* Madison: University of Wisconsin Press, 1965.

Law

Matthieu J-C. Moss

The United States of America, a former colony of the British Empire, has a legal heritage descended from the English common law system. The American legal system maintains law and order; manages large populations, commerce, and the wealth of the nation; and reflects American culture. Through judicial decisions and legislative action, the law has evolved to remain up-to-date and to represent contemporary society. Consequently, the U.S. Constitution, one of the governing documents of American law, functions as a living organic law, a product of the American experience. An understanding of the American legal system requires an examination of the common law system, how it evolved, and how it came to the United States of America.

Common law refers to the system of laws developed in England and adopted by most of the English-speaking world. Common law uses the concept of stare decisis (let the decision stand) as a basis for its system, with past decisions serving as a high source of authority. Judges draw their decisions from existing principles of law, thus reflecting the living values, attitudes, and ethical ideas of the people. English common law developed purely as a product of English constitutional development. By contrast, most countries of continental Europe and the nations settled by them employ the civil law system—the other principal legal system of the democratic world. Civil law rests on Roman law, which was extended to the limits of the Roman Empire. Islamic law, the third major legal system, relies on the Koran, as interpreted by tradition and juristic writings.

During the reign of Henry II (1154–1189), England adopted a system of royal courts and common law throughout the country. The Judicature Act of 1873 further consolidated a series of statutes and overturned the whole classical structure of the English courts. In the early thirteenth century, the Normans, under William the Conqueror, took to England their laws, which descended from the Scandinavian conquerors of western France. Anglo-Saxon law at that time was well established in England, but the Normans offered refined administrative skills. They established a system of government to deal with the highly decentralized British shires, bringing all the English counties under one common rule. The colonists carried this system of laws to the British colonies in the New World.

The early American legal system adhered to English law but gradually changed over the centuries. Law emerged from the necessary customs and morals of society, even though the colonial judicial system of the eighteenth century in the United States remained notably English. The common law evolved from the customs of the royal courts, though as the legal system developed, previous cases became a source of law. The skeleton of colonial law was shaped in the courts but followed English practice. Unlike the situation in the English system, though, the colonies started off with one court that passed necessary laws. Until 1776, law libraries contained mainly English documents and William Blackstone's *Commentaries on the Laws of England* (1765–1769), a concise and updated resource covering the basics of English law that is still employed today. Early American law literature remained quite sparse.

Although many of the old English laws and traditions prevailed in the colonies, no standardized law existed there. Each colony developed its own system of law, as each state does today (allowing for the existence of the Quebec provincial and Louisiana state legal systems). In 1776, the colonies declared themselves independent. The founding fathers drew up the Articles of Confederation, but they proved unsatisfactory. After the failure of the Articles due to a lack of taxing power, delegates to the Constitutional Convention drafted the federal Constitution that the states signed in 1787. The states also drew up their own constitutions, and federal courts served as the courts of appeal for major state courts. Ultimately, debates developed as to whether the common law system should be overthrown.

Doubts existed as to whether the English common law system would come to dominate North America. With the different nations that were colonizing the North American continent came varying legal systems: The British, French, and Spanish and even the Dutch in Delaware carried with them their own legal cultures and heritages as they settled into their respective territories across the continent. However, by the turn of the nineteenth century, the common law system had taken a firm hold in the United States, and there was little risk that it would be supplanted by the French Napoleonic Code, the only real alternative. Just two remnants of the French legal system continue today in two of France's old colonies—the Province of Quebec in Canada and the State of Louisiana.

By the middle of the nineteenth century, the preconditions for a separate and distinct American jurisprudence had been achieved. Enough time had elapsed since the Declaration of Independence for an American legal heritage to develop. American precedence had been built up, legal texts had been written, and lawyers had been trained in the United States. The American legal system was not yet completely autonomous, and judges still referred to English law for precedents where American law was lacking, but those areas became fewer and fewer as the years went by. One clear distinction came with the transition in land laws. In England the legal system facilitated land inheritance through primogeniture. A significant break came in the 1850s when the United States rejected the notion of passing on all land to the eldest son. This decision reflected the emergence of a legal system independent from English law.

Legal Terms and Applications

Two types of court cases—civil and criminal—exist in the United States. Plaintiffs initiate civil cases, in which a company or an individual sues for financial reparations, whereas the state prosecutes criminal cases, which involve punishments of fines or imprisonment. Common law and equity (whereby both parties benefit) remain separate in that equity deals with more than simply financial reparations. In England, the Courts of Chancery and the Star Chamber, which deal with equity matters, have the authority to force people to undertake certain actions, such as selling property—something that is not done in a civil case. Equity receiverships allow courts to take possession of assets and redistribute them. In the United States, the process of equity receivership was not dealt with until the formulation of stable bankruptcy laws in 1898.

Most legal thought develops institutionally, not individually, through processes occurring in the courtroom and legislative chambers. Legislation, which is promulgated in the legislative branch of the government, involves a new rule or law that has just taken effect and specifies when the law is applicable. Case law, by contrast, is retroactive. Taxes offer a good case study in this regard. With legislation, individuals can only be taxed on money they have earned from the moment the law was passed, whereas with a case law, a ruling can deem that individuals owe the government back taxes. For this reason, courts must take into account the effects their decisions will have; consequently, courts usually issue conservative decisions.

A contract constitutes a binding agreement that two or more individuals or entities enter into—an enforceable promise that is to be carried out at a future date. Two types of contracts exist. A contract of sale is the most common and is usually made instantaneously, as when purchasing goods. The second involves a more complicated transaction, usually associated with a trading or commercial situation, involving a guarantee to provide goods or services in the future. In Anglo-American law, contracts can be formal (written documents) or informal (implied in speech or writing). A stable society requires both types of contracts.

For almost 700 years, the jury system has been an important part of the legal system. There are two types of juries. The petit jury hears both civil cases (to establish damages that will be awarded) and criminal cases (to establish guilt). The grand jury, which functions as an accusatory body, establishes, based on evidence presented to it, whether a case warrants trial. The jury system is much criticized for being flawed because jurors tend to make their decisions based on emotion rather than rational thought. Presently, the grand jury exists in only half the United States and in the federal courts.

Commerce Clause

The commerce clause, as presented in the U.S. Constitution, gives the government the power "to regulate commerce with foreign nations, and among the several states, and

Supreme Court Chief Justice John Marshall. (Library of Congress.)

with the Indian tribes." In order to regulate enormously powerful business corporations, to carry forward programs of social welfare and economic justice, to safeguard the rights of individual citizens, and to allow that diversity of state legislation so necessary in a federal system of government, the Supreme Court eventually defined what constituted commerce.

The period from 1824 to 1937 saw several important events in the adjudication of the commerce clause before the Supreme Court. *Gibbons v. Ogden* (1824) was the first case in which the Court interpreted and applied that particular clause of the U.S. Constitution. The commerce clause came about because states erected barriers to protect manufacturers within their borders. *Gibbons v. Ogden* emerged because the state of New York prevented Thomas Gibbons, a resident of Elizabethtown, New Jersey, from running his ferry service between New Jersey and New York, in competition with the ferry service of Col. Aaron Ogden of New York. Lawyers argued the steamboat case in front of the Supreme Court in February 1824. Daniel Webster and William Wirt (the U.S. attorney general from 1817 to 1829) represented qGibbons, and Thomas J. Oakley and Thomas A. Emmet represented Ogden. Webster argued that the federal government retained the sole authority over commerce and that the states lacked the power to enact laws affecting it. Emmet, for his part, argued for a narrow definition of commerce. He contended that Congress might have an incidental power to regulate navigation but only insofar as that navigation occurred for the limited purposes of commerce. Emmet argued that the individual states had always exercised the power of making material regulations respecting commerce.

Robert F. Wagner guided so many key New Deal bills through the U.S. Senate that he was dubbed the "legislative pilot of the New Deal." (Library of Congress.)

On March 2, 1824, Justice John Marshall handed down his decision. He rejected the premise that the expressly granted powers of the Constitution should be constructed strictly. He took the word *commerce* and gave it a broad definition, he extended the federal power to regulate commerce within state boundaries, and he gave wide scope to the Constitution grant in applying these powers.

Following the *Gibbons v. Ogden* case, the Supreme Court presided over the watershed case *Cooley v. Board of Wardens of the Port of Philadelphia* (1852), which cleared up questions raised in the *Gibbons v. Ogden* decision. First, the Supreme Court held that certain subjects of national importance demanded uniform congressional regulation, whereas others of strictly local concern properly remained under the jurisdiction of state regulation. Second and perhaps most important, the Court gave itself great power by becoming the final arbitrator in decisions that would affect the core of the American federal system. The commerce clause has proven extremely important in America's legal history because through it, the government has exercised a tremendous amount of centralized authority. Using the commerce clause, the government could weld the diverse parts of the country into a single nation.

As a result of *Cooley v. Board of Wardens*, states were able to impose tariffs on shipping through their territories, but the courts would strike down laws if state regulation favored local businesses. On February 4, 1887, Congress passed the Interstate Commerce Act to regulate rail rates, which were running rampant. It also established the five-person Interstate Commerce Commission (ICC), but the act could not properly enforce the Interstate Commerce Act until the passage of the Hepburn Act in 1906, the Mann-Elkins Act of 1910, and the Federal Transportation Act of 1920. Around 1900, Congress used the commerce clause to regulate the national economy and certain businesses as well. The Supreme Court, in the process, gave an expanded interpretation of the scope of national authority contained in that delegated power, but it never gave complete free rein to the commerce clause, which led to the rise of the doctrine of dual federalism.

The concept of dual federalism involves the notion that the national government functions as one of two powers and that the two levels of government—national and state—operate as sovereign and equal entities within their respective spheres. With dual federalism, state powers expanded. And as a direct consequence of dual federalism, the federal government could not regulate child labor: The Supreme Court reasoned that child labor remained purely a local matter, keeping it out of the regulatory reach of the federal government.

With the New York Stock Market crash in 1929 and the onset of the Great Depression, the Court reversed its policy on dual federalism. To deal with the depression, President Franklin D. Roosevelt implemented his reforms in economics, agriculture, banking and finance, manufacturing, and labor, all of which involved statutes that the Court had struck down before. Congress passed the National Labor Act (Wagner Act) on July 5, 1935, regulating labor-management relations in industry and creating the National Labor Relations Board (NLRB). *National Labor Relations Board v. Jones & Laughlin* (1937) became the first test case before the Supreme Court. The circuit courts had ruled in favor of the Jones & Laughlin Steel Corporation of Pittsburgh, citing *Carter v. Carter Coal Co.,* which distinguished between production and commerce. The Supreme Court did not uphold this distinction, and as a result, the NLRB was able to order companies to desist from certain labor practices if they adversely affected commerce in any way. By the end of 1938, the authority of the NLRB extended to companies that were wholly intrastate, that shipped goods in interstate commerce, or that provided essential services for the instrumentation of commerce.

The two other important cases dealing with the commerce clause were *United States v. Darby* (1941) and *Wickard v. Filburn* (1942). The rulings from these cases resolved the confusion surrounding the commerce clause once and for all. The Supreme Court found that the clause "could reach any individual activity, no matter how insignificant in itself, if, when combined with other similar activities, it exerted a 'substantial economic effect' on interstate commerce." The Court did away with the old distinction between commerce and production, bringing manufacturing, mining, and agriculture into—and making them inseparable from—commerce. The Supreme Court also did away with the constitutional doctrine of dual federalism and denied states the power to limit the delegated powers of the federal government.

Since 1937, the Court's interpretation of the commerce clause has given Congress broad and sweeping powers to regulate labor-management relations. By the end of 1942, the Supreme Court had also given Congress extensive authority to regulate commerce, but this authority did not extend to the insurance industry because insurance was deemed more of a contract than a business. The Court refused to hear cases dealing with insurance until 1944 in *United States v. South-Eastern Underwriters Association*, a case in which Justice Hugo L. Black held that both the commerce clause and the Sherman Anti-Trust Act could be applied to the insurance business.

Bankruptcy Law

Bankruptcy law in the United States gives more favorable treatment to debtors than to creditors. Moreover, the courts view bankruptcy not as a last resort but rather as another option to resolve financial difficulties. Famous individuals declare bankruptcy quite frequently and for different reasons; for example, they may use bankruptcy to get out of a contract.

Another characteristic of U.S. bankruptcy law is that lawyers are used to declare bankruptcy, whereas in other nations, bankruptcy decisions are made through an administrative process. A bankruptcy judge oversees the process in the United States, and both the debtor and the creditor usually retain counsel. By contrast, in England, another market-based economy, an administrator supervises the process, and the debtor (whether an individual or a business) rarely has the option of being represented by counsel. This is an interesting development, given the fact that when U.S. bankruptcy laws were first enacted in 1800, they resembled the English laws almost exactly.

Two types of bankruptcies exist in the U.S. legal system—one for individuals and another for corporations. For individuals, Chapter 7 bankruptcy involves a straight liquidation, whereby all of the individual's assets are liquidated and used to pay off creditors. The court then relieves the debtor of his or her entire burden. An individual may also file a Chapter 13 bankruptcy. This chapter of the Bankruptcy Code provides for a rehabilitation case, whereby the debtor pays a portion of the debt over a period of three to five years—making this a less stigmatizing form of bankruptcy. Thus, an individual has two options when declaring bankruptcy: either liquidation (Chapter 7) or rehabilitation (Chapter 13). In both cases, the debtor can retain certain assets in order to be able to make a fresh start. A debtor or creditor can initiate a bankruptcy claim, but most of the time, such claims are made voluntarily by the debtor.

As with individual bankruptcy, a company can file for either liquidation or reorganization. For the corporation, Chapter 7 involves liquidation, but it is complete and with no exemptions. Chapter 11 allows for the rehabilitation of companies. On occasion, individuals can invoke Chapter 11 and small businesses can file Chapter 13 bankruptcies.

In the late eighteenth century, bankruptcy law involved an ideological struggle between opposing groups. On the one hand, Alexander Hamilton and the Federalists believed that the future of America lay with commerce and that bankruptcy laws were essential to protect both creditors and debtors; they argued that these laws would encourage credit, thereby fueling commercial growth. Thomas Jefferson and the Republicans, on the other hand, feared that a federal bankruptcy law would erode the importance of farmer's property rights and shift power from the state to the federal court.

Debates raged throughout the nineteenth century on such issues as whether only debtors could invoke bankruptcy laws. Congress enacted three bankruptcy laws (in 1800, 1841, and 1867) but repealed each of them a few years later, since legislators had hastily formulated the acts to respond to grave economic distress. The bankruptcy legislation of 1898, however, had staying power. In the end, the nation's first large-scale corporate reorganization, which involved the bankruptcy of many railroads during the 1890s, resulted in stable bankruptcy laws. The courts, not Congress, dealt with this problem, creating a process known as equity receivership.

Congress amended U.S. bankruptcy laws most recently in the Bankruptcy Act of 2005, signed into law on October 17, 2005. The act required debtors with incomes over a certain level to repay creditors instead of simply discharging the debt and must wait a minimum of eight years, up from six years, before being eligible to file for bankruptcy again. It also required the completion of mandatory credit counseling from an approved agency 180 days prior to filing a bankruptcy petition as well as a second post-petition course on personal financial management. The law also allowed for the interception of income tax refunds and the reporting of back due child support, the withholding of a debtor's income to repay a loan from an ERISA qualified pension plan sponsored by the debtor's employer, and allows landlord's to continue the eviction process against a tenant if the eviction order was obtained prior to the tenant filing his or her bankruptcy petition. The Bankruptcy Act of 2005 also expands the definition of student loans to comply with the definition for such loans as provided under the Internal Revenue Code. One of the most significant portions of the act involves changes involving the discharge of credit card debt. A debtor who owes one creditor a debt of more than $500 for luxury goods purchased within 90 days of filing a bankruptcy petition or obtained a cash advance of more than $750 within 70 days of the filing cannot have those debts discharged; luxury goods are defined to exclude those goods and services reasonably necessary for support or maintenance.

Effective U.S. bankruptcy laws went through three eras. The first involved the enactment of the 1898 Bankruptcy Act and the perfection of the equity receivership technique for large-scale reorganizations. The Great Depression and the New Deal marked the second era, during which bankruptcy reforms reinforced and expanded the general bankruptcy practice and completely reshaped the landscape of large-scale corporate reorganization. The enactment of the 1978 Bankruptcy Code and the revitalization of bankruptcy practice initiated the final era.

Antitrust Law

Today, antitrust law shapes the policy of almost every large company in the world. Following World War II, the United States wanted to impose its antitrust tradition on the rest of the world. Contradictions existed between nations, as most industrial countries tolerated (or even encouraged) cartels whereas the United States banned them. The antitrust concept has a hallowed place in American economic and political life. Antitrust legislation focuses on preventing collusion among competing firms hoping to raise prices and hinder competition. European markets, by contrast, set minimum prices and cooperated with cartels. This policy protected the smaller firms, stabilized markets, and kept the overall economy stable.

In the 50 years before World War II, nations backed away from the idea of economic competition as promoting the common good. The pace of the retreat, at first gradual, picked up with the outbreak of World War I. The expansion of cartels was among the chief manifestations of this trend, and cartels played an ever-growing role in domestic and international trade and by 1939 had become a major factor in the world economy. The United States remained the only country of the industrialized world to reject the notion of cartels, and it reacted to cartels abroad by increasing tariff barriers. Americans respected the efficiency of big business but feared its economic and political powers. They placed great confidence in economic competition as a check on the power of big business, and they looked askance at cartels. As a result, Washington regulated the activities of large firms, outlawing cartels and imposing other restrictions on companies.

Congress passed the Sherman Anti-Trust Act of 1890 as the first measure directed against big business. In 1914, during the administration of President Woodrow Wilson, Congress also passed the Clayton Anti-Trust and Federal Trade Commission Acts. With the Great Depression, however, Franklin Roosevelt secured passage of the National Industrial Recovery Act (NIRA), which suspended the antitrust laws and allowed cartels during the economic downturn under "codes of conduct for each industry." In his second term, Roosevelt went on a strong antitrust crusade, creating the Temporary National Economic Committee (TNEC) and the Justice Department's Antitrust Division, headed by Thurman Arnold. Before the outbreak of war in Europe in 1939, Arnold concentrated on domestic conditions. But the war forced him to pay more attention to foreign affairs. His Antitrust Division operated constructively in peacetime, but he failed to see the importance of cartels in wartime, when free market rules are suspended and close cooperation is needed. Although the government retreated from its antitrust position during the war, Washington would pick it up again afterward.

With the onset of World War II, American firms participating in cartels experienced difficulties, as did those involved in the antitrust drive. Since the United States remained technically neutral, cartel agreements with German firms remained in place. American businesses did not sever their ties because of the advantages gained, such as access to innovations, and Congress did not suspend cartel agreements because if it had, the executive branch would have had to admit that war with

Germany remained a possibility. Furthermore, the need to coordinate mobilization and placate the business community led to sharp restrictions on the antitrust drive.

After World War II, the United States began to focus its attention on foreign cartels. A small group associated with the Antitrust Division of the Justice Department took an interest in foreign affairs and used the division's position in the world to attack foreign cartels, believing that Europe's failures resulted from its lack of an antitrust tradition. But domestic markets outside the United States facilitated cartels because they remained necessary to the smaller economies. According to Wyatt Wells, in his work *Antitrust and the Formation of the Postwar World*, the successful export of the antitrust concept depended on economic development abroad. After 1945, the nations of Western Europe integrated their markets, stabilized their currencies, and built or reinforced democratic governments. In this context, companies could afford competition, and most European governments responded to Washington's urging and enacted antitrust statutes roughly comparable to those in American law. Yet in the absence of favorable conditions—for example, in Japan—antitrust foundered.

The postwar attack on cartels was advanced, in part, under the banner of free trade. However, long-term goals such as commercial liberalization would have to wait, as nations simply tried to stabilize the postwar world economy. They created the International Trade Organization (ITO) to deal with this concern, and few firms (the De Beers diamond cartel and shipping businesses being the notable exceptions) escaped the blows dealt by the U.S. courts. In the early 1950s, as Western nations achieved a measure of prosperity, cartel policy also achieved a certain level of equilibrium. Radical decartelization failed in Japan and Germany, but court decisions in the United States had struck the seriously weakened international cartels. Monopoly remained suspect, and cartels were largely forbidden, but big business would continue as long as competition persisted. In practice, some cartels were allowed to exist if they could cite special circumstances or command substantial political support.

Legal Education

In the early days of the colonies, lawyers played a small role and were generally unwelcome; indeed, pleading for hire was prohibited by the Massachusetts *Body of Liberties* (1641). Over time, however, lawyers came to fulfill two important functions in the legal system: providing advice and practicing advocacy. Today, some lawyers specialize in courtroom work (like English barristers), and others work in their offices (like English solicitors/attorneys). In Britain, the two specializations remained separate, though this is not the case in the United States. In America, lawyers receive training at law schools, which are usually affiliated with a university, whereas in Britain, they train at one of the four Inns of Court, a combination of law school and professional organization.

The history of the law school in the United States differs from that of legal education in the rest of the common law system. Only in North America can a law school function completely apart from the rest of the university with which it is affiliated.

Before the Civil War, law schools played a minor role in the training of lawyers. The trend of educating attorneys in law schools began only in the early years of the twentieth century, and it developed for numerous reasons, mainly to achieve higher standards, establish standardization, and exclude immigrants from the field. (The American Bar Association [ABA] and the American Association of Law Schools [AALS] wanted to exclude immigrants because they did not espouse the values of the dominant Anglo-Saxon Protestants.) Clearly, the raising of standards played an important role, for elite lawyers (like elites in other fields of the time) wished to establish more rigorous academic instruction.

The ABA and AALS campaigned on two fronts: (1) to increase standards required of accredited universities and (2) to secure legislation that would impose these higher standards. Not until 1928 did states require attorneys to attend law school before practicing in the field. This mandatory policy largely involved competition with schools that taught law on a part-time basis or at night that could not meet the required standards. These schools fiercely resisted any attempt at change, but the economic situation of the Great Depression forced many of them to shut down.

With the closure of the "lesser" law schools, the ABA and AALS had the freedom to implement a legal training system of their choosing. The bar exam became compulsory, and without passing it, lawyers could not practice in any state. The standards of the bar rose, making it more difficult to pass the exam. Harvard University played a large part in setting these standards. Christopher Columbus Langdell, the first dean of the Harvard Law School, promoted graduate professional education for lawyers in order to elevate the Harvard program from mediocrity to distinction. Other universities quickly followed suit by establishing law schools of their own or by bringing independent institutions under their auspices. Acceptance into law school became more selective, especially with the implementation of the Law School Admission Test (LSAT) in 1948.

Today's law schools in the United States produce considerable legal writings in their law reviews. Most of these schools publish journals, and eminent lawyers and law professors write the lead articles. These works are probably more valuable than any other secondary legal source. Indeed, doctrinal writing holds an important place as a secondary source of law in the Anglo-American legal system.

Conclusion

The American legal system, once intrinsically linked with English law, has come into its own over the past couple of centuries. Today, it has become a model for many of the emerging democracies. Through the legal and legislative branches of the government, American law has adequately managed the commerce and the wealth of the nation, while also reflecting American values. At the turn of the twentieth century, antitrust legislation, bankruptcy legislation, and the commerce clause all emerged to deal with the rise of big business. In addition, modern American law schools successfully train American lawyers, thus maintaining an independent American legal tradition.

References

Benson, Paul R., Jr. *The Supreme Court and the Commerce Clause, 1937–1970*. New York: Dunellen Publishing, 1970.

Billias, George Athan, ed. *Law and Authority in Colonial America: Selected Essays*. Barre, MA: Barre Publishers, 1965.

Friedman, Lawrence M. *A History of American Law*. New York: Simon and Schuster, 1973.

Horwitz, Morton J. *The Transformation of American Law, 1780–1860*. New York: Oxford University Press, 1992.

Kempin, Frederick G., Jr. *Historical Introduction to Anglo-American Law in a Nutshell*. St. Paul, MN: West Publishing, 1973.

Schwartz, Bernard. *The Law in America: A History*. New York: McGraw-Hill, 1974.

Skeely, David A., Jr. *Debt's Dominion: A History of Bankruptcy Law in America*. Princeton, NJ: Princeton University Press, 2001.

The Standard Legal Law Library. "Recent Changes in Bankruptcy Laws: An Overview of the Bankruptcy Act of 2005." Available: http://www.standardlegal.com/law-library/Recent-Bankruptcy-Law-Changes.html; accessed December 2, 2009.

Stevens, Robert. *Law School: Legal Education in America from the 1850s to the 1980s*. Chapel Hill: University of North Carolina Press, 1983.

Wells, Wyatt. *Antitrust and the Formation of the Postwar World*. New York: Columbia University Press, 2002.

Monetary Policy

David T. Flynn

Monetary policy is the branch of economic policy that attempts to achieve goals such as stabilizing employment and prices as well as fostering economic growth through the manipulation of the monetary system; it achieves these goals by employing certain variables, among them the supply of money, the level and term structure of interest rates, and the overall availability of credit in the economy. Modern central banks, such as the Federal Reserve system (the Fed), have a variety of policy goals. Although most focus on price stability, the Federal Reserve strives to meet six different, legislatively mandated goals: (1) price stability, (2) financial market stability, (3) high employment, (4) economic growth, (5) foreign exchange stability, and (6) interest rate stability.

Money is anything generally accepted in exchange for goods or services or in the payment of debts. Money also has three functions: It serves as a medium of exchange, as a unit of account, and as a store of value. A medium of exchange is an item that facilitates exchange between parties; a unit of account is the standard for assessing value or price; and a store of value is an asset function for money. Money fits into the national economy in many ways. The government finances its spending by taxing, by borrowing through the issuing of bonds, and by printing money. There are other beneficial aspects to monetary policy as well, such as interest rate management. The goals of monetary policy were similar even before the existence of the Fed.

To understand monetary policy, one must understand interest rates. According to the relationship known as the Fisher equation, nominal interest rates (the rates that are quoted in the financial market) can be broken down into two separate parts—the real interest rate (i.e., the real cost of borrowing) and peoples' expectations of inflation, with inflation defined as a sustained increase in the general level of prices. Roughly speaking, the nominal interest rate is equal to the real interest rate plus expected inflation.

For a substantial portion of its history, the United States operated on a specie standard, with other currency (such as banknotes or Treasury notes) being convertible into specie (gold or silver). The price of gold was fixed in terms of dollars, which meant that any other countries that guaranteed the convertibility of currency—that is, any other countries on a gold standard—had a fixed exchange rate relationship with the United States. The price-specie flow mechanism would then keep the exchange rates balanced. A fall in prices in the United States caused by an aggregate demand shock or an increase in aggregate supply meant that U.S. goods were relatively cheap compared to foreign goods. This situation resulted in an increase in foreign demand for U.S. goods and larger flows of gold into the country to pay for larger purchases of goods. The increased gold stock in the United States boosted the money supply, and as a result, the price level would rise to its original level.

Policy goals are seldom achieved directly, and the enactment of monetary policy thus comes through the manipulation of the bank system. Specifically, the monetary policy authority changes the level of reserves in the banking system, influencing the ability of banks to provide credit to customers. Increases in reserves lead to increases in credit availability, which is expansionary, and the reverse process leads to contraction. Even without an official central bank, governments enact policy in this fashion.

The British North American Colonies

The North American colonies of England experienced several changes in monetary policy. Specie was the legal tender for international payments and was equated with wealth and power. Each colony had its own pound (£) as the unit of account, with a mandated exchange rate of £133.33 colonial to £100 sterling. The colonies did attempt to manage their exchange rates and attract gold to the borders by selling items to foreign countries directly instead of through Britain. They also experimented with paper money, which was considered legal tender for domestic transactions only. Of course, the institutions developed to operate this policy were not the same as the ones existing today. For instance, there was no central bank, such as the Federal Reserve Bank system, to oversee the colonial money supply. Instead, each colony ran its own independent policy, and as a result, the supply of paper notes in any colony typically included the notes of bordering colonies; this situation led to difficulties in defining the money supply and problems in terms of price level in the region. The individuals responsible for operating fiscal policy, government spending, and taxing decisions also made the monetary policy decisions. There was a perceived shortfall of media of exchange at this time, and the notes were to add liquidity to the economy. The media included paper notes issued by the colonial government; any minted gold and silver coins in circulation, both foreign and domestic; and sterling bills of exchange. The notes were issued as mortgages, typically a loan of up to one-half the value of pledged property. The government accepted the notes in payment for the loan but also imposed taxes at the same time, for which the notes were legal tender. In this way, the government would be able to retire the notes and avoid inflation. Unfortunately, retirements and issues were at times excessive, leading to large increases in the value of notes in circulation and fluctuations in the price level, though this was not universal. In fact, price-level fluctuations did not match well the changes in the stock of money in many colonies. There is serious debate about why this was the case, centering on the idea of the backing for the currency. The future tax receipts were considered as the backing of the currency, much like gold is when the country is on a gold standard. Disputes focus on the issues of exchange rates and the credibility of taxing authorities.

The Revolutionary War provides another early lesson in monetary policy. The Continental Congress acted as the government for the rebelling colonies and needed to finance the war effort. Lacking the ability to tax and unable to issue bonds, the Congress turned to a third option—printing money, the now famous Continental. The Continental Congress issued excessive amounts of the notes, to the point that they depreciated dramatically: thus the phrase "Not worth a Continental." In all, continental currency, state paper notes, and quartermaster certificates totaled nearly $400 million, which clearly contributed to inflation. The debate over this currency can be cast in the same light as the one over the colonial government note issues, in which the value of the currency wildly fluctuated.

The First and Second Banks of the United States

With great effort and skill, Treasury Secretary Alexander Hamilton convinced Congress to approve the First Bank of the United States in 1791, with a 20-year charter. There were serious political concerns about the operations of the First Bank, particularly the lack of state control over a branch bank operating within the state's borders. It also seemed unfair to many that state banks would be forced to compete against a national commercial bank. Despite its name, the First Bank was not to have the same functions and goals as a modern central bank; instead, it would increase the productive capacity of the economy. The bank would be large and have operations in many states and therefore would provide a uniform paper currency throughout the United States. At the same time, it would also maintain the government's credit. The bulk of the bank's capitalization took the form of government bonds, which provided an additional benefit to the government. By holding a portion of the debt as capital, the bank helped keep government borrowing costs—the interest rates on government debt—low.

The First Bank did not realize its full potential as a commercial bank, but this was the result of a prudent strategy. The complaints already mentioned would have multiplied if the First Bank branches had made large numbers of loans, taking business from state-chartered banks. The First Bank did, however, take some actions that resembled those of a central bank. For instance, if general financial market conditions dictated a reduction in available credit, the First Bank would present accumulated notes of other banks for redemption in specie, forcing those banks to further reduce their note issues because they now had a smaller reserve of specie. If the First Bank deemed looser credit conditions were necessary, it could expand its own lending operations, either to businesses or to banks, and create a multiplied expansion of bank credit. The First Bank could also affect this policy by declining to present banknotes for redemption in specie. The large government deposits and larger than normal reserve holdings of the First Bank of the United States allowed for the bank's adoption of this function. The First Bank then conducted monetary policy by manipulating the specie holdings, or reserves, of other banks in the nation. The bank performed its functions well throughout its charter, but because of the continued political contro-versy, particularly on the constitutionality of the First Bank, its charter was not renewed upon expiration. The Treasury then became the primary economic policy-maker for the U.S. government.

In the absence of the First Bank, the Treasury came to rely on the state banks. Treasury deposits in state banks led to expansions of bank credit and eventually infla-tion and problems with the payment system in the United States. The financing of the War of 1812 increased the Treasury debt and contributed to the expansion of bank credit. The Treasury notes functioned as bank reserves, since they were a partial legal tender and national money, and this led to a large expansion in available bank credit and in the number of banks. The inflation caused problems with convertibility, an export of gold and silver to other countries, and a concentration of domestic deposits of gold and silver in the Northeast, as banks in that region did not have such a high number of banknotes in circulation.

The note issues were so excessive that the Treasury accepted banknotes as pay-ment because a failure to do so would lead to a financial crisis and bank failures. The supporters of a new national bank pointed to the improved security that would exist in the banking sector as a significant reason to establish a new institution. The Treasury, in particular, endorsed the idea of a national bank to aid in a return to more stable monetary and financial conditions.

The United States was concerned with resuming the specie convertibility of banknotes in 1816, and it was into this policy era that the Second Bank of the United States entered. Treasury Secretary William H. Crawford recognized the role of the Treasury notes in the large issues of bank paper notes. As government receipts increased in the period after the War of 1812, the Treasury was able to retire a signifi-cant number of its notes, which reduced bank reserves and led to a decrease in avail-able bank credit and note issue. The deflation that ensued moved the Second Bank toward the resumption of specie payments. In this way, the Treasury was acting as a modern central bank, directing monetary policy and using the Second Bank as a scapegoat to take the complaints of bankers, businesses, and debtors hurt by the decline in prices and economic activity.

Initially, the Second Bank had the same role as the First Bank—providing a source of demand for government debt. The Treasury was the active player in mon-etary policy, adjusting its issues of debt and levels of deposits in the banking system. Later in the life of the Second Bank, Nicholas Biddle implemented monetary policy through the bank. He did not come to the bank with these ideas but rather developed them after examining the institution's practices and the financial conditions in the United States. The banking system at the time was based on the convertibility of bank-issued paper currency, or notes, into gold. In an effort to guarantee both the security and the soundness of the banking system, as well as control the level of currency in circulation, the Second Bank undertook to control banknote issues. As the depository institution of the federal government, the Second Bank had a larger source of funds to use than the rest of the banking system. As such, it came to hold a large number of commercial banknotes. If leaders of the Second Bank felt that the note issues of any commercial bank were excessive (or nearly excessive), they could threaten to present sufficient amounts of the bank's paper currency in their possession for payment in specie. If the bank did not have a sufficient reserve of gold available, they would be forced to suspend conversion—essentially, they would fail. Through this mechanism, the Second Bank was able to use its gold reserves to exert significant control over the banking system, but it was exactly this ability that caught the attention of many legislators who abhorred this authority in general and especially in a nonelected official such as the president of the Bank of the United States, who was appointed. The ability to conduct monetary policy was also a political liability, as many were concerned that there was the potential for much to go wrong with an inept or "evil" person in control of the bank.

From the post–Civil War era to the founding of the Federal Reserve, the Department of the Treasury was responsible for monetary policy management in the United States. To finance the Civil War, the Union had an option not truly available to the Confederacy—issuing bonds. Unfortunately, the large issues of bonds would drive up the costs of borrowing by raising the interest rate. As it had done with the First and Second Banks, the government looked to create a demand for its debt. It did this through the National Bank system. The capital of the banks in this system could be U.S government debt, which created a demand for the bonds. To get banks to switch from state charters to national bank charters required further legislation. The state banks were doing fine and did not see any reason to adopt more stringent federal rules in their operations. To provide an incentive for the banks to switch charters, the government imposed a prohibitive tax of 10 percent on state banknote issues. The costs were so high that many switched their charters. It was through adjustments in the level of Treasury deposits in the banking system that policy changes were enacted. These changes also altered the level of reserves in the system and either expanded or contracted the available amount of bank credit. This situation would lead to an adjustment throughout the entire banking sector, which would change the prevailing credit conditions and result, it was hoped, in achievement of the desired policy goal. A significant change in the banking system came as part of the Union's effort to finance the Civil War.

The Federal Reserve Bank System before the Great Depression

When members of Congress created the Federal Reserve Bank system, they intended to reduce the seasonal fluctuations observed in the economy over the course of a year and to end the cycle of panics in the financial system; the system experienced major banking crises in 1873, 1884, 1890, 1893, and 1907. The Fed was to meet these goals by providing an elastic currency. The credit flowing from the Federal Reserve to the commercial banking sector would counter the normal cyclical behavior of the economy and smooth out fluctuations in economic performance and activity. The only tool available to the Fed was the discounting of eligible securities. Through this process, banks would increase reserves and have more credit available when needed, for example, during a recession.

World War I was an early challenge for the monetary policy of the Fed. Although initially not directly involved in the conflict, the United States supplied the warring parties with goods, which resulted in a large inflow of gold to the country. The Fed did not have sufficient stocks of securities to sterilize, or offset, the increase in money supply. Sterilization would involve the government selling securities for gold, which would reduce the reserves in the system. The only option was to increase the discount rate, though the Fed did not do that. The gold influx stopped when the United States entered the war and provided its Allies with credit for purchases. At this time, the young central bank agreed to an accommodation policy with the Treasury, wherein the Fed kept government borrowing costs low in order to assist with the war effort. The accommodation created an expansionary environment for bank credit, which led to acceleration of inflation. The gold standard eventually triggered an export of gold from the United States, which reduced the supply of money. The Fed did not take action until 1920, when outflows of gold reached critical levels. The Fed raised the discount rate, which stopped the exodus of gold but, in turn, led to a decrease in the price level and economic activity and a recession in 1920 and 1921.

During the 1920s, the Fed discovered its second policy tool—open market operations, or the purchase and sale of government securities. Although these operations were known before the 1920s, they were used only as a source of revenue for the Fed, not as part of a monetary policy. Gradually, the effect of purchases on interest rates was noticed. The connection between the bank reserves and a fractional reserve system led to the conclusion that if the Fed purchased securities from commercial banks, that would lead to an increase in bank reserves and the ability of banks to increase credit in the economy through the multiple expansion of deposits and loans and thus lower interest rates. Despite its importance, this understanding was not always used appropriately in the 1920s to offset expansions in the money supply.

The Federal Reserve System and the Great Depression

The Fed's failure to end stock market speculation early in the 1920s led to a large run-up in stock prices, which it felt unable to stop. The Fed was not able to help strengthen the weakening economy for fear of feeding the speculation in equities. Moral suasion proved ineffective, and eventually, the Fed signaled its policy change by raising the discount rate. The economic hardship of the Great Depression is well documented: nearly 25 percent unemployment; a reduction in the U.S. capital stock; and a dramatic weakness in the banking sector, with thousands of bank failures and millions in lost deposits. The inaction of the Fed at that time can be explained as the result of a battle between policy camps. Pro-cyclical supporters urged no action; countercyclical advocates urged an expansionary, countercyclical policy. International conditions required the Fed to increase the discount rate in order to return gold to the United States and increase the reserves in many banks. The banks held some of these reserves as excess reserves—a cushion to ensure their ability to meet depositor demands for liquidity. The Fed misinterpreted this sign, believing that

The Liberty Loan Choir performs on the steps of City Hall in New York City during the third Liberty Loan campaign in April 1918. (National Archives.)

banks found inadequate lending opportunities, and it failed to adopt a policy stance that led to further expansion.

Many of the institutional changes that occurred during the Great Depression affected monetary policy and the Fed directly. Congress gave the Fed its last policy tool—the ability to set reserve requirements. There were significant changes in the banking sector, including the separation of commercial bank activities, life insurance, and brokerage activities. The Federal Deposit Insurance Corporation (FDIC) guaranteed the deposits of customers up to a maximum amount. The United States abandoned the gold standard and saw the price of a troy ounce of gold in dollars increase nearly 70 percent to $35. Gold flowed back into the United States, and as a result, the money supply expanded. The creation of deposit insurance also increased peoples' confidence in the banking system, and so cash flowed back into banks. In addition, the expansion in reserves led to an increase in excess reserves, or the funds

"Even a little can help a lot - *NOW*"

Buy U.S. WAR STAMPS BONDS

U.S. War Stamp and Bonds poster from 1942 encourages families to support the war effort. (Library of Congress.)

the banks held to provide extra liquidity. The Fed misinterpreted this increase as a sign of few acceptable lending options and decided to conduct open market sales in order to reduce the risk of inflation in the future.

World War II presented a significant challenge for the Fed, just as World War I had. Before America entered the hostilities, there was a buildup of gold in the United States as European nations and citizens sent gold overseas for purchases and security. The Treasury also requested that the Fed adopt an accommodation policy once again, though the effects on the price level were less than those that occurred in World War I. Inflation remained low in this instance because of the entry of the United States into the war in 1941. The inflationary pressures did not have sufficient time to build, and the economy experienced a mix of price controls and public saving because of a reduced availability of consumer goods. In addition, the Treasury's efforts to finance the war led to patriotic calls for sacrifice and saving, for example, through the purchase of war bonds.

After the war, several factors combined to increase the level of inflation: People spent the accumulated savings and wealth from the war period; the Fed continued to accommodate Treasury borrowing to keep the cost of funds low; and the government adopted the Employment Act of 1946, making it the duty of the government, including the Fed, to maintain employment at a high level. The Bretton

Woods system of exchange rates, which centered on narrow bands for fluctuations with the U.S. dollar fixed in terms of gold, came into existence and was thought to be strong enough to prevent the transmission of crisis as had occurred in the 1930s. To help maintain the system of exchange rates and keep international financial flows moving, the International Monetary Fund (IMF) was created.

Monetary policy became more active in the 1950s as inflation increased because of U.S. government buildup and expenditures for the Korean War. The Fed was certain that the accommodation policy was at least partly to blame. The Fed and the Treasury agreed to lift the accommodation policy, although the Treasury made the Fed promise not to allow rates to rise too quickly. The 1950s saw open market operations become the primary tool of monetary policy.

The Fed also became more concerned about targets for monetary policy at this time and looked to measures such as free reserves, or bank excess reserves less discount loans. High levels of free reserves represented a relaxed policy conducive to expansion, since banks had more reserves available to use in making loans. The Fed's other target, short-term interest rates, functioned little better because of the increase in the public's inflationary expectations. As a result, the Fed was constantly feeding the cycle rather than muting it. These concerns dogged the Fed over the entire course of the 1960s.

The Federal Reserve since the 1960s

The Fed's policy record did not improve much in the early 1970s, despite the recognition by many economists that a pro-cyclical policy did not work. Arthur Burns became chair of the Federal Reserve's Board of Governors in 1970 and adjusted the Fed's focus to monetary aggregates (that is, everything in the financial sector, including savings accounts and money market accounts). Unfortunately, the Fed was about to discover that some choices of targets were inconsistent and would force policy to be pro-cyclical once again. The Fed used two sets of targets, one for the monetary aggregates and one for short-term interest rates, the federal funds rate. The problem was the bandwidth adopted for the two separate targets. The monetary aggregate growth rates were typically quite large, whereas the bandwidth for the federal funds rate tended to be smaller. The result was that although the Fed thought it targeted the aggregates, it was actually focusing on the short-term interest rates. As economic events caused market rates to rise outside the prescribed bandwidth, the Fed would conduct open market purchases to add credit to the system and lower the interest rate. The side effect of this policy was that it also increased the monetary base and reserves in the banking system. The multiple expansion of deposits led to larger levels of the monetary aggregates than targeted and an increase in inflation, which tended to result in an increase in market interest rates again.

In 1979, with the appointment of Paul Volcker to the position of chair of the Board of Governors, the Fed began a long fight against inflation and the expectations of inflation in the economy. Volcker de-emphasized the interest rate targets of the Fed to allow them to rise. To slow inflation, the economy needed to experience a slowdown. Part of the difficulty in this process was the lack of Federal Reserve credibility.

Despite numerous previous attempts at reducing inflation, monetary policy did not seem capable of reaching this goal. People were unsure whether the current Fed policy would actually reduce the level of inflation permanently, and consequently, adjustment was quite difficult. Also at question was whether the Fed would stick to its policy or recant in the face of public pressure and economic weakness. Additional complicating factors at the time were financial innovation and regulation.

The high interest rates of the 1970s led to a process known as disintermediation, as people withdrew their deposits from banks with rate ceilings set lower than the market rate or completely disallowed, as on demand deposits. People and companies attempted to hold as little in transactions accounts as possible. Money market mutual funds were a popular destination for these monies. Banks countered with negotiable order of withdrawal (NOW) and automatic transfer from savings (ATS) accounts that paid market rates, but it was not really enough. The 1982 Garn-St. Germain Depository Institutions Act introduced money market deposit accounts (MMDAs), which had no interest rate ceilings. The Depository Institutions Deregulation and Monetary Control Act (DIDMCA) of 1980 extended Fed reserve requirements to all depository institutions and allowed nonmember banks access to the Fed's discount window. Financial and technological innovations diminished the predictive power of relationships between monetary aggregates and other economic variables of interest to monetary policymakers.

The 1980s saw the adoption of a borrowed reserves target, that is, discount loans. As interest rates rise, there is an incentive for banks to increase their borrowing from the central bank to boost their levels of reserves available for lending. To offset this upward pressure on interest rates, the Fed conducted open market purchases in an effort to increase the available supply of credit and lower the interest rate. Although the interest rates were under tighter control, the open market purchases resulted in an increase in the money supply. The large fluctuations in money supply caused by this target led the Fed to abandon its M1 target in the late 1980s and eventually its M2 in the 1990s. (M1 is a measure of the U.S. money stock that consists of currency held by the public, travelers' checks, demand deposits, and other checkable deposits, including negotiable order of withdrawal [NOW] and automatic transfer service [ATS] account balances and share draft account balances at credit unions. M2 is M1 plus savings accounts and small-denomination time deposits, plus shares in money market mutual funds [other than those restricted to institutional investors], plus overnight Eurodollars and repurchase agreements.)

The 1990s brought new challenges to the Fed. The recession of 1990 and 1991 was an important economic event, and the fear of a slow recovery or a prolonged recession resulted in the Fed maintaining a low federal funds rate of 3 percent. The easy credit policy provided banks with the reserves they needed to make loans and expand economic activity. The Fed was still wary of inflation expectations, however, and in the mid-1990s, when it was clear that the economy was recovering, it increased the federal funds rate to 6 percent. This move has been termed a preemptive strike against inflation. The Fed was signaling to financial markets that it was still wary of inflation and would take the necessary steps to prevent its return, so much so that it would not let expectations of inflation take root in the economy.

The stock market decline in the year 2000 and the terrorist attacks of September 11, 2001, have posed additional problems for the Fed. To complicate matters, the accounting practices of American corporations and several large bankruptcies resulted in instability in the financial markets for much of the years 2001 and 2002. At this point, the Fed must attempt to balance several of its goals, such as achieving financial market stability and price stability. The federal funds rate stands at historically low levels in an attempt to foster a sustained recovery in the American economy. The active and early response of the Fed to the problems of 2000–2001 prevented prolonged recession and economic crisis. As the economy showed signs of strengthening in 2004, the Federal Reserve increased the short-term interest rate. However, that rate increase was not followed by a similar increase in long-term interest rates as such rate changes had done from 1971 to 2002. Fed Chairman Alan Greenspan noted that this shift had occurred because of an unintended reserve currency savings abroad as countries such as China and other emerging developing nations pursued economic policies that dramatically increased the amount of their exports, which purchasing nations paid for in dollars. This change in their policies had begun in the early 1990s and by 2003 the enormous amount of reserve currency savings resulted in declines in the long-term securities interest rates. This development left the Federal Reserve with little power to slow down the frenzy within the mortgage and housing industries, a development that left the door open for the housing bubble that burst in August 2007.

During the current recession, which began in 2007, the Federal Reserve maintained a "soft money" policy as it attempted to stimulate the U.S. economy during the financially difficult times. Rates remained low throughout 2008 and 2009 as the crisis deepened, affecting the financial services and stock markets as well as businesses and labor. With the continued increase in bank failures, which went from three in 2007 to 25 in 2008 before jumping to 140 in 2009, as well as rising unemployment, which reached into the double-digits in October 2009, the Federal Reserve will most likely maintain an easy money policy with low interest rates for some time to come.

One of the primary concerns among many members of Congress as well as economic analysts was recently articulated by retired Federal Reserve Chair Alan Greenspan. In a speech presented at a meeting of the Council on Foreign Affairs in New York in October 2009, Greenspan observed that many financial services institutions had been allowed to become "too big to fail," and that the Federal Reserve had adopted that doctrine in 2008 when it arranged the bailout of several giant banking, investment, and insurance institutions. Consequently, he cautioned, it would be very "difficult to repair their credibility on that" when the time came to increase interest rates as the economy strengthened "because when push came to shove, they didn't stand up" to the corporate giants and might be tempted to pursue easy money policies that would end the current recession, which was caused by the bursting of the house bubble, but in effect create a future bubble in another industry.

During the renomination hearings for the current Fed Chairman Ben Bernanke, which started at the end of 2009, many congressional members and financial analysts called for Bernanke's replacement with a hard money chairman. In addition, the Senate drafted legislation that would strip the Federal Reserve of its supervisory power of banks and would also redefine its central role in maintaining financial stability.

Only time will tell if Congress shifts control of U.S. monetary policy from the Federal Reserve Bank to some other agency or entity and if that occurs whether the policies pursued thereafter will prove as beneficial to the U.S. economy as they have throughout the majority of the time the Federal Reserve has determined monetary policy.

References

Calomiris, Charles. "Institutional Failure, Monetary Scarcity, and the Depreciation of the Continental." *Journal of Economic History*, vol. 48, no. 1 (March 1988): 47–68.

Friedman, Milton, and Anna J. Schwartz. *A Monetary History of the United States, 1867–1960*. Princeton, NJ: Princeton University Press, 1963.

Goodfriend, Marvin. "Monetary Policy Comes of Age: A 20th Century Odyssey." *Economic Quarterly* (Federal Reserve Bank of Richmond, Virginia), vol. 83, no. 1 (Winter 1997): 543.

Goodfriend, Marvin. "The Phases of U.S. Monetary Policy: 1987 to 2001." *Economic Quarterly* (Federal Reserve Bank of Richmond, Virginia), vol. 88, no. 4 (Fall 2002): 1–17.

Greenspan, Alan. "The Fed Didn't Cause the Housing Bubble," *Wall Street Journal*, March 11, 2009. Available: http://online.wsj.com/article/SB123672965 066989281.html; accessed December 30, 2009.

Meulendyke, Ann-Marie. *U.S. Monetary Policy and Financial Markets*. 3rd ed. New York: Federal Reserve Bank of New York, 1998.

Mishkin, Frederic S. *The Economics of Money, Banking, and Financial Markets*. 6th ed. New York: Addison-Wesley, 2003, ch. 18.

New York Times. "Greenspan Calls to Break Up Banks 'Too Big to Fail.' " October 5, 2009. Available: http://dealbook.blogs.nytimes.com/2009/10/15/greenspan -break-up-banks-too-big-to-fail/; accessed December 30, 2009.

Pearce, David W. *The MIT Dictionary of Modern Economics*. 4th ed. Cambridge, MA: MIT Press, 1995.

Smith, Bruce D. "American Colonial Monetary Regimes: The Failure of the Quantity Theory and Some Evidence in Favor of an Alternate View." *Canadian Journal of Economics*, vol. 18 (1985): 531–565.

Timberlake, Richard. *Monetary Policy in the United States: An Intellectual and Institutional History*. Chicago: University of Chicago Press, 1993.

Walton, Gary M., and Hugh Rockoff. *History of the American Economy*. 9th ed. Fort Worth, TX: South-Western Thomson Learning, 2002.

Wicker, Elmus. "Colonial Monetary Standards Contrasted: Evidence from the Seven Years' War." *Journal of Economic History*, vol. 45 (1985): 869–884.

Money Laundering

Trifin J. Roule

Money laundering is the process by which the proceeds of crime are transferred through the financial system to conceal their illicit origins and make the illegal profits appear to be legitimate funds. The laundering of these illicit assets is routinely linked to criminal acts that generate significant proceeds, such as drug trafficking, extortion, prostitution, and people smuggling. Additionally, white-collar crimes, such as fraud, insider trading, and tax evasion, are frequently associated with laundering schemes. In recent years, considerable attention has also been devoted to deterring terrorist groups from laundering illicit profits through banking and nonbanking institutions. Each of these groups has utilized financial institutions in the United States to launder illicit assets and fund future criminal or terrorist acts. Moreover, the immense sum of illicit money laundered through U.S. financial institutions, more than $100 billion annually, has the potential to damage the reputation of individual financial sectors, such as the banking industry or brokerage houses, that depend on the perception that financial transactions are conducted under the highest legal and ethical standards. Money launderers also negatively affect communities by reducing tax revenues, competing unfairly with legitimate businesses, and diminishing the amount of funds devoted to economic development and social programs.

The Laundry Cycle

The conversion of illicit assets into seemingly legitimate funds is known as the laundry cycle. The laundry cycle consists of three distinct stages: (1) placement, the process of introducing the illegal assets into the financial system through a series of transactions, including deposits and wire transfers; (2) layering, the process of engaging in a series of conversions or movements to distance the funds from their illicit origins; and (3) integration, by which, after successfully completing the placement and layering of illicit assets, the funds are reintroduced as legitimate earnings. Each stage may involve single or multiple transactions. The most common technique for laundering illicit profits is a process known as "smurfing," which entails the structured placement of illicit funds into financial institutions in amounts that are below the threshold levels for recognizing suspicious or unusual deposits. Other widespread forms of laundering include cross-border currency smuggling and the funneling of illicit profits through loosely regulated casinos. Money is also routinely laundered through brokerage houses, jewelry dealers, automobile dealerships, and insurance companies. Once the money is laundered, the assets are typically used to fund future criminal acts or purchase real estate, luxury goods, and legitimate businesses.

Laundering Illicit Funds in the United States

The placement of illegal profits in legitimate ventures dates to the beginning of the Republic, when individuals used illicit earnings to purchase real estate, livestock, or high-priced goods. Until the early twentieth century, enforcement efforts were largely directed at traditional criminal offenses, such as smuggling and theft, that generated modest amounts of illicit income; little attention was devoted to the funds generated from criminal acts. Although the eighteenth and nineteenth centuries were replete with examples of schemes to place criminal assets in U.S. financial institutions, no legislation was passed to combat financial crimes, and the funds were usually kept in banks and later reinvested in the economy without fear of confiscation. This situation changed during the Prohibition era, when law enforcement agencies showed a growing concern over the immense sums of illegal assets that funded sophisticated criminal enterprises. Throughout the 1920s and 1930s, organized criminal groups led by crime bosses, such as Mayer Lansky and Al Capone, routinely avoided paying income taxes by investing illegal profits in legitimate businesses. The illicit profits earned through prostitution, drug trafficking, and the production and distribution of alcohol were invested in legitimate, cash-based businesses, such as clothes laundries and restaurants. Thus, the illicit earnings were commingled with the licit revenues received from seemingly legitimate businesses. The first known usage of the expression *money laundering* by American enforcement and regulatory agencies occurred during the Watergate scandal in the 1970s, but money laundering was not criminalized in the United States until the passage of the Money Laundering Control Act of 1986.

Early Efforts to Combat Money Laundering

The continued growth of organized crime in the United States throughout the twentieth century demanded action from the U.S. government. In an effort to tackle the rising number of criminal gangs, including East Coast mob families, Congress passed three pieces of legislation from the mid-1950s until the early 1960s to combat illicit finance schemes. The first was the Laundering of Monetary Instruments Act of 1956. This law criminalized the act of knowingly transferring unlawfully obtained assets through financial institutions; further, the act of concealing or disguising the source or ownership of illicit funds also became a crime. One year later, Congress passed the Monetary Transactions in Property Derived from Specified Unlawful Activity Act of 1957, which established penalties for "attempts to engage in a monetary transaction in criminally derived property that is of a value greater than $10,000." The law also set penalties for violating the statute: For funneling illicit proceeds through financial institutions, these penalties included (1) a fine of $500,000 or imprisonment for up to 10 years or (2) a fine and imprisonment. The third major piece of legislation to combat money laundering was the Prohibition of Unlicensed Money Transmitting Businesses Act of 1960; it would be the last measure of its type enacted for a decade. This law was designed to assure oversight of the numerous money transmitter businesses in the United States, including many that failed to register with state governments. The act mandated registration but did not address other regulatory issues, such as record-keeping requirements. Ultimately, it had little effect because prosecutors had to prove the defendant knew that the money transmitter was unlicensed, that state law required a license, and that the operation of an unlicensed business was a criminal offense.

The U.S. Response to the Narcotics-Trafficking Boom

The first major effort by the United States to curtail the laundering of illicit assets occurred in 1970 with the passage of the Bank Secrecy Act (BSA). The BSA was enacted for two reasons: first, to improve detection and investigation of tax violations, including white-collar crimes, and second, to respond to reports that organized criminal groups that oversaw lucrative narcotics-trafficking routes were transporting large amounts of currency across U.S. borders. In an effort to curtail bulk cash smuggling, the BSA was designed to create a paper trail for large currency transactions and establish stringent regulatory reporting standards. Most important, the law directed financial institutions to introduce record-keeping requirements. And through the new currency transaction report (CTR) regime, the statute required such institutions to notify the Internal Revenue Service of any individual who withdrew or deposited more than $10,000 in a single day.

Soon after the passage of the BSA, the momentum to combat illicit finance schemes waned. The Watergate scandal, economic concerns, and the growing enmity between the United States and the Soviet Union effectively overshadowed additional efforts against money laundering for more than a decade. However, by the mid-1980s, the substantial rise in narcotics trafficking caused immense concern over the mounting number of illicit finance schemes and resulted in a sustained effort by Congress to construct a comprehensive regime to tackle money laundering. With the introduction of the Money Laundering Control Act of 1986 (MLCA) as a part of the Anti-Drug Abuse Act of 1986, Congress enacted sweeping changes to curtail the structured deposits, or smurfing, of illicit assets. Most important, the legislation criminalized money laundering and established three new criminal offenses for money-laundering activities through banking or nonbanking institutions. The new offenses included knowingly helping to launder money from a criminal activity, engaging in a transaction of more than $10,000 that involved property from a criminal activity, and structuring transactions to avoid BSA reporting. Moreover, the statute established strict penalties for convicted launderers, including imprisonment for a maximum of 20 years and fines up to $500,000 or two times the amount laundered. The law also granted the Internal

Revenue Service the power to seize property involved in the breach of money-laundering laws. Finally, the legislation bolstered regulatory and enforcement efforts by mandating the reporting of suspicious or unusual transactions through the submission of a suspicious activity report (SAR). The form was designed to specifically report instances of structured deposits in U.S. financial institutions.

The MLCA was the first important statute passed to combat money laundering in over a decade. The new legislation, however, lacked instruments to promote international cooperation in the fight against money laundering. After a debate on the deficiencies of the MLCA, Congress passed the Anti-Drug Abuse Act of 1988, which reinforced efforts to fight money laundering in several ways, especially through the establishment of channels to facilitate cooperation with foreign regulatory and enforcement agencies. The statute granted the Department of the Treasury the right to negotiate bilateral international agreements to promote the exchange of information related to illicit finance schemes. The new law also significantly increased civil, criminal, and forfeiture sanctions for laundering crimes, and it authorized the forfeiture of "any property, real or personal, involved in a transaction or attempted transaction in violation of laws." Additionally, the legislation increased the criminal penalty for tax evasion when the funds at issue were connected with criminal activity.

The growing narcotics trade in the Americas and Asia in the 1980s demonstrated that crime had become global, and criminal groups were routinely utilizing rapid advances in technology and the globalization of the financial services industry to launder illicit assets. Changes in banking activities necessitated increased cooperation between the United States and foreign jurisdictions in order to monitor illegal cash flows. The Crime Control Act, which was passed by Congress in 1990, enhanced enforcement efforts by permitting federal banking agencies (such as the Federal Reserve Board and the Federal Deposit Insurance Corporation) to request the assistance of a foreign banking authority in conducting any investigation, examination, or enforcement action. The United States also signed a large number of mutual legal assistance treaties (MLATs), which are negotiated by the Department of State in cooperation with the Department of Justice to facilitate cooperation in criminal matters, including money laundering and asset forfeiture. The MLATs are designed to promote the exchange of evidence and information in criminal matters and are extremely useful as a means of obtaining banking and other financial records. International assistance was further extended with the passage of the Federal Deposit Insurance Corporation Improvement Act of 1991, which permitted U.S. authorities to disclose information obtained in the course of exercising their supervisory or examination authority to foreign bank regulatory officials.

International cooperation has been strongly promoted at all levels of the U.S. government, and the United States has often taken a leadership role in international efforts devoted to combating money laundering. For example, the United States is a signatory to the 1988 UN Convention against Illicit Traffic in Narcotic Drugs and Psychotropic Substances (Vienna Convention), which calls on nations to criminalize money laundering; assure that bank secrecy is not a barrier to criminal investigations; and promote the removal of legislative impediments to investigation, prosecution, and international cooperation. The United States is also a member of the Financial Aid Task Force (FATF), which was created at the economic summit of the major industrialized countries in 1989. The FATF is an intergovernmental body that develops and promotes national legislative and regulatory reforms to combat money laundering. Composed of representatives from 29 countries, the FATF has compiled and issued 40 recommendations to assist states in tackling money-laundering schemes, specifically addressing record-keeping requirements, the mandatory reporting of suspicious or large financial transactions, the identification of beneficial ownership, and the elimination of anonymous accounts. The United States has also promoted the need for conventions and declarations designed to unite the global financial centers in the fight against laundering schemes. As a result, U.S. financial institutions adhere to the nonbinding 1988 Basil Declaration, which encourages all banks to ensure that persons conducting business with their institutions are properly identified, illicit transactions are discouraged, and cooperation with law enforcement agencies in financial investigations is achieved with alacrity.

The U.S. Response to the BCCI Scandal

Domestic efforts to assure adequate oversight of U.S. financial transactions were proven to be largely inadequate with the uncovering of the Bank of Credit and Commerce International (BCCI) scandal in 1991. BCCI was a Pakistani-managed, Middle East–financed international private bank with branches in over 70 countries, including the United States, and assets of over $20 billion. Investigators were shocked at the number of jurisdictions involved in the scandal (the United States among them) and the secrecy provisions that permitted BCCI to conduct a series of criminal acts and funnel illicit profits through front companies in the Cayman Islands to U.S. and European banks. In response to the BCCI revelations, Congress passed the Housing and Community Development Act of 1992, often referred to as the Annunzio-Wylie Anti-Money Laundering Act. This statute requires financial institutions and their employees to report any suspicious transactions that may be relevant to a possible violation of a law or regulation, and it specifically protects those parties from any civil suits arising from the submission of such reports. The legislation further mandates financial institutions to carry out programs to thwart money laundering by addressing training and due diligence concerns, and it authorizes financial institutions to maintain stringent record-keeping procedures. The statute also requires each financial institution to designate a compliance officer and conduct routine audits to assess the adequacy of in-house programs to curb money laundering.

In addition, the statute strengthens penalties for depository institutions found guilty of money laundering. Under the Annunzio-Wylie Anti-Money Laundering Act, the Federal Deposit Insurance Corporation and the Department of the Treasury are granted the power to act as comptroller for an insured depository institution that is found guilty of any money-laundering offense or a criminal Bank Secrecy Act violation. On receipt of written notification from the attorney general that a national bank or an agency of a foreign bank has been found guilty of money laundering, a comptroller appointed by the U.S. government schedules a hearing to determine whether to revoke the bank's charter. The decision to terminate the charter is based on a set of factors, including whether the senior executive officers had knowledge of the illicit activity and whether the bank had policies and procedures in place to prevent money laundering; the institution's level of cooperation with agencies investigating the alleged offense is also considered. Finally, to assure adequate cooperation between governmental agencies that investigate money-laundering offenses, the Annunzio-Wylie Anti-Money Laundering Act established the BSA Advisory Group, which includes representatives from the Treasury and Justice Departments and the Office of National Drug Control Policy, as well as other interested persons and financial institutions.

The last major statute on money laundering to be passed before the turn of the century was the Money Laundering Suppression Act of 1994. Until the passage of this measure, criminals routinely utilized unregulated brokerage or securities firms to launder illicit assets. This act amended the BSA by requiring nonbank financial institutions, such as brokerage firms, to submit to a series of reporting requirements. These firms, however, remained loosely regulated and failed to institute self-policing measures to combat money-laundering schemes. As a result, organized criminal groups continued to launder illicit proceeds until the passage of the Money Laundering Abatement and Anti-Terrorist Financing Act of 2001, which mandated stringent reporting requirements for security firms and brokerage houses.

The Criminal Response to U.S. Efforts to Combat Money Laundering

In response to the nearly decade-long strengthening of the U.S. financial sector, criminal groups devised a series of new schemes to avoid increasingly rigorous reporting requirements. Instead of directly challenging the capabilities of U.S. financial institutions in combating money laundering, criminal networks began to deposit illicit proceeds abroad and transfer the assets to the United States through a series of wire transfers. Especially problematic was their use of offshore financial centers, including a number of jurisdictions in the Caribbean and South Pacific. These centers are composed of institutions that restrict access to the offshore sector to nonresidents. Most of the offshore banking institutions lack stringent regulatory regimes, and they provide clients with anonymous accounts for the placement of assets. The offshore nonbanking institutions, such as insurance agencies and security brokers, are particularly troubling because they lack even the most rudimentary oversight mechanisms. Throughout the 1990s, the offshore sector was a safe haven for the deposit of criminal assets and a desirable location for individuals determined to evade home-country tax regimes. On countless occasions, funds from offshore zones were later transferred through U.S. financial institutions.

Another means utilized throughout the 1990s to avoid money-laundering oversight mechanisms was the highly successful Black Market Peso Exchange System (BMPE), a trade-based regime that depends on commercial traffic between the United

States and Colombia to launder profits from the sale of illegal drugs in America. The process begins when a Colombian drug organization sells narcotics in the United States in exchange for U.S. currency. That currency is sold to a Colombian black market peso broker's agent in the United States. Once the dollars are delivered to the U.S.-based agent, the peso broker in Colombia deposits the agreed-on equivalent in Colombian pesos into the organization's account in Colombia. The Colombian broker now has a pool of laundered dollars to sell to Colombian importers. These importers then use the dollars to purchase goods, either from the United States or from other markets, that are transported to Colombia. Law enforcement agencies estimate that the black market peso exchange launders between $3 billion and $6 billion annually.

Another area of concern is the routine passage of illicit funds through wire transfer services. The enormous volume of financial transactions conducted through U.S. banking and nonbanking institutions routinely facilitates money-laundering schemes and hinders effective regulation of banking activities. Every day, in fact, the U.S. financial system handles more than 700,000 wire transfers, valued at over $2 trillion. Determining which of these transactions might be related to money laundering creates an immense problem for both private-sector institutions and law enforcement or regulatory agencies. The massive amount of funds transferred through U.S. financial institutions provided a means to cloak the transfer of billions of illicit dollars in the late 1990s via a number of U.S. banks, including the Bank of New York. The so-called Bank of New York scandal demonstrated that launderers could move tens of billions of dollars through a couple of computers housed at an unregistered money-transmission business that had full access to the Bank of New York's international wire transfer services.

White-collar criminals also routinely use wire transfer services provided by off-shore financial institutions. After an extensive investigation, the Federal Reserve and its chair, Alan Greenspan, concluded that the offshore location of Long Term Capital Management, a hedge fund based in the Cayman Islands, had prevented U.S. regulators from realizing that the entity had accumulated leverage amounting to more than $1 trillion and used U.S. banks to finance the huge risks involved in the hedge fund. The collapse of Long Term Capital Management resulted in increased pressure on offshore zones from U.S. regulatory bodies. Most of the jurisdictions responded by increasing oversight of wire transfers to the United States and other global financial centers.

With the increased attention on traditional banking mechanisms such as wire transfers, the laundering of illicit funds was expanded to nonregulated sectors throughout the 1990s. For instance, alternative remittance, or underground, banking systems emerged as new means to avoid attracting the attention of regulatory and law enforcement personnel in the United States. The very nature of the alternative remittance system makes it extremely difficult to monitor and track the flow of money. One example is the *hawala* system, which, in its simplest form, consists of two persons in distant locations communicating by phone, fax, or email. No money is exchanged between the hawala brokers themselves, only between the brokers and the customers, and the broker does not maintain records of the transactions. The anonymity and secrecy of the remittance transactions facilitates the transfer of illicit funds linked to a variety of criminal activities, including money laundering, corruption of government officials, and tax evasion. In 2001 the use of hawala was linked by U.S. law enforcement agencies to a number of terrorist financing schemes.

In an effort to curtail abuses of wire services and the offshore sector, black market peso schemes, and the rise of alternative remittance systems, the U.S. government initiated a comprehensive plan to assure adequate oversight of U.S. institutions; it also devised long-range plans to combat the growing number of illicit finance schemes. On October 15, 1998, Congress passed the Money Laundering and Financial Crimes Strategy Act. The legislation called on the president, acting in consultation with the secretary of the treasury and the attorney general, to develop a national strategy for combating money laundering and related financial crimes. The first national strategy was to be sent to Congress in 1999 and updated annually.

The U.S. Response to International Terrorism Financing

After the terrorist attacks on the United States on September 11, 2001, the government launched a series of significant initiatives to thwart money laundering and terrorist financing. Like criminal networks, terrorist groups commingle illicit revenues with legitimate funds drawn from the profits of commercial enterprises, as well as charitable donations from witting and unwitting sympathizers. Although tracking terrorist financial transactions is more difficult than following the money trails of mainstream criminal groups, both terrorists and conventional criminals use similar methods to launder assets through U.S. financial institutions.

In an effort to curtail terrorist finance passing through financial institutions located in the United States, President George W. Bush signed into law on October 26, 2001, the most significant financial crimes legislation since the Bank Secrecy Act of 1970. The new statute, known as the Money Laundering Abatement and Anti-Terrorist Financing Act of 2001, contains substantial amendments to previous money-laundering laws. Notably, Title III of the new measure—the United and Strengthening America by Providing Appropriate Tools Required to Intercept and Obstruct Terrorism Act of 2001, commonly known as the Patriot Act—includes comprehensive regulatory and enforcement provisions that affect the daily operations of U.S. banking and nonbanking financial institutions.

The legislation mandates that U.S. financial institutions establish programs to thwart money laundering, and it expands the reporting of SARs to brokers and dealers and a number of other financial sectors. The Patriot Act requires every financial institution, including such previously unregulated sectors as hedge funds and commercial loan and finance companies, to maintain programs of this type. Some 25 different categories of financial institutions are required to develop internal policies, procedures, and controls; designate compliance officers; conduct ongoing employee training programs; and perform independent audit functions to test programs. The measure also sets toughened standards for due diligence and for customer identification and verification, mandating extremely intrusive obligations to identify the ownership of institutions and assets deemed to be high-risk. High-risk accounts and transactions subject

President George W. Bush speaks to the media about the Patriot Act extension prior to departing the White House for Camp David on December 22, 2005. Congress passed a one-month extension of the act later that day. (The White House.)

to enhanced due diligence include most offshore banks (other than those in a group of jurisdictions approved by the U.S. Federal Reserve); accounts involving foreign senior political figures, families, and friends; and private banking accounts defined as accounts or sets of accounts involving $1 million or more managed on behalf of identifiable individuals or groups of individuals.

Other salient provisions of Title III of the Patriot Act include the following:

- Section 311, which gives the United States the authority to apply graduated, proportionate measures against a foreign jurisdiction, foreign financial institution, type of transaction, or account that the secretary of the Treasury determines to be a "primary money laundering concern."

- Section 313, which generally prohibits U.S. financial institutions from maintaining a correspondent account in the United States for a foreign shell bank, that is, a foreign bank that does not have a physical presence in any country. The provision also generally requires financial institutions to take reasonable steps to ensure that foreign banks with correspondent accounts do not use those accounts to indirectly provide banking services to a foreign shell bank.

- Section 319, which allows the secretary of the Treasury or the attorney general to subpoena records of a foreign bank that maintains a correspondent account in the

United States. The subpoena can request any records relating to the account, including records located in a foreign country that involve the deposit of funds into the foreign bank.

- Section 359, which brings informal banking systems, such as hawalas, under the Bank Secrecy Act.

- Section 362, which requires the secretary of the Treasury to establish a secure network to (1) allow financial institutions to file Bank Secrecy Act reports electronically through the secure network and (2) provide financial institutions with alerts regarding suspicious activities.

- Section 1006, which amends the Immigration and Nationality Act to exclude aliens engaged in or seeking to engage in money laundering as described in U.S. law or those that aid, abet, assist, or collude in such activity. This section also requires the secretary of state to establish a watch list identifying persons worldwide who are known for or suspected of money laundering.

The United States also signed two important international agreements after the September 11, 2001, attacks to assist in the international effort to combat money-laundering offenses. In October 2001 the United States agreed to adhere to the newly adopted UN Security Council Resolution 1373 (UNSCR 1373), a binding document that requires all UN member states to

- Criminalize the use or collection of funds intended or known to be intended for terrorism;

- Immediately freeze funds, assets, or economic resources of persons who commit, attempt to commit, or facilitate terrorist acts and entities owned or controlled by them;

- Prohibit nationals or persons within their territories from aiding or providing any aid to persons and entities involved in terrorism;

- Refrain from providing any form of support to entities or persons involved in terrorism; and

- Deny safe haven to (1) those who finance, plan, support, or commit terrorist acts and (2) individuals who themselves provide safe havens for such persons.

Moreover, each UN member state is required to submit progress reports, providing information as to how it has implemented UNSCR 1373.

In another effort to support the international fight against financial crimes, the United States pledged to implement the Eight Special FATF Recommendations to combat terrorist finance. The recommendations require FATF members to complete the following:

- Ratify and implement the 1999 UN International Convention for the Suppression of the Financing of Terrorism and UNSCR 1373.

- Criminalize the financing of terrorism, terrorist acts, and terrorist organizations and ensure that such offenses are designated as money-laundering predicate offenses.

- Implement measures to freeze, without delay, funds or other assets of terrorists, those who finance terrorism, and terrorist organizations in accordance with the UN resolutions relating to the prevention and suppression of the financing of terrorist acts.

- Subject financial institutions or other businesses or entities to obligations designed to combat money laundering.

- Offer another country, on the basis of a treaty, arrangement, or other mechanism for mutual legal assistance or information exchange, the greatest possible measure of assistance in connection with criminal, civil enforcement, and administrative investigations, inquiries, and proceedings relating to the financing of terrorism, terrorist acts, and terrorist organizations.

- Take measures to ensure that persons or legal entities, including agents, that provide a service for the transmission of money or value, including transmission through an informal money or value transfer system or network, be licensed or registered and subject to all the FATF recommendations that apply to banks and nonbank financial institutions.

- Require financial institutions, including money remitters, to include accurate and meaningful originator information (name, address, and account number) on funds transfers and related messages that are sent. Further, the information should remain with the transfer or related message through the payment chain.

- Review the adequacy of laws and regulations that relate to entities that can be abused for the financing of terrorism. Nonprofit organizations are particularly vulnerable, and countries should ensure that such organizations could not be misused by terrorist organizations posing as legitimate entities.

Conclusion

Generally, the U.S. provisions regarding money-laundering offenses and forfeiture are sound and are actively used. After the passage of a series of statutes in this regard, criminal networks increasingly relied on nonbanking institutions to launder illicit profits. The effectiveness of U.S. policy in establishing a regime to combat money laundering is evidenced by the fact that fees charged by criminals to assist in money-laundering schemes have risen dramatically since 1985. These fees totaled 6 percent before 1986, but the increased risk involved with laundering illicit assets thereafter resulted in fees of more than 25 percent. Nevertheless, launderers are employing increasingly sophisticated schemes to place criminal assets in U.S. financial institutions. The immense size and sophistication of the financial service sector in the United States continue to provide enormous opportunity for criminal and terrorist groups to pass funds through U.S. banking and nonbanking institutions.

The attacks on the United States in September 2001 resulted in massive changes in terms of the efforts undertaken to tackle the money-laundering problem. Investigations into a number of terrorist acts have established a clear link between illicit finance schemes and the funding of attacks on civilian populations across the globe. Consequently, the United States strengthened legislation related to money laundering and increased the oversight of nonbanking institutions. Although the legislative amendments were initiated by terrorist attacks in the United States, improved oversight of U.S. financial institutions will also result in an increase in asset seizures and arrests of individuals engaged in organized criminal activity and white-collar crimes.

Since the mid-1950s, legislation has been designed to curtail criminal activities and assure U.S. citizens that domestic financial transactions are based on the highest ethical standards. For the foreseeable future, legislative and law enforcement efforts will focus on the urgent need to prevent illicit funds from entering the United States to underwrite attacks on American citizens.

References

Cassard, Marcel. *The Role of the Off-Shore Centers in International Financial Mediation.* Washington, DC: International Monetary Fund Working Paper, 1994.

Fabre, Guilhem. *Criminal Prosperity: Drug Trafficking, Money Laundering, and Financial Crisis after the Cold War.* London: Curzon Press, 2002.

Gilmore, William C. *Dirty Money: The Evolution of Money-Laundering Counter-Measures.* 2nd ed. Strasbourg, France: Council of Europe Press, 1995.

Hinterseer, Kris. *Criminal Finance: The Political Economy of Money Laundering in a Comparative Legal Context.* Boston: Kluwer Law International, 2002.

Parlour, Richard, ed. *Butterworths International Guide to Money Laundering: Law and Practice.* London: Butterworths, 1995.

Savla, Sandeep. *Money Laundering and Financial Intermediaries.* Boston: Kluwer Law International, 2001.

Savona, Ernesto. *European Money Trails.* The Netherlands: Harwood Academic Publishers, 1999.

Savona, Ernesto. *Responding to Money Laundering: International Perspectives.* Toronto: Harwood Academic Publishers, 1997.

Science and Technology

Ann Johnson

One of the central questions of economic policy explores how the government can foster economic growth. Although expanding the borders of a nation or its resources promises to create growth, politicians cannot easily control the circumstances or consequences of such expansion. As a result, economic thinkers have often focused on policies that the state can control more easily—including those related to the progress of science and technology. Economists and policymakers have frequently posited a causal relationship between new technologies and economic growth, often looking to Britain's industrialization as an example. In Great Britain, the scientific revolution of Isaac Newton and Robert Boyle in the late seventeenth century led to the Industrial Revolution of the late eighteenth century and created Britain's unparalleled economic supremacy in the nineteenth century. Although causality in this chain of events remains hotly disputed by many historians, the correlation between the growth of science and technology, on the one hand, and the national economy, on the other, cannot be simply dismissed—economic and technological developments accompany one another. Consequently, this Baconian equation—whereby science yields technology, which yields economic growth—has always been and continues to be an unwritten assumption of economic policy. Attacks on this formula in the post–World War II period have not dissuaded economic policymakers from building programs to encourage the development of science and technology in the name of national growth.

The ways in which scientific and technological development has been fostered have differed over time. The differences often hinge on how significant a role the federal government plays in the business life of the nation. Consequently, for most of America's history, the government's involvement in science and technology has waxed and waned, increasing in periods of crisis (such as wartime) and decreasing in periods of less urgent need. Furthermore, the kinds of activities the government has undertaken in the name of science remain quite diverse, from intellectual property law to military investment, from education to the direct funding of research.

Science and Technology in the Eighteenth and Nineteenth Centuries

Economic policy as it applies to science and technology extends back to the nation's very beginnings and the ratification of the U.S. Constitution. The Constitution mentions science once in Article 1, Section 8 and states that Congress has the power "to promote the Progress of Science and useful Arts, by securing for limited Times to Authors and Inventors the exclusive Right to their respective Writings and Discoveries." To do this, George Washington signed the country's first patent act into effect on July 31, 1790. According to this act, the federal government could grant patents for "any useful art, manufacture, engine, machine, or device, or any improvement thereon not before known or used." A three-member patent board, which included Thomas Jefferson (the first patent examiner and secretary of state), Secretary of War Henry Knox, and Attorney General Edmund Randolph, granted the patents. Each applicant had to supply a specification, a drawing, or preferably a model and pay a nominal fee. The board decided the duration of each patent, up to a maximum of 14 years. In addition, it established penalties for patent infringements.

The system created by the Patent Law of 1790 relied heavily on the secretary of state's oversight and involvement. Since this responsibility conflicted with the numerous other duties of the position, Jefferson strove to change the system. Furthermore, with only 55 patents approved between 1790 and 1793, patent applicants expressed dissatisfaction with the delays in issuing patents caused by the competing demands on the patent examiner's time. Consequently, Congress passed a new patent act in 1793. This legislation left the administration of patents in the secretary of state's office but created a registration system under which patents were granted pro forma upon the completion of the required paperwork, ensuring the granting of virtually every patent. By the 1830s, complaints against this system had mounted, and the 1836 Patent Act further revised the system. The Patent Act codified standards for the approval of patents—definitions that persist to the present day. Essentially, it required that inventions had to be novel, useful, and non-obvious to a practitioner skilled in the relevant area. In many ways, the 1836 system combined the scrutiny of the 1790 system with the bureaucracy of the 1793 act.

The government's first involvement in creating an institution for the study of science came with Jefferson's election to the presidency in 1800. Jefferson advocated a national institution for the sciences, which would generate graduates who could put their knowledge to work for the common good. Although the new president initially opposed the creation of a national military academy, his opposition waned when he realized that with the right personnel, his institution for science and a national military academy could operate as one and the same entity. Further, he recognized that a military academy would attract far less political and regional opposition than a national university.

Congress established the U.S. Military Academy at the garrison at West Point, New York, in March 1802. The academy operated as a continuation of a military school that had been in existence at West Point since 1796, albeit without the endorsement of the federal government. Superintendent Jonathan Williams, a man of the Enlightenment who had assisted his great-uncle Benjamin Franklin in numerous experiments, headed the school. Williams had also traveled extensively in France and knew French scientific and military institutions, including the Ecole Polytechnique—the model for the U.S.

Military Academy. Jefferson clearly chose Williams to head West Point on the basis of his scientific reputation.

Williams's tenure at West Point was rocky, however, because of his efforts to create a scientific, as well as a military, institution. He established the U.S. Military Philosophical Society, a scientific society open to civilians that he hoped would become a leading organization for the production and dissemination of new scientific knowledge. The society's membership rolls included Jefferson, James Madison, James Monroe, John Quincy Adams, John Marshall, Robert Fulton, and Eli Whitney, among others. Although the society never achieved the distinction in science that its illustrious membership promised, West Point nonetheless did become the leading educational institution for science and especially engineering in the antebellum period.

At least until West Point graduates proved their mettle in the Mexican-American War (1846–1848), the academy had to survive periods of wavering federal support, as well as outright hostility from some members of Congress. Many Americans underestimated the scientific importance of West Point, but it did produce the nation's most important promoter of science in the nineteenth century—Alexander Dallas Bache (class of 1825)—and an overwhelming majority of the nation's university-trained engineers, many of whom went on to hold important positions in the construction of the nation's infrastructure. West Point produced more scientists and engineers than science education colleges themselves.

In the early nineteenth century, technology assumed an increasingly central role in the nation, particularly in terms of the industry and commerce. Engineers constructed roads, canals, and harbors to facilitate domestic and international trade, and inventors developed, patented, and sold the machines that underpinned the industrial and agricultural development of the nation. The government maintained a laissez-faire policy relative to this technological development. But with technological progress inevitably came technological difficulties, forcing the government to eventually adjudicate and prevent disasters. The first technology to require government intervention for public safety involved the steam engine. The invention and diffusion of the steamboat in the early nineteenth century played an important role in opening up the commerce of the nation to the western territory, which was reachable through the country's extensive rivers. The steamboat made river transportation fast and inexpensive. But by the 1830s, the United States experienced a rash of steam-boiler explosions, victims of which numbered in the hundreds. Yet no government agency with the authority to investigate the accidents existed.

As long as the public used high-pressure steam engines, accidents continued. Scientists in the private sector realized that this problem had become a subject ripe for empirical study. Alexander Dallas Bache, then a professor at the University of Pennsylvania, organized an investigation into the causes of boiler explosions at the Franklin Institute, a privately endowed organization in Philadelphia. After a six-year study, the institute found that most explosions occurred because of negligence; in other words, they were preventable. The Franklin Institute's report called on the government to develop some sort of regulatory legislation and advocated inspections, licensing, and penalties for noncompliance. However, all attempts to get legislation passed in Congress failed, with arguments over the constitutionality, efficacy, and expense of such regulation stalling passage. Then, in July 1838, a bill was passed that provided for licensing, certification, and the appointment of regional inspectors without financial ties to manufacture. Furthermore, it established liability for owners and operators in the case of accidents. However, since the act did not specify the inspection criteria, inspectors enforced the laws haphazardly across the nation. No one liked the law as it was passed, and it failed to prevent accidents, as evidenced by the 70 explosions that occurred between 1841 and 1848.

In 1852, Congress returned to the issue of regulation. Sen. John Davis of Massachusetts worked with engineers to construct more effective legislation. The bill Davis introduced proved quite similar to the recommendations of the Franklin Institute's 1836 report. Davis's 1852 bill met resistance from a small but vocal number of Congress members who opposed any kind of interference in commerce. To them, regulation threatened private property rights. Nonetheless, the bill passed, and a new role for government had begun. In some ways, the 1852 bill became a model for the regulation of technology, setting manufacturing standards, operating standards, a system of annual inspections, and licensing procedures for engineers. Congress authorized stiff penalties for noncompliance, especially for fraudulent and falsified documentation. Inspection boards investigated accidents. This legislation established a precedent that has justified further regulatory oversight of new technologies to the present day.

Despite the willingness of Congress to consider a more active role in the nation's technology, support for the development of new science and technology remained a foreign notion. For example, congressional reluctance to involve the government in the pursuit of science, regardless of the economic costs, delayed the creation of the Smithsonian Institution. In his will, James Smithson, a wealthy British bachelor, bequeathed his entire estate to the United States for the purpose of developing "an establishment for the increase and diffusion of knowledge among men." He did not specify any other stipulation in the bequest, so Congress debated whether to accept the gift and what to establish using the half million dollars. Finally, in August 1846, Congress passed a bill for this project, providing a secretary, a board of regents, and a building that would include space for laboratories, libraries, museums, lecture rooms, and an art gallery. Clearly, a wide range of activities were planned for this endeavor, but Congress had not decided exactly what role the government might take in the sponsorship of science, even without the expenditure of tax dollars. Bache served as the sole scientist on the board, and under his direction, the Smithsonian moved toward becoming an institution of scientific research. He ensured this trajectory when he appointed his friend Joseph Henry, a professor of physics at Princeton, as the institution's first director. Under Henry's management, despite constant struggles about funding and direction, the Smithsonian became a precedent-setting private foundation that supported scientific research as its primary goal, rather than as a by-product of other priorities.

The American Civil War presented the federal government with new and unprecedented military and technological problems, from ironclad ships to steam engines to submarines. It also presented an opportunity for those pushing for a greater federal role in the direction and funding of science and engineering. War changed the climate in Congress, making legislators much more receptive to the idea of encouraging research, though, ironically, the cost of fighting the war meant that funds for scientific research almost disappeared. During the Civil War, the federal government approved several institutions that would exert a lasting influence on science into the twentieth century, including the Department of Agriculture, the National Academy of Sciences, and the Morrill system of land-grant colleges. Congress created the Department of Agriculture from the agricultural division of the Patent Office, which was responsible for patenting plants. Although headed by a chemist, the department's scientific mission would become subjugated to the demands of American farmers until well into the twentieth century.

The Morrill Act also bridged the divide between science and farming. Vermont Republican Justin Morrill had become convinced that the nation was failing to provide useful knowledge to its farmers and workers. He imagined that new educational institutions would improve America's productivity by making practical scientific and technical education accessible to all. After years of fighting between northerners and southerners, he drafted a bill in 1862 that offered 30,000 acres of federal land to each state for each senator and representative to create "at least one college where the leading object shall be hellip; . . . to teach such branches of learning as are related to agriculture and the mechanic arts." States could either designate existing universities to fulfill this function, as in the case of Wisconsin, or found new institutions, such as the University of California. After the war, southern states divided the appropriation between separate agricultural and mechanical colleges for whites and blacks. The colleges created by the act became sites for the pursuit of new knowledge in engineering and agriculture. For agriculture, the 1887 Hatch Act furthered this mission by allocating funds for agricultural experiment stations operated in conjunction with the land-grant schools.

Of the developments in the Civil War era, the National Academy of Sciences possessed the most direct mission in terms of supporting and directing scientific research. Bache had been arguing since the 1840s for an American equivalent to the French Academie des Sciences—to support research through government subsidy, centrally organize and coordinate research in the nation's interest, and advise the government on scientific and engineering issues. By 1862, with Congress seemingly interested in authorizing greater government activity in science and with the pressing need for expert advice about military technologies, Bache decided the time was right to pursue his notion of the academy. To do so, he secured the support of Massachusetts senator Henry Wilson. On March 3, 1863, Wilson presented the act to incorporate the National Academy of the Sciences, which required approval from Congress but no appropriation, and it passed. The National Academy of the Sciences Act named the 50 charter members of the academy who would remain members for life, a move that elicited some ire from the American scientific community, particularly since the new members represented Bache's interests in the physical sciences more often than they represented the numerically larger community of natural historians. Even among those elected to the academy, considerable discontent existed. But following the lead of Joseph Henry, who accepted his nomination as a member despite his dislike of the autocratic setup of the academy and its prescribed membership, all nominees for membership eventually accepted their appointments.

Controversy over the origins of the National Academy of Sciences soon gave way to a more devastating congressional apathy. Despite the fact that Congress had chartered the academy, it failed to consult with it for scientific and technical advice. In fact, only seven requests were made to the academy during the war, and the Treasury and Navy Departments resisted paying the expenses of the committees that had formed within the academy to study specific issues.

Economic policy regarding science and technology in nineteenth-century America continued to be characterized more by belief than action. American politicians and scientists alike commonly believed that technological progress would lead to a more prosperous nation. However, politicians remained wary of claiming that the federal government should assume responsibility for pursuing scientific and technological research. Scientists, for their part, wanted to avoid offering the government any real control over scientific endeavors. So, while admitting that science and technology had a central role to play in the economic life of the nation, neither scientists nor politicians were willing to coordinate a partnership between science, technology, and the government.

Science and Technology in the Twentieth Century

The 1901 founding of the industrial research laboratory at General Electric (GE) set a new tone for science and technology at the beginning of a new century. GE's lab was neither the first nor the only industrial research laboratory in the United States, and the industrial research laboratory was not a uniquely American development. Still, GE's reputation, the size of its research arm, and its high visibility helped establish a growing tradition of commercial research facilities. Industrial research labs represented a new alliance between science, technology, and industry in America. The corporate pursuit of research and development (R&D) helped set the new tone: Science no longer functioned as an esoteric activity pursued only at universities and by private scientific societies, but instead it became germane to the economic life of General Electric and therefore the nation. This development promised to produce a national attitude more conducive to government interest in scientific and industrial research. In addition, intellectuals such as Charles Sanders Pierce and John Dewey trusted technology to improve the life of the nation, both socially and economically. Those politicians who resisted greater government involvement in science often did so not because they doubted science's economic promise but rather because they came from a laissez-faire ideological position—believing that the government should not interfere in the market and that supporting research was interference. According to this view, GE and other large corporations should have set up large industrial research facilities precisely because their work involved a business mission. Although national interests required successful companies, they argued, the government should not directly aid those companies.

But national defense proved another matter altogether, and in that sphere, the notion of governmental involvement met no resistance. As a result, scientists advocating more government support often heightened their efforts during wartime. This dynamic occurred during both world wars. Although the federal government did create new agencies related to scientific and technological research—such as the National Bureau of Standards (1901), which became the government's first physical laboratory during peacetime—Congress established nearly all the agencies with scientific missions under the cloud of war.

In 1915, the promise of the airplane as a military tool helped create support for an agency devoted to the study of aeronautical research. Attaching it to a naval appropriations bill, Congress created the National Advisory Committee for Aeronautics, or NACA, "to direct the scientific study of the problems of flight." Although only $5,000 was appropriated for research, the move to direct federal support for research in any field constituted a notable change from congressional attitudes in the past. NACA's board consisted of 12 members appointed by the president, though notably no one from the aircraft industry received an appointment until 1939. NACA originally operated as a committee to provide technological advice and as such reported directly to the president, but it gradually evolved into more of a research agency. In 1917, NACA set up its primary research facility, Langley Field in Hampton Roads, Virginia; others would follow. NACA became a model agency that was largely devoted to research into civilian flight, and the military branches took control of their own research. In addition to its work in aeronautical research, NACA helped gain passage for bills such as the Kelly Air Mail Act of 1925, which authorized the use of private companies for airmail delivery, acting essentially as a government subsidy of the nascent commercial air travel industry. The Air Commerce Act of 1926 created the Bureau of Aeronautics within the Department of Commerce, which provided regulatory oversight of the whole air industry, in ways not entirely dissimilar to earlier steam-boiler regulation. In 1958, NACA became the National Aeronautics and Space Administration, or NASA.

The success of NACA as a site for limited government-sponsored research notwithstanding, prominent scientists had greater visions for the marriage between federal support and scientific research. Early in the twentieth century, George Ellery Hale, founder and director of the Mount Wilson Observatory in Pasadena, California, and one of the founders of the California Institute of Technology, saw the war in Europe as an opportunity to promote American science. He presented a plan to the National Academy of Sciences in April 1916: If the United States proceeded to go to war with Germany, the academy would offer its services and resources to the president. This plan received a unanimous endorsement by the membership of the academy, and the academy planned to send a delegation to Woodrow Wilson. A group of five imminent scientists met with the president and stressed the importance of science to the nation's defense. Wilson agreed to involve the academy in the creation of an arsenal of science. Back at the academy, the National Research Council, or NRC, was formed to promote cooperation between research institutions and leading scientists and engineers in universities, industry, government, and the military.

Hale's plan was highly centralized, investing a great deal of power in the NRC. Consequently, it generated some resistance, though it also made the secrecy needed for wartime more manageable. Hale intended to work directly with the president instead of through any intermediary institutions. For this reason, he also sought the approval of Wilson's 1916 Republican opponent, Charles Evans Hughes; Hale wanted to ensure the NRC's position regardless of who won the 1916 election. However, like Bache before him, he sought the cooperation but not the oversight of the government. His National Research Council would contract to perform and coordinate research for the government, but it would not operate as a government agency. As a result, the NRC continued to be funded by private gifts, just as the National Academy of Sciences had. Given the short duration of the war after the United States entered into it, little time remained to test these arrangements.

In March 1918, Hale worked to make the National Research Council and its connections to government permanent. He wanted to do this through an executive order, so that the NRC could remain a private organization without governmental control. Wilson agreed and signed an order in May 1918 to make the NRC a permanent executive scientific advisory council. Hale reorganized the NRC for peacetime in 1919 and placed the research focus on pure, instead of industrial, research. As the United States retreated into its isolationist position, Congress cut funding, and the NRC's connections with government, especially the military, suffered.

The NRC reinforced the role of American universities as the frontline institutions in scientific research. In the face of extremely limited governmental support, the council also worked closely with the growing number of philanthropic patrons of science, such as the Carnegie Institution and the Rockefeller and Guggenheim Foundations.

During the Great Depression of the 1930s, even the small amount of funding that had supported limited scientific research dried up. Debates about whether technology, by increasing productivity, had increased unemployment changed the public's impression of technology. The Progressive Era's unparalleled faith in technological progress vanished, replaced by a suspicion that technology had contributed to the dire circumstances of the period. However, policy changed with Franklin Delano Roosevelt's New Deal. The Works Progress Administration (WPA), committed to finding jobs for skilled people, ended up supporting some scientific research and many engineering projects. By 1938, most federal spending on science (including technology and agriculture) had been restored to pre-depression levels. And as the United States grew closer to war, the WPA moved into defense projects, with increasing scientific and technological components.

War again provided a significant catalyst for government interest in scientific research, and like Hale and Bache in wars fought previously, one individual played a prominent role in creating a new vision of scientific and technological cooperation with the government. In 1939, Vannevar Bush went to Washington from his position as a dean at the Massachusetts Institute of Technology (MIT) to head the Carnegie Institution, one of the philanthropies primarily involved in funding scientific research. Bush received an appointment as the chair of NACA. An electrical engineer, he possessed a centralized, hierarchical vision of science. Concerned about Germany's aggression in Europe, he supported military modernization and preparedness.

Bush took the lead in organizing science for war. He approached Harry Hopkins, Roosevelt's closest adviser, in May 1940 with a plan to mobilize and coordinate

Headquarters of the National Academy of Sciences in Washington, D.C., ca. 1909–1932. (Library of Congress.)

researchers under nongovernmental experts like himself. Hopkins saw Bush as the man who could harness America's considerable technical resources in the national interest. By June Roosevelt had created the National Defense Research Committee (NDRC), and the president began to delegate science and technology policy to Bush. In hindsight, it is clear that, with the NDRC, the mobilization of scientific and technological resources began a full year and a half before the United States entered World War II. When the government needed science to advance the war effort, science was ready.

Whereas earlier attempts by scientists to contribute to war efforts had been more promise than action, science played a much more important role in World War II. In May 1941, Bush headed the Office of Scientific Research and Defense (OSRD), a newly created agency put in charge of the NDRC. This office, though providing scientific and technological R&D for the military, remained under civilian control. Bush sought out scientists, engineers, and technicians; offered over 9,000 draft deferments; and placed people where their skills and experiences would be most useful. The OSRD also contracted research to additional private, university, and government institutions, and Bush could move projects between institutions. The OSRD oversaw most of the important technological developments of the war, from radar to the proximity fuse—with the notable exception of the Manhattan Project, which began as an OSRD project but, for reasons of budget and secrecy, was transferred to the Army Corps of Engineers, where it essentially functioned autonomously. In addition to Bush's OSRD, the military branches themselves spawned new R&D capabilities during the war. These agencies often quarreled with the OSRD over personnel and projects. Still, Congress rarely limited funding in the war years, and the federal R&D budget (including agriculture) grew from $74.1 million in 1940 to $1.59 billion in 1945. The government spent over $2 billion on research during World War II—not including the Manhattan Project—divided roughly equally between the army, the navy, the army air corps, and the OSRD.

The size of the federal government swelled during the war, and although it did contract afterward, it did not shrink all the way back to prewar levels. Vannevar Bush wanted to ensure a continued partnership between his researchers and the government. However, he hoped to make certain that scientists, not politicians or bureaucrats, made the key decisions about what research to pursue. Like Hale, he envisioned government support without government supervision. However, the Keynesian vision of the state's role in the economy came into conflict with Bush's vision. If Bush argued that scientific research played a central role in economic and technological development, which he did, then it would be hard for him to convince the government to leave the direction of that research to a small, elite committee. As argued by Harley Kilgore of West Virginia, Bush's opponent in the debates about the structure of the National Science Foundation, something with such a strong influence on the nation's economic future belonged in democratic hands. For five years, from 1945 to 1950, Bush and Kilgore engaged in a high-profile debate over the government's role in the sponsorship of science. They agreed that the government should aid R&D spending, but they disagreed about just how much direction and oversight the federal government should provide. Kilgore advocated a central agency to direct and fund research in the interest of economic growth. Bush wanted an agency controlled by scientists, with basic science as their priority.

Meanwhile, others in Congress remained less supportive of funding science and instead sought policies to create an economic environment in which market forces would encourage companies to invest in R&D. They contended that private R&D should be supported by university research, which could be funded to a lesser extent by the government. In its 1947 report, the president's Scientific Research Board called for the nation to spend 1 percent of its national income on R&D. By the 1950s this level of funding had become a standard expectation.

In May 1950, a month and half before the beginning of the Korean War, President Harry Truman signed the National Science Foundation (NSF) Act. The act fixed the structure of the NSF, which would be supervised by a board appointed by the president that would share power with a director. Alan Waterman, the chief scientist at the Office of Naval Research, became the first director of the NSF. Hardly the dictator Bush feared, Waterman worked cooperatively and deferentially with scientists in the academy. Through the NSF, the federal government sponsored research, but scientists at nongovernmental institutions, principally universities, would perform the work. In addition, the NSF supported the kind of basic research that Bush had promoted in his report *Science, the Endless Frontier*. During the five-year fight for the NSF, other new and existing institutions and agencies, such as the National Institutes for Health and the Atomic Energy Commission, had taken over many of the functions that Kilgore had imagined for the NSF. However, the orientation to so-called pure science left the NSF vulnerable to questions about its utility—Congress often wanted more concrete commitments about the benefits of funding basic science. The NSF faced extinction in 1952 and fought for its existence in its first several years.

The NSF's worries ended in 1957 with the Soviet Union's launch of their *Sputnik* satellite. To many Americans, *Sputnik* became a technological symbol of Moscow's growing and aggressive power. The United States had been developing a similar satellite since 1955, under the navy's Project Vanguard. In fact, the country successfully launched *Explorer 1* only three months after *Sputnik* in 1958. But the impact of seeing the Soviets arrive first in space cannot be underestimated. The government's science policy in response to *Sputnik* encompassed several dimensions, all of which justified considerable increases in funding. In the wake of *Sputnik*, the federal government created new agencies, increased the funding and visibility of old agencies, and constructed initiatives for scientific and technological education. In 1958, Congress created NASA, which, as mentioned, was a transformation of NACA. NASA constituted the most visible government response to *Sputnik*. In addition, the National Defense Education Act created a student loan program; provided financial assistance for instruction in science, mathematics, and foreign languages; and gave fellowships for graduate training in science and engineering. By 1960, spurred by the Cold War, the federal government had clearly taken responsibility for funding scientific research.

Between 1958 and 1968, federal funding of science remained high. Private investment in R&D grew more regularly and steadily than the more volatile federal expenditure. Still, the federal share of national R&D investment hovered around 63 percent from 1960 to 1985. NASA expenses accounted for a considerable proportion of federal expenditures and peaked in 1968, in the wake of John F. Kennedy's pledge to send a man to the moon in the decade of the 1960s. The effort to achieve that goal, called Project Apollo, cost $25.4 billion and ultimately succeeded with the 1968 orbit of the moon and the 1969 lunar landing of *Apollo 11*.

However, just as spending on science reached unprecedented levels, Bush's vision of pure science in the national interest came under fire. In 1965 the Department of Defense sponsored its own study of the efficacy of scientific research, called Project Hindsight. The report, issued in 1969, examined the development of 20 weapon systems and overwhelmingly credited targeted, applied research, not Bush's pure research, for their development. Although there was some criticism of Project Hindsight—including a refutation by the NSF—the study changed the policy climate, casting a much more favorable light on targeted research.

The Vietnam conflict also affected R&D spending. Although public opposition to the war and to the military more generally cast a shadow over defense research, military procurement channeled money to the defense industry and its R&D. Some new

Astronaut Edward White becomes the first American man to walk in space during the Gemini IV mission on June 9, 1965. (National Aeronautics and Space Administration.)

military technologies had been developed under federal contracts, but others emerged more independently. Procurement acted as another way for the government to direct R&D. For example, in 1962, the federal government purchased the entire output of integrated circuits in their initial year of production. Many of these technologies also worked their way into public, nonmilitary applications, from television to the computer to the microwave. In the twentieth century, the aircraft industry oversaw particularly successful transfers of technology from military to civilian applications.

The end of the Cold War in 1991 caused considerable confusion in terms of science and technology policy. The Cold War had given policymakers a clear national security imperative for the R&D funding, and the generally strong postwar economy ensured access to the necessary funds. Even after the stagnant economy of the 1970s, President Ronald Reagan's emphasis on national defense nearly returned defense-related R&D to its 1960s levels. By 1986, defense expenditures peaked at 69 percent of the federal R&D budget. Combining the public and private sectors, two-thirds of the $120 billion spent on R&D funded defense work. Still, by 1992, defense spending as a proportion of total R&D had only shrunk to 60 percent. Even President Bill Clinton, who claimed to favor R&D with more direct technological consequences, sought only for civilian R&D to achieve parity with military R&D by 1998. Yet the reduction in defense research brought consequences. As the national security basis of the federal investment in science eroded, so did congressional interest in supporting large scientific research projects. The 1993 collapse of support for the $8 billion superconducting supercollider would become the most visible casualty.

In the postwar period, as expenses grew, so did Congress's interest in adjudicating scientific and technological budget allocations. By the 1960s, concerns arose that Congress members lacked the expertise to make these technical decisions and that they needed better access to expert advice, much like the president had had from organizations such as the National Academy of Sciences since the Civil War. Emilio Daddario, a Connecticut Democrat and chair of the congressional Subcommittee on Science, Research, and Development, called for a study of Congress's access to technical advice and information. He found that although a system of scientific and technical advisers for the executive branch existed, the legislative branch lacked such accommodation. Daddario began to push for an advisory agency for Congress. However, his interests remained more than organizational—he hoped Congress could take a greater role in managing technology, especially moderating its negative environmental consequences. For Daddario, the promising tool was technology assessment, and the agency he sought for Congress would take a leading role in such efforts. He introduced his legislation in 1970 and immediately encountered resistance, with most of the opposition aimed directly at the regulatory dimension of technology assessment. Although Daddario was no longer in the House when it was formed, Congress created the Office of Technology Assessment (OTA) in 1972 as a supplement to the General Accounting Office. When OTA began operating in 1974, Daddario became its chair. In practice, the OTA served as an advisory body for the Congress, and Daddario's hopes for true technology assessment failed to materialize. Following the 1994 Republican takeover of Congress, congressional action eliminated the OTA.

During the 20-year existence of the OTA, the president's system of science advisers also underwent several changes. In 1976, the Office of Science and Technology Policy was created to "serve as a source of scientific and technological analysis and judgment for the President with respect to major policies, plans, and programs of the Federal Government." George H. Bush's President's Committee of Advisors on Science and Technology (PCAST) provided further support to the chief executive. This committee coordinated access to experts in the private sector and academic community, particularly on matters of technological development, setting scientific research priorities, and reforming math and science education. President Bill Clinton created another group, the National Science and Technology Council (NSTC), in 1993 to coordinate federal R&D. This council, which was to report to the vice president, followed clear goals for federal investments in science and technology. George W. Bush reformed PCAST in 2001 when he created the President's Council of Advisors on Science and Technology (PCAST 2001), in large part to provide advice and aid in decisions about stem-cell research. Each of these groups operated with specific issues in mind, and the subtle differences and hierarchies between these advisory bodies created room to discuss controversial subjects. Unlike the OTA, whose ineffectiveness at investigating controversial problems stemmed from its dependent political position, the presidential committees operated independently and, generally, in limited time frames.

The history of science and technology policy in the United States is necessarily multifaceted because so many factors affect the development of scientific and technological knowledge. The most direct influence in this field remains federal funding, but that funding often comes with federal control, which scientific and technological practitioners have often resisted. In addition, national security continues to be the most common rationale for federal research support, and that orientation clearly affects the nature of the science and technology produced. Federal support in the education of both highly trained technical personnel and the public also plays an important role in a nation's ability to produce science and engineering advances. In the twentieth century, the role of private corporations in the pursuit of scientific knowledge grew increasingly important, and government policies, such as taxation, had the capacity to affect the methods and levels of private research support. In the case of existent technologies, federal and state regulation clearly influences both regional and national economies. Lastly, matter related to intellectual property law should not be dismissed as critical factors in technological development, as recent issues in technology transfer and pharmaceutical patenting have shown.

References

Ambrose, Stephen E. *Duty, Honor, Country: A History of West Point*. Baltimore, MD: Johns Hopkins University Press, 1966.

Bruce, Robert. *The Launching of Modern American Science, 1846–1876*. New York: Alfred A. Knopf, 1987.

Burke, John G. "Bursting Boilers and the Federal Power." *Technology and Culture*, vol. 7, no. 1 (January 1966): 1–23.

Bush, Vannevar. *Science, the Endless Frontier*. Washington, DC: U.S. Government Printing Office, 1945.

Dupree, A. Hunter. *Science in the Federal Government: A History of Policies and Activities to 1940.* Cambridge, MA: Harvard University Press, Belknap Press, 1957.

Galbraith, John Kenneth. *The New Industrial State.* 4th ed. Boston: Houghton Mifflin, 1985.

Hart, David M. *Forged Consensus: Science, Technology, and Economic Policy in the United States, 1921–1953.* Princeton, NJ: Princeton University Press, 1998.

Kealey, Terrence. *The Economic Laws of Scientific Research.* New York: St. Martin's Press, 1996.

Kevles, Daniel J. "The National Science Foundation and the Debate over Postwar Research Policy." *Isis*, vol. 68 (1977): 5–27.

Kevles, Daniel J. *The Physicists: The History of a Scientific Community in Modern America.* New York: Alfred A. Knopf, 1978.

Kunkle, Gregory C. "New Challenge or the Past Revisited? The Office of Technology Assessment in Historical Context." *Technology in Society*, vol. 17, no. 2 (1995): 175–197.

Landau, Ralph, and Dale W. Jorgensen. *Technology and Economic Policy.* Cambridge, MA: Ballinger, 1986.

Licht, Walter. *Industrializing America: The Nineteenth Century.* Baltimore, MD: Johns Hopkins University Press, 1995.

Pursell, Carroll. *The Machine in America: A Social History of Technology.* Baltimore, MD: Johns Hopkins University Press, 1995.

Rosenberg, Nathan, and David C. Mowery. *Technology and the Pursuit of Economic Growth.* Cambridge: Cambridge University Press, 1989.

Shapley, Deborah. "Clintonizing Science Policy." *Bulletin of Atomic Scientists*, December 1993. Available: http://www.thebulletin.org/issues/1993/d93/d93 Shapley.html; accessed May 2, 2003.

Walterscheid, Edward C. *To Promote the Progress of Useful Arts: American Patent Law and Administration, 1798–1836.* Littleton, CO: Fred Rothman, 1998.

Slavery

Avery Plaw

Even today, roughly 150 years since its demise as a legal institution, American slavery remains a focus of controversy, albeit of a rather different character than that which preceded its extinction. In the mid-1800s Southern planters passionately defended the morality of their "peculiar institution" against equally impassioned denunciations by (mostly Northern) abolitionists. Planters insisted that the system of slave labor was good and right not only for themselves and their communities but also for the slaves. The abolitionists, however, long ago won the day both on the field of battle and on the field of public discourse, and few if any will take up the challenge of a moral defense of slavery today. That particular controversy over slavery, which troubled the American conscience for so long, is over.

The controversies that swirl around slavery today are of a more historical and technical nature. Why did the slave system of labor, for example, embed itself so deeply in the American South while gradually disappearing in virtually every other New World colony? Was American slavery comparatively humane, at least relative to other New World systems of slavery? Did American slaves live in materially worse conditions than free industrial workers in the North? Did slaves benefit substantially from the value that they produced? Was the American slave-labor system inefficient in comparison with "free" agricultural labor? Was American slavery moribund by the eve of the Civil War, or was it dynamic and expanding? In short, setting aside the issue of its morality, was slavery at least economically rational?

Much of the controversy that has surrounded these questions—and the consequent impulse to reexamine the evidence relating to them—was instigated by the publication of Robert Fogel and Stanley Engerman's *Time on the Cross: The Economics of American Negro Slavery* in 1974. In this groundbreaking text, the authors attacked the two contending approaches that had dominated scholarship on American slavery up to that period. The first approach was exemplified by the well-known American historian Ulrich B. Phillips, particularly in his classic *American Negro Slavery* (1918). Phillips's study focused almost exclusively on white slaveowners and their organization and management of the slave system of labor. Regarding the slaves themselves, he infamously remarked that whites helped the slaves to become as good as they were. Phillips's approach can be summarized as a view of slavery through the owners' eyes, and his work falls into a category that is sometimes called the literature of slave domination. No doubt this approach was not merely ideologically satisfactory from the perspective of white Southerners but also convenient from the perspective of historians, as slaveowners left a much wider array of artifacts and records from which a picture of a time and place could be reconstructed than did illiterate slaves with few possessions. Working from such material does seem likely, however, to produce a very one-sided account of the American experience of slavery.

The alternate approach to which Fogel and Engerman equally responded was, in a sense, the mirror opposite of the first approach. It could be called the literature of slave victimization, and it is probably best represented in Stanley M. Elkins's *Slavery: A Problem in American Institutional and Intellectual Life* (1959). Instead of seeing slavery through the owners' eyes, this approach attempted to reconstruct something of the slaves' own experience of slavery. Elkins noted that, in contrast to Brazil and the Caribbean Islands, the American South experienced no large and sustained slave revolts, and he tried to explain this absence by arguing that the American slave-labor system in the South, especially the Deep South, was, from the slave's perspective, harsher than the comparable systems in the Caribbean and in South America. Elkins argued that Southern slavery was similar to Nazi concentration camps in the sense of constituting a "total experience" that utterly isolated the individual slave, cutting off all meaningful social relations except with the paternal figure of the owner as "the good father." The individual slave was thus rendered psychologically defenseless and then systematically transformed into what Elkins termed a "Sambo"—a docile and childlike creature who identified with the very master who was the source of his emasculation. In a way, Elkins's book and the enormous literature that it spawned re-created the same picture of "the slave as the object of the Master's will" that lay at the heart of Phillips's book but now revealed from a different perspective.

Fogel and Engerman responded to the literatures of domination and victimization by stressing two main themes. On the one hand, their analysis emphasized the resilience of African Americans trapped within the slave system and the spaces of autonomy and distinctive culture they were able to carve out and preserve for themselves within the system. On the other hand, they argued that slavery itself was not based simply on irrational or archaic domination or victimization but rather on an economically rational and highly effective system of (exploitative) production. They employed new econometric techniques to engineer a careful reassessment of the extensive raw statistical data on slavery, and they argued that their analysis revealed that, contrary to received wisdom, the American slave was not lazy but worked as hard as the white laborer. Although critics of slavery argued that the system was inefficient, the authors found that slave agriculture was actually 35 percent more efficient than free agriculture. Moreover, the purchase of a slave was a highly rational investment, just the same as an investment in a manufacturing company. Further, the authors noted, slavery continued as an economically viable and even expanding system up to the Civil War. Finally and perhaps most problematically, Fogel and Engerman argued that the costs of owning a slave amounted to 90 percent of the profit derived from his or her labor.

Many historians and economists have disputed Fogel and Engerman's analysis and conclusions, but some have come to their defense, and Fogel and Engerman themselves have, in the intervening years, published several books of essays and evidence supporting their initial claims. The result has been a large and diverse literature. What this literature reveals broadly, without retracing the specific lines of argument, is that although there is a good deal of general evidence supporting most of Fogel and Engerman's analysis, especially their more strictly economic conclusions, there are also enormous regional and historical disparities underlying the American experience of slavery, which are masked by an aggregate quantitative focus. Statistical analysis needs to be balanced with historical, regional, and microlevel examination if it is to be illuminating. Although microlevel analyses of individual plantations are somewhat beyond the parameters of this short interpretive essay, a brief historical overview sensitive to regional divergences and the evolution of slavery over time should help to contextualize Fogel and Engerman's findings.

Historical Overview

American slavery was a system of labor based on ownership of persons rather than on consent and contract. It applied almost exclusively to blacks (mainly Africans or people of African extraction). It ended formally in 1865 with the Northern victory in the Civil War and the passage of the Thirteenth Amendment to the U.S. Constitution. The more difficult and controversial question is when slavery effectively began as a general system of labor in the British colonies that would eventually become the United States. Slavery was, of course, permitted virtually everywhere in the colonies during most of the seventeenth century, and it was formally legal throughout the colonies by 1750 (when Georgia overturned its short-lived antislavery statutes of 1733). But until the Anglo-Dutch War (1664–1667), the slave trade was dominated by the Portuguese and the Dutch, and there was little commerce with the American colonies. Records show that one Dutch captain sold 20 slaves in Virginia in 1619, but this transaction seems to have been rather exceptional. Although the historical records are unclear about the numbers of black slaves in the early colonies, the scholarly consensus is that although they were not unknown, they were a rarity. In general, the colonists showed a marked preference for importing indentured servants from Europe to fill their growing demands for labor. African slaves were considered too expensive, too difficult to acclimatize and train, and too time-consuming to supervise in comparison with European servants. The American colonists did experiment with using native Indians as slaves (for example, the government of South Carolina in 1708 estimated the colony had 1,400 Indian slaves in a total population of 12,580), but they were frustrated by cultural barriers (the men frequently refused to perform agricultural tasks they regarded as women's work), the proximity of escape, and the vulnerability of natives to European diseases. The initial experiment with slavery was a failure.

In the latter part of the seventeenth century, however, the economic incentives concerning the importation of labor began to change. This shift in incentives had three main causes. First, there was an enormous increase in the demand for labor. In the Virginia colony, for example, the highly labor-intensive tobacco agriculture took off economically while at the same time the overall population of the colony and of those attempting tobacco cultivation tripled in the years from 1750 to 1800. The demand for labor correspondingly increased. Second, political stabilization and economic growth in Europe and particularly the United Kingdom led to a sharp reduction in the availability of indentured servants as well as a sharp rise in the cost of importing them. Third, the successful English war against the Dutch and the consequent British takeover of the Dutch slave trade led to a sharp reduction in the price and an increase in the availability of African slaves to American colonists. Historian Russel Menard, for example, has calculated that the comparative price of African slaves to indentured servants fell between 1674 and 1791 from a ratio of 2.88 to 1 to 1.83 to 1. When the permanence of slave labor (and the slaves' progeny) is factored into these comparative costs, it is easy to see why the colonists began to rationally opt for slave labor over the importation of indentured servants.

The result of this combination of a new structure of incentives and the new accessibility of the African slaves was the development of a triangular system of trade. Ships would typically depart from ports such as Liverpool and Boston loaded with weapons, manufactured goods, and rum and sail for the coast of northwest Africa, where they would trade these goods with coastal forts, sometimes called factories, and local tribes in exchange for slaves. The ships would then sail for the New World laden with a human cargo that would later be sold in South America (most notoriously in Brazil), in the Caribbean Islands (for instance, Saint Domingue [later Haiti], Jamaica, Cuba, or Bermuda), or in the American colonies. Historian Philip Curtin estimated in 1969 that, despite the expiration of between 5 and 20 percent of the human cargo (mainly in the infamous "middle passage" portion of the journey), around 9.5 million Africans were transported as slaves to the New World. Current estimates range as high as 11 million. Around 85 percent of the slaves transported to the New World were sold in Brazil and many more in the Caribbean Islands (Jamaica, for example, is estimated to have imported 750,000 slaves to work on its sugar plantations). Before the banning of the slave trade by Congress in 1808, the American colonies (and later the United States) probably imported somewhere between 600,000 and 650,000 slaves, about 6 percent of the New World total.

It is estimated that by 1680, the American colonies, though still overwhelmingly white, contained around 7,000 African slaves. By 1790, however, the population of African slaves in the colonies had increased almost a hundred times, to close to 700,000. By 1810, the number had risen to 1.1 million and, by 1860, on the eve of the Civil War, the population stood at almost 4 million. The rapidly rising number of slaves in the United States begs an important question, which, in turn, illuminates one of the highly distinctive characteristics of American slavery. If only around 650,000 slaves were imported into the States and if the trade was ended in 1808, what accounts for the fast and continuing growth of the slave population? The answer is simply that, unlike virtually every other slave society in the New World (except Bermuda), the American slave population grew naturally through reproduction, and it grew very rapidly—by four times between 1810 and 1860 alone. The remarkable character of this feature of American slavery can be illustrated by briefly comparing the demographics of slavery in America and in Jamaica. Of the 750,000 slaves imported into Jamaica, only 311,000 remained at the time of emancipation in 1834, whereas the smaller population imported into America had already grown well into the millions.

A number of factors have been cited to explain the remarkable fertility of the American slave population, four of which have received the most attention. First, the food self-sufficiency of the American mainland is thought to have allowed slave-owners to provide their slaves with a larger, healthier, and more consistent diet than was practicable for most other New World slave populations. After all, the owners had an important vested interest in the health and strength of their slaves. Second, the absence of tropical diseases has been frequently identified as an important con-tributor to the high growth rate of the slave population. Third, the fact that slaves in America were largely involved in the cultivation of tobacco, rice, and later cotton rather than sugar (with the exception of a few large plantations in Louisiana) is thought to help explain a comparatively lower mortality rate, which contributed to the rate of overall population growth. Sugar cultivation typically exposed workers to grim and harsh conditions and an exhausting pace of labor, which raised mortality rates and permitted little time for raising families. Finally, it is often pointed out that there was a self-reenforcing quality to the natural growth of a slave population. In short, although the initially imported populations tended to be, for obvious reasons, disproportionately male, reproduction over generations tended to rapidly balance out the gender gap, encouraging further population growth.

Of course, slaveowners also had a vested interest in the numerical increase of their slaves for the simple reason that it augmented their property and personal worth and the amount of labor under their control. It has correspondingly sometimes been argued that owners deliberately bred their slaves (or bred *with* their slaves) as a sort of investment. Although there can be no doubt that many slaveowners often took ad-vantage of their female property and that at least some of them encouraged shorter lactation periods (often only a year), which encouraged more rapidly renewed fertil-ity, there is little evidence that these behaviors were carried out systematically in a manner that would explain the pervasive phenomenon of natural population growth. Moreover, many of the same behaviors were recorded in other slave societies, in which the population shrank precipitously.

At any rate, regardless of the precise explanation (and it is likely, in fact, some combination of all the factors mentioned here), the phenomenon of rapid natural population growth is a distinctive and unambiguously established feature of American slavery, which tends broadly to support Fogel and Engerman's thesis that American slaves enjoyed a significantly better material condition than slaves elsewhere in the New World. Two further important and distinctive features of American slavery may be noted at this point. First, most owners tended to run or at least to personally oversee their own business affairs (as compared to the phenomenon of absentee ownership that characterized the bulk of New World slavery). Second, African slaves were always dispersed in America among a large

A nineteenth-century painting of a Southern cotton plantation near the Mississippi River. This romanticized depiction of plantation life shows the production of cotton through slave labor and the wealth of the Southern cotton aristocracy. (Library of Congress.)

white population. Even in the South, slaves never accounted for much more than a third of the total population, whereas in much of the Caribbean, they ended up outnumbering whites by ratios as high as 10 to 1. Still, although these statistical generalities are useful in establishing a framework for exploring American slavery, they also conceal a great deal of the very real diversity that developed on the ground. To understand that diversity, it is essential to distinguish the growth of different regional concentrations of slave labor organized around the cultivation of different crops.

As Table 7 illustrates, the slave population was by no means evenly spread through the colonies, and indeed, following the War of Independence, African American slavery quickly became a wholly Southern phenomenon. In 1790, the Northern states contained just over 40,000 slaves (mainly concentrated in New York State and Rhode Island) out of a broader population of 697,897, accounting in total for just under 6 percent of the American slave population as a whole. By 1860, however, slavery had been effectively eliminated in the North, whereas the total slave population, now entirely in the South, continued to rise to close to 4 million.

Table 7. Slave population and distribution, 1790 and 1860

	1790	1860
United States	697,897 (17.8%)*	3,953,760 (12.6%)
North	40,370 (2.1%)	64[†](0.0%)
Regional share	5.8%	0.0%
South	657,527 (33.5%)	3,953,696 (32.1%)
Regional share	94.2%	100.0%
Upper South	521,169 (32.0%)	1,530,229 (22.1%)
Regional share	74.7%	38.7%
Deep South	136,358 (41.1%)	2,423,467 (44.8%)
Regional share	19.5%	61.3%
Upper South by state		
Delaware	8,887 (15.0%)	1,798 (1.6%)
Maryland	103,036 (32.2%)	87,189 (12.7%)
District of Columbia		3,185 (4.2%)
Virginia	293,427 (39.2%)	490,865 (30.7%)
North Carolina	100,572 (25.5%)	331,059 (33.4%)
Kentucky	11,830 (16.2%)	225,483 (19.5%)
Missouri		114,931 (9.7%)
Tennessee	3,417 (9.5%)	275,719 (24.8%)
Deep South by state		
South Carolina	107,094 (43.0%)	402,406 (57.2%)
Georgia		462,198 (43.7%)
Florida		61,745 (44.0%)
Arkansas		111,115 (25.5%)
Alabama		435,080 (45.1%)
Louisiana	16,544 (51.6%)[‡]	331,726 (46.9%)
Mississippi		436,631 (55.2%)
Texas		182,566 (30.2%)

*Parenthetical numbers represent percentage of local population.

[†]Includes 18 lifetime apprentices in New Jersey.

[‡]In 1785; not included in regional or nation totals.

Source: http://fisher.lib.viriginia.edu/cgi-local/censusbin/census/cen.pl?year=790; http://fisher.lib.virginia.edu/cgi-local/censusbin/cen.pl?year=860.

Even within the South, however, slaves were not evenly distributed. In 1790, a little under half of the slave population (293,427) was concentrated in Virginia (accounting for close to 40 percent of the state's total population), with Maryland, North Carolina, and South Carolina accounting for most of the other half. By 1860, slavery had expanded geographically along with the South. Although Virginia and North Carolina continued to lead the states of the Upper South and South Carolina and Georgia continued to be among the leading states of the Deep South (with well over half of South Carolina's population being made up by slaves), Alabama, Mississippi, and Louisiana had also emerged as major slave states, and, equally important, the institution had infiltrated every Southern state.

The distribution of slaves throughout the United States and its change over time reflected basic economic realities on the ground. In the pre-independence period, the colonies could be usefully divided into three basic groups: the North, the Upper South, and the Deep South. The primary early demand for slaves was concentrated in Virginia, Maryland, and the upper part of North Carolina and was mostly driven by the development of commercial tobacco farming, which grew rapidly through the latter part of the seventeenth century, increasing from exports of 20,000 pounds in 1619 to 38 million pounds in 1700. Toward the end of the century, South Carolina and later Georgia emerged as a second major source of demand for slaves as the commercial farming of rice developed in the low country, growing from exports of 12,000 pounds in 1698 to 18 million pounds in 1730 and 83 million pounds in 1770.

Finally, at the turn of the century and into the antebellum period, technological advances such as the harnessing of steam power and the invention of the cotton gin in 1793 resulted in a sharply rising demand, particularly in England, for cotton, a crop for which the conditions of the Deep South were particularly well suited. Although America exported only 3,000 bales of cotton in 1790, total exports rose to 178,000 bales by 1810 and surpassed 4 million bales by 1860. The cultivation of cotton initially was restricted to South Carolina and Georgia but quickly expanded into newly settled states, such as Arkansas, Florida, Texas, and, most prominently, Alabama, Mississippi, and Louisiana, which together grew more than half of the nation's cotton by 1834. The highly labor-intensive character of cotton cultivation generated an insatiable demand for labor. The steep growth of the cotton industry and its rapid expansion westward through the Deep South correspondingly help to account for both for the spread of slavery throughout the states of the South, especially the Deep South, and the remarkable increase in the numbers of slaves working in these states.

The distinctive character of the intensive slavery that emerged with the opening of the Deep Southwest suggests a final sub-distinction that is useful to keep in mind. The Deep Southeast continued to mix limited cotton cultivation with traditional rice and indigo cultivation, whereas the Deep Southwest concentrated on intensive cotton cultivation. The resulting demand for labor in the Deep Southwest generated high prices for slaves and resulted in enormous sales of slaves "down the river"—farther into the West and deeper into the South. Although statistics are not precise, scholars estimate that over a million slaves were sent westward between 1790 and 1860—perhaps up to twice as many as made the transatlantic passage.

The danger of being sold down the river into the "new" South represented a genuine horror for slaves, not only because of the trauma of adjusting to unknown owners and the separation from family that was often implied, usually permanently, but also because of the rumors they heard of a harsher and more brutal slavery awaiting them in the West. The rumors were not wrong. It was generally better to be a slave in the Southeast than in the Southwest, although rice cultivation in the Southeast was probably worse than tobacco cultivation in the Upper South or the kind of slavery that had developed in the North. This state of affairs evolved for sound economic reasons. With the dearth of labor in the West and the enormous profits to be made on cotton exports, planters worked the slaves that they could get as hard as they could. In short, there were undoubtedly important differences in the character of slavery in the regions that have been distinguished in this essay, and these differences of character changed over time.

In broad terms, the situation of slaves worsened from North to South and from East to West. In the North, where commercial cultivation of cash crops was never the focus of the economy, slavery remained relatively marginal, although the slave population rose by 1790, just before slavery was legally prohibited, to around 20 percent of the total population in some regions of states such as New York and Rhode Island. Slaves were used in domestic service, in skilled crafts, and as day labor. Some slaves were also used in larger commercial projects—they cultivated wheat along the banks of the Hudson River or raised horses and dairy cows in Rhode Island—but there remains little evidence in these cases of the extensive use of the harsh discipline and cruel punishments employed throughout the South. Slaveholdings were typically small, rarely exceeding five, and slaves worked with or under their owners and usually enjoyed a significant degree of autonomy in arranging their lives outside the workplace—choosing a spouse and raising a family. The conditions of work were generally good by comparison with those in the South, and the proportion of free blacks was comparatively high and rose continually through the post-independence period, already reaching over 40 percent of the total Northern black population by 1790.

In the latter part of the eighteenth century, the obvious implications of the War of Independence, fought in the name of a right of all men to "liberty," had a deep impact on Northern views of slavery. Although the founding fathers (many of them among the largest slaveholders of their time) compromised with powerful slaveowner interests in drafting the Constitution and so declined to constitutionally abolish slavery, they did indicate an intention to banish the slave trade in 20 years' time, a number of slave states in the meantime acted on their own to do this, including Virginia in 1778. The War of Independence produced a reorientation of attitude in the North, which led to laws outlawing slavery in all Northern states by 1804, although some of these included gradualist features.

In the Upper South, as Table 8 indicates, slaves typically lived in larger holdings than in the North but distinctly smaller holdings than in the Deep South (around half as large), especially once Louisiana (purchased in 1803), with its large sugar plantations, is factored in. The smaller size of holdings reflects the fact that tobacco, the predominant cash crop in the Upper South, could be cultivated successfully in small or medium-sized plots. In general, tobacco farming was less labor-intensive than rice or cotton cultivation, and it did not expose laborers to the health risks associated with working in rice fields in the midsummer. Most of these slaves worked in small groups either directly or indirectly under the supervision of their owners and thus were less often and less thoroughly subject to professional overseers and drivers. The smaller scale of production did not demand the rigid systems of rules characteristic of large plantations and the harsh punishments associated with those rules. Moreover, in the second half of the eighteenth century, land exhaustion led to a tobacco crisis, and many planters turned all or part of their fields toward the cultivation of other, even less labor-intensive crops, such as wheat. On average, the food and habitation provided for slaves were simple but adequate and certainly better than the crowded collective dwellings and more regimented life farther south and west. Finally, as the overall slave population shifted from transported Africans to native-born slaves, with

Table 8. Median holdings of slaves in the South by state

	1790	1850	1860
Louisiana		38.9	49.3
South Carolina	36.2	38.2	38.9
Mississippi		33.0	35.0
Alabama		29.9	33.4
Florida		28.5	28.4
Georgia		26.0	26.4
Arkansas		18.4	23.4
North Carolina	13.3	18.6	19.3
Virginia	17.4	18.1	18.8
Texas		14.9	17.6
Tennessee		15.2	15.1
Maryland	15.5	12.2	14.0
Kentucky		10.3	10.4
Missouri		8.6	8.3
Delaware		5.7	6.3
Total Deep South		30.9	32.5
Total Upper South		15.3	15.6
Total South		20.6	20.3

Source: Lewis C. Gray, *History of Agriculture in the Southern United States to 1860* (Washington, DC: Carnegie Institute of Washington, 1933), pp. 530–531. Reprinted with permission.

slaves thus becoming more fully socialized into the life of the Upper South and gaining the confidence of their owners, slaves were frequently allowed a good deal of independence in organizing their personal affairs.

Finally, Elkins in particular makes a convincing case that slavery in the Deep South, both in the East and especially in the West, was particularly harsh, although the further claim that it was worse than the forms of slavery that developed in South America and the Caribbean remains problematic. It is difficult to systematically quantify these differences, but extensive anecdotal evidence suggests that demands on slaves were greater, life was more rigidly and intrusively organized, and punishments were more severe and more frequently employed in the large slaveholdings of the Deep South. In general, the intensity of economic exploitation of the slave-labor systems seems to have been comparatively higher, especially in the early period of western expansion.

As slavery in the South became increasingly isolated through the later antebellum period, however, the most harsh and brutal features of the system were moderated or at least de-emphasized, and the distinctive characteristics of American slavery began to coalesce into the "peculiar institution" that the South defended in the Civil War. To begin with, Southerners found themselves increasingly alone. In 1750, slavery extended throughout the American colonies and indeed through virtually all of the New World. By 1850, however, the North had done away with slavery, and in the Western Hemisphere, only Brazil and the Spanish islands of Cuba and Puerto Rico retained it. At the same time, a strong abolition movement developed both in the North and, to a much more limited extent, in the South (mostly among Quakers). Finally, two great religious revivals that swept across the South instigated growing

Slaves escape by way of the Underground Railroad. An informal network of abolitionists, the Underground Railroad helped guide fugitive slaves to safety across the Canadian border or into free states during the years prior to the American Civil War. (Library of Congress.)

concern with the spiritual condition and humane treatment of the slave population. Both the Great Awakening of the 1730s and 1740s and a second wave of religious revivalism that ran through the South in the 1770s and 1780s emphasized the "equality of all souls before God" and thus led, by the turn of the century, to an increasingly widespread concern with the moral implications of slavery; in some cases, they even led to direct antislavery agitation in the South itself (particularly among Methodists and Baptists in the Upper South). This last development, however, should not be overexaggerated. Explicit abolitionism never developed into a significant mainstream movement within the South itself. Nonetheless, as a result of the increasing isolation of slavery in the American South, the widespread calls for abolition in the North, and at least the emergence of doubts and concerns about slavery in the South, Southern slaveowners (who never made up a majority of the white population, even in the South) were increasingly called on to explicitly defend their "peculiar institution."

These external pressures on slavery were complemented by a number of internal developments, and together, they generated a gradual shift through the antebellum period from an aggressive and nakedly exploitative form of slavery to a more moderate and paternalistic slavery across the South, although important regional disparities in terms of harshness remained. In the first place, the slave population itself was becoming more and more pervasively American-born, particularly following the ban of the slave trade in 1804. As Fogel and Engerman argued, the foreign-born proportion of the black population in America had fallen to around 20 percent by 1800, and it fell off further as imports were banned. American-born slaves did not generally require the same extreme measures to "break their spirits" as many of the adult Africans who had been sold into slavery and transported to America. Their socialization typically occurred more smoothly and gradually while they were growing up, and although a background regime of discipline was certainly deemed necessary, flogging (or whipping) generally proved adequate. Punishment did not need to take the flagrant and brutal forms, such as branding, castration, amputation, and hanging, that were often required to "break in" new slaves or to make examples of those who refused to accept their new status. Finally, the passage of the Eighth Amendment to the U.S. Constitution, prohibiting cruel and unusual punishment, may have also contributed to the progressive shift away from the harshest forms of slave discipline.

A second distinctive feature of American slavery also influenced the later antebellum character of slavery in the South. Southern owners were typically resident owners, and even in the larger slaveholdings of the Deep South, as more slaves were born in the States, they increasingly knew and were personally known by their owners. The Southern slaveowners in the late antebellum period continually emphasized their care and concern for their slaves, and it was common to hear a slaveowner describe these slaves as "my people." Indeed, slaveowners' professions of "love" for their people filled the literature of the time. Moreover, slavery was increasingly defended as a tutelary situation, which above all benefited the slaves themselves. No doubt, much of this talk of care and concern was hypocritical hyperbole, all of which never stopped most slaveowners from extracting extensive profit from the labor of their property. Yet it is important that many Southern slaveowners made at least superficial efforts to improve the condition of "their people" (although often in a manner designed to reinforce their dependence on their masters), either by improving their habitations, food, clothing, and skills; by rewarding them when they performed noteworthy services; by allowing them greater leisure and more autonomy over their leisure time; or by assigning them greater responsibilities when warranted, often involving the supervision or direction of other slaves.

There is evidence, then, of a general improvement in the material conditions of Southern slaves, particularly in the late antebellum period. In some cases, indeed, their material condition may have compared favorably, particularly in the Upper South, with that of industrial workers in the North, as Fogel and Engerman insisted. Thus, it is ironic that the war to end slavery may have been fought at just the time when slavery was reaching its least onerous stage. The point that must, however, be borne in mind is that slavery remained slavery—a degraded and morally repugnant condition, regardless of any marginal improvements in slaves' material welfare.

The growing strength of abolitionism in the North along with the decline of the Whig Party opened the way in the 1850s for the emergence of the new Republican Party, with strong antislavery sensibilities. Drawing on the growing concentration of population in the industrialized North, as well as division and disaffection in the South, the Republican Party presidential candidate, Abraham Lincoln, defeated Stephen Douglas, the (Northern) Democratic candidate, in the 1860 election. Despite Lincoln's assurances that, to preserve the integrity of the Union, he would refrain from outlawing slavery, seven Southern states had seceded from the Union by the time of his inauguration in March 1861. Then, on April 12, 1861, South Carolina fired on Fort Sumter. The Civil War, which would ultimately lead to the elimination of American slavery, had begun.

Conclusion

With a basic historical and regional sense of the development of American slavery, it may now be productive to return to some of the continuingly controversial questions with which this essay began. Why did the slave system of labor, for example, embed itself so deeply in the American South while gradually disappearing in virtually every other New World colony? The answer must be, as is so often the case, a combination of factors: the continuously high demand for and corresponding scarcity of labor throughout America's colonial and antebellum history; the emergence and rapid growth of a manageable population of native-born slaves; the commercial success of American slave-based cultivation; and the continuing dispersion of slaves among a majority white population, which militated against any organized, armed resistance. All of these factors contribute to explaining the resilience and longevity of American slavery.

Did American slaves live in materially worse conditions than free industrial workers in the North? Did slaves benefit substantially from the value that they produced? The answer here is that sometimes they benefited, and sometimes they were materially better off, depending on which regions and historical periods of slavery are under consideration and which industrial workers, living where and when, are taken as a basis of comparison. Slaves in the post-independence North or late antebellum South may have done moderately well on some such material comparisons, and this finding may also help to explain why American slavery survived for so long. But even where they did compare favorably, the comparison only reveals a misleadingly tiny aspect of the slaves' overall condition. Slaves were the explicit and legal property of others, an indefensibly degraded moral condition that has no comparator among Northern industrial workers.

Was American slavery comparatively humane, at least relative to other New World systems of slavery? In general, it probably was, and this was likely another factor contributing to its longevity, although results would likely vary somewhat depending on region and period (if not according to individual owners). Early American slavery in the low lands of Georgia or the sugar plantations of early-nineteenth-century Louisiana may not have been noticeably more humane than slavery in Bermuda, for example.

Finally, American slavery ultimately outlasted slavery almost everywhere else in the New World, and it is unlikely that it was more humane than any free system of contract labor.

Was the American slave-labor system inefficient in comparison with "free" agricultural labor? Historians Alfred Conrad and John Meyer reversed much of the received wisdom about low slave-labor productivity and profitability by showing that the rate of return produced by an average male slave on Southern antebellum plantations was typically between 5 and 8 percent of his initial cost annually (falling to 2 to 5 percent in the exhausted lands of the eastern seaboard and rising as high as 10 to 13 percent on the best lands in Mississippi, Alabama, and South Carolina), with a slightly lower rate for female slaves. They further argued that these numbers compare favorably, on average, with the vast bulk of both agriculture and industrial concerns in the North. This analysis helps to explain the rapid economic growth of the antebellum South. Fogel and Engerman later revisited Conrad and Meyer's analysis in detail, and in what probably remains the most comprehensive and compelling examination of slave-labor profitability, they determined that Conrad and Meyer had somewhat underestimated the level of profitability for male and especially female slaves. Their revised conclusion was an approximately 10 percent aggregate rate of annual return for both male and female slaves. Again, this rate compared favorably with both successful agricultural and industrial concerns in the North. Although Fogel and Engerman's conclusions are still disputed by many scholars and may legitimately be accused of slanting far more to the antebellum than the colonial period, a consensus seems to be emerging that slave cultivation was generally far more profitable than was previously thought and was probably not only a better investment than free Northern agriculture but also likely comparable with some more successful industrial investments.

Was American slavery moribund by the eve of the Civil War, or was it dynamic and expanding? Between the War of Independence and the Civil War, nine new states adopted the system of slave labor, and vast new territories came under its control. Slavery virtually monopolized the cultivation of America's biggest and most valuable export, cotton. In 1854, Congress's Kansas-Nebraska Act opened up Northern states, which had been closed to slavery by the Northwest Ordinance. Meanwhile, the Southern economy was growing much faster than the economies of England, France, or Brazil throughout the late antebellum period. There can be little question, then, that slavery was not only healthy in America in the 1850s, but also rapidly growing. Indeed, it was the threat posed by the rapid expansion of slavery that galvanized the North to take the drastic action of electing a Republican president. Lincoln himself argued, in a speech in Springfield, Illinois, on June 16, 1858, that the United States had to quickly confront the slavery question once and for all, or all would ultimately succumb to its temptations—the Union had to be "all slave or all free," for "a house divided cannot stand."

Finally, setting aside the issue of its morality, was slavery at least economically rational? Unquestionably, it was. Slavery was stable and highly profitable and could, at times at least, be arguably beneficial in a material sense to those subjected to it (in comparison to comparable free labor). The market could coexist as easily with a slave-labor system as it could with a contract-labor system in the North. The choice to invest in slavery, to practice slavery, and to legalize and defend slavery was fully rational in economic terms.

The moral of this long story, then, is simply this: The American experience with slavery illustrates that the market is morally neutral—it can reward and encourage morally abhorrent institutions as easily as morally laudable ones. The market itself is in no sense a dependable moral guide. Attention must be paid to the way that culture, politics, and law shape the dynamics of the market, and the consequences of market interactions must be carefully examined to avoid such disasters in the future.

References

Berlin, Ira. *Slaves without Masters: The Free Negro in the Antebellum South*. New York: Vintage Books, 1974.

Elkins, Stanley M. *Slavery: A Problem in American Institutional and Intellectual Life*. Chicago: University of Chicago Press, 1959.

Fogel, Robert William. *Without Consent or Contract: The Rise and Fall of American Slavery*. New York: W. W. Norton, 1989.

Fogel, Robert William, and Stanley L. Engerman, eds. *Time on the Cross: The Economics of American Negro Slavery*. London: Little, Brown, 1974.

Fogel, Robert William, and Stanley L. Engerman, eds. *Time on the Cross, Volume 2: Evidence and Methods—a Supplement*. London: Little, Brown, 1974.

Fogel, Robert William, and Stanley L. Engerman, eds. *Without Consent or Contract: The Rise and Fall of American Slavery—Technical Papers: Markets and Production, Volume 1*. New York: W. W. Norton, 1992.

Fogel, Robert William, and Stanley L. Engerman, eds. *Without Consent or Contract: The Rise and Fall of American Slavery: Conditions of Slave Life and the Transition to Freedom—Technical Papers, Volume 2*. New York: W. W. Norton, 1992.

Fogel, Robert William, Ralph A. Galantine, and Richard L. Manning, eds. *Without Consent or Contract: The Rise and Fall of American Slavery—Evidence and Methods*. New York: W. W. Norton, 1992.

Gray, Lewis C. *History of Agriculture in the Southern United States to 1860*. Gloucester, MA: P. Smith, 1958.

Gutman, Herbert G. *Slavery and the Numbers Game: A Critique of* Time on the Cross. Chicago: University of Illinois Press, 1975.

Kolchin, Peter. *Unfree Labor: American Slavery and Russian Serfdom*. Cambridge, MA: Harvard University Press, Belknap Press, 1987.

Kolchin, Peter. *American Slavery: 1619–1687*. New York: Hill and Wang, 1993.

Phillips, Ulrich B. *American Negro Slavery*. Baton Rouge: Louisiana State University Press, 1966.

White, John, and Ralph Willett, eds. *Slavery in the American South*. London: Longman, 1970.

Stock Market

Aaron Z. Pitluck

Astock market is a market for the trade of securities and other financial instruments. Like a market in books, transcription services, or labor, a stock market need not have a geographic reference, and it can be more or less fragmented into autonomous markets. More abstractly, the term *stock market* refers to aggregate supply and aggregate demand forces for securities. The supply of such securities is generally fixed, although new securities are issued from time to time by extant and new public and private corporate organizations. The principal actors in stock markets are investors (representing themselves or clients), brokers (who act as intermediaries between investors and the exchange and who may, on some exchanges, trade for themselves as well as their clients), and regulators (who, depending on the exchange, may be either the brokers themselves or quasi-public or public bodies). In contrast to the abstract stock market, a stock exchange is the organization and institution at which trading in stocks takes place—for example, the New York Stock Exchange.

A wide variety of institutionalist scholars have made the reasonable argument that economic markets require certain legal, social, political, or cultural institutions in order to function. For example, the Nobel Prize–winning economic historian Douglass C. North has argued throughout his career that what distinguishes European and American economies from those in the developing world are the superior economic institutions in the former. Such institutions can be formal (for instance, legal property rights or government economic policies) or informal (for instance, norms, culture, or ideology). As North and others have contended, superior institutions structure human interactions so as to promote economic efficiency, minimize uncertainty, and thereby promote economic growth.

Recent research by Rafael La Porta, Florencio Lopez-de-Silanes, and Andrei Shleifer (1999) has made a persuasive case for the necessity of certain basic institutions for the operation of a stock market. These scholars created a database of 49 countries that describes each nation's basic shareholder rights, creditor rights, and quality of law enforcement. Through a systematic comparison of the countries' legal rights and the quality of their stock markets, La Porta and colleagues argued that only countries with a legal system that protects minority shareholder rights can allow dispersed ownership of corporations to occur and thus have a thriving stock market. The argument, as outlined in the first paragraph of their work, is quite intuitive. Who would voluntarily purchase an equity share in a corporation without legal protection from the majority shareholders (or from the controlling management), so as to ensure that the company will continue to behave as it has in the past? The scholars' intuitive finding was that only countries with strong minority investor protection legislation also have vibrant stock markets.

An older and more historical literature agrees, as popularized in Michel Albert's global best-seller *Capitalism versus Capitalism* and in the academic research of Mark J. Roe. These authors described a world in which countries can choose to adopt one of two types of financial systems. One financial system is like that of Germany or Japan and is characterized by concentrated ownership of corporations and bank-based capital markets. The other system features dispersed ownership of corporations within vibrant stock markets, as exemplified by the United States and United Kingdom. John C. Coffee Jr. summarized the conventional wisdom of the two opposing forms of financial markets that we see in the world today. The German model, he said, operates on a consolidated basis controlled by blockholders and wealthy individuals with little accountability except to some large banks. The antithesis is the American model, a decentralized system controlled by the Securities and Exchange Commission with its stringent disclosure and reporting rules and enforcement capabilities.

And yet, Coffee noted, the U.S. stock market, the paragon of a dispersed ownership system, had strong securities markets in the eighteenth and nineteenth centuries but lacked *stringent reporting requirements and openness within the markets*. Moreover, the nineteenth-century stock market in the United States not only lacked federal or state legal protections but also generally lacked an uncorrupt judiciary or legislature; this was especially true in New York City, where the political machine both selected and controlled local judges. Through the placement of bribes or the movement of lawsuits between competing state jurisdictions, powerful economic actors had wide latitude to ensure that the few extant laws concerning the stock market were interpreted in their favor.

The Early Stock Market

The early U.S. stock market was geographically fragmented and operated without the benefits of exchanges or security-specific legislation. Today, the term *broker* is narrowly defined in securities markets as one who specializes in the purchase and sale of securities, but the word had a far broader meaning in the late 1700s. Brokers in the early Republic were generalist middlemen who brought together buyers and sellers and profited from a transaction's commission. It was common for brokers to not only buy and sell securities but also insure cargo, run a private lottery, and act as business partners in private banks, issuing their own notes to be used as currency. With the exception of shipbuilding and pig-iron production, there was practically no manufacturing at that time, so most businesspeople were, in fact, brokers. Brokers were concentrated where wealth was concentrated—in the port cities of New York, Boston, and the nation's temporary capital, Philadelphia.

The early national stock market was an ad hoc and transient creation of brokers who facilitated the trading of securities from their separate offices or by meeting in the streets. In 1781, for example, a New Yorker who wished to purchase equity in the new Bank of North America (the country's first blue-chip investment) could do so only from other New York traders with the aid of one of the handful of brokers' offices and curb traders located in the city. For a New Yorker to trade with a Philadelphian, he would need to travel to Philadelphia himself or have his broker communicate with that city.

The First Catalyst of Development

Shortly after independence, the country was in financial chaos and fragmented, with hundreds of private banks issuing their own currencies. The Continental Congress had issued fiat money, known as Continentals, of unproven value and paid for arms with forced loans. In addition, the government had gone deeply in debt to France and the Netherlands in order to finance the Revolution.

In the 1790s, Secretary of the Treasury Alexander Hamilton restructured America's debts by paying off the country's creditors (both foreign and domestic) and the debts of state governments by issuing new bonds in the name of the federal government. Market analysts viewed this positively; the young country had enormous growth potential, and the new national government was portraying itself by its actions as fiscally responsible to its creditors. As a result, the United States had the highest credit rating in Europe, with its bonds typically selling at 10 percent premium over par (face value). This massive issuance of high-quality public debt securities dramatically altered the national stock market but provided both quality listings as well as a large supply that was met with increased demand. Trading volume surged, and many brokers abandoned other forms of brokerage to concentrate on the lucrative trading of government bonds. As a by-product of fiscal prudence, Hamilton single-handedly created the nation's first stock market bubble. (A bubble is created when stocks become overvalued, and when the bubble bursts, the prices fall quickly and dramatically.)

The price bubble surged further with the issuance of stock in the country's first central bank, the Bank of the United States. Manipulation in the unregulated stock market was simple to accomplish and a common practice. Hamilton's former assistant at the Treasury, William Duer, profited mightily with market manipulation that suggested there were syndicates stretching to the highest levels of government. The bubble finally collapsed in March 1792, and brokers returned to their former businesses as generalist middlemen—but not without seeing profound institutional change. The bubble's high trading volume provided sufficient motivation for the more successful brokers to form exclusive trading cartels with fixed commissions. This situation resulted in the creation of the Philadelphia Stock Exchange, organized in 1790. And, in 1792, with the Buttonwood Agreement, a group of New York brokers formed the symbolic ancestor of the New York Stock Exchange.

In the development of the U.S. stock market, a repeated pattern can be detected: war financed with a rapid buildup of government debt, an increase of demand due to the government's reasonable debt management, and an escalation of trading in response to this increase in supply. In each time period, such a pattern has led to an expansion of the brokerage industry.

Another stock market bubble was created when the United States entered the fiscally and militarily disastrous War of 1812. Government debt rose from $45 million in 1811 to $127 million just four years later. This escalation was partly financed with high inflation. The rising debt and inflation as well as a proliferation of state-chartered banks all contributed not only to additional monetary chaos but also to a brisk business in the trading of both government debt and the monies of private and state-chartered banks—particularly in Philadelphia, where the large banks and the more organized Philadelphia Stock Exchange were located.

The Civil War debt created a decadent atmosphere of unprecedented wealth from unprecedented trading volume on Wall Street. The Union government borrowed on an extraordinary scale; the national debt rose from $64.8 million in 1861 to $2.755 billion in 1865, an increase by a factor of 42. By the war's end, the interest payments alone were twice the size of annual government expenditures before the war. This debt was in large part financed through the sale of federal bonds in the world's first mass sale of securities to individuals. By 1865, approximately 5 percent of the population of the North had purchased bonds. World War I and its debt created a similar pattern, as did World War II (although the stock market boom itself was delayed until after the war's end).

In sum, the skyrocketing government debt dramatically increased the supply of securities that could be traded and acted as a powerful stimulus for stock market development. These surges of investment volume occurred irrespective of the quantity or quality of economic regulation in each time period. The fiscally responsible financing of war repeatedly resulted in a high amount of investment.

Capital-Intensive Corporations and Speculative Industries

In addition to war and government debt, the U.S. stock market experienced rapid development from the growth of capital-intensive industries (for example, financial services, canal building, and the railroad industry) as well as speculative industries (for example, speculative mining and speculative Internet technologies). This essay will examine the effect on U.S. stock markets of the following industries, in rough chronological order: financial corporations, speculative mining ventures, and transportation corporations.

Financial Corporations

The banking and insurance industries dominated the eighteenth- and early-nineteenth-century stock market because of their sheer numbers. Such early corporations date at least as far back as 1791 with the widely distributed publicly traded Bank of the United States, which was chartered as the country's first central bank. An exceptional proliferation of regional banks (many corporately held and publicly traded on stock markets) was prompted by three unusual economic policies of the early United States. First, previous to the Civil War, there was no federal currency, and thus, private banks and many other organizations issued their own. Second, state governments subscribed to a strategy of mercantilism that opposed other states' banks from competing within their own borders, while at the same time frequently collecting bribes and indulging in other corrupt practices in the granting of banking licenses. This situation created segmented financial and money markets. Third, because of competing ideologies and national political maneuvers, the federal government's two attempts at creating a central bank failed. The effect was an enormous demand for banking services (including the use of currency)—a demand that was unfulfilled by the government. The early private banks were often diversely owned corporations listed on the stock market. It is instructive to note that as late as 1836, of the 81 corporations listed on the New York Stock Exchange, 38 were banks and 32 were insurance companies whereas only 8 were railroads and canal companies. In sum, the segmented state markets, with politicized licensing requirements, resulted not only in monopoly profits in financial services such as banking but also in the growth of U.S. stock markets that traded securities in these corporations.

Mining

Like the California gold rush itself, the speculation of mining corporations was conducted with little information in the gamble for great riches. Security prices boomed and collapsed based on rumors, purported news, expert opinions, new complications, and so on. The history of mining securities is an excellent case study of two competing pressures on regulators. On one hand, there was the pressure to maintain a stock exchange with relatively high-quality listings. On the other hand, there was the high volume and corresponding profitable commissions that could be realized by lowering listing standards and including the trading of highly speculative securities.

Historically, the established U.S. exchanges have tended to eschew such listings, thereby facilitating the creation and flowering of competing stock exchanges with lower listing standards. As mineral discoveries dried up, these competing mining exchanges rapidly folded. The established exchanges, though they lost a great deal of business during the boom, nevertheless survived and prospered or merged in later years.

The 1860s were years of wealth and misery, laying the foundation for the inequality and corruption of the Gilded Age. The era suffered the slaughter of soldiers and civilians during the Civil War and also saw a series of major discoveries of precious metals in the West. This combination of newfound money in the mountains and the rise and fall of gold prices during successive Confederate and Union victories resulted in volatile markets in precious metals—and also enormous opportunities for speculative profit. In New York City, demand for trading gold or for the speculative purchase of moneymaking mines was so great that the established exchanges were unable to cope with the volume. Many brokers were earning $800 to $10,000 per day from trading commissions alone, at a time when $1,500 per year was a middle-class income. The demand for trading was so great that daytime trading in the downtown stock exchanges spilled over into the evening in fashionable uptown hotels. After the Civil War, 24-hour securities trading would not return to New York for well over a century.

Despite this surge in volume, the more established exchanges, such as the New York Stock and Exchange Board (NYS&EB), briefly even refused to trade in gold (as it was viewed as unpatriotic), and the NYS&EB continued to refuse to list the more speculative mining ventures, which, of course, meant most of them. As a result, several new stock exchanges formed in New York City to compete with the established ones, among them Gilpin's Gold Exchange in 1862, Gallaher's Evening Exchange in uptown hotels in 1864, the New York Mining Stock Board in 1864, the Petroleum Stock Exchange in 1864, and the Wishart and Company's Petroleum Exchange in 1865. The high volume also created the necessity for continuous auction trading rather than twice-daily auctions at 10:30 a.m. and 2:30 p.m. But even this financial innovation was resisted by the NYS&EB until a competing exchange forced it to adopt the practice and merge with the competitor.

Outside New York, approximately 25 stock exchanges opened in the 1860s. The majority of them were mining stock exchanges, primarily formed in 1863 and 1864 in California and Nevada. These western exchanges were located near the mines seeking financing. The Nevada exchanges were ephemeral, tending to close during the local depression of 1864 and 1865. In the Mississippi Valley, exchanges were set up in Chicago, Cincinnati, St. Louis, and New Orleans to cater primarily to local investors and local businesses and specializing in speculation of gold trading. However, with the exception of Chicago (with its vast trunk lines of railroad), the Mississippi Valley cities that served as conduits for gold were hampered during the Civil War. Although most of the exchanges were short-lived, they paved the way for the creation of new exchanges in later years. As a result, each major city with an exchange that opened in the 1860s found itself with an exchange during the Roaring Twenties.

Transportation

More speculative than finance but generally with a higher amount and quality of information than mining stocks, the transportation industry and its high capital requirements dramatically developed the U.S. stock market.

One of eighteenth-century America's gravest political and economic dilemmas was the high cost of overland transportation. The well-settled eastern seaboard had only expensive access to the agricultural produce of the West via two river networks. Moreover, routes without rivers were terribly costly. Before 1825, it would take three weeks and $120 for a ton of flour (worth $40) to leave Buffalo and reach New York City, effectively quadrupling the cost.

The Erie Canal was an elegant proposal to solve this political economic problem. The engineering task was monumental, however. The proposed route from Lake Erie to the Hudson River was 363 miles long and would descend through 83 locks and 555 feet. The entire canal, 44 feet wide and 4 feet deep, was to be dug by hand. Were that same bag of flour to float via a canal between Buffalo and New York City, it would take a mere eight days at a cost of $6. To provide food and goods in one-third the time and at one-twentieth the prior cost would transform New York City and its environs into a growth engine. The canal was by far the boldest engineering project prior to the Civil War.

In 1792, two corporations were chartered to complete the Erie Canal project. This arrangement was not unusual. In fact, two-thirds of all chartered corporations between the Revolution and 1801 were formed to complete infrastructure projects such as bridges, turnpikes, canals, and wharves. Their stock was rarely in demand, for the projects could tie up capital for years and the charters frequently restricted the tolls that could be charged. Moreover, such infrastructure projects were frequently fraught with labor, management, and engineering difficulties. Purchasers of stock in these corporations frequently either viewed the investment as civic philanthropy or viewed the infrastructure as an indirect means of improving the value of their businesses or land. The Erie Canal, constructed under such uncertainty and risk, could not be fully financed through the stock market, even with the New York State government promising to purchase shares. Insufficient demand for the stock led to the project being underfinanced. Engineering and management difficulties compounded the problem, and both corporations failed.

Several decades later, after lengthy debate in New York's state legislature and after suave politicking by the mayor of New York City, DeWitt Clinton, the state agreed to build the canal itself and finance it with bonds secured by the state's credit. The Erie Canal bonds were marketed as low-risk securities because of the state guarantee to honor the bonds regardless of whether the canal was completed or not or profitable or not. The issue was an enormous success, with 42 separate flotations between 1817 and 1825. Despite the doubts of many that the canal could ever be completed, it was finished in only eight years, thanks, in part, to the adequate financing provided by state-secured bonds.

The successive financing of other canals was similar to that for the Erie Canal. State and municipal bonds were sold overseas through merchant bankers' personal networks or through the Second Bank of the United States. Between 1815 and 1860, total expenditures on canals was an estimated $188 million, of which 73 percent was raised through the sales of state and municipal bonds.

The creation of railroad tracks and a steam engine capable of speeds of up to 18 miles per hour transformed the economics of transit on a scale equivalent to the canals. Unlike the canals, however, the early railroads were not nearly as constrained by nature's topography. The earliest railroads of the 1840s and 1850s were short local lines intended to more rapidly connect a town with a river or port. These roads were generally financed locally by the sale of corporate bonds, which were purchased by the businesses and families located along the route. The railroad company would organize public meetings, circulate petitions, canvas from door to door, and organize propaganda parades and other public functions. For residents with little cash, bonds were frequently sold in return for labor or goods, and loans were offered for the purchase of bonds using the family farm or property as collateral.

The demand for railroads and the entrepreneurial energy to create them quickly outstripped such local financing and was, of course, ineffective on routes passing through unsettled territories. By the mid-1850s, numerous investment banks had opened in New York City specializing in the trade of railroad bonds to European investors. In the years following the Civil War, between 1865 and 1873, railroad mileage doubled, and the total capital invested more than tripled. By the Civil War, the financing of railroads had been transformed so that such investment bankers became critical middlemen. Investment bankers designed the menu of financial instruments with which to purchase existing tracks and build connections between them, underwrote the new issues, and orchestrated syndicates to disseminate the securities to bankers and wealthy investors.

In the post–Civil War decades of the nineteenth century, the railroad industry was easily the largest consumer of capital on the nation's stock exchanges. Unfortunately, the rapid construction of railroad track was creating ruinous competition. During the 1880s, approximately 75,000 miles of track were laid, by far the largest amount ever built anywhere in the world in any decade. By the late 1890s, the industry began consolidating through a combination of foreclosure sales, mergers, and acquisitions organized by the great investment banks, such as the House of Morgan, or through alliances between competitors cemented with cross-ownership of equity and interlocking directorships.

The Peak of Nongovernmental Regulation and Continued Abuse

During the 50 years from 1880 to the end of the Roaring Twenties, the U.S. political economy was dramatically transformed by increased urbanization and large-scale migration to the cities, the creation of great industrial and manufacturing corporations, and the consolidation and concentration of corporate power. Between 1897 and 1904, 4,277 U.S. firms consolidated into 257 corporations. The largest was unquestionably U.S. Steel, as engineered by J. P. Morgan and a syndicate of investment bankers.

Shortly after 1900, new forms of equity began to be sold on the stock market by the investment banking houses, including dual class stocks, voting trusts, and pyramid holding company structures. The effect was to further separate stock ownership from voting rights; majority stock ownership was no longer necessary to control a corporation. Since the beginning of U.S. stock markets, control of a corporation by stock ownership had been a partial illusion given the ability to manipulate many corporations' stock prices and dilute share ownership at will. But with the institutionalization of these new forms of stock, corporate control became a fiction entirely unrelated to stock ownership. By 1930, a famous study by Adolf A. Berle and Gardiner C. Means determined that in 21 percent of the 200 largest corporations, such legal devices, rather than majority share ownership, held corporate control. In 1925, it was exposed that agents owning less than 5 percent of the total stock controlled several leading corporations.

Under such extreme circumstances, why would individuals invest in the stock market without minority rights protections or even an uncorrupt judiciary to protect them? A partial answer involves the existence of powerful representatives to protect investors' interests. In the large railroad corporations and large merged manufacturing corporations, the great investment banking houses acquired seats on the boards of directors. By holding these directorships, the money trusts represented their clients' interests, monitored the controlling management, and, most important, protected the value of their investors' share ownership by preventing predatory raids by outsiders seeking to purchase controlling shares without paying a premium for acquiring control.

A second institution functioning as a substitute for insufficient minority rights protection was the self-regulation of stock exchanges where securities were traded. For example, in 1868, in response to the battle for ownership and control of the Erie Railroad, the New York Stock Exchange (NYSE) required that all listed corporations divulge yearly financial information so that investors could appraise the value of those corporations. In practice, this was ineffectual until the development of double-entry bookkeeping, the accounting industry, and the credentialing of accountants in the 1890s. A more successful example of the way in which investors were protected by new stock exchange regulations was the NYSE's implementation of the bright-line rules in the 1920s. These rules included prohibiting listed corporations from issuing nonvoting common stock or permitting a transfer of corporate control without an explicit shareholder vote. However, the alleged strengths of self-regulation should not be exaggerated. In retrospect, it was largely ineffective in preventing market manipulation, profitable trading based on insider information, or abuse by brokers of trading in front of their client's orders. In sum, despite the inability of the NYSE (or other stock exchanges, for that matter) to prevent market manipulation and the abuse of broker's power over their customers, the NYSE took clear steps toward making corporate financial information transparent and a few steps toward shareholder democracy.

An Attempt at State Regulation

Prior to 1933, with the significant exception of the federal postal laws that contained antifraud provisions, there was no federal regulation of the national stock market or the states' stock exchanges. Stocks were traded like any other commodity, in spite of significant differences between financial markets and other product markets.

Despite a century of reports by historians, journalists, and industry commentators about notorious public stock market scandals, cases of grievous yet licit market manipulation, and numerous acts of fraud; despite similar findings by the congressionally established Industrial Commission in 1900 and again in 1902; despite the 1913 public reports by the congressionally established Pujo Committee or the popular summary of the committee's findings by jurist Louis Brandeis in *Other People's Money*, the public debate in each case did not lead to federal government legislation.

States, however, took the lead with so-called blue-sky laws, intended to protect investors from fraudulent investments—speculative schemes that had no more basis than so many feet of blue sky (as described by Supreme Court Justice Joseph McKenna in 1917).

Broadly speaking, such nineteenth-century state legislation was almost exclusively designed to regulate the business activities of corporations chartered by the state. Only rarely did legislation seek to regulate the securities transactions themselves. For example, the first blue-sky law was enacted by a progressive bank commissioner in Kansas in 1911. Kansas's merit-based regime required that all securities of businesses incorporated in the state had to be licensed by the state. Moreover, the bank commissioner was permitted to withhold licenses not only to businesses that were deemed fraudulent but also even to those deemed to be a poor investment and unable, therefore, to promise a fair return for investors. Thus, Kansas's blue-sky law, though allegedly designed to prevent fraud within the state, contained wide powers to ensure the quality of listed companies incorporated in Kansas. Within two years, 23 states adopted their own blue-sky statutes and, by 1933, every state with the exception of Nevada had also adopted some form of blue-sky legislation.

In practice, such legislation was ineffectual. States had no means of enforcing the legislation against financiers residing out of state. Moreover, the states failed to create administrations charged with investigation and enforcement. By the early 1930s, only eight states had full-time commissions charged with enforcing blue-sky laws. A skeptic could easily argue that the main practical effect of blue-sky laws was providing an additional source of state revenue through securities licensing.

This is not to say that blue-sky laws were inconsequential. They produced numerous pragmatic case studies of merit-based securities licensing. And when the first federal legislation was enacted, it closely mirrored extant blue-sky legislation.

The Era of Federal Regulation

The reversal of the long-standing federal government policy of laissez-faire with regard to securities markets was reversed during President Franklin Roosevelt's first hundred days and the avalanche of legislation enacted in that period to pull the United States out of the Great Depression. When federal legislation of the national stock market began in 1933, it was rapid and radical. Within the space of just 15 months, the federal government implemented the Securities Act, the Glass-Steagall Act, and the Securities Exchange Act. These three acts in concert required material financial information about corporations to be disclosed in annual financial reports and quarterly earnings statements (what the NYSE and individual state blue-sky laws had tried to do with only partial success). They created a new federal administrative organization to oversee securities markets, the Securities and Exchange Commission (SEC), something states with blue-sky laws generally failed to do. And they legislated the full separation of commercial and investment banking, thereby forcing banks to choose to either

Distressed investors and speculators mobbed the New York Stock Exchange in 1929 in the wake of the great stock market crash. (Library of Congress.)

take deposits and provide commercial loans or engage in the lucrative business of originating and distributing corporate securities as investment bankers.

In 1934, the NYSE, under its elected president, Richard Whitney, attempted self-reform so as to convince the public that further federal legislation was unnecessary. The NYSE governors voted to prohibit market manipulation syndicates, forbade specialist brokers from giving inside information to others, and prohibited brokers from purchasing options in stocks for which they made a market. In the public's mind, such late reforms merely amounted to an admission of grave moral failures on Wall Street. Whitney proved to be a poor role model for the moral stature of Wall Street: In 1938, he was indicted for defrauding his wife's trust, for stealing from the New York Yacht Club (for which he was treasurer), stealing from his brokerage clients' accounts, and even embezzling from a fund for widows and orphans of deceased NYSE members (for which he had been appointed a trustee).

The Postwar Stock Market

Prior to the 1940s, stock brokerage firms were uniformly small boutique companies of perhaps 50 accounts or less; their clients were primarily the friends and family of the brokerage's partners. But in the early years following World War II, firms such as Merrill Lynch pioneered a mass-market business model featuring small accounts and a high trading volume. By the end of the 1940s, Merrill Lynch was the largest brokerage house on Wall Street. By 1960, its gross income was nearly four times the size of the second-biggest brokerage house and roughly as large as the next four firms combined. Players in the industry referred to Merrill's 540,000 accounts as the thundering herd. Individual investors participating in the stock market tripled between the war and the mid-1960s, and they doubled again over the following 20 years.

Capital poured into the U.S. stock market after the war, not only from the reentry of the middle classes into the stock market but also because of the inflow of institutional investors. Previously, institutional investors were concerned about the uncertain value of listed corporations and wary of the routinely practiced market manipulation and insider trading. But one by one, they reappraised the developing stock market. With the institutionalization of uniform and comparable quarterly earnings between corporations, the accuracy of that information confirmed by independent auditors, and the market's first constraints on market manipulation and insider trading given the surveillance of the Securities and Exchange Commission, institutional investors determined that the stock market was no longer as risky or uncertain as it had been in the past.

The new records of high trading volume, although welcome, were drowning the smaller and less administratively capable brokerage houses. Not all brokerage houses could afford the transition from paper trades to electronic trading. In 1975, with the elimination of fixed commissions on trading, the volume of trading increased further—but at the expense of weaker brokerage firms that drowned in the paperwork. Expensive mistakes were routinely made. Money was lost. In December 1968, investigators discovered that $4.1 billion in securities simply could not be accounted for.

As a result, brokerage houses with fewer accounts and undercapitalized or administratively disadvantaged houses began to go bankrupt or merge with more successful brokerage firms. The federal government stepped in again in 1970 and founded the Securities Investor Protection Corporation to insure customer funds placed with brokers. In return for this valuable protection, stock brokerage companies were later subjected to greater surveillance, auditing, and regulatory requirements.

In the last quarter of the twentieth century, numerous economic sectors were deregulated, including the railroad, airline, utility, and telecommunications industries. By 1999, when the Financial Services Modernization Act was enacted, the death knell of the Glass-Steagall Act of 1933 had been sounded. Over time, the regulatory power of the Securities and Exchange Commission, that other great creation of 1933, has swelled and ebbed with strong or weak presidentially appointed chairpersons. Moreover, although the stock market has grown in complexity and size, the

SEC has, in recent years, been unable to keep pace with its strong surveillance, investigation, and prosecution goals because of an insufficient budget set by Congress.

It is reasonable to believe that this power imbalance between financial capital and its regulators led, in 2001, to the $50 billion collapse of Enron Corporation, the largest bankruptcy in U.S. corporate history, because of fraudulent accounting and securities market manipulation. Yet Enron pales in comparison to the largest one-year loss in U.S. corporate history, which occurred when AOL Time Warner wrote off nearly $100 billion from its books in 2002 because of excessively creative accounting in previous years.

It is a paradox of eighteenth- and nineteenth-century stock market development that investors were repeatedly willing to invest with so little oversight. The second half of the twentieth century demonstrated that federal regulation and oversight could create a stock market with sufficient protections so as to significantly encourage institutional and individual investors to invest. The fundamental regulatory question for much of the twenty-first century will be how to successfully reregulate after 25 years of experimentation with deregulation.

References

Abolafia, Mitchel Y. *Making Markets: Opportunism and Restraint on Wall Street.* Cambridge, MA: Harvard University Press, 1996.

Banner, Stuart. *Anglo-American Securities Regulation: Cultural and Political Roots, 1690–1860.* Cambridge: Cambridge University Press, 1998.

Burk, James. *Values in the Marketplace: The American Stock Market under Federal Securities Law.* New York: Aldine de Gruyter, 1992.

Carosso, Vincent P. *Investment Banking in America: A History.* Cambridge, MA: Harvard University Press, 1970.

Chandler, Alfred Dupont. *The Visible Hand: The Managerial Revolution in American Business.* Cambridge, MA: Harvard University Press, Belknap Press, 1977.

Chernow, Ron. *The House of Morgan: An American Banking Dynasty and the Rise of Modern Finance.* New York: Simon and Schuster, 1990.

Coffee, John C., Jr. "The Rise of Dispersed Ownership: The Roles of Law and the State in the Separation of Ownership and Control." *Yale Law Journal*, vol. 111 (2001): 1–82.

Gabaldon, Theresa A. "John Law, with a Tulip, in the South Seas: Gambling and the Regulation of Euphoric Market Transactions." *Journal of Corporation Law*, vol. 26, no. 2 (Winter 2001): 225–284.

Gordon, John Steele. *The Great Game: The Emergence of Wall Street as a World Power, 1653–2000.* New York: Simon and Schuster, 2000.

Hayes, Samuel L., III. *Wall Street and Regulation.* Cambridge, MA: Harvard Business School Press, 1987.

La Porta, Rafael, Florencio Lopez-de-Silanes, and Andrei Shleifer. "Corporate Ownership around the World." *Journal of Finance*, vol. 54, no. 2 (April 1999): 471–517.

Levitt, Arthur. *Take on the Street: What Wall Street and Corporate America Don't Want You to Know; What You Can Do to Fight Back*. New York: Pantheon, 2002.

North, Douglass C. *Institutions, Institutional Change, and Economic Performance*. Cambridge: Cambridge University Press, 1990.

Roe, Mark J. "Political Preconditions to Separating Ownership from Control." *Stanford Law Review*, vol. 539 (2000–2001): 539–606.

Roe, Mark J. "Political Theory of American Corporate Finance." *Columbia Law Review*, vol. 91, no. 1 (January 1991): 10–67.

Sears, Marian V. *Mining Stock Exchanges, 1860–1930: A Historical Survey*. Missoula: University of Montana Press, 1973.

Seligman, Joel. *The Transformation of Wall Street: A History of the Securities and Exchange Commission and Modern Corporate Finance*. Rev. ed. Boston: Northeastern University Press, 1995.

Shiller, Robert J. *Irrational Exuberance*. Princeton, NJ: Princeton University Press, 2000.

Smith, George David, and Richard Sylla. "The Transformation of Financial Capitalism: An Essay on the History of American Capital Markets." *Financial Markets, Institutions, and Instruments*, vol. 2, no. 2 (May 1993): 1–61.

Werner, Walter, and Steven T. Smith. *Wall Street*. New York: Columbia University Press, 1991.

Taxation

Theo Edwin Maloy

Taxes are compulsory payments to a government based on financial criteria that indicate capacity to pay. Tax payments differ from prices because they lack any connection to a specific purchase of a governmental good or service. Taxpayers do not contribute on the basis of their sense of civic pride or duty. Congress establishes tax statutes and administrative regulations through a political process. Some taxes may have quasi-market effects, especially those designed so that the heaviest users of a governmental good or service pay the majority of its cost.

The three primary measures of the taxpayer's capacity to bear a tax burden include income, purchases or sales, and property ownership or wealth. The U.S. government relies on corporate and individual income taxes, and the Social Security tax, levied on payrolls, has become an additional income-type tax. The federal government levies neither a general sales tax nor a property tax; however, it does collect selective excise taxes on some items and customs duties on imported products. Taxes on the purchase or sale of goods and services remain the largest source of state revenues. All states have either a sales or gross receipts tax, and almost all have a general sales tax as well. A great majority of states also levy individual income taxes and/or corporate income taxes. Fewer than half levy a general property tax. Although property taxes constitute the majority of local tax revenues, localities also levy general sales taxes, selective excise taxes, individual income taxes, and corporate income taxes. State laws authorize municipalities to establish local tax rates.

Some taxes discourage an undesirable individual or business activity, but a tax levied for revenue proves adequate if it can generate sufficient revenues at socially acceptable rates. A zero percent tax would raise no revenue. A 100 percent tax also would raise no revenue because no one would engage in an activity that delivered all of the proceeds to government. Thus, taxing agencies utilize a rate-to-revenue curve to determine or estimate any tax. Depending on the rate-to-revenue curve, either a tax increase or a tax reduction could generate greater or lesser revenues.

Tax adequacy has both long-term and short-term aspects. A tax with cyclical aspects will collect adequate revenues during short-term economic fluctuations. Property taxes have cyclical stability, whereas general sales taxes and corporate income taxes are less stable. Although a tax system must deliver adequate revenues during cyclical economic downturns in order to finance public assistance expenditures, it must also increase revenues as an economy expands in order to meet the growing demands for government services.

In *The Wealth of Nations*, Adam Smith proposed four principles of taxation (italics added):

1. *The subjects* of every state ought to contribute toward the support of the government, as nearly as possible, in proportion to their respective abilities; that is, in proportion to the revenue which they respectively enjoy under the protection of the state.

2. *The tax* that each individual is bound to pay ought to be certain and not arbitrary. The time of payment, the manner of payment, the quantity to be paid, ought all to be clear and plain to the contributor, and to every other person.

3. *Every tax* ought to be levied at a time or in the manner, in which it is most likely to be convenient for the contributor to pay it.

4. *Every tax* ought to be so contrived as both to take out and to keep out of the pockets of the people as little as possible, over and above what it brings into the public treasury of the state.

Smith believed that tax laws should be adopted in an open legislative process and based on objective and explicit criteria that are understandable and fair to all taxpayers.

Economists George Break and Joseph Pechman declared that taxation was wealth redistribution accomplished without disrupting other economic activities. In addition to transferring purchasing power from the private sector to the public sector, taxes redistribute purchasing power within the private sector.

Since a tax system creates winners and losers, tax policy must determine who will bear the tax burden. Officials can levy taxes according to the benefit the taxpayer receives or according to the taxpayer's ability to pay. A benefit-received system operates as a quasi-market, with individuals paying for government services that they want and use. However, two problems exist with a benefit-received system. First, many government agencies provide services (such as social assistance) even though the recipients cannot purchase them. Second, many government services, including the safety provided by police patrols, benefit all residents although only some of the residents pay for them. Some benefit-based selective excise taxes, such as those levied on motor fuels or automobile tires, remain closely linked to the use of a governmental good or service, such as a highway. Many Americans accept use taxes if the tax burden remains consistent with the taxpayer's usage—that is, they will not use public services if the low taxes create wasteful oversupplies, and they will not utilize a public service if the tax rate exceeds the value of the service in their minds. However, since some consumers cannot pay the tax and since some services benefit those who do not share the cost, the adoption of the ability-to-pay principle remains necessary.

The ability-to-pay approach requires the development of sliding-scale fees and a determination of the distribution of the tax bill among taxpayers. Horizontal equity considers equal treatment of taxpayers who have equal capacities to pay taxes. Vertical equity concerns the proper relationship between the relative tax burdens paid by individuals and different capacities to pay taxes. A tax structure becomes regressive if tax rates are lower in high-ability groups than in low-ability groups. It is proportional if tax rates remain equal for all groups. Progressive tax rates charge higher rates for high-ability (higher-income) groups than for low-ability (lower-income) groups. Thus, a proportional rate does not alter a population's income distribution, a regressive rate transfers wealth to higher-ability individuals, and a progressive rate transfers wealth to lower-ability individuals. Increasing collection rates can decrease equity because taxing payrolls remains convenient, but higher-income individuals have more interest, dividend, rental, and capital gain incomes, which are difficult to locate and tax.

Accounting records disclose who makes tax payments, but the distribution may not accurately show the final impact of the tax burden. Both businesses and individuals make tax payments, and those bearing the initial tax impact may shift a portion of the tax burden by changing prices or by altering purchasing behavior. A tax paid by a business may lower the owners' profits, the management's salaries, the suppliers' prices, or the employees' salaries or benefits. Or it may raise the prices that customers pay.

Business taxes include property taxes, income taxes, gross receipts taxes, franchise taxes, licenses, severance taxes, document and stock transfer taxes, and miscellaneous business and occupation taxes. Taxes on individuals include property taxes, income taxes, retail sales taxes, and selective excise taxes. In all cases, the final and total responsibility for personal taxes belongs to an individual, owner, manager, employer, employee, or customer. State and local governments favor taxes on business because the ultimate burden of such taxes may fall on owners or customers who live outside the state or municipality. However, an attempt to put the majority of a government's tax burden on businesses could cause the businesses to move to another jurisdiction. The area's economy would suffer, so state and local governments weigh the impact that taxes have on economic development and job creation. Officials often compare tax types and rates to those of neighboring governments and offer tax concessions if businesses will relocate into a given jurisdiction. Access to raw materials or markets; the availability of skilled or unskilled labor; convenient air, ground, or water transportation; and a variety of production costs may have an equal or greater influence on business-location decisions, but elected and appointed government officials eagerly offer tax incentives as part of an industrial development package. Tax considerations often may determine the choice of a final location, but they are unlikely to influence the choice of a general area. If officials offer no tax incentives and a business locates elsewhere, voter dissatisfaction might occur if the area's economy declines. Consequently, officials often offer incentives such as tax abatements, exemptions, or credits in exchange for industrial location or job creation.

The tax burden includes both the tax bill and the cost of calculating and paying the tax. A complicated tax system increases compliance costs, compliance problems, and governmental administrative duties and expenses. Changes in the tax system increase the cost of compliance, and they prohibit effective business and personal planning.

A broader-based tax, which places a tax on larger sums of money, can raise greater amounts of revenue with a lower tax rate, causing fewer economic dislocations. Higher tax rates may induce individuals to choose to enjoy more leisure time instead of working more hours, or the higher rate may cause workers to work more hours to replace the income taken by the taxes. High tax rates on specific types of business organizations, production techniques, and distribution or marketing systems may cause owners to quit an industry or change their firm's methods. Business owners or individuals may also alter their after-tax rates of return by modifying their investment types or techniques and savings rates.

Income Taxes

Because of a U.S. Supreme Court ruling that declared the personal income tax unconstitutional, Congress agreed upon and sent out to the states the Sixteenth Amendment, which sanctions an income tax, which was ratified in 1913. During World War II, the levy became a mass tax at a rate that applied to the majority of the population. The national government also uses payroll taxes to finance the social insurance system, including Social Security and Medicare.

The federal government defines income as the money or other gain received in a given period of time by an individual, corporation, or other economic entity for labor, goods, or services or from property, natural resources, investments, or operations. However, any government can establish its own definition of income. In fact, the government defines income and decides what sums are exempted, how the amounts are manipulated, and by what rates the defined income is multiplied or divided. The basic tax calculation equals the total income less adjustments, including deductions and exclusions, multiplied by a percentage rate obtained from a tax schedule, less any tax credits. Partnerships or proprietorships usually pay the same tax as the individual. Governments can designate the income or payroll tax to be levied on the employer, the employee, or a combination of both, although the employers can place the final impact on employees by adjusting salaries or benefits. Nevertheless, income remains an important measure of tax capacity, and governments can adopt exemptions, deductions, or credits to adjust the tax base in light of family size, physical or mental infirmities, or economic circumstances. The income tax's broad base allows for the collection of large revenues without making unacceptable impacts on the overall economy. However, the adjustments complicate the income tax, making it expensive to administer, and most taxpayers have a difficult time understanding the complicated tax structure. Aspects of the tax system also discourage saving and investment and specifically discourage investment in certain sectors of the economy. Since the federal government taxes corporate profits as well as investors' dividends from profits, the United States doubly taxes corporate profits paid out in dividends.

Personal deductions, subtracted from total income, can improve horizontal and vertical equity by adjusting the tax base. Deductions for uncontrollable expenditures, such as medical or property casualty losses; for meritorious expenditures, such as charitable or religious contributions; and for expenditures necessary to generate income, such as travel expenses, union dues, or work uniforms, can lower the tax obligation. Tax credits are subtracted from a calculated tax liability. Credits can be refundable, meaning the taxpayer receives a payment from the government, or they can be nonrefundable, meaning they can only be subtracted from a tax liability. A credit can be given for an entire expenditure or for some portion of it.

Congress taxes corporations as legal persons. A depreciation schedule uses a formula to allocate portions of the cost of long-lived assets to particular years in order to create a deduction similar to the individual's deductions for the cost of earning income. Similarly, nations and states must calculate the portion of a corporation's income subject to the jurisdiction's tax system.

Consumption Taxes

Taxes on wages, goods, and services operate as broad-based taxes that raise large amounts of revenues with low tax rates. Consumption taxes provide a way for governments to collect revenues from persons with high taxpaying capacities but low current incomes. States and localities collect a majority of their revenues from general sales or selective excise taxes. States cannot tax expenditures in interstate commerce, but purchases may be taxed at the destination of the purchase rather than at the location of the seller.

A general sales tax applies to all transactions, with possible exceptions such as prescription medicines or food for at-home consumption. An excise tax applies to specific transactions, such as purchases of tobacco, alcohol, or motor fuels. Excise tax revenues, levied as unit taxes on each item purchased or ad valorem taxes as a percentage of the purchase price, grow slowly because the unit taxes do not reflect increasing prices. The tax is collected from a purchaser or from the manufacturer, who then raises the sale price to recapture all or part of the tax levy. An excise tax can be adopted to discourage the use of a particular item, such as the sumptuary taxes on tobacco and alcohol; it can be adopted as a quasi-price for a government service, as is the case with the benefit-based tax on motor fuels as a quasi-price of highways; or it can be used as a method of taxing extraordinary taxpaying capacity, as with hotel and motel lodging taxes. Excise taxes can also be applied to business purchases—for example, the regulatory and environmental taxes on chemicals that contribute to environmental pollution. With both sales taxes and excise taxes, revenues can be collected for the general support of the government, or they may be earmarked for a specific government function.

Retail sales taxes are ad valorem taxes either on consumers' purchases or on merchants' gross receipts. Final determination of purchases and the associated payment of taxes falls primarily on the purchaser. Business purchases of raw materials, components and materials, or equipment used in production are exempted because to tax those items would raise finished goods' prices and increase inflation. The taxation of commercial purchases between businesses would also lead to increased mergers of suppliers and manufacturers.

Purchases of services are often exempted from sales taxes, often for purely historical reasons. In addition, business purchases of specific professional services are exempted because taxing the purchases from professionals would encourage the practice of moving the services into the organization rather than making purchases from outside the organization. Commodity exemptions for purchases of consumer goods such as prescription medicines, food for at-home consumption, and sometimes clothes are politically popular because they make up higher percentages of the purchases made by low-income families and because these are necessary, not discretionary, expenditures.

Property Taxes

Local governments rely heavily on the revenue derived from property taxes. States developed taxes on goods and services because during the Great Depression, property taxes, which were the predominant revenue source at the time, could not be collected. Subdivisions within states, such as counties and special districts, are greatly dependent on property taxes for their operating revenues.

Property taxes are not wealth taxes because some items of personal property are exempted. In addition, the tax on a home is based on the gross value, which is not adjusted for any mortgage liability. Some properties are taxed twice, which occurs, for example, when a corporation's assets are taxed and then an owner's corporate stock, representing a share of the assets, is taxed.

Taxed property can be either real property, including real estate and improvements on the land, or personal property, including machinery, automobiles, jewelry, and stocks and bonds. Some jurisdictions tax personal property more heavily than real property. Many others exempt personal property from the tax assessment. Even more jurisdictions tax businesses' property at higher rates than individuals' property. Intangible property, such as stocks and bonds, may be exempted from property taxation, or it may be taxed at a different rate than tangible property, such as machinery or automobiles.

Property tax rates are often determined as part of the jurisdiction's annual budget process, with the rate set at the level necessary to create adequate revenues to finance governmental activities, including debt service. Property taxes on real estate are based on assessments in order to determine the tax base. One standard of assessment, market value, is the cash price that the real property would bring in a competitive and open market, but the value is hypothetical because most property is not for sale in such a market. Sales of comparable properties can be used to estimate a property's value. Some jurisdictions assess value on a cost-summation approach, with each building characteristic having a predetermined dollar value and with the sum adjusted for the property's age and depreciation. Many jurisdictions assess the property base on its current usage, and they often have different tax rates for different property uses, including lower rates for agricultural land. Although most states have some system of periodic reassessment, others revalue real estate only when it is sold, leading to very different tax levies on adjoining and otherwise identical properties that have been sold in different years. Real property can be assessed yearly; every piece of property can be assessed in the same year on a periodic schedule; or the jurisdiction can divide the property into groups, with the groups being assessed in a rotation. In all cases, new construction would be immediately assessed.

Property tax relief is offered in the form of reductions in the tax base, preferential rates, or tax credits. A homestead exemption reduces the tax base for an owner who lives on a property. Veterans and the elderly often receive tax exemptions. The exemptions are popular, but other property owners' taxes are increased to create adequate tax revenues. Businesses and industries often receive tax rebates or exemptions for industrial development or job creation. Churches, charities, and other governments do not pay property taxes. Many jurisdictions have adopted circuit-breaker systems to refund property taxes if they become an excessive part of low-income individuals' expenditures. Some jurisdictions defer property taxes on real estate owned by the elderly but calculate the growing liability and recoup the sum from the person's estate. Many jurisdictions tax agricultural property at a lower rate than residential or industrial property, but when the real estate is converted to another use, the deferred taxes from a specific number of years are collected.

Property can be assessed at its calculated value or at some percentage of the calculated value. If the property were assessed at its calculated value, a tax rate would be established. If the property were assessed at a fraction of its calculated value, possibly half of the market value, the tax rate would be adjusted, possibly to twice the existing rate. Fractional adjustment can lead to taxpayer confusion when a taxpayer believes that the low assessment means that a tax bill is being similarly reduced. Because property taxes require assessment, confusing fractional assessment can produce differing assessments in different areas of the same jurisdiction, either by accident or by favoritism.

Property owners receive a statement each year detailing the amount of property taxes that they pay to each jurisdiction in which they live, including the city, the county, the school districts, and all of the special districts. Similarly, taxpayers each year calculate their income tax payments and submit tax returns detailing all of their tax liabilities. Although sales taxes once were deductible from the federal income tax, there is no reason today for taxpayers to total the consumption taxes that they pay. Property taxes and income taxes generate significant taxpayer dissatisfaction, but consumption taxes receive comparatively little attention.

Among the industrialized nations, the United States is a low-tax country, with total taxes being approximately 30 percent of the gross domestic product (GDP). The average in industrialized nations is approximately 40 percent of the GDP.

References

Mikesell, John. *Fiscal Administration: Analysis and Applications for the Public Sector.* 5th ed. Fort Worth, TX: Harcourt, Brace, 1999.

O'Brien, D. P., ed. *The History of Taxation.* Brookfield, VT: Pickering and Chatto, 1999.

Ratner, Sidney. *A Political and Social History of Federal Taxation, 1789–1913.* New York: W. W. Norton, 1942.

Trade Policy

Josh Pratt

Benjamin Franklin once said, "No nation was ever ruined by trade." As America's most savvy commerce expert and the man who negotiated the nation's first commercial agreement, Franklin possessed the wisdom to render such a judgment. He had observed his land's trade policies under three distinct governments and gained insights from their successes and failures. Throughout the centuries after his passing, the United States has continued to embrace the spirit—if not always the practice—of his philosophy concerning the goodness of trade.

Trade Policy and the Colonial Experience

As feudalism declined in Europe in the period after the Renaissance, the ideology of mercantilism quickly replaced it. Striving for economic self-sufficiency and a favorable balance of trade through the influx of bullion and the establishment of overseas colonies, most of the European great powers allowed their colonies little freedom in matters of foreign trade. England and its colonies proved an exception. Civil and international wars as well as haphazard colonization initially left England's politicians with little time for or interest in regulating the trade of the British colonies. Although American colonists, like all British subjects, were barred from challenging the East India Company's monopoly on trade with Asia, no legal restrictions prevented them from trading with the French West Indies, the Dutch West Indies, the British West Indies, or the Spanish West Indies. Legal barriers prevented the colonists from conducting trade with adversarial nations, but these restrictions seldom proved effective. In fact, much of the currency circulating in the American colonies came from trade with forbidden areas, with the tacit consent of many royal customs officers.

The 12 years between 1660 and 1672 saw the first etchings of a British trade policy in the American colonies as Parliament passed the Acts of Trade and Navigation. Reflecting the dominant mercantilist ideology in that era, the acts created a list of enumerated articles legally traded only with Britain. Initially, the enumerated goods included tobacco, sugar, and cotton, but between 1705 and 1722, Parliament expanded the list to include rice, molasses, furs, and naval stores. The enumerated articles list continued to expand until the beginning of the American Revolution, at which time salt fish was the only significant nonenumerated good.

Such laws did not prevent America's trade relations with the Indian tribes to the west. These tribes served as some of the earliest trading partners of the American colonists, and regular trade became established throughout the sixteenth and seventeenth centuries. The Narragansett Indians in particular prized European-style manufactures and tools for their utility, superior design, and value as status symbols. The Narragansetts initially exchanged furs for the goods. Such trade proved lucrative for both sides while furs maintained their tremendous popularity in Europe, but many tribes found themselves stuck with an unfavorable balance of trade when the value of their furs plummeted but their dependence on European goods remained steady. Other tribes traded heavily with Massachusetts colonists for firearms, ammunition, and alcohol both before and after the colony passed a law in 1633 that fixed the penalty for selling arms to Indians at £10 per gun, £5 for powder, and 40s. for shot.

The outbreak of King Philip's War (1675–1676) between colonists and Indians drastically changed the nature of trade with the native peoples. Colonial leaders, desperate for a means of generating revenue to fill the coffers emptied by the war, began to tacitly permit the practice of selling captured Indians into foreign slavery in 1675. At first, this slave trade satisfied colonial leaders' needs; the market rate for captured natives averaged £3 per Indian, and Massachusetts's colonists alone obtained a remarkable £387.13 for 188 Indian slaves sold to foreigners. Even Indians living peaceably in colonial hamlets often found themselves "captured" by their colonist neighbors and sold into slavery. Although never fully legal, the practice of selling Indians into slavery ceased only as a result of market forces: As foreigners heard New Englanders' allegations that the Indians of King Philip's War were "subtle, bloody, and dangerous," they feared the risk of owning them; ultimately, Indian slaves became almost entirely unmarketable.

Although the American colonies eventually could not trade in Indian slaves, the African slave market persisted throughout the colonial period. American ships obtained West Africans, and shipmasters sold them as slaves in the West Indies. With the profits from their cargo, the shipmasters purchased molasses and sold it upon their return to New England. New Englanders converted this molasses into the rum that was used to purchase more slaves in the West African market, thus continuing the triangular trade. By 1750, half of the 340 ships in Newport, Rhode Island, were engaged in the slave trade.

To understand the potential magnitude of this trade, it should be noted that in 1750, Massachusetts alone contained 63 rum distilleries producing 12,500 hogsheads (757,500 gallons) of rum. The cost of a man in West Africa equaled 115 gallons of rum. The market for rum proved so vast that, in 1752, a Yankee captain who wanted to fill his sloop with rum before traveling to West Africa five weeks in the future was told by his agent that the demand for rum so exceeded its supply that it would be at least three months before the liquor would be available. The British colonists' rum choked out their French competitors' alcoholic products in West Africa.

The end of the Seven Years' War between the French and the British forced England to reconsider its treatment of the American colonies in terms of their foreign trade. The war had depleted the royal treasury, and the colonies had done little to help out financially. Parliament began to regulate strictly America's trade. It tightened customs collections, which had previously been considered especially lax, and found long lists of items in the Acts of Trade and Navigation that could produce revenue for the Crown. Parliament also ruled that American exports to the European continent first had to be cleared through a British port, which swelled shipping costs beyond any hope for profit.

Ironically, perhaps the worst blow to American trade actually came from a lowering of tax rates. The import tax on non-English molasses had previously stood at 6d. per gallon, but customs officers had always collected a much lower rate. Parliament cut the official rate to 3d. per gallon on paper but warned of strict enforcement—and this combination of events drove the taxes to twice their previous rate in practice. All this effectively restricted molasses imports to that obtained from the British West Indies alone. Cash reserves melted away, and the export market slowed dramatically. The restrictive trade acts became collectively known as the Sugar Act.

Parliament followed the Sugar Act with another tax, the Stamp Act, which called for a duty on a variety of paper items in the colonies. Opposition to the Stamp Act flared among the colonists, who resented the fact that Parliament had not recognized their objections to the new tax. Further, after the implementation of the Sugar Act, many colonists had already begun to reject the theoretical notions of British sovereignty over the colonies. The Stamp Act hastened the spread of such ideas.

On the eve of the Revolution, in protest against the Sugar Act and other restrictive trade acts against the colonies, 900 American merchants agreed to boycott British imports until Parliament repealed the Stamp and Sugar Acts. Scared British merchants forced an irate Parliament to take action and, by 1766, the Stamp Act became void and the molasses tax fell to insignificant levels. However, the colonists remained angered over Prime Minister William Pitt's requirement that all colonial exports had to pass through British ports, and anger turned into outrage over a new order that the New England colonies could only trade with England or the British West Indies. Then, in 1773, Parliament noticed that the popularity in the colonies of imported tea from Britain presented an opportunity for revenue growth. Parliament levied a tariff on tea imports, incorrectly assuming that the colonists would not mind the duty because it allowed the price of British tea to remain at levels below those of smuggled Dutch tea. Opposition to this act proved overwhelming and resulted in the Boston Tea Party as well as other forms of opposition that made a clash between Britain and its American colonies inevitable.

Trade Policy from Independence to 1815

Early on, the federal government took a lax attitude toward trade regulation. The Articles of Confederation, operational from 1781 until 1789, forbade Congress from concluding any commercial treaty that would limit the states' rights to customs duties. In effect, Congress avoided rendering decisions on foreign trade policy matters. Foreign nations wishing to conduct commerce with the former American colonies now found that they had to negotiate individual trade treaties with each of the newly empowered American states, a process that proved cumbersome for foreigners and discouraged international trade. In 1789, the ratification of the Constitution drastically changed the direction that the Articles of Confederation had set for America's trade policy. The Constitution clearly permitted Congress to levy and collect taxes, and the first Congress quickly imposed a customs tariff to collect revenue for the fledgling government.

In the 1790s, the U.S. economy boomed and foreign trade became a source of American optimism. By this decade, Virginia and the Carolinas recovered their prewar volume of exports in tobacco, naval stores, and rice. Additionally, a poor harvest in France provided a favorable grain market for the middle states. England demonstrated its willingness to become an American rice and tobacco marketplace as trade between the two nations flourished. Restless Jamaican and Barbadian citizens aided American shipmasters as they smuggled goods onto those two islands. No longer forbidden to trade with Asia by the monopoly powers of the British East India Company, northern shipowners participated in a booming trade with Calcutta, India, and Canton, China. In 1789, America conducted more trade in these two cities than any other nation save for Britain.

As foreign trade became increasingly important to the new nation, Treasury Secretary Alexander Hamilton issued the "Report on Privileges and Restrictions on the Commerce of the United States in Foreign Countries" to detail America's current foreign trade relationships and proffer to Congress a trade policy. At this time, the largest U.S. exports were breadstuffs, tobacco, rice, and wood. Great Britain purchased more American exports than any other nation, taking in approximately twice as many American goods as French items and more than four times as many products as Spain or Portugal. However, America's imports from these nations lacked proportion with its exports; the U.S. import relationship with Great Britain rose to 7 times as much as that with France and 50 times as much as that with Spain (see Tables 9 and 10).

The "Report on Privileges" showed that American firms faced barriers to trading with European nations and especially with their colonies. These countries imposed heavy barriers to trade in Europe and prohibited much of America's commerce with their colonies. The Jefferson administration's recommendations to remedy this

Table 9. Exports to various nations, 1789–1790

Spain and its dominions	$2,005,905
Portugal and its dominions	1,283,462
France and its dominions	4,698,735
Great Britain and its dominions	9,363,416
United Netherlands and its dominions	1,963,880
Denmark and its dominions	224,415
Sweden and its dominions	47,240

Table 10. Imports from various nations, 1789–1790

Spain and its dominions	$335,110
Portugal and its dominions	95,763
France and its dominions	2,068,348
Great Britain and its dominions	15,285,428
United Netherlands and its dominions	1,172,692
Denmark and its dominions	351,364
Sweden and its dominions	14,325

situation included promoting free trade through friendly agreements or, if necessary, by imposing countervailing tariffs and barriers against these countries.

Jefferson removed the excise tax on distilled liquors to make them more affordable relative to imports, but this action had the undesirable consequence of making the federal government even more dependent on tariff revenues. As aggressive European powers in the early nineteenth century continued to discriminate against American commerce and violate U.S. claims to neutral commercial rights, Jefferson and his successor, James Madison, both experimented with trade sanctions, including embargoes and nonintercourse, to remedy the problem. (The nonintercourse sanction meant that America would not trade with England or France but would trade with everyone else. Also, America would resume trade with the first of these two countries to promise to respect America's rights as a nation, and then it would declare war on the other country.) However, the federal government's dependence on customs income and the subsequent decline in foreign trade before the War of 1812 caused national leaders to resort to bolder measures for the restoration of foreign trade and neutral rights.

Trade Policy from 1815 to the Civil War

The Anglo-American Commercial Treaty of 1815 ended the British policy of discriminating against U.S. ships in British markets. This accursed barrier removed, the United States could return to the course of expanding foreign trade that its leaders had pursued before the war. Thus, President Madison shocked the nation when he rallied for a protective tariff in February 1815.

American foreign trade policy began to shift markedly from its free trade leanings before the War of 1812 to the origins of the American System in the years immediately after it. A national consensus emerged that demanded the development of a manufacturing base diverse enough to secure American independence from foreign military and trade conflicts. As long as mercantilist systems prevailed throughout the world, the leaders of the United States in this era believed that the nation had to pursue a similar policy.

The Democratic Party promoted a higher tariff policy to protect and facilitate American manufacturing. Henry Clay and John C. Calhoun, congressional leaders in the years after the War of 1812, also pressed for heavy protective tariffs for

A political cartoon lampoons the "cursed Ograbme" (embargo spelled backwards). The Embargo Act of 1807 eliminated U.S. trade with other nations, with the intent of forcing England and France to respect the neutral trading rights of the United States. The act was repealed in 1809, as it had failed to end either action by England or France, but instead caused a disruption of the U.S. economy and the revitalization of Federalist protest against the Republicans. (Lossing, Benson J., *The Pictorial Field-Book of the War of 1812*, 1868.)

manufactured goods, even though both men represented states that surely would have benefited from increased foreign trade. Politicians viewed the tariff not as a device for overcharging American consumers in the short term but instead as a means of stimulating investment in the United States and reaping the full benefits of production and consumption at home. That tariffs during this era also provided the government with a steady stream of revenue must have been viewed as a boon to such politicians.

In 1816, as a result of these and other arguments in favor of trade restrictions, Congress passed the nation's first protective tariff. Duties of 30 percent on iron products and 25 percent on cotton and woolen goods were set in place. President James Monroe advocated broad tariff increases in his message to Congress in 1822, and Henry Clay also helped to persuade Congress to raise tariffs again in 1824. Then, the Tariff Act of 1828, also known as the Tariff of Abominations, raised tariffs to their highest rates in American history. Under this act, average rates on durable goods hovered around 61.7 percent.

The Tariff of Abominations opened up a debate between advocates of free trade and proponents of protectionism that would continue throughout the century. The South Carolina nullification crisis induced Clay to engineer a tariff reduction in 1833, which cut tariff rates to 20 percent over nine years. This tariff deviated from the hitherto dominant protectionist philosophy, but the depression of 1837 caused a swing back to a more protective tariff in 1842. In the 40 years from 1821 to 1861, the high-tariff position generally dominated that of free trade.

Nevertheless, in the decades between the War of 1812 and the Civil War, both exports and imports flourished despite the high tariffs. Cotton exports soared 1,300 percent, and tobacco exports doubled. At the same time, the expectation that tariffs would stimulate internal investment came to fruition as private investment in textiles and other import-competing industries increased greatly.

A greater exporting prowess in the South and a changing sentiment toward lower tariffs in the 1840s induced Democrats to shift their party position in favor of tariffs for revenue purposes only, a position close to the free trade stance in the 1800s. In 1854, Democrats negotiated a Canadian reciprocity treaty that allowed for limited free trade. However, because that treaty covered only raw materials, Canada increased its import duties on U.S. manufactures, and American fishing and lumber industries suffered. Democrats also obtained highly biased treaties that provided Americans with virtually unlimited trading privileges in the nations of Japan and China as well as in the Middle East and Africa.

Thus, the debate over tariffs and free trade also served to divide the nation between the free trade, agrarian South and the protectionist, manufacture-driven North. The last president elected before the outbreak of the Civil War, Abraham Lincoln, advocated a high tariff. He believed that free trade would inevitably lead to low wages and financial ruin. After the Civil War began, Secretary of the Treasury Salmon Chase encouraged Congress to double customs duties to pay for the expense of the war.

Trade Policy from the Civil War to World War I

Immediately after the Civil War, the United States experienced a tremendous economic expansion that again changed the nation's attitude toward foreign trade. Finished manufactures, which made up half of all imports before the Civil War, fell to less than a third of all imports 20 years later. American exports became increasingly prevalent in the world markets. The people were convinced that selling, buying, and investing in foreign markets would prove crucial to the economic wealth and development of the nation. More specifically, Americans felt that overproduction and unemployment, which became all too familiar during the severe depressions of the 1890s, could be prevented by opening up foreign markets to American agricultural and manufacturing surpluses. Foreign commerce became a symbol of national power, the navy and the foreign service industry expanded to protect business interests, and citizens called for an imperialist and activist foreign policy.

Latin America became fertile soil for businesses seeking to exploit the desire of Americans for greater foreign trade. Bananas were especially popular at home after the Civil War, and entrepreneurs found Latin America to have ideal growing conditions for that crop. Although most were never legally American colonies, the nations of Central America, South America, and the Caribbean kowtowed to extremely powerful businesses backed by the American government. Companies such as United Fruit and Standard Fruit negotiated land concessions, tax exemptions, the use of national resources, and the free import of numerous products with host governments. These companies also imported their own labor forces, constructed company towns, and built the entire infrastructure for modern communities in the areas that they dominated.

Soon, the United States had acquired an informal empire in this region, based on economic and political control rather than colonial annexation. American companies controlled the tariff revenues, budgets, foreign debts, and internal investments of a plethora of Latin American countries. Although bananas and coffee often would account for 80 percent of the exports from Central American countries at the time, U.S. conglomerates owned almost all of the concession taxes and import rights on these products. This Central American trade became so important that in 1913, when the Senate Finance Committee debated the proposed Underwood-Simmons Tariff, it found that a meager $.05 tariff on bananas would generate $1 million a year for the federal government. However, the public backlash against taxing these Central American imports proved so strong that Congress removed the banana tariff from the tariff bill.

America's imperial experience in Asia lacked the power that it had in Latin America. England became a prospective colonizer of China long before the United States had the capacity to dominate the region, and by the late nineteenth century, most European empires had carved a sphere of influence for themselves in China, to the exclusion of U.S. interests. Although ambitious American traders profited greatly as opium-peddling middlemen between the warring Chinese and English in the mid-eighteenth century, legitimate American businesses saw that they had been shut out of China in the years following the Civil War. To combat this combination of barriers, President William McKinley's expansionist secretary of state, John Hay, issued the first "Open Door note," which committed America to free trade in Asia and urged all European nations to follow suit.

Hay feared that China's antiforeigner Boxer Rebellion of 1900 would give foreign powers a reason to overturn the Open Door notes and strengthen their spheres of influence in China, so the United States justified sending military forces to China under the Open Door policy. Later, as Russia and Japan fought the Russo-Japanese War for Chinese territorial conquest, President Theodore Roosevelt feared that the belligerents would disrupt American commerce in China. Roosevelt used the Open Door notes as motivation to bring the warring parties to the peace table.

John Milton Hay was a poet, novelist, and historian as well as U.S. Secretary of State under Presidents William McKinley and Theodore Roosevelt, when he helped introduce the "Open Door" policy in China. (Library of Congress.)

In 1909, Roosevelt's successor, President William Howard Taft, supplemented the Open Door notes with the policy of "dollar diplomacy," which increased U.S. trade abroad by supporting American enterprises and investments in China. Also, in 1909, Japan and Russia violated the Open Door policy without U.S. retaliation, and U.S. commercial enterprises began to reduce their investment in China. By 1913, President Woodrow Wilson's preoccupation with isolationism and the European conflict caused him to abandon the Open Door policy.

Despite the widely held belief that America should rely on foreign trade to increase its world power and domestic economy, laissez-faire sentiments fell into disfavor again after the Civil War. Indeed, in the waning years of the nineteenth century, high protectionism garnered some of its most fervent support in American history. In the 1880 election, tariffs became the sole divisive issue between the high tariff Republican candidate James Garfield and the free trade Democratic candidate Winfield S. Hancock. Garfield's narrow victory ensured that tariffs would continue to increase; indeed, high tariffs caused Treasury surpluses every year from 1866 to 1888. President Grover Cleveland, the first Democrat elected after the Civil War, thought the Treasury surplus was highly undesirable for the American people and sought to reverse the postwar trend of escalating tariffs. But Congress proved unwilling to lower tariffs, and Benjamin Harrison's defeat of Cleveland in the 1888 election made the passage of the Tariff of 1888 and the McKinley Tariff (1890) inevitable. Protectionists dropped the pretense that fledgling industries required high tariffs for protection. Instead, they argued that high tariffs would reduce the Treasury surplus by making imports unbearably costly for the American public.

At the turn of the twentieth century, tariff revisionist groups began to form and attempt to lobby the government for a change in trade policy. These organizations generally supported tariffs based on reciprocity and urged the federal government to create a commission to oversee the process in a scientific manner. The National Tariff Commission Association (NTCA), the lobbying organization that worked for the creation of the Tariff Board and strove to see it modeled after the German tariff commission, was the most influential of these groups. Presidents Theodore Roosevelt and William Taft both supported the revisionists in their quest for lower rates. Indeed, Taft so vehemently supported the Payne-Aldrich Tariff of 1909, the first act addressing tariff rates since the Dingley Act of 1897, that he agreed to the Sixteenth Amendment (which provided for a national income tax) just to gain the Democrats' support for the tariff reduction.

World War I accelerated the growth of America's international commerce. European and Asian warring states all sought access to U.S. resources. Exports to the Allies quickly began to soar, rising from $825 million in 1914 to $3.2 billion by 1916. Trade between the Central Powers and the United States fell off dramatically after Britain blockaded Germany in the beginning of the war. Germany cried out for the United States to stop selling munitions to England and complained that Washington showed a bias toward the Allies in its extension of war loans. U.S. officials curtly replied that a reduction in trade with the Allies would not compromise America's neutrality, a position that reflected President Wilson's disapproval of America simply being the well-paid arsenal of the Allies.

Virtually all trade with the Central Powers ceased with the October 6, 1917, passage of the Trading with the Enemy Act, which forbade commerce with enemy nations or their associates. The act gave the Wilson administration the power to impose an embargo on imports from enemy nations, and the War Trade Board became authorized to prevent trade with the enemy. Congress clearly intended to use this act against the Central Powers. The act also authorized censorship of foreign newspapers.

Trade Policy in the Interwar Period

After World War I, the exporting prowess that the United States had gained during the war endured, and American products proved competitive in world markets beyond what had seemed possible only years before. U.S. trade during the war enriched the nation, and its continuation after the war made possible the Roaring Twenties. Europe desperately struggled to rebuild, and American goods made that goal possible. World War I had rendered the United States a creditor nation, with many more goods flowing from America into Europe than vice versa. Relatively high tariffs intensified the imbalance of payments between the Continent and the United States.

An unfavorable balance of trade between Europe and the United States, coupled with increased competition from goods flowing out of Asia and Latin America and agricultural production slumps, signaled problems for American exports. A depression began in October 1929 and, in June 1930, Congress intensified America's foreign trade slump by passing the Hawley-Smoot Tariff Act. This piece of legislation raised tariffs to their highest level since the Tariff of Abominations over 100 years before, with agricultural and some manufacturing goods receiving the greatest tariff increases. Congressional motives for this increase stemmed from a "beggar thy neighbor" policy, as governmental leaders who desired to stop the economic slump domestically cared little for the effects of the tariffs on the economies of other nations. However, other countries soon levied reciprocal tariffs against American goods, which further depressed world trade.

President Franklin D. Roosevelt waited until 1934 to ask Congress for legislation to allow negotiation with other countries for lower tariffs. He received the Reciprocal Trade Agreements Act in the summer of 1934. Secretary of State Cordell Hull believed that this precursor to the 1948 General Agreement on Tariffs and Trade (GATT) would reverse the high-tariff policies that he thought had wreaked havoc on American exporting.

As a severe depression developed at home, President Roosevelt set about tackling America's problems abroad. Between 1935 and 1941, Congress passed what became known as the Neutrality Acts, which imposed an arms and loan embargo against all warring states. Roosevelt, strongly supportive of the Allies but aware that the American public wished to avoid direct involvement in a war, allowed trade policy to dictate foreign policy by attempting twice in 1939 to persuade Congress to repeal the Neutrality Acts and allow for economic intermediation with the Allies. Congress grudgingly acceded on the second attempt and removed the arms embargo but added the stipulation that arms be sold on a "cash-and-carry" basis only. On August 2, 1940, Roosevelt signed an executive order to trade destroyers for military bases, and on March 11 of the following year, Congress authorized a lend-lease proposal after Britain could no longer come up with the cash necessary to purchase American weapons for war. Twenty-six days later, Congress authorized its first lend-lease package, earmarking $7 billion for the Allies. Roosevelt froze all Axis assets in the United States in June 1941.

Just as Germany lost its battle with England for a share of wartime trade with America, Japan, too, found that U.S. trade policy was a dangerous substitute for foreign policy. In the pre–World War II era, Japan remained utterly dependent on the United States for much of the products it required to pursue its belligerent policy in Asia. After going against U.S. wishes and pressuring France to allow Japanese troops to enter French Indochina, Japan found itself the target of an American embargo on U.S. iron and steel. In July 1941, Japan further extended its troops in Asia, forcing the United States to freeze all Japanese assets and implement an embargo against the island nation on all products except for food and cotton. Without trade with countries under the U.S. economic sphere of dominion, Japan lost access to 66 percent of its export market and 39 percent of its imports. Far more significantly, Japan imported 84 percent and 80 percent of its oil from the United States in the years 1938 and 1940,

Table 11. Average tariffs on industrial products (in percentages)

	Pre–Uruguay round	Post–Uruguay round
By country/region		
Developed countries' imports from:		
World	6.2	3.7
North America	5.1	2.8
Latin America	4.9	3.3
Western Europe	6.4	3.5
Central and Eastern Europe	4.0	2.4
Africa	2.7	2.0
Asia	7.7	4.9
Developing countries' imports from:		
World	20.5	14.4
North America	23.2	15.7
Latin America	27.6	18.5
Western Europe	25.8	18.3
Central and Eastern Europe	18.4	15.1
Africa	12.3	8.0
Asia	17.8	12.7
By product		
All industrial products	6.3	3.8
Fish and fish products	6.1	4.5
Wood, pulp, paper, and furniture	3.5	1.1
Textiles and clothing	15.5	12.1
Leather, rubber, and footwear	8.9	7.3
Metals	3.7	1.4
Chemicals and photographic supplies	6.7	3.7
Transport equipment	7.5	5.8
Nonelectric machinery	4.8	1.9
Electric machinery	6.6	3.5
Mineral products and precious stones	2.3	1.1

respectively. Without U.S. oil, Japan anticipated exhausting its supply in one and a half to two years. The Japanese prime minister, Tojo, considered the embargo an act of war because a lack of oil would destroy the imperial navy even as it rested in port. In his diary, he described America's high post–World War I tariff policies and the pre–World War II economic blockade as inflicting a mortal blow to Japan.

Trade Policy from World War II to the Present

Roosevelt's fear of the revival of the protectionism and high tariffs that contributed to the depression and war in the first half of the century led him to take preventative measures. In 1947 and 1948, the administration of his successor, Harry S Truman, helped develop the GATT, which further liberalized trade by gradually reducing and eliminating tariffs, subsidies, quotas, and other trade barriers. In October 1962, Congress passed the Trade Expansion Act at the behest of President John F. Kennedy, allowing the president to cut tariffs by up to 50 percent over five years and to remove many tariffs altogether on goods traded between Western Europe and the United States. This act gave the executive branch leverage in the Kennedy Round of GATT negotiations, which ran from 1964 to 1967, and it also served as an extension of U.S. foreign policy in its pressure on the Soviet Union. The Kennedy Round modified GATT rules and allowed for the lowering of rates across the board instead of on a product-by-product basis. The United States lowered its tariffs on a variety of products. European nations failed to reciprocate by lowering their trade barriers, and in many cases, they increased rates through less visible but equally potent forms of trade restrictions. The most recent round of GATT negotiations, the Uruguay Round (1986–1994), cut tariffs by 34 percent on average (see Table 11). The Uruguay Round agreement revised the rules regarding dumping and export subsidies, and it eliminated voluntary export restrictions (VERs) and extended intellectual property rights internationally. Finally, the Uruguay Round ended the GATT and created in its place the World Trade Organization (WTO), which now supervises the implementation of trade agreements and settles trade disputes.

Members of both the GATT and WTO organized around the liberal economic principles of nondiscrimination and fair national treatment of imports. The goals of these two organizations focused on lowering trade barriers and enacting a rules-based trading system. The GATT and WTO did, however, allow for conditions under which trade restrictions remained permissible. Today, member nations can discriminate against nonmember nations, retaliate against unfairly trading member nations, and establish preferential trading areas that provide trade benefits in excess of the terms of GATT and WTO. Further, certain escape clauses or safeguards permit the temporary exemption of some industries from the rules of trade restrictions.

It was not simply a desire to return to normalcy that led American leaders to encourage trade. The emergence of a bipolar postwar world and the conflict between the communist Soviet Union and capitalist United States meant that America again needed a strong economic base. When Mao Zedong declared China a communist state, President Truman resisted becoming involved in mainland Asian affairs. But the outbreak of the Korean War caused the United States to stress Taiwanese trade and economic development as another Asian check to communist designs in the region. The United States became Taiwan's biggest trading partner until the 1970s, when Taiwan diversified its commercial relations.

China viewed the exchange of military systems between the United States and Taiwan as an extension of a hostile U.S. foreign policy. It struggled to remain closed to U.S. trade until 1999, when entrance into the WTO induced Chinese leaders to open their market to the United States and lower tariffs in exchange for support of China's WTO bid. Both countries reached an agreement to phase out quotas on Chinese textiles by 2005.

After World War II, America helped reconstruct the Japanese economy as a capitalist bulwark against Soviet ambitions in Asia. Japan remained the biggest trading partner of the United States for several decades. Although America held a favorable balance of trade with Japan during the early postwar years, by the 1970s, this trade balance had shifted. America, which had proved a willing dumping ground for

Japanese products while asking little in return, suddenly demanded that Japan rescind its highly stringent import regulations and open its markets to American goods. The Japanese government found that it could placate the United States by implementing voluntary export restrictions against the products that America wished to restrict. In 1971, Japan enacted VERs against textiles, followed in later years by steel and chemicals, then against consumer electronics, automobiles, metal-working machines, and, most recently, against computer chips.

Voluntary export restraints benefited Japan on a deeper level than simply appeasing the United States. VERs essentially represent a collusion between two governments, and Japan stood to gain much economically by implementing them with Washington's consent. Had the United States simply levied a tariff against the Japanese goods that threatened U.S. businesses, the federal government would have received the tariff revenues, which would have amounted to the difference between the world price and the U.S. tariff-heightened market price. But by voluntarily restricting the supply of their goods, the Japanese theoretically could contract the world supply and effectively drive up the world price for those goods. Japanese manufacturers would effectively absorb the higher profits created by their government's collusive agreement with the United States. This approach would work particularly well in postwar Japan, whose government remained dominated by the interests of government and large business partnerships known as *zaibatsu*. The close relationship between government and industry in Japan made VERs a viable response to U.S. pressure.

The VERs proved effective, helping the yen to appreciate relative to the dollar and causing the Japanese trade surplus with the United States to fall. But they also created long-term difficulties for the United States. In addition to causing the sacrifice of potential tariff revenues to the Japanese government, the VERs also lowered the opportunity cost of the foreign industries for diversifying into another type of manufacture. When they agreed to restrict the export of small automobiles, Japanese businesses found it profitable to begin exporting midsize cars and trucks. Although U.S. trade negotiators pursued short-term U.S. interests, the U.S.-requested VERs have created more problems for domestic industry in the long run.

Nevertheless, Japan's red tape and its outright ban on certain American imports still angers many Americans. Although Japan remains the largest importer of certain U.S. farm products, not until 1991 did it allow the importation of U.S. beef and citrus products. Enormous tariffs, such as a 70 percent tariff on American beef, still hinder foreign trade between the two nations. U.S. firms clamor against regulations such as the so-called Big Store Law, which prevents large chain stores from operating in Japan, as well as the "closed system" under which the Japanese government exerts protectionism with the consent of domestic big business. These artificial barriers to trade extend monopoly-like powers to domestic industries at the expense of foreign competitors and are seen by many as an unfair restriction of free trade.

The European Union (EU) has proven to be a barb in postwar trade relations between Europe and America. Since 1989, the EU has banned the import of bananas and hormone-treated beef and has not heeded U.S. and WTO objections. In 1999, the United States took action, levying retaliatory tariffs of 100 percent against 15 EU products. As Europe and the United States continue to compete with one another for global trade power, the further liberalization of trade between the two regions remains uncertain.

Although Canada and Mexico are America's largest and third-largest trading partners, respectively, no serious effort at integrating trade between the three partners has existed since efforts were made toward the Canadian reciprocity treaty of 1854. In 1989, the widely hailed Canada-U.S. Free Trade Agreement (CUFTA) began the process of eliminating all bilateral tariffs either immediately or in equal annual steps. Momentum encouraging free trade generated the North American Free Trade Agreement (NAFTA) of 1992, which created a free trade zone between Mexico, Canada, and the United States. Since it began the 15-year process of eliminating tariffs between the three partners in 1994, NAFTA has created a free trade area rivaling the EU in terms of GDP and population encompassed. Although some difficulties still hamper the implementation of the agreement, the transition has generally been smooth.

Such cooperative trade agreements represent a worldwide trend in the postwar era toward the liberalization of trade. In casting off many of the conservative trade ideologies of the past and paying little heed to Marxist critiques, industrialized nations are seeking to reduce most trade barriers with their biggest trading partners. Some of this reduction in protectionism may have resulted from governments' increased awareness that protection may force costs on society and even on the domestic industries receiving protection. In addition to the previously discussed flaws of VERs, all forms of trade protection may result in the misallocation of factors of production into industries in which they are utilized less efficiently. Further, industries believing that a government may be willing to extend protection will see potentially great gains in diverting otherwise productive resources into lobbying efforts against the government. Finally, as economists Neil Vousden and Neil Campbell argue, industries characterized by little competition often will not make the effort to succeed in their fields, a phenomenon known as x-efficiency.

What of the future of American trade liberalization in the Western Hemisphere? In 1995 a group of 34 trade ministers from North, South, and Central America met to create a free trade area of the Americas (FTAA), which would be developed through an evolution of the continents' many subregional trade agreements. If realized, this trade liberalization effort would be the most ambitious example of economic cooperation to date. Additionally, the United States, through participating in the Asia Pacific Economic Cooperation Forum (APEC), has worked toward achieving free trade in the Asia-Pacific region by the year 2020. These goals, if accomplished, would fundamentally change the way America conducts trade through the first quarter of the twenty-first century.

References

Butler, Michael A. *Cautious Visionary: Cordell Hull and Trade Reform, 1933–1937*. Kent, OH: Kent State University Press, 1998.

Eckes, Alfred E. *Opening America's Market: U.S. Foreign Policy since 1776*. Chapel Hill: University of North Carolina Press, 1995.

Eckes, Alfred, Richard L. Brinkman, and William A. Lovett. *U.S. Trade Policy: History, Theory, and the WTO*. Armonk, NY: M. E. Sharpe, 1999.

Gibson, Martha L. *Conflict amid Consensus in American Trade Policy*. Washington, DC: Georgetown University Press, 2000.

Hane, Mikoso. *Modern Japan*. Boulder, CO: Westview Press, 2001.

Jenkins, Virginia S. *Bananas: An American History*. Washington, DC: Smithsonian Institution Press, 2000.

Lancaster, B. *The American Revolution*. Boston: Houghton Mifflin, 2001.

Lepore, Jill. *The Name of War*. New York: Vintage Books, 1998.

Morrison, S. E., H. S. Commager, and W. E. Leuchtenburg. *The Growth of the American Republic*. Vol. 1. 7th ed. New York: Oxford University Press, 1980.

Orne, William A. *Understanding NAFTA: Mexico, Free Trade, and the New North America*. Austin: University of Texas Press, 1996.

Pastor, Robert A. *Congress and the Politics of U.S. Foreign Economic Policy 1929–1976*. Berkeley: University of California Press, 1980.

Pope-Hennessy, James. *Sins of the Fathers: The Atlantic Slave Traders*. London: Phoenix Press, 2000.

Spence, Jonathan D. *The Search for Modern China*. 2nd ed. New York: W. W. Norton, 1999.

Transportation Policy

Joseph A. Devine

Transportation policy remains of vital importance because it lies at the heart of the American economy. A synergistic relationship exists between the transportation industries and the rest of the economy. Systems and methods of moving goods and people have driven the American economy forward, and advances in the general economy have propelled improvements in transportation. Transportation developments have been determined by geographic factors and human actions. Some of the human actions affecting transportation have been unthinking responses to the "invisible hand" of the market or to other unplanned factors, but many changes have resulted from conscious policy decisions made by the government at all levels and sometimes by nongovernmental policymakers, such as the heads of large corporations or unions.

Transportation Policy in the Colonial Period

Geography often determines how people and freight move from one place to another. During the colonial period, before the Industrial Revolution came to America, geographic factors such as the deep estuaries and navigable rivers along the Atlantic coast far outweighed human policy, but nevertheless, colonists consciously adopted some noteworthy policies to control transportation between the populations of the seaboard colonies and the six other areas with which they traded: the European continent, the Caribbean Islands, the interior inhabited by Native Americans, Africa (especially West Africa), French Canada, and the Spanish American borderlands. Government policies modified or limited relations with all six regions but almost never as effectively as the policymakers desired. The Navigation Acts provide the most famous example of such regulations. First in 1651, when Oliver Cromwell controlled England, and then in 1660 after the Restoration, England tried to ensure that trade into and out of the American colonies would be carried on English ships manned mainly by English sailors (with the understanding that "English" included colonial Americans). Exporting "enumerated" goods such as tobacco to the continent of Europe and, after 1663, importing most European goods occurred only through England. When the Caribbean Islands concentrated on sugar production in the second half of the seventeenth century and those islands became a major market for New England fish and the middle colony cereals, Parliament tried to channel North American foodstuffs to the British West Indies rather than to the French or Dutch West

Indies. The Molasses Act of 1733, an attempt to direct North American ships to Jamaica, Barbados, and other British islands, imposed a prohibitive duty of 6d. per gallon on molasses imported from non-British islands, but the chicanery of American merchants and the greed of bribable customs collectors nullified the act.

At various times, the imperial government and individual provinces established policies concerning trade and transportation with areas other than Europe or the Caribbean. In the seventeenth century, the English government gave the Royal African Company a monopoly over the sordid business of transporting slaves from Africa to the New World. Ironically, by the end of the eighteenth century, the British nation, which had become the dominant carrier in the transatlantic slave business, experienced an awakening of conscience, and the British navy began to effectively patrol against slavers. Freight to and from the other three areas mentioned—the interior of North America, Canada, and nearby Spanish territories—was carried by packhorses, wagons, canoes, or sailing vessels and at different times fell subject to a combination of provincial, British, or foreign laws, with widely varying degrees of effectiveness. Provincial governments regularly licensed traders who transported rum, firearms, and trade goods to Native Americans—sometimes to prevent an outrageous exploitation of these people and sometimes to protect favored traders from interlopers from a different province.

The American Revolutionary War shifted most major policy decisions about transportation from London to the new nation, but the formation of the American transportation policy has never been entirely free from the policies of foreign nations. For instance, England retained some say about U.S. transportation policy long after the Revolution. The British negotiators of the Treaty of Paris of 1783 obtained a provision giving Britain navigation rights on the Mississippi. Much later, in the 1846 Clayton-Bulyer Treaty, Britain secured equal rights to control any future trans-isthmian canal Americans might build, a right it retained until the 1901 Hay-Pauncefote Treaty. Even in the late twentieth and early twenty-first centuries, Britain, along with its 14 European Union colleagues, has had a voice in U.S. transportation policies over such issues as landing rights of American airlines and mergers of transportation companies; an example of the latter is the recent merger of Chrysler with Daimler-Benz, a leading manufacturer in America of heavy-duty trucks and school buses.

Transportation Policy in the Early Republic

Upon achieving independence, Americans rejoiced in their expansive new country, but several major transportation issues confronted policymakers. These problems included inadequate access to the two great waterways that could afford easy transportation across much of North America—the Mississippi/Ohio and the Great Lakes/St. Lawrence systems; the Appalachian barrier to communications between the eastern and western halves of the United States; and poor north-south roads along the eastern seaboard.

To the frustration of Americans, full access to the Mississippi/Ohio and the Great Lakes/St. Lawrence systems remained tantalizingly just out of reach. For years to come, American policymakers sought to make those two great systems provide effective transportation. The challenge proved particularly great in the pre-railroad age, when only waterways could economically transport high-volume, low-value farm products for distances greater than 20 or 30 miles.

The Paris peace settlement of the 1780s gave the United States the eastern side of the Mississippi Valley down to Florida, but Florida, controlled by Britain since 1763, reverted back to Spain. Spain knew that if farmers living on the three-eighths of American soil drained by the Mississippi, the Ohio, and their tributaries had access to the world's oceans through New Orleans, a flood of settlers would spill over into Louisiana and Texas, leading to a spread of American power. Therefore, Spain resolutely resisted the efforts of John Jay and other American diplomats to let American rafts and flatboats float down to New Orleans to connect with shipping on Lake Pontchartrain. America's inability to change Spain's attitude caused many frontierspeople to support the new U.S. Constitution, since a stronger national government would be more capable of pressuring Spain into negotiating navigation rights. In 1795, New Orleans finally became incorporated in America's transportation system when Spain acquiesced to Pinckney's Treaty out of fear that if it did not unlock New Orleans, Americans would ally with George III, their former king, and seize the city. So Pinckney's Treaty opened up the Ohio and Mississippi Valleys, but Spain's cession of New Orleans and Louisiana to powerful France in 1800 again threatened to stifle the West. President Thomas Jefferson remained determined to enable western farmers to transport their produce through New Orleans. He told Robert R. Livingston and James Monroe that the United States should "marry the British fleet and nation" if Napoleon would not sell New Orleans. The crisis ended in 1803 when Napoleon agreed to sell New Orleans and all of Louisiana. With the political problem solved, the question became how to turn the "father of waters" into a practical, two-way highway. Over the next two centuries, steamboats (and their diesel successors) and the dams, locks, navigation aids, and dredging of the Corps of Engineers fulfilled this goal.

The history of transportation policies in regard to the Great Lakes and the St. Lawrence River differs from that of the Mississippi. Very different geography, British control of the St. Lawrence, and the eagerness of merchants and investors in New York City, Philadelphia, and Baltimore to bridge the Appalachian barrier between the East and the West created transportation routes into the middle of the country. These new routes diminished the interest of American politicians in Montreal and Quebec as possible entrepôts of the Midwest. Several geographic considerations made the St. Lawrence less important than the Mississippi as an outlet to saltwater: Most of the rivers in the middle of the country flowed south into the Mississippi, not into the Great Lakes; the lakes and the St. Lawrence froze in the winter; and an impassible obstacle, Niagara Falls, existed between Lake Erie and Lake Ontario until the Welland Canal provided a bypass in 1829. Not until the mid-twentieth century, during President Dwight D. Eisenhower's administration, did American policymakers join with Canada in developing the St. Lawrence Seaway (1959) to make the St. Lawrence a practical outlet for mid-America.

In the early nineteenth century, Thomas Jefferson's secretary of the treasury, Albert Gallatin, proposed a grand system of canals and turnpikes to connect eastern river systems with the trans-Appalachian Ohio/Mississippi system and to provide north-south roads to supplement seaboard coastal shipping. The National Road (or Cumberland Pike), which initially (in 1818) connected the Potomac at Cumberland, Maryland, with the Ohio at Wheeling, Virginia, and later was extended at each end to Baltimore and central Illinois, is a tangible result of Gallatin's plan. Two twentieth-century highways, U.S. 40 and Interstate 70, followed the route of that first federal highway. But, by the 1830s, the job of developing transportation routes across the Appalachians shifted from the federal government to states and seaboard cities. Henry Clay and President John Quincy Adams, proponents of the American System that would have given the federal government responsibility for developing a transportation system, lost control of the national government to Andrew Jackson (president from 1829 to 1837) and his followers, who favored a limited federal role. Jackson demonstrated his attitude most famously with his "Maysville veto" (1830), a refusal to spend federal funds on a highway. In the 1830s, the national government handed over maintenance of the National Road to the states through which it ran. The prevailing consensus was that the formation of an American transportation policy should be decentralized.

Rivers and Canals

Before the Civil War, East Coast ports vied with each other to extend their hinterlands across the Appalachians. Investors and local leaders wanted the produce of the Midwest to reach world markets through their cities rather than via New Orleans and the Mississippi or by the St. Lawrence. Clearly, New York City became far more successful than its rivals, and the Erie Canal served as the foundation of its success.

In all of American history, the decision to build the Erie Canal may be the most significant example of a well-conceived transportation policy. As early as the 1740s, New York's lieutenant governor, Cadwallader Colden, had realized that a canal through the Mohawk Valley could connect the Hudson to Lake Erie and thereby expand New York City's hinterland to encompass the heart of the continent. In the early 1800s, as New Yorkers planned to build the canal, the federal government declined to participate in the project. President James Madison had constitutional scruples about whether the federal government should undertake such a project—especially since it would not benefit Virginia—so it became an undertaking of solely the state government of New York. DeWitt Clinton, its most vociferous supporter, won the backing of the state legislature (and the governorship for himself) and began construction on July 4, 1817. When the canal opened in 1825, it ran 363 miles from Lake Erie at Buffalo to Albany on the Hudson, and its impact on New York City, 150 miles downriver from Albany, became apparent immediately. Western grain went through New York City, and manufactures and immigrants headed for Ohio, Indiana, and Illinois traveled up the Hudson from the city.

The opening of the Erie Canal in 1825 after eight years of construction. The Erie Canal was the longest canal of its time, running through the New York wilderness and linking Lake Erie to the Hudson River. (Library of Congress.)

The success of the Erie Canal stimulated Boston, Philadelphia, Baltimore, and Charleston to attempt to duplicate New York's achievement. Pennsylvania's rugged Allegheny Mountains between Philadelphia and Pittsburgh yielded no pathway for a canal crossing, so Philadelphians persuaded the state legislature to underwrite the Main Line system. Instead of a single canal like the Erie, Pennsylvania's Main Line connected Philadelphia on the Delaware River to Pittsburgh at the Ohio with a mix of canals, railroads, and inclined planes. (Inclined planes used steam-powered winches placed on the tops of ridges to pull flatcars up railroad tracks.) The Main Line system, a brave effort that enthralled Charles Dickens with its scenic views, proved a colossal economic failure.

Railroads

Also a failure, the Chesapeake and Ohio Canal, financed by investors from the Baltimore/Washington region, did not breach Maryland's mountains and never reached its second namesake. By the 1830s, most of New York's rivals realized that their best hope of reaching the other side of the Appalachians depended on the new

In 1862, the U.S. Congress chartered the Central Pacific Railroad to build east from Sacramento, and the Union Pacific Railroad to build west from Omaha. Here, workers join the tracks at Promontory Point in Utah in 1869, creating the first transcontinental railroad. (National Archives and Records Administration.)

British invention—railroads. On July 4, 1828, investors at Baltimore watched Charles Carroll of Carrolton, Maryland, a signer of the Declaration of Independence, inaugurate a new transportation age as he turned the first shovelful of dirt to begin construction of the Baltimore and Ohio Railroad. In the early 1830s, the longest single railroad line in the world, the Charleston and Hamburg, stretched from Charleston, South Carolina, toward the Mississippi. In the 1850s, Philadelphians, having given up on the Main Line system, completed the Pennsylvania Railroad to connect the City of Brotherly Love with Pittsburgh. But unfortunately for all of New York City's rivals, by the time their railroads reached the beginnings of the Ohio/Mississippi system on the other side of the mountains, New York merchants had two western rail connections of their own. The Erie Railroad, completed in 1851, ran from the Hudson to Lake Erie along the latitude of the Pennsylvania–New York border and, by the middle of the 1850s, the steamboat operator Cornelius Vanderbilt had tied together a series of small railroads between Albany and Buffalo into the New York Central, which soon had connections into Manhattan.

By the time of the Civil War, maps of the U.S. transportation system showed a vast array of railroads and a few key canals—of which the Erie remained by far the most important, for it carried from the Midwest to New York more freight than the combined total carried by all the major railroads that crossed the mountains. Four key railroad trunk lines existed: the Erie and the New York Central ran from Lake Erie to New York City, the Pennsylvania ran from Pittsburgh to Philadelphia, and the Baltimore and Ohio ran from Wheeling to Baltimore; each of the four had subsidiaries or partners that continued into the heartland. In the South, a railroad route from Charleston to Memphis had been built, and the Boston and Albany brought Boston in touch with the West, albeit over one of New York's railroads. But as George Rogers Taylor and other transportation historians have noted, America's railroads and canals were not the product of a carefully planned national transportation policy. They had resulted from a series of rival policies, with each financed and supported by individuals and concerns representing parochial interests that had little or no care about a national transportation policy. No uniform gauge existed on American railroads. In cities such as Philadelphia, Richmond, or Pittsburgh, transferring cargo from one railroad to another required the use of a horse and wagon because "connecting" railroad companies often did not physically join each other. The national government did become interested in transportation policy in a limited capacity when officials authorized the use of army engineers to survey the line of the Baltimore and Ohio and when Congress approved a grant of federal land to finance the Illinois Central's route from Chicago to New Orleans in 1850. But between the administrations of Thomas Jefferson and Abraham Lincoln, local investors and city and state governments continued to make the key decisions about transportation policy.

After the election of Lincoln and the Civil War, even though states, municipalities, and private investors continued to have considerable input concerning transportation policy, major decisions occurred at the national level. The two biggest issues in the last third of the nineteenth century involved the building of railroads between the heartland and the Pacific Coast and determining how much public regulation should be exercised over the railroad companies that had become so dominant in the American economy. At a time when railroads had no competition from motor vehicles or airplanes, they employed more people than the U.S. government, and more money was invested in them than in all of America's manufacturing.

By the 1850s, many people had foreseen a rail connection between the Mississippi Valley and California. Jefferson Davis, secretary of war in Franklin Pierce's administration, ordered a study of possible routes, and just five years after Mexico had ceded a huge part of its territory in the treaty ending the Mexican-American War of 1846 to 1848, negotiators persuaded Mexico to sell the Gadsden Purchase to the United States. The purchase ceded the Gila Valley to the United States, a good southern route to California. Before the United States lurched into the Civil War and during the war as well, several general assumptions developed about what the policy should be in regard to a Pacific railroad. Because of the vast distances, sparse population, and rugged terrain involved, private investors could not bear the entire cost of construction; government aid would be required, and it had to come from the national government, not from states. Furthermore, people believed a Pacific railroad should be a privately owned entity, not a government-operated route like the Erie Canal or the failed Pennsylvania Main Line. When Americans first started envisioning a transcontinental railroad, no one could foresee the construction of as many railroads as would be built by 1893—five!

In the 1850s, every major city in the Mississippi Valley, from New Orleans northward, hoped to become the terminus of the transcontinental railroad. When President Lincoln signed legislation chartering two companies, the Union Pacific and the Central Pacific, to build the rail connection between the center of the country and California, the South had already seceded, eliminating any possibility of a route from New Orleans or Memphis. The Pacific Railway Act of 1862, and an amending law in 1864, chartered two private companies, the Central Pacific and the Union Pacific, to construct the railway. The Union Pacific built from Omaha westward, and initially, the Central Pacific was to build from Sacramento 150 miles into Nevada. However, effective lobbying by the Central Pacific brought authorization (in 1866) for that railroad to go indefinitely eastward until it met the tracks of the Union Pacific. The joining of the two lines occurred on May 10, 1869, at Promontory Point, Utah Territory, in a celebrated ceremony that was instantly reported to the entire nation by telegraph. Congress gave generous land grants and cash loans to the Central Pacific and Union Pacific and to three other transcontinental railroad companies that were soon chartered: The Southern Pacific joined San Francisco to New Orleans in 1883; the Northern Pacific connected St. Paul and Portland, Oregon, in 1883; and the Atchinson, Topeka, and Santa Fe reached southern California in 1888. In return for the generous help of the nation, the railroads committed to carrying troops for half fare, a provision the nation appreciated during World War II (after which the discount ended). A fifth transcontinental line, the Great Northern, completed between St. Paul and Seattle by James J. Hill in 1893, was built when the nation no longer felt compelled to give railroads huge land grants. By the end of the nineteenth century, many Americans thought national policy had been much too favorable to the railroads, and disgust over the Crédit Mobilier scandal and other reports of unsavory corporate influence on members of Congress increased the dissatisfaction. (Crédit Mobilier was a company established by the Union Pacific Railroad and received contracts to construct its rail lines. Company stock was given to members of Congress, who then granted land and federal subsidies to the company to increase their profits. The involvement of prominent politicians was exposed in 1872 and 1873, with several resigning from office as a result.) But historians have not reached a consensus about the wisdom of the policy of giving great gifts of land to expedite construction of the western railroads.

Now, in the twenty-first century, when almost all long-distance passenger travel occurs by automobiles or airplanes and when trains no longer carry most freight, it is hard to envision how much railroads dominated both freight and passenger business in the late nineteenth century. However, because railroads had overbuilt, extending their lines into places with too few customers to maintain a profit, and because managers looted many companies, even in the age of railroad dominance, railroad bankruptcies were very common, especially during the economic downturns of 1873 and 1893. Yet, despite the weak financial condition of many lines, the public became convinced that the railroads still took advantage of their customers. Farmers in states such as Kansas or Minnesota, many served by only a single railroad, resented paying higher freight rates than shippers between Chicago and New York. They thought the only explanation for higher rates west of the Mississippi and the still higher rates west of the Missouri was that competition between the several trunk lines running east from Chicago kept rates low, whereas out on the prairies, the lack of competition allowed companies to gouge their captive clients. Farmers in Texas, a state that had given considerable public land to the railroads, were infuriated by the rail companies' failure to complete their lines in the time required by their charters. Everywhere, Americans wondered if the free railroad passes given to members of Congress and other legislators constituted bribes, designed to persuade them to ignore unfair rates. The public's unhappiness with railroads in the late nineteenth century led to a national policy of strictly regulating and supervising railroads, which was destined to endure into the last quarter of the twentieth century. When railroads had a natural monopoly, it made sense for the public to intervene in the absence of competition, but the country's determination to control railroads persisted long after real competition developed from automobiles and trucks running on government-financed highways and airplanes taking off from publicly built airports.

The national policy of strictly controlling the railroad industry took root in the 1870s with the so-called Granger Laws—laws passed by Midwestern farming states to regulate railroads. Those laws, named after a farmer's organization, the National Grange of the Patrons of Husbandry, eventually ran afoul of the interstate commerce clause in the Constitution. When an 1886 Supreme Court decision (the *Wabash* case) drastically limited states' ability to regulate intrastate commerce that had interstate links, Congress gave the federal government jurisdiction over railroad traffic. The Interstate Commerce Act of 1887 mandated fair rates for interstate railroad traffic and established the quasi-judicial Interstate Commerce Commission (ICC) to supervise railroads. Congress approved the act by a vote of 219 to 49 in the House of Representatives and 43 to 15 in the Senate, indicating strong public support for it. The creation of the ICC constituted a landmark in the evolution of national transportation policy, but a series of court decisions over the next quarter century undermined the ICC's effectiveness. Not until the Progressive Era, during the presidencies of Theodore Roosevelt, William Howard Taft, and Woodrow Wilson, did the ICC effectively control railroads. The 1903 Elkins Act forbade secret rebates to favored shippers. The Hepburn Act of 1906, one of Roosevelt's most important reforms, gave the ICC power to actually set railroad rates (subject to appeal in the courts) and extended its jurisdiction to express companies and oil pipelines. During World War I, the federal government took total control of railroad operations after bad weather and inept distribution of freight cars caused a breakdown in the nation's rail system.

A 1921 Model T Ford, parked near the White House. (Library of Congress.)

After the war, however, railroad operations returned to prewar conditions, but the government retained a high degree of control over the railroads. For the next 60 years, the ICC opposed the railroads' efforts to fight truckers for freight by slashing rates, and the government's antitrust policies discouraged railroad mergers and consolidations.

In the early twentieth century, just when the public began insisting on strict regulation of the apparently monopolistic railroads, two new technologies—the automobile and the airplane—emerged, for which new transportation policies had to be devised.

Automobiles

Although an experimental automobile was demonstrated in France in 1769, the first really modern cars were invented in Germany in 1886. Despite being steadily improved in succeeding years, autos remained unreliable and expensive until Henry Ford introduced his Model T in 1908, a truly revolutionary advance over earlier vehicles. Remarkably sturdy, easily repairable, and priced at $825 initially—and sold for under $300 in the 1920s—it was within the reach of the middle class. Ford's

Model T and a range of cars produced by over 200 other manufacturers brought a public clamor for good roads, and governments at every level responded. From the 1830s to the early years of the 1900s, the federal government had contributed little to America's roads, but from Woodrow Wilson's administration to the present, it has consistently played a major role in the building and maintaining of America's highways.

Wilson signed the Federal Aid Road Act in 1916, laying the foundation of the federal highway policy. This act, which had epochal implications for federal-state relations because of its matching-dollar provision, offered cooperating states $5 million in 1917 and an additional $5 million each year thereafter (culminating in $25 million in 1921) if they would spend a dollar of state money for each dollar they received from the federal government. Allocation of the 50:50 matching dollars to the 48 states occurred according to a formula based equally on area, population, and post road mileage. For nearly a hundred years, the federal government has appropriated highway money to states under such a matching-dollar system, but the ratio between federal and state dollars has varied greatly, sometimes going to 90:10 for parts of the interstate system. The formulas, always the subject of intense political debate, have become far more complicated than the original one based on population, area, and post roads. The most important of the federal highway matching-dollar programs, the interstate system launched in 1956 during Eisenhower's administration, began after fierce debates. The creation of that system required major decisions about transportation policy. Should trucks pay fuel and tire taxes comparable to the real estate taxes railroads paid to states and localities? Should truckers' fuel taxes be as high in relation to their vehicle weight as passenger car fuel taxes were to the weight of automobiles? Should most of the interstates be toll roads paid for by users? Americans answered all these questions in the negative.

Airplanes

The Wright brothers realized one of humanity's greatest dreams in 1903. News of their flight spread speedily, and within a quarter century, large numbers of Americans had seen airplanes thanks to the barnstormers who seemingly flew into every hamlet. Although airlines and airplane manufacturers operated as private industries, a consensus developed that government at the national, state, and local levels should establish policies that would help this exciting new form of transportation—all the more so after World War I demonstrated the military significance of airplanes. The earliest planes were marvels, but they were not very efficient. Not until the first modern airliner, the Douglas DC-3, began flying in 1935 was it possible for an airline to make a profit just from the passengers its planes carried. In the 1920s, under the pretense that the U.S. Post Office had a desperate need to speed mail through the air, the federal government began awarding airmail contracts to airlines. This stimulus and the creation of a system of navigation aids with federally paid air controllers became as vital to the airlines as federal land grants had been for the Union Pacific and Central Pacific Railroads in the 1860s, and few among the public begrudged that help.

States and localities assisted the airlines by constructing airports and not charging the airlines for the total cost. And in the mid-twentieth century, to ensure that airlines made money, the Federal Aviation Administration limited the number of airline routes and regulated ticket prices.

In the last third of the twentieth century, a fundamental change in national transportation policy occurred as the nation adopted deregulation—although it would be more accurate to describe this as a policy of less regulation. In 1978, President Jimmy Carter approved legislation deregulating the airline industry. Total deregulation had not occurred—federal inspectors continued to enforce rules about safety and proper maintenance, and the actual flights of air carriers remained under the watchful eyes of air controllers. Deregulation actually meant a virtual end to restrictions on who could serve which routes and what prices airlines could charge for tickets. The results proved dramatic. Increased competition, lowered ticket prices, and passenger mileage more than doubled. New airlines sprang into existence, and some airlines, most notably Southwest, flourished. But all did not. Bankruptcy or forced takeover became the fate of some of the famous pioneering airlines, such as Pan American, TWA, and Eastern.

Jimmy Carter's administration also deregulated the railroad industry with the 1980 Staggers Act, named for a congressman from West Virginia—a state whose coal companies had long chafed under the railroads' inability to cut freight rates without going through the onerous process of obtaining ICC approval. Even before the Staggers Act, the federal government had begun easing its antitrust policies to permit the railroad industry to merge troubled lines, and it had agreed to let the railroads shed their unprofitable passenger service to local governments' transit systems or, in the case of long-distance service, to a federally supported quasi-governmental agency, Amtrak (founded in 1970). A series of mergers resulted in two giant railroad companies, the Union Pacific and the Burlington Northern Santa Fe, controlling the West's historical routes from the center of the country to California; two other giants, CSX and Norfolk Southern, dominating railroad traffic east of the Mississippi; and two medium-sized railroads, Kansas City Southern and Illinois Central (the latter a subsidiary of a Canadian railroad), operated in between the western and eastern giants. As part of the trend toward less regulation, President Bill Clinton signed a law in 1995 that curtailed some of the ICC's powers, dividing its remaining responsibilities between the Surface Transportation Board and the Federal Highway Administration and terminating the ICC itself. In that same year, a federal trucking deregulation superseded most state trucking regulations.

As the United States proceeded into the twenty-first century, national transportation policy rested on the assumption that much of the regulation that had developed since the late-nineteenth-century days of the Granger Laws unduly hampered American economic development. Recent trends continue to move toward some sort of deregulation, but that does not mean railroads, airlines, trucks, passenger cars, tugboats and barges, and pipelines operate in a totally laissez-faire state. Through the power of the purse, in such laws as the Intermodal Surface Transportation Act of 1991 and its 2001 successor, the national government continues to mold transportation policy. Using the threat of withholding highway funds, for example, Washington has successfully pressured states to enact laws requiring the use of seat belts and curbing driving under the influence of alcohol.

In the coming years, debates about transportation policy will center on certain key issues. How far should deregulation proceed? How should the nation weigh the social benefits of Amtrak against its inability to be self-supporting? In the urban areas, how should federal money be divided between mass transit and highways? What is the relationship between transportation policy and urban sprawl? How should transportation policy relate to petroleum policy?

References

Bilstein, Roger E. *Flight in America*. Baltimore, MD: Johns Hopkins University Press, 1984.

Goddard, Stephen B. *Getting There*. Chicago: University of Chicago Press, 1994.

Nevins, Allan, with Frank E. Hill. *Ford*. 3 vols. New York: Scribner's, 1954–1963.

Taylor, George Rogers. *The Transportation Revolution, 1815–1860*. New York: Holt, Rinehart and Winston, 1951.

Urbanization

Eileen Robertson-Rehberg

Urbanization involves an ongoing process of social and economic transformation resulting in and maintaining high-density population concentrations. The U.S. Bureau of the Census defines an area with a population concentration of 2,500 as urban land. Early urban areas (predating 1850) were associated with centers of finance and modes of transportation such as ships and railroads. In the mid-western and northeastern United States, many urban centers expanded at the turn of the twentieth century when immigrant populations from Europe and migrant populations from more rural areas moved into the factory cities of the Northeast for economic opportunities in mass industry and commercial districts.

At first, the urban expansion of the nineteenth century and early twentieth century occurred in an unplanned manner. The industrialized American city of the late eighteenth and early nineteenth centuries prompted economic growth, and the forces of trade and commerce created both advantages and disadvantages for the urban dwellers. Prior to mass industry and modern transportation systems, the maximum expansion of an urban population remained relatively small, around 30,000—enough to maintain a social cohesion within the urban geography. With the advent of industrialization, as cities expanded beyond former proportions with populations of various cultural and ethnic characteristics, component neighborhoods developed according to the social and economic attributes of the resident population. As a result, social cohesion became more characteristic within neighborhood boundaries, and neighborhood locations took on patterns that distinguished the wealthy from the poor. Wealthier neighborhoods were located near commercial districts or in suburban locations, whereas low-income neighborhoods often developed near the factories where residents worked.

The three essential components of the city were the factory, the railroad, and the slum. According to the Tenement House Commission of 1894, around the turn of the twentieth century in New York City, three out of five residents lived in slum neighborhoods. Experts define the term *slums* as urban development areas and poor neighborhoods; more typically, they are described as working-class neighborhoods characterized by deteriorating and overcrowded housing. However, new tenement apartments, built by investors to maximize the number of people per square foot with minimal ventilation, also made up part of the slum landscape. In the beginning of the twentieth century, some Americans responded to slum development by attempting to alter the behaviors of workers through such measures as closing down saloons, teaching immigrants to behave like Americans, increasing police forces to maintain order, and providing health services to prevent contagious diseases from spreading into more affluent neighborhoods. Therefore, this period of urbanization became characterized by urban administration and charitable organizations that treated poverty-ridden slum neighborhoods as elements of diseases, something to be controlled, contained, and reformed (hence the term *blight* for working-class sections of the urban environment). By the 1920s housing investigations and urban zoning were incorporated in the functions of many local urban administrations. But investigations often were limited to reporting on the immoral and unsanitary behaviors of individuals rather than criticizing the owners of slum housing who profited from the rental properties.

Urban studies, conducted in the 1930s, relied on the ideology and methods of analysis that developed in an age of emergent sociological studies; these studies were dominated by the work of Charles Darwin in the field of biology and then Herbert Spencer and Social Darwinism. Spencer's basic Darwinian premise held that everything in the universe starts out incoherently and gradually becomes coherent. Therefore, it was argued, human society and the urban hierarchy, from rich to poor, developed as part of a natural order of things. Those who were most successful had superior skills in the division of labor and subsequently reaped rewards through differences in the wage structure and in the quality of urban housing. Experts described the emergence of a variety of urban neighborhoods, from the slums to the mansions of the rich, as functional in natural Darwinistic models of the human evolution of inferior and superior social groups, often identified by race or cultural attributes. Establishing the classical tradition in urban studies based on Darwinian ideology, Robert E. Park and E. W. Burgess provided a seminal work, *The City*, on urban development theory in the field of human ecology. There, the relationship between social changes, group mobility, and housing quality became established. In an article titled "Succession: An Ecological Concept," Park explained his notion of cities and growth as the movement of populations to natural areas. Cities were locations that grew like rings on a tree, with the growth based on the social characteristics of populations. In fact, the analogy of tree rings is a biological reference that presumed human society had two levels of natural organization that determined growth—the biotic (natural) and the cultural. The biotic occurred in the unthinking realm of human existence that was analogous to plants, where plants have natural areas of development based on unthinking natural competition. For Park, all else with regard to humans and the social order remained cultural.

Park and Burgess based their work on economic ideas of evolutionary change as the product of competition resulting in the survival of the fittest, another Darwinian concept. Processes of neighborhood development began, they contended, with the commercial development of the city. Component neighborhoods surrounding the commerce of the city competed for space. The relationship between unique resident groups and their status in the division of labor, so necessary to the economy and efficiency of the city, determined the relative status for each neighborhood. The less necessary or redundant the labor was, the lower the quality and value of the neighborhood. However, they noted that these changes had dimensions limited by preexisting structural or cultural formations that created the larger collective civilization. Park found that society, in its biotic and cultural forms, took on territorial dimensions, whereby some cultures lived in poorer inner-city areas near industrial sites and other cultures lived in more desirable urban and suburban areas. He likened this phenomenon to Darwin's web of life, which, in human dimensions, took on the particularly human characteristics of survival of the fittest within the framework of laws and customs. In the human ecology model for urban development, there was a parallel theory fundamental to economics at that time. In *Introduction to Economic History* (1922), Norman Scott Brien Gras outlined the entire story of economic history as evolutionary stages manifested in metropolitan society, the economy, and the natural laws of human nature and competition.

Based on the work of Burgess and Park, economists often describe the ideas of social mobility, housing, and labor as the natural order of human activity, tied to the characteristics and behaviors of social groups. Such arguments underpinned public and private policies that guided institutions to discriminate against minority communities. In the 1940s, Amos Hawley took the focus of analysis away from the "natural" abilities of particular social groups and instead examined human ecology as it adapted to the demands of a capitalist system. Although Hawley discussed the urban model of community development as clusters or neighborhoods identified by residents characterized by divisions of labor, his theory defined community as part of a social system that was primarily economic in its dimensions. Similar to Park and Burgess, Hawley observed that a community functions as a society that takes shape around the local economy, similar to an organism that takes shape around its particular function. But Hawley regarded the economic system, not culture or human nature, as the ultimate determinant of the internal development of the community. In spite of his differences with the Park and Burgess work, Hawley described the community's development in urban society using evolutionary references to the natural world, much as succession theory did. His term *system* development was analogous to the development of a biological system. Hawley regarded a society as a formation interdependent between a population and the capitalist environment—similar to the system of an organism in formation in a particular environment. The circulation of the system remained dependent on the way that capital maximized the operation of the system toward profit. In Hawley's view, capital interacted with people in the system, just like the rest of the environment, and it was responsible for the characteristics of community development. He prioritized the capitalist economy as an external environmental factor and a source of contention to assimilate within the system in order to take on particular and useful dimensions. Hawley proposed that the development of the urban system should be scientifically examined as a way of understanding a capitalist society and its methods of circulation and evolution as it entered the system and reformed the community. He regarded the capitalist economy as invasive and sometimes counterproductive in social formation and advocated for an ecological approach to class analysis. The environment did not exist as a deterministic evolutionary process in this case, he said, but was part of an interactive and inter-dependent economic process.

Hawley explicitly stated the economic dynamics in a human ecology of change. In fact, any theory of the communities formed as people come together in a particular place cannot dismiss the economically interdependent relationship. In this sense, households, neighborhoods, and communities operate as interdependent economic units, and within the community, each household creates a value. Economists describe households and the places within which they live as subunits of neighborhoods within a larger community and the sustaining economic system. The logic seems clear in terms of the literature on slums in the twentieth century. People with poor wages lived in poor dwellings. Therefore, society and the various neighborhoods in the community environment of the urban work world will change as work opportunities change. In terms of the industrial economy, the booming demand for workers during both world wars and the populations that migrated into the urban areas for jobs where opportunities and the demand for labor opened up caused the urban character to expand and change. In periods of depression, the reverse process would occur. As work opportunities decreased, some neighborhoods would become more vulnerable than others to adverse effects. In many cases, low-skilled labor in the manufacturing sector realized the changing tide of the economy first.

Changes in the urban economy and society appeared before World War II. Without effective housing programs for inner-city neighborhoods, many buildings continued to deteriorate. The U.S. Housing Act of 1937 defined the term *slum* as "any area where dwellings predominate, which, by reason of dilapidation, overcrowding, faulty arrangement or design, lack of ventilation, light or sanitation facilities, or any combination of these factors are detrimental to safety, health, or morals." In the 1930s, the federal legislation designed to address urban slums came under the short-lived Public Works Administration and public housing programs. Subsidized public housing developed as a new legislative concept that was never popular with strong lobbies such as the National Association of Real Estate Boards (NAREB). In the 1950s public housing programs came under heavy attack in the hearings led by Sen. Joseph McCarthy, where they were depicted as part of a socialist or communist policy agenda.

Slum neighborhoods in cities throughout the nation remained neglected because of opposition to government housing programs for the poor. But there was no similar opposition to other federal housing programs aimed at private home ownership. Subsidized loans for homes helped to bail out failing banks at a time when many Americans attributed economic depression and previous economic hardships to the devastating effects of business cycles in the capitalist system—a situation that led many to question the viability of such a system. So the government gave the economy a source of growth by subsidizing the private home market. Specifically, in the 1930s, the federal government provided incentives for home ownership in the form of subsidies, including support for contractors who built large suburban communities. Subsidized home ownership also shifted economic growth and employment from the city to the suburbs, leaving inner-city residents with limited opportunities for jobs or affordable, quality housing. By the time the Great Depression ended, some major precedents had been set that would create the basis for all future developments in housing legislation.

The housing legislation of the 1930s bailed out banks, provided opportunities for home ownership, and quieted much of the social unrest of the times. But the critical response to the challenges of the day provided a form of long-term legislation for home ownership and housing that led to "suburbanization," at a time when transportation made it feasible to establish residential neighborhoods farther from factories. These compound developments led to a population decline in the major cities of the Midwest and Northeast. Subsidized housing loans helped to create massive suburbs in the periphery of urban centers, and new transportation infrastructures redeveloped cities in response to the demand for automobile travel in an era marked by the commuter relationship between suburbia and the city financial center. Eventually, as critical masses located outside city boundaries, the financial industry and economic growth followed as nodes of suburban financial centers, as opposed to the former model of central finance in inner-city commercial and financial districts. But subsidized home ownership remained exclusively for white city dwellers. Many people of color found their communities were left behind; they clustered in poor neighborhoods and found their job opportunities had decreased.

Urbanization in the 1950s occurred as a result of public and private policies for investment and the perception of the characteristics of poverty associated with the inner-city minorities and a variety of problems that existed only in certain urban neighborhoods—the other America. In the classical tradition, the other America included a population that existed outside the economic and social mainstream of the rest of the nation. The classical theory of urban development lacked a critical perspective discussed in the work of David Harvey (1973), a prominent author on city planning and social justice issues. Urban planning and zoning had a history of maintaining the "city beautiful" with parks and eliminating or degrading poor neighborhoods in the interest of new transportation systems to convey suburban populations to jobs and shopping in the core city. The poor and minorities were restricted to certain zones and kept out of wealthier neighborhoods to preserve property values. Raymond Mohl noted that American planning focused on the needs of city officials and businesspeople instead of the lower classes—the opposite of European planning, which incorporated all aspects of the city. Social concerns continued to drive urban planning in Europe, whereas in the United States, the movement focused on real estate values and re-creating the aristocratic city.

Harvey's work on the topic of urban development contributed greatly to changing ideas about the natural processes of housing deterioration and real estate investments in rental properties. Harvey described urbanization as a development in modern history within the context of an environment of local power and business interests. He coined the term *redlining* in describing discrimination and the banking system and the related aspects of rental property and landlord disinvestments that existed both in urban planning and in federal and local guidelines for lending. In Harvey's analysis, nothing natural or evolutionary brought about urban decay. Rather, these developments occurred as the result of human decisions made within institutions that condoned racism by singling out communities of color as high-risk neighborhoods that could not qualify for the loans necessary to their development.

In the 1950s, a neoclassical analysis of urban neighborhoods and slums ignored the social justice issues Harvey raised. Milton Friedman provided the theoretical basis for eminent domain in his classic work *Democracy and Freedom* (1963), in which he described the forced removal of particular urban neighborhoods and their populations as a necessary plan for the improvement of the entire city. According to Friedman, as local governments selected neighborhoods for purposes of redevelopment, a decrease in low-income housing led to the displacement of poor populations. But the social consequences for slum residents translated into gains for the greater community as luxury apartments and commercial buildings replaced dilapidated buildings surrounded by business districts. City planners typically referred to slum residents as part of a cost-benefit equation, whereby the slum dweller as a social deviant required scarce municipal resources in the form of services. As Friedman saw it, the result increased taxes and neighborhood effects that compromised property values and caused the flight of the middle class. In addition to the consumption of scarce services, the slum dweller existed outside the social and economic norms of the larger community and was thus responsible for the physical condition of the slum neighborhood. Friedman noted that slums fulfilled their requirements by providing basic housing to unproductive or underproductive members of society.

The Friedman analysis failed to provide a historical context for the accumulated problems of segregated zoning, preferences in home loans, community disinvestments, or the real estate interests of absentee landlords. The fact was that poor communities and largely communities of color found themselves permanently displaced as city officials destroyed entire neighborhoods for the purposes of slum clearance when investors found that new commercial buildings for banks, offices, and luxury apartments could increase the value of inner-city property and bring a better return on their real estate investments.

In the works of both Hawley and Harvey, the lack of a critical perspective led to viable alternatives to the classical economics of evolutionary urban development. Hawley addressed the factors of capital accumulation in a capitalist society, and Friedman acknowledged important factors regarding urban economies, unemployment, and the slums. For his part, Harvey brought to the fore the fact that communities of color were excluded from housing opportunities during the period of suburbanization and that many urban communities became zoned or redlined into areas that were denied access to loans; further, he argued that these developments occurred as the result of a public policy calculated in a racist institutional environment and were lobbied for by powerful interests. However, in their differing versions of urbanization, all three authors discussed the logic of natural competition and the inability of certain groups to adapt. It should be noted that Harvey's and Friedman's arguments were advanced in a time when federal programs set the stage for urban riots—violent uprisings that occurred throughout major cities. The chaos of urban riots led to a more organized community activism that was an outgrowth of city development issues and public policy. Activist planners—students of the social justice argument who were concerned with issues of equity and social justice in the city—took up the cause of urban activism.

In the 1970s and 1980s, the social justice approach to urbanization failed to account for the reality that an economic shift had limited job opportunities in the city. Suburbanization, transportation, and technological changes created new locations for economic development outside the city. Urbanization under inner-city activism contributed to an inner-city population that was dependent on increases in public welfare and bereft of opportunities for social mobility. The failure of social programs, the findings of the McGone Commission on the Watts riots (in 1965), and President Lyndon Johnson's Kerner Commission's investigations into the large number of people of color acting against local symbols of white American society in 1967 challenged the limitations of the social justice model. In the 1970s these findings led to theories of "spatial mismatch"—theories that examined inner-city population locations and economic growth as two distinct and separate developments that led to a mismatch of jobs and people seeking jobs. Both commission reports discussed the problems of residential segregation that contributed to a lack of access to the economic growth that shifted from the city to the suburbs. A contributing work on this issue, written by John F. Kain and titled "The Effect of the Ghetto on the Distribution and Level of Nonwhite Employment in Urban Areas," acknowledged that as certain groups received access and opportunity to move to the suburbs, so did the economy. Cities that were formerly the centers of industrial production moved to the periphery of postindustrial developments around employment associated with jobs such as those in services and high technology. By the 1970s and 1980s, theories of spatial mismatch became tangible explanations for increases in urban decay and urban poverty. The central business districts of urban areas saw retail increasingly move to megamalls in suburban areas, and inner-city core businesses and employment continued to decline. The inner-city poverty rate, which had been decreasing, began to rise. Large portions of the population in cities were simply left behind, and inner-city people of color who never escaped poverty found their opportunities were even more limited.

In "The Spatial Mismatch Hypothesis: Three Decades Later," Kain discussed the historical and statistical warfare between proponents and opponents of the spatial mismatch theory. The basis for the theory was that housing discrimination led to the residential isolation of minority populations, which denied them access to employment opportunities. William Julius Wilson revived the theory in his book *The Truly Disadvantaged: The Inner City, the Underclass and Public Policy*. Wilson's work revisited the idea that inner-city poverty was the result of a racial group being isolated from opportunity because of a disparity between the locations of residences and job opportunities. Bennett Harrison discounted this argument by using empirical evidence to demonstrate the prevalence of the "dual labor market" in the postindustrial era. In his analysis, Harrison concluded that lack of skills, not spatial dislocation, created the problem. Inner-city minority populations did not possess the skills to adapt to the new technological industries that were replacing older, less-skilled industrial production lines. Therefore, in a dual labor market—one for the less skilled and one for those with higher-level technological skills—the compensation for the skilled workers proved adequate, whereas that for individuals without skills remained less secure and certainly less rewarding; in turn, this situation reduced the unskilled worker's capacity to find and keep a job.

Spatial mismatch provides an analysis of the factors of unemployment and wages based on the history of housing discrimination. Harrison argued that changes in the requirements for skilled labor had put inner-city minorities in poverty. But in both cases, the opportunity structure of employment for communities of color remained limited, either by a lack of educational opportunities or a lack of economic opportunities. And in any case, housing and investment opportunities were limited, putting inner-city communities at risk for high unemployment and poor housing conditions.

Sen. Daniel Patrick Moynihan offered a radical departure from the notion of institutional discrimination. The Moynihan argument concluded that the problems could be traced to the dysfunctional and pathological culture of the minority population typically found in African American, inner-city neighborhoods. The aberrant urban culture was primarily distinguished by the prevalence of female-headed households, crime, and out-of-wedlock births, all of which caused the deterioration of inner-city neighborhoods. Whereas spatial mismatch acknowledged the compounded problems of institutionalized and historical racism, Moynihan's arguments established a basis for social welfare reforms designed to encourage responsible behaviors (marriage and employment), rather than institutional reforms and civil rights.

David Bartlet, David Elesh, Ira Goldstein, George Leon, and William Yancey, in their work "Islands in the Stream: Neighborhoods and the Political Economy of the City," examined the political economy of urbanization in a work on the postindustrial city. The authors outlined the history of redlining and disinvestments for urban communities of color throughout the period of industrial flight in the 1970s and 1980s to dispel evolutionary notions concerning urban populations. They provided the basis for a continued discussion of urbanization as located in a period of de-urbanization in the absence of institutional reforms. Their argument held that the continued discriminatory practices of financial institutions and government policies accelerated the decline of specific neighborhoods in the period of transition that occurred as industries moved from urban centers to other regions or nations. At that time, the phrase *postindustrial economy* was often used to describe a major trend in evolutionary urban changes in the Western world. In the literature, *post-industrialism* meant the process whereby losses in mass-manufacturing jobs were replaced with jobs in high-technology or service industries. The postindustrial age was incorporated into postmodern theories of a society that moved in social stages through major changes in production. Modern societies invested in the technology for mass production, and postmodern societies moved out of mass production and into the information age with more advanced computer technology. In this developmental model, service industries were seen to operate as the predominant sources for employment in the postindustrial/modern age. In "Neighborhoods and the Political Economy," the authors described the city as various neighborhoods, not in the biotic system of the evolutionary economics of natural development but as a composite of neighborhoods within an urban environment, where officials and investors continued to target certain neighborhoods for redevelopment. Neighborhoods became *islands in the stream*, a phrase used to describe areas within a city context as changing and interrelated entities. These neighborhoods were part of the circulation of labor, investments, and disinvestments that was organized by the various levels of governance in relationship to the larger context of the economy affecting the city. The discussion was posed as an alternative to a more simplistic and classical version of a monocentric city, or the city that grows "naturally" from the central business district to surrounding areas, like the rings in a tree. The deindustrialization and urbanization processes of the postindustrial cities coincide with the reindustrialization and urbanization of other areas, generally from the northeastern and mid-western industrial cities of the United States to the southern and the Sun Belt states. By the 1970s, the movement and transformation of industry required changes in local government initiatives and practical and theoretical changes in planning that left some neighborhoods in economic and social disintegration.

The theories of postmodern industrial societies influenced the planning principles of urban development. The success of urban land-use strategies became measured by their capacity to prepare cities for future development in order to conform to the needs of service industries in the information age. Downtowns in large cities built new businesses and offices for corporate headquarters and financial services with computerized and centralized operations. Such plans have led to residential development for the modern aristocrat, the cosmopolitan urbanite, in a period when cities seek to revitalize and to increase populations with gentrified neighborhoods. In this case, the political economy of the city, rather than the science of nature and evolution, shapes urbanization. Even more classical authors of urban theory acknowledge that, as economic growth creates obsolescent spaces in postindustrial cities, revitalization plans displace poor populations considered obsolescent in the new industrial technologies. By contrast, spatial mismatch theories also describe the obsolescence of low-skilled populations. Therefore, urbanization would appear to be a natural and functional operation of society and the economy, combined with the more political dimensions of urban management on the part of government administration.

Even if the economic principles of the free market are the only standard by which to examine urbanization and its development, the contradictions are still remarkable because government policy and administration have directed urbanization. Government interventions, such as those in the Great Depression, have compensated for financial and social failures in the free market. Public subsidies for home ownership and transportation infrastructure have determined urban development. And planning and targeted public investments continue to influence the demographics of urban centers. The continued presence of poor neighborhoods, characterized by low-income groups and decreasing property values, serves as an impetus for urban redevelopment and the fluctuation of populations, moving back and forth from the suburban to the urban and from one region to another as the economy and jobs shift and as housing locations become targeted for change. This is an evolutionary model, but the stages function as part of a decision-making process that has equated human development with profits in industry and housing and provided few opportunities for social mobility for those left behind in poor urban neighborhoods.

References

Bartlet, David, David Elesh, Ira Goldstein, George Leon, and William Yancey. "Islands in the Stream: Neighborhoods and the Political Economy of the City." In Irwin Altman and Abraham Wandersman, eds., *Neighborhood and Community Environments*. New York: Plenum Press, 1987.

Bluestone, Barry, and Bennett Harrison. *The Deindustrialization of America: Plant Closings, Community Abandonment, and the Dismantling of Basic Industry*. New York: Basic Books, 1982.

Clark, David. *Post-Industrial America: A Geographical Perspective*. New York: Methuen, 1985.

Friedman, Milton. *Capitalism and Freedom*. Chicago: University of Chicago Press, 1962.

Gras, Norman Scott Brien. *Introduction to Economic History*. New York: Harper and Brothers, 1922.

Hall, Peter. "The Turbulent Eighth Decade: Challenges to American City Planning." *Journal of the American Planning Association*, vol. 55, no. 3 (1989): 275–282.

Harvey, David. *Social Justice and the City*. London: Edward Arnold, 1973.

Hawley, Amos. *Human Ecology: A Theory of Community Structure*. New York: Ronald Press, 1950.

Kain, J. F. "The Spatial Mismatch Hypothesis: Three Decades Later." *Housing Policy Debate*, vol. 3, no. 2 (1992): 371–462.

Kleinberg, Benjamin. *Urban America in Transformation: Perspectives on Urban Policy and Development*. Thousand Oaks, CA: Sage Publications, 1995.

Mohl, Raymond A. *Urban Policy in Twentieth Century America*. New Brunswick, NJ: Rutgers University Press, 1993.

Moynihan, Daniel P. "Toward a National Urban Policy." In Daniel P. Moynihan, ed., *Toward a National Urban Policy*. New York: Basic Books, 1970.

Park, R. E. "Succession, an Ecological Concept." *American Sociological Review*, vol. 1, no. 2 (1936): 171–181.

Radford, Gail. *Modern Housing in America: Policy Struggles in the New Deal Era*. Chicago: Columbia University Press, 1996.

Weiss, Marc A. *The Rise of the Community Builders: The American Real Estate Industry and Urban Land Use Planning*. New York: Columbia University Press, 1987.

Wilson, William J. *When Work Disappears: The World of the New Urban Poor*. New York: Random House, 1997.

War

G. David Price

The relationship of war to economic policy has been a two-way street throughout American history. The dynamics of wars have greatly affected the country's economic policy, and scholars often see at least some of the causes of America's wars as related to its economic policy. At first, the colonies that would become the United States were bound by the mercantilist economic policies of the British Empire, which frequently led the British to war with rival European empires. That situation eventually proved unbearable, resulting in the War of American Independence and a new set of economic policies. During the antebellum period, war and economic policy were almost always geared toward establishing American dominance and control over Native American land and turning it into surplus-producing farmland. As the Industrial Revolution progressed in the latter part of the nineteenth century, economic policies to aid industrialization came to drive American military action. By the end of the century, America was involved in wars to increase its share of the world's markets, not to expand the amount of the North American mainland that it settled. Eventually, the goal of increasing America's share of world markets gave way to a desire to restructure the basis upon which the global economy operated. Both these policies caused conflict, but slowly, America's preferred economic policies for the world economy triumphed. Despite this success, the United States still uses—and must use—military means to maintain the hegemony of its vision of appropriate economic policy.

From Colony to Republic, 1580s through the 1780s

As noted, economic policy dominated America's history from the beginning. The very settlement of North America and the Caribbean by the English began as part of England's adoption of a mercantilist economic policy. Settling North America contributed to that policy by providing the markets and raw materials that England needed to achieve the mercantilist goal of trade surpluses. The process of settlement produced frequent conflicts. Native peoples resisted the loss of land and resources to settlers, sparking countless wars between the groups. And rival European powers tried to control the same areas that England did, leading to a series of wars between the major European countries.

As time wore on, these wars between the British and the Native Americans and the British and their European rivals merged. This outcome was most apparent in the aptly named French and Indian War, a conflict that proved to be a critical turning point in British policy toward what would ultimately become the United States. Both sides made extensive use of Native Americans during the war. The British and their American colonists prevailed in the war, giving the British Empire authority over all of mainland North America east of the Mississippi River except for Florida. Britain was now free from the interference of European rivals in its development and exploitation of its North American colonies.

Britain's colonists, however, proved to be a new obstacle to the Crown's plan, for their vision of the future of North America was increasingly divergent from that of the home country after the French and Indian War. The colonists supported an economic policy of expansion and settlement on Native American lands. The primary goal of the British, by contrast, was to ensure that North America play its role in the trade patterns of the empire. Settlement on Native American land interfered with this plan by creating potential conflicts that could easily disrupt the established trade patterns between Britain and either its colonies or its Native American allies. To prevent that outcome, the British government issued the Proclamation of 1763, which prohibited the colonists from settling on much of the land over which Britain recently had gained control, directly contradicting the desires and expectations of the colonists.

The damaged forward section of the U.S. battleship *Maine* following its sinking. In 1911, army engineers built a coffer dam around the wreckage, pumping out the water and allowing the wreckage to be studied. (Naval Historical Center.)

As if that were not galling enough to the colonists, the British began tightening up enforcement of the mercantilist policies that ensured that the trading relationship between the colonies and Britain worked in Britain's favor. Earlier British governments had created a series of laws known as the Navigation Acts to accomplish this; however, enforcement of these laws had been lax because previous generations of British officials held an attitude of salutary neglect toward their New World possessions. This attitude changed dramatically after the French and Indian War, and the British government began to enforce laws such as the Navigation Acts more vigorously. These measures were designed to limit the types of products that the colonists could produce, forcing them to provide surplus raw materials for export and to import manufactured goods and agricultural products that could not be grown in British North America. The linchpin of the system was the requirement that all this trade had to pass through ports in Britain. These policies limited the diversity of the colonial economic structure and ensured that all trade throughout the British Empire passed through the hands of British-based merchants.

Resentment over these new policies was one of the issues that led 13 of Britain's North American colonies to declare independence from the Crown in 1776 and form the United States. Even while mired in its War of Independence, the government of the new country made dramatic reversals of British economic policy. States began giving citizens who were willing to help in the war grants of land that had been put off-limits by the Proclamation of 1763. People who took the land grants now had a vested interest in the success of the war. If it failed, their land grants would be worthless.

Instead of all trade having to go through Britain, the new government allowed direct trade with any country except Britain. This exception was a foreshadowing of a common American policy during times of war and conflict—embargoing trade against the country's foes. When the dust settled after the chaos of the War of Independence and early attempts at forming a government, a new United States of America emerged; its Constitution gave the central government the power to determine economic policy and make decisions regarding war.

The Early Republic, 1790s through the 1830s

Almost immediately, the new government of the United States found itself faced with wars on multiple fronts. In 1789, the French Revolution and the Napoleonic Wars broke out, engulfing the major states of Europe. Both sides engaged in activities bordering on piracy, which many Americans saw as provocation for war. Although President George Washington tried to pursue a policy of neutrality, how to respond to these conflicts became a contentious issue for the emerging factions of American politics, the Federalists and the Democratic-Republicans.

The Federalists hoped to make America the junior partner in a British-dominated global economy, and going to war against Britain was obviously not conducive to achieving that goal. The first step toward bringing about the Federalist policy was the negotiation of Jay's Treaty. This treaty put American trade with Britain on a most-favored-nation status, closely tying together British and American trade. It also contained promises from Britain to refrain from the types of provocative acts that had led to calls for war. With the country's trade tied to Britain and the reasons for war against that nation muted, the Federalists next tried to further cement the Anglo-American alliance by leading the country to war with Britain's enemy, France. Highlighting provocative French actions, Federalists tried to scare up war hysteria in what became known as the quasi-war with France. Their attempt failed, and they lost power to the Democratic-Republicans in the election of 1800.

The Democratic-Republicans felt that American policy should be based on the ideas of freedom of the seas and the right of neutral countries to carry on trade without harassment by belligerent countries. Ironically, to bring this about, they pursued a policy of setting up embargoes against belligerent countries, thereby denying American merchants the freedom to work out trade arrangements with their counterparts in warring countries. The embargoes were poorly and inconsistently implemented and incredibly unpopular. Worse, they proved economically devastating. Despite this failure, the policy of embargoing countries to accomplish foreign policy objectives became a mainstay of American diplomacy.

To obtain support for the embargoes, the Democratic-Republicans whipped up war hysteria, particularly against Britain. This hysteria, combined with continued British provocation, led President James Madison to declare war against Britain in 1812. America's motives and aims in the War of 1812 illustrate important points about Democratic-Republican economic policy. Geographic expansion to get more farmland so that future generations could live as yeoman farmers was the primary concern of the Democratic-Republicans. They believed a successful war with Britain would solidify American control over areas such as the Louisiana Purchase (which the Democratic-Republicans had obtained for the United States peacefully) and perhaps lead to the addition of British-held territory to the United States. The war ended in a stalemate in December 1814, although many historians conclude that America's respectable showing in it ensured that European powers would not seize the unsettled American lands west of the Mississippi River.

Wars with European powers were not the only conflicts that Americans faced in this period. The policy of allowing settlement on Native American land led to a series of small-scale frontier wars. The Native Americans were often aided by Britain and Spain, the two countries that claimed the North American mainland outside the United States. Despite these conflicts and the deaths of thousands of settlers and tens of thousands of Native Americans, the U.S. government continued unabated to pursue its policy of conquest and expansion in Native American lands. Although it took until the 1830s before the last Native American tribes were moved west of the Mississippi River, the policy of turning their land into American settlements, through warfare if necessary, continued with great success throughout the period. This process would be repeated after the Civil War, when widespread interest in the settlement of the Louisiana Purchase area began. Changes in warfare technology made it even easier then for the U.S. government to push the Native Americans aside.

Be Careful What You Ask For: Manifest Destiny and Civil War, 1830s through the 1860s

By the 1830s, many American political leaders spoke of the United States having a "Manifest Destiny" to expand, by force if necessary, across the continent to the Pacific Ocean. This ethic was an intensification of the previous policy of taking land and opening it up for settlement. Control of the West Coast was also seen as important by the merchant class, which was trying to gain markets and products in East Asia. Fulfilling this destiny would bring the United States into armed conflict not only with Native Americans but also with the new country of Mexico. Ultimately, the success in those conflicts would leave America with new, internal conflicts to address, which were only resolved by the most damaging war the United States ever fought—the American Civil War.

In an attempt to dilute the Native American population with Anglos, the Mexican government began a policy of encouraging American citizens to settle in its northern frontier areas, especially Texas. Soon, the number of Americans in much of the Mexican northern frontier greatly exceeded the number of Mexicans. Conflict arose when the Mexican government began to enforce its prohibition of slavery in Texas. In 1836, the Americans successfully revolted and established an independent Texas, which sought admission to the United States. Although domestic political considerations prevented the Texans' request from being accepted until 1845, many U.S. citizens felt that the controversy between American Texans and Mexico would be the catalyst that would allow the nation to complete its Manifest Destiny mission.

This belief was well founded. As soon as the United States annexed Texas, Mexico, which had never fully accepted the independence of Texas, began mobilizing troops and sending them to a disputed border region. The United States responded by dispatching troops there as well. Inevitably, this led to skirmishes and casualties, which the administration of President James Polk used as justification for war. The United States won the war and added much of Mexico's northern frontier to its holdings, completing the southern part of its Manifest Destiny project. A treaty with Britain, ratified in 1845, divided the Oregon Territory between the United States and Britain, giving America control over the areas needed to complete its Manifest Destiny goals in the more northern latitudes.

The Polk administration's acquisition of such large amounts of territory created a serious problem for the American political system. The expansion of slavery had become an increasingly controversial issue since the Missouri Compromise, which allowed Missouri to enter the Union as a slave state and Maine as a free state and established 36°30′ as the northern boundary for slavery in the United States. The addition of new territory opened this issue up once again. Generally speaking, Americans' positions on the expansion of slavery fell along regional and economic lines, with Southerners supportive of it and Northerners opposed.

The country's economic development had led to regional economic specialization, which also caused people in different regions to support different economic policies. Northerners, increasingly reliant on manufacturing as their economic base, favored high tariffs to protect the domestic market from foreign competition. They also felt the revenue generated from those tariffs should be used to fund public works and infrastructure projects, known as "internal improvements," that would facilitate the movement of goods within the United States. Southerners generally held opposing views on economic policy. They believed tariffs should be low and that the federal government should not fund internal improvements. Those living in the western frontier areas often leaned toward the Northerners' position. The issue of expanding slavery clearly tipped the balance in the western frontier toward that position in this sectional conflict. A local economy dominated by large plantations worked by slaves was generally incompatible with the lifestyle of the yeoman family farmer, a way of life that was sought by many on the frontier.

These regional cleavages about the country's economic policies deepened throughout the 1850s. After the election of 1860 showed that the North and the western frontier had firmly lined up against the South, the South attempted to secede from the rest of the nation and establish its own country in which it could follow the economic policies it favored. This precipitated the American Civil War. And just as the divisions that led to the Civil War were, in large measure, about economic policy, the war's outcome radically changed the direction of American economic policy.

In terms of economic policy, the primary winners of the American Civil War were the emerging industrialists of the North. The scale of the war and the mobilization efforts dwarfed previous American military endeavors. Congress gave generous subsidies to railroads to ensure that the transportation infrastructure needed to coordinate and prosecute the war would be available. Furthermore, contracts with the Union army greatly enriched several Northern industries. Although the American military's consumption had always had economic benefits, the Civil War brought such consumption to unprecedented heights.

The Civil War also settled the regional conflicts over the direction of American economic policy. The federal government laid the groundwork to continue its subsidization of railroad construction after the war through the Pacific Railroad Act. Slavery was abolished, forcing a redefinition of labor practices in large-scale agricultural enterprises. The Morrill Tariff, passed during the Civil War, began a policy of high tariffs to protect domestic manufacturers—an approach that would persist for over 50 years. In short, economic policy, which had previously operated largely in accord with the wishes of Southerners by condoning slavery and opposing high tariffs and internal improvements, underwent a dramatic reversal to favor those policies desired by Northern industrialists.

Empire Versus Free Trade, 1870s through the 1930s

The generation after the Civil War had only minimal experience with military conflicts, none of which touched the Civil War in terms of its sheer horror and intensity. There were, to be sure, campaigns to subdue the last remaining Native Americans west of the Mississippi River. But these campaigns, though devastating to the Native Americans, involved little mobilization effort on the part of U.S. government. And unlike previous conflicts in which state militias had to be activated, the post-1865 Indian wars were handled entirely by the very small permanent, professional army that the United States maintained. Although the goal of these campaigns was the same as that embodied in the pre–Civil War policy of conquering land and expanding settlement, they were more about finishing up unfinished business rather than a resurgent domination of pro-agrarian economic policy.

The first major initiative spawned by the post–Civil War, proindustrialist economic policy that led to conflict was the attempt to gain an empire. Although Americans were busy putting down the last Native American resistance to white settlement, many other industrial countries were dividing the world's markets into formal and informal empires in an era known as the age of imperialism. Americans seemed oblivious to this subjugation of the world's markets until the depression of 1893, when some of them saw increased exports as a way to revive declining American industrial production and reduce price-crippling agricultural surpluses. America's tariffs had provoked retaliatory tariffs from other industrial countries, and the age of imperialism had closed off almost all the markets of the nonindustrial world, leaving the United States with few opportunities to export its surpluses.

American policymakers came up with two contradictory solutions to this problem. One was to ask the other industrial countries to abandon their empires and allow international trade to operate along the free trade principles first articulated in Secretary of State John Hay's Open Door notes. Although other countries politely paid lip service to Hay's principles, they made no fundamental change in how international economic relations were conducted.

At the same time, the U.S. government asked other countries to give up the economic privileges of their empires even as it was establishing an empire of its own. Citing the human rights abuses perpetrated by the Spanish colonial administration against the Cubans it governed, American media and policymakers whipped up anti-Spanish war fervor. When an American battleship, provocatively sent to Cuba to intimidate the Spanish, mysteriously blew up in the waters of Havana's harbor, the public demanded war, and the administration of President William McKinley quickly complied, asking for a declaration of war in April 1898. The United States easily won the Spanish-American War, and Spain ceded control of all its remaining overseas possessions outside of Africa to the United States.

The taking of Spain's colonial empire represented a fundamental change in America's economic goals in warfare. Previously, lands acquired by the United States were more or less cleared of the native populations and opened to settlement. This was not the case with the lands obtained from Spain. In fact, the way in which the United States established its rule over these areas was designed to discourage large-scale American migration and settlement. Cuba was made a nominally independent country, although with the Platt Amendment, the United States claimed the right to overthrow and replace any Cuban government with which it disagreed. The Philippines were made a direct colony of the United States. In regard to Puerto Rico, the Foraker Act created a new category (the unincorporated territory) that explicitly prohibited the process of territorial self-government and opportunity for statehood that had traditionally been observed. These policies suggest that America's desire was not to settle these areas; rather, it was to establish control of the economic activity and markets in them. To grow, an agrarian economy needs to bring more land under cultivation, but an industrial economy needs access to raw materials and markets. The policies practiced during and after the Spanish-American War suggest that American policymakers were shaping war policy to meet the needs of the country's changing economy.

American policymakers found ample opportunity to create economic policies to further economic growth during World War I. Much like the situation during the French Revolution and the Napoleonic Wars, the United States first followed a policy of neutrality and trade, and combatants on both sides again engaged in aggressive acts to disrupt American trade with their enemies. Eventually, again as in the earlier conflicts, these acts led America to enter into the war.

The U.S. government encouraged American businesses to take advantage of the increased opportunities for trade brought about by the war. As a neutral nation with an impressive productive capacity, the United States began supplying belligerent countries with many of the goods their war-diminished economies could not provide. Soon, both sides laid mines in shipping lanes, the British imposed a blockade around their enemies, and Germany announced a policy of unrestricted submarine warfare. Although the U.S. government protested these actions, it came down much harder on Germany, and American economic interaction increasingly favored the Allies. When the Allies no longer had the foreign exchange to buy American goods, the U.S. government allowed American banks to loan Allied governments money so they could continue their purchases. By 1917, the U.S. economy and many private banks and businesses had a vested interest in an Allied victory because of these economic ties.

This vested interest, created by American economic policy, appeared to be threatened in early 1917 by the Central Powers' increasing dominance over Russia, one of the Allies. Also, the Germans became more aggressive with their unrestricted submarine warfare, sinking three American ships in less than a week in March 1917. These developments led President Woodrow Wilson to seek a war declaration from Congress, which he received in April 1917.

The ideas of the Progressive movement heavily influenced wartime domestic economic policy in the United States. An expanded income tax was used to finance a sizable amount of the war effort. The Progressive notion of civic participation imbued the government's efforts to get the public to limit consumption of scarce resources and to buy bonds to finance the portion of the war that tax revenues could not. Using the regulatory boards established by the Progressives as a model, the government established the War Industries Board, which basically had the power to make all production, resource allocation, pricing, and labor decisions for industries critical to the war effort. Although the power was used only sporadically and for short periods of time, this was an important new development in wartime economic policy. For the first time in American history, the government claimed the right to run private-sector industry in times of national emergency.

Wilson devised a set of policies called the Fourteen Points of Peace to convince the public to support the war. These policies were to be a blueprint for how countries should conduct relations with one another after the war. Economic policy was very prominent in Wilson's plan. The Fourteen Points reiterated American economic policies such as the Open Door and the right of neutrals to trade unmolested in times of war.

The war ended favorably for the Allies and, in 1919, they drew up the Treaty of Versailles to reestablish peaceful and cooperative patterns of international relations. Wilson had hoped his Fourteen Points would be the basis for the treaty. Although the other industrial countries still largely paid only lip service to the Open Door policy, they did agree to accept Wilson's idea of the League of Nations, an organization that pledged to defend the rights of countries to carry out commerce in international waters. The league also set up a mechanism, the mandate system, that was designed to move nonindustrial countries from being ruled directly as colonies to formal independence. Ironically, although the league was Wilson's idea, the U.S. Congress chose not to join it, depriving the organization of the primary voice that sought to liberalize the world economy.

Despite these moves toward realizing the American vision of an international economy increasingly run by free trade principles, the United States itself followed policies that contradicted that aim during the 1920s and 1930s. As a result of the disruption of international trade patterns during World War I, Americans picked up a substantial market share in Latin America, which had been under the informal economic control of Britain since the early 1800s. To maintain control of these markets, the United States engaged in a series of small military interventions to remove Latin American governments that were practicing policies counter to that control. So, even as the United States was urging other countries to surrender economic control of their empires, it was unwilling to participate in the vehicle it had established to facilitate that end and it was creating its own informal empire in Latin America.

The outbreak of World War II led to substantial change in American economic policy. During the mid-1930s, a series of laws called the Neutrality Acts were passed, designed to cut off economic interaction between the United States and warring countries. The hope was that this move would prevent situations like those that contributed to America's entry into World War I. When World War II actually started in the late 1930s, the United States not only ignored or changed these laws but also clearly used economic policy to favor one side in the conflict. The most obvious examples of this are the Lend-Lease program and the embargo against Japan. Under the Lend-Lease program, the United States gave Germany's enemies surplus military equipment to use in the war effort. America had just started a massive military buildup, so it now had a great deal of "surplus" military equipment. America's policy was intended to make the country, as President Franklin D. Roosevelt described it, the "arsenal of democracy." The United States would use its economic might to equip other countries, which would do the actual fighting against the tyrannical forces around the world.

The United States began to use economic coercion against Japan to get it to end its war against China. By Summer 1941, Washington had cut off all trade with Japan. Americans thought this economic pressure would force Japanese leaders to do as the U.S. government wished, since America was Japan's primary source of petroleum. Instead, the pressure led the Japanese to devise a plan to seize the oil-rich Dutch East Indies. To prevent American interference with that plan, the Japanese military felt it was necessary to destroy the U.S. Pacific Fleet and seize the American colony of the Philippines. The attack on Pearl Harbor was the first step in the plan, and with it came American entry into the war.

The war effort resulted in a wide range of radical economic changes. The policies followed during World War I were revived and expanded. Government agencies such as the War Production Board and the Office of War Mobilization took near complete control of the economy. By the end of the war, government spending accounted for almost half of the country's gross national product (GNP). Wages and prices were controlled by the government, as was the consumption of many goods through rationing. Many New Deal policies found expression in the war. Executive Order 8802 prohibited employment discrimination by firms with war contracts, and other regulations virtually required union membership for those in war-related industries. As a result, union membership rose by over 50 percent to almost 15 million by the war's end. The Commodity Credit Corporation became the model for a U.S. policy dubbed the "warehouse war," which sought to corner the global market in strategic commodities in order to deprive the enemy of them. Although these policies proved to be temporary, they demonstrate how vital economic policy is in situations of total war.

Creating and Maintaining a Liberal Global Economy

As World War II drew to a close, American policymakers turned their energies toward finding an economic policy that would help prevent future worldwide conflicts. Not surprisingly, their solution called for the world to embrace free market capitalism and the free trade principles of the Open Door system. Much of the world, however, had little interest in such policies. The stiffest resistance came from the communist Soviet Union, which was able to help spread communism to several places in Europe and Asia in the years after World War II. A new type of war, the Cold War, erupted as a consequence. The Cold War was often described as fundamentally being a clash of economic ideologies—U.S. capitalism versus Soviet communism. Each side devoted its foreign policy to making its economic policies the basis for the world economy.

Economic policy provided many tactics employed in waging the Cold War. The United States used economic aid to shore up anticommunist governments. The most famous example of that was the Marshall Plan, by which Congress authorized the expenditure of several billion dollars to rebuild the war-ravaged economic infrastructure of Western Europe. This tactic established economic aid to foreign countries as a permanent

The second of the World Trade Center towers collapses after it was hit by an airplane in a terrorist attack on September 11, 2001, in New York. (UPI.)

tool of American diplomacy. However, the United States was quick to use military and economic coercion against those countries that did not support its economic vision in the Cold War. Some leaders who pursued economic policies contrary to America's wishes were overthrown, such as Mohammed Mossadeq of Iran and Salvador Allende of Chile. Others faced embargoes, such as Gamal Abdel Nasser in Egypt and Fidel Castro in Cuba.

Using economic policy to win the Cold War sometimes led to policies that seemed counterintuitive to America's overall goal of making the world economy run along the lines of free trade and capitalism. The General Agreement on Tariffs and Trade (GATT), an institution designed to bring freer trade to the global economy, became a vehicle for economically tying countries to the United States through trade agreements. Global free trade gave way to trade bound to America.

The Cold War had important influences on the domestic economic policy of the United States. For instance, the Keynesian revolution in economic policy was essentially completed by the Cold War as governments accepted the theory that deficit spending was necessary to offset business cycles that included high unemployment and slow business growth. Government spending increased to fund the military necessary to fight the war, including an enormously expensive arms race with the Soviet Union and large-scale American military interventions in Korea and Vietnam. President Lyndon B. Johnson's decision not to raise taxes to pay for involvement in Vietnam led to serious economic difficulties by the early 1970s, prompting his successor to try to impose government controls over the economy (most notably, a temporary wage-and-price freeze). The Cold War also provided some justification for expanding and maintaining the Keynesian welfare state that began with the New Deal. Keeping the population stable and prosperous took on greater saliency with the dynamics of the Cold War, and a larger welfare state aided that process.

The Cold War began to fizzle out in 1989 as the Communist governments of the Soviet Union and Eastern Europe collapsed. Even in the war's latter days, it was increasingly apparent that the next likely battlefield, both for combat and economic policy, would be the oil fields of the Middle East. Middle Eastern countries flexed their economic muscle during the 1970s, spearheading huge price increases that drove crude oil prices from $2 per barrel to $32 per barrel. Such dramatic price increases on this vital commodity wreaked havoc on the economies of the industrial countries of the world, America's Cold War allies. This scenario foreshadowed the importance of the oil-rich Middle East in the post–Cold War era.

The bulk of America's warfare and military operations in the 1990s were devoted to maintaining control of and stability in those oil-rich Middle Eastern areas. Unfortunately, these aims were somewhat contradictory. The post–Cold War problems of the Middle East began with the 1990 Iraqi invasion of Kuwait. In what became known as the Gulf War, the United States obtained a UN sanction to lead a military operation designed to drive out Iraq and restore Kuwait's independence. The United States was concerned that Iraq would control too much of the world's oil supply if it kept control of Kuwait and that it might be tempted to seize Kuwait's oil-rich neighbors. After forcing the Iraqis out, the United States maintained tens of thousands of troops in the oil kingdoms of the Persian Gulf to prevent an Iraqi attack. The presence of these troops, however, offended religious extremists in the Arab world, who responded by forming a terrorist network called Al Qaeda. Al Qaeda launched a series of attacks against the United States, culminating in the assaults on the World Trade Center and the Pentagon on September 11, 2001. These attacks, which killed over 3,000 Americans, led President George W. Bush to declare the War on Terror. Between September 2001 and the end of 2009, Congress has appropriated $864 billion for the global war on terror with the funds used for military operations, base security, foreign aid and embassy costs, reconstruction, and veterans health care costs. During that same period, the United States has conducted three key military-related operations in the war on terrorism worldwide: (1) Operation Enduring Freedom (OEF) involving Afghanistan and other counter-terrorism operations, which received 20 percent of the already allocated funding; (2) Operation Iraqi Freedom, which received 74 percent of the funding (OFI); and (3) Operation Noble Eagle, which provides enhancement of security at military bases and accounts for 3 percent of the funding with the other 1 percent applied to other expenses. At the beginning of 2009, the administration requested additional supplemental appropriation funding from Congress, which if passed would increase the total cost of the war on terror to $941 billion.

Critics of the War on Terror argue that the United States should remove its troops from Iraq and Afghanistan and that the dollars spend on the War on Terror are being wasted, whereas they should be spent instead on domestic economic programs. Supporters of the War on Terror argue that by exporting the fighting abroad, the United States has been safer since no successful terrorist attacks have occurred on American soil since the War on Terror began. They also point to the significant negative impact that the September 11, 2001, had on the U.S. economy and, especially during the current recession, the nation cannot afford another such financial disaster on time of the recession.

Although Democrat presidential candidate Barack Obama promised the withdrawal of U.S. forces from Iraq within months if he was elected, that has not occurred since he took office in January 2009. It is unlikely that U.S. troops will be withdrawn from anti-terrorist operations worldwide anytime soon, especially after the attempted detonation of an explosive device by a Nigerian Islamic-radicalized national en route from Amsterdam to Detroit, Michigan, on Christmas Day 2009 and in light of an increase presence of Al Qaeda in the country of Yemen recently.

References

Chan, S., and C. A. Drury, eds. *Sanctions as Economic Statecraft: Theory and Practice*. New York: St. Martin's Press, 2000.

Cohen, Stephen D. *Fundamentals of U.S. Foreign Trade Policy: Economics, Politics, Laws, and Issues*. Boulder, CO: Westview Press, 2003.

Collins, Robert M. *More: The Politics of Economic Growth in Postwar America*. New York: Oxford University Press, 2000.

Congressional Research Office. "CRS Report for Congress: The Cost of Iraq, Afghanistan, and Other Global War on Terror Operations Since 9/11," RL33110 (May 15, 2009).

Dykstra, David L. *The Shifting Balance of Power: American-British Diplomacy in North America, 1842–1848*. Lanham, MD: University Press of America, 1999.

Eisner, Marc Allen. *From Warfare State to Welfare State: World War I, Compensatory State-Building, and the Limits of the Modern Order*. University Park: Pennsylvania State University Press, 2000.

Hawley, Ellis W. *The Great War and the Search for a Modern Order: A History of the American People and Their Institutions, 1917–1933*. New York: St. Martin's Press, 1979.

Hoge J., and G. Rose, eds. *How Did This Happen? Terrorism and the New War*. New York: Public Affairs, 2002.

Hoge, J., and F. Zakaria, eds. *The American Encounter: The United States and the Making of the Modern World: Essays from 75 Years of Foreign Affairs*. New York: Basic Books, 1997.

Jennings, Frances. *Empire of Fortune: Crowns, Colonies, and Tribes in the Seven Years' War in America*. New York: Norton, 1988.

Jones, Howard. *Crucible of Power: A History of American Foreign Relations to 1913*. Wilmington, DE: SR Books, 2002.

Liska, George. *Expanding Realism: The Historical Dimension of World Politics*. Lanham, MD: Rowman and Littlefield, 1998.

Marshall, P., and G. Williams. *The British Atlantic Empire before the American Revolution*. London: Cass, 1980.

Ninkovich, Frank A. *The United States and Imperialism*. Malden, MA: Blackwell, 2001.

Nobles, G. *American Frontiers: Cultural Encounters and Continental Conquest*. New York: Hill and Wang, 1997.

Pletcher, David M. *The Diplomacy of Involvement: American Economic Expansion across the Pacific, 1784–1900*. Columbia: University of Missouri Press, 2001.

Reyna, S., and R. Downs. *Deadly Developments: Capitalism, States, and War*. Amsterdam: Gordon and Breach, 1999.

Rhodes, Benjamin D. *United States Foreign Policy in the Interwar Period, 1918–1941: The Golden Age of American Diplomatic and Military Complacency*. Westport, CT: Praeger, 2001.

Solnit, Rebecca. *Savage Dreams: A Journey into the Hidden Wars of the American West*. San Francisco: Sierra Club, 1994.

Zakaria, Fareed. *From Wealth to Power: The Unusual Origins of America's World Role*. Princeton, NJ: Princeton University Press, 1998.

Welfare State

Kathleen A. Tobin

During the first half of the twentieth century, the United States experienced a tremendous expansion in its welfare programs at the federal level, developing into what is termed the "welfare state." During the 1950s and 1960s, this expansion continued even further, increasing programs such as Social Security and Aid to Families with Dependent Children. A new understanding of social reform, poverty, and state responsibility helped to influence the creation of welfare programs beginning in the Progressive Era, but two disparate economic trends aided in putting this new philosophy into action. First, the effects of the Great Depression created a greater atmosphere of need, placing unprecedented demands on any programs already in place and resulting in the creation of new programs. Once the welfare state became fixed, expectations of assistance for the less fortunate rose in America, and though this subject was greatly debated, post–World War II prosperity allowed for the continued and often increased funding of programs. But although the welfare state as we have come to know it evolved comparatively quickly in the last century, it had established roots long before.

Much of the sentiment and practical measures present in the modern welfare state appeared in the English Poor Laws of the sixteenth and seventeenth centuries. As English society shifted from feudalism to a wage-based economy, the lower classes no longer enjoyed the guarantee of security that they once held. Under feudalism, the serf could rely on—for better or worse—a lasting relationship with his or her master. Although wage earners enjoyed more freedom, they lacked a guarantee of economic security. When jobless, they often turned to begging or stealing. In response, the landed gentry encouraged passage of legislation compelling people to work for a living and punishing those caught begging or giving money or goods to beggars.

As the English economy transformed into one based on the production of wool for a larger market, population and social shifts demanded that society pay more attention to the poor. First, the enclosure system, which gave large tracts of land to sheep raisers, forced the small landowners off their land and into urban areas. In addition, the growing economy encouraged the migration of potential workers into regions where they hoped to find work but could not. At the same time, Henry VIII, in his break from the Catholic Church, worked to abolish monasteries, institutions that for centuries had been largely responsible for addressing the needs of the poor. During the sixteenth century, Parliament passed a series of laws in this arena, essentially taking a harsh position against those in need, but by 1600 some attitudes and terminology regarding poverty began to change. Parliament had designed earlier legislation to punish vagabonds and beggars, but the Act of 1597 focused on the "relief of the poor." The Elizabethan Poor Law of 1601 served as a model and was fundamentally unchanged for centuries. Though the measure was enacted at the national level, local officials carried it out, emphasizing work and family responsibility. As with a number of institutions, English Poor Law was transplanted in the American colonies.

The colonies had comparatively fewer poor than did the home country. The availability of land and access to it—either by ownership or through common grazing rights—and the need for labor left fewer people without a means to live. However, America remained far from a paradise, and many arrived in the colonies ill or otherwise unable to work. Subsequent generations eventually produced more individuals with physical or mental problems that prevented them from working. In addition, comparatively few individuals amassed substantial wealth in the early years of the colonies, which placed the responsibility of poor relief on those with moderate means. As a result, colonial assemblies enacted poor laws similar to those in England.

The laws varied from colony to colony, as the economies, social structure, and needs differed. For example, colonies such as Virginia depended on large numbers of indentured servants, who often struggled financially once their contracts of service ended. Able-bodied adults often "bonded out," whereas parents placed their children in apprenticeship programs. In southern colonies, free education remained virtually nonexistent, but in colonies such as Massachusetts, which was much more "community-minded" from its foundation, education functioned as a means of creating productive citizens. Port cities, such as New York, developed legislation to address issues involved with the incoming poor, and various urban centers experienced an influx of desperate people who had fled from the frontier after encountering serious problems there, such as the Indian wars. Although laws varied from place to place, most all were influenced by religious beliefs, which generally viewed the poor with pity and considered them deserving of help. In many cases, assistance originated in the local church or parish.

As the nation evolved in its early years of independence, new ideas of welfare appeared as well. The French and Indian War and the American Revolution had l eft large numbers of widows and children in the various colonies and new states, a situation that demanded new attention to funding. Religious groups, such as the Quakers, became well known for their efforts to support those in need, as did certain nonreligious organizations, such as nationality groups (representing immigrants from Scotland, Ireland, Germany, and France) and fraternal societies. Public aid and individual philanthropy originated from seemingly endless sources and in many forms. Furthermore, the revolutionary philosophy, which declared universal human rights, drew increasing attention to the needs of all people. Although the war itself disrupted the implementation of many programs, the sentiment supporting assistance expanded.

Immediately following the Revolutionary War, the poor laws themselves remained essentially the same; retaining their variations from state to state, they were transplanted into the new territories. Frontier issues such as housing, school construction, and Indian relations helped to shape whatever legislation was deemed necessary. In 1790 townships in the newly created Northwest Territory gained jurisdiction over the poor and responsibility for distribution of relief, a structure that continued when the region divided into the various states of Ohio, Michigan, Indiana, Illinois, and Wisconsin. The Revolution brought about a more significant change in the southern states, where the churches had primarily accepted responsibility for poor relief. The war brought greater separation between church and state, which encouraged states to place poor relief under civil jurisdiction in the South.

One of the most complex notions regarding the responsibility for poor relief in the United States developed during the early years of nationhood. In the decades before the Civil War, the demand for states' rights resulted in a continued fragmentation of relief programs. The U.S. Constitution's general welfare clause (Article 1, Section 8) stated that "the Congress shall have power to lay and collect taxes, duties, imposts and excises, to pay the debts and provide for the common defence and general welfare of the United States," but many argued over the founders' intention. Though that single clause might have given the federal government ultimate power in developing and sustaining a national system of poor relief from the start, the strength of the defenders of states' rights effectively limited the role played by the federal government in this case. At the same time, Americans developed a sense of national identity, which included ethics of individualism and self-reliance, promoting the idea that anyone could make a living if willing to do so. Territorial expansion and economic growth advanced this notion as possibilities for individual economic independence grew. Overall, Americans seemed to prefer voluntary philanthropy to public programs when the need to provide relief arose. The separation of church and state, combined with the fervor of the Second Great Awakening, resulted in competition between numerous religious denominations, each with its own hospitals, orphanages, and schools.

New population theories inspired by the work of Thomas Malthus at the dawn of the nineteenth century, originating in Europe but international in scope, often argued against poor relief. One of the greatest fears—which has continued into the twenty-first century—was that offering assistance would encourage the poor to have more children. Population theorists insisted that refusing them aid would force them to limit their family size. Though such arguments held less weight in land-rich America, the notion that poor laws contributed to overpopulation took root in the United States as well. In addition, classical economists believed there was a finite amount of capital available to support the working class and that money spent on assistance would take away from the wage-earning pool. These beliefs, combined with nineteenth-century ideals of individualism and industriousness, resulted in a sharp decline in support for public assistance.

Renaissance, Reformation, and Enlightenment philosophies, which had challenged the notion of poverty as inevitable, helped to lay the groundwork for reform movements that shaped early-nineteenth-century American society. But though reformers sought real improvement in the conditions of the poor, they also worked within an atmosphere in which the poor were increasingly blamed for their own poverty. Before the early nineteenth century, the idea that "the poor will always be with us" existed alongside the notion that society should address the needs of the poor. During the early 1800s, reformers attempted to put into action a kind of democracy that coexisted with individual responsibility. Only in a minority of cases did Americans see people in need as "worthy" of assistance, and a large percentage of those were put to work in workhouses.

People in need of assistance lived and worked under watchful eyes. Society housed those deemed unable to provide for themselves, such as the permanently disabled, in institutions, often in horrid conditions. Social reformers recommended the development of workhouses and almshouses as more humane and effective means of dealing with the poor. New York's secretary of state, J. V. N. Yates, provided one of the nation's most influential documents supporting this move. Commissioned in 1834 by the state legislature to survey the state of poor relief, he reported tremendous problems and proposed to correct the situation by placing the poor in institutions. Within a short time, various states had constructed almshouses (Massachusetts alone had 219 by 1860), but reformers subsequently reported the existence of inhumane conditions in a number of them.

Social reformers sought both state and federal assistance in addressing the poor housing conditions. Dorothea Dix fought one of the more pronounced battles in her effort to obtain federal funding to address the needs of the mentally ill who were often held under inhumane conditions in almshouses and jails. After years of research and lobbying, she finally convinced both houses of Congress in 1854 to pass legislation appropriating land for the construction of adequate mental hospitals. However, President Franklin Pierce vetoed the legislation because he feared the idea of making the federal government the "greatest almoner of public charity throughout the United States," a move he saw as contrary to the U.S. Constitution. The federal government had previously given land grants to a number of efforts considered to be social welfare projects, but Pierce's comments set the tone for federal resistance on the welfare front. On the state and municipal levels, surveys of poverty continued, but private charities distributed most of the funds.

The Civil War placed unforeseen demands on charity organizations, which failed to meet all of the needs of people affected by the conflict. Unprecedented concerns about public health and medical care issues demanded much attention, spurring the creation of the U.S. Sanitary Commission. Led and staffed primarily by women, the commission provided supplies and services to meet the critical demands for medical treatment of injured individuals. The Sanitary Commission not only served as a foundation for subsequent developments in the field of medicine but also demonstrated that provisions for assistance were possible and desirable on a national scale. Furthermore, the conclusion of the Civil War brought about a philosophical and political shift that strengthened the position of the federal government relative to issues of states' rights.

The establishment of the Freedmen's Bureau (Bureau of Refugees, Freedmen, and Abandoned Lands) in 1864 as the nation's first federal welfare agency demonstrated the willingness and ability of the federal government to address welfare needs when the local governments failed to do so. Though dismantled in 1872, the bureau helped to establish schools for more than a half million freed slaves, operating under the philosophy that education could serve as the means to escape poverty. It also supported medical care, the maintenance of hospitals, and assistance in land distribution. The act that established the bureau signaled the first solid attempt by the federal government to take responsibility for social welfare. At the same time, however, American economic philosophy discouraged such a role.

During the nineteenth century, broad-based industrial capitalism left workers increasingly dependent on larger forces for employment, but laissez-faire attitudes in business and government provided little protection for workers who were injured or laid off, with the poor being generally neglected. Adam Smith's free market economic philosophy reigned, and officials viewed regulations designed to protect workers as an imposition and generally detrimental to the natural balance of a free and profitable economy. Much resistance existed to any government demands that business provide for the welfare of their workers, especially at the federal level. Many Americans criticized the idea of taxing the wealthy to provide for the indigent because it interfered with the natural laws of economics.

Social Darwinists, who applied elements of the survival of the fittest concept to business, also applied them to society, justifying the existence of poor people as a factor of natural selection. In other words, they believed that the poor became poor because they did not have the inherent qualities necessary to become wealthy. Social Darwinists argued that "do-gooders" should ignore individuals with disabilities or illnesses that many believed contributed to poverty. In their view, charitable aid only hurt society, as it allowed the weaker to survive. Reformers, by contrast, believed that providing assistance to all Americans in need was a fundamental role in a democracy. Yet even reformers blamed individuals, personal circumstances, or character flaws for poverty in the nineteenth century. With the best intentions, the Society for the Prevention of Pauperism and similar groups attempted to help the poor overcome any shortcomings that had led them to a life of poverty.

The subsequent development of charity organization societies in the 1870s featured the use of scientific management principles to address social ills and provide individuals with "scientific charity." Still, ideas inherent in the American work ethic and Social Darwinism abounded. Mutual-aid societies (including secret societies, sick and funeral benefit societies, and life insurance societies) that had promoted fraternity and association since the early nineteenth century continued to thrive. They served as vehicles to collect contributions and distribute relief to those in need of aid, and they did so with fewer stigmas attached. By the late nineteenth century, Americans viewed both private and public charity as patronizing, with the needy placed in a position of inferiority, but they considered fraternal societies far more egalitarian because those giving and those receiving coexisted on more equal terms.

The dawn of the twentieth century brought a wealth of reforms, inspired by Progressives who sought to apply scientific principles, modern understanding, and democratic ideals to the task of improving conditions in the changing American city.

Rapid urbanization, industrialization, and immigration resulted in demands on housing and health services, and though many groups sought changes at the municipal level, some changes took place through congressional legislation. Proponents of proposals for federal mandates addressed social welfare issues by employing models from Germany and Great Britain, where reform at the national level had made great strides. Unions urged the federal government to force businesses to put protective measures in place. In 1912, the American Association for Labor Legislation proposed compulsory health insurance, which would have required disability, hospitalization, maternity care, and burial benefits to be financed by employers, workers, and taxpayers.

But the United States resisted the adoption of programs that had found success in other countries. By 1884, Germany had implemented a broad social insurance system, and other Europeans subsequently followed. However, the United States opted for a system of "welfare capitalism," in which corporations periodically implemented measures that would pacify workers by providing benefits. Refusing to take orders from the government or from labor unions, company owners gradually began to provide just enough in insurance policies and pensions to prevent litigation and strikes. In reality, workers did not always have access to promised benefits, since the law had not mandated them. And workers often viewed the company store system—in which companies provided stores, homes, and recreational facilities for their employees—as feudalistic, making them even more dependent on the companies and living at the mercy of factory owners who controlled every aspect of their lives.

Still, the turn of the twentieth century saw the beginning of increased focus on social welfare and reform. Writers such as Upton Sinclair, who vividly depicted the horrid lives of immigrants working in Chicago's meatpacking industry in *The Jungle*, shed light on social ills in a way that eventually drew a significant government response. That work alone receives credit for inspiring the Pure Food and Drug Act of 1906. But such writings also influenced reforms in housing, factory conditions, and child labor.

Children drew much attention in social reform programs, as the state assumed an increasing responsibility for their welfare. With new attitudes toward education, certification, and professionalization, modern "experts" addressed public health concerns through nutrition, disease prevention, and education programs and even juvenile courts. They argued that a failure to address needs beginning in early childhood could prove costly—monetarily and otherwise—to society at large. The year 1912 marked the creation of the U.S. Children's Bureau, a significant shift toward the nationalization of welfare. The Children's Bureau took up causes of maternal and child health, maternal and child mortality rates, and health provisions for mothers and children in poor urban and rural areas.

The country's entrance into World War I altered the role of the federal government considerably. The government expanded its powers during the Great Depression and World War II, but the foundations for such expansion developed during World War I. A peacetime economy was transformed into a wartime economy largely through the creation of the War Industries Board, as well as the U.S. Food Administration, the National War Labor Board, the U.S. Railroad Administration, the

U.S. Fuel Administration, and so on. These agencies would fix prices and control production and resources at the federal level, all for the good of the nation and the war effort.

This new position of the federal government had a significant impact on its approach to welfare programs. First, the creation of federal agencies with substantial powers to address needs permeated the arena of social welfare. In addition, the government transmitted information and scientific knowledge gathered in the war effort to the civilian sector. For example, social workers noted that the prevention of many of society's ills required addressing the needs of America's children—such as nutrition, health care, education, and juvenile courts, as mentioned earlier. The Progressive Era had brought attention to social ills that often seemed too costly to solve, but reformers insisted that prevention programs involving children were a good investment and saved dollars in the long run. When the government began a program to provide detailed physical examinations for draftees into the armed forces, experts found that many disabilities (or problems termed "defects" at the time) could have been prevented by improved care during pregnancy and early childhood. As a result, the Children's Bureau expanded programs in public health. This sense of federal responsibility would continue after the war. In 1921, women's groups successfully lobbied for passage of the Sheppard-Towner Maternity and Infancy Act, allocating federal funds to create maternity and pediatric clinics.

Though during the first few decades of the twentieth century the nation experienced a growing sense of duty in terms of addressing the needs of the poor, society was unprepared to handle the demands of the Great Depression. In October 1929, the stock market crashed, setting off a downward spiral of the economy that would raise unemployment rates to unprecedented levels. State, municipal, and private philanthropic agencies inadequately addressed the burden of relief, as the needs exceeded their resources. As the depression set in, tax revenues and donations diminished, forcing the federal government to assume responsibility and initiate new programs. President Herbert Hoover instituted plans for public works programs that would rely on cooperation from the various states, but such programs could not provide immediate solutions to the growing number of unemployed. The Hoover administration also established the President's Committee for Employment, but it would limit itself to overseeing state, local, and private relief programs. Those programs lacked the resources necessary, given the severity of the situation, and directors of the programs lobbied Washington for a federal relief program. Despite much resistance, Congress and the president granted authority to the Reconstruction Finance Corporation (RFC) to make $300 million in loans available to the states for unemployment relief. However, the program proved ineffective, largely because of a lack of federal regulations on administering the money. Hoover received heavy criticism for his unwillingness to take strong action as president when the economy collapsed.

In 1932, the American electorate blamed Hoover for failing to confront the depression effectively and voted in Franklin Delano Roosevelt. In his first 100 days, Roosevelt convinced Congress to implement a vast array of programs to address difficulties across the American economy, including banking, agriculture, and industry.

In an unprecedented move, the government created the Federal Emergency Relief Administration (FERA) to provide assistance to the unemployed. It abolished the existing loans established through the RFC under Hoover, replacing them with grants, and strengthened administrative powers to oversee the program.

Myriad other programs followed. In November 1933, Congress created the Civil Works Administration (CWA), a work relief program designed to put at least half of the nation's unemployed to work. In 1934, the government replaced the CWA with the Emergency Work Relief Program, which, in turn, the Works Progress Administration (WPA) replaced. During that time, the WPA employed an average of 2 million Americans per month. To address the special needs of young men and boys—who, experts warned, could cause significant problems in society if left idle for too long—the federal government designed the Civilian Conservation Corps (CCC). The War Department supervised the CCC work camps, and the Departments of Agriculture and the Interior planned projects that primarily put them to work in reforestation and flood control.

Even as various programs successfully assisted those in need, members of Congress recommended implementing something more long term. Members proposed the Lundeen Bill, or the Workers' Unemployment, Old Age and Social Insurance Bill, to provide unemployment benefits at prevailing wages for all those who were unemployed through no fault of their own. But many Americans viewed the legislation as too far-reaching. The economic tradition of the United States had seen periods of significant layoffs, and would see layoffs in the future. To suggest that the federal government should assume responsibility for all people involuntarily unemployed seemed unimaginable. Instead, Congress passed the Social Security Act of 1935. Though more specific and more limited, that measure signaled a historic turning point in the shift toward general, long-term federal responsibility in providing for Americans who found themselves in need. In addition to providing a kind of social insurance for retirement in old age, the act established a program of federal grants-in-aid to states providing assistance to the elderly, the blind, and dependent children.

Though it has remained the cornerstone of social welfare in the United States, the Social Security Act met with significant resistance from a variety of critics. Ideological and political differences among supporters of Social Security acted as obstacles to developing a unified lobbying force. In addition, conservatives argued that such a program too closely mirrored the welfare programs of a more nationalist and socialist nature that were then expanding in other countries—something feared during the rise of Hitler and Stalinist Russia. And American businesspeople opposed an increase in taxes to support such a program while the economy continued to struggle.

One of the most significant influences in developing the Social Security Act of 1935 came from the Townsend movement, a grassroots force spearheaded by Francis Townsend, a physician. Townsend served as a powerful advocate for the elderly, whom he believed needed protection from destitution. Although many social welfare programs had historically centered on the needs of children, Townsend and his supporters effectively brought the needs of the elderly to the nation's attention. Calls for "old-age insurance" had gained some attention during the 1920s, but they gained momentum during the depression as pensions voluntarily established by companies suddenly went bankrupt. In addition, the elderly had formed a powerful lobbying group that cut across class lines. They did not represent a small group of poor or underprivileged. Rather, they represented all but the very wealthy, who could afford not to work even in old age. But Congress did not limit the Social Security Act to helping the elderly. Very important, it established the first federal program to aid dependent children—a program that would see significant expansion in the 1960s—and it recognized severe physical disabilities such as blindness as obstacles to gainful employment.

The 1930s' trend toward federal responsibility for the welfare of the American people did not cease when the depression ended. Instead, the long-term policies expanded during the subsequent period of prosperity. America's entrance into World War II helped to boost the economy by shifting it to one based on war production. Though ultimately advantageous for economic rebirth and individual income, industrial and agricultural restructuring resulted in a tremendous dislocation and relocation of workers, raising new concerns about housing and settlement. These changes appeared especially pronounced among minorities. White workers received a warm welcome into areas that needed workers, but the loss of potential workers into the military forced companies to draw from pools of women, blacks, and Latinos in order to fill positions. When minorities moved into industrial areas in hopes of finding employment, they encountered racism and discriminatory housing policies, making resettlement difficult. Because bosses generally preferred to hire Caucasian women, minorities often remained unemployed, forcing the federal government to reexamine its new welfare policies. Furthermore, the employment of women inspired a remarkable—though short-lived—federal child care program.

The GI Bill remains the most significant piece of wartime "welfare" legislation. Federally sponsored benefits for the families of soldiers who were killed or disabled already existed, but this bill went further. It was passed principally in order to honor those who served in the war, but it also helped to ensure national stability. Advocates warned of massive social and economic instability when millions of veterans began to seek jobs during a critical period of economic restructuring, as the country shifted from wartime to peacetime production. The GI Bill offered educational assistance to returning veterans and loans for the purchase of a home, business, or farm. The program eased resettlement in a way that would not harm an already fragile economy, and it reflected the more general trend toward a growing role for the federal government in welfare.

During the 1950s, economic prosperity drew new criticism of the Social Security system, with some people contending that Americans no longer needed it. However, the system kept expanding. President Harry S Truman worked to continue this and other New Deal programs initiated by Roosevelt and see them grow under what he called his Fair Deal. He supported an increase in the minimum wage, an expansion of Social Security, and new public works projects. In addition, he proposed federally funded slum clearance and the construction of low-income housing. He even went as far as proposing federal aid for education and a system of national health care, neither of which passed. But even under the more conservative Republican administration of President Dwight D. Eisenhower, the nation witnessed a massive expansion of Social Security. Disabled workers became eligible for social insurance benefits, and states obtained federal public assistance. And in what would become a historic move, Eisenhower authorized the creation of the Department of Health, Education, and Welfare.

The postwar period brought tremendous economic prosperity to the nation, which lasted into the 1950s. Poverty had seemingly become invisible. American optimism tended to gloss over any economic shortcomings that might have existed, and there was little debate about poverty. Although poverty still existed, confident depictions of prosperity served to place American economics on the side of good in the struggle against communism. Late in the decade, however, all that began to change. In his *Affluent Society* (1958), economist John Kenneth Galbraith extolled the virtues of economic progress but painted a less than perfect picture of American society. In *The Other America* (1962), Michael Harrington went further in exposing the seriousness of economic injustice within various segments of American society. Both of these works influenced new attacks on poverty.

Under John F. Kennedy's administration, poverty resurfaced as an evil to be confronted. His successor, Lyndon B. Johnson, made such an effort a primary goal, and within six months of taking office, he outlined his War on Poverty. By August 1964, Johnson convinced Congress to pass the Economic Opportunity Act, which created antipoverty programs under the direction of a new federal agency, the Office of Economic Opportunity (OEO). Johnson's War on Poverty sparked a heated debate, and many questioned its effectiveness. Conservative critics argued that the programs were unnecessary and costly and would create a dependency for people who should be working harder to find their own success. Others argued that Johnson had taken on too much by even suggesting that the nation might see a victory over poverty through the creation of federally funded programs. Defenders of Johnson's policies maintained that they did see some success and that the country would have experienced greater results if the government had not spent so much money on the Vietnam War. In fact, some programs did achieve success, remaining in place for decades. The Job Corps, a work-training program for young people, and Head Start, an early childhood education program, proved quite effective.

Richard Nixon responded to critics of the "welfare mess" by dismantling many of the programs begun under the War on Poverty. But under the Nixon administration, a quiet revolution took place and demonstrated the strength of the federal government's role in social welfare. In 1965, Congress allocated some 42 percent of the federal budget for defense and only 25 percent for social welfare—the basis for protests surrounding America's priorities. However, by 1975, defense expenditures accounted for only 25 percent of the federal budget, whereas welfare expenditures had reached 43 percent. Even with the fiscal demands of the Vietnam War and with the new conservative Republican administration, welfare expenditures rose.

The election of Ronald Reagan in 1980 introduced a new kind of conservatism with the dawn of a new decade—a conservatism, not only in foreign policy but also in domestic policy, that would attack social welfare. A disillusioned American public saw that the federal government had not eradicated poverty and described liberal economic and social policies begun in the 1960s as failures. Reagan campaigned and won on the basis of this disillusionment, and he offered a new plan for a better economic future for all Americans. His economic policy—referred to as Reaganomics—called for severe tax cuts, which he maintained would provide greater incentives for hard work, stimulate individual productivity, and thereby improve the American economy. He promised he would not cut welfare programs designed to protect the truly needy, insisting that a "safety net" would remain in place. However, he excluded Aid to Families with Dependent Children and Food Stamps from this plan. He did defend Social Security and Medicare, which benefited all Americans regardless of income. He converted other programs into a system of "block grants," by which the federal government granted money to various states for welfare needs. His administration also eliminated federal revenue sharing, which had been established in the 1960s to address housing, health, and nutrition needs in poor communities. He met his goals of bringing to an end the welfare bureaucracy in Washington and decreasing welfare expenditures.

The George H. W. Bush administration promised a kinder, gentler America, but the new president continued many of Reagan's policies. He opposed tax hikes and encouraged states to maintain welfare responsibilities. In addition, he called on states to act as "laboratories" experimenting with new and often controversial programs that would discourage dependency on welfare and provide alternative incentives for self-improvement. He also carried on Reagan's theme of privatization, encouraging private charities and other organizations to provide social services instead of local, state, or federal governments. He often made references to America's "1,000 points of light"—or volunteers who would provide assistance to those who were less fortunate.

The election of Bill Clinton introduced the possibility of new approaches to federal responsibility for social welfare. First Lady Hillary Clinton espoused the idea that "it takes a village to raise a child," suggesting that society should take a more active role in seeing to the welfare of individuals. But such a philosophy came under attack. In the first few months of the Clinton administration, proposals for health care reform, whereby the federal government would more directly provide adequate health care for Americans, met defeat. The conflict over social welfare concerns intensified with the election of a Republican majority in Congress in 1994 and the positioning of outspoken conservative Newt Gingrich as Speaker of the House. Gingrich and House Republicans strongly supported what they termed a "Contract with America," which would bring an end to entitlement welfare and place the blame on unmarried mothers, who were said to demonstrate a lack of personal responsibility in creating lives of welfare dependency for themselves. In essence, the same arguments used some 200 years before—that relief tended to make people lazy and encouraged the poor to have even more children—persisted.

Although social programs in education, health care, and family leave have expanded and have become expected in other industrialized nations of the world, the United States has continued to take a comparatively conservative stance, relying on individual responsibility and privately funded charities. The fear that able people will refuse to work, depending on the government for something to which they consider themselves entitled, had persisted. Above all, welfare policy makers have worked diligently to convince American taxpayers that only the "deserving" will receive benefits.

References

Axinn, June, and Mark J. Stern. *Social Welfare: A History of the American Response to Need.* Boston: Allyn and Bacon, 2001.

Beito, David T. *From Mutual Aid to the Welfare State: Fraternal Societies and Social Services, 1890–1967.* Chapel Hill: University of North Carolina Press, 2000.

Berkowitz, Edward, and Kim McQuaid. *Creating the Welfare State: The Political Economy of Twentieth-Century Reform.* New York: Praeger, 1988.

DiNitto, Diana M. *Social Welfare: Politics and Public Policy.* Boston: Allyn and Bacon, 2000.

Dobelstein, Andrew W. *Moral Authority, Ideology, and the Future of American Social Welfare.* Boulder, CO: Westview Press, 1999.

Eisner, Mark Allen. *From Warfare State to Welfare State: World War I, Compensatory State-Building, and the Limits of the Modern Order.* University Park: Pennsylvania State University Press, 2000.

Galbraith, John Kenneth. *The Affluent Society.* 2nd ed. Boston: Houghton Mifflin, 1969.

Gensler, Howard, ed. *The American Welfare System: Origins, Structure, and Effects.* Westport, CT: Praeger, 1996.

Ginsberg, Leon. *Understanding Social Problems, Policies, and Programs.* Columbia: University of South Carolina Press, 1996.

Harrington, Michael. *The Other America: Poverty in the United States.* New York: Macmillan, 1969.

Hombs, Mary Ellen. *Welfare Reform: A Reference Handbook.* Santa Barbara, CA: ABC-CLIO, 1996.

Johnson, Louise C., Charles L. Schwartz, and Donald S. Tate. *Social Welfare: A Response to Human Need.* Boston: Allyn and Bacon, 1997.

Karger, Howard Jacob, and David Stoesz. *American Social Welfare Policy: A Pluralist Approach.* New York: Longman, 1998.

Katz, Michael B. *In the Shadow of the Poorhouse: A Social History of Welfare in America.* New York: Basic Books, 1997.

Katz, Michael B. *The Price of Citizenship: Redefining the American Welfare State.* New York: Metropolitan Books, 2001.

Kronenwetter, Michael. *Welfare State America: Safety Net or Social Contract?* New York: Franklin Watts, 1993.

Miles, Arthur P. *An Introduction to Public Welfare.* Boston: D. C. Heath, 1949.

Noble, Charles. *Welfare As We Knew It: A Political History of the American Welfare State.* New York: Oxford University Press, 1997.

Popple, Philip R., and Leslie Leighninger. *Social Work, Social Welfare, and American Society.* Boston: Allyn and Bacon, 1999.

Singleton, Jeff. *The American Dole: Unemployment Relief and the Welfare State in the Great Depression.* Westport, CT: Greenwood Press, 2000.

Trattner, Walter. *Crusade for the Children: A History of the National Child Labor Committee and Child Labor Reform in America.* Chicago: Quadrangle Books, 1970.

Trattner, Walter. *From Poor Law to Welfare State: A History of Social Welfare in America.* New York: Free Press, 1999.

Zijderveld, Anton C. *The Waning of the Welfare State: The End of Comprehensive State Succor.* New Brunswick, NJ: Transaction Books, 1999.

Primary Source Documents

Primary Source Documents

Ordinance of the Northwest Territory (1787)

Passed on July 13, 1787, the Ordinance of the Northwest Territory, commonly referred to as the Northwest Ordinance, established the procedures by which the western lands ceded to the national government by the states would form territorial governments. Congress appointed a governor, secretary, and three judges to administer the territory until the number of voting citizens reached 5,000. At that point the citizens elected a legislature. When the population increased to 60,000, the territory could apply for statehood on an equal basis with the other states. The ordinance also guaranteed the validity of contracts, prohibited individuals born in the territory from becoming slaves, and ensured freedom of religion. The passage of this act encouraged investors and settlers to migrate to the region.

Source: www.law.ou.edu/aku/ordinance.html.

An ordinance for the government of the Territory of the United States northwest of the river Ohio.

SECTION 1. Be it ordained by the United States on Congress assembled, That the said territory, for the purpose of temporary government, be one district, subject, however, to be divided into two districts, as future circumstances may, in the opinion of Congress, make it expedient.

SEC. 2. Be it ordained by the authority aforesaid, That the estates both of resident and non-resident proprietors in the said territory, dying intestate, shall descend to, and be distributed among, their children and the descendants of a deceased child in equal parts, the descendants of a deceased child or grandchild to take the share of their deceased parent in equal parts among them; and where there shall be no children or descendants, then in equal parts to the next of kin in equal degree; and among collaterals, the children of a deceased brother or sister of the intestate shall have, in equal parts among them, their deceased parent's share; and there shall, in no case, be a distinction between kindred of the whole and half blood; saving in all cases to the widow of the intestate, her third part of the real estate for life, and one-third part of the personal estate; and this law relative to descents and dower, shall remain in full force until altered by the legislature of the district. And until the governor and judges shall adopt laws as hereinafter mentioned, estates in the said territory may be devised or bequeathed by wills in writing, signed and sealed by him or her in whom the estate may be, (being of full age), and attested by three witnesses; and real estates may be conveyed by lease and release, or bargain and sale, signed, sealed, and delivered by the person, being of full age, in whom the estate may be, and attested by two witnesses, provided such wills be duly proved, and such conveyances be acknowledged, or the execution thereof duly proved, and be recorded within one year after proper magistrates, courts, and registers, shall be appointed for that purpose; and personal property may be transferred by delivery, saving, however to the French and Canadian inhabitants, and other settlers of the Kaskaskies, Saint Vincents, and the neighboring villages, who have heretofore professed themselves citizens of Virginia, their laws and customs now in force among them, relative to the descent and conveyance of property.

SEC. 3. Be it ordained by the authority aforesaid, That there shall be appointed, from time to time, by Congress, a governor, whose commission shall continue in force for the term of three years, unless sooner revoked by Congress; he shall reside in the district, and have a freehold estate therein, in one thousand acres of land, while in the exercise of his office.

SEC. 4. There shall be appointed from time to time, by Congress, a secretary, whose commission shall continue in force for four years, unless sooner revoked; he shall reside in the district, and have a freehold estate therein, in five hundred acres of land, while in the exercise of his office. It shall be his duty to keep and preserve the acts and laws passed by the legislature, and the public records of the district, and the proceedings of the governor in his executive department, and transmit authentic copies of such acts and proceedings every six months to the Secretary of Congress. There shall also be appointed a court, to consist of three judges, any two of whom to form a court, who shall have a common-law jurisdiction, and reside in the district, and have each therein a freehold estate, in five hundred acres of land, while in the exercise of their offices; and their commissions shall continue in force during good behavior.

SEC. 5. The governor and judges, or a majority of them, shall adopt and publish in the district such laws of the original States, criminal and civil, as may be necessary, and best suited to the circumstances of the district, and report them to Congress from time to time, which laws shall be in force in the district until the organization of the general assembly therein, unless disapproved of by Congress; but afterwards the legislature shall have authority to alter them as they shall think fit.

SEC. 6. The governor, for the time being, shall be commander-in-chief of the militia, appoint and commission all officers in the same below the rank of general officers; all general officers shall be appointed and commissioned by Congress.

SEC. 7. Previous to the organization of the general assembly the governor shall appoint such magistrates, and other civil officers, in each county or township, as he shall find necessary for the preservation of the peace and good order in the same. After the general assembly shall be organized the powers and duties of magistrates and other civil officers shall be regulated and defined by the said assembly; but all magistrates and other civil officers, not herein otherwise directed, shall, during the continuance of this temporary government, be appointed by the governor.

SEC. 8. For the prevention of crimes and injuries, the laws to be adopted or made shall have force in all parts of the district, and for the execution of process, criminal and civil, the governor shall make proper divisions thereof; and he shall proceed, from time to time, as circumstances may require, to lay out the parts of the district in which the Indian titles shall have been extinguished, into counties and townships, subject, however, to such alterations as may thereafter be made by the legislature.

SEC. 9. So soon as there shall be five thousand free male inhabitants, of full age, in the district, upon giving proof thereof to the governor, they shall receive authority, with time and place, to elect representatives from their counties or townships, to represent them in the general assembly: PROVIDED, That for every five hundred free male inhabitants there shall be one representative, and so on, progressively, with the number of free male inhabitants, shall the right of representation increase, until the number of representatives shall amount to twenty-five; after which the number and proportion of representatives shall be regulated by the legislature: PROVIDED, That no person be eligible or qualified to act as a representative, unless he shall have been a citizen of one of the United States three years, and be a resident in the district, or unless he shall have resided in the district three years; and, in either case, shall likewise hold in his own right, in fee simple, two hundred acres of land within the same: PROVIDED ALSO, That a freehold in fifty acres of land in the district, having been a citizen of one of the States, and being resident in the district, or the like freehold and two years' residence in the district, shall be necessary to qualify a man as an elector of a representative.

SEC. 10. The representatives thus elected shall serve for the term of two years; and in case of the death of a representative, or removal from office, the governor shall issue a writ to the county or township, for which he was a member, to elect another in his stead, to serve for the residue of the term.

SEC. 11. The general assembly, or legislature, shall consist of the governor, legislative council, and a house of representatives. The legislative council shall consist of five members to continue in office five years, unless sooner removed by Congress; any three of whom to be a quorum; and the members of the council shall be nominated and appointed in the following manner, to wit: As soon as representatives shall be elected the governor shall appoint a time and place for them to meet together, and when meet they shall nominate ten persons, resident in the district, and each possessed of a freehold in five hundred acres of land, and return their names to Congress, five of whom Congress shall appoint and commission to serve as aforesaid; and whenever a vacancy shall happen in the council, by death or removal from office, the house of representatives shall nominate two persons, qualified as aforesaid, for each vacancy, and return their names to Congress, one of whom Congress shall appoint and commission for the residue of the term; and every five years, four months at least before the expiration of the time of service of the members of the council, the said house shall nominate ten persons, qualified as aforesaid, and return their names to Congress, five of whom Congress shall appoint and commission to serve as members of the council five years, unless sooner removed. And the governor, legislative council, and house of representatives shall have authority to make laws in all cases for the good government of the district, not repugnant to the principles and articles in this ordinance established and declared. And all bills, having passed by a majority in the house, and by a majority in the council, shall be referred to the governor for his assent; but no bill, or legislative act whatever, shall be of any force without his assent. The governor shall have power to convene, prorogue, and dissolve the general assembly when, in his opinion, it shall be expedient.

SEC. 12. The governor, judges, legislative council, secretary, and such other officers as Congress shall appoint in the district, shall take an oath or affirmation of fidelity, and of office; the governor before the President of Congress, and all other officers before the governor. As soon as a legislature shall be formed in the district, the council and house assembled, in one room, shall have authority, by joint ballot, to elect a delegate to Congress, who shall have a seat in Congress, with a right of debating, but not of voting, during this temporary government.

SEC. 13. And for extending the fundamental principles of civil and religious liberty, which form the basis whereon these republics, their laws and constitutions, are erected; to fix and establish those principles as the basis of all laws, constitutions, and governments, which forever hereafter shall be formed in the said territory; to provide, also, for the establishment of States, and permanent government therein, and for their admission to a share in the Federal councils on an equal footing with the original States, at as early periods as may be consistent with the general interest.

SEC. 14. It is hereby ordained and declared, by the authority aforesaid, that the following articles shall be considered as articles of compact, between the original States and the people and States in the said territory, and forever remain unalterable, unless by common consent, to wit:

ARTICLE I

No person, demeaning himself in a peaceable and orderly manner, shall ever be molested on account of his mode of worship, or religious sentiments, in the said territory.

ARTICLE II

The inhabitants of the said territory shall always be entitled to the benefits of the writs of habeas corpus, and of the trial by jury; of a proportionate representation of the people in the legislature, and of judicial proceedings according to the course of the common law. All persons shall be bailable, unless for capital offences, where the proof shall be evident, or the presumption great. All fines shall be moderate; and no cruel or unusual punishments shall be inflicted. No man shall be deprived of his liberty or property, but by the judgment of his peers, or the law of the land, and should the public exigencies make it necessary, for the common preservation, to take any person's property, or to demand his particular services, full compensation shall be made for the same. And, in the just preservation of rights and property, it is understood and declared, that no law ought ever to be made or have force in the said territory, that shall, in any manner whatever, interfere with or affect private contracts, or engagements, bona fide, and without fraud previously formed.

ARTICLE III

Religion, morality, and knowledge being necessary to good government and happiness of mankind, schools and the means of education shall forever be encouraged. The utmost good faith shall always be observed towards the Indians; their lands and property shall never be taken from them without their consent; and in their property, rights, and liberty they never shall be invaded or disturbed, unless in just and lawful wars authorized by Congress; but laws founded in justice and humanity shall, from time to time, be made, for preventing wrongs being done to them, and for preserving peace and friendship with them.

ARTICLE IV

The said territory, and the States which may be formed therein, shall forever remain a part of this confederacy of the United States of America, subject to the Articles of Confederation, and to such alterations therein as shall be constitutionally made; and to all the acts and ordinances of the United States in Congress assembled, conformable thereto. The inhabitants and settlers in the said territory shall be subject to pay a part of the Federal debts, contracted, or to be contracted, and a proportional part of the expenses of government to be apportioned on them by Congress, according to the same common rule and measure by which apportionments thereof shall be made on the other States; and the taxes for paying their proportion shall be laid and levied by the authority and direction of the legislatures of the districts, or districts, or new States, as in the original States, within the time agreed upon by the United States in Congress assembled. The legislatures of those districts, or new States, shall never interfere with the primary disposal of the soil by the United States in Congress assembled, nor with any regulations Congress may find necessary for securing the title in such soil to the bona fide purchasers. No tax shall be imposed on lands the property of the United States; and in no case shall non-resident proprietors be taxed higher than residents. The navigable waters leading into the Mississippi and Saint Lawrence, and the carrying places between the same shall be common highways, and forever free, as well to the inhabitants of the said territory as to the citizens of the United States, and those of any other States that may be admitted into the confederacy, without any tax, impost, or duty therefor.

ARTICLE V

There shall be formed in the said territory not less than three nor more than five States; and the boundaries of the States, as soon as Virginia shall alter her act of cession and consent to the same, shall become fixed and established as follows, to wit: The western State, in the said territory, shall be bounded by the Mississippi, the Ohio, and the Wabash rivers; a direct line drawn from the Wabash and Post Vincents, due north, to the territorial line between the United States and Canada; and by the said territorial line to the Lake of the Woods and Mississippi. The middle State shall be bounded by the said direct line, the Wabash from Post Vincents to the Ohio, by the Ohio, by direct line drawn due north from the mouth of the Great Miami to the said territorial line and by the said territorial line. The eastern State shall be bounded by the last mentioned direct line, the Ohio, the Pennsylvania, and the said territorial line: PROVIDED, HOWEVER, And it is further understood and declared, that the boundaries of these three States shall be subject so far to be altered, that, if Congress shall hereafter find it expedient, they shall have authority to form one or two States in that part of the said territory which lies north of an east and west line drawn through the southerly bend or extreme of Lake Michigan. And whenever any of the said States shall have sixty thousand free inhabitants therein, such State shall be admitted, by its delegates, into the Congress of the United States, on an equal footing with the original States, in all respects whatever; and shall be at liberty to form a permanent constitution and State government; PROVIDED, The constitution and government, so to be formed, shall be republican, and in conformity to the principles contained in these articles, and, so far as it can be consistent with the general interest of the confederacy, such admission shall be allowed at an earlier period, and when there may be a less number of free inhabitants in the State than sixty thousand.

ARTICLE VI

There shall be neither slavery nor involuntary servitude in the said territory, otherwise than in the punishment of crimes, whereof the party shall have been duly convicted: PROVIDED ALWAYS, That any person escaping into the same, from whom labor or service is lawfully claimed in any one of the original States, such fugitive may be lawfully reclaimed, and conveyed to the person claiming his or her labor or service as aforesaid.

Be it ordained by the authority aforesaid, That the resolutions of the 23rd of April, 1784, relative to the subject of this ordinance, be, and the same are hereby, repealed, and declared null and void.

Done by the United States, in Congress assembled, the 13th day of July, in the year of our Lord 1787, and of their sovereignty and independence the twelfth.

Report on the Subject of Manufactures (1791)

On December 5, 1791, Secretary of the Treasury Alexander Hamilton submitted his Report on the Subject of Manufactures *to Congress. Hamilton argued that the United States needed to develop domestic manufacturing as a means of protecting its economic freedom. As a supplier of raw materials for industrial England and other European powers, the United States remained dependent on foreign governments in economic matters. Hamilton pointed out that if the United States would initiate a protective tariff, then investors would contribute to the development of industries within the country. These enterprises could take advantage of the internal availability of natural resources. Although there were not enough workers for a large number of these factories, Hamilton pointed out that such a policy would also encourage immigration and thereby eliminate the problem of a "scarcity of hands." Although Congress failed to implement all of Hamilton's proposals, after the War of 1812 the first protective tariff was passed. "Protectionism," as Hamilton's philosophy became known, continued in the United States until the post–World War II era. Consequently, the nation developed into an industrialized country instead of an agricultural one.*

Source: American Memory: A Century of Lawmaking for a New Nation: U.S. Congressional Documents and Debates, 1774–1875, Annals of Congress, 2nd Congress, pp. 971–1035, http://www.loc.gov. Errors that appear in the following reflect the document as transcribed on this Internet site.

The Secretary of the Treasury, in obedience to the order of the House of Representatives, of the 15th day of January 1790, has applied his attention, at as early a period as his other duties would permit, to the subject of Manufactures; and particularly to the means of promoting such as will tend to render the United States, independent of foreign nations, for military and other essential supplies. And he there(upon) respectfully submits the following Report.

The expediency of encouraging manufactures in the United States, which was not long since deemed very questionable, appears at this time to be pretty generally admitted. The embarrassments, which have obstructed the progress of our external trade, have led to serious reflections on the necessity of enlarging the sphere of our domestic commerce: the restrictive regulations, which in foreign markets abridge the vent of the increasing surplus or our Agricultural produce, serve to beget an earnest desire, that a more extensive demand for that surplus may be created at home: And the complete success, which has rewarded manufacturing enterprise, in some valuable branches, conspiring with the promising symptoms, which attend some less mature essays, in others, justify a hope, that the obstacles to the growth of this species of industry are less formidable that they were apprehended to be; and that it is not difficult to find, in its further extension: a full indemnification for any external disadvantages, which are or may be experienced, as well as an accession of resources, favorable to national independence and safety.

There still are, nevertheless, respectable patrons of opinions, unfriendly to the encouragement of manufacturers. The following are, substantially, the arguments, by which these opinions are defended.

"In every country (say those who entertain them) Agriculture is the most beneficial and *productive* object of human industry. This position, generally, if not universally true, applies with peculiar emphasis to the United States, on account of their immense tracts of fertile territory, uninhabited and unimproved. Nothing can afford so advantageous an employment for capital and labour, as the conversion of this extensive wilderness into cultivated farms. Nothing equally with this, can contribute to the population, strength and real riches of the country."

"To endeavor by the extraordinary patronage of Government, to accelerate the growth of manufactures, is in fact, to endeavor, by force and art, to transfer the natural current of industry, from a more, to a less beneficial channel. Whatever has such a tendency must necessarily be unwise. Indeed it can hardly ever be wise in a government, to attempt to give a direction to the industry of its citizens. This, under the quick-sighted guidance of private interest, will, if left to itself, infallibly find its own way to the most profitable employment: and 'tis by such employment, that the public prosperity will be more effectually promoted. To leave industry to itself, therefore, is, in almost every case, the soundest as well as the simplest policy."

"This policy is not only recommended to the United States, by considerations which affect all nations, it is, in a manner, dictated to them by the imperious force of a very peculiar situation. The smallness of their population compared with their territory—the constant allurements of emigration from the settled to the unsettled parts of the country—the facility with which the less independent condition of a artisan can be exchanged for the more independent condition of a farmer, these and similar causes conspire to produce, and for a length of time must continued to occasion, a scarcity of hands for manufacturing occupation, and dearness of labor generally. To these disadvantages for the prosecution of manufactures, a deficiency of pecuniary capital being added, the prospect of a successful competition with the manufactures of Europe must be regarded as little less than desperate. Extensive manufactures can only be the offspring of a redundant, at least of a full population. Till the latter shall characterise the situation of the county, 'tis vain to hope for the former."

"If, contrary to the natural course of things, an unseasonable and premature spring can be given to certain fabrics, by heavy duties, prohibitions, bounties, or by other forced expedients; this will only be to sacrifice the interests of the community to those of particular classes. Besides the misdirection of labour, a virtual monopoly will be given to the persons employed on such fabrics: and an enhancement of price, the inevitable consequence of every monopoly, must be defrayed at the expence of the other parts of society. It is far preferable, that those persons should be engaged in the cultivation of the earth, and that we should procure, in exchange for its productions, the commodities, with which foreigners were able to supply us in greater perfection, and upon better terms."

This mode of reasoning is founded upon facts and principles, which have certainly respectable pretensions. If it had governed the conduct of nations, more generally than it has done, there is room to suppose, that it might have carried them faster to prosperity and greatness, than they have attained by the pursuit of maxims too widely opposite. Most general theories, however, admit of numerous exceptions, and there are few, if any, of the political kind, which do not blend a considerable portion of error, with the truths they inculcate.

In order to an accurate judgment how far that which has been just stated ought to be deemed liable to a similar imputation, it is necessary to advert carefully to the considerations, which plead in favor of manufactures, and which appear to recommend the special and positive encouragement of them; in certain cases, and under certain reasonable limitations.

It ought readily to be conceded that the cultivation of the earth—as the primary and most certain source of national supply—as the immediate and chief source of subsistence to a man—as the principal source of those materials which constitute the nutriment of other kinds of labor—as including a state more favourable to the freedom and independence of the human mind—one, perhaps, most conducive to the multiplication of the human species—has *intrinsically a strong claim to pre-eminence over every other kind of industry.*

But, that is has a title to any thing like an exclusive predilection, in any country, ought to be admitted with great caution. That is even more productive than every other branch of Industry requires more evidence, than has yet been given in support of the position. That its real interests, precious and important as without the help of exaggeration and importance, they truly are, will be advantaged, rather than injured by the due encouragement of manufactures, may, it is believed, be satisfactorily demonstrated. And it is also believed that the expediency of such encouragement in a general view may be shewn to be recommended by the most cogent and persuasive motives of national policy.

It has been maintained, that Agriculture is, not only, the most productive, but the only productive species of industry. The reality of this suggestion in either aspect has, however, not been verified by any accurate detail of facts and calculations; and the general arguments, which are adduced to prove it, are rather subtil and paradoxical, than solid or convincing.

Those which maintain its exclusive productiveness are to this effect.

Labour, bestowed upon the cultivation of land produces enough, not only to replace all the necessary expences incurred in the business, and to maintain the persons who are employed in it, but to afford together with the *ordinary profit* on the stock and capital of the Farmer, a nett surplus, or *rent* for the landlord or proprietor of the soil. But the labor of Artificers does nothing more, than replace the Stock which employees them (or which furnishes materials tools and wages) and yield the *ordinary profit* of that Stock. It yields nothing equivalent to the *rent* of the land and labour of the country. The additional value given to those parts of the produce of land, which are wrought into manufacturers, is counterbalanced by the value of those other parts of that produce, which are consumed by the manufacturers. It can therefore only be by saving, or *parsimony*, not by the positive *productiveness* of their labour, that the classes of Artificers can in any degree augment the revenue of the Society.

To this it has been answered—

I—"That inasmuch as it is acknowledged, that manufacturing labour reproduces a value equal to that which is expended or consumed in carrying it on, and continues in existence the original Stock or capital employed—it ought on that account alone, to escape being considered as wholly unproductive: That though is should be admitted, as alleged, that the consumption of the produce of the soil, by the classes of Artificers or Manufacturers, is exactly equal to the value added by there labour to the materials upon with it is exerted; yet it would not thence follow, that it added nothing to the Revenue of the Society, or to the aggregate value of the annual produce of its land and labour. If the consumption for any given period amounted to a *given sum* in the *increased* value of the produce manufactured, in the same period, to a *like sum*, the total amount of the consumption and production during that period, will be equal to the *two sums*, and consequently double the value of the agriculture produce consumed. And though the increment of value produced by the classes of Artificers should at no time exceed the value of the produce of the land consumed by them, yet there would be at every moment, in consequence of labour, a greater value of goods in the market then would exist independent of it."

II—"That the position, that Artificers can augment the revenue of a Society, only by parsimony, is true, in no other sense, than in one, which is equally applicable to Husbandmen or Cultivators. It may be alike affirmed of all these classes, that the fund acquired by there labor destined for their support is not, in an ordinary way, more than equal to it. And hence it will follow, that augmentations of the wealth or capital of the community (except in the instances of some extraordinary dexterity or skill) can only proceed, with respect to any of them, from the savings of the more thrifty and parsimonious."

III—"That the annual produce of the land and labour of a country can be encreased, in two ways—by some improvement in the *productive powers* of the useful labour, which actually exists within it, or by some increase in the quantity of such labour:

That with regard to the first, the labour of Artificers being capable of greater subdivision in simplicity of operation, within that of Cultivators, it is susceptible, in a proportionably greater degree, of improvement in its *productive powers*, whether to be derived from an accession of Skill, or from the application of ingenious machinery; in which particular, therefore, the labour employed in the cultural of land can pretend to no advantage over that engaged in manufactures: That with regard to an augmentation of the quantity of useful labuor, this, excluding adventitious circumstances, must depend essentially upon an increase of *capital*, which again must depend upon the savings made out of the revenues of those, who furnish or manage *that*, which is at any time employed, whether in Agricultural or Manufactures, or in any other way."

But while the *exclusive* productiveness of Agricultural labour has been thus denied and refuted, the superiority of its productiveness has been conceded without hesitation. As this concession involves a point of considerable magnitude, in relation to maxims of public administration, the grounds which it rests are worthy of a distinct and particular examination.

One of the arguments made use of, in support of the idea maybe pronounced both quaint and superficial. It amounts to this—That in the productions of the soil, nature co-operates with man; and that the effect of their joint labour must be greater than that of the labour of man alone.

This, however, is far from being a necessary inference. It is very conceivable, that the labor of man alone laid out upon a work, requiring great skill and art to bring it to perfection, may be more productive, *in value*, than the labour of nature and man combined, when directed toward more simple operations and objects: And when it is recollected to what an extent the Agency of nature, in the application of the mechanical powers, is made auxiliary to the prosecution of manufactures, the suggestion, which has been noticed, loses even the appearance of plausibility.

It might also be observed, with a contrary view, that the labour employed in Agriculture is in a great measure periodical and occasional, depending on the seasons, liable to various and long intermissions; while that occupied in many manufactures is constant and regular, extending through the year, embracing in some instances night as well as day. It is also probable, that there are among the cultivators of land more examples of remissness, than among artificers. The farmer, from the peculiar fertility of his land, or some other favorable circumstance, may frequently obtain a livelihood, even with a considerable degree of carelessness in the mode of cultivation; but the artisan can with difficulty effect the same object, without exerting himself pretty equally with all those, who are engaged in the same pursuit. And if it may likewise be assumed as a fact, that manufactures open a wider field to exertions of ingenuity than agriculture, it would not be a strained conjecture, that the labour employed in the former, being at once more *constant*, more uniform, and more ingenious, than that which is employed in the latter, will be found at the same time more productive.

But it is not meant to lay stress on observations of this nature—they ought only to serve as a counterbalance to those of a similar complexion. Circumstances so vague and general, as well as so abstract, can afford little instruction in a matter of this kind.

Another, and that which seems to be the principal argument offered for the superior productiveness of Agricultural labour, turns upon the allegation, that labour employed on manufactures yields nothing equivalent to the rent of land; or to that nett surplus, as it is called, which accrues to the proprietor of the soil.

But this distinction, important as it has been deemed, appears rather *verbal* than *substantial.*

It is easily discernable, that what in the first instance is divided into two parts under the denominations of the *ordinary profit* of the Stock of the farmer and *rent* to the landlord, is in the second instance united under the general appellation of the *ordinary profit* on the Stock of the Undertaker; and that this formal or verbal distribution constitutes the whole difference in the two cases. It seems to have been overlooked, that the land is itself a Stock or capital, advanced or lent by its owner to the occupier or tenant, and that the rent he receives is only the ordinary profit of a certain Stock in land, not managed by the proprietor himself, but by another to whom he leads or lets it, and who on his part advances a second capital to stock & improve the land, upon which he also receives the usual profit. The rent of the landlord and the profit of the farmer are therefore nothing more than the *ordinary profits* of *two* capitals, belonging to *two* different persons, and united in the cultivation of a farm: As in the other case, the surplus which arises upon any manufactory, after replacing the expences of carrying it on, answers to the ordinary profits of *one* or *more* capitals engaged in the persecution of such manufactory. It is said *one* or *more* capitals; because, in fact the same thing which is contemplated, in the case of the farm, sometimes happens in that of a manufactory. There is one, who furnishes a part of the capital, or lends a part of the money, by which it is carried on, and another, who carries it on, with the addition of his own capital. Out of the surplus, which remains, after defraying expences, an interest is paid to the money-lender for the portion of the capital furnished by him, which exactly agrees with the rent paid to the landlord; and the residue of that surplus constitutes the profit of the undertaker or manufacturer, and agrees with what is denominated the ordinary profits on the Stock of the farmer. Both together make the ordinary profits of two capitals (employed in a manufactory; as in the other case the rent of the landlord and the revenue of the farmer compose the ordinary profits of two Capitals) employed in the cultivation of a farm.

The rent therefore accruing to the proprietor of the land, far from being a criterion of *exclusive* productiveness, as has been argued, is no criterion even of superior productiveness. The question must still be, whether the surplus, after defraying expences of a *given capital* employed in the *purchase* and *improvement* of a piece of land, is greater or less, than that of a like capital employed in the prosecution of a manufactory: or whether the *whole value produced* from a *given capital* and a *given quantity* of *labour*, employed in one way, be greater or less, than the *whole value produced* from an *equal capital* and an *equal quantity* of *labour* employed in the other way: or rather, perhaps whether the business of Agriculture or that of Manufactures will yield the greatest product, according to a *compound ratio* of the quantity of the Capital and the quantity of labour, which are employed in the one or in the other.

The solution of either of these questions is not easy; it involves numerous and complicated details, depending on an accurate knowledge of the objects to be compared. It is not known that the comparison has ever yet been made upon sufficient data properly ascertained and analised. To be able to make it on the present occasion with satisfactory precision would demand more previous enquiry and investigation, than there has been hitherto either leisure or opportunity to accomplish.

Some essays however have been made towards acquiring the requisite information; which have rather served to throw doubt upon, than to confirm the Hypothesis, under examination: But it ought to be acknowledged, that they have been too little diversified, and are too imperfect, to authorise a definitive conclusion either way; leading rather to probable conjecture than to certain deduction. They render it probable, there are various branches of manufactures, in which a given Capital will yield a greater *total* product, and a considerably greater *nett* product, than an equal capital invested in the purchase and improvement of lands; and that there are also *some* branches, in which both the *gross* and the *nett* produce will exceed that of Agricultural industry; according to a compound ratio of capital and labour: But it is on this last point, that there appears to be the greatest room for doubt. It is far less difficult to infer generally, that the *nett produce* of Capital engaged in manufacturing enterprises is greater than that of Capital engaged in Agriculture.

In stating these results, the purchase and improvement of lands, under previous cultivation are alone contemplated. The comparison is more in favour of Agriculture, when it is made with reference to the settlement of new and waste lands; but an argument drawn from so temporary a circumstance could have no weight in determining the general question concerning the permanent relative productiveness of the two species of industry. How far it ought to influence the policy of the United States, on the score of particular situation, will be averted to in another place.

The foregoing suggestions are *not designed to inculcate an opinion that manufacturing industry is more productive than that of Agriculture.* They are intended rather to shew that the reverse of this proposition is not ascertained; that the general arguments which are brought to establish it are not satisfactory; and consequently that a supposition of the superior productiveness of Tillage ought to be no obstacle to listening to any substantial inducements to the encouragement of manufactures, which may be otherwise perceived to exist, through an apprehension, that they may have a tendency to divert labour from a more to a less profitable employment.

It is extremely probable, that on a full and accurate devellopment of the matter, on the ground of fact and calculation, it would be discovered that there is no material difference between the aggregate productiveness of the one, and of the other kind of industry; and that the propriety of the encouragements, which may in any case be proposed to be given to either ought to be determined upon considerations irrelative to any comparison of that nature.

II But without contending for the superior productiveness of Manufacturing Industry, it may conduce to a better judgment of the policy, which ought to be pursued respecting its encouragement, to contemplate the subject, under some additional aspects, tending not only to confirm the idea, that this kind of industry has been improperly represented as unproductive in itself; but [to] evince in addition that the establishment and diffusion of manufactures have the effect of rendering the total mass of useful and productive labor in a community, *greater than it would otherwise be.* In prosecuting this discussion, it may be necessary briefly to resume and review some of the topics, which have been already touched.

To affirm, that the labour of the Manufacturer is unproductive, because he consumes as much of the produce of land, as he adds value to the raw materials which he manufactures, is not better founded, than it would be to affirm, that the labour of the farmer, which furnishes materials to the manufacturer, is unproductive, *because he consumes an equal value of manufactured articles.* Each furnishes a certain portion of the produce of his labor to the other, and each destroys a correspondent proportion of the produce of the labour of the other. In the mean time, the maintenance of two Citizens, instead of one, is going on; the State has two members instead of one; and they together consume twice the value of what is produced from the land.

If instead of a farmer and artificer, there were a farmer only, he would be under the necessity of devoting a part of his labour to the fabrication of cloathing and other articles, which he would procure of the artificer, in the case of there being such a person; and of course he would be able to devote less labor to the cultivation of his farm; and would draw from it a proportionably less product. The whole quantity of production, in this state of things, in provisions, raw materials and manufactures, would certainly not exceed in value the amount of what would be produced in provisions and raw materials only, if there were an artificer as well as a farmer.

Again—if there were both an artificer and a farmer, the latter would be left at liberty to pursue exclusively the cultivation of his farm. A greater quantity of provisions and raw materials would of course be produced—equal at least—as has been already observed, to the whole amount of the provisions, raw materials and manufactures, which would exist on a contrary supposition. The artificer, at the same time would be going on in the production of manufactured commodities; to an amount sufficient not only to repay the farmer, in those commodities, for the provisions and materials which were procured from him, but to furnish the Artificer himself with a supply of similar commodities for his own use. Thus then, there would be two quantities or values in existence, instead of one; and the revenue and consumption would be double in one case, what it would be in the other.

If in place of both these suppositions, there were supposed to be two farmers, and no artificer, each of whom applied a part of his labour to the culture of land, and another part to the fabrication of Manufactures—in this case, the portion of the labour of both bestowed upon land would produce the same quantity of provisions and raw materials only, as would be produced by the intire sum of the labour of one applied in the same manner, and the portion of the labour of both bestowed upon manufactures, would produce the same quantity of manufactures only, as would be produced by the intire sum of the labour of one applied in the same manner. Hence the produce of the labour of the two farmers would not be greater than the produce of the labour of the farmer and artificer; and hence, it results, that the labour of the artificer is as positively productive as that of the farmer, and, as positively, augments the revenue of the Society.

The labour of the Artificer replaces to the farmer that portion of his labour, with which he provides the materials of exchange with the Artificer, and which he would otherwise have been compelled to apply to manufactures: and while the Artificer thus enables the farmer to enlarge his stock of Agricultural industry, a portion of which he purchases for his own use, *he also supplies himself with the manufactured articles of which he stands in need.*

He does still more—Besides this equivalent which he gives for the portion of Agricultural labour consumed by him, and this supply of manufactured commodities for his own consumption—he furnishes still a surplus, which compensates for the use of the Capital advanced either by himself or some other person, for carrying on the business. This is the ordinary profit of the Stock employed in the manufactory, and is, in every sense, as effective an addition to the income of the Society, as the rent of land.

The produce of the labour of the Artificer consequently, may be regarded as composed of three parts; one by which the provisions for his subsistence and the materials for his work are purchased of the farmer, one by which he supplies himself with manufactured necessaries, and a third which constitutes the profit on the Stock employed. The two last portions seem to have been overlooked in the system, which represents manufacturing industry as barren and unproductive.

In the course of the preceding illustrations, the products of equal quantities of the labour of the farmer and artificer have been treated as if equal to each other. But this is not to be understood as intending to assert any such precise equality. It is merely a manner of expression adopted for the sake of simplicity and perspicuity. Whether the value of the produce of the labour of the farmer be somewhat more or less, than that of the artificer, is not material to the main scope of the argument, which hitherto has only aimed at shewing, that the one, as well as the other, occasions a possitive augmentation of the total produce and revenue of the Society.

It is now proper to proceed a step further, and to enumerate the principal circumstances, from which it may be inferred—That manufacturing establishments not only occasion a possitive augmentation of the Produce and Revenue of the Society, but that they contribute essentially to rendering then greater than they could possibly be, without such establishments. These circumstances are—

1. The division of Labour.
2. An extension of the use of Machinery.
3. Additional employment to classes of the community not ordinarily engaged in the business.
4. The promoting of emigration from foreign Countries.
5. The furnishing greater scope for the diversity of talents and dispositions which discriminate men from each another.
6. The affording a more ample and various field of enterprize.
7. The creating in some instances a new, and securing in all, a more certain and steady demand for the surplus produce of the soil.

Each of these circumstances has a considerable influence upon the total mass of industrious effort in a community. Together, they add to it a degree of energy and effect, which are not easily conceived. Some comments upon each of them, in the order in which they have been stated, may serve to explain their importance.

I. As to the Division of Labour.

It has justly been observed, that there is scarcely any thing of greater moment in the œconomy of a nation, than the proper division of labour. The seperation of occupations causes each to be carried to a much greater perfection, than it could possible acquire, if they were blended. This arises principally from three circumstances.

1st—The greater skill and dexterity naturally resulting from a constant and undivided application to a single object. It is evident, that these properties must increase, in proportion to the separation and simplification of objects and the steadiness of the attention devoted to each; and must be less, in proportion to the complication of objects, and the number among which the attention is distracted.

2nd. The œconomy of time—by avoiding the loss of it, incident to a frequent transition from one operation to another of a different nature. This depends on various circumstances—the transition itself—the orderly disposition of the implements, machines and materials employed in the operation to be relinquished—the preparatory steps to the commencement of a new one—the interruption of the impulse, which the mind of the workman acquires, from being engaged in a particular operation—the distractions hesitations and reluctances, which attend the passage from one kind of business to another.

3rd. An extension of the use of Machinery. A man occupied on a single object will have it more in his power, and will be more naturally led to exert his imagination in devising methods to facilitate and abrige labour, than if he were perplexed by a variety of independent and dissimilar operations. Besides this, the fabrication of Machines, in numerous instances, becoming itself a distinct trade, the Artist who follows it, has all the advantages which have been enumerated, for improvement in his particular art; and in both ways the invention and application of machinery are extended.

And from these causes united, the mere separation of the occupation of the cultivator, from that of the Artificer, has the effect of augmenting the *productive powers* of labour, and with them, the total mass of the produce or revenue of a Country. In this single view of the subject, therefore, the utility of Artificers or Manufactures, towards promoting an increase of productive industry, is apparent.

II. As to an extension of the use of Machinery a point which though partly anticipated requires to be placed in one or two additional lights.

The employment of Machinery forms an item of great importance in the general mass of national industry 'Tis an artificial force brought in aid of the natural force of man; and, to all the purposes of labour, is an increase of hands; an accession of strength, *unencumbered too by the expence of maintaining the laborer.* May it not therefore be fairly inferred, that those occupations, which give greatest scope to the use of this auxiliary, contribute most to the general Stock of industrious effort, and, in consequence, to the general product of industry?

It shall be taken for granted, and the truth of the position referred to observation, that manufacturing pursuits are susceptible in a greater degree of the application of machinery, than those of Agriculture. If so all the difference is lost to a community, which, instead of manufacturing for itself, procures the fabrics requisite to its supply from other Countries. The substitution of foreign for domestic manufactures is a transfer to foreign nations of the advantages accruing from the employment of Machinery, in the modes in which it is capable of being employed, with most utility and to the greatest extent.

The Cotton Mill invented in England, within the last twenty years, is a signal illustration of the general proposition, which has been just advanced. In consequence of it, all the different processes for spining Cotton are performed by means of Machines, which are put in motion by water, and attended chiefly by women and Children; [and by a smaller] number of [persons, in the whole, than are] requisite in the ordinary mode of spinning. And it is an advantage of great moment that the operations of this mill continue with convenience, during the night, as well as through the day. The prodigious affect of such a Machine is easily conceived. To this invention is to be attributed essentially the immense progress, which has been so suddenly made in Great Britain in the various fabrics of Cotton.

III. As to the additional employment of classes of the community, not ordinarily engaged in the particular business.

This is not among the least valuable of the means, by which manufacturing institutions contribute to augment the general stock of industry and production. In places where those institutions prevail, besides the persons regularly engaged in them, they afford occasional and extra employment to industrious individuals and families, who are willing to devote the leisure resulting from the intermissions of their ordinary pursuits to collateral labours, as a resource of multiplying their acquisitions or [their] enjoyments. The husbandman himself experiences a new source of profit and support from the encreased industry of his wife and daughters; invited and stimulated by the demands of the neighboring manufactories.

Besides this advantage of occasional employment to classes having different occupations, there is another of a nature allied to it [and] of a similar tendency. This is—the employment of persons who would otherwise be idle (and in many cases a burthen on the community), either from the byass of temper, habit, infirmity of body, or some other cause, indisposing, or disqualifying them for the toils of the Country. It is worthy of particular remark, that, in general, women and Children are rendered more useful and the latter more early useful by manufacturing establishments, than they would otherwise be. Of the number of persons employed in the Cotton Manufactories of Great Britain, it is computed the 4/7 nearly are women and children; of whom the greatest proportion are children and many of them of a very tender age.

And thus it appears to be one of the attributes of manufactures, and one of no small consequence, to give occasion to the exertion of a greater quantity of Industry, even by the *same number* of persons, where they happen to prevail, than would exist, if there were no such establishments.

IV. As to the promoting of emigration from foreign Countries.

Men reluctantly quit one course of occupation and livelihood for another, unless invited to it by very apparent and proximate advantages. Many, who would go from one country to another, if they had a prospect of continuing with more benefit the callings, to which they have been educated, will often not be tempted to change their situation, by the hope of doing better, in some other way. Manufacturers, who listening to the powerful invitations of a better price for their fabrics, or their labour, of greater cheapness of provisions and raw materials, of an exemption from the chief part of the taxes burthens and restraints, which they endure in the old world, of greater personal independence and consequence, under the operation of a more equal government, and of what is far more precious than mere religious toleration—a perfect equality of religious privileges; would probably flock from Europe to the United States to pursue their own trades or professions, if they were once made sensible of the advantages they would enjoy, and were inspired with an assurance of encouragement and employment, will, with difficulty, be induced to transplant themselves, with a view to becoming Cultivators of Land.

If it be true then, that it is the interest of the United States to open every possible [avenue to] emigration from abroad, it affords a weighty argument for the encouragement of manufactures; which for the reason just assigned, will have the strongest tendency to multiply the inducements to it.

Here is perceived an important resource, not only for extending the population, and with it the useful and productive labour of the country, but likewise for the prosecution of manufactures, without deducting from the number of hands, which might otherwise be drawn to tillage; and even for the indemnification of Agriculture for such as might happen to be diverted from it. Many, whom Manufacturing views would induce to emigrate, would afterwards yield to the temptations, which the particular situation of this Country holds out to Agricultural pursuits. And while Agriculture would in other respects derive many signal and unmingled advantages, from the growth of manufactures, it is a problem whether it would gain or lose, as to the article of the number of persons employed in carrying it on.

V. As to the furnishing greater scope for the diversity of talents and dispositions, which discriminate men from each other.

This is a much more powerful mean of augmenting the fund of national Industry than may at first sight appear. It is a just observation, that minds of the strongest and most active powers for their proper objects fall below mediocrity and labour without effect, if confined to uncongenial pursuits. And it is thence to be inferred, that the results of human exertion may be immensely increased by diversifying its objects. When all the different kinds of industry obtain in a community, each individual can find his proper element, and can call into activity the whole vigour of his nature. And the community is benefitted by the services of its respective members, in the manner in which each can serve it with most effect.

If there be any thing in a remark often to be met with—namely that there is, in the genius of the people of this country, a peculiar aptitude for mechanic improvements, it would operate as a forcible reason for giving opportunities to the exercise of that species of talent, by the propagation of manufactures.

VI. As to the affording a more ample and various field for enterprise.

This also is of greater consequence in the general scale of national exertion, than might perhaps on a superficial view be supposed, and has effects not altogether dissimilar from those of the circumstance last noticed. To cherish and stimulate the activity of the human mind, by multiplying the objects of enterprise, is not among the least considerable of the expedients, by which the wealth of a nation may be promoted. Even things in themselves not positively advantageous, sometimes becomes so, by their tendency to provoke exertion. Every new scene which is opened to the busy nature of man to rouse and exert itself, is the addition of a new energy to the general stock of effort.

The spirit of enterprise, useful and prolific as it is, must necessarily be contracted or expanded in proportion to the simplicity or variety of the occupations and productions, which are to be found in a Society. It must be less in a nation of mere cultivators, than in a nation of cultivators and merchants; less in a nation of cultivators and merchants, than in a nation of cultivators, artificers and merchants.

VII. As to the creating, in some instances, a new, and securing in all a more certain and steady demand, for the surplus produce of the soil.

This is among the most important of the circumstances which have been indicated. It is a principal mean, by which the establishment of manufactures contributed to an augmentation of the produce or revenue of a country, and has an immediate and direct relation to the prosperity of Agriculture.

It is evident, that the exertions of the husbandman will be steady or fluctuating, vigorous or feeble, in proportion to the steadiness or fluctuation, adequateness, or inadequateness of the markets on which he must depend, for the vent of the surplus, which may be produced by his labour; and that such surplus in the ordinary course of things will be greater or less in the same proportion.

For the purpose of this vent, a domestic market is greatly to be preferred to a foreign one; because it is in the nature of things, far more to be relied upon.

It is a primary object of the policy of nations, to be able to supply themselves with subsistence from their own soils; and manufacturing nations, as far as circumstances permit, endeavor to procure, from the same source, the raw materials necessary for their own fabrics. This disposition, urged by the spirit of monopoly, is sometimes even carried to an injudicious extreme. It seems not always to be recollected, that nations, who have neither mines nor manufactures, can only obtain the manufactured articles, of which they stand in need, by an exchange of the products of their soils; and that, if those who can best furnish them with such articles are unwilling to give a due course to this exchange, they must of necessity make every possible effort to manufacture for themselves, the effect of which is that the manufacturing nations abrige the natural advantages of their situation, through an unwillingness to permit the Agricultural countries to enjoy the advantages of theirs, and sacrifice the interests of a mutually beneficial intercourse to the vain project of *selling every thing and buying nothing.*

But it is also a consequence of the policy, which has been noted, that the foreign demand for the products of Agricultural Countries, is, in a great degree, rather casual and occasional, than certain or constant. To what extent injurious interruptions of the demand for some of the staple commodities of the United States, may have been experienced, from that cause, must be referred to the judgment of those who are engaged in carrying on the commerce of the country; but it may be safely assumed, that such interruptions are at times very inconveniently felt, and that cases not unfrequently occur, in which markets are so confined and restricted, as to render the demand very unequal to the supply.

Independently likewise of the artificial impediments, which are created by the policy in question, there are natural causes tending to render the external demand for the surplus of Agricultural nations a precarious reliance. The differences of seasons, in the countries, which are the consumers make immense differences in the produce of their own soils, in different years; and consequently in the degrees of their necessity for foreign supply. Plentiful harvests with them, especially if similar ones occur at the same time in the countries, which are the furnishers, occasion of course a glut in the markets of the latter.

Considering how fast and how much the progress of new settlements in the United States must increase the surplus produce of the soil, and weighing seriously the tendency of the system, which prevails among most of the commercial nations of Europe; whatever dependence may be placed on the force of national circumstances to counteract the effects of an artificial policy; there appear strong reasons to regard the foreign demand for that surplus as too uncertain a reliance, and to desire a substitute for it, in an extensive domestic market.

To secure such a market, there is no other expedient, than to promote manufacturing establishments. Manufacturers who constitute the most numerous class, after the Cultivators of land, are for that reason the principal consumers of the surplus of their labour.

This idea of an extensive domestic market for the surplus produce of the soil is of the first consequence. It is of all things, that which most effectually conduces to a flourishing state of Agriculture. If the effect of manufactories should be to detach a portion of the hands, which would otherwise be engaged in Tillage, it might possibly cause a smaller quantity of lands to be under cultivation but by their tendency to procure a more certain demand for the surplus produce of the soil, they would, at the same time, cause the lands which were in cultivation to be better improved and more productive. And while, by their influence, the condition of each individual farmer would be meliorated, the total mass of Agricultural production would probably be increased. For this must evidently depend as much, if not more, upon the degree of improvement; than upon the number of acres under culture.

It merits particular observation, that the multiplication of manufactories not only furnishes a Market for those articles, which have been accustomed to be produced in abundance, in a country; but it likewise creates a demand for such as were either unknown or produced in inconsiderable quantities. The bowels as well as the surface of the earth are ransacked for articles which were before neglected. Animals, Plants and Minerals acquire an utility and value, which were before unexplored.

The foregoing considerations seem sufficient to establish, as general propositions, That it is the interest of nations to diversify the industrious pursuits of the individuals, who compose them—That the establishment of manufactures is calculated not only to increase the general stock of useful and productive labour; but even to improve the state of Agriculture in particular; certainly to advance the interests of those who are engaged in it. There are other views, that will be hereafter taken of the subject, which it is conceived, will serve to confirm these inferences.

III Previously to a further discussion of the objections to the encouragement of manufactures which had been stated, it will be of use to see what can be said, in reference to the particular situation of the United States, against the conclusions appearing to result from what has been already offered.

It may be observed, and the idea is of no inconsiderable weight, that however true it might be, that a State, which possessing large tracts of vacant and fertile territory, was at the same time secluded from foreign commerce, would find its interest and the interest of Agriculture, in diverting a part of its population from Tillage to Manufactures; yet it will not follow, that the same is true of a State, which having such vacant and fertile territory, has at the same time ample opportunity of procuring from abroad, on good terms, all the fabrics of which it stands in need, for the supply of its inhabitants. The power of doing this at least secures the great advantage of a division of labour; leaving the farmer free to pursue exclusively the culture of his land, and enabling him to procure with its products the manufactured supplied requisite either to his wants or to his enjoyments. And though it should be true, that in settled countries, the diversification of Industry is conducive to an increase in the productive powers of labour, and to an augmentation of revenue and capital; yet it is scarcely conceivable that there can be any [thing] of so solid and permanent advantage to an uncultivated and unpeopled country as to convert its wastes into cultivated and inhabited districts. If the Revenue, in the mean time, should be less, the Capital, in the event, must be greater.

To these observations, the following appears to be a satisfactory answer—

1. If the system of perfect liberty to industry and commerce were the prevailing system of nations—the arguments which dissuade a country in the predicament of the United States, from the zealous pursuits of manufactures would doubtless have great force. It will not be affirmed, that they might not be permitted, with few exceptions, to serve as a rule of national conduct. In such a state of things, each country would have the full benefit of its peculiar advantages to compensate for its deficiencies or disadvantages. If one nation were in condition to supply manufactured articles on better terms than another, that other might find an abundant indemnification in a superior capacity to furnish the produce of the soil. And a free exchange, mutually beneficial, of the commodities which each was able to supply, on the best terms, might be carried on between them, supporting in full vigour the industry of each. And though the circumstances which have been mentioned and others, which will be unfolded hereafter render it probable, that nations merely Agricultural would not enjoy the same degree of opulence, in proportion to their numbers, as those united manufactures with agriculture: yet the progressive improvement of the lands of the former might, in the end, atone for an inferior degree of opulence in the mean time: and in a case in which opposite considerations are pretty equally balanced, the option ought perhaps always to be, in favour of leaving Industry to its own direction.

But the system which has been mentioned, is far from characterising the general policy of Nations. [The prevalent one has been regulated by an opposite spirit.]

The consequence of it is, that the United States are to a certain extent in the situation of a country precluded from foreign Commerce. They can indeed, without difficulty obtain from abroad the manufactured supplies, of which they are in want; but they experience numerous and very injurious impediments to the emission and vent of their own commodities. Nor is this the case in reference to a single foreign nation only. The regulations of several countries, with which we have the most extensive intercourse, throw serious obstructions in the way of the principal staples of the United States.

In such a position of things, the United States cannot exchange with Europe on equal terms; and the want of reciprocity would render them the victim of a system, which should induce them to confine their views to Agriculture and refrain from Manufactures. A constant and encreasing necessity, on their part, for the commodities of Europe, and only a partial and occasional demand for their own, in return, could not but expose them to a state of impoverishment, compared with the opulence to which their political and natural advantages authorise them to aspire.

Remarks of this kind are not made in the spirit of complaint. 'Tis for the nations, whose regulations are alluded to, to judge for themselves, whether, by aiming at too much they do not lose more than they gain. 'Tis for the United States to consider by what means they can render themselves least dependent, on the combinations, right or wrong of foreign policy.

It is no small consolation, that already the measures which have embarrassed our Trade, have accelerated internal improvements, which upon the whole have bettered our affairs. To diversify and extend these improvements is the surest and safest method of indemnifying ourselves for any inconveniences, which those or similar measures have a tendency to beget. If Europe will not take from us the products of our soil, upon terms consistent with out interest, the natural remedy is to contract as fast as possible our wants of her.

2. The conversion of their waste into cultivated lands is certainly a point of great moment in the political calculations of the United States. But the degree in which this may possibly be retarded by the encouragement of manufactories does not appear to countervail the powerful inducements to affording that encouragement.

An observation made in another place is of a nature to have great influence upon this question. If it cannot be denied, that the interests even of Agriculture may be advanced more by having such of the lands of a state as are occupied under good cultivation, than by having a greater quantity occupied under a must inferior cultivation, and if Manufactories, for the reasons assigned, must be admitted to have a tendency to promote a more steady and vigorous cultivation of the lands occupied than would happen without them— it will follow, that they are capable of indemnifying a country for a diminution of the progress of new settlements; and may serve to increase both the capital [value] and the income of its lands, even though they should abrige the number of acres under Tillage.

But it does, by no means, follow, that the progress of new settlements would be retarded by the extension of Manufactures. The desire of being an independent proprietor of land is founded on such strong principles in the human breast, that where the opportunity of becoming so is as great as it is in the United States, the proportion will be small of those, whose situations would otherwise lead to it, who would be diverted from it towards Manufactures. And it is highly probable, as already intimated, that the accessions of foreigners, who originally drawn over by manufacturing views would afterwards abandon them for Agricultural, would be more than equivalent for those of our own Citizens, who might happen to be detached from them.

The remaining objections to a particular encouragement of manufactures in the United States now require to be examined.

One of these turns on the proposition, that Industry, if left to itself, will naturally find its way to the most useful and profitable employment: whence it is inferred, that manufactures without the aid of government will grow up as soon and as fast, as the natural state of things and the interest of the community may require.

Against the solidity of this hypothesis, in the full latitude of the terms, very cogent reasons may be offered. These have relation to—the strong influence of habit and the spirit of imitation—the fear of want of success in untried enterprises—the intrinsic difficulties incident to first essays towards a competition with those who have previously attained to perfection in the business to be attempted—the bounties premiums and other artificial encouragements, with which foreign nations second the exertions of their own Citizens in the branches, in which they are to be rivalled.

Experience teaches, that men are often so much governed by what they are accustomed to see and practice, that the simplest and most obvious improvements, in the [most] ordinary occupations, are adopted with hesitation, reluctance and by slow graduations. The spontaneous transition to new pursuits, in a community long habituated to different ones, may be expected to be attended with proportionably greater difficulty. When former occupations ceased to yield a profit adequate to the subsistence of their followers, or when there was an absolute deficiency of employment in them, owing to the superabundance of hands, changes would ensue; but these changes would be likely to be more tardy than might consist with the interest either of individuals or of the Society. In many cases they would not happen, while a bare support could be ensured an adherence to ancient courses; though a resort to a more profitable employment might be practicable. To produce the desireable changes, as early as may be expedient, may therefore require the incitement and patronage of government.

The apprehension of failing in new attempts is perhaps a more serious impediment. There are dispositions apt to be attracted by the mere novelty of an undertaking—but these are not always those best calculated to give it success. To this, it is of importance that the confidence of cautious sagacious capitalists both citizens and foreigners, should be excited. And to inspire this description of persons with confidence, it is essential, that they should be made to see in any project, which is new, and for that reason alone, if, for no other, precarious, the prospect of such a degree of countenance and support from government, as may be capable of overcoming the obstacles, inseperable from first experiments.

The superiority antecedently enjoyed by nations, who have preoccupied and perfected a branch of industry, constitutes a more formidable obstacle, than either of those, which have been mentioned, to the introduction of the same branch into a country, in which it did not before exist. To maintain between the recent establishments of one country and the long matured establishments of another country, a competition upon equal terms, both as to quality and price, is in most cases impracticable. The disparity in the one, or in the other, or in both, must necessarily be so considerable as to forbid a successful rivalship, without the extraordinary aid and protection of government.

But the greatest obstacle of all to the successful prosecution of a new branch of industry in a country, in which it was before unknown, consists, as far as the instances apply, in the bounties premiums and other aids which are granted, in a variety of cases, by the nations, in which the establishments to be imitated are previously introduced. It is well known (and particular examples in the course of this report will be cited) that certain nations grant bounties on the exportation of particular commodities, to enable their own workmen to undersell and supplant all competitors, in the countries to which those commodities are sent. Hence the undertakers of a new manufacture have to contend not only with the natural disadvantages of a new undertaking, but with the gratuities and remunerations which other governments bestow. To be enabled to contend with success, it is evident, that the interference and aid of their own government are indispensable.

Combinations by those engaged in a particular branch of business in one country, to frustrate the first efforts to introduce it into another, by temporary sacrifices, recompensed perhaps by extraordinary indemnifications of the government of such country, are believed to have existed, and are not to be regarded as destitute of probability. The existence or assurance of aid from the government of the country, in which the business is to be introduced, may be essential to fortify adventurers against the dread of such combinations, to defeat their effects, if formed and to prevent their being formed, by demonstrating that they must in the end prove fruitless.

Whatever room there may be for an expectation that the industry of a people, under the direction of private interest, will upon equal terms find out the most beneficial employment for itself, there is none for a reliance, that it will struggle against the force of unequal terms, or will of itself surmount all the adventitious barriers to a successful competition, which may have been erected either by the advantages naturally acquired from practice and previous possession of the ground, or by those which may have sprung from positive regulations and an artificial policy. This general reflection might alone suffice as an answer to the objection under examination; exclusively of the weighty considerations which have been particularly urged.

The objections of the pursuit of manufactures in the United States, which next present themselves to discussion, represent an impracticability of success, arising from three causes—scarcity of hands—dearness of labour—want of capital.

The two first circumstances are to a certain extent real, and within due limits, ought to be admitted as obstacles to the success of manufacturing enterprize in the United States. But there are various considerations, which lessen their force, and tend to afford an assurance that they are not sufficient to prevent the advantageous prosecution of many very useful and extensive manufactories.

With regard to scarcity of hands, the fact itself must be applied with no small qualification to certain parts of the United States. There are large districts, which may be considered as pretty fully peopled; and which notwithstanding a continual drain for distant settlement, are thickly interspersed with flourishing and increasing towns. If these districts have not already reached the point, at which the complaint of scarcity of hands ceases, they are not remote from it, and are approaching fast towards it: And having perhaps fewer attractions to agriculture, than some other parts of the Union, they exhibit a proportionally stronger tendency towards other kinds of industry. In these districts, may be discerned, no inconsiderable maturity for manufacturing establishments.

But there are circumstances, which have been already noticed with another view, that materially diminish every where the effect of a scarcity of hands. These circumstances are—the great use which can be made of women and children; on which point a very pregnant and instructive fact has been mentioned—the vast extension given by late improvements to the employment of Machines, which substituting the Agency of fire and water, has prodigiously lessened the necessity for manual labor—the employment of persons ordinarily engaged in other occupations, during the seasons, or hours of leisure; which, besides giving occasion to the exertion of a greater quantity of labour by the same number of persons, and thereby encreasing the general stock of labour, as has been elsewhere remarked, may also be taken into the calculation, as a resource for obviating the scarcity of hands—lastly the attraction of foreign emigrants. Whoever inspects, with a careful eye, the composition of our towns will be made sensible to what an extent this resource may be relied upon. This exhibits a large proportion of ingenious and valuable workmen, in different arts and trades, who, by expatriating from Europe, have improved their own condition, and added to the industry and wealth of the United States. It is a natural inference from the experience, we have already had, that as soon as the United States shall present the countenance of a serious prosecution of Manufactures—as soon as foreign artists shall be made sensible that the state of things here affords a moral certainty of employment and encouragement—competent numbers of European workmen will transplant themselves, effectually to ensure the success of the design. How indeed can it otherwise happen considering the various and powerful inducements, which the situation of this country offers; addressing themselves to so many strong passions and feelings, to so many general and particular interests?

It may be affirmed therefore, in respect to hands for carrying on manufactures, that we shall in a great measure trade upon a foreign Stock; reserving our own, for the cultivation of our lands and the manning of our Ships; as far as character and circumstances [shall] incline. It is not unworthy of remark, that the objection to the success of manufactures, deduced from the scarcity of hands, is alike applicable to Trade and Navigation; and yet these are perceived to flourish, without any sensible impediment from that cause.

As to the dearness of labour (another of the obstacles alledged) this has relation principally to two circumstances, one that which has been just discussed, or the scarcity of hands, the other, the greatness of profits.

As far as it is a consequence of the scarcity of hands, it is mitigated by all the considerations which have been adduced as lessening that deficiency.

It is certain too, that the disparity in this respect, between some of the most manufacturing parts of Europe and a large proportion of the United States, is not nearly so great as is commonly imagined. It is also much less in regard to Artificers and manufacturers than in regard to country labourers; and while a careful comparison shews, that there is, in this particular, much exaggeration; it is also evident that the effect of the degree of disparity, which does truly exist, is diminished in proportion to the use which can be made of machinery.

To illustrate this last idea—Let it be supposed, that the difference of price, in two Countries, of a given quantity of manual labour requisite to the fabrication of a given article is as 10; and that some *mechanic power* is introduced into both countries, which performing half the necessary labour, leaves only half to be done by hand, it is evident, that the difference in the cost of the fabrication of the article in question, in the two countries, as far as it is connected with the price of labour, will be reduced from 10. to 5, in consequence of the introduction of that *power.*

This circumstance is worthy of the most particular attention. It diminishes immensely one of the objections most strenuously urged, against the success of manufactures in the United States.

To procure all such machines as are known in any part of Europe, can only require a proper provision and due pains. The knowledge of several of the most important of them is already possessed. The preparation of them here, is in most cases, practicable on nearly equal terms. As far as they depend on Water, some superiority of advantages may be claimed, from the uncommon variety and greater cheapness of situations adapted to Mill seats, with which different parts of the United States abound.

So far as the dearness of labour may be a consequence of the greatness of profits in any branch of business, it is no obstacle of its success. The Undertaker can afford to pay the price.

There are grounds to conclude the undertakers of Manufacturers in this Country can at this time afford to pay higher wages to the workmen they may employ than are paid to similar workmen in Europe. The prices of foreign fabrics, in the markets of the United States, which will for a long time regulate the prices of the domestic ones, may be considered as compounded of the following ingredients—The first cost of materials, including the Taxes, if any, which are paid upon them where they are made: the expence of grounds, building machinery and tools: the wages of the persons employed in the manufactory: the profits on the capital or Stock employed: the commissions of Agents to purchase them where they are made; the expence of transportation to the United States [including insurance and other incidental charges;] the taxes or duties, if any [and fees of office] which are paid on their exportation: the taxes or duties [and fees of office] which are paid on their importation.

As to the first of these items, the cost of materials, the advantage upon the whole, is at present on the side of the United States, and the difference, in their favor, must increase, in proportion as a certain and extensive domestic demand shall induce the proprietors of land to devote more of their attention to the production of those materials. It ought not to escape observation, in a comparison on this point, that some of the principal manufacturing Countries in Europe are much more dependent on foreign supply for the materials of the manufactures, than would be the United States, who are capable of supplying themselves, with a greater abundance, as well as a greater variety of the requisite materials.

As to the second item, the expence of grounds buildings machinery and tools, an equality at least may be assumed; since advantages in some particulars will counterbalance temporary disadvantages in others.

As to the third item, or the article of wages, the comparison certainly turns against the United States, though as before observed not in so great a degree as is commonly supposed.

The fourth item is alike applicable to the foreign and to the domestic manufacture. It is indeed more properly a *result* than a particular, to be compared.

But with respect to all the remaining items, they are alone applicable to the foreign manufacture, and in the strictest sense extraordinaries; constituting a sum of extra change on the foreign fabric, which cannot be estimated, at less than [from 15 to 30] per Cent. on the cost of it at the manufactory.

This sum of extra charge may confidently be regarded as more than a Counterpoise for the real difference in the price of labour; and is a satisfactory proof that manufactures may prosper in defiance of it in the United States. To the general allegation, connected with the circumstances of scarcity of hands and dearness of labour, that extensive manufactures can only grow out of a redundant or full population, it will be sufficient, to answer generally, that the fact has been otherwise—That the situation alleged to be an essential condition of success, has not been that of several nations, at periods when they had already attained to maturity in a variety of manufactures.

The supposed want of Capital for the prosecution of manufactures in the United States is the most indefinite of the objections which are usually opposed to it.

It is very difficult to pronounce any thing precise concerning the real extent of the monied capital of a Country, and still more concentrating the proportion which it bears to the objects that invite employment of Capital. It is not less difficult to pronounce how far the *effect* of any given quantity of money, as capital, or in other words, as a medium for circulating the industry and property of a nation, may be encreased by the very circumstance of the additional motion, which is given to it by the new objects of employment. That effect, like the momentum of descending bodies, may not improperly be represented, as in a compound ratio to *mass* and *velocity*. It seems pretty certain, that a given sum of money, in a situation, in which the quick impulses of commercial activity were little felt, would appear inadequate to the circulation of as great a quantity of industry and property, as in one, in which their full influence was experienced.

It is not obvious, why the same objection might not as well be made to external commerce as to manufactures; since it is manifest that our immense tracts of land occupied and unoccupied are capable of giving employment to more capital than is actually bestowed upon them. It is certain, that the United States offer a vast field for the advantageous employment of Capital; but it does not follow, that there will not be found, in one way or another, a sufficient fund for the successful prosecution of any species of industry which is likely to prove truly beneficial.

The following considerations are of a nature to remove all inquietude on the score of want of Capital.

The introduction of Banks, as has been shewn on another occasion has a powerful tendency to extend the active Capital of a Country. Experience of the Utility of these Institutions is multiplying them in the United States. It is probable that they will be established wherever they can exist with advantage; and wherever, they can be supported, if administered with prudence, they will add new energies to all pecuniary operations.

The aid of foreign Capital may safely, and, with considerable latitude be taken into calculation. Its instrumentality has been long experienced in our external commerce; and it has begun to be felt in various other modes. Not only our funds, but our Agriculture and other internal improvements have been animated by it. It has already in a few instances extended even to our manufactures.

It is a well known fact, that there are parts of Europe, which have more Capital, than profitable domestic objects of employment. Hence, among other proofs, the large loans continually furnished to foreign states. And it is equally certain that the capital of other parts may find more profitable employment in the United States, than at home. And notwithstanding there are weighty inducements to prefer the employment of capital at home even at less profit, to an investment of it abroad, though with greater gain, yet these inducements are overruled either by a deficiency of employment or by a very material difference in profit. Both these Causes operate to produce a transfer of foreign capital to the United States. 'Tis certain, that various objects in this country hold out advantages, which are with difficulty to be equalled elsewhere; and under the increasingly favorable impressions, which are entertained of our government, the attractions will become more and More strong. These impressions will prove a rich mine of prosperity to the Country, if they are confirmed and strengthened by the progress of our affairs. And to secure this advantage, little more is now necessary, than to foster industry, and cultivate order and tranquility, at home and abroad.

It is not impossible, that there may be persons disposed to look with a jealous eye on the introduction of foreign Capital, as if it were an instrument to deprive our own citizens of the profits of our own industry: But perhaps there never could be a more unreasonable jealousy. Instead of being viewed as a rival, it ought to be Considered as a most valuable auxiliary; conducing to put in Motion a greater Quantity of productive labour, and a greater portion of useful enterprise than could exist without it. It is at least evident, that in a Country situated like the United States, with an infinite fund of resources yet to be unfolded, every farthing of foreign capital, which is laid out in internal ameliorations, and in industrious establishments of a permanent nature, is a precious acquisition.

And whatever be the objects which originally attract foreign Capital, when once introduced, it may be directed towards any purpose of beneficial exertion, which is desired. And to detain it among us, there can be no expedient so effectual as to enlarge the sphere, within which it may be usefully employed: Though induced merely with views to speculations in the funds, it may afterwards be rendered subservient to the Interests of Agriculture, Commerce & Manufactures.

But the attraction of foreign Capital for the direct purpose of Manufactures ought not to be deemed a chimerial expectation. There are already examples of it, as remarked in another place. And the examples, if the disposition be cultivated can hardly fail to multiply. There are also instances of another kind, which serve to strengthen the expectation. Enterprises for improving the Public Communications, by cutting canals, opening the obstructions in Rivers and erecting bridges, have received very material aid from the same source.

When the Manufacturing Capitalist of Europe shall advert to the many important advantages, which have been intimated, in the Course of this report, he cannot but perceive very powerful inducements to a transfer of himself and his Capital to the United States. Among the reflections, which a most interesting peculiarity of situation is calculated to suggest, it cannot escape his observation, as a circumstance of Moment in the calculation, that the progressive population and improvement of the United States, insure a continually increasing domestic demand for the fabrics which he shall produce, not to be affected by any external casualties or vicissitudes.

But while there are Circumstances sufficiently strong to authorise a considerable degree of reliance on the aid of foreign Capital towards the attainment of the object in view, it is satisfactory to have good grounds of assurance, that there are domestic resources of themselves adequate to it. It happens, that there is a species of Capital actually existing within the United States, which relieves from all inquietude on the score of want of Capital—This is the funded Debt.

The effect of a funded debt, as a species of Capital, has been Noticed upon a former Occasion; but a more particular elucidation of the point seems to be required by the stress which is here laid upon it. This shall accordingly be attempted.

Public Funds answer the purpose of Capital, from the estimation in which they are usually held by Monied men; and consequently from the Ease and dispatch with which they can be turned into money. This capacity of prompt convertibility into money causes a transfer of stock to be in a great number of Cases equivalent to a payment in coin. And where it does not happen to suit the party who is to receive, to accept a transfer of Stock, the party who is to pay, is never at a loss to find elsewhere a purchaser of his Stock, who will furnish him in lieu of it, with the Coin of which he stands in need. Hence in a sound and settled state of the public funds, a man possessed of a sum in them can embrace any scheme of business, which offers, with as much confidence as if he were possessed of an equal sum in Coin.

This operation of public funds as capital is too obvious to be denied; but it is objected to the Idea of their operating as an *augmentation* of the Capital of the community, that they serve to occasion the *destruction* of some other capital to an equal amount.

The Capital which alone they can be supposed to destroy must consist of—The annual revenue, which is applied to the payment of Interest on the debt, and to the gradual redemption of the principal—The amount of the Coin, which is employed in circulating the funds, or, in other words, in effecting the different alienations which they undergo.

But the following appears to be the true and accurate view of this matter.

1st. As to the point of the Annual Revenue requisite for Payment of interest and redemption of principal.

As a determinate proportion will tend to perspicuity in the reasoning, let it be supposed that the annual revenue to be applied, corresponding with the modification of the 6 per Cent stock of the United States, is in the ratio of eight upon the hundred, that is in the first instance six on Account of interest, and two on account of Principal.

Thus far it is evident, that the Capital destroyed to the capital created, would bear no greater proportion, than 8 to 100. There would be withdrawn from the total mass of other capitals a sum of eight dollars to be paid to the public creditor; while he would be possessed of a sum of One Hundred dollars, ready to be applied to any purpose, to be embarked in any enterprize, which might appear to him eligible. Here then the *Augmentation* of Capital, or the excess of that which is produced, beyond that which is destroyed is equal to Ninety two dollars. To this conclusion, it may be objected, that the sum of Eight dollars is to be withdrawn annually, until the whole hundred is extinguished, and it may be inferred, that in the process of time a capital will be destroyed equal to that which is at first created.

But it is nevertheless true, that during the whole of the interval, between the creation of the Capital of 100 dollars, and its reduction to a sum not greater than that of the annual revenue appropriated to its redemption—there will be a greater active capital in existence than if no debt had been Contracted. The sum drawn from other Capitals *in any one year* will not exceed eight dollars; but there will be *at every instance of time* during the whole period, in question a sum corresponding *with so much of the principal*, as remains *unredeemed*, in the hands of some person, or other, employed, or ready to be employed in some profitable undertaking. There will therefore constantly be more capital, in capacity to be employed, than capital taken from employment. The excess for the first year has been stated to be Ninety two dollars; it will diminish yearly, but there always will be an excess, until the principal of the debt is brought to a level with the *redeeming annuity*, that is, in the case which has been assumed by way of example, to *eight dollars*. The reality of this excess becomes palpable, if it is supposed, as often happens, that the citizen of a foreign Country imports into the United States 100 dollars for the purchase of an equal sum of public debt. Here is an absolute augmentation of the mass of Circulating Coin to the extent of 100 dollars. At the end of a year the foreigner is presumed to draw back eight dollars on account of his Principal and Interest, but he still leaves, Ninety two of his original Deposit in circulation, as he in like manner leaves Eighty four at the end of the second year, drawing back then also the annuity of Eight Dollars: And thus the Matter proceeds; The capital left in circulation diminishing each year, and coming nearer to the level of the annuity drawnback. There are however some differences in the ultimate operation of the part of the debt, which is purchased by foreigners, and that which remains in the hands of citizens. But the general effect in each case, though in different degrees, is to add to the active capital of the Country.

Hitherto the reasoning has proceeded on a concession of the position, that there is a destruction of some other capital, to the extent of the annuity appropriated to the payment of the Interest and the redemption of the principal of the deb(t) but in this, too much has been conceded. There is at most a temp(orary) transfer of some other capital, to the amount of the Annuity, from those who pay to the Creditor who receives; which he again restor(es) to the circulation to resume the offices of capital. This he does ei(ther) immediately by employing the money in some branch of Industry, or mediately by lending it to some other person, who does so employ (it) or by spending it on his own maintenance. In either sup(position) there is no destruction of capital, there is nothing more (than a) suspension of its motion for a time; that is, while it is (passing) from the hands of those who pay into the Public coffers, & thence (through) the public Creditor into some other Channel of circulation. (When) the payments of interest are periodical and quick and made by instrumentality of Banks the diversion or suspension of capita(l) may almost be denominated momentary. Hence the deduction on this Account is far less, than it at first sight appears to be.

There is evidently, as far as regards the annuity no destruction nor transfer of any other Capital, than that por(tion) of the income of each individual, which goes to make up the Annuity. The land which furnishes the Farmer with the s(um) which he is to contribute remains the same; and the like m(ay) be observed of other Capitals. Indeed as far as the Tax, w(hich) is the object of contribution (as frequently happens, when it doe(s) not oppress, by its weight) may have been a Motive to *greate(r) exertion* in any occupation; it may even serve to encrease the contributory Capital: This idea is not without importanc(e) in the general view of the subject.

It remains to see, what further deduction out to be mad(e) from the capital which is created, by the existence of the Debt; on account of the coin, which is employed in its circulation. This is susceptible of much less precise calculation, than the Article which has been just discussed. It is impossible to say what proportion of coin in necessary to carry on the alienations which any species of property usually undergoes. The quantity indeed varies according to circumstances. But it may still without hesitation be pronounced, from the quickness of the rotation, or rather of the transitions, that the *medium* of circulation always bears but a small proportion to the amount of the *property* circulated. And it is thence satisfactorily deductible, that the coin employed in the Negociations of the funds and which serves to give them activity, as capital, is incomparably less than the sum of the debt negotiated for the purposes of business.

It ought not, however, to be omitted, that the negotiation of the funds becomes itself a distinct business; which employs, and by employing diverts a portion of the circulating coin from other pursuits. But making due allowance for this circumstance there is no reason to conclude, that the effect of the diversion of coin in the whole operation bears any considerable proportion to the amount of the Capital to which it gives activity. The sum of the debt in circulation is continually at the Command, of any useful enterprise—the coin itself which circulates it, is never more than momentarily suspended from its ordinary functions. It experiences an incessant and rapid flux and reflux to and from the Channels of industry to those of speculations in the funds.

There are strong circumstances in confirmation of this Theory. The force of Monied Capital which has been displayed in Great Britain, and the height to which every species of industry has grown up under it, defy a solution from the quantity of coin which that kingdom has ever possessed. Accordingly it has been Coeval with its funding system, the prevailing opinion of the men of business, and of the generality of the most sagacious theorists of that country, that the operation of the public funds as capital has contributed to the effect in question. Among ourselves appearances this far favour the same Conclusion. Industry in general seems to have been reanimated. There are symptoms indicating an extension of our Commerce. Our navigation has certainly of late had a Considerable spring, and there appears to be in many parts of the Union a command of capital, which till lately, since the revolution at least, was unknown. But it is at the same time to be acknowledged, that other circumstances have concurred, (and in a great degree) in producing the present state of things, and that the appearances are not yet sufficiently decisive, to be entirely relied upon.

In the question under discussion, it is important to distinguish between an *absolute increase of Capital, or an accession of real wealth*, and *an artificial increase of Capital*, as an engine of business, or as an instrument of industry and Commerce. In the first sense, a funded debt has no pretensions to being deemed an increase in Capital; in the last, it has pretensions which are not easy to be controverted. Of a similar nature is bank credit and in an inferior degree, every species of private credit.

But though a funded debt is not in the first instance, an absolute increase of Capital, or an augmentation of real wealth; yet by serving as a New power in the operation of industry, it has within certain bounds a tendency to increase the real wealth of a Community, in like manner as money borrowed by a thrifty farmer, to be laid out in the improvement of his farm may, in the end, add to his Stock of real riches.

There are respectable individuals, who from a just aversion to an accumulation of Public debt, are unwilling to concede to it any kind of utility, who can discern no good to alleviate the ill with which they suppose it pregnant; who cannot be persuaded that it ought in any sense to be viewed as an increase of capital lest it should be inferred, that the more debt the more capital, the greater the burthens the greater the blessings of the community.

But it interests the public Councils to estimate every object as it truly is; to appreciate how far the good in any measure is compensated by the ill; or the ill by the good, Either of them is seldom unmixed.

Neither will it follow, that an accumulation of debt is desirable, because a certain degree of it operates as capital. There may be a plethora in the political, as in the Natural body; There may be a state of things in which any such artificial capital is unnecessary. The debt too may be swelled to such a size, as that the greatest part of it may cease to be useful as a Capital, serving only to pamper the dissipation of idle and dissolute individuals: as that the sums required to pay the Interest upon it may become oppressive, and beyond the means, which a government can employ, consistently with its tranquility, to raise them; as that the resources of taxation, to face the debt, may have been strained too far to admit of extensions adequate to exigencies, which regard the public safety.

Where this critical point is, cannot be pronounced, but it is impossible to believe, that there is not such a point.

And as the vicissitudes of Nations beget a perpetual tendency to the accumulation of debt, there ought to be in every government a perpetual, anxious and unceasing effort to reduce that, which at any time exists, as fast as shall be practicable consistently with integrity and good faith.

Reasonings on a subject comprehending ideas so abstract and complex, so little reducible to precise calculation as those which enter into the question just discussed, are always attended with a danger of running into fallacies. Due allowance ought therefore to be made for this possibility. But as far as the Nature of the subject admits of it, there appears to be satisfactory ground for a belief, that the public funds operate as a resource of capital to the Citizens of the United States, and, if they are a resource at all, it is an extensive one.

To all the arguments which are brought to evince the impracticability of success in manufacturing establishments in the United States, it might have been a sufficient answer to have referred to the experience of what has been already done. It is certain that several important branches have grown up and flourished with a rapidity which surprises: affording an encouraging assurance of success in future attempts: of these it may not be improper to enumerate the most considerable.

I. Of Skins.	Tanned and tawed leather dressed skins, shoes, boots and Slippers, harness and sadlery of all kinds. Portmanteau's and trunks, leather breeches, gloves, muffs and tippets, parchment and Glue.
II. Of Iron.	Barr and Sheet Iron, Steel, Nail—rods & Nails, implem(ents) of husbandry, Stoves, pots and other household utensils, the steel and Iron work of carriages and for Shipbuildin(g,) Anchors, scale beams and Weights & Various tools of Artificers, arms of different kinds; though the manufacture of these last has of late diminished for want of demand.
III. Of Wood.	Ships Cabinet Wares and Turnery, Wool and Cotton ca(rds) and other Machinery for manufactures and husband(ry,) Mathematical instruments, Coopers wares of every kind.
IV. Of flax & Hemp.	Cables, sail-cloth, Cordage, Twine and pack-thread.
V.	Bricks and course tiles & Potters Wares.
VI.	Ardent Spirits, and malt liquors.
VII.	Writing and printing Paper, sheathing and wrapping Paper, pasteboards, fillers or press papers, paper hangings.
VIII.	Hats of furr and Wool and of mixtures of both, Womens Stuff and Silk shoes.
IX.	Refined Sugars.
X.	Oils of Animals and seeds; Soap, Spermaceti and Tallow Candles.
XI.	Copper and brass wares, particularly utensils for distillers, Sugar refiners and brewers, And—Irons and other Articles for household Use, philosophical apparatus.
XII.	Tin Wares, for most purposes of Ordinary use.
XIII.	Carriages of all kinds

XIV.	Snuff, chewing & smoking Tobacco.
XV.	Starch and Hairpowder.
XVI.	Lampblack and other painters colours.
XVII.	Gunpowder

Besides manufactories of these articles which are carried on as regular Trades, and have attained to a considerable degree of maturity, there is a vast scene of household manufacturing, which contributes more largely to the supply of the Community, than could be imagined; without having made it an object of particular enquiry. This observation is the pleasing result of the investigation, to which the subject of the report has led, and is applicable as well to the Southern as to the middle and Northern States; great quantities of coarse cloths, coatings, serges, and flannels, linsey Woolseys, hosiery of Wool, cotton & thread, coarse fustians, jeans and Muslins, check(ed) and striped cotton and linen goods, bed ticks, Coverlets and Counterpanes, Tow linens, coarse shirtings, sheetings, toweling and table linen, and various mixtures of wool and cotton, and of Cotton & flax are made in the household way, and in many instances to an extent not only sufficient for the supply of the families in which they are made, but for sale, and (even in some cases) for exportation. It is computed in a number of districts the 2/3 3/4 and even 4/5 of all the clothing of the Inhabitants are made by themselves. The importance of so great a progress, as appears to have been made in family Manufactures, within a few years, both in a moral and political view, renders the fact highly interesting.

Neither does the above enumeration comprehend all the articles, that are manufactured as regular Trades. Many others occur, which are equally well established, but which not being of equal importance have been omitted. And there are many attempts still in their Infancy, which though attended with very favorable appearances, could not have been properly comprized in an enumeration of manufactories, already established. There are other articles also of great importance, which tho' strictly speaking manufactures are omitted, as being immediately connected with husbandry: such are flour, pot & pearl ash, Pitch, tar, turpentine and the like.

There remains to be noticed an objection to the encouragement of manufactures, of a nature different from those which question the probability of success. This is derived from its supposed tendency to give a monopoly of advantages to particula(r) classes at the expence of the rest of the community, who, it is affirmed, would be able to procure the requisite supplies of manufactured articles on better terms from foreigners, than from our own Citizens, and who it is alledged, are reduced to a necessity of paying an enhanced price for whatever they want, by every measure, which obstructs the free competition of foreign commodi(es).

It is not an unreasonable supposition, that measures, which serve to abridge the free competition of foreign Articles, have a tendency to occasion an enhancement of prices and it is not to be denied that such is the effect in a number of Cases, but the fact does not uniformly correspond with the theory. A reduction of prices has in several instances immediately succeeded the establishment of a domestic manufacture. Whether it be that foreign Manufacturers endeavor to suppla(nt) by underselling our own, or whatever else be the cause, the effect has been such as is stated, and the reverse of what mig(ht) have been expected.

But though it were true, that the immedi(ate) and certain effect of regulations controuling the competition of foreign with domestic fabrics was an increase of price, it is universally true, that the contrary is the ultimate effect with every successful manufacture. When a domestic manufacture has attainted to perfection, and has engaged in the prosecution of it a competent number of Persons, it invariably becomes cheaper. Being free from the heavy charges, which attend the importation of foreign commodities, it can be afforded, and accordingly seldom or never fails to be sold Cheaper, in process of time, than was the foreign Article for which it is a substitute. The internal competition, which takes place, soon does away every thing like Monopoly, and by degrees reduces the price of the Article to the *minimum* of a reasonable profit on the Capital employed. This accords with the reason of the thing and with experience.

Whence it follows, that it is the interest of a community with a view to eventual and permanent œconomy, to encourage the growth of manufactures. In a national view, a temporary enhancement of price must always be well compensated by a permanent reduction of it.

It is a reflection, which may with propriety be indulged here, that this eventual diminution of the prices of manufactured Articles; which is the result of internal manufacturing establishments, has a direct and very important tendency to benefit agriculture. It enables the farmer, to procure with a smaller quantity of his labour, the manufactured produce of which he stan(ds) in need, and consequently increases the value of his income and property.

The objections which are commonly made to the expediency of encouraging, and to the probability of succeeding in manufacturing pursuits, in the United states, having now been discussed; the Considerations which have appeared in the Course of the discussion, recommending that species of industry to the patronage of the Government, will be materially strengthened by a few general and some particular topics, which have been naturally reserved for subsequent Notice.

I There seems to be a moral certainty, that the trade of a country which is both manufacturing and Agricultural will be more lucrative and prosperous, than that of a Counry, which is, merely Agricultural.

One reason for this is found in that general effort of nations (which has been already mentioned) to procure from their own soils, the articles of prime necessity requisite to their own consumption and use; and which serves to render their demand for a foreign supply of such articles in a great degree occasional and contingent. Hence, while the necessities of nations exclusively devoted to Agriculture, for the fabrics of manufacturing st(ates) are constant and regular, the wants of the latter for the products of the former, are liable to very considerable fluctuations and interruptions. The great inequalities resulting from difference of seasons, have been elsewhere remarked: This uniformity of deman(d) on one side, and unsteadiness of it, on the other, must necessarily ha(ve) a tendency to cause the general course of the exchange of commodit(ies) between the parties to turn to the disadvantage of the merely agricultural States. Peculiarity of situation, a climate and soil ada(pted) to the production of peculiar commodities, may, sometimes, contradi(ct) in the rule; but there is every reason to believe that it will be fou(nd) in the Main, a just one.

Another circumstance which gives a superiority of commercial advantages to states, that manufact(ure) as well as cultivate, consists in the more numerous attractions, which a more diversified market offers to foreign Customers, and greater scope, which it affords to mercantile enterprise. It is (a) position of indisputable truth in Commerce, depending too on very obvious reasons, that the greatest resort will ever be to those mar(ts) where commodities, while equally abundant, are most various. Each difference of kind holds out an additional inducement. And it is a position not less clear, that the field of enterprise must be enlarged to the Merchants of a Country, in proportion (to) the variety as well as the abundance of commodities which they find at home for exportation to foreign Markets.

A third circumstance, perhaps not inferior to either of the other two, conferring the superiority which has been stated has relation to the stagnations of demand for certain commodities which at some time or other interfere more or less with the sale of all. The Nation which can bring to Market, but few articles is likely to be more quickly and sensibly affected by such stagnations, than one, which is always possessed of a great variety of commodities. The former frequently finds too great a proportion of its stock of materials, for sale or exchange, lying on hand—or is obliged to make injurious sacrifices to supply its wants of foreign articles, which are *Numerous* and *urgent* in proportion to the smallness of he number of its own. The latter commonly finds itself indemnified, by the high prices of some articles, for the low prices of others— and the Prompt and advantageous sale of those articles which are in demand enables its merchant the better to wait for a favorable change, in respect to those which are not. There is ground to believe, that a difference of situation, in this particular, has immensely different effect(ts) upon the wealth and prosperity of Nations.

From these circumstances collectively, two important inferences are to be drawn, one, that there is always a higher probability of a favorable balance of Trade, in regard to countries in which manufactures founded on the basis of a thriving Agriculture flourish, than in regard to those, which are confined wholly or almost wholly to Agriculture; the other (which is also a consequence of the first) that countries of the former description are likely to possess more pecuniary wealth, or money, than those of the later.

Facts appear to correspond with this conclusion. The importations of manufactured supplies seem invariably to drain the merely Agricultural people of their wealth. Let the situation of the manufacturing countries of Europe be compared in this particular, with that of Countries which only cultivate, and the disparity will be striking. Other causes, it is true, help to Account for this disparity between some of them; and among these causes, the relative state of Agriculture; but between others of them, the most prominent circumstance of dissimilitude arises from the Comparative state of Manufactures. In corroboration of the same idea, it ought not to escape remark, that the West India Islands, the soils of which are the most fertile, and the Nation, which in the greatest degree supplies the rest of the world, with the precious metals, exchange to a loss with almost every other Country.

As far as experience at home may guide, it will lead to the same conclusion. Previous to the revolution, the quantity of coin, possessed by the colonies, which now compose the United states, appeared, to be inadequate to their circulation; and their debt to Great-Britain was progressive. Since the Revolution, the States, in which manufactures have most increased, have recovered fastest from the injuries of the late War, and abound most in pecuniary resources.

It ought to be admitted, however in this as in the preceding case, that causes irrelative to the state of manufactures account, in a degree, for the Phœnomena remarked. The continual progress of new settlements has a natural tendency to occasion an unfavorable balance of Trade; though it indemnifies for the inconvenience, by that increase of the national capital which flows from the conversion of waste into improved lands: And the different degrees of external commerce, which are carried on by the different States, may make material differences in the comparative state of their wealth. The first circumstance has reference to the deficien(cy) of coin and the increase of debt previous to the revolution; the last to the advantages which the most manufacturing states appear to have enjoyed, over the others, since the termination of the late War.

But the uniform appearance of an abundance of specie, as the concomitant of a flourishing state of manufacture(s) and of the reverse, where they do not prevail, afford a strong presumption of their favourable operations upon the wealth of a Country.

Not only the wealth; but the independence and security of a Country, appear to be materially connected with the prosperity of manufactures. Every nation, with a view to those great objects, ought to endeavor to possess within itself all the essentials of national supply. These comprise the means of *Subsistence habitation clothing* and *defence.*

The possession of these is necessary to the perfection of the body politic, to the safety as well as to the welfare of the society; the want of either, is the want of an important organ of political life and Motion; and in the various crises which await a state, it must severely feel the effects of such deficiency. The extreme embarrassments of the United States during the late War, from an incapacity of supplying themselves, are still matter of keen recollection: A future war might be expected again to exemplify the mischiefs and dangers of a situation, to which that incapacity is still in too great a degree applicable, unless changed by timely and vigorous exertion. To effect this change as fast as shall be prudent, merits all the attention and all the Zeal of our Public Councils; 'tis the next great work to be accomplished.

The want of a Navy to protect our external commerce, as long as it shall Continue, must render it a peculiarly precarious reliance, for the supply of essential articles, and must serve to strengthen prodigiously the arguments in favour of manufactures.

To these general Considerations are added some of a more particular nature.

Our distance from Europe, the great fountain of manufactured supply, subjects us in the existing state of things, to inconvenience and loss in two Ways.

The bulkiness of those commodities which are the chief productions of the soil, necessarily imposes very heavy charges on their transportation, to distant markets. These charges, in the Cases, in which the nations, to whom our products are sent, maintain a Competition in the supply of their own markets, principally fall upon us, and form material deductions from the primitive value of the articles furnished. The charges on manufactured supplies, brought from Europe are greatly enhanced by the same circumstance of distance. These charges, again, in the cases in which our own industry maintains no competition, in our own markets, also principally fall upon us; and are an additional cause of extraordinary deduction from the primitive value of our own products; these bei(ng) the materials of exchange for the foreign fabrics, which we consume.

The equality and moderation of individual prope(rty) and the growing settlements of new districts, occasion in this country an unusual demand for coarse manufactures; The charges of which being greater in proportion to their greater bulk augment the disadvantage, which has been just described.

As in most countries domestic supplie(s) maintain a very considerable competition with such foreign productions of the soil, as are imported for sale; if the extensive establishment of Manufactories in the United states does not create a similar competition in respect to manufactured articles, it appears to be clearly deducible, from the Considerations which have been mentioned, that they must sustain a double loss in their exchanges with foreign Nations; strongly conducive to an unfavorable balance of Trade, and very prejudicial to their Interests.

These disadvantages press with no small weight, on the landed interest of the Country. In seasons of peace, they cause a serious deduction from the intrinsic value of the products of the soil. In the time of a War, which shou'd either involve ourselves, or another nation, possessing a Considerable share of our carrying trade, the charges on the transportation of our commodities, bulky as most of them are, could hardly fail to prove a grievous burthen to the farmer; while obliged to depend in so great degree as he now does, upon foreign markets for the vent of the surplus of his labour.

As far as the prosperity of the Fisheries of the United states is impeded by the want of an adequate market, there arises another special reason for desiring the extension of manufactures. Besides the fish, which in many places, would be likely to make a part of the subsistence of the persons employed; it is known that the oils, bones and skins of marine animals, are of extensive use in various manufactures. Hence the prospect of an additional demand for the produce of the Fisheries.

One more point of view only remains in which to Consider the expediency of encouraging manufactures in the United states.

It is not uncommon to meet with an opin(ion) that though the promoting of manufactures may be the interest of a part of the Union, it is contrary to that of another part. The Northern & southern regions are sometimes represented as having adverse interests in this respect. Those are called Manufacturing, these Agricultural states; and a species of opposition is imagined to subsist between the Manufacturing a(nd) Agricultural interests.

This idea of an opposition between those two interests is the common error of the early periods of every country, but experience gradually dissipates it. Indeed they are perceived so often to succour and to befriend each other, that they come at length to be considered as one: a supposition which has been frequently abused and is not universally true. Particular encouragements of particular manufactures may be of a Nature to sacrifice the interests of landholders to those of manufacturers; But it is nevertheless a maxim well established by experience, and generally acknowledged, where there has been sufficient experience, that the *aggregate* prosperity of manufactures, and the *aggregate* prosperity of Agriculture are intimately connected. In the Course of the discussion which has had place, various weighty considerations have been adduced operating in support of that maxim. Perhaps the superior steadiness of the demand of a domestic market for the surplus produce of the soil, is alone a convincing argument of its truth.

Ideas of a contrariety of interests between the Northern and southern regions of the Union, are in the Main as unfounded as they are mischievous. The diversity of Circumstances on which such contrariety is usually predicated, authorises a directly contrary conclusion. Mutual wants constitute one of the strongest links of political connection, and the extent of the(se) bears a natural proportion to the diversity in the means of mutual supply.

In proportion as the mind is accustomed to trace the intimate connexion of interest, which subsists between all the parts of a Society united under the *same* government—the infinite variety of channels which serve to Circulate the prosper(ity) of each to and through the rest—in that proportion will it be little apt to be disturbed by solicitudes and Apprehensions which originate in local discriminations. It is a truth as important as it is agreeable, and one to which it is not easy to imagine exceptions, that every thing tending to establish *substantial* and *permanent order*, in the affairs of a Country, to increase the total mass of industry and opulence, is ultimately beneficial to every part of it. On the Credit of this great truth, an acquiescence may safely be accorded, from every quarter, to all institutions & arrangements, which promise a confirmation of public order, and an augmentation of National Resource.

But there are more particular considerations which serve to fortify the idea, that the encouragement of manufactures in the interest of all parts of the Union. If the Northern and middle states should be the principal scenes of such establishments, they would immediately benefit the more southern, by creating a demand for productions; some of which they have in common with the other states, and others of which are either peculiar to them, or more abundant, or of better quality, than elsewhere. These productions, principally are Timber, flax, Hemp, Cotton, Wool, raw silk, Indigo, iron, lead, furs, hides, skins and coals. Of these articles Cotton & Indigo are peculiar to the southern states; as are hitherto *Lead & Coal*. Flax and Hemp are or may be raised in greater abundance there, than in the More Northern states, and the Wool of Virginia is said to be of better quality than that of any other state: a Circumstance rendered the more probable by the reflection that Virginia embraces the same latitudes with the finest Wool Countries of Europe. The Climate of the south is also better adapted to the production of silk.

The extensive cultivation of Cotton can perhaps hardly be expected, but from the previous establishment of domestic Manufactories of the Article; and the surest encouragement and vent, for the others, would result from similar establishments in respect to them.

If then, it satisfactorily appears, that it is the Interest of the United states, generally, to encourage manufactures, it merits particular attention, that there are circumstances, which Render the present a critical moment for entering with Zeal upon the important business. The effort cannot fail to be materially seconded by a considerable and encreasing influx of money, in consequence of foreign speculations in the funds— and by the disorders, which exist in different parts of Europe.

The first circumstance not only facilita(tes) the execution of manufacturing enterprises; but it indicates them as a necessary mean to turn the thing itself to advantage, and to prevent its being eventually an evil. If useful employment be not found for the Money of foreigners brought to the country to be invested (i)n purchase(s) of the public debt, it will quickly be reexported to defray the expence of an extraordinary consumption of foreign luxuries; and distressing drains of our specie may hereafter be experienced to pay the interest and redeem the principal of the purchased debt.

This useful employment too ought to be of a Nature to produce solid and permanent improvements. If the money merely serves to give temporary spring to foreign commerce; as it cannot procure new and lasting outlets for the products of the Country; there will be no real or durable advantage gained. As far as it shall find its way in Agricultural ameliorations, in opening canals, and in similar improvements, it will be productive of substantial utility. But there is reason to doubt, whether in such channels it is likely to find sufficient employment, and still more whether many of those who possess it, would be as readily attracted to objects of this nature, as to manufacturing pursuits; which bear greater analogy to those to which they are accustomed, and to the spirit generated by them.

To open the one field, as well as the other, will at least secure a better prospect of useful employment, for whatever accession of money, there has been or may be.

There is at the present juncture a certain fermentation of mind, a certain activity of speculation and enterprise which if properly directed may be made subservient to useful purposes; but which if left entirely to itself, may be attended with pernicious effects.

The disturbed state of Europe, inclining its citizens to emigration, the requisite workmen, will be more easily acquired, than at another time; and the effect of multiplying the opportunities of employment to those who emigrate, may be an increase of the number and extent of valuable acquisitions to the population arts and industry of the Country. To find pleasure in the calamities of other nations, would be criminal; but to benefit ourselves, by opening an asylum to those who suffer, in consequence of them, is as justifiable as it is pol(itic.)

A full view having now been taken of the inducements to the promotion of Manufactures in the United states, accompanied with an examination of the principal objections which are commonly urged *in opposition*, it is proper in the next place, to consider the means, by which it may be effected, as introductory to a Specification of the objects which in the present state of things appear the most fit to be encouraged, and of the particular measures which it may be adviseable to adopt, in respect to each.

In order to a better judgment of the Means proper to be resorted to by the United states, it will be of use to Advert to those which have been employed with success in other Countries. The principal of these are.

I Protecting duties—or duties on those foreign articles which are the rivals of the domestic ones, intended to be encouraged.

Duties of this Nature evidently amount to a virtual bounty on the domestic fabrics since by enhancing the charges on foreign Articles, they enable the National Manufacturers to undersell all their foreign Competitors. The propriety of this species of encouragement need not be dwelt upon; as it is not only a clear result from the numerous topics which have been suggested, but is sanctioned by the laws of the United states in a variety of instances; it has the additional recommendat(ion) of being a resource of revenue. Indeed all the duties imposed on imported articles, though with an exclusive view to Revenue, have the effect in Contemplation, and except where they fall on raw materials wear a beneficent aspect towards the manufactures of the Country.

II Prohibitions of rival articles or duties equivalent to prohibitions.

This is another and an efficacious mean of encouraging national manufactures, but in general it is only fit to be employed when a manufacture, has made such a progress and is in so many hands as to insure a due competition, and an adequate supply on reasonable terms. Of duties equivalent to prohibitions, there are examples in the Laws of the United States, and there are other Cases to which the principle may be advantageously extended, but they are not numero(us).

Considering a monopoly of the domestic market to its own manufacturers as the reigning policy of manufacturing Nations, a similar policy on the part of the United states in every proper instance, is directed, it might almost be said, by the principles of distributive justice; certainly by the duty of endeavouring to secure to their own Citizens a reciprocity of advantages.

III Prohibitions of the exportation of the materials of manufactures.

The desire of securing a cheap and plentiful supply for the national workmen, and, where the article is either peculiar to the Country, or a peculiar quality there, the jealousy of enabling foreign workmen to rival those of the nation, with its ow(n) Materials, are the leading motives to this species of regulation. (It) ought not to be affirmed, that it is in no instance proper, but it is certainly one which ought to be adopted with great circumspect(ion) and only in very plain Cases. It is seen at once, that its immedi(ate) operation, is to abridge the demand and keep down the price of the produce of some other branch of industry, generally speaking, of Agriculture, to the prejudice of those, who carry it on; and tho(ough) if it be really essential to the prosperity of any very important nati(onal) Manufacture, it may happen that those who are injured in the first instance, may be eventually indemnified, by the superior (steadiness) of an extensive domestic market, depending on that prosperity; yet in a matter, in which there is so much room for nice and difficult combinations, in which such considerations combat each other, prudence seems to dictate, that the expedient in question, ought to be indulged with a sparing hand.

IV Pecuniary bounties

This has been found one of the most efficacious means of encouraging manufactures, and it is in some views, the best. Though it has not yet been practiced by the

Government of the United states (unless the allowance on the exportation of dried an pickled Fish and salted meat could be considered as a bounty) and though it is less favored by public opinion that some other modes.

Its advantages, are these—

1. It is a species of encouragement more positive and direct than any other, and for that very reason, has a more immediate tendency to stimulate and uphold new enterprises, increasing the chances of profit, and diminishing the risks of loss, in the first attempts.

2. It avoids the inconvenience of a temporary augmentation of price, which is incident to some other modes, or it produces it to a less degree; either by making no addition to the charges on the rival foreign article, as in the Case of protecting duties, or by making a small addition. The first happens when the fund for the bounty is derived from a different object (which may or may not increase the price of some other article, according to the nature of that object) the second, when the fund is derived from the same or a similar object of foreign manufacture. One per cent duty on the foreign article converted into a bounty on the domestic, will have an equal effect with a duty of two per Cent, exclusive of such bounty; and the price of the foreign commodity is liable to be raised, in the one Case, in the proportion of 1 per Cent; in the other, in that of two per Cent. Indeed the bounty when drawn from another source is calculated to promote a reduction of price, because without laying any new charge on the foreign article, it serves to introduce a competition with it, and to increase the total quantity of the article in the Market.

3. Bounties have not like high protecting duties, a tendency to produce scarcity. An increase of price is not always the immediate, though, where the progress of a domestic Manufacture does not counteract a rise, it is commonly the ultimate effect of an additional duty. In the interval, between the laying of the duty and a proportional increase of price, it may discourage importation, by interfering with the profits to be expected from the sale of the article.

4. Bounties are sometimes not only the best, but the only proper expedient, for uniting the encouragement of a new object of agriculture, with that of a new object of manufacture. It is the Interest of the farmer to have the production of the raw material promoted, by counteracting the interference of the foreig(n) material of the same kind. It is the interest of the manufactu(rer) to have the material abundant and cheap. If prior to the domes(tic) production of the Material, in sufficient quantity, to supply the manufacturer on good terms; a duty be laid upon the importation of it from abroad, with a view to promote the raising of it at home, the Interests both of the Farmer and Manufacturer will be disserved. By either destroying the requisite supply, or raising the price of the article, beyond what can be afforded to be given for it, by the Conductor of an infant manufacture it is abandoned or fails; an(d) there being no domestic manufactories to create a demand for t(he) raw material, which is raised

by the farmer, it is in vain, that the Competition of the like foreign articles may have been destroy(ed).

It cannot escape notice, that a duty upon the importation of (an) articles can not otherwise aid the domestic production of it, than giving the latter greater advantages in the home market. It ca(n) have no influence upon the advantageous sale of the article produced, in foreign markets; no tendency, there(fore) to promote its exportation.

The true way to conciliate these two interests, is to lay a duty on foreign *manufactures* of the material, the growth of which is desired to be encouraged, and to apply the produce of that duty by way of bounty, either upon the production of the material itself or upon its manufacture at home or upon both. In this disposition of the thing, the Manufacturer commences his enterprise under every advantage, which is attainable, as to quantity or price, of the raw material: And the Farmer if the bounty be immediately to him, is enabled by it to enter into a successful competition with the foreign material; if the bounty be to the manufacturer on so much of the domestic material as he consumes, the operation is nearly the same; he has a motive of interest to prefer the domestic Commodity, if of equal quality, even at a higher price than the foreign, so long as the difference of price is any thing short of the bounty which is allowed upon the article.

Except the simple and ordinary kinds of household Manufactures, or those for which there are very commanding local advantages, pecuniary bounties are in most cases indispensable to the introduction of a new branch. A stimulus and a support not less powerful and direct is generally speaking essential to the overcoming of the obstacles which arise from the Competitions of superior skill and maturity elsewhere. Bounties are especially essential, in regard to articles, upon which those foreigners, who have been accustomed to supply a Country, are in the practice of granting them.

The continuance of bounties on manufactures long established must almost always be of questionable policy: Because a presumption would arise in every such Case, that there were natural and inherent impediments to success. But in new undertakings, they are as justifiable, as they are oftentimes necessary.

There is a degree of prejudice against bounties from an appearance of giving away the pubic money, without an immediate consideration, and from a supposition, that they serve to enrich particular classes, at the expence of the Community.

But neither of these sources of dislike will bear a serious examination. There is no purpose, to which public money can be more beneficially applied, than to the acquisition of a new and useful branch of industry; no Consideration more valuable than a permanent addition to the general stock of productive labour.

As to the second source of objection, it equally lies against other modes of encouragement, which are admitted to be eligible. As often as a duty upon a foreign article makes an addition to its price, it causes an extra expence to the Community, for the benefit of the domestic manufacturer. A bounty does no more: But it is the Interest of the society in each case, to submit to a temporary expence, which is more than compensated, by an increase of industry and Wealth, by an augmentation of resources and independence; & by the circumstance of eventual cheapness, which has been noticed in another place.

It would deserve attention, however, in the employment of this species of encouragement in the United states, as a reason for moderating the degree of it in the instances, in which it might be deemed eligible, that the great distance of this country from Europe imposes very heavy charges on all the fabrics which are brought from thence, amounting from [15 to 30] per Cent on their value, according to their bulk.

A Question has been made concerning the Constitutional right of the Government of the United States to apply this species of encouragement, but there is certainly no good foundation for such a question. The National Legislature has express authority "To lay and Collect taxes, duties, imposts and excises, to pay the debts and provide for the *Common defence* and *general welfare*" with no other qualifications than that all duties, imposts and excises, shall be *uniform* throughout the United states, that no capitation or other direct tax shall be laid unless in proportion to numbers ascertained by a census or enumeration taken on the principles prescribed in the Constitution, and that "no tax or duty shall be laid on articles exported from any state." These three qualifications excepted, the power to *raise money* is *plenary*, and *indefinite;* and the objects to which it may be *appropriated* are no less comprehensive, than the payment of the public debts and the providing for the common defence and *"general Welfare."* The terms *"general Welfare"* were doubtless intended to signify more than was expressed or imported in those which Preceded; otherwise numerous exigencies incident to the affairs of a Nation would have been left without a provision. The phrase is as comprehensive as any that could have been used; because it was not fit that the constitutional authority of the Union, to appropriate its revenues shou'd have been restricted within narrower limits than the "General Welfare" and because this necessarily embraces a vast variety of particulars, which are susceptible neither of specification nor of definition.

It is therefore of necessity left to the discretion of the National Legislature, to pronounce, upon the subjects, which concern the general Welfare, and for which under that description, an appropriation of money is requisite and proper. And there seems to be no room for a doubt that whatever concerns the general Interests of *learning* of *Agriculture* of *Manufactures* and of *Commerce* are within the sphere of the national Councils *as far as regards an application of Money.*

The only qualification of the generallity of the Phrase in question, which seems to be admissible, is this—That the object to which an appropriation of money is to be made *General* and not *local;* its operation extending in fact, or by possibility, throughout the Union, and not being confined to a particular spot.

No objection ought to arise to this construction from a supposition that it would imply a power to do whatever else should appear to Congress conducive to the General Welfare. A power to appropriate money with this latitude which is granted too in *express terms* would not carry a power to do any other thing, not authorized in the constitution, either expressly or by fair implication.

V Premiums

These are of a Nature allied to bounties, though distinguishable from them, in some important features.

Bounties are applicable to the whole quantity of an article produced, or manufactured, or exported, and involve a correspondent expence. Premiums serve to reward some particular excellence or superiority, some extraordinary exertion or skill, and are dispensed on(ly) in a small number of cases. But their effect is to stimulate gener(al) effort. Contrived so as to be both honorary and lucrative, they address themselves to different passions; touching the chords as well of emulation as of Interest. They are accordingly a very economical mean of exciting the enterprise of a Whole Community.

There are various Societies in different countries, whose object is the dispensation of Premiums for the encouragemen(t) of *Agriculture Arts manufactures* and *Commerce;* and though they are for the most part voluntary associations, with comparatively slender funds, their utility has been immense. Much has been done by this mean in great Britain: Scotland in particular owes materially to it a prodigious amelioration of Condition. From a similar establishment in the United states, supplied and supported by the Government of the Union, vast benefits might reasonably be expected. Some further ideas on this head, shall accordingly be submitted, in the conclusion of this report.

VI The Exemption of the Materials of manufactures from duty.

The policy of that Exemption as a general rule, particularly in reference to new Establishments, is obvious. It can hardly ever be advisable to add the obstructions of fiscal burthens to the difficulties which naturally embarrass a new manufacture; and where it is matured and in condition to become an object of revenue, it is generally speaking better that the fabric, than the Material should be the subject of Taxation. Ideas of proportion between the quantum of the tax and the value of the article, can be more easily adjusted, in the former, than in the latter case. An argument for exemptions of this kind in the United States, is to be derived from the practice, as far as their necessities have permitted, of those nations whom we are to meet as competitors in our own and in foreign Markets.

There are however exceptions to it; of which some examples will be given under the next head.

The Laws of the Union afford instances of the observance of the policy here recommended, but it will probably be found adviseable to extend it to some other Cases. Of a nature, bearing some affinity to that policy is the regulation which exempts from duty the tools and implements, as well as the books, cloths and household furniture of foreign artists, who come to reside in the United states; an advantage already secured to them by the Laws of the Union, and which, it is, in every view, proper to Continue.

VII Drawbacks of the duties which are imposed on the Materials of Manufactures.

It has already been observed as a general rule that duties on those materials, ought with certain exceptions to be foreborne. Of these exceptions, three cases occur, which may serve as examples—one—where the material is itself, an object of general or extensive consumption, and a fit and productive source of revenue: Another, where a manufacture of a simpler kind [the competition of which with a like domestic article is desired to be restrained,] partakes of the Nature of a raw material, from being capable, by a further process to be converted into a manufacture of a different kind, the introduction of growth of which is desired to be encouraged; a third where the Material itself is a production of the Country, and in sufficient abundance to furnish cheap and plentiful supply to the national Manufacturer.

Under the first description comes the article of Molasses. It is not only a fair object of revenue; but being a sweet, it is just that the consumers of it should pay a duty as well as the Consumer(s) of sugar.

Cottons and linens in their White state fall under the second description. A duty upon such as are imported is proper to promote the domestic Manufacture of similar articles in the same state. A drawback of that duty is proper to encourage the printing and staining at home of those which are brought from abroad: When the first of these manufac(tures) has attained sufficient maturity in a Country, to furnish a full supply for (the) second, the utility of the drawback ceases.

The article of Hemp either now does or may be expected soon to exemplify the third Case, in the United states.

Where duties on the materials of manufactures are not laid for the purpose of preventing a competition with some domestic production, the same reasons which recommend, as a general rule, the exemption of those materials from duties, would recommend as a like General rule, the allowance of draw backs, in favor of the manufacturer. Accordingly such drawbacks are familiar in countries which systematically pursue the business of manufactures; which furnishes an argument for the observance of a similar policy in the United states; and the Idea has been adopted by the laws of the Union in the stances of salt and Molasses. It is believed that it will be found advantageous to extend it to some other Articles.

VIII The encouragement of new inventions and discoveries, at home, and of the introduction into the United States of such as may have been made in other countries; particularly those, which relate to machinery.

This is among the most useful and unexceptionable of the aids, which can be given to
manufactures. The usual means of that encouragement are pecuniary rewards, and,
for a time, exclusive privileges. The first must be employed, according to the occasion, and the utiity of the invention, or discovery: For the last, so far as respects
"authors and inventors" provision has been made by Law. But it is desireable in
regard to improvements and secrets of extraordinary value, to be able to extend the
same benefit to Introducers, as well as Authors and Inventors; a policy which has
been practiced with advantge in other countries. Here, however, as in some other
cases, there is cause to regret, that the competency of the authority of the National
Government to the *good*, which might be done, is not without a question. Many aids
might be given to industry; many internal improvements of primary magnitude might
be promoted, by an authority operating throughout the Union, which cannot be
effected, as well, if at all, by an authority confined within the limits of a single state.

But if the legislature of the Union cannot do all the good, that might be wished, it is at
least desirable, that all may be done, which is practicable. Means for promoting the
introduction of foreign improvements, though less efficaciously than might be
accomplished with more adequate authority, will form a part of the plan intended to
be submitted in the close of this report.

It is customary with manufacturing nations to prohibit, under severe penalties, the
exportation of implements and machines, which they have either invented or
improved. There are already objects for a similar regulation in the United States;
and others may be expected to occur from time to time. The adoption of it seems to
be dictated by the principle of reciprocity. Great liberality, in such respects, might
better comport with the general spirit of the country; but a selfish and exclusive policy
in other quarters will not always permit the free indulgence of a spirit, which would
place us upon an unequal footing. As far as prohibitions tend to prevent foreign competitors from deriving the benefit of the improvements made at home, they tend to
increase the advantages of those by whom they may have been introduced; and operate as an encouragement to exertion.

IX Judicious regulations for the inspection of manufactured commodities.

This is not among the least important of the means, by which the prosperity of manufactures may be promoted. It is indeed in many cases one of the most essential. Contributing to prevent frauds upon consumers at home and exporters to foreign countries—to
improve the quality & preserve the character of the national manufactures, it cannot fail
to aid the expeditious and advantageous Sale of them, and to serve as a guard against

successful competition from other quarters. The reputation of the flour and lumber of some states, and of the Pot ash of others has been established by an attention to this point. And the like good name might be procured for those articles, wheresoever produced, by a judicious and uniform system of Inspection; throughout the ports of the United States. A like system might also be extended with advantage to other commodities.

X The facilitating of pecuniary remittances from place to place is a point of considerable moment to trade in general, and to manufactures in particular; by rendering more easy the purchase of raw materials and provisions and the payment for manufactured supplies. A general circulation of Bank paper, which is to be expected from the institution lately established will be a most valuable mean to this end. But much good would also accrue from some additional provisions respecting inland bills of exchange. If those drawn in one state payable in another were made negotiable, everywhere, and interest and damages allowed in case of protest, it would greatly promote negotiations between the Citizens of different states, by rendering them more secure; and, with it the convenience and advantage of the Merchants and manufacturers of each.

XI The facilitating of the transportation of commodities.

Improvements favoring this object intimately concern all the domestic interests of a community; but they may without impropriety be mentioned as having an important relation to manufactures. There is perhaps scarcely any thing, which has been better calculated to assist the manufactures of Great Britain, then the ameliorations of the public roads of that Kingdom, and the great process which has been of late made in opening canals. Of the former, the United States stand much in need; and for the latter they present uncommon facilities.

The symptoms of attention to the improvement of inland Navigation, which have lately appeared in some quarters, must fill with pleasure every breast warmed with a true Zeal for the prosperity of the Country. These examples, it is to be hoped, will stimulate the exertions of the Government and the Citizens of every state. There can certainly be no object, more worthy of the cares of the local administrations; and it were to be wished, that there was no doubt of the power of the national Government to lend its direct aid, on a comprehensive plan. This is one of those improvements, which could be prosecuted with more efficacy by the whole, than by any part or parts of the Union. There are cases in which the general interest will be in danger to be sacrificed to the collission of some supposed local interests. Jealousies, in matters of this kind, are as apt to exist, as they are apt to be erroneous.

The following remarks are sufficiently judicious and pertinent to deserve a literal quotation. "Good roads, canals, and navigable rivers, by diminishing the expence of carriage, put the *remote parts of a country* more nearly upon a level with those in the neighborhood of the town. They are *upon that account* the greatest of all improvements. They encourage the cultivation of the remote, which must always be the most extensive circle of the country. They are advantageous to the Town by breaking down the monopoly of the country in its neighborhood. They are advantageous *even to that part of the Country.* Though they introduce some rival commodities into the old Market, they open many new markets to its produce. Monopoly besides is a great enemy to good management, which can never be universally established, but in consequence of that free and universal competition, which forces every body to have recourse to it for the sake of self defence. It is not more than Fifty years ago that *some of the countries in the neighborhood of London petitioned the Parliament, against the extension of the turnpike roads, into the remoter counties. Those remoter counties, they pretended, from the cheapness of Labor, would be able to sell their grass and corn cheaper in the London Market, than themselves, and they would thereby reduce their rents and ruin their cultivation.* Their rents however have risen and their cultivation has been improved, since that time.

Specimens of a spirit, similar to that which governed the counties here spoken of present themselves too frequently to the eye of an impartial observer, and render it a wish of patriotism, that the body in the Country, in whose councils a local or partial spirit is least likely to predominate, were at liberty to pursue and promote the general interest, in those instances, in which there might be danger of the interference of such a spirit.

The foregoing are the principal of the means, by which the growth of manufactures is ordinarily promoted. It is, however, not merely necessary, that the measures of government, which have a direct view to manufactures, should be calculated to assist and protect them, but that those which only collaterally affect them, in the general course of the administration, should be gaurded from any peculiar tendency to injure them.

There are certain species of taxes, which are apt to be oppressive to different parts of the community, and among other ill effects have a very unfriendly aspect towards manufactures. All Poll or Capitation taxes are of this nature. They either proceed, according to a fixed rate, which operates unequally, and injuriously to the industrious poor; or they vest a discretion in certain officers, to make estimates and assessments which are necessarily vague, conjectural and liable to abuse. They ought therefore to be abstained from, in all but cases of distressing emergency.

All such taxes (including all taxes on occupations) which proceed according to the amount of capital *supposed* to be employed in a business, or of profits *supposed* to be made in it are unavoidably hurtful to industry. It is in vain, that the evil may be endeavoured to be mitigated by leaving it, in the first instance, in the option of the party to be taxed, to declare the amount of his capital or profits.

Men engaged in any trade of business have commonly weighty reasons to avoid disclosures, which would expose, with any thing like accuracy, the real state of their affairs.

They most frequently find it better to risk oppression, than to avail themselves of so inconvenient a refuge. And the consequence is, that they often suffer oppression.

When the disclosure too, if made, is not definitive, but controulable by the discretion, or in other words, by the passions & prejudices of the revenue officers, it is not only an ineffectual protection, but the possibility of its being so is an additional reason for not resorting to it.

Allowing to the public officers the most equitable dispositions; yet where they are to exercise a discretion, without certain data, they cannot fail to be often misled by appearances. The quantity of business, which seems to be going on, is, in a vast number of cases, a very deceitful criterion of the profits which are made; yet it is perhaps the best they can have, and it is the one, on which they will most naturally rely. A business therefore which may rather require aid, from the government, than be in a capacity to be contributory to it, may find itself crushed by the mistaken conjectures of the Assessors of taxes.

Arbitrary taxes, under which denomination are comprised all those, that leave the *quantum* of the tax to be raised on each person, to the *discretion* of certain officers, are as contrary to the genius of liberty as to the maxims of industry. In this light, they have been viewed by the most judicious observers on government; who have bestowed upon them the severest epithets of reprobation; as constituting one of the worst features usually to be met with in the practice of despotic governments.

It is certain at least, that such taxes are particularly inimical to the success of manufacturing industry, and ought carefully to be avoided by a government, which desires to promote it.

The great copiousness of the subject of this Report has insensibly led to a more lengthy preliminary discussion, than was originally contemplated, or intended. It appeared proper to investigate principles, to consider objections, and to endeavour to establish the utility of the thing proposed to be encouraged; previous to a specification of the objects which might occur, as meriting or requiring encouragement, and of the measures, which might be proper, in respect to each. The first purpose having been fulfilled, it remains to pursue the second. In the selection of objects, five circumstances seem intitled to particular attention; the capacity of the Country to furnish the raw material —the degree in which the nature of the manufacture admits of a substitute for manual labour in machinery—the facility of execution—the extensiveness of the uses, to which the article can be applied—its subserviency to other interests, particularly the great one of national defence. There are however objects, to which these circumstances are little applicable, which for some special reasons, may have a claim to encouragement.

A designation of the principal raw material of which each manufacture is composed will serve to introduce the remarks upon it. As, in the first place—

Iron

The manufactures of this article are entitled to preeminent rank. None are more essential in their kinds, nor so extensive in their uses. They constitute in whole or in part the implements or the materials or both of almost every useful occupation. Their instrumentality is everywhere conspicuous.

It is fortunate for the United States that they have peculiar advantages for deriving the full benefit of this most valuable material, and that they have every motive to improve it, with systematic care. It is to be found in various parts of the United States, in great abundance and of almost every quality; and fuel the chief instrument in manufacturing, it is both cheap and plenty. This particularly applies to Charcoal; but there are productive coal mines already in operation, and strong indications, that the material is to be found in abundance, in a variety of places.

The inquiries to which the subject of this report has led have been answered with proofs that manufactories of Iron, though generally understood to be extensive, are far more so than is commonly supposed. The kinds, in which the greatest progress has been made, have been mentioned in another place, and need not be repeated; but there is little doubt that every other kind, with due cultivation, will rapidly succeed. It is worthy of remark that several of the particular trades, of which it is the basis, are capable of being carried on without the aid of large capitals.

Iron works have very greatly increased in the United States and are prosecuted, with much more advantage than formerly. The average price before the revolution was about Sixty four Dollars per Ton—at present it is about Eighty; a rise which is chiefly to be attributed to the increase of manufactures of the material.

The still further extension and multiplication of such manufactures will have the double effect of promoting the extraction of the Metal itself, and of converting it to a greater number of profitable purposes.

Those manufactures too united in a greater degree, than almost any others, the several requisites, which have been mentioned, as proper to be consulted in the selection of objects.

The only further encouragement of manufactories of this article, the propriety of which may be considered as unquestionable, seems to be an increase of the duties on foreign rival commodities.

Steel is a branch, which has already made a considerable progress, and it is ascertained that some new enterprizes, on a more extensive scale, have been lately set on foot. The facility of carrying it to an extent, which will supply all internal demands, and furnish a considerable surplus for exportation cannot be doubted. The duty upon the importation of this article, which is at present seventy five cents per Cwt., may it is conceived be safely and advantageously extended to 100 Cents. It is desirable, by decisive arrangements, to second the efforts, which are making in so very valuable a branch.

The United States already in a great measure supply themselves with Nails & Spikes. They are able, and ought certainly, to do it intirely. The first and most laborious operation, in this manufacture is performed by water mills; and of the persons afterwards employed a great proportion are boys, whose early habits of industry are of importance to the community, to the present support of this families, and to their own future comfort. It is not less curious than true, that in certain parts of the country, the making of Nails is an occasional family manufacture.

The expendiency of an additional duty on these materials is indicated by an important fact. About one million 800,000 pounds of them were imported into the United States in the course of a year ending the 30th. of September 1790. A duty of two Cents per lb would, it is presumable, speedily put an end to so considerable an importation. And it is in every view proper that an end should be put to it.

The manufacture of these articles, like that of some others, suffers from the carelessness and dishonesty of a part of those who carry it on. An inspection in certain cases might tend to correct the evil. It will deserve consideration whether a regulation of this sort cannot be applied, without inconvenience, to the exportation of the articles either to foreign countries, or from one state to another.

The implements of husbandry are made in several States in great abundance. In many places it is done by the common blacksmiths. And there is no doubt that an ample supply for the whole country can with great ease be procured among ourselves.

Various kinds of edged tools for the use of Mechanics are also made; and a considerable quantity of hollow wares; though the business of castings has not yet attained the perfection which might be wished. It is however improving, and as there are respectable capitals in good hands, embarked in the prosecution of those branches of iron manufactories, which are yet in their infancy, they may all be contemplated as objects not difficult to be acquired.

To ensure the end, it seems equally safe and prudent to extend the duty *ad valorem* upon all manufactures of Iron, or of which iron is the article of chief value, to ten per Cent.

Fire arms and other military weapons may it is conceived, be placed without inconvenience in the class of articles rates at 15 per Cent. There are already manufactories of these articles, which only require the stimulus of a certain demand to render them adequate to the supply of the United States.

It would also be a material aid to manufactories of this nature, as well as a mean of public security, if provision should be made for an annual purchase of military weapons, of home manufacture to a certain determinate extent, in order to the formation of Arsenals; and to replace from time to time such as should be withdrawn from use, so as always to have in store the quantity of each kinds, which should be deemed a competent supply.

But it may hereafter deserve legislative consideration, whether manufactories of all the necessary weapons of war ought not to be established, on account of the Government itself. Such establishments are agreeable on the usual practice of Nations and that practice seems founded on sufficient reason.

There appears to be an improvidence, in leaving these essential instruments of national defence to the casual speculations of individual adventure; a resource which can less be relied upon, in this case than in most others; the articles in question not being objects of ordinary and indispensable private consumption or use. As a general rule, manufactories on the immediate account of Government are to be avoided; but this seems to be one of the few exceptions, which that rule admits, depending on very special reasons.

Manufactures of Steel, generally, or of which steel is the article of chief value, may with advantage be placed in the class of goods rated at 7 ½ per Cent. As manufactures of this kind have not yet made any considerable progress, it is a reason for not rating them as high as those of iron; but as this material is the basis of them, and as their extension is not less practicable, than important, it is desirable to promote it by a somewhat higher duty than the present.

A question arises, how far it might be expedient to permit the importation of iron in pigs and bars free from duty. It would certainly be favourable to manufactures of the article; but the doubt is whether it might not interfere with its production.

Two circumstances, however, abate if they do not remove apprehension, on this score; one is, the considerable increase of price, which has been already remarked, and which renders it probable, that the free admission of foreign iron would not be inconsistent with an adequate profit to the proprietors of Iron Works; the other is, the augmentation of demand, which would be likely to attend the increase in manufactures of the article, in consequence of the additional encouragements proposed to be given. But caution nevertheless in a matter of this kind is most adviseable. The measure suggested ought perhaps rather to be contemplated, subject to the lights of further experience, than immediately adopted.

Copper

The manufactures of which this article is susceptible are also of great extent and utility. Under this description, those of brass, of which it is the principal ingreedient, are intended to be included.

The material is a natural production of the Country. Mines of Copper have actually been wrought, and with profit to the undertakers, though it is not known, that any are now in this condition. And nothing is easier, than the introduction of it, from other countries, on moderate terms, and in great plenty.

Coppersmiths and brass founders, particularly the former, are numerous in the United States; some of whom carry on business to a respectable extent.

To multiply and extend manufactories of the materials in question is worthy of attention and effort. In order to this, it is desireable to facilitate a plentiful supply of the materials. And a proper mean to this end is to place them in the class of free articles. Copper in plates and brass are already in this predicament, but copper in pigs and bars is not—neither is *lapis calaminaris*, which together with *copper* and *charcoal*, constitute the component ingredients of brass. The exemption from duty, by parity of reason, ought to embrace all such of these articles, as are objects of importation. An additional duty, on brass wares, will tend to the general end in view. These now stand at 5 per Cent, while those of tin, pewter and copper are rates at 7 ½. There appears to be a propriety in every view in placing brass wares upon the same level with them; and it merits consideration whether the duty upon all of them ought not to be raised to 10 per Cent.

Lead

There are numerous proofs, that this material abounds in the United States, and requires little to unfold it to an extent, more than equal to every domestic occasion. A prolific mine of it has long been open in the South Western parts of Virginia, and under a public administration, during the late war, yielded a considerable supply for military use. This is now in the hands of individuals, who not only carry it on with spirit; but have established manufactories of it, at Richmond, in the same State.

The duties, already laid upon the importation of this article, either in its unmanufactured, or manufactured state, ensure it a decisive advantage in the home market—which amounts to considerable encouragement. If the duty on pewter wares should be raised it would afford a further encouragement. Nothing else occurs as proper to be added.

Fossil Coal

This, as an important instrument of manufactures, may without impropriety be mentioned among the subjects of this Report.

A copious supply of it would be of great consequence to the iron branch: As an article of household fuel also it is an interesting production; the utility of which must increase in proportion to the decrease of wood, by the progress of settlement and cultivation. And its importance to navigation, as an immense article of transportation coastwise, is signally exemplified in Great Britain.

It is known, that there are several coal mines in Virginia, now worked; and appearances of their existence are familiar in a number of places.

The expediency of a bounty on all the species of coal of home production, and of premiums, on the opening of new mines, under certain qualifications, appears to be worthy of particular examination. The great importance of the article will amply justify a reasonable expence in this way, if it shall appear to be necessary to and shall be thought it likely to answer the end.

Wood

Several manufactures of this article flourish in the United States. Ships are no where built in greater perfection, and cabinet wares, generally, are made little if at all inferior to those of Europe. Their extent is such as to have admitted of considerable exportation.

An exemption from duty of the several kinds of wood ordinarily used in these manufactures seem to be all, that is requisite, by way of encouragement. It is recommended by the consideration of a similar policy being pursued in other countries, and by the expediency of giving equal advantages to our own workmen in wood. The abundance of Timber proper for ship building in the United States does not appear to be an objection to it. The increasing scarcity and the growing importance of that article, in the European countries, admonish the United States to commerce, and systematically to pursue, measures for the preservation of their stock. Whatever may promote the regular establishment of the Magazines of Ship Timber is in various views desirable.

Skins

There are scarcely any manufactories of greater importance, than of this article. Their direct and very happy influence upon Agriculture, by promoting the raising of Cattle of different kinds, is a very material consideration.

It is pleasing too, to observe the extensive progress they have made in their principal branches; which are so far matured as almost to defy foreign competition. Tanneries in particular are not only carried on as a regular business, innumerous instances and in various parts of the Country; but they constitute in some places a valuable item of incidental family manufactures.

Representations however have been made, importing the expediency of further encouragement to the Leather-Branch in two ways—one by increasing the duty on the manufactures of it, which are imported—the other by prohibiting the exportation of bark. In support of the latter it is alleged that the price of bark, chiefly in consequence of large exportations, has risen within a few years from [about three Dollars to four dollars and a half per cord.]

These suggestions are submitted rather as intimations, which merit consideration, than as matters, the propriety of which is manifest. It is not clear, that an increase of duty is necessary: and in regard to the prohibition desired, there is no evidence of any considerable exportation hitherto; and it is most probable, that whatever augmentation of price may have taken place, is to be attributed to an extension of the home demand from the increase of manufactures, and to a decrease of the supply in consequence of the progress of Settlement; rather than to the quantities which have been exported.

It is mentioned however, as an additional reason for the prohibition, that one species of the bark usually exported is in some sort peculiar to the country, and the material of a very valuable dye, of great use in some other manufactures, in which the United States have begun a competition.

There may also be this argument in favor of an increase of duty. The object is of importance enough to claim decisive encouragement and the progress, which has been made, leaves no room to apprehend any inconvenience on the score of supply from such an increase.

It would be of benefit to this branch, if glue which is now rated at 5 perCent, were made the object of an excluding duty. It is already made in large quantities at various tanneries; and like paper, is an entire œconomy of materials, which if not manufactured would be left to perish. It may be placed with advantage in the class of articles paying 15 perCent.

Grain

Manufactures of the several species of this article have a title to peculiar favor; not only because they are most of them immediately connected with the subsistence of the citizens; but because they enlarge the demand for the most precious products of the soil.

Though flour may with propriety be noticed as a manufacture of Grain, it were useless to do it, but for the purpose of submitting the expediency of a general system of inspection, throughout the ports of the United states; which, if established upon proper principles, would be likely to improve the quality of our flour every where, and to raise its reputation in foreign markets. There are however considerations which stand in the way of such an arrangement.

Ardent spirits and malt liquors are, next to flour, the two principal manufactures of Grain. The first has made a very extensive, the last a considerable progress in the

United States. In respect to both, an exclusive possession of the home market ought to be secured to the domestic manufacturers; as fast as circumstances will admit. Nothing is more practicable & nothing more desireable.

The existing laws of the United States have done much towards attaining this valuable object; but some additions to the present duties, on foreign distilled spirits, and foreign malt liquors, and perhaps an abatement of those on home made spirits, would more effectually secure it; and there does not occur any very weighty objection to either.

An augmentation of the duties on imported spirits would favour, as well as the distillation of Spirits from molasses, as that from Grain. And to secure to the nation the benefit of the manufacture, even of foreign materials, is always of great, though perhaps of secondary importance.

A strong impression prevails in the minds of those concerned in distilleries (including too the mot candid and enlightened) that greater differences in the rates of duty on foreign and domestic spirits are necessary, completely to secure the successful manufacture of the latter; and there are fact which entitle this impression to attention.

It is known, that the price of molasses for some years past, has been successively rising in the West India Markets, owing partly to competition, which did not formerly exist, and partly to an extension of demand in this country; and it is evident, that the late disturbances in those Islands, from which we draw our principal supply, must so far interfere with the production of the article, as to occasion a material enhancement of price. The destruction and devastation attendant on the insurrection in Hispaniola, in particular, must not only contribute very much to that effect, but may be expected to give it some duration. These circumstances, and the duty of three cents per Gallon on molasses, may render it difficult for the distillers of that material to maintain with adequate profit a competition, with the rum brought from the West Indies, the quality of which is so considerably superior.

The consumption of Geneva or Gin in this country is extensive. It is not long since distilleries of it have grown up among us, to any importance. They are now becoming of consequence, but being still in their infancy, they require protection.

It is represented, that the price of some of the materials is greater here, than in Holland, from which place large quantities are brought, the price of labour considerably greater, the capitals engaged in the business there much larger, than those which are employed here, the rate of profits, at which the Undertakers can afford to carry it on, much less—the prejudices, in favor of imported Gin, strong. These circumstances are alleged to outweigh the charges, which attend the bringing of the Article, from Europe to the United states and the present difference of duty, so as to obstruct the prosecution of the manufacture, with due advantage.

Experiment could perhaps alone decide with certainty the justness of the suggestions, which are made; but in relation to branches of manufacture so important, it would seem inexpedient to hazard an unfavourable issue, and better to err on the side of too great, than of too small a difference, in the particular in question.

It is therefore submitted, that an addition of two cents per Gallon be made to the duty on imported spirits of the first class of proof, with a proportionable increase on those of higher proof; and that a deduction of one cent per Gallon be made from the duty on spirits distilled within the United states, beginning with the first class of proof, and a proportionable deduction from the duty on those of higher proof.

It is ascertained, that by far the greatest part of the malt liquors consumed in the United States are the produce of domestic breweries. It is desireable, and, in all likelihood, attainable, that the whole consumption should be supplied by ourselves.

The malt liquors, made at home, though inferior to the best are equal to a great part of those, which have been usually imported. The progress already made is an earnest of what may be accomplished. The growing competition is an assurance of improvement. This will be accelerated by measures, tending to invite a greater capital into this channel of employment.

To render the encouragement to domestic breweries decisive, it may be adviseable to substitute to the present rates of duty eight cents per gallon generally; and it will deserve to be considered as a guard against evasions, whether there ought not to be a prohibition of their importation, except in casks of considerable capacity. It is to be hoped, that such a duty would banish from the market, foreign malt liquors of inferior quality; and that the best kind only would continue to be imported till it should be supplanted, by the efforts of equal skill or care at home.

Till that period, the importation so qualified would be an useful stimulous to improvement: And in the mean time, the payment of the increased price, for the enjoyment of a luxury, in order to the encouragement of a most useful branch of domestic industry, could not reasonably be deemed a hardship.

As a further aid to the manufactures of grain, though upon a smaller scale, the article of Starch, hair powder and wafers, may with great propriety be placed among those, which are rate at 15 perCent. No manufactures are more simple, nor more completely within the reach of a full supply, from domestic sources, and it is a policy, as common as it is obvious, to make them the objects either of prohibitory duties, or of express prohibition.

Flax and Hemp

Manufactures of these articles have so much affinity to each other, and they are so often blended, that they many with advantage be considered in conjunction. The importance of the linnin branch to agriculture—its precious effects upon household industry—the ease, with which the materials can be produced at home to any requisite extend—the great advances, which have been already made, in the coarser fabricks of them, expecially in the family way, constitute claims, of peculiar force, to the patronage of the government.

This patronage may be afford in various ways; by promoting the growth of the materials; by increasing the impediments to an advantageous competition of rival foreign articles; by direct bounties or premiums upon the home manufacture.

First. As to promoting the growth of the materials.

In respect to hemp, something has been already done by the high duty upon foreign hemp. If the facilities for domestic production were not unusually great, the policy of the duty, on the foreign raw material, would be highly questionable, as interfering with the growth of manufactures of it. But making the proper allowances for those facilities, and with an eye to the future and natural progress, of the country, the measure does not appear, upon the whole, exceptionable. A strong wish naturally suggests itself, tha(t) some method could be devised of affording a more direct encouragement to the growth both of flax and hemp; such as would be effectual, and at the same time not attended with too great inconveniences. To this end, bounties and premiums offer themselves to *consideration;* but no modification of them has yet occurred, which would not either hazard too much expence, or operate unequally in reference to the circumstances of different parts of the Union, and which would not be attended with very great difficulties in the execution.

Secondly—

As to encreasing the impediments to an advantageous competition of rival foreign articles.

To this purpose, an augmentation of the duties on importation is the obvious expedient; which, in regard to certain articles, appears to be recommended by sufficient reasons.

The principal of these articles is Sail cloth; one intimately connected with navigation and defence; and of which a flourishing manufactory is established at Boston and very promising ones at several other places.

It is presumed to be both safe and adviseable to place this in the class of articles rated at 10 Per cent. A strong reason for it results from the consideration that a bounty of two pence sterling per ell is allowed, in Great Britain, upon the exportation of the sail cloth manufactured in that Kingdom.

It would likewise appear to be good policy to raise the duty to 7 ½ perCent on the following articles. Drillings, Osnaburghs, Ticklenburghs, Dowlas, Canvas, Brown Rolls,

Bagging, and upon all other linnens the first cost of which at the place of exportation does not exceed 35 cents per yard. A bounty of 12 ½ per Cent, upon an average on the exportation of such similar linens from Great-Britain encourages the manufacture of them in that country and increases the obstacles to a successful competition in the countries to which they are sent.

The quantities of tow and other household linnens manufactured in different parts of the United States and the expectations, which are derived from some late experiments, of being able to extend the use of labour-saving machines, in the coarser fabrics of linnen, obviate the danger of inconvenience, from an increase of the duty upon such articles, and authorize a hope of speedy and complete success to the endeavours, which may be used for procuring an internal supply.

Thirdly. As to direct bounties, or premiums upon the manufactured articles.

To afford more effectual encouragement to the manufacture, and at the same time to promote the cheapness of the article for the benefit of navigation, it will be of great use to allow a bounty of two Cents per yard on all Sail Cloth, which is made in the United States from materials of their own growth. This would also assist the Culture of those materials. An encouragement of this kind if adopted ought to be established for a moderate term of years, to invite to new undertakings and to an extension of the old. This is an article of importance enough to warrant the employment of extraordinary means in its favor.

Cotton

There is something in the texture of this material, which adapts it in a peculiar degree to the application of Machines. The signal Utility of the mill for spinning of cotton, not long since invented in England, has been noticed in another place; but there are other machines scarcely inferior in utility which, in the different manufactories of this article are employed either exclusively, or with more than ordinary effect. This very important circumstance recommends the fabricks of cotton, in a more particular manner, to a country in which a defect of hands constitutes the greatest obstacles to success.

The variety and extent of the uses to which the manufactures of this article are applicable is another powerful argument in their favor.

And the faculty of the United States to produce the raw material in abundance, & of a quality, which though alledged to be inferior to some that is produced in other quarters, is nevertheless capable of being used with advantage, in many fabrics, and is probably susceptible of being carried, by a more experienced culture, to much greater perfection—suggests an additional and a very cogent inducement to the vigorous pursuit of the cotton branch, in its several subdivisions.

How much has been already done has been stated in a preceding part of this report.

In addition to this, it may be announced, that a society is forming with a capital which is expected to be extended to at lease half a million of dollars; on behalf of which measures are already in train for prosecuting on a large scale, the making and printing of cotton goods.

These circumstances conspire to indicate the expediency of removing any obstructions, which may happen to exist, to the advantageous prosecution of the manufactories in question, and of adding such encouragements, as may appear necessary and proper.

The present duty of three cents per lb. on the foreign raw material, is undoubtedly a very serious impediment to the progress of those manufactories.

The injurious tendency of similar duties either prior to the establishment, or in the infancy of the domestic manufacture, of the article, as it regards the manufacture, and their worse than inutility, in relation to the home production of the material itself, have been anticipated particularly in discussing the subject of pecuniary bounties.

Cotton has not the same pretensions, with hemp, to form an exception to the general rule.

Not being, like hemp an universal production of the Country it affords less assurance of an adequate internal supply; but the chief objection arises from the doubts; which are entertained concerning the quality of the national cotton. It is alledged, that the fibre of it is considerably shorter and weaker, than that of some other places; and it has been observed as a general rule, that the nearer the place of growth to the Equator, the better the quality of the cotton. That which comes from Cayenne, Surrinam and Demarara is said to be preferable, even at a material difference of price, to the Cotton of the Islands.

While a hope may reasonably be indulged, that with due care and attention the national cotton may be made to approach nearer than it now does to that of regions, somewhat more favored by climate; and while facts authorize an opinion, that very great use may be made of it, and that it is a resource which gives greater security to the cotton fabrics of this country, than can be enjoyed by any which depends wholly on external supply it will certainly be wise, in every view, to let our infant manufactures have the full benefit of the best materials on the cheapest terms.

It is obvious that the necessity of having such materials is proportioned to the unskilfulness and inexperience of the workmen employed, who if inexpert, will not fail to commit great waste, where the materials they are to work with are of an indifferent kind.

To secure to the national manufactures so essential an advantage, a repeal of the present duty on imported cotton is indispensible.

A substitute for this, far more encouraging to domestic production, will be to grant a bounty on the national cotton, when wrought at a home manufactory; to which a bounty on the exportation of it may be added. Either or both would do much more towards promoting the growth of the article, than the merely nominal encouragement, which it is proposed to abolish. The first would also have a direct influence in encouraging the manufacture.

The bounty which has been mentioned as existing in Great Britain, upon the exportation of coarse linnens not exceeding a certain value, applies also to certain discriptions of cotton goods of similar value.

This furnishes an additional argument for allowing to the national manufacturers the species of encouragement just suggested, and indeed for adding some other aid.

One cent per yard, not less than of a given width, on all goods of cotton, or of cotton and linnen mixed, which are manufactured in the United States; with the addition of one cent per lb weight of the material; if made of national cotton; would amount to an aid of considerable importance, both to the production and to the manufacture of that valuable article. And it is conceived, that the expence would be well justified by the magnitude of the object.

The printing and staining of cotton goods is known to be a distinct business from the fabrication of them. It is one easily accomplished and which, as it adds materially to the value of the article in its white state, and prepares it for a variety of new uses, is of importance to be promoted.

As imported cottons, equally with those which are made at home, may be objects of this manufacture, it will merit consideration, whether the whole, or a part of the duty, on the white goods, ought not to be allowed to be drawn back in favor of those, who print or stain them. This measure would certainly operate as a powerful encouragement to the business; and though it may in a degree counteract the original fabrication of the articles it would probably more than compensate for this disadvantage, in the rapid growth of a collateral branch, which is of a nature sooner to attain to maturity. When a sufficient progress shall have been made, the drawback may be abrogated; and by that time the domestic supply of the articles to be printed or stained will have been extended.

If the duty of 7 ½ per Cent on certain kinds of cotton goods were extended to all goods of cotton, or of which it is the principal material, it would probably more than counterbalance the effect of the drawback proposed, in relation to the fabrication of the article. And no material objection occurs to such an extension. The duty then considering all the circumstances which attend goods of this description could not be deemed inconveniently high; and it may be inferred from various causes that the prices of them would still continued moderate.

Manufactories of cotton goods, not long since established at Beverly, in Massachusetts, and at Providence in the state of Rhode Island and conducted with a perseverence corresponding with the patriotic motives which began them, seem to have overcome the first obstacles to success; producing corduroys, velverets, fustians, jeans, and other similar articles of a quality, which will bear a comparison with the like articles brought from Manchester. The one at Providence has the merit of being the first in introducing [into the United States] the celebrated cotton mill; which not only furnishes materials for that manufactory itself, but for the supply of private families for household manufacture.

Other manufactories of the same material; as regular businesses, have also been begun at different places in the state of Connecticut, but all upon a smaller scale, than those above mentioned. Some essays are also making in the printing and staining of cotton goods. There are several small establishments of this kind already on foot.

Wool

In a country, the climate of which partakes of so considerable a proportion of winter, as that of a great part of the United States, the woolen branch cannot be regarded, as inferior to any, which relates to the cloathing of the inhabitants.

Household manufactures of this material are carried on, in different parts of the United States, to a very interesting extent; but there is only one branch, which, as a regular business, can be said to have acquired maturity. This is the making of hats.

Hats of wool, and of wool mixed with fur, are made in large quantities, in different States; & nothing seems wanting, but an adequate supply of materials, to render the manufacture commensurate with the demand.

A promising essay, towards the fabrication of cloths, cassimires and other woolen goods, is likewise going on at *Hartford* in Connecticut. Specimens of the different kinds which are made, in the possession of the Secretary, evince that these fabrics have attained a very considerable degree of perfection. Their quality certainly surpasses anything, that could have been looked for, in so short a time, and under so great disadvantages; and conspires with the scantiness of the means, which have been at the command of the directors, to form the eulogium of that public spirit, perseverence and judgment, which have been able to accomplish so much.

To cherish and bring to maturity this precious embryo must engage the most ardent wishes—and proportionable regret, as far as the means of doing it may appear difficult or uncertain.

Measures, which should tend to promote an abundant supply of wool, of good quality, would probably afford the most efficacious aid, that present circumstances permit.

To encourage the raising and improving the breed of sheep, at home, would certainly be the most desireable expedient, for the purpose; but it may not be alone sufficient, especially as it is yet a problem, whether our wool be capable of such a degree of improvement, as to render it fit for the finer fabrics.

Premiums would probably be found the best means of promoting the domestic, and bounties the foreign supply. The first may be within the compass of the institution hereafter to be submitted—The last would require a specific legislative provision. If any bounties are granted they ought of course to be adjusted with an eye to quality, as well as quantity.

A fund for the purpose may be derived from the addition of 2 ½ per Cent, to the present rate of duty, on Carpets and Carpeting; an increase, to which the nature of the Articles suggests no objection, and which may at the same time furnish a motive the more to the fabrication of them at home; towards which some beginnings have been made.

Silk

The production of this Article is attended with great facility in most parts of the United States. Some pleasing essays are making in Connecticut, as well towards that, as towards the Manufacture of what is produced. Stockings, Hankerchiefs Ribbons & Buttons are made though as yet but in small quantities.

A Manufactory of Lace upon a scale not very extensive has been long memorable at Ipswich in the State of Massachusetts.

An exemption of the material from the duty, which it now pays on importation, and premiums upon the production, to be dispensed under the direction of the Institution before alluded to, seem to be the only species of encouragement adviseable at so early a stage of the thing.

Glass

The Materials for making Glass are found every where. In the United States there is no deficiency of them. The sands and Stones called Tarso, which include flinty and chrystalline substances generally, and the Salts of various plants, particularly of the Sea Weed Kali or Kelp constitute the essential ingredients. An extraordinary abundance of Fuel is a particular advantage by this Country for such manufactures. They, however, require large Capitals and involve much manual labour.

Different manufactories of Glass are not on foot in the United States. The present duty of 12 ½ per Cent on all imported articles of glass amount to a considerable encouragement of those Manufactories. If any thing in addition is judged eligible, the most proper would appear to be a direct bounty, on Window Glass and black Bottles.

The first recommends itself as an object of general convenience; the last adds to that character, the circumstance of being an important item in breweries. A Complaint is made of great deficiency in this respect.

Gun Powder

No small progress has been of late made in the manufacture of this very important article: It may indeed be considered as already established; but its high importance renders its further extension very desireable.

The encouragements, which it already enjoys, are a duty of 10 per Cent on the foreign rival article, and an exemption of Salt petre one of the principal ingredients of which it is composed, from duty. A like exemption of Sulphur, another chief ingredient, would appear to be equally proper. No quantity of this Article has yet been produced, from internal sources. The use made of it in finishing the bottoms of Ships, is an additional inducement to placing it in the class of free goods. Regulations for the careful inspection of the article would have a favourable tendency.

Paper

Manufactories of paper are among those which are Arrived at the greatest maturity in the United States, and are most adequate to national supply. That of paper hangings is a branch, in which respectable progress has been made.

Nothing material seems wanting to the further success of this valuable branch which is already protected by a competent duty on similar imported Articles.

In the enumeration of the several kinds, made subject to that duty, Sheathing and Cartridge paper have been omitted. These, being the most simple manufactures of the sort, and necessary to military supply, as well as Ship building, recommend themselves equally with those of other descriptions, to encouragement, and appear to be as fully within the compass of domestic exertions.

Printed books

The great number of presses disseminated throughout the Union, seem to afford an assurance, that there is not need of being indebted to foreign Countries for the printing of the Books, which are used in the United States. A duty of ten per Cent instead of five, which is now charged upon the Article, would have a tendency to aid the business internally.

It occurs, as an objection to this, that it may have an unfavourable aspect towards literature, by raising the prices of Books in universal use in private families Schools and other Seminaries of learning. But the difference it is conceived would be without effect.

As to Books which usually fill the Libraries of the wealthier classes and of professional Men, such as Augmentation of prices, as might be occasioned by an additional duty of five per Cent would be too little felt to be an impediment to the acquisition.

And with regard to books which may be specially imported for the use of particular seminaries of learning, and of public libraries, a total exemption from duty would be adviseable, which would go far towards obviating the objection just mentioned. They are now subject to a duty of 5 per Cent.

As to the books in most general family use, the constancy and universality of the demand would insure exertions to furnish them at home and the means are compleatly adequate. It may also be expected ultimately, in this as in other cases, that the extension of the domestic manufacture would conduce to the cheapness of the article.

It ought not to pass unremarked, that to encourage the printing of books is to encourage the manufacture of paper.

Refined Sugars and Chocolate

Are among the number of extensive and prosperous domestic manufactures.

Drawbacks of the duties upon the materials, of which they are respectively made, in cases of exportation, would have a beneficial influence upon the manufacture, and would conform to a precedent, which has been already furnished, in the instance of molasses, on the exportation of distilled spirits.

Cocoa the raw material now pays a duty of one cent per lb., while chocolate which is a prevailing and very simple manufacture, is comprised in a mass of articles rated at no more than five per Cent.

There would appear to be a propriety in encouraging the manufacture, by a somewhat higher duty, on its foreign rival, than is paid on the raw material. Two cents per lb. on imported chocolate would, it is presumed, be without inconvenience.

The foregoing heads comprise the most important of the several kinds of manufactures, which have occurred as requiring, and, at the same time, as most proper for public encouragement; and such measures for affording it, as have appeared best calculated to answer the end, have been suggested.

The observations, which have accompanied this delineation of objects, supercede the necessity of many supplementary remarks. One or two however may not be altogether superfluous.

Bounties are in various instances proposed as one species of encouragement.

It is a familiar objection to them, that they are difficult to be managed and liable to frauds. But neither that difficulty nor this danger seems sufficiently great to countervail the advantages of which they are productive, when rightly applied. And it is presumed to have been shewn, that they are in some cases, particularly in the infancy of new enterprises indispensable.

It will however be necessary to guard, with extraordinary circumspection, the manner of dispensing them. The requisite precautions have been thought of; but to enter into the detail would swell this report, already voluminous, to a size too inconvenient.

If the principle shall not be deemed inadmissible the means of avoiding an abuse of it will not be likely to present insurmountable obstacles. There are useful guides from practice in other quarters.

It shall therefore only be remarked here, in relation to this point, that any bounty, which may be applied to the *manufacture* of an article, cannot with safety extend beyond those manufactories, at which the making of the article is a *regular trade*.

It would be impossible to annex adequate precautions to a benefit of that nature, if extended to every private family, in which the manufacture was incidentally carried on, and its being a merely incidental occupation which engages a portion of time that would otherwise be lost, it can be advantageously carried on, without so special an aid.

The possibility of a diminution of the revenue may also present itself, as an objection to the arrangements, which have been submitted.

But there is no truth, which may be more firmly relied upon, than the interests of the revenue are promoted, by whatever promotes an increase of National industry and wealth.

In proportion to the degree of these, is the capacity of every country to contribute to the public Treasury; and where the capacity to pay is increased, or even is not decreased, the only consequence of measures, which diminish any particular resource is a change of the object. If by encouraging the manufacture of an article at home, the revenue, which has been wont to accrue from its importation, should be lessened, an indemnification can easily be found, either out of the manufacture itself, or from some other object, which may be deemed more convenient.

The measures however, which have been submitted, taken aggregately, will for a long time to come rather augment than decrease the public revenue.

There is little room to hope, that the progress of manufactures, will so equally keep pace with the progress of population, as to prevent, even, a gradual augmentation of the product of the duties on imported articles.

As, nevertheless, an abolition in some instances, and a reduction in others of duties, which have been pledged for the public debt, is proposed, it is essential, that is should be accompanied with a competent substitute. In order to this, it is requisite, that all the additional duties which shall be laid, be appropriated in the first instance, to replace all defalcations, which may proceed from any such abolition or diminution. It is evident, at first glance, that they will not only be adequate to this, but will yield a considerable surplus.

This surplus will serve.

First. To constitute a fund for paying the bounties which shall have been decreed.

Secondly. To constitute a fund for the operations of a Board, to be established, for promoting Arts, Agriculture, Manufactures and Commerce. Of this institution, different intimations have been given, in the course of this report. An outline of a plan for it shall now be submitted.

Let a certain annual sum, be set apart, and placed under the management of Commissioners, not less than three, to consist of certain Officers of the Government and their Successors in Office.

Let these Commissioners be empowered to apply the fund confided to them—to defray the expences of the emigration of Artists, and Manufacturers in particular branches of extraordinary importance—to induce the prosecution and introduction of useful discoveries, inventions and improvements, by proportionate rewards, judiciously held out and applied—to encourage by premiums both honorable and lucrative the exertions of individuals, And of classes, in relation to the several objects, they are charged with promoting—and to afford such other aids to those objects, as may be generally designated by law.

The Commissioners to render [to the Legislature] an annual account of their transactions and disbursements; and all such sums as shall not have been applied to the purposes of their trust, at the end of every three years, to revert to the Treasury. It may also be enjoined upon them, not to draw out the money, but for the purpose of some specific disbursement.

It may moreover be of use, to authorize them to receive voluntary contributions; making it their duty to apply them to the particular objects for which they may have been made, if any shall have been designated by the donors.

There is reasons to believe, that the progress of particular manufactures has been much retarded by the want of skilful workmen. And it often happens that the capitals employed are not equal to the purposes of bringing from abroad workmen of a superior kind. Here, is case worthy of it, the auxiliary agency of Government would in all probability be useful. There are also valuable workmen, in every branch, who are prevented from emigrating solely by the want of means. Occasional aids to such persons properly administered might be a source of valuable acquisitions of the country.

The propriety of stimulating by rewards, the invention and introduction of useful improvements, is admitted without difficulty. But the success of attempts in this way must evidently depend much on the manner of conducting them. It is probable, that the placing of the dispensation of those rewards under some proper discretionary direction, where they may be accompanied by *collateral expedients*, will serve to give them the surest efficacy. It seems impracticable to apportion, by general rules, specific compensations for discoveries of unknown and disproportionate utility.

The great use which may be made of a fund of this mature to procure and import foreign improvements is particularly obvious. Among these, the article of machines would form a most important item.

The operation and utility of premiums have been adverted to; together with the advantages which have resulted from the dispensation, under the direction of certain public and private societies. Of this some experience has been had in the instance of the Pennsylvania society, [for the Promotion of Manufactures and useful Arts;] but the funds of that association have been too contracted to produce more than a very small portion of the good to which the principles of it would have led. It may confidently be affirmed that there is scarcely any thing, which has been devised, better calculated to excite a general spirit of improvement than the institutions of this nature. They are truly invaluable.

In countries where there is a great private wealth much may be effected by the voluntary contributions of patriotic individuals, but in a community situated like that of the

United States, the public purse must supply the deficiency of private resource. In what can it be so useful as in prompting and improving the efforts of industry?

All which is humbly submitted
Alexander Hamilton
Secretary of the Treasury

Treaty between the United States of America and the French Republic with Conventions (Louisiana Purchase, 1803)

The Louisiana Purchase opened up the western expansion of the United States. In 1803, Thomas Jefferson instructed his special envoy Robert Livingston to negotiate with the French for access to the port of New Orleans once it was learned that the Spanish were in the process of ceding the territory back to the French. The possibility for Americans to ship goods down the Mississippi River and from there transship the products to the eastern seaboard or other parts of the world determined the economic future of the new settlers in the Ohio Valley region. Napoleon, embroiled in a war with Great Britain for dominance over Europe, decided to sell Louisiana after the slave revolt on Haiti. His plan was initially to use Louisiana as the breadbasket for the slaves on his sugar plantations. Livingston agreed to the $15 million purchase price without authorization, but the Senate ratified the treaty anyway.

Source: http://www.imu.edu/madison/louisianapurchase/treatytext.htm.

The President of the United States of America and the First Consul of the French Republic in the name of the French People desiring to remove all Source of misunderstanding relative to objects of discussion mentioned in the Second and fifth articles of the Convention of the 8th Vendémiaire on 9/30 September 1800 relative to the rights claimed by the United States in virtue of the Treaty concluded at Madrid the 27 of October 1795, between His Catholic Majesty & the Said United States, & willing to Strengthen the union and friendship which at the time of the Said Convention was happily reestablished between the two nations have respectively named their Plenipotentiaries to wit The President of the United States, by and with the advice and consent of the Senate of the Said States; Robert R. Livingston Minister Plenipotentiary of the United States and James Monroe Minister Plenipotentiary and Envoy extraordinary of the Said States near the Government of the French Republic; And the First Consul in the name of the French people, Citizen Francis Barbé Marbois Minister of the public treasury who after having respectively exchanged their full powers have agreed to the following Articles.

Article I

Whereas by the Article the third of the Treaty concluded at St Ildefonso the 9th Vendémiaire on 1st October 1800 between the First Consul of the French Republic and his Catholic Majesty it was agreed as follows.

"His Catholic Majesty promises and engages on his part to cede to the French Republic six months after the full and entire execution of the conditions and Stipulations herein relative to his Royal Highness the Duke of Parma, the Colony or Province of Louisiana with the Same extent that it now has in the hand of Spain, & that it had when France possessed it; and Such as it Should be after the Treaties subsequently entered into between Spain and other States."

And whereas in pursuance of the Treaty and particularly of the third article the French Republic has an incontestible title to the domain and to the possession of the said Territory—The First Consul of the French Republic desiring to give to the United States a strong proof of his friendship doth hereby cede to the United States in the name of the French Republic for ever and in full Sovereignty the said territory with all its rights and appurtenances as fully and in the Same manner as they have been acquired by the French Republic in virtue of the above mentioned Treaty concluded with his Catholic Majesty.

Article II

In the cession made by the preceding article are included the adjacent Islands belonging to Louisiana all public lots and Squares, vacant lands and all public buildings, fortifications, barracks and other edifices which are not private property.—The Archives, papers & documents relative to the domain and Sovereignty of Louisiana and its dependences will be left in the possession of the Commissaries of the United States, and copies will be afterwards given in due form to the Magistrates and Municipal officers of such of the said papers and documents as may be necessary to them.

Article III

The inhabitants of the ceded territory shall be incorporated in the Union of the United States and admitted as soon as possible according to the principles of the federal Constitution to the enjoyment of all these rights, advantages and immunities of citizens of the United States, and in the mean time they shall be maintained and protected in the free enjoyment of their liberty, property and the Religion which they profess.

Article IV

There Shall be Sent by the Government of France a Commissary to Louisiana to the end that he do every act necessary as well to receive from the Officers of his Catholic

Majesty the Said country and its dependences in the name of the French Republic if it has not been already done as to transmit it in the name of the French Republic to the Commissary or agent of the United States.

Article V

Immediately after the ratification of the present Treaty by the President of the United States and in case that of the first Consul's shall have been previously obtained, the commissary of the French Republic shall remit all military posts of New Orleans and other parts of the ceded territory to the Commissary or Commissaries named by the President to take possession—the troops whether of France or Spain who may be there shall cease to occupy any military post from the time of taking possession and shall be embarked as soon as possible in the course of three months after the ratification of this treaty.

Article VI

The United States promise to execute Such treaties and articles as may have been agreed between Spain and the tribes and nations of Indians until by mutual consent of the United States and the said tribes or nations other Suitable articles Shall have been agreed upon.

Article VII

As it is reciprocally advantageous to the commerce of France and the United States to encourage the communication of both nations for a limited time in the country ceded by the present treaty until general arrangements relative to commerce of both nations may be agreed on; it has been agreed between the contracting parties that the French Ships coming directly from France or any of her colonies loaded only with the produce and manufactures of France or her Said Colonies; and the Ships of Spain coming directly from Spain or any of her colonies loaded only with the produce or manufactures of Spain or her Colonies shall be admitted during the Space of twelve years in the Port of New-Orleans and in all other legal ports-of-entry within the ceded territory in the Same manner as the Ships of the United States coming directly from France or Spain or any of their Colonies without being Subject to any other or greater duty on merchandize or other or greater tonnage than that paid by the citizens of the United States.

During that Space of time above mentioned no other nation Shall have a right to the Same privileges in the Ports of the ceded territory—the twelve years Shall commence three months after the exchange of ratifications if it Shall take place in France or three months after it Shall have been notified at Paris to the French Government if it Shall take place in the United States; It is however well understood that the object of the above article is to favour the manufactures, Commerce, freight and navigation of France and of Spain So far as relates to the importations that the French and Spanish Shall make into the Said Ports of the United States without in any Sort affecting the regulations that the United States may make concerning the exportation of the produce and merchandize of the United States, or any right they may have to make Such regulations.

Article VIII

In future and for ever after the expiration of the twelve years, the Ships of France shall be treated upon the footing of the most favoured nations in the ports above mentioned.

Article IX

The particular Convention Signed this day by the respective Ministers, having for its object to provide for the payment of debts due to the Citizens of the United States by the French Republic prior to the 30th Sept. 1800 (8th Vendé miaire an 9) is approved and to have its execution in the Same manner as if it had been inserted in this present treaty, and it Shall be ratified in the same form and in the Same time So that the one Shall not be ratified distinct from the other.

Another particular Convention Signed at the Same date as the present treaty relative to a definitive rule between the contracting parties is in the like manner approved and will be ratified in the Same form, and in the Same time and jointly.

Article X

The present treaty Shall be ratified in good and due form and the ratifications Shall be exchanged in the Space of Six months after the date of the Signature by the Ministers Plenipotentiary or Sooner if possible.

In faith whereof the respective Plenipotentiaries have Signed these articles in the French and English languages; declaring nevertheless that the present Treaty was originally agreed to in the French language; and have thereunto affixed their Seals.

Done at Paris the tenth day of Floreal in the eleventh year of the French Republic; and the 30th of April 1803.

Robt R Livingston [seal]
Jas. Monroe [seal]
Barbé Marbois [seal]

A CONVENTION BETWEEN THE UNITED STATES OF AMERICA AND THE FRENCH REPUBLIC

The President of the United States of America and the First Consul of the French Republic in the name of the French people, in consequence of the treaty of cession of Louisiana which has been Signed this day; wishing to regulate definitively every thing which has relation to the Said cession have authorized to this effect the Plenipotentiaries, that is to say the President of the United States has, by and with the advice and consent of the Senate of the Said States, nominated for their Plenipotentiaries, Robert R. Livingston, Minister Plenipotentiary of the United States, and James Monroe, Minister Plenipotentiary and Envoy-Extraordinary of the Said United States, near the Government of the French Republic; and the First Consul of the French Republic, in the name of the French people, has named as Pleniopotentiary of the Said Republic the citizen Francis Barbé Marbois: who, in virtue of their full powers, which have been exchanged this day, have agreed to the following articles:

Article 1

The Government of the United States engages to pay to the French government in the manner Specified in the following article the sum of Sixty millions of francs independant of the Sum which Shall be fixed by another Convention for the payment of the debts due by France to citizens of the United States.

Article 2

For the payment of the Sum of Sixty millions of francs mentioned in the preceding article the United States shall create a Stock of eleven millions, two hundred and fifty thousand Dollars bearing an interest of Six per cent: per annum payable half yearly in London Amsterdam or Paris amounting by the half year to three hundred and thirty Seven thousand five hundred Dollars, according to the proportions which Shall be determined by the French Government to be paid at either place: The principal of the Said Stock to be reimbursed at the treasury of the United States in annual payments of not less than three millions of Dollars each; of which the first payment Shall commence fifteen years after the date of the exchange of ratifications:—this Stock Shall be transferred to the government of France or to Such person or persons as Shall be authorized to receive it in three months at most after the exchange of ratifications of this treaty and after Louisiana Shall be taken possession of the name of the Government of the United States.

It is further agreed that if the French Government Should be desirous of disposing of the Said Stock to receive the capital in Europe at Shorter terms that its measures for that purpose Shall be taken So as to favour in the greatest degree possible the credit of the United States, and to raise to the highest price the Said Stock.

Article 3

It is agreed that the Dollar of the United States Specified in the present Convention shall be fixed at five francs 3333/100000 or five livres eight Sous tournois.

The present Convention Shall be ratified in good and due form, and the ratifications Shall be exchanged the Space of Six months to date from this day or Sooner if possible.

In faith of which the respective Plenipotentiaries have Signed the above articles both in the french and english languages, declaring nevertheless that the present treaty has been originally agreed on and written in the french language; to which they have hereunto affixed their Seals.

Done at Paris the tenth of Floreal eleventh year of the french Republic, 30th April 1803.

Robt R Livingston [seal]
Jas. Monroe [seal]
Barbé Marbois [seal]

CONVENTION BETWEEN THE UNITED STATES OF AMERICA AND THE FRENCH REPUBLIC

The President of the United States of America and the First Consul of the French Republic in the name of the French People having by a Treaty of this date terminated all difficulties relative to Louisiana, and established on a Solid foundation the friendship which unites the two nations and being desirous in complyance with the Second and fifth Articles of the Convention of the 8th Vendémiaire ninth year of the French Republic (30th September 1800) to Secure the payment of the Sums due by France to the citizens of the United States have respectively nominated as Plenipotentiaries that is to Say The President of the United States of America by and with the advise and consent of their Senate Robert R. Livingston Minister Plenipotentiary and James Monroe Minister Plenipotentiary and Envoy Extraordinary of the Said States near the Government of the French Republic: and the First Consul in the name of the French People the Citizen Francis Barbé Marbois Minister of the public treasury; who after having exchanged their full powers have agreed to the following articles.

Article 1

The debts due by France to citizens of the United States contracted before the 8th Vendémiaire ninth year of the French Republic (30th September 1800) Shall be paid according to the following regulations with interest at Six per Cent; to commence from the period when the accounts and vouchers were presented to the French Government.

Article 2

The debts provided for by the preceding Article are those whose result is comprised in the conjectural note annexed to the present Convention and which, with the interest cannot exceed the Sum of twenty millions of Francs. The claims comprised in the Said note which fall within the exceptions of the following articles, Shall not be admitted to the benefit of this provision.

Article 3

The principal and interests of the Said debts Shall be discharged by the United States, by orders drawn by their Minister Plenipotentiary on their treasury, these orders Shall be payable Sixty days after the exchange of ratifications of the Treaty and the Conventions Signed this day, and after possession Shall be given of Louisiana by the Commissaries of France to those of the United States.

Article 4

It is expressly agreed that the preceding articles Shall comprehend no debts but Such as are due to citizens of the United States who have been and are yet creditors of France for Supplies for embargoes and prizes made at Sea, in which the appeal has been properly lodged within the time mentioned in the Said Convention 8th Vendémiaire ninth year, (30th Sept 1800).

Article 5

The preceding Articles Shall apply only, First: to captures of which the council of prizes Shall have ordered restitution, it being well understood that the claimant cannot have recourse to the United States otherwise than he might have had to the Government of the French republic, and only in case of insufficiency of the captors—2d the debts mentioned in the Said fifth Article of the Convention contracted before the 8th Vendé miaire an 9/30th September 1800 the payment of which has been heretofore claimed of the actual Government of France and for which the creditors have a right to the protection of the United States;—the Said 5th Article does not comprehend prizes whose condemnation has been or Shall be confirmed: it is the express intention of the contracting parties not to extend the benefit of the present Convention to reclamations of American citizens who Shall have established houses of Commerce in France, England or other countries than the United States in partnership with foreigners, and who by that reason and the nature of their commerce ought to be regarded as domiciliated in the places where Such house exist.—All agreements and bargains concerning merchandize, which Shall not be the property of American citizens, are equally excepted from the benefit of the said Conventions, Saving however to Such persons their claims in like manner as if this Treaty had not been made.

Article 6

And that the different questions which may arise under the preceding article may be fairly investigated, the Ministers Plenipotentiary of the United States Shall name three persons, who Shall act from the present and provisionally, and who shall have full power to examine, without removing the documents, all the accounts of the different claims already liquidated by the Bureaus established for this purpose by the French Republic, and to ascertain whether they belong to the classes designated by the present Convention and the principles established in it or if they are not in one of its exceptions and on their Certificate, declaring that the debt is due to an American Citizen or his representative and that it existed before the 8th Vendémiaire 9th year/ 30 September 1800 the debtor shall be entitled to an order on the Treasury of the United States in the manner prescribed by the 3d Article.

Article 7

The Same agents Shall likewise have power, without removing the documents, to examine the claims which are prepared for verification, and to certify those which ought to be admitted by uniting the necessary qualifications, and not being comprised in the exceptions contained in the present Convention.

Article 8

The Same agents shall likewise examine the claims which are not prepared for liquidation, and certify in writing those which in their judgment ought to be admitted to liquidation.

Article 9

In proportion as the debts mentioned in these articles Shall be admitted they Shall be discharged with interest at Six per Cent: by the Treasury of the United States.

Article 10

And that no debt shall not have the qualifications above mentioned and that no unjust or exorbitant demand may be admitted, the Commercial agent of the United States at Paris or such other agent as the Minister Plenipotentiary or the United States Shall think proper to nominate shall assist at the operations of the Bureaus and cooperate in the examinations of the claims; and if this agent Shall be of the opinion that any debt is not completely proved, or if he shall judge that it is not comprised in the principles of the fifth article above mentioned, and if notwithstanding his opinion the Bureaus established by the french Government should think that it ought to be liquidated, he shall transmit his observations to the board established by the United States, who, without removing documents, shall make a complete examination of the debt and vouchers which Support it, and report the result to the Minister of the United States.—The Minister of the United States Shall transmit his observations in all Such cases to the Minister of the treasury of the French Republic, on whose report the French Government Shall decide definitively in every case.

The rejection of any claim Shall have no other effect than to exempt the United States from the payment of it, the French Government reserving to itself, the right to decide definitively on Such claim So far as it concerns itself.

Article 11

Every necessary decision Shall be made in the course of a year to commence from the exchange of ratifications, and no reclamation Shall be admitted afterwards.

Article 12

In case of claims for debts contracted by the Government of France with citizens of the United States Since the 8th Vendé miaire 9th year/30 September 1800 not being comprised in this Convention may be pursued, and the payment demanded in the Same manner as if it had not been made.

Article 13

The present convention Shall be ratified in good and due form and the ratifications Shall be exchanged in Six months from the date of the Signature of the Ministers Plenipotentiary, or Sooner if possible.

In faith of which, the respective Ministers Plenipotentiary have signed the above Articles both in the french and english languages, declaring nevertheless that the present treaty has been originally agreed on and written in the french language, to which they have hereunto affixed their Seals.

Done at Paris, the tenth of Floreal, eleventh year of the French Republic. 30th April 1803.

Robt R Livingston [seal]
Jas. Monroe [seal]
Barbé Marbois [seal]

Treaty of Guadalupe Hidalgo (1848)

The Treaty of Guadalupe Hidalgo ended the Mexican War between the United States and Mexico. Signed on February 2, 1848, the treaty established the southern boundary of the United States as the Rio Grande River. Mexico agreed to cede to the United States all of its land known as California and New Mexico—an area that comprises present-day California, Nevada, Utah, parts of Arizona, New Mexico, Colorado, and Wyoming. In exchange the United States offered $15 million in compensation to Mexico and assumed the debts of the Mexican government to U.S. citizens. The following year, gold was discovered in California. The natural resources and availability of this land greatly impacted the U.S. economy.

Source: http://www.yale.edu/lawweb/avalon/diplomacy/mexico/guadhida.htm.

TREATY OF PEACE, FRIENDSHIP, LIMITS, AND SETTLEMENT BETWEEN THE UNITED STATES OF AMERICA AND THE UNITED MEXICAN STATES CONCLUDED AT GUADALUPE HIDALGO, FEBRUARY 2, 1848; RATIFICATION ADVISED BY SENATE, WITH AMENDMENTS, MARCH 10, 1848; RATIFIED BY PRESIDENT, MARCH 16, 1848; RATIFICATIONS EXCHANGED AT QUERETARO, MAY 30, 1848; PROCLAIMED, JULY 4, 1848.

IN THE NAME OF ALMIGHTY GOD

The United States of America and the United Mexican States animated by a sincere desire to put an end to the calamities of the war which unhappily exists between the two Republics and to establish Upon a solid basis relations of peace and friendship, which shall confer reciprocal benefits upon the citizens of both, and assure the concord, harmony, and mutual confidence wherein the two people should live, as good neighbors have for that purpose appointed their respective plenipotentiaries, that is to say: The President of the United States has appointed Nicholas P. Trist, a citizen of the United States, and the President of the Mexican Republic has appointed Don Luis Gonzaga Cuevas, Don Bernardo Couto, and Don Miguel Atristain, citizens of the said Republic; Who, after a reciprocal communication of their respective full powers, have, under the protection of Almighty God, the author of peace, arranged, agreed upon, and signed the following:

Treaty of Peace, Friendship, Limits, and Settlement between the United States of America and the Mexican Republic.

ARTICLE I

There shall be firm and universal peace between the United States of America and the Mexican Republic, and between their respective countries, territories, cities, towns, and people, without exception of places or persons.

ARTICLE II

Immediately upon the signature of this treaty, a convention shall be entered into between a commissioner or commissioners appointed by the General-in-chief of the forces of the United States, and such as may be appointed by the Mexican Government, to the end that a provisional suspension of hostilities shall take place, and that, in the places occupied by the said forces, constitutional order may be reestablished, as regards the political, administrative, and judicial branches, so far as this shall be permitted by the circumstances of military occupation.

ARTICLE III

Immediately upon the ratification of the present treaty by the Government of the United States, orders shall be transmitted to the commanders of their land and naval forces, requiring the latter (provided this treaty shall then have been ratified by the Government of the Mexican Republic, and the ratifications exchanged) immediately to desist from blockading any Mexican ports and requiring the former (under the same condition) to commence, at the earliest moment practicable, withdrawing all troops of the United States then in the interior of the Mexican Republic, to points that shall be selected by common agreement, at a distance from the seaports not exceeding thirty leagues; and such evacuation of the interior of the Republic shall be completed with the least possible delay; the Mexican Government hereby binding itself to afford every facility in its power for rendering the same convenience to the troops, on their march and in their new positions, and for promoting a good understanding between them and the inhabitants. In like manner orders shall be dispatched to the persons in charge of the custom houses at all ports occupied by the forces of the United States, requiring them (under the same condition) immediately to deliver possession of the same to the persons authorized by the Mexican Government to receive it, together with all bonds and evidences of debt for duties on importations and on exportations, not yet fallen due. Moreover, a faithful and exact account shall be made out, showing the entire amount of all duties on imports and on exports, collected at such custom-houses, or elsewhere in Mexico, by authority of the United States, from and after the day of ratification of this treaty by the Government of the Mexican Republic; and also an account of the cost of collection; and such entire amount, deducting only the cost of collection, shall be delivered to the Mexican Government, at the city of Mexico, within three months after the exchange of ratifications.

The evacuation of the capital of the Mexican Republic by the troops of the United States, in virtue of the above stipulation, shall be completed in one month after the orders there stipulated for shall have been received by the commander of said troops, or sooner if possible.

ARTICLE IV

Immediately after the exchange of ratifications of the present treaty all castles, forts, territories, places, and possessions, which have been taken or occupied by the forces of the United States during the present war, within the limits of the Mexican Republic, as about to be established by the following article, shall be definitely restored to the said Republic, together with all the artillery, arms, apparatus of war, munitions, and other public property, which were in the said castles and forts when captured, and which shall remain there at the time when this treaty shall be duly ratified by the Government of the Mexican Republic. To this end, immediately upon the signature of this treaty, orders shall be dispatched to the American officers commanding such castles and forts, securing against the removal or destruction of any such artillery, arms, apparatus of war, munitions, or other public property. The city of Mexico, within the inner line of entrenchments surrounding the said city, is comprehended in the above stipulation, as regards the restoration of artillery, apparatus of war, & c.

The final evacuation of the territory of the Mexican Republic, by the forces of the United States, shall be completed in three months from the said exchange of ratifications, or sooner if possible; the Mexican Government hereby engaging, as in the foregoing article to use all means in its power for facilitating such evacuation, and rendering it convenient to the troops, and for promoting a good understanding between them and the inhabitants.

If, however, the ratification of this treaty by both parties should not take place in time to allow the embarcation of the troops of the United States to be completed before the commencement of the sickly season, at the Mexican ports on the Gulf of Mexico, in such case a friendly arrangement shall be entered into between the General-in-Chief of the said troops and the Mexican Government, whereby healthy and otherwise suitable places, at a distance from the ports not exceeding thirty leagues, shall be designated for the residence of such troops as may not yet have embarked, until the return of the healthy season. And the space of time here referred to as, comprehending the sickly season shall be understood to extend from the first day of May to the first day of November.

All prisoners of war taken on either side, on land or on sea, shall be restored as soon as practicable after the exchange of ratifications of this treaty. It is also agreed that if any Mexicans should now be held as captives by any savage tribe within the limits of the United States, as about to be established by the following article, the Government of the said United States will exact the release of such captives and cause them to be restored to their country.

ARTICLE V

The boundary line between the two Republics shall commence in the Gulf of Mexico, three leagues from land, opposite the mouth of the Rio Grande, otherwise called Rio Bravo del Norte, or Opposite the mouth of its deepest branch, if it should have more than one branch emptying directly into the sea; from thence up the middle of that river, following the deepest channel, where it has more than one, to the point where it strikes the southern boundary of New Mexico; thence, westwardly, along the whole southern boundary of New Mexico (which runs north of the town called Paso) to its western termination; thence, northward, along the western line of New Mexico, until it intersects the first branch of the river Gila; (or if it should not intersect any branch of that river, then to the point on the said line nearest to such branch, and thence in a direct line to the same); thence down the middle of the said branch and of the said river, until it empties into the Rio Colorado; thence across the Rio Colorado, following the division line between Upper and Lower California, to the Pacific Ocean.

The southern and western limits of New Mexico, mentioned in the article, are those laid down in the map entitled "Map of the United Mexican States, as organized and defined by various acts of the Congress of said republic, and constructed according to the best authorities. Revised edition. Published at New York, in 1847, by J. Disturnell," of which map a copy is added to this treaty, bearing the signatures and seals of the undersigned Plenipotentiaries, And, in order to preclude all difficulty in tracing upon the ground the limit separating Upper from Lower California, it is agreed that the said limit shall consist of a straight line drawn from the middle of the Rio Gila, where it unites with the Colorado, to a point on the coast of the Pacific Ocean, distant one marine league due south of the southernmost point of the port of San Diego, according to the plan of said port made in the year 1782 by Don Juan Pantoja, second sailing-master of the Spanish fleet, and published at Madrid in the year 1802, in the atlas to the voyage of the schooners Sutil and Mexicana; of which plan a copy is hereunto added, signed and sealed by the respective Plenipotentiaries.

In order to designate the boundary line with due precision, upon authoritative maps, and to establish upon the ground land-marks which shall show the limits of both republics, as described in the present article, the two Governments shall each appoint a commissioner and a surveyor, who, before the expiration of one year from the date of the exchange of ratifications of this treaty, shall meet at the port of San Diego, and proceed to run and mark the said boundary in its whole course to the mouth of the Rio Bravo del Norte. They shall keep journals and make out plans of their operations; and the result agreed upon by them shall be deemed a part of this treaty, and shall have the same force as if it were inserted therein. The two Governments will amicably agree regarding what may be necessary to these persons, and also as to their respective escorts, should such be necessary.

The boundary line established by this article shall be religiously respected by each of the two republics, and no change shall ever be made therein, except by the express and free consent of both nations, lawfully given by the General Government of each, in conformity with its own constitution.

ARTICLE VI

The vessels and citizens of the United States shall, in all time, have a free and uninterrupted passage by the Gulf of California, and by the river Colorado below its confluence with the Gila, to and from their possessions situated north of the boundary line defined in the preceding article; it being understood that this passage is to be by navigating the Gulf of California and the river Colorado, and not by land, without the express consent of the Mexican Government.

If, by the examinations which may be made, it should be ascertained to be practicable and advantageous to construct a road, canal, or railway, which should in whole or in part run upon the river Gila, or upon its right or its left bank, within the space of one marine league from either margin of the river, the Governments of both republics will form an agreement regarding its construction, in order that it may serve equally for the use and advantage of both countries.

ARTICLE VII

The river Gila, and the part of the Rio Bravo del Norte lying below the southern boundary of New Mexico, being, agreeably to the fifth article, divided in the middle between the two republics, the navigation of the Gila and of the Bravo below said boundary shall be free and common to the vessels and citizens of both countries; and neither shall, without the consent of the other, construct any work that may impede or interrupt, in whole or in part, the exercise of this right; not even for the purpose of favoring new methods of navigation. Nor shall any tax or contribution, under any denomination or title, be levied upon vessels or persons navigating the same or upon merchandise or effects transported thereon, except in the case of landing upon one of their shores. If, for the purpose of making the said rivers navigable, or for maintaining them in such state, it should be necessary or advantageous to establish any tax or contribution, this shall not be done without the consent of both Governments.

The stipulations contained in the present article shall not impair the territorial rights of either republic within its established limits.

ARTICLE VIII

Mexicans now established in territories previously belonging to Mexico, and which remain for the future within the limits of the United States, as defined by the present treaty, shall be free to continue where they now reside, or to remove at any time to the Mexican Republic, retaining the property which they possess in the said territories, or disposing thereof, and removing the proceeds wherever they please, without their being subjected, on this account, to any contribution, tax, or charge whatever.

Those who shall prefer to remain in the said territories may either retain the title and rights of Mexican citizens, or acquire those of citizens of the United States. But they shall be under the obligation to make their election within one year from the date of the exchange of ratifications of this treaty; and those who shall remain in the said territories after the expiration of that year, without having declared their intention to retain the character of Mexicans, shall be considered to have elected to become citizens of the United States.

In the said territories, property of every kind, now belonging to Mexicans not established there, shall be inviolably respected. The present owners, the heirs of these, and all Mexicans who may hereafter acquire said property by contract, shall enjoy with respect to it guarantees equally ample as if the same belonged to citizens of the United States.

ARTICLE IX

The Mexicans who, in the territories aforesaid, shall not preserve the character of citizens of the Mexican Republic, conformably with what is stipulated in the preceding article, shall be incorporated into the Union of the United States and be admitted at the proper time (to be judged of by the Congress of the United States) to the enjoyment of all the rights of citizens of the United States, according to the principles of the Constitution; and in the mean time, shall be maintained and protected in the free enjoyment of their liberty and property, and secured in the free exercise of their religion without restriction.

ARTICLE X

[Stricken out by the United States Amendments]

ARTICLE XI

Considering that a great part of the territories, which, by the present treaty, are to be comprehended for the future within the limits of the United States, is now occupied by savage tribes, who will hereafter be under the exclusive control of the Government of the United States, and whose incursions within the territory of Mexico would be prejudicial in the extreme, it is solemnly agreed that all such incursions shall be forcibly restrained by the Government of the United States whensoever this may be necessary; and that when they cannot be prevented, they shall be punished by the said Government, and satisfaction for the same shall be exacted all in the same way, and with equal diligence and energy, as if the same incursions were meditated or committed within its own territory, against its own citizens.

It shall not be lawful, under any pretext whatever, for any inhabitant of the United States to purchase or acquire any Mexican, or any foreigner residing in Mexico, who may have been captured by Indians inhabiting the territory of either of the two republics; nor to purchase or acquire horses, mules, cattle, or property of any kind, stolen within Mexican territory by such Indians.

And in the event of any person or persons, captured within Mexican territory by Indians, being carried into the territory of the United States, the Government of the latter engages and binds itself, in the most solemn manner, so soon as it shall know of such captives being within its territory, and shall be able so to do, through the faithful exercise of its influence and power, to rescue them and return them to their country or deliver them to the agent or representative of the Mexican Government. The Mexican authorities will, as far as practicable, give to the Government of the United States notice of such captures; and its agents shall pay the expenses incurred in the maintenance and transmission of the rescued captives; who, in the mean time, shall be treated with the utmost hospitality by the American authorities at the place where they may be. But if the Government of the United States, before receiving such notice from Mexico, should obtain intelligence, through any other channel, of the existence of Mexican captives within its territory, it will proceed forthwith to effect their release and delivery to the Mexican agent, as above stipulated.

For the purpose of giving to these stipulations the fullest possible efficacy, thereby affording the security and redress demanded by their true spirit and intent, the Government of the United States will now and hereafter pass, without unnecessary delay, and always vigilantly enforce, such laws as the nature of the subject may require. And, finally, the sacredness of this obligation shall never be lost sight of by the said Government, when providing for the removal of the Indians from any portion of the said territories, or for its being settled by citizens of the United States; but, on the contrary, special care shall then be taken not to place its Indian occupants under the necessity of seeking new homes, by committing those invasions which the United States have solemnly obliged themselves to restrain.

ARTICLE XII

In consideration of the extension acquired by the boundaries of the United States, as defined in the fifth article of the present treaty, the Government of the United States engages to pay to that of the Mexican Republic the sum of fifteen millions of dollars.

Immediately after the treaty shall have been duly ratified by the Government of the Mexican Republic, the sum of three millions of dollars shall be paid to the said Government by that of the United States, at the city of Mexico, in the gold or silver coin of Mexico. The remaining twelve millions of dollars shall be paid at the same place, and in the same coin, in annual installments of three millions of dollars each, together with interest on the same at the rate of six per centum per annum. This interest shall begin to run upon the whole sum of twelve millions from the day of the ratification of the present treaty by the Mexican Government, and the first of the installments shall be paid at the expiration of one year from the same day. Together with each annual installment, as it falls due, the whole interest accruing on such installment from the beginning shall also be paid.

ARTICLE XIII

The United States engage, moreover, to assume and pay to the claimants all the amounts now due them, and those hereafter to become due, by reason of the claims already liquidated and decided against the Mexican Republic, under the conventions between the two republics severally concluded on the eleventh day of April, eighteen hundred and thirty-nine, and on the thirtieth day of January, eighteen hundred and forty-three; so that the Mexican Republic shall be absolutely exempt, for the future, from all expense whatever on account of the said claims.

ARTICLE XIV

The United States do furthermore discharge the Mexican Republic from all claims of citizens of the United States, not heretofore decided against the Mexican Government, which may have arisen previously to the date of the signature of this treaty; which discharge shall be final and perpetual, whether the said claims be rejected or be allowed by the board of commissioners provided for in the following article, and whatever shall be the total amount of those allowed.

ARTICLE XV

The United States, exonerating Mexico from all demands on account of the claims of their citizens mentioned in the preceding article, and considering them entirely and forever canceled, whatever their amount may be, undertake to make satisfaction for the same, to an amount not exceeding three and one-quarter millions of dollars. To ascertain the validity and amount of those claims, a board of commissioners shall be established by the Government of the United States, whose awards shall be final and conclusive; provided that, in deciding upon the validity of each claim, the board shall be guided and governed by the principles and rules of decision prescribed by the first and fifth articles of the unratified convention, concluded at the city of Mexico on the twentieth day of November, one thousand eight hundred and forty-three; and in no case shall an award be made in favour of any claim not embraced by these principles and rules.

If, in the opinion of the said board of commissioners or of the claimants, any books, records, or documents, in the possession or power of the Government of the Mexican Republic, shall be deemed necessary to the just decision of any claim, the commissioners, or the claimants through them, shall, within such period as Congress may designate, make an application in writing for the same, addressed to the Mexican Minister of Foreign Affairs, to be transmitted by the Secretary of State of the United States; and the Mexican Government engages, at the earliest possible moment after the receipt of such demand, to cause any of the books, records, or documents so specified, which shall be in their possession or power (or authenticated copies or extracts of the same), to be transmitted to the said Secretary of State, who shall immediately deliver them over to the said board of commissioners; provided that no such application shall be made by or at the instance of any claimant, until the facts which it is expected to prove by such books, records, or documents, shall have been stated under oath or affirmation.

ARTICLE XVI

Each of the contracting parties reserves to itself the entire right to fortify whatever point within its territory it may judge proper so to fortify for its security.

ARTICLE XVII

The treaty of amity, commerce, and navigation, concluded at the city of Mexico, on the fifth day of April, a.d. 1831, between the United States of America and the United Mexican States, except the additional article, and except so far as the stipulations of the said treaty may be incompatible with any stipulation contained in the present treaty, is hereby revived for the period of eight years from the day of the exchange of ratifications of this treaty, with the same force and virtue as if incorporated therein; it being understood that each of the contracting parties reserves to itself the right, at any time after the said period of eight years shall have expired, to terminate the same by giving one year's notice of such intention to the other party.

ARTICLE XVIII

All supplies whatever for troops of the United States in Mexico, arriving at ports in the occupation of such troops previous to the final evacuation thereof, although subsequently to the restoration of the custom-houses at such ports, shall be entirely exempt from duties and charges of any kind; the Government of the United States hereby engaging and pledging its faith to establish and vigilantly to enforce, all possible guards for securing the revenue of Mexico, by preventing the importation, under cover of this stipulation, of any articles other than such, both in kind and in quantity, as shall really be wanted for the use and consumption of the forces of the United

States during the time they may remain in Mexico. To this end it shall be the duty of all officers and agents of the United States to denounce to the Mexican authorities at the respective ports any attempts at a fraudulent abuse of this stipulation, which they may know of, or may have reason to suspect, and to give to such authorities all the aid in their power with regard thereto; and every such attempt, when duly proved and established by sentence of a competent tribunal, They shall be punished by the confiscation of the property so attempted to be fraudulently introduced.

ARTICLE XIX

With respect to all merchandise, effects, and property whatsoever, imported into ports of Mexico, whilst in the occupation of the forces of the United States, whether by citizens of either republic, or by citizens or subjects of any neutral nation, the following rules shall be observed:

(1) All such merchandise, effects, and property, if imported previously to the restoration of the custom-houses to the Mexican authorities, as stipulated for in the third article of this treaty, shall be exempt from confiscation, although the importation of the same be prohibited by the Mexican tariff.

(2) The same perfect exemption shall be enjoyed by all such merchandise, effects, and property, imported subsequently to the restoration of the custom-houses, and previously to the sixty days fixed in the following article for the coming into force of the Mexican tariff at such ports respectively; the said merchandise, effects, and property being, however, at the time of their importation, subject to the payment of duties, as provided for in the said following article.

(3) All merchandise, effects, and property described in the two rules foregoing shall, during their continuance at the place of importation, and upon their leaving such place for the interior, be exempt from all duty, tax, or imposts of every kind, under whatsoever title or denomination. Nor shall they be there subject to any charge whatsoever upon the sale thereof.

(4) All merchandise, effects, and property, described in the first and second rules, which shall have been removed to any place in the interior, whilst such place was in the occupation of the forces of the United States, shall, during their continuance therein, be exempt from all tax upon the sale or consumption thereof, and from every kind of impost or contribution, under whatsoever title or denomination.

(5) But if any merchandise, effects, or property, described in the first and second rules, shall be removed to any place not occupied at the time by the forces of the United States, they shall, upon their introduction into such place, or upon their sale or consumption there, be subject to the same duties which, under the Mexican laws, they would be required to pay in such cases if they had been imported in time of

peace, through the maritime custom-houses, and had there paid the duties conformably with the Mexican tariff.

(6) The owners of all merchandise, effects, or property, described in the first and second rules, and existing in any port of Mexico, shall have the right to reship the same, exempt from all tax, impost, or contribution whatever.

With respect to the metals, or other property, exported from any Mexican port whilst in the occupation of the forces of the United States, and previously to the restoration of the custom-house at such port, no person shall be required by the Mexican authorities, whether general or state, to pay any tax, duty, or contribution upon any such exportation, or in any manner to account for the same to the said authorities.

ARTICLE XX

Through consideration for the interests of commerce generally, it is agreed, that if less than sixty days should elapse between the date of the signature of this treaty and the restoration of the custom houses, conformably with the stipulation in the third article, in such case all merchandise, effects and property whatsoever, arriving at the Mexican ports after the restoration of the said custom-houses, and previously to the expiration of sixty days after the day of signature of this treaty, shall be admitted to entry; and no other duties shall be levied thereon than the duties established by the tariff found in force at such custom-houses at the time of the restoration of the same. And to all such merchandise, effects, and property, the rules established by the preceding article shall apply.

ARTICLE XXI

If unhappily any disagreement should hereafter arise between the Governments of the two republics, whether with respect to the interpretation of any stipulation in this treaty, or with respect to any other particular concerning the political or commercial relations of the two nations, the said Governments, in the name of those nations, do promise to each other that they will endeavour, in the most sincere and earnest manner, to settle the differences so arising, and to preserve the state of peace and friendship in which the two countries are now placing themselves, using, for this end, mutual representations and pacific negotiations. And if, by these means, they should not be enabled to come to an agreement, a resort shall not, on this account, be had to reprisals, aggression, or hostility of any kind, by the one republic against the other, until the Government of that which deems itself aggrieved shall have maturely considered, in the spirit of peace and good neighbourship, whether it would not be better that such difference should be settled by the arbitration of commissioners appointed on each side, or by that of a friendly nation. And should such course be proposed by either party, it shall be acceded to by the other, unless deemed by it altogether incompatible with the nature of the difference, or the circumstances of the case.

ARTICLE XXII

If (which is not to be expected, and which God forbid) war should unhappily break out between the two republics, they do now, with a view to such calamity, solemnly pledge themselves to each other and to the world to observe the following rules; absolutely where the nature of the subject permits, and as closely as possible in all cases where such absolute observance shall be impossible:

(1) The merchants of either republic then residing in the other shall be allowed to remain twelve months (for those dwelling in the interior), and six months (for those dwelling at the seaports) to collect their debts and settle their affairs; during which periods they shall enjoy the same protection, and be on the same footing, in all respects, as the citizens or subjects of the most friendly nations; and, at the expiration thereof, or at any time before, they shall have full liberty to depart, carrying off all their effects without molestation or hindrance, conforming therein to the same laws which the citizens or subjects of the most friendly nations are required to conform to. Upon the entrance of the armies of either nation into the territories of the other, women and children, ecclesiastics, scholars of every faculty, cultivators of the earth, merchants, artisans, manufacturers, and fishermen, unarmed and inhabiting unfortified towns, villages, or places, and in general all persons whose occupations are for the common subsistence and benefit of mankind, shall be allowed to continue their respective employments, unmolested in their persons. Nor shall their houses or goods be burnt or otherwise destroyed, nor their cattle taken, nor their fields wasted, by the armed force into whose power, by the events of war, they may happen to fall; but if the necessity arise to take anything from them for the use of such armed force, the same shall be paid for at an equitable price. All churches, hospitals, schools, colleges, libraries, and other establishments for charitable and beneficent purposes, shall be respected, and all persons connected with the same protected in the discharge of their duties, and the pursuit of their vocations.

(2) In order that the fate of prisoners of war may be alleviated all such practices as those of sending them into distant, inclement or unwholesome districts, or crowding them into close and noxious places, shall be studiously avoided. They shall not be confined in dungeons, prison ships, or prisons; nor be put in irons, or bound or otherwise restrained in the use of their limbs. The officers shall enjoy liberty on their paroles, within convenient districts, and have comfortable quarters; and the common soldiers shall be disposed in cantonments, open and extensive enough for air and exercise and lodged in barracks as roomy and good as are provided by the party in whose power they are for its own troops. But if any officer shall break his parole by leaving the district so assigned him, or any other prisoner shall escape from the limits of his cantonment after they shall have been designated to him, such individual, officer, or other prisoner, shall forfeit so much of the benefit of this article as provides for his liberty on parole or in cantonment. And if any officer so breaking his parole or any

common soldier so escaping from the limits assigned him, shall afterwards be found in arms previously to his being regularly exchanged, the person so offending shall be dealt with according to the established laws of war. The officers shall be daily furnished, by the party in whose power they are, with as many rations, and of the same articles, as are allowed either in kind or by commutation, to officers of equal rank in its own army; and all others shall be daily furnished with such ration as is allowed to a common soldier in its own service; the value of all which supplies shall, at the close of the war, or at periods to be agreed upon between the respective commanders, be paid by the other party, on a mutual adjustment of accounts for the subsistence of prisoners; and such accounts shall not be mingled with or set off against any others, nor the balance due on them withheld, as a compensation or reprisal for any cause whatever, real or pretended. Each party shall be allowed to keep a commissary of prisoners, appointed by itself, with every cantonment of prisoners, in possession of the other; which commissary shall see the prisoners as often as he pleases; shall be allowed to receive, exempt from all duties and taxes, and to distribute, whatever comforts may be sent to them by their friends; and shall be free to transmit his reports in open letters to the party by whom he is employed.

And it is declared that neither the pretense that war dissolves all treaties, nor any other whatever, shall be considered as annulling or suspending the solemn covenant contained in this article. On the contrary, the state of war is precisely that for which it is provided; and, during which, its stipulations are to be as sacredly observed as the most acknowledged obligations under the law of nature or nations.

ARTICLE XXIII

This treaty shall be ratified by the President of the United States of America, by and with the advice and consent of the Senate thereof; and by the President of the Mexican Republic, with the previous approbation of its general Congress; and the ratifications shall be exchanged in the City of Washington, or at the seat of Government of Mexico, in four months from the date of the signature hereof, or sooner if practicable.

In faith whereof we, the respective Plenipotentiaries, have signed this treaty of peace, friendship, limits, and settlement, and have hereunto affixed our seals respectively. Done in quintuplicate, at the city of Guadalupe Hidalgo, on the second day of February, in the year of our Lord one thousand eight hundred and forty-eight.

N. P. TRIST
LUIS P. CUEVAS
BERNARDO COUTO
MIGL. ATRISTAIN

* * *

Article IX was modified and Article X was stricken by the U.S. Congress. The following are the original articles. An explanation or agreement of why the articles were stricken, known as the protocol of Querétaro, is also included below.

* * *

ARTICLE IX

The Mexicans who, in the territories aforesaid, shall not preserve the character of citizens of the Mexican Republic, conformably with what is stipulated in the preceding Article, shall be incorporated into the Union of the United States, and admitted as soon as possible, according to the principles of the Federal Constitution, to the enjoyment of all the rights of citizens of the United States. In the mean time, they shall be maintained and protected in the enjoyment of their liberty, their property, and the civil rights now vested in them according to the Mexican laws. With respect to political rights, their condition shall be on an equality with that of the inhabitants of the other territories of the United States; and at least equally good as that of the inhabitants of Louisiana and the Floridas, when these provinces, by transfer from the French Republic and the Crown of Spain, became territories of the United States.

The same most ample guaranty shall be enjoyed by all ecclesiastics and religious corporations or communities, as well in the discharge of the offices of their ministry, as in the enjoyment of their property of every kind, whether individual or corporate. This guaranty shall embrace all temples, houses and edifices dedicated to the Roman Catholic worship; as well as all property destined to its support, or to that of schools, hospitals and other foundations for charitable or beneficent purposes. No property of this nature shall be considered as having become the property of the American Government, or as subject to be, by it, disposed of or diverted to other uses.

Finally, the relations and communication between the Catholics living in the territories aforesaid, and their respective ecclesiastical authorities, shall be open, free and exempt from all hindrance whatever, even although such authorities should reside within the limits of the Mexican Republic, as defined by this treaty; and this freedom shall continue, so long as a new demarcation of ecclesiastical districts shall not have been made, conformably with the laws of the Roman Catholic Church.

ARTICLE X

All grants of land made by the Mexican government or by the competent authorities, in territories previously appertaining to Mexico, and remaining for the future within the limits of the United States, shall be respected as valid, to the same extent that the same grants would be valid, to the said territories had remained within the limits of Mexico.

But the grantees of lands in Texas, put in possession thereof, who, by reason of the circumstances of the country since the beginning of the troubles between Texas and the Mexican Government, may have been prevented from fulfilling all the conditions of their grants, shall be under the obligation to fulfill the said conditions within the periods limited in the same respectively; such periods to be now counted from the date of the exchange of ratifications of this Treaty: in default of which the said grants shall not be obligatory upon the State of Texas, in virtue of the stipulations contained in this Article.

The foregoing stipulation in regard to grantees of land in Texas, is extended to all grantees of land in the territories aforesaid, elsewhere than in Texas, put in possession under such grants; and, in default of the fulfillment of the conditions of any such grant, within the new period, which, as is above stipulated, begins with the day of the exchange of ratifications of this treaty, the same shall be null and void.

THE PROTOCOL OF QUERÉTARO

In the city of Queretaro on the twenty sixth of the month of May eighteen hundred and forty-eight at a conference between Their Excellencies Nathan Clifford and Ambrose H. Sevier Commissioners of the United States of America, with full powers from their Government to make to the Mexican Republic suitable explanations in regard to the amendments which the Senate and Government of the said United States have made in the treaty of peace, friendship, limits and definitive settlement between the two Republics, signed in Guadalupe Hidalgo, on the second day of February of the present year, and His Excellency Don Luis de la Rosa, Minister of Foreign Affairs of the Republic of Mexico, it was agreed, after adequate conversation respecting the changes alluded to, to record in the present protocol the following explanations which Their aforesaid Excellencies the Commissioners gave in the name of their Government and in fulfillment of the Commission conferred upon them near the Mexican Republic.

First.

The American Government by suppressing the IXth article of the Treaty of Guadalupe and substituting the III article of the Treaty of Louisiana did not intend to diminish in any way what was agreed upon by the aforesaid article IXth in favor of the inhabitants of the territories ceded by Mexico. Its understanding that all of that agreement is contained in the IIId article of the Treaty of Louisiana. In consequence, all the privileges and guarantees, civil, political and religious, which would have been possessed by the inhabitants of the ceded territories, if the IXth article of the Treaty had been retained, will be enjoyed by them without any difference under the article which has been substituted.

Second.

The American Government, by suppressing the Xth article of the Treaty of Guadalupe did not in any way intend to annul the grants of lands made by Mexico in the ceded territories. These grants, notwithstanding the suppression of the article of the Treaty, preserve the legal value which they may possess; and the grantees may cause their legitimate titles to be acknowledged before the American tribunals.

Conformably to the law of the United States, legitimate titles to every description of property personal and real, existing in the ceded territories, are those which were legitimate titles under the Mexican law in California and New Mexico up to the 13th of May 1846, and in Texas up to the 2d March 1836.

Third.

The Government of the United States by suppressing the concluding paragraph of article XIIth of the Treaty, did not intend to deprive the Mexican Republic of the free and unrestrained faculty of ceding, conveying or transferring at any time (as it may judge best, the sum of the twelve millions of dollars which the same Government of the United States is to deliver in the places designated by the amended article.

And these explanations having been accepted by the Minister of Foreign Affairs of the Mexican Republic, he declared in name of his Government that with the understanding conveyed by them, the same Government would proceed to ratify the Treaty of Guadalupe as modified by the Senate and Government of the United States. In testimony of which their Excellencies the aforesaid Commissioners and the Minister have signed and sealed in quintuplicate the present protocol.

[Seal] A. H. Sevier
[Seal] Nathan Clifford
[Seal] Luis de la Rosa

Gadsden Purchase Treaty (1853)

In 1853, just five years after the signing of the Treaty of Guadalupe Hidalgo, the United States negotiated the purchase of a narrow strip of land in the Mesilla Valley of northern Mexico. The Gadsden Purchase, named after U.S. negotiator James Gadsden, covered approximately 30,000 square miles. Mexico received $10 million in compensation from the United States. Used for the southern route of the railroad to the Pacific, this land currently is located in the southern portions of Arizona and New Mexico.

Source: http://www.yale.edu/lawweb/avalon/diplomacy/mexico/mx1853.htm.

BY THE PRESIDENT OF THE UNITED STATES OF AMERICA

A PROCLAMATION.

WHEREAS a treaty between the United States of America and the Mexican Republic was concluded and signed at the City of Mexico on the thirtieth day of December, one thousand eight hundred and fifty-three; which treaty, as amended by the Senate of the United States, and being in the English and Spanish languages, is word for word as follows:

IN THE NAME OF ALMIGHTY GOD:

The Republic of Mexico and the United States of America desiring to remove every cause of disagreement which might interfere in any manner with the better friendship and intercourse between the two countries, and especially in respect to the true limits which should be established, when, notwithstanding what was covenanted in the treaty of Guadalupe Hidalgo in the year 1848, opposite interpretations have been urged, which might give occasion to questions of serious moment: to avoid these, and to strengthen and more firmly maintain the peace which happily prevails between the two republics, the President of the United States has, for this purpose, appointed James Gadsden, Envoy Extraordinary and Minister Plenipotentiary of the same, near the Mexican government, and the President of Mexico has appointed as Plenipotentiary "ad hoc" his excellency Don Manuel Diez de Bonilla, cavalier grand cross of the national and distinguished order of Guadalupe, and Secretary of State, and of the office of Foreign Relations, and Don Jose Salazar Ylarregui and General Mariano Monterde as scientific commissioners, invested with full powers for this negotiation, who, having communicated their respective full powers, and finding them in due and proper form, have agreed upon the articles following:

ARTICLE I.

The Mexican Republic agrees to designate the following as her true limits with the United States for the future: retaining the same dividing line between the two Californias as already defined and established, according to the 5th article of the treaty of Guadalupe Hidalgo, the limits between the two republics shall be as follows: Beginning in the Gulf of Mexico, three leagues from land, opposite the mouth of the Rio Grande, as provided in the 5th article of the treaty of Guadalupe Hidalgo; thence, as defined in the said article, up the middle of that river to the point where the parallel of 31° 47′ north latitude crosses the same; thence due west one hundred miles; thence south to the parallel of 31° 20′ north latitude; thence along the said parallel of 31° 20′ to the 111th meridian of longitude west of Greenwich; thence in a straight line to a point on the Colorado River twenty English miles below the junction of the Gila and Colorado rivers; thence up the middle of the said river Colorado until it intersects the present line between the United States and Mexico.

For the performance of this portion of the treaty, each of the two governments shall nominate one commissioner, to the end that, by common consent the two thus nominated, having met in the city of Paso del Norte, three months after the exchange of the ratifications of this treaty, may proceed to survey and mark out upon the land the dividing line stipulated by this article, where it shall not have already been surveyed and established by the mixed commission, according to the treaty of Guadalupe, keeping a journal and making proper plans of their operations. For this purpose, if they should judge it necessary, the contracting parties shall be at liberty each to unite to its respective commissioner, scientific or other assistants, such as astronomers and surveyors, whose concurrence shall not be considered necessary for the settlement and of a true line of division between the two Republics; that line shall be alone established upon which the commissioners may fix, their consent in this particular being considered decisive and an integral part of this treaty, without necessity of ulterior ratification or approval, and without room for interpretation of any kind by either of the parties contracting.

The dividing line thus established shall, in all time, be faithfully respected by the two governments, without any variation therein, unless of the express and free consent of the two, given in conformity to the principles of the law of nations, and in accordance with the constitution of each country respectively.

In consequence, the stipulation in the 5th article of the treaty of Guadalupe upon the boundary line therein described is no longer of any force, wherein it may conflict with that here established, the said line being considered annulled and abolished wherever it may not coincide with the present, and in the same manner remaining in full force where in accordance with the same.

ARTICLE II.

The government of Mexico hereby releases the United States from all liability on account of the obligations contained in the eleventh article of the treaty of Guadalupe Hidalgo; and the said article and the thirty-third article of the treaty of amity, commerce, and navigation between the United States of America and the United Mexican States concluded at Mexico, on the fifth day of April, 1831, are hereby abrogated.

ARTICLE III.

In consideration of the foregoing stipulations, the Government of the United States agrees to pay to the government of Mexico, in the city of New York, the sum of ten millions of dollars, of which seven millions shall be paid immediately upon the exchange of the ratifications of this treaty, and the remaining three millions as soon as the boundary line shall be surveyed, marked, and established.

ARTICLE IV.

The provisions of the 6th and 7th articles of the treaty of Guadalupe Hidalgo having been rendered nugatory, for the most part, by the cession of territory granted in the first article of this treaty, the said articles are hereby abrogated and annulled, and the provisions as herein expressed substituted therefor. The vessels, and citizens of the United States shall, in all time, have free and uninterrupted passage through the Gulf of California, to and from their possessions situated north of the boundary line of the two countries. It being understood that this passage is to be by navigating the Gulf of California and the river Colorado, and not by land, without the express consent of the Mexican government; and precisely the same provisions, stipulations, and restrictions, in all respects, are hereby agreed upon and adopted, and shall be scrupulously observed and enforced by the two contracting governments in reference to the Rio Colorado, so far and for such distance as the middle of that river is made their common boundary line by the first article of this treaty.

The several provisions, stipulations, and restrictions contained in the 7th article of the treaty of Guadalupe Hidalgo shall remain in force only so far as regards the Rio Bravo del Forte, below the initial of the said boundary provided in the first article of this treaty; that is to say, below the intersection of the 31° 47′ parallel of latitude, with the boundary line established by the late treaty dividing said river from its mouth upwards, according to the fifth article of the treaty of Guadalupe.

ARTICLE V.

All the provisions of the eighth and ninth, sixteenth and seventeenth articles of the treaty of Guadalupe Hidalgo, shall apply to the territory ceded by the Mexican Republic in the first article of the present treaty, and to all the rights of persons and property, both civil and ecclesiastical, within the same, as fully and as effectually as if the said articles were herein again recited and set forth.

ARTICLE VI.

No grants of land within the territory ceded by the first article of this treaty bearing date subsequent to the day—twenty-fifth of September—when the minister and subscriber to this treaty on the part of the United States, proposed to the Government of Mexico to terminate the question of boundary, will be considered valid or be recognized by the United States, or will any grants made previously be respected or be considered as obligatory which have not been located and duly recorded in the archives of Mexico.

ARTICLE VII.

Should there at any future period (which God forbid) occur any disagreement between the two nations which might lead to a rupture of their relations and reciprocal peace, they bind themselves in like manner to procure by every possible method the adjustment of every difference; and should they still in this manner not succeed, never will they proceed to a declaration of war, without having previously paid attention to what has been set forth in article twenty-one of the treaty of Guadalupe for similar cases; which article, as well as the twenty-second is here reaffirmed.

ARTICLE VIII.

The Mexican Government having on the 5th of February, 1853, authorized the early construction of a plank and railroad across the Isthmus of Tehuantepec, and, to secure the stable benefits of said transit way to the persons and merchandise of the citizens of Mexico and the United States, it is stipulated that neither government will interpose any obstacle to the transit of persons and merchandise of both nations; and at no time shall higher charges be made on the transit of persons and property of citizens of the United States, than may be made on the persons and property of other foreign nations, nor shall any interest in said transit way, nor in the proceeds thereof, be transferred to any foreign government.

The United States, by its agents, shall have the right to transport across the isthmus, in closed bags, the mails of the United States not intended for distribution along the line of communication; also the effects of the United States government and its citizens, which may be intended for transit, and not for distribution on the isthmus, free of custom-house or other charges by the Mexican government. Neither passports nor letters of security will be required of persons crossing the isthmus and not remaining in the country.

When the construction of the railroad shall be completed, the Mexican government agrees to open a port of entry in addition to the port of Vera Cruz, at or near the terminus of said road on the Gulf of Mexico.

The two governments will enter into arrangements for the prompt transit of troops and munitions of the United States, which that government may have occasion to send from one part of its territory to another, lying on opposite sides of the continent.

The Mexican government having agreed to protect with its whole power the prosecution, preservation, and security of the work, the United States may extend its protection as it shall judge wise to it when it may feel sanctioned and warranted by the public or international law.

ARTICLE IX.

This treaty shall be ratified, and the respective ratifications shall be exchanged at the city of Washington within the exact period of six months from the date of its signature, or sooner, if possible.

In testimony whereof, we, the plenipotentiaries of the contracting parties, have hereunto affixed our hands and seals at Mexico, the thirtieth (30th) day of December, in the year of our Lord one thousand eight hundred and fifty-three, in the thirty-third year of the independence of the Mexican republic, and the seventy-eighth of that of the United States.

JAMES GADSDEN,
MANUEL DIEZ DE BONILLA
JOSE SALAZAR YLARBEGUI
J. MARIANO MONTERDE,

And whereas the said treaty, as amended, has been duly ratified on both parts, and the respective ratifications of the same have this day been exchanged at Washington, by WILLIAM L. MARCY, Secretary of State of the United States, and SENOR GENERAL DON JUAN N. ALMONTE, Envoy Extraordinary and Minister Plenipotentiary of the Mexican Republic, on the part of their respective Governments:

Now, therefore, be it known that I, FRANKLIN PIERCE, President of the United States of America, have caused the said treaty to be made public, to the end that the same, and every clause and article thereof, may be observed and fulfilled with good faith by the United States and the citizens thereof.

In witness whereof I have hereunto set my hand and caused the seal of the United States to be affixed.

Done at the city of Washington, this thirtieth day of June, in the year of our Lord one thousand eight hundred and fifty-four, and of the Independence of the United States the seventy-eighth.

BY THE PRESIDENT:
FRANKLIN PIERCE,
W. L. MARCY, Secretary of State.

Homestead Act (1862)

Signed into law by the Northern Republican Congress during the Civil War, the Homestead Act allowed individuals who never raised arms against the United States to acquire 160 acres of public land for a nominal filing fee after five years of residency or for $1.25 per acre after just six months of residency. Between 1862 and 1986, more than 25 percent of all public lands were disposed of under this act. The total number of acres amounted to 287,500,000. Homesteaders, enticed by the opportunity to receive free land, helped settle the West.

Source: Congressional Globe online, 37th Congress, 2nd session, pp. 352–353, http://www.loc.gov.

An act to Secure Homesteads to actual Settlers on the Public Domain.

Be it enacted by the Senate and House of Representatives of the United States of America in Congress assembled, That any person who is the head of a family, or who has arrived at the age of twenty-one years, and is a citizen of the United States, or who shall have filed his declaration of intention to become such, as required by the naturalization laws of the United States, and who has never borne arms against the United States Government or given aid and comfort to its enemies, shall, from and after the first of January, eighteen hundred and sixty-three, be entitled to enter one quarter section or a less quantity of unappropriated public lands, upon which said person may have filed a preemption claim, or which may, at the time the application is made, be subject to preemption at one dollar and twenty-five cents, or less, per acre; or eighty acres or less of such unappropriated lands, at two dollars and fifty cents per acre, to be located in a body, in conformity to the legal subdivisions of the public lands, and after the same shall have been surveyed: Provided, That any person owning and residing on land may, under the provisions of this act, enter other land lying contiguous to his or her said land, which shall not, with the land so already owned and occupied, exceed in the aggregate, one hundred and sixty acres.

Section 2. And be it further enacted, That the person applying for the benefit of this act shall, upon application to the register of the land office in which he or she is about to make such entry, make affidavit before the said register or receiver that he or she is the head of a family, or is twenty-one years or more of age, or shall have performed service in the army or navy of the United States, and that he has never borne arms against the Government of the United States or given aid and comfort to its enemies, and that such application is made for his or her exclusive use and benefit, and that said entry is made for the purpose of actual settlement and cultivation, and not either directly or indirectly for the use or benefit of any other person or persons whomsoever; and upon filing the said affidavit with the register or receiver, and on payment of ten dollars, he or she shall thereupon be permitted to enter the quantity of land specified: Provided, however, That no certificate shall be given or patent issued therefor until the expiration of five years from the date of such entry; and if, at the expiration of such time, or at any time within two years thereafter, the person making such entry; or, if he be dead, his widow; or in case of her death, his heirs or devisee; or in the case of a widow making such entry, her heirs or devisee, in the case of her death; shall prove by two credible witnesses that he, she, or they have resided upon or cultivated the same for the term of five years immediately succeeding the time of filing the affidavit aforesaid, and shall make affidavit that no part of said land has been alienated, and he has borne true allegiance to the Government of the United States; then, in such case, he, she, or they, if at that time a citizen of the United States, shall be entitled to a patent, as in other cases provided for by law: And, provided, further, That in case of the death of both father and mother, leaving an infant child, or children, under twenty-one years of age, the right and fee shall enure to the benefit of said infant child or children; and the executor, administrator, or guardian may, at any time within two years after the death of the surviving parent, and in accordance with the laws of the State in which such children for the time being have their domicil, sell said land for the benefit of said infants, but for no other purpose; and the purchaser shall acquire the absolute title by the purchase, and be entitled to a patent from the United States, on payment of the office fees and sum of money herein specified.

Section 3. And be it further enacted, That the register of the land office shall note all such applications on the tract books and plats of his office, and keep a register of all such entries, and make return thereof to the General Land Office, together with the proof upon which they have been founded.

Section 4. And be it further enacted, That no lands acquired under the provisions of this act shall in any event become liable to the satisfaction of any debt or debts contracted prior to the issuing of the patent therefor.

Section 5. And be it further enacted, That if, at any time after the filing of the affidavit, as required in the second section of this act, and before the expiration of the five years aforesaid, it shall be proven, after due notice to the settler, to the satisfaction of the register of the land office, that the person having filed such affidavit shall have actually changed his or her residence, or abandoned the said land for more than six months at any time, then and in that event the land so entered shall revert to the government.

Section 6. And be it further enacted, That no individual shall be permitted to acquire title to more than one quarter section under the provisions of this act; and that the Commissioner of the General Land Office is hereby required to prepare and issue such rules and regulations, consistent with this act, as shall be necessary and proper to carry its provisions into effect; and that the registers and receivers of the several land offices shall be entitled to receive the same compensation for any lands entered under the provisions of this act that they are now entitled to receive when the same quantity of land is entered with money, one half to be paid by the person making the application at the time of so doing, and the other half on the issue of the certificate by the person to whom it may be issued; but this shall not be construed to enlarge the maximum of compensation now prescribed by law for any register or receiver: Provided, That nothing contained in this act shall be so construed as to impair or interfere in any manner whatever with existing preemption rights: And provided, further, That all persons who may have filed their applications for a preemption right prior to the passage of this act, shall be entitled to all privileges of this act: Provided, further, That no person who has served or may hereafter serve, for period of not less than fourteen days in the army or navy of the United States, either regular or volunteer, under the laws thereof, during the existence of an actual war, domestic or foreign, shall be deprived of the benefits of this act of account of not having attained the age of twenty-one years.

Section 7. And be it further enacted, That the fifth section of the act entitled "An act in addition to an act more effectually to provide for the punishment of certain crimes against the United States, and for other purposes," approved the third of March, in the year eighteen hundred and fifty-seven, shall extend to all oaths, affirmations, and affidavits, required or authorized by this act.

Section 8. And be it further enacted, That nothing in this act shall be so construed as to prevent any person who has availed him or herself of the benefits of the first section of this act, from paying the minimum price, or the price to which the same may have graduated, for the quantity of land so entered at any time before the expiration of the five years, and obtaining a patent therefor from the government, as in other cases provided by law, on making proof of settlement and cultivation as provided by existing laws granting preemption rights.

Approved, May 20, 1862.

Emancipation Proclamation (1863)

On January 1, 1863, President Abraham Lincoln declared that all slaves in areas of open rebellion were free. Although the Emancipation Proclamation did not have any immediate effect on the status of slaves in the Confederacy, after the Civil War the United States abolished slavery with the ratification of the Thirteenth Amendment to the Constitution. The end of slavery produced a dramatic impact on the economic structure of the South. Individuals lost a large portion of their wealth as slaves received their freedom, with no compensation to the prior owners. Consequently, the primary asset of the Southern whites remained the land, which they rented out to former slaves who became tenant farmers, commonly referred to as sharecroppers.

Source: http://www.yale.edu/lawweb/avalon/emancipa.htm.

By the President of the United States of America: A Proclamation.

Whereas, on the twenty-second day of September, in the year of our Lord one thousand eight hundred and sixty-two, a proclamation was issued by the President of the United States, containing, among other things, the following, to wit:

"That on the first day of January, in the year of our Lord one thousand eight hundred and sixty-three, all persons held as slaves within any State or designated part of a State, the people whereof shall then be in rebellion against the United States, shall be then, thenceforward, and forever free; and the Executive Government of the United States, including the military and naval authority thereof, will recognize and maintain the freedom of such persons, and will do no act or acts to repress such persons, or any of them, in any efforts they may make for their actual freedom.

"That the Executive will, on the first day of January aforesaid, by proclamation, designate the States and parts of States, if any, in which the people thereof, respectively, shall then be in rebellion against the United States; and the fact that any State, or the people thereof, shall on that day be, in good faith, represented in the Congress of the United States by members chosen thereto at elections wherein a majority of the qualified voters of such State shall have participated, shall, in the absence of strong countervailing testimony, be deemed conclusive evidence that such State, and the people thereof, are not then in rebellion against the United States."

Now, therefore I, Abraham Lincoln, President of the United States, by virtue of the power in me vested as Commander-in-Chief, of the Army and Navy of the United States in time of actual armed rebellion against the authority and government of the United States, and as a fit and necessary war measure for suppressing said rebellion, do, on this first day of January, in the year of our Lord one thousand eight hundred and sixty-three, and in accordance with my purpose so to do publicly proclaimed for the full period of one hundred days, from the day first above mentioned, order and designate as the States and parts of States wherein the people thereof respectively, are this day in rebellion against the United States, the following, to wit: Arkansas, Texas, Louisiana, (except the Parishes of St. Bernard, Plaquemines, Jefferson, St. John, St. Charles, St. James Ascension, Assumption, Terrebonne, Lafourche, St. Mary, St. Martin, and Orleans, including the City of New Orleans) Mississippi, Alabama, Florida, Georgia, South Carolina, North Carolina, and Virginia, (except the forty-eight counties designated as West Virginia, and also the counties of Berkley, Accomac, Northampton, Elizabeth City, York, Princess Ann, and Norfolk, including the cities of Norfolk and Portsmouth), and which excepted parts, are for the present, left precisely as if this proclamation were not issued.

And by virtue of the power, and for the purpose aforesaid, I do order and declare that all persons held as slaves within said designated States, and parts of States, are, and henceforward shall be free; and that the Executive government of the United States, including the military and naval authorities thereof, will recognize and maintain the freedom of said persons.

And I hereby enjoin upon the people so declared to be free to abstain from all violence, unless in necessary self-defence; and I recommend to them that, in all cases when allowed, they labor faithfully for reasonable wages.

And I further declare and make known, that such persons of suitable condition, will be received into the armed service of the United States to garrison forts, positions, stations, and other places, and to man vessels of all sorts in said service.

And upon this act, sincerely believed to be an act of justice, warranted by the Constitution, upon military necessity, I invoke the considerate judgment of mankind, and the gracious favor of Almighty God.

In witness whereof, I have hereunto set my hand and caused the seal of the United States to be affixed.

Done at the City of Washington, this first day of January, in the year of our Lord one thousand eight hundred and sixty three, and of the Independence of the United States of America the eighty-seventh.

By the President: ABRAHAM LINCOLN
WILLIAM H. SEWARD, Secretary of State.

Timber Culture Act (1873)

Although the Homestead Act encouraged Americans to settle in certain parts of the West, Congress also recognized the need to encourage growth of timber on the prairies. Under the Timber Culture Act, settlers could claim an additional 160 acres of public land in the region for a small fee if they planted one-quarter of the land in trees. This policy not only enticed settlers onto the Great Plains, which would become the breadbasket of the United States, but also prevented soil erosion.

Source: Public Statutes at Large, Vol. 17, p. 602.

An Act to encourage the Growth of Timber on western Prairies.

Be it enacted by the Senate and the House of Representatives of the United States of America in Congress assembled, That any person who shall plant, protect, and keep in a healthy, growing condition for ten years forty acres of timber, the trees thereon not being more than twelve feet apart each way on any quarter-section of any of the public lands of the United States shall be entitled to a patent for the whole of said quarter-section at the expiration of said ten years, on making proof of such fact by not less than two credible witnesses; Provided, That only one quarter in any section shall be thus granted.

Section 2. That the person applying for the benefit of this act shall, upon application to the register of the land-office in which he or she is about to make such entry, make affidavit before said register or receiver that said entry is made for the cultivation of timber, and upon filing said affidavit with said register and receiver, and on payment of ten dollars, he or she shall thereupon be permitted to enter the quantity of land specified: Provided however, That no certificate shall be given at patent issue therefor until after the expiration of at least ten years from the date of such entry; and if at the expiration of such time, or at any time within three years thereafter, the person making such entry, or if he or she be dead, his or her heirs or legal representatives, shall prove by two credible witnesses that he, she, or they have planted, and not for less than ten years have cultivated and protected such quantity and character of timber as aforesaid, they shall receive the patent for such quarter-section of land.

Section 3. That if at any time after the filing of said affidavit, and prior to the issuing of the patent for said land, it shall be proven after due notice to the party making such entry and claiming to cultivate such timber, to the satisfaction of the register of the land-office that such person has abandoned or failed to cultivate, protect and keep in good condition such timber, then, and in that event, said land shall revert to the United States.

Section 4. That each and every person who, under the provisions of an act entitled "An act to secure homesteads to actual settlers on the public domain" approved May twentieth, eighteen hundred and sixty-two, or any amendment thereto, having a homestead on said public domain, who at the end of the third year of his or her residence thereon, shall have had under cultivation, for two years, one acre of timber, the trees thereon not being more than twelve feet apart each way, and in a good, thrifty condition, for each and every sixteen acres of said homestead, shall upon due proof of said fact by two credible witnesses receive his or her patent for said homestead.

Section 5. That no land acquired under provisions of this act shall, in any event, become liable to the satisfaction of any debt or debts contracted prior to the issuing of patent therefor.

Section 6. That the commissioner of the general land-office is hereby required to prepare and issue such rules and regulations, consistent with this act, as shall be necessary and proper to carry its provisions into effect; and the registers and the receivers of the several land-offices shall be entitled to receive the same compensation for any lands entered under the provisions of this that they are now entitled to receive when the quantity of land is entered without money.

Section 7. That the fifth section of the act entitled "An act in addition to an act to punish crimes against the United States, and for other purposes" approved March third, eighteen hundred and fifty-seven, shall extend to all oaths, affirmations, and affidavits required or authorized by this act.

Approved, March 3, 1873.

Timber and Stone Culture Act (1878)

Like the Homestead and Timber Culture Acts, the Timber and Stone Culture Act allowed Americans settlers to obtain another 160 acres of public land. Under this legislation, the land could be purchased for $1.25 per acre. Only land located in *the far western states fell under lands available under this act. Since much of the land remained unfit for cultivation, the government offered it for sale at a reduced rate.*

Source: Public Statutes at Large, Vol. 20, pp. 89–91.

An act for the sale of timber lands in the States of California, Oregon, Nevada, and in Washington Territory.

Be it enacted by the Senate and House of Representatives of the United States of America in Congress assembled, That surveyed public lands of the United States within the States of California, Oregon and Nevada and in Washington Territory, not included within military, Indian, or other reservations of the United States, valuable chiefly for timber, but unfit for cultivation, and which have not been offered at public sale according to law, may be sold to citizens of the United States, or persons who have declared their intention to become such, in quantities not exceeding one hundred and sixty acres to any one person or associations of persons, at the minimum price of two dollars and fifty cents per acre; and lands valuable chiefly for stone may be sold on the same terms as timber lands: Provided, That nothing herein contained shall defeat or impair any bona-fide claim under any law of the United States, or authorize the sale of any mining claim, or the improvements of any bona-fide settler, or lands containing gold, silver, cinnabar, copper, or coal, or lands selected by said States under any law of the United States donating lands for internal improvements, education, or other purposes: And provided further, That none of the rights conferred by the act approved July twenty-six, eighteen hundred and sixty-six, entitled "An act granting the right of way to ditch and canal owners over the public lands, and for other purposes," shall be abrogated by this act; and all patents granted shall be subject to any vested and accrued water rights, or rights to ditches and reservoirs used in connection with such water rights, as may have been acquired under and by the provisions of said act; and such rights shall be expressly reserved in any patent issued under this act.

Sec. 2. That any person desiring to avail himself of the provisions of this act shall file with the register of the proper district a written statement in duplicate, one of which is to be transmitted to the General Land Office, designating by legal subdivisions the particular tract of land he desires to purchase, setting forth that the same is unfit for cultivation, and valuable chiefly for its timber or stone; that it is uninhabited; contains no mining or other improvements, except for ditch or canal purposes, where any such do exist, save such as were made by or belong to the applicant, nor, as deponent verily believes, any valuable deposit of gold, silver, cinnabar, copper, or coal; that deponent had made no other application under this act; that he does not apply to purchase the same on speculation, but in good faith to appropriate it to his own exclusive use and benefit; and that he has not, directly or indirectly, made any agreement or contract, in any way or manner, with any person or persons whatsoever, by which the title which he may acquire from the government of the United States should inure, in whole or in part, to the benefit of any person except himself; which statement must be verified by the oath of the applicant before the register or the receiver of the land-office within the district where the land is situated; and if any person taking such oath shall swear falsely in the premises, he shall be subject to all the pains and penalties of perjury, and shall forfeit the money which he may have paid for said lands, and all right and title to the same; and any grant or conveyance which he may have made, except in the hands of the bona-fide purchasers, shall be null and void.

Sec. 3. That upon the filing of said statement, as provided in the second section of this act, the register of the land office, shall post a notice of such application embracing a description of the land by legal subdivisions, in his office, for a period of sixty days, and shall furnish the applicant a copy of the same for publication, at the expense of such applicant, in a newspaper published nearest the location of the premises, for a like period of time; and after the expiration of said sixty days, if no adverse claim shall have been filed, the person desiring to purchase shall furnish to the register of the land-office satisfactory evidence, first, that said notice of the application prepared by the register as aforesaid was duly published in a newspaper as herein required; secondly, that the land is of the character contemplated in this act, unoccupied and without improvements, other than those excepted, either mining or agricultural, and that it apparently contains no valuable deposits of gold, silver, cinnabar, copper, or coal; and upon payment to the proper officer of the purchase money of said land, together with the fees of the register and the receiver, as provided for in case of mining claims in the twelfth section of the act approved May tenth, eighteen hundred and seventy-two, the applicant may be permitted to enter said tract, and, on the transmission to the General Land Office of the papers and testimony in the case, a patent shall issue thereon: Provided, That any person having a valid claim to any portion of the land may object, in writing, to the issuance of a patent to lands so held by him, stating the nature of his claim thereto; and evidence shall be taken, and the merits of said objection shall be determined by the officers of the land-office, subject to appeal, as in other land cases. Effect shall be given to the foregoing provisions of this act by regulations to be prescribed by the Commissioner of the General Land Office.

Sec. 4. That after the passage of this act it shall be unlawful to cut, or cause or procure to be cut, or wantonly destroy, any timber growing on any lands of the United States, in said States and Territory or remove, or cause to be removed, any timber from said public lands, with intent to export or dispose of the same; and no owner, director, or agent of any railroad, shall knowingly transport the same, or any lumber manufactured therefrom; and any person violating the provisions of this section shall be guilty of a misdemeanor, and, on conviction, shall be fined for every such offense a sum not less than one hundred nor more than one thousand dollar: Provided, That nothing herein contained shall prevent any miner or agriculturist from clearing his land in the ordinary working of his mining claim, or preparing his farm for tillage, or from taking the timber necessary to support his improvements, or the taking of the timber for the use of the United States; and the penalties herein provided shall not take effect until ninety days after the passage of this act.

Sec. 5. That any person prosecuted in said States and Territory for violating section two thousand four hundred and sixty-one of the Revised Statutes of the United States who is not prosecuted for cutting timber for export from the United States, may be relieved from further prosecution and liability therefor upon payment, into the court wherein such action is pending, of the sum of two dollars and fifty cents per acre for all lands on which he shall have cut or caused to be cut timber, or removed or caused to be removed the same: Provided, That nothing contained in this section shall be construed as granting to the person hereby relieved the title to said lands for said payment; but he shall have the right to purchase the same upon the same terms and conditions as other persons, as provided hereinbefore in this act: And further provided, that all moneys collected under this act shall be covered into the Treasury of the United States. And section four thousand seven hundred and fifty-one of the Revised Statutes is hereby repealed, so far as it relates to the States and Territory herein named.

Sec 6. That all acts and parts of this act inconsistent with the provisions of this act are hereby repealed.

Approved, June 3, 1878.

Sherman Anti-Trust Act (1890)

Initially passed to prevent big business from forming monopolies, the Sherman Anti-Trust Act resulted in a case against the sugar company E. C. Knight and Company. Although the sugar producer controlled 98 percent of the market, the Supreme Court ruled that a monopoly did not exist. However, the act was used successfully against the American Railway Union during the 1894 Pullman strike, when all railroad employees went out on strike. In 1914, Congress passed the Clayton Anti-Trust Act, which was afterwards used to bust up the trusts.

Source: Public Statutes at Large, Vol. 26, pp. 209–210.

An act to protect trade and commerce against unlawful restraints and monopolies.

Be it enacted by the Senate and the House of Representatives of the United States of America in Congress assembled,

Sec. 1. Every contract, combination in the form and trust or otherwise, or conspiracy, in restraint of trade or commerce among the United States, or with foreign nations, is hereby declared to be illegal. Every person who shall make any such contract or engage in any such combination or conspiracy, shall be deemed guilty of a misdemeanor, and, on conviction thereof, shall be punished by fine not exceeding five thousand dollars, or by imprisonment not exceeding one year, or by both said punishments, in the discretion of the court.

Sec. 2. Every person who shall monopolize, or attempt to monopolize, or combine or conspire with any other person or persons, to monopolize any part of the trade or commerce among the several States, or with foreign nations, shall be deemed guilty of a misdemeanor, and, on conviction thereof, shall be punished by fine not exceeding five thousand dollars, or by imprisonment not exceeding one year, or both said punishments, in the discretion of the court.

Sec. 3. Every contract, combination in form of trust or otherwise, or conspiracy, in restraint of trade or commerce in any Territory of the United States or of the District of Columbia, or in restraint of trade and commerce between any such Territory and another, or between any such Territory or Territories and any State or States or the District of Columbia, or with foreign nations, or between the District of Columbia and any State or States or foreign nations, is hereby declared illegal. Every person who shall make any such contract or engage in any such combination or conspiracy, shall be deemed guilty of a misdemeanor, and, on conviction thereof, shall be punished by fine not exceeding five thousand dollars, or by imprisonment not exceeding one year, or by both said punishments, in the discretion of the court.

Sec. 4. The several circuit courts of the United States are hereby invested with jurisdiction to prevent and restrain violations of this act; and it shall be the duty of the several district attorneys of the United States, in their respective districts, under the direction of the Attorney General, to institute proceedings in equity to prevent and restrain such violations. Such proceedings may be by way of petition setting forth the case and praying that such violation shall be enjoined or otherwise prohibited. When the parties complained of shall have been duly notified of such petition the court shall proceed, as soon as may be, to the hearing and determination of the case; and pending such petition and before final decree, the court may at any time make such temporary restraining order or prohibition as shall be deemed just in the premises.

Sec. 5. Whenever it shall appear to the court before which any proceeding under section four of this act may be pending, that the ends of justice require that the other parties should be brought before the court, the court may cause them to be summoned, whether they reside in the district in which the court is held or not; and subpoenas to that end may be served in any district by the marshal thereof.

Sec. 6. Any property owned under any contract or by any combination, or pursuant to any conspiracy (and being the subject thereof) mentioned in section one of this act, and being in the course of transportation from one State to another, or to a foreign country, shall be forfeited to the United States, and may be seized and condemned by like proceedings as those provided by law for the forfeiture, seizure, and condemnation of property imported into the United States contrary to law.

Sec. 7. Any person who shall be injured in his business or property by any other person or corporation by reason of anything forbidden or declared to be unlawful by this act, may sue therefor in any circuit court of the United States in the district in which the defendant resides or is found, without respect to the amount in controversy, and shall recover three fold the damages by him sustained, and the costs of suit, including a reasonable attorney's fee.

Sec. 8. That the word "person," or "persons," wherever used in this act shall be deemed to include corporations and associations existing under or authorized by the laws of either the United States, the laws of any of the Territories, or the laws of any State, or the laws of any foreign country.

Approved, July 2, 1890.

Panama Canal Treaty of 1903

The construction of the Panama Canal opened up trade between the Pacific and the Atlantic Oceans for the United States as well as the rest of the world. Although prior to the building of the canal ships circumvented South America to reach the other ocean, the canal reduced the amount of time and cost of shipping goods. The United States controlled a 10-mile-wide strip of land along the 40-mile canal until 1978, when the canal was ceded back to the country of Panama, effective December 31, 1999.

Source: http://www.owecc.net/his/09/panama_canal_treaty.htm.

Concluded November 18, 1903; ratification advised by the Senate February 23, 1904; ratified by President February 25, 1904; ratifications exchanged February 26, 1904; proclaimed February 26, 1904. (U.S. Stats., vol. 33.)

The United States of America and the Republic of Panama being desirous to insure the construction of a ship canal across the Isthmus of Panama to connect the Atlantic and Pacific oceans, and the Congress of the United States of America having passed an act approved June 28, 1902, in furtherance of that object, by which the President of the United States is authorized to acquire within a reasonable time the control of the necessary territory of the Republic of Colombia, and the sovereignty of such territory being actually vested in the Republic of Panama, the high contracting parties have resolved for that purpose to conclude a convention and have accordingly appointed as their plenipotentiaries,

The President of the United States of America, John Hay, Secretary of State, and

The Government of the Republic of Panama, Philippe Bunau-Varilla, Envoy Extraordinary and Minister Plenipotentiary of the Republic of Panama, thereunto specially empowered by said government, who after communicating with each other their respective full powers, found to be in good and due form, have agreed upon and concluded the following articles:

ARTICLE I

The United States guarantees and will maintain the independence of the Republic of Panama.

ARTICLE II

The Republic of Panama grants to the United States in perpetuity the use, occupation and control of a zone of land and land under water for the construction maintenance, operation, sanitation and protection of said Canal of the width of ten miles extending to the distance of five miles on each side of the center line of the route of the Canal to be constructed; the said zone beginning in the Caribbean Sea three marine miles from mean low water mark and extending to and across the Isthmus of Panama into the Pacific ocean to a distance of three marine miles from mean low water mark with the proviso that the cities of Panama and Colon and the harbors adjacent to said cities, which are included within the boundaries of the zone above described, shall not be included within this grant. The Republic of Panama further grants to the United States in perpetuity the use, occupation and control of any other lands and waters outside of the zone above described which may be necessary and convenient for the construction, maintenance, operation, sanitation and protection of the said Canal or of any auxiliary canals or other works necessary and convenient for the construction, maintenance, operation, sanitation and protection of the said enterprise.

The Republic of Panama further grants in like manner to the United States in perpetuity all islands within the limits of the zone above described and in addition thereto the group of small islands in the Bay of Panama, named, Perico, Naos, Culebra and Flamenco.

ARTICLE III

The Republic of Panama grants to the United States all the rights, power and authority within the zone mentioned and described in Article II of this agreement and within the limits of all auxiliary lands and waters mentioned and described in said Article II which the United States would possess and exercise if it were the sovereign of the territory within which said lands and waters are located to the entire exclusion of the exercise by the Republic of Panama of any such sovereign rights, power or authority.

ARTICLE IV

As rights subsidiary to the above grants the Republic of Panama grants in perpetuity to the United States the right to use the rivers, streams, lakes and other bodies of water within its limits for navigation, the supply of water or water-power or other purposes, so far as the use of said rivers, streams, lakes and bodies of water and the waters thereof may be necessary and convenient for the construction, maintenance, operation, sanitation and protection of the said Canal.

ARTICLE V

The Republic of Panama grants to the United States in perpetuity a monopoly for the construction, maintenance and operation of any system of communication by means of canal or railroad across its territory between the Caribbean Sea and the Pacific Ocean.

ARTICLE VI

The grants herein contained shall in no manner invalidate the titles or rights of private land holders or owners of private property in the said zone or in or to any of the lands or waters granted to the United States by the provisions of any Article of this treaty, nor shall they interfere with the rights of way over the public roads passing through the said zone or over any of the said lands or waters unless said rights of way or private rights shall conflict with rights herein granted to the United States in which case the rights of the United States shall be superior. All damages caused to the owners of private lands or private property of any kind by reason of the grants contained in this treaty or by reason of the operations of the United States, its agents or employees, or by reason of the construction, maintenance, operation, sanitation and protection of the said Canal or of the works of sanitation and protection herein provided for, shall be appraised and settled by a joint Commission appointed by the Governments of the United States and the Republic of Panama, whose decisions as to such damages shall be final and whose awards as to such damages shall be paid solely by the United States. No part of the work on said Canal or the Panama railroad or on any auxiliary works relating thereto and authorized by the terms of this treaty shall be prevented, delayed or impeded by or pending such proceedings to ascertain such damages. The appraisal of said private lands and private property and the assessment of damages to them shall be based upon their value before the date of this convention.

ARTICLE VII

The Republic of Panama grants to the United States within the limits of the cities of Panama and Colon and their adjacent harbors and within the territory adjacent thereto the right to acquire by purchase or by the exercise of the right of eminent domain, any lands, buildings, water rights or other properties necessary and convenient for the construction, maintenance, operation and protection of the Canal and of any works of sanitation, such as the collection and disposition of sewage and the distribution of water in the said cities of Panama and Colon, which in the discretion of the United States may be necessary and convenient for the construction, maintenance, operation, sanitation and protection of the said Canal and railroad. All such works of sanitation, collection and disposition of sewage and distribution of water in the cities of Panama and Colon shall be made at the expense of the United States, and the Government of the United States, its agents or nominees shall be authorized to impose and collect water rates and sewerage rates which shall be sufficient to provide for the payment of interest and the amortization of the principal of the cost of said works within a period of fifty years and upon the expiration of said term of fifty years the system of sewers and water works shall revert to and become the properties of the cities of Panama and Colon respectively, and the use of the water shall be free to the inhabitants of Panama and Colon, except to the extent that water rates may be necessary for the operation and maintenance of said system of sewers and water.

The Republic of Panama agrees that the cities of Panama and Colon shall comply in perpetuity with the sanitary ordinances whether of a preventive or curative character prescribed by the United States and in case the Government of Panama is unable or fails in its duty to enforce this compliance by the cities of Panama and Colon with the sanitary ordinances of the United States the Republic of Panama grants to the United States the right and authority to enforce the same.

The same right and authority are granted to the United States for the maintenance of public order in the cities of Panama and Colon and the territories and harbors adjacent thereto in case the Republic of Panama should not be, in the judgment of the United States, able to maintain such order.

ARTICLE VIII

The Republic of Panama grants to the United States all rights which it now has or hereafter may acquire to be property of the New Panama Canal Company and the Panama Railroad Company as a result of the transfer of sovereignty from the Republic of Colombia to the Republic of Panama over the Isthmus of Panama and authorizes the New Panama Canal Company to sell and transfer to the United States its rights, privileges, properties and concessions as well as the Panama Railroad and all the shares or part of the shares of that company; . . . the public lands situated outside of the zone described in Article II of this treaty now included in the concessions to both said enterprises and not required in the construction or operation of the Canal shall revert to the Republic of Panama except any property now owned by or in the possession of said companies within Panama or Colon or the ports or terminals thereof.

ARTICLE IX

The United States agrees that the ports at either entrance of the Canal and the waters thereof, and the Republic of Panama agrees that the towns of Panama and Colon shall be free for all time so that there shall not be imposed or collected custom house tolls, tonnage, anchorage, lighthouse, wharf, pilot, or quarantine dues or any other charges or taxes of any kind upon any vessel using or passing through the Canal or belonging to or employed by the United States, directly or indirectly, in connection with the construction, maintenance, operation, sanitation and protection of the main Canal, or auxiliary works, or upon the cargo, officers, crew, or passengers of any such vessels, except such tolls and charges as may be imposed by the United States for the use of the Canal and other works, and except tolls and charges imposed by the Republic of Panama upon merchandise destined to be introduced for the consumption of the rest of the Republic of Panama, and upon vessels touching at the ports of Colon and Panama and which do not cross the Canal.

The Government of the Republic of Panama shall have the right to establish in such ports and in the towns of Panama and Colon such houses and guards as it may deem necessary to collect duties on importations destined to other portions of Panama and to prevent contraband trade. The United States Shall have the right to make use of the towns and harbors of Panama and Colon as places of anchorage, and for making repairs, for loading, unloading, depositing, or transshipping cargoes either in transit or destined for the service of the Canal and for other works pertaining to the Canal.

ARTICLE X

The Republic of Panama agrees that there shall not be imposed any taxes, national, municipal, departmental, or of any other class, upon the Canal, the railways and auxiliary works, tugs and other vessels employed in the service of the Canal, store houses, work shops, offices, quarters for laborers, factories of all kinds, warehouses, wharves, machinery and other works, property, and effects appertaining to the Canal or railroad and auxiliary works, or their officers or employees, situated within the cities of Panama and Colon, and that there shall not be imposed contributions or charges of a personal character of any kind upon officers, employees, laborers, and other individuals in the service of the Canal and railroad and auxiliary works.

ARTICLE XI

The United States agrees that the official dispatches of the Government of the Republic of Panama shall be transmitted over any telegraph and telephone lines established for canal purposes and used for public and private business at rates not higher than those required from officials in the service of the United States.

ARTICLE XII

The Government of the Republic of Panama shall permit the immigration and free access to the lands and workshops of the Canal and its auxiliary works of all employees and workmen of Whatever nationality under contract to work upon or seeking employment upon or in any wise connected with the said Canal and its auxiliary works, with their respective families, and all such persons shall be free and exempt from the military service of the Republic of Panama.

ARTICLE XIII

The United States may import at any time into the said zone and auxiliary lands, free of custom duties, imposts, taxes, or other charges, and without any restrictions, any and all vessels, dredges, engines, cars, machinery, tools, explosives, materials, supplies, and other articles necessary and convenient in the construction, maintenance, operation, sanitation and protection of the Canal and auxiliary works, and all provisions, medicines, clothing, supplies and other things necessary and convenient for the officers, employees, workmen and laborers in the service and employ of the United States and for their families. If any such articles are disposed of for use outside of the zone and auxiliary lands granted to the United States and within the territory of the Republic, they shall be subject to the same import or other duties as like articles imported under the laws of the Republic of Panama.

ARTICLE XIV

As the price or compensation for the rights, powers and privileges granted in this convention by the Republic of Panama to the United States, the Government of the United States agrees to pay to the Republic of Panama the sum of ten million dollars ($10,000,000) in gold coin of the United States on the exchange of the ratification of this convention and also an annual payment during the life of this convention of two hundred and fifty thousand dollars ($250,000) in like gold coin, beginning nine years after the date aforesaid.

The provisions of this Article shall be in addition to all other benefits assured to the Republic of Panama under this convention.

But no delay or difference of opinion under this Article or any other provisions of this treaty shall affect or interrupt the full operation and effect of this convention in all other respects.

ARTICLE XV

The joint commission referred to in Article VI shall be established as follows:

The President of the United States shall nominate two persons and the President of the Republic of Panama shall nominate two persons and they shall proceed to a decision; but in case of disagreement of the Commission (by reason of their being equally divided in conclusion) an umpire shall be appointed by the two Governments who shall render the decision. In the event of the death, absence, or incapacity of a Commissioner or Umpire, or of his omitting, declining or ceasing to act, his place shall be filled by the appointment of another person in the manner above indicated. All decisions by a majority of the Commission or by the Umpire shall be final.

ARTICLE XVI

The two Governments shall make adequate provision by future agreement for the pursuit, capture, imprisonment, detention and delivery within said zone and auxiliary lands to the authorities of the Republic of Panama of persons charged with the commitment of crimes, felonies or misdemeanors without said zone and for the pursuit, capture, imprisonment, detention and delivery without said zone to the authorities of the United States of persons charged with the commitment of crimes, felonies and misdemeanors within said zone and auxiliary lands.

ARTICLE XVII

The Republic of Panama grants to the United States the use of all the ports of the Republic open to commerce as places of refuge for any vessels employed in the Canal enterprise, and for all vessels passing or bound to pass through the Canal which may be in distress and be driven to seek refuge in said ports. Such vessels shall be exempt from anchorage and tonnage dues on the part of the Republic of Panama.

ARTICLE XVIII

The Canal, when constructed, and the entrances thereto shall be neutral in perpetuity, and shall be opened upon the terms provided for by Section I of Article three of, and in conformity with all the stipulations of, the treaty entered into by the Governments of the United States and Great Britain on November 18, 1901.

ARTICLE XIX

The Government of the Republic of Panama shall have the right to transport over the Canal its vessels and its troops and munitions of war in such vessels at all times without paying charges of any kind. The exemption is to be extended to the auxiliary railway for the transportation of persons in the service of the Republic of Panama, or of the police force charged with the preservation of public order outside of said zone, as well as to their baggage, munitions of war and supplies.

ARTICLE XX

If by virtue of any existing treaty in relation to the territory of the Isthmus of Panama, whereof the obligations shall descend or be assumed by the Republic of Panama, there may be any privilege or concession in favor the Government or the citizens and subjects of a third power relative to an interoceanic means of communication which in any of its terms may be incompatible with the terms of the present convention, the Republic of Panama agrees to cancel or modify such treaty in due form, for which purpose it shall give to the said third power the requisite notification within the term of four months from the date of the present convention, and in case the existing treaty contains no clause permitting its modification or annulment, the Republic of Panama agrees to procure its modification or annulment in such form that there shall not exist any conflict with the stipulations of the present convention.

ARTICLE XXI

The rights and privileges granted by the Republic of Panama to the United States in the preceding Articles are understood to be free of all anterior debts, liens, trusts, or liabilities, or concessions or privileges to other Governments, corporations, syndicates or individuals, and consequently, if there should arise any claims on account of the present concessions and privileges or otherwise, the claimants shall resort to the Government of the Republic of Panama and not to the United States for any indemnity or compromise which may be required.

ARTICLE XXII

The Republic of Panama renounces and grants to the United States the participation to which it might be entitled in the future earnings of the Canal under Article XV of the concessionary contract with Lucien N. B. Wyse now owned by the New Panama Canal Company and any and all other rights or claims of a pecuniary nature arising under or relating to said concession, or arising under or relating to the concessions to the Panama Railroad Company or any extension or modification thereof; and it likewise renounces, confirms and grants to the United States, now and hereafter, all the rights and property reserved in the said concessions which otherwise would belong to Panama at or before the expiration of the terms of ninety-nine years of the concessions granted to or held by the above mentioned party and companies, and all right, title and interest which it now has or many hereafter have, in and to the lands, canal, works, property and rights held by the said companies under said concessions or otherwise, and acquired or to be acquired by the United States from or through the New Panama Canal Company, including any property and rights which might or may in the future either by lapse of time, forfeiture or otherwise, revert to the Republic of Panama, under any contracts or concessions, with said Wyse, the Universal Panama Canal Company, the Panama Railroad Company and the New Panama Canal Company.

The aforesaid rights and property shall be and are free and released from any present or reversionary interest in or claims of Panama and the title of the United States thereto upon consummation of the contemplated purchase by the United States from the New Panama Canal (company, shall be absolute, so far as concerns the Republic of Panama, excepting always the rights of the Republic specifically secured under this treaty.

ARTICLE XXIII

If it should become necessary at any time to employ armed forces for the safety or protection of the Canal, or of the ships that make use of the same, or the railways and auxiliary works, the United States shall have the right, at all times and in its discretion, to use its police and its land and naval forces or to establish fortifications for these purposes.

ARTICLE XXIV

No change either in the Government or in the laws and treaties of the Republic of Panama shall, without the consent of the United States, affect any right of the United States under the present convention, or under any treaty stipulation between the two countries that now exists or may hereafter exist touching the subject matter of this convention.

If the Republic of Panama shall hereafter enter as a constituent into any other Government or into any union or confederation of states, so as to merge her sovereignty or independence in such Government, union or confederation, the rights of the United States under this convention shall not be in any respect lessened or impaired.

ARTICLE XXV

For the better performance of the engagements of this convention and to the end of the efficient protection of the Canal and the preservation of its neutrality, the Government of the Republic of Panama will sell or lease to the United States lands adequate and necessary for naval or coaling stations on the Pacific coast and on the western Caribbean coast of the Republic at certain points to be agreed upon with the President of the United States.

ARTICLE XXVI

This convention when signed by the Plenipotentiaries of the Contracting Parties shall be ratified by the respective Governments and the ratifications shall be exchanged at Washington at the earliest date possible.

In faith whereof the respective Plenipotentiaries have signed the present convention in duplicate and have hereunto affixed their respective seals.

Done at the City of Washington the 18th day of November in the year of our Lord nineteen hundred and three.

JOHN HAY
P. BUNAU VARILLA

Federal Reserve Act (1913)

The Federal Reserve Act established the modern banking system of the United States. Designed to provide elasticity of the money supply and as a lender of last resort for banks, the Federal Reserve (Fed) regulates the money supply by increasing or decreasing interest rates. The Fed also acts as a clearinghouse for financial transactions. During its nine decades of operation, the policies of the Fed helped stabilize the U.S. economy.

Source: Public Statutes at Large, Vol. 38, Part I, pp. 251–275.

An Act to provide for the establishment of Federal reserve banks, to furnish an elastic currency, to afford means of rediscounting commercial paper, to establish a more effective supervision of banking in the United States, and for other purposes.

Be it enacted by the Senate and the House of Representatives of the United States of America in Congress assembled, That the short title of this Act shall be the "Federal Reserve Act."

Whenever the word "bank" is used in this Act, the word shall be held to include State bank, banking association, and trust company, except where national banks or Federal reserve banks are specifically referred to.

The terms "national bank" and "national banking association" used in this Act shall be held to be synonymous and interchangeable. The term "member bank" shall be held to mean any national bank, State bank, or bank or trust company which has become a member of one of the reserve banks created by this Act. The term "board" shall be held to mean Federal Reserve Boards; the term "district" shall be held to mean Federal Reserve district; the term "reserve bank" shall be held to mean Federal reserve bank.

FEDERAL RESERVE DISTRICTS.

Sec. 2. As soon as practicable, the Secretary of the Treasury, the Secretary of Agriculture and the Comptroller of the Currency, acting as "The Reserve Bank Organization Committee," shall designate not less than eight nor more than twelve cities to be known as Federal Reserve cities, and shall divide the continental United States, excluding Alaska, into districts, each district to contain only one of such Federal reserve cities. The determination of said organization committee shall not be subject to review except by the Federal Reserve Board when organized: Provided, That the districts shall be apportioned with due regard to the convenience and customary course of business and shall not necessarily be coterminous with any State or States. The districts thus created may be readjusted and new districts may from time to time be created by the Federal Reserve Board, not to exceed twelve in all. Such districts shall be known as Federal reserve districts and may be designated by number. A majority of the organization committee shall constitute a quorum with authority to act.

Said organization committee shall be authorized to employ counsel and expert aid, to take testimony, to send for persons and papers, to administer oaths, and to make such investigation as may be deemed necessary by the said committee in determining the reserve districts and in designating the cities within such districts where such Federal reserve banks shall be severally located. The said committee shall supervise the organization in each of the cities designated of a Federal reserve bank, which shall include in its title the name of the city in which it is situated, as "Federal Reserve Bank of Chicago."

Under regulations to be prescribed by the organization committee, every national banking association in the United States is hereby required, and every eligible bank in the United States and every trust company within the District of Columbia, is hereby authorized to signify in writing, within sixty days after the passage of this Act, its acceptance of the terms and provisions hereof. When the organization committee shall have designated the cities in which the Federal reserve banks are to organized, and fixed the geographical limits of the Federal reserve districts, every national banking association within that district shall be required within thirty days after notice from the organization committee, to subscribe to the capital stock of such Federal reserve bank in a sum equal to six per centum of the paid-up capital stock and surplus of such bank, one-sixth of the subscription to be payable on call of the organization committee or of the Federal Reserve Board, one-sixth within three months and one-sixth within six months thereafter, and the remainder of the subscription, or any part thereof, shall be subject to call when deemed necessary by the Federal Reserve Board, said payments to be in gold or gold certificates.

The shareholders of every Federal reserve bank shall be held individually responsible, equally and ratably, and not for one another, for all contracts, debts, and engagements of such bank to the extent of the amount of their subscription to such stock at the par value thereof in addition to the amount subscribed, whether such subscriptions have been paid up in whole or in part, under the provisions of this Act.

Any national bank failing to signify its acceptance of the terms of this Act within the sixty days aforesaid, shall cease to act as a reserve agent, upon thirty days notice, to be given within the discretion of the said organization committee or of the Federal Reserve Board.

Should any national banking association in the United States now organized fail within one year after the passage of this Act to become a member bank or fail to comply with any of the provisions of this Act applicable thereto, all of the rights, privileges, and franchises of such association granted to it under the national-bank Act, or under provisions of this Act, shall be thereby forfeited. Any noncompliance with or violation of this Act shall, however, be determined and adjudged by any court of the United States of competent jurisdiction in a suit brought for that purpose in the district or territory in which such bank is located, under direction of the Federal Reserve Board, by the Comptroller of the Currency in his own name before the association shall be declared dissolved. In cases of such noncompliance or violation, other than the failure to become a member bank under the provisions of this Act, every director who participated in or assented to the same shall be held liable in his personal or individual capacity for all the damages which said bank, its shareholders, or any other person shall have sustained in consequence of such violation.

Such dissolution shall not take away or impair any remedy against such corporation, its stockholders or officers, for any liability or penalty which shall have been previously incurred.

Should the subscriptions by banks to the stock of said Federal reserve banks or any one or more of them be, in the judgment of the organization committee, insufficient to provide the amount of capital required therefor, then and in that event the said organization committee may, under conditions and regulations to be prescribed by it, offer to public subscription at par an amount of stock in said Federal reserve banks, or any one or more of them, as said committee shall determine, subject to the same conditions as to payment and stock liability as provided for member banks.

No individual, copartnership, or corporation other than a member bank of its district shall be permitted to subscribe for or to hold at any time more than $25,000 par value of stock in any Federal reserve bank. Such stock shall be known as public stock and may be transferred on the books of the Federal reserve bank by the chairman of the board of directors at such bank.

Should the total subscriptions by banks and the public to the stock of said Federal reserve banks, or any one or more of them, be, in the judgment of the organization committee, insufficient to provide the amount of capital required therefor, then and in that event the said organization committee shall allot to the United States such an amount of said stock as said committee shall determine. Said United States stock shall be paid for at par out of any money in the Treasury not otherwise appropriated, and shall be held by the Secretary of the Treasury and disposed of for the benefit of the United States in such manner, at such times, and at such price, not less than par, as the Secretary of the Treasury shall determine.

Stock not held by member banks shall not be entitled to voting power.

The Federal Reserve Board is hereby empowered to adopt and promulgate rules and regulations governing the transfers of said stock.

No Federal reserve bank shall commence business with a subscribed capital less than $4,000,000. The organization of reserve districts and Federal reserve cities shall not be construed as changing the present status of reserve cities and central reserve cities, except in so far as this Act changes the amount of reserves that may be carried with approved reserve agents located therein. The organization committee shall have power to appoint such assistants and incur such expenses in carrying out the provisions of this Act as it shall be deemed necessary; and such expenses shall be payable by the Treasurer of the United States upon voucher approved by the Secretary of the Treasury, and the sum of $100,000, or so much thereof as may be necessary, is hereby appropriated, out of the moneys in the Treasury not otherwise appropriated, for the payment of such expenses.

BRANCH OFFICES.

Sec. 3. Each Federal reserve bank shall establish branch banks within the Federal reserve district in which it is located and may do so in the district of any Federal reserve bank which may have been suspended. Such branches shall be operated by a board of directors under rules and regulations approved by the Federal Reserve Board. Directors of branch banks shall possess the same qualifications as directors of the Federal reserve banks. Four of said directors shall be selected by the reserve bank and three by the Federal Reserve Board, and they shall hold office during the pleasure, respectively, of the parent bank and the Federal Reserve Board. The reserve bank shall designate one of the directors as manager.

FEDERAL RESERVE BANKS.

Sec. 4. When the organization committee shall have established Federal reserve districts as provided in section two of this Act, a certificate shall be filed with the Comptroller of the Currency showing the geographical limits of such districts and the Federal reserve city designated in each of such districts.

The Comptroller of the Currency shall thereupon cause to be forwarded to each national bank located in each district, and to other banks declared to be eligible by the organization committee which may apply therefor, an application blank in form to be approved by the organization committee, which blank shall contain a resolution to be adopted by the board of directors of each bank executing such application, authorizing a subscription to the capital stock of the Federal reserve bank organizing in that district in accordance with the provisions of this Act.

When the minimum amount of capital stock prescribed by this Act for the organization of any Federal reserve bank shall have been subscribed and allotted, the organization committee shall designate any five banks of those whose applications have been received, to execute a certificate of organization, and thereupon the banks so designated shall, under their seals, make an organization certificate which shall specifically state the name of such Federal reserve bank, the territorial extent of the district over which the operations of such Federal reserve bank are to be carried on, the city and the State in which said bank is to located, the amount of capital stock and the number of shares into which the same is divided, the name and place of doing business of each bank executing such certificate, and of all banks which have subscribed to the capital stock of such Federal reserve bank and the number of shares subscribed by each, and the fact that the certificate is made to enable those banks executing same, and all banks which have subscribed or may thereafter subscribe to the capital stock of such Federal reserve bank, to avail themselves of the advantages of this Act.

The said organization certificate shall be acknowledged before a judge of some court of record or notary public; and shall be, together with the acknowledgment thereof, authenticated by the seal of such court, or notary, transmitted to the Comptroller of the Currency, who shall file, record and carefully preserve the same in his office.

Upon the filing of such certificate with the Comptroller of the Currency as aforesaid, the said Federal reserve bank shall become a body corporate and as such, and in the name designated in such organization certificate, shall have power—

First. To adopt and use a corporate seal.

Second. To have succession for a period of twenty years from its organization unless it is sooner dissolved by an Act of Congress, or unless its franchise becomes forfeited by some violation of law.

Third. To make contracts.

Fourth. To sue and be sued, complain and defend, in any court of law or equity.

Fifth. To appoint by its board of directors, such officers and employees as are not otherwise provided for in this Act, to define their duties, require bonds of them and fix the penalty thereof, and to dismiss at pleasure such officers or employees.

Sixth. To prescribe by its board of directors, by in-laws not inconsistent with law, regulating the manner in which its general business may be conducted, and the privileges granted to it by law may be exercised and enjoyed.

Seventh. To exercise by its board of directors, or duly authorized officers or agents, all powers specifically granted for the provisions of this Act and such incidental powers as shall be necessary to carry on the business of banking within the limitations prescribed by this Act.

Eighth. Upon deposit with the Treasurer of the United States of any bonds of the United States in the manner provided existing law relating to national banks, to receive from the Comptroller of the Currency circulating notes in blank, registered and countersigned as provided by law, equal in amount to the par value of the bonds so deposited, such notes to be issued under the same conditions and provisions of law as relate to the issue of circulating notes of national banks secured by bonds of the United States bearing the circulating privilege, except that the issue of such notes shall not be limited to the capital stock of such Federal reserve bank.

But no Federal reserve bank shall transact any business except such as is incidental and necessarily preliminary to its organization until it has been authorized by the Comptroller of the Currency to commence business under the provisions of this Act.

Every Federal reserve bank shall be conducted under the supervision and control of a board of directors.

The board of directors shall perform the duties usually appertaining to the office of directors of banking associations and all such duties as are prescribed by law.

Said board shall administer the affairs of said bank fairly and impartially and without discrimination in favor or against any member bank or banks and shall, subject to the provisions of law and the orders of the Federal Reserve Board, extend to each member bank such discounts, advancements and accommodations as may be safely and reasonably made with due regard for the claims and demands of other member banks.

Such board of directors shall be selected as hereinafter specified and shall consist of nine members, holding office for three years, and divided into three classes, designated as classes A, B, and C.

Class A shall consist of three members, who shall be chosen by and be representative of the stock-holding banks.

Class B shall consists of three members, who at the time of their election shall be actively engaged in their district in commerce, agriculture or some other industrial pursuit.

Class C shall consist of three members who shall be designated by the Federal Reserve Board. When the necessary subscriptions to the Capital stock have been obtained for the organization of any Federal reserve bank, the Federal Reserve Board shall appoint the class C directors and shall designate one of such directors as chairman of the board to be selected. Pending the designation of such chairman, the organization committee shall exercise the power and duties appertaining to the office of chairman in the organization of such Federal reserve bank.

No Senator or Representative in Congress shall be a member of the Federal Reserve Board or an officer or a director of a Federal reserve bank.

No director of class B shall be an officer, director, or employee of any bank.

No director of class C shall be an officer, director, employee, or stockholder of any bank.

Directors of class A and B shall be chosen in the following manner:

The chairman of the board of directors of the Federal reserve bank of the district in which the bank is situated or, pending the appointment of such chairman, the organization of such chairman, the organization committee shall classify the member banks of the districts into three groups or divisions. Each group shall contain as nearly as may be one-third of the aggregate number of the member banks of the district and shall consist, as nearly as may be, of banks of similar capitalization. The groups shall be designated by number by the chairman.

At a regularly called meeting of the board of directors of each member bank in the district it shall elect by ballot a district reserve elector and shall certify his name to the chairman of the board of directors of the Federal reserve bank of the district. The chairman shall make lists of the district reserve electors thus named by banks in each of the aforesaid three groups and shall transmit one list to each elector in each group. Each member bank shall be permitted to nominate to the chairman one candidate for director of class A and one candidate for class B. The candidates so nominated shall be listed by the chairman, indicating by whom nominated, and a copy of said list shall, within fifteen days after its completion, be furnished by the chairman to each elector.

Every elector shall, within fifteen days after the receipt of the said list, certify to the chairman his first, second, and other choices of a director of class A and B, respectively, upon a preferential ballot, on a form furnished by the chairman of the board of directors of the Federal reserve bank of the district. Each elector shall make a cross opposite the name of the first, second, and other choices for a director of class A and for a director of class B, but shall not vote more than one choice for any candidate.

Any candidate having a majority of all votes cast in the column of first choice shall be declared elected. If no candidate have a majority of all the votes in the first column, then there shall be added together the votes cast by the electors for such candidates in the second column and the votes cast for the several candidates in the first column. If any candidate then have a majority of the electors voting, by adding together the first and second choices, he shall be declared elected. If no candidate have a majority of electors voting when the first and second choices shall have been added, then the votes cast in the third column from other choices shall be added together in like manner, and the candidate then having the highest number of votes shall be declared elected. An immediate report of election shall be declared.

Class C directors shall be appointed by the Federal Reserve Board. They shall have been for at least two years residents of the district for which they are appointed, one of whom shall be designated by said board as chairman of the board of directors of the Federal reserve bank and as "Federal reserve agent." He shall be a person of tested banking experience; and in addition to his duties as chairman of the board of directors of the federal reserve bank he shall be required to maintain under regulations to be established by the Federal Reserve Board a local office of said board on the premises of the Federal reserve bank. He shall make regular reports to the Federal Reserve Board, and shall act as its official representative for the performance of the functions conferred upon it by this Act. He shall receive an annual compensation to be fixed by the Federal Reserve Board and paid monthly by the Federal reserve bank to which he is designated. One of the directors of class C, who shall be a person of tested banking experience, shall be appointed by the Federal Reserve Board as deputy chairman and deputy Federal reserve agent to exercise the powers of the chairman of the board and Federal reserve agent in case of absence or disability of his principal.

Directors of Federal reserve banks shall receive, in addition to any compensation otherwise provided, a reasonable allowance for necessary expenses in attending meetings of their respective boards, which amount shall be paid by the respective Federal reserve banks. Any compensation that may be provided by board of directors of Federal reserve banks for directors, officers or employees shall be subject to the approval of the Federal Reserve Board.

The Reserve Bank Organization Committee may, in organizing Federal reserve banks, call such meetings of bank directors in the several districts as may be necessary to carry out the purposes of this Act, and may exercise the functions herein conferred upon the chairman of the board of directors of each Federal reserve bank pending the complete organization of such bank.

At the first meeting of the full board of directors of each Federal reserve bank, it shall be the duty of the directors of classes A, B, and C respectively, to designate one of the members of each class whose term of office shall expire in one year from the first of January nearest to date of such meeting, one whose term of office shall expire at the end of two years from said date, and one whose term of office shall expire at the end of three years from said date. Thereafter every director of a Federal reserve bank chosen as hereinbefore provided shall hold office for a term of three years. Vacancies that may occur in the several classes of directors of Federal reserve banks may be filled in the manner provided for the original selection of such directors, such appointees to hold office for the unexpired terms of their predecessors.

STOCK ISSUES; INCREASE AND DECREASE OF CAPITAL.

Sec. 5. The capital stock of each Federal reserve bank shall be divided into shares of $100 each. The outstanding capital stock shall be increased from time to time as member banks increase their capital stock and surplus or as additional banks become members, and may be decreased as member banks reduce their capital stock or surplus or cease to be members. Shares of the capital stock of Federal reserve banks owned by member banks shall not be transferred or hypothecated. When a member bank increases its capital stock or surplus, it shall thereupon subscribe for an additional amount of capital stock of the Federal reserve bank of its district equal to six per centum of the said increase, one-half of said subscription to be paid in the manner hereinbefore provided for original subscription, and one-half subject to call of the Federal Reserve Board. A bank applying for stock in a Federal reserve bank at any time after the organization thereof must subscribe for an amount of the capital stock of the Federal reserve bank equal to six per centum of the paid-up capital stock and surplus of said applicant bank, paying therefor its par value plus one-half of one per centum a month from the period of the last dividend. When the capital stock of any Federal reserve bank shall have been increased either on account of the increase of capital stock of member banks or on account of the increase in the number of member banks, the board of directors shall cause to be executed a certificate to the Comptroller of the Currency showing the increase in capital stock, the amount paid in, and by whom paid. When a member bank reduces its capital stock it shall surrender a proportionate amount of its holdings in the capital of said Federal reserve bank, and when a member bank voluntarily liquidates it shall surrender all of its holdings of the capital stock of said Federal reserve bank and be released from its stock subscription not previously called. In either case the shares surrendered shall be canceled and the member bank shall receive in payment therefor, under regulations to be prescribed by the Federal Reserve Board, a sum equal to its cash-paid subscriptions on the shares surrounded and one-half of one per centum a month from the period of the last dividend, not to exceed the book value thereof, less any liability of such member bank to the Federal reserve bank.

Sec. 6. If any member bank shall be declared insolvent and a receiver appointed therefor, the stock held by it in said Federal reserve bank shall be canceled, without impairment of its liability, and all cash-paid subscriptions on said stock, with one-half of one per centum per month from the period of last dividend, not to exceed the book value thereof, shall be first applied to all debts of the insolvent member bank to the Federal reserve bank, and the balance, if any, shall be paid to the receiver of the insolvent bank. Whenever the capital stock of a Federal reserve bank is reduced, either on account of reduction in capital stock of any member bank or of the liquidation or insolvency of such bank, the board of directors shall cause to be executed a certificate to the Comptroller of the Currency showing such reduction of capital stock and the amount repaid to such bank.

DIVISION OF EARNINGS.

Sec. 7. After all necessary expenses of a Federal reserve bank have been paid or provided for, the stockholders shall be entitled to receive an annual dividend of six per centum on the paid-in capital stock, which dividend shall be cumulative. After the aforesaid dividend claims have been fully met, all the net earnings shall be paid to the United States as a franchise tax, except that one-half of such net earnings shall be paid into a surplus fund until it shall amount to forty per centum of the paid-in capital stock of such bank.

The net earnings derived by the United States from Federal reserve banks shall, in the discretion of the Secretary, be used to supplement the gold reserve held against outstanding United States notes, or shall be applied to the reduction of the outstanding bonded indebtedness of the United States under regulations to be prescribed by the Secretary of the Treasury. Should a Federal reserve bank be dissolved or go into liquidation, any surplus remaining, after the payment of all debts, dividend requirements as hereinbefore provided, and the par value of the stock, shall be paid to and become the property of the United States and shall be similarly applied.

Federal reserve banks, including the capital stock and surplus therein, and the income derived therefrom shall be exempt from Federal, State, and local taxation, except taxes in real estate.

Sec. 8. Section fifty-one hundred and fifty-four, United States Revised Statutes, is hereby amended to read as follows:

Any bank incorporated by special law of any State or of the United States or organized under the general laws of any State or of the United States and having an unimpaired capital sufficient to entitle it to become a national banking association under the provisions of the existing laws may, by the vote of the shareholders owning not less than fifty-one per centum of the capital stock of such bank or banking association, with the approval of the Comptroller of the Currency be converted into a national banking association, with any name approved by the Comptroller of the Currency:

Provided, however, That said conversion shall not be in contravention of the State law. In such case the articles of association and organization certificate may be executed by a majority of the directors of the bank or banking institution, and the certificate shall declare that the owners of fifty-one per centum of the capital stock have authorized the directors to make such certificate and to change or convert the bank or banking institution into a national association. A majority of the directors, after executing the articles of association and the organization certificate, shall have the power to execute all other papers and do whatever may be required to make its organization perfect and complete as a national association. The shares of any such bank may continue to be for the same amount as they were before the conversion, and the directors may continue to be directors of the association until others are elected or appointed in accordance with the provisions of the statutes of the United States. When the Comptroller has given to such bank or banking association a certificate that the provisions of this Act have been complied with, such bank or banking association, and all its stockholders, officers, and employees, shall have the same powers and privileges, and shall be subject to the same duties, liabilities, and regulations, in all respects, as shall have been prescribed by the Federal Reserve Act and by the national banking Act for associations originally organized as national banking associations.

STATE BANKS AS MEMBERS.

Sec. 9. Any bank incorporated by special law of any State, or organized under the general laws of any State or of the United States, may make application to the reserve bank organization committee, pending organization, and thereafter to the Federal Reserve Board for the right to subscribe to the stock of the Federal reserve bank organized or to be organized within the Federal reserve district where the applicant is located. The organization committee or the Federal Reserve Board, under such rules and regulations as it may prescribe, subject to the provisions of this section, may permit the applying bank to become a shareholder in the Federal reserve bank of the district in which the applying bank is located. Whenever the organization committee or the Federal Reserve Board shall permit the applying bank to become a stockholder in the Federal reserve bank of the district, stock shall be issued and paid for under the rules and regulations in this Act provided for national banks which become stockholders in Federal reserve banks.

The organization committee or the Federal Reserve Board shall establish by-laws for the general government of its conduct in acting upon applications made by the State banks and banking associations and trust companies for stock ownership in Federal reserve banks. Such by-laws shall require applying banks not organized under Federal law to comply with the reserve and capital requirements and to submit to the examination and regulation prescribed by the organization committee or by the Federal Reserve Board. No applying bank shall be admitted to membership in a Federal reserve bank unless it possesses a paid-up unimpaired capital sufficient to entitle it to become a national banking association in the place where it is situated, under the provisions of the national banking Act.

Any bank becoming a member of the Federal reserve bank under the provisions of this section shall, in addition to the regulations and restrictions hereinbefore provided, be required to conform to the provisions of law imposed on the national banks respecting the limitation of liability which may be incurred by any person, firm, or corporation to such banks, the prohibition against making purchase of loans on stock of such banks, and the withdrawal or impairment of capital, or the payment of unearned dividends, and to such rules and as the Federal Reserve Board may, in pursuance thereof, prescribe.

Such banks, and the officers, agents, and employees thereof, shall also be subject to the provisions of and to the penalties prescribed by sections fifty-one hundred and ninety-eight, fifty-two hundred, fifty-two hundred and one, and fifty-two hundred and eight, and fifty-two hundred and nine of the Revised Statutes. The member banks shall also be required to make reports of the conditions and of the payments of dividends to the comptroller, as provided in sections fifty-two hundred and eleven and fifty-two hundred and twelve of the Revised Statutes, and shall be subject to the penalties prescribed by section fifty-two hundred and thirteen for the failure to make such report.

If at any time it shall appear to the Federal Reserve Board that a member bank has failed to comply with the provisions of this section or the regulations of the federal Reserve Board, it shall be within the power of the said board, after hearing, to require such bank to surrender its stock in the Federal reserve bank; upon such surrender the Federal reserve bank shall pay the cash-paid subscriptions to the said stock with interest at the rate of one-half of one per centum per month, computed from the last dividend, if earned, not to exceed the book value thereof, less any liability to said Federal reserve bank, except the subscription liability not previously called, which shall be canceled, and said Federal reserve bank shall, upon notice from the Federal Reserve Board, be required to suspend said bank from further privileges of membership, and shall within thirty days of such notice cancel and retire its stock and make payment therefor in the manner herein provided. The Federal Reserve Board may restore membership upon due proof of compliance with the conditions imposed by this section.

FEDERAL RESERVE BOARD.

Sec. 10. A Federal Reserve Board is hereby created which shall consist of seven members, including the Secretary of the Treasury and the Comptroller of the Currency, who shall be members ex officio, and five members appointed by the President of the United States, by and with the advice and consent of the Senate. In selecting the five appointive members of the Federal Reserve Board, not more than one of whom shall be selected from any one Federal reserve district, the President shall have due regard to a fair representation of the different commercial, industrial and geographical divisions of the country. The five members of the Federal Reserve Board appointed by the President and confirmed as aforesaid shall devote their entire time to the business of the Federal Reserve Board and shall each receive an annual salary of $12,000, payable monthly with actual necessary traveling expenses, and the Comptroller of the Currency, as ex officio member of the Federal Reserve Board, shall, in addition to the salary now paid him as Comptroller of the Currency, receive the sum of $7,000 annually for his services as member of said board.

The members of said board, the Secretary of the Treasury, the Assistant Secretaries of the Treasury, and the Comptroller of the Currency shall be ineligible during the time they are in office and for two years thereafter to hold any office, position, or employment in any member bank. Of the five members thus appointed by the President at least two shall be persons experienced in banking or finance. One shall be designated by the President to serve for two, one for four, one for six, one for eight, and one for ten years, and thereafter each member so appointed shall serve for a term of ten years unless sooner removed for cause by the President. Of the five persons thus appointed, one shall be designated by the President as governor and one as vice governor of the Federal Reserve Board. The governor of the Federal Reserve Board, subject to its supervision, shall be the active executive officer. The Secretary of the Treasury may assign offices in the Department of the Treasury for the use of the Federal Reserve Board. Each member of the Federal Reserve Board shall within fifteen days after notice of appointment make and subscribe to the oath of office.

The Federal Reserve Board shall have the power to levy semiannually upon the Federal reserve banks, in proportion to their capital stock and surplus, an assessment sufficient to pay its estimated expenses and the salaries of its members and employees for the half year succeeding the levying of such assessment, together with any deficit carried forward from the preceding half year.

The first meeting of the Federal Reserve Board shall be held in Washington, District of Columbia, as soon as may be after the passage of this Act, at a date to be fixed by the Reserve Bank Organization Committee. The Secretary of the Treasury shall be ex officio chairman of the Federal Reserve Board. No member of the Federal Reserve Board shall be an officer or director of any bank, banking institution, trust company, of Federal reserve bank nor hold stock in any bank, banking institution, or trust company; and before entering upon his duties as a member of the Federal Reserve Board he shall certify under oath to the Secretary of the Treasury that he has complied with this requirement. Whenever a vacancy shall occur, other than by expiration of term, among the five members of the Federal Reserve Board appointed by the President, as above provided, a successor shall be appointed by the President, with the advice and consent of the Senate, to fill such vacancy, and when appointed he shall hold office for the unexpired term of the member whose place he is selected to fill.

The President shall have the power to fill all vacancies that may happen on the Federal Reserve Board during the recess of the Senate, by granting commissions which shall expire thirty days after the next session of the Senate convenes.

Nothing in this Act contained shall be construed as taking away any powers heretofore vested by law in the Secretary of the Treasury which relate to the supervision, management, and control of the Treasury Department and bureaus under such department, and wherever any power vested by this Act in the Federal Reserve Board or the Federal reserve agents appears to conflict with the powers of the Secretary of the Treasury, such powers shall be exercised subject to the supervision and control of the Secretary.

The Federal Reserve Board shall annually make a full report of its operations to the Speaker of the House of Representatives, who shall cause the same to be printed for the information of the Congress.

Section three hundred and twenty-four of the Revised Statutes shall be amended so as to read as follows: There shall be in the Department of the Treasury a bureau charged with the execution of all laws passed by Congress relating to the issue and regulation of national currency secured by the United States bonds and, under the general supervision of the Federal Reserve Board, of all Federal reserve notes, the chief officer of which bureau shall be called the Comptroller of Currency and shall perform his duties under the general directions of the Secretary of the Treasury.

Sec. 11. The Federal Reserve Board shall be authorized and empowered:

(a) To examine at its discretion the accounts, books and affairs of each Federal reserve bank and of each member bank and to require such statements and reports as it may deem necessary. The said board shall publish once each week a statement showing the condition of each Federal reserve bank and a consolidated statement for all Federal reserve banks. Such statements shall show in detail the assets and liabilities of the Federal reserve banks, single and combined, and shall furnish full information regarding the character of the money held as reserve and the amount, nature and maturities of the paper and other investments owned or held by Federal reserve banks.

(b) To permit, or, on the affirmative vote of at least five members of the Reserve Board to require Federal reserve banks to rediscount the discounted paper of other Federal reserve banks at rates of interest to be fixed by the Federal Reserve Board.

(c) To suspend for a period not exceeding thirty days, and from time to time to renew such suspension for periods not exceeding fifteen days, any reserve requirement specified in this Act: Provided, That it shall establish a graduated tax upon the amounts by which the reserve requirements of this Act may be permitted to fall below the level hereinafter specified: And provided further, That when the gold reserve held against Federal reserve notes falls below forty per centum the Federal Reserve Board shall establish a graduated tax of not more than one per centum per annum upon such deficiency until the reserve falls to thirty-two and one-half per centum, and when said reserve falls below thirty-two and one-half per centum, a tax at the rate increasingly of not less than one and one-half per centum per annum upon each two and one-half per centum or fraction thereof that such reserve falls below thirty-two and one-half per centum. The tax shall be paid by the reserve bank, but the reserve bank shall add an amount equal to said tax to the rates of interest and discount fixed by the Federal Reserve Board.

(d) To supervise and regulate the bureau under the charge of the Comptroller of the Currency the issue and retirement of Federal reserve notes, and to prescribe rules and regulations under which such notes may be delivered by the Comptroller to the Federal reserve agents applying therefor.

(e) To add to the number of cities classified as reserve and central reserve cities under existing law in which national banking associations are subject to the reserve requirements set forth in section twenty of this Act; or to reclassify existing reserve and central reserve cities or to terminate their designation as such.

(f) To suspend or remove any officer or director of any Federal reserve bank, the cause of such removal to be forthwith communicated in writing by the Federal Reserve Board to the removed officer or director and to said bank.

(g) To require the writing off of doubtful or worthless assets upon the books and balance sheets of Federal reserve banks.

(h) To suspend, for the violation of any of the provisions of this Act, the operations of any Federal reserve bank, to take possession thereof, administer the same during the period of suspension, and, when deemed advisable, to liquidate or reorganize such bank.

(i) To require bonds of Federal reserve agents, to make regulations for the safeguarding of all collateral, bonds, Federal reserve notes, money or property of any kind deposited in the hands of such agents, and said board shall perform the duties, functions, or services specified in this Act, and make all rules and regulations necessary to enable said board effectively to perform the same.

(j) To exercise general supervision over said Federal reserve banks.

(k) To grant by special permit to national banks applying therefor, when not in contravention of State or local law, the right to act as trustee, executor, administrator, or registrar of stocks and bonds under such rules and regulations as the said board may prescribe.

(l) To employ such attorneys, experts, assistants, clerks, or other employees as may be deemed necessary to conduct the business of the board. All salaries and fees shall be fixed in advance by said board and shall be paid in the same manner as the salaries of the members of said board. All such attorneys, experts, assistants, clerks, and other employees shall be appointed without regard to the provisions of the Act of January sixteenth, eighteen hundred and eighty-three (volume twenty-two, United States Statutes at Large, page four hundred and three), and amendments thereto, or any rule or regulation made in pursuance thereof: Provided, That nothing herein shall prevent the President from placing said employees in the classified service.

FEDERAL ADVISORY COUNCIL.

Sec 12. There is hereby created a Federal Advisory Council, which shall consist of as many members as there are Federal reserve districts. Each Federal reserve bank by its board of directors shall annually select from its own Federal reserve district one member of said council, who shall receive such compensation and allowances as may be fixed by his board of directors subject to the approval of the Federal Reserve Board. The meetings of said advisory council shall be held at Washington, District of Columbia, at least four times each year, and oftener if called by the Federal Reserve Board. The council may in addition to the meetings above provided for hold such other meetings in Washington, District of Columbia, or elsewhere, as it may deem necessary, may select its own officers and adopt its own methods of procedure, and a majority of its members shall constitute a quorum for the transaction of business.

Vacancies in the council shall be filled by the respective reserve banks, and members selected to fill vacancies, shall serve for the unexpired term.

The Federal Advisory Council shall have power, by itself or through its officers, (1) to confer directly with the Federal Reserve Board on general business conditions; (2) to make oral or written representations concerning matters within the jurisdiction of said board; (3) to call for information and to make recommendations in regards to discount rates, rediscount business, note issues, reserve conditions in the various districts, the purchase of gold or securities by reserve banks, open-market operations by said banks, and the general affairs of the reserve banking system.

POWERS OF FEDERAL RESERVE BANKS.

Sec. 13. Any Federal reserve bank may receive from any of its member banks, and from the United States, deposits of current funds in lawful money, national-bank notes, Federal reserve notes, or checks and drafts upon solvent member banks, payable upon presentation; or, solely for exchange purposes, may receive from other Federal reserve banks deposits of current funds in lawful money, national-bank notes, or checks and drafts upon solvent member or other Federal reserve banks, payable upon presentation.

Upon the indorsement of any of its member banks, with a waiver of demand, notice and protest by such bank, any Federal reserve bank may discount notes, drafts, and bills of exchange arising out of actual commercial transactions; that is, notes, drafts, and bills of exchange issued or drawn for agricultural, industrial, or commercial purposes, or the proceeds of which have been used, or are to be used, for such purposes, the Federal Reserve Board to have the right to determine or define the character of the paper thus eligible for discount, within the meaning of this Act. Nothing in this Act contained shall be construed to prohibit such notes, drafts, and bills of exchange, secured by staple agricultural products, or other goods, wares, or merchandise from being eligible for such discount; but such definition shall not include notes, drafts, or bills covering merely investments or issued or drawn for the purpose of carrying or trading in stocks, bonds, or other investment securities, except bonds and notes of the Government of the United States. Notes, drafts, and bills admitted to discount under the terms of this paragraph must have a maturity at the time of discount of not more than ninety days: Provided, That notes, drafts, and bills drawn or issued for agricultural purposes or based on live stock and having a maturity not exceeding six months may be discounted in an amount to be limited to a percentage of the capital of the Federal reserve bank, to be ascertained and fixed by the Federal Reserve Board.

Any Federal reserve bank may discount acceptances which are based on the importation or exportation of goods and which have a maturity at time of discount of not more than three months, and indorsed by at least one member bank. The amount of acceptances so discounted shall at no time exceed one-half the paid-up capital stock and surplus of the bank for which the rediscounts are made.

The aggregate of such notes and bills bearing the signature or indorsement of any one person, company, firm, or corporation rediscounted for any one bank shall at no time exceed ten per centum of the unimpaired capital and surplus of said bank; but this restriction shall not apply to the discount of bills of exchange drawn in good faith against actually existing values.

Any member bank may accept drafts or bills of exchange drawn upon it and growing out of transactions involving the importation or exportation of goods not more than six months sight to run; but no bank shall accept such bills to an amount equal at any time in the aggregate to more than one-half of its paid-up capital stock and surplus.

Section fifty-two hundred and two of the Revised Statutes of the United States is hereby amended so as to read as follows: No national banking association shall at any time be indebted, or in any way liable, to an amount exceeding the amount of its capital stock at such time actually paid in and remaining undiminished by losses or otherwise, except on account of demands of the nature following:

First. Notes of circulation.

Second. Moneys deposited with or collected by the association.

Third. Bills of exchange or drafts drawn against money actually on deposit to the credit of the association, or due thereto.

Fourth. Liabilities to the stockholders of the association for dividends and reserve profits.

Fifth. Liabilities incurred under the provisions of the Federal Reserve Act.

The rediscount by any Federal reserve bank of any bills receivable and of domestic and foreign bills of exchange, and of acceptances authorized by this Act, shall be subject to such restrictions, limitations, and regulations as may be imposed by the Federal Reserve Board.

OPEN-MARKET OPERATIONS.

Sec. 14. Any Federal reserve bank may, under rules and regulations prescribed by the Federal Reserve Board, purchase and sell in the open market, at home or abroad, either from or to domestic or foreign banks, firms, corporations, or individuals, cable transfers and bankers' acceptances and bills of exchange of the kinds and maturities by this Act made eligible for rediscount, with or without the indorsement of a member bank.

Every Federal reserve bank shall have power:

(a) To deal in gold coin and bullion at home or abroad, to make loans thereof, exchange Federal reserve notes for gold, gold coin or bullion, giving therefor, when necessary, acceptable security, including the hypothecation of United States bonds or other securities which Federal reserve banks are authorized to hold;

(b) To buy and sell, at home or abroad, bonds and notes of the United States, and bills, notes, revenue bonds, and warrants with a maturity from date of purchase of not exceeding six months, issued in anticipation of the collection of taxes or in anticipation of the receipt of assured revenues by any State, county, district, political subdivision, or municipality in the continental United States, including irrigation, drainage and reclamation districts, such purchases to be made in accordance with rules and regulations prescribed by the Federal Reserve Board;

(c) To purchase from member banks and to sell, with or without its indorsement, bills of exchange arising out of commercial transactions, as hereinbefore defined;

(d) To establish from time to time, subject to review and determination of the Federal Reserve Board, rates of discount to be charged by the Federal reserve bank for each class of paper, which shall be fixed with a view of accommodating commerce and business;

(e) To establish accounts with other Federal reserve banks for exchange purposes and, with the consent of the Federal Reserve Board, to open and maintain banking accounts in foreign countries, appoint correspondents, and establish agencies in such countries wheresoever it may deem best for the purpose of purchasing, selling, and collecting bills of exchange, and to buy and sell with or without its endorsement, through such correspondents or agencies, bills of exchange arising out of actual commercial transactions which have not more than ninety days to run and which bear the signature of two or more reasonable parties.

GOVERNMENT DEPOSITS.

Sec. 15. The moneys held in the general fund of the Treasury except the five per centum fund for the redemption of outstanding national-bank notes and the funds provided in this Act for the redemption of Federal reserve notes may, upon the direction of the Secretary of the Treasury, be deposited in Federal reserve banks, which banks, when required by the Secretary of the Treasury, shall act as fiscal agents of the United States; and the revenues of the Government or any part thereof may be deposited in such banks, and disbursements may be made by checks drawn against such deposits.

No public funds of the Philippine Islands, or of the postal savings, or any Government funds, shall be deposited in the continental United States in and bank not belonging to the system established by this Act: Provided, however, That nothing in this Act shall be construed to deny the right of the Secretary of the Treasury to use member banks as depositories.

NOTE ISSUES.

Sec. 16. Federal reserve notes, to be issued at the discretion of the Federal Reserve Board for the purpose of making advances to Federal reserve banks through the Federal reserve agents as hereinafter set forth and for no other purpose, are hereby authorized. The said notes shall be obligations of the United States and shall be receivable by all national and member banks and Federal reserve banks and for all taxes, customs, and other public dues. They shall be redeemed in gold on demand at the Treasury Department of the United States, in the city of Washington, District of Columbia, or in gold or lawful money at any Federal reserve bank.

Any Federal reserve bank may make application to the local Federal reserve agent for such amount of the Federal reserve noted hereinbefore provided for as it may require. Such application shall be accompanied with a tender to the local Federal reserve agent of collateral in amount equal to the sum of the Federal reserve notes thus applied for and issued pursuant to such application. The collateral security thus offered shall be notes and bills, accepted for rediscount under the provisions of section thirteen of this Act, and the Federal reserve agent shall each day notify the Federal Reserve Board of all issues and withdrawals of Federal reserve notes to and by the Federal reserve bank to which it is accredited. The said Federal Reserve Board may at any time call upon a Federal reserve bank for additional security to protect the Federal reserve notes issued to it.

Every Federal reserve bank shall maintain reserves in gold or lawful money of not less than thirty-five per centum against its deposits and reserves in gold of not less than forty per centum against its Federal reserve notes in actual circulation, and not offset by gold or lawful money deposited with the Federal reserve agent. Notes so paid out shall bear upon their faces a distinctive letter and serial number, which shall be assigned by the Federal Reserve Board to each Federal reserve bank. Whenever Federal reserve notes issued through one Federal reserve bank shall be received by another Federal reserve bank they shall be promptly returned for credit or redemption to the Federal reserve bank through which they were originally issued. No Federal reserve bank shall pay out notes issued through another under penalty of a tax of ten per centum upon the face value of notes so paid out. Notes presented for redemption at the Treasury of the United States shall be paid out of the redemption fund and returned to the Federal reserve banks through which they were originally issued, and thereupon such Federal reserve bank shall, upon demand of the Secretary of the Treasury, reimburse such redemption fund in lawful money or, if such Federal reserve notes have been redeemed by the Treasurer in gold or gold certificates, then such funds shall be reimbursed to the extent deemed necessary by the Secretary of the Treasury in gold or gold certificates, and such Federal reserve bank shall, so long as any of its Federal reserve notes remain outstanding, maintain with the Treasurer in gold an amount sufficient in the judgment of the Secretary to provide for all redemptions to be made by the Treasurer. Federal reserve notes received by the Treasury, otherwise than for redemption, may be exchanged for gold out of the redemption fund hereinafter provided and returned to the reserve bank through which they were originally issued, or they may be returned to such bank for the credit of the United States. Federal reserve notes unfit for circulation shall be returned by the Federal reserve agents to the Comptroller of the Currency for cancellation and destruction.

The Federal Reserve Board shall require each Federal reserve bank to maintain on deposit in the Treasury of the United States a sum in gold sufficient in the judgment of the Secretary of the Treasury for the redemption of the Federal reserve notes issued to such bank, but in no event less than five per centum; but such deposit of gold shall be counted and included as part of the forty per centum reserve hereinbefore required. The board shall have the right, acting through the Federal reserve agent, to grant in whole or in part or to reject entirely the application of any Federal reserve bank for Federal reserve notes; but to the extent that such application may be granted the Federal Reserve Board shall, through its local Federal reserve agent, supply Federal reserve notes to the bank so applying, and such bank shall be charged with the amount of such notes and shall pay such rate of interest on said amount as may be established by the Federal Reserve Board, and the amount of such Federal reserve notes so issued to any such bank shall, upon delivery, together with such notes of such Federal reserve bank as may be issued under section eighteen of this Act upon security of United States two per centum Government bonds, become a first and paramount lien on all the assets of such bank.

Any Federal reserve bank may at any time reduce its liability for outstanding Federal reserve notes by depositing, with the Federal reserve agent, its Federal reserve notes, gold, gold certificates, or lawful money of the United States. Federal reserve notes so deposited shall not be reissued, except upon compliance with the conditions of an original issue.

The Federal reserve agent shall hold such gold, gold certificates, or lawful money available exclusively for exchange for the outstanding Federal reserve notes when offered by the reserve bank of which he is a director. Upon the request of the Secretary of the Treasury the Federal Reserve Board shall require the Federal reserve agent to transmit so much of said gold to the Treasury of the United States as may be required for the exclusive purpose of the redemption of such notes.

Any Federal reserve bank may at its discretion withdraw collateral deposited with the local Federal reserve agent for the protection of its Federal reserve notes deposited with it and shall at the same time substitute therefor other like collateral of equal amount with the approval of the Federal reserve agent under regulations to be prescribed by the Federal Reserve Board.

In order to furnish suitable notes for circulation as Federal reserve notes, the Comptroller of the Currency shall, under the direction of the Secretary of the Treasury, cause plates and dies to be engraved in the best manner to guard against counterfeits and fraudulent alterations, and shall have printed therefrom and numbered such quantities of such notes of the denominations of $5, $10, $20, $50, $100, as may be required to supply the Federal reserve banks. Such notes shall be in form and tenor as directed by the Secretary of the Treasury under the provisions of this Act and shall bear the distinctive numbers of the several reserve banks through which they are issued.

When such notes have been prepared, they shall be deposited in the Treasury, or in the subtreasury or mint of the United States nearest the place of business of each Federal reserve bank and shall be held for the use of such bank subject to the order of the Comptroller of the Currency for their delivery, as provided for by this Act.

The plates and dies to be procured by the Comptroller of Currency for the printing of such circulating notes shall remain under his control and direction, and the expenses necessarily incurred in executing the laws relating to the procuring of such notes, and all other expenses incidental to their issue and retirement, shall be paid by the Federal reserve banks, and the Federal Reserve Board shall include in its estimate of expenses levied against the Federal reserve banks a sufficient amount to cover the expenses herein provided for.

The examination of plates, dies, bed pieces, and so forth, and regulations relating to such examination of plates, dies, and so forth, of national-bank notes provided for in section fifty-one hundred and seventy-four Revised Statutes, is hereby extended to include notes herein provided for.

Any appropriation heretofore made out of the general funds of the Treasury for engraving plates and dies, the purchase of distinctive paper, or to cover any other expense in connection with the printing of national-bank notes or notes provided for by the Act of May thirtieth, nineteen hundred and eight, and any distinctive paper that may be on hand at the time of the passage of this Act may be used in the discretion of the Secretary for the purposes of this Act, and should the appropriations heretofore made be insufficient to meet the requirements of this Act in addition to circulating notes provided for by existing law, the Secretary is hereby authorized to use so much of any funds in the Treasury not otherwise appropriated for the purpose of furnishing the notes aforesaid: Provided, however, That nothing in this section contained shall be construed as exempting national banks or Federal reserve banks from their liability to reimburse the United States for any expenses incurred in printing and issuing circulating notes.

Every Federal reserve bank shall receive on deposit at par from member banks or from Federal reserve banks checks and drafts drawn upon any of its depositors, and when remitted by a Federal reserve bank, checks and drafts drawn by any depositor in any other Federal reserve bank or member bank upon funds to the credit of said depositor in said reserve bank or member bank. Nothing herein contained shall be construed as prohibiting a member bank from charging its actual expense incurred in collecting and remitting funds, or for the exchange sold to its patrons. The Federal Reserve Board shall, by rule, fix the charges to be collected by the member banks from its patrons whose checks are cleared through the Federal reserve bank and the charge which may be imposed for the service and clearing or collection rendered by the Federal reserve bank. The Federal Reserve Board shall make and promulgate from time to time regulations governing the transfer of funds and charges therefor among Federal reserve banks and their branches, and may at their discretion exercise the functions of a clearing house for such Federal reserve banks, or may designate a Federal reserve bank to exercise such functions, and may also require each such bank to exercise the functions of a clearing house for its member banks.

Sec. 17. So much of the provisions of section fifty-one hundred and fifty-nine of the Revised Statutes of the United States, and section four of the Act of June twentieth, eighteen hundred and seventy-four, and section eight of the Act of July twelfth, eighteen hundred and eighty-two, and of any other provisions of existing statutes as require that before any national banking associations shall be authorized to commence banking business it shall transfer and deliver to the Treasurer of the United States a stated amount of United States registered bonds is hereby repealed.

REFUNDING BONDS.

Sec. 18. After two years from the passage of this Act, and at any time during a period of twenty years thereafter, any member bank desiring to retire the whole or any part of its circulating notes, may file with the Treasurer of the United States an application to sell for its account, at par and accrued interest, United States bonds securing circulation to be retired.

The Treasurer shall, at the end of each quarterly period, furnish the Federal Reserve Board with a list of such applications, and the Federal Reserve Board may, in its discretion, require the Federal reserve banks to purchase such bonds from the banks whose applications have been filed with the Treasurer at least ten days before the end of any quarterly period at which the Federal Reserve Board may direct the purchase to be made: Provided, That Federal reserve banks shall not be permitted to purchase an amount to exceed $25,000,000 of such bonds in any one year, and which amount shall include bonds acquired under section four of this Act by the Federal reserve bank.

Provided further, That the Federal Reserve Board shall allot to each Federal reserve bank such proportion of such bonds as the capital and surplus of such bank shall bear to the aggregate capital and surplus of all the Federal reserve banks.

Upon notice from the Treasurer of the amount of bonds so sold for its account, each member bank shall duly assign and transfer, in writing, such bonds to the Federal reserve bank purchasing the same, and such Federal reserve bank shall, thereupon, deposit lawful money with the Treasurer of the United States for the purchase price of such bonds, and the Treasurer shall pay to the member bank selling such bonds any balance due after deducting a sufficient sum to redeem its outstanding notes secured by such bonds, which notes shall be canceled and permanently retired when redeemed.

The Federal reserve banks purchasing such bonds shall be permitted to take out an amount of circulating notes equal to the par value of such bonds.

Upon the deposit with the Treasurer of the United States of bonds so purchased, or any bonds with the circulating privilege acquired under section four of this Act, any Federal reserve bank making such deposit in the manner provided by existing law, shall be entitled to receive from the Comptroller of the Currency circulating notes in blank, registered and countersigned as provided by law, equal in amount to the par value of the bonds so deposited. Such notes shall be the obligations of the Federal reserve bank procuring the same, and shall be in form prescribed by the Secretary of the Treasury, and to the same tenor and effect as national-bank notes now provided by law. They shall be issued and redeemed under the same terms and conditions as national-bank notes except that they shall not be limited to the amount of the capital stock of the Federal reserve bank issuing them.

Upon application of any Federal reserve bank, approved by the Federal Reserve Board, the Secretary of the Treasury may issue, in exchange for United States two per centum gold bonds bearing the circulation privilege, but against which no circulation is outstanding, one-year notes of the United States without the circulation privilege, to an amount not to exceed one-half of the two per centum bonds so tendered for exchange, and thirty-year three per centum gold bonds without the circulation privilege for the remainder of the two per centum bonds so tendered: Provided, That at the time of such exchange the Federal reserve bank obtaining such one-year gold notes shall enter into an obligation with the Secretary of the Treasury binding itself to purchase from the United States for gold at the maturity of such one-year notes, an amount equal to those delivered in exchange for such bonds, if so requested by the Secretary, and at each maturity of one-year notes so purchased by such Federal reserve bank, to purchase from the United States such an amount of one-year notes as the Secretary may tender to such bank, not to exceed the amount issued to such bank in the first instance, in exchange for the two per centum United States gold bonds; said obligation to purchase at maturity such notes shall continue in force for a period not to exceed thirty years.

For the purpose of making the exchange herein provided for, the Secretary of the Treasury is authorized to issue at par Treasury notes in coupon or registered form as he may prescribe in denominations of one hundred dollars, or any multiple thereof, bearing interest at the rate of three per centum per annum, payable quarterly, such Treasury notes to be payable not more than one year from the date of their issue in gold coin of the present standard value, and to be exempt as to principal and interest from the payment of all taxes and duties of the United States except as provided by this Act, as well as from taxes in any form by or under any State, municipal, or local authorities. And for the same purpose, the Secretary is authorized and empowered to issue United States gold bonds at par, bearing three per centum interest payable thirty years from date of issue, such bonds to be of the same general tenor and effect and to be issued under the same general terms and conditions as the United States three per centum bonds without the circulation privilege now issued and outstanding.

Upon application of any Federal reserve bank, approved by the Federal Reserve Board, the Secretary may issue at par such three per centum bonds in exchange for the one-year gold notes herein provided for.

BANK RESERVES.

Sec. 19. Demand deposits within the meaning of this Act shall comprise all deposits payable within thirty days, and time deposits shall comprise all deposits payable after thirty days, and all savings accounts and certificates of deposit which are subject to not less than thirty days' notice before payment.

When the Secretary of the Treasury shall have officially announced, in such manner as he may elect, the establishment of a Federal reserve bank in any district, every sub-scribing member bank shall establish and maintain reserves as follows:

(a) A bank not in a reserve or central reserve city as now or hereafter defined shall hold and maintain reserves equal to twelve per centum of the aggregate amount of its demand deposits and five per centum of its time deposits, as follows:

In its vaults for a period of thirty-six months after said date five-twelfths thereof and permanently thereafter four-twelfths.

In the Federal reserve bank of its district, for a period of twelve months after said date, two-twelfths, and for each succeeding six months an additional one-twelfth, until five-twelfths have been so deposited, which shall be the amount permanently required.

For a period of thirty-six months after said date the balance of the reserves may be held in its own vaults, or in the Federal reserve bank, or in national banks in reserve or central reserve cities as now defined by law.

After said thirty-six months' period said reserves, other than those hereinbefore required to be held in the vaults of the member bank and in the Federal reserve bank, shall be held in the vaults of the member bank or in the Federal reserve bank, or in both, at the option of the member bank.

(b) A bank in a reserve city, as now or hereafter defined, shall hold and maintain reserves equal to fifteen per centum of the aggregate amount of its demand deposits and five per centum of its time deposits, as follows:

In its vaults for a period of thirty-six months after said date six-fifteenths thereof, and permanently thereafter five-fifteenths.

In the Federal reserve bank of its district for a period of twelve months after the date aforesaid at least three-fifteenths, and for each succeeding six months an additional one-fifteenth, until six-fifteenths have been so deposited, which shall be the amount permanently required.

For a period of thirty-six months after said date the balance of the reserves may be held in its own vaults, or in the Federal reserve bank, or in national banks in reserve or central reserve cities as now defined by law.

After thirty-six months' period all of said reserves, except those hereinbefore required to be held permanently in the vaults of the member bank and in the Federal reserve bank, shall be held in its vaults or in the Federal reserve bank, or in both, at the option of the member bank.

(c) A bank in a central reserve city, as now or hereafter defined, shall hold and maintain a reserve equal to eighteen per centum of the aggregate amount of its demand deposits and five per centum of its time deposits, as follows:

In its vaults six-eighteenths thereof.

In the Federal reserve bank seven-eighteenths.

The balance of said reserves shall be held in its own vaults or in the Federal reserve bank, at its option.

Any Federal reserve bank may receive from the member banks as reserves, not exceeding one-half of each installment, eligible paper as described in section fourteen properly indorsed and acceptable to the said reserve bank.

If a State bank or trust company is required by law of its State to keep its reserves either in its own vaults or with another State bank or trust company, such reserve deposits so kept in such State bank or trust company shall be construed, within the meaning of this section, as if they were reserve deposits in a national bank in a reserve or central reserve city for a period of three years after the Secretary of the

Treasury shall have officially announced the establishment of a Federal reserve bank in the district in which such State bank or trust company is situate. Except as thus provided, no member bank shall keep on deposit with any nonmember bank a sum in excess of ten per centum of its own paid-up capital and surplus. No member bank shall act as the medium or agent of a nonmember bank in applying for or receiving discounts from a Federal reserve bank under the provisions of this Act except by permission of the Federal Reserve Board.

The reserve carried by a member bank with a Federal reserve bank may, under the regulations and subject to such penalties as may be described by the Federal Reserve Board, be checked against and withdrawn by such member bank for the purpose of meeting existing liabilities: Provided, however, That no bank shall at any time make new loans or shall pay any dividends unless and until the total reserve required by law is fully restored.

In estimating the reserves required by this Act, the net balance of amounts due to and from other banks shall be taken as the basis for ascertaining the deposits against which the reserves shall be determined. Balances in reserve banks due to member banks shall, to the extent herein provided, be counted as reserves.

National banks located in Alaska or outside the continental United States may remain nonmember banks, and shall in that event maintain reserves and comply with all the conditions now provided by law regulating them; or said banks, except in the Philippine Islands, may, with the consent of the Reserve Board, become member banks of any one of the reserve districts, and shall, in that event, take stock, maintain reserves, and be subject to all the other provisions of this Act.

Sec. 20. So much of sections two and three of the Act of June twentieth, eighteen hundred and seventy-four, entitled "An Act fixing the amount of United States notes, providing for a redistribution of the national-bank currency, and for other purposes," as provides that the fund deposited by any national banking association with the Treasurer of the United States for the redemption of its notes shall be counted as a part of its lawful reserve as provided in the Act aforesaid, is hereby repealed. And from and after the passage of this Act such fund of five per centum shall in no case be counted by any national banking association as a part of its lawful reserve.

BANK EXAMINATIONS.

Sec. 21. Section fifty-two hundred and forty, United States Revised Statutes, is amended to read as follows:

The Comptroller of the Currency, with the approval of the Secretary of the Treasury, shall appoint examiners who shall examine every member bank at least twice in each calendar year and oftener if considered necessary: Provided, however, That the

Federal Reserve Board may authorize examination by the State authorities to be accepted in the case of State banks and trust companies and may at any time direct the holding of a special examination of State banks or trust companies that are stockholders in any Federal reserve bank, or of any other member bank, shall have power to make a thorough examination of all the affairs of the bank and in so doing so he shall have power to administer oaths and to examine any of the officers and agents thereof under oath and shall make a full and detailed report of the condition of said bank to the Comptroller of the Currency.

The Federal Reserve Board, upon the recommendation of the Comptroller of the Currency, shall affix the salaries of all bank examiners and make report thereof to Congress. The expense of the examinations herein provided for shall be assessed by the Comptroller of the Currency upon the banks examined in proportion to assets or resources held by the banks upon the dates of examination of the various banks.

In addition to the examinations made and conducted by the Comptroller of the Currency, every Federal reserve bank may, with the approval of the Federal reserve agent or the Federal Reserve Board, provide for special examination of member banks within its district. The expenses of such examinations shall be borne by the bank examined. Such examinations shall be so conducted as to inform the Federal reserve bank of the condition of its member banks and of the lines of credit which are being extended by them. Every Federal reserve bank shall at times furnish to the Federal Reserve Board such information as may be demanded concerning the condition of any member bank within the district of the said Federal reserve bank.

No bank shall be subject to visitatorial powers other than such as are authorized by law, or vested in the courts of justice or such as shall be or shall have been exercised or directed by Congress, or by either House thereof or by any committee of Congress or of either House duly authorized.

The Federal Reserve Board shall, at least once a year, order an examination of each Federal reserve bank, and upon joint application of ten member banks the Federal Reserve Board shall order a special examination and report of the condition of any Federal reserve bank.

Sec. 22. No member bank or any officer, director, or employee thereof shall hereafter make any loan or grant any gratuity to any bank examiner. Any bank officer, director, or employee violating this provision shall be deemed guilty of a misdemeanor and shall be imprisoned not exceeding one year or fined not more than $5,000, or both; and may be fined a further sum equal to the money so loaned or gratuity given. Any examiner accepting a loan or gratuity from any bank examined by him or from an officer, director, or employee thereof shall be guilty of a misdemeanor and shall be imprisoned not exceeding one year or fined not more than $5,000, or both; and may be fined a further sum equal to the money so loaned or gratuity given; and shall forever thereafter be disqualified from holding office as a national-bank examiner. No national-bank examiner shall perform any other service for compensation while holding such office for any bank or officer, director, or employee thereof.

Other than the usual salary or director's fee paid to any officer, director, or employee of a member bank and other than a reasonable fee paid by said bank to such officer, director, or employee for services rendered to such bank, no officer, director, employee, or attorney of a member bank shall be a beneficiary of or receive, directly or indirectly, any fee, commission, gift, or other consideration for or in connection with any transaction or business of the bank. No examiner, public or private, shall disclose the names of the borrowers or the collateral for loans of a member bank to other than the proper officers of such bank without first having obtained the express permission in writing from the Comptroller of the Currency, or from the board of directors of such bank, except when ordered to do so by a court of competent jurisdiction, or by direction of the Congress of the United States, or of either House thereof, or any committee of Congress or of either House duly authorized. Any person violating any provision of this section shall be punished by a fine not exceeding $5,000 or by imprisonment not exceeding one year, or both.

Except as provided in existing laws, this provision shall not take effect until sixty days after the passage of this Act. The stockholders of every national banking association shall be held individually responsible for all contracts, debts, and engagements of such association, each to the amount of his stock therein, at the par value thereof in addition to the amount invested in such stock. The stockholders in any national banking association who shall have transferred their shares or registered the transfer thereof within sixty days next before the date of the failure of such association to meet its obligations, or with knowledge of such impending failure, shall be liable to the same extent as if they had made no such transfer, to the extent that the subsequent transferee fails to meet such liability; but this provision shall not be construed to affect in any way any recourse which such shareholders might otherwise have against those in whose names such shares are registered at the time of such failure.

LOANS OF FARM LANDS.

Sec. 24. Any national banking association not situated in a central reserve city may make loans secured by improved and unencumbered farm land, situated within its Federal reserve district, but no such loan shall be made for a longer time than five years, nor for an amount exceeding fifty per centum of the actual value of the property offered as security. Any such bank may make such loans in an aggregate sum equal to twenty-five per centum of its capital and surplus or to one-third of its time deposits and such banks may continue hereafter as heretofore to receive time deposits and to pay interest on the same.

The Federal Reserve Board shall have the power from time to time to add to the list of cities in which national banks shall not be permitted to make loans secured upon real estate in the manner described in this section.

FOREIGN BRANCHES.

Sec. 25. Any banking association possessing a capital and surplus of $1,000,000 or more may file application with the Federal Reserve Board, upon such conditions and under such regulations as may be prescribed by the said board, for the purpose of securing authority to establish branches in foreign countries or dependencies of the United States for the furtherance of the foreign commerce of the United States, and to act, if required to do so, as fiscal agents of the United States. Such application shall specify, in addition to the name and capital of the banking association filing it, the place or places where the banking operations proposed are to be carried on, and the amount of capital set aside for the conduct of its foreign business. The Federal Reserve Board shall have the power to approve or to reject such application if, in its judgment, the amount of capital proposed to be set aside for the conduct of foreign business is inadequate, or if for other reasons the granting of such application is deemed inexpedient.

Every national banking association which shall receive authority to establish foreign branches shall be required at all times to furnish information concerning the condition of such branches to the Comptroller of the Currency upon demand, and the Federal Reserve Board may order special examinations of the said foreign branches at such time or times as it may deem best. Every national banking association shall conduct the accounts of each foreign branch independently of the accounts of other foreign branches established by it and of its home office, and shall at the end of each fiscal period transfer to its general ledger the profit or loss accruing at each branch as a separate item.

Sec. 26. All provisions of law inconsistent with or superseded by any of the provisions of this Act are to the extent and to that extent only hereby repealed: Provided, Nothing in this Act contained shall be construed to repeal the parity provision or provisions contained in an Act approved March fourteenth, nineteen hundred, entitled "An Act to define and fix the standard of value, to maintain the parity of all forms of money issued or coined by the United States, to refund the public debt, and for other purposes," and the Secretary of the Treasury may for the purpose of maintaining such parity and to strengthen the gold reserve, borrow gold on the security of United States bonds authorized by section two of the Act last referred to or for one-year gold notes bearing interest at a rate not to exceed three per centum per annum, or sell the same if necessary to obtain gold. When the funds of the Treasury on hand justify, he may purchase and retire such outstanding bonds and notes.

The provisions of the Act of May thirtieth, nineteen hundred and eight, authorizing national currency associations, the issue of additional national-bank circulation, and creating a National Monetary Commission, which expires by limitation under the terms of such Act on the thirtieth day of June, nineteen hundred and fourteen, are hereby extended to June thirtieth, nineteen hundred and fifteen, and sections fifty-one hundred and fifty-three, fifty-one hundred and seventy-two, fifty-one hundred and ninety-one, and fifty-two hundred and fourteen of the Revised Statutes of the United States, which were amended by the Act of May thirtieth, nineteen hundred and eight, are hereby reenacted to read as such sections read prior to May thirtieth, nineteen hundred and eight, subject to such amendments or modifications as are prescribed in this Act: Provided, however, That section nine of the Act first referred to in this section is hereby amended so as to change the tax rates fixed in said Act by making the portion applicable thereto read as follows:

National banking associations having circulating notes secured otherwise than by bonds of the United States, shall pay for the first three months a tax at the rate of three per centum per annum upon the average amount of such of their notes in circulation as are based upon the deposit of such securities, and afterwards an additional tax rate of one-half of one per centum per annum for each month until a tax of six per centum per annum is reached, and thereafter such tax of six per centum per annum upon the average amount of such notes.

Sec. 28. Section fifty-one hundred and forty-three of the Revised Statutes is hereby amended and reenacted to read as follows: Any association formed under this title may, by the vote of the shareholders owning two thirds of its capital stock, reduce its capital to any sum not below the amount required by this title to authorize the formation of associations; but no such reduction shall be allowable which will reduce the capital of the association below the amount required for its outstanding circulation, nor shall any reduction be made until the amount of the proposed reduction has been reported to the Comptroller of the Currency and such reduction has been approved by the said Comptroller of the Currency and by the Federal Reserve Board, or by the organization committee pending the organization of the Federal Reserve Board.

Sec. 29. If any clause, sentence, paragraph, or part of this Act shall for any reason be adjudged by any court of competent jurisdiction to be invalid, such judgment shall not affect, impair, or invalidate the remainder of this Act, but shall be confined in its operation to the clause, sentence, paragraph, or part thereof directly involved in the controversy in which such judgment shall have been rendered.

Sec. 30. The right to amend, alter, or repeal this Act is hereby expressly reserved.

Approved, December 23, 1913.

Clayton Anti-Trust Act (1914)

Passed by Congress in 1914, the Clayton Anti-Trust Act was designed to modify the Sherman Anti-Trust Act. Companies could no longer conclude exclusive sales agreements or have interlocking directorates. Labor unions and farmer's cooperatives did not fall under this act. This piece of legislation prevented the formation of new monopolies and allowed the courts to disassemble existing trusts.

Source: Public Statutes at Large, Vol. 38 Part I, pp. 730–740.

An Act To supplement existing laws against unlawful restraints and monopolies, and for other purposes.

Be it enacted by the Senate and the House of Representatives of the United States in Congress assembled, That "antitrust laws," as used herein, includes the Act entitled "An Act to protect trade and commerce against unlawful restraints and monopolies," approved July second, eighteen hundred and ninety; sections seventy-three to seventy-seven, inclusive, of an Act entitled "An Act to reduce taxation, to provide revenue for the Government, and for other purposes," of August twenty-seventh, eighteen hundred and ninety-four; an Act entitled "An Act to amend sections seventy-three and seventy-six of the Act of August twenty-seventh, eighteen hundred and ninety-four, entitled 'An Act to reduce taxation, to provided revenue for the Government, and for other purposes,' " approved February twelfth, nineteen hundred and thirteen; and also this Act. "Commerce," as used herein, means trade or commerce among the several States and with foreign nations, or between the District of Columbia or any Territory of the United States and any State, Territory, or foreign nation, or between any insular possessions or other places under the jurisdiction of the United States, or between any such possessions or place and any State or Territory of the United States or the District of Columbia or any foreign nation, or within the District of Columbia or any Territory or any insular possession or other place under the jurisdiction of the United States: Provided, That nothing in this Act contained shall apply to the Philippine Islands. The word "person" or "persons" whenever used in this Act shall be deemed to include corporations and associations existing under or authorized by the laws of either the United States, the laws of any of the Territories, the laws of any State, or the laws of any foreign country.

Sec. 2. That it shall be unlawful for any person engaged in commerce, in the course of such commerce, either directly or indirectly to discriminate in price between different purchasers of commodities, which commodities are sold for use, consumption, or resale within the United States or any Territory thereof or the District of Columbia or any insular possession or other place under the jurisdiction of the United States, where the effect of such discrimination may be to substantially lessen competition or tend to create a monopoly in any line of commerce: Provided, That nothing herein contained shall prevent discrimination in price between purchasers of commodities on account of differences in the grade, quality, or quantity of the commodity sold, or that makes only due allowance for difference in the cost of selling or transportation, or discrimination in price in the same or different communities made in good faith to meet competition: And provided further, That nothing herein contained shall prevent persons engaged in selling goods, wares, or merchandise in commerce from selecting their own customers in bona fide transactions and not in restraint of trade.

Sec. 3. That it shall be unlawful for any person engaged in commerce, in the course of such commerce, to lease or make a sale or contract for sale of goods, wares, or merchandise, machinery, supplies or other commodities, whether patented or unpatented, for use, consumption or resale within the United States or any Territory thereof or the District of Columbia or any insular possession or other place under the jurisdiction of the United States, or fix a price charged therefor, or discount from, or rebate upon, such price, on the condition, agreement or understanding that the lessee or purchaser thereof shall not use or deal in the goods, wares, merchandise, machinery, supplies or other commodities of a competitor or competitors of the lessor or seller, where the effect of such lease, sale, or contract for sale or such condition, agreement or understanding may be to substantially lessen competition or tend to create a monopoly in any line of commerce.

Sec. 4. That any person who shall be injured in his business or property by reason of anything forbidden in the antitrust laws may sue therefor in any district court of the United States in the district in which the defendant resides or is found or has an agent, without respect to the amount in controversy, and shall recover threefold the damages by him sustained, and the cost of suit, including a reasonable attorney's fee.

Sec. 5. That a final judgment or decree hereafter rendered in any criminal prosecution or in any suit or proceeding in equity brought by or on behalf of the United States under the antitrust laws to the effect that a defendant has violated said laws shall be prima facie evidence against such defendant in any suit or proceeding brought by any other party against such defendant under said laws as to all matters respecting which said judgment or decree would be an estoppel as between the parties thereto: Provided, This section shall not apply to consent judgments or decrees entered before any testimony has been taken: Provided further, This section shall not apply to consent judgments or decrees rendered in criminal proceedings or suits in equity, now pending, in which the taking of testimony has been commenced but has not been concluded, provided such judgments or decrees are rendered before any further testimony is taken.

Whenever any suit or proceeding in equity or criminal prosecution is instituted by the United States to prevent, restrain or punish violations of any of the antitrust laws, the running of the statute of limitations in respect of each and every private right of action arising under said laws and based in whole or in part on any matter complained of in said suit or proceeding shall be suspended during the pendency thereof.

Sec. 6. That the labor of a human being is not a commodity or article of commerce. Nothing contained in the antitrust laws shall be construed to forbid the existence and operation of labor, agricultural, or horticultural organizations, instituted for the purposes of mutual help, and not having capital stock or conducted for profit, or to forbid or restrain individual members of such organizations from lawfully carrying out the legitimate objects thereof; nor shall such organizations, or the members thereof, be held or construed to be illegal combinations or conspiracies in restraint of trade, under the antitrust laws.

Sec. 7. That no corporation engaged in commerce shall acquire, directly or indirectly, the whole or any part of the stock or other share capital of another corporation engaged also in commerce, where the effect of such acquisition may be to substantially lessen competition between the corporation whose stock is so acquired and the corporation making the acquisition, or to restrain such commerce in any section or community, or tend to create a monopoly of any line of commerce. No corporation shall acquire, directly or indirectly, the whole or any part of the stock or other share capital of two or more corporations engaged in commerce where the effect of such acquisition, or the use of such stock by the voting or granting of proxies or otherwise, may be to substantially lessen competition between such corporations, or any of them, whose stock or other share capital is so acquired, or to restrain such commerce in any section or community, or tend to create a monopoly of any line of commerce.

This section shall not apply to corporations purchasing such stock solely for investment and not using the same by voting or otherwise to bring about, or in attempting to bring about, the substantial lessening of competition. Nor shall anything contained in this section prevent a corporation engaged in commerce from causing the formation of subsidiary corporations for the actual carrying on of their immediate lawful business, or the natural and legitimate branches or extensions thereof, or from owning and holding all or a part of the stock of such subsidiary corporations, when the effect of such formation is not to substantially lessen competition.

Nor shall anything herein contained be construed to prohibit any common carrier subject to the laws to regulate commerce from aiding in the construction of branches or short lines so located as to become feeders to the main line of the company so aiding in such construction or from acquiring or owning all or any part of the stock of such branch lines, nor to prevent any such common carrier from acquiring and owning all or any part of the stock of a branch or short line constructed by an independent company where there is no substantial competition between the company owning the main line acquiring the property or an interest therein, nor to prevent such common carrier from extending any of its lines through the medium of the acquisition of stock or otherwise of any other such common carrier where there is no substantial competition between the company extending its lines and the company whose stock, property, or an interest therein is so acquired.

Nothing contained in this section shall be held to affect or impair any right heretofore legally acquired: Provided, That nothing in this section shall be held or construed to authorize or make lawful anything heretofore prohibited or made illegal by the anti-trust laws, nor to exempt any person from the penal provisions thereof or the civil remedies therein provided.

Sec. 8. That from and after two years from the date of the approval of this Act no person shall at the same time be a director or other officer or employee of more than one bank, banking association or trust company, organized or operating under the laws of the United States, either of which has deposits, capital, surplus, and undivided profits aggregating more than $5,000,000; and no private banker or person who is a director in any bank or trust company, organized and operating under the laws of a State, having deposits, capital, surplus, and undivided profits aggregating more than $5,000,000, shall be eligible to be a director in any bank or banking association organized or operating under the laws of the United States. The eligibility of a director, officer, or employee under the foregoing provisions shall be determined by the average amount of deposits, capital, surplus, and undivided profits as shown in the official statements of such bank, banking association, or trust company filed as provided by law during the fiscal year preceding the date set for the annual election of directors, and when a director, officer, or employee has been elected or selected in accordance with the provisions of this Act it shall be lawful for him to continue as such for one year thereafter under said election or employment.

No bank, banking association or trust company, organized or operating under the laws of the United States, in any city incorporated town or village of more than two hundred thousand inhabitants, as shown by the last preceding decennial census of the United States, shall have as a director or other officer or employee any private banker or any director or other officer or employee of any other bank, banking association or trust company located in the same place: Provided, That nothing in this section shall apply to mutual savings banks not having a capital stock represented by shares: Provided further, That a director or other officer or employee of such bank, banking association, or trust company may be a director or other officer or employee of not more than one other bank or trust company organized under the laws of the United States or any State where the entire capital stock is owned by stockholders in the other: And provided further, That nothing contained in this section shall forbid a director of class A of a Federal reserve bank, as defined in the Federal Reserve Act, from being an officer or director or both an officer and director in one member bank.

That from and after two years from the date of the approval of this Act no person at the same time shall be a director in any two or more corporations, any one of which has capital, surplus, and undivided profits aggregating more than $1,000,000, engaged in whole or in part in commerce, other than banks, banking associations, trust companies and common carriers subject to the Act to regulate commerce, approved February fourth, eighteen hundred and eighty-seven, if such corporations are or shall have been theretofore, by virtue of their business and location of operation, competitors, so that the elimination of competition by agreement between them would constitute a violation of any of the provisions of any of the antitrust laws. The eligibility of a director under the foregoing provision shall be determined by the aggregate amount of the capital, surplus, and undivided profits, exclusive of dividends declared but not paid to stockholders, at the end of the fiscal year of said corporation next preceding the election of directors, and when a director has been elected in accordance with the provisions of this Act it shall be lawful for him to continue as such for one year thereafter.

When any person elected or chosen as a director or officer or selected as an employee of any bank or other corporation subject to the provisions of this Act is eligible at the time of his election or selection to act for such bank or other corporation in such capacity his eligibility to act in such capacity shall not be affected and he shall not become or be deemed amenable to any of the provisions hereof by reason of any change in the affairs of such bank or other corporation from whatsoever cause, whether specifically excepted by any of the provisions hereof or not, until the expiration of one year from the date of his election or employment.

Sec. 9. Every president, director, officer or manager of any firm, association or corporation engaged in commerce as a common carrier, who embezzles, steals, abstracts or willfully misapplies, or willfully permits to be misapplied, any of the moneys, funds, credits, securities, property or assets of such firm, association or corporation, arising or accruing from, or used in, such commerce, in whole or in part, or willfully converts the same to his own use or to the use of another, shall be deemed guilty of a felony and upon conviction shall be fined not less than $500 or confined in the penitentiary not less than one year nor more than ten years, or both, in the discretion of the court.

Prosecutions hereunder may be in the district court of the United States for the district wherein the offense may have been committed. That nothing in this section shall be held to take away or impair the jurisdiction of the courts of the several States under the laws thereof; and a judgment of conviction or acquittal on the merits under the laws of any State shall be a bar to any prosecution hereunder for the same act or acts.

Sec. 10. That after two years from the approval of this Act no common carrier engaged in commerce shall have any dealings in securities, supplies or other articles of commerce, or shall make or have any contracts for construction or maintenance of any kind, to the amount of more than $50,000, in the aggregate, in any one year, with another corporation, firm, partnership or association when the said common carrier shall have upon its board of directors or as its president, manager or as its purchasing or selling officer, or agent in the particular transaction, any person who is at the same time a director, manager, or purchasing or selling officer of, or who has any substantial interest in, such other corporation, firm, partnership or association, unless and except such purchases shall be made from, or such dealings shall be with, the bidder whose bid is the most favorable to such common carrier, to be ascertained by competitive bidding under regulations to be prescribed by rule or otherwise by the Interstate Commerce Commission. No bid shall be received unless the name and address of the bidder or the names and addresses of the officers, directors and general managers thereof, if the bidder be a corporation, or of the members, if it be a partnership or firm, be given with the bid.

Any person who shall, directly or indirectly, do or attempt to do anything to prevent anyone from bidding or shall do any act to prevent free and fair competition among the bidders or those desiring to bid shall be punished as prescribed in this section in the case of an officer or director. Every such common carrier having such transactions or making any such purchases shall within thirty days after making the same file with the Interstate Commerce Commission a full and detailed statement of the transaction showing the manner of the competitive bidding, and the names and addresses of the directors and officers of the corporations and the members of the firm or partnership bidding; and whenever the said commission shall, after investigation or hearing, have reason to believe that the law has been violated in and about the said purchases and documents and its own view or findings regarding the transaction to the Attorney General.

If any common carrier shall violate this section it shall be fined not exceeding $25,000; and every such director, agent, manager or officer thereof who shall have knowingly voted for or directed the act constituting such violation or who shall have aided or abetted in such violation shall be deemed guilty of a misdemeanor and shall be fined not exceeding $5,000, or confined in jail not exceeding one year, or both, in the discretion of the court.

Sec. 11. That the authority to enforce compliance with sections two, three, seven and eight of this Act by the persons respectively subject to is hereby vested; in the Interstate Commerce Commission where applicable to common carriers, in the Federal Reserve Boards where applicable to banks, banking associations and trust companies, and in the Federal Trade Commission where applicable to all other character of commerce, to be exercised as follows:

Whenever the commission or board vested with jurisdiction thereof shall have reason to believe that any person is violating or has violated any of the provisions of sections, two, three, seven and eight of this Act, it shall issue and serve upon such a complaint stating its charges in that respect, and containing a notice of a hearing upon a day and place therein fixed at least thirty days after the service of said complaint. The person so complained of shall have the right to appear at the place and time so fixed and show cause why an order should not be entered by the commission or board requiring such person to cease and desist from the violation of the law so charged in said complaint. Any person may make application, and upon good cause shown may be allowed by the commission or board, to intervene and appear in said proceeding by counsel or in person. The testimony in any such proceeding shall be reduced to writing and filed in the office of the commission or board. If upon such hearing the commission or board, as the case may be, shall be of the opinion that any of the provisions of said sections have been or are being violated, it shall make a report in writing in which it shall state its findings as to the facts, and shall issue and cause to be served on such person an order requiring such person to cease and desist from such violations, and divest itself of the stock held or rid itself of the directors chosen contrary to the provisions of sections seven and eight of this Act, if any there be, in the manner and within the time fixed by said order. Until a transcript of the record in such hearing shall have been filed in a circuit court of appeals of the United States, as hereinafter provided, the commission or board may at any time, upon such notice and in any such manner as it shall deem proper, modify or set aside, in whole or in part, any report or any order made or issued by it under this section.

If such person fails or neglects to obey such order of the commission or board while the same is in effect, the commission or board may apply to the circuit court of appeals of the United States, within any circuit where the violation complained of was or is being committed or where such person resides or carries on business, for the enforcement of its order, and shall certify and file with its application a transcript of the entire record in the proceeding, including all the testimony taken and the report and order of the commission or board. Upon such filing of the application and transcript the court shall cause notice thereof to be served upon such person and thereupon shall have jurisdiction of the proceeding and of the question determined therein, and shall have power to make and enter upon the pleadings, testimony, and proceedings set forth in such transcript a decree affirming, modifying, or setting aside the order of the commission or board. The findings of the commission or board as to the facts, if supported by testimony, shall be conclusive. If either party shall apply to the court for leave to adduce additional evidence, and shall show to the satisfaction of the court that such additional evidence is material and that there were reasonable grounds for the failure to adduce such evidence in the proceeding before the commission or board, the court may order such additional evidence to be taken before the commission or board and to be adduced upon the hearing in such manner and upon such terms and conditions as to the court may seem proper. The commission or board may modify its findings as to the facts, or make new findings, by reason of the additional evidence so taken, and it shall file such modified or new findings, which, if supported by testimony, shall be conclusive, and its recommendation, if any, for the modification or setting aside of its original order, with the return of such additional evidence. The judgment and decree of the court shall be final, except that the same shall be subject to review by the Supreme Court upon certiorari as provided in section two hundred and forty of the Judicial Code.

Any party required by such order of the commission or board to cease and desist from a violation charge may obtain a review of such order in said circuit court of appeals by filing in the court a written petition praying that the order of the commission or board be set aside. A copy of such petition shall be forthwith served upon the commission or board, and thereupon the commission or board forthwith shall certify and file in the court a transcript of the record as hereinbefore provided. Upon the filing of the transcript the court shall have the same jurisdiction to affirm, set aside, or modify the order of the commission or board as in the case of an application by the commission or board for the enforcement of its order, and the findings of the commission or board as to the facts, if supported by testimony, shall in like manner be conclusive.

The jurisdiction of the circuit court of appeals of the United States to enforce, set aside, or modify orders of the commission or board shall be exclusive. Such proceedings in the circuit court of appeals shall be given precedence over other cases pending therein, and shall be in every way expedited. No order of the commission or board or the judgment of the court to enforce the same shall in any wise relieve or absolve any person from any liability under the antitrust Acts.

Complaints, orders, and other processes of the commission or board under this section may be served by anyone duly authorized by the commission or board, either (a) by delivering a copy thereof to the person to be served, or to a member of the partnership to be served, or to the president, secretary, or other executive officer or a director of the corporation to be served; or (b) by leaving a copy thereof at the principal place of business of such person; or (c) by registering and mailing a copy thereof addressed to such person at his principal office or place of business. The verified return by the person so serving said complaint, order, or other process setting forth the manner of said service shall be proof of the same, and the return post-office receipt for said complaint, order, or other process registered and mailed as aforesaid shall be proof of the service of the same.

Sec. 12. That any suit, action, or proceeding under the antitrust laws against a corporation may be brought not only in the judicial district whereof it is an inhabitant, but also on any district wherein it may be found or transacts business; and all process in such cases may be served in the district of which it is an inhabitant, or wherever it may be found.

Sec. 13. That in any suit, action, or proceeding brought by or on behalf of the United States subpoenas for witnesses who are required to attend a court of the United States in any judicial district in any case, civil or criminal, arising under the antitrust laws may run into any other district: Provided, That in civil cases no writ of subpoena shall issue for witnesses living out of the district in which the court is held at a greater distance than one hundred miles from the place of holding the same without the permission of the trial court being first had upon proper application and cause shown.

That whenever a corporation shall violate any of the penal provisions of the antitrust laws, such violation shall be deemed to be also that of the individual directors, officers, or agents of such corporation who shall have authorized, ordered, or done any of the acts constituting in whole or in part such violation, and such violation shall be deemed a misdemeanor, and upon conviction therefor of any such director, officer, or agent he shall be punished by a fine of not exceeding $5,000 or by imprisonment for not exceeding one year, or by both, in the discretion of the court.

Sec. 15. That the several district courts of the United States are hereby invested with jurisdiction to prevent and restrain violations of this Act, and it shall be the duty of the several district attorneys of the United States, in their respective districts, under the direction of the Attorney General, to institute proceedings in equity to prevent and restrain such violations. Such proceedings may be by way of petition setting forth the case and praying that such violation shall be enjoined or otherwise prohibited. When the parties complained of shall have been duly notified of such petition, the court shall proceed, as soon as may be, to the hearing and determination of the case; and pending such petition, and before the final decree, the court may at any time make such restraining order or prohibition as shall be deemed just in the premises. Whenever it shall appear to the court before which any such proceeding may be pending that the ends of justice require that other parties should be brought before the court, the court may cause them to be summoned, whether they reside in the district in which the court is held or not, and subpoenas to that end may be served in any district by the marshal thereof.

Sec. 16. That any person, firm, corporation, or association shall be entitled to sue for and have injunctive relief, in any court of the United States having jurisdiction over the parties, against threatened loss or damage by a violation of the antitrust laws, including sections two, three, seven and eight of this Act, when and under the same conditions and principles as injunctive relief against threatened conduct that will cause loss or damage is granted by courts of equity, under the rules governing such proceedings, and upon the execution of proper bond against damages for an injunction improvidently granted and a showing that the danger of irreparable loss or damage is immediate, a preliminary injunction may issue: Provided, That nothing herein contained shall be construed to entitle any person, firm, corporation, or association, except the United States, to bring suit in equity for injunctive relief against any common carrier subject to the provisions of this Act to regulate commerce, approved February fourth, eighteen hundred and eighty-seven, in respect of any matter subject to the regulation, supervision, or other jurisdiction of the Interstate Commerce Commission.

Sec. 17. That no preliminary injunction shall be issued without notice to the opposite party. No temporary restraining order shall be granted without notice to the opposite party unless it shall be clearly appear from specific facts shown by affidavit or by the verified bill that immediate and irreparable injury, loss, or damage will result to the applicant before notice can be served and a hearing had therein. Every such temporary restraining order shall be indorsed with the date and hour of issuance, shall be forthwith filed in the clerk's office and entered of record, shall define the injury and state why it is irreparable and why the order was granted without notice, and shall by its terms expire within such time after entry, not to exceed ten days, as the court or judge may fix, unless within the time so fixed the order is extended for a like period for good cause shown, and the reasons for such extension shall be entered of record. In case a temporary restraining order shall be granted without notice in the contingency specified, the matter of the issuance of a preliminary injunction shall be set down for a hearing at the earliest possible time and shall take precedence of all matters except older matters of the same character; and when the same comes up for hearing the party obtaining the temporary restraining order shall proceed with the application for a preliminary injunction, and if he does not do so the court shall dissolve the temporary restraining order. Upon two days' notice to the party obtaining such temporary restraining order the opposite party may appear and move the dissolution or modification of the order, and in that event the court or judge shall proceed to hear and determine the motion as expeditiously as the ends of justice may require.

Section two hundred and sixty-three of an Act entitled "An Act to codify, revise, and amend the laws relating to the judiciary," approved March third, nineteen hundred and eleven, is hereby repealed. Nothing in this section contained shall be deemed to alter, repeal, or amend section two hundred and sixty-six of an Act entitled "An Act to codify, revise, and amend the laws relating to the judiciary," approved March third, nineteen hundred and eleven.

Sec. 18. That, except as otherwise provided in section 16 of this Act, no restraining order or interlocutory order of injunction shall issue, except upon the giving of security by the applicant in such sum as the court or judge may deem proper, conditioned upon the payment of such costs and damages as may be incurred or suffered by any party who may be found to have been wrongfully enjoined or restrained thereby.

Sec. 19. That every order of jurisdiction or restraining order shall set forth the reasons for the issuance of the same, shall be specific in terms, and shall describe in reasonable detail, and not by reference to the bill of complaint or other document, the act or acts sought to be restrained, and shall be binding only upon the parties to the suit, their officers, agents, servants, employees, and attorneys, or those in active concert or participating with them, and who shall, by personal service or otherwise, have received actual notice of the same.

Sec. 20. That no restraining order or injunction shall be granted by any court of the United States, or a judge or the judges thereof, in any case between an employer and employees, or between employers and employees, or between employees, or between persons employed and persons seeking employment, involving, or growing out of, a dispute concerning terms or conditions of employment, unless necessary to prevent irreparable injury to property, or to a property right, of the party making the application, for which injury there is no adequate remedy at law, and such property or property right must be described with particularity in the application, which must be in writing and sworn to by the applicant or by his agent or attorney.

And no such restraining order or conjunction shall prohibit any person or persons, whether singly or in concert, from terminating any relation of employment, or from ceasing to perform any work or labor, or from recommending, advising, or persuading others by peaceful means so to do; or from attending at any place where any such person or persons may lawfully be, for the purpose of peacefully obtaining or communicating information, or from peacefully persuading any person to work or to abstain from working; or from ceasing to patronize or to employ any party to such dispute, or from recommending, advising, or persuading others by peaceful and lawful means to do so; or from paying or giving to, or withholding from, any person engaged in such dispute, any strike benefits or other moneys or things of value; or from peaceably assembling in a lawful manner, and for lawful purposes; or for doing any act or thing which might lawfully be done in the absence of such dispute by any party thereto; nor shall any of the acts specified in this paragraph be considered or held to be violations of any law of the United States.

Sec. 21. That any person who shall willfully disobey any lawful writ, process, order, rule, decree, or command of any district court of the United States or any court of the District of Columbia by doing any act or thing therein, or thereby forbidden to be done by him, if the act or thing so done by him be of such character as to constitute a criminal offense under any statute of the United States, or under the laws of any State in which the act was committed, shall be proceeded against for his said contempt as hereinafter provided.

Sec. 22. That whenever it shall be made to appear to any district court or judge thereof, or to any judge therein sitting, by the return of a proper officer on lawful process, or upon the affidavit of some credible person, or by information filed by any district attorney, that there is reasonable ground to believe that any person has been guilty of such contempt, the court or judge thereof, or any judge therein sitting, may issue a rule requiring the said person so charged to show cause upon a day certain why he should not be punished therefor, which rule, together with a copy of the affidavit or information, shall be served upon the person charged, with sufficient promptness to enable him to prepare for and make return to the order at the time fixed therein. If upon or by such return, in the judgment of the court, the alleged contempt be not sufficiently purged, a trial shall be directed at a time and place fixed by the court: Provided, however, That if the accused, being a natural person, fail or refuse to make return to the rule to show cause, an attachment may issue against his person to compel an answer, and in case of his continued failure or refusal, or if for any reason it be impracticable to dispose of the matter on the return day, he may be required to give reasonable bail for his attendance at the trial and his submission to the final judgment of the court. Where the accused is a body corporate, an attachment for the sequestration of its property may be issued upon like refusal or failure to answer.

In all cases within the purview of this Act such trial may be by the court, or, upon demand of the accused, by a jury; in which latter event the court may impanel a jury from the jurors then in attendance, or the court or the judge thereof in chambers may cause a sufficient number of jurors to be selected and summoned, as provided by law, to attend at the time and place of trial, at which time a jury shall be selected and impaneled as upon a trial for misdemeanor; and such trial shall conform, as near as may be, to the practice in criminal cases prosecuted by indictment or upon information.

If the accused be found guilty, judgment shall be entered accordingly, prescribing the punishment, either by fine or imprisonment, or both, in the discretion of the court. Such fine shall be paid to the United States or to the complainant or other party injured by the act constituting the contempt, or may, where more than one is so damaged, be divided or apportioned among them as the court may direct, but in no case shall the fine to be paid to the United States exceed, in case the accused is a natural person, the sum of $1,000, nor shall such imprisonment exceed the term of six months: Provided, That in any case the court or a judge thereof may, for good cause shown, by affidavit or proof taken in open court or before such judge and filed with the papers in the case, dispense with the rule to show cause, and may issue an attachment for the arrest of the person charged with contempt; in which event such person, when arrested, shall be brought before such court or a judge thereof without unnecessary delay and shall be admitted to bail in a reasonable penalty for his appearance to answer to the charge or for trial for the contempt; and thereafter the proceedings shall be the same as provided herein in case the rule had issued in the first instance.

Sec. 23. That the evidence taken upon the trial of any persons so accused may be preserved by bill of exceptions, and any judgment of conviction may be reviewed upon writ of error in all respects as now provided by law in criminal cases, and may be affirmed, reversed, or modified as justice may require. Upon the granting of such writ of error, execution of judgment shall be stayed, and the accused, if thereby sentenced to imprisonment, shall be admitted to bail in such reasonable sum as may be required by the court, or by any justice, or any judge of any district court of the United States or any court of the district of Columbia.

Sec. 24. That nothing herein contained shall be construed to relate to contempts committed in the presence of the court, or so near thereto as to obstruct the administration of justice, nor to contempts committed in disobedience of any lawful writ, process, order, rule, decree, or command entered in any suit or action brought or prosecuted in the name of, or on behalf of, the United States, but the same, and all other cases of contempt not specifically embraced within section twenty-one of this Act, may be punished in conformity to the usages at law and in equity now prevailing.

Sec. 25. That no proceeding for contempt shall be instituted against any person unless begun within one year from the date of the act complained of; nor shall any such proceeding be a bar to any criminal prosecution for the same act or acts; but nothing herein contained shall affect any proceedings in contempt pending at the time of the passage of this Act.

Sec. 26. If any clause, sentence, paragraph, or part of this Act shall, for any reason, be adjudged by any court of competent jurisdiction to be invalid, such judgment shall not affect, impair, or invalidate the remainder thereof, but shall be confined in its operation to the clause, sentence, paragraph, or part thereof directly involved in the controversy in which said judgment shall have been rendered.

Approved, October 15, 1914.

Federal Trade Commission (1915)

The Federal Trade Commission (FTC), established as an independent government agency in 1915, enforces antitrust laws and ensures that American businesses engage in fair competition. The five-member commission focuses on the prevention of interlocking directorates, monitors the acquisition of capital stock, and deals with issues such as false advertising. The FTC also enforces the Trust in Lending Act. The only industries that the commission does not have jurisdiction over are banks and common carriers.

Source: Public Statutes at Large, Vol. 38 Part I, pp. 717–724.

An Act To create a Federal Trade Commission, to define its powers and duties, and for other purposes.

Be it enacted by the Senate and the House of Representatives of the United States of America in Congress assembled, That a commission is hereby created and established, to be known as the Federal Trade Commission (hereinafter referred to as the commission), which shall be composed of five commissioners, who shall be appointed by the President, by and with the advice and consent of the Senate. Not more than three of the commissioners shall be members of the same political party. The first commissioners appointed shall continue in office for terms of three, four, five, six, and seven years, respectively, from the date of the taking effect of this Act, the term of each to be designated by the President, but their successors shall be appointed for terms of seven years, except that any person chosen to fill a vacancy shall be appointed only for the unexpired term of the commissioner whom he will succeed. The commissioner shall choose a chairman from its own membership. No commissioner shall engage in any other business, vocation, or employment. Any commissioner may be removed by the President for inefficiency, neglect of duty, or malfeasance in office. A vacancy in the commission shall not impair the right of the remaining commissioners to exercise all the powers of the commission. The commission shall have an official seal, which shall be judicially noticed.

Sec. 2. That each commissioner shall receive a salary of $10,000 a year, payable in the same manner as the salaries of the judges of the courts of the United States. The commission shall appoint a secretary, who shall receive a salary of $5,000 a year, payable in like manner, and it shall have the authority to employ and fix the compensation of such attorneys, special experts, examiners, clerks, and other employees as it may from time to time find necessary for the proper performance of its duties and as may be from time to time appropriated for by Congress.

With the exception of the secretary, a clerk to each commissioner, the attorneys, and such special experts and examiners as the commission may from time to time find necessary for the conduct of its work, all employees of the commission shall be part of the classified civil service, and shall enter the service under such rules and regulations as may be prescribed by the Civil Service Commission.

All of the expenses of the commission, including all necessary expenses for transportation incurred by the commissioners or by employees under their orders, in making any investigation, or upon official business in any other places than in the city of Washington, shall be allowed and paid on the presentation of itemized vouchers therefor approved by the commission.

Until otherwise provided by law, the commission may rent suitable offices for its use.

The Auditor for the State and other Departments shall receive and examine all accounts of expenditures of the commission.

Sec. 3. That upon the organization of the commission and election of its chairman, the Bureau of Corporations and the offices of Commissioner and Deputy Commissioner of Corporations shall cease to exist; and all pending investigations and proceedings of the Bureau of Corporations shall be continued by the commission.

All clerks and employees of the said bureau shall be transferred to and become clerks and employees of the commission at their present grades and salaries. All records, papers, and property of the said bureau shall become records, papers, and property of the commission, and all unexpected funds and appropriations for the use and maintenance of the said bureau, including any allotment already made to it by the Secretary of the Commerce from the contingent appropriation for the Department of Commerce for the fiscal year nineteen hundred and fifteen, or from the departmental printing fund for the fiscal year nineteen hundred and fifteen, shall become funds and appropriations available to be extended by the commission in the exercise of the powers, authority, and duties conferred on it by this Act.

The principal office of the commission shall be in the city of Washington, but it may meet and exercise all its powers at any other place. The commission may, by one or more of its members, or by such examiners as it may designate, prosecute any inquiry necessary to its duties in any part of the United States.

Sec. 4. That the words defined in this section shall have the following meaning when found in this Act, to wit: "Commerce" means commerce among the several States or with foreign nations, or in any Territory of the United States or in the District of Columbia, or between any such Territory and another, or between any such Territory and any State or foreign nation, or between the District of Columbia and any State or Territory or foreign nation.

"Corporation" means any company or association incorporated or unincorporated, which is organized to carry on business for profit and has shares of capital or capital stock, and any company or association, incorporated or unincorporated, without shares of capital or capital stock, except partnerships, which is organized to carry on business for its own profit or that of its members.

"Documentary evidence" means all documents, papers, and correspondence in existence at and after the passage of this Act.

"Acts to regulate commerce" means the Act entitled "An Act to regulate commerce," approved February fourteenth, eighteen hundred and eighty-seven, and all Acts amendatory thereof and supplementary thereto.

"Antitrust acts" means the Act entitled "An Act to protect trade and commerce against unlawful restraints and monopolies," approved July second, eighteen hundred and ninety; also the sections seventy-three to seventy-seven, inclusive, of an Act entitled "An Act to reduce taxation, to provide revenue for the Government, and for other purposes," approved August twenty-seventh, eighteen hundred and ninety-four; and also the Act entitled "An Act to amend sections seventy-three and seventy-six of the Act of August twenty-seventh, eighteen hundred and ninety-four, entitled 'An Act to reduce taxation, to provide revenue for the Government, and for other purposes,' " approved February twelfth, nineteen hundred and thirteen.

Sec. 5. That unfair methods of competition in commerce are hereby declared unlawful. The commission is hereby empowered and directed to prevent persons, partnerships, or corporations, except banks, and common carriers subject to the Acts to regulate commerce, from using unfair methods of competition in commerce.

Whenever the commission shall have reason to believe that any such person, partnership, or corporation has been or is using any unfair method of competition in commerce, and if it shall appear to the commission that a proceeding by it in respect thereof would be to the best interest of the public, it shall issue and serve upon such person, partnership, or corporation a complaint stating its charges in that respect, and containing a notice of a hearing upon a day and a place therein fixed at least thirty days after the service of said complaint. The person, partnership, or corporation so complained of shall have the right to answer at the place and time so fixed and show cause why an order should not be entered by the commission requiring such person, partnership, or corporation to cease and desist from the violation of the law so charged in said complaint. Any person, partnership, or corporation may make application, and upon good cause shown may be allowed by the commission, to intervene and appear in said proceeding shall be reduced to writing and filed in the office of the commission. If upon such hearing the commission shall be of the opinion that the method of competition in question is prohibited by this Act, it shall make a report in writing in which it shall state its findings as to the facts, and shall issue and cause to be served on such person, partnership, or corporation an order requiring such person, partnership, or corporation to cease and desist from using such method of competition. Until a transcript of the record in such hearing shall have been filed in a circuit court of appeals of the United States, as hereinafter provided, the commission may at any time, upon such notice and in such manner as it shall deem proper, modify or set aside, in whole or in part, any report or any order made or issued by it under this section.

If such person, partnership, or corporation fails or neglects to obey such order of the commission while the same is in effect, the commission may apply to the circuit court of appeals of the United States, within any circuit where the method of competition in question was used or where such person, partnership, or corporation resides or carries on business, for the enforcement of its order, and shall certify and file with its application a transcript of the entire record in the proceeding, including all the testimony taken and the report and order of the commission. Upon such filing of the application and transcript the court shall cause notice thereof to be served upon such person, partnership, or corporation and thereupon shall have jurisdiction of the proceeding and of the question determined therein, and shall have the power to make and enter upon the pleadings, testimony, and proceedings set forth in such transcript a decree affirming, modifying, or setting aside the order of the commission. The findings of the commission as to the facts, if supported by testimony, shall be inclusive. If either party shall apply to the court for leave to adduce additional evidence, and shall show to the satisfaction of the court that such additional evidence is material and that there is reasonable grounds for the failure to adduce such evidence in the proceeding before the commission, the court may order such additional evidence to be taken before the commission and to be adduced upon the hearing in such manner and upon such terms and conditions as the court may deem proper. The commission may modify its findings as to the facts, or make new findings, by reason of the additional evidence so taken, and it shall file such modified or new findings, which, if supported by testimony, shall be conclusive, and its recommendation, if any, for the modification or setting aside of its original order, with the return of such additional evidence. The judgment and decree of the court shall be final, except that the same shall be subject to review by the Supreme Court upon certiorari as provided in section two hundred and forty of the Judicial Code.

Any party required by such order of the commission to cease and desist from using such method of competition may obtain a review of such order in said circuit court of appeals by filing in the court a written petition praying that the order of the commission be set aside. A copy of such petition shall be forthwith served upon the commission, and thereupon the commission forthwith shall certify and file in the court a transcript of the record as hereinbefore provided. Upon the filing of the transcript the court shall have the same jurisdiction to affirm, set aside, or modify the order of the commission as in the case of an application by the commission for the enforcement of its order, and the findings of the commission as to the facts, if supported by testimony, shall in like manner be conclusive.

The jurisdiction of the circuit court of appeals of the United States to enforce, set aside, or modify orders of the commission shall be exclusive.

Such proceedings in the circuit court of appeals shall be given precedence over other cases pending therein, and shall be in every way expedited. No order of the commission or judgment of the court to enforce the same shall in any wise relieve or absolve any person, partnership, or corporation from any liability under the antitrust acts.

Complaints, orders, and other processes of the commission under this section may be served by anyone duly authorized by the commission, either (a) by delivering a copy thereof to the person to be served, or to a member of the partnership to be served, or to the president, secretary, or other executive officer or a director of the corporation to be served; or (b) by leaving a copy thereof at the principal office or place of business of such person, partnership, or corporation; or (c) by registering and mailing a copy thereof addressed to such person, partnership, or corporation at his or its principal office or place of business. The verified return by the person so serving said complaint, order, or other process setting forth the manner of said service shall be proof of the same, and the return post-office receipt for said complaint, order, or other process registered and mailed as aforesaid shall be proof of the service of the same.

Sec. 6. That the commission shall also have the power—

(a) To gather and compile information concerning, and to investigate from time to time the organization, business, conduct, practices, and management of any corporation engaged in commerce, excepting banks and common carriers subject to the Act to regulate commerce, and its relation to other corporations and to individuals, associations, and partnerships.

(b) To require, by general or special orders, corporations engaged in commerce, excepting banks, and common carriers subject to the Act to regulate commerce, or any class of them, or any of them, respectively, to file with the commission in such form as the commission may prescribe annual or special, or both annual and special, reports or answers in writing to specific questions, furnishing to the commission such information as it may require as to the organization, business, conduct, practices, management, and relation to other corporations, partnerships, and individuals of the respective corporations filing such reports or answers in writing. Such reports and answers shall be made under oath, or otherwise, as the commission may prescribe, and shall be filed with the commission within such reasonable period as the commission may prescribe, unless additional time be granted in any case by the commission.

(c) Whenever a final decree has been entered against any defendant corporation in any suit brought by the United States to prevent and restrain any violation of the antitrust Acts, to make investigation, upon its own initiative, of the manner in which the decree has been or is being carried out, and upon the application of the Attorney General it shall be his duty to make such investigation. It shall transmit to the Attorney General a report embodying its findings and recommendations as result of any such investigation, and the report shall be made public in the discretion of the commission.

(d) Upon the direction of the President or either House of Congress to investigate and report the facts relating to any alleged violations of the antitrust Acts by any corporation.

(e) Upon the application of the Attorney General to investigate and make recommendations for the readjustment of the business of any corporation alleged to be violating the antitrust Acts in order that the corporation may thereafter maintain its organization, management, and conduct of business in accordance with law.

(f) To make public from time to time such portions of the information obtained by it hereunder, except trade secrets and names of customers, as it shall deem expedient in the public interest; and to make annual and special reports to the Congress and to submit therewith recommendations for additional legislation; and to provide for the publication of its reports and decisions in such form and manner as may be best adapted for public information and use.

(g) From time to time to classify corporations and to make rules and regulations for the purpose of carrying out the provisions of this Act.

(h) To investigate, from time to time, trade conditions in and with foreign countries where associations, combinations, or practices of manufacturers, merchants, or traders, or other conditions, may affect the foreign trade of the United States, and to report to Congress thereon, with such recommendations as it deems advisable.

Sec. 7. That in any suit in equity brought by or under the direction of the Attorney General as provided in the antitrust Acts, the court may, upon the conclusion of the testimony therein, if it shall be then of opinion that the complainant is entitled to relief, refer said suit to the commission, as a master in chancery, to ascertain and report an appropriate form of decree therein. The commission shall proceed upon such notice to the parties and under such rules of procedure as the court may prescribe, and upon the coming in of such report such exceptions may be filed and such proceedings had in relation thereto as upon the report of a master in other equity causes, but the court may adopt or reject such report, in whole or in part, and enter such decree as the nature of the case may in its judgment require.

Sec. 8. That the several departments and bureaus of the Government when directed by the President shall furnish with the commission, upon its request, all records, papers, and information in their possession relating to any corporation subject to any of the provisions of this Act, and shall detail from time to time such officials and employees to the commission as he may direct.

Sec. 9. That for the purposes of this Act the commission, or its duly authorized agent or agents, shall at all reasonable times have access to, for the purpose of examination, and the right to copy any documentary evidence of any corporation being investigated or proceeded against; and the commission shall have the power to require by subpoena the attendance and testimony of witnesses and the production of all such documentary evidence relating to any matter under investigation. Any member of the commission may sign subpoenas, and members and examiners of the commission may administer oaths and affirmations, examine witnesses, and receive evidence.

Such attendance of witnesses, and the production of such documentary evidence, may be required from any place in the United States, at any designated place of hearing. And in case of disobedience to a subpoena the commission may invoke the aid of any court of the United States in requiring the attendance and testimony of witnesses and the production of documentary evidence.

Any of the district courts of the United States within the jurisdiction of which such inquiry is carried on may, in case of contumacy or refusal to obey a subpoena issued to any corporation or other person, issue an order requiring such corporation or other person to appear before the commission, or to produce the documentary evidence if so ordered, or to give evidence touching the matter in question; and any failure to obey such order of the court may be punished by such court as a contempt thereof.

Upon the application of the Attorney General of the United States, at the request of the commission, the district courts of the United States shall have the jurisdiction to issue writs of mandamus commanding any person or corporation to comply with the provisions of this Act or any order of the commission made in pursuance thereof.

The commission may order testimony to be taken by deposition in any proceeding or investigation pending under this Act at any stage of such proceeding or investigation. Such depositions may be taken before any person designated by the commission and having power to administer oaths. Such testimony shall be reduced to writing by the person taking the deposition, or under his direction, and shall then be subscribed by the deponent. Any person may be compelled to appear and depose and to produce documentary evidence in the same manner as witnesses may be compelled to appear and testify and produce documentary evidence before the commission as herein provided.

Witnesses summoned before the commission shall be paid the same fees and mileage that are paid witnesses in the courts of the United States, and witnesses whose depositions are taken and the persons taking the same shall severally be entitled to the same fees as are paid for like services in the courts of the United States.

No person shall be excused from attending and testifying or from producing documentary evidence before the commission or in obedience to the subpoena of the commission on the ground or for the reason that the testimony or evidence, documentary or otherwise, required of him may tend to criminate him or subject him to a penalty or forfeiture. But no natural person shall be prosecuted or subjected to any penalty or forfeiture for or on account of any transaction, matter, or thing concerning which he may testify, or produce evidence, documentary or otherwise, before the commission in obedience to a subpoena issued by it: Provided, That no natural person so testifying shall be exempt from prosecution and punishment for perjury committed in so testifying.

Sec. 10. That any person who shall neglect or refuse to attend and testify, or to answer any lawful inquiry, or to produce documentary evidence, if in his power to do so, in obedience to the subpoena or lawful requirement of the commission, shall be guilty of an offense and upon conviction thereof by a court of competent jurisdiction shall be punished by a fine of not less than $1,000 nor more than $5,000, or by imprisonment for not more than one year, or by both such fine and imprisonment.

Any person who shall willfully make, or cause to be made, any false entry or statement of fact in any report required to be made under this Act, or who shall willfully make, or cause to be made, any false entry in any account, record, or memorandum kept by any corporation subject to this Act, or who shall willfully neglect or fail to make, or to cause to be made, full, true, and correct entries in such accounts, records, or memoranda of all facts and transactions appertaining to the business of such corporation, or who shall willfully remove out of the jurisdiction of the United States, or willfully mutilate, alter, or by other means falsify any documentary evidence of such corporation, or who shall willfully refuse to submit to the commission or to any of its authorized agents, for the purpose of inspection and taking copies, any documentary evidence of such corporation in his possession or within his control, shall be deemed guilty of an offense against the United States, and shall be subject, upon conviction in any court of the United States of competent jurisdiction, to a fine of not less than $1,000 nor more than $5,000, or to imprisonment for a term not more than three years, or to both such fine and imprisonment.

If any corporation required by this Act to file any annual or special report shall fail to do so within the time fixed by the commission for filing the same, and such failure shall continue for thirty days after notice of such default, the corporation shall forfeit to the United States the sum of $100 for each and every day of the continuance of such failure, which forfeiture shall be payable into the Treasury of the United States, and shall be recoverable in a civil suit in the name of the United States brought in the district where the corporation has its principal office or in any district in which it shall do business. It shall be the duty of the various district attorneys, under the direction of the Attorney General of the United States, to prosecute for the recovery of forfeitures. The costs and expenses of such prosecution shall be paid out of the appropriation for the expenses of the courts of the United States.

Any officer or employee of the commission who shall make public any information obtained by the commission without its authority, unless directed by a court, shall be deemed guilty of a misdemeanor, and, upon conviction thereof, shall be punished by a fine not exceeding $5,000, or by imprisonment not exceeding one year, or by fine and imprisonment, in the discretion of the court.

Sec. 11. Nothing contained in this Act shall be construed to prevent or interfere with the enforcement of the provisions of the antitrust Acts or the Acts to regulate commerce, nor shall anything contained in this Act be construed to alter, modify, or repeal the said antitrust Act or the Acts to regulate commerce or any part or parts thereof.

Approved, September 26, 1914.

Franklin D. Roosevelt on Hawley-Smoot Tariff (1932)

During the election of 1932, in a speech in Sioux City, Iowa, Democratic presidential candidate Franklin D. Roosevelt blamed President Herbert Hoover for the Great Depression because he signed the Hawley-Smoot Tariff into law. Roosevelt claimed that the tariff caused the Great Depression, although Hoover argued that other events around the world precipitated the crisis.

Source: Roosevelt, Franklin D. *The Public Papers and Addresses of Franklin D. Roosevelt, 1928–1932.* Vol. 1. New York: Random House, 1938.

Mr. Chairman, my friends in Sioux City, my friends in this great State, and, indeed, all of you through the country who are listening on the radio tonight, let me tell you first of all that I appreciate this remarkable welcome that you have given me, and I appreciate, too, the performance put on by the mounted patrol of my fellow Shriners.

Two weeks ago, when I was heading toward the Coast, I presented before an audience in the City of Topeka, what I conceived to be the problem of agriculture in these United States, with particular reference to the Middle West and West, and what the Government of the Nation can do to meet that problem of ours.

I have been highly gratified to receive from all parts of the country and particularly from farm leaders themselves, assurances of their hearty support and promises of co-operation, in the efforts that I proposed to improve the deplorable condition into which agriculture has fallen. The meeting of this farm problem of ours is going to be successful only if two factors are present.

The first is a sympathetic Administration in Washington, and the second is the hearty support and patient cooperation of agriculture itself and its leaders.

I cannot avoid a word concerning this plight of agriculture—what it means to all. It means that the product of your labor brings just half of what it brought before the war. It means that no matter how hard you work and how long and how carefully you save, and how much efficiency you apply to your business, you face a steadily diminishing return. As a farm leader said to me, you have been caught like a man in a deep pit, helpless in the grip of forces that are beyond your control. Still, my friends, it has meant that in spite of the maxims that we have learned when we were in school, that we ought to work and save, to be prudent and be temperate, in spite of all of the rest of the homely virtues, the return on these virtues has belied the hopes and the promises on which you and I were raised.

That is one of the tragic consequences of this depression. The things that we were taught have not come true. We were taught to work and we have been denied the opportunity to work. We were taught to increase the products of our labor and we have found that while the products increase the return has decreased. We were taught to bring forth the fruits of the earth, and we have found that the fruits of the earth have found no market.

The results of our labor, my friends, have been lost in the smash of an economic system that was unable to fulfill its purposes.

It is a moral as well as an economic question that we face—moral because we want to reestablish the standards that in times past were our goal. We want the opportunity to live in comfort, reasonable comfort, out of which we may build our spiritual values. The consequences of poverty bring a loss of spiritual and moral values. And even more important is the loss of the opportunity that we hope to give to the younger generation. We want our children to have a chance for an education, for the sound development of American standards to be applied in their daily lives at play and work. Those opportunities can come only if the condition of agriculture is made more prosperous.

Now, the farmer—and when I speak of the farmer I mean not only you who live in the corn belt, but also those in the East and the Northwest who are in the dairy business, those in the South who are raising cotton, and those on the plains who are raising cattle and sheep, and those in the many sections of the country who are raising cattle, all kinds of things, small fruits and big fruits—in other words, the farmer in the broad sense, has been attacked during this past decade simultaneously from two sides. On the one side the farmer's expenses, chiefly in the form of increased taxes, have been going up rather steadily during the past generation, and on the other side, he has been attacked by a constantly depreciating farm dollar during the past twelve years, and it seems to be nothing less than old-fashioned horse sense to seek means to circumvent both of these attacks at the same time. That means, first, for us to seek relief for him from the burden of his expense account and, second, to try to restore the purchasing power of his dollar by getting for him higher prices for the products of the soil.

Now, those two great purposes are, quite frankly, the basis of my farm policy, and I have definitely connected both of them with the broadest aspects of a new national economy, something that I like to label in simpler words, "A New Deal," covering every part of the Nation, and covering industry and business as well as farming, because I recognize, first of all, that from the soil itself springs our ability to restore our trade with the other Nations of the world.

First of all, I want to discuss with you one of the angles of the mounting expenses of agriculture in practically every community and in every State—the problem of taxes which we have to pay.

Let us examine the proportion of our expenditures that goes to the various divisions of Government. Half of what you and I pay for the support of the Government—in other words, on the average in this country fifty cents out of every dollar—goes to local government, that is, cities, townships, counties and lots of other small units; and the other half, the other fifty cents, goes to the State and Nation.

This fifty cents that goes to local government, therefore, points to the necessity for attention to local government. As a broad proposition you and I know we are not using our present agencies of local government with real economy and efficiency. That means we must require our public servants to give a fuller measure of service for what they are paid. It means we must eliminate useless office holders. It means every public official, every employee of local government must determine that he owes it to the country to cooperate in the great purpose of saving the taxpayers' money.

But it means more than that, my friends. I am going to speak very frankly to you. There are offices in most States that are provided for in the Constitution and laws of some of the States, offices that have an honorable history but are no longer necessary for the conduct of Government. We have too many tax layers, and it seems to me relief can come only through resolute, courageous cutting.

Some of you will ask why I, a candidate for the office of president of the United States, am talking to you about changes in local government. Now, it is perfectly clear that the president has no legal or constitutional control over the local government under which you people live. The President has, nevertheless, my friends, the right and even the duty of taking a moral leadership in this national task because it is a national problem, because in its scope it covers every State, and any problem that is national in this broader sense creates a national moral responsibility in the President of the United States himself.

And I propose to use this position of high responsibility to discuss up and down the country, in all seasons and at all times, the duty of reducing taxes, or increasing the efficiency of Government, of cutting out the underbrush around out governmental structure, of getting the most public service for every dollar paid in taxation. That I pledge you, and nothing I have said in the campaign transcends in importance this covenant with the taxpayers of the United States.

Now, of the other half dollar of your taxes, it is true that part goes to the support of State Governments. I am not going to discuss that end. In this field also I believe that substantial reductions can be made. While the President rightly has no authority over State budgets, he has the same moral responsibility of national leadership for generally lowered expenses, and therefore for generally lowered taxes.

It is in the field of the Federal Government that the office of President can, of course, make itself most directly and definitely felt. Over 30 percent of your tax dollar goes to Washington, and in their field also, items such as the interest can be accomplished. There are, of course, items such as the interest on the public debt which must be paid each year, and which can be reduced only through a reduction of the debt itself, by the creation of a surplus in the place of the present deficit in the national treasury, and it is perhaps worth while that I should tell you that I spent nearly eight years in Washington during the Administration of Woodrow Wilson, and that during those eight years I had a fair understanding of the problem of the national expenses, and that I knew first hand many of the details of actual administration of the different departments. Later in this campaign, I proposed to analyze the enormous increase in the growth of what you and I call bureaucracy. We are not getting an adequate return for the money we are spending in Washington, or to put it another way, we are spending altogether too much money for Government services that are neither practical nor necessary. And then, in addition to that, we are attempting too many functions. We need to simplify what the Federal Government is giving to the people.

I accuse the present Administration of being the greatest spending Administration in peace times in all our history. It is an Administration that has piled bureau on bureau, commission on commission, and has failed to anticipate the dire needs and the reduced earning power of the people. Bureaus and bureaucrats, commissions and commissioners have been retained at the expense of the taxpayer.

Now, I read in the past few days in the newspapers that the President is at work on a plan to consolidate and simplify the Federal bureaucracy. My friends, four long years ago, in the campaign of 1928, he, as a candidate, proposed to do this same thing. And today, once more a candidate, he is still proposing, and I leave you to draw your own inferences.

And on my part I ask you very simply to assign to me the task of reducing the annual operating expenses of your national Government.

Now I come to the other half of the farmer's problem, the increase of the purchasing power of the farm dollar. I have already gone at length into the emergency proposals relating to our major crops, and now I want to discuss in more detail a very important factor, a thing known as the tariff, and our economic relationship to the rest of this big round world.

From the beginning of our Government, one of the most difficult questions in our economic life has been the tariff. But it is a fact that it is now so interwoven with our whole economic structure, and that structure is such an intricate and delicate pattern of causes and effects, that tariff revision must be undertaken, with scrupulous care and only on the basis of established facts.

I have to go back in history a little way. In the course of his 1928 campaign, the present Republican candidate for President with great boldness laid down the propositions that high tariffs interfere only slightly, if at all, with our export or our import trade, that they are necessary to the success of agriculture and afford essential farm relief; that they do not interfere with the payments of debts by other Nations to us, and that they are absolutely necessary to the economic formula which he proposed at that time as the road to the abolition of poverty. And I must pause here for a moment to observe that the experience of the past four years has unhappily demonstrated the error, the gross, fundamental, basic error of every single one of those propositions—but four years ago!—that every one of them has been one of the effective causes of the present depression; and finally that no substantial progress toward recovery from this depression, either here or abroad, can be had without a forthright recognition of those errors.

And so I am asking effective action to reverse the disastrous policies which were based on them. As I have elsewhere remarked, the 1928 Republican leadership prosperity promise was based on the assertion that although our agriculture was producing a surplus far in excess of our power to consume, and that, due to the mass and automatic machine production of today, our industrial production had also passed far beyond the point of domestic consumption, nevertheless, we should press forward to increase industrial production as the only means of maintaining prosperity and employment. And the candidate of that year insisted that, although we could not consume all those things at home, there was some kind of unlimited market for our rapidly increasing surplus in export trade, and he boldly asserted that on this theory we were on the verge of the greatest commercial expansion in history. I do not have to tell you the later history of that.

And then, in the spring of 1929, ostensibly for the purpose of enacting legislation for the relief of agriculture, a special session of Congress was called, and the disastrous fruit of that session was the notorious and indefensible Grundy-Smoot-Hawley tariff.

As to the much-heralded purpose of that special session for the relief of agriculture, the result, my friends, was a ghastly jest. The principal cash crops of our farms are produced much in excess of our domestic requirements. And we know that no tariff on a surplus crop, no matter how high the wall—1,000 percent, if you like—has the slightest effect on raising the domestic price of that crop. Why, the producers of all those crops are so effectively thrust outside the protection of our tariff walls as if there were no tariff at all. But we still know that the tariff does protect the price of industrial products and raises them above world prices, as the farmer with increasing bitterness has come to realize. He sells on a free trade basis; he buys in a protected market. The higher industrial tariffs go, my friends, the greater is the burden of the farmer.

Now, the first effect of the Grundy tariff was to increase or sustain the cost of all that agriculture buys, but the harm to our whole farm production did not stop there.

The destructive effect of the Grundy tariff on export markets has not been confined to agriculture. It has ruined our export trade in industrial products as well. Industry, with its foreign trade cut off, naturally began to look to the home market—a market supplied for the greater part by the purchasing power of farm families—but for reasons that you and I know, it found that the Grundy tariff had reduced the buying power of the farmer.

So what happened? Deprived of any American market, the other industrial Nations in order to support their own industries, and take care of their own employment problem, had to find new outlets. In that quest they took to trade agreements with other countries than ourselves and also to the preservation of their own domestic markets against importations by trade restrictions of all kinds. An almost frantic movement toward self-contained nationalism began among other Nations of the world, and of course the direct result was a series of retaliatory and defensive measures on their part, in the shape of tariffs and embargoes and import quotas and international arrangements. Almost immediately international commerce began to languish. The export markets for our industrial and agricultural surplus began to disappear altogether.

In the year 1929, a year before the enactment of the Grundy tariff, we exported 54.8 percent of all the cotton produced in the United States—more than one-half. That means, Mr. Cotton Grower, that in 1929 every other row of your cotton was sold abroad. And you, the growers of wheat, exported 17 percent of your wheat, but your great foreign market had been largely sacrificed; and so, with the grower of rye, who was able to disposed of 20 percent of his crop to foreign markets. The grower of leaf-tobacco had a stake of 41 percent of his income overseas, and one-third of the lard production, 33 percent, was exported in the year 1929. Where does that come in? Well, it concerns the corn grower because some of us, even from the East, know that corn is exported in the shape of lard.

How were your interests taken care of? Oh, they gave you a tariff on corn—chicken feed—literally and figuratively, but those figures show how vitally you are interested in the preservation, perhaps I had better say the return, of our export trade.

Now, the ink on the Hawley-Smoot-Grundy tariff bill was hardly dry before foreign Nations commenced their program of retaliation. Brick for brick they built their walls against us. They learned the lesson from us. The villainy we taught them they practiced on us.

And the Administration in Washington had reason to know that would happen. It was warned. While the bill was before Congress, our State Department received 160 protests from 33 other nations, many of whom after the passage of the bill erected their own tariff walls to the detriment or destruction of much of our export trade.

Well, what is the result? In two years, from 1930 to May, 1932, to escape the penalty on the introduction of American-made goods, American manufacturers have established in foreign countries 258 separate factories; 48 of them in Europe; 12 in Latin American; 28 in the Far East, and 71 across the border in Canada. The Prime Minister of Canada said in a recent speech that a factory is moving every day of the year from the United States into Canada, and he assured those at the recent conferences at Ottawa that the arrangements made there with Great Britain and other colonies would take $250,000,000 of Canadian trade that would otherwise go to the United States. So you see, my friends, what that tariff bill did there was to put more men on the street here, and to put more people to work outside our borders.

Now, there was a secondary and perhaps even more disastrous effect of Grundyism. Billions of dollars of debts are due to this country from abroad. If the debtor Nations cannot export goods, they must try to pay in gold. But we started such a drain on the gold reserves of the other Nations as to force practically all of them off the gold standard. What happened? The value of the money of each of these countries relative to the value of our dollar declined alarmingly and steadily. It took more Argentine pesos to buy an American plow. It took more English shillings to buy an American bushel of wheat, or an American bale of cotton.

Why, they just could not buy goods with their money. These goods then were thrown back upon our markets and prices fell still more.

And so, summing up, this Grundy tariff has largely extinguished the export markets for our industrial and our farm surplus; it has prevented the payment of public and private debts to us and the interest thereon, increasing taxation to meet the expense of our Government, and finally it has driven our factories abroad.

The process still goes on, my friends. Indeed, it may be only in its beginning. The Grundy tariff still retains its grip on the throat of international commerce.

There is no relief in sight, and certainly there can be no relief if the men in Washington responsible for this disaster continue in power. And I say to you, in all earnestness and sincerity, that unless and until this process is reversed throughout the world, there is no hope for full economic recovery, or for true prosperity in this beloved country of ours.

The essential trouble is that the Republican leaders thought they had a good patent on the doctrine of unscaleable tariff walls and that no other Nation could use the same idea. Well, either that patent has expired or else never was any good anyway; or else, one other alternative, all the other Nations have infringed on our patent and there is no court to which we can take our case. It was a stupid, blundering idea, and we know it today and we know it has brought disaster.

Do not expect our adroit Republican friends to admit this. They do not. On the contrary, they have adopted the boldest alibi in the history of politics. Having brought this trouble on the world, they now seek to avoid all responsibility by blaming the foreign victims for their own economic blundering. They say that all of our troubles come from abroad and that the Administration is not in the least to be held to answer. This excuse is a classic of impertinence. If ever a condition was more clearly traceable to two specific American-made causes, it is the depression of this country and the world. Those two causes are interrelated. The second one, in point of time, is the Grundy tariff. The first one is the fact that by improvident loans to "backward and crippled countries," the policy of which was specifically recommended by the President, we financed practically our entire export trade and the payment of interest and principal to us by our debtors, and even in part, the payment of German reparations.

When we began to diminish that financing in 1929 the economic structure of the world began to totter.

If it be fair to ask, What does the Democratic Party propose to do in the premises?

The platform declares in favor of a competitive tariff which means one which will put the American producers on a market equality with their foreign competitors, one that equalizes the difference in the cost of production, not a prohibitory tariff back of which domestic producers may combine to practice extortion of the American public.

I appreciate that the doctrine thus announced is not widely different from that preached by Republican statesmen and politicians, but I do know this, that the theory professed by them is that the tariff should equalize the difference in the cost of production as between this country and competitive countries, and I know that in practice that theory is utterly disregarded. The rates that are imposed are far in excess of any such difference, looking to total exclusion of imports—in other words, prohibitory rates.

Of course the outrageously excessive rates in that bill as it became law, must come down. But we should not lower them beyond a reasonable point, a point indicated by common sense and facts. Such revision of the tariff will injure no legitimate interest. Labor need have no apprehensions concerning such a course, for labor knows by long and bitter experience that the highly protected industries pay not one penny higher wages than the non-protected industries, such as the automobile industry, for example.

But, my friends, how is reduction to be accomplished? In view of present world conditions, international negotiation is the first, the most practical, the most common-sense, and the most desirable method. We must consent to the reduction to some extent of some of our duties in order to secure a lowering of foreign tariff walls over which a larger measure of our surplus may be sent.

I have not the fear that possesses some timorous minds that we should get the worst of it in such reciprocal arrangements. I ask if you have no faith in our Yankee tradition of good old-fashioned trading? Do you believe that our early instincts for successful barter have degenerated or atrophied? I do not think so. I have confidence that the spirit of the stalwart traders still permeates our people, that the red blood of the men who sailed our Yankee clipper ships around the Horn and Cape of Good Hope in the China trade still courses in our veins. I cannot picture Uncle Sam as a supine, white-livered, flabby-muscled old man, cooling his heels in the shade of our tariff walls. We may not have the astuteness in some forms of international diplomacy that our more experienced European friends have, but when it comes to good old-fashioned barter and trade—whether it be goods or tariff—my money is on the American. My friends, there cannot and shall not be any foreign dictation of our tariff policies, but I am willing and ready to sit down around the table with them.

And next, my friends, the Democrats propose to accomplish the necessary reduction through the agency of the Tariff Commission.

I need not say to you that one of the most deplorable features of tariff legislation is the log-rolling process by which it has been effected in Republican and Democratic Congresses. Indefensible rates are introduced through an understanding, usually implied rather than expressed among members, each of whom is interested in one or more individual items. Yet, it is a case of you scratch my back and I will scratch yours.

Now, to avoid that as well as other evils in tariff making, a Democratic Congress in 1916 passed, and a Democratic President approved, a bill creating a bipartisan Tariff Commission, charged with the duty of supplying the Congress with accurate and full information upon which to base tariff rates. That Commission functioned as a scientific body until 1922, when by the incorporation of the so-called flexible provisions of the Act it was transformed into a political body. Under those flexible provisions—reenacted in the Grundy tariff of 1930—the Commission reports not to a Congress but to the President, who is then empowered on its recommendation to raise or lower the tariff rates by as much as 50 percent. At the last session of Congress—this brings us down to date—by the practically unanimous action of the Democrats of both houses, aided by liberal-minded Republicans led by Senator Norris, of Nebraska, a bill was passed by the Congress, but vetoed by the President, which, for the purpose of preventing log-rolling provided that if a report were made by the Tariff Commission on a particular item, with a recommendation as to the rates of duty, a bill to make effective that rate would not be subject to amendment in the Congress so as to include any other items not directly affected by the change proposed in the bill. And in that way each particular tariff rate proposed would be judged on its merits alone. If that bill had been signed by the President of the United States, log-rolling would have come to an end.

I am confident in the belief that under such a system rates adopted would generally be so reasonable that there would be very little opportunity for criticism or even caviling as to them. I am sure that it is not that any duties are imposed that complaint is made, for despite the effort, repeated in every campaign, to stigmatize the Democratic Party as a free trade party, there never has been a tariff act passed since the Government came into existence, in which the duties were not levied with a view to giving the American producer an advantage over his foreign competitor. I think you will agree with me that the difference in our day between the two major parties in respect to their leadership on the subject of the tariff is that the Republican leaders, whatever may be their profession, would put the duties so high as to make them practically prohibitive—and on the other hand that the Democratic leaders would put them as low as the preservation of the prosperity of American industry and American agriculture will permit.

Another feature of the bill to which reference has been made, a feature designed to obviate tariff log-rolling, contemplated the appointment of a public counsel who should be heard on all applications for changes in rates whether for increases sought by producers, sometimes greedy producers, or for decreases asked by importers, equally often actuated by purely selfish motives. And I hope some such change may speedily be enacted. It will have my cordial approval because, my friends, it means that the average citizen would have some representation.

Now, just a few words in closing. I want to speak to you of one other factor which enters into the dangerous emergency in which you farmers find yourselves at this moment. For more than a year I have spoken in my State and in other States of the actual calamity that impends on account of farm mortgages. Ever since my nomination on the first day of July, I have advocated immediate attention and immediate action looking to the preservation of the American home to the American farmer. But I recognize that I am not at the head of the National Administration nor shall I be until the March 4th next. Today I read in the papers that for the first time, so far as I know, the Administration of President Hoover has discovered the fact that there is such a thing as a farm mortgage or a home mortgage.

I do not have to tell you that, with the knowledge of conditions in my State which ranks fifth or sixth among the agricultural States of the Union and with the knowledge I have gleaned on this trip from coast to coast, I realize to the full the seriousness of the farm mortgage situation. And at least we can take a crumb of hope from his proposal for just another conference, a conference of some kind at least to discuss the situation. Seriously, my friends, all that I can tell you is that with you I deplore, I regret the inexcusable, the reprehensible delay of Washington, not for months alone, but for years. I have already been specific on this subject, upon mortgages, in my Topeka speech. All that I can promise you between now and the fourth of March is that I will continue to preach the plight of the farmer who is losing his home. All I can do is to promise you that when the authority of administration and recommendation to Congress is placed in my hands I will do everything in my power to bring the relief that is so long overdue. I shall not wait until the end of a campaign, I shall not wait until I have spent four years in the White House.

Herbert Hoover's Response to Franklin D. Roosevelt on Hawley-Smoot Tariff (1932)

During the presidential campaign of 1932, President Herbert Hoover tried to counter Roosevelt's argument that the Hawley-Smoot Tariff created the Great Depression. He pointed out that protectionist measures were implemented by the newly formed countries of Europe years before the passage of Hawley-Smoot. He eloquently argued that the cause of the depression remained rooted in Europe. But voters did not listen to his message and Franklin D. Roosevelt was elected. With Roosevelt's election, the United States government shifted to deficit spending, which continues to this day.

Source: Hoover, Herbert, and Calvin Coolidge. *Campaign Speeches of 1932.*Garden City, NY: Doubleday, Herbert & Company, 1933, pp. 80–109.

I spoke at Des Moines about agriculture. My remarks this evening will be largely directed to employment and to the wage and salary earners. I propose to review what the Administration has done and the measures and policies it has in action together with the relation of these policies to those of our opponents. As President of the United States, I have the duty to speak to workers, but I also have a certain personal right to speak.

When I talk to you tonight about labor I speak not out of academic imaginings but from sharp personal experience. I have looked at these human problems, not only from the fireside of one who has returned from a day's work with his own hands but I know the problem that haunts the employer through the night, desperate to find the money with which to meet the week's pay roll. In public service during years I have had to look at these problems from the point of view of the national welfare as a whole.

The people of a free nation have a right to ask their government, "Why has our employment been interrupted? What measures have been taken in our protection? What has been done to remove the obstacles from the return of our work to us?" They not only have a right to ask these questions but to have an answer. I am here tonight to give that answer.

During the past three years our economic system has received the most terrific shock and dislocation which, had not strong action been taken by your government, would have imperiled the Republic and the whole hope of recovery. It has affected business, industry, employment, and agriculture alike. It is appropriate to report that while many of our measures are directed to the protection and assistance of particular groups, yet all are in the same boat and all must come to shore together. And how are they to get to shore? By listening to those who manifestly display a lack of knowledge of the character of the storm and of the primary problems of navigation? By boring holes in the bottom of the boat? By throwing overboard the measures designed to meet the storm and which are proving their effectiveness?

Our opponents have been going up and down the land repeating the statement that the sole or major origins of this disruption of this world-wide hurricane came from the United States through the wild floatation of securities and the stock market speculation in New York three years ago, together with the passage of the Smoot-Hawley tariff bill, which took place 9 months after the storm broke.

I proposed to discuss this assertion.

First. Because it can be proved absolutely untrue.

Second. Because the United States did not bring this calamity upon the world. The United States is not the oppressor of the world.

Third. Because it can be demonstrated to be founded upon a complete misunderstanding of what has happened in the world.

Fourth. Because any party which exhibits such a lack of economic understanding upon which to base national politics should not be trusted with the fate of 25,000,000 American families. They should not be trusted to command the battle against the most gigantic economic emergency with which our people have ever been confronted, and to bring that battle to victorious issue in the reestablishment of the functioning of our economic machine.

This thesis of the opposition as to the origin of our troubles is a wonderful explanation for political purposes. I would be glad, indeed, if all the enormous problems in the world could be simplified in such a fashion. If that were all that has been the matter with us, we could have recovered from this depression two years ago instead of fighting ever since that time against the most destructive force which we have ever met in the whole history of the United States—and I am glad to say fighting victoriously.

Nowhere do I find the slightest reference in all the statements of the opposition party to the part played by the greatest war in history, the inheritances from it, the fears and panics and dreadful economic catastrophes which have developed from these causes in foreign countries, or the idea that they may have had the remotest thing to do with the calamity against which this administration is fighting day and night.

The leaders of the Democratic Party appear to be entirely in ignorance of the effect of the killing or incapacitating of 40,000,000 of the best youth of the earth, or of the stupendous cost of war—a sum of $300,000,000,000, or a sum nearly equal to the value of all the property in the United States, or the stupendous inheritance of debt, with its subsequent burden of taxes on scores of nations, with their stifling effect upon recuperation of industry and commerce or paralyzing effect upon world commerce by the continued instability of currencies and budgets.

Democratic leaders have apparently not yet learned of the political instability that arose all over Europe from the harsh treaties which ended the war from time to time paralyzed confidence. They have apparently never heard of the continuing economic dislocation from the transfer on every frontier of great masses of people from their former economic setting.

They apparently have not heard of the continuing dislocation of the stream of economic life which has been caused by the carving of 12 new nations from 3 old empires. These nations have a rightful aspiration to build their own separate economic systems; they naturally have surrounded themselves with tariffs and other national protections and have thereby diverted the long-established currents of trade. I presume, however, that if our Democrat leaders should hear of these nine new tariff walls introduced into the world some 14 years ago they would lay them at the door of the Smoot-Hawley bill passed 12 years later.

They apparently have not heard of the increase of standing armies of the world from two to five million men, with consequent burdens upon the taxpayer and the constant threat to the peace of the world.

Democratic leaders apparently ignore the effect upon us of the revolution among 300,000,000 people in China or the agitations amongst 160,000,000 people in Russia. They have ignored the effect of Russia's dumping into the world the commodities taken from its necessitous people in a desperate effort to secure money with which to carry on—shall I call it—a new deal.

The Democratic leaders apparently have never heard that there has been gigantic over-production of rubber in the Indies, of sugar in Cuba, of coffee in Brazil, of cocoa in Ecuador, of copper in the Congo, of lead in Burma, overproduction of zinc in Australia, overproduction of oil from new discoveries in the United States, Russia, Sumatra, and Venezuela; and likewise the effect of the introduction into the world of gigantic areas of new wheatlands in the Argentine and in Canada; new cotton lands in Egypt. In each and every case these enormous overproductions, far beyond consumption even in boom times, have crashed into the immutable law of supply and demand and brought collapse in prices and with it a train of bankruptcies and destruction of buying power for American goods.

They appear not to recognize that these forces finally generated economic strangulations, fears, and panic, the streams of which precipitated another long series of world-wide disasters.

The Democratic leaders apparently never heard that there followed revolutions in Spain and Portugal, Brazil, the Argentine, Chile, Peru, Ecuador, Siam, with attempts at revolution in a dozen other countries, resulting in their partial or practical repudiation of debt and the constant decrease in buying power for our goods.

They seem not to know that the further accumulation of all these causes and dislocations finally placed a strain upon the weakened economic systems of Europe until one by one they collapsed in failure of their gold standards and the partial or total repudiation of debts. They would hold the American people ignorant that every one of these nations in their financial crises imposed direct or indirect restrictions on the import of goods in order to reduce expenditures of their people. They call these "reprisals" against the Smoot-Hawley tariff bill.

They apparently have never heard of the succeeding jeopardy in which our Nation was put through these destructions of world commerce, or the persistent dumping of securities into the American market from these panic-stricken countries; the gigantic drains upon our gold and exchange; or the consequent fear that swept over our people, causing them to draw from our bank resources $1,500,000,000, all of which contracted credit, resulted in demand for payment of debts right and left, and thwarted our every effort for industrial recovery.

Yet in the face of all these tremendous facts, our Democratic friends leave the impression with the American people that the prime cause of this disaster was the boom in flotations and stock prices and a small increase in American tariffs.

Such an impression is unquestionably sought by the Democratic candidate when he says:

"That bubble burst first in the land of its origin—the United States. The major collapse abroad followed. It was not simultaneous with ours."

I do not underrate the distressing losses to millions of our people or the weakening of our strength from the mania of speculation and flotation of securities, but I may incidentally remark that the state governments have the primary responsibility to protect their citizens in these matters and that the vast majority of such transactions originated or took place in the State of New York.

But as to the accuracy of the statement I have quoted I may call your attention to a recent bulletin of the highly respected National Bureau of Economic Research, in which it is shown that this depression in the world began in 11 countries, having a population of 600,000,000 people, before it even appeared in our country, instead of the bubble having "first burst in the United States." Their report shows that the depression in eight other countries, with a population of another 600,000,000 people, started at the same time with ours. In fact, the shocks from the continued economic earthquakes in these other countries carried our prices far below the values they would otherwise have sunk to, with all its train of greatly increased losses, perils, and unemployment.

Our opponents demand to know why the governmental leaders of business men over the world did not foresee the approach of these disintegrating forces. That answer is simple. The whole world was striving to overcome them, but finally they accumulated until certain countries could no longer stand the strain, and their people, suddenly overtaken by fear and panic, through hoarding and exporting their capital for safety, brought down their own houses and these disasters spread like a prairie fire through the world. No man can foresee the coming fear or panic, or the extent of this effect. I did not notice any Democratic Jeremiahs.

So much for the beginnings and forces moving in this calamity.

I now come to the amazing statements that the tariff bill of 1930 has borne a major influence in this debacle.

I quote from the Democratic candidate:

"The Hawley-Smoot tariff is one of the most important factors in the present world-wide depressions."

"The tariff has done so much to destroy foreign trade as to make foreign trade virtually impossible."

I shall analyze the accuracy of these statements not only because I should like to get before my countrymen a picture of the lack of understanding which the Democratic Party has of world trade, but also for the further reasons that it is of vital importance to labor that, as our opponents have this obsession, it means that if they are intrusted with control of our government they intend to break down the protective tariff which is the very first line of defense of the American standard of living against these new forces.

It requires a collection of dull facts to demonstrate the errors in these bald assertions by Democratic leaders.

At the beginning I may repeat that this tariff bill was not passed until nine months after the economic depression began in the United States and also not until 20 other countries had already gone into the depression.

The Democratic Party seldom mentions that 66 per cent of our imports are free of duty, but that is the fact. From half to two-thirds of the trade of the world is in nondutiable goods—that is, mostly raw materials; another part is in luxuries, upon which all nations collect tariffs for revenue; another part, and probably less than one-third of the whole, is in competitive goods so far as the importing nation is concerned and therefore subject to protective tariffs.

The trade of the world has distressingly diminished under the impact of these successive dislocations abroad. But the decrease is almost exactly the same in the free goods everywhere as in the dutiable goods. That is the case in the United States.

If the Smoot-Hawley tariff reduced our imports of dutiable goods, what was it that reduced the two-thirds of non-dutiable goods?

If we explore a little further, we would find from the Tariff Commission that the total duties collected in a comparable year represent 16 per cent of the total imports, this being an increase from 13.8 per cent of the previous tariffs. In other words, the effect of the new tariff shows an increase of 2.2 per cent. This is the margin with which they say we have pulled down foreign governments, created tyrannies, financial shocks, and revolutions.

I may mention that upon the same basis the McKinley duties were 23 per cent; the Dingley duties were 25.8 per cent; the Payne-Aldrich duties were 19.3 per cent of the whole of our imports—all compared with the 16 per cent of the present tariff— and yet they produced in foreign countries no revolutions, no financial crises, and did not destroy the whole world, nor destroy American foreign trade.

And I may explore the facts further. The 5-year average of the import trade of the United States before the depression was about 12 per cent of the whole world import trade. This they would say that 2.2 per cent increase applied to one-eighth of the world's imports has produced this catastrophe.

I can explore this in still another direction. I remind you that we levy tariffs upon only one-third of our imports. I also remind you that the actual increases made in the Smoot-Hawley Act covered one-quarter of the dutiable imports. I may also remind you that our import trade is only one-eighth of the import trade of the world. So they would have us believe this world catastrophe and this destruction of foreign trade happened because the United States increased tariffs on one-fourth of one-third of one-eighth of the world's imports. Thus we pulled down the world, so they tell us, by increased on less than 1 per cent of the goods being imported by the world.

And I may explore the responsibility of the tariffs still further. My opponent has said that it—

"Started such a drain on the gold reserves of the principal countries as to force practically all of them off the gold standard."

At Des Moines I defended the American people from this guilt. I pointed out that it happens there had been no drain of gold from Europe, which is the center of this disturbance, but on the contrary, that Europe's gold holdings have increased every year since the Smoot-Hawley tariff was passed.

My fellow citizens, I could continue for hours in an analysis of mistaken statements and misinformation from the opposition. But I assure you that this country is not to blame for the catastrophes that have come on the world. The American people did not originate the age-old controversies of Europe. We did not inaugurate the Great War or the panics in Europe.

No, my friends, the increase of duties collected by the United States by 2.2 per cent calculated on all the goods we import did not bring about the debacle in the world. If every country in the world were to increase the duty upon their imports by 2.2 per cent tomorrow, but if at the same time they would also adopt domestic policies which would bring about release of the energies and progress of their people—if they would support confidence in the world, then the world's, as well as our own, international commerce would thrive and boom beyond any dimensions that we ever dreamed of.

I dwell on this point, not only because I believe it is important to correct current misstatements of our opponents but because the policies of our opponents are founded upon misconceptions of the utmost gravity for the future of the United States. If it were not a matter of such utter gravity for the future of the United States, I should treat them not in a sense of seriousness but in a sense of humor. There is a vital determination before the American people as to whether there shall be placed in power over the destinies of 120,000,000 of people a party which so lacks a penetration into the forces active in the world and the dangers and responsibilities that arise from them. . . .

I wish for a moment to return to the tariff. There is no measure in the whole economic gamut more vital to the American workingman and the farmer today than the maintenance of the protective tariff. I stand on that principle of protection. Our opponents are opposed to that principle. They propose "a competitive tariff for revenue." They propose to do this in the face of the fact that in the last year currencies of competing nations have depreciated by going off the gold standard and consequently wages have been lowered in 30 competing countries. This is a flat issue which every farmer and workman in the United States should consider from the point of view of his home and his living.

That it is the intention of the Democratic candidate to reduce the tariffs—on all commodities—must be clear from these typical expressions in respect to the present tariff used in this campaign—"Wicked and exorbitant tariff," "its outrageous rates," "almost prohibitive tariffs," "the notorious and indefensible Smoot-Hawley tariff," "the excessive rates of that bill must come down," "until the tariff is lowered," "our policy calls for lower tariffs."

Do you want to compete with laborers whose wages in his own money are only sufficient to buy from one-eighth to one-third of the amount of bread and butter which you can buy at the present rate of wages? That is the plain question. It does not require a great deal of ingenious argument to support its correct answer. It is true we have the most gigantic market in the world today, surrounded by nations clamoring to get in. But it has been my belief—and it is still my belief—that we should protect this market for our own labor; not surrender it to the labor of foreign countries as the Democratic party proposes to do.

Lyndon B. Johnson's Great Society Speech (1964)

The civil rights movement of the 1950s and early 1960s shed light on the economic plight of African Americans as well as that of other less prosperous sectors of the United States. The Johnson Administration proposed a series of programs designed to address the needs of the poor, especially in the areas of education, health care, and housing. President Lyndon B. Johnson outlined the new policy, known as the Great Society, in a speech at the University of Michigan on May 22, 1964.

Source: Johnson, Lyndon B. Public Papers of the President of the United States, Lyndon B. Johnson, 1963–1964 online. Book I, pp. 704–707. http://coursesa.matrix .msu.edu/~hst306/documents/great.htm.

President Lyndon B. Johnson's Remarks at the University of Michigan on May 22, 1964.

President Hatcher, Governor Romney, Senators McNamara and Hart, Congressmen Meader and Staebler, and other members of the fine Michigan delegation, members of the graduating class, my fellow Americans:

It is a great pleasure to be here today. This university has been coeducational since 1870, but I do not believe it was on the basis of your accomplishments that a Detroit high school girl said, "In choosing a college, you first have to decide whether you want a coeducational school or an educational school."

Well, we can find both here at Michigan, although perhaps at different hours.

I came out here today very anxious to meet the Michigan student whose father told a friend of mine that his son's education had been a real value. It stopped his mother from bragging about him.

I have come today from the turmoil of your Capital to the tranquility of your campus to speak about the future of your country.

The purpose of protecting the life of our Nation and preserving the liberty of our citizens is to pursue the happiness of our people. Our success in that pursuit is the test of our success as a Nation.

For a century we labored to settle and to subdue a continent. For half a century we called upon unbounded invention and untiring industry to create an order of plenty for all of our people.

The challenge of the next half century is whether we have the wisdom to use that wealth to enrich and elevate our national life, and to advance the quality of our American civilization.

Your imagination, your initiative, and your indignation will determine whether we build a society where progress is the servant of our needs, or a society where old values and new visions are buried under unbridled growth. For in your time we have the opportunity to move not only toward the rich society and the powerful society, but upward to the Great Society.

The Great Society rests on abundance and liberty for all. It demands an end to poverty and racial injustice, to which we are totally committed in our time. But that is just the beginning.

The Great Society is a place where every child can find knowledge to enrich his mind and to enlarge his talents. It is a place where leisure is a welcome chance to build and reflect, not a feared cause of boredom and restlessness. It is a place where the city of man serves not only the needs of the body and the demands of commerce but the desire for beauty and the hunger for community.

It is a place where man can renew contact with nature. It is a place which honors creation for its own sake and for what it adds to the understanding of the race. It is a place where men are more concerned with the quality of their goals than the quantity of their goods.

But most of all, the Great Society is not a safe harbor, a resting place, a final objective, a finished work. It is a challenge constantly renewed, beckoning us toward a destiny where the meaning of our lives matches the marvelous products of our labor.

So I want to talk to you today about three places where we begin to build the Great Society—in our cities, in our countryside, and in our classrooms.

Many of you will live to see the day, perhaps 50 years from now, when there will be 400 million Americans—four-fifths of them in urban areas. In the remainder of this century urban population will double, city land will double, and we will have to build homes, highways, and facilities equal to all those built since this country was first settled. So in the next 40 years we must rebuild the entire urban United States.

Aristotle said: "Men come together in cities in order to live, but they remain together in order to live the good life." It is harder and harder to live the good life in American cities today.

The catalog of ills is long: there is the decay of the centers and the despoiling of the suburbs. There is not enough housing for our people or transportation for our traffic. Open land is vanishing and old landmarks are violated.

Worst of all expansion is eroding the precious and time honored values of community with neighbors and communion with nature. The loss of these values breeds loneliness and boredom and indifference.

Our society will never be great until our cities are great. Today the frontier of imagination and innovation is inside those cities and not beyond their borders.

New experiments are already going on. It will be the task of your generation to make the American city a place where future generations will come, not only to live but to live the good life.

I understand that if I stayed here tonight I would see that Michigan students are really doing their best to live the good life.

This is the place where the Peace Corps was started. It is inspiring to see how all of you, while you are in this country, are trying so hard to live at the level of the people.

A second place where we begin to build the Great Society is in our countryside. We have always prided ourselves on being not only America the strong and America the free, but America the beautiful. Today that beauty is in danger. The water we drink, the food we eat, the very air that we breathe, are threatened with pollution. Our parks are overcrowded, our seashores overburdened. Green fields and dense forests are disappearing.

A few years ago we were greatly concerned about the "Ugly American." Today we must act to prevent an ugly America.

For once the battle is lost, once our natural splendor is destroyed, it can never be recaptured. And once man can no longer walk with beauty or wonder at nature his spirit will wither and his sustenance be wasted.

A third place to build the Great Society is in the classrooms of America. There your children's lives will be shaped. Our society will not be great until every young mind is set free to scan the farthest reaches of thought and imagination. We are still far from that goal.

Today, 8 million adult Americans, more than the entire population of Michigan, have not finished 5 years of school. Nearly 20 million have not finished 8 years of school. Nearly 54 million—more than one-quarter of all America—have not even finished high school.

Each year more than 100,000 high school graduates, with proved ability, do not enter college because they cannot afford it. And if we cannot educate today's youth, what will we do in 1970 when elementary school enrollment will be 5 million greater than 1960? And high school enrollment will rise by 5 million. College enrollment will increase by more than 3 million.

In many places, classrooms are overcrowded and curricula are outdated. Most of our qualified teachers are underpaid, and many of our paid teachers are unqualified. So we must give every child a place to sit and a teacher to learn from. Poverty must not be a bar to learning, and learning must offer an escape from poverty.

But more classrooms and more teachers are not enough. We must seek an educational system which grows in excellence as it grows in size. This means better training for our teachers. It means preparing youth to enjoy their hours of leisure as well as their hours of labor. It means exploring new techniques of teaching, to find new ways to stimulate the love of learning and the capacity for creation.

These are three of the central issues of the Great Society. While our Government has many programs directed at those issues, I do not pretend that we have the full answer to those problems.

But I do promise this: We are going to assemble the best thought and the broadest knowledge from all over the world to find those answers for America. I intend to establish working groups to prepare a series of White House conferences and meetings—on the cities, on natural beauty, on the quality of education, and on other emerging challenges. And from these meetings and from this inspiration and from these studies we will begin to set our course toward the Great Society.

The solution to these problems does not rest on a massive program in Washington, nor can it rely solely on the strained resources of local authority. They require us to create new concepts of cooperation, a creative federalism, between the National Capital and the leaders of local communities.

Woodrow Wilson once wrote: "Every man sent out from his university should be a man of his Nation as well as a man of his time."

Within your lifetime powerful forces, already loosed, will take us toward a way of life beyond the realm of our experience, almost beyond the bounds of our imagination.

For better or for worse, your generation has been appointed by history to deal with those problems and to lead America toward a new age. You have the chance never before afforded to any people in any age. You can help build a society where the demands of morality, and the needs of the spirit, can be realized in the life of the Nation.

So, will you join in the battle to give every citizen the full equality which God enjoins and the law requires, whatever his belief, or race, or the color of his skin?

Will you join in the battle to give every citizen an escape from the crushing weight of poverty?

Will you join in the battle to make it possible for all nations to live in enduring peace—as neighbors and not as mortal enemies?

Will you join in the battle to build the Great Society, to prove that our material progress is only the foundation on which we will build a richer life of mind and spirit?

There are those timid souls who say this battle cannot be won; that we are condemned to a soulless wealth. I do not agree. We have the power to shape the civilization that we want. But we need your will, your labor, your hearts, if we are to build that kind of society.

Those who came to this land sought to build more than just a new country. They sought a new world. So I have come here today to your campus to say that you can make their vision our reality. So let us from this moment begin our work so that in the future men will look back and say: It was then, after a long and weary way, that man turned the exploits of his genius to the full enrichment of his life.

Thank you. Goodby.

Panama Canal Treaty of 1977

After 13 years of negotiations, the U.S. government, during the administration of Jimmy Carter, concluded a treaty that gradually shifted control of the Panama Canal to the government of Panama. The United States, after constructing the canal and collecting the tolls for decades, turned over authority on December 31, 1999. The treaty signified the end of an era. The economic ramifications of this agreement included the loss of revenue and the end of yearly rent payments to Panama. Many Americans argued against the ratification of the treaty on the grounds that, in time of war, the United States was not guaranteed right of passage through the canal.

Source: http://www.state.gov/p/wha/rlnks/11936.htm.

The United States of America and the Republic of Panama, Acting in the spirit of the Joint Declaration of April 3, 1964, by the Representatives of the Governments of the United States of America and the Republic of Panama, and of the Joint Statement of Principles of February 7, 1974, initialed by the Secretary of State of the United States of America and the Foreign Minister of the Republic of Panama, and Acknowledging the Republic of Panama's sovereignty over its territory, Have decided to terminate the prior Treaties pertaining to the Panama Canal and to conclude a new Treaty to serve as the basis for a new relationship between them and, accordingly, have agreed upon the following:

Article I: Abrogation of Prior Treaties and Establishment of a New Relationship

- 1. Upon its entry into force, this Treaty terminates and supersedes:
    - (a) The Isthmian Canal Convention between the United States of America and the Republic of Panama, signed at Washington, November 18, 1903;
    - (b) The Treaty of Friendship and Cooperation signed at Washington, March 2, 1936, and the Treaty of Mutual Understanding and Cooperation and the related Memorandum of Understandings Reached, signed at Panama, January 25, 1955, between the United States of America and the Republic of Panama;
    - (c) All other treaties, conventions, agreements, and exchanges of notes between the United States of America and the Republic of Panama

concerning the Panama Canal, which were in force prior to the entry into force of this Treaty; and

(d) Provisions concerning the Panama Canal, which appear in other treaties, conventions, agreements, and exchanges of notes between the United States of America and the Republic of Panama, which were in force prior to the entry into force of this Treaty.

- 2. In accordance with the terms of this Treaty and related agreements, the Republic of Panama, as territorial sovereign, grants to the United States of America, for the duration of this Treaty, the rights necessary to regulate the transit of ships through the Panama Canal, and to manage, operate, maintain, improve, protect and defend the Canal. The Republic of Panama guarantees to the United States of America the peaceful use of the land and water areas which it has been granted the rights to use for such purposes pursuant to this Treaty and related agreements.

- 3. The Republic of Panama shall participate increasingly in the management and protection and defense of the Canal, as provided in this Treaty.

- 4. In view of the special relationship established by this Treaty, the United States of America and the Republic of Panama shall cooperate to assure the uninterrupted and efficient operation of the Panama Canal.

Article II: Ratification, Entry into Force, and Termination

- 1. The Treaty shall be subject to ratification in accordance with the constitutional procedures of the two Parties. The instruments of ratification of this Treaty shall be exchanged at Panama at the same time as the instruments of ratification of the Treaty Concerning the Permanent Neutrality and Operation of the Panama Canal, signed this date, are exchanged. This Treaty shall enter into force, simultaneously with the Treaty Concerning the Permanent Neutrality and Operation of the Panama Canal, six calendar months from the date of the exchange of the instruments of ratification.

2. This Treaty shall terminate at noon, Panama time, December 31, 1999.

Article III: Canal Operation and Management

- 1. The Republic of Panama, as territorial sovereign, grants to the United States of America the rights to manage, operate, and maintain the Panama Canal, its complementary works, installations, and equipment and to provide for the orderly transit of vessels through the Panama Canal. The United States of America accepts the grant of such rights and undertakes to exercise them in accordance with this Treaty and related agreements.

2. In carrying out the foregoing responsibilities, the United States of America may:

   ○ (a) Use for the aforementioned purposes, without cost except as provided in this Treaty, the various installations and areas (including the Panama

Canal) and waters, described in the Agreement in Implementation of this Article, signed this date, as well as such other areas and installations as are made available to the United States of America under this Treaty and related agreements, and take the measures necessary to ensure sanitation of such areas;

(b) Make such improvements and alterations to the aforesaid installations and areas as it deems appropriate, consistent with the terms of this Treaty;

(c) Make and enforce all rules pertaining the passage of vessels through the Canal and other rules with respect to navigation and maritime matters, in accordance with this Treaty and related agreements. The Republic of Panama will lend its cooperation, when necessary, in the enforcement of such rules;

(d) Establish, modify, collect and retain tolls for the use of the Panama Canal, and other charges, and establish and modify methods of their assessment;

(e) Regulate relations with employees of the United States Government;

(f) Provide supporting services to facilitate the performance of its responsibilities under this Article;

(g) Issue and enforce regulations for the exercise of the rights and responsibilities of the United States of America under this Treaty and related agreements. The Republic of Panama will lend its cooperation, when necessary, in the enforcement of such rules; and

(h) Exercise any other right granted under this Treaty, or otherwise agreed upon between the two Parties.

3. Pursuant to the foregoing grant of rights, the United States of America shall, in accordance with the terms of this Treaty and the provisions of United States law, carry out its responsibilities by means of a United States Government agency called the Panama Canal Commission, which shall be constituted by and in conformity with the laws of the United States of America.

○ (a) The Panama Canal Commission shall be supervised by a Board composed of nine members, five of whom shall be nationals of the United States of America, and four of whom shall be Panamanian nationals proposed by the Republic of Panama for appointment to such positions by the United States of America in a timely manner.

(b) Should the Republic of Panama request the United States of America to remove a Panamanian national from membership on the Board, the United States of America shall agree to such request. In that event, the Republic of Panama shall propose another Panamanian national for appointment by the United States of America to such position in a timely manner. In case of removal of a Panamanian member of the Board on the initiative of the United States of America, both Parties will consult in advance in order to reach agreement concerning such removal, and the Republic of Panama shall propose another Panamanian national for appointment by the United States of America in his stead.

(c) The United States of America shall employ a national of the United States of America as Administrator of the Panama Canal Commission, and a Panamanian national as Deputy Administrator, through December 31, 1989. Beginning January 1, 1990, a Panamanian national shall be employed as the Administrator and a national of the United States of America shall occupy the position of Deputy Administrator. Such Panamanian nationals shall be proposed to the United States of America by the Republic of Panama for appointment to such positions by the United States of America.

(d) Should the United States of America remove the Panamanian national from his position as Deputy Administrator, or Administrator, the Republic of Panama shall propose another Panamanian national for appointment to such position by the United States of America.

4. An illustrative description of the activities the Panama Canal Commission will perform in carrying out the responsibilities and rights of the United States of America under this Article is set forth at the Annex. Also set forth in the Annex are procedures for the discontinuance or transfer of those activities performed prior to the entry into force of this Treaty by the Panama Canal Company or the Canal Zone Government which are not to be carried out by the Panama Canal Commission.

5. The Panama Canal Commission shall reimburse the Republic of Panama for the costs incurred by the Republic of Panama in providing the following public services in the Canal operation areas and in housing areas set forth in the Agreement in Implementation of Article III of this Treaty and occupied by both United States and Panamanian citizen employees of the Panama Canal Commission: police, fire protection, street maintenance, street lighting, street cleaning, traffic management and garbage collection. The Panama Canal Commission shall pay the Republic of Panama the sum of ten million United States dollars (US$10,000,000) per annum for the foregoing services. It is agreed that every three years from the date that this Treaty enters into force, the costs involved in furnishing said services shall be reexamined to determine whether adjustment of the annual payment should be made because of inflation and other relevant factors affecting the cost of such services.

6. The Republic of Panama shall be responsible for providing, in all areas comprising the former Canal Zone, services of a general jurisdictional nature

such as customs and immigration, postal services, courts and licensing, in accordance with this Treaty and related agreements.

7. The United States of America and the Republic of Panama shall establish a Panama Canal Consultative Committee, composed of an equal number of high-level representatives of the United States of America and the Republic of Panama, and which may appoint such subcommittees as it may deem appropriate. This Committee shall advise the United States of America and the Republic of Panama on matters of policy affecting the Canal's operation. In view of both Parties' special interest in the continuity and efficiency of the Canal operation in the future, the Committee shall advise on matters such as general tolls policy, employment and training policies to increase the participation of Panamanian nationals in the operation of the Canal, and international policies on matters concerning the Canal. The Committee's recommendations shall be transmitted to the two Governments, which shall give such recommendations full consideration in the formulation of such policy decisions.

8. In addition to the participation of Panamanian nationals at high management levels of the Panama Canal Commission, as provided for in paragraph 3 of this Article, there shall be growing participation of Panamanian nationals at all other levels and areas of employment in the aforesaid commission, with the objective of preparing, in an orderly and efficient fashion, for the assumption by the Republic of Panama of full responsibility for the management, operation and maintenance of the Canal upon the termination of this Treaty.

9. The use of the areas, waters and installations with respect to which the United States of America is granted rights pursuant to this Article, and the rights and legal status of United States Government agencies and employees operating in the Republic of Panama pursuant to this Article, shall be governed by Agreement in Implementation of this Article, signed this date.

10. Upon entry into force of this Treaty, the United States Government agencies known as the Panama Canal Company and the Canal Zone Government shall cease to operate within the territory of the Republic of Panama that formerly constituted the Canal Zone.

Article IV: Protection and Defense

- 1. The United States of America and the Republic of Panama commit themselves to protect and defend the Panama Canal. Each Party shall act, in accordance with its constitutional processes, to meet the danger resulting from an armed attack or other actions which threaten the security of the Panama Canal or of ships transiting it.

  2. For the duration of this Treaty, the United States of America shall have primary responsibility to protect and defend the Canal. The rights of the

United States of America to station, train, and move military forces within the Republic of Panama are described in the Agreement in Implementation of this Article, signed this date. The use of areas and installations and the legal status of the armed forces of the United States of America in the Republic of Panama shall be governed by the aforesaid Agreement.

3. In order to facilitate the participation and cooperation of the armed forces of both Parties in the protection and defense of the Canal, the United States of America and the Republic of Panama shall establish a Combined Board comprised of an equal number of senior military representatives of each Party. These representatives shall be charged by their respective governments with consulting and cooperating on all matters pertaining to the protection and defense of the Canal, and with planning for actions to be taken in concert for that purpose. Such combined protection and defense arrangements shall not inhibit the identity or lines of authority of the armed forces of the United States of America or the Republic of Panama. The Combined Board shall provide for coordination and cooperation concerning such matters as:

    ○ (a) The preparation of contingency plans for the protection and defense of the Canal based upon the cooperative efforts of the armed forces of both Parties;

    (b) The planning and conduct of combined military exercises; and

    (c) The conduct of United States and Panamanian military operations with respect to the protection and defense of the Canal.

4. The Combined Board shall, at five-year intervals throughout the duration of this Treaty, review the resources being made available by the two Parties for the protection and defense of the Canal. Also, the Combined Board shall make appropriate recommendations to the two Governments respecting projected requirements, the efficient utilization of available resources of the two Parties, and other matters of mutual interest with respect to the protection and defense of the Canal.

5. To the extent possible consistent with its primary responsibility for the protection and defense of the Panama Canal, the United States of America will endeavor to maintain its armed forces in the Republic of Panama in normal times at a level not in excess of that of the armed forces of the United States of America in the territory of the former Canal Zone immediately prior to the entry into force of this Treaty.

Article V: Principle of Non-Intervention

Employees of the Panama Canal Commission, their dependents and designated contractors of the Panama Canal Commission, who are nationals of the United States of America, shall respect the laws of the Republic of Panama and shall abstain from any activity incompatible with the spirit of this Treaty. Accordingly, they shall abstain from any political activity in the Republic of Panama as well as from any intervention in the internal affairs of the Republic of Panama. The United States of America shall take all measures within its authority to ensure that the provisions of this Article are fulfilled.

Article VI: Protection of the Environment

- 1. The United States of America and the Republic of Panama commit themselves to implement this Treaty in a manner consistent with the protection of the natural environment of the Republic of Panama. To this end, they shall consult and cooperate with each other in all appropriate ways to ensure that they shall give due regard to the protection and conservation of the environment.

- 2. A Joint Commission on the Environment shall be established with equal representation from the United States and the Republic of Panama, which shall periodically review the implementation of this Treaty and shall recommend as appropriate to the two Governments ways to avoid or, should this not be possible, to mitigate the adverse environmental impacts which might result from their respective actions pursuant to the Treaty.

- 3. The United States of America and the Republic of Panama shall furnish the Joint Commission on the Environment complete information on any action taken in accordance with this Treaty which, in the judgment of both, might have a significant effect on the environment. Such information shall be made available to the Commission as far in advance of the contemplated action as possible to facilitate the study by the Commission of any potential environmental problems and to allow for consideration of the recommendation of the Commission before the contemplated action is carried out.

Article VII: Flags

- 1. The entire territory of the Republic of Panama, including the areas the use of which the Republic of Panama makes available to the United States of America pursuant to this Treaty and related agreements, shall be under the flag of the Republic of Panama, and consequently such flag always shall occupy the position of honor.

- 2. The flag of the United States of America may be displayed, together with the flag of the Republic of Panama, at the headquarters of the Panama Canal Commission, at the site of the Combined Board, and as provided in the Agreement in Implementation of Article IV of this Treaty.

- 3. The flag of the United States of America also may be displayed at other places and on some occasions, as agreed by both Parties.

Article VIII: Privileges and Immunities

- 1. The installations owned or used by the agencies or instrumentalities of the United States of America operating in the Republic of Panama pursuant to this Treaty and related agreements, and their official archives and documents, shall be inviolable. The two Parties shall agree on procedures to be followed in the conduct of any criminal investigation at such locations by the Republic of Panama.

2. Agencies and instrumentalities of the Government of the United States of America operating in the Republic of Panama pursuant to this Treaty and related agreements shall be immune from the jurisdiction of the Republic of Panama.

3. In addition to such other privileges and immunities as are afforded to employees of the United States Government and their dependents pursuant to this Treaty, the United States of America may designate up to twenty officials of the Panama Canal Commission who, along with their dependents, shall enjoy the privileges and immunities accorded to diplomatic agents and their dependents under international law and practice. The United States of America shall furnish to the Republic of Panama a list of the names of said officials and their dependents, identifying the positions they occupy in the Government of the United States of America, and shall keep such list current at all times.

Article IX: Applicable Laws and Law Enforcement

- 1. In accordance with the provisions of this Treaty and related agreements, the law of the Republic of Panama shall apply in the areas made available for the use of the United States of America pursuant to this Treaty. The law of the Republic of Panama shall be applied to matters or events which occurred in the former Canal Zone prior to the entry into force of this Treaty only to the extent specifically provided in prior treaties and agreements.

2. Natural or juridical persons who, on the date of entry into force of this Treaty, are engaged in business or non-profit activities at locations in the former Canal Zone may continue such business or activities at those locations under the same terms and conditions prevailing prior to the entry into force of this Treaty for a thirty-month transition period from its entry into force. The Republic of Panama shall maintain the same operating conditions as those applicable to the aforementioned enterprises prior to the entry into force of this Treaty in order that they may receive licenses to do business in the Republic of Panama subject to their compliance with the requirements of its law. Thereafter, such persons shall receive the same treatment under the law of the Republic of Panama as similar enterprises already established in the rest of the territory of the Republic of Panama without discrimination.

3. The rights of ownership, as recognized by the United States of America, enjoyed by natural or juridical private persons in buildings and other improvements to real property located in the former Canal Zone shall be recognized by the Republic of Panama in conformity with its laws.

4. With respect to buildings and other improvements to real property located in the Canal operating areas, housing areas or other areas subject to the licensing procedure established in Article IV of the Agreement in Implementation of Article III of this Treaty, the owners shall be authorized to continue using the land upon which their property is located in accordance with the procedures established in that Article.

5. With respect to buildings and other improvements to real property located in areas of the former Canal Zone to which the aforesaid licensing procedure is not applicable, or may cease to be applicable during the lifetime or upon termination of this Treaty, the owners may continue to use the land upon which their property is located, subject to the payment of a reasonable charge to the Republic of Panama. Should the Republic of Panama decide to sell such land, the owners of the buildings or other improvements located thereon shall be offered a first option to purchase such land at a reasonable cost. In the case of non-profit enterprises, such as churches and fraternal organizations, the cost of purchase will be nominal in accordance with the prevailing practice in the rest of the territory of the Republic of Panama.

6. If any of the aforementioned persons are required by the Republic of Panama to discontinue their activities or vacate their property for public purposes, they shall be compensated at fair market value by the Republic of Panama.

7. The provisions of paragraphs 2–6 above shall apply to natural or juridical persons who have been engaged in business or non-profit activities at locations in the former Canal Zone for at least six months prior to the date of signature of this Treaty.

8. The Republic of Panama shall not issue, adopt or enforce any law, decree, regulation, or international agreement or take any other action which purports to regulate or would otherwise interfere with the exercise on the part of the United States of America of any right granted under this Treaty or related agreements.

9. Vessels transiting the Canal, and cargo, passengers and crews carried on such vessels shall be exempt from any taxes, fees, or other charges by the Republic of Panama. However, in the event such vessels call at a Panamanian port, they may be assessed charges thereto, such as charges for services provided to the vessel. The Republic of Panama may also require the passengers and crew disembarking from such vessels to pay such taxes, fees and charges as are established under Panamanian law for persons entering its territory. Such taxes, fees and charges shall be assessed on a nondiscriminatory basis.

10. The United States of America and the Republic of Panama will cooperate in taking such steps as may from time to time be necessary to guarantee the security of the Panama Canal Commission, its property, its employees and their dependents, and their property, the Forces of the United States of

America and the members thereof, the civilian component of the United States Forces, the dependents of members of the Forces and civilian component, and their property, and the contractors of the Panama Canal Commission and of the United States Forces, their dependents, and their property. The Republic of Panama will seek from its Legislative Branch such legislation as may be needed to carry out the foregoing purposes and to punish any offenders.

11. The Parties shall conclude an agreement whereby nationals of either State, who are sentenced by the courts of the other State, and who are not domiciled therein, may elect to serve their sentences in their State of nationality.

Article X: Employment with the Panama Canal Commission

- 1. In exercising its rights and fulfilling its responsibilities as the employer, the United States of America shall establish employment and labor regulations which shall contain the terms, conditions and prerequisites for all categories of employees of the Panama Canal Commission. These regulations shall be provided to the Republic of Panama prior to their entry into force.

2. (a) The regulations shall establish a system of preference when hiring employees, for Panamanian applicants possessing the skills and qualifications required for employment by the Panama Canal Commission. The United States of America shall endeavor to ensure that the number of Panamanian nationals employed by the Panama Canal Commission in relation to the total number of its employees will conform to the proportion established for foreign enterprises under the law of the Republic of Panama.

   - (b) The terms and conditions of employment to be established will in general be no less favorable to persons already employed by the Panama Canal Company or Canal Zone Government prior to the entry into force of this Treaty, than those in effect immediately prior to that date.

3. (a) The United States of America shall establish an employment policy for the Panama Canal Commission that shall generally limit the recruitment of personnel outside the Republic of Panama to persons possessing requisite skills and qualifications which are not available in the Republic of Panama.

   - (b) The United States of America will establish training programs for Panamanian employees and apprentices in order to increase the number of Panamanian nationals qualified to assume positions with the Panama Canal Commission, as positions become available.

   - (c) Within five years from the entry into force of this Treaty, the number of United States nationals employed by the Panama Canal Commission who were previously employed by the Panama Canal Company shall be at least twenty percent less than the total number of United States nationals working for the Panama Canal Company immediately prior to the entry into force of this Treaty.

    (d) The United States of America shall periodically inform the Republic of Panama, through the Coordinating Committee, established pursuant to the Agreement in Implementation of Article III of this Treaty, of available positions within the Panama Canal Commission. The Republic of Panama shall similarly provide the United States of America any information it may have as to the availability of Panamanian nationals claiming to have skills and qualifications that might be required by the Panama Canal Commission, in order that the United States of America may take this information into account.

4. The United States of America will establish qualification standards for skills, training, and experience required by the Panama Canal Commission. In establishing such standards, to the extent they include a requirement for a professional license, the United States of America, without prejudice to its right to require additional professional skills and qualifications, shall recognize the professional licenses issued by the Republic of Panama.

5. The United States of America shall establish a policy for the periodic rotation, at a maximum of every five years, of United States citizen employees and other non-Panamanian employees, hired after the entry into force of this Treaty. It is recognized that certain exceptions to the said policy of rotation may be made for sound administrative reasons, such as in the case of employees holding positions requiring certain non-transferable or non-recruitable skills.

6. With regard to wages and fringe benefits, there shall be no discrimination on the basis of nationality, sex, or race. Payments by the Panama Canal Commission of additional remuneration, or the provision of other benefits, such as home leave benefits, to United States nationals employed prior to entry into force of this Treaty, or to persons of any nationality, including Panamanian nationals who are thereafter recruited outside of the Republic of Panama and who change their place of residence, shall not be considered to be discrimination for the purpose of this paragraph.

7. Persons employed by the Panama Canal Commission or Canal Zone Government prior to the entry into force of this Treaty, who are displaced from their employment as a result of the discontinuance by the United States of America of certain activities pursuant to this Treaty, will be placed by the United States of America, to the maximum extent feasible, in other appropriate jobs with the Government of the United States in accordance with United States Civil Service regulations. For such persons who are not United States nationals, placement efforts will be confined to United States Government activities located within the Republic of Panama. Likewise, persons previously employed in activities for which the Republic of Panama

assumes responsibility as a result of this Treaty will be continued in their employment to the maximum extent feasible by the Republic of Panama. The Republic of Panama shall, to the maximum extent feasible, ensure that the terms and conditions of employment applicable to personnel employed in the activities for which it assumed responsibility are not less favorable than those in effect immediately prior to the entry into force of this Treaty. Non– United States nationals employed by the Panama Canal Company or Canal Zone Government prior to the entry into force of this Treaty who are involuntarily separated from their positions because of the discontinuance of an activity by reason of this Treaty, who are not entitled to an immediate annuity under the United States Civil Service Retirement System, and for whom continued employment in the Republic of Panama by the Government of the United States of America is not practicable, will be provided special job placement assistance by the Republic of Panama for employment in positions for which they may be qualified by experience and training.

8. The Parties agree to establish a system whereby the Panama Canal Commission may, if deemed mutually convenient or desirable by the two Parties, assign certain employees of the Panama Canal Commission, for a limited period of time, to assist in the operation of activities transferred to the responsibility of the Republic of Panama as a result of this Treaty or related agreements. The salaries and other costs of employment of any such persons assigned to provide such assistance shall be reimbursed to the United States of America by the Republic of Panama.

9. (a) The right of employees to negotiate collective contracts with the Panama Canal Commission is recognized. Labor relations with employees of the Panama Canal Commission shall be conducted in accordance with forms of collective bargaining established by the United States of America after consultation with employee unions. (b) Employee unions shall have the right to affiliate with international labor organizations.

10. The United States of America will provide an appropriate early optional retirement program for all persons employed by the Panama Canal Company or Canal Zone Government immediately prior to the entry into force of this Treaty. In this regard, taking into account the unique circumstances created by the provisions of this Treaty, including its duration, and their effect upon such employees, the United States of America shall, with respect to them:

    o (a) determine that conditions exist which invoke applicable United States law permitting early retirement annuities and apply such law for a substantial period of the duration of the treaty;

    (b) seek special legislation to provide more liberal entitlement to, and calculation of, retirement annuities than is currently provided for by law.

Article XI: Provisions for the Transition Period

- 1. The Republic of Panama shall reassume plenary jurisdiction over the former Canal Zone upon entry into force of this Treaty and in accordance with its terms. In order to provide for an orderly transition to the full application of the jurisdictional arrangements established by this Treaty and related agreements, the provisions of this Article shall become applicable upon the date this Treaty enters into force, and shall remain in effect for thirty calendar months. The authority granted in this Article to the United States of America for this transition period shall supplement, and is not intended to limit, the full application and effect of the rights and authority granted to the United States of America elsewhere in this Treaty and in related agreements.

  2. During this transition period, the criminal and civil laws of the United States of America shall apply concurrently with those of the Republic of Panama in certain of the areas and installations made available for the use of the United States of America pursuant to this Treaty, in accordance with the following provisions:

      ○ (a) The Republic Panama permits the authorities of the United States of America to have the primary right to exercise criminal jurisdiction over United States citizen employees of the Panama Canal Commission and their dependents, and members of the United States Forces and civilian component and their dependents, in the following cases:

        ■ (i) for any offense committed during the transition period within such areas and installations, and

          (ii) for any offense committed prior to that period in the former Canal Zone.

      ○ The Republic of Panama shall have the primary right to exercise jurisdiction over all other offenses committed by such persons, except as otherwise agreed.

      ○ (b) Either Party may waive its primary right to exercise jurisdiction in a specific case or category of cases.

  3. The United States of America shall retain the right to exercise jurisdiction in criminal cases relating to offenses committed prior to the entry into force of this Treaty in violation of the laws applicable in the former Canal Zone.

  4. For the transition period, the United States of America shall retain police authority and maintain a police force in the aforementioned areas and installations. In such areas, the police authorities of the United States of America may take into custody any person not subject to their primary jurisdiction if such person is believed to have committed or to be committing an offense against applicable laws or regulations, and shall promptly transfer custody to the police authorities of the Republic of Panama. The United States of America and the Republic of Panama shall establish joint police

patrols in agreed areas. Any arrests conducted by a joint patrol shall be the responsibility of the patrol member or members representing the Party having primary jurisdiction over the person or persons arrested.

5. The courts of the United States of America and related personnel, functioning in the former Canal Zone immediately prior to the entry into force of this Treaty, may continue to function during the transition period for the judicial enforcement of the jurisdiction to be exercised by the United States of America in accordance with this Article.

6. In civil cases, the civilian courts of the United States of America in the Republic of Panama shall have no jurisdiction over new cases of a private civil nature, but shall retain full jurisdiction during the transition period to dispose of any civil cases, including admiralty cases, already instituted and pending before the courts prior to the entry into force of this Treaty.

7. The laws, regulations, and administrative authority of the United States of America applicable in the former Canal Zone immediately prior to the entry into force of this Treaty shall, to the extent not inconsistent with this Treaty and related agreements, continue in force for the purpose of the exercise by the United States of America of law enforcement and judicial jurisdiction only during the transition period. The United States of America may amend, repeal or otherwise change such laws, regulations and administrative authority. The two Parties shall consult concerning procedural and substantive matters relative to the implementation of this Article, including the disposition of cases pending at the end of the transition period and, in this respect, may enter into appropriate agreements by an exchange of notes or other instrument.

8. During this transition period, the United States of America may continue to incarcerate individuals in the areas and installations made available for the use of the United States of America by the Republic of Panama pursuant to this Treaty and related agreements, or to transfer them to penal facilities in the United States of America to serve their sentences.

Article XII: A Sea-Level Canal or a Third Lane of Locks

- 1. The United States of America and the Republic of Panama recognize that a sea-level canal may be important for international navigation in the future. Consequently, during the duration of this Treaty, both Parties commit themselves to study jointly the feasibility of a sea-level canal in the Republic of Panama, and in the event they determine that such a waterway is necessary, they shall negotiate terms, agreeable to both Parties, for its construction.

2. The United States of America and the Republic of Panama agree on the following:

   ○ a) No new interoceanic canal shall be constructed in the territory of the Republic of Panama during the duration of this Treaty, except in accordance with the provisions of this Treaty, or as the two Parties may otherwise agree; and

    (b) During the duration of this Treaty, the United States of America shall not negotiate with third States for the right to construct an interoceanic canal on any other route in the Western Hemisphere, except as the two Parties may otherwise agree.

3. The Republic of Panama grants to the United States of America the right to add a third lane of locks to the existing Panama Canal. This right may be exercised at any time during the duration of this Treaty, provided that the United States of America has delivered to the Republic of Panama copies of the plans for such construction.

4. In the event the United States of America exercises the right granted in paragraph 3 above, it may use for that purpose, in addition to the areas otherwise made available to the United States of America pursuant to this Treaty, such other areas as the two Parties may agree upon. The terms and conditions applicable to Canal operating areas made available by the Republic of Panama for the use of the United States of America pursuant to Article III of this Treaty shall apply in a similar manner to such additional areas.

5. In the construction of the aforesaid works, the United States of America shall not use nuclear excavation techniques without the previous consent of the Republic of Panama.

Article XIII: Property Transfer and Economic Participation by the Republic of Panama

- 1. Upon termination of this Treaty, the Republic of Panama shall assume total responsibility for the management, operation, and maintenance of the Panama Canal, which shall be turned over in operating condition and free of liens and debts, except as the two Parties may otherwise agree.

  2. The United States of America transfers, without charge, to the Republic of Panama all right, title and interest the United States of America may have with respect to all real property, including non-removable improvements thereon, as set forth below:

    ○ (a) Upon the entry into force of this Treaty, the Panama Railroad and such property that was located in the former Canal Zone but that is not within the land and water areas the use of which is made available to the United States of America pursuant to this Treaty. However, it is agreed that the transfer on such date shall not include buildings and other facilities, except housing, the use of which is retained by the United States of America pursuant to this Treaty and related agreements, outside such areas;

        (b) Such property located in an area or a portion thereof at such time as the use by the United States of America of such area or portion thereof ceases pursuant to agreement between the two Parties.

(c) Housing units made available for occupancy by members of the Armed Forces of the Republic of Panama in accordance with paragraph 5(b) of Annex B to the Agreement in Implementation of Article IV of this Treaty at such time as such units are made available to the Republic of Panama.

(d) Upon termination of this Treaty, all real property and non-removable improvements that were used by the United States of America for the purposes of this Treaty and related agreements and equipment related to the management, operation and maintenance of the Canal remaining in the Republic of Panama.

3. The Republic of Panama agrees to hold the United States of America harmless with respect to any claims which may be made by third parties relating to rights, title and interest in such property.

4. The Republic of Panama shall receive, in addition, from the Panama Canal Commission a just and equitable return on the national resources which it has dedicated to the efficient management, operation, maintenance, protection and defense of the Panama Canal, in accordance with the following:

o (a) An annual amount to be paid out of Canal operating revenues computed at a rate of thirty hundredths of a United States dollar (US$0.30) per Panama Canal net ton, or its equivalency, for each vessel transiting the Canal after the entry into force of this Treaty, for which tolls are charged. The rate of thirty hundredths of a United States dollar (US$0.30) per Panama Canal net ton, or its equivalency, will be adjusted to reflect changes in the United States wholesale price index for total manufactured goods during biennial periods. The first adjustment shall take place five years after entry into force of this Treaty, taking into account the changes that occurred in such price index during the preceding two years. Thereafter, successive adjustments shall take place at the end of each biennial period. If the United States of America should decide that another indexing method is preferable, such method shall be proposed to the Republic of Panama and applied if mutually agreed.

(b) A fixed annuity of ten million United States dollars (US$10,000,000) to be paid out of Canal operating revenues. This amount shall constitute a fixed expense of the Panama Canal Commission.

(c) An annual amount of up to ten million United States dollars (US$10,000,000) per year, to be paid out of Canal operating revenues to the extent that such revenues exceed expenditures of the Panama Canal Commission including amounts paid pursuant to this Treaty. In the event Canal operating revenues in any year do not produce a surplus sufficient to cover this payment, the unpaid balance shall be paid from operating surpluses in future years in a manner to be mutually agreed.

Article XIV: Settlement of Disputes

In the event that any question should arise between the Parties concerning the interpretation of this Treaty or related agreements, they shall make every effort to resolve the matter through consultation in the appropriate committees established pursuant to this Treaty and related agreements, or, if appropriate, through diplomatic channels. In the event the Parties are unable to resolve a particular matter through such means, they may, in appropriate cases, agree to submit the matter to conciliation, mediation, arbitration, or such other procedure for the peaceful settlement of the dispute as they may mutually deem appropriate. DONE at Washington, this 7th day of September, 1977 in duplicate, in the English and Spanish languages, both texts being equally authentic.

Annex: Procedures for the Cessation or Transfer of Activities Carried Out by the Panama Canal Company and the Canal Zone Government and Illustrative List of the Functions That May Be Performed by the Panama Canal Commission

- 1. The laws of the Republic of Panama shall regulate the exercise of private economic activities within the areas made available by the Republic of Panama for the use of the United States of America pursuant to this Treaty. Natural or juridical persons who, at least six months prior to the date of signature of this Treaty, were legally established and engaged in the exercise of economic activities in accordance with the provisions of paragraphs 2–7 of Article IX of this Treaty.

  2. The Panama Canal Commission shall not perform governmental or commercial functions as stipulated in paragraph 4 of this Annex, provided, however, that this shall not be deemed to limit in any way the right of the United States of America to perform those functions that may be necessary for the efficient management, operation and maintenance of the Canal.

  3. It is understood that the Panama Canal Commission, in the exercise of the rights of the United States of America with respect to the management, operation and maintenance of the Canal, may perform functions such as are set forth below by way of illustration:

    - a. Management of the Canal enterprise.

      b. Aids to navigation in Canal waters and in proximity thereto.

      c. Control of vessel movement.

      d. Operation and maintenance of the locks.

      e. Tug service for the transit of vessels and dredging for the piers and docks of the Panama Canal Commission.

      f. Control of the water levels in Gatun, Alajuela (Madden), and Miraflores Lakes.

      g. Non-commercial transportation services in Canal waters.

h. Meteorological and hydrographic services.

i. Admeasurement.

j. Non-commercial motor transport and maintenance.

k. Industrial security through the use of watchmen.

l. Procurement and warehousing.

m. Telecommunications.

n. Protection of the environment by preventing and controlling the spillage of oil and substances harmful to human or animal life and of the ecological equilibrium in areas used in operation of the Canal and the anchorages.

o. Non-commercial vessel repair.

p. Air conditioning services in Canal installations.

q. Industrial sanitation and health services.

r. Engineering design, construction and maintenance of Panama Canal Commission installations.

s. Dredging of the Canal channel, terminal ports and adjacent waters.

t. Control of the banks and stabilizing of the slopes of the Canal.

u. Non-commercial handling of cargo on the piers and docks of the Panama Canal Commission.

v. Maintenance of public areas of the Panama Canal Commission, such as parks and gardens.

w. Generation of electric power.

x. Purification and supply of water.

y. Marine salvage in Canal waters.

z. Such other functions as may be necessary or appropriate to carry out, in conformity with this Treaty and related agreements, the rights and responsibilities of the United States of America with respect to the management, operation and maintenance of the Panama Canal.

4. The following activities and operations carried out by the Panama Canal Company and the Canal Zone Government shall not be carried out by the Panama Canal Commission, effective upon the dates indicated herein:

   ○ (a) Upon the date of entry into force of this Treaty:

     ▪ (i) Wholesale and retail sales, including those through commissaries, food stores, department stores, optical shops and pastry shops;

     (ii) The production of food and drink, including milk products and bakery products;

     (iii) The operation of public restaurants and cafeterias and the sale of articles through vending machines;

(iv) The operation of movie theaters, bowling alleys, pool rooms and other recreational and amusement facilities for the use of which a charge is payable;

(v) The operation of laundry and dry cleaning plants other than those operated for official use;

(vi) The repair and service of privately owned automobiles or the sale of petroleum or lubricants thereto, including the operation of gasoline stations, repair garages and tire repair and recapping facilities, and the repair and service of other privately owned property, including appliances, electronic devices, boats, motors, and furniture;

(vii) The operation of cold storage and freezer plants other than those operated for official use;

(viii) The operation of freight houses other than those operated for official use;

(ix) The operation of commercial services to and supply of privately owned and operated vessels, including the constitution of vessels, the sale of petroleum and lubricants and the provision of water, tug services not related to the Canal or other United States Government operations, and repair of such vessels, except in situations where repairs may be necessary to remove disabled vessels from the Canal;

(x) Printing services other than for official use;

(xi) Maritime transportation for the use of the general public;

(xii) Health and medical services provided to individuals, including hospitals, leprosariums, veterinary, mortuary and cemetery services;

(xiii) Educational services not for professional training, including schools and libraries;

(xiv) Postal services;

(xv) Immigration, customs and quarantine controls, except those measures necessary to ensure the sanitation of the Canal;

(xvi) Commercial pier and dock services, such as the handling of cargo and passengers; and

(xvii) Any other commercial activity of a similar nature, not related to the management, operation or maintenance of the Canal.

- (b) Within thirty calendar months from the date of entry into force of this Treaty, governmental services such as:

  - (i) Police;

  (ii) Courts; and

  (iii) Prison system.

5. (a) With respect to those activities or functions described in paragraph 4 above, or otherwise agreed upon by the two Parties, which are to be assumed by the Government of the Republic of Panama or by private persons subject to its authority, the two Parties shall consult prior to the discontinuance of such activities or functions by the Panama Canal Commission to develop appropriate arrangements for the orderly transfer and continued efficient operation or conduct thereof.

     ○ (b) In the event that appropriate arrangements cannot be arrived at to ensure the continued performance of a particular activity or function described in paragraph 4 above which is necessary to the efficient management, operation or maintenance of the Canal, the Panama Canal Commission may, to the extent consistent with the other provisions of this Treaty and related agreements, continue to perform such activity or function until such arrangements can be made.

United States Senate Modifications (Incorporated Into the June 1978 Instruments of Ratification)

(a) RESERVATIONS:

- (1) Pursuant to its adherence to the principle of nonintervention, any action taken by the United States of America in the exercise of its rights to assure that the Panama Canal shall remain open, neutral, secure, and accessible, pursuant to the provisions of the Panama Canal Treaty, the Treaty Concerning the Permanent Neutrality and Operation of the Panama Canal, and the resolutions of ratification thereto, shall be only for the purpose of assuring that the Canal shall remain open, neutral, secure, and accessible, and shall not have as its purpose or be interpreted as a right of intervention in the internal affairs of the Republic of Panama or interference with its political independence or sovereign integrity.

- (2) The instruments of ratification of the Panama Canal Treaty to be exchanged by the United States of America and the Republic of Panama shall each include provisions whereby each Party agrees to waive its rights and release the other Party from its obligations under paragraph 2 of Article XII of the Treaty.

- (3) Notwithstanding any provision of the Treaty, no funds may be drawn from the Treasury of the United States of America for payments under paragraph 4 of Article XIII without statutory authorization.

- (4) Any accumulated unpaid balance under paragraph 4(c) of Article XIII of the Treaty at the date of termination of the Treaty shall be payable only to the extent of any operating surplus in the last year of the duration of the Treaty, and nothing in such paragraph may be constructed as obligating the United States of America to pay, after the date of the termination of the Treaty, any such unpaid balance which shall have accrued before such date.

(5) Exchange of the instruments of ratification of the Panama Canal Treaty and of the Treaty Concerning the Permanent Neutrality and Operation of the Panama Canal shall not be effective earlier than March 31, 1979, and such Treaties shall not enter into force prior to October 1, 1979, unless legislation necessary to implement the provisions of the Panama Canal Treaty shall have been enacted by the Congress of the United States of America before March 31, 1979.

(6) After the date of entry into force of the Treaty, the Panama Canal Commission shall, unless otherwise provided by legislation enacted by the Congress of the United States of America, be obligated to reimburse the Treasury of the United States of America, as nearly as possible, for the interest cost of the funds or other assets directly invested in the Commission by the Government of the United States of America and for the interest cost of the funds or other assets directly invested in the predecessor Panama Canal Company by the Government of the United States of America and not reimbursed before the date of entry into force of the Treaty. Such reimbursement for such interest costs shall be made at a rate determined by the Secretary of the Treasury of the United States of America and at annual intervals to the extent earned, and if not earned, shall be made from subsequent earnings. For purposes of this reservation, the phrase "funds or other assets directly invested" shall have the same meaning as the phrase "net direct investment" has under section 62 of title 2 of the Canal Zone Code.

(b) UNDERSTANDINGS:

• (1) Before the first day of the three-year period beginning on the date of entry into force of the Treaty and before each three-year period following thereafter, the two Parties shall agree upon the specific levels and quality of services, as are referred to in paragraph 5 of Article III of the Treaty, to be provided during the following three-year period and, except for the first three-year period, on the reimbursement to be made for the costs of such services, such services to be limited to such as are essential to the effective functioning of the Canal operating areas and the housing areas referred to in paragraph 5 of Article III. If payments made under paragraph 5 of Article III for the preceding three-year period, including the initial three-year period, exceed or are less than the actual costs to the Republic of Panama for supplying, during such period, the specific levels and quality of services agreed upon, then the Panama Canal Commission shall deduct from or add to the payment required to be made to the Republic of Panama for each of the following three years one-third of such excess or deficit, as the case may be. There shall be an independent and binding audit, conducted by an auditor mutually selected by both Parties, of any costs of services disputed by the two Parties pursuant to the reexamination of such costs provided for in this understanding.

(2) Nothing in paragraph 3, 4, or 5 of Article IV of the Treaty may be construed to limit either the provisions of the first paragraph of Article IV providing that each Party shall act, in accordance with its constitutional processes, to meet danger threatening the security of the Panama Canal, or the provisions of paragraph 2 of Article IV providing that the United States of America shall have primary responsibility to protect and defend the Canal for the duration of the Treaty.

(3) Nothing in paragraph 4(c) of Article XIII of the Treaty shall be construed to limit the authority of the United States of America, through the United States Government agency called the Panama Canal Commission, to make such financial decisions and incur such expenses as are reasonable and necessary for the management, operation, and maintenance of the Panama Canal. In addition, toll rates established pursuant to paragraph 2(d) of Article III need not be set at levels designed to produce revenues to cover the payment to the Republic of Panama described in paragraph 4(c) of Article XIII.

(4) Any agreement concluded pursuant to paragraph II of Article IX of the Treaty with respect to the transfer of prisoners shall be concluded in accordance with the constitutional processes of both Parties.

(5) Nothing in the Treaty, in the Annex or Agreed Minute relating to the Treaty, or in any other agreement relating to the Treaty obligates the United States of America to provide any economic assistance, military grant assistance, security supporting assistance, foreign military sales credits, or international military education and training to the Republic of Panama.

(6) The President shall include all reservations and understandings incorporated by the Senate in this resolution of ratification in the instrument of ratification to be exchanged with the Government of the Republic of Panama.

Treaty Concerning the Permanent Neutrality and Operation of the Panama Canal

The United States of America and the Republic of Panama have agreed upon the following:

Article I

The Republic of Panama declares that the Canal, as an international transit waterway, shall be permanently neutral in accordance with the regime established in this Treaty. The same regime of neutrality shall apply to any other international waterway that may be built either partially or wholly in the territory of the Republic of Panama.

Article II

The Republic of Panama declares the neutrality of the Canal in order that both in time of peace and in time of war it shall remain secure and open to peaceful transit by the vessels of all nations on terms of entire equality, so that there will be no discrimination against any nation, or its citizens or subjects, concerning the conditions or charges of transit, or for any other reason, and so that the Canal, and therefore the Isthmus of Panama, shall not be the target of reprisals in any armed conflict between other nations of the world. The foregoing shall be subject to the following requirements:

- (a) Payment of tolls and other charges for transit and ancillary services, provided they have been fixed in conformity with the provisions of Article III (c);
- (b) Compliance with applicable rules and regulations, provided such rules and regulations are applied in conformity with the provisions of Article III;
- (c) The requirement that transiting vessels commit no acts of hostility while in the Canal; and
- (d) Such other conditions and restrictions as are established by this Treaty.

Article III

- 1. For purposes of the security, efficiency and proper maintenance of the Canal the following rules shall apply:
  - (a) The Canal shall be operated efficiently in accordance with conditions of transit through the Canal, and rules and regulations that shall be just, equitable and reasonable, and limited to those necessary for safe navigation and efficient, sanitary operation of the Canal;
  - (b) Ancillary services necessary for transit through the Canal shall be provided;
  - (c) Tolls and other charges for transit and ancillary services shall be just, reasonable, equitable and consistent with the principles of international law;
  - (d) As a pre-condition of transit, vessels may be required to establish clearly the financial responsibility and guarantees for payment of reasonable and adequate indemnification, consistent with international practice and standards, for damages resulting from acts or omissions of such vessels when passing through the Canal. In the case of vessels owned or operated by a State or for which it has acknowledged responsibility, a certification by that State that it shall observe its obligations under international law to pay for damages resulting from the act or omission of such vessels when passing through the Canal shall be deemed sufficient to establish such financial responsibility;

(e) Vessels of war and auxiliary vessels of all nations shall at all times be entitled to transit the Canal, irrespective of their internal operation, means of propulsion, origin, destination or armament, without being subjected, as a condition of transit, to inspection, search or surveillance. However, such vessels may be required to certify that they have complied with all applicable health, sanitation and quarantine regulations. In addition, such vessels shall be entitled to refuse to disclose their internal operation, origin, armament, cargo or destination. However, auxiliary vessels may be required to present written assurances, certified by an official at a high level of the government of the State requesting the exemption, that they are owned or operated by that government and in this case are being used only on government non-commercial service.

- 2. For the purposes of this Treaty, the terms "Canal," "vessel of war," "auxiliary vessel," "internal operation," "armament" and "inspection" shall have the meanings assigned them in Annex A to this Treaty.

Article IV

The United States of America and the Republic of Panama agree to maintain the regime of neutrality established in this Treaty, which shall be maintained in order that the Canal shall remain permanently neutral, notwithstanding the termination of any other treaties entered into by the two Contracting Parties.

Article V

After the termination of the Panama Canal Treaty, only the Republic of Panama shall operate the Canal and maintain military forces, defense sites and military installations within its national territory.

Article VI

- 1. In recognition of the important contributions of the United States of America and of the Republic of Panama to the construction, operation, maintenance, and protection and defense of the Canal, vessels of war and auxiliary vessels of those nations shall, notwithstanding any other provisions of this Treaty, be entitled to transit the Canal irrespective of their internal operation, means of propulsion, origin, destination, armament or cargo carried. Such vessels of war and auxiliary vessels will be entitled to transit the Canal expeditiously.

- 2. The United States of America, so long as it has responsibility for the operation of the Canal, may continue to provide the Republic of Colombia toll-free transit through the Canal for its troops, vessels and materials of war. Thereafter, the Republic of Panama may provide the Republic of Colombia and the Republic of Costa Rica with the right of toll-free transit.

Article VII

- 1. The United States of America and the Republic of Panama shall jointly sponsor a resolution in the Organization of American States opening to accession by all nations of the world the Protocol to this Treaty whereby all the signatories will adhere to the objective of this Treaty, agreeing to respect the regime of neutrality set forth herein.
  2. The Organization of American States shall act as the depositary for this Treaty and related instruments.

Article VIII

This Treaty shall be subject to ratification in accordance with the constitutional procedures of the two Parties. The instruments of ratification of this Treaty shall be exchanged at Panama at the same time as the instruments of ratification of the Panama Canal Treaty, signed this date, are exchanged. This Treaty shall enter into force, simultaneously with the Panama Canal Treaty, six calendar months from the date of the exchange of the instruments of ratification.

DONE at Washington, this 7th day of September, 1977, in the English and Spanish languages, both texts being equally authentic.

Annex A

- 1. "Canal" includes the existing Panama Canal, the entrances thereto and the territorial seas of the Republic of Panama adjacent thereto, as defined on the map annexed hereto (Annex B), and any other interoceanic waterway in which the United States of America is a participant or in which the United States of America has participated in connection with the construction or financing, that may be operated wholly or partially within the territory of the Republic of Panama, the entrances thereto and the territorial seas adjacent thereto.
  2. "Vessel of war" means a ship belonging to the naval forces of a State, and bearing the external marks distinguishing warships of its nationality, under the command of an officer duly commissioned by the government and whose name appears in the Navy List, and manned by a crew which is under regular naval discipline.
  3. "Auxiliary vessel" means any ship, not a vessel of war, that is owned or operated by a State and used, for the time being, exclusively on government non-commercial service.
  4. "Internal operation" encompasses all machinery and propulsion systems, as well as the management and control of the vessel, including its crew. It does not include the measures necessary to transit vessels under the control of pilots while such vessels are in the Canal.

5. "Armament" means arms, ammunition, implements of war and other equipment of a vessel which possesses characteristics appropriate for use for warlike purposes.

6. "Inspection" includes on-board examination of vessel structure, cargo, armament and internal operation. It does not include those measures strictly necessary for admeasurement, nor those measures strictly necessary to assure safe, sanitary transit and navigation, including examination of deck and visual navigation equipment, nor in the case of live cargoes, such as cattle or other livestock, that may carry communicable diseases, those measures necessary to assure that health and sanitation requirements are satisfied. United States Senate Modifications (Incorporated Into the June 1978 Instruments of Ratification)

(a) AMENDMENTS

- (1) At the end of Article IV, insert the following:

  "A correct and authoritative statement of certain rights and duties of the Parties under the foregoing is contained in the Statement of Understanding issued by the Government of the United States of America on October 14, 1977, and by the Government of the Republic of Panama on October 18, 1977, which is hereby incorporated as an integral part of this Treaty, as follows:

  " 'Under the Treaty Concerning the Permanent Neutrality and Operation of the Panama Canal (the Neutrality Treaty), Panama and the United States have the responsibility to assure that the Panama Canal will remain open and secure to ships of all nations. The correct interpretation of this principle is that each of the two countries shall, in accordance with their respective constitutional processes, defend the Canal against any threat to the regime of neutrality, and consequently shall have the right to act against any aggression or threat directed against the Canal or against the peaceful transit of vessels through the Canal.

  " 'This does not mean, nor shall it be interpreted as, a right of intervention of the United States in the internal affairs of Panama. Any United States action will be directed at insuring that the Canal will remain open, secure, and accessible, and it shall never be directed against the territorial integrity or political independence of Panama.' "

  (2) At the end of the first paragraph of Article VI, insert the following:

  "In accordance with the Statement of Understanding mentioned in Article IV above: 'The Neutrality Treaty provides that the vessels of war and auxiliary vessels of the United States and Panama will be entitled to transit the Canal expeditiously. This is intended, and it shall so be interpreted, to assure the transit of such vessels through the Canal as quickly as possible, without any impediment, with expedited treatment, and in case of need or emergency, to go to the head of the line of vessels in order to transit the Canal rapidly.' "

(b) CONDITIONS:

- (1) Notwithstanding the provisions of Article V or any other provision of the Treaty, if the Canal is closed, or its operations are interfered with, the United States of America and the Republic of Panama shall each independently have the right to take such steps as each deems necessary, in accordance with its constitutional processes, including the use of military force in the Republic of Panama, to reopen the Canal or restore the operations of the Canal, as the case may be.

   (2) The instruments of ratification of the Treaty shall be exchanged only upon the conclusion of a Protocol of Exchange, to be signed by authorized representatives of both Governments, which shall constitute an integral part of the Treaty documents and which shall include the following:

   "Nothing in the Treaty shall preclude the Republic of Panama and the United States of America from making, in accordance with their respective constitutional processes, any agreement or arrangement between the two countries to facilitate performance at any time after December 31, 1999, of their responsibilities to maintain the regime of neutrality established in the Treaty, including agreements or arrangements for the stationing of any United States military forces or the maintenance of defense sites after that date in the Republic of Panama that the Republic of Panama and the United States of America may deem necessary or appropriate."

(c) RESERVATIONS:

- 1) Before the date of entry into force of the Treaty, the two Parties shall begin to negotiate for an agreement under which the American Battle Monuments Commission would, upon the date of entry into force of such agreement and thereafter, administer, free of all taxes and other charges and without compensation to the Republic of Panama and in accordance with the practices, privileges, and immunities associated with the administration of cemeteries outside the United States of America by the American Battle Monuments Commission, including the display of the flag of the United States of America, such part of Corozal Cemetery in the former Canal Zone as encompasses the remains of citizens of the United States of America.

   (2) The flag of the United States of America may be displayed, pursuant to the provisions of paragraph 3 of Article VII of the Panama Canal Treaty, at such part of Corozal Cemetery in the former Canal Zone as encompasses the remains of citizens of the United States of America.

(3) The President—

○ (A) shall have announced, before the date of entry into force of the Treaty, his intention to transfer, consistent with an agreement with the Republic of Panama, and before the date of termination of the Panama Canal Treaty, to the American Battle Monuments Commission the administration of such part of Corozal Cemetery as encompasses the remains of citizens of the United States of America; and

(B) shall have announced, immediately after the date of exchange of instruments of ratification, plans, to be carried out at the expense of the Government of the United States of America, for

■ (i) removing, before the date of entry into force of the Treaty, the remains of citizens of the United States of America from Mount Hope Cemetery to such part of Corozal Cemetery as encompasses such remains, except that the remains of any citizen whose next of kin objects in writing to the Secretary of the Army not later than three months after the date of exchange of the instruments of ratification of the Treaty shall not be removed; and

(ii) transporting to the United States of America for reinterment, if the next of kin so requests, not later than thirty months after the date of entry into force of the Treaty, any such remains encompassed by Corozal Cemetery and, before the date of entry into force of the Treaty, any remains removed from Mount Hope Cemetery pursuant to subclause (i); and

(C) shall have fully advised, before the date of entry into force of the Treaty, the next of kin objecting under clause (B) (i) of all available options and their implications.

(4) To carry out the purposes of Article III of the Treaty of assuring the security, efficiency, and proper maintenance of the Panama Canal, the United States of America and the Republic of Panama, during their respective periods of responsibility for Canal operation and maintenance, shall, unless the amount of the operating revenues of the Canal exceeds the amount needed to carry out the purposes of such Article, use such revenues of the Canal only for purposes consistent with the purposes of Article III.

(d) UNDERSTANDING:

• (1) Paragraph 1 (c) of Article III of the Treaty shall be construed as requiring, before any adjustment in tolls for use of the Canal, that the effects of any such toll adjustment on the trade patterns of the two Parties shall be given full consideration, including consideration of the following factors in a manner consistent with the regime of neutrality:

○ (A) the costs of operating and maintaining the Panama Canal;

(B) the competitive position of the use of the Canal in relation to other
means of transportation;

(C) the interests of both Parties in maintaining their domestic fleets;

(D) the impact of such an adjustment on the various geographic areas of
each of the two Parties; and

(E) the interests of both Parties in maximizing their international
commerce. The United States of America and the Republic of Panama
shall cooperate in exchanging information necessary for the
consideration of such factors.

- (2) The agreement "to maintain the regime of neutrality established in this
Treaty" in Article IV of the Treaty means that either of the two Parties to
the Treaty may, in accordance with its constitutional processes, take
unilateral action to defend the Panama Canal against any threat, as
determined by the Party taking such action.

- (3) The determination of "need or emergency" for the purpose of any vessel
of war or auxiliary vessel of the United States of America or the
Republic of Panama going to the head of the line of vessels in order to
transit the Panama Canal rapidly shall be made by the nation operating
such vessel.

- (4) Nothing in the Treaty, in Annex A or B thereto, in the Protocol relating to
the Treaty, or in any other agreement relating to the Treaty, obligates the
United States of America to provide any economic assistance, military grant
assistance, security supporting assistance, foreign military sales credits, or
international military education and training to the Republic of Panama.

- (5) The President shall include all amendments, conditions, reservations, and
understandings incorporated by the Senate in this resolution of ratification
in the instrument of ratification to be exchanged with the Government of the
Republic of Panama.

Ronald Reagan's Remarks and a Question and Answer Session with Reporters on the Air Traffic Controllers' Strike (1981)

During the Pullman Strike of 1894 the government forced American Railway Union members, who the U.S. attorney general claimed were in violation of the Sherman Anti-Trust Act, to return to work after the railway system shut down when all railroad employees joined the strike. The importance of the transportation system caused the government to intercede. The same problem occurred in 1981 when members of the Air Traffic Controllers Union, in violation of their contract, called for a strike, a tactic intended to ground all planes in the United States. President Ronald Reagan warned the union that he would fire all air traffic controllers who went out on strike and he did so when they ignored his warning; he explained his actions in a press conference on August 3, 1981.

Source: http://www.reagan.utexas.edu/resource/speeches/1981/8038/a.htm.

August 3, 1981

The President. This morning at 7 a.m. the union representing those who man America's air traffic control facilities called a strike. This was the culmination of 7 months of negotiations between the Federal Aviation Administration and the union. At one point in these negotiations agreement was reached and signed by both sides, granting a $40 million increase in salaries and benefits. This is twice what other government employees can expect. It was granted in recognition of the difficulties inherent in the work these people perform. Now, however, the union demands are 17 times what had been agreed to—$681 million. This would impose a tax burden on their fellow citizens which is unacceptable.

I would like to thank the supervisors and controllers who are on the job today, helping to get the nation's air system operating safely. In the New York area, for example, four supervisors were scheduled to report for work, and 17 additionally volunteered. At National Airport a traffic controller told a newsperson he had resigned from the union and reported to work because, "How can I ask my kids to obey the law if I don't?" This is a great tribute to America.

Let me make one thing plain. I respect the right of workers in the private sector to strike. Indeed, as president of my own union, I led the first strike ever called by that union. I guess I'm maybe the first one to ever hold this office who is a lifetime member of an AFL-CIO union. But we cannot compare labor-management relations in the private sector with government. Government cannot close down the assembly line. It has to provide without interruption the protective services which are government's reason for being.

It was in recognition of this that the Congress passed a law forbidding strikes by government employees against the public safety. Let me read the solemn oath taken by each of these employees, a sworn affidavit, when they accepted their jobs: "I am not participating in any strike against the Government of the United States or any agency thereof, and I will not so participate while an employee of the Government of the United States or any agency thereof."

It is for this reason that I must tell those who fail to report for duty this morning they are in violation of the law, and if they do not report for work within 48 hours, they have forfeited their jobs and will be terminated.

Q[uestion]. Mr. President, are you going to order any union members who violate the law to go to jail?

The President. Well, I have some people around here, and maybe I should refer that question to the Attorney General.

Q[uestion]. Do you think that they should go to jail, Mr. President, anybody who violates this law?

The President. I told you what I think should be done. They're terminated.

The Attorney General: Well, as the President has said, striking under these circumstances constitutes a violation of the law, and we intend to initiate in appropriate cases criminal proceedings against those who have violated the law.

Q[uestion]. How quickly will you initiate criminal proceedings, Mr. Attorney General?

The Attorney General: We will initiate those proceedings as soon as we can.

Q[uestion]. Today?

The Attorney General: The process will be underway probably by noon today.

Q[uestion]. Are you going to try and fine the union $1 million per day?

The Attorney General: Well, that's the prerogative of the court. In the event that any individuals are found guilty of contempt of a court order, the penalty for that, of course, is imposed by the court.

Q[uestion]. How much more is the government prepared to offer the union?

The Secretary of Transportation. We think we had a very satisfactory offer on the table. It's twice what other Government employees are going to get—11.4 percent. Their demands were so unreasonable there was no spot to negotiate, when you're talking to somebody 17 times away from where you presently are. We do not plan to increase our offer to the union.

Q[uestion]. Under no circumstances?

The Secretary of Transportation. As far as I'm concerned, under no circumstance.

Q[uestion]. Will you continue to meet with them?

The Secretary of Transportation. We will not meet with the union as long as they're on strike. When they're off of strike, and assuming that they are not decertified, we will meet with the union and try to negotiate a satisfactory contract.

Q[uestion]. Do you have any idea how it's going at the airports around the country?

The Secretary of Transportation. Relatively, it's going quite well. We're operating somewhat in excess of 50 percent capacity. We could increase that. We have determined, until we feel we're in total control of the system, that we will not increase that. Also, as you probably know, we have some rather severe weather in the Midwest, and our first priority is safety.

Q[uestion]. What can you tell us about possible decertification of the union and impoundment of its strike funds?

The Secretary of Transportation. There has been a court action to impound the strike fund of $3.5 million. We are going before the National Labor Relations Authority this morning and ask for decertification of the union.

Q[uestion]. When you say that you're not going to increase your offer, are you referring to the original offer or the last offer which you've made? Is that still valid?

The Secretary of Transportation. The last offer we made in present value was exactly the same as the first offer. Mr. Poli (Robert Poli, Professional Air Traffic Controllers Organization) asked me about 11 o'clock last evening if he could phase the increase in over a period of time. For that reason, we phased it in over a longer period of time. It would have given him a larger increase in terms of where he would be when the next negotiations started, but in present value it was the $40 million originally on the table.

Q[uestion]. Mr. Attorney General, in seeking criminal action against the union leaders, will you seek to put them in jail if they do not order these people back to work?

The Attorney General. Well, we will seek whatever penalty is appropriate under the circumstances in each individual case.

Q[uestion]. Do you think that is an appropriate circumstance?

The Attorney General. It is certainly one of the penalties that is provided for in the law, and in appropriate cases, we could very well seek that penalty.

Q[uestion]. What's appropriate?

The Attorney General. Well, that depends upon the fact of each case.

Q[uestion]. What makes the difference?

Q[uestion]. Can I go back to my "fine" question? How much would you like to see the union fined every day?

The Attorney General. Well, there's no way to answer that question. We would just have to wait until we get into court, see what the circumstances are, and determine what position we would take in the various cases under the facts as they develop.

Q[uestion]. But you won't go to court and ask the court for a specific amount?

The Attorney General. Well, I'm sure we will when we reach that point, but there's no way to pick a figure now.

Q[uestion]. Mr. President, will you delay your trip to California or cancel it if the strike is still on later this week?

The President. If any situation should arise that would require my presence here, naturally I will do that. So, that will be a decision that awaits what's going to happen. May I just—because I have to be back in there for another appointment—may I just say one thing on top of this? With all this talk of penalties and everything else, I hope that you'll emphasize, again, the possibility of termination, because I believe that there are a great many of those people—and they're fine people—who have been swept up in this and probably have not really considered the result—the fact that they had taken an oath, the fact that this is now in violation of the law, as that one supervisor referred to with regard to his children. And I am hoping that they will in a sense remove themselves from the lawbreaker situation by returning to their posts.

I have no way to know whether this had been conveyed to them by their union leaders, who had been informed that this would be the result of a strike.

Q[uestion]. Your deadline is 7 o'clock Wednesday morning for them to return to work?

The President. Forty-eight hours.

The Secretary of Transportation. It's 11 o'clock Wednesday morning.

Q[uestion]. Mr. President, why have you taken such strong action as your first action? Why not some lesser action at this point?

The President. What lesser action can there be? The law is very explicit. They are violating the law. And as I say, we called this to the attention of their leadership. Whether this was conveyed to the membership before they voted to strike, I don't know. But this is one of the reasons why there can be no further negotiation while this situation continues. You can't sit and negotiate with a union that's in violation of the law.

The Secretary of Transportation. And their oath.

The President. And their oath.

Q[uestion]. Are you more likely to proceed in the criminal direction toward the leadership than the rank and file, Mr. President?

The President. Well, that again is not for me to answer.

Q[uestion]. Mr. Secretary, what can you tell us about the possible use of military air controllers—how many, how quickly can they get on the job?

The Secretary of Transportation. In answer to the previous question, we will move both civil and criminal, probably more civil than criminal, and we now have papers in the U.S. attorneys offices, under the Attorney General, in about 20 locations around the country where would be involved two or three principal people.

As far as the military personnel are concerned, they are going to fundamentally be backup to the supervisory personnel. We had 150 on the job, supposedly, about a half-hour ago. We're going to increase that to somewhere between 700 and 850.

Q[uestion]. Mr. Secretary, are you ready to hire other people should these other people not return?

The Secretary of Transportation. Yes, we will, and we hope we do not reach that point. Again as the President said, we're hoping these people come back to work. They do a fine job. If that does not take place, we have a training school, as you know. We will be advertising. We have a number of applicants right now. There's a waiting list in terms of people that want to be controllers, and we'll start retraining and reorganize the entire FAA traffic controller group.

Q[uestion]. Just to clarify, is your deadline 7 a.m. Wednesday or 11 o'clock?

The Secretary of Transportation. It's 11 a.m. Wednesday. The President said 48 hours, and that would be 48 hours.

Q[uestion]. If you actually fire these people, won't it put your air traffic control system in a hole for years to come, since you can't just cook up a controller in—[inaudible]?

The Secretary of Transportation. That obviously depends on how many return to work. Right now we're able to operate the system. In some areas, we've been very gratified by the support we've received. In other areas, we've been disappointed. And until I see the numbers, there's no way I can answer that question.

Q[uestion]. Mr. Lewis, did you tell the union leadership when you were talking to them that their members would be fired if they went out on strike?

The Secretary of Transportation. I told Mr. Poli yesterday that the President gave me three instructions in terms of the firmness of the negotiations: one is there would be no amnesty; the second there would be no negotiations during the strike; and third is that if they went on strike, these people would no longer be government employees.

Q[uestion]. Mr. Secretary, you said no negotiations. What about informal meetings of any kind with Mr. Poli?

The Secretary of Transportation. We will have no meetings until the strike is terminated with the union.

Q[uestion]. Have you served Poli at this point? Has he been served by the Attorney General?

The Attorney General. In the civil action that was filed this morning, the service was made on the attorney for the union, and the court has determined that that was appropriate service on all of the officers of the union.

Q[uestion]. My previous question about whether you're going to take a harder line on the leadership than rank and file in terms of any criminal prosecution, can you give us an answer on that?

The Attorney General. No, I can't answer that except to say that each case will be investigated on its own merits, and action will be taken as appropriate in each of those cases.

Q[uestion]. Mr. Lewis, do you know how many applications for controller jobs you have on file now?

The Secretary of Transportation. I do not know. I'm going to check when I get back. I am aware there's a waiting list, and I do not have the figure. If you care to have that, you can call our office, and we'll tell you. Also, we'll be advertising and recruiting people for this job if necessary.

Q[uestion]. Mr. Secretary, how long are you prepared to hold out if there's a partial but not complete strike?

The Secretary of Transportation. I think the President made it very clear that as of 48 hours from now, if the people are not back on the job, they will not be government employees at any time in the future.

Q[uestion]. How long are you prepared to run the air controller system—[inaudible]?

The Secretary of Transportation. For years, if we have to.

Q[uestion]. How long does it take to train a new controller, from the waiting list?

The Secretary of Transportation. It varies; it depends on the type of center they're going to be in. For someone to start in the system and work through the more minor office types of control situations till they get to, let's say, a Chicago or a Washington National, it takes about 3 years. So in this case, what we'll have to do if some of the major metropolitan areas are shut down or a considerable portion is shut down, we'll be bringing people in from other areas that are qualified and then start bringing people through the training schools in the smaller cities and smaller airports.

Q[uestion]. Mr. Secretary, have you definitely made your final offer to the union?

The Secretary of Transportation. Yes, we have.

Q[uestion]. Thank you.

NOTE: The President read the statement to reporters at 10:55 a.m. in the Rose Garden at the White House.

Byron L. Dorgan's Senate Speech Opposing Financial Services Modernization Act (Gramm-Leach-Bliley) (1999)

With the failure of thousands of banks following the Stock Market Crash of 1929, Congress enacted the Glass-Steagall Act, imposing restrictions on the financial industry and prohibiting banks from underwriting insurance policies or selling securities. The banking, insurance, and financial services industries were not allowed to engage in the economic activities of either of the other two industries until passage of the Gramm-Leach-Bliley Act, often referred to as the Financial Services Modernization Act, on November 4, 1999. Just before the vote in the Senate, Senator Byron L. Dorgan (D-ND) gave a speech on the floor of the Senate in which he predicted that the measure would result in a future economic crisis, one that indeed struck the commercial and investment banking industry a decade later in 2008. He warned that increased concentration and mergers in the financial industry would result in the growth of businesses "too big to fail," and "raises the likelihood of future massive taxpayer bailouts."

Source: Congressional Record, 106th Congress, pp. S13896–S13897.

MR. DORGAN. Mr. President, I come to the floor in a circumstance where I will not support the legislation that is before the Senate today. Before I describe the reasons for that, let me say I certainly admire the craftsmanship and the legislative skills of the Senator from Texas and the Senator from Maryland, and so many others who have played a role in bringing this legislation to the floor. Frankly, I did not think they were going to get it done, but they did.

In the final hours of the Congress, they bring a piece of legislation to the floor—it is called financial services modernization. I know they feel passionately and strongly it is the right thing to do. For other reasons, I feel very strongly it is the wrong thing to do. I do not come to denigrate their work. We have a philosophical disagreement about this legislation, and I want to describe why.

This legislation repeals some of the major provisions of the Glass-Steagall Act named after Senator Carter Glass from Virginia, and Henry Steagall, a Congressman from Alabama, the primary authors. It will allow banks and security underwriters to affiliate with one another. It also repeals similar provisions in other banking laws to allow banks and insurance firms to marry up. It will permit many new kinds of financial services to be conducted within a financial holding company or a national bank subsidiary.

I want to describe why I think in many ways this effort is some legislative version of back to the future. I believe when this legislation is enacted—and it is expected it will be—we will see immediately even a greater level of concentration and merger activity in the financial services industries.

When there is this aggressive move toward even greater concentration—and the concentration we have seen recently ought to be alarming to all of us—but when this increased concentration occurs, we ought to ask the question: Will this be good for the consumer, or will it hurt the consumer? We know it will probably be good for those who are combining and merging. They do that because it is in their interest. But will it be in the public's interest? Will the consumer be better served by larger and larger companies?

Bank mergers, in fact, last year held the top spot in the value of all mergers: More than $250 billion in bank mergers deals last year. That is $250 billion out of $1.6 trillion in merger deals. Of the banks in this country, 10 companies hold about 30 percent of all domestic deposits and are expected to hold more than 40 percent of all domestic assets should the pending bank mergers that now exist be approved.

After news that there was a compromise on this financial services modernization bill in the late hours, a compromise that there was going to be a bill passed by Congress, I noted the stock values of likely takeover targets jumped in some cases by more than $7 a share. That ought to tell us what is on the horizon.

Clearly this legislation is not concerned about the rapid rate of consolidation in our financial services industries. The conference report that is before us dropped even a minimal House bill provision that would have required an annual General Accounting Office report to Congress on market concentration in financial services over the next 5 years. Even that minimal step that was in the House bill was dropped in this conference report.

What does it mean if we have all this concentration and merger activity? The bigger they are, the less likely this Government can allow them to fail. That is why we have a doctrine in this country with some of our larger banks—and that "some" is a growing list—of something called "too big to fail." A few years ago, we had only 11 banks in America that were considered by our regulators so big they would not be allowed to fail. Their failure would be catastrophic to our economy and so, therefore, they cannot fail.

The list of too big to fail banks has grown actually. Now it is 21 banks. There are 21 banks that are now too big to fail in this country.

We are also told by the Federal Reserve Board that the largest megabanks in this country, so-called LCBOs, the large complex banking organizations, need customized supervision because their complexity and size have reached a scale and diversity that would threaten the stability of financial markets around the world in the event of failure.

Let me read something from the Federal Reserve Bank president from Richmond. This is a Fed regional bank president saying this:

Here's the risk: when a bank's balance sheet has been weakened by financial losses, the safety net creates adverse incentives that economists usually refer to as a "moral hazard." Since the bank is insured, its depositors will not necessarily rush to withdraw deposits even if knowledge of the bank's problems begins to spread.

Because the bank is too big to fail.

In these circumstances, the bank has an incentive to pursue relatively risky loans and investments in hope that higher returns will strengthen its balance sheets and ease the difficulty. If the gamble fails, the insurance fund and ultimately taxpayers are left to absorb the losses. I am sure you remember that not very long ago, the S&L [Savings & Loan] bailout bilked taxpayers for well over $100 billion.

Again, quoting the president of the Richmond Federal Reserve Bank:

The point I want to make in the context of bank mergers is that the failure of a large, merged banking organization could be very costly to resolve. Additionally, the existence of such organizations could exacerbate the so-called too-big-to-fail problem and the risks it prevents. Consequently, I believe the current merger wave has intensified the need for a fresh review of the safety net—specifically the breadth of the deposit insurance coverage—with an eye towards reform.

This bill addresses a lot of issues. But it does nothing, for example, to deal with megabanks engaged in risky derivatives trading. I do not know if many know it, but we have something like $33 trillion in value of derivatives held by U.S. commercial banks in this country.

Federally-insured banks in this country are trading in derivatives out of their own proprietary accounts. You could just as well put a roulette wheel in the bank lobby. That is what it is. I offered amendments on the floor of the Senate when this bill was originally here to stop bank speculation in derivatives in their own proprietary accounts and also to take a look at some sensible regulation of risky hedge funds, but those amendments were rejected. You think there is not risk here? There is dramatic risk, and it is increasing. This piece of legislation acts as if it does not exist. It ignores it.

A philosopher and author once said: Those who cannot remember the past are condemned to repeat it. We have a piece of legislation on the floor today that I hope very much for the sake of not only those who vote for it and believe in it but for the American people who will eventually have to pick up the pieces—I hope this works.

Fusing together of the idea of banking, which requires not just safety and soundness to be successful but the perception of safety and soundness, with other inherently risky speculative activity is, in my judgment, unwise.

I do not usually quote William Safire. I guess I have done it a couple of times on the floor of the Senate. I suppose we all look for things that are comforting to our point of view. But William Safire wrote a piece three days ago in the *New York Times*:

Americans are unaware that Congress and the President have just agreed to put us all at extraordinary financial and personal risk.

Then he talks about the risk. The risk of allowing the coupling of inherently risky enterprises with our banking system, that requires the perception of safety and soundness, I personally think is unwise. I do not denigrate those who believe otherwise. There is room for disagreement. I may be dead wrong.

It may be that I am hopelessly old-fashioned. But I just do not think we should ignore the lessons learned in the 1930s, when we had this galloping behavior by people who believed nothing was ever going to go wrong and you could do banking and securities and all this together—just kind of put it in a tossed salad; it would be just fine—and then we saw, of course, massive failures across this country. And people understood that we did something wrong here: We allowed the financial institutions, and especially the banks in this country, to be involved in circumstances that were inherently risky. It was a dumb thing to do.

The result was, we created barriers saying: Let's not let that happen again. Let's never let that happen again. And those barriers are now being torn down with a bill called financial services modernization.

I remember a couple of circumstances that existed more recently. I was not around during the bank failures of the 1930s. I was not around for the debate that persuaded a Congress to enact Glass-Steagall and a range of other protections. But I was here when, in the early 1980s, it was decided that we should expand opportunities for savings and loans to do certain things. And they began to broker deposits and they took off. They would take a sleepy little savings and loan in some town, and they would take off like a Roman candle. Pretty soon they would have a multi-billion-dollar organization, and they would decide they would use the organization to park junk bonds in. We had a savings and loan out in California that had over 50 percent of its assets in risky junk bonds.

Let me describe the ultimate perversion, the hood ornament on stupidity. The U.S. Government owned nonperforming junk bonds in the Taj Mahal Casino. Let me say that again. The U.S. Government ended up owning nonperforming junk bonds in the Taj Mahal Casino in Atlantic City. How did that happen? The savings and loans were able to buy junk bonds. The savings and loans went belly up. The junk bonds were not performing. And the U.S. Government ended up with those junk bonds.

Was that a perversion? Of course it was. But it is an example of what has happened when we decide, under a term called modernization, to forget the lessons of the past, to forget there are certain things that are inherently risky, and they ought not be fused or merged with the enterprise of banking that requires the perception and, of course, the reality—but especially the perception—of safety and soundness.

Last year, we had a failure of a firm called LTCM, Long-Term Capital Management. It was an organization run by some of the smartest people in the world, I guess, in the area of finance. They had Nobel laureates helping run this place. They had some of the smartest people on Wall Street. They put together a lot of money. They had this hedge fund, unregulated hedge fund. They had invested more than $1 trillion in derivatives in this fund—more than $1 trillion in derivatives value.

Then, with all of the smartest folks around, and all this money, and an enormous amount of leverage, when it looked as if this firm was going to go belly up, just flat broke, guess what happened. On a Sunday, Mr. Greenspan and the Federal Reserve Board decided to convene a meeting of the corresponding banks and others who had an interest in this, saying: "You have to save Long-Term Capital Management. You have to save this hedge firm. If you don't, there will be catastrophic results in the economy."

The hit will be too big.

You have this unregulated risky activity out there in the economy, and you have one firm that has $1 trillion in derivative values and enormous risk, and, with all their brains, it doesn't work. They are going to go belly up. Who bears the burden for that? The Federal Government, the Federal Reserve Board.

We have the GAO [Government Accounting Office] doing an investigation to find out the circumstances of all that. I am very interested in this no-fault capitalism that exists with respect to Long-Term Capital Management. Who decides what kind of capitalism is no-fault capitalism? And when and how and is there a conflict of interest here?

The reason I raise this point is, this will be replicated again and again and again, as long as we bring bills to the floor that talk about financial services modernization and refuse to deal with the issue of thoughtful and sensible regulation of things such as hedge funds and derivatives and as long as we bring bills to the floor that say we can connect and couple, we can actually hitch up, inherently risky enterprises with the core banking issues in this country.

I hear about fire walls and affiliates, all these issues. I probably know less about them than some others; I admit that. But I certainly know, having studied and read a great deal about the lessons of history, there are some things that are not old-fashioned; there are some notions that represent transcendental truths. One of those, in my judgment, is that we are, with this piece of legislation, moving towards greater risk. We are almost certainly moving towards substantial new concentration and mergers in the financial services industry that are deliberately and certainly, with this legislation, moving towards inheriting much greater risk in our financial services industries.

I regret I cannot support the legislation. But let me end where I began because this is not one of those issues where I don't respect those who have a different view. I said when I started—I say as I close—there was a great deal of legislative skill exhibited on the part of those who put this together. I didn't think they were going to get this done, frankly. I wish they hadn't, but they did. That is a testament to their skill.

I don't know whether I am right or wrong on this issue. I believe fervently that 2 years, 5 years, 10 years from now, we will look back at this moment and say: We modernized the financial services industry because the industry did it itself and we needed to move ahead and draw a ring around it and provide some guidance, some rules and regulations. I also think we will, in 10 years time, look back and say: We should not have done that because we forgot the lessons of the past; those lessons represent timeless truths that were as true in the year 2000 or 2010 as they were in the year 1930 or 1935.

Again, I cannot vote for this legislation. My hope is that history will prove me wrong and that this will not pose the kind of difficulties and risks I fear it will for the American people.

One final point: With respect to the regulation of risky hedge funds, and especially the issue dealing with the value of derivatives in this country—$33 trillion, a substantial amount of it is held by the 25 largest banks in this country, a substantial amount being traded in proprietary accounts of those banks—we must do something to address those issues. That kind of risk overhanging the financial institutions of this country one day, with a thud, will wake everyone up and lead them to ask the question: Why didn't we understand that we have to do something about that? How on Earth could we have thought that would continue to exist without a massive problem for the American people and for its financial system?

I yield the floor.

Economic Stimulus Act of 2008

On January 3, 2008, President George W. Bush and Congress attempted to jumpstart the stalled U.S. economy with the passage of the Economic Stimulus Act. Under Title I of the Act, Congress authorized the payment of rebates to individual taxpayers (not estates, trusts, or corporations), ranging in amounts from $300 to $1,200 per household at an estimated cost from $50 to $150 million, as well as through incentives for business investment in the form of credit allowances for certain assets of up to either $250,000 or $800,000, depending on Internal Revenue Service classification. Under Title II, the Act increased the authorized limitations on the maximum original principle mortgage obligation for both the Federal National Mortgage Association (Fannie Mae) and Federal Home Loan Mortgage Corporation (Freddie Mac) as well as the Federal Home Agency (FHA) by an amount of up to 125 percent more than the limits previously imposed for 2008. The FHA limit increased from 125 percent for a one-residence dwelling to up to 175 percent over the previously authorized median price level for 2008. In the case of mortgages purchased by Fannie Mae and Freddie Mac, the Secretary of Housing and Urban Development was granted discretionary power to make additional upward increases of up to $100,000 over the new limit created by this act itself. Title II also specifies the sense of Congress as to the importance that both Fannie Mae and Freddie Mac have for the liquidity of the U.S. housing market. Congress passed this act in January 2008, after the housing bubble ruptured with the sub-prime mortgage crisis in 2007 and before the apex of the mortgage crisis with the near collapse of Fannie Mae and Freddie Mac in mid-2008.

Source: Congressional Record, Economic Stimulus Act of 2008, 110th Congress, H.R. 5140, http://thomas.loc.gov/cgi-bin/query/D?c110:5:./temp/~c110CH6uBB:: (accessed October 10, 2009).

One Hundred Tenth Congress of the United States of America

AT THE SECOND SESSION

Begun and held at the City of Washington on Thursday, the third day of January, two thousand and eight

An Act to provide economic stimulus through recovery rebates to individuals, incentives for business investment, and an increase in conforming and FHA loan limits.

Be it enacted by the Senate and House of Representatives of the United States of America in Congress assembled,

SECTION 1. SHORT TITLE; TABLE OF CONTENTS.

(a) Short Title-This Act may be cited as the 'Economic Stimulus Act of 2008'.

(b) Table of Contents-The table of contents of this Act is as follows:

Sec.1. Short title; table of contents.

TITLE I—RECOVERY REBATES AND INCENTIVES FOR BUSINESS INVESTMENT

Sec.101.2008 recovery rebates for individuals.

Sec. 102. Temporary increase in limitations on expensing of certain depreciable business assets.

Sec. 103. Special allowance for certain property acquired during 2008.

TITLE II—HOUSING GSE AND FHA LOAN LIMITS

Sec. 201. Temporary conforming loan limit increase for Fannie Mae and Freddie Mac.

Sec. 202. Temporary loan limit increase for FHA.

TITLE III—EMERGENCY DESIGNATION

Sec. 301. Emergency designation.

TITLE I—RECOVERY REBATES AND INCENTIVES FOR BUSINESS INVESTMENT

SEC. 101. 2008 RECOVERY REBATES FOR INDIVIDUALS.

(a) In General- Section 6428 of the Internal Revenue Code of 1986 is amended to read as follows:

SEC. 6428. 2008 RECOVERY REBATES FOR INDIVIDUALS.

(a) In General-In the case of an eligible individual, there shall be allowed as a credit against the tax imposed by subtitle A for the first taxable year beginning in 2008 an amount equal to the lesser of—

(1) net income tax liability, or

(2) $600 ($1,200 in the case of a joint return).

(b) Special Rules-

(1) IN GENERAL-In the case of a taxpayer described in paragraph (2)—

(A) the amount determined under subsection (a) shall not be less than $300 ($600 in the case of a joint return), and

(B) the amount determined under subsection (a) (after the application of subparagraph (A)) shall be increased by the product of $300 multiplied by the number of qualifying children (within the meaning of section 24(c)) of the taxpayer.

(2) TAXPAYER DESCRIBED- A taxpayer is described in this paragraph if the taxpayer—

(A) has qualifying income of at least $3,000, or

(B) has—

(i) net income tax liability which is greater than zero, and

(ii) gross income which is greater than the sum of the basic standard deduction plus the exemption amount (twice the exemption amount in the case of a joint return).

(c) Treatment of Credit-The credit allowed by subsection (a) shall be treated as allowed by subpart C of part IV of subchapter A of chapter 1.

(d) Limitation Based on Adjusted Gross Income-The amount of the credit allowed by subsection (a) (determined without regard to this subsection and subsection (f)) shall be reduced (but not below zero) by 5 percent of so much of the taxpayer's adjusted gross income as exceeds $75,000 ($150,000 in the case of a joint return).

(e) Definitions- For purposes of this section—

(1) QUALIFYING INCOME-The term 'qualifying income' means—

(A) earned income,

(B) social security benefits (within the meaning of section 86(d)), and

(C) any compensation or pension received under chapter 11, chapter 13, or chapter 15 of title 38, United States Code.

(2) NET INCOME TAX LIABILITY-The term 'net income tax liability' means the excess of—

(A) the sum of the taxpayer's regular tax liability (within the meaning of section 26(b)) and the tax imposed by section 55 for the taxable year, over

(B) the credits allowed by part IV (other than section 24 and subpart C thereof) of subchapter A of chapter 1.

(3) ELIGIBLE INDIVIDUAL- The term 'eligible individual' means any individual other than—

(A) any nonresident alien individual,

(B) any individual with respect to whom a deduction under section 151 is allowable to another taxpayer for a taxable year beginning in the calendar year in which the individual's taxable year begins, and

(C) an estate or trust.

(4) EARNED INCOME- The term 'earned income' has the meaning set forth in section 32(c)(2) except that—

(A) subclause (II) of subparagraph (B)(vi) thereof shall be applied by substituting 'January 1, 2009' for 'January 1, 2008', and

(B) such term shall not include net earnings from self-employment which are not taken into account in computing taxable income.

    (5) BASIC STANDARD DEDUCTION; EXEMPTION AMOUNT-The terms 'basic standard deduction' and 'exemption amount' shall have the same respective meanings as when used in section 6012(a).

(f) Coordination With Advance Refunds of Credit-

    (1) IN GENERAL- The amount of credit which would (but for this paragraph) be allowable under this section shall be reduced (but not below zero) by the aggregate refunds and credits made or allowed to the taxpayer under sub section (g). Any failure to so reduce the credit shall be treated as arising out of a mathematical or clerical error and assessed according to section 6213(b)(1).

    (2) JOINT RETURNS- In the case of a refund or credit made or allowed under subsection (g) with respect to a joint return, half of such refund or credit shall be treated as having been made or allowed to each individual filing such return.

(g) Advance Refunds and Credits-

    (1) IN GENERAL- Each individual who was an eligible individual for such individual's first taxable year beginning in 2007 shall be treated as having made a payment against the tax imposed by chapter 1 for such first taxable year in an amount equal to the advance refund amount for such taxable year.

    (2) ADVANCE REFUND AMOUNT- For purposes of paragraph (1), the advance refund amount is the amount that would have been allowed as a credit under this section for such first taxable year if this section (other than subsection (f) and this subsection) had applied to such taxable year.

    (3) TIMING OF PAYMENTS-The Secretary shall, subject to the provisions of this title, refund or credit any overpayment attributable to this section as rapidly as possible. No refund or credit shall be made or allowed under this subsection after December 31, 2008.

    (4) NO INTEREST-No interest shall be allowed on any overpayment attributable to this section.

(h) Identification Number Requirement-

    (1) IN GENERAL-No credit shall be allowed under subsection (a) to an eligible individual who does not include on the return of tax for the taxable year—

        (A) such individual's valid identification number,

        (B) in the case of a joint return, the valid identification number of such individual's spouse, and

        (C) in the case of any qualifying child taken into account under subsection (b)(1)(B), the valid identification number of such qualifying child.

    (2) VALID IDENTIFICATION NUMBER- For purposes of paragraph (1), the term 'valid identification number' means a social security number issued to an individual by the Social Security Administration. Such term shall not include a TIN issued by the Internal Revenue Service.'.

(b) Administrative Amendments-

    (1) DEFINITION OF DEFICIENCY- Section 6211(b)(4)(A) of the Internal Revenue Code of 1986 is amended by striking 'and 53(e)' and inserting '53(e), and 6428'.

(2) MATHEMATICAL OR CLERICAL ERROR AUTHORITY- Section 6213(g) (2)(L) of such Code is amended by striking 'or 32' and inserting '32, or 6428'.

(c) Treatment of Possessions-

(1) PAYMENTS TO POSSESSIONS-

(A) MIRROR CODE POSSESSION-The Secretary of the Treasury shall make a payment to each possession of the United States with a mirror code tax system in an amount equal to the loss to that possession by reason of the amendments made by this section. Such amount shall be determined by the Secretary of the Treasury based on information provided by the government of the respective possession.

(B) OTHER POSSESSIONS-The Secretary of the Treasury shall make a payment to each possession of the United States which does not have a mirror code tax system in an amount estimated by the Secretary of the Treasury as being equal to the aggregate benefits that would have been provided to residents of such possession by reason of the amendments made by this section if a mirror code tax system had been in effect in such possession. The preceding sentence shall not apply with respect to any possession of the United States unless such possession has a plan, which has been approved by the Secretary of the Treasury, under which such possession will promptly distribute such payment to the residents of such possession.

(2) COORDINATION WITH CREDIT ALLOWED AGAINST UNITED STATES INCOME TAXES-No credit shall be allowed against United States income taxes under section 6428 of the Internal Revenue Code of 1986 (as amended by this section) to any person—

(A) to whom a credit is allowed against taxes imposed by the possession by reason of the amendments made by this section, or

(B) who is eligible for a payment under a plan described in paragraph (1)(B).

(3) DEFINITIONS AND SPECIAL RULES-

(A) POSSESSION OF THE UNITED STATES- For purposes of this subsection, the term 'possession of the United States' includes the Commonwealth of Puerto Rico and the Commonwealth of the Northern Mariana Islands.

(B) MIRROR CODE TAX SYSTEM- For purposes of this subsection, the term 'mirror code tax system' means, with respect to any possession of the United States, the income tax system of such possession if the income tax liability of the residents of such possession under such system is determined by reference to the income tax laws of the United States as if such possession were the United States.

(C) TREATMENT OF PAYMENTS- For purposes of section 1324(b)(2) of title 31, United States Code, the payments under this subsection shall be treated in the same manner as a refund due from the credit allowed under section 6428 of the Internal Revenue Code of 1986 (as amended by this section).

(d) Refunds Disregarded in the Administration of Federal Programs and Federally Assisted Programs- Any credit or refund allowed or made to any individual by reason of section 6428 of the Internal Revenue Code of 1986 (as amended by this section) or by reason of subsection (c) of this section shall not be taken into account as income and shall not be taken into account as resources for the month of receipt and the following two months, for purposes of determining the eligibility of such individual or any other individual for benefits or assistance, or the amount or extent of benefits or assistance, under any Federal program or under any State or local program financed in whole or in part with Federal funds.

(e) Appropriations to Carry Out Rebates-

(1) IN GENERAL- Immediately upon the enactment of this Act, the following sums are appropriated, out of any money in the Treasury not otherwise appropriated, for the fiscal year ending September 30, 2008:

(A) DEPARTMENT OF THE TREASURY-

(i) For an additional amount for 'Department of the Treasury—Financial Management Service—Salaries and Expenses', $64,175,000, to remain available until September 30, 2009.

(ii) For an additional amount for 'Department of the Treasury—Internal Revenue Service—Taxpayer Services', $50,720,000, to remain available until September 30, 2009.

(iii) For an additional amount for 'Department of the Treasury—Internal Revenue Service—Operations Support', $151,415,000, to remain available until September 30, 2009.

(B) SOCIAL SECURITY ADMINISTRATION- For an additional amount for 'Social Security Administration—Limitation on Administrative Expenses', $31,000,000, to remain available until September 30, 2008.

(2) REPORTS- No later than 15 days after enactment of this Act, the Secretary of the Treasury shall submit a plan to the Committees on Appropriations of the House of Representatives and the Senate detailing the expected use of the funds provided by paragraph (1)(A). Beginning 90 days after enactment of this Act, the Secretary of the Treasury shall submit a quarterly report to the Committees on Appropriations of the House of Representatives and the Senate detailing the actual expenditure of funds provided by paragraph (1)(A) and the expected expenditure of such funds in the subsequent quarter.

(f) Conforming Amendments-

(1) Paragraph (2) of section 1324(b) of title 31, United States Code, is amended by inserting 'or 6428' after 'section 35'.

(2) Paragraph (1) of section 1(i) of the Internal Revenue Code of 1986 is amended by striking subparagraph (D).

(3) The item relating to section 6428 in the table of sections for subchapter B of chapter 65 of such Code is amended to read as follows:

Sec. 6428. 2008 recovery rebates for individuals.'.

SEC. 102. TEMPORARY INCREASE IN LIMITATIONS ON EXPENSING OF CERTAIN DEPRECIABLE BUSINESS ASSETS.

(a) In General- Subsection (b) of section 179 of the Internal Revenue Code of 1986 (relating to limitations) is amended by adding at the end the following new paragraph:

(7) INCREASE IN LIMITATIONS FOR 2008- In the case of any taxable year beginning in 2008—

(A) the dollar limitation under paragraph (1) shall be $250,000,

(B) the dollar limitation under paragraph (2) shall be $800,000, and

(C) the amounts described in subparagraphs (A) and (B) shall not be adjusted under paragraph (5).'.

(b) Effective Date- The amendment made by this section shall apply to taxable years beginning after December 31, 2007.

SEC. 103. SPECIAL ALLOWANCE FOR CERTAIN PROPERTY ACQUIRED DURING 2008.

(a) In General- Subsection (k) of section 168 of the Internal Revenue Code of 1986 (relating to special allowance for certain property acquired after September 10, 2001, and before January 1, 2005) is amended—

(1) by striking 'September 10, 2001' each place it appears and inserting 'December 31, 2007',

(2) by striking 'September 11, 2001' each place it appears and inserting 'January 1, 2008',

(3) by striking 'January 1, 2005' each place it appears and inserting 'January 1, 2009', and

(4) by striking 'January 1, 2006' each place it appears and inserting 'January 1, 2010'.

(b) 50 Percent Allowance- Subparagraph (A) of section 168(k)(1) of such Code is amended by striking '30 percent' and inserting '50 percent'.

(c) Conforming Amendments-

(1) Subclause (I) of section 168(k)(2)(B)(i) of such Code is amended by striking 'and (iii)' and inserting '(iii), and (iv)'.

(2) Subclause (IV) of section 168(k)(2)(B)(i) of such Code is amended by striking 'clauses (ii) and (iii)' and inserting 'clause (iii)'.

(3) Clause (i) of section 168(k)(2)(C) of such Code is amended by striking 'and (iii)' and inserting, '(iii), and (iv)'.

(4) Clause (i) of section 168(k)(2)(F) of such Code is amended by striking '$4,600' and inserting '$8,000'.

(5)(A) Subsection (k) of section 168 of such Code is amended by striking paragraph (4).

(B) Clause (iii) of section 168(k)(2)(D) of such Code is amended by striking the last sentence.

(6) Paragraph (4) of section 168(l) of such Code is amended by redesignating subparagraphs (A), (B), and (C) as subparagraphs (B), (C), and (D) and

inserting before subparagraph (B) (as so redesignated) the following new subparagraph:

(A) BONUS DEPRECIATION PROPERTY UNDER SUBSECTION (k)-
Such term shall not include any property to which section 168(k) applies.'

(7) Paragraph (5) of section 168(l) of such Code is amended—

(A) by striking 'September 10, 2001' in subparagraph (A) and inserting 'December 31, 2007', and

(B) by striking 'January 1, 2005' in subparagraph (B) and inserting 'January 1, 2009'.

(8) Subparagraph (D) of section 1400L(b)(2) of such Code is amended by striking 'January 1, 2005' and inserting 'January 1, 2010'.

(9) Paragraph (3) of section 1400N(d) of such Code is amended—

(A) by striking 'September 10, 2001' in subparagraph (A) and inserting 'December 31, 2007', and

(B) by striking 'January 1, 2005' in subparagraph (B) and inserting 'January 1, 2009'.

(10) Paragraph (6) of section 1400N(d) of such Code is amended by adding at the end the following new subparagraph:

(E) EXCEPTION FOR BONUS DEPRECIATION PROPERTY UNDER SECTION 168(k)- The term 'specified Gulf Opportunity Zone extension property' shall not include any property to which section 168(k) applies.'.

(11) The heading for subsection (k) of section 168 of such Code is amended—

(A) by striking 'September 10, 2001' and inserting 'December 31, 2007', and

(B) by striking 'January 1, 2005' and inserting 'January 1, 2009'.

(12) The heading for clause (ii) of section 168(k)(2)(B) of such Code is amended by striking 'PRE-JANUARY 1, 2005' and inserting 'PRE-JANUARY 1, 2009'.

(d) Effective Date- The amendments made by this section shall apply to property placed in service after December 31, 2007, in taxable years ending after such date.

TITLE II—HOUSING GSE AND FHA LOAN LIMITS

SEC. 201. TEMPORARY CONFORMING LOAN LIMIT INCREASE FOR FANNIE MAE AND FREDDIE MAC.

(a) Increase of High Cost Areas Limits for Housing GSEs- For mortgages originated during the period beginning on July 1, 2007, and ending at the end of December 31, 2008:

(1) FANNIE MAE- With respect to the Federal National Mortgage Association, notwithstanding section 302(b)(2) of the Federal National Mortgage Association Charter Act (12 U.S.C. 1717(b)(2)), the limitation on the maximum original principal obligation of a mortgage that may be purchased by the Association shall be the higher of—

(A) the limitation for 2008 determined under such section 302(b)(2) for a residence of the applicable size; or

(B) 125 percent of the area median price for a residence of the applicable size, but in no case to exceed 175 percent of the limitation for 2008 determined under such section 302(b)(2) for a residence of the applicable size.

    (2) FREDDIE MAC- With respect to the Federal Home Loan Mortgage Corporation, notwithstanding section 305(a)(2) of the Federal Home Loan Mortgage Corporation Act (12 U.S.C. 1454(a)(2)), the limitation on the maximum original principal obligation of a mortgage that may be purchased by the Corporation shall be the higher of—

        (A) the limitation determined for 2008 under such section 305(a)(2) for a residence of the applicable size; or

        (B) 125 percent of the area median price for a residence of the applicable size, but in no case to exceed 175 percent of the limitation determined for 2008 under such section 305(a)(2) for a residence of the applicable size.

(b) Determination of Limits- The areas and area median prices used for purposes of the determinations under subsection (a) shall be the areas and area median prices used by the Secretary of Housing and Urban Development in determining the applicable limits under section 202 of this title.

(c) Rule of Construction- A mortgage originated during the period referred to in subsection (a) that is eligible for purchase by the Federal National Mortgage Association or the Federal Home Loan Mortgage Corporation pursuant to this section shall be eligible for such purchase for the duration of the term of the mortgage, notwithstanding that such purchase occurs after the expiration of such period.

(d) Effect on Housing Goals- Notwithstanding any other provision of law, mortgages purchased in accordance with the increased maximum original principal obligation limitations determined pursuant to this section shall not be considered in determining performance with respect to any of the housing goals established under section 1332, 1333, or 1334 of the Housing and Community Development Act of 1992 (12 U.S.C. 4562-4), and shall not be considered in determining compliance with such goals pursuant to section 1336 of such Act (12 U.S.C. 4566) and regulations, orders, or guidelines issued thereunder.

(e) Sense of Congress- It is the sense of the Congress that the securitization of mortgages by the Federal National Mortgage Association and the Federal Home Loan Mortgage Corporation plays an important role in providing liquidity to the United States housing markets. Therefore, the Congress encourages the Federal National Mortgage Association and the Federal Home Loan Mortgage Corporation to securitize mortgages acquired under the increased conforming loan limits established in this section, to the extent that such securitizations can be effected in a timely and efficient manner that does not impose additional costs for mortgages originated, purchased, or securitized under the existing limits or interfere with the goal of adding liquidity to the market.

SEC. 202. TEMPORARY LOAN LIMIT INCREASE FOR FHA.

(a) Increase of High-Cost Area Limit- For mortgages for which the mortgagee has issued credit approval for the borrower on or before December 31, 2008, sub-paragraph (A) of section 203(b)(2) of the National Housing Act (12 U.S.C. 1709 (b)(2)(A)) shall be considered (except for purposes of section 255(g) of such

Act (12 U.S.C. 1715z-20(g))) to require that a mortgage shall involve a principal obligation in an amount that does not exceed the lesser of—

(1) in the case of a 1-family residence, 125 percent of the median 1-family house price in the area, as determined by the Secretary; and in the case of a 2-, 3-, or 4-family residence, the percentage of such median price that bears the same ratio to such median price as the dollar amount limitation determined for 2008 under section 305(a)(2) of the Federal Home Loan Mortgage Corporation Act (12 U.S.C. 1454(a)(2)) for a 2-, 3-, or 4-family residence, respectively, bears to the dollar amount limitation determined for 2008 under such section for a 1-family residence; or

(2) 175 percent of the dollar amount limitation determined for 2008 under such section 305(a)(2) for a residence of the applicable size (without regard to any authority to increase such limitation with respect to properties located in Alaska, Guam, Hawaii, or the Virgin Islands);

except that the dollar amount limitation in effect under this subsection for any size residence for any area shall not be less than the greater of: (A) the dollar amount limitation in effect under such section 203(b)(2) for the area on October 21, 1998; or (B) 65 percent of the dollar amount limitation determined for 2008 under such section 305(a)(2) for a residence of the applicable size. Any reference in this subsection to dollar amount limitations in effect under section 305(a)(2) of the Federal Home Loan Mortgage Corporation Act means such limitations as in effect without regard to any increase in such limitation pursuant to section 201 of this title.

(b) Discretionary Authority- If the Secretary of Housing and Urban Development determines that market conditions warrant such an increase, the Secretary may, for the period that begins upon the date of the enactment of this Act and ends at the end of the date specified in subsection (a), increase the maximum dollar amount limitation determined pursuant to subsection (a) with respect to any particular size or sizes of residences, or with respect to residences located in any particular area or areas, to an amount that does not exceed the maximum dollar amount then otherwise in effect pursuant to subsection (a) for such size residence, or for such area (if applicable), by not more than $100,000.

(c) Publication of Area Median Prices and Loan Limits- The Secretary of Housing and Urban Development shall publish the median house prices and mortgage principal obligation limits, as revised pursuant to this section, for all areas as soon as practicable, but in no case more than 30 days after the date of the enactment of this Act. With respect to existing areas for which the Secretary has not established area median prices before such date of enactment, the Secretary may rely on existing commercial data in determining area median prices and calculating such revised principal obligation limits.

TITLE III—EMERGENCY DESIGNATION
SEC. 301. EMERGENCY DESIGNATION.

For purposes of Senate enforcement, all provisions of this Act are designated as emergency requirements and necessary to meet emergency needs pursuant to section 204 of S. Con. Res. 21 (110th Congress), the concurrent resolution on the budget for fiscal year 2008.

> Speaker of the House of Representatives.
> Vice President of the United States and
> President of the Senate.

New York Fed's Summary of Financing Agreement of JPMorgan Chase's Acquisition of Bear Sterns (2008)

Just over six months after the 2007 mortgage crisis sent the U.S. economy into a liquidity crisis and credit crunch, Bear Stearns, the nation's fifth-largest investment bank, became the first major investment firm to find itself on the brink of bankruptcy, despite the fact that it had sound collateral assets available to use as security for new capital financial loans but was still unable to arrange for new loans. Fearing that the bankruptcy of Bear Stearns would send a shockwave through the financial markets and the whole U.S. economy if allowed to fail, Federal Reserve Chair Ben Bernanke and Treasury Secretary Henry Paulson Jr. arranged the immediate sale of Bear Stearns to JPMorgan Chase, with the U.S. government providing $29 billion to JPMorgan Chase, thereby assuming the risk of the less liquid assets of Bear Stearns. Below is a summary of the terms and conditions of the arrangements between the New York Federal Reserve Bank and JPMorgan Chase.

Source: Federal Reserve Bank of New York, Press Release, "Summary of Terms and Conditions Regarding JPMorgan Chase Facility," March 24, 2008, http://www.newyorkfed.org/newsevents/news/markets/2008/rp080324b.html.

The Federal Reserve Bank of New York ("New York Fed") has agreed to lend $29 billion in connection with the acquisition of The Bear Stearns Companies Inc. by JPMorgan Chase & Co.

The loan will be against a portfolio of $30 billion in assets of Bear Stearns, based on the value of the portfolio as marked to market by Bear Stearns on March 14, 2008.

JPMorgan Chase has agreed to provide $1 billion in funding in the form of a note that will be subordinated to the Federal Reserve note. The JPMorgan Chase note will be the first to absorb losses, if any, on the liquidation of the portfolio of assets.

The New York Fed loan and the JPMorgan Chase subordinated note will be made to a Delaware limited liability company ("LLC") established for the purpose of holding the Bear Stearns assets. Using a single entity (the LLC) will ease administration of the portfolio and will remove constraints on the money manager that might arise from retaining the assets on the books of Bear Stearns.

The loan from the New York Fed and the subordinated note from JPMorgan Chase will each be for a term of 10 years, renewable by the New York Fed.

The rate due on the loan from the New York Fed is the primary credit rate, which currently is 2.5 percent and fluctuates with the discount rate. The rate on the subordinated note from JPMorgan Chase is the primary credit rate plus 450[*] basis points (currently, a total of 7 percent).

BlackRock Financial Management Inc. has been retained by the New York Fed to manage and liquidate the assets.

The Federal Reserve loan is being provided under the authority granted by section 13(3) of the Federal Reserve Act. The Board authorized the New York Fed to enter into this loan and made the findings required by section 13(3) at a meeting on Sunday, March 16, 2008.

Repayment of the loans will begin on the second anniversary of the loan, unless the Reserve Bank determines to begin payments earlier. Payments from the liquidation of the assets in the LLC will be made in the following order (each category must be fully paid before proceeding to the next lower category):

- to pay the necessary operating expenses of the LLC incurred in managing and liquidating the assets as of the repayment date;
- to repay the entire $29 billion principal due to the New York Fed;
- to pay all interest due to the New York Fed on its loan;
- to repay the entire $1 billion subordinated note due to JPMorgan Chase;
- to pay all interest due to JPMorgan Chase on its subordinated note;
- to pay any other non-operating expenses of the LLC, if any.

Any remaining funds resulting from the liquidation of the assets will be paid to the New York Fed.

Correction: A previous version of this document incorrectly stated the rate on the subordinated note from JPMorgan Chase as the primary credit rate plus 475 basis points. It is the primary credit rate plus 450 basis points.

U.S. Treasury Fact Sheet on Fannie Mae and Freddie Mac Bailout (2008)

In August 2007, the housing bubble burst in the United States, caused by the sub-prime mortgage crisis. The nation's economic situation worsened over the next year, with a major liquidity crisis and credit crunch spreading from the mortgage industry to the investment banking markets. In March 2008, the New York Federal Reserve Bank concluded an agreement with JPMorgan Chase in which JPMorgan Chase purchased Bear Stearns, the nation's fifth-largest investment firm, in exchange for a $29 billion loan from the New York Fed in an effort to prevent the economic crisis from spiraling further out of control. Shortly thereafter, the Federal Reserve Chair and Treasury Secretary realized that the government would also have to bailout the two Government Sponsored Enterprises (GSEs) mortgage giants Fannie Mae and Freddie Mac, which held $5 trillion in mortgage-backed securities and were on the verge of bankruptcy. The terms of the $100 billion credit facility to each of the two GSEs, which the GSEs can repay and then borrow against repeatedly as a revolving line of credit, included a requirement that they reduce their mortgage-backed securities portfolios down to $850 billion by the end of 2009, and then a further 10 percent annually until the amount was only $250 billion.

Source: U.S. Treasury Department Office of Public Affairs, Fact Sheet: Treasury Senior Preferred Stock Purchase Agreement, September 7, 2009, accessed online at http://docs.google.com/gview?a=v&q=cache:on7twCQpleQJ:www.treas.gov/press/ releases/reports/pspa_factsheet_090708%2520hp1128.pdf+FACT+SHEET: +TREASURY+SENIOR+PREFERRED+STOCK+PURCHASE+AGREEMENT &hl=en&gl=us&sig=AFQjCNHhpn0ZrSWtrsBXK1nL8j0p2k-Mkg.

Fannie Mae and Freddie Mac debt and mortgage backed securities outstanding today amount to about $5 trillion, and are held by central banks and investors around the world. Investors have purchased securities of these government sponsored enterprises in part because the ambiguities in their Congressional charters created a perception of government backing. These ambiguities fostered enormous growth in GSE debt outstanding and the breadth of these holdings pose a systemic risk to our financial system. Because the U.S. government created these ambiguities, we have a responsibility to both avert and ultimately address the systemic risk now posed by the scale and breadth of the holdings of GSE debt and mortgage backed securities.

To address our responsibility to support GSE debt and mortgage backed securities holders, Treasury entered into a Senior Preferred Stock Purchase Agreement with each GSE which ensures that each enterprise maintains a positive net worth. This measure adds to market stability by providing additional security to GSE debt holders—senior and subordinated—and adds to mortgage affordability by providing additional confidence to investors in GSE mortgage-backed securities. This commitment also eliminates any mandatory triggering of receivership.

These agreements are the most effective means of averting systemic risk and contain terms and conditions to protect the taxpayer. They are more efficient than a one-time equity injection, in that Treasury will use them only as needed and on terms that the Treasury deems appropriate.

These agreements provide significant protections for the taxpayer, in the form of senior preferred stock with a liquidation preference, an upfront $1 billion issuance of senior preferred stock with a 10 percent coupon from each GSE, quarterly dividend payments, warrants representing an ownership stake of 79.9 percent in each GSE going forward, and a quarterly fee starting in 2010.

Terms of the Agreements:

- The agreements are contracts between the Department of the Treasury and each GSE. They are indefinite in duration and have a capacity of $100 billion each, an amount chosen to demonstrate a strong commitment to the GSEs' creditors and mortgage backed security holders. This number is unrelated to the Treasury's analysis of the current financial conditions of the GSEs.

- If the Federal Housing Finance Agency determines that a GSE's liabilities have exceeded its assets under generally accepted accounting principles, Treasury will contribute cash capital to the GSE in an amount equal to the difference between liabilities and assets. An amount equal to each such contribution will be added to the senior preferred stock held by Treasury, which will be senior to all other preferred stock, common stock or other capital stock to be issued by the GSE. These agreements will protect the senior and subordinated debt and the mortgage backed securities of the GSEs. The GSE's common stock and existing preferred shareholders will bear any losses ahead of the government.

- In exchange for entering into these agreements with the GSEs, Treasury will immediately receive the following compensation:
  - $1 billion of senior preferred stock in each GSE
  - Warrants for the purchase of common stock of each GSE representing 79.9 percent of the common stock of each GSE on a fully-diluted basis at a nominal price

- The senior preferred stock shall accrue dividends at 10 percent per year. The rate shall increase to 12 percent if, in any quarter, the dividends are not paid in cash, until all accrued dividends have been paid in cash.

- The senior preferred stock shall not be entitled to voting rights. In a conservatorship, voting rights of all stockholders are vested in the Conservator.

- Beginning March 31, 2010, the GSEs shall pay the Treasury on a quarterly basis a periodic commitment fee that will compensate the Treasury for the explicit support provided by the agreement. The Secretary of the Treasury and the Conservator shall determine the periodic commitment fee in consultation with the Chairman of the Federal Reserve. This fee may be paid in cash or may be added to the senior preferred stock.

- The following covenants apply to the GSEs as part of the agreements.
  - Without the prior consent of the Treasury, the GSEs shall not:
    - Make any payment to purchase or redeem its capital stock, or pay any dividends, including preferred dividends (other than dividends on the senior preferred stock)
    - Issue capital stock of any kind
    - Enter into any new or adjust any existing compensation agreements with "named executive officers" without consulting with Treasury
    - Terminate conservatorship other than in connection with receivership
    - Sell, convey or transfer any of its assets outside the ordinary course of business except as necessary to meet their obligation under the agreements to reduce their portfolio of retained mortgages and mortgage backed securities
    - Increase its debt to more than 110% of its debt as of June 30, 2008
    - Acquire or consolidate with, or merge into, another entity.

- Each GSE's retained mortgage and mortgage backed securities portfolio shall not exceed $850 billion as of December 31, 2009, and shall decline by 10 percent per year until it reaches $250 billion.

AIG's Statement on Bailout Agreement with New York Federal Reserve (2008)

Beginning in August 2007, a mortgage crisis sent the U.S. economy into a recession. By early 2008, the resulting tightening of financial markets produced a liquidity crisis and credit crunch and the government moved to bailout the failing investment firm of Bear Stearns through a merger with JPMorgan Chase, which included a $29 billion credit facility agreement with the purchasing firm. On September 7, the government bailed out the two giant mortgage Government-Sponsored Enterprises (GSEs), Fannie Mae and Freddie Mac, with the issuance of a $100 billion revolving credit facility to each. The next week, the international insurance and financial giant American International Group (AIG) was forced to raise an additional $14.5 billion after the company's credit rating was lowered because of its record second quarter unrealized loss of $26.2 billion. One day later, on September 16, 2008, the Federal Reserve pledged $85 billion to AIG in exchange for a 79.9 percent equity stake in the *company. The bailout was justified on the basis that AIG, an insurer of property, casualty, and life insurance operating in 130 countries and jurisdictions through the world's largest network, was "too big to fail" On September 23, 2008, New York Federal Reserve Bank and AIG finalized the following terms and conditions of the bailout agreement. Two months later, the AIG bailout rose to $150 billion, its interest rate was lowered, and the repayment period extended by three years after the company announced its 2007–2008 unrealized loss on credit-default swaps amounted to $33.2 billion.*

Source: AIG Press Release, "AIG Signs Definitive Agreement with Federal Reserve Bank of New York for $85 Billion Credit Facility," September 23, 2008, http://media.corporate-ir.net/media_files/irol/76/76115/releases/092408.pdf.

NEW YORK, September 23, 2008–

American International Group, Inc. (AIG) today announced that it has signed a definitive agreement with the Federal Reserve Bank of New York for a two-year, $85 billion revolving credit facility. Interest will accrue at a rate based on 3-month LIBOR plus 8.50 percent. The facility provides for an initial gross commitment fee of 2 percent of the total facility on the closing date. AIG will also pay a commitment fee on undrawn amounts at the rate of 8.50 percent per annum. Interest and the commitment fees are generally payable through an increase in the outstanding balance under the facility.

AIG is required to repay the facility from, among other things, the proceeds of certain asset sales and issuances of debt or equity securities. These mandatory repayments permanently reduce the amount available to be borrowed under the facility. Under the agreement, AIG will issue a new series of Convertible Participating Serial Preferred Stock to a trust that will hold the Preferred Stock for the benefit of the United States Treasury. The Preferred Stock will be entitled to participate in any dividends paid on the common stock, with the payments attributable to the Preferred Stock being approximately, but not in excess of, 79.9% of the aggregate dividends paid. The Preferred Stock will vote with the common stock on all matters, and will hold approximately, but not in excess of, 79.9 percent of the aggregate voting power. The Preferred Stock will be convertible into common stock following a special shareholders meeting to amend AIG's restated certificate of incorporation.

Borrowings under the facility are conditioned on the Federal Reserve Bank of New York being reasonably satisfied with, among other things, AIG's corporate governance. The facility contains customary affirmative and negative covenants, including a requirement to maintain a minimum amount of liquidity and a requirement to use reasonable efforts to cause the composition of the Board of Directors of AIG to be satisfactory to the trust holding the Preferred Stock within 10 days after the establishment of the trust.

AIG Chairman and Chief Executive Officer Edward M. Liddy said, "AIG made an exhaustive effort to address its liquidity needs through private sector financing, but was unable to do so in the current environment. This facility was the company's best alternative. We are pleased to have finalized the terms of the facility, and are already developing a plan to sell assets, repay the facility and emerge as a smaller but profitable company. Importantly, AIG's insurance subsidiaries remain strong, liquid and well-capitalized."

The facility will be secured by a pledge of the capital stock and assets of certain of AIG's subsidiaries, subject to exclusions for certain property the pledge of which is not permitted by AIG debt instruments, as well as exclusions of assets of regulated subsidiaries, assets of foreign subsidiaries and assets of special purpose vehicles.

It should be noted that the remarks made in this press release may contain projections concerning financial information and statements concerning future economic performance and events, plans and objectives relating to management, operations, products and services, and assumptions underlying these projections and statements. It is possible that AIG's actual results and financial condition may differ, possibly materially, from the anticipated results and financial condition indicated in these projections and statements. Factors that could cause AIG's actual results to differ, possibly materially, from those in the specific projections and statements are discussed in Item 1A. Risk Factors of AIG's Annual Report on Form 10-K for the year ended December 31, 2007, and in Item 2. Management's Discussion and Analysis of Financial Condition and Results of Operations of AIG's Quarterly Report on Form 10-Q for the period ended June 30, 2008. AIG is not under any obligation (and expressly disclaims any such obligations) to update or alter its projections and other statements whether as a result of new information, future events or otherwise.

American International Group, Inc. (AIG), a world leader in insurance and financial services, is the leading international insurance organization with operations in more than 130 countries and jurisdictions. AIG companies serve commercial, institutional and individual customers through the most extensive worldwide property-casualty and life insurance networks of any insurer. In addition, AIG companies are leading providers of retirement services, financial services and asset management around the world. AIG's common stock is listed on the New York Stock Exchange, as well as the stock exchanges in Ireland and Tokyo.

George W. Bush's "Our Economy Is in Danger" Speech (2008)

On September 24, 2008, President George W. Bush gave the following nationally televised speech addressing the economic crisis and discussing the administration's financial rescue plan. The speech came on the heels of the worst week in U.S.

economic history since the Great Depression. After Bush's speech, in which he stressed the urgency required in passing legislation to address the escalating crisis, Congress enacted the $700 billion Emergency Economic Stabilization Act on October 3, 2008.

Source: White House Press Office, September 24, 2008.

PRESIDENT: Good evening. This is an extraordinary period for America's economy.

Over the past few weeks, many Americans have felt anxiety about their finances and their future. I understand their worry and their frustration.

We've seen triple-digit swings in the stock market. Major financial institutions have teetered on the edge of collapse, and some have failed. As uncertainty has grown, many banks have restricted lending, credit markets have frozen, and families and businesses have found it harder to borrow money.

We're in the midst of a serious financial crisis, and the federal government is responding with decisive action.

We boosted confidence in money market mutual funds and acted to prevent major investors from intentionally driving down stocks for their own personal gain.

Most importantly, my administration is working with Congress to address the root cause behind much of the instability in our markets.

Financial assets related to home mortgages have lost value during the house decline, and the banks holding these assets have restricted credit. As a result, our entire economy is in danger.

So I propose that the federal government reduce the risk posed by these troubled assets and supply urgently needed money so banks and other financial institutions can avoid collapse and resume lending.

This rescue effort is not aimed at preserving any individual company or industry. It is aimed at preserving America's overall economy.

It will help American consumers and businesses get credit to meet their daily needs and create jobs. And it will help send a signal to markets around the world that America's financial system is back on track.

I know many Americans have questions tonight: How did we reach this point in our economy? How will the solution I propose work? And what does this mean for your financial future?

These are good questions, and they deserve clear answers.

First, how did our economy reach this point? Well, most economists agree that the problems we're witnessing today developed over a long period of time. For more than a decade, a massive amount of money flowed into the United States from investors abroad because our country is an attractive and secure place to do business.

This large influx of money to U.S. banks and financial institutions, along with low interest rates, made it easier for Americans to get credit. These developments allowed more families to borrow money for cars, and homes, and college tuition, some for the first time. They allowed more entrepreneurs to get loans to start new businesses and create jobs.

Unfortunately, there were also some serious negative consequences, particularly in the housing market. Easy credit, combined with the faulty assumption that home values would continue to rise, led to excesses and bad decisions.

Many mortgage lenders approved loans for borrowers without carefully examining their ability to pay. Many borrowers took out loans larger than they could afford, assuming that they could sell or refinance their homes at a higher price later on.

Optimism about housing values also led to a boom in home construction. Eventually, the number of new houses exceeded the number of people willing to buy them. And with supply exceeding demand, housing prices fell, and this created a problem.

Borrowers with adjustable-rate mortgages, who had been planning to sell or refinance their homes at a higher price, were stuck with homes worth less than expected, along with mortgage payments they could not afford.

As a result, many mortgage-holders began to default. These widespread defaults had effects far beyond the housing market.

See, in today's mortgage industry, home loans are often packaged together and converted into financial products called mortgage-backed securities. These securities were sold to investors around the world.

Many investors assumed these securities were trustworthy and asked few questions about their actual value. Two of the leading purchasers of mortgage-backed securities were Fannie Mae and Freddie Mac.

Because these companies were chartered by Congress, many believed they were guaranteed by the federal government. This allowed them to borrow enormous sums of money, fuel the market for questionable investments, and put our financial system at risk.

The decline in the housing market set off a domino effect across our economy. When home values declined, borrowers defaulted on their mortgages, and investors holding mortgage-backed securities began to incur serious losses.

Before long, these securities became so unreliable that they were not being bought or sold. Investment banks, such as Bear Stearns and Lehman Brothers, found themselves saddled with large amounts of assets they could not sell. They ran out of money needed to meet their immediate obligations, and they faced imminent collapse.

Other banks found themselves in severe financial trouble. These banks began holding on to their money, and lending dried up, and the gears of the American financial system began grinding to a halt.

With the situation becoming more precarious by the day, I faced a choice, to step in with dramatic government action or to stand back and allow the irresponsible actions of some to undermine the financial security of all.

I'm a strong believer in free enterprise, so my natural instinct is to oppose government intervention. I believe companies that make bad decisions should be allowed to go out of business.

Under normal circumstances, I would have followed this course. But these are not normal circumstances. The market is not functioning properly. There has been a widespread loss of confidence, and major sectors of America's financial system are at risk of shutting down.

The government's top economic experts warn that, without immediate action by Congress, America could slip into a financial panic and a distressing scenario would unfold.

More banks could fail, including some in your community. The stock market would drop even more, which would reduce the value of your retirement account. The value of your home could plummet. Foreclosures would rise dramatically.

And if you own a business or a farm, you would find it harder and more expensive to get credit. More businesses would close their doors, and millions of Americans could lose their jobs.

Even if you have good credit history, it would be more difficult for you to get the loans you need to buy a car or send your children to college. And, ultimately, our country could experience a long and painful recession.

Fellow citizens, we must not let this happen. I appreciate the work of leaders from both parties in both houses of Congress to address this problem and to make improvements to the proposal my administration sent to them.

There is a spirit of cooperation between Democrats and Republicans and between Congress and this administration. In that spirit, I've invited Senators McCain and Obama to join congressional leaders of both parties at the White House tomorrow to help speed our discussions toward a bipartisan bill.

I know that an economic rescue package will present a tough vote for many members of Congress. It is difficult to pass a bill that commits so much of the taxpayers' hard-earned money.

I also understand the frustration of responsible Americans who pay their mortgages on time, file their tax returns every April 15th, and are reluctant to pay the cost of excesses on Wall Street.

But given the situation we are facing, not passing a bill now would cost these Americans much more later.

Many Americans are asking, how would a rescue plan work? After much discussion, there's now widespread agreement on the principles such a plan would include.

It would remove the risk posed by the troubled assets, including mortgage-backed securities, now clogging the financial system. This would free banks to resume the flow of credit to American families and businesses.

Any rescue plan should also be designed to ensure that taxpayers are protected. It should welcome the participation of financial institutions, large and small. It should make certain that failed executives do not receive a windfall from your tax dollars.

It should establish a bipartisan board to oversee the plan's implementation, and it should be enacted as soon as possible.

In close consultation with Treasury Secretary Hank Paulson, Federal Reserve Chairman Ben Bernanke, and SEC Chairman Chris Cox, I announced a plan on Friday.

First, the plan is big enough to solve a serious problem. Under our proposal, the federal government would put up to $700 billion taxpayer dollars on the line to purchase troubled assets that are clogging the financial system.

In the short term, this will free up banks to resume the flow of credit to American families and businesses, and this will help our economy grow.

Second, as markets have lost confidence in mortgage-backed securities, their prices have dropped sharply, yet the value of many of these assets will likely be higher than their current price, because the vast majority of Americans will ultimately pay off their mortgages.

The government is the one institution with the patience and resources to buy these assets at their current low prices and hold them until markets return to normal.

And when that happens, money will flow back to the Treasury as these assets are sold, and we expect that much, if not all, of the tax dollars we invest will be paid back.

The final question is, what does this mean for your economic future? Well, the primary steps—purpose of the steps I've outlined tonight is to safeguard the financial security of American workers, and families, and small businesses. The federal government also continues to enforce laws and regulations protecting your money.

The Treasury Department recently offered government insurance for money market mutual funds. And through the FDIC, every savings account, checking account, and certificate of deposit is insured by the federal government for up to $100,000.

The FDIC has been in existence for 75 years, and no one has ever lost a penny on an insured deposit, and this will not change.

Once this crisis is resolved, there will be time to update our financial regulatory structures. Our 21st-century global economy remains regulated largely by outdated 20th-century laws.

Recently, we've seen how one company can grow so large that its failure jeopardizes the entire financial system.

Earlier this year, Secretary Paulson proposed a blueprint that would modernize our financial regulations. For example, the Federal Reserve would be authorized to take a closer look at the operations of companies across the financial spectrum and ensure that their practices do not threaten overall financial stability.

There are other good ideas, and members of Congress should consider them. As they do, they must ensure that efforts to regulate Wall Street do not end up hampering our economy's ability to grow.

In the long run, Americans have good reason to be confident in our economic strength. Despite corrections in the marketplace and instances of abuse, democratic capitalism is the best system ever devised.

It has unleashed the talents and the productivity and entrepreneurial spirit of our citizens. It has made this country the best place in the world to invest and do business. And it gives our economy the flexibility and resilience to absorb shocks, adjust, and bounce back.

Our economy is facing a moment of great challenge, but we've overcome tough challenges before, and we will overcome this one.

I know that Americans sometimes get discouraged by the tone in Washington and the seemingly endless partisan struggles, yet history has shown that, in times of real trial, elected officials rise to the occasion.

And together we will show the world once again what kind of country America is: a nation that tackles problems head on, where leaders come together to meet great tests, and where people of every background can work hard, develop their talents, and realize their dreams.

Thank you for listening. May God bless you.

George W. Bush's Speech on Efforts to Restore Economic Stability (2008)

Seven days after Congress passed the Emergency Economic Stabilization Act of 2008, President George W. Bush gave the following speech in which he attempted to restore confidence in U.S. financial markets. The focus of the speech was on the efforts being made by his administration to restore economic stability.

Source: White House Press Office, October 10, 2008.

THE PRESIDENT: Good morning. Over the past few days, we have witnessed a startling drop in the stock market—much of it driven by uncertainty and fear. This has been a deeply unsettling period for the American people. Many of our citizens have serious concerns about their retirement accounts, their investments, and their economic well-being.

Here's what the American people need to know: that the United States government is acting; we will continue to act to resolve this crisis and restore stability to our markets. We are a prosperous nation with immense resources and a wide range of tools at our disposal. We're using these tools aggressively.

The fundamental problem is this: As the housing market has declined, banks holding assets related to home mortgages have suffered serious losses. As a result of these losses, many banks lack the capital or the confidence in each other to make new loans. In turn, our system of credit has frozen, which is keeping American businesses from financing their daily transactions—and creating uncertainty throughout our economy.

This uncertainty has led to anxiety among our people. And that is understandable—that anxiety can feed anxiety, and that can make it hard to see all that is being done to solve the problem. The federal government has a comprehensive strategy and the tools necessary to address the challenges in our economy. Fellow citizens: We can solve this crisis—and we will.

Here are the problems we face and the steps we are taking:

First, key markets are not functioning because there's a lack of liquidity—the grease necessary to keep the gears of our financial system turning. So the Federal Reserve has injected hundreds of billions of dollars into the system. The Fed has joined with central banks around the world to coordinate a cut in interest rates. This rate cut will allow banks to borrow money more affordably—and it should help free up additional credit necessary to create jobs, and finance college educations, and help American families meet their daily needs. The Fed has also announced a new program to provide support for the commercial paper market, which is freezing up. As the new program kicks in over the next week or so, it will help revive a key source of short-term financing for American businesses and financial institutions.

Second, some Americans are concerned about whether their money is safe. So the Federal Deposit Insurance Corporation and the National Credit Union Administration have significantly expanded the amount of money insured in savings accounts, and checking accounts, and certificates of deposit. That means that if you have up to $250,000 in one of these insured accounts, every penny of that money is safe. The Treasury Department has also acted to restore confidence in a key element of America's financial system by offering government insurance for money market mutual funds.

Thirdly, we are concerned that some investors could take advantage of the crisis to illegally manipulate the stock market. So the Securities and Exchange Commission has launched rigorous enforcement actions to detect fraud and manipulation in the market. The SEC is focused on preventing abusive practices, such as putting out false information to drive down particular stocks for personal gain. Anyone caught engaging in illegal financial activities will be prosecuted.

Fourth, the decline in the housing market has left many Americans struggling to meet their mortgages and are concerned about losing their homes. My administration has launched two initiatives to help responsible borrowers keep their homes. One is called HOPE NOW, and it brings together homeowners and lenders and mortgage servicers, and others to find ways to prevent foreclosure. The other initiative is aimed at making it easier for responsible homeowners to refinance into affordable mortgages insured by the Federal Housing Administration. So far, these programs have helped more than 2 million Americans stay in their home. And the point is this: If you are struggling to meet your mortgage, there are ways that you can get help.

With these actions to help to prevent foreclosures, we're addressing a key problem in the housing market: The supply of homes now exceeds demand. And as a result, home values have declined. Once supply and demand balance out, our housing market will be able to recover—and that will help our broader economy begin to grow.

Fifth, we've seen that problems in the financial system are not isolated to the United States. They're also affecting other nations around the globe. So we're working closely with partners around the world to ensure that our actions are coordinated and effective. Tomorrow, I'll meet with the finance ministers from our partners in the G7 and the heads of the International Monetary Fund and World Bank. Secretary Paulson will also meet with finance ministers from the world's 20 leading economies. Through these efforts, the world is sending an unmistakable signal: We're in this together, and we'll come through this together.

And finally, American businesses and consumers are struggling to obtain credit, because banks do not have sufficient capital to make loans. So my administration worked with Congress to quickly pass a $700 billion financial rescue package. This new law authorizes the Treasury Department to use a variety of measures to help bank [sic] rebuild capital—including buying or insuring troubled assets and purchasing equity of financial institutions. The Department will implement measures that have maximum impact as quickly as possible. Seven hundred billion dollars is a significant amount of money. And as we act, we will do it in a way that is effective.

The plan we are executing is aggressive. It is the right plan. It will take time to have its full impact. It is flexible enough to adapt as the situation changes. And it is big enough to work.

The federal government will continue to take the actions necessary to restore stability to our financial markets and growth to our economy. We have an outstanding economic team carrying out this effort, led by Secretary of the Treasury Hank Paulson, Federal Reserve Chairman Ben Bernanke, SEC Chairman Chris Cox, and FDIC Chair Sheila Bair. I thank them and their dedicated teams for their service during this important moment in our country's history.

This is an anxious time, but the American people can be confident in our economic future. We know what the problems are, we have the tools we need to fix them, and we're working swiftly to do so. Our economy is innovative, industrious and resilient because the American people who make up our economy are innovative, industrious and resilient. We all share a determination to solve this problem—and that is exactly what we're going to do. May God bless you.

Statement of Treasury Secretary Henry M. Paulson Jr. on Actions to Protect the U.S. Economy (2008)

After the worst week on Wall Street since the Great Depression, within weeks Congress passed the Emergency Economic Stabilization Act on October 3, 2008. The act granted authority to Secretary of Treasury Henry M. Paulson Jr. to restore liquidity and stability to the U.S. financial system through the use of a $700 billion *fund designed to protect the assets of American citizens and jobs. On October 14, 2008, Treasury Secretary Henry M. Paulson Jr. announced that $250 billion of the $700 billion would be used to provide capital to U.S. banks and thrifts in an attempt to loosen up the availability of credit desperately needed by American businesses and individuals. The following is Paulson's statement on the Treasury's plan to provide capital to financial institutions through the purchase of equity shares in U.S. banks and thrifts.*

Source: U.S. Department of Treasury Press Release, "Statement by Secretary Henry M. Paulson Jr. on Actions to Protect the U.S. Economy," HP-1205, October 14, 2008, http://www.treas.gov/press/releases/hp1205.htm.

Treasury today issued the following statement by Secretary Henry M. Paulson, Jr. on actions to protect the economy and restore confidence and stability to our financial markets:

America is a strong nation. We are a confident and optimistic people. Our confidence is born out of our long history of meeting every challenge we face. Time and time again our nation has faced adversity and time and time again we have overcome it and risen to new heights. This time will be no different.

Today, there is a lack of confidence in our financial system – a lack of confidence that must be conquered because it poses an enormous threat to our economy. Investors are unwilling to lend to banks, and healthy banks are unwilling to lend to each other and to consumers and businesses.

In recent weeks, the American people have felt the effects of a frozen financial system. They have seen reduced values in their retirement and investment accounts. They have worried about meeting payrolls and they have worried about losing their jobs. Families all across our Nation have gone through long days and long nights of concern about their financial situations today, and their financial situations tomorrow. Without confidence that their most basic financial needs will be met, Americans lose confidence in our economy, and this is unacceptable.

President Bush has directed me to consider all necessary steps to restore confidence and stability to our financial markets and get credit flowing again. Ten days ago Congress gave important new tools to the Treasury, the Federal Reserve, and the FDIC to meet the challenges posed to our economy. My colleagues and I are working creatively and collaboratively to deploy these tools and direct our powers at this disruption to our economy.

Today we are taking decisive actions to protect the U.S. economy. We regret having to take these actions. Today's actions are not what we ever wanted to do – but today's actions are what we must do to restore confidence to our financial system.

Today I am announcing that the Treasury will purchase equity stakes in a wide array of banks and thrifts. Government owning a stake in any private U.S. company is objectionable to most Americans – me included. Yet the alternative of leaving businesses and consumers without access to financing is totally unacceptable. When financing isn't available, consumers and businesses shrink their spending, which leads to businesses cutting jobs and even closing up shop.

To avoid that outcome, we must restore confidence in our financial system. The first step in that effort is a plan to make capital available on attractive terms to a broad array of banks and thrifts, so they can provide credit to our economy. From the $700 billion financial rescue package [Emergency Economic Stabilization Act], Treasury will make $250 billion in capital available to U.S. financial institutions in the form of preferred stock. Institutions that sell shares to the government will accept restrictions on executive compensation, including a clawback provision and a ban on golden parachutes during the period that Treasury holds equity issued through this program. In addition, taxpayers will not only own shares that should be paid back with a reasonable return, but also will receive warrants for common shares in participating institutions. We expect all participating banks to continue and to strengthen their efforts to help struggling homeowners who can afford their homes avoid foreclosure. Foreclosures not only hurt the families who lose their homes, they hurt neighborhoods, communities and our economy as a whole.

While many banks have suffered significant losses during this period of market turmoil, many others have plenty of capital to get through this period, but are not positioned to lend as widely as is necessary to support our economy. Our goal is to see a wide array of healthy institutions sell preferred shares to the Treasury, and raise additional private capital, so that they can make more loans to businesses and consumers across the nation. At a time when events naturally make even the most daring investors more risk-averse, the needs of our economy require that our financial institutions not take this new capital to hoard it, but to deploy it.

Nine large financial institutions have already agreed to participate in this program. They have agreed to sell preferred shares to the U.S. government, on the same terms that will be available to a broad array of small and medium-sized banks and thrifts across the nation. These are healthy institutions, and they have taken this step for the good of the U.S. economy. As these healthy institutions increase their capital base, they will be able to increase their funding to U.S. consumers and businesses.

I am joined here this morning by [Federal Reserve] Chairman [Ben] Bernanke and [FDIC] Chairman [Sheila C.] Bair, who have also taken extraordinary actions to support investor confidence in our financial system, so that funds will again flow through our banks to the U.S. economy. Each of them will describe their actions.

Combined, our actions are extensive, powerful and transformative. They demonstrate that the government will do what is necessary to restore the flow of funds on which our economy depends and will act to avoid, where possible, the failure of any systemically important institution.

These three steps significantly strengthen financial institutions and improve their access to funding, enabling them to increase financing of the consumption and business investment that drive U.S. economic growth. Market participants here and around the world can take confidence from the powerful actions taken today and our broad commitment to the health of the global financial system.

We are acting with unprecedented speed taking unprecedented measures that we never thought would be necessary. But they are necessary to get our economy back on an even keel, and secure the confidence and future of our markets, our economy and the economic well-being of all Americans.

U.S. Secretary of Treasury Henry Paulson's Remarks on Troubled Assets Relief Program (TARP) (2008)

On November 12, 2008, the U.S. Treasury Department issued the following prepared text of Treasury Secretary Henry Paulson's remarks about the financial crisis that began in 2007, the efforts made since that time to restore economic stability, the resulting passage of the $700 billion Emergency Economic Stabilization Act and its immediate impact, as well as future economic considerations under review.

Source: U.S. Department of Treasury, November 12, 2008, http://www.ustreas.gov/press/releases/hp1265.htm.

Washington, D.C.

Good morning. I will provide an update on the state of the financial system, our economy, and our strategy for continued implementation of the financial rescue package.

Current State of Global Financial System

The actions taken by Treasury, the Federal Reserve and the FDIC in October have clearly helped stabilize our financial system. Before we acted, we were at a tipping point. Credit markets were largely frozen, denying financial institutions, businesses and consumers access to vital funding and credit. U.S. and European financial institutions were under extreme pressure, and investor confidence in our system was dangerously low.

We also acted quickly and in coordination with colleagues around the world to stabilize the global financial system. Going into the Annual IMF/World Bank meetings in early October, I made clear that we would use the financial rescue package granted by Congress to purchase equity directly from financial institutions - the fastest and most productive means of using our new authorities to stabilize our financial system. We launched our capital purchase program the following week when we announced that nine of the largest U.S. financial institutions, holding approximately 55 percent of U.S. banking assets would sell $125 billion in preferred stock to the Treasury. At the same time, the FDIC announced it would temporarily guarantee all newly issued senior unsecured debt of participating organizations for up to three years. In addition, the FDIC provided an unlimited guarantee on non-interest bearing transaction accounts that expires at the end of next year.

As I assess where we are today, I believe we have taken the necessary steps to prevent a broad systemic event. Both at home and around the world we have already seen signs of improvement. Our system is stronger and more stable than just a few weeks ago. Although this is a major accomplishment, we have many challenges ahead of us. Our financial system remains fragile in the face of an economic downturn here and abroad, and financial institutions' balance sheets still hold significant illiquid assets. Market turmoil will not abate until the biggest part of the housing correction is behind us. Our primary focus must be recovery and repair.

Housing and Mortgage Finance

Overall, we are in a better position than we were, but we must address the continued challenges of a weak economy, especially the housing correction and lending contraction.

On housing, we have worked aggressively to avoid preventable foreclosures and keep mortgage financing available. In October 2007, we helped establish the HOPE NOW Alliance, a coalition of mortgage servicers, investors and counselors, to help struggling homeowners avoid preventable foreclosures. HOPE NOW created a streamlined protocol to assist struggling borrowers who could afford their homes with a loan modification. The industry is now helping 200,000 homeowners a month avoid foreclosure. In addition, HUD has created new programs to complement existing FHA options, and to refinance a larger number of struggling borrowers into affordable FHA mortgages.

Most significantly, we acted earlier this year to prevent the failure of Fannie Mae and Freddie Mac, the housing GSEs that now touch over 70 percent of mortgage originations. I clearly stated at that time three critical objectives: providing stability to financial markets, supporting the availability of mortgage finance, and protecting taxpayers - both by minimizing the near term costs to the taxpayer and by setting policymakers on a course to resolve the systemic risk created by the inherent conflict in the GSE structure.

Fortunately we acted, citing concerns about both the quality and quantity of GSE capital. Unfortunately, our actions proved all too necessary. The GSEs were failing, and if they did fail, it would have materially exacerbated the recent market turmoil and more profoundly impacted household wealth: from family budgets, to home values, to savings for college and retirement.

Earlier this week, Fannie Mae reported a record loss, including write-downs of its deferred tax assets that make up a significant portion of its capital. We monitor closely the performance of both Fannie Mae and Freddie Mac, and both are performing within the range of our expectations. The magnitude of the losses at Fannie Mae were within the range of what we expected, and further confirms the need for our strong actions.

Eight weeks ago, Treasury took responsibility for supporting the agency debt securities and the agency MBS [Mortgage-Backed Securities] through a preferred stock purchase agreement that guarantees a positive net worth in each enterprise - effectively, a guarantee on GSE debt and agency MBS. We also established a credit facility to provide the GSEs the strongest possible liquidity backstop. As the enterprises go through this difficult housing correction we will, as needed and promised, purchase preferred shares under the terms of that agreement. The U.S. government honors its commitments, and investors can bank on it.

When we took action in September, I said that we would be entering a "time out" - a period where the new President and Congress must decide what role government in general, and the GSEs in particular, should play in the housing market. In my view, government support needs to be either explicit or non-existent, and structured to resolve the conflict between public and private purposes. And policymakers must address the issue of systemic risk. In the weeks ahead, I will share some thoughts outlining my views on long term reform.

In the meantime, the GSEs now operate on stable footing. They have strong government support backing both future capital and liquidity needs. We have stabilized the GSEs and limited systemic risk, and our authorities provide us with additional flexibility to use as necessary to accomplish our objectives.

Implementing the Financial Rescue Package

More recently, we have also taken extraordinary steps to support our financial markets and financial institutions. As credit markets froze in mid-September, the Administration asked Congress for broad tools and flexibility to rescue the financial system. We asked for $700 billion to purchase troubled assets from financial institutions. At the time, we believed that would be the most effective means of getting credit flowing again.

During the two weeks that Congress considered the legislation, market conditions worsened considerably. It was clear to me by the time the bill was signed on

October 3rd that we needed to act quickly and forcefully, and that purchasing troubled assets - our initial focus - would take time to implement and would not be sufficient given the severity of the problem. In consultation with the Federal Reserve, I determined that the most timely, effective step to improve credit market conditions was to strengthen bank balance sheets quickly through direct purchases of equity in banks.

Of course, before that time, the only instances in which Treasury had taken equity positions was in rescuing a failing institution. Both the preferred stock purchase agreement for Fannie Mae and Freddie Mac, and the Federal Reserve's secured lending facility for AIG came with significant taxpayer protections and conditions. As we planned a capital purchase plan to support the overall financial system by strengthening balance sheets of a broad array of healthy banks, the terms had to be designed to encourage broad participation, balanced to ensure appropriate taxpayer protection and not impede the flow of private capital.

Capital Purchase Plan

We announced a plan on October 14th to purchase up to $250 billion in preferred stock in federally regulated banks and thrifts. By October 26th we had $115 billion out the door to eight large institutions. In Washington that is a land-speed record from announcing a program to getting funds out the door. We now have approved dozens of additional applications, and investments are being made in approved institutions. Although we are moving very quickly it will take time to complete legal contracts and execute investments in the significant number of institutions who meet the eligibility requirements and are approved, but we are on the path to getting this done.

Although this program's primary purpose is stabilizing our financial system, banks must also continue lending. During times like these with a slowing economy and some deterioration in credit conditions, even the healthiest banks tend to become more risk-averse and restrain lending, and regulators' actions have reinforced this lending restraint in the past. With a stronger capital base, our banks will be more confident and better positioned to play their necessary role to support economic activity. Today banking regulators issued a statement emphasizing that the extraordinary government actions taken by the Fed, Treasury, and FDIC to stabilize and strengthen the banking system are not merely one-sided; all banks - not just those participating in the Capital Purchase Program - have benefited, so they all also have responsibilities in the areas of lending, dividend and compensation policies, and foreclosure mitigation. I commend this action and I am particularly focused on the importance of prudent bank lending to restore our economic growth.

Since announcing the Capital Purchase Program, we have been examining a wide range of ideas that can further strengthen the financial system and get lending going again to support the broader economy. First and foremost, because the system remains fragile, we must continue to stand ready to prevent systemic failures. That is the basis for Monday's action to purchase preferred shares in AIG. The stability of our system remains the highest priority.

We must also allow markets and institutions to absorb the extensive array of new policies put in place in a very short period of time. The injection of up to $250 billion of capital into individual banks, the FDIC's temporary guarantee of bank debt and the Federal Reserve's multiple liquidity facilities for banks, money funds and commercial paper issuers have all significantly enhanced liquidity and helped improve market conditions.

Priorities for Remaining TARP Funds

We have evaluated options for most effectively deploying the remaining TARP funds, and have identified three critical priorities. First, we must continue to reinforce the stability of the financial system, so that banks and other institutions critical to the provision of credit are able to support economic recovery and growth. Although the financial system has stabilized, both banks and non-banks may well need more capital given their troubled asset holdings, projections for continued high rates of foreclosures and stagnant U.S. and world economic conditions. Second, the important markets for securitizing credit outside of the banking system also need support. Approximately 40 percent of U.S. consumer credit is provided through securitization of credit card receivables, auto loans, and student loans and similar products. This market, which is vital for lending and growth, has for all practical purposes ground to a halt. Addressing these two priorities will have powerful impacts on the overall financial system, the strength of our financial institutions and the availability of consumer credit. Third, we continue to explore ways to reduce the risk of foreclosure.

Over these past weeks we have continued to examine the relative benefits of purchasing illiquid mortgage-related assets. Our assessment at this time is that this is not the most effective way to use TARP funds, but we will continue to examine whether targeted forms of asset purchase can play a useful role, relative to other potential uses of TARP resources, in helping to strengthen our financial system and support lending. But other strategies I will outline will help to alleviate the pressure of illiquid assets.

Further Strategies

First, we are designing further strategies for building capital in financial institutions. Stronger capital positions will enable financial institutions to better manage the illiquid assets on their books and better ensure that they remain healthy. Any future program should maintain our principle of encouraging participation of healthy institutions while protecting taxpayers. We are carefully evaluating programs which would further leverage the impact of a TARP investment by attracting private capital, potentially through matching investments. In developing a potential matching program, we will also consider capital needs of non-bank financial institutions not eligible for the current capital program; broadening access in this way would bring both benefits and challenges. Non-bank financial institutions provide credit that is essential to U.S. businesses and consumers. However, many are not directly regulated and are active in a wide range of businesses, and taxpayer protections in a program of this sort would be more difficult to achieve. Also before embarking on a second capital purchase program, the first one must be completed, and we have to assess its impact and use this information to evaluate the size and focus of an additional program in light of existing economic and market conditions.

Second, we are examining strategies to support consumer access to credit outside the banking system. To date, Fed, FDIC and Treasury programs have been targeted at our banking system, and the non-bank consumer finance sector continues to face difficult funding issues. Specifically, the asset-backed securitization market has played a critical role for many years in lowering the cost and increasing the availability of consumer finance. This market is currently in distress, costs of funding have skyrocketed and new issue activity has come to a halt. Today, the illiquidity in this sector is raising the cost and reducing the availability of car loans, student loans and credit cards. This is creating a heavy burden on the American people and reducing the number of jobs in our economy. With the Federal Reserve we are exploring the development of a potential liquidity facility for highly-rated AAA asset-backed securities. We are looking at ways to possibly use the TARP to encourage private investors to come back to this troubled market, by providing them access to federal financing while protecting the taxpayers' investment. By doing so, we can lower costs and increase credit availability for consumers. Addressing the needs of the securitization sector will help get lending going again, helping consumers and supporting the U.S. economy. While this securitization effort is targeted at consumer financing, the program we are evaluating may also be used to support new commercial and residential mortgage-backed securities lending.

Third, we are examining strategies to mitigate mortgage foreclosures. In crafting the financial rescue package, we and the Congress agreed that Treasury would use its leverage as a major purchaser of troubled mortgages to work with servicers and achieve more aggressive mortgage modification standards. Now that we are not planning to purchase illiquid mortgage assets, we must find another way to meet that commitment.

FDIC Chairman Bair has given us a model, in the mortgage modification protocol she developed with IndyMac Bank. Through the end of October, the FDIC has completed loan modifications for 3,500 borrowers, with several thousand more modifications currently being processed. These modifications have reduced payments for participating homeowners by an average of $380 month, or about 23 percent. We have worked with the FHFA, the GSEs, HUD and the Hope Now alliance who yesterday announced a streamlined industry-wide modification program that for the first time adopts an explicit affordability target similar to the model pioneered at IndyMac. With this commitment, the GSEs and large portfolio investors are setting a new industry standard for foreclosure mitigation. Potentially hundreds of thousands more struggling borrowers will be enabled to stay in their homes at an affordable monthly mortgage payment.

Beyond these efforts, there has been significant work to design and evaluate a number of proposals to induce further modifications. Each of these would, however, require substantial government subsidies. The FDIC, for example, has developed a proposal that Treasury and others in the Administration continue to discuss. I believe it is an important idea. As we evaluate the merits of any new proposal, we also will have to identify and justify the means to finance it. We must be careful to distinguish this type of assistance, which essentially involves direct spending, from the type of invest-ments that are intended to promote financial stability, protect the taxpayer, and be recovered under the TARP legislation. Maximizing loan modifications, nonetheless, is a key part of working through the housing correction and maintaining the quality of communities across the nation, and we will continue working hard to make progress here.

We will continue to pursue the three strategies I have just outlined: how best to strengthen the capital base of our financial system; how best to support the asset-backed securitization market that is critical to consumer finance, and how to increase foreclosure mitigation efforts. All of these strategies are important, but ensuring the financial system has sufficient capital is essential to getting credit flowing to consum-ers and businesses and that is where the bulk of the remaining TARP funds should be deployed—in a program to support the system and as a contingency reserve for addressing any unforeseen systemic events.

We are focused on developing and preparing programs which can be implemented for each of these strategies. We will continue to brief President-elect Obama's transition team on all of these issues.

Global Challenge

Of course managing through this market turmoil while mitigating the impact of the credit crisis is a global as well as a national issue. We in the U.S. are well aware and humbled by our own failings and recognize our special responsibility to the global economy. The U.S. housing correction exposed gaping shortcomings in the outdated U.S. regulatory system, shortcomings in other regulatory regimes and excesses in U.S. and European financial institutions. These institutions found them-selves with large holdings of structured products, including complex and opaque mortgage-backed securities. Some European institutions were characterized by high leverage, exposure to their own housing markets, exposure to Central European insti-tutions, weak business models or overly aggressive expansion, while others faced weaknesses because of inadequate depositor protection systems. It should not be surprising that after 13 months of stress in the global capital markets, banks from the U.S. to the U.K., from Germany to Iceland, from Russia to France, had difficulties that exposed some of these weaknesses for the first time. For some of these banks, this proved to be a hurdle too high and government action was necessary to support financial stability.

In that regard the G7 Finance Ministers meeting last month represented a major turning point in stabilizing the global financial system as the ministers came together to support a number of powerful strategies that were soon turned into effective actions in the United States and Europe. It is also clear that our first priority must be recovery and repair. And of course we must take strong actions to fix our system so that the world does not have to suffer something like this ever again. The Leaders summit President Bush will be hosting this weekend marks a very important step in what will be an ongoing process of recovery and reform.

And to adequately reform our system, we must make sure we fully understand the nature of the problem which will not be possible until we are confident it is behind us. Of course, it is already clear that we must address a number of significant issues, such as improving risk management practices, compensation practices, oversight of mortgage origination and the securitization process, credit rating agencies, OTC derivative market infrastructure and regulatory policies, practices and regimes in our respective countries. And we recognize that our financial institutions and our markets are global, but our regulatory regimes are national, so we will examine how best to improve cooperation and information sharing to foster global financial system stability.

But let us not forget one fundamental issue which lies at the heart of our problems. Over a period of years, persistent and growing global imbalances fueled a dramatic increase in capital flows, low interest rates, excessive risk taking and a global search for return. Those excesses cannot be attributed to any single nation. There is no doubt that low U.S. savings are a significant factor, but the lack of consumption and accumulation of reserves in Asia and oil-exporting countries and structural issues in Europe have also fed the imbalances.

If we only address particular regulatory issues - as critical as they are - without addressing the global imbalances that fueled recent excesses, we will have missed an opportunity to dramatically improve the foundation for global markets and economic vitality going forward. The pressure from global imbalances will simply build up again until it finds another outlet.

The nations attending this weekend's summit represent the 20 largest economies in the world over 77 percent of global GDP. President Bush is convening this group of countries to discuss and address problems such as global imbalances, making regulatory regimes more effective, fostering cooperation among regulators, and reforming international institutions to better address today's global economy. We can't simply task the IMF, the FSF or other International Financial Institutions to solve the problems, unless member nations all see that they have a shared interest in a solution. There are no easy answers, because until we reach a consensus on a broad-based reform agenda, we will not reach a solution. This weekend provides an opportunity for nations to take an important step, but only one step, on the necessary path to reform.

Conclusion

The road ahead, for the U.S. economy and the global economy, is full of challenges. And it will take strong leadership to address them. I am confident the United States, under this and the next Administration, will rise to these challenges. I will do everything I can to put us on the right path, both by working diligently through the end of my term and by working closely to ensure the smoothest possible transition.

Federal Reserve Governor Randall S. Kroszner's "The Community Reinvestment Act and the Recent Mortgage Crisis" Speech (2008)

When the economic recession started with the sub-prime mortgage crisis in August 2007, the Community Reinvestment Act (CRA) became the target of many critics who argued that the legislation was the root cause of the current economic crisis, claiming that the requirements placed on banks to make credit available in low-income areas resulted in a proliferation of risky mortgages that sparked the current mortgage crisis when these mortgages went into default. The Federal Reserve, in partnership with The Brookings Institution, conducted a study in all areas across the country to determine what role, if any, the act might have played. On December 3, 2008, Federal Reserve Governor Randall S. Kroszner gave the following speech at the Board of Governors of the Federal Reserve System's conference "At the Confronting Concentrated Poverty Policy Forum" in Washington, D.C., in which he noted that there was no evidence to support the charges against the CRA.

Source: Board of Governors of the Federal Reserve System, December 3, 2008, accessed online at http://www.federalreserve.gov/newsevents/speech/kroszner20081203a.htm.

Good morning. I am pleased to welcome you to the Board and even more pleased to introduce today's discussion of the study conducted by the Federal Reserve System's Community Affairs program in partnership with The Brookings Institution, *The Enduring Challenge of Concentrated Poverty in America: Case Studies from Communities across the U.S.*

As you have heard, this report represents an extraordinary and comprehensive effort by staff in all 12 Reserve Banks and at the Board of Governors to explore the problem of concentrated poverty. The 16 case studies in the report represent urban and rural areas, immigrant and Native American communities, as well as older "weak" market cities and newer "strong" market areas. By covering a wide variety of communities, the report adds depth and texture to the existing literature on poverty and offers important insights regarding the relationship between public services and private investment.

For those who may not be familiar with the Federal Reserve System's Community Affairs function, this report illustrates one of the many ways in which it supports the System's objectives for economic growth by promoting community development and fair and impartial access to credit. The System's strength in research, together with its unique structure, makes it particularly well suited to pursue this kind of work.

The Community Affairs program takes advantage of the 12 Federal Reserve Banks located in different regions of the country to gather information on local conditions and to conduct outreach and education efforts through regular contact with financial institutions and market intermediaries. The System's network of Community Affairs staff works with lenders, community organizations, and local governments to identify trends and issues affecting low- and moderate-income neighborhoods. This communication with both financial markets and communities allows the Federal Reserve to act as a bridge between the private and public sectors.

The System's reputation for high-quality research, outreach, and analysis and its regional presence made these 16 case studies and the comparative analysis possible. This report makes an important contribution to the literature on the dynamics of poor people living in poor communities by recognizing the existence and persistence of concentrations of poverty beyond the urban areas where it has been well documented. Indeed, the study confirms that poverty persists in places, such as rural and suburban communities, where it is not so easily seen.

The report also identifies the existing avenues for bringing poor people and communities into the economic mainstream. This topic is at the center of today's discussions. The Federal Reserve, together with the other federal financial regulatory agencies, has had some experience in addressing the credit needs of underserved communities, using the Community Reinvestment Act (CRA) as our guide. CRA encourages financial institutions not only to extend mortgage, small business, and other types of credit to lower-income neighborhoods and households, but also to provide investments and services to lower-income areas and people as part of an overall effort to build the capacity necessary for these places to thrive.

Some critics of the CRA contend that by encouraging banking institutions to help meet the credit needs of lower-income borrowers and areas, the law pushed banking institutions to undertake high-risk mortgage lending. We have not yet seen empirical evidence to support these claims, nor has it been our experience in implementing the law over the past 30 years that the CRA has contributed to the erosion of safe and sound lending practices. In the remainder of my remarks, I will discuss some of our experiences with the CRA. I will also discuss the findings of a recent analysis of mortgage-related data by Federal Reserve staff that runs counter to the charge that the CRA was at the root of, or otherwise contributed in any substantive way, to the current subprime crisis.

Regulatory Efforts to Meet Credit Needs in Underserved Markets

In the 1970s, when banking was still a local enterprise, the Congress enacted the CRA. The act required the banking regulators to encourage insured depository institutions—that is, commercial banks and thrifts—to help meet the credit needs of their entire community, including low- and moderate-income areas. The CRA does not stipulate minimum targets or goals for lending, investments, or services. Rather, the law provides incentives for financial institutions to help meet the credit needs of lower-income people and areas, consistent with safe and sound banking practices, and commensurately provides them favorable CRA consideration for those activities. By requiring regulators to make CRA performance ratings and evaluations public and to consider those ratings when reviewing applications for mergers, acquisitions, and branches, the Congress created an unusual set of incentives to promote interaction between lenders and community organizations.

Given the incentives of the CRA, bankers have pursued lines of business that had not been previously tapped by forming partnerships with community organizations and other stakeholders to identify and help meet the credit needs of underserved communities. This experimentation in lending, often combined with financial education and counseling and consideration of nontraditional measures of creditworthiness, expanded the markets for safe lending in underserved communities and demonstrated its viability; as a result, these actions attracted competition from other financial services providers, many of whom were not covered by the CRA. There are many fine examples of community development lending and investment activities designed to address needs in the poorest of areas, including many of those highlighted by the case studies in this report.

During trips to the regional Federal Reserve Banks and Branches, I have spent a lot of time visiting areas with high concentrations of poverty. For many years, the Fed has promoted community banking services for the unbanked and underbanked population. It was gratifying for me to find that financial services were accessible in, for example, central Cleveland, thanks to the efforts of one local bank that offers check-cashing services at much lower rates than competing nonbank check cashers. Similarly, in the Little Haiti neighborhood in Miami, another case-study community that I had the opportunity to visit last year, one banking institution has committed to serving the neighborhood's unbanked residents by hiring Creole-speaking staff to promote a prosperity campaign built around the Earned Income Tax Credit.

I am sure that today's luncheon speaker, Tom Barrett, mayor of Milwaukee, could share similar observations about a local financial institution serving that case-study neighborhood by providing low-income residents complimentary electronic income tax filing combined with financial education seminars, innovative credit repair programs, and low-cost banking services. These services benefit lower-income customers by providing a simple means of accessing Earned Income and Homestead Tax Credits and the services necessary to maximize the benefits of these programs.

In addition to providing financial services to lower-income people, banks also provide critical community development loans and investments to address affordable housing and economic development needs. These activities are particularly effective because they leverage the resources available to communities from public subsidies and tax credit programs that are targeted to lower-income people. In just the past two years, banks have reported making over $120 billion in community development loans nationwide. This figure does not capture the full extent of such lending, because smaller institutions are not required to report community development loans to their regulators.

Evidence on CRA and the Subprime Crisis

Over the years, the Federal Reserve has prepared two reports for the Congress that provide information on the performance of lending to lower-income borrowers or neighborhoods—populations that are the focus of the CRA. These studies found that lending to lower-income individuals and communities has been nearly as profitable and performed similarly to other types of lending done by CRA-covered institutions. Thus, the long-term evidence shows that the CRA has not pushed banks into extending loans that perform out of line with their traditional businesses. Rather, the law has encouraged banks to be aware of lending opportunities in all segments of their local communities as well as to learn how to undertake such lending in a safe and sound manner.

Recently, Federal Reserve staff has undertaken more specific analysis focusing on the potential relationship between the CRA and the current subprime crisis. This analysis was performed for the purpose of assessing claims that the CRA was a principal cause of the current mortgage market difficulties. For this analysis, the staff examined lending activity covering the period that corresponds to the height of the subprime boom.

The research focused on two basic questions. First, we asked what share of originations for subprime loans is related to the CRA. The potential role of the CRA in the subprime crisis could either be large or small, depending on the answer to this question. We found that the loans that are the focus of the CRA represent a very small portion of the subprime lending market, casting considerable doubt on the potential contribution that the law could have made to the subprime mortgage crisis.

Second, we asked how CRA-related subprime loans performed relative to other loans. Once again, the potential role of the CRA could be large or small, depending on the answer to this question. We found that delinquency rates were high in all neighborhood income groups, and that CRA-related subprime loans performed in a comparable manner to other subprime loans; as such, differences in performance between CRA-related subprime lending and other subprime lending cannot lie at the root of recent market turmoil.

In analyzing the available data, we focused on two distinct metrics: loan origination activity and loan performance. With respect to the first question concerning loan originations, we wanted to know which types of lending institutions made higher-priced loans, to whom those loans were made, and in what types of neighborhoods the loans were extended.[5] This analysis allowed us to determine what fraction of subprime lending could be related to the CRA.

Our analysis of the loan data found that about 60 percent of higher-priced loan originations went to middle- or higher-income borrowers or neighborhoods. Such borrowers are not the populations targeted by the CRA. In addition, more than 20 percent of the higher-priced loans were extended to lower-income borrowers or borrowers in lower-income areas by independent nonbank institutions—that is, institutions not covered by the CRA.

Putting together these facts provides a striking result: Only 6 percent of all the higher-priced loans were extended by CRA-covered lenders to lower-income borrowers or neighborhoods in their CRA assessment areas, the local geographies that are the primary focus for CRA evaluation purposes. This result undermines the assertion by critics of the potential for a substantial role for the CRA in the subprime crisis. In other words, the very small share of all higher-priced loan originations that can reasonably be attributed to the CRA makes it hard to imagine how this law could have contributed in any meaningful way to the current subprime crisis.

Of course, loan originations are only one path that banking institutions can follow to meet their CRA obligations. They can also purchase loans from lenders not covered by the CRA, and in this way encourage more of this type of lending. The data also suggest that these types of transactions have not been a significant factor in the current crisis. Specifically, less than 2 percent of the higher-priced and CRA-credit-eligible mortgage originations sold by independent mortgage companies were purchased by CRA-covered institutions.

I now want to turn to the second question concerning how CRA-related subprime lending performed relative to other types of lending. To address this issue, we looked at data on subprime and alt-A mortgage delinquencies in lower-income neighborhoods and compared them with those in middle- and higher-income neighborhoods to see how CRA-related loans performed.[7] An overall comparison revealed that the rates for all subprime and alt-A loans delinquent 90 days or more is high regardless of neighborhood income. This result casts further doubt on the view that the CRA could have contributed in any meaningful way to the current subprime crisis.

Unfortunately, the available data on loan performance do not let us distinguish which specific loans in lower-income areas were related to the CRA. As noted earlier, institutions not covered by the CRA extended many loans to borrowers in lower-income areas. Also, some lower-income lending by institutions subject to the law was outside their local communities and unlikely to have been motivated by the CRA.

To learn more about the relative performance of CRA-related lending, we conducted more detailed analyses to try to focus on performance differences that might truly arise as a consequence of the rule as opposed to other factors. Attempting to adjust for other relevant factors is challenging but worthwhile to try to assess the performance of CRA-related lending. In one such analysis, we compared loan delinquency rates in neighborhoods that are right above and right below the CRA neighborhood income eligibility threshold. In other words, we compared loan performance by borrowers in two groups of neighborhoods that should not be very different except for the fact that the lending in one group received special attention under the CRA.

When we conducted this analysis, we found essentially no difference in the performance of subprime loans in Zip codes that were just below or just above the income threshold for the CRA. The results of this analysis are not consistent with the contention that the CRA is at the root of the subprime crisis, because delinquency rates for subprime and alt-A loans in neighborhoods just below the CRA-eligibility threshold are very similar to delinquency rates on loans just above the threshold, hence not the subject of CRA lending.

To gain further insight into the potential relationship between the CRA and the subprime crisis, we also compared the recent performance of subprime loans with mortgages originated and held in portfolio under the affordable lending programs operated by NeighborWorks America (NWA). As a member of the board of directors of the NWA, I am quite familiar with its lending activities. The NWA has partnered with many CRA-covered banking institutions to originate and hold mortgages made predominantly to lower-income borrowers and neighborhoods. So, to the extent that such loans are representative of CRA-lending programs in general, the performance of these loans is helpful in understanding the relationship between the CRA and the subprime crisis. We found that loans originated under the NWA program had a lower delinquency rate than subprime loans. Furthermore, the loans in the NWA affordable lending portfolio had a lower rate of foreclosure than prime loans. The result that the loans in the NWA portfolio performed better than subprime loans again casts doubt on the contention that the CRA has been a significant contributor to the subprime crisis.

The final analysis we undertook to investigate the likely effects of the CRA on the subprime crisis was to examine foreclosure activity across neighborhoods grouped by income. We found that most foreclosure filings have taken place in middle- or higher-income neighborhoods; in fact, foreclosure filings have increased at a faster pace in middle- or higher-income areas than in lower-income areas that are the focus of the CRA.

Two key points emerge from all of our analysis of the available data. First, only a small portion of subprime mortgage originations are related to the CRA. Second, CRA- related loans appear to perform comparably to other types of subprime loans. Taken together, as I stated earlier, we believe that the available evidence runs counter to the contention that the CRA contributed in any substantive way to the current mortgage crisis.

Conclusions

Our findings are important because neighborhoods and communities affected by the economic downturn will require the active participation of financial institutions. Considering the situation today, many neighborhoods that are not currently the focus of the CRA are also experiencing great difficulties. Our recent review of foreclosure data suggested that many middle-income areas currently have elevated rates of foreclosure filings and could face the prospect of falling into low-to-moderate income status. In fact, 13 percent of the middle-income Zip codes have had foreclosure-rate filings that are above the overall rate for lower-income areas.

Helping to stabilize such areas not only benefits families in these areas but also provides spillover benefits to adjacent lower-income areas that are the traditional target of the CRA. Recognizing this, the Congress recently underscored the need for states and localities to undertake a comprehensive approach to stabilizing neighborhoods hard-hit by foreclosures through the enactment of the new Neighborhood Stabilization Program (NSP). The NSP permits targeting of federal funds to benefit families up to 120 percent of area median income in those areas experiencing rising foreclosures and falling home values.

In conclusion, I believe the CRA is an important model for designing incentives that motivate private-sector involvement to help meet community needs. The CRA has, in fact, been helpful in alleviating the financial isolation of many areas of concentrated poverty, but as our report illustrates, there is much more that could be done in these communities. Contrary to the assertions of critics, the evidence does not support the view that the CRA contributed in any substantial way to the crisis in the subprime mortgage market. Today's discussion is an important first step in the process of identifying other initiatives and areas of cooperation between government and the private sector that will effectively address the continuing challenge of poverty in the United States.

Barack Obama's Remarks on Recovery Act of 2009

After taking office on January 21, 2009, Barack Obama proposed that Congress enact a new stimulus package because of the continued economic downtown in the U.S. economy, which began back in August 2007. On January 25, a stimulus bill was introduced into the House of Representatives. The final version of the measure, known as The American Recovery and Reinvestment Act of 2009, was agreed on by both the House and the Senate on February 13, 2009. The $787 billion stimulus package made funds available in the areas of education, health care, and infrastructure, including the energy sector, as well as tax cuts for the low-income, expansion of unemployment benefits, and other social programs. In addition, the act authorized the use of federal funds to assist state and local fiscal stabilization for the budget year ending on September 30, 2009. President Obama signed the bill into law while hosting an economic forum in Denver, Colorado, on February 17, 2009.

Source: CNN Politics. Obama's Remarks on Signing the Stimulus Plan. February 17, 2009, http://articles.cnn.com/2009-02-17/politics/obama.stimulus.remarks_1 _economic-stimulus-bill-sign-today-speaker-pelosi?_s=PM:POLITICS.

Today does not mark the end of our economic troubles. Nor does it constitute all of what we must do to turn our economy around. But it does mark the beginning of the end—the beginning of what we need to do to create jobs for Americans scrambling in the wake of layoffs, to provide relief for families worried they won't be able to pay next month's bills and to set our economy on a firmer foundation, paving the way to long-term growth and prosperity.

The American Recovery and Reinvestment Act that I will sign today, a plan that meets the principles I laid out in January, is the most sweeping economic recovery package in our history. It is the product of broad consultations—and the recipient of broad support—from business leaders, unions and public interest groups, the Chamber of Commerce, the National Association of Manufacturers, Democrats and Republicans, mayors as well as governors.

It is a rare thing in Washington for people with such different viewpoints to come together and support the same bill, and on behalf of our nation, I thank them for it, including your two outstanding new senators, Michael Bennet and Mark Udall.

I also want to thank my vice president, Joe Biden, for working behind the scenes from the very start to make this recovery act possible. I want to thank Speaker Pelosi and

Harry Reid for acting so quickly and proving that Congress could step up to this challenge. I want to thank Max Baucus, chairman of the Finance Committee, without whom none of this would have happened. And I want to thank all the committee chairs and members of Congress for coming up with a plan that is both bold and balanced enough to meet the demands of this moment. The American people were looking to them for leadership, and that is what they provided.

What makes this recovery plan so important is not just that it will create or save 3½ million jobs over the next two years, including nearly 60,000 in Colorado. It's that we are putting Americans to work doing the work that America needs done in critical areas that have been neglected for too long, work that will bring real and lasting change for generations to come.

Because we know we can't build our economic future on the transportation and information networks of the past, we are remaking the American landscape with the largest new investment in our nation's infrastructure since Eisenhower built an interstate highway system in the 1950s.

Because of this investment, nearly 400,000 men and women will go to work rebuilding our crumbling roads and bridges, repairing our faulty dams and levees, bringing critical broadband connections to businesses and homes in nearly every community in America, upgrading mass transit and building high-speed rail lines that will improve travel and commerce throughout the nation.

Because we know America can't out-compete the world tomorrow if our children are being out-educated today, we are making the largest investment in education in our nation's history. It's an investment that will create jobs building 21st-century classrooms, libraries and labs for millions of children across America. It will provide funds to train a new generation of math and science teachers while giving aid to states and school districts to stop teachers from being laid off and education programs from being cut.

In New York City alone, 14,000 teachers who were set to be let go may now be able to continue pursuing their critical mission. It's an investment that will create a new $2,500 annual tax credit to put the dream of a college degree within reach for middle class families and make college affordable for seven million students, helping more of our sons and daughters aim higher, reach farther and fulfill their God-given potential.

Because we know that spiraling health care costs are crushing families and businesses alike, we are taking the most meaningful steps in years towards modernizing our health care system. It's an investment that will take the long overdue step of computerizing America's medical records, to reduce the duplication and waste that costs billions of health care dollars and the medical errors that every year cost thousands of lives.

Further, thanks to the action we have taken, 7 million Americans who lost their health care along with their jobs will continue to get the coverage they need, and roughly 20 million more can breathe a little easier, knowing that their health care won't be cut due to a state budget shortfall. And an historic commitment to wellness initiatives will keep millions of Americans from setting foot in the doctor's office for purely preventable diseases.

Taken together with the enactment earlier this month of a long-delayed law to extend health care to millions more children of working families, we have done more in 30 days to advance the cause of health reform than this country has done in a decade.

Because we know we can't power America's future on energy that's controlled by foreign dictators, we are taking a big step down the road to energy independence and laying the groundwork for a new green energy economy that can create countless well-paying jobs. It's an investment that will double the amount of renewable energy produced over the next three years and provide tax credits and loan guarantees to companies like Namaste Solar, a company that will be expanding, instead of laying people off, as a result of the plan I am signing.

In the process, we will transform the way we use energy. Today, the electricity we use is carried along a grid of lines and wires that dates back to Thomas Edison, a grid that can't support the demands of clean energy. This means we're using 19th- and 20th-century technologies to battle 21st-century problems like climate change and energy security.

It also means that places like North Dakota can produce a lot of wind energy but can't deliver it to communities that want it, leading to a gap between how much clean energy we are using and how much we could be using.

The investment we are making today will create a newer, smarter electric grid that will allow for the broader use of alternative energy. We will build on the work that's being done in places like Boulder, Colorado, a community that is on pace to be the world's first Smart Grid city. This investment will place Smart Meters in homes to make our energy bills lower, make outages less likely and make it easier to use clean energy.

It's an investment that will save taxpayers over $1 billion by slashing energy costs in our federal buildings by 25 percent and save working families hundreds of dollars a year on their energy bills by weatherizing over 1 million homes. And it's an investment that takes the important first step towards a nationwide transmission superhighway that will connect our cities to the windy plains of the Dakotas and the sunny deserts of the Southwest.

Even beyond energy, from the National Institutes of Health to the National Science Foundation, this recovery act represents the biggest increase in basic research funding in the long history of America's noble endeavor to better understand our world. Just as President Kennedy sparked an explosion of innovation when he set America's sights on the moon, I hope this investment will ignite our imagination once more, spurring new discoveries and breakthroughs that will make our economy stronger, our nation more secure and our planet safer for our children.

While this package is mostly composed of critical investments, it also includes aid to state and local governments to prevent layoffs of firefighters or police recruits—recruits like the ones in Columbus, Ohio, who were told that instead of being sworn in as officers, they would be let go.

It includes help for those hardest hit by our economic crisis, like the nearly 18 million Americans who will get larger unemployment checks in the mail. And about a third of this package comes in the form of tax cuts—the most progressive in our history—not only spurring job creation but putting money in the pockets of 95 percent of all hardworking families.

Unlike tax cuts we've seen in recent years, the vast majority of these tax benefits will go not to the wealthiest Americans but to the middle class, with those workers who make the least benefiting the most. And it's a plan that rewards responsibility, lifting 2 million Americans from poverty by ensuring that anyone who works hard does not have to raise a child below the poverty line.

As a whole, this plan will help poor and working Americans pull themselves into the middle class in a way we haven't seen in nearly 50 years.

What I am signing, then, is a balanced plan with a mix of tax cuts and investments. It is a plan that's been put together without earmarks or the usual pork-barrel spending. And it is a plan that will be implemented with an unprecedented level of transparency and accountability.

With a recovery package of this scale comes a responsibility to assure every taxpayer that we are being careful with the money they work so hard to earn. That's why I am assigning a team of managers to ensure that the precious dollars we have invested are being spent wisely and well. We will hold the governors and local officials who receive money to the same high standards. And we expect you, the American people, to hold us accountable for the results. That is why we have created recovery.gov, so every American can go online and see how their money is being spent.

As important as the step we take today is, this legislation represents only the first part of the broad strategy we need to address our economic crisis. In the coming days and weeks, I will be launching other aspects of the plan. We will need to stabilize, repair and reform our banking system and get credit flowing again to families and businesses.

We will need to end a culture where we ignore problems until they become full-blown crises instead of recognizing that the only way to build a thriving economy is to set and enforce firm rules of the road. We must stem the spread of foreclosures and falling home values for all Americans and do everything we can to help responsible homeowners stay in their homes, something I will talk more about tomorrow.

And while we need to do everything in the short-term to get our economy moving again, we must recognize that having inherited a trillion-dollar deficit, we need to begin restoring fiscal discipline and taming our exploding deficits over the long-term.

None of this will be easy. The road to recovery will not be straight and true. It will demand courage and discipline and a new sense of responsibility that has been missing, from Wall Street to Washington. There will be hazards and reverses along the way. But I have every confidence that if we are willing to continue doing the difficult work that must be done—by each of us and by all of us—then we will leave this struggling economy behind us, and come out on the other side, more prosperous as a people.

For our American story is not—and has never been—about things coming easy. It's about rising to the moment when the moment is hard, converting crisis into opportunity and seeing to it that we emerge from whatever trials we face stronger than we were before. It's about rejecting the notion that our fate is somehow written for us, and instead laying claim to a destiny of our own making.

That is what earlier generations of Americans have done, and that is what we are doing today.

Thank you.

Barack Obama's State of the Union Speech on Economic Crisis and Recovery Efforts (2009)

On February 24, 2009, President Obama delivered the following speech to a joint session of Congress. He commented on the passage of the American Recovery and Reinvestment Act of 2009 and how his administration was acting swiftly to loosen up the flow of credit, which was needed to infuse the economy and restore confidence in order to break the downward turn that continued over the previous year-and-a-half.

Source: White House Press Office, January 24, 2009.

PRESIDENT: Madam Speaker, Mr. Vice President, members of Congress, the First Lady of the United States—she's around here somewhere.

I have come here tonight not only to address the distinguished men and women in this great chamber, but to speak frankly and directly to the men and women who sent us here.

I know that for many Americans watching right now, the state of our economy is a concern that rises above all others. And rightly so. If you haven't been personally affected by this recession, you probably know someone who has—a friend; a neighbor; a member of your family. You don't need to hear another list of statistics to know that our economy is in crisis, because you live it every day. It's the worry you wake up with and the source of sleepless nights. It's the job you thought you'd retire from but now have lost; the business you built your dreams upon that's now hanging by a thread; the college acceptance letter your child had to put back in the envelope. The impact of this recession is real, and it is everywhere.

But while our economy may be weakened and our confidence shaken, though we are living through difficult and uncertain times, tonight I want every American to know this: We will rebuild, we will recover, and the United States of America will emerge stronger than before.

The weight of this crisis will not determine the destiny of this nation. The answers to our problems don't lie beyond our reach. They exist in our laboratories and our universities; in our fields and our factories; in the imaginations of our entrepreneurs and the pride of the hardest-working people on Earth. Those qualities that have made America the greatest force of progress and prosperity in human history we still possess in ample measure. What is required now is for this country to pull together, confront boldly the challenges we face, and take responsibility for our future once more.

Now, if we're honest with ourselves, we'll admit that for too long, we have not always met these responsibilities—as a government or as a people. I say this not to lay blame or to look backwards, but because it is only by understanding how we arrived at this moment that we'll be able to lift ourselves out of this predicament.

The fact is our economy did not fall into decline overnight. Nor did all of our problems begin when the housing market collapsed or the stock market sank. We have known for decades that our survival depends on finding new sources of energy. Yet we import more oil today than ever before. The cost of health care eats up more and more of our savings each year, yet we keep delaying reform. Our children will compete for jobs in a global economy that too many of our schools do not prepare them for. And though all these challenges went unsolved, we still managed to spend more money and pile up more debt, both as individuals and through our government, than ever before.

In other words, we have lived through an era where too often short-term gains were prized over long-term prosperity; where we failed to look beyond the next payment, the next quarter or the next election. A surplus became an excuse to transfer wealth to the wealthy instead of an opportunity to invest in our future. Regulations were gutted for the sake of a quick profit at the expense of a healthy market. People bought homes they knew they couldn't afford from banks and lenders who pushed those bad loans anyway. And all the while, critical debates and difficult decisions were put off for some other time on some other day.

Well that day of reckoning has arrived, and the time to take charge of our future is here.

Now is the time to act boldly and wisely—to not only revive this economy, but to build a new foundation for lasting prosperity. Now is the time to jumpstart job creation, re-start lending, and invest in areas like energy, health care, and education that will grow our economy, even as we make hard choices to bring our deficit down. That is what my economic agenda is designed to do, and that is what I'd like to talk to you about tonight.

It's an agenda that begins with jobs.

As soon as I took office, I asked this Congress to send me a recovery plan by President's Day that would put people back to work and put money in their pockets. Not because I believe in bigger government—I don't. Not because I'm not mindful of the massive debt we've inherited—I am. I called for action because the failure to do so would have cost more jobs and caused more hardship. In fact, a failure to act would have worsened our long-term deficit by assuring weak economic growth for years. And that's why I pushed for quick action. And tonight, I am grateful that this Congress delivered, and pleased to say that the American Recovery and Reinvestment Act is now law.

Over the next two years, this plan will save or create 3.5 million jobs. More than 90 percent of these jobs will be in the private sector—jobs rebuilding our roads and bridges; constructing wind turbines and solar panels; laying broadband and expanding mass transit.

Because of this plan, there are teachers who can now keep their jobs and educate our kids. Health care professionals can continue caring for our sick. There are 57 police officers who are still on the streets of Minneapolis tonight because this plan prevented the layoffs their department was about to make.

Because of this plan, 95 percent of working households in America will receive a tax cut—a tax cut that you will see in your paychecks beginning on April 1.

Because of this plan, families who are struggling to pay tuition costs will receive a $2,500 tax credit for all four years of college. And Americans—and Americans who have lost their jobs in this recession will be able to receive extended unemployment benefits and continued health care coverage to help them weather this storm.

Now, I know there are some in this chamber and watching at home who are skeptical of whether this plan will work. And I understand that skepticism. Here in Washington, we've all seen how quickly good intentions can turn into broken promises and wasteful spending. And with a plan of this scale comes enormous responsibility to get it right.

And that's why I've asked Vice President [Joe] Biden to lead a tough, unprecedented oversight effort—because nobody messes with Joe. I—isn't that right? They don't mess with you. I have told each of my Cabinet, as well as mayors and governors across the country, that they will be held accountable by me and the American people for every dollar they spend. I've appointed a proven and aggressive Inspector General to ferret out any and all cases of waste and fraud. And we have created a new website called recovery.gov so that every American can find out how and where their money is being spent.

So the recovery plan we passed is the first step in getting our economy back on track. But it is just the first step. Because even if we manage this plan flawlessly, there will be no real recovery unless we clean up the credit crisis that has severely weakened our financial system.

I want to speak plainly and candidly about this issue tonight, because every American should know that it directly affects you and your family's well-being. You should also know that the money you've deposited in banks across the country is safe; your insurance is secure; you can rely on the continued operation of our financial system. That's not the source of concern.

The concern is that if we do not restart lending in this country, our recovery will be choked off before it even begins.

You see—you see, the flow of credit is the lifeblood of our economy. The ability to get a loan is how you finance the purchase of everything from a home to a car to a college education; how stores stock their shelves, farms buy equipment, and businesses make payroll.

But credit has stopped flowing the way it should. Too many bad loans from the housing crisis have made their way onto the books of too many banks. And with so much debt and so little confidence, these banks are now fearful of lending out any more money to households, to businesses, or even to each other. And when there is no lending, families can't afford to buy homes or cars. So businesses are forced to make layoffs. Our economy suffers even more, and credit dries up even further.

That is why this administration is moving swiftly and aggressively to break this destructive cycle, to restore confidence, and restart lending.

And we will do so in several ways. First, we are creating a new lending fund that represents the largest effort ever to help provide auto loans, college loans, and small business loans to the consumers and entrepreneurs who keep this economy running.

Second—second, we have launched a housing plan that will help responsible families facing the threat of foreclosure lower their monthly payments and refinance their mortgages. It's a plan that won't help speculators or that neighbor down the street who bought a house he could never hope to afford, but it will help millions of Americans who are struggling with declining home values—Americans who will now be able to take advantage of the lower interest rates that this plan has already helped to bring about. In fact, the average family who refinances today can save nearly $2,000 per year on their mortgage.

Third, we will act with the full force of the federal government to ensure that the major banks that Americans depend on have enough confidence and enough money to lend even in more difficult times. And when we learn that a major bank has serious problems, we will hold accountable those responsible, force the necessary adjustments, provide the support to clean up their balance sheets, and assure the continuity of a strong, viable institution that can serve our people and our economy.

I understand that on any given day, Wall Street may be more comforted by an approach that gives bank bailouts with no strings attached, and that holds nobody accountable for their reckless decisions. But such an approach won't solve the problem. And our goal is to quicken the day when we restart lending to the American people and American business, and end this crisis once and for all.

And I intend to hold these banks fully accountable for the assistance they receive, and this time, they will have to clearly demonstrate how taxpayer dollars result in more lending for the American taxpayer. This time—this time, CEOs won't be able to use taxpayer money to pad their paychecks, or buy fancy drapes, or disappear on a private jet. Those days are over.

Still, this plan will require significant resources from the federal government—and, yes, probably more than we've already set aside. But while the cost of action will be great, I can assure you that the cost of inaction will be far greater, for it could result in an economy that sputters along for not months or years, but perhaps a decade. That would be worse for our deficit, worse for business, worse for you and worse for the next generation. And I refuse to let that happen.

Now, I understand that when the last administration asked this Congress to provide assistance for struggling banks, Democrats and Republicans alike were infuriated by the mismanagement and the results that followed. So were the American taxpayers. So was I. So I know how unpopular it is to be seen as helping banks right now, especially when everyone is suffering in part from their bad decisions. I promise you—I get it.

But I also know that in a time of crisis, we cannot afford to govern out of anger, or yield to the politics of the moment. My job—our job—is to solve the problem. Our job is to govern with a sense of responsibility. I will not send—I will not spend a single penny for the purpose of rewarding a single Wall Street executive, but I will do whatever it takes to help the small business that can't pay its workers, or the family that has saved and still can't get a mortgage.

That's what this is about. It's not about helping banks—it's about helping people. It's not about helping banks; it's about helping people. Because when credit is available again, that young family can finally buy a new home. And then some company will hire workers to build it. And then those workers will have money to spend. And if they can get a loan, too, maybe they'll finally buy that car, or open their own business. Investors will return to the market, and American families will see their retirement secured once more. Slowly, but surely, confidence will return and our economy will recover.

So I ask this Congress to join me in doing whatever proves necessary. Because we cannot consign our nation to an open-ended recession. And to ensure that a crisis of this magnitude never happens again, I ask Congress to move quickly on legislation that will finally reform our outdated regulatory system. It is time—it is time to put in place tough, new common-sense rules of the road so that our financial market rewards drive and innovation, and punishes short-cuts and abuse.

The recovery plan and the financial stability plan are the immediate steps we're taking to revive our economy in the short term. But the only way to fully restore America's economic strength is to make the long-term investments that will lead to new jobs, new industries, and a renewed ability to compete with the rest of the world. The only way this century will be another American century is if we confront at last the price of our dependence on oil and the high cost of health care; the schools that aren't preparing our children and the mountain of debt they stand to inherit. That is our responsibility.

In the next few days, I will submit a budget to Congress. So often, we've come to view these documents as simply numbers on a page or a laundry list of programs. I see this document differently. I see it as a vision for America—as a blueprint for our future.

My budget does not attempt to solve every problem or address every issue. It reflects the stark reality of what we've inherited—a trillion-dollar deficit, a financial crisis, and a costly recession.

Given these realities, everyone in this chamber—Democrats and Republicans—will have to sacrifice some worthy priorities for which there are no dollars. And that includes me.

But that does not mean we can afford to ignore our long-term challenges. I reject the view that says our problems will simply take care of themselves; that says government has no role in laying the foundation for our common prosperity.

For history tells a different story. History reminds us that at every moment of economic upheaval and transformation, this nation has responded with bold action and big ideas. In the midst of civil war, we laid railroad tracks from one coast to another that spurred commerce and industry. From the turmoil of the Industrial Revolution came a system of public high schools that prepared our citizens for a new age. In the wake of war and depression, the GI Bill sent a generation to college and created the largest middle class in history. And a twilight struggle for freedom led to a nation of highways, an American on the moon, and an explosion of technology that still shapes our world.

In each case, government didn't supplant private enterprise; it catalyzed private enterprise. It created the conditions for thousands of entrepreneurs and new businesses to adapt and to thrive.

We are a nation that has seen promise amid peril, and claimed opportunity from ordeal. Now we must be that nation again. That is why, even as it cuts back on programs we don't need, the budget I submit will invest in the three areas that are absolutely critical to our economic future: energy, health care, and education.

It begins with energy.

We know the country that harnesses the power of clean, renewable energy will lead the 21st century. And yet, it is China that has launched the largest effort in history to make their economy energy-efficient. We invented solar technology, but we've fallen behind countries like Germany and Japan in producing it. New plug-in hybrids roll off our assembly lines, but they will run on batteries made in Korea.

Well, I do not accept a future where the jobs and industries of tomorrow take root beyond our borders—and I know you don't, either. It is time for America to lead again.

Thanks to our recovery plan, we will double this nation's supply of renewable energy in the next three years. We've also made the largest investment in basic research funding in American history—an investment that will spur not only new discoveries in energy, but breakthroughs in medicine and science and technology.

We will soon lay down thousands of miles of power lines that can carry new energy to cities and towns across this country. And we will put Americans to work making our homes and buildings more efficient so that we can save billions of dollars on our energy bills.

But to truly transform our economy, to protect our security, and save our planet from the ravages of climate change, we need to ultimately make clean, renewable energy the profitable kind of energy. So I ask this Congress to send me legislation that places a market-based cap on carbon pollution and drives the production of more renewable energy in America. That's what we need. And to support—to support that innovation, we will invest $15 billion a year to develop technologies like wind power and solar power, advanced biofuels, clean coal, and more efficient cars and trucks built right here in America.

Speaking of our auto industry, everyone recognizes that years of bad decision-making and a global recession have pushed our automakers to the brink. We should not, and will not, protect them from their own bad practices. But we are committed to the goal of a retooled, reimagined auto industry that can compete and win. Millions of jobs depend on it. Scores of communities depend on it. And I believe the nation that invented the automobile cannot walk away from it.

None of this will come without cost, nor will it be easy. But this is America. We don't do what's easy. We do what's necessary to move this country forward.

And for that same reason, we must also address the crushing cost of health care.

This is a cost that now causes a bankruptcy in America every thirty seconds. By the end of the year, it could cause 1.5 million Americans to lose their homes. In the last eight years, premiums have grown four times faster than wages. And in each of these years, 1 million more Americans have lost their health insurance. It is one of the major reasons why small businesses close their doors and corporations ship jobs overseas. And it's one of the largest and fastest-growing parts of our budget.

Given these facts, we can no longer afford to put health care reform on hold. We can't afford to do it. It's time.

Already, we've done more to advance the cause of health care reform in the last thirty days than we've done in the last decade. When it was days old, this Congress passed a law to provide and protect health insurance for 11 million American children whose parents work full-time. Our recovery plan will invest in electronic health records and new technology that will reduce errors, bring down costs, ensure privacy, and save lives. It will launch a new effort to conquer a disease that has touched the life of nearly every American, including me, by seeking a cure for cancer in our time. And—and it makes the largest investment ever in preventive care, because that's one of the best ways to keep our people healthy and our costs under control.

This budget builds on these reforms. It includes a historic commitment to comprehensive health care reform—a down payment on the principle that we must have quality, affordable health care for every American. It's a commitment—it's a commitment that's paid for in part by efficiencies in our system that are long overdue. And it's a step we must take if we hope to bring down our deficit in the years to come.

Now, there will be many different opinions and ideas about how to achieve reform, and that's why I'm bringing together businesses and workers, doctors and health care providers, Democrats and Republicans to begin work on this issue next week.

I suffer no illusions that this will be an easy process. Once again, it will be hard. But I also know that nearly a century after Teddy Roosevelt first called for reform, the cost of our health care has weighed down our economy and our conscience long enough. So let there be no doubt: Health care reform cannot wait, it must not wait, and it will not wait another year.

The third challenge we must address is the urgent need to expand the promise of education in America.

In a global economy where the most valuable skill you can sell is your knowledge, a good education is no longer just a pathway to opportunity—it is a prerequisite.

Right now, three-quarters of the fastest-growing occupations require more than a high school diploma. And yet, just over half of our citizens have that level of education. We have one of the highest high school dropout rates of any industrialized nation. And half of the students who begin college never finish.

This is a prescription for economic decline, because we know the countries that out-teach us today will out-compete us tomorrow. That is why it will be the goal of this administration to ensure that every child has access to a complete and competitive education—from the day they are born to the day they begin a career. That is a promise we have to make to the children of America.

Already, we've made an historic investment in education through the economic recovery plan. We've dramatically expanded early childhood education and will continue to improve its quality, because we know that the most formative learning comes in those first years of life. We've made college affordable for nearly seven million more students—seven million. And we have provided the resources necessary to prevent painful cuts and teacher layoffs that would set back our children's progress.

But we know that our schools don't just need more resources. They need more reform. That is why this budget creates new teachers—new incentives for teacher performance; pathways for advancement, and rewards for success. We'll invest in innovative programs that are already helping schools meet high standards and close achievement gaps. And we will expand our commitment to charter schools.

It is our responsibility as lawmakers and as educators to make this system work. But it is the responsibility of every citizen to participate in it. So tonight, I ask every American to commit to at least one year or more of higher education or career training. This can be community college or a four-year school; vocational training or an apprenticeship. But whatever the training may be, every American will need to get more than a high school diploma. And dropping out of high school is no longer an option. It's not just quitting on yourself, it's quitting on your country – and this country needs and values the talents of every American. That's why we will support—we will provide the support necessary for all young Americans to complete college and meet a new goal: By 2020, America will once again have the highest proportion of college graduates in the world. That is a goal we can meet. That's a goal we can meet.

Now, I know that the price of tuition is higher than ever, which is why if you are willing to volunteer in your neighborhood or give back to your community or serve your country, we will make sure that you can afford a higher education. And to encourage a renewed spirit of national service for this and future generations, I ask Congress to send me the bipartisan legislation that bears the name of Senator Orrin Hatch, as well as an American who has never stopped asking what he can do for his country—Senator Edward Kennedy.

These education policies will open the doors of opportunity for our children. But it is up to us to ensure they walk through them. In the end, there is no program or policy that can substitute for a parent—for a mother or father who will attend those parent/teacher conferences, or help with homework, or turn off the TV, put away the video games, read to their child. I speak to you not just as a President, but as a father, when I say that responsibility for our children's education must begin at home. That is not a Democratic issue or a Republican issue. That's an American issue.

There is, of course, another responsibility we have to our children. And that's the responsibility to ensure that we do not pass on to them a debt they cannot pay. That is critical. I agree, absolutely. See, I know we can get some consensus in here. With the deficit we inherited, the cost—the cost of the crisis we face, and the long-term challenges we must meet, it has never been more important to ensure that as our economy recovers, we do what it takes to bring this deficit down. That is critical.

Now, I'm proud that we passed a recovery plan free of earmarks—and I want to pass a budget next year that ensures that each dollar we spend reflects only our most important national priorities.

And yesterday, I held a fiscal summit where I pledged to cut the deficit in half by the end of my first term in office. My administration has also begun to go line by line through the federal budget in order to eliminate wasteful and ineffective programs. As you can imagine, this is a process that will take some time. But we have already identified $2 trillion in savings over the next decade.

In this budget—in this budget, we will end education programs that don't work and end direct payments to large agribusiness that don't need them. We'll eliminate— we'll eliminate the no-bid contracts that have wasted billions in Iraq—and reform— and reform our defense budget so that we're not paying for Cold War-era weapons systems we don't use. We will—we will root out—we will root out the waste and fraud and abuse in our Medicare program that doesn't make our seniors any healthier. We will restore a sense of fairness and balance to our tax code by finally ending the tax breaks for corporations that ship our jobs overseas.

In order to save our children from a future of debt, we will also end the tax breaks for the wealthiest 2 percent of Americans. Now, let me be clear—let me be absolutely clear, because I know you'll end up hearing some of the same claims that rolling back these tax breaks means a massive tax increase on the American people: If your family earns less than $250,000 a year—a quarter million dollars a year—you will not see your taxes increased a single dime. I repeat: Not one single dime. Not a dime. In fact, the recovery plan provides a tax cut—that's right, a tax cut—for 95 percent of working families. And by the way, these checks are on the way.

Now, to preserve our long-term fiscal health, we must also address the growing costs in Medicare and Social Security. Comprehensive health care reform is the best way to strengthen Medicare for years to come. And we must also begin a conversation on how to do the same for Social Security, while creating tax-free universal savings accounts for all Americans.

Finally, because we're also suffering from a deficit of trust, I am committed to restoring a sense of honesty and accountability to our budget. That is why this budget looks ahead 10 years and accounts for spending that was left out under the old rules—and for the first time, that includes the full cost of fighting in Iraq and Afghanistan. For seven years, we have been a nation at war. No longer will we hide its price.

Along with our outstanding national security team, I'm now carefully reviewing our policies in both wars, and I will soon announce a way forward in Iraq that leaves Iraq to its people and responsibly ends this war.

And with our friends and allies, we will forge a new and comprehensive strategy for Afghanistan and Pakistan to defeat al Qaeda and combat extremism. Because I will not allow terrorists to plot against the American people from safe havens halfway around the world. We will not allow it.

As we meet here tonight, our men and women in uniform stand watch abroad and more are readying to deploy. To each and every one of them, and to the families who bear the quiet burden of their absence, Americans are united in sending one message: We honor your service, we are inspired by your sacrifice, and you have our unyielding support.

To relieve the strain on our forces, my budget increases the number of our soldiers and Marines. And to keep our sacred trust with those who serve, we will raise their pay, and give our veterans the expanded health care and benefits that they have earned.

To overcome extremism, we must also be vigilant in upholding the values our troops defend—because there is no force in the world more powerful than the example of America. And that is why I have ordered the closing of the detention center at Guantanamo Bay, and will seek swift and certain justice for captured terrorists. Because living our values doesn't make us weaker, it makes us safer and it makes us stronger. And that is why I can stand here tonight and say without exception or equivocation that the United States of America does not torture. We can make that commitment here tonight.

In words and deeds, we are showing the world that a new era of engagement has begun. For we know that America cannot meet the threats of this century alone, but the world cannot meet them without America. We cannot shun the negotiating table, nor ignore the foes or forces that could do us harm. We are instead called to move forward with the sense of confidence and candor that serious times demand.

To seek progress towards a secure and lasting peace between Israel and her neighbors, we have appointed an envoy to sustain our effort. To meet the challenges of the 21st century—from terrorism to nuclear proliferation; from pandemic disease to cyber threats to crushing poverty—we will strengthen old alliances, forge new ones, and use all elements of our national power.

And to respond to an economic crisis that is global in scope, we are working with the nations of the G20 to restore confidence in our financial system, avoid the possibility of escalating protectionism, and spur demand for American goods in markets across the globe. For the world depends on us having a strong economy, just as our economy depends on the strength of the world's.

As we stand at this crossroads of history, the eyes of all people in all nations are once again upon us—watching to see what we do with this moment; waiting for us to lead.

Those of us gathered here tonight have been called to govern in extraordinary times. It is a tremendous burden, but also a great privilege—one that has been entrusted to few generations of Americans. For in our hands lies the ability to shape our world for good or for ill.

I know that it's easy to lose sight of this truth — to become cynical and doubtful; consumed with the petty and the trivial. But in my life, I have also learned that hope is found in unlikely places; that inspiration often comes not from those with the most power or celebrity, but from the dreams and aspirations of Americans who are anything but ordinary.

I think of Leonard Abess, a bank president from Miami who reportedly cashed out of his company, took a $60 million bonus, and gave it out to all 399 people who worked for him, plus another 72 who used to work for him. He didn't tell anyone, but when the local newspaper found out, he simply said, "I knew some of these people since I was seven years old. It didn't feel right getting the money myself."

I think about—I think about Greensburg—Greensburg, Kansas, a town that was completely destroyed by a tornado, but is being rebuilt by its residents as a global example of how clean energy can power an entire community—how it can bring jobs and businesses to a place where piles of bricks and rubble once lay. "The tragedy was terrible," said one of the men who helped them rebuild. "But the folks here know that it also provided an incredible opportunity."

I think about Ty'Sheoma Bethea, the young girl from that school I visited in Dillon, South Carolina—a place where the ceilings leak, the paint peels off the walls, and they have to stop teaching six times a day because the train barrels by their classroom. She had been told that her school is hopeless, but the other day after class she went to the public library and typed up a letter to the people sitting in this chamber. She even asked her principal for the money to buy a stamp. The letter asks us for help, and says, "We are just students trying to become lawyers, doctors, congressmen like yourself and one day president, so we can make a change to not just the state of South Carolina but also the world. We are not quitters." That's what she said. We are not quitters.

These words—these words and these stories tell us something about the spirit of the people who sent us here. They tell us that even in the most trying times, amid the most difficult circumstances, there is a generosity, a resilience, a decency, and a determination that perseveres; a willingness to take responsibility for our future and for posterity.

Their resolve must be our inspiration. Their concerns must be our cause. And we must show them and all our people that we are equal to the task before us.

I know—look, I know that we haven't agreed on every issue thus far. There are surely times in the future where we will part ways. But I also know that every American who is sitting here tonight loves this country and wants it to succeed. I know that. That must be the starting point for every debate we have in the coming months, and where we return after those debates are done. That is the foundation on which the American people expect us to build common ground.

And if we do—if we come together and lift this nation from the depths of this crisis; if we put our people back to work and restart the engine of our prosperity; if we confront without fear the challenges of our time and summon that enduring spirit of an America that does not quit, then someday years from now our children can tell their children that this was the time when we performed, in the words that are carved into this very chamber, "something worthy to be remembered."

Thank you. God bless you, and may God bless the United States of America.

Barack Obama's Remarks on the American Automotive Industry Bailout (2009)

President Barack Obama made the following remarks on the American automotive industry bailouts on March 30, 2009. He discussed the Auto Task Force, the government-backed Warrantee Commitment Program, and the viability assessments for General Motors and Chrysler Corporations. He also introduced the idea of the Cash for Clunkers program.

Source: White House Office of the Press Secretary. Remarks by the President on the American Automotive Industry. March 30, 2009, http://www.whitehouse.gov/the _press_office/Remarks-by-the-President-on-the-American-Automotive-Industry-3/30/09/.

Good morning everybody.

One of the challenges we've confronted from the beginning of this administration is what to do with the state of the struggling auto industry. In recent months, my Auto Task Force has been reviewing requests by General Motors and Chrysler for additional government assistance, as well as plans developed by each of these companies to restructure, to modernize, and to make themselves more competitive. Our evaluation is now complete. But before I lay out what needs to be done going forward, I want to say a few words about where we are and what led us to this point.

It will come as no surprise that some Americans who have suffered most during this recession have been those in the auto industry and those working for companies that support it. Over the past year, our auto industry has shed over 400,000 jobs, not only at plants that produce cars, but at the businesses that produce the parts that go into them and the dealers that sell and repair them. More than one in ten Michigan residents is out of work—the most of any state. And towns and cities across the great Midwest have watched unemployment climb higher than it's been in decades.

The pain being felt in places that rely on our auto industry is not the fault of our workers; they labor tirelessly and desperately want to see their companies succeed. It's not the fault of all the families and communities that supported manufacturing plants throughout the generations. Rather, it's a failure of leadership—from Washington to Detroit—that led our auto companies to this point.

Year after year, decade after decade, we've seen problems papered over and tough choices kicked down the road, even as foreign competitors outpaced us. Well, we've reached the end of that road. And we, as a nation, cannot afford to shirk responsibility any longer. Now is the time to confront our problems head-on and do what's necessary to solve them.

We cannot, and must not, and we will not let our auto industry simply vanish. This industry is like no other—it's an emblem of the American spirit; a once and future symbol of America's success. It's what helped build the middle class and sustained it throughout the 20th century. It's a source of deep pride for the generations of American workers whose hard work and imagination led to some of the finest cars the world has ever known. It's a pillar of our economy that has held up the dreams of millions of our people. And we cannot continue to excuse poor decisions. We cannot make the survival of our auto industry dependent on an unending flow of taxpayer dollars. These companies—and this industry—must ultimately stand on their own, not as wards of the state.

And that's why the federal government provided General Motors and Chrysler with emergency loans to prevent their sudden collapse at the end of last year—only on the condition that they would develop plans to restructure. In keeping with that agreement, each company has submitted a plan to restructure. But after careful analysis, we've determined that neither goes far enough to warrant the substantial new investments that these companies are requesting.

And so today I'm announcing that my administration will offer GM and Chrysler a limited additional period of time to work with creditors, unions, and other stakeholders to fundamentally restructure in a way that would justify an investment of additional taxpayer dollars. During this period they must produce plans that would give the American people confidence in their long-term prospects for success.

Now, what we're asking for is difficult. It will require hard choices by companies. It will require unions and workers who have already made extraordinarily painful concessions to do more. It'll require creditors to recognize that they can't hold out for the prospect of endless government bailouts. It'll have to—it will require efforts from a whole host of other stakeholders, including dealers and suppliers. Only then can we ask American taxpayers who have already put up so much of their hard-earned money to once more invest in a revitalized auto industry.

But I'm confident that if each are willing to do their part, if all of us are doing our part, then this restructuring, as painful as it will be in the short term, will mark not an end, but a new beginning for a great American industry—an auto industry that is once more out-competing the world; a 21st century auto industry that is creating new jobs, unleashing new prosperity, and manufacturing the fuel-efficient cars and trucks that will carry us towards an energy-independent future. I am absolutely committed to working with Congress and the auto companies to meet one goal: The United States of America will lead the world in building the next generation of clean cars.

And no one can deny that our auto industry has made meaningful progress in recent years—and this doesn't get talked about often enough. Some of the cars made by American workers right now are outperforming the best cars made abroad. In 2008, the North American Car of the Year was a GM. This year, Buick tied for first place as the most reliable car in the world. Our companies are investing in breakthrough technologies that hold the promise of new vehicles that will help America end its addiction to foreign oil.

But our auto industry is not moving in the right direction fast enough to succeed in a very tough environment. So let me discuss what measures need to be taken by each of the auto companies requesting taxpayer assistance, and I'll start with General Motors.

GM has made a good faith effort to restructure over the past several months—but the plan that they've put forward is, in its current form, not strong enough. However, after broad consultation with a range of industry experts and financial advisors, I'm absolutely confident that GM can rise again, providing that it undergoes a fundamental restructuring. As an initial step, GM is announcing today that Rick Wagoner is stepping aside as Chairman and CEO. This is not meant as a condemnation of Mr. Wagoner, who's devoted his life to this company and has had a distinguished career; rather, it's a recognition that will take new vision and new direction to create the GM of the future.

In this context, my administration will offer General Motors adequate working capital over the next sixty days. And during this time, my team will be working closely with GM to produce a better business plan. They must ask themselves: Have they consolidated enough unprofitable brands? Have they cleaned up their balance sheets, or are they still saddled with so much debt that they can't make future investments? Above all, have they created a credible model for how not only to survive, but to succeed in this competitive global market?

Let me be clear: The United States government has no interest in running GM. We have no intention of running GM. What we are interested in is giving GM an opportunity to finally make those much-needed changes that will let them emerge from this crisis a stronger and more competitive company

The situation at Chrysler is more challenging. It's with deep reluctance but also a clear-eyed recognition of the facts that we've determined, after careful review, that Chrysler needs a partner to remain viable. Recently, Chrysler reached out and found what could be a potential partner—the international car company Fiat, where the current management team has executed an impressive turnaround. Fiat is prepared to transfer its cutting-edge technology to Chrysler and, after working closely with my team, has committed to build—building new fuel-efficient cars and engines right here in the United States. We've also secured an agreement that will ensure that Chrysler repays taxpayers for any new investments that are made before Fiat is allowed to take a majority ownership stake in Chrysler.

Still, such a deal would require an additional investment of taxpayer dollars, and there are a number of hurdles that must be overcome to make it work. I'm committed to doing all I can to see if a deal can be struck in a way that upholds the interests of American taxpayers. And that's why we'll give Chrysler and Fiat thirty days to overcome these hurdles and reach a final agreement—and we will provide Chrysler with adequate capital to continue operating during that time. If they are able to come to a sound agreement that protects American taxpayers, we will consider lending up to $6 billion to help their plan succeed. But if they and their stakeholders are unable to reach such an agreement, and in the absence of any other viable partnership, we will not be able to justify investing additional tax dollars to keep Chrysler in business.

Now, while Chrysler and GM are very different companies with very different paths forward, both need a fresh start to implement the restructuring plan they develop. That may mean using our bankruptcy code as a mechanism to help them restructure quickly and emerge stronger. Now, I want everybody to be clear about this. I know that when people hear the word "bankruptcy" it can be unsettling, so let me explain exactly what I mean. What I'm talking about is using our existing legal structure as a tool that, with the backing of the U.S. government, can make it easier for General Motors and Chrysler to quickly clear away old debts that are weighing them down so that they can get back on their feet and onto a path to success; a tool that we can use, even as workers staying on the job building cars that are being sold.

What I'm not talking about is a process where a company is simply broken up, sold off, and no longer exists. We're not talking about that. And what I'm not talking about is a company that's stuck in court for years, unable to get out.

So it's my hope that the steps I'm announcing today will have a salutary effect—will go a long way forward towards answering many of the questions that people have about the future of GM and Chrysler.

But just in case there's still nagging doubts; let me say it as plainly as I can: If you buy a car from Chrysler or General Motors, you will be able to get your car serviced and repaired, just like always. Your warranty will be safe. In fact, it will be safer than it's ever been, because starting today, the United States government will stand behind your warranty.

But we must also recognize that the difficulties facing this industry are due in no small part to the weaknesses in our economy as a whole. And therefore, to support demand for auto sales during this period, I'm directing my team to take several steps.

First, we will ensure that Recovery Act funds to purchase government cars get out as quickly as possible and work through the budget process to accelerate other federal fleet purchases, as well.

Second, we'll accelerate our efforts through the Treasury Department's Consumer and Business Lending Initiative. And we are working intensively with the auto finance companies to increase the flow of credit to both consumers and dealers.

Third, the IRS is launching a campaign to alert consumers of a new tax benefit for auto purchases made between February 16 and the end of this year—if you buy a car anytime this year, you may be able to deduct the cost of any sales and excise taxes. And this provision could save families hundreds of dollars and lead to as many as 100,000 new car sales.

Finally, several members of Congress have proposed an even more ambitious incentive program to increase car sales while modernizing our auto fleet. And such fleet modernization programs, which provide a generous credit to consumers who turn in old, less fuel-efficient cars and purchase cleaner cars, have been successful in boosting auto sales in a number of European countries. I want to work with Congress to identify parts of the Recovery Act that could be trimmed to fund such a program, and make it retroactive starting today.

Now, let there be no doubt, it will take an unprecedented effort on all our parts—from the halls of Congress to the boardroom, from the union hall to the factory floor—to see the auto industry through these difficult times. And I want every American to know that the path I'm laying out today is our best chance to make sure that the cars of the future are built where they've always been built—in Detroit and across the Midwest—to make America's auto industry in the 21st century what it was in the 20th century—unsurpassed around the world. The path has been chosen after consulting with other governments that are facing this crisis. We've worked closely with the government of Canada on GM and Chrysler, as both those companies have extensive operations there. The Canadian government has indicated its support for our approach and will be announcing their specific commitments later today.

While the steps I'm taking will have an impact on all Americans, some of our fellow citizens will be affected more than others. So I'd like to speak directly to all those men and women who work in the auto industry or live in countless communities that depend on it. Many of you have been going through tough times for longer than you care to remember. And I won't pretend that the tough times are over. I can't promise you there isn't more difficulty to come.

But what I can promise you is this: I will fight for you. You're the reason I'm here today. I got my start fighting for working families in the shadows of a shuttered steel plant. I wake up every single day asking myself what can I do to give you and working people all across this country a fair shot at the American Dream.

When a community is struck by a natural disaster, the nation responds to put it back on its feet. While the storm that has hit our auto towns is not a tornado or a hurricane, the damage is clear, and we must likewise respond. And that's why today I'm designating a new Director of Recovery for Auto Communities and Workers to cut through the red tape and ensure that the full resources of our federal government are leveraged to assist the workers, communities, and regions that rely on our auto industry. Edward Montgomery, a former Deputy Labor Secretary, has agreed to serve in this role.

And together with Labor Secretary Solis and my Auto Task Force, Ed will help provide support to auto workers and their families, and open up opportunity to manufacturing communities in Michigan and Ohio and Indiana and every other state that relies on the auto industry.

They will have a strong advocate in Ed. He will direct a comprehensive effort that will help lift up the hardest-hit areas by using the unprecedented levels of funding available in our Recovery Act and throughout our government to create new manufacturing jobs and new businesses where they're needed most—in your communities. And he will also lead an effort to identify new initiatives we may need to help support your communities going forward.

These efforts, as essential as they are, are not going to make everything better overnight. There are jobs that won't be saved. There are plants that may not reopen. There's little I can say that can subdue the anger or ease the frustration of all whose livelihoods hang in the balance because of failures that weren't theirs.

But there's something I want everybody to remember. Remember that it is precisely in times like these—in moments of trial and moments of hardship—that Americans rediscover the ingenuity and resilience that makes us who we are; that made the auto industry what it once was and what it will be again; that sent those first mass-produced cars rolling off the assembly lines; that built an arsenal of democracy that propelled America to victory in the Second World War; and that powered our economic prowess in the first American century.

Because I know that if we can tap into that same ingenuity and resilience right now, if we can carry one another through this difficult time and do what must be done, then we will look back and say that this was the moment when the American auto industry shed its old ways, marched into the future, remade itself, and once more became an engine of opportunity and prosperity not only in Detroit, not only in our Midwest, but all across America.

I'm confident we can make that happen, but we've got a lot of work to do. Thank you. Thank you everybody.

Bibliography

Books and Articles

Abbott, George C. *Sugar*. New York: Routledge, 1990.

Abolafia, Mitchel Y. *Making Markets: Opportunism and Restraint on Wall Street*. Cambridge, MA: Harvard University Press, 1996.

Abrams, Ann Uhry. *The Pilgrims and Pocahontas: Rival Myths of American Origin*. Boulder, CO: Westview Press, 1999.

Adams, Gordon. *The Iron Triangle*. New Brunswick, NJ: Transaction Books, 1982.

Adler-Karlsson, Gunnar. *Western Economic Warfare 1947–1967*. Stockholm: Almquist and Wiksell, 1968.

Ahmad, J. J., E. Lutz, and S. El Sarafy. *Environmental Accounting for Sustainable Development*. Washington, DC: World Bank, 1989.

Aldcroft, D. H., and M. J. Oliver. *Exchange Rate Regimes in the Twentieth Century*. Cheltenham, England: Edward Elgar, 1998.

Alexander, Alison, James Owers, and Rod Carveth. *Media Economics: Theory and Practice*. Hillsdale, NJ: L. Erlbaum Associates, 1993.

Alexander, Donald, ed. *Telecommunications Policy: Have Regulators Dialed the Wrong Number?* Westport, CT: Praeger, 1997.

Alogoskoufis, G. "Monetary Accommodation, Exchange Rate Regimes, and Inflation Persistence." *Economic Journal*, vol. 102 (May 1992): 461–480.

Altschiller, Donald, ed. *Affirmative Action*. New York: H. W. Wilson, 1991.

Amato, Giulano. *Antitrust and the Bounds of Power: The Dilemma of Liberal Democracy in the History of the Market*. Oxford: Hart Publishing, 1997.

Ambrose, Stephen E. *Duty, Honor, Country: A History of West Point*. Baltimore, MD: Johns Hopkins University Press, 1966.

Ambrose, Stephen E. *The Education of a Politician*. Vol. 1, *Nixon*. New York: Simon and Schuster, 1987–1991.

Amin, Samir. *Spectres of Capitalism: A Critique of Current Intellectual Fashions*. New York: Monthly Review Press, 1998.

Amott, Teresa, and Michael D. Calhoun, with Don Reeves. *Let's Get Real about Welfare*. Silver Spring, MD: Bread for the World Occasional Paper no. 5, 1995.

Anderson, Clay J. *A Half-Century of Federal Reserve Policymaking, 1914–1964*. Philadelphia: Federal Reserve Bank of Philadelphia, 1964.

Anderson, Fred. *Crucible of War*. New York: Alfred A. Knopf, 2000.

Andrew, John A. *Lyndon Johnson and the Great Society*. Chicago: I. R. Dee, 1998.

Anguizola, G. A. *Philippe Bunau-Varilla: The Man behind the Panama Canal*. Chicago: Nelson-Hall, 1980.

Appleby, Joyce. *Capitalism and a New Social Order: The Republican Vision of the 1790s*. New York: New York University Press, 1984.

Applegate, Edd. *Personalities and Products: A Historical Perspective on Advertising in America*. Westport, CT: Greenwood Press, 1998.

Arber, Edward, ed. *A Transcript of the Registers of the Company of Stationers of London, 1554–1640* A.D. 5 vols. New York: P. Smith, 1950.

Arendell, Terry. *Mothers and Divorce: Legal, Economic, and Social Dilemmas*. Berkeley: University of California Press, 1986.

Arkes, Adley. *Bureaucracy, the Marshall Plan, and the National Interest*. Princeton, NJ: Princeton University Press, 1973.

Arthur, John A. *Invisible Sojourners: African Immigrant Diaspora in the United States*. Westport, CT: Praeger, 2000.

Axinn, June, and Mark J. Stern. *Social Welfare: A History of the American Response to Need*. Boston: Allyn and Bacon, 2001.

Baepler, Paul, ed. *White Slaves, African Master: An Anthology of American Barbary Captivity Narratives*. Chicago: University of Chicago Press, 1999.

Baicker, Katherine, Claudia Goldin, and Lawrence F. Katz. "A Distinctive System: Origins and Impact of U.S. Unemployment Compensation." In Michael D. Bordo, Claudia Goldin, and Eugene N. White, eds., *The Defining Moment: The Great Depression and the American Economy in the Twentieth Century*. Chicago: University of Chicago Press, 1998.

Bailey, Stephen K. *Congress Makes a Law: The Story behind the Employment Act of 1946*. New York: Columbia University Press, 1950.

Bailey, Thomas A. "Was the Election of 1900 a Mandate on Imperialism?" *Mississippi Valley Historical Review*, vol. 24 (June 1937): 43–52.

Bain, Joe. *Barriers to New Competition*. Cambridge, MA: Harvard University Press, 1956.

Bairoch, Paul. *Economics and World History: Myths and Paradoxes*. Chicago: University of Chicago Press, 1993.

Baker, C. Edwin. *Advertising and a Democratic Press*. Princeton, NJ: Princeton University Press, 1994.

Baker, Wendy. *NASA: America in Space*. New York: Crescent Books, 1986.

Baldwin, Sidney. *Poverty and Politics: The Rise and Decline of the Farm Security Administration*. Chapel Hill: University of North Carolina Press, 1968.

Banner, Stuart. *Anglo-American Securities Regulation: Cultural and Political Roots, 1690–1860*. Cambridge: Cambridge University Press, 1998.

Baranoff, Dalit. "Shaped by Risk: Fire Insurance in America 1790–1920." PhD dissertation. Baltimore, MD: Johns Hopkins University, 2003.

Baranoff, Etti. *Risk Management and Insurance*. New York: John Wiley and Sons, 2003.

Barber, W. J. *Designs within Disorder: Franklin Roosevelt, the Economists, and the Shaping of American Economic Policy, 1933–1945*. New York: Cambridge University Press, 1996.

Barfield, Claude E. *Free Trade, Sovereignty, Democracy: The Future of the World Trade Organization*. Washington, DC: American Enterprise Institute, 2001.

Barker, Charles A. *Henry George*. New York: Oxford University Press, 1955.

Barrett, Jay Amos. *Evolution of the Ordinance of 1787*. New York: Arno Press, 1971.

Barry, Patricia D. *Mental Health and Mental Illness*. Philadelphia: Lippincott-Raven, 1998.

Bartlet, David, David Elesh, Ira Goldstein, George Leon, and William Yancey. "Islands in the Stream: Neighborhoods and the Political Economy of the City." In Irwin Altman and Abraham Wandersman, eds., *Neighborhood and Community Environments*. New York: Plenum Press, 1987.

Bassett, Ross Knox. *To the Digital Age: Research Labs, Start-up Companies, and the Rise of MOS Technology*. Baltimore, MD: Johns Hopkins University Press, 2002.

Baum, Lawrence. *The Transformation of American Law 1870–1960: The Crisis of Legal Orthodoxy*. New York: Oxford University Press, 1992.

Baum, Lawrence. *The Supreme Court*. Washington, DC: Congressional Quarterly Press, 2001.

Baxter, Maurice G. *Henry Clay and the American System*. Lexington: University Press of Kentucky, 1995.

Bean, William Bennett. *Walter Reed: A Biography*. Charlottesville: University Press of Virginia, 1982.

Becker, Robert A. *Revolution, Reform, and the Politics of American Taxation*. Baton Rouge: Louisiana State University Press, 1980.

Beisner, Robert L. *Twelve against Empire: The Anti-Imperialists, 1898–1900*. Chicago: University of Chicago Press, 1985.

Beisner, Robert L. *From the Old Diplomacy to the New 1865–1900*. Wheeling, IL: Harlan Davidson, 1986.

Beito, David T. *From Mutual Aid to the Welfare State: Fraternal Societies and Social Services, 1890–1967*. Chapel Hill: University of North Carolina Press, 2000.

Bell, Stephanie, "Can Taxes and Bonds Finance Government Spending?" *Journal of Economic Issues*, vol. 34, no. 3 (2000): 603–620.

Bellush, Bernard. *The Failure of the NRA*. New York: Norton, 1975.

Bemis, Samuel Flagg. *The Diplomacy of the American Revolution.* Bloomington: Indiana University Press, 1957.

Benedict, Michael Les. "Laissez-Faire and Liberty: A Re-Evaluation of the Meaning and Origins of Laissez-Faire Constitutionalism." *Law History Review,* vol. 3 no. 2 (Fall 1985): 293–332.

Benedict, Murray R. *Farm Policies of the United States, 1790–1950: A Study of Their Origins and Development.* New York: Twentieth Century Fund, 1953.

Bennett, David. *The Party of Fear: From Nativist Movements to the New Right in American History.* Chapel Hill: University of North Carolina Press, 1988.

Bennett, Michael J. *When Dreams Came True: The GI Bill and the Making of Modern America.* Washington, DC: Brassey's, 1996.

Benson, Paul R., Jr. *The Supreme Court and the Commerce Clause, 1937–1970.* New York: Dunellen Publishing, 1970.

Bent, A. E., and R. A. Rossum. "Urban Administration and Collective Bargaining." In Alan Edward Bent and Ralph A. Rossum, eds., *Urban Administration: Management, Politics, and Change.* Port Washington, NY: Kennikat Press, 1976.

Benton, Ted, ed. *The Greening of Marxism.* New York: Guilford Press, 1996.

Berg, Maxine. *The Age of Manufacturers, 1700–1820: Industry, Innovation, and Work in Britain.* New York: Routledge, 1994.

Bergsten, C. Fred. *Global Economic Leadership and the Group of Seven.* Washington, DC: Institute for International Economics, 1996.

Berk, Gerald. *Alternative Tracks: The Constitution of the American Industrial Order, 1865–1917.* Baltimore, MD: Johns Hopkins University Press, 1994.

Berkowitz, Edward, and Kim McQuaid. *Creating the Welfare State: The Political Economy of Twentieth-Century Reform.* New York: Praeger, 1988.

Berlin, Ira. *Slaves without Masters: The Free Negro in the Antebellum South.* New York: Vintage Books, 1974.

Bernstein, Michael A. *The Great Depression.* Cambridge: Cambridge University Press, 1987.

Bertrand, Hermann von. *Negotiating NAFTA: A Mexican Envoy's Account.* Westport, CT: Praeger, 1997.

Bertsch, Gary K., ed. *Controlling East-West Trade and Technology Transfer.* Durham, NC: Duke University Press, 1988.

Billias, George Athan, ed. *Law and Authority in Colonial America: Selected Essays.* Barre, MA: Barre Publishers, 1965.

Billington, Ray Allen. *Westward Expansion: A History of the American Frontier.* New York: Macmillan, 1967.

Bilstein, Roger E. *Flight in America.* Baltimore, MD: Johns Hopkins University Press, 1984.

Bilstein, Roger E. *The American Aerospace Industry*. New York: Twayne Publishers, 1996.

Binns, Tristan Boyer. *FEMA: Federal Emergency Management Agency*. Chicago: Heinemann, 2002.

Bittlingmayer, George. "Economics and 100 Years of Antitrust: Introduction." *Economic Inquiry*, vol. 30, no. 2 (1992): 203–206.

Blackford, Mansel, and Austin Kerr. *Business Enterprise in American History*. 2nd ed. New York: Houghton Mifflin, 1990.

Blainey, Geoffrey. *The Causes of War*. New York: Free Press, 1988.

Blair, John M. *The Control of Oil*. New York: Pantheon, 1976.

Blank, Rebecca M., and David E. Card. "Recent Trends in Insured and Uninsured Unemployment: Is There an Explanation?" *Quarterly Journal of Economics*, vol. 106 (November 1991): 1157–1189.

Blinder, Alan. *Economic Policy and the Great Stagflation*. New York: Academic Press, 1979.

Blinder, Alan. *Hard Heads, Soft Hearts: Tough-Minded Economics for a Just Society*. New York: Addison-Wesley, 1987.

Blodgett, Geoffrey. *The Gentle Reformers: Massachusetts Democrats in the Cleveland Era*. Cambridge MA: Harvard University Press, 1966.

Bloodworth, William A., Jr. *Upton Sinclair*. New York: Macmillan, 1977.

Bloomfield, Lincoln P. *In Search of American Foreign Policy*. New York: Oxford University Press, 1974.

Bluestone, Barry, and Bennett Harrison. *The Deindustrialization of America: Plant Closings, Community Abandonment, and the Dismantling of Basic Industry*. New York: Basic Books, 1982.

Blum, Albert A. *A History of the American Labor Movement*. Washington, DC: American Historical Association, 1972.

Blum, John Morton. *V Was for Victory*. San Diego, CA: Harcourt Brace Jovanovich, 1976.

Board of Governors of the Federal Reserve System. *The Federal Reserve System: Purposes and Functions*. Washington, DC: U.S. Government Printing Office, 1994.

Bodnar, John. *The Transplanted*. Bloomington: Indiana University Press, 1985.

Bollier, David. *Citizen Action and Other Big Ideas: A History of Ralph Nader and the Modern Consumer Movement*. Washington, DC: Center for the Study of Responsive Law, 1991.

Bordo, M. D., and L. Jonung. *Monetary Regimes, Inflation, and Monetary Reform*. Stockholm: Stockholm School of Economics Reprint Series, no. 156, 1996.

Borjas, George J. "The Economics of Immigration." *Journal of Economic Literature*, vol. 32, no. 4 (December 1994): 1667–1717.

Boskin, Michael J. *Reagan and the Economy.* San Francisco: ICS Press, 1987.

Bottomore, Tom. *Classes in Modern Society.* New York: Vintage Books, 1991.

Braudel, Fernand. *The Perspective of the World: Civilization and Capitalism, 15th–18th Century.* London: Collins, 1984.

Brazelton, W. Robert. "The Economics of Leon Hirsch Keyserling." *Journal of Economic Perspectives*, vol. 11, no. 4 (Fall 1997): 189–197.

Brewer, John. *The Sinews of Power: War, Money, and the English State, 1688–1783.* Cambridge, MA: Harvard University Press, 1990.

Bridenbaugh, Carl. *Vexed and Troubled Englishmen 1590–1642.* New York: Oxford University Press, 1968.

Bridges, Hal. "The Robber Baron Concept in American History." *Business History Review*, vol. 32 (Spring 1958): 1–13.

Brittan, Samuel. *A Restatement of Economic Liberalism.* Atlantic Highlands, NJ: Humanities Press International, 1988.

Brock, Gerald. *Telecommunications Policy for the Information Age: From Monopoly to Competition.* Cambridge, MA: Harvard University Press, 1994.

Brodie, Bernard. *War and Politics.* New York: Macmillan, 1973.

Brodley, Joseph F. "Post-Chicago Economics and Workable Legal Policy." *Antitrust Law Journal*, vol. 63, no. 2 (1995): 683.

Brodsky, Alyn. *Grover Cleveland: A Study in Character.* New York: St. Martin's Press, 2000.

Bromberg, Joan Lisa. *NASA and the Space Industry.* Baltimore, MD: Johns Hopkins University Press, 1999.

Bromley, Simon. *American Hegemony and World Oil.* University Park: Pennsylvania State University Press, 1991.

Brooks, David. "Supply-Side Squabbles." *National Review*, vol. 38 (October 24, 1986): 28–33.

Brown, D. Clayton. *Electricity for Rural America.* Westport, CT: Greenwood Press, 1980.

Brown, E. Cary. "Fiscal Policy in the Thirties: A Reappraisal." *American Economic Review*, vol. 46, no. 5 (1956): 875–879.

Brown, Roger H. *Redeeming the Republic: Federalists, Taxation, and the Origins of the Constitution.* Baltimore, MD: Johns Hopkins University Press, 1993.

Brown, Thomas. *Oil on Ice: Alaskan Wilderness at the Crossroads.* San Francisco: Sierra Club, 1971.

Browne, William P. *Private Interests, Public Policy, and American Agriculture.* Lawrence: University Press of Kansas, 1988.

Broz, J. Lawrence. *The International Origins of the Federal Reserve System.* Ithaca, NY: Cornell University Press, 1997.

Bruce, Neil. *Public Finance and the American Economy.* Boston, MA: Addison-Wesley, 2001.

Bruce, Robert V. *The Launching of Modern American Science, 1846–1876.* New York: Alfred A. Knopf, 1987.

Bruce, Robert V. *1877: Year of Violence.* Chicago: I. R. Dee, 1989.

Bruchey, Stuart W. *Enterprise: The Dynamic Economy of a Free People.* Cambridge, MA: Harvard University Press, 1990.

Bryan, Frank, and John McClaughry. *The Vermont Papers: Recreating Democracy on a Human Scale.* Post Mills, VT: Chelsea Green Publishing, 1989.

Buchanan, James, and Richard Wagner. *Democracy in Deficit.* New York: Academic Press, 1977.

Buck, Solon Justus. *The Granger Movement: A Study of Agricultural Organization and Its Political, Economic, and Social Manifestations, 1870–1880.* Cambridge, MA: Harvard University Press, 1913.

Burdette, Franklin L. *The Republican Party: A Short History.* New York: Nostrand, 1972.

Burk, James. *Values in the Marketplace: The American Stock Market under Federal Securities Law.* New York: Aldine de Gruyter, 1992.

Burke, John G. "Bursting Boilers and the Federal Power." *Technology and Culture,* vol. 7, no. 1 (January 1966): 1–23.

Burner, David, and Thomas West. *The Torch Is Passed: The Kennedy Brothers and American Liberalism.* New York: Brandywine Press, 1984.

Burnham, Walter D. "The Legacy of George Bush: Travails of an Understudy." In Gerald M. Pomper, ed., *The Election of 1992.* Chatham, NJ: Chatham House Publishers, 1992.

Burns, A. F. "Some Essentials of International Monetary Reform." *Federal Reserve Bulletin,* vol. 58, no. 6 (June 1972): 545–549ff.

Burns, A. F. *Reflections of an Economic Policy Maker: Speeches and Congressional Statements 1969–1978.* Washington, DC: American Enterprise Institute, 1978.

Burns, Helen M. *The American Banking Community and New Deal Banking Reforms: 1933–1935.* Westport, CT: Greenwood Press, 1974.

Bush, Vannevar. *Science, the Endless Frontier.* Washington, DC: U.S. Government Printing Office, 1945.

Butkiewicz, James L., Kenneth J. Koford, and Jeffrey B. Miller, eds. *Keynes' Economic Legacy: Contemporary Economic Theories.* New York: Praeger, 1986.

Butler, Michael A. *Cautious Visionary: Cordell Hull and Trade Reform, 1933–1937.* Kent, OH: Kent State University Press, 1998.

Cahn, Steven, ed. *The Affirmative Action Debate.* New York: Routledge, 2002.

Callahan, North. *TVA: Bridge over Troubled Waters.* South Brunswick, NJ: A. S. Barnes, 1980.

Calomiris, Charles. "Institutional Failure, Monetary Scarcity, and the Depreciation of the Continental." *Journal of Economic History*, vol. 48, no. 1 (March 1988): 47–68.

Campagna, Anthony S. *The Economic Consequence of the Vietnam War*. New York: Praeger, 1991.

Campbell, Ballard C. *The Growth of American Government*. Bloomington: Indiana University Press, 1995.

Campbell, Charles S. *The Transformation of American Foreign Relations*. New York: Harper and Row, 1976.

Campbell-Kelly, Martin, and William Aspray. *Computer: A History of the Information Machine*. New York: Basic Books, 1996.

Carlson, Leonard A. *Indians, Bureaucrats, and Land: The Dawes Act and the Decline of Indian Farming*. Westport, CT: Greenwood Press, 1981.

Carlton, Frank Tracy. *Economic Influences upon Educational Progress in the United States, 1820–1850*. New York: Teachers College Press, 1966.

Carosso, Vincent P. *Investment Banking in America: A History*. Cambridge, MA: Harvard University Press, 1970.

Carothers, Doris. *Chronology of the Federal Emergency Relief Administration, May 12, 1933, to December 31, 1935*. New York: Da Capo Press, 1971.

Carothers, Jo Dale. "Protection of Intellectual Property on the World Wide Web: Is the Digital Millennium Copyright Act Sufficient?" *Arizona Law Review*, vol. 41 (Fall 1999): 937–961.

Carranza, Mario Esteban. *South American Free Trade Area or Free Trade Area of the Americas?* Burlington, VT: Ashgate, 2000.

Carson, Carol S. "The History of the United States National Income and Product Accounts: The Development of an Analytical Tool." *Review of Income and Wealth*, series 21 (1975): 153–181.

Carson, Richard L. *Comparative Economic Systems*. Armonk, NY: M. E. Sharpe, 1990.

Cassard, Marcel. *The Role of the Off-Shore Centers in International Financial Mediation*. Washington, DC: International Monetary Fund Working Paper, 1994.

Chamberlain, Lawrence H. *The President, Congress, and Legislation*. New York: Columbia University Press, 1946.

Chambers, John Whiteclay, II. *The American Military History*. New York: Oxford University Press, 1999.

Chan, S., and C. A. Drury, eds. *Sanctions as Economic Statecraft: Theory and Practice*. New York: St. Martin's Press, 2000.

Chandler, Alfred Dupont. *The Visible Hand: The Managerial Revolution in American Business*. Cambridge, MA: Harvard University Press, Belknap Press, 1977.

Chandler, Lester V. *Benjamin Strong, Central Banker*. New York: Arno Press, 1978.

Chandler, William U. *The Myth of TVA: Conservation and Development in the Tennessee Valley, 1933–1983*. Cambridge, MA: Ballinger, 1984.

Chatfield, Charles. *The American Peace Movement: Ideals and Activism*. New York: Twayne Publishers, 1992.

Chernow, Ron. *The House of Morgan: An American Banking Dynasty and the Rise of Modern Finance*. New York: Simon and Schuster, 1990.

Chernow, Ron. *The Warbugs: The Twentieth Century Odyssey of a Remarkable Jewish Family*. Ithaca, NY: Cornell University Press, 1993.

Chernow, Ron. "The New Deal's Gift to Wall Street." *Wall Street Journal*, November 11, 1999.

Cherry, Shelia. "Green Machine." *Insight*, vol. 16, no. 45 (December 4, 2000): 24.

Chesler, Phyllis, and Emily Jane Goodman. *Women, Money, and Power*. New York: William Morrow, 1976.

Chessman, G. Wallace. *Theodore Roosevelt and the Politics of Power*. Prospect Heights, IL: Waveland Press, 1994.

Chisum, Donald S. *Principles of Patent Law: Cases and Materials*. 2nd ed. New York: Foundation Press, 2001.

Christie, Ian R. *Crisis of Empire: Great Britain and the American Colonies, 1754–1783*. New York: W. W. Norton, 1966.

Cicchetti, Charles J. *Alaskan Oil: Alternative Routes and Markets*. Baltimore, MD: Johns Hopkins University Press, 1972.

Clark, David. *Post-Industrial America: A Geographical Perspective*. New York: Methuen, 1985.

Clark, Ronald W. *Edison: The Man Who Made the Future*. New York: G. P. Putnam, 1977.

Clement, Norris C. *North American Economic Integration: Theory and Practice*. Northampton, MA: Edward Elgar Publishing, 1999.

Clements, Kendrick A. *The Presidency of Woodrow Wilson*. Lawrence: University Press of Kansas, 1992.

Clements, Kendrick A. *Hoover, Conservation, and Consumerism: Engineering the Good Life*. Lawrence: University Press of Kansas, 2000.

Clouse, Jerry A. *The Whiskey Rebellion*. Harrisburg: Pennsylvania Historical and Museum Commission, 1994.

Clowse, Barbara Barksdale. *Brainpower for the Cold War: The Sputnik Crisis and National Defense Education Act of 1958*. Westport, CT: Greenwood Press, 1981.

Coats, A. W. "The American Economic Association and the Economics Profession." *Journal of Economic Literature*, vol. 23 (1985): 1697–1727.

Cobb, James C. *The Most Southern Place on Earth: The Mississippi Delta and the Roots of Regional Identity*. New York: Oxford University Press, 1992.

Cochrane, Willard W. *The Development of American Agriculture: A Historical Analysis*. Minneapolis: University of Minnesota Press, 1993.

Cochrane, Willard W., and C. Ford Runge. *Reforming Farm Policy: Toward a National Agenda*. Ames: Iowa State University Press, 1992.

Cochrane, Willard W., and Mary E. Ryan. *American Farm Policy, 1948–1973*. Minneapolis: University of Minnesota Press, 1976.

Coffee, John C., Jr. "The Rise of Dispersed Ownership: The Roles of Law and the State in the Separation of Ownership and Control." *Yale Law Journal*, vol. 111 (2001): 1–82.

Cohen, Andrew, and Beth Heinsohn. *The Department of Defense*. New York: Chelsea House, 1990.

Cohen, Stephen D. *Fundamentals of U.S. Foreign Trade Policy: Economics, Politics, Laws, and Issues*. Boulder, CO: Westview Press, 2003.

Cohen, Warren, ed. *The Cambridge History of American Foreign Relations*. London: Cambridge University Press, 1993.

Coit, Margaret L. *John C. Calhoun: American Portrait*. Boston: Houghton Mifflin, 1950.

Colander, David C., and Harry Landreth, eds. *The Coming of Keynesianism to America: Conversations with the Founders of Keynesian Economics*. Cheltenham, England: Edward Elgar, 1996.

Cole, Donald B. *The Presidency of Andrew Jackson*. Lawrence: University Press of Kansas, 1993.

Cole, Wayne S. *Senator Gerald P. Nye and American Foreign Relations*. Westport, CT: Greenwood Press, 1980.

Coleman, D. C., ed. *Revisions in Mercantilism*. London: Methuen, 1969.

Coleman, Kenneth, ed. *A History of Georgia*. Athens: University of Georgia Press, 1977.

Coletta, Paola E. *The Presidency of William Howard Taft*. Lawrence: University Press of Kansas, 1973.

Collins, Robert M. *More: The Politics of Economic Growth in Postwar America*. New York: Oxford University Press, 2000.

Compton, Eric N. *The New World of Commercial Banking*. Lexington, MA: Lexington Books, 1987.

Confessore, Nicholas. "Green Herring," *The American Prospect*, vol. 43 (March 1, 1999): 41.

Conot, Robert E. *A Streak of Luck: The Life and Legend of Thomas Alva Edison*. New York: Seaview Books, 1979.

Conway, M. Margaret, David W. Ahern, and Gertrude A. Steuernagel. *Women and Public Policy: A Revolution in Progress*. Washington, DC: Congressional Quarterly Press, 1999.

Conway, Thomas A. *The ABC of the Townsend Plan*. New York: H. W. Wilson, 2000.

Coombs, C. A. *The Arena of International Finance*. New York: John Wiley and Sons, 1976.

Cooper, John Milton, Jr. *Pivotal Decades: The United States, 1900–1920*. New York: W. W. Norton, 1990.

Cope, Megan. "Responsibility, Regulation, and Retrenchment: The End of Welfare?" In Lynn A. Staeheli, Janet E. Kodras, and Colin Flint, eds., *State Devolution in America*. Beverly Hills, CA: Sage Publications, 1997.

Corder, J. Kevin. *Central Bank Autonomy: The Federal Reserve System in American Politics*. New York: Garland Publishing, 1998.

Cordery, Stacy A. *Theodore Roosevelt: In the Vanguard of the Modern*. Belmont, CA: Wadsworth, 2003.

Cordesman, Anthony. *U.S. Government Efforts to Create a Homeland Defense Capability: Program Budget and Overview*. Washington, DC: Center for Strategic and International Studies, December 2000.

Corwin, E. S. "The Schechter Case—Landmark or What?" *New York University Law Quarterly Review*, vol. 13 (1936): 151–190.

Countryman, Edward. *Americans: A Collision of Histories*. New York: Hill and Wang, 1996.

Cowan, Ruth Schwartz. *A Social History of American Technology*. New York: Oxford University Press, 1997.

Crabb, Cecil V., Jr. *Policymakers and Critics: Conflicting Theories of American Foreign Policy*. New York: Praeger, 1976.

Crawford, Margaret L. *Building the Workingman's Paradise: The Design of American Company Towns*. New York: Verso, 1993.

Critchlow, Donald T. *Studebaker: The Life and Death of an American Corporation*. Bloomington: Indiana University Press, 1996.

Crunden, Robert M. *Ministers of Reform: The Progressives' Achievement in American Civilization, 1889–1920*. New York: Basic Books, 1982.

Culbert, Jeff. *The Open Mythology of the Green Party Politics*. North York, Ontario: York University, 1996.

Cunningham, Noble E. *The Jeffersonian Republicans: The Formation of Party Organization, 1789–1801*. Chapel Hill: University of North Carolina Press, published for the Institute of Early American History and Culture at Williamsburg, Virginia, 1957.

Curry, Earl R. *Hoover's Dominican Diplomacy and the Origins of the Good Neighbor Policy*. New York: Garland Publishing, 1979.

Curtin, Philip D. *The Rise and Fall of the Plantation Complex: Essays in Atlantic History*. New York: Cambridge University Press, 1990.

Curtis, James. *Mind's Eye, Mind's Truth: FSA Photography Reconsidered*. Philadelphia: Temple University Press, 1989.

Cushman, Barry. *Rethinking the New Deal Court: The Structure of a Constitutional Revolution*. New York: Oxford University Press, 1998.

Czech, Brian, and Paul R. Krausman. *The Endangered Species Act: History, Conservation, Biology, and Public Policy*. Baltimore, MD: Johns Hopkins University Press, 2001.

Dallek, Robert K. *The American Style of Foreign Policy: Cultural Politics and Foreign Affairs*. New York: Alfred A. Knopf, 1983.

Dangerfield, George. *The Era of Good Feelings*. New York: Harcourt, Brace and World, 1952.

Dangerfield, George. *The Awakening of American Nationalism 1815–1828*. New York: Harper and Row, 1965.

David, Andrew. *Famous Supreme Court Cases*. Minneapolis, MN: Lerner Publishing, 1980.

Davidson, Roger H., and Sar A. Levitan. *Antipoverty Housekeeping: The Administration of the Economic Opportunity Act*. Ann Arbor, MI: Institute of Labor and Industrial Relations, 1968.

Davies, Glyn. *A History of Money from Ancient Times to the Present Day*. Cardiff: University of Wales Press, 2002.

Davis, Jack E. *The Civil Rights Movement*. Malden, MA: Blackwell, 2001.

Davis, Kenneth. *FDR, the New Deal Years, 1933–37: A History*. New York: Random House, 1986.

Daynes, Byron W., and Glen Sussman. *The American Presidency*. Upper Saddle River, NJ: Prentice-Hall, 2001.

De Angelis, Massimo. *Keynesianism, Social Conflict, and Political Economy*. London: Macmillan, 2000.

DeGruson, Gene, ed. *The Lost First Edition of Upton Sinclair's* The Jungle. Memphis, TN: Peachtree Publishers, 1988.

Dell, Floyd. *Upton Sinclair: A Study in Social Protest*. New York: AMS Press, 1970.

Denison, Edward F. *Trends in American Economic Growth, 1915–1982*. Washington, DC: Brookings Institution, 1982.

Destler, I. M. *American Trade Politics*. 2nd ed. Washington, DC: Institute for International Economics, 1992.

de Tocqueville, Alexis. *Democracy in America*, ed. J. P. Mayer; trans. George Lawrence. New York: Perennial Library, 1988.

de Vries, G. M. *Balance of Payments Adjustment, 1945 to 1986: The IMF Experience*. Washington, DC: International Monetary Fund, 1987.

Dewing, Arthur S. *Corporate Promotions and Reorganizations*. New York: Harper and Row, 1969.

Dewson, Mary W., to Mr. C. W. Dunning. Letter. "Objections to the Candy Manufac-turing Code." Attached Testimony from Hearing of March 13, 1934. Democratic National Committee–Women's Division Correspondence–General (Box no. 5) Folder: Consumers' Advisory Board of NRA 1933–1935. Franklin D. Roosevelt Library, Hyde Park, New York, March 19, 1934.

Diamond, R. *Nixon: The Third Year of His Presidency.* Washington, DC: Congressional Quarterly Press, 1972.

Dickerson, O. M. *The Navigation Acts and the American Revolution.* Philadelphia: University of Pennsylvania Press, 1951.

DiNitto, Diana M. *Social Welfare: Politics and Public Policy.* Boston: Allyn and Bacon, 2000.

Dinnerstein, Leonard, and David M. Reimers. *Ethnic Americans.* New York: Columbia University Press, 1999.

Dobelstein, Andrew W. *Moral Authority, Ideology, and the Future of American Social Welfare.* Boulder, CO: Westview Press, 1999.

Dobson, Alan P. *U.S. Economic Statecraft for Survival, 1933–1991: Of Sanctions, Embargoes, and Economic Warfare.* New York: Routledge, 2002.

Dobyns, Kenneth W. *The Patent Office Pony: A History of the Early Patent Office.* Spotsylvania, VA: Sergeant Kirkland's Press, 1999.

Doerflinger, Thomas. *A Vigorous Spirit of Enterprise: Merchants and Economic Development in Revolutionary Philadelphia.* Chapel Hill: University of North Carolina Press, 1986.

Dolan, Ronald E., and Robert L. Worden, eds. *Japan: A Country Study.* 5th ed. Washington, DC: U.S. Government Printing Office, 1992.

Donner, Irah. "The Copyright Clause of the U.S. Constitution: Why Did the Framers Include It with Unanimous Approval?" *American Journal of Legal History*, vol. 36, no. 3 (1992): 361–378.

Dorfman, Joseph. *The Economic Mind in American Civilization.* New York: Viking Press, 1946.

Draper, Theodore. *A Very Thin Line: The Iran-Contra Affairs.* New York: Hill and Wang, 1991.

Dubofsky, Melvyn. *We Shall Be All: A History of the Industrial Workers of the World.* Urbana: University of Illinois Press, 1988.

Dubofsky, Melvyn. *Hard Work: The Making of Labor History.* Urbana: University of Illinois Press, 2000.

Duggan, Michael A. *Antitrust and the U.S. Supreme Court, 1829–1980: A Compen-dium of Supreme Court Decisions Dealing with Restraint of Trade and Monopoly.* New York: Federal Legal Publications, 1981.

Dulles, Foster Rhea. *America's Rise to World Power.* New York: Harper and Row, 1954.

Dulles, Foster Rhea, and Melvyn Dubofsky. *Labor in America: A History*. Wheeling, IL: Harlan Davidson, 1993.

Duncan, Stephen M. *Citizen Warriors: America's National Guard and Reserve Forces and the Politics of National Security*. Novato, CA: Presidio, 1997.

Dunkman, William E. *Money, Credit, and Banking*. New York: Random House, 1970.

Dupree, A. Hunter. *Science in the Federal Government: A History of Policies and Activities to 1940*. Cambridge, MA: Harvard University Press, Belknap Press, 1957.

Durr, Clifford J. *The Early History of Defense Plant Corporation*. Washington, DC: Committee on Public Administration Cases, 1950.

Dykstra, David L. *The Shifting Balance of Power: American-British Diplomacy in North America, 1842–1848*. Lanham, MD: University Press of America, 1999.

Eckes, Alfred E. *Opening America's Market: U.S. Foreign Policy since 1776*. Chapel Hill: University of North Carolina Press, 1995.

Eckes, Alfred, Richard L. Brinkman, and William A. Lovett. *U.S. Trade Policy: History, Theory, and the WTO*. Armonk, NY: M. E. Sharpe, 1999.

Eden, Robert. *The New Deal and Its Legacy: Critique and Reappraisal*. New York: Greenwood Press, 1989.

Eisner, Marc Allen. *From Warfare State to Welfare State: World War I, Compensatory State-Building, and the Limits of the Modern Order*. University Park: Pennsylvania State University Press, 2000.

Eisner, Robert. *How Real Is the Federal Deficit?* New York: Free Press, 1986.

Eisner, Robert. *The Total Income System of Accounts*. Chicago: University of Chicago Press, 1989.

Eisner, Robert. *The Misunderstood Economy: What Counts and How to Count It*. Boston, MA: Harvard Business School Press, 1994.

Elder, Witt, ed. *The Supreme Court A to Z: A Ready Reference Encyclopedia*. Washington, DC: Congressional Quarterly Press, 1993.

Elias, Stephen, and Richard Stim. *Patent, Copyright, and Trademark*. Berkeley, CA: Nolo, 2002.

Elkins, Stanley M. *Slavery: A Problem in American Institutional and Intellectual Life*. Chicago: University of Chicago Press, 1959.

Ellis, Richard E. *The Union at Risk: Jacksonian Democracy, States' Rights, and the Nullification Crisis*. New York: Oxford University Press, 1987.

Emanuel, Steven. *Constitutional Law*. Larchmont, NY: Emanuel Law Outlines, 1987.

Emert, Phyllis Raybin. *Colonial Triangular Trade: An Economy Based on Human Misery*. Carlisle, MA: Discovery Enterprises, 1995.

Emminger, O. "The D-Mark in the Conflict between Internal and External Equilibrium, 1948–75." Princeton, NJ: International Finance Section, Department of Economics, Princeton University, 1977.

Engelman, Fred L. *The Peace of Christmas Eve*. New York: Harcourt, Brace and World, 1962.

Engerman, Stanley L., and Robert E. Gallman, eds. *The Cambridge Economic History of the United States*. 3 vols. Cambridge: Cambridge University Press, 1996–2000.

Ewalt, Patricia L. *Social Policy: Reform, Research, and Practice*. Washington, DC: NASW Press, 1997.

Fabian, Ann. *Card Sharps and Bucket Shops: Gambling in Nineteenth-Century America*. New York: Routledge, 1999.

Fabre, Guilhem. *Criminal Prosperity: Drug Trafficking, Money Laundering, and Financial Crisis after the Cold War*. London: Curzon Press, 2002.

Fainstein, S. *Restructuring the City: The Political Economy of Urban Development*. New York: Longman, 1983.

Faulk, Odie B. *Too Far North, Too Far South*. Los Angeles, CA: Westernlore Press, 1967.

Faulkner, Harold U. *The Decline of Laissez-Faire 1897–1917*. New York: Holt, Rinehart and Winston, 1951.

Fehrenbacher, Don E. *The Era of Expansion, 1800–1848*. New York: John Wiley and Sons, 1969.

Fein, Melanie L. "What Does It Mean to Banking: Regulating Cyberspace?" *Bank Management*, vol. 71 (September–October 1995): 8–14.

Feldman, Douglas A., and Julia Wang Miller, eds. *The AIDS Crisis: A Documentary History*. Westport, CT: Greenwood Press, 1998.

Feldman, Ron. "Changes in Farmer Mac's Charter," *Choices: The Magazine of Food, Farm, and Resource Issues*. vol. 11, no. 3 (1996): 8–12.

Feldstein, Martin, ed. *American Economic Policy in the 1980s*. Chicago: University of Chicago Press, 1994.

Feller, Daniel. *The Jacksonian Promise: America, 1815–1840*. Baltimore, MD: Johns Hopkins University Press, 1995.

Ferguson, E. James. *The Power of the Purse: A History of American Public Finance, 1776–1789*. Chapel Hill: University of North Carolina Press, 1961.

Ferguson, Niall. *The Cash Nexus*. New York: Basic Books, 2001.

Ferrell, Robert H. *American Diplomacy: The Twentieth Century*. New York: Norton, 1988.

Findlay, Ronald. *The Triangular Trade and the Atlantic Economy of the Eighteenth Century*. Princeton, NJ: International Finance Section, Department of Economics, Princeton University, 1990.

Fine, Sidney. *Laissez-Faire and the General Welfare State*. Ann Arbor: University of Michigan Press, 1966.

Fink, Leon. *Workingmen's Democracy: The Knights of Labor and American Politics.* Urbana: University of Illinois Press, 1983.

Fischer, Thomas C. *The United States, the European Union, and the "Globalization" of World Trade: Allies or Adversaries?* Westport, CT: Quorum, 2000.

Fishback, Price V., and Shawn Everett Kantor. *A Prelude to the Welfare State: The Origins of Workers' Compensation.* Chicago: University of Chicago Press, 2000.

Fisher, Gordon M. "The Development and History of the Poverty Thresholds." *Social Security Bulletin*, vol. 55 (Winter 1992): 3–14.

Fisk, Catherine L. "Working Knowledge: Trade Secrets, Restrictive Covenants in Employment, and the Rise of Corporate Intellectual Property, 1800–1920." *Hastings Law Journal*, vol. 52 (2001): 441–535.

Fite, Gilbert C. *American Farmers: The New Minority.* Bloomington: Indiana University Press, 1981.

Fite, Gilbert C. *Cotton Fields No More: Southern Agriculture, 1865–1980.* Lexington: University Press of Kentucky, 1984.

Fitzgerald, Frances. *Way Out There in the Blue.* New York: Simon and Schuster, 2000.

Fleming, Donald, and Bernard Bailyn, eds. *The Intellectual Migration: Europe and America, 1930–1960.* Cambridge, MA: Harvard University Press, Belknap Press, 1969.

Fleming, Susan Hall. "OSHA at 30." *Job Safety and Health Quarterly*, vol. 12 (Spring 2001): 23–32.

Flemming, Thomas. *The Berlin Wall.* Munich: Hagen Koch, 1988.

Flink, James J. *The Automobile Age.* Cambridge, MA: MIT Press, 1990.

Flippen, J. Brooks. *Nixon and the Environment.* Albuquerque: University of New Mexico Press, 2000.

Fogel, Robert William. *Without Consent or Contract: The Rise and Fall of American Slavery.* New York: W. W. Norton, 1989.

Fogel, Robert William, and Stanley Engerman, eds. *A Reinterpretation of American Economic History.* New York: Harper and Row, 1971.

Fogel, Robert William, and Stanley Engerman, eds. *Time on the Cross: The Economics of American Negro Slavery.* London: Little, Brown, 1974.

Fogel, Robert William, and Stanley Engerman, eds. *Time on the Cross, Volume 2: Evidence and Methods—a Supplement.* London: Little, Brown, 1974.

Fogel, Robert William, and Stanley Engerman, eds. *Without Consent or Contract: The Rise and Fall of American Slavery—Technical Papers: Markets and Production. Volume 1.* New York: W. W. Norton, 1992.

Fogel, Robert William, and Stanley Engerman, eds. *Without Consent or Contract: The Rise and Fall of American Slavery: Conditions of Slave Life and the Transition to Freedom—Technical Papers, Volume 2.* New York: W. W. Norton, 1992.

Fogel, Robert William, Ralph A. Galantine, and Richard L. Manning, eds. *Without Consent or Contract: The Rise and Fall of American Slavery—Evidence and Methods*. New York: W. W. Norton, 1992.

Folbre, Nancy, and Barnet Wagman. "Counting Housework: Revised Estimates of Real Product in the United States, 1800–1860." *Journal of Economic History*, vol. 53 (1993): 275–288.

Folsom, Burton W., Jr. "Robber Barons Have Been Unfairly Denigrated." In William Dudley, ed., *The Industrial Revolution: Opposing Viewpoints*. San Diego, CA: Greenhaven Press, 1998.

Folsom, Ralph Haughwout. *NAFTA in a Nutshell*. St. Paul, MN: West Group, 1999.

Foner, Eric. *Free Soil, Free Labor, Free Men: The Ideology of the Republican Party before the Civil War*. New York: Oxford University Press, 1970.

Foner, Eric. *Reconstruction: America's Unfinished Revolution, 1863–1877*. New York: Harper and Row, 1988.

Foner, Eric. *The Story of American Freedom*. New York: Norton, 1999.

Foner, Philip S. *A History of the Labor Movement in the United States*. 4 vols. New York: International Publishers, 1955–1975.

Foner, Philip S. *The Great Labor Uprising of 1877*. New York: Monad Press, 1977.

Forbes, John Douglas. *J. P. Morgan, Jr., 1867–1943*. Charlottesville: University Press of Virginia, 1981.

Foreman, Grant. *Indian Removal: The Emigration of the Five Civilized Tribes of Indians*. Norman: University of Oklahoma Press, 1953.

Forster, Cornelius P. *The Uncontrolled Chancellor: Charles Townshend and His American Policy*. Providence: Rhode Island Bicentennial Foundation, 1978.

Foster, John. *Class Struggle and the Industrial Revolution*. London: Weidenfeld and Nicolson, 1974.

Fouda, Safaa A. "Liquid Fuels from Natural Gas." *Scientific American*, vol. 278, no. 3 (March 1998): 74–77.

Fox, Elaine. "The Modernization of Antitrust: A New Equilibrium." *Cornell Law Review*, vol. 66 (1981): 1140–1156.

Fox, Kel M. "Aftosa: The Campaign against Foot-and-Mouth Disease in Mexico, 1946–1951." *Journal of Arizona History*, vol. 38, no. 1 (1997): 23–40.

Fox, Stephen. *The Mirror Makers: A History of American Advertising and Its Creators*. Chicago: University of Illinois Press, 1997.

Franko, Patrice M. *Toward a New Security Architecture in the Americas: The Strategic Implications of the FTAA*. Washington, DC: Center for Strategic and International Studies, 2000.

Fraser, James W. *The School in the United States: A Documentary History*. Boston: McGraw-Hill, 2001.

Freedman, Lawrence. *The Evolution of Nuclear Strategy*. New York: St. Martin's Press, 1989.

Freehling, William W. *Prelude to Civil War: The Nullification Movement in South Carolina 1816–1832*. New York: Harper and Row, 1966.

Friedman, Lawrence M. *A History of American Law*. New York: Simon and Schuster, 1973.

Friedman, Milton. *Capitalism and Freedom*. Chicago: University of Chicago Press, 1962.

Friedman, Milton. *An Economist's Protest*. Glen Ridge, NJ: Thomas Horton, 1972.

Friedman, Milton. *Essays in Positive Economics*. Chicago: University of Chicago Press, 1953.

Friedman, Milton. *There's No Such Thing as a Free Lunch*. LaSalle, IL: Open Court, 1975.

Friedman, Milton, and R. V. Roosa. *The Balance of Payments: Free versus Fixed Exchange Rates*. Washington, DC: American Enterprise Institute for Public Policy Research, 1967.

Friedman, Milton, and Anna J. Schwartz. *A Monetary History of the United States, 1867–1960*. Princeton, NJ: Princeton University Press, 1963.

Frisch, Morton. *Alexander Hamilton and the Political Order*. Lanham, MD: University Press of America, 1991.

Frumkin, Norman. *Guide to Economic Indicators*. Armonk, NY: M. E. Sharpe, 1994.

Fry, Michael, ed. *Adam Smith's Legacy: His Place in the Development of Modern Economics*. New York: Routledge, 1992.

Funigiello, Philip J. *American-Soviet Trade in the Cold War*. Chapel Hill: University of North Carolina Press, 1988.

Furer, Howard B. *"The Fuller Court, 1888–1910,"* in *The Supreme Court in American Life*. Vol. 5. Millwood, NY: Associated Faculty Press, 1986.

Gabaldon, Theresa A. "John Law, with a Tulip, in the South Seas: Gambling and the Regulation of Euphoric Market Transactions." *Journal of Corporation Law*, vol. 26, no. 2 (Winter 2001): 225–284.

Gabe, Jonathan, David Kelleher, and Gareth Williams, eds. *Challenging Medicine*. New York: Routledge, 1994.

Gabel, David. "Competition in a Network Industry: The Telephone Industry, 1894–1910." *Journal of Economic History*, vol. 54, no. 3 (September 1994): 543.

Galbraith, John Kenneth. *The Affluent Society*. 2nd ed. Boston: Houghton Mifflin, 1969.

Galbraith, John Kenneth. *The Great Crash, 1929*. Boston: Houghton Mifflin, 1972.

Galbraith, John Kenneth. "Keynes, Roosevelt, and the Complementary Revolutions." In Harold L. Wattel, ed., *The Policy Consequences of John Maynard Keynes*. Armonk, NY: M. E. Sharpe, 1985.

Galbraith, John Kenneth. *The New Industrial State*. 4th ed. Boston: Houghton Mifflin, 1985.

Gans, Herbert J. *The Levittowners: Ways of Life and Politics in a New Suburban Community*. New York: Pantheon, 1967.

Gardner, Richard N. *Sterling-Dollar Diplomacy in Current Perspective: The Origins and the Prospects of Our International Economic Order*. New York: Columbia University Press, 1980.

Garraty, John A. *The New Commonwealth, 1877–1890*. New York: Harper and Row, 1968.

Garraty, John A. *Unemployment in History: Economic Thought and Public Policy*. New York: Harper and Row, 1978.

Garrow, David J., ed. *The Montgomery Bus Boycott and the Women Who Started It: The Memoir of Jo Ann Gibson Robinson*. Knoxville: University of Tennessee Press, 1987.

Gates, Paul Wallace. *Agriculture and the Civil War*. New York: Alfred A. Knopf, 1965.

Gates, Paul Wallace. *History of Public Land Law Development*. Washington, DC: U.S. Government Printing Office, 1968.

Gates, Paul Wallace. *Public Land Policies: Management and Disposal*. New York: Arno Press, 1979.

Geisst, Charles R. *100 Years of Wall Street*. New York: McGraw-Hill, 2000.

Gelfand, Mark I. *A Nation of Cities*. New York: Oxford University Press, 1975.

Gensler, Howard, ed. *The American Welfare System: Origins, Structure, and Effects*. Westport, CT: Praeger, 1996.

Gibson, Martha L. *Conflict amid Consensus in American Trade Policy*. Washington, DC: Georgetown University Press, 2000.

Giddens, Anthony. *The Class Structure of Modern Society*. London: Hutchinson, 1973.

Gilderhus, Mark. *The Second Century: U.S.–Latin American Relations since 1889*. New York: Scholastic Resources, 1999.

Gilmore, William C. *Dirty Money: The Evolution of Money-Laundering Counter-Measures*. 2nd ed. Strasbourg, France: Council of Europe Press, 1995.

Gilpin, Robert. *War and Change in World Politics*. New York: Cambridge University Press, 1981.

Gilpin, Robert. *Global Political Economy: Understanding the International Economic Order*. Princeton: Princeton University Press, 2001.

Ginsberg, Leon. *Understanding Social Problems, Policies, and Programs*. Columbia: University of South Carolina Press, 1996.

Glynn, Patrick. *Closing Pandora's Box*. New York: New Republic Books, 1992.

Goddard, Stephen B. *Getting There*. Chicago: University of Chicago Press, 1994.

Goldin, Claudia. "Labor Markets in the Twentieth Century." In Stanley L. Engerman and Robert E. Gallman, eds., *The Cambridge History of the United States*. Vol. 3. New York: Cambridge University Press, 1996.

Goldin, Claudia, and Robert A. Margo. "The Great Compression: The Wage Structure in the United States at Mid-Century." *Quarterly Journal of Economics*, vol. 107 (February 1992): 1–34.

Goldman, Ralph Morris. *The Democratic Party in American Politics*. New York: Macmillan, 1966.

Goldstein, Judith. *Ideas, Interests, and American Trade Policy*. Ithaca, NY: Cornell University Press, 1993.

Goldstein, Morris. *The Exchange Rate System and the IMF: A Model Agenda*. Washington, DC: Institute for International Economics, 1995.

Golembiewski, R. T., and M. White. *Cases in Public Management*. Boston: Houghton Mifflin, 1983.

Goodfriend, Marvin. "Monetary Policy Comes of Age: A 20th Century Odyssey." *Economic Quarterly* (Federal Reserve Bank of Richmond, Virginia), vol. 83, no. 1 (Winter 1997): 543.

Goodfriend, Marvin. "The Phases of U.S. Monetary Policy: 1987 to 2001." *Economic Quarterly* (Federal Reserve Bank of Richmond, Virginia), vol. 88, no. 4 (Fall 2002): 1–17.

Goodman, Jane. *Women, Money, and Power*. New York: William Morrow, 1976.

Goodwyn, Lawrence. *The Populist Movement: A Short History of the Agrarian Revolt in America*. New York: Oxford University Press, 1978.

Goralski, Robert, and Russell Freeburg. *Oil and War*. New York: William Morrow, 1987.

Gordon, Colin. *New Deals: Business, Labor, and Politics in America, 1920–1935*. New York: Cambridge University Press, 1994.

Gordon, John Steele. *The Great Game: The Emergence of Wall Street As a World Power, 1653–2000*. New York: Simon and Schuster, 2000.

Gould, Lewis L. *The Presidency of William McKinley*. Lawrence: Regents Press of Kansas, 1980.

Graham, Bradley. *Hit to Kill*. New York: Public Affairs, 2001.

Grant, H. Roger. *Insurance Reform: Consumer Action in the Progressive Era*. Ames: Iowa State University Press, 1979.

Gras, Norman Scott Brien. *Introduction to Economic History*. New York: Harper and Brothers, 1922.

Gray, Colin S. *House of Cards*. Ithaca, NY: Cornell University Press, 1992.

Gray, Lewis C. *History of Agriculture in the Southern United States to 1860*. Gloucester, MA: P. Smith, 1958.

Gray, Wayne B., and Carol Adaire Jones. "Are OSHA Health Inspections Effective? A Longitudinal Study of the Manufacturing Sector." *Review of Economics and Statistics*, vol. 73 (August 1991): 504–508.

Greene, John Robert. *The Presidency of George Bush*. Lawrence: University Press of Kansas, 2000.

Greenwood, Michael J., and John M. McDowell. "Differential Economic Opportunity, Transferability of Skills, and Immigration to the United States and Canada," *Review of Economics and Statistics*, vol. 73, no. 4 (November 1991): 612–623.

Greider, William. *Secrets of the Temple: How the Federal Reserve Runs the Country*. New York: Simon and Schuster, 1987.

Grey, Lewis C. *History of Agriculture in the Southern United States to 1860*. Washington, DC: Carnegie Institution of Washington, 1933.

Griess, Thomas, ed. *Early American Wars and Military Institutions*. New York: Avery, 1986.

Grimes, Alan P. *Democracy and the Amendments to the Constitution*. Lexington, MA: Lexington Books, 1978.

Griswold, Wesley S. *The Night the Revolution Began*. Brattleboro, VT: Stephen Green Press, 1972.

Griswold del Castillo, Richard. *The Treaty of Guadalupe Hidalgo: A Legacy of Conflict*. Norman: University of Oklahoma Press, 1990.

Grobb, Gerald. *Workers and Utopia: A Study of Ideological Conflict in the American Labor Movement, 1865–1900*. Chicago: Quadrangle Books, 1961.

Groh, Lynn. *Walter Reed, Pioneer in Medicine*. Champaign, IL: Garrard Publishing, 1971.

Gropman, Alan, ed. *The Big L: American Logistics in World War II*. Washington, DC: National Defense University Press, 1997.

Grotton, Martha V., ed. *Congress and the Nation*. Vol. 5, 1977–1980, Government Series. Washington, DC: Congressional Quarterly Press, 1981.

Guelzo, Allen G. *Lincoln: Redeemer President*. Grand Rapids, MI: W. B. Eerdmans, 1999.

Gutek, Gerald Lee. *Education and Schooling in America*. Englewood Cliffs, NJ: Prentice-Hall, 1988.

Gutman, Herbert G. *Slavery and the Numbers Game: A Critique of* Time on the Cross. Chicago: University of Illinois Press, 1975.

Hadjimichalakis, Michael. *The Federal Reserve, Money, and Interest Rates: The Volcker Years and Beyond*. New York: Praeger, 1984.

Haggerty, Richard A., ed. *Dominican Republic and Haiti: Country Studies*. 2nd ed. Washington, DC: U.S. Government Printing Office, 1991.

Hair, William Ivy. *The Kingfish and His Realm: The Life and Times of Huey P. Long*. Baton Rouge: Louisiana State University Press, 1991.

Hall, John, and Patrick Joyce, eds. *Reworking Class*. Ithaca, NY: Cornell University Press, 1987.

Hall, Kermit L., ed. *The Oxford Companion to the Supreme Court of the United States*. New York: Oxford University Press, 1992.

Hall, Kermit L., ed. *The Oxford Guide to United States Supreme Court Decisions*. New York: Oxford University Press, 2001.

Hall, Peter. "The Turbulent Eighth Decade: Challenges to American City Planning." *Journal of the American Planning Association*, vol. 55, no. 3 (1989): 275–282.

Hall, Ronald, Alasdair Smith, and Loukas Tsoukalis, eds. *Competitiveness and Cohesion in EU Policies*. New York: Oxford University Press, 2001.

Hamilton, Alexander. *The Papers of Alexander Hamilton, Volumes VI–X*. New York: Columbia University Press, 1963.

Hamilton, Alexander, James Madison, and John Jay. *The Federalist Papers*. New York: Bantam Books, 1987.

Hammond, Bray. *Banks and Politics in America from the Revolution to the Civil War*. Princeton, NJ: Princeton University Press, 1957.

Hammond, Bray. *Sovereignty and an Empty Purse: Banks and Politics in the Civil War*. Princeton, NJ: Princeton University Press, 1970.

Handlin, Oscar. *The Uprooted*. Boston: Little, Brown, 1973.

Hane, Mikoso. *Modern Japan*. Boulder, CO: Westview Press, 2001.

Hansen, Alvin. *Full Recovery or Stagnation*. New York: Norton and Norton, 1938.

Hansen, John Mark. *Gaining Access: Congress and the Farm Lobby, 1919–1981*. Chicago: University of Chicago Press, 1991.

Hardach, Gerd. *The First World War, 1914–1918*. Berkeley: University of California Press, 1977.

Hargrove, Edwin C., and Samuel A. Morley, eds. *The President and the Council of Economic Advisers: Interviews with CEA Chairmen*. Boulder, CO: Westview Press, 1984.

Hargrove, Erwin C. *Prisoners of Myth: The Leadership of the Tennessee Valley Authority 1933–1990*. Knoxville: University of Tennessee Press, 2001.

Harl, Neal. *The Farm Debt Crisis of the 1980s*. Ames: Iowa State University Press, 1990.

Harper, Lawrence A. *The English Navigation Laws*. New York: Octagon Books, 1964.

Harrington, Michael. *The Other America: Poverty in the United States*. New York: Macmillan, 1969.

Harrington, Scott E. "Insurance Rate Regulation in the 20th Century." *Journal of Risk and Insurance*, vol. 19, no. 2 (Winter 2000): 204–218.

Harris, Leon A. *Upton Sinclair: American Rebel*. New York: Thomas Y. Crowell, 1975.

Harris, Robert G., and C. Jeffrey Kraft. "Meddling Through: Regulating Local Telephone Competition in the United States," *Journal of Economic Perspectives*, vol. 11, no. 4 (Fall 1997): 93–112.

Harrison, Mark, ed. *The Economics of World War II*. New York: Cambridge University Press, 2000.

Harryvan, A. G., and J. van der Harst, eds. *Documents on European Union*. New York: St. Martin's Press, 1997.

Hart, David M. *Forged Consensus: Science, Technology, and Economic Policy in the United States, 1921–1953*. Princeton, NJ: Princeton University Press, 1998.

Hartung, William. *Corporate Welfare for Weapons Makers*. Washington, DC: Cato Institute, 1999.

Harvey, David. *Social Justice and the City*. London: Edward Arnold, 1973.

Harvey, William H. *Coin's Financial School up to Date*. Chicago: Coin Publishing, 1895.

Harvey, William H. *Coin's Financial School*. Reprinted with introduction by Richard Hofstadter. Cambridge, MA: Harvard University Press, 1963.

Haupt, Georges. *Aspects of International Socialism, 1871–1914*. Cambridge: Cambridge University Press, 1986.

Havrilesky, Thomas. *The Pressures on American Monetary Policy*. Boston: Kluwer, 1993.

Hawley, Amos. *Human Ecology: A Theory of Community Structure*. New York: Ronald Press, 1950.

Hawley, Ellis W. *The Great War and the Search for a Modern Order: A History of the American People and Their Institutions, 1917–1933*. New York: St. Martin's Press, 1979.

Hayek, Friedrich. *The Constitution of Liberty*. Chicago: University of Chicago Press, 1960.

Hayek, Friedrich. *The Road to Serfdom*. Chicago: University of Chicago Press, 1980.

Hayes, Jimmy. Letter to Henry Sirgo. December 7, 1994.

Hayes, Samuel L., III. *Wall Street and Regulation*. Cambridge, MA: Harvard Business School Press, 1987.

Hays, R. Allen. *The Federal Government and Urban Housing: Ideology and Change in Public Policy*. 2nd ed. Albany: State University of New York, 1995.

Hays, Samuel P. *Conservation and the Gospel of Efficiency: The Progressive Conservation Movement, 1890–1920*. Cambridge, MA: Harvard University Press, 1959.

Hays, Samuel P. *Beauty, Health, and Permanence: Environmental Politics in the United States, 1955–1985*. New York: Cambridge University Press, 1987.

Hazlett, Thomas. "The Legislative History of the Sherman Act Re-Examined." *Economic Inquiry*, vol. 30, no. 2 (1992): 263–276.

Heilbroner, Robert, and Peter Bernstein. *The Debt and the Deficit: False Alarms, Real Possibilities*. New York: Norton, 1989.

Heilbroner, Robert L., and Aaron Singer. *The Economic Transformation of America: 1600 to Present*. San Diego, CA: Harcourt Brace Jovanovich, 1984.

Heinrichs, Waldo. *Threshold of War*. Oxford: Oxford University Press, 1990.

Heisey, D. Ray. "Slavery: America's Irrepressible Conflict." In Dewitte Holland, ed., *America in Controversy: History of American Public Address*. Dubuque, IA: W. C. Brown, 1973.

Helms, Douglas, and Susan Flader, eds. *The History of Soil and Water Conservation*. Berkeley: University of California Press, 1985.

Henderson, James W. *Health Economics and Policy*. Cincinnati, OH: South-Western Press, 2002.

Herbst, Jurgen. *The Once and Future School: Three Hundred and Fifty Years of American Secondary Education*. New York: Routledge, 1996.

Herda, D. J., and Margaret L. Madden. *Energy Resources: Towards a Renewable Future*. New York: Franklin Watts, 1991.

Herman, Sondra R. *Eleven against Empire: Studies in American Internationalist Thought, 1898–1921*. Stanford, CA: Stanford University Press, 1969.

Hibbard, Benjamin Horace. *A History of the Public Land Policies*. Madison: University of Wisconsin Press, 1965.

Hickey, Donald R. *The War of 1812: A Forgotten Conflict*. Urbana: University of Illinois Press, 1989.

Hidy, Ralph W., and Muriel E. Hidy. *Pioneering in Big Business 1882–1911*. New York: Harper and Brothers, 1955.

Higham, John. *Strangers in the Land: Patterns of American Nativism, 1860–1925*. New York: Atheneum, 1968.

Himmelberg, Robert F. *The Origins of the National Recovery Administration*. New York: Fordham University Press, 1976.

Hinterseer, Kris. *Criminal Finance: The Political Economy of Money Laundering in a Comparative Legal Context*. Boston: Kluwer Law International, 2002.

Hinton, Harold B. *Cordell Hull: A Biography*. Garden City, NY: Doubleday, Doran, 1942.

Hirschman, Albert O. *A Propensity to Self-Subversion*. Cambridge, MA: Harvard University Press, 1995.

Hobsbawm, Eric. *The Age of Revolution, 1789–1848*. New York: Mentor, 1962.

Hoffman, Ronald. *Peace and the Peacemakers*. Charlottesville: University Press of Virginia, 1986.

Hofstadter, Richard, ed. *The Paranoid Style in American Politics and Other Essays*. New York: Alfred A. Knopf, 1965.

Hogan, Michael J. *The Marshall Plan: America, Britain, and the Reconstruction of Western Europe, 1947–1952.* New York: Cambridge University Press, 1987.

Hoge J., and G. Rose, eds. *How Did This Happen? Terrorism and the New War.* New York: Public Affairs, 2002.

Hoge, J., and F. Zakaria, eds. *The American Encounter: The United States and the Making of the Modern World: Essays from 75 Years of Foreign Affairs.* New York: Basic Books, 1997.

Holland, James W. *Andrew Jackson and the Creek War.* Tuscaloosa: University of Alabama Press, 1990.

Holli, Melvin G. "Urban Reform." In Lewis L. Gould, ed., *The Progressive Era.* Syracuse, NY: Syracuse University Press, 1974.

Holsti, Ole R., and James S. Rosenau. *American Leadership in World Affairs.* Boston: Allen and Unwin, 1984.

Holt, Marilyn Irvin. *Linoleum, Better Babies, and the Modern Farm Woman, 1890–1930.* Albuquerque: University of New Mexico Press, 1995.

Holt, Michael F. *The Rise and Fall of the American Whig Party: Jacksonian Politics and the Onset of the Civil War.* New York: Oxford University Press, 1999.

Hombs, Mary Ellen. *Welfare Reform: A Reference Handbook.* Santa Barbara, CA: ABC-CLIO, 1996.

Hoogenboom, Ari. *Outlawing the Spoils: A History of the Civil Service Reform Movement, 1865–1883.* Urbana: University of Illinois Press, 1961.

Hoogenboom, Ari, and Olive Hoogenboom. *A History of the ICC: From Panacea to Palliative.* New York: Norton, 1976.

Horan, James David. *The Pinkertons: The Detective Dynasty That Made History.* New York: Crown Publishers, 1967.

Horman, Robert D. *Reforming the International Monetary System: From Roosevelt to Reagan.* New York: Foreign Policy Association, 1987.

Horsman, Reginald. *The Causes of the War of 1812.* New York: A. S. Barnes, 1962.

Horsman, Reginald. *The War of 1812.* New York: Alfred A. Knopf, 1969.

Horsman, Reginald. *The New Republic: The United States of America, 1789–1815.* New York: Longman, 2000.

Horwitz, Morton J. *The Transformation of American Law, 1780–1860.* New York: Oxford University Press, 1992.

Horwitz, Morton J. *The Transformation of American Law, 1870–1960: The Crisis of Legal Orthodoxy.* New York: Oxford University Press, 1992.

Horwitz, Steven. *Monetary Evolution, Free Banking, and Economic Order.* Boulder, CO: Westview Press, 1992.

Hovenkamp, Herbert. *Enterprise and American Law, 1836– 1937.* Cambridge, MA: Harvard University Press, 1991.

Hovenkamp, Herbert. *Federal Antitrust Policy: The Law of Competition and Its Practice*. St Paul, MN: West Group, 1999.

Howe, Daniel W. *The Political Culture of the American Whigs*. Chicago: University of Chicago Press, 1979.

Howell, Thomas R., et al. *Steel and the State: Government Intervention and Steel's Structural Crisis*. Boulder, CO: Westview Press, 1988.

Hower, Ralph M. *The History of an Advertising Agency: N. W. Ayer and Son at Work, 1869–1949*. Cambridge, MA: Harvard University Press, 1949.

Hubbert, M. King. *Nuclear Energy and the Fossil Fuels, in Drilling and Production Practice in 1956*. Washington, DC: American Petroleum Institute, 1957.

Huefner, Robert P., and Margaret P. Battin, eds. *Changing to National Health Care: Ethical and Policy Issues*. Salt Lake City: University of Utah Press, 1992.

Hughes, Jonathan R. T. *The Governmental Habit Redux: Economic Controls from Colonial Times to the Present*. Princeton, NJ: Princeton University Press, 1991.

Hull, Cordell. *The Memoirs of Cordell Hull*. New York: Macmillan, 1948.

Hund, Gaillard, and John Brown Scott, eds. *Debates in the Federal Convention of 1787* reported by James Madison. In "The Avalon Project at the Yale Law School: Documents in Law, History, and Diplomacy." New York: Oxford University Press, 1920.

Hurt, R. Douglas. *Agricultural Technology in the Twentieth Century*. Manhattan, KS: Sunflower University Press, 1991.

Hurt, R. Douglas. *American Agriculture: A Brief History*. Ames: Iowa State University Press, 1994.

Ingebretsen, Mark. *Nasdaq: A History of the Market That Changed the World*. Roseville, CA: Prima, 2002.

Irons, Peter. *A People's History of the United States*. New York: Viking, 1999.

Irwin, Douglas A. *Free Trade under Fire*. Princeton, NJ: Princeton University Press, 2002.

Irwin, Manley, and James McConnaughey. "Telecommunications," In Walter Adams and James Brock, eds., *The Structure of American Industry*. Upper Saddle River, NJ: Prenctice-Hall, 2001.

Isaacs, Jeremy, and Taylor Downing. *The Cold War*. Boston: Little, Brown, 1999.

Isenberg, Andrew C. *The Destruction of the Bison: An Environmental History, 1750–1920*. New York: Cambridge University Press, 2000.

Jackson, Donald. *Great American Bridges and Dams*. New York: John Wiley and Sons, 1988.

Jackson, Kenneth T. *Crabgrass Frontier*. New York: Oxford University Press, 1985.

Jacobs, Eva, and Stephanie Shipp. "How Family Spending Has Changed in the U.S." *Monthly Labor Review*, vol. 113, no. 3 (March 1990): 20–27.

Jacoby, Daniel. *Laboring for Freedom: A New Look at the History of Labor in America.* Armonk, NY: M. E. Sharpe, 1998.

Jaffe, Steven H. "Yale Moses Beach." In Kenneth T. Jackson, ed., *The Encyclopedia of New York History.* New Haven, CT: Yale University Press, 1995.

James, Harold. *International Monetary Cooperation since Bretton Woods.* New York: Oxford University Press, 1996.

Jay, Martin. *Marxism and Totality: The Adventures of a Concept from Lukacs to Habermas.* Berkeley: University of California Press, 1984.

Jeansonne, Glen. *Messiah of the Masses: Huey P. Long and the Great Depression.* New York: Harper Collins, 1993.

Jeffers, Harry Paul. *An Honest President: The Life and Presidencies of Grover Cleveland.* New York: William Morrow, 2000.

Jeffries, John C. *Justice Lewis F. Powell, Jr.: Biography.* New York: Scribner's, 1994.

Jehl, Douglas. "Curse of the Winds Turns to Farmer's Blessing." *New York Times,* November 26, 2000.

Jenkins, Virginia S. *Bananas: An American History.* Washington, DC: Smithsonian Institution Press, 2000.

Jennings, Frances. *Empire of Fortune: Crowns, Colonies, and Tribes in the Seven Years' War in America.* New York: Norton, 1988.

Jennings, Jan, ed. *Roadside America: The Car in Design and Culture.* Ames: Iowa State University Press, 1990.

Jensen, Merrill. *The Articles of Confederation.* Madison: University of Wisconsin Press, 1940.

Jeong, Ho-Won. "The Struggle for Wider Participation," In Chadwick F. Alger, ed., *The Future of the United Nations System: Potential for the Twenty-first Century.* Tokyo: United Nations University Press, 1998.

Johnson, Allen, ed. *Dictionary of American Biography.* Vols. 2, 3, and 5. New York: Scribner's, 1929.

Johnson, David S., John M. Rogers, and Lucilla Tan. "A Century of Family Budgets in the United States." *Monthly Labor Review,* vol. 124, no. 5 (May 2001): 28–45.

Johnson, Herbert A. *John Jay, Colonial Lawyer.* New York: Garland Publishing, 1989.

Johnson, Leland. "Technological Advance and Market Structure in Domestic Telecommunications." *American Economic Review,* vol. 60, no. 2 (May 1970): 204–208.

Johnson, Louise C., Charles L. Schwartz, and Donald S. Tate. *Social Welfare: A Response to Human Need.* Boston: Allyn and Bacon, 1997.

Johnson, Lyndon B. *The Vantage Point: Perspectives of the Presidency.* New York: Holt, Rinehart and Winston, 1971.

Johnson, Peter. *The Government of Money: Monetarism in Germany and the United States*. Ithaca, NY: Cornell University Press, 1998.

Johnston, J. Bennett. Letter to Henry Sirgo. December 12, 1994.

Jones, David A. *History of Criminology: A Philosophical Perspective*. Westport, CT: Greenwood Press, 1986.

Jones, Howard. *Abraham Lincoln and a New Birth of Freedom*. Lincoln: University of Nebraska Press, 1999.

Jones, Howard. *Crucible of Power: A History of American Foreign Relations to 1913*. Wilmington, DE: SR Books, 2002.

Jones, Peter d'A., ed. *The Robber Barons Revisited: Problems in American Civilization*. Lexington, MA: D. C. Heath, 1968.

Joseph, Joan. *Political Corruption*. New York: Pocket Books, 1974.

Josephson, Matthew. *Edison: A Biography*. New York: McGraw-Hill, 1959.

Judge, Edward H., and John W. Langdon. *A Hard and Bitter Peace: A Global History of the Cold War*. Englewood Cliffs, NJ: Prentice-Hall, 1996.

Kadlec, Daniel. "Bank on Change." *Time*, November 8, 1999.

Kain, J. F. "The Spatial Mismatch Hypothesis: Three Decades Later." *Housing Policy Debate*, vol. 3, no. 2 (1992): 371–462.

Kaplan, Edward S. *American Trade Policy, 1923–1995*. Westport, CT: Greenwood Press, 1996.

Kaplan, Lawrence S. *NATO and the United States: The Enduring Alliance*. New York: Twayne Publishers, 1994.

Karger, Howard Jacob, and David Stoesz. *American Social Welfare Policy: A Pluralist Approach*. New York: Longman, 1998.

Karnow, Stanley. *In Our Image: America's Empire in the Philippines*. New York: Ballantine Books, 1990.

Kaspi, André. *Les Américains*. Paris: Le Seuil, 1998.

Kassinger, Ruth. *U.S. Census: A Mirror of America*. Austin, TX: Raintree Steck-Vaughn, 1999.

Kasson, John. *Civilizing the Machine: Technology and Republican Values in America, 1776–1900*. New York: Penguin, 1977.

Katz, Michael B. *In the Shadow of the Poorhouse: A Social History of Welfare in America*. New York: Basic Books, 1997.

Katz, Michael B. *The Price of Citizenship: Redefining the American Welfare State*. New York: Metropolitan Books, 2001.

Kaufman, Burton I. *The Oil Cartel Case*. Westport, CT: Greenwood Press, 1978.

Kaysen, Carl, and Donald Turner. *Antitrust Policy: An Economic and Legal Analysis*. Cambridge, MA: Harvard University Press, 1959.

Kealey, Terrence. *The Economic Laws of Scientific Research*. New York: St. Martin's Press, 1996.

Keegan, John. *The First World War*. New York: Alfred A. Knopf, 1999.

Keest, Kathleen E. *Truth in Lending*. Boston: National Consumer Law Center, 1995.

Keever, David B., ed. *Interactive Management and Defense Advanced Research Projects Agency*. Fairfax, VA: Institute for Advanced Study in the Integrative Sciences, George Mason University, 1990.

Keller, Morton. *The Life Insurance Enterprise, 1885–1910: A Study in the Limits of Corporate Power*. Cambridge, MA: Belknap Press, 1963.

Keller, Morton. *Regulating a New Economy: Public Policy and Economic Change in America, 1900–1933*. Cambridge, MA: Harvard University Press, 1990.

Kelly, Barbara M. *Expanding the American Dream: Building and Rebuilding Levittown*. Albany: State University of New York Press, 1993.

Kelly, William Boland. *Studies in United States Commercial Policy*. Chapel Hill: University of North Carolina Press, 1963.

Kempin, Frederick G., Jr. *Historical Introduction to Anglo-American Law in a Nutshell*. St. Paul, MN: West Publishing, 1973.

Kendrick, John W., ed. *The New System of National Accounts*. Boston: Kluwer Academic Publishers, 1996.

Kennedy, Paul. *The Rise and Fall of the Great Powers*. New York: Vintage Books, 1987.

Kennedy, Susan Estabrook. *The Banking Crisis of 1933*. Lexington: University of Kentucky Press, 1973.

Kent, Frank R. *The Democratic Party: A History*. New York: Century Co., 1928.

Kessides, Christine. *The Contributions of Infrastructure to Economic Development: A Review of Experience and Policy Implications*. Washington, DC: World Bank, 1993.

Kessner, Thomas. *The Golden Door and Jewish Immigrant Mobility in New York City, 1880–1915*. New York: Oxford University Press, 1977.

Ketchem, Ralph, ed. *The Anti-Federalist Papers and the Constitutional Convention Debates*. New York: New American Library, 1986.

Kettl, Donald. *Leadership at the Fed*. New Haven, CT: Yale University Press, 1986.

Kevles, Daniel J. "The National Science Foundation and the Debate over Postwar Research Policy." *Isis*, vol. 68 (1977): 5–27.

Kevles, Daniel J. *The Physicists: The History of a Scientific Community in Modern America*. New York: Alfred A. Knopf, 1978.

Key, V. O. *Politics, Parties, and Pressure Groups*. New York: Crowell, 1964.

Keylor, William R. *The Twentieth Century World: An International History*. New York: Oxford University Press, 2001.

Keyssar, Alexander. *Out of Work: The First Century of Unemployment in Massachusetts*. Cambridge: Cambridge University Press, 1986.

Killick, John. *The United States and European Reconstruction, 1945–1960*. Edinburgh, UK: Keele University Press, 1997.

Kindleberger, Charles. *The World in Depression, 1929–1939*. Berkeley: University of California Press, 1973.

Kindleberger, Charles. *Manias, Panics, and Crashes: A History of Financial Crises*. New York: Basic Books, 1978.

Kirby, Jack Temple. *Rural Worlds Lost: The American South 1920–1960*. Baton Rouge: Louisiana State University Press, 1987.

Kirshner, O., ed. *The Bretton Woods–GATT System: Retrospect and Prospect after Fifty Years*. London: M. E. Sharpe, 1996.

Kittross, John, ed. *Documents in American Telecommunications Policy*. 2 vols. New York: Arno Press, 1977.

Klebaner, Benjamin J. *American Commercial Banking: A History*. Boston: Twayne Publishers, 1990.

Kleinberg, Benjamin. *Urban America in Transformation: Perspectives on Urban Policy and Development*. Thousand Oaks, CA: Sage Publications, 1995.

Kliebard, Herbert M. *Schooled to Work: Vocationalism and the American Curriculum, 1876–1946*. New York: Teachers College Press, 1999.

Kline, Mary-Jo, ed. *Alexander Hamilton: A Biography in His Own Words*. New York: Newsweek Books, 1973.

Knepper, George W. *Ohio and Its People*. Kent, OH: Kent State University Press, 1997.

Knight, Carol Lynn H. *The American Colonial Press and the Townshend Crisis 1766–70*. Lewiston, NY: Edward Mellen Press, 1990.

Knox, John Jay. *A History of Banking in the United States*. New York: Bradford Rhodes, 1903.

Koistinen, Paul. *The Military-Industrial Complex*. New York: Praeger, 1980.

Kolakowski, Leszek. *Main Currents of Marxism*. 3 vols. Oxford: Oxford University Press, 1978.

Kolchin, Peter. *Unfree Labor: American Slavery and Russian Serfdom*. Cambridge, MA: Harvard University Press, Belknap Press, 1987.

Kolchin, Peter. *American Slavery: 1619–1687*. New York: Hill and Wang, 1993.

Kolko, Gabriel. *The Triumph of Conservatism: A Reinterpretation of American History, 1900–1916*. Chicago: Quadrangle Books, 1963.

Kopcke, Richard, and Lynn Browne, eds. *The Evolution of Monetary Policy and the Federal Reserve System over the Past Thirty Years: A Conference in Honor of Frank E. Morris*. Boston: Federal Reserve Bank of Boston, 2000.

Koppel, Ross. *Alzheimer's Disease: The Costs to U.S. Businesses in 2002.* Wyncote, PA: Alzheimer's Association, 2002.

Kosterlit, Julie. "Siblings Fat and Sassy," *National Journal*, May 13, 2000.

Kousser, J. Morgan. *The Shaping of Southern Politics: Suffrage Restriction and the Establishment of the One-Party South, 1880–1910.* New Haven, CT: Yale University Press, 1974.

Kovacic, William E. "The Influence of Economics on Antitrust Law." *Economic Inquiry*, vol. 30, no. 2 (1992): 294–306.

Kregel, J. A. "Budget Deficits, Stabilization Policy, and Liquidity Preference." In Fausto Vicarelli, ed. *Keynes's Relevance Today.* Philadelphia: University of Pennsylvania Press, 1985.

Kronenwetter, Michael. *Welfare State America: Safety Net or Social Contract?* New York: Franklin Watts, 1993.

Krooss, Herman, and Martin Blyn. *A History of Financial Intermediaries.* New York: Random House, 1971.

Krugman, Paul. *Peddling Prosperity.* New York: W. W. Norton, 1994.

Kulikoff, Allan. *The Agrarian Origins of American Capitalism.* Charlottesville: University Press of Virginia, 1992.

Kuniholm, Bruce R. *The Origins of the Cold War in the Near East: Great-Power Conflict and Diplomacy in Iran, Turkey, and Greece.* Princeton, NJ: Princeton University Press, 1980.

Kunkle, Gregory C. "New Challenge or the Past Revisited? The Office of Technology Assessment in Historical Context." *Technology in Society*, vol. 17, no. 2 (1995): 175–197.

Kunz, Diane B. *Butter and Guns: America's Cold War Economic Diplomacy.* New York: Free Press, 1997.

Kuppenheimer, L. B. *Albert Gallatin's Vision of Democratic Stability.* Westport, CT: Praeger, 1996.

Kuznets, Simon. "Economic Growth and Income Inequality." *American Economic Review*, vol. 45, no. 1 (March 1955): 1–28.

Labarre, Benjamin Woods. *The Boston Tea Party.* New York: Oxford University Press, 1964.

Lacey, Dan. *The Essential Immigrant.* New York: Hippocrene Books, 1990.

LaFeber, Walter. *The Panama Canal.* Rev. ed. New York: Oxford University Press, 1989.

LaFeber, Walter. *The American Search for Opportunity, 1865–1913.* Cambridge: Cambridge University Press, 1993.

LaFeber, Walter. *The American Age: United States Foreign Policy at Home and Abroad since 1750.* 2nd ed. New York: Norton, 1994.

Laird, Pamela Walker. *Advertising Progress: American Business and the Rise of Consumer Marketing*. Baltimore, MD: Johns Hopkins University Press, 1998.

Lancaster, B. *The American Revolution*. Boston: Houghton Mifflin, 2001.

Landau, Ralph, and Dale W. Jorgensen. *Technology and Economic Policy*. Cambridge, MA: Ballinger, 1986.

Lane, Kris E. *Pillaging the Empire: Piracy in the Americas, 1500–1750*. Armonk, NY: M. E. Sharpe, 1998.

Lapati, Americo D. *Education and the Federal Government: A Historical Record*. New York: Mason/Charter, 1975.

Lapidus, Nancy. *HUD House*. Bloomington, IN: First Books Library, 2002.

La Porta, Rafael, Florencio Lopez-de-Silanes, and Andrei Shleifer. "Corporate Ownership around the World." *Journal of Finance*, vol. 54, no. 2 (April 1999): 471–517.

Lapsley, James T. *Bottled Poetry: Napa Winemaking from Prohibition to the Modern Era*. Berkeley: University of California Press, 1996.

Larson, Henrietta M. "The Rise of Big Business in the Oil Industry." In *Oil's First Century: Papers Given at the Centennial Seminar on the History of the Petroleum Industry*, comp. and ed. staff of *Business History Review*. Boston: Harvard Graduate School of Business Administration, 1960.

Lash, Joseph P. *Dealers and Dreamers: A New Look at the New Deal*. New York: Doubleday, 1988.

Latner, Richard B. *The Presidency of Andrew Jackson*. Athens: University of Georgia Press, 1979.

Laudon, Kenneth, and Carol Guercio Traver. *E-Commerce: Business, Technology, Society*. Boston: Addison-Wesley, 2002.

Laurie, Bruce. *Artisans into Workers: Labor in Nineteenth-Century America*. New York: Hill and Wang, 1989.

Lebergott, Stanley. *Manpower in Economic Growth: The American Record since 1800*. New York: McGraw-Hill, 1964.

Leebaert, Derek. *The Fifty-Year Wound: The True Price of America's Cold War Victory*. New York: Little, Brown, 2002.

Legg, Keith R. *Politics and the International System: An Introduction*. New York: Harper and Row, 1971.

Leopold, Richard W. *The Growth of American Foreign Policy*. New York: Alfred A. Knopf, 1962.

Lepore, Jill. *The Name of War*. New York: Vintage Books, 1998.

Lerner, Abba. "Functional Finance and the Federal Debt." *Social Research*, vol. 10, no. 1 (1944): 10–51.

Lerner, Abba. *The Economics of Employment*. New York: McGraw-Hill, 1951.

Leslie, Douglas. *Labor Law*. St. Paul, MN: West Publishing, 1986.

Leuchtenburg, William Edward. *Franklin D. Roosevelt and the New Deal, 1932–1940*. New York: Harper and Row, 1963.

Leuchtenburg, William Edward. *Franklin D. Roosevelt: A Profile*. New York: Hill and Wang, 1967.

Levitt, Arthur. *Take on the Street: What Wall Street and Corporate America Don't Want You to Know; What You Can Do to Fight Back*. New York: Pantheon, 2002.

Levy, Michael E., et al. *Federal Budget Deficits and the U.S. Economy*. New York: The Conference Board, 1984.

Libbey, James K. *Russian-American Economic Relations*. Gulf Breeze, FL: Academic International Press, 1999.

Libecap, Gary D. "The Rise of the Chicago Packers and the Origins of Meat Inspection and Antitrust." *Economic Inquiry*, vol. 30, no. 2 (1992): 242–262.

Licht, Walter. *Industrializing America: The Nineteenth Century*. Baltimore, MD: Johns Hopkins University Press, 1995.

Lichtenstein, Nelson. *State of the Union: A Century of American Labor*. Princeton, NJ: Princeton University Press, 2002.

Liebovich, Louis W. *Bylines in Despair: Herbert Hoover, the Great Depression, and the U.S. Media*. Westport, CT: Praeger, 1994.

Liebowitz, Stan J., and Stephen E. Margolis. *Winners, Losers, and Microsoft*. Oakland, CA: Independent Institute, 1999.

Lilly, Claude C. "A History of Insurance Regulation in the United States." *CPCU [Chartered Property Casualty Underwriter] Annals*, vol. 29 (June 1976): 99–115.

Lindert, Peter H. *International Economics*. Homewood, IL: R. D. Irwin, 1991.

Link, Arthur S. *Woodrow Wilson and the Progressive Era, 1910–1917*. New York: Harper and Row, 1954.

Link, Arthur S., and Richard L. McCormick. *Progressivism*. Arlington Heights, IL: Harlan Davidson, 1983.

Liska, George. *Expanding Realism: The Historical Dimension of World Politics*. Lanham, MD: Rowman and Littlefield, 1998.

Livesay, Harold C. *Andrew Carnegie and the Rise of Big Business*. Boston: Little, Brown, 1975.

Livingston, James. *Origins of the Federal Reserve System: Money, Class, and Corporate Capitalism, 1890–1913*. New York: Arno Press, 1978.

Lofgren, Don J. *Dangerous Premises: An Insider's View of OSHA Enforcement*. Ithaca: ILR Press, 1989.

Long, Doris E. *Unfair Competition and the Lanham Act*. Washington, DC: Bureau of National Affairs, 1993.

Lowrie, Allen, and Michael D. Max. "The Extraordinary Promise and Challenge of Gas Hydrates." *World Oil*, vol. 220, no. 9 (September 1999): 49–57.

Lugar, Richard G., and R. James Woolsey. "The New Petroleum." *Foreign Affairs*, vol. 78, no. 1 (January/February 1999): 88–103.

MacAvoy, Paul W., ed. *Deregulation and Privatization in the United States*. Edinburgh, Scotland: Edinburgh University Press, 1995.

MacKinnon, James. "It's Not Easy Being Green." *New Age Journal*, vol. 16, no. 6 (September 1, 1999): 76.

Madison, James H., ed. *Heartland: Comparative Histories of the Midwestern States*. Bloomington: Indiana University Press, 1990.

Magrath, C. Peter. *Yazoo: Law and Politics in the New Republic, Case of* Fletcher v. Peck. Providence, RI: Brown University Press, 1966.

Maier, Pauline. *From Resistance to Revolution: Colonial Radicals and the Development of American Opposition to Britain, 1765–1776*. New York: Alfred A. Knopf, 1972.

Mann, Charles C. "Who Will Own Your Next Good Idea?" *Atlantic Monthly*, vol. 282, no. 3 (September 1998): 57–64.

Manne, Henry G., ed. *Economic Policy and the Regulation of Corporate Securities*. Washington, DC: American Enterprise Institute for Public Policy Research, 1969.

Manthy, Robert S. *Natural Resource Commodities—A Century of Statistics: Prices, Output, Consumption, Foreign Trade, and Employment in the United States, 1870–1973*. Baltimore, MD: Johns Hopkins University Press, 1978.

Marcus, G. J. *The Age of Nelson*. New York: Viking, 1971.

Marglin, Stephen A., and Juliet B. Schor, eds. *The Golden Age of Capitalism: Reinterpreting the Postwar Experience*. Oxford: Clarendon Press, 1991.

Markusen, Ann, and Joel Yudken. *Dismantling the Cold War Economy*. New York: Basic Books, 1992.

Marsh, G. Rogge. "The Environmental Realities of Petroleum Exploration." In Richard Steinmetz, ed., *The Business of Petroleum Exploration*. Tulsa, OK: American Association of Petroleum Geologists, 1992.

Marshall, Alfred. *Principles of Economics*. New York: Macmillan, 1890.

Marshall, P., and G. Williams. *The British Atlantic Empire before the American Revolution*. London: Cass, 1980.

Martin, Albro. *James J. Hill and the Opening of the Northwest*. New York: Oxford University Press, 1976.

Martin, Joel W. *Sacred Revolt: The Muskogees Struggle for a New World*. Boston: Beacon Press, 1991.

Martin, Jonathan. "Exxon." In Adele Hast, ed., *International Directory of Company Histories*. Chicago: St. James Press, 1988–1996.

Martin, Justin. *Greenspan, the Man Behind the Money*. Cambridge, MA: Perseus Publishing, 2000.

Mastanduno, Michael. *Economic Containment: CoCom and the Politics of East-West Trade*. Ithaca, NY: Cornell University Press, 1992.

Matusow, Allen J. *The Unraveling of America: A History of Liberalism in the 1960s*. New York: Harper and Row, 1984.

Mayer, Thomas. *Monetary Policy and the Great Inflation in the United States: The Federal Reserve and the Failure of Macroeconomic Policy, 1965–1979*. Northampton, MA: Edward Elgar, 1999.

McCloskey, Robert G. *The American Supreme Court*. Chicago: University of Chicago Press, 2000.

McClure, Arthur F., James Riley Chrisman, and Perry Mock. *Education for Work: The Historical Evolution of Vocational and Distributive Education in America*. Rutherford, NJ: Fairleigh Dickinson University Press, 1985.

McClure, Charles R. *Linking the U.S. National Technical Information Service with Academic and Public Libraries*. Norwood, NJ: Ablex, 1986.

McConnell, Campbell R. *Economics: Principles, Problems, and Policies*. New York: McGraw-Hill, 1963.

McCraw, Thomas K. *TVA and the Power Fight, 1933–1939*. Philadelphia: Lippincott, 1971.

McCraw, Thomas K. *Prophets of Regulation*. Cambridge, MA: Harvard University Press, 1984.

McCulley, Richard. *Banks and Politics during the Progressive Era: The Origins of the Federal Reserve System, 1897–1913*. New York: Garland Publishing, 1997.

McCullough, David. *The Path between the Seas: The Creation of the Panama Canal, 1870–1914*. New York: Simon and Schuster, 1977.

McCusker, John J. *How Much Is That in Real Money? A Historical Price Index for Use as a Deflator of Money Values in the Economy of the United States*. 2nd ed. Worcester, MA: American Antiquarian Society, 2001.

McCusker, John J. *Mercantilism and the Economic History of the Early Modern Atlantic World*. Cambridge: Cambridge University Press, 2001.

McDonald, Forrest. *A Constitutional History of the United States*. New York: Franklin Watts, 1982.

McElroy, Robert. *Grover Cleveland: The Man and the Statesman*. New York: Harper and Brothers, 1923.

McFarland, Gerald W. "Partisanship of Non-Partisan Dorman B. Eaton and the Genteel Reform Tradition." *Journal of American History*, vol. 54 (1968): 806–822.

McFarland, M. Carter. *Federal Government and Urban Problems: HUD: Successes, Failures, and the Fate of Our Cities*. Boulder, CO: Westview Press, 1978.

McGuire, Robert A. *To Form a More Perfect Union: A New Economic Interpretation of the Constitution of the United States*. New York: Oxford University Press, 2001.

McHugh, Tom. *The Time of the Buffalo*. New York: Alfred A. Knopf, 1972.

McKenzie, Richard B. *Trust on Trial: How the Microsoft Case Is Reframing the Rules of Competition*. Cambridge, MA: Perseus Publishing, 2001.

McLean, John G., and Robert William Haigh. *The Growth of Integrated Oil Companies*. Boston: Division of Research, Graduate School of Business Administration, Harvard University, 1954.

McMath, Robert C. *American Populism: A Social History, 1877–1898*. New York: Hill and Wang, 1993.

McNamara, Peter. *Political Economy and Statesmanship: Smith, Hamilton, and the Foundation of the Commercial Republic*. DeKalb: Northern Illinois University Press, 1998.

McNeil, William C. *American Money and the Weimar Republic: Economics and Politics on the Eve of the Great Depression*. New York: Columbia University Press, 1986.

Meehan, Eugene J. "The Evolution of Public Housing Policy." In J. Paul Mitchell, ed., *Federal Housing Policy and Programs: Past and Present*. New Brunswick, NJ: Center for Urban Policy Research, 1985, pp. 287–318.

Meeropol, Michael. *Surrender, How the Clinton Administration Completed the Reagan Revolution*. Ann Arbor: University of Michigan Press, 1998.

Merk, Frederick. *Manifest Destiny and Mission in American History*. Westport, CT: Greenwood Press, 1963.

Merkel, Philip L. "Going National: The Life Insurance Industry's Campaign for Federal Regulation after the Civil War." *Business History Review*, vol. 65 (Autumn 1991): 528–553.

Merry, Henry J. *Five-Branch Government: The Full Measure of Constitutional Checks and Balances*. Urbana: University of Illinois Press, 1980.

Meulendyke, Ann-Marie. *U.S. Monetary Policy and Financial Markets*. 3rd ed. New York: Federal Reserve Bank of New York, 1998.

Meyer, Balthasar Henry. *A History of the Northern Securities Case*. New York: Da Capo Press, 1972.

Meyer, Warren G., ed. *Vocational Education and the Nation's Economy*. Washington, DC: American Vocational Association, 1977.

Middlekauff, Robert. *Bacon's Rebellion*. Chicago: Rand McNally, 1964.

Middlekauff, Robert. *The Glorious Cause: The American Revolution, 1763–1789*. New York: Oxford University Press, 1982.

Mikesell, John. *Fiscal Administration: Analysis and Applications for the Public Sector*. 5th ed. Fort Worth, TX: Harcourt, Brace, 1999.

Mikesell, Raymond Frech. *The Bretton Woods Debates: A Memoir*. Princeton, NJ: International Finance Section, Department of Economics, Princeton University, 1994.

Miles, Arthur P. *An Introduction to Public Welfare.* Boston: D. C. Heath, 1949.

"Millennium Copyright Act Sufficient," *Arizona Law Review*, vol. 41 (Fall 1999): 937–961.

Miller, Stephen. *Excellence and Equity: The National Endowment for the Humanities.* Lexington: University Press of Kentucky, 1984.

Millis, H. A., and E. C. Brown. *From the Wagner Act to Taft-Hartley.* Chicago: University of Chicago Press, 1950.

Millman, Joel. *The Other Americans.* New York: Viking, 1997.

Milward, Alan S. *War, Economy, and Society 1939–1945.* Berkeley: University of California Press, 1977.

Minsky, Hyman P. *Can "It" Happen Again?* Armonk, NY: M. E. Sharpe, 1982.

Mishkin, Frederic S. *The Economics of Money, Banking, and Financial Markets.* 6th ed. New York: Addison-Wesley, 2003, ch. 18.

Mitchell, Betty Lou. "Prophet without Honor: A Biography of Edmund Ruffin." PhD dissertation, University of Massachusetts, 1979.f

Mitchell, Bridger, and Ingo Vogelsand. *Telecommunications Competition: The Last Ten Miles.* Cambridge, MA: MIT Press, 1997.

Mitchell, Broadus. *A Preface to Economics.* New York: Henry Holt, 1932.

Mitchell, John G. "Urban Sprawl: The American Dream?" *National Geographic*, vol. 200, no. 1 (July 2001): 48–74.

Mitten, Christopher. *Shawn Fanning: Napster and the Music Revolution.* Brookfield, CT: Twenty-First Century Books, 2002.

Moen, Jon, and Ellis W. Tallman. "The Bank Panic of 1907: The Role of Trust Companies." *Journal of Economic History*, vol. 52 (September 1992): 611–630.

Moggridge, D. E. *Maynard Keynes: An Economist's Biography.* London: Routledge, 1992.

Mohl, Raymond A. *Urban Policy in Twentieth Century America.* New Brunswick, NJ: Rutgers University Press, 1993.

Montgomery, David. *The Fall of the House of Labor: The Workplace, the State, and American Labor Activism, 1865–1925.* New York: Cambridge University Press, 1987.

Moore, Carl H. *The Federal Reserve System: A History of the First 75 Years.* Jefferson, NC: McFarland, 1990.

Morales Carrión, Arturo. *Puerto Rico: A Political and Cultural History.* New York: Norton, 1983.

Morgan, Edmund S., and Helen Morgan. *The Stamp Act Crisis.* New York: Collier, 1962.

Morgan, Kenneth. *Slavery and Servitude in Colonial North America: A Short History.* New York: New York University Press, 2001.

Morganthau, Hans. *In Defense of the National Interest*. New York: Alfred A. Knopf, 1952.

Morris, Irwin. *Congress, the President, and Federal Reserve: The Politics of American Monetary Policy-Making*. Ann Arbor: University of Michigan Press, 2000.

Morris, Richard B., ed. *John Jay*. New York: Harper and Row, 1975.

Morrison, S. E., H. S. Commager, and W. E. Leuchtenburg. *The Growth of the American Republic*. Vol. 1. 7th ed. New York: Oxford University Press, 1980.

Mosler, Warren. *Soft Currency Economics*. West Palm Beach, FL: AVM, 1995.

Motor Vehicles Manufacturers Association. *Motor Vehicle Facts and Figures*. Detroit, MI: Automobile Manufacturers Association, annual publication.

Moynihan, Daniel Patrick. *Maximum Feasible Misunderstanding: Community Action in the War on Poverty*. New York: Free Press, 1969.

Moynihan, Daniel Patrick. "Toward a National Urban Policy." In Daniel P. Moynihan. ed., *Toward a National Urban Policy*. New York: Basic Books, 1970.

Mucciaroni, Gary. *The Political Failure of Employment Policy, 1945–1982*. Pittsburgh, PA: University of Pittsburgh Press, 1990.

Mueller, Dennis C. "Lessons from the United States' Antitrust History." *International Journal of Industrial Organization*, vol. 14 (1996): 415–445.

Nadiri, I. *Innovations and Technological Spillovers*. National Bureau of Economic Research (NBER) Working Paper no. 4423. Boston: NBER, 1993.

Nash, Gerald. *The Crucial Era: The Great Depression and World War II, 1929–1945*. 2nd ed. New York: Waveland Press, 1998.

National Endowment for the Arts: 1965–2000: A Brief Chronology of Federal Involvement in the Arts. Washington, DC: National Endowment for the Arts, 2000.

Nelson, Daniel. *Shifting Fortunes: The Rise and Decline of American Labor from the 1820s to the Present*. Chicago: I. R. Dee, 1997.

Nelson, Daniel. *Unemployment Insurance: The American Experience, 1915–1935*. Madison: University of Wisconsin Press, 1969.

Nelson, John R., Jr. *Liberty and Property: Political Economy and Policy Making in the New Nation 1789–1812*. Baltimore, MD: Johns Hopkins University Press, 1987.

Nester, William. *The First Global War*. Westport, CT: Praeger, 2000.

Neth, Mary C. *Preserving the Family Farm: Women, Community, and the Foundations of Agribusiness in the Midwest, 1900–1940*. Baltimore, MD: Johns Hopkins University Press, 1995.

Nettels, Curtis P. *The Emergence of a National Economy, 1775–1815*. New York: Holt, Rinehart and Winston, 1962.

Nevins, Allan. *John D. Rockefeller*. New York: Scribner's, 1940.

Nevins, Allan. *Study in Power: John D. Rockefeller, Industrialist and Philanthropist.* New York: Scribner's, 1953.

Nevins, Allan, with Frank E. Hill. *Ford.* 3 vols. New York: Scribner's, 1954–1963.

Newbery, David M. *Privatization, Restructuring, and Regulation of Network Utilities.* Cambridge, MA: MIT Press, 1999.

Nichols, Jeannette P. "Bryan's Benefactor: Coin Harvey and His World." *Ohio Historical Quarterly*, vol. 67 (October 1958): 299–325.

Nieman, Donald G., ed. *The Freedmen's Bureau and Black Freedom.* Vol. 2, *African-American Life in the Post-Emancipation South, 1861–1900.* New York: Garland Publishing, 1994.

Niemark, Marilyn Kleinberg. *The Hidden Dimensions of Annual Reports: Sixty Years of Social Conflict at General Motors.* Princeton, NJ: Markus Wiener, 1995.

Ninkovich, Frank A. *The United States and Imperialism.* Malden, MA: Blackwell, 2001.

Niven, John. *Martin Van Buren: The Romantic Age of American Politics.* New York: Oxford University Press, 1983.

Nixon, Edgar B. *Franklin D. Roosevelt and Conservation.* Hyde Park, NY: Franklin D. Roosevelt Library, 1957.

Nixon, R. M. *Six Crises.* London: W. H. Allen, 1962.

Nixon, R. M. *The Dollar and World Liquidity.* New York: Random House, 1967.

Nixon, R. M. *The Real War.* New York: Warner, 1980.

Noble, Charles. *Welfare As We Knew It: A Political History of the American Welfare State.* New York: Oxford University Press, 1997.

Nobles, G. *American Frontiers: Cultural Encounters and Continental Conquest.* New York: Hill and Wang, 1997.

Nolan, Janne. *Guardians of the Arsenal.* New York: Basic Books, 1989.

Nordin, D. Sven. *Rich Harvest: A History of the Grange, 1867–1900.* Jackson: University Press of Mississippi, 1974.

North, Douglass C. *Institutions, Institutional Change, and Economic Performance.* Cambridge: Cambridge University Press, 1990.

Norton, Hugh S. *The Employment Act and the Council of Economic Advisers, 1946–1976.* Columbia: University of South Carolina Press, 1977.

Nove, Alec. *The Economics of Feasible Socialism.* London: Allen and Unwin, 1983.

Nugent, Walter. *Into the West: The Story of Its People.* New York: Alfred A. Knopf, 1999.

Nye, Russell B. *Fettered Freedom: Civil Liberties and the Slave Controversy, 1830–1860.* East Lansing: Michigan State University Press, 1963.

O'Brien, D. P., ed. *The History of Taxation.* Brookfield, VT: Pickering and Chatto, 1999.

O'Conner, Patricia Ann, ed. "Congress and the Nation." *Congressional Quarterly*, vol. 4 (1977): 201, 203.

O'Connor, Martin, ed. *Is Capitalism Sustainable? Political Economy and the Politics of Ecology*. New York: Guilford Press, 1994.

Olson, James Stuart. *The Ethnic Dimension in American History*. New York: St. Martin's Press, 1979.

Olson, James Stuart, ed. *Historical Dictionary of the New Deal: From Inauguration to Preparation for War*. Westport, CT: Greenwood Press, 1985.

Olufs, Dick W., III. *The Making of Telecommunications Policy*. Boulder, CO: Lynne Rienner Publishers, 1999.

O'Neill, Timothy J. *Bakke and the Politics of Equality*. Middletown, CT: Wesleyan University Press, 1985.

O'Neill, William L. *A Democracy at War: America's Fight at Home and Abroad in World War II*. New York: Free Press, 1993.

Onuf, Peter S. *Statehood and Union: A History of the North-West Ordinance*. Bloomington: Indiana University Press, 1987.

Opie, John. *Nature's Nation: An Environmental History of the United States*. Ft. Worth, TX: Harcourt, Brace, 1998.

Orne, William A. *Understanding NAFTA: Mexico, Free Trade, and the New North America*. Austin: University of Texas Press, 1996.

O'Sullivan, John, and Edward F. Keuchel. *American Economic History: From Abundance to Constraint*. New York: Markus Wiener, 1989.

Oubre, Claude F. *Forty Acres and a Mule: The Freedmen's Bureau and Black Land Ownership*. Baton Rouge: Louisiana State University Press, 1978.

Pacelle, Richard L., Jr. *The Transformation of the Supreme Court's Agenda: From the New Deal to the Reagan Administration*. Boulder, CO: Westview Press, 1991.

Paige, Sean. "Green Like Me." *Insight*, vol. 14, no. 46 (December 14, 1998): 16.

Paine, Arthur Elijah. *The Granger Movement in Illinois*. Urbana: University of Illinois Press, 1904.

Pan American Union. *In the Service of the Americas: Fiftieth Anniversary of the Pan American Union, April 14, 1940*. Washington, DC: Pan American Union, 1940.

Panogopoulos, E. P. *Essays on the History and Meaning of Checks and Balances*. Lanham, MD: University Press of America, 1986.

Papke, David Ray. *The Pullman Case: The Clash of Labor and Capital in Industrial America*. Lawrence: University Press of Kansas, 1999.

Park, R. E. "Succession, an Ecological Concept." *American Sociological Review*, vol. 1, no. 2 (1936): 171–181.

Parker, William B. *The Life and Public Services of Justin Smith Morrill*. New York: Da Capo Press, 1971.

Parkerson, Donald Hugh, and Jo Ann Parkerson. *Transitions in American Education: A Social History of Teaching*. New York: Routledge Falmer, 2001.

Parlour, Richard, ed. *Butterworths International Guide to Money Laundering: Law and Practice*. London: Butterworths, 1995.

Parmet, Herbert. *George Bush: The Life of a Lone Star Yankee*. New York: Scribner's, 1997.

Parrini, Carl P. *Heir to Empire: United States Economic Diplomacy, 1916–1923*. Pittsburgh, PA: University of Pittsburgh Press, 1969.

Parrish, Michael. *Anxious Decades: America in Prosperity and Depression, 1920–1941*. New York: W. W. Norton, 1992.

Pastor, Robert A. *Congress and the Politics of U.S. Foreign Economic Policy 1929–1976*. Berkeley: University of California Press, 1980.

Pastor, Robert A. *Not Condemned to Repetition: The United States and Nicaragua*. 2nd ed. Boulder, CO: Westview Press, 2002.

Patinkin, Don. *Money, Interest, and Prices: An Integration of Monetary and Value Theory*. New York: Random House, 1965.

Patrick, William. *The Food and Drug Administration*. New York: Chelsea House, 1988.

Patterson, James. *Grand Expectations: The United States, 1945–1974*. New York: Oxford University Press, 1996.

Patterson, Thomas G., and J. Garry Clifford. *America Ascendant: U.S. Foreign Relations since 1939*. Lexington, MA: D. C. Heath, 1995.

Patterson, Thomas G., and Dennis Merrill, eds. *Major Problems in American Foreign Relations since 1914*. Vol. 2. Lexington, MA: D. C. Heath, 1995.

Paxton, John, and John Wroughton. *Smuggling*. London: Macmillan, 1971.

Pearce, David W. *The MIT Dictionary of Modern Economics*. 4th ed. Cambridge, MA: MIT Press, 1995.

Peltzman, Sam, and Clifford Winston, eds. *Deregulation of Network Industries: What's Next?* Washington, DC: American Enterprise Institute and Brookings Institution Joint Center for Regulatory Studies, 2000.

Pérez, Louis A. *Cuba: Between Reform and Revolution*. New York: Oxford University Press, 1988.

Pérez, Louis A. *The War of 1898: The United States and Cuba in History and Historiography*. Chapel Hill: University of North Carolina Press, 1998.

Perkins, Dexter. *The American Approach to Foreign Policy*. Cambridge, MA: Harvard University Press, 1962.

Perkins, Edwin J. *American Public Finance and Financial Services, 1700–1815*. Columbus: Ohio State University Press, 1994.

Perloff, Jeffrey. *Microeconomics*. Reading, MA: Addison-Wesley, 1999.

Perritt, H. Hardy. "Robert Barnwell Rhett's Speech, July 4, 1859." In J. Jeffery Auer, ed., *Antislavery and Disunion, 1858–1861: Studies in the Rhetoric of Compromise and Conflict*. New York: Harper and Row, 1963.

Peterson, Merrill D. *Olive Branch and Sword: The Compromise of 1833*. Baton Rouge: Louisiana State University Press, 1982.

Peterson, Merrill D. *The Great Triumvirate: Webster, Clay, and Calhoun*. New York: Oxford University Press, 1987.

Peterson, Peter G. *Facing Up: How to Rescue the Economy from Crushing Debt and Restore the American Dream*. New York: Simon and Schuster, 1993.

Petulla, Joseph M. *American Environmental History*. 2nd ed. Columbus, OH: Merrill Publishing, 1988.

Phillips, Ulrich B. *American Negro Slavery*. Baton Rouge: Louisiana State University Press, 1966.

Pickens, Donald K. "Truman's Council of Economic Advisers and the Legacy of New Deal Liberalism." In William T. Levantrosser, ed., *Harry S. Truman, the Man from Independence*. New York: Greenwood Press, 1986, pp. 245–263.

Pickens, Donald K. "The CEA and the Burden of New Deal Liberalism." In Bernard J. Firestone and Robert C. Vogt, eds., *Lyndon Baines Johnson*. New York: Greenwood Press, 1988, pp. 191–204.

Pickens, Donald K. "Leon Keyserling and Integrative Liberalism." *Red River Historical Journal*, vol. 1 (October 2000): 44–74.

Pike, Frederick B. *FDR's Good Neighbor Policy: Sixty Years of Generally Gentle Chaos*. Austin: University of Texas Press, 1995.

Piketty, Thomas, and Emmanuel Saez. "Income Inequality in the United States, 1913–1998." National Bureau of Economic Research Working Paper no. 8467, September 2001.

Pisani, Donald J. *To Reclaim a Divided West: Water, Law, and Public Policy, 1848–1902*. Albuquerque: University of New Mexico Press, 1992.

Pit, Fenna, and Willem Van Vliet. "Public Housing in the United States." In Elizabeth Huttman and Willem Van Vliet, eds., *Handbook of Housing and the Built Environment in the United States*. New York: Greenwood Press, 1988.

Plano, Jack C., and Milton Greenberg. *The American Political Dictionary*. 11th ed. Fort Worth, TX: Harcourt College Publishers, 2002.

Pletcher, David M. *The Diplomacy of Involvement: American Economic Expansion across the Pacific, 1784–1900*. Columbia: University of Missouri Press, 2001.

Poguntke, Thomas. *From Nuclear Building Sites to Cabinet: The Career of the German Green Party*. Keele, Germany: Keele University Press, 2001.

Polanyi, Karl. *The Great Transformation: The Political and Economic Origins of Our Time*. Boston: Beacon Press, 2001.

Pollin, Robert, and Stephanie Luce. *The Living Wage: Building a Fair Economy.* New York: New Press, 1998.

Pomeroy, Earl, and Carole Olson Gates. "State and Federal Regulation of the Business of Insurance." *Journal of Risk and Insurance*, vol. 19, no. 2 (Winter 2000): 179–188.

Pope-Hennessy, James. *Sins of the Fathers: The Atlantic Slave Traders.* London: Phoenix Press, 2000.

Popple, Philip R., and Leslie Leighninger. *Social Work, Social Welfare, and American Society.* Boston: Allyn and Bacon, 1999.

Porter, Edward. "Are We Running Out of Oil?" Discussion Paper no. 081. Washington, DC: American Petroleum Institute, 1995.

Portes, Alejandro, and Ruben G. Rumbaut. *Immigrant America.* Berkeley: University of California Press, 1990.

Posner, Richard A. *Antitrust Cases, Economic Notes, and Other Materials.* St. Paul, MN: West Publishing, 1981.

Poulantzas, Nicos. *Political Power and Social Classes.* London: New Left Books, 1973.

Prager, Robin A. "The Effects of Horizontal Mergers on Competition: The Case of the Northern Securities Company." *Rand Journal of Economics*, vol. 23 (Spring 1992): 123–133.

Pratt, Julius W. *The Expansionists of 1898.* Chicago: Quadrangle Books, 1964.

Preeg, Ernest H. *Traders and Diplomats: An Analysis of the Kennedy Round of Negotiations under the General Agreement on Tariffs and Trade.* Washington: Brookings Institution, 1970.

Prestbo, John, ed. *Markets Measure: An Illustrated History of America Told through the Dow Jones Industrial Average.* New York: Dow Jones, 1999.

Preston, Diana. *The Boxer Rebellion: The Dramatic Story of China's War on Foreigners That Shook the World in the Summer of 1900.* New York: Walker, 2000.

Prince, Carl E. *The Federalists and the Origins of the U.S. Civil Service.* New York: New York University Press, 1977.

Prucha, Paul. *The Great Father: The United States Government and the American Indians.* Lincoln: University of Nebraska Press, 1984.

Pulliam, John D., and James Van Patten. *History of Education in America.* Englewood Cliffs, NJ: Merrill, 1995.

Pursell, Carroll. *The Machine in America: A Social History of Technology.* Baltimore, MD: Johns Hopkins University Press, 1995.

Putnam, Robert D., and Nichols Bayne. *Hanging Together: Cooperation and Conflict in the Seven-Power Summits.* Cambridge, MA: Harvard University Press, 1987.

Quester, George. *American Foreign Policy: The Lost Consensus.* New York: Praeger, 1982.

Radford, Gail. *Modern Housing in America: Policy Struggles in the New Deal Era.* Chicago: Columbia University Press, 1996.

Rainsford, George N. *Congress and Higher Education in the Nineteenth Century.* Knoxville: University of Tennessee Press, 1972.

Rakove, Jack. *The Beginnings of National Politics: An Interpretive History of the Continental Congress.* New York: Alfred A. Knopf, 1979.

Rasmussen, Wayne D. *Taking the University to the People: Seventy-five Years of Cooperative Extension.* Ames: Iowa State University Press, 1989.

Ratner, Sidney. *A Political and Social History of Federal Taxation, 1789–1913.* New York: W. W. Norton, 1942.

Ravitch, Diane. *The Troubled Crusade: American Education, 1945–1980.* New York: Basic Books, 1983.

Rayback, Joseph G. *A History of American Labor.* New York: Free Press, 1966.

Rayback, Joseph G. *Free Soil: The Extension of 1848.* Lexington: University Press of Kentucky, 1971.

Rayport, Jeffrey, and Bernard Jaworski. *e-Commerce.* Boston: McGraw-Hill, 2001.

Rediker, Marcus. *Between the Devil and the Deep Blue Sea: Merchant Seamen, Pirates, and the Anglo-American Maritime World.* New York: Cambridge University Press, 1987.

Redlich, Fritz. *The Molding of American Banking: Men and Ideas.* New York: Hafner, 1947 and 1951.

Reid, T. R. *Congressional Odyssey: The Saga of a Senate Bill.* San Francisco: W. H. Freeman, 1980.

Reimers, David M. *Still the Golden Door: The Third World Comes to America.* New York: Columbia University Press, 1992.

Reisman, David. *Economic Thought and Political Theory.* Boston: Kluwer Academic Publishers, 1994.

Remini, Robert V. *Andrew Jackson and the Bank War: A Study in the Growth of Presidential Power.* New York: W. W. Norton, 1967.

Remini, Robert V. *Henry Clay: Statesman for the Union.* New York: W. W. Norton, 1991.

Remini, Robert V. *Andrew Jackson.* New York: Harperennial, 1999.

Reyna, S., and R. Downs. *Deadly Developments: Capitalism, States, and War.* Amsterdam: Gordon and Breach, 1999.

Reynolds, David R. *One World Divisible: A Global History since 1945.* New York: W. W. Norton, 2000.

Reynolds, Morgan O. *The History and Economics of Labor Unions.* College Station: Texas A&M University Press, 1985.

Rezneck, Samuel. *Business Depressions and Financial Panics: Essays in American Business and Economic History.* New York: Greenwood Press, 1968.

Rhodes, Benjamin D. *United States Foreign Policy in the Interwar Period, 1918–1941: The Golden Age of American Diplomatic and Military Complacency.* Westport, CT: Praeger, 2001.

Rice, Bradley Robert. *Progressive Cities: The Commission Government Movement in America, 1901–1920.* Austin: University of Texas Press, 1977.

Richardson, Heather Cox. *The Greatest Nation of the Earth: Republican Economic Policies during the Civil War.* Cambridge, MA: Harvard University Press, 1997.

Rideout, Walter B. *The Radical Novel in the United States, 1900–1951: Some Relationships of Literature and Society.* Cambridge, MA: Harvard University Press, 1956.

Robbins, Roy M. *Our Landed Heritage: The Public Domain, 1776–1936.* Princeton, NJ: Princeton University Press, 1942.

Robinson, Kenneth L. *Farm and Food Policies and Their Consequences.* Englewood Cliffs, NJ: Prentice-Hall, 1989.

Rockoff, Hugh. *Drastic Measures: A History of Wage and Price Controls in the United States.* New York: Cambridge University Press, 1984.

Rockoff, Hugh. "Banking and Finance, 1789–1914." In Stanley L. Engerman and Robert E. Gallman, eds., *The Cambridge Economic History of the United States.* Vol. 2: *The Long Nineteenth Century.* New York: Cambridge University Press, 2000.

Rodgers, Harrell R. *American Poverty in a New Era of Reform.* Armonk, NY: M. E. Sharpe, 2000.

Roe, Mark J. "Political Theory of American Corporate Finance." *Columbia Law Review,* vol. 91, no. 1 (January 1991): 10–67.

Roe, Mark J. "Political Preconditions to Separating Ownership from Control." *Stanford Law Review,* vol. 539 (2000–2001): 539–606.

Rogowsky, Robert A., et al. *Trade Liberalization: Fears and Facts.* Westport, CT: Praeger, 2001.

Romer, Christina D. "New Estimates of Prewar Gross National Product and Unemployment." *Journal of Economic History,* vol. 46 (1986): 341–352.

Ronen, Simcha. *Comparative and Multinational Management.* Washington, DC: Library of Congress, 1986.

Rose, Edward J. *Henry George.* New York: Twayne Publishers, 1968.

Rose, Kenneth W. "John D. Rockefeller." In John A. Garraty and Mark C. Caernes, eds., *American National Biography.* New York: Oxford University Press, 1999.

Rose, Mark H. *Interstate Express Highway Politics 1941–1989.* Knoxville: University of Tennessee Press, 1990.

Rosenberg, Nathan, and David C. Mowery. *Technology and the Pursuit of Economic Growth.* Cambridge: Cambridge University Press, 1989.

Ross, Earle Dudley. *Democracy's College: The Land-Grant Movement in the Formative State.* New York: Arno Press, 1969.

Rothbard, Murray N. *The Panic of 1819: Reactions and Policies*. New York: Columbia University Press, 1962.

Rothman, Hal. *The Greening of a Nation? Environmentalism in the United States since 1945*. Ft. Worth, TX: Harcourt, Brace, 1998.

Rotzoll, Kim B., and James E. Haefner, with Steven R. Hall. *Advertising in Contemporary Society: Perspectives toward Understanding*. 3rd ed. Chicago: University of Illinois Press, 1996.

Rowan, Richard Wilmer. *The Pinkertons: A Detective Dynasty*. Boston: Little, Brown, 1931.

Rowe, Leo Stanton. *The Pan American Union and the Pan American Conferences, 1890–1940*. Washington, DC: Pan American Union, 1940.

Roy, William G. "The Politics of Bureaucratization and the United States Bureau of Corporations." *Journal of Political and Military Sociology*, vol. 10 (1982).

Roy, William G. *Socializing Capital: The Rise of The Large Industrial Corporation in America*. Princeton, NJ: Princeton University Press, 1997.

Rubin, Dale F. "Public Aid to Professional Sports Teams." *Toledo Law Review*, vol. 30 (Spring 1999): 393–418.

Rudolph, Frederick. *The American College and University: A History*. New York: Alfred A. Knopf, 1968.

Russell, Charles Edward. *The Greatest Trust in the World*. New York: Ridgway-Thayer, 1905.

Sacharin, Ken. *Attention: How to Interrupt, Yell, Whisper, and Touch Consumers*. New York: John Wiley and Sons, 2001.

Sachs, Wolfgang. "The Archaeology of the Development Idea." *Interculture*, vol. 23, no. 4 (1990).

Sale, Kirkpatrick. *The Green Revolution: The American Environmental Movement, 1962–1992*. New York: Hill and Wang, 1993.

Sampson, Anthony. *The Seven Sisters*. New York: Viking, 1975.

Samuel, Lawrence R. *Brought to You By: Postwar Television Advertising and the American Dream*. Austin: University of Texas Press, 2001.

Samuelson, Pamela. "The Originality Standard for Literary Works under U.S. Copyright Law." *American Journal of Comparative Law*, vol. 42 (1994): 393–397.

Samuelson, Paul A., William D. Nordhaus, and Michael J. Mandel. *Economics*. New York: McGraw-Hill, 1995.

Samuelson, Robert J. *The Good Life and Its Discontents: The American Dream in the Age of Entitlement, 1945–1995*. New York: Time Books, 1995.

Sanders, Elizabeth. *Roots of Reform: Farmers, Workers, and the American State, 1877–1917*. Chicago: University of Chicago Press, 1999.

Sassoon, Donald. *One Hundred Years of Socialism: The West European Left in the Twentieth Century*. New York: New Press, 1996.

Saunders, Robert M. *In Search of Woodrow Wilson: Beliefs and Behavior*. Westport, CT: Greenwood Press, 1998.

Savage, James D. *Balanced Budgets and American Politics*. Ithaca, NY: Cornell University Press, 1988.

Savla, Sandeep. *Money Laundering and Financial Intermediaries*. Boston: Kluwer Law International, 2001.

Savona, Ernesto. *Responding to Money Laundering: International Perspectives*. Toronto: Harwood Academic Publishers, 1997.

Savona, Ernesto. *European Money Trails*. The Netherlands: Harwood Academic Publishers, 1999.

Schelling, Thomas C., and Morton H. Halperin. *Strategy and Arms Control*. New York: Twentieth Century Fund, 1961.

Schieber, Sylvester J., and John B. Shoven. *The Real Deal: The History and Future of Social Security*. New Haven, CT: Yale University Press, 1999.

Schild, Georg. *Bretton Woods and Dumbarton Oaks: American Economic and Political Postwar Planning in the Summer of 1944*. New York: St. Martin's Press, 1995.

Schirmer, Daniel B. *Republic or Empire: American Resistance to the Philippine War*. Cambridge, MA: Schenkman, 1972.

Schneider, Gary, and James Perry. *Electronic Commerce*. Boston: Thompson Learning, 2001.

Schoenbrun, David. *Triumph in Paris: The Exploits of Benjamin Franklin*. New York: Harper and Row, 1976.

Schoultz, Lars. *Beneath the United States: A History of U.S. Policy toward Latin America*. Cambridge, MA: Harvard University Press, 1998.

Schroeder, Paul W. *The Transformation of European Politics, 1763–1848*. Oxford: Oxford University Press, 1994.

Schudson, Michael. *Advertising, the Uneasy Persuasion: Its Dubious Impact on American Society*. New York: Basic Books, 1984.

Schurr, Sam H., Calvin C. Burwell, Warren D. Devine, and Sidney Sonenblum. *Electricity in the American Economy: Agent of Technological Progress*. Westport, CT: Greenwood Press, 1990.

Schurr, Sam H., and Bruce C. Netschert. *Energy in the American Economy, 1850–1975: An Economic Study of Its History and Prospects*. Baltimore, MD: Johns Hopkins University Press, 1960.

Schwantes, Carlos A. *Coxey's Army: An American Odyssey*. Lincoln: University of Nebraska Press, 1985.

Schwartz, Bernard. *The Law in America: A History.* New York: McGraw-Hill, 1974.

Schwartz, Bernard. *A History of the Supreme Court.* New York: Oxford University Press, 1993.

Schweikart, Larry. *Banking in the American South from the Age of Jackson to Reconstruction.* Baton Rouge: Louisiana State University Press, 1988.

Schweitzer, Robert L., ed. *United States Policy toward Cuba: Tighten or Lift the Embargo?* Washington, DC: United States Global Strategy Council, 1995.

Schwengel, Fred. *The Republican Party: Its Heritage and History.* Washington, DC: Acropolis Books, 1987.

Scott, Ivan. *Upton Sinclair, the Forgotten Socialist.* Lewiston, NY: Edward Mellen Press, 1997.

Sears, Marian V. *Mining Stock Exchanges, 1860–1930: A Historical Survey.* Missoula: University of Montana Press, 1973.

Seely, Bruce E. *Building the American Highway System: Engineers as Policy Makers.* Philadelphia: Temple University Press, 1987.

Seligman, Joel. *The Transformation of Wall Street: A History of the Securities and Exchange Commission and Modern Corporate Finance.* Rev. ed. Boston: Northeastern University Press, 1995.

Sellers, Charles. *The Market Revolution: Jacksonian America, 1815–1846.* New York: Oxford University Press, 1991.

Sgori, Peter P. *The Purchase of Alaska, March 3, 1867: Bargain at Two Cents an Acre.* New York: Franklin Watts, 1975.

Sheingate, Adam D. *The Rise of the Agricultural Welfare State: Institutions and Interest Group Power in the United States, France, and Japan.* Princeton, NJ: Princeton University Press, 2001.

Shenk, David. *Data Smog: Surviving the Information Glut.* San Francisco: Harper Edge, 1997.

Shepperd, William G. *The Economics of Industrial Organization.* Englewood Cliffs, NJ: Prentice-Hall, 1979.

Sherman, Howard J., and David X. Kola. *Business Cycles and Forecasting.* New York: Harper Collins, 1996.

Shiers, George, ed. *The Development of Wireless to 1920.* New York: Arno Press, 1977.

Shiers, George, ed. *The Electric Telegraph: An Historical Anthology.* New York: Arno Press, 1977.

Shiers, George, ed. *The Telephone: An Historical Anthology.* New York: Arno Press, 1977.

Shiller, Robert J. *Irrational Exuberance.* Princeton, NJ: Princeton University Press, 2000.

Shook, Dale N. *William G. McAdoo and the Development of National Economic Policy: 1913–1918*. New York: Garland Publishing, 1987.

Shultz, G. P., and K. W. Dam. *Economic Policy beyond the Headlines*. New York: W. W. Norton, 1977.

Siegel, Adrienne. *The Marshall Court, 1801–1835*. Millwood, NY: Associated Faculty Press, 1987.

Siegel, Barry, ed. *Money in Crisis: The Federal Reserve, the Economy, and the Monetary Reform*. San Francisco: Pacific Institute for Public Policy Research, 1984.

Siegel, Martin. *The Taney Court, 1836–1864*. Millwood, NY: Associated Faculty Press, 1987.

Silverstein, Ken. "Candidate Nader." *Mother Jones*, vol. 25, no. 4 (July 1, 2000): 60.

Simonds, William Adams. *Henry Ford: His Life, His Work, His Genius*. New York: Bobbs-Merrill, 1943.

Sinclair, Upton. *The Autobiography of Upton Sinclair*. New York: Harcourt, Brace and World, 1962.

Singer, H. W. "Editorial: The Golden Age of the Keynesian Consensus—The Pendulum Swings Back." *World Development*, vol. 25, no. 3 (1997): 293–297.

Singleton, Jeff. *The American Dole: Unemployment Relief and the Welfare State in the Great Depression*. Westport, CT: Greenwood Press, 2000.

Skeely, David A., Jr. *Debt's Dominion: A History of Bankruptcy Law in America*. Princeton, NJ: Princeton University Press, 2001.

Skeet, Ian. *OPEC: Twenty-five Years of Prices and Politics*. Cambridge: Cambridge University Press, 1988.

Skidelsky, Robert. *John Maynard Keynes*. 3 vols. London: Macmillan, 1983–2000.

Skitol, Robert A. "The Shifting Sands of Antitrust Policy: Where It Has Been, Where It Is Now, Where It Will Be in Its Third Century." *Cornell Journal of Law and Public Policy*, vol. 9, no. 1 (Fall 1999): 239–266.

Sklar, Martin J. *The Corporate Reconstruction of American Capitalism, 1890–1916: The Market, the Law, and Politics*. New York: Cambridge University Press, 1988.

Slaughter, Thomas P. *The Whiskey Rebellion: Frontier Epilogue to the American Revolution*. New York: Oxford University Press, 1986.

Smith, Adam. *An Inquiry into the Nature and Causes of the Wealth of Nations*. London: Printed for W. Strahan and T. Cadell, 1776.

Smith, Bruce D. "American Colonial Monetary Regimes: The Failure of the Quantity Theory and Some Evidence in Favor of an Alternate View." *Canadian Journal of Economics*, vol. 18 (1985): 531–565.

Smith, George David, and Richard Sylla. "The Transformation of Financial Capitalism: An Essay on the History of American Capital Markets." *Financial Markets, Institutions, and Instruments*, vol. 2, no. 2 (May 1993): 1–61.

Smith, Jean Edward. *John Marshall: Definer of a Nation*. New York: Henry Holt, 1998.

Smith, Katherine R. "Congress Again Considers 'Green' Payments to Farmers." *Issues in Science and Technology*, vol. 17, no. 3 (2001): 26.

Smith, Marian L. "Overview of INS History." In George T. Kurian, ed., *A Historical Guide to the U.S. Government*. New York: Oxford University Press, 1998.

Smith, Olivia J., ed. *Aging in America*. New York: H. W. Wilson, 2000.

Smith, R. Elberton. *The Army and Economic Mobilization*. Washington, DC: U.S. Government Printing Office, 1959.

Sobel, Robert. *The Big Board: A History of the New York Stock Market*. New York: Free Press, 1965.

Sobel, Robert. *AMEX: A History of the American Stock Exchange, 1921–1971*. New York: Weybright and Talley, 1972.

Solganick, Allen. "The Robber Baron Concept and Its Revisionists." *Science and Society*, vol. 49 (Summer 1965): 17–23.

Solnit, Rebecca. *Savage Dreams: A Journey into the Hidden Wars of the American West*. San Francisco: Sierra Club, 1994.

Somers, Herman M. *Presidential Agency: The Office of War Mobilization and Reconversion*. New York: Greenwood Press, 1969.

Somervill, Barbara A. *Andrew Jackson*. Minneapolis, MN: Compass Point Books, 2003.

Sparrow, Bartholomew H. *From the Outside In*. Princeton, NJ: Princeton University Press, 1996.

Spear, Donald P. "California Besieged: The Foot-and-Mouth Epidemic of 1924." *Agricultural History*, vol. 56 (July 1982): 528–541.

Spence, Jonathan D. *The Search for Modern China*. 2nd ed. New York: W. W. Norton, 1999.

Spiegel, Henry William. *The Growth of Economic Thought*. Durham, NC: Duke University Press, 1994.

Spulber, Nicholas. *Managing the American Economy: From Roosevelt to Reagan*. Bloomington: Indiana University Press, 1989.

Stagg, J. C. A. *Mr. Madison's War: Politics, Diplomacy, and Warfare in the Early American Republic, 1783–1830*. Princeton, NJ: Princeton University Press, 1983.

Stanwood, Edward. *American Tariff Controversies in the Nineteenth Century*. New York: Russell and Russell, 1967.

Starr, Chauncey, and Philip C. Ritterbush. *Science, Technology, and the Human Prospect: Proceedings of the Edison Centennial Symposium*. New York: Pergamon Press, 1980.

Steamer, Robert J. *The Supreme Court in Crisis: A History of Conflict*. Amherst: University of Massachusetts Press, 1971.

Steele, Ian K. *Politics of Colonial Policy: The Board of Trade in Colonial Administration 1696–1720*. Oxford: Clarendon Press, 1968.

Steeples, Douglas, and David Whitten. *Democracy in Desperation: The Depression of 1893*. Westport, CT: Greenwood Press, 1998.

Steger, Manfred B. *Globalism: The New Market Ideology*. Lanham, MD: Rowman and Littlefield, 2002.

Stein, Herbert. *The Fiscal Revolution in America*. Rev. ed. Washington, DC: American Enterprise Institute, 1990.

Stein, Herbert. *Presidential Economics: The Making of Economic Policy from Roosevelt to Clinton*. Washington, DC: American Enterprise Institute, 1994.

Stein, Herbert. *On the Other Hand . . . Essays on Economics, Economists, and Politics*. Washington, DC: American Enterprise Institute, 1995.

Stephanson, Anders. *Manifest Destiny: American Expansion and the Empire of Right*. New York: Hill and Wang, 1995.

Stephenson, Nathaniel Wright. *Nelson W. Aldrich: A Leader in American Politics*. New York: Scribner's, 1930.

Sterk, Steward P. "Rhetoric and Reality in Copyright Law." *Michigan Law Review*, vol. 94, no. 5 (1996): 1197–1249.

Stevens, Joseph E. *Hoover Dam: An American Adventure*. Norman: University of Oklahoma Press, 1988.

Stevens, Robert. *Law School: Legal Education in America from the 1850s to the 1980s*. Chapel Hill: University of North Carolina Press, 1983.

Stevenson, Jonathon. *Preventing Conflict: The Role of the Bretton Woods Institutions*. New York: Oxford University Press, 2000.

Stigler, George J. *The Theory of Price*. New York: Macmillan, 1947.

Stockman, David A. *Triumph of Politics: How the Reagan Revolution Failed*. New York: Harper and Row, 1986.

Stone, Alan. *Economic Regulation and the Public Interest: The Federal Trade Commission in Theory and Practice*. Ithaca, NY: Cornell University Press, 1977.

Stone, Richard D. *The Interstate Commerce Commission and the Railroad Industry: A History of Regulatory Policy*. New York: Praeger, 1991.

Stover, John F. *American Railroads*. Chicago: University of Chicago Press, 1997.

Strachan, Hew. *The First World War: Volume 1*. Oxford: Oxford University Press, 2001.

Strouse, Jean. *Morgan: American Financier*. New York: Random House, 1999.

Stuart, Pamela B. *The Federal Trade Commission*. New York: Chelsea House, 1991.

Stuart, Reginald. *Half-Way Pacifist: Thomas Jefferson's View of War*. Toronto: University of Toronto Press, 1978.

Sullivan, Lawrence A. "Post-Chicago Economics: Economists, Lawyers, Judges, and Enforcement Officials in a Less Determinate Theoretical World." *Antitrust Law Journal*, vol. 63, no. 2 (1995): 669–674.

Summers, Festus. *William L. Wilson and Tariff Reform*. New Brunswick, NJ: Rutgers University Press, 1953.

Sussman, Gennifer. *The St. Lawrence Seaway: History and Analysis of a Joint Water Highway*. Washington, DC: National Planning Association, 1978.

Sweeney, John J., and David Kusnet. *America Needs a Raise: Fighting for Economic Security and Social Justice*. New York: Replica Books, 2000.

Sweet, William. *Great Lakes States: Trouble in America's Industrial Heartland*. Washington, DC: Congressional Quarterly Editorial Research Reports, 1980.

Sylla, Richard. "American Banking and Growth in the Nineteenth Century: A Partial View of the Terrain." *Explorations in Economic History*, vol. 9 (1971–1972): 197–227.

Takaki, Ronald. *A Different Mirror*. Boston: Little, Brown, 1993.

Talbot, Ross B., and Don F. Hadwinger. *The Policy Process in American Agriculture*. San Francisco: Chandler Publishing, 1968.

Tansill, Charles C. *The Purchase of the Danish West Indies*. Baltimore, MD: Johns Hopkins University Press, 1932.

Tap, Bruce. *Over Lincoln's Shoulder*. Lawrence: University Press of Kansas, 1998.

Tassey, G. *Technology and Economic Growth: Implications for Federal Policy*. National Institute of Standards and Technology (NIST) Planning Report 95-3. Washington, DC: U.S. Department of Commerce, 1995.

Tate, Merze. *The United States and the Hawaiian Kingdom*. New Haven, CT: Yale University Press, 1965.

Taussig, Frank W. *Tariff History of the United States*. 8th ed. Cambridge, MA: Harvard University Press, 1931.

Taylor, Benjamin, and Fred Witney. *Labor Relations Law*. Englewood Cliffs, NJ: Prentice-Hall, 1987.

Taylor, George Rogers. *The Transportation Revolution, 1815–1860*. New York: Holt, Rinehart and Winston, 1951.

Taylor, George Rogers, ed. *Jackson vs. Biddle's Bank: The Struggle over the Second Bank of the United States*. Lexington, MA: D. C. Heath, 1972.

Taylor, John M. *William Henry Seward: Lincoln's Right Hand*. New York: Harper Collins, 1991.

Teaford, Jon C. *Cities of the Heartland: The Rise and Fall of the Industrial Midwest*. Bloomington: Indiana University Press, 1994.

Tedlow, Richard S. "Advertising and Public Relations." In Glenn Porter, ed., *Encyclopedia of American Economic History, Volume 2*. New York: Scribner's, 1980.

Tedlow, Richard S. *The Rise of the American Business Corporation*. Philadelphia: Harwood Academic Publishers, 1991.

Teles, Steven. *Whose Welfare? AFDC and Elite Politics*. Lawrence: University Press of Kansas, 1996.

Temin, Peter. *The Jacksonian Economy*. New York: W. W. Norton, 1969.

Temin, Peter. *Did Monetary Forces Cause the Great Depression?* New York: Norton, 1976.

Temin, Peter. *Lessons from the Great Depression*. Cambridge, MA: MIT Press, 1989.

Terrill, Tom E. *The Tariff, Politics, and American Foreign Policy: 1874–1901*. Westport, CT: Greenwood Press, 1973.

Thorelli, Hans B. *The Federal Antitrust Policy: The Origination of an American Tradition*. Baltimore, MD: Johns Hopkins University Press, 1955.

Thornton, Mark. *The Economics of Prohibition*. Salt Lake City: University of Utah Press, 1991.

Thornton, Richard C. *The Nixon-Kissinger Years*. New York: Paragon, 1989.

Thornton, Richard C. *The Carter Years*. New York: Paragon, 1991.

Tilly, Louise A., and Patricia Gurin, eds. *Women, Politics, and Change*. New York: Russell Sage Foundation, 1990.

Timberlake, Richard. *The Origins of Central Banking in the United States*. Cambridge, MA: Harvard University Press, 1978.

Timberlake, Richard. *Monetary Policy in the United States: An Intellectual and Institutional History*. Chicago: University of Chicago Press, 1993.

Tindall, George Brown, and David Emory Shi. *America: A Narrative History*. New York: W. W. Norton, 1999.

Tomlins, Christopher L. *The State and the Unions: Labor Relations, Law, and the Organized Labor Movement in America, 1880–1960*. Cambridge: Cambridge University Press, 1985.

Tompkins, E. Berkeley. "The Old Guard: A Study of Anti-Imperialist Leadership." *Historian*, vol. 30 (May 1968): 360–388.

Trattner, Walter. *Crusade for the Children: A History of the National Child Labor Committee and Child Labor Reform in America*. Chicago: Quadrangle Books, 1970.

Trattner, Walter. *From Poor Law to Welfare State: A History of Social Welfare in America*. New York: Free Press, 1999.

Trefousee, Hans L. *The Radical Republicans*. New York: Alfred A. Knopf, 1969.

Trefousee, Hans L. *Lincoln's Design for Emancipation*. Philadelphia: Lippincott, 1975.

Tucker, Robert. *Empire of Liberty: The Statecraft of Thomas Jefferson.* New York: Oxford University Press, 1990.

Tucker, Spencer C. *The Great War, 1914–1918.* Bloomington: Indiana University Press, 1998.

Twain, Mark. Quoted in the *New York Times*, December 10, 1889.

Tyack, David B., Thomas James, and Aaron Benavot. *Law and the Shaping of Public Education, 1785–1954.* Madison: University of Wisconsin Press, 1987.

Tyler, Poyntz, ed. *Securities, Exchanges, and the SEC.* New York: H. W. Wilson, 1965.

Unger, Irwin. *The Greenback Era: A Social and Political History of America.* Princeton, NJ: Princeton University Press, 1964.

Unger, Irwin. *The Best of Intentions: The Triumph and Failure of the Great Society under Kennedy, Johnson, and Nixon.* New York: Doubleday, 1996.

"The United Nations Children's Fund." *Yearbook of the United Nations.* New York: United Nations, 2000.

Urwin, Derek W. *The Community of Europe: A History of European Integration since 1945.* New York: Longman, 1995.

Utley, Jonathan G. *Going to War with Japan, 1937–1941.* Knoxville: University of Tennessee Press, 1985.

Vaitheeswaran, Vejay. "Energy: A Brighter Future." *The Economist*, February 10, 2001.

Van Deusen, Glyndon G. *William Henry Seward.* New York: Oxford University Press, 1967.

Van Deusen, Glyndon G. *The Jacksonian Era 1828–1848.* Prospect Heights, IL: Waveland Press, 1992.

Vietor, Richard. *Contrived Competition: Regulation and Deregulation in America.* Cambridge, MA: Harvard University Press, 1994.

Vinovskis, Maris A. *Education, Society, and Economic Opportunity: A Historical Perspective on Persistent Issues.* New Haven, CT: Yale University Press, 1995.

Viscusi, W. Kip, John M. Vernon, and Joseph E. Harrington Jr. *Economics of Regulation and Antitrust.* 3rd ed. Cambridge, MA: MIT Press, 2000.

Vogelsang, Ingo, and Glenn Woroch. "Local Telephone Service: A Complex Dance of Technology, Regulation, and Competition." In Larry Duetsch, ed., *Industry Studies.* Armonk, NY: M. E. Sharpe, 1998.

Vohra, Ranbir. *China's Path to Modernization.* Upper Saddle River, NJ: Prentice-Hall, 2000.

Volcker, P., and T. Gyohten. *Changing Fortunes: The World's Money and the Threat to American Leadership.* New York: Times Books, 1992.

Wachhorst, Wyn. *Thomas Alva Edison: An American Myth.* Cambridge, MA: MIT Press, 1980.

Wagner, Tim. "Insurance Rating Bureaus." *Journal of Risk and Insurance*, vol. 19, no. 2 (Winter 2000): 189–203.

Wallerstein, Immanuel. *Mercantilism and the Consolidation of the European World Economy, 1600–1750*. New York: Academic Press, 1980.

Wallerstein, Immanuel. *The Modern World System III: The Second Era of Great Expansion of the Capitalist World-Economy, 1730–1840s*. New York: Academic Press, 1989.

Walters, Ray. *Albert Gallatin*. New York: Macmillan, 1957.

Walterscheid, Edward C. *To Promote the Progress of Useful Arts: American Patent Law and Administration, 1798–1836*. Littleton, CO: Fred Rothman, 1998.

Walton, Gary M., and Hugh Rockoff. *History of the American Economy*. 9th ed. Fort Worth, TX: South-Western Thomson Learning, 2002.

Ware, Susan. *Beyond Suffrage: Women in the New Deal*. Cambridge, MA: Harvard University Press, 1981.

Warne, Colston E. *The Pullman Boycott of 1894: The Problem of Federal Intervention*. Boston: D. C. Heath, 1955.

Warner, Aaron W., Mathew Forstater, and Sumner M. Rosen, eds. *Commitment to Full Employment: The Economics and Social Policy of William S. Vickrey*. Armonk, NY: M. E. Sharpe, 2000.

War Production Board. *Industrial Mobilization for War*. Westport, CT: Greenwood Press, 1970.

Warshaw, Shirley Anne. *The Keys to Power: Managing the Presidency*. New York: Longman, 2000.

Washburn, Wilcomb A. *The Governor and the Rebel: A History of Bacon's Rebellion*. Chapel Hill: University of North Carolina Press, published for the Institute of Early American History and Culture at Williamsburg, Virginia, 1957.

Watson, Harry, L. *Liberty and Power: The Politics of Jacksonian America*. New York: Hill and Wang, 1990.

Web, Stephen Saunders. *1676: The End of American Independence*. New York: Alfred A. Knopf, 1984.

Weber, Christopher. *". . . Good as Gold"? How We Lost Our Gold Reserves and Destroyed the Dollar*. Berryville, VA: George Edward Durell Foundation, 1988.

Weeks, Lewis G. "Where Will Energy Come from in 2059?" *Petroleum Engineer for Management*, vol. 31 (August 1959): 53–69.

Weil, David. "If OSHA Is So Bad, Why Is Compliance So Good?" *Rand Journal of Economics*, vol. 27 (Autumn 1996): 618–640.

Weir, David. "The Reliability of Historical Macroeconomic Data for Comparing Cyclical Stability." *Journal of Economic History*, vol. 46 (1986): 353–365.

Weiss, Marc A. *The Rise of the Community Builders: The American Real Estate Industry and Urban Land Use Planning*. New York: Columbia University Press, 1987.

Weiss, Thomas G., D. P. Forsythe, and Roger A. Coate. *The United Nations and Changing World Politics*. Boulder, CO: Westview Press, 1994.

Welch, John L. "Modernizing for the Millennium: The 1999 Amendments to the Trademark Law." *Intellectual Property Today*, vol. 7, no. 1 (January 2000): 24–33.

Welch, Richard E. *Response to Imperialism: The United States and the Philippine American War, 1898–1902*. Chapel Hill: University of North Carolina Press, 1972.

Welch, Richard E. *The Presidencies of Grover Cleveland*. Lawrence: University Press of Kansas, 1988.

Wells, Wyatt C. *Economist in an Uncertain World: Arthur F. Burns and the Federal Reserve, 1970–78*. New York: Columbia University Press, 1994.

Wells, Wyatt C. *Antitrust and the Formation of the Postwar World*. New York: Columbia University Press, 2002.

Werner, Walter, and Steven T. Smith. *Wall Street*. New York: Columbia University Press, 1991.

Weslager, C. A. *The Stamp Act Congress*. Newark: University of Delaware Press, 1976.

White, Eugene N. "Banking and Finance in the Twentieth Century." In Stanley L. Engerman and Robert E. Gallman, eds., *The Cambridge Economic History of the United States*. Vol. 3: *The Twentieth Century*. New York: Cambridge University Press, 2000.

White, Henry K. "The Pacific Railway Debts." *Journal of Political Economy*, vol. 2 (June 1894): 424–452.

White, John, and Ralph Willett, eds. *Slavery in the American South*. London: Longman, 1970.

White, Leonard D. *The Republican Era: A Study in Administrative History*. New York: Macmillan, 1965.

White, Ron, and Michael White. *MP3 Underground*. Indianapolis, IN: Que Corp., 2001.

Wicker, Elmus. *Federal Reserve and Monetary Policy, 1917–1933*. New York: Random House, 1966.

Wicker, Elmus. "Colonial Monetary Standards Contrasted: Evidence from the Seven Years' War." *Journal of Economic History*, vol. 45 (1985): 869–884.

Wilburn, Jean Alexander. *Biddle's Bank: The Crucial Years*. New York: Columbia University Press, 1967.

Wilcox, Clair, and William G. Shepherd. *Public Policies toward Business.* 5th ed. Homewood, IL: Richard D. Irwin, 1975.

Wilkinson, J. Harvie. *From Brown to Bakke: The Supreme Court and School Integration.* New York: Oxford University Press, 1979.

Williams, Ernest William. *The Regulation of Rail-Motor Rate Competition.* New York: Harper, 1958.

Williams, Frances Leigh. *A Founding Family.* New York: Harcourt Brace Jovanovich, 1978.

Williams, Frederick D. *The Northwest Ordinance.* East Lansing: Michigan State University Press, 1989.

Williams, Neville. *Contraband Cargoes: Seven Centuries of Smuggling.* New York: Longmans, 1959.

Williams, T. Harry. *Lincoln and the Radicals.* Madison: University of Wisconsin Press, 1941.

Williamson, J. *The Failure of World Monetary Reform.* London: Nelson, 1977.

Williamson, Oliver E. *Antitrust Economics: Mergers, Contracting, and Strategic Behavior.* Oxford: Blackwell, 1987.

Wilson, Kevin G. *Deregulating Telecommunications: U.S. and Canadian Telecommunications, 1840–1997.* Lanham, MD: Rowman and Littlefield, 2000.

Wilson, William J. *When Work Disappears: The World of the New Urban Poor.* New York: Random House, 1997.

Winkler, Allan M. *Home Front U.S.A: America during World War II.* 2nd ed. Wheeling, IL: Harlan Davidson, 2000.

Wirt, Frederick M., and Grant Harman, eds. *Education, Recession, and the World Village: A Comparative Political Economy of Education.* London: Falmer Press, 1986.

Wolman, Paul. *Most Favored Nation: The Republican Revisionists and U.S. Tariff Policy, 1897–1912.* Chapel Hill: University of North Carolina Press, 1992.

Woodward, Bob. *Maestro: Greenspan's Fed and the American Boom.* New York: Simon and Schuster, 2001.

Woolley, John. *Monetary Politics: The Federal Reserve and the Politics of Monetary Policy.* New York: Cambridge University Press, 1984.

World Bank. *World Bank Development Report 1999–2000.* Oxford: Oxford University Press, 2000.

World Intellectual Property Organization. *The First Twenty-five Years of the World Intellectual Property Organization, from 1967 to 1992.* Geneva: International Bureau of Intellectual Property, 1992.

Worster, Donald. *Dust Bowl: The Southern Plains in the 1930s.* Oxford: Oxford University Press, 1979.

Worster, Donald, ed. *American Environmentalism: The Formative Period, 1860–1915*. New York: John Wiley and Sons, 1973.

Wray, J. Harry. *Sense and Non-Sense: American Culture and Politics*. Upper Saddle River, NJ: Prentice-Hall, 2001.

Wray, L. Randall, *Understanding Modern Money*. Cheltenham, England: Edward Elgar, 1998.

Wright, Eric Olin. *Class, Crisis, and the State*. London: New Left Books, 1978.

Wright, Jim. Interview with Henry Sirgo. Fort Worth, Texas, April 10, 1998.

Wright, John R. *Interest Groups and Congress: Lobbying, Contributions, and Influence*. Boston: Allyn and Bacon, 1996.

Wueschner, Silvano. *Charting Twentieth Century Monetary Policy: Herbert Hoover and Benjamin Strong, 1917–1927*. Westport, CT: Greenwood Press, 1999.

Yergin, Daniel. *The Prize: The Epic Quest for Oil, Money, and Power*. New York: Simon and Schuster, 1991.

You, Jong-il. *The Bretton Woods Institutions: Evolution, Reform, and Change*. Seoul: Korea Development Institute, 2000.

Young, Warren. *Atomic Energy Costing*. Norwell, MA: Kluwer Press, 1998.

Zahniser, Marvin R. *Charles Cotesworth Pinckney*. Chapel Hill: University of North Carolina Press, 1967.

Zakaria, Fareed. *From Wealth to Power: The Unusual Origins of America's World Role*. Princeton, NJ: Princeton University Press, 1998.

Zeiler, Thomas W. *Free Trade, Free World: The Advent of GATT*. Chapel Hill: University of North Carolina Press, 1999.

Zieger, Robert H. *American Workers, American Unions, 1920–1985*. Baltimore, MD: Johns Hopkins University Press, 1994.

Zijderveld, Anton C. *The Waning of the Welfare State: The End of Comprehensive State Succor*. New Brunswick, NJ: Transaction Books, 1999.

Zink, Harry. *City Bosses in the United States: A Study of Twenty Municipal Bosses*. Durham, NC: Duke University Press, 1930.

Zundel, Alan F. *Declarations of Dependency: The Civic Republican Tradition in U.S. Poverty Policy*. Albany, NY: State University of New York Press, 2000.

Web sites

African Methodist Episcopal Church Review. Reprinted by the Ohio Historical Society, "The African-American Experience in Ohio, 1850–1920," vol. 6, no. 3 (January 1890). Available: http://dbs.ohiohistory.org/africanam/page.cfm?ID=2387.

American Economic Association. http://www.vanderbilt.edu/AEA/; accessed January 15, 2003.

"ARPA-DARPA: The History of the Name." April 18, 2001. Available: http://www.darpa.mil//; accessed September 17, 2001.

AT&T Labs—Research. http://www.research.att.com/~amo; accessed June 16, 2000.

Bureau of Land Management. http://www.blm.gov/natacq/pls02/pls1-2_02.pdf; accessed June 29, 2003.

Bureau of the Census. http://www.census.gov; accessed January 3, 2003.

Center for Immigration Studies. http://www.cis.org; accessed September 2, 2002.

CNN Politics. Obama's Remarks on Signing the Stimulus Plan. February 17, 2009, http://articles.cnn.com/2009-02-17/politics/obama.stimulus.remarks _1_economic-stimulus-bill-sign-today-speaker-pelosi?_s=PM:POLITICS.

Congressional Research Service. "Summary of the American Clean Energy and Security Act of 2009." Available: http://www.govtrack.us/congress/bill.xp d?bill=h111-2454&tab=summary; accessed November 27, 2009.

Cooperative State Research, Education, and Extension Service of USDA (REEUSDA). "Bankhead-Jones Act of 1935." June 29, 1935. Available: http:// www.reeusda.gov/1700/legis/bkjones.htm; accessed December 21, 2002.

"DARPA over the Years." April 18, 2001. Available: http://www.darpa.mil/; accessed September 17, 2001.

DARPA. "Technology Transition." January 1997. Available: http://www.darpa.mil/; accessed September 17, 2001.

The Debates in the Federal Constitution of 1787. Available: http://www.constitution .org/dfc/dfc_0818.htm; accessed June 27, 2003.

Defense Advanced Research Projects Administration. Available: www.darpa.mil/ mto; accessed February 9, 2003.

Defense Manufacturing in 2010 and Beyond, Meeting the Changing Needs of National Defense. Appendix A. National Academy Press, 1999. Available: http:// www.nap.edu/readingroom/books/defman/app_appa.html; accessed September 17, 2001.

Department of Veterans Affairs (VA). "The GI Bill: From Roosevelt to Montgomery: GI Bill History." No date. Available: http://www.gibill.va.gov/education/GI_ Bill.htm; accessed October 15, 2002.

eMarketer. "Newspapers Join in Twitter Conversation." Available: http:// www.emarketer.com/Article.aspx?R=1007442; accessed December 28, 2009.

"EPA Timeline." January 10, 2003. Available: http://www.epa.gov/; accessed February 2, 2003.

"Facts and Figures: The Internet Economy Indicators." September 12, 2002. Available: http://www.internetindicators.com/facts.html; accessed September 12, 2002.

Federal Deposit Insurance Corporation, "Failed Bank List." Available: http:// www.fdic.gov/bank/individual/failed/banklist.html; accessed December 26, 2009.

Federal Pell Grant Program. *Biennial Evaluation Report, FY 93–94.* Chapter 501. Available: http://www.ed.gov/pubs/Biennial/501.html; accessed November 27, 2002.

Federation for American Immigration Reform. http://www.fairus.org; accessed September 21, 2002.

Fishback, Price V. "Workers' Compensation." In Robert Whaples, ed., EH.Net Encyclopedia. August 15, 2001. Available: http://www.eh.net/encyclopedia/fishback.workers.compensation.php; accessed February 2, 2002.

Fishback, Price V. "Workers' Compensation." In Robert Whaples, ed., *EH.Net Encyclopedia*. August 15, 2001. Available: http://www.eh.net/encyclopedia/fishback.workers.compensation.php; accessed October 5, 2002.

"Greenpeace History." No date. Available: http://www.greenpeacecanada.org; accessed September 7, 2001.

Greenspan, Alan. "The Fed Didn't Cause the Housing Bubble," *Wall Street Journal*. (March 11, 2009) Available: http://online.wsj.com/article/SB123672965066989281.html; accessed December 30, 2009.

Higher Education Resource Hub (HERH). "Land-Grant Act: History and Institutions." No date. Available: http://www.higher-ed.org/resources/morrill_acts.htm; accessed March 1, 2002.

http://fisher.lib.virginia.edu/cgi-local/censusbin/census/cen.pl?year=790.

http://fisher.lib.virginia.edu/cgi-local/censusbin/cen.pl?year=860.

Immigration and Naturalization Service. http://www.usdoj.gov/ins; accessed September 1, 2002.

"Inside Greenpeace: History and Mission." September 7, 2001. Available: http://www.greenpeaceusa.org/; accessed September 7, 2001.

Introduction to the Debates in the Federal Convention of 1787 by James Madison. Available: http://www.constitution.org/dfc/dfc_0001.htm; accessed June 27, 2003.

Jaffe, Matthew. "Ben Bernanke Wins Fed Reappointment Vote in Senate Banking Committee," ABCNews/Money. http://abcnews.go.com/Business/ben-bernanke-reappointment-federal-reserve-bank-senate-banking/story?id=9362540; accessed December 18, 2009.

Killeen, Kieran, and John Sipple. *School Consolidation and Transportation Policy: An Empirical and Institutional Analysis*. Randolph, VT: Rural School and Community Trust, April 2000. Available: www.ruralchallenge.org; accessed May 30, 2001.

Lewis, Jack. "The Birth of EPA." November 1985. Available: http://www.epa.gov/; accessed September 17, 2001.

"London Greenpeace: A History of Peace, Protest, and Campaigning." No date. Available: http://www.mcspotlight.org/people/biogs/london_grnpeace.html; accessed September 7, 2001.

MacMeekin, Dan. *Island Law: The Insular Cases*. November 26, 2002. Available: http://www.macmeekin.com/Library/Insular%20Cases.htm#Verdugo; accessed December 28, 2002.

Martin, James J. "Charles Beard: A Tribute." *Journal of Historical Review.* 1981. Available: http://www.ihr.org/jhr/v03/v03p239_Martin.html; accessed September 6, 2001.

McAdoo, William Gibbs. "American Rights." *American Leaders Speak: Recordings from World War I and the 1920 Election, 1918–1920.* Sound recording, no date. Available: http://lcweb2.loc.gov/; accessed August 18, 2002.

Medicaid: A Brief Summary, Health Care Financing Agency. 2001. Available: http://http://cms.hhs.gov/medicaid/.

Microsoft. www.microsoft.com; accessed February 9, 2003.

Mississippi State University (MSSTATE), Department of Agricultural Information Science and Education. "Development of Vocational Education in Agriculture: The Smith-Hughes Act of 1917." Available: http://www.ais.ms-state.edu/AEE/8593/unit4/tsld022.htm; accessed October 16, 1998.

Mulhauser, Dana. "Student Aid Rose Sharply over the Past Four Years, Study Finds." *Chronicle of Higher Education*, July 31, 2001. Available: http://www.chronicle.com/daily/2001/07/2001073101n.htm; accessed June 3, 2002.

Murphy, Sharon Ann. "Life Insurance in the United States through World War I." In Robert Whaples, ed., *EH.Net Encyclopedia.* August 15, 2002. Available: http://www.eh.net/encyclopedia/murphy.life.insurance.us.php; accessed August 15, 2002.

National Center for Education Statistics (NCES). "Education and the Economy: An Indicators Report." 1997. Available: http://www.nces.ed.gov/pubs97/97939.html; accessed September 24, 2002.

National Center for Education Statistics (NCES). *Digest of Education Statistics, 2000.* Chapter 4, "Federal Programs for Education and Related Activities." 2000. Available: http://www.nces.ed.gov/pubsearch/digest/ch4.html#1; accessed September 24, 2002.

National Endowment for the Humanities. http://www.neh.fed.us; accessed February 15, 2003.

National Immigration Forum. http://www.immigrationforum.org; accessed September 1, 2002.

New York Times. "Greenspan Calls to Break Up Banks 'Too Big to Fail'," October 5, 2009. Available: http://dealbook.blogs.nytimes.com/2009/10/15/greenspan-break-up-banks-too-big-to-fail/; accessed December 30, 2009.

North Carolina State University (NCSU), Department of Agricultural and Extension Education. "More than Sows, Cows, and Plows," January 13, 1999. Available: http://www.cals.ncsu.edu/agexed/aee501/show2/tsld005.htm; accessed October 21, 2002.

Odlyzko, Andrew. "The History of Communications and Its Implications for the Internet." U.S. Department of Labor. No date. Available: www.dol.gov; accessed January 23, 2003.

Odlyzko, Andrew. "Technology Is Transforming the U.S. Economy." U.S. Department of Labor. No date. Available: www.dol.gov; accessed January 23, 2003.

"Policy Analysis: Abstracts of the Chapters Memory, Reason, and Imagination: A Quarter Century of Pell Grants." The College Board. No date. Available: http://www.collegeboard.org/policy/html/topics.html; accessed October 17, 2002.

Shapley, Deborah. "Clintonizing Science Policy." *Bulletin of Atomic Scientists*, December 1993. Available: http://www.thebulletin.org/issues/1993/d93/d93 Shapley.html; accessed May 2, 2003.

Shiffman, Denise. "Obama's Rivals Should Steal From His Social Playbook: Web Strategy Forges Deep, Wide Connections," Advertising Act. Available: http://adage.com/campaigntrail/post?article_id=126336; accessed December 28, 2009.

Texas A&M University, College of Education (TAMU). "Vocational Education Legislation from 1950–1990." 1990. Available: http://www.coe.tamu.edu/~epsy/cded/becky1.htm; accessed October 29, 2002.

Texas A&M University, College of Education (TAMU). "Summary of Selected Federal Legislation Preceding the Smith-Hughes Act of 1917 to 1946." 1997. Available: http://www.coe.tamu.edu/~epsy/cded/owre1.htm; accessed November 13, 2002.

The Standard Legal Law Library. "Recent Changes in Bankruptcy Laws: An Overview of the Bankruptcy Act of 2005." Available: http://www.standardlegal.com/law-library/Recent-Bankruptcy-Law-Changes.html; accessed December 2, 2009.

University of Calgary. "The Impact of the Telephone on Society Today." No date. Available: http://www.ucalgary.ca/~dabrent/380/webproj/index380.html; accessed September 28, 2002.

University of Kentucky (UKY). "The Morrill Act and the Land-Grant Colleges." No date. Available: http://www.uky.edu/CampusGuide/land-grant.html; accessed July 22, 2002.

U.S. Army Armor Center, "History of Fort Knox." No date. Available: http://www.knox.army.mil/history.stm; accessed January 29, 2002.

U.S. Bureau of Economic Analysis. www.bea.gov; accessed February 22, 2003.

U.S. Census Bureau. *Historical Poverty Tables—People*. Table 3. 2001. Available: http://www.census.gov/hhes/poverty/histpov/hstpov3.html; accessed June 12, 2002.

U.S. Census Bureau. *Poverty Thresholds in 2000, by Size of Family and Number of Related Children under 18 Years*. 2001. Available: http://www.census.gov/hhes/poverty/threshld/thresh00.html; accessed July 15, 2002.

U.S. Census Bureau. *U.S. Trade Balance with Japan*. 2003. Available: http://www.census.gov/foreign-trade/balance/5880.html; accessed July 16, 2003.

U.S. Census Bureau, Population Division. http://www.census/gov/population/www/documentation/twps0029/tab02.html.

U.S. Constitution, article 1, section 8, clause 8. Available: http://www.constitution/ dfc/dfc_0905.htm.

U.S. Copyright Office. "The Digital Millennium Copyright Act of 1998 Summary." December 1998. Available: www.loc.gov/copyright/legislation/dmca.pdf; accessed September 15, 2001.

U.S. Department of Agriculture Economic Research Service. "Lenders and Financial Markets: Farmer Mac." 2001. Available: http://www.ers.usda.gov/briefing/Financial Markets/LendersFarmerMac.htm; accessed January 18, 2002.

U.S. Department of Education (ED). "The Federal Role in Education." April 2, 2003. Available: http://www.ed.gov/offices/OUS/fedrole.html; accessed April 5, 2003.

U.S. Department of Energy. *Energy in the United States, 1635–2000*. April 2002. Available: http://www.eia.doe.gov/emeu/aer; accessed June 20, 2002.

U.S. Department of Justice. "Public Comments and Plaintiff's Response: United States of America vs Aluminum Company of America and Alumax, Inc." No date. Available: http://www.usdoj.gov/atr/cases/f1900/1948.htm; accessed July 15, 2003.

U.S. Department of Justice Antitrust Case Filings. "United States v. Microsoft Current Case." No date. Available: http://www.usdoj.gov/atr/cases/ms_index.htm; accessed July 14, 2003.

U.S. Department of Labor Bureau of Labor Statistics. "Economic News Release: Employment Situation." Available: www.bls.gov, accessed December 24, 2009.

U.S. Department of Labor Wage and Hour Division. "History of Federal Minimum Wage Rates Under the Fair Labor Standards Act, 1938-2009." Available: www.dol.gov/whd/minwage/chart.htm; accessed December 12, 2009.

U.S. Department of Treasury, November 12, 2008, http://www.ustreas.gov/press/ releases/hp1265.htm.

"Watching YouTube: News, Research, and Statistics about Online Video and the 'Tube." Available: http://www.strangelove.com/blog/2009/08/video-ad -spending-projected-699-million-2009/; accessed December 28, 2009.

Weingroff, Richard F. "Federal-Aid Highway Act of 1956: Creating the Interstate System." U.S. Department of Transportation, Federal Highway Administration. April 28, 2003. Available: http://www.fhwa.dot.gov/infrastructure/rw96e.htm; accessed April 28, 2003.

Whitehouse. http://www.whitehouse.gov; accessed June 1, 2003.

White House Office of the Press Secretary. Remarks by the President on the American Automotive Industry. March 30, 2009, http://www.whitehouse.gov/the_press_ office/Remarks-by-the-President-on-the-American-Automotive-Industry-3/30/09/.

Williamson, Debra Aho. "Social Network Advertising: Trends for 2010." *eMarketer*. Available: http://www.emarketer.com/blog/index.php/social-network-advertising- trends-2010/; accessed December 28, 2009.

World Health Organization. "Bovine Spongiform Encephalopathy Fact Sheet." Updated November 2002. Available: http://www.who.int/inf-fs/en/fact113.html; accessed September 4, 2001.

World Intellectual Property Organization. www.wipo.org; accessed September 2, 2002.

Zebib, Mohammad. "The Regulatory Road to Interstate Banking in the U.S.: Era of the National Bank Act, 1864–1900." *Delta Business Review*, vol. 5, no. 1. Available: http://cber.nlu.edu/DBR/ZEBIB.htm; accessed December 27, 2002.

Government Documents

A.L.A. Schechter Poultry Corp. et al. v. United States, 295 U.S. 495 (1935).

An Act to Secure Homesteads to Actual Settlers on the Public Domain. U.S. Statutes at Large 12 (1863): 392–393.

An Analysis of Export Control of U.S. Technology, a DOD Perspective: A Report of the Defense Science Board Task Force on Export of U.S. Technology—the "Bucy Report." Washington, DC: U.S. Government Printing Office, 1976.

"Bill Easing Credit Designed to Recruit Young Farmers." *Congressional Quarterly* (August 8, 1992): 2351.

Board of Governors of the Federal Reserve System. *The Federal Reserve System: Purposes and Functions.* Washington, DC: Government Printing Office, 1994.

Buckley v. Vallejo, 424 U.S. 1 (1976).

Bureau of Economic Analysis. *Balance of Payments of the United States: Concepts, Data Sources, and Estimating Procedures.* Washington, DC: U.S. Government Printing Office, 1990.

Bureau of the Census. *Historical Statistics of the United States: Colonial Times to 1957.* Washington, DC: U.S. Government Printing Office, 1960.

Bureau of National Affairs (BNA). *Equal Pay for Equal Work: Federal Equal Pay Law of 1963.* Washington, DC: BNA, 1963.

Citizens United v. Federal Election Commission, 558 U.S. ___ (2010).

Clinton, William J. "Statement on Signing the Federal Agricultural Improvement and Reform Act of 1996." *Weekly Compilation of Presidential Documents* 32, no. 14 (1996): 614.

Congressional Research Office. "CRS Report for Congress: The Cost of Iraq, Afghanistan, and Other Global War on Terror Operations Since 9/11," RL33110 (May 15, 2009).

Davis v. Federal Election Commission, No. 7-320 (June 26, 2008).

Digital Millennium Copyright Act. U.S. Statutes at Large 112 (1998): 2860.

Downes v. Bidwell, 182 U.S. 244 (1901).

Economic Opportunity Act of 1964. U.S. Statutes at Large 78 (1965): 508.

"Economic Report of the President." Washington, DC: U.S. Government Printing Office, 1999.

Energy Information Administration. *Twenty-fifth Anniversary of the 1973 Oil Embargo: Energy Trends since the First Major U.S. Energy Crisis.* Washington, DC: U.S. Government Printing Office, 1998.

Export Control Act. U.S. Statutes at Large 63 (1949): 7.

Federal Deposit Insurance Corporation (FDIC). *A Brief History of Deposit Insurance in the United States.* Washington, DC: FDIC, 1998.

Federal Election Commission v. Wisconsin Right to Life, Inc., 551 U.S. 449 (2007).

FEMA: The Federal Emergency Management Agency. Washington, DC: FEMA, 2001.

Food, Agriculture, Conservation, and Trade Act of 1990. U.S. Statutes at Large 104 (1990): 1388.

Horseshoe Bend National Military Park, Alabama: Official Guide and Map. Washington, DC: U.S. Department of the Interior, 1993.

House Committee on International Relations. *Implementation of the Iran Nonproliferation Act of 2000.* Washington, DC: U.S. Government Printing Office, 2001.

Hunt, Commonwealth v. 45, Mass. (4 Met.) 111, 38 Amer. Dec. 346 (1842): 1, 2.

McConnell v. Federal Election Commission, 540 U.S. 93 (2003).

Mutual Defense Assistance Control Act. U.S. Statutes at Large 65 (1952): 644.

Northern Securities Company v. United States, 193 U.S. 197 (1904).

Privatization: Lessons Learned by State and Local Government. Washington, DC: U.S. General Accounting Office, 1997.

Register of Debates. Senate, 20th Cong., 1st sess., 1828.

Senate Subcommittee on International Trade and Finance. *Reauthorization of the Export Administration Act.* Washington, DC: U.S. Government Printing Office, 2000.

Session Laws of American States and Territories prior to 1900. Microfiche. Westport, CT: Redgrave Information Resources Corporation, 1998.

Shelley v. Kraemer, 334 U.S. 1 (1948).

The Student Guide: Financial Aid 2001–2002. Student Financial Assistance. U.S. Department of Education. Washington, DC: U.S. Government Printing Office, 2002.

United States Patent Act. U.S. Statutes at Large 1 (1793): 318–323.

United States Trademark Act. U.S. Statutes at Large 21 (1881): 502.

United States Trademark Acts. U.S. Statutes at Large 33 (1905): 724.

U.S. Department of Agriculture. *Credit in Rural America.* Washington, DC: U.S. Government Printing Office, 2001.

U.S. Department of Agriculture Economic Research Service. "Can Federal Action Improve Efficiency in the Market for Farm Loans?" Agriculture Information Bulletin no. 724-01, 1996.

U.S. Department of Commerce. *NOAA's Climate Observations and Services*. Silver Spring, MD: National Oceanic and Atmospheric Administration, 2001.

U.S. Department of State. *Foreign Assistance Act of 1961*. Washington, DC: U.S. Government Printing Office, 1982.

U.S. House of Representatives. *Farmer Mac Reform Act of 1995*. Washington, DC: U.S. Government Printing Office, 1996.

U.S. Information Agency (USIA). *United States Information Agency: A Commemoration*. Washington, DC: USIA, 2000.

U.S. Senate. *Nomination of Paul A. Volcker*. Hearing before the Committee on Banking, Housing, and Urban Affairs. 96th Cong., 1st sess., July 30, 1979.

U.S. Senate. *Report of the Subcommittee on the Constitution, Committee on the Judiciary*. Washington, DC: U.S. Government Printing Office, 1985.

U.S. Statutes at Large 28 (1895): 422–423.

About the Editor and Contributors

Editor

Cynthia L. Clark, PhD, teaches at the University of Texas at Arlington in Arlington, Texas. Her field of specialization is modern U.S. history with an emphasis on political and economic issues.

Contributors

Albert Atkins is a Professor in the Business Department at Argosy University, Orange, California.

Dalit Baranoff is a PhD student in the History Department at Johns Hopkins University, Baltimore, Maryland.

John Barnhill is a civil servant and independent scholar in Yukon, Oklahoma.

Daniel K. Blewett is a reference librarian, College of DuPage, Glen Ellyn, Illinois.

Julie A. Bogdan is an independent historian residing in Herkimer, New York.

John D. Buenker is a Professor of History and Ethnic Studies in the History Department at the University of Wisconsin–Parkside, Kenosha, Wisconsin.

James T. Carroll is an Associate Professor of History at Iona College, New Rochelle, New York.

Susan Coleman is an Instructor of Political Science in the Department of History and Political Science at West Texas A&M University, Canyon, Texas.

Robert C. Cottrell is a Professor in the History and American Studies Department at California State University, Chico, California.

Deana Covel is an MA student in the History Department at the University of Texas at Arlington, Arlington, Texas.

Joseph A. Devine is a Professor in the History Department at Stephen F. Austin State University, Nacogdoches, Texas.

Robert Dimand is a Professor in the Economics Department at Brock University, Saint Catharines, Ontario, Canada.

Scott R. DiMarco is Director of Library Services at Herkimer County Community College in Herkimer, New York.

Lisa A. Ennis is a librarian in the Russell Library at Georgia College and State University, Milledgeville, Georgia.

Ann Harper Fender is a Professor in the Economics Department at Gettysburg, College, Gettysburg, Pennsylvania.

Brooks Flippen is an Associate Professor in the Department of Social Sciences at Southeastern Oklahoma State University, Durant, Oklahoma.

David T. Flynn is an Assistant Professor in the Economics Department at the University of North Dakota, Grand Forks, North Dakota.

Mathew Forstater is an Assistant Professor in the Department of Economics, University of Missouri, Kansas City, Missouri.

John K. Franklin is an Adjunct Instructor in the Humanities Department at Graceland University, Lamori, Iowa.

Mark Frezzo is a PhD candidate in the Sociology Department at Binghampton University, Binghampton, New York, and is a Lecturer in Sociology and Geography at SUNY, Cortland.

W. Chad Futrell is a PhD student in the Development Sociology Department at Cornell University, Ithaca, New York.

Peter S. Genovese is a PhD student in the History Department at Bowling Green State University, Bowling Green, Ohio.

Eli Goldstein is a PhD candidate in the Department of Economics at Bar-Ilan University, Rishion Le-Zion, Israel.

Robert Herren is a Professor of Agribusiness and Applied Economics in the Economics Department at North Dakota State University, Fargo, North Dakota.

Charles F. Howlett is an Adjunct Professor at Adelphi University, West Islip, New York, and an advanced placement teacher for the Amityville Public Schools, New York Public Schools.

Ann Johnson is an Assistant Professor in the History Department at Fordham University, New York City.

Russell Douglass Jones is a Lecturer in the History and Philosophy Department at Eastern Michigan University, Ypsilanti, Michigan.

Fadhel Kaboub is a PhD candidate in the Economics Department at University of Missouri–Kansas City, Kansas City, Missouri.

Jonah Katz is a PhD student in the History Department at Drake University, Des Moines, Iowa.

Everett W. Kindig is an Associate Professor in the History Department, Midwestern State University, Wichita Falls, Texas.

Thibaut Kleiner is an official in the Competition Directorate General of the European Commission, Brussels, Belgium.

Robert Leeson is an Associate Professor in the Economics Department at Murdoch University, Perth, Australia.

Keith A. Leitich is an independent scholar residing in Seattle, Washington.

James K. Libbey is an Associate Professor in Humanities and Social Sciences Department, Embry-Riddle Aeronautical University, Dayton Beach, Florida.

Theo Edwin Maloy is an Assistant Professor of Public Administration in the Department of History and Political Science, West Texas A&M University, Canyon, Texas.

John Marino is Manager of Research and Cultural Affairs with the National Italian American Foundation, Washington, D.C.

Peter Hans Matthews is an Associate Professor in the Department of Economics at Middlebury College, Middlebury, Vermont.

James E. McWilliams is an Associate Professor in the History Department at Southwest Texas State University, San Marcos, Texas.

Michael A. Meeropol is a Professor and Chair of the Department of Economics at Western New England College in Wilbraham, Massachusetts.

Karen A. J. Miller is an Associate Professor in the Department of History at Oakland University, Rochester, Michigan.

Keith L. Miller is an independent scholar living in Philadelphia, Pennsylvania.

Matthieu J-C. Moss is an MA student in the History Department at the Ohio University, Athens, Ohio.

Michael V. Namarato is a Professor in the Department of History at the University of Mississippi, University, Mississippi.

Caryn E. Neumann is a PhD candidate in the Department of History at Ohio State University, Columbus, Ohio.

Shannon Daniel O'Bryan is a PhD student in the History Department at the University of Tennessee, Knoxville, Tennessee.

Lisa L. Ossian is an Instructor in the Humanities at Southwestern Community College in Creston, Iowa.

Laura Seeley Pangallozzi is a PhD candidate in the Department of Urban Planning at Rutgers University, Camden, New Jersey.

James D. Perry is a defense analyst at the Science Applications International Corp., McLean, Virginia.

Donald K. Pickens is a Professor in the History Department at the University of North Texas, Denton, Texas.

Aaron Z. Pitluck is a PhD candidate in the Sociology Department at the University of Wisconsin–Madison, Madison, Wisconsin.

Avery Plaw is an Assistant Professor of Political Science at Concordia University, Montreal, Canada.

John Grady Powell is a student in the Economics Department at Furman University, Greenville, South Carolina.

Josh Pratt is a Masters student in Business Administration at Price College of Business, University of Oklahoma, Oklahoma City, Oklahoma.

Christopher A. Preble is the Director of Foreign Policy Studies at the Cato Institute, Washington, DC.

G. David Price is an Assistant Professor in the Social and Behavioral Sciences Department at Santa Fe Community College, Gainesville, Florida.

Eric Pullin is an Instructor in the College of Business at Cardinal Stritch University, Milwaukee, Wisconsin.

Peter Rainow, PhD, is an independent scholar living in Foster City, California.

John David Rausch Jr. is an Assistant Professor of Political Science at West Texas A&M University, Canyon, Texas.

Ty M. Reese is an Assistant Professor in the Department of History at the University of North Dakota, Grand Forks, North Dakota.

Eileen Robertson-Rehberg, PhD, is the Assistant Director of the Carl Frost Center for Social Science Research, Social Science Division of Hope College, Holland, Michigan.

Robert Rook is an Associate Professor and Chair of the Department of History at Fort Hays State University, Hays, Kansas.

Trifin J. Roule is an assistant editor of the *Journal of Money Laundering Control*, Pittsburgh, Pennsylvania.

Margaret Sankey is a PhD student in the History Department at Auburn University, Auburn, Alabama.

Simone Selva is a PhD student in the Department of History of Society and Institutions at the State University of Milan, Milan, Italy.

Sayuri Shimizu is an Associate Professor in the History Department at Michigan State University, Rochester, Michigan.

David B. Sicilia is an Associate Professor Department of History at the University of Maryland, College Park, Maryland.

Henry B. Sirgo is a Professor of Political Science in the Department of Social Sciences at McNeese State University, Lake Charles, Louisiana.

Steven E. Siry is a Professor in the Department of History at Baldwin-Wallace College, Berea, Ohio.

T. Jason Soderstrum is a graduate student in the History Department at Iowa State University, Roland, Iowa.

Mary Stockwell is an Associate Professor in the History Department at Lourdes College, Sylvania, Ohio.

R. Jake Sudderth is a graduate student in the School of Arts and Sciences at Columbia University, New York City.

Robert P. Sutton is a Professor in the History Department at Western Illinois University, Macomb, Illinois.

Pavlina R. Tcherneva is an Associate Director, Center for Full Employment and Price Stability in the Economics Department at the University of Missouri–Kansas City, Kansas City, Missouri.

Saranna R. Thornton is an Associate Professor in the Department of Economics, Hampden-Sydney College, Hampden-Sydney, Virginia.

Kathleen A. Tobin is an Assistant Professor in the School of Liberal Arts and Social Sciences at Purdue University–Calumet, Hammond, Indiana.

Zdravka K. Todorova is a graduate student in the Economics Department of the University of Missouri at Kansas City, Kansas City, Missouri.

Richard Toye is a Lecturer in the History Department at Homerton College, University of Cambridge, Cambridge, England.

David Treviño teaches History at Donna Klein Jewish Academy in Boca Raton, Florida.

Elaine C. Prange Turney is a Lecturer in the History Department at Northwest Vista College, San Antonio, Texas.

Eugene Van Sickle is a PhD student in the History Department at West Virginia University, Morgantown, West Virginia.

David E. Walker is a Professor of Communication Studies at Middle Tennessee State University, Murfreesboro, Tennessee.

David W. Waltrop is a PhD student in the Department of History at the University of Maryland–Baltimore County, Baltimore, Maryland.

Tony Ward is a Professor in the Department of Economics at Brock University, Saint Catharines, Ontario, Canada.

Wyatt Wells is an Associate Professor in the History Department at Auburn University Montgomery, Montgomery, Alabama.

Leigh Whaley is an Associate Professor in Department of History and Classics, Acadia University, Wolfville, Nova Scotia, Canada.

Robert Whaples is an Associate Professor in the Department of Economics at Wake Forest University, Winston-Salem, North Carolina.

Sandra L. Willett is a student in the English Department at the University of Central Oklahoma, Edmond, Oklahoma.

Ben Wynne is an Instructor in the History Department at the University of Mississippi, Oxford, Mississippi.

Warren Young is an Associate Professor in the Economics Department at Bar Ilan University, Ramat Gan, Israel.

Guoqiang Zheng is an Assistant Professor in the Department of History at Angelo State University, San Angelo, Texas.

Index

debt creates large trading volume, 823

and development of new technologies, 769–70

economic devastation of the South, 105, 108–9, 542, 586

effects on federal economic policy, 62, 143, 239, 586, 596, 619, 640, 724–25, 861

and Emancipation Proclamation, 156–57, 198

financed with legal paper currency, 303–5, 380, 471, 573, 640

first income tax levied during, 356

foreign policy during, 394, 419, 824–25

and immigration, 653

legislation passed during, 6, 229, 297, 303–5, 365, 369, 427, 432, 638, 724–25, 839–40

and Pinkerton Detective Agency, 354

"The Civil War" public television documentary, 307

Civil Works Administration (CWA), 78–79, 175, 317, 515, 716, 877

Clark, Grenville, 148

Clark, John Bates, 589

Clark, Maurice B., 382–83

Clark, Thomas, 702

Clark, William, 202, 271

Class, 78–79

crime as issue, 115

differences revealed, 129

reductionism, 79

violent struggle promoted by IWW, 240

Classical economics theory, 125, 199, 531, 851

and Adam Smith, 265

compared to political economy theory, 265

supply-side principle, 420

Classical-liberal economic system, 495

Classical paradigm, 260

Clay, Henry (1777–1852), 80–81, 824

and American system, 31, 586, 651, 836

attempts to acquire Canada, 65

and Distribution Act (1836), 137, 723

Maysville Road Bill (1830), 279

and national bank, 42, 251

negotiates Missouri Compromise, 401

and nullification crisis, 184, 326, 423

Speaker of the House, 251, 326

and Treaty of Ghent, 435, 473

Whig Party leader, 20, 251, 475, 821

Clayton, Henry De Lamar, 81

Clayton Act (1950), 524

Clayton Anti-Trust Act (1914), 525

amendments to, 527, 530

document, 1037–49

enforces Sherman Anti-Trust Act, 81, 398, 524

and Federal Trade Commission, 22–23, 179, 524, 643, 738

purpose of, 62, 263, 417, 439, 550

Clayton-Bulwer Treaty (1850), 227, 834

Clean Air Acts (1965, 1970), 28, 60, 459, 648

Clean Water Restoration Act (1966), 216

Clearinghouses, 540

Cleveland, Grover (1837–1908), 82, 575

attempts tariff reform, 281, 365, 443, 478, 825

efforts to counter bossism, 107

expands forest reserves, 190, 726

and Panic of 1892, 210, 398

and Pullman strike, 82, 367

refuses to annex Hawaiian islands, 225, 419

Clinton, Bill. See Clinton, William Jefferson

Clinton, DeWitt, 639, 802, 836

Clinton, George, 128

Clinton, Hillary Rodham, 287, 507, 705, 880

Clinton, William Jefferson (1946–), 60, 83–85, 123, 219, 287, 386, 551, 845

agricultural policy, 10

and American Inventors Protection Act, 16

and antitrust enforcement, 23

budget for AIDS, 2, 137

created National Science and Technology Council, 779

economic policy, 450, 533, 648, 778

Speech Opposing Financial Services
Modernization Act (Gramm-Leach-
Bliley) (1999) (document)
Fire insurance, 308, 665–72
Firemen's Magazine (periodical), 122
Fireside chats of Franklin D. Roosevelt,
283–84
Firestone, Harvey S., 151
Fish, Jim, 318
Fish and Wildlife Service conservation
policies, 99
Fisher, Irving, 207, 589
Fisher equation, 742
Fitzhugh, George, 402
Fixed currency exchange rates, 182,
405
Flagler, Henry M., 383
The Fleischmann Yeast Hour radio
advertising, 501
Fletcher v. Peck (1810), 180, 491, 692
Flex acres, 180–81
Floating exchange rates, 181–82
Florida, 46, 61, 115, 188, 191, 270, 354,
356, 383, 434, 481, 613, 638, 703, 788,
835, 857
Flynn, Elizabeth Gurley, 240
FMD. *See* Foot and mouth disease
Fogel, Robert, 781
FOMC. *See* Federal Open Market
Committee
Food
consumer spending, 102
prices lowered, 9
Food, Agriculture, Conservation, and Trade
Act (1990), 181
Food and Drug Administration (FDA),
182–83, 455, 459
Food for Peace Program, 450
Food safety laws, 254
Food Security Act (1985), 169, 520
Food stamp program (USDA), 163, 360,
518–19
Foot and mouth disease (FMD), 183
Foraker Act (1900), 140, 863
Forbes, Francis, 685
Force Act (1833), 183–84, 251, 364, 423
Ford, Gerald R., 131, 219, 414, 604

Ford, Henry (1863–1947), 27, 151, 184–85,
611, 715, 842
attempts to acquire Muscle Shoals plant,
299, 426
and Edison, 610
installment plan established, 113
Ford Motor Company, 27, 185, 552, 611–12
Fordney-McCumber Tariff (1922), 8, 20,
185, 225, 282
exempts farm cooperatives from antitrust
prosecution, 514
wipes out reductions of
Underwood-Simmons Tariff Act, 444
Foreign Affairs and Restructuring Act
(1998), 461
Foreign aid programs
entwined with foreign policy, 634
for increased globalization, 206
lend-lease assistance to Allied powers
(World War II), 172
through USAID, 450
Foreign Assistance Act (1948), 92, 450
Foreign competition
farmers protected from, 8
operating without, 62
Foreign direct investment, 298
Foreign policy, U.S., 186–90, 632–35
dollar diplomacy, 138–39
and economic policy, 864
of embargoing, 858
formulated on economics, 634, 651
global involvement based on opposition
to Soviet Union, 633
ideological period, 632
isolationism, 249–50
noninvolvement reversed with lend-lease
plan, 267–68
realistic period, 632
of Republican Party, 379
Republican Party perceived
as superior, 128
utopian period, 632
under William Seward, 394
Foreign trade. *See* Trade policy
Forest Homestead Law (1906), 726
Forest Reserve Act (1891), 190, 725, 727
Forest Service, U.S., 99, 614, 715

Immigration Act (1924), 233, 656
Immigration Act (1965), 234
Immigration Act (1990), 662
Immigration Act (Johnson-Reid Act)
(1924), 233, 656
Immigration and Nationality Act (1952),
657, 662
amended by Patriot Act, 763
Immigration and Naturalization Bureau,
453, 456
Immigration policy, 650–64
Chinese exclusion, 653
effects of September 11, 2001, 662, 664
exclusion (1914–1965), 655–57
first great wave (1830–1860), 652–53
quotas, 656–58, 662
reforms, 657, 660
responsibility of federal government, not
states, 654
restrictiveness, 656
for talented and meritorious
individuals, 657
tied to labor market demands, 657
Immigration Reform and Control Act
(1986), 657, 662
Imperialism, 23, 379
Import and export indexes, as economic
indicators, 145
Imports
duties, 62, 281
duties reduced/increased by executive
branch, 376
illegal (smuggling), 406–7
impost (tax), 104
restrictions on the United States by Cuba, 116
sugar, 126, 139, 225, 354, 420
taxes to generate revenue, 381
from various nations (1789–1790), 821
(table)
Impost, as source of income for Continental
Congress, 104, 141, 243, 297–98,
691–92, 872
Impress, of U.S. sailors into Royal Navy,
128, 187, 254, 435, 436, 472
Income
inequality, 85
measured with CPI, 101

Income tax, 810, 812, 813–14, 816
declared unconstitutional, 356–57
as direct tax, 356
established with Underwood-Simmons
Tariff Act, 443
finances World War I effort, 863
graduated, 62, 280, 358, 444
included in Wilson-Gorman
Tariff Act, 478
indexed to CPI's inflation rate, 102
linked to wealth, 474
negative, 167
personal, 62, 231
progressive, 474
sanctioned by Sixteenth Amendment, 398
Indentured servitude, 235, 650, 709
Independent Officers Appropriation Act
(1934), 148
Indianapolis, Indiana, 215–16, 620
Indian confederation, in War of
1812, 472
Indian New Deal, 236
Indian policy, 235–37
Indian Removal Act (1830), 431
Indian Reorganization Act (1934), 59
Indian reservation system
under Dawes Severalty Act, 122
termination of, 236
Indians
assimilation policy, 235–36
forced removal of, 431
treaty to open Ohio for settlement, 436
tribes as trading partners
with colonists, 818
used as slaves, experimentally, 783.
See also Bureau of Indian Affairs;
Native Americans
Indian wars
handled by U.S. army, 862
and U.S. policy of expansion into Native
American lands, 857
Individualism
of laissez-faire economics, 265
and poor relief, 872
Indochina, 253, 827
Indonesia, 332–34, 338
Industrial heartland, 237

Riots, 78, 82, 233, 430, 456, 465

Rivers, transportation policy, 836–37

Robber barons, 381–82

The Robber Barons: The Great American Capitalists (Josephson), 382

Roberts, Owen, 700

Robinson-Patman Act (1936), 524, 530

Robotics, and ATO programs, 3

Rockefeller, John D. (1839–1937), 382–83, 523
  as captain of industry, 66–67
  and Clayton Anti-Trust Act, 81
  operating without threat of foreign competition, 62
  political power, 240
  as robber baron, 381–82
  Standard Oil monopoly, 332, 415

Rockefeller Foundation, 383

Rockingham, Marquis of, 18, 321, 415

Roe, Mark J., 797

Roe v. Wade, 358

Roger's Rangers, 197

Rogue states, 418
  and deployment of missile defense systems, 134
  economic controls over, 166

Rolfe, John (1585–1622), 383

Romania, 323

Ronald Reagan's Remarks and a Question and Answer Session with Reporters on the Air Traffic controller's Strike (1981) (document), 1107–1113

Roosa, Robert, 181

Roosevelt, Eleanor, 79, 384, 480

Roosevelt, Franklin D. (FDR) (1882–1945), 191, 224, 260, 269, 384–86, 395
  and advertising, 501
  Aid to Dependent Children, 11, 360
  and anti-trust legislation, 529
  Banking Act (1933), 37, 38, 451, 544
  bans U.S. private ownership of gold, 577
  Chamber of Congress criticizes, 451
  creates FDIC, 36, 39, 544
  declares noninterventionist Latin America policy, 211
  and Economy Act (1933), 148
  and Emergency Price Control Act, 158, 331
  encourages settlement and irrigation in western United States, 317–18
  establishes FERA, 174–75, 877
  Fireside chats, 283–84
  fixes price of gold, 117, 207, 208, 209, 577
  G.I. Bill of Rights, 393, 599, 878
  Keynesian economic policies, 126, 259, 366
  and labor, 311, 451, 456, 470, 715
  lend-lease plan, 267
  minimum wage requirements implemented, 293
  New Deal, 36, 39, 44, 76, 79, 176, 310, 313, 316–17, 390–92, 451, 456, 646, 701, 735, 773–74
  opposes Hawley-Smoot Tariff, 226, 379, speech (document), 1057–67
  public housing programs, 459–60
  Reciprocal Trade Agreements Act, 194, 226, 232, 365, 376, 827
  Reconstruction Finance Corp., 38, 360
  reforms Federal Reserve system, 39, 544, 624
  responds to agricultural crisis, 5, 9, 99, 142, 171, 347, 361, 409, 515
  Rural Electrification Administration, 389
  silver purchase policy opposition, 86
  Security and Exchange Commission, creation of, 318, 805
  Smith-Connally Act passed over veto, 404
  Social Security Act, 408–9, 429, 445, 451, 877
  supports TVA project, 300, 426
  Union Party opposes re-election, 429
  World War II, 331, 332, 334, 456, 473, 483, 488, 827

Roosevelt, Theodore (1858–1919), 204, 386–88, 506
  conservation policies, 99, 725
  designates forest reserves, 190
  efforts to counter bossism, 107